ENCYCLOPEDIA OF THE U.S. PRESIDENCY

A HISTORICAL REFERENCE

VOLUME V

—◦◦◦◦—

Hoover–Nixon
1929–1974

ENCYCLOPEDIA OF THE U.S. PRESIDENCY

A HISTORICAL REFERENCE

VOLUME V

—\\\\—

Hoover–Nixon
1929–1974

Edited by
Nancy Beck Young, Ph.D.

☑ Facts On File
An Infobase Learning Company

ENCYCLOPEDIA OF THE U.S. PRESIDENCY: A HISTORICAL REFERENCE

Facts On File, Inc.
An imprint of Infobase Learning
132 West 31st Street
New York NY 10001

Library of Congress Cataloging-in-Publication Data

Encyclopedia of the U.S. presidency / [edited by] Nancy Beck Young.
p. cm.
Includes bibliographical references and index.
ISBN 978-0-8160-6744-2
1. Presidents—United States—Encyclopedias, Juvenile. 2. Presidents—United
States—History—Encyclopedias, Juvenile. 3. United States—Politics and
government—Encyclopedias, Juvenile. I. Young, Nancy Beck.
JK517.E53 2011   352.230973'03—dc22
2010020746

Facts On File books are available at special discounts when purchased in bulk
quantities for businesses, associations, institutions, or sales promotions.
Please call our Special Sales Department in New York
at (212) 967-8800 or (800) 322-8755.

You can find Facts On File on the World Wide Web at
http://www.infobaselearning.com

Excerpts included herewith have been reprinted by permission of
the copyright holders; the author has made every effort to contact
copyright holders. The publisher will be glad to rectify, in future editions,
any errors or omissions brought to its notice.

Text design and composition by Erika K. Arroyo
Cover printed by Yurchak Printing, Landisville, Pa.
Book printed and bound by Yurchak Printing, Landisville, Pa.
Date printed: December 2012
Printed in the United States of America

10 9 8 7 6 5 4 3 2 1

This book is printed on acid-free paper.

Contents

VOLUME V

Major Events and Issues vi
Documents xiii
Special Features: First Ladies,
Vice Presidents, and Social History xv

HERBERT C. HOOVER 1

Biography of Herbert C. Hoover 3
Presidential Election of 1928 11
Hoover Administration (1929–1933) 17
Major Events and Issues 30
Documents 50

FRANKLIN D. ROOSEVELT 55

Biography of Franklin D. Roosevelt 57
Presidential Election of 1932 67
Presidential Election of 1936 78
Presidential Election of 1940 83
Presidential Election of 1944 92
Roosevelt Administration (1933–1945) 99
Major Events and Issues 121
Documents 176

HARRY S. TRUMAN 191

Biography of Harry S. Truman 193
Presidential Election of 1948 201
Truman Administration (1945–1953) 208
Major Events and Issues 223
Documents 249

DWIGHT D. EISENHOWER 255

Biography of Dwight D. Eisenhower 257
Presidential Election of 1952 265
Presidential Election of 1956 272
Eisenhower Administration (1953–1961) .. 277
Major Events and Issues 294
Documents 317

JOHN F. KENNEDY 325

Biography of John F. Kennedy 327
Presidential Election of 1960 335
Kennedy Administration (1961–1963) 343
Major Events and Issues 354
Documents 381

LYNDON B. JOHNSON 389

Biography of Lyndon B. Johnson 391
Presidential Election of 1964 402
Johnson Administration (1963–1969) 411
Major Events and Issues 426
Documents 450

RICHARD M. NIXON 459

Biography of Richard M. Nixon 461
Presidential Election of 1968 476
Presidential Election of 1972 485
Nixon Administration (1969–1974) 492
Major Events and Issues 510
Documents 539

Major Events and Issues

HOOVER ADMINISTRATION (1929–1933) **30**

Agricultural Marketing Act (1929)

Air Mail Act (1930)

American Gothic, by Grant Wood (1930)

Bonus March (1932)

Camp Rapidan

Corporatism

Drought of 1930–1931

Emergency Relief and Construction Act (1932)

Empire State Building Completed (1931)

Federal Farm Board

Federal Home Loan Bank Act (1932)

Great Depression

Individualism

Lindbergh Baby Kidnapping (1932)

London Naval Conference (1930)

Look Homeward, Angel, by Thomas Wolfe (1929)

Moratorium on Reparations and War Debts (1931)

Museum of Modern Art Opens (1929)

National Institute of Health Act (1930)

Near v. Minnesota (1931)

Norris-LaGuardia Act (1932)

Pecora Wall Street Investigation (1932–1934)

President's Emergency Committee for Employment

President's Mountain School

President's Organization on Unemployment Relief (1931)

Press Relations

Reconstruction Finance Corporation Act (1932)

St. Valentine's Day Massacre (1929)

Scottsboro Case

Smoot-Hawley Tariff (1930)

The Sound and the Fury, by William Faulkner (1929)

South American Trip (1928–1929)

Stimson Doctrine (1932)

Stock Market Crash (1929)

Supreme Court Appointments

Swope Plan (1931)

Veterans Administration Created (1930)

White House Conference on Child Health and Welfare (1930)

Wickersham Commission on Law Enforcement (1929–1931)

World Disarmament Conference (1932)

ROOSEVELT ADMINISTRATION (1933–1945) **121**

Agricultural Adjustment Act (1933)

Air War in Europe (1942–1943)

Alien Registration Act (1940)

Antimonopoly Policies

Appalachian Spring, by Aaron Copland (1944)

Assassination of Huey Long (1935)

Atlantic Charter (1941)

Banking Act (1933)

Banking Act (1935)

Barden-LaFollette Act (1943)

Bataan Death March (1942)

Battle of the Atlantic (1940–1943)

Battle of the Coral Sea (1942)

Battle of Corregidor (1941–1942)

Battle of Guadalcanal (1942–1943)

Battle of Iwo Jima (1945)

Battle of the Java Sea (1942)

Battle of Leyte Gulf (1944)

Battle of Midway (1942)

Battle of Okinawa (1945)

Battle of the Philippine Sea (1944)

Berlin Olympics (1936)

Board of Economic Warfare

Bonneville Dam

Bracero Program

Brain Trust

Bretton Woods Agreement (1944)

Burke-Wadsworth Selective Service Training Act (1940)

Cairo Conference (1943)

Casablanca Conference (1943)

China-Burma-India Theater (1942–1945)

Civil Aeronautics Act (1938)

Civil Works Administration

Civilian Conservation Corps (1933–1942)

Communications Act (1934)

D-Day and the Battle for Northwest Europe (1944–1945)

Detroit Race Riot (1943)

Dumbarton Oaks Conference (1944)

Dust Bowl

Economy Act (1933)

Edwards v. California (1941)

Emergency Banking Relief Act (1933)

Executive Reorganization

Fair Employment Practices Committee

Fair Labor Standards Act (1938)

Farm Security Administration (1937–1946)

Federal Emergency Relief Administration

Flood Control Act (1936)

Guffey-Snyder Act (1935)

Hatch Act (1939)

Home Owners' Loan Act (1933)

Indian Reorganization Act (1934)

Internment of Japanese Americans

Italian Campaign (1943–1945)

Jewish Refugee Crisis

Lend-Lease Act (1941)

Life Magazine First Published by Henry Luce (1936)

Manhattan Project

National Industrial Recovery Act (1933)

National Labor Relations Act (1935)

National War Labor Board

National Youth Administration (1935–1943)

Native Son, by Richard Wright (1940)

Natural Gas Act (1938)

Neutrality Acts (1935–1939)

North African Campaign (1942–1943)

Office of Price Administration (1941–1947)

Office of Production Management

Office of War Information (1942–1945)

Office of War Mobilization

Pearl Harbor Attack (1941)

Porgy and Bess, by George Gershwin (1935)

Public Utility Holding Company Act (1935)

Public Works Administration

Recession of 1937

Reciprocal Trade Agreements Act (1934)

Reconstruction Finance Corporation

Resettlement Administration

Ruml Plan (1943)

Rural Electrification Administration (1935–1994)

Securities and Exchange Commission

Servicemen's Readjustment Act (1944)

Sinking of the *Panay* (1937)

Sit-down Strikes (1936–1937)

Smith v. Allwright (1944)

Social Security Act (1935)

Soil Conservation and Domestic Allotment Act (1935)

Strange Fruit, by Lillian Smith (1944)

Supreme Court Reorganization Plan (1937)

Teheran Conference (1943)

Tennessee Valley Authority

Tokyo Air Raids (1945)

Twenty-first Amendment (1933)

United States v. Curtiss-Wright Export Corporation (1936)

U.S.A., by John Dos Passos (1930s)

War Manpower Commission

War of the Worlds, Radio Broadcast by Orson Welles (1938)

War Production Board (1942–1945)

Wealth Tax Act (1935)

West Coast Hotel Co. v. Parrish (1937)

Works Progress Administration

Yalta Conference (1945)

Zoot Suit Riots (1943)

TRUMAN ADMINISTRATION (1945–1953) 223

Aid to Greece and Turkey

Atomic Energy Act (1946)

Berlin Blockade and Airlift (1948–1949)

Bombing of Hiroshima and Nagasaki (1945)

The Catcher in the Rye, by J. D. Salinger (1951)

Civil Rights Program

Common Sense Baby and Child Care, by Benjamin Spock (1946)

Containment Policy

Death of a Salesman, by Arthur Miller (1949)

Defense Production Act (1950)

Dennis v. United States (1951)

Desegregation of the Military

Displaced Persons Act (1948)

Economic Reconversion

Election of 1946

Employment Act (1946)

Fair Deal

Farmers Home Administration Act (1946)

Federal Airport Act (1946)

Federal Rent Control Act (1948)

Firing of General MacArthur (1951)

Fulbright Act (1946)

Hiss Case (1948–1950)

Hospital Survey and Construction Act (1946)

Housing Act (1949)

Integration of the Brooklyn Dodgers (1947)

Kefauver Crime Committee (1950–1951)

Korean War (1950–1953)

Legislative Reorganization Act (1946)

Long Telegram (1946)

Loyalty Security Program

Marshall Plan

McCarran Internal Security Act (1950)

McCarran-Walter Immigration Act (1952)

McCarthyism

McCarthy's Speech in Wheeling, West Virginia (1950)

National Mental Health Act (1946)

National School Lunch Act (1946)

National Security Act (1947)

National Security Council Document 68 (1950)

North Atlantic Treaty Organization

Potsdam Conference (1945)

Price Controls

Recognition of Israel (1948)

Rosenberg Case (1950–1953)

San Francisco Conference (1945)

Selective Service Act (1948)

Sexual Behavior in the Human Male, by Alfred Kinsey (1948)

Shelley v. Kraemer (1948)

Sweat v. Painter (1950)

Taft-Hartley Act (1947)

Truman Era Scandals

Twenty-second Amendment (1951)

Youngstown Sheet and Tube Company v. Sawyer (1952)

EISENHOWER ADMINISTRATION (1953–1961) 294

Army-McCarthy Hearings (1954)

Atomic Energy Act (1954)

Atoms for Peace

Battle of Dien Bien Phu (1954)

Berlin Crisis

Bricker Amendment

Brown v. Board of Education of Topeka, Kansas (1954)

CIA Intervention in Guatemala (1954)

CIA Intervention in Iran (1953)

Civil Rights Act (1957)

Civil Rights Act (1960)

Communist Control Act (1954)

Defense Reorganization Act (1958)

Dixon-Yates Scandal

Domino Theory

Eisenhower Doctrine (1957)

Farewell Address (1961)

Formosa (Taiwan) Resolution (1955)

Geneva Accords (1954)

Geneva Conference (1954)

Khrushchev Visit (1959)

Landrum-Griffin Act (1959)

Lebanon, Intervention in

Little Rock Crisis (1957)

Modern Republicanism

Montgomery Bus Boycott (1955–1956)

National Aeronautics and Space Act (1958)

National Defense Education Act (1958)

National Interstate and Defense Highways Act (1956)

New Look

Open Skies

Oppenheimer Case (1954)

SEATO Established (1954)

Soil Bank Act (1956)

Southern Manifesto (1956)

Sputnik (1957)

Submerged Lands Act (1953)

Suez Crisis (1956)

Taiwan Strait Crises (1954–1955 and 1958)

U-2 Crisis (1960)

KENNEDY ADMINISTRATION (1961–1963) 354

Abington School District v. Schempp (1963)

Alliance for Progress

Arms Control and Disarmament Act (1961)

Assassination of President Kennedy (1963)

Baker v. Carr (1962)

Battle of Ap Bac (1963)

Bay of Pigs (1961)

Berlin Crisis

Birmingham Church Bombing (1963)

Birmingham Riots (1963)

Buddhist Uprising in Vietnam (1963)

Civil Rights Policies

Clean Air Act (1963)

Communications Satellite Act (1962)

Community Mental Health Centers Act (1963)

Coup Against Ngo Dinh Diem (1963)

Cuban Missile Crisis (1962)

Education Legislation

Engel v. Vitale (1962)

Equal Pay Act (1963)

Farm Policy

The Feminine Mystique, by Betty Friedan (1963)

First U.S. Space Flight (1961)

Freedom Rides (1961)

Gideon v. Wainwright (1963)

Health Professions Education Assistance Act (1963)

Housing Act (1961)

Kefauver-Harris Drug Amendments (1962)

Kennedy v. Mendoza-Martinez (1963)

Laotian Crisis

Limited Test Ban Treaty (1963)

Manpower Development and Training Act (1962)

Mapp v. Ohio (1961)

March on Washington for Jobs and Freedom
(1963)

Minimum Wage Legislation (1961)

Mutual Educational and Cultural Exchange Act
(1961)

New Frontier

Peace Corps

Pop Art Movement

President's Commission on the Status of
Women

Rules Committee Fight (1961)

Silent Spring, by Rachel Carson (1962)

Space Program

Steel Crisis (1962)

Strategic Hamlet Program (1962)

Tax Cut Proposals

Trade Expansion Act (1962)

University of Mississippi Integration Crisis
(1962)

Vienna Summit (1961)

Vietnam War

Vocational Education Act (1963)

JOHNSON ADMINISTRATION
(1963–1969) **426**

1968 Democratic National Convention

Act to Eliminate the Gold Reserve against
Federal Reserve Notes (1968)

Age Discrimination in Employment Act (1967)

Agent Orange

Air Quality Control Act (1967)

Alcoholic Rehabilitation Act (1968)

American Independent Party Emerges (1968)

Antiwar March on the Pentagon (1967)

Assassination of Malcolm X (1965)

Assassination of Martin Luther King, Jr. (1968)

Assassination of Robert F. Kennedy (1968)

Battle of Hue (1968)

Beautification Program

Body Counts

Child Nutrition Act (1966)

Civil Rights Act (1964)

Civil Rights Act (1968)

Comprehensive Health Planning Act (1966)

Department of Housing and Urban
Development Act (1965)

Department of Transportation Act (1966)

Detroit Riot (1967)

Drug Abuse Control Amendments (1965)

Duncan v. Louisiana (1968)

Economic Opportunity Act (1964)

Economic Opportunity Amendments (1967)

Elementary and Secondary Education Act
(1965)

Federal Cigarette Labeling and Advertising Act
(1965)

Food and Agriculture Act (1965)

Food Stamp Act (1964)

Freedom of Information Act (1966)

Ginzburg v. United States (1966)

Great Society

Griswold v. Connecticut (1965)

Gulf of Tonkin Resolution (1964)

Head Start

Heart of Atlanta Motel v. United States (1964)

Higher Education Act (1965)

Historic Preservation Act (1966)

Ho Chi Minh Trail

Housing and Urban Development Act (1965)

Housing and Urban Development Act (1968)

Immigration and Nationality Act Amendments
(1965)

"Johnson Treatment"

Katzenbach v. McClung (1964)

Kerner Commission

Maddox and *C. Turner Joy* Attacks (1964)

Marines Landed at Danang (1965)

Media Relations

Medicaid Act (1965)

Medicare Act (1965)

Miranda v. Arizona (1966)

Mississippi Burning Trial *(United States v. Price
et al.)* (1966)

Model Cities Program

Motor Vehicle Air Pollution Control Act (1965)

My Lai Massacre (1968)

Narcotic Addict Rehabilitation Act (1966)

National Foundation on the Arts and Humanities Act (1965)

National Traffic and Motor Vehicle Safety Act (1966)

Newark Riot (1967)

New Left/Antiwar Movement

New York City Blackout (1965)

New York Times v. Sullivan (1964)

Nuclear Nonproliferation Treaty (1968–1970)

Omnibus Crime Control and Safe Streets Act (1968)

Operation Rolling Thunder (1965–1968)

Poor People's March on Washington (Poor People's Campaign) (1968)

Pueblo Incident (1968)

Reynolds v. Sims (1964)

Selma Protests (1965)

Sheppard v. Maxwell (1966)

Siege of Khe Sanh (1967–1968)

Six-Day War (1967)

Space Program

Supreme Court Appointments

Terry v. Ohio (1968)

Tet Offensive (1968)

Trial of Lenny Bruce (1964)

Unsafe At Any Speed, by Ralph Nader (1965)

Urban Mass Transportation Act (1964)

Voting Rights Act (1965)

War on Poverty

Warren Commission

Water Quality Control Act (1965)

Watts Riot (1965)

Wilderness Act (1964)

NIXON ADMINISTRATION (1969–1974) **510**

Affirmative Action Policy

Antiballistic Missile Systems Treaty (1972)

Antiwar March, Washington, D.C. (1971)

Apollo 11 Lands on the Moon (1969)

Assassination Attempt Against George Wallace (1972)

"Battle of the Sexes" (1973)

Branzburg v. Hayes (1972)

Cambodian Bombings and Invasion

Charles Manson Murders (1969)

Chicago 8 Trial (1969–1970)

Child Nutrition Act Amendments (1972)

Christmas Bombings (1972)

Clean Air Act (1970)

Coastal Zone Management Act (1972)

Comprehensive Drug Abuse Prevention and Control Act (1970)

Comprehensive Employment and Training Act (1973)

Congressional Budget and Impoundment Control Act (1974)

Consumer Product Safety Act (1972)

Détente

Easter Offensive (1972)

Emergency Petroleum Allocation Act (1973)

Endangered Species Act (1973)

Equal Credit Opportunity Act (1974)

Family Educational Rights and Privacy Act (1974)

Federal Election Campaign Act (1971)

Federal Water Pollution Control Act Amendments (1972)

Frontiero v. Richardson (1973)

Furman v. Georgia (1972)

General Revenue Sharing

Hanoi Hilton

Housing and Community Development Act (1974)

Impeachment Hearings and Resignation of President Nixon (1974)

Jackson State College Shootings (1970)

Kennedy Center for the Performing Arts Opens (1971)

Kent State University Shootings (1970)

Kidnapping of Patricia Hearst (1974)

Milliken v. Bradley (1974)

Moratorium Demonstrations (1969)

Napalm

National Environmental Policy Act (1969)

National Mass Transportation Assistance Act (1974)

New York Times Co. v. United States (1971)

Occupational Safety and Health Act (1970)

Oil Embargo (1973–1974)

Organized Crime Control Act (1970)

Paris Peace Talks

Plumbers

Public Health Cigarette Smoking Act (1970)

Railway Passenger Service Act (1970)

Regional Rail Reorganization Act (1973)

Rehabilitation Act (1973)

Roe v. Wade (1973)

Safe Drinking Water Act (1974)

San Antonio Independent School District v. Rodriguez (1973)

Saturday Night Massacre (1973)

Skylab Mission (1973)

Stonewall Inn Riots (1969)

Supplemental Security Income Program

Supreme Court Appointments

Swann v. Charlotte-Mecklenburg Board of Education (1971)

Tax Reform Act (1969)

Title IX of the Education Amendments (1972)

Title X of the Public Health Service Act (1970)

Trade Act (1974)

Trans-Alaska Pipeline Authorization Act (1973)

Twenty-sixth Amendment (1971)

United States v. Nixon (1974)

U.S. Troops Evacuate Vietnam (1973)

Vietnamization Policy

Visit to China (1972)

Wage and Price Controls (1971)

War Powers Act (1973)

White House Tapes

Woodstock Music Festival (1969)

Documents

HOOVER ADMINISTRATION **50**

President Herbert C. Hoover, Inaugural Address, March 4, 1929

President Hoover, Statement on Public Works and Unemployment, January 3, 1930

President Hoover, Veto of the Muscle Shoals Resolution, March 3, 1931

President Hoover, Statement about Signing the Reconstruction Finance Corporation Act, January 22, 1932

ROOSEVELT ADMINISTRATION **176**

President Franklin D. Roosevelt, Inaugural Address, March 4, 1933

President Roosevelt, Fireside Chat on Banking, March 12, 1933

President Roosevelt, Press Conference [about *Schechter Poultry Corp. v. United States*], May 31, 1935

President Roosevelt, Address at Barnesville, Georgia, August 11, 1938

President Roosevelt, State of the Union Address [regarding the "Four Freedoms"], January 6, 1941

President Roosevelt, Address to Congress Requesting a Declaration of War with Japan, December 8, 1941

President Roosevelt, Excerpts from the Press Conference on D-Day, June 6, 1944

Joint Statement of Roosevelt, Churchill, and Stalin at the Yalta Conference, February 11, 1945

TRUMAN ADMINISTRATION **249**

President Harry S. Truman, Statement Announcing the Use of the Atomic Bomb at Hiroshima, August 6, 1945

White House Statement Concerning Controls Over the Price and Distribution of Meat, May 3, 1946

President Truman, Special Message to Congress on Greece and Turkey: The Truman Doctrine, March 12, 1947

President Truman, Radio Address to the American People on the Veto of the Taft-Hartley Bill, June 20, 1947

President Truman, Statement Announcing Recognition of the State of Israel, May 14, 1948

President Truman, Address to the American People on the Situation in Korea, July 19, 1950

EISENHOWER ADMINISTRATION **317**

President Dwight D. Eisenhower, Statement upon Signing the Submerged Lands Act, May 22, 1953

President Eisenhower, Letter to the Shah of Iran Concerning the Settlement of the Oil Problem, released August 5, 1954; dated August 4, 1954

President Eisenhower, Statement upon Signing the Communist Control Act, August 24, 1954

President Eisenhower, Telegram to Senator Russell of Georgia Regarding the Use of Federal Troops at Little Rock, September 27, 1957

President Eisenhower, News Conference regarding *Sputnik*, October 9, 1957

President Eisenhower, Farewell Address to the American People, January 17, 1961

KENNEDY ADMINISTRATION 381

President John F. Kennedy, Inaugural Address, January 20, 1961

President Kennedy, Statement Concerning Interference with the Freedom Riders in Alabama, May 20, 1961

President Kennedy, Radio and Television Report to the American People on the Soviet Arms Buildup in Cuba, October 22, 1962

President Kennedy, Commencement Address at American University in Washington, June 10, 1963

President Kennedy, News Conference [regarding Vietnam], November 14, 1963

JOHNSON ADMINISTRATION 450

President Lyndon B. Johnson, Remarks upon Arrival at Andrews Air Force Base, November 22, 1963

President Johnson, "Let us Continue" Address Before a Joint Session of Congress, November 27, 1963

President Johnson, Address Following Renewed Aggression in the Gulf of Tonkin, August 4, 1964

President Johnson, Special Message to Congress: The American Promise, March 15, 1965

President Johnson, News Conference, April 1, 1965

President Johnson, Address to the Nation Announcing Steps to Limit the War in Vietnam and Reporting His Decision Not to Seek Reelection, March 31, 1968

NIXON ADMINISTRATION 539

President Richard M. Nixon, Telegram to the Crew of *Apollo 9,* March 13, 1969

President Nixon, Letter to President Ho Chi Minh of the Democratic Republic of Vietnam, November 3, 1969

President Nixon, Statement on the Deaths of Four Students at Kent State University, May 4, 1970

President Nixon, Address to the Nation Outlining a New Economic Policy: "The Challenge of Peace," August 15, 1971

President Nixon, Question-and-Answer Session at the Annual Convention of the Associated Press Managing Editors Association, November 17, 1973

President Nixon, Address to the Nation Announcing His Decision to Resign the Office of President of the United States, August 8, 1974

SPECIAL FEATURES

First Ladies

Lou Henry Hoover 4
Eleanor Roosevelt 58
Bess Truman 194
Mamie Eisenhower 258
Jacqueline Kennedy 328
Lady Bird Johnson 392
Pat Nixon 462

Vice Presidents

Charles Curtis 12
John Nance Garner 68
Henry A. Wallace 86
Alben Barkley 204
Hubert H. Humphrey 404
Spiro T. Agnew 480

Social History

Lou Henry Hoover, the Rise of Girl Scouting, and the Rapidan Plan
   for Depression Relief 20
Roosevelt, the Fireside Chats, and the Rise of Radio 100
Truman, Housing Policy, and the Rise of Levittown 209
Ike Loves Lucy: Eisenhower and the Rise of Television 278
The Kennedys and the Baby Boom 345
The Johnsons, Beautification, and the New Environmentalism 414
Nixon and Elvis: The Story Behind the Picture 492

Herbert C. Hoover

August 10, 1874–October 20, 1964

Thirty-first President of the United States
March 4, 1929–March 4, 1933

≈≥ HERBERT C. HOOVER ≥≈

Place of Birth: West Branch, Iowa

Date of Birth: August 10, 1874

Places of Residence: Iowa, California

Class Background: poor

Father's Career: blacksmith and farm implement dealer

Mother's Career: homemaker

Number of Siblings: two

Religion: Quaker

Education: graduated Stanford University, 1895

Political Party: Republican

Military Service: none

Spouse: Lou Henry Hoover

Spouse's Education: graduated from Stanford University, 1898

Spouse's Career: public service, leader of numerous women's voluntary associations, homemaker

Number of Children: two

Sports and Hobbies: fishing, medicine ball

Career Prior to the Presidency: mining engineer, founder and director of the Commission for Relief in Belgium during World War I, head of the Food Administration during World War I, member of federal and international economic organizations, secretary of commerce

Age upon Entering the White House: 54 years, 206 days

Reason for Leaving the White House: was defeated for a second term by Franklin D. Roosevelt

Career after the Presidency: chair of the first and second Hoover Commission, writer, public speaker

Date of Death: October 20, 1964

Cause of Death: bleeding from upper gastrointestinal tract, strained vascular system

Last Words: unknown

Burial Site: West Branch, Iowa

Value of Estate at Time of Death: unknown, in the millions

BIOGRAPHY OF HOOVER

Son of Jesse and Hulda Minthorn Hoover, Herbert Clark Hoover was born in West Branch, Iowa, on August 10, 1874. His father was a blacksmith and a farm implement dealer and his mother was a homemaker. When young Herbert was just six years old, his father died of a heart attack, and his mother sought comfort in her Quaker faith. Because she performed religious work for the Quakers, Hulda Hoover was often away from home. Four years after her husband's death she contracted pneumonia when traveling home from a revival meeting. Her death left Herbert and his siblings, Theodore and May, orphans and they were sent to live with different relatives.

When Herbert, just 11 years old, left in November 1885 to live with his aunt and uncle, John and Laura Minthorn, in Oregon, he took the values of his rural midwestern Quaker upbringing with him. Simple attire and a frank, brusque manner characterized the young man, and he retained these habits for the remainder of his life. He had also picked up an appreciation for education. He approached his studies and the problems he encountered from a rational perspective. Along with these traits, Hoover had gained from his religion a social conscience. He believed in peace, and he wanted society to improve its treatment of American Indians, prisoners, and African Americans. The pragmatic tendencies within Hoover caused him also to appreciate the importance of the business community to society. As an adult, then, he mixed Quaker tenets with the realities of the mining and engineering world. He smoked, swore, drank alcohol, and fished on Sundays.

The Minthorns ran a preparatory school, which young Herbert attended for three years. He also worked for the Oregon Land Company at his uncle's behest. Hoover enjoyed the trade and took classes to prepare himself for a career in business. He sought further education at the newly created Stanford University, entering its pioneer class in 1891. Because his academic credentials were not sufficient, Hoover took remedial classes to ensure his success at Stanford. He studied geology, and he benefited from the opportunity to work summers with the U.S. Geological Survey. Hoover proved himself something of an entrepreneur at college, serving as student body treasurer, working a paper route, building a laundry service, and improving the profits for athletic events. While a student, he also met the woman who would become his life partner, fellow geology major and outdoorswoman Lou Henry.

Herbert Hoover from childhood to early adulthood. From left, the future president appears at around age five in West Branch, Iowa; a schoolboy of 12 in 1886 in Newberg, Oregon; at the age of 17 shortly before entering Stanford University; and as a young mining engineer in 1904 at the age of 30. *(Associated Press)*

LOU HENRY HOOVER

(1874–1944) *first lady of the United States, March 4, 1929–March 4, 1933*

Born on March 29, 1874, to Florence Weed Henry and Charles Delano Henry, Lou Henry was the oldest of two daughters. A younger sister, Jean, was born in 1882. Lou Henry's father was a banker and her mother was a homemaker. The Henry family lived in Waterloo, Iowa, until the mid-1880s when they migrated to California. Throughout her childhood, Lou enjoyed an atypical upbringing. She frequently went camping, fishing, and hiking with her father. These experiences gave her a life-long appreciation of nature.

Lou's parents encouraged her to transcend the normative gender roles of late 19th-century America in other ways. When she finished her public schooling, she enrolled first at Los Angeles Normal School and then at San Jose Normal School. She graduated in 1893 with a teaching certificate. Unsure of her career direction, Lou worked at her father's bank for about a year. When she heard a Stanford University geology professor give a public lecture, Lou discovered an intellectual outlet that meshed perfectly with her personality and her love of the outdoors. She matriculated to Stanford that fall, where she met fellow geology major Herbert Hoover. After discovering their common Iowa background, their passion for geology, and their affection for the outdoors, the two developed a close relationship, which they sustained through correspondence after Herbert's graduation in 1895 and Lou's in 1898.

Gender stereotyping influenced the job search for the couple. While Herbert quickly worked his way up to supervisor for all Chinese mining operations at the British firm of Bewick, Moreing and Company, Lou could not find a position befitting her education. She even lamented to a friend that her life would be so much better if her degree, an A.B., stood for a boy. After a year of fruitless job searching and volunteer work with the American Red Cross, she considered returning to Stanford for graduate work, but her plans changed when Herbert telegraphed her a marriage proposal. The two were wed in a civil ceremony on February 10, 1899, and their honeymoon took place aboard ship on the way to China.

Lou savored life in Asia, learning Chinese and developing a life-long interest in collecting fine Chinese porcelain. In 1900, Lou and Herbert, who were living in Tientsin (now Tianjin), found themselves in the middle of the Boxer Rebellion, an uprising against foreigners engaged in business and missionary work in China. Westerners in Tientsin built barricades, and Lou Henry Hoover, in anticipation of her work in future crises, rode her bicycle around the barricades, carried a weapon, treated the sick, and helped run a dairy.

In 1902, the Hoovers moved to London, where Herbert assumed a partnership in Bewick, Moreing. In the decade that

Lou Henry Hoover *(Library of Congress)*

Hoover continued his courtship of Lou Henry after he graduated from Stanford. The couple communicated via letters and telegrams, and Hoover even used the latter to propose marriage in 1899. Lou Henry and Herbert Hoover married in a civil ceremony at her parents' home on February 10 of that year. They spent their honeymoon aboard a ship to China where Herbert Hoover was working in the mining industry.

Hoover began his career in the mining profession as a day laborer in California. His work ethic earned him a promotion. By March 1897 the London firm of Bewick, Moreing hired him to find new gold mines in western Australia. Hoover

built a successful record, and in two years he was promoted to chief engineer for the Chinese Engineering and Mining Company. There he developed several significant coal mines. The Hoovers' stay in China coincided with the Boxer Rebellion, an uprising against foreigners engaged in business and missionary work in China. During this conflict, Hoover secured the title to these mines. Bewick, Moreing compensated him with a partnership, which necessitated a move to London. Once the couple relocated to London, they had two sons: Herbert Charles Hoover, Jr., was born on August 4, 1903, and Allan Henry Hoover was born on July 17, 1907.

followed, Lou and Herbert had two sons and began raising their family: Herbert Charles Hoover, Jr., was born on August 4, 1903, and Allan Henry Hoover was born on July 17, 1907. Additionally, Lou oversaw a joint translation project with her husband, converting the 16th-century mining text, *De Re Metallica,* from Latin into English.

When World War I started in 1914, the Hoovers' lives changed forever. Philanthropic work and public service became the focus for both Lou and Herbert. Herbert became the director of the Commission for Relief in Belgium. Lou undertook parallel voluntary duties: She helped stranded American tourists gain safe passage from London back to the United States, she gave speeches in the United States to raise money for Belgian relief, and she helped facilitate the sale of Belgian lace in the United States, with the proceeds going to Belgian relief efforts. When the United States entered the war in 1917, Herbert became director of the newly created Food Administration, a part of the wartime bureaucracy of the Woodrow Wilson administration. Lou adapted well to life in Washington, D.C. She created and funded the Food Administration Club—a place offering wholesome lodging, food, and entertainment—for single women employed in various wartime agencies. Also during these years Lou Hoover became involved with the Girl Scouts.

Following Warren G. Harding's election as president, Herbert Hoover became secretary of commerce in 1921, a position he held for the next eight years through Calvin Coolidge's administration. During these years, Lou Henry Hoover served as the national president of the Girl Scouts between 1922 and 1925. She fine-tuned the organization's governmental structure, upgraded its financial security, and helped expand its favorable public image. She also held leadership posts with the fledgling National Amateur Athletic Federation and the Women's Division of the National Amateur Athletic Federation. With both organizations she championed the idea of play for play's sake as opposed to competing to win.

Following her husband's election to the presidency in 1928, Lou Henry Hoover combined traditional and modern approaches to her new post as first lady. She revolutionized White House entertaining by moving away from long, formal receiving lines to more informal clustered gatherings of guests. She understood that entertaining could serve the political needs of her husband's presidency and made decisions about who to invite to luncheons and dinners accordingly. She worked with an assistant to compile a history of the White House and its furnishings. Most important, she entertained Jessie DePriest, the wife of newly elected representative Oscar Stanton DePriest (R-IL), at a White House tea. Knowing the event would be controversial because the DePriests were African American, Hoover went to great lengths to ensure the tea would be unknown to the wider world before its staging. Still, the aftermath of the tea brought considerable negative public reaction, revealing the extent of racial prejudice in the country. This innovative civil rights stand was not the only first lady first for Lou Henry Hoover. She also was the first first lady to speak on the radio, a communication medium she used frequently during her husband's presidency to address significant public issues. She designed the presidential retreat at Camp Rapidan, Virginia, and she helped fund and build a school for nearby impoverished mountain children. Most important, she used her connections with Girl Scouting and other women's voluntary associations to develop a program for depression relief, which was run out of the East Wing of the White House. This reactive approach took the many pleas for assistance that poured into her White House office, investigated their merit, and sought the appropriate local agency to provide the necessary care for those individuals with valid problems.

After her husband's defeat in his 1932 reelection bid, Lou Henry Hoover welcomed the opportunity to return to her beloved Palo Alto, California. She continued her activism with the Girl Scouts, serving another term as the organization's president between 1935 and 1937. She also helped found Friends of Music at Stanford University, and she gave advice to conservative Republican women who shared her disdain for the Franklin D. Roosevelt administration. She died from a heart attack on January 7, 1944.

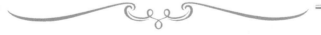

Hoover's primary responsibilities involved significant travel around the world to develop new mines. He developed silver, lead, and zinc mines in Myanmar (then known as Burma), zinc mines in Australia, and copper mines and petroleum fields in Russia. He became a millionaire from his work as a mining engineer. The last decade of the 19th century and the first 14 years of the 20th century proved the apex for the foreign mining industry, and Hoover was among the key players abroad. He became known as the doctor of sick mines, and he, often with his growing family, traveled the globe numerous times to diagnose and repair ailing operations. He undertook several publishing opportunities. He cooperated with Lou Henry Hoover on the translation of *De Re Metallica* from the 16th-century Latin original to English, he wrote articles about technical and financial issues pertinent to mining, and he authored a popular textbook, *Principles of Mining.* This work revealed his corporatist philosophy regarding the need for balancing the needs of laborers with the needs of managers and owners. Finally, Hoover served as president of the American Institute of Mining and Metallurgical Engineers.

Once World War I began in 1914, Hoover never again worked in the private sector. He accepted no salary for this or any of his subsequent public endeavors. He devoted the remainder of his life to public service in one form or another. His first meaningful endeavor was as head of the Commission for Relief in Belgium (CRB). After conversations with Walter Hines Page, the American ambassador to the Court of St. James in Great Britain, Belgian banking officials, and other representatives of neutral nations, Hoover made it his mission to work on behalf of Belgian relief. Concurrently with this responsibility, he spent the initial weeks of the war working with British officials to secure the safe return of American travelers to the United States. When the German army overran Belgium between August and October of 1914, it took all available food resources for its own needs. Without outside intervention, the Belgian people faced starvation. The German government disallowed any provisioning for the Belgian people that might appear to aid the French and the British. Only a relief effort undertaken by neutral nations could gain German approval. Hoover's duties included significant negotiation with both the Allied and the Central Powers, substantial fundraising work, efforts to purchase and distribute food and medicine, and public relations activities. Over the next four years, the CRB fed 9 million Belgians and later 2 million French citizens in the German-occupied north of France. Of Hoover's efforts, an appreciative Page remarked to President WOODROW WILSON: "Simple, modest, energetic little man who began his career in California and will end it in Heaven, and he doesn't want anyone's thanks."

After the United States declared war on Germany in 1917, President Wilson asked Hoover to assume leadership of the U.S. Food Administration, a government agency created for the express purpose of overseeing a voluntary rationing program and ensure distribution of food resources to those entities that needed it the most. Wilson tapped Hoover for this important post because of his reputation with the CRB, and he accepted. Hoover drew on his experiences with the CRB and emphasized volunteerism, both in terms of rationing food and fuel and in terms of staffing the new bureaucratic agency. Regarding the latter, Hoover employed numerous volunteers to assist with the work of the Food Administration. He oversaw the development of standardized package sizing. While he abhorred the notion of mandatory price controls, Hoover nonetheless helped implement the Lever Food Control Act of 1917, which established the long-term price of wheat. His failure to do anything about the escalating price of cotton, a fiber but not a foodstuff and not covered in wartime legislation, proved politically problematic for President Wilson and other Democrats. He also established meaningful relationships with the key businesses involved in food production, encouraging them to standardize their business practices. His goal was to control exorbitant business profits, but these methods failed. Finally, Hoover and his family encouraged food conserva-

tion by setting an example of their eating habits for the rest of the nation. Lou Henry Hoover cooperated with a leading women's magazine to publish information about the menus served at the Hoover table. He received wide commendation for his effective leadership.

Germany surrendered in 1918, and during the postwar period, Hoover became the director general of the American Relief Administration in Europe, a post he held from 1919 to 1920. European food needs in the immediate postwar period became a testing ground for Hoover. He saw the deprivations across the European continent as offering a perfect opportunity for meeting the dilemma posed by the overproduction of American foodstuffs. He lobbied Congress to provide $100 million in credit to the Allies for the purchase of agricultural produce from the United States. While working in this capacity, Hoover also played a critical role in the economic reconversion of Europe, helping to reestablish the infrastructure of capitalism. Hoover contended that food relief should also be provided to Germany, and he encouraged journalists to push for American acceptance of this program. Between 1919 and 1923, Hoover also oversaw food relief to the new Soviet Union, which suffered a devastating famine. He did so despite his extreme distaste for Bolshevism.

In each of these endeavors, Hoover amassed a successful public record, drawing the attention of the Republican Party and the Democratic Party, both of which wanted him to run for president under their respective banners in 1920. Hoover declined, but when WARREN G. HARDING, a Republican, became president in 1921, he accepted an appointment as secretary of commerce, a post he held until he became president of the United States eight years later. In the late 1910s and early 1920s, the years when Hoover first gained wide attention, he began publicizing his progressive but individualistic social philosophy. *American Individualism*, a book Hoover published in 1922, laid out his social and political beliefs: muted class distinctions, meritocracy, scientific expertise, civil liberties, and equality of opportunity. He also advocated numerous progressive causes, among which were a federal employment service, a home loan bank, a minimum wage, equal pay for men and women, the elimination of child labor, and a 48-hour work week.

Hoover became one of the most prominent figures in Washington during the 1920s, turning the Department of Commerce into an example of modern efficiency. Significant programs carried out during Hoover's tenure at the Commerce Department included modern theorizing about the business cycle, promoting industrial standardization, instituting federal regulations for the new radio and aeronautics industries, and providing federal supervision of foreign loans. For these and other endeavors as secretary of commerce, Hoover used the problems of the war era as a barometer to gauge the reform needs of the country. Expertise, voluntary regulation, and reliance on public conferences proved some of the most important tools Hoover used to implement his vision as secretary of commerce. He encouraged farmers to experiment with cooperative mar-keting and he argued against the various export debenture plans prominent in Congress, the most popular of which was the McNary-Haugen bill. (The export debenture plans

BIOGRAPHICAL TIME LINE

1874
August 10 Herbert Hoover is born in West Branch, Iowa.

1885
November 10 An orphaned Hoover moves to Oregon to live with his aunt and uncle, John and Laura Minthorn.

1895
May 26 Hoover graduates from Stanford University with a degree in geology, a member of the pioneering class.

1897
March Hoover is hired by the London firm of Bewick, Moreing and Co. to find new gold mines in western Australia.

1899
February 10 Hoover marries Lou Henry.

1901
December 18 Hoover is named a partner in Bewick, Moreing and Co.

1914
November 5 Hoover heads up the Commission for Relief in Belgium.

1917
President Woodrow Wilson asks Hoover to assume leadership of the U.S. Food Administration, a government agency created for the express purpose of overseeing a voluntary rationing program and ensure distribution of food resources to those entities that needed it the most.

1919
July 12 Hoover forms the American Relief Administration in postwar Europe.

1919–1923
Hoover oversees food relief for the new Soviet Union, which suffered a devastating famine.

1921
March 5 President Warren G. Harding appoints Hoover secretary of commerce, a position he holds until 1928.

1922
Hoover publishes *American Individualism*, laying out his social and political beliefs: muted class distinctions, meritocracy, scientific expertise, civil liberties, and equality of opportunity.

1928
November 6 Hoover is elected president of the United States.

1929
March 4 Hoover is inaugurated president.

1932
November 8 Hoover loses his reelection bid to Franklin Roosevelt.

1933
March 4 Hoover's last day as president.

1947
July 17 President Harry S. Truman appoints Hoover chairman of the Commission on Organization of the Executive Branch of Government (the Hoover Commission).

1949
Hoover turns in the Hoover Commission Report.

1955
The second Hoover Commission turns in its report to President Dwight Eisenhower.

1964
October 20 Hoover dies in New York City.

promised higher earnings for American farmers. Architects of the various plans argued that the higher prices on the domestic market could be achieved by encouraging traders to sell more agricultural produce abroad, thereby eliminating the domestic glut. Exporters would be encouraged to sell abroad by means of certificates, commonly called debentures, with a cash value to be used for payment of customs duties on any imported good. The holders of the debentures could use them or sell them to importers. The government would not cash the debentures but would see a decrease in customs duties from such a plan.) He achieved mixed results in seeking improved working conditions for industry. Hoover spent much time working with water development projects. He helped create the Colorado River Commission, a dam building endeavor, and he worked for the creation of the St. Lawrence Seaway (completed in 1959 after overcoming much political opposition). For the business community, Hoover pushed for creation of trade associations.

In 1928, CALVIN COOLIDGE announced that he would not run for reelection, opening the way for Hoover to enter the race. His extensive popularity made him a favorite even before the Republicans met in convention to name a candidate, and Hoover easily bested his opponents for the nomination. In addition to his many accomplishments during wartime and as secretary of commerce, his role in providing relief after the devastating 1927 flood along the Mississippi River helped boost his public image. The general election in 1928 pitted Hoover against Alfred E. Smith, a New York City Democrat who was then governor of the Empire State. Whereas Hoover, with his rural, Protestant roots, appealed to middle-American sensibilities, Smith's urban, Irish-Catholic identity troubled many in the country critical of the demographic shifts raised by the massive immigration of the last half century. Hoover played into the country's ethnocultural divide by supporting Prohibition while Smith campaigned as an avowed opponent of temperance. During the campaign, Hoover made numerous hopeful statements about the economy, for example promising, "given a chance to go forward with the policies of the last eight years, and we shall soon with the help of God be in sight of the day when poverty will be banished from this Nation." Hoover's victory can be understood as a last gasp for the traditional political alignment of the country, for Smith's competitiveness suggested the likelihood of a significant partisan realignment.

During Hoover's presidency, Lou and Herbert Hoover's elder son, Herbert, Jr., contracted tuberculosis. This disease of the lungs often lasted several years, and it was characterized by excessive coughing, general malaise, and fever. The most common treatment involved convalescence in a sanatorium, ideally located in a dry climate. Furthermore doctors recommended sleeping outdoors or at least with the windows open. Because President Hoover could not tolerate the thought of his son recuperating far away in the desert South-

west, Herbert, Jr. spent his recovery in Asheville, North Carolina. President Hoover had time for only one visit, though. Herbert, Jr.'s wife, Margaret, and their two children lived in the White House for the duration of the treatment. At the same time, Hoover's younger son, Allan, was a student at Stanford University and rarely even visited the White House.

Not only was the presidency filled with personal crisis for the Hoover family, but also it came to be dominated by one of the biggest crises in the nation's history—the GREAT DEPRESSION. From his March 4, 1929, inauguration through the late summer, Hoover was able to define his work in the White House. The AGRICULTURAL MARKETING ACT was passed, creating the FEDERAL FARM BOARD. Debate commenced on the SMOOT-HAWLEY TARIFF, which was not enacted until 1930 and which implemented a protective tariff.

Once the stock market crashed in October, the nation's economic woes dominated politics in Washington, D.C., and across the nation for the rest of his presidency. Even though Hoover was far more activist than any of his predecessors who faced economic panics, he was never again fully in control of the events his administration faced. Still, Hoover advocated public works spending as a curative for the economic woes. He pushed for two different federal agencies to coordinate relief (the PRESIDENT'S EMERGENCY COMMITTEE FOR EMPLOYMENT and its successor, the PRESIDENT'S ORGANIZATION ON UNEMPLOYMENT RELIEF) as well as the Reconstruction Finance Corporation to loan money to troubled banks, industries, and railroads. Because his rather dour demeanor prevented him from connecting directly with the American people in showing that he understood the human extent of the nation's suffering, Hoover garnered a reputation for not caring about the miseries engendered by the depression.

Ultimately, Hoover's foreign policy became tied to the Great Depression, but early in his administration he worked to better U.S. relations with Latin America. He played a role in the London Naval Disarmament Conference of 1930, but once market conditions worsened, he argued that because the depression was worldwide in origin it similarly needed a global solution.

His fatal error was the decision in 1932 to order the U.S. Army to remove the Bonus Marchers, veterans of World War I, from their encampments in and around Washington, D.C. These individuals had marched from across the country to the nation's capital to lobby for the early payment of the World War I soldiers' bonus, but many lawmakers and the president had been cool to their presence. The firefight that resulted helped ensure FRANKLIN D. ROOSEVELT's victory over Hoover in the presidential election of 1932.

When the Hoovers left Washington in 1933, Herbert Hoover turned his attention to writing. His 1934 book, *The Challenge to Liberty,* cautioned that the New Deal would result in fascism. His eight-volume publication, *Addresses Upon the American Road,* published between 1936 and 1961

President-elect Herbert Hoover and his wife Lou are seated at a table, joined by their family on November 9, 1928. Standing behind Hoover *(left)* is his son, Allan Hoover. His daughter-in-law, Margaret Hoover, stands next to her husband, Herbert Hoover, Jr., while their daughter, Peggy Ann Hoover, sits with her grandmother. *(Associated Press)*

further developed Hoover's criticisms of Roosevelt and the New Deal. *America's First Crusade,* published in 1941, laid out Hoover's perspective on how to achieve peace in the world and his opposition to U.S. participation in World War II (Hoover supported intervention after Pearl Harbor). His other significant literary endeavor was the publication of his memoirs in three volumes (1951–52). Additional publica-

tions included a book about Woodrow Wilson and a multivolume treatise on American relief activities.

Hoover enjoyed one of the longest post-presidential careers—31 years—but neither the Republicans nor the Democrats wanted much to do with the man whom many Americans blamed for the misery of the depression. As such, Hoover devoted much time and money to private charitable work. He raised tens of millions of dollars for various causes. He became involved with the Boys Clubs of America. Hoover had little to do with the federal government until World War II reproduced some of the same problems with which Hoover had contended in Belgium and France during World War I. In the pre- and postwar periods, Hoover assisted Presidents Franklin D. Roosevelt and HARRY S. TRUMAN with food relief policy.

Hoover did not approve of dropping the atomic bomb on Japan to end World War II. Rather, he argued in favor of an unconditional surrender by Japan and believed that a strong Soviet role in Asia and Eastern Europe were in America's best interest. Hoover did not fall into either dominant camp of interventionism or isolationism in the postwar period. He was less concerned with the supposed threat of communism than most Americans in or out of politics. Convinced of the dominance of American capitalism throughout the world,

Hoover worried little about the dangers posed by Soviet communism. Hoover argued that the example of American economic and political success was a much more successful weapon against communism than either the creation of the North Atlantic Treaty Organization or the battles waged in fighting the Korean War. Likewise, Hoover opposed U.S. intervention in Vietnam.

Hoover's most significant public service after he left the presidency came with his chairmanship of the two Commissions on Organization of the Executive Branch of the Government (1947–49 and 1953–55). So associated was he with these two endeavors that they were known in public as the Hoover Commissions. The impetus for these commissions came from the political problems posed by a burgeoning bureaucracy that ensued in the wake of World War II and the Korean War. The first Hoover Commission issued its report to President Truman in 1949, and it has been regarded

Following his death on October 20, 1964, former president Herbert Hoover lay in state at the U.S. Capitol. Above, President Lyndon Johnson bows his head after placing a wreath on the bier. *(Library of Congress)*

as a success. It examined in-depth the wartime expansion of the federal government and issued recommendations on how more results could be accomplished with less money. Approximately 70 percent of the proposals were enacted into law. The second Hoover Commission issued its report to President DWIGHT D. EISENHOWER in 1955, but received lower marks than the previous endeavor, largely because its recommendations were considered to be too conservative. Hoover complained that Eisenhower gave less attention to his proposals than had Truman in the previous decade. Nonetheless, officials in the administration of President JOHN F. KENNEDY in the early 1960s praised the report for its cost-saving proposals.

Before his death on October 20, 1964, Hoover helped establish the Herbert Hoover Presidential Library at West Branch, Iowa, and the Hoover Institution on War, Revolution, and Peace at Stanford University. In the years between 1933 when he left the presidency and his death in 1964, Hoover remade himself from failed politician blamed by many for the Great Depression to respected elder statesman. After Truman called him back into public service, Hoover became an unofficial adviser to presidents of both political parties. He worked eight to 12 hours a day almost until his death. His complex legacy remains important for those who wish to understand the transformations that the United States underwent in the 20th century.

PRESIDENTIAL ELECTION OF 1928

The 1928 presidential election both reached back to the past and forward to the future. The radio functioned as the principal campaign communications tool employed by the two candidates, marking the first time this new medium played a major role in American politics. Republican candidate Herbert Hoover and Democratic candidate Alfred E. Smith each embodied various components of modernity. Hoover, as a mining engineer, embodied the new faith in scientific progress and technology while Smith, through his Catholicism and his Irish immigrant background as well as his New York City roots, encapsulated the emerging politics of plurality and diversity. The forces of tradition also played a role in the symbolism of the campaign. Hoover suggested that his victory could bring a return to America's rural past, and rural voters overwhelmingly rejected Smith and the urban vision he brought before the voters. Whereas Hoover was uncomfortable in the role of candidate, Smith thrived on interaction with the voters. Even Republicans complained of Hoover's conventional demeanor and attire.

Republicans did not lack for aspirants for the presidency in 1928 nor were the most common names discussed men without talent. In fact, the reverse was true. The field included Vice President Charles G. Dawes, former Illinois governor Frank Lowden, Supreme Court justice and former secretary of state Charles Evans Hughes, World War I military hero General John J. Pershing, and several influential senators, among whom were George W. Norris (Nebraska), James E. Watson (Indiana), CHARLES CURTIS (Kansas), and Guy D. Goff (West Virginia). Compared to these individuals, Herbert Hoover had amassed but a scant resumé of political accomplishment, having never been elected to a single office or even run a campaign.

Hoover possessed, however, a significant record of accomplishment, having enjoyed a successful career as a mining engineer, planned the relief of occupied Belgium and guided the Food Administration both during World War I, and served as commerce secretary during the 1920s in the administrations of Presidents WARREN G. HARDING and CALVIN COOLIDGE. As a result, he quickly became the favorite for his party's nomination when the conventioneers arrived in Kansas City, Missouri, in mid-June 1928. Among his positive traits were a behind-the-scenes work ethic and a disdain for "politics" and a nonpartisan approach to public policy together with his administrative acumen, his humanitarianism, and his commitment to scientific expertise and efficiency. Furthermore, Hoover outstripped his Republican adversaries in political fund-raising, organization, and public recognition.

Delegates from farm states opposed the Hoover candidacy despite the fact that the Iowan shared much of their rural outlook. In one key area, though, Hoover failed the agricultural bloc: He opposed any and all export debenture plans to inflate prices on the domestic market by encouraging increased exports with the provision of certificates that could be used to cover import duties on any good being shipped to the United States. Hoover's moderation ran counter to the agrarian radicalism of the late 19th and early 20th centuries. Even this difference prompted little in the way of convention fireworks. Instead, the keynote address proved dull as did the report from the Resolutions Committee. Only the permanent chairman provided some excitement, promising conventioneers that the Republicans would be ready to meet the challenge posed by the Democratic candidate, as yet unknown. Even though Hoover meddled little in the drafting of the party's platform, the document proved satisfactory to the candidate. It called for the continuation of Prohibition, a cooperative farm policy, government efficiency, reduced spending, continued tariff protection, assistance for labor, and positive foreign relations.

On the third day of the convention proceedings, the roll call of states began for the purpose of choosing the nominee. The Alabama delegation yielded to California so that the delegation from Hoover's adopted state—he had lived in California and attended college at Stanford—could be the first to nominate him for the presidency. While the demonstration

CHARLES CURTIS

(1860–1936) *vice president of the United States, March 4, 1929–March 4, 1933*

Charles Curtis was born on January 25, 1860, to Orren Arms Curtis, a soldier, and Ellen Gonville Pappan, a quarter-blood Kansa (Kaw) Indian. This heritage made Curtis the only person with Indian blood elected to the vice presidency. Curtis spent the majority of his formative years under the care of his paternal grandmother, Permelia Hubbard Curtis, because his mother died in 1863 and his father was frequently away from home. In 1866, his maternal grandmother, Julie Gonville Pappan, took Curtis to live with her on the Kaw Indian Reservation near Council Grove, Kansas. Young Charles returned to his grandmother Curtis's home a few years later as a result of the Kaw removal to Indian Territory and the closing of the school he attended.

Educated in Topeka, Kansas, Charles Curtis worked a number of odd jobs as a youth until he was admitted to the bar in 1881. Three years later, he married Anna E. Baird, and the couple had three children: Permelia, Harry King, and Leona. In addition to the practice of law, Curtis became involved in real estate development in part as a result of inheriting Indian allotment land from his grandmother. Curtis's investments proved profitable, and he used his experience as evidence to argue in favor of land allotments as a path to Indian assimilation.

Politics also attracted Curtis's attention, and he became involved in the local Republican Party. His first elected office, county attorney for Shawnee County, came in 1884, and the recent enactment of Prohibition by the Kansas legislature provided Curtis the opportunity to attract significant public attention to his position. He closed the now illegal bars operating in the state capital.

In 1892, at the height of the Populist movement, Curtis nonetheless gained election to the U.S. House of Representatives as a conservative Republican. He possessed a gift for speaking directly with the people, and he arranged his office operations to give priorities to constituent service issues such as Civil War pension requests. His half sister, Dolly Gann, was the secretary in his office responsible for this particular job, and the index card system she maintained on Kansas was remarkably thorough. These factors, combined with his attention to constituents' needs, made him a formidable candidate at each election.

Curtis used his Indian heritage to facilitate his political career, making Indian issues a centerpiece of his legislative strat-

Charles Curtis *(Library of Congress)*

was planned, it was also heartfelt. The chairman of the California delegation was a close friend of Hoover's, and he extolled the presumptive nominee's many positive characteristics. With Hoover's more serious contenders—Dawes, Lowden, Hughes, and Pershing—out of the race after they had calculated the impossibility of besting the popular secretary of commerce, all that remained was the nomination of the remaining candidates, none of whom had a chance, and the tallying of state delegation votes to make official the Hoover nomination. His first ballot victory was nearly unanimous. Instead of naming his choice for the vice presidency, Hoover left the decision up to the convention, and the delegates tapped Senator Curtis of Kansas. Curtis initially opposed the idea, going so far as to question whether or not Hoover subscribed to ortho-

dox Republican views, but he ultimately congratulated the nominee and accepted the vice-presidential nomination. The Republican platform endorsed the policies of Calvin Coolidge, and it included a call for frugal government, a protective tariff, opposition to the cancellation of foreign debts, and support for efforts to ensure permanent world peace.

The Democrats gathered in Houston, Texas, for their convention two weeks after the Republican conclave. Managing to avoid a repeat of the calamitous 1924 convention when it had taken delegates an unprecedented 103 ballots to decide on a nominee, the Democrats selected New York governor Alfred E. Smith on the first ballot. Smith enjoyed a unique biography in American politics. While numerous leaders had risen from humble, rural roots, Smith was the first national egy. This point, though, was paradoxical because Curtis had been removed from the Kaw tribe years earlier in 1878 for failure to participate in tribal affairs and move to Indian Territory. That decision had resulted in part from his maternal grandmother's advice that he separate from the tribe. Legislation bearing his name, the Curtis Act of 1898, proved an important turning point in the history of Indian politics. It eliminated tribal courts, disbanded the Five Civilized Tribes (the Cherokees, Choctaws, Creeks, Seminoles, and Chickasaws) that had been removed from the southeastern United States in the 1820s and 1830s to present-day Oklahoma, and helped ensure that Oklahoma would become a state in 1907. As such, the Curtis Act was the most important piece of Indian legislation between 1887 and 1934.

In 1903, Curtis became chair of the House Committee on Indian Affairs. Contradictions abounded in his Indian policy. While he defended the rights of Indian women and children of Indian and white parentage, Curtis also worked as an attorney for the energy companies that exploited Indians, taking their mineral rights with little or no compensation in return. In other ways, his Indian politics were self-serving: He oversaw the allotments for the Kaw tribe, an act that regained him his tribal membership and a right to a portion of the Kaw allotment that was dispensed in 1902. His political style in all of these dealings was to work behind the scenes. Curtis viewed formal debate, either in committee or on the House floor, as counterproductive when compared with political deal making.

Curtis remained in the House of Representatives until 1907 when the Kansas state legislature elected him to the U.S. Senate to fill an unexpired term that ran from mid-January to early March 1907. The legislature also elected him to the full six-year term beginning in March 1907. He was defeated in 1912 when he sought reelection to the post largely because he had supported the high-tariff Payne-Aldrich Act of 1909. That law had brought a split in the Republican Party between progressives, who opposed high tariffs, and conservatives, who supported them. (The Seventeenth Amendment to the Constitution, having been passed by Congress in 1912 and ratified in 1913, provided for popular election of U.S. senators.) In 1914, however, Curtis regained a U.S. Senate seat when the voters of Kansas sent him back to Washington, D.C. Reelected in 1920 and 1926, Curtis remained in the Senate until 1929 when he became vice president. As a senator, Curtis worked with and ultimately entered the leadership. He chaired the Senate Rules Committee, gained the post of party whip in 1915, and remained in that position until 1924, when, upon the death of Senate Majority Leader Henry Cabot Lodge, he was elevated to that office.

Ambitious for the presidency, Curtis opposed Herbert Hoover for the Republican nomination in 1928, arguing that Hoover could never win. Many in Washington assumed Curtis was President Calvin Coolidge's choice for the Republican nomination, and even Hoover privately noted Curtis "was a natural selection for Mr. Coolidge's type of mind." After Hoover gained the nomination, Curtis was named as the vice-presidential candidate. Republican managers at the convention wanted a farm state candidate for the number two spot on the ticket, especially since Hoover did not have the best reputation among agrarians. The presidential candidate had first earned the enmity of the farm bloc during World War I with his policies at the Food Administration and had further angered the interest group with his opposition to farm relief plans such as the McNary-Haugen bill in the 1920s. Curtis spent his four years as vice president chairing Senate deliberations and hosting official functions, neither of which called for the use of his horse-trading approach to politics. While Curtis did attend cabinet meetings, he was not a consequential figure in the Hoover presidency. He nonetheless remained on the ballot with Hoover in 1932. After his defeat for reelection as vice president, Curtis practiced law in Washington, D.C., until his death on February 8, 1936.

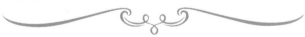

political figure who came from a background of urban poverty. Born in a tenement near the Brooklyn Bridge, Smith had worked as a newsboy and a fishmonger before gaining entry into the world of politics through Tammany Hall, the infamous political machine. He served 12 years in the New York State Assembly, and four terms as governor of New York from 1919 to 1920 and 1923 to 1928. He was the first Roman Catholic and the first Irish American to run for president on a major party ticket.

Northeastern Democrats helped maneuver Smith's nomination. He was chosen despite the fact that party regulars were not favorable to Smith's candidacy. Only fellow New Yorker FRANKLIN D. ROOSEVELT conveyed any enthusiasm for the nominee. Other Democratic contenders included Senators James A. Reed (Missouri) and Walter F. George (Georgia), Representatives William A. Ayers (Indiana) and Cordell Hull (Tennessee), Houston businessman Jesse H. Jones, Huston Thompson of Colorado, Atlee Pomerene of Ohio, and Evans Woollen of Indiana. As had been true for the Republicans, agricultural policy and Prohibition attracted significant attention from the delegates. Smith's image as an urban politician led the farm bloc to distrust him. The Prohibition issue came to the fore when Smith told the convention of his opposition to the Eighteenth Amendment, ratified in 1919, that had led to the outlawing of alcohol throughout the country. Southern Democrats, the base of the party, could not accept Smith's opposition to Prohibition nor were they keen on his Irish Catholic identity. Thus, ethnocultural issues

Democrats nominated New York governor Al Smith at their national convention in Houston, Texas, in 1928. Smith lost the election to Herbert Hoover. *(Library of Congress)*

trumped the substance of Smith's essential conservatism—a point of agreement with Democrats from the South—in determining the fate of his candidacy. Although he had supported some elements of the progressive agenda, namely improved factory regulations, better housing conditions, and expanded public welfare programs, Smith also adhered to several notable conservative positions: He opposed woman suffrage, expansion of the federal government bureaucracy and the federal budget, and government intrusion into the business world. These positions made him more conservative than the Republican nominee. Likewise, the Democratic platform declared in favor of states' rights, against what it termed the corruption of the Republican Party, support for efficient management of public funds, and study of the growing unemployment problem.

Hoover's political naiveté had little impact on his race for the presidency because his administrative and organizational skills along with his public image overcame this weakness. He worked to gain the support of Republican leaders at the state level, and he replaced key Republican strategists with loyal supporters and built a well-oiled machine before the official campaign kick-off on August 11, 1928. On that date, Hoover received, and accepted, his official notification of the nomination at a ceremony held at the Stanford University football stadium before an audience of 70,000. Hoover's speech reached an even larger audience of 30 million listeners courtesy of a radio transmission. Despite his emotionless delivery, the content was weighty, and Americans in and out of the stadium assessed the speech as proof of Hoover's political gravitas. Among the issues Hoover developed were cooperative agricultural marketing, collective bargaining for labor, water power development, and an end to boom-and-bust economic cycles. Hoover also articulated his philosophy of American CORPORATISM, which balanced the interests of business, labor, and government, and his belief in volunteerism and INDIVIDUALISM.

As stodgy as Hoover was on the hustings, Smith proved himself to be a colorful and dramatic campaigner. He drew on his past experience as an actor to make his speeches all

that much more powerful and convincing for each audience he addressed. Smith disdained modern advertising technology, preferring instead to appeal directly to the voters with uncomplicated and frank rhetoric that was both humorous and educational. Gesticulating often, his energetic and extemporaneous style of speech highlighted his New York City heritage. Despite his background with Tammany Hall, the New York City political machine often known for corruption, Smith campaigned for government modernization. Even though Smith drew large crowds for his many speeches, one journalist cautioned readers not to take that fact as evidence of a pending Smith victory. Smith, the journalist argued, drew large crowds composed more of curiosity seekers than of committed voters. Furthermore, the radio rendered Smith's speaking style less than appealing to voters in the listening audience. Instead of capturing his folksy appeal, the radio made Smith sound tinny and unpleasant. While the new communications device de-emphasized substantive politics in stressing the politics of style, neither candidate exhibited much flair on the radio. It is unlikely, however, that this had much effect on the outcome of the election as only urban Americans were able to follow the campaign on the radio in 1928. Few radio stations then existed in rural areas. According to the 1930 census, just over 40 percent of American households had radios.

Hoover and Smith competed for the support of the major social and economic groups. Their struggle to win the backing of the business community was telling. Hoover relied on his connections with the trade associations to boost his candidacy. Smith gained favor from industry when he appointed John Raskob of General Motors as his national campaign chairman. However, he did not best Hoover in the pursuit of this constituency. Evidence of that fact comes from Franklin Roosevelt's efforts to bring Julius Barnes, the chairman of the board of the Chamber of Commerce, into the Smith camp. Roosevelt told Barnes that Hoover had renounced his commitment to Wilsonian progressivism. Barnes would have none of it. His anger at Roosevelt indicated the depth of the business commitment to Hoover. Labor divided in its support for the two candidates. Hoover enjoyed the respect of many within the labor movement for his opposition to the injunction to prevent strikes. While small-scale farmers distrusted Hoover, national farm leaders backed the Republican candidate. Former Bull Moose progressives also split in their support of Hoover, with some accepting him as an heir to THEODORE ROOSEVELT and others distrusting his connections with the business community.

Between August 11 and November 2, Hoover delivered six major campaign speeches in which he articulated versions of his August 11 acceptance speech. Each speech took into account the particular interests of the audience. For example, in rural areas Hoover emphasized agrarian themes and in urban areas he stressed the importance of public works projects for unemployment relief.

The most negative component of the campaign involved Republican demagoguery over the issue of Smith's Catholicism. The numerous examples of intolerance were important not because they changed the course of the election but because they reflected and amplified the prejudices endemic within American society. Given the political alignment of the country almost any Republican would have defeated Smith that November. The press fulminated at length about the dangers of a Catholic president. Some went so far as to argue that Catholics were inherently immoral. Put "a Christian in the White House," one campaign button read, implying that Catholics were not genuinely

Christian. Others charged that the pope would dominate a Catholic president. More important, a speech arranged by the Republican Speaker's Bureau before an audience of Protestant clergy members in Ohio included venomous comments about the malevolence of Catholicism. When the public reacted negatively to these tactics, Hoover and the Republicans disavowed responsibility for the speech. Hoover tried to have it both ways. He enjoyed any benefits the anti-Catholic harangue brought to his campaign while publicly calling for fair play in the contest.

Exacerbating the widespread religious bigotry was Smith's urban, ethnic identity and his opposition to Prohibition. These ethnocultural issues generated much passion among voters, both northern Republicans and southern Democrats. For some, such facts served as proof of Smith's lower-class status and concomitant lack of qualifications for the presidency. In fact, Hoover campaign advertisements for women's magazines pitted LOU HENRY HOOVER's middle-class respectability against Catherine Smith's roots in the Lower East Side of New York City. Because these issues proved especially troublesome to southerners, the Hoover campaign stressed the ethnocultural issues below the Mason-Dixon line in hopes of breaking the Democratic lock on the "Solid South."

Turnout on election day, November 6, 1928, was exceedingly high with 67.5 percent of the electorate voting. Furthermore, Hoover's popular and Electoral College vote totals exceeded all past presidential winners. In the former, Hoover

This E. W. Kemble drawing shows a joust between Republican candidate Herbert Hoover, riding on the Republican elephant, and Democratic candidate Al Smith, riding on the Tammany Tiger, during the 1928 presidential election. *(Library of Congress)*

Republican presidential nominee Herbert Hoover addresses a crowd in Elizabethon, Tennessee, on October 8, 1928. *(Associated Press)*

bested Smith 21,433,113 to 15,017,684 and, in the latter, 444 to 87. Socialist candidate Norman M. Thomas received 267,478 popular votes and no Electoral College votes. Hoover swept every region of the country except the South, but even there he made inroads, winning Florida, Tennessee, North Carolina, Kentucky, and Virginia. Although debates about religion played a role in the contest, the deciding factors in Hoover's favor were his public image, his long record of accomplishment, his efficient campaign organization, and the economic prosperity enjoyed under Republican administrations in the 1920s. The most significant trends for the future of American politics established in the election occurred on the Democratic side. Smith carried cities that before had typically voted Republican. Furthermore, he bested Hoover in the 50 most urban counties in the country. Finally, Smith broke the Republican lock on the Northeast, winning Massachusetts and Rhode Island. His Catholicism, while not decisive to the 1928 contest, nonetheless symbolized the emergence of the Democratic Party as the voice for urban, immigrant concerns.

HOOVER ADMINISTRATION (1929–1933)

The weather on March 4, 1929, was cold and drizzly in the nation's capital, but it failed to dampen Herbert Hoover's spirits. "We want to see a nation built of homeowners and farm owners," he declared in his inaugural address as the nation's 31st president. "We want to see more and more of them insured against death and accident, unemployment and old age. We want them all secure." He promised Americans a "New Day" that would see the elimination of poverty in the land. Journalists found much to celebrate about the former wunderkind of the engineering world, who had spent the last decade and a half of his life in public service, overseeing massive food distribution to war-torn Europe and serving as secretary of commerce during eight prosperous years.

National and international economic developments, however, combined with Hoover's political style would make the fulfillment of this promise almost impossible. Both Herbert and Lou Henry Hoover believed that self-promotion

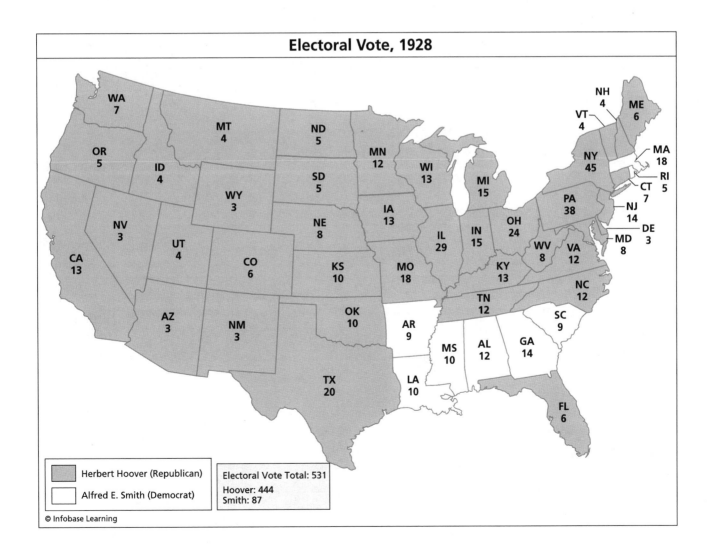

Electoral Vote, 1928

Legend:
- Herbert Hoover (Republican)
- Alfred E. Smith (Democrat)

Electoral Vote Total: 531
Hoover: 444
Smith: 87

© Infobase Learning

1928 Election Statistics

State	Number of Electors	Total Popular Vote	Elec Vote R	Elec Vote D	Pop Vote R	Pop Vote D	Pop Vote S	Margin of Victory Votes	Margin of Victory % Total Vote
Alabama	12	248,981		12	2	1	3	7,071	2.84%
Arizona	3	91,254	3		1	2	-	13,996	15.34%
Arkansas	9	197,726		9	2	1	3	41,412	20.94%
California	13	1,796,656	13		1	2	3	547,958	30.50%
Colorado	6	392,242	6		1	2	3	120,741	30.78%
Connecticut	7	553,031	7		1	2	3	44,574	8.06%
Delaware	3	104,602	3		1	2	3	33,506	32.03%
Florida	6	253,674	6		1	2	3	42,404	16.72%
Georgia	14	229,158		14	2	1	3	30,234	13.19%
Idaho	4	151,541	4		1	2	3	44,396	29.30%
Illinois	29	3,107,489	29		1	2	3	455,324	14.65%
Indiana	15	1,421,314	15		1	2	4	285,599	20.09%
Iowa	13	1,009,489	13		1	2	4	244,259	24.20%
Kansas	10	713,200	10		1	2	3	320,669	44.96%
Kentucky	13	941,274	13		1	2	3	177,664	18.87%
Louisiana	10	215,833		10	2	1	-	113,495	52.58%
Maine	6	262,171	6		1	2	3	98,744	37.66%
Maryland	8	528,348	8		1	2	3	77,853	14.74%
Massachusetts	18	1,577,823		18	2	1	3	17,192	1.09%
Michigan	15	1,372,082	15		1	2	3	568,634	41.44%
Minnesota	12	970,976	12		1	2	3	164,526	16.94%
Mississippi	10	151,692		10	2	1	-	97,386	64.20%
Missouri	18	1,500,721	18		1	2	3	171,518	11.43%
Montana	4	194,108	4		1	2	3	34,722	17.89%
Nebraska	8	547,144	8		1	2	3	147,786	27.01%
Nevada	3	32,417	3		1	2	-	4,237	13.07%
New Hampshire	4	196,757	4		1	2	3	34,689	17.63%
New Jersey	14	1,548,195	14		1	2	3	309,123	19.97%
New Mexico	3	118,014	3		1	2	-	21,434	18.16%
New York	45	4,405,626	45		1	2	3	103,481	2.35%
North Carolina	12	635,150	12		1	2	-	62,696	9.87%
North Dakota	5	239,867	5		1	2	3	24,793	10.34%
Ohio	24	2,508,346	24		1	2	3	763,336	30.43%
Oklahoma	10	618,427	10		1	2	3	174,872	28.28%
Oregon	5	319,942	5		1	2	3	96,118	30.04%
Pennsylvania	38	3,150,610	38		1	2	3	987,796	31.35%
Rhode Island	5	237,194		5	2	1	-	1,451	0.61%
South Carolina	9	68,605		9	2	1	3	56,842	82.85%
South Dakota	5	261,865	5		1	2	4	54,943	20.98%
Tennessee	12	363,473	12		1	2	3	28,045	7.72%
Texas	20	717,797	20		1	2	3	27,782	3.87%
Utah	4	176,603	4		1	2	3	13,633	7.72%
Vermont	4	135,191	4		1	2	-	45,964	34.00%
Virginia	12	305,358	12		1	2	3	24,463	8.01%
Washington	7	500,840	7		1	2	4	179,072	35.75%
West Virginia	8	642,752	8		1	2	4	111,767	17.39%
Wisconsin	13	1,016,831	13		1	2	3	93,946	9.24%
Wyoming	3	82,835	3		1	2	3	23,449	28.31%
Total	531	36,815,224	444	87	1	2	3	6,415,429	17.43%

Hoover Republican		Smith Democratic		Thomas Socialist		Others	
120,725	48.49%	127,796	51.33%	460	0.18%	0	0.00%
52,533	57.57%	38,537	42.23%	0	0.00%	184	0.20%
77,784	39.34%	119,196	60.28%	429	0.22%	317	0.16%
1,162,323	64.69%	614,365	34.19%	19,595	1.09%	373	0.02%
253,872	64.72%	133,131	33.94%	3,472	0.89%	1,767	0.45%
296,614	53.63%	252,040	45.57%	3,019	0.55%	1,358	0.25%
68,860	65.83%	35,354	33.80%	329	0.31%	59	0.06%
144,168	56.83%	101,764	40.12%	4,036	1.59%	3,706	1.46%
99,368	43.36%	129,602	56.56%	124	0.05%	64	0.03%
97,322	64.22%	52,926	34.93%	1,293	0.85%	0	0.00%
1,769,141	56.93%	1,313,817	42.28%	19,138	0.62%	5,393	0.17%
848,290	59.68%	562,691	39.59%	3,871	0.27%	6,462	0.45%
623,570	61.77%	379,311	37.57%	2,960	0.29%	3,648	0.36%
513,672	72.02%	193,003	27.06%	6,205	0.87%	320	0.04%
558,734	59.36%	381,070	40.48%	837	0.09%	633	0.07%
51,160	23.70%	164,655	76.29%	0	0.00%	18	0.01%
179,923	68.63%	81,179	30.96%	1,068	0.41%	1	0.00%
301,479	57.06%	223,626	42.33%	1,701	0.32%	1,542	0.29%
775,566	49.15%	792,758	50.24%	6,262	0.40%	3,237	0.21%
965,396	70.36%	396,762	28.92%	3,516	0.26%	6,408	0.47%
560,977	57.77%	396,451	40.83%	6,774	0.70%	6,774	0.70%
27,153	17.90%	124,539	82.10%	0	0.00%	0	0.00%
834,080	55.58%	662,562	44.15%	3,739	0.25%	340	0.02%
113,300	58.37%	78,578	40.48%	1,667	0.86%	563	0.29%
345,745	63.19%	197,959	36.18%	3,434	0.63%	6	0.00%
18,327	56.54%	14,090	43.46%	0	0.00%	0	0.00%
115,404	58.65%	80,715	41.02%	465	0.24%	173	0.09%
925,285	59.77%	616,162	39.80%	4,866	0.31%	1,882	0.12%
69,645	59.01%	48,211	40.85%	0	0.00%	158	0.13%
2,193,344	49.79%	2,089,863	47.44%	107,332	2.44%	15,087	0.34%
348,923	54.94%	286,227	45.06%	0	0.00%	0	0.00%
131,441	54.80%	106,648	44.46%	936	0.39%	842	0.35%
1,627,546	64.89%	864,210	34.45%	8,683	0.35%	7,907	0.32%
394,046	63.72%	219,174	35.44%	3,924	0.63%	1,283	0.21%
205,341	64.18%	109,223	34.14%	2,720	0.85%	2,658	0.83%
2,055,382	65.24%	1,067,586	33.89%	18,647	0.59%	8,995	0.29%
117,522	49.55%	118,973	50.16%	0	0.00%	699	0.29%
5,858	8.54%	62,700	91.39%	47	0.07%	0	0.00%
157,603	60.18%	102,660	39.20%	443	0.17%	1,159	0.44%
195,388	53.76%	167,343	46.04%	631	0.17%	111	0.03%
372,324	51.87%	344,542	48.00%	722	0.10%	209	0.03%
94,618	53.58%	80,985	45.86%	954	0.54%	46	0.03%
90,404	66.87%	44,440	32.87%	0	0.00%	347	0.26%
164,609	53.91%	140,146	45.90%	250	0.08%	353	0.12%
335,844	67.06%	156,772	31.30%	2,615	0.52%	5,609	1.12%
375,551	58.43%	263,784	41.04%	1,313	0.20%	2,104	0.33%
544,205	53.52%	450,259	44.28%	18,213	1.79%	4,154	0.41%
52,748	63.68%	29,299	35.37%	788	0.95%	0	0.00%
21,433,113	58.22%	15,017,684	40.79%	267,478	0.73%	96,949	0.26%

of charitable and philanthropic works constituted inappropriate, self-serving behavior. They preferred that their private financial donations and their organizing efforts on behalf of worthy causes remain anonymous. They did not perform good deeds for the sake of improving their public reputations but because the work needed to be done for the betterment of society. This approach carried over to Hoover's political career, and when the stock market crashed in October 1929, which plunged the nation into the worst economic depression in history, Hoover was never able to adequately explain to the American people either his perspective on the crisis or his policies to relieve the nation's economic woes. Indeed, the majority of Americans came to view the four years of Hoover's presidency as an unmitigated failure. Such a view, though, is too harsh a verdict because many of the depression relief and recovery policies that Hoover tentatively adopted served as the foundation for FRANKLIN D. ROOSEVELT's New Deal in 1933.

To begin his administration on an amicable note, Hoover balanced various interests and sections in the selection of his cabinet, and its overriding characteristic was its administrative fluency not its progressive allegiances. To appease con-

---

LOU HENRY HOOVER, THE RISE OF GIRL SCOUTING, AND THE RAPIDAN PLAN FOR DEPRESSION RELIEF

Perhaps more than any of the other women's voluntary organizations with which she was affiliated, the Girl Scouts embodied perfectly Lou Henry Hoover's belief in individualism, activism, the natural world, and the empowerment of women. During World War I, when her husband, future president Herbert Hoover, was overseeing food relief for Europe, Lou Henry Hoover became interested in the girl scouting movement. She addressed a local Girl Scout group on November 21, 1917, about the importance of food conservation. That speaking engagement spawned a lifetime interest in the nascent organization. Initially, Hoover's involvement in scouting was minimal and local. She was a troop leader in Washington, D.C., for 10 years. Her attachment to scouting resulted from her atypical childhood in which she enjoyed hiking, fishing, camping, and other outdoor activities. Scouting also provided a counterbalance to urbanization and industrialization, which Hoover believed important given the shifts within American society.

Juliette Gordon Low first created the American Girl Scout organization in 1912; by 1920, it had 70,000 members. Eighteen girls from Savannah, Georgia, attended the first meeting. Low hoped the organization would aid the physical, mental, and spiritual development of girls regardless of social class. She wanted to bring girls out of their isolated homes and into a larger community. Low developed her ideas for girl scouting from her 1911 meeting with Sir Robert Baden-Powell, the founder of the Boy Scouts and the Girl Guides in England. Girl Scouts tutored young women in both traditional homemaking and in the skills necessary for successful professional careers. In that way the Girl Scout movement reflected the changed circumstances in which women arranged and organized their lives in the early 20th century.

In 1922, Hoover became the national president of the Girl Scouts. She held that post until 1925. Under her direction the organization improved its financial operations, democratized its governance, and worked to improve its public image. She championed the Lone Scouting program, which provided a scouting outlet for young girls living in isolated regions where the population was insufficient to support traditional troops. Furthermore, she developed a leadership training program to make sure the organization could keep pace with the demands for additional scouting troops. Finally, she helped establish the Girl Scouts National Little House as a homemaking laboratory in Washington, D.C.

Hoover worked with girl scouting in numerous ways while first lady, but the most ambitious involved her Rapidan Plan. She wanted to turn the Girl Scouts into a voluntary army for depression relief. In the fall of 1931, Hoover called a meeting of Girl Scout leaders at Camp Rapidan, the presidential retreat she had built with her husband in the Blue Ridge Mountains of Virginia. The national leaders who attended left the conclave full of ideas for using volunteerism to tackle the relief problems in their local communities. Because Hoover called this strategy meeting some weeks before the Girl Scouts annual convention, she knew that she and other backers of the Rapidan Plan would have another opportunity to gain converts. Hoover told the conventioneers that they must devote their troops' activities to the serious, service work of scouting. She gave examples of what some troops were already doing. Troops that participated in the Rapidan Plan often coordinated their efforts with the President's Organization on Unemployment Relief and with scouting officials. The primary areas of scouting relief work under the Rapidan Plan included food, clothing, medical care, and Christmas relief. While the Rapidan Plan had little impact on the depression, it provided a significant boon for girl scouting. The Girl Scout troops that participated in the relief efforts gained a greater sense of service to the larger community. Furthermore, the social awareness that the Rapidan Plan brought to the economic misery of the depression made the organization seem all that much more relevant. As such, membership in the Girl Scouts increased by almost 20,000 from 1931 to 1932.

Hoover's inauguration, March 4, 1929 *(Library of Congress)*

servative, old guard Republicans, Hoover retained Andrew Mellon as secretary of the treasury, a post he had held since the beginning of the WARREN G. HARDING administration in 1921. Mellon's fiscal conservatism and his opposition to high taxes were well known in 1929. When Hoover could not get his first choice for secretary of agriculture—Republican senator Charles McNary of Oregon, an advocate of export debentures (the provision of certificates, commonly called debentures, to exporters of agricultural produce that could be used for payment of customs duties on any imported good) for increasing domestic farm income—he settled for Arthur Hyde, the governor of Missouri. He named James W. Good, a loyal campaigner in 1928, secretary of war. When he died in December 1929, undersecretary of war Patrick J. Hurley replaced him. Walter Brown became postmaster general. Ray Lyman Wilbur, a friend since their undergraduate days at Stanford, was named secretary of the interior. The governor

general of the Philippines, Henry Stimson, became secretary of state. Other cabinet appointments included Attorney General William D. Mitchell, Secretary of Labor James J. Davis, Secretary of the Navy Charles Francis Adams, and Secretary of Commerce Robert P. Lamont.

Hoover began his presidency with high hopes to take action on numerous issues. He wanted to reform the nation's judiciary, provide better enforcement of Prohibition, encourage synchronization between government and business, expand educational opportunities, improve public health, and provide enhanced international means for maintaining world peace.

The politics of reform dominated the spring and summer of 1929 for the Hoover administration. He called for additional civil service protections for federal workers, the termination of private oil and gas leases on government lands (such practices had led to significant public controversy, specifically the Teapot Dome scandal during the Harding administration), a federal investigation and prosecution of Chicago-based mobster Al Capone, an expansion of the national park and national forest system, a special session of Congress to implement agricultural relief, tax cuts for low-income Americans, expanded government services for veterans, the creation of an antitrust division in the Justice Department, improved air mail service, the creation of the Federal Bureau of Prisons, reform of the Bureau of Indian Affairs, dam construction in the Tennessee Valley and in central California, federal loans for urban slum clearance, the creation of a federal Department of Education, and a pension program for elderly Americans. Of this ambitious laundry list of domestic reforms, Hoover succeeded in implementing all but the last four: dam construction, slum clearance, establishing a Department of Education, and instituting pensions for the elderly.

The first year of the Hoover presidency also witnessed other accomplishments. He agreed with progressive politi-

cians that the sizable refunds from income, estate, and gift taxes should be publicized so that voters could learn who had benefited from the changes to tax law in the 1920s. Likewise, Hoover arranged for the names of those who lobbied for judicial appointments to be known by the public. Hoover sought various protections for the civil liberties of individuals. Of special concern were those involved in labor strife, charged with political subversion, Prohibition violations, or victims of racial discrimination. He also advocated for improved conditions for American Indians, children's health, and housing.

During the spring of 1929, Hoover fulfilled his promise to bring Congress into special session to deal with the nation's agricultural and tariff problems. The AGRICULTURAL MARKETING ACT of 1929 established the FEDERAL FARM BOARD. Both the legislation and the new agency followed from Hoover's theory of CORPORATISM, which called for industry to engage in self-regulation, while avoiding the artificial price supports favored by progressive Republicans

---

ADMINISTRATION TIME LINE

1929

March 4 Herbert Hoover is inaugurated president.

March 7 President Hoover calls a special session of Congress to convene April 15 to work on agricultural and tariff issues.

May Wickersham Commission on Law Enforcement is named.

June 15 Hoover signs the Agricultural Marketing Act into law, establishing the Federal Farm Board with a $500 million budget.

September 3 The height of the 1920s bull market is reached.

September 5 Stock market prices begin to fall.

October 29 On "Black Tuesday" the stock market crashes and signals the start of the Great Depression.

November 19 Hoover begins meeting with business, labor, and government leaders to address the depression. The president seeks maintenance of current employment and wage levels.

1930

January–April The London Naval Disarmament Conference is held.

April 22 The three-power naval treaty among Great Britain, Japan, and the United States, a by-product of the London Naval Disarmament Conference, is signed.

April 29 Air Mail Act is passed allowing the postmaster general to issue airmail contracts without competitive bidding.

June 17 Hoover signs the Smoot-Hawley Tariff, which increases rates on agricultural imports and provides protections for the industrial sector.

July 21 The Veterans Administration is created.

October 21 Hoover creates the President's Emergency Committee for Employment, a cabinet committee on unemployment.

November 19 Hoover convenes the White House Conference on Child Health and Welfare.

December 20 Congress passes drought relief legislation.

1931

June 1 In *Near v. Minnesota,* the Supreme Court finds Minnesota's "gag law" restricted the First

and opposed by the president. Thus, the focus was on creating and encouraging farmer cooperatives and efficiency in agriculture. Lawmakers also considered tariff legislation to protect farmers, who had been suffering throughout the 1920s from an agricultural depression. The Smoot-Hawley bill, as it was named, was amended to protect manufacturing as well. The bill became more and more problematic the longer Congress debated it, and the legislation was not passed until 1930. Hoover refused to play an active role in the legislative deliberations, and the proposed legislation became a catch-all for the special interests of the members of Congress. The tariff revisions became all that much more protective and food prices soared as a result. The Smoot-Hawley Tariff raised rates approximately 40 to 50 percent on agricultural produce and also included protectionist schedules for industrial production. This nationalist approach to trade policy, aiming to protect domestic producers from foreign competition, worsened the Great Depression.

Perhaps the greatest irony of Hoover's presidency is the blame that was heaped on him for causing, or at least not properly tackling, the Great Depression. Actually, as early as 1925, Hoover had warned of serious economic consequences for the nation if stock market speculation was left unchecked. President Coolidge ignored such warnings from his secretary of commerce. As president-elect, Hoover cautioned the Federal Reserve Board that interest rate increases were needed to halt the unhealthy speculation. Hoover even called for journalists in newspapers and radio to warn against the dangerous investment trends. However, such an activist approach to the operations of the free market was unheard of for American presidents, and Hoover soon backtracked from his warnings as his presidency progressed. Common perceptions held that if presidents issued such alerts they could trigger economic panic.

The STOCK MARKET CRASH in the fall of 1929 propelled the onset of the Great Depression. The speculative bubble, which had fueled much of the economic growth of the 1920s,

---

Amendment's protections for freedom of the press.

June 20 President Hoover announces a one-year moratorium on all debts incurred during World War I.

August 19 Hoover creates the President's Organization for Unemployment Relief from the old President's Emergency Committee for Employment.

December 7 President Hoover asks Congress to pass legislation creating the Reconstruction Finance Corporation to rescue the financial services industry.

1932

January 7 The Stimson Doctrine is issued. Secretary of State Henry Stimson calls for a policy of nonrecognition of any and all territorial changes resulting from Japan's military actions in Manchuria.

January 22 Hoover signs legislation creating the Reconstruction Finance Corporation.

February 2 The World Disarmament Conference opens in Geneva, Switzerland.

March 23 Hoover signs the Norris-LaGuardia Act, granting workers the right to join labor unions and limiting use of the federal injunction against strikers.

June 21 Hoover signs the Federal Home Loan Bank Act.

July 21 The Emergency Relief and Construction Act is passed providing loans to the states and funds for public works.

July 28 Hoover orders the U.S. Army to clear the Bonus Marchers out of Washington, D.C.

November 8 Hoover loses his reelection bid for the presidency.

1932–1934

The Senate Banking Committee directs its chief counsel, Ferdinand Pecora, to run an investigation into the practices of Wall Street bankers as they related to the onset of the Great Depression.

1933

March 4 Hoover spends his last day as president.

As president, Hoover tried to address many issues, including better enforcement of Prohibition. Here, New York City deputy police commissioner John A. Leach watches agents pour liquor into a sewer following a raid. *(Library of Congress)*

burst when the unstable credit mechanisms for stock purchases became unsustainable. Since investors had borrowed against the value of stocks at excessively inflated prices, they could not remain in the market when prices on those same stocks tumbled. Instead, investors were left with what amounted to an unsecured debt with no hope of recouping their initial purchase, let alone any profit. Large bankers had tried to stave off the crash by buying up stocks, but the economic powers of market correction were stronger than the bankers. On October 29, 1929, a day commonly known as Black Tuesday, over 16 million shares were traded at rock-bottom prices. In a single day, sellers lost over $30 billion in paper value.

The country had survived several financial panics in the 19th century—1808, 1819, 1837, 1857, 1873, and 1893—and four in the early 20th century—1907, 1910, 1913, and 1914.

The expectations for presidential behavior remained largely the same during this century and a quarter of economic fluctuation; the public and politicians alike believed that boom-and-bust cycles were inevitable parts of the capitalist, industrial economic system and should be endured without governmental intervention. In the fall of 1929, though, Hoover refused to accept this traditional approach to economic misery. He believed the federal government should play a role in thwarting an economic collapse.

Hoover used strategies much like those he had employed in the last 15 or so years he had spent in public service, namely, persuading those with the means to do so to fund voluntary relief programs, calling conferences to educate the public about relief measures, and establishing commissions assigned to research the problems facing the country. He began by inviting business, agricultural, and labor leaders to a series of conferences to map efforts to achieve recovery. This approach melded well with Hoover's approach to corporatism and with his understanding of INDIVIDUALISM. It also harkened back to the 1921 conference on unemployment that he oversaw as President Harding's secretary of commerce. In 1929, he wanted employers to hold the line on wages and he wanted workers to withdraw demands for pay increases. He secured assurances from the leaders of both groups that they would do so. Railroad and utility executives pledged to the president that they would undertake new construction projects in 1930.

Likewise, Hoover pushed both the federal and state governments to continue with construction projects. Finally, he asked Congress both for a tax cut and for increased spending on public works.

Journalists and newspaper editors approved. As the new year approached, Hoover received positive reviews for his economic activism. These assessments were not wrong, and throughout his term, Hoover employed economically legitimate strategies to fight the growing depression. That he failed only puts him on a par with his successor, Franklin D. Roosevelt, who likewise could not solve the riddle of the depression. It ultimately took the overheated military

This Clifford Kennedy Berryman cartoon from December 1929 shows the difficulties the Hoover White House faced in reforming the nation's tariff laws. The Smoot-Hawley Tariff that Congress ultimately passed in June 1930 proved problematic and worsened the deepening economic depression. *(Library of Congress)*

economy of World War II in the early 1940s to pull the country above the economic levels attained during the 1920s before the crash.

In his first annual message to Congress in December 1929, Hoover laid out a comprehensive plan for recovery. Banking reform, resource conservation, public works, and housing proposals were geared toward the progressives and moderates in Congress while government economy programs, calls for a balanced budget, and tax cuts played to the old guard conservatives. Public works projects won continued backing from Hoover as the depression worsened. By fiscal year 1931 (which began on July 1, 1931), approximately $200 million in additional spending had been devoted to public works. Likewise, railroads and public utilities increased their investment expenditures by $500 million from 1929 to 1930. Hoover took so much encouragement from these developments that he rejected unemployment relief proposals coming from within his administration. Part of the problem resulted from the overlooked decline in private construction outlays.

In keeping with his corporatist, individualist style, Hoover relied on appointed committees to bring about voluntary relief at the local level. In October 1930 he created the PRESIDENT'S EMERGENCY COMMITTEE FOR EMPLOYMENT, and in August 1931 he renamed it the PRESIDENT'S ORGANIZATION FOR UNEMPLOYMENT RELIEF in hopes that its effectiveness would improve. Because the new committee had essentially the same responsibilities as the first, little changed as to results. He named a host of other committees and boards to bring about decentralized action that would solve the problems posed by the depression. Each of these commissions sought in one way or another to encourage voluntary cooperation. Two privately financed entities that he appointed included the Timber Conservation Board and the Federal Oil Conservation Board. The federal boards he created included the Federal Drought Relief Committee, the National Credit Corporation, the Citizen's Reconstruction Organization, the Federal Employment Stabilization Board, and the Federal Power Commission. None had coercive economic power because Hoover disdained such intervention. In fact, the more the depression worsened, the greater grew Hoover's faith in volunteerism. He led by example, especially regarding his own salary. When Hoover entered public service in 1914 he renounced a salary, noting that accepting compensation would change the meaning of his work from that of public service. He continued that practice for the remainder of his public career. When he served as secretary of commerce and president, though, he had to take a salary. He deposited the money into a separate account and, as he explained to a reporter in 1937, "distributed it where I thought it would do the most good. Part of it went to supplement the salaries of men who worked under me and whom the government paid less than I thought they were worth. Part of it went to charities."

Because the Great Depression proved so widespread, deep, and intractable, the majority of the Hoover presidency was spent dealing with domestic concerns. Nonetheless, Hoover did not ignore foreign policy. Even before his inauguration, Hoover took a good will trip to South America. He applied Quaker notions of negotiation rather than relying on the use of force to achieve his diplomatic ends. He sought good relations with Central and South America, U.S. participation in the World Court and the League of Nations, and enactment of a host of disarmament agreements. Instead of calling for the use of troops to counter Japan's invasion of Manchuria in 1931, Hoover worked with Secretary of State Henry Stimson to develop a policy of nonrecognition for territory gained through aggression, which emerged as the STIMSON DOCTRINE. While the 1930 LONDON NAVAL CONFERENCE achieved some success, the 1932 WORLD DISARMAMENT CONFERENCE at Geneva achieved few tangible results.

Once the depression worsened, the economic crisis became central to Hoover's foreign policy. In 1931, significant financial institutions in Europe collapsed, creating a credit crunch. In light of these developments, Great Britain went off the gold standard. These actions fed into Hoover's belief that the depression was international in origin. As such, he sought both international and domestic solutions, including a one-year moratorium on repayment of Allied debts to the United States and payment of German reparations stemming from World War I, preservation for the U.S. dollar of the gold standard and higher interest rates in the United States.

Voters in the 1930 midterm elections focused far more on the sour economy than on Hoover's foreign or domestic policy initiatives. Even though many of Hoover's proposals, limited as they were, had been successful, it was hard for voters to get beyond the statistics on unemployment, bank failures, and other economic indices. In 1930, unemployment had reached almost 9 percent, up from just over 3 percent before the crash. Additionally, there were more than 1,300 bank failures that year alone. Moreover, the Democratic Party ably exploited the situation, attacking the Smoot-Hawley Tariff, the dismal agricultural earnings, Hoover's failure to address the DROUGHT OF 1930–31, his support for Prohibition (some politicians had begun to argue for its repeal as a depression relief measure), his internationalism, and his seeming lack of concern for individual deprivation and misery. The result was a Democratic gain of seats in the House of Representatives sufficient to give the party control of the lower chamber.

Scholars who have studied the Great Depression have yet to agree on what caused the stock market to crash in 1929 and how it led to more than a decade of misery. Theories vary from placing blame on international forces, instability remaining from World War I, problems within the American banking industry, stock speculation, and congressional inaction on Hoover's reform proposals. These were explanations favored by the president, but his critics have added another potential cause to the list: adoption of the protectionist Smoot-Hawley Tariff. Still, other forces must also be considered, including the glut of consumer goods on the market and the corresponding decline of large purchases (such as automobiles and household appliances), a decade-long agricultural depression, a widening gap between workers' wages and corporate profits, bank investment and speculation in the stock market, and the lack of any social safety net for the unemployed.

Hoover refused to support any sort of purposeful management of his image before the public. He never understood the increasing importance of celebrity and image in American politics and public life. The most notable example of this trend was the public's fascination in 1927 with Charles Lindbergh's solo flight across the Atlantic Ocean. Hoover would have none of the new exploitation of image for the sake of policy. For example, one day when he happened upon some boys playing baseball, he stopped to watch and visit. Aides recommended that he return the following day so that the photographer could capture the wholesome scene, but he declined. Nor would he allow the media to print pictures of his family. More important, he was unwilling to publicize his private endeavors toward depression relief, and he opposed news coverage of the donation of his salary to assist the poor. He also raised $500,000 for the 1930 White House Conference on Child Health and Welfare. Furthermore, Herbert and Lou Henry Hoover collaborated on a long-term philanthropic project near their Blue Ridge Mountain retreat, Camp Rapidan. The local mountaineers had no accessible school for their children, so the Hoovers built, equipped, and maintained one with privately donated funds.

Hoover's belief in self-reliant individualism and community cooperation had helped secure his success with wartime relief efforts in Belgium, with stewardship of the Commerce Department in the 1920s, and with the provision of aid during the 1927 Mississippi River flood, but such an approach failed during his term as president. The public had approved of his approach to each of these earlier crises, but when he applied the same philosophy to the Great Depression, he faced a significant backlash when those efforts appeared to be too limited and piecemeal, and when they failed to bring results. Hoover stridently defended his belief that voluntary acts of relief far exceeded a government dole; such payments, he believed, would destroy the recipient's spirit and self-reliance and ultimately democracy itself. The public never knew of the president's anxious concern for the suffering that beset Hoover on a daily basis. Instead, through the media the public was presented with the image of a president on the defensive, denying the extent of the suffering caused by the depression. For example, he denied that any were starving in the country. Combined with Hoover's dour public persona, such comments made him the butt of countless jokes.

Aspects of Hoover's personality contributed to his political failures. He did not deal well with divergent views. A simple explanation is that his incredibly successful career and his own confidence in his abilities caused him to have little tolerance for those who proffered other views. This personality trait had deeper roots, though. Hoover's view of public service paralleled his view of philanthropy. He believed in the increasingly outmoded notion of disinterested public service. A self-made millionaire, Hoover had little time for politicians who used their public offices for personal reward. This high-mindedness made it difficult for Hoover to fit into the political milieu of the nation's capital, where less honorable mores often prevailed.

In other ways, Hoover never learned the fine art of political behavior. A self-styled "technocrat" who believed that experts could resolve problems big and small, he did not appreciate the necessity for negotiation to craft effective legislation and public policy. Hoover had little stomach for the small talk and the affirmations of mutual admiration, often false, exchanged among political operators. Nor was he comfortable with the back-slapping and meaningless praise that politicians routinely employed. Most important, the sense that he disliked any political opposition made it difficult for loyalists, let alone critics, to discuss policy options with him. In less prosaic ways, Hoover suffered politically. While he had gained the Republican nomination in 1928 on the first ballot, conservatives in the party never completely trusted him because he had loyally served President Wilson's Democratic administration during World War I. Likewise, Hoover earned the disdain of Republican progressives because he was not willing to adopt their agrarian policies for increasing farm income. Furthermore, Democrats had little incentive to work with the president, especially after the depression worsened. Running against Hoover seemed a sure strategy for political success.

The creation of the Reconstruction Finance Corporation became the centerpiece of Hoover's depression recovery strategy. Created in January 1932, this agency reflected Hoover's belief corporatism in serving to counter demands for direct federal government relief payments to the unemployed. The Reconstruction Finance Corporation made loans to banks, railroads and other entities as well as for local relief projects and public works programs to protect the infrastructure of the American economy. Hoover believed this strategy would provide the unemployed what they needed most: jobs in the businesses that had been saved from bankruptcy. Furthermore, he contended that the Reconstruction Finance Corporation would, through a revival of credit, help restore public faith in the economy. The design of this agency reflected the tensions between Hoover's economic intervention—he was the first president to provide for direct federal involvement in the nation's economic machinery during peacetime—and his desire to avoid overly radical solutions—he maintained that the Reconstruction Finance Corporation should be temporary. It also reflected his belief that credit problems were more significant than the human misery engendered by starvation and unemployment since he refused any plans for the Reconstruction Finance Corporation to make large loans for direct relief. Although many historians and economists eventually endorsed the Hoover methods as being more sound than any of the congressional calls then being made for welfare, the approach nonetheless heightened Hoover's image of lacking empathy for the individual sufferer during the depression.

Just as Hoover lost the faith of the people so also did he lose any semblance of a working relationship with Congress. However, Hoover never really professed much faith in the ability of Congress to address the issues of the depression. Especially after the 1930 midterm elections when Democrats regained control of the House of Representatives, congressional cooperation was difficult for Hoover to obtain. Lawmakers increasingly advocated direct federal relief payments to the unemployed, but for Hoover there was no compromise on this issue. The EMERGENCY RELIEF AND CONSTRUCTION ACT of 1932 contained none of the congressional proposals for a dole, instead providing loans to the states and for public works funding. Critics of the administration have nonetheless argued that Hoover's support for this measure signaled his acknowledgment that his policies had failed. The most significant example of legislative-executive discord came with the battle over early payment of the bonus to veterans of World War I. The bonus episode, coming in the summer of 1932 and ending in a military firefight between veterans of the army and the army itself, virtually guaranteed that Hoover would fail to win reelection that fall.

On hearing of the bonus debacle, Franklin D. Roosevelt quipped that the 1932 presidential election was all but won. Even Hoover initially saw little to be gained from an active campaign, planning only three speeches. The spirit of competition, though, pushed the embattled president out on the campaign trail, where Lou Henry Hoover proved to be his most effective weapon. The first lady routinely drew favorable crowd responses with a smile, a wave, and occasionally a few words of greeting. Not surprisingly, Herbert Hoover's campaign remarks, namely, that economic conditions could

With three days to go before the election, a huge crowd gathers in Peoria, Illinois, to hear President Hoover on November 5, 1932.
(© Bettmann/CORBIS)

CABINET, COURT, AND CONGRESS

Cabinet Members

Secretary of State
Henry L. Stimson, 1929–33

Secretary of War
James W. Good, 1929
Patrick J. Hurley, 1929–33

Secretary of the Treasury
Andrew W. Mellon, 1929–32
Ogden L. Mills, 1932–33

Postmaster General
Walter F. Brown, 1929–33

Attorney General
William DeWitt Mitchell, 1929–33

Secretary of the Interior
Ray L. Wilbur, 1929–33

Secretary of Agriculture
Arthur M. Hyde, 1929–33

Secretary of the Navy
Charles F. Adams, 1929–33

Secretary of Commerce
Robert P. Lamont, 1929–32
Roy D. Chapin, 1932–33

Secretary of Labor
James J. Davis, 1929–30
William N. Doak, 1930–33

Supreme Court Appointments

*(Nominated for Chief Justice)

Name	Confirmation Vote	Dates of Service
*Charles Evans Hughes	Confirmed, 52–26	1930–41
John Parker	Rejected, 39–41	
Owen Roberts	Confirmed, Voice Vote	1930–45
Benjamin Cardozo	Confirmed, Voice Vote	1932–38

Legislative Leaders

Congress	Speaker of the House	State	Party
71st Congress (1929–31)	Nicholas R. Longworth	Ohio	Republican
72nd Congress (1931–33)	John Nance Garner	Texas	Democrat

Congress	House Majority Leader	State	Party
71st Congress (1929–31)	John Q. Tilson	Connecticut	Republican
72nd Congress (1931–33)	Henry T. Rainey	Illinois	Democrat

Congress	House Minority Leader	State	Party
71st Congress (1929–31)	John Nance Garner	Texas	Democrat
72nd Congress (1931–33)	Bertrand H. Snell	New York	Republican

Congress	House Democratic Whip	State	Party
71st Congress (1929–31)	John McDuffie	Alabama	Democrat
72nd Congress (1931–33)	John McDuffie	Alabama	Democrat

Congress	House Republican Whip	State	Party
71st Congress (1929–31)	Albert H. Vestal	Indiana	Republican
72nd Congress (1931–33)	Carl G. Bachmann	West Virginia	Republican

Congress	Senate Majority Leader	State	Party
71st Congress (1929–31)	James E. Watson, Jr.	Indiana	Republican
72nd Congress (1931–33)	James E. Watson, Jr.	Indiana	Republican

Congress	Senate Minority Leader	State	Party
71st Congress (1929–31)	Joseph T. Robinson	Arkansas	Democrat
72nd Congress (1931–33)	Joseph T. Robinson	Arkansas	Democrat

be much worse than they were, inspired few voters. The only thing that motivated Hoover to carry on in the face of openly hostile crowds was his fear of Roosevelt's supposed radicalism. The election results that November surprised no one. Hoover carried just six states and he became the first incumbent president to be defeated for reelection in 40 years.

The resounding victory for Roosevelt made the remaining months of Hoover's presidency that much more difficult. Investors unsure of the economic changes that would come with the Roosevelt administration worried about the future of the gold standard. Hoover bought into these concerns and tried in a letter to get Roosevelt to agree to several policy positions: a balanced budget, a fight against inflation, and prevention of dissemination of information about Reconstruction Finance Corporation loans. The president-elect refused to make any statement that would limit his future options or decisions. Nor was Roosevelt willing to agree to joint action with Hoover to forestall the run on the banks that was causing significant distress throughout much of the country. Hoover proposed that the Federal Reserve Board provide guarantees for depositors' accounts, and the board responded with a call to temporarily close the nation's banks. Before taking the latter course, Hoover sought Roosevelt's cooperation, but again, the president-elect wanted no part of such a plan before taking office in his own right on March 4, 1933. Hoover continued lobbying Roosevelt up until the day of the inauguration, but he received nothing for his efforts beyond the president-elect's statement that the governors of the individual states were free to act on their own.

Thus ended the Hoover presidency. His legacy, though, is more complex than that of the image of an uncaring, reserved technocrat with which he is associated. Much of what Hoover proposed and fought for during his administration served as the foundation for programs generally associated with Roosevelt and the New Deal: the Reconstruction Finance Corporation was the funding mechanism for the New Deal, agricultural support programs, and sustained public works investment. Few who lived through the Great Depression were able to acknowledge the relationship between the Hoover and Roosevelt administrations. Instead, Americans in the 1930s were only too willing to believe the worst about Herbert Hoover. That he lived until 1964 allowed him ample opportunity to revive his pre-presidential image.

MAJOR EVENTS AND ISSUES

Agricultural Marketing Act (1929)   American farmers experienced depressed earnings throughout the 1920s, and

numerous legislative panaceas were offered in Congress, with the common aim of guaranteeing parity for agriculture with industry through a federal subsidy program. Most common were the export-debenture plans to raise agricultural prices on the domestic market by providing debentures, or certificates, to exporters for use against customs duties on any imported good, the most popular of which was the McNary-Haugen bill (named for its sponsors, Senator Charles McNary [R-OR] and Representative Gilbert Haugen [R-IA]), that provided government subsidies for crops sold overseas at less than the value of production. President Hoover abhorred these approaches, advocating instead a farm board with authority to loan money to farm cooperatives that would then assist farmers in more efficient production and marketing methods. He promised western lawmakers that he would help push reform legislation through Congress, but the McNary-Haugen Act did not please this constituency. Its provisions—creation of the FEDERAL FARM BOARD and a $500 million revolving fund for loans to agricultural cooperatives—disappointed congressional lawmakers from agricultural states because it provided few additional powers to the federal government and its terms were vague.

Air Mail Act (1930)   Air freight carriers had been using planes to transport the mail since the mid-1920s. By 1929, various pilot groups had organized, and 61 passenger lines and 47 airmail lines operated in the United States. The volume of airmail exceeded 7 million pounds that year. The Air Mail Act of 1930, President Hoover argued, would benefit the country by encouraging the development of new industries, specifically air passenger service.

The postmaster general, Walter Brown, drafted the legislation, which he and the president hoped would unify the industry. Their approach to this legislation stemmed from Hoover's beliefs that businesses in the same industry should cooperate for the sake of efficiency. As commerce secretary in the 1920s, Hoover had favored the establishment of cooperative associations within industries that he hoped would abet modernization of the economy. Hoover was never a classic conservative who believed in unfettered competition. Brown viewed the prevalence of outdated equipment and lax safety standards the result of competition for government airmail subsidies. Instead, he believed airlines should look to passenger service for profits.

Under the 1930 legislation, the postmaster general gained new power to issue airmail contracts without competitive bidding. Additionally, the use of space rather than weight to assess postage rates encouraged airlines to invest in new equipment. Brown and Hoover wanted to implement regulated competition into this fledgling industry, and the spate of mergers and consolidations within the airline industry gave rise to many of the larger airlines that dominated U.S. aviation for the better part of the 20th century.

American Gothic, by Grant Wood (1930)   First exhibited at the Art Institute of Chicago in 1930, Grant Wood's painting *American Gothic* won a $300 prize. The painting, eventually one of the most famous in the United States, depicted a farmer and his unmarried daughter standing outside a Gothic Revival—style white farmhouse. An Iowan, Wood was inspired by the Northern Renaissance art he had studied on multiple trips to Europe. With its representational landscape—and dour-looking figures—*American Gothic* exemplified the Regionalist style, which stood in opposition to European abstract art. Wood denied that his painting was intended as satire of an insular midwestern culture. The often-parodied painting has alternatively been read as a celebration of rural American values.

Bonus March (1932)   In 1924, Congress passed legislation providing for payment of Adjusted Service Certificates, an insurance policy popularly known as the bonus, to veterans of World War I, which were scheduled to come due in 1945. With the onset of the GREAT DEPRESSION and the rise of unemployment among former soldiers, however, several members of Congress, most notably Representative Wright Patman (D-TX), introduced legislation in 1929 for immedi-

American Gothic by Grant Wood *(©Danita Delimont/Alamy)*

ate payment of the bonus. Fiscal conservatives criticized the measure as inflationary, and President Hoover threatened a veto.

Approximately 20,000 impoverished veterans (along with women and children), under the leadership of Walter Waters, a World War I sergeant from Portland, Oregon, marched to Washington, D.C., in the spring of 1932 to lobby for the bonus. The march began in Portland, Oregon, and the veterans named themselves the Bonus Expeditionary Force (after the American Expeditionary Force of World War I). They rode the rails and survived on handouts. Once they arrived in Washington in June and July, the veterans camped both on the Anacostia Flats and in unoccupied buildings, scheduled for demolition, in the business district near Capitol Hill. They regularly held large marches and rallies along Pennsylvania Avenue. Both President Hoover and the first lady quietly ensured necessary food and supplies were made available to the disadvantaged veterans, but the president refused any meeting, public or otherwise, with the group.

After the legislation passed the House but failed in the Senate, Hoover authorized $100,000 to pay for the marchers' return transportation home. While many left the nation's capital, a core group remained through the summer and continued their pressure for immediate payment of the bonus. Pelham D. Glassford, Washington, D.C., superintendent of police, had managed to keep the peace among the marchers, but when demands for their removal from the abandoned buildings intensified, the situation became untenable and fears of violence spread. Confusion remains as to whether the police or district commissioners asked for federal assistance to remove the marchers. Secretary of War Patrick Hurley requested Hoover to declare martial law, but Hoover refused, instead commanding Hurley to remove the marchers from the buildings to their nearby camps. Hurley ordered the army chief of staff, General Douglas MacArthur, to push the veterans across the river to Anacostia.

Using tanks, guns, and tear gas, MacArthur exceeded Hoover's orders and tried to push the marchers even farther away from Capitol Hill. The specter of soldiers firing on ex-soldiers proved disastrous—and deadly. One death and significant negative public press resulted from the firefight, which quickly assumed political implications with the presidential election just months away. Most poignant was the stabbing by one of the soldiers of a seven-year-old boy who wanted to retrieve his pet rabbit before leaving the area in question. While MacArthur publicly celebrated his preeminent role in thwarting what he wrongly believed was a revolution that threatened the government, in reality the episode characterized the depth of economic misery in the nation. In the end, it mattered little that MacArthur had exceeded Hoover's orders. This debacle helped ensure Hoover's defeat in the election of November 1932.

Veterans march in Washington, D.C., on April 8, 1932, demanding their bonus. The violent effort to disperse the bonus marchers three months later doomed President Hoover's bid for reelection. *(Library of Congress)*

Camp Rapidan   Built in the Blue Ridge Mountains of Virginia about 90 miles southwest of Washington, D.C., Camp Rapidan was the first retreat built exclusively for the relaxation purposes of the president. President Hoover and his wife, LOU HENRY HOOVER, spent more than $200,000 of their own money to construct and maintain this weekend fishing camp. Lou Henry Hoover planned and oversaw the construction. Opened in the summer of 1929, the facility consisted of 24 buildings made of pine and designed to be habitable from early spring through late autumn. Campers enjoyed numerous modern conveniences: electricity, telephone service, regular newspaper delivery, and air mail service. Both Hoovers used the camp in both official and unofficial capacities. The president invited members of Congress and economic advisers to Camp Rapidan to debate policy. He entertained British prime minister Ramsay MacDonald at the camp. Lou Henry Hoover used the camp to conduct Girl Scout business. The Hoovers donated the camp to the Shenandoah National Park, and visitors can tour those structures that have been restored to their 1931 appearance.

Corporatism   *Corporatism* is a term that many historians have employed in trying to understand the policies of the Hoover administration (1929–33) regarding government, labor, and business. Even though President Hoover did not use the term himself, he wrote and thought extensively about the issues involved in the concept as early as 1922 when he published the booklet, *American Individualism.* From Hoover's perspective, society's advance depended on a balance of power between government, business, and labor. From this balance, cooperation could and would result that would ensure better social organization. Decentralization was another significant component of Hoover's corporatism, which was moderate in contrast with those corporatists who wished for compulsory, private cartels.

By the time Hoover became president in 1929, though, trends in the American political economy rendered it almost impossible to achieve, let alone sustain, this precarious balance between government, business, and labor because the lines that divided these elements of society had become dis-

Lou Hoover and a girl scout during a Girl Scouts picnic at Camp Rapidan *(Library of Congress)*

torted beyond recognition. Put simply, the style of corporatism that Hoover practiced was too old-fashioned for the complexities of the modern American economy. It took the GREAT DEPRESSION to write the final obituary for Hoover's corporatism. During the 1930s, a pluralist approach to liberal welfare statism filled the vacuum.

Drought of 1930–1931   In the summer of 1930, a severe drought struck in the Midwest, specifically the Ohio River and the Mississippi River valleys and continued into 1931. Crops were destroyed, livestock was in jeopardy, and water resources literally dried up. The threat of famine was very real for the farmers in the region, who depended on the land for their sustenance. President Hoover faced this problem much like he had tackled Belgian relief during World War I and the Mississippi River flooding in 1927. To bring the situation under control, he called for investigations into the severity of the problem and asked governors of the affected states to meet with him. The president also called for railroads to lower freight rates, banks to expand credit, and the Red Cross

to facilitate voluntary relief. Hoover drew criticism when he offered a meager sum to be used for a crop seed and animal feed federal loan fund. Lawmakers in the affected region called for a $60 million loan fund, but Hoover proposed just $25 million. Furthermore, Hoover rejected any provision for the loan fund to cover food relief for people. In the end, the president bowed to congressional pressure and accepted a $65 million relief package. The question of relief for human starvation was sidestepped. The measure said nothing about whether or not people could use the funds for their own needs, but in practice, the funds were used for people to buy food as well as for livestock feed and crop seed relief.

Emergency Relief and Construction Act (1932)   After the Reconstruction Finance Corporation failed to bring about substantial relief from the depression, President Hoover considered more liberal measures in the late spring and summer of 1932. In July, he signed the Emergency Relief and Construction Act, the most extensive public works relief legislation to date, which, by its very existence, acknowledged the failures of both private and public relief at the state and local levels. Much debate occurred before a compromise bill could be drafted. Some lawmakers preferred direct federal aid to the states. Others argued for federal loans to the states, and still others contended federal bonds were the solution. Each proposal, though, threatened the economy in significant ways, either further unbalancing the budget or increasing the federal debt. None promised to shore up confidence in the federal government, which was flagging in part because of the outflow of gold reserves from the country.

Preservation of the nation's credit underlay the drafting of the Emergency Relief and Construction Act, which ultimately provided for $1.5 billion in funds for construction of income-producing public projects, $300 million worth of loans to the states for direct relief, and $200 million to help fund the liquidation of banks that were closing. Lawmakers required that information on all loans be reported to Congress. Impact of this legislation was scant because the depression was worsening and because national attention was focused on the upcoming presidential election. Equally important to the failures of this legislation was the skepticism with which officials in the Hoover administration viewed it. Substantial oversight and thrifty distribution policies governed usage of the funds that were made available for relief and public works. When state governors applied for loans under this program they had to sign oaths of poverty pledging that their coffers were tapped out and undergo degrading scrutiny in which federal officials looked for ways to reduce the loan amount.

Empire State Building Completed (1931)   The construction of the Empire State Building began in March 1930 in New York City when Walter Chrysler of the Chrysler Corporation and John Jakob Raskob of the General Motors Corporation both sought to construct the world's tallest building. The Chrysler Building was finished first, in 1930, and, at a height of 1,046 feet (319 m) and 77 stories, held the honor of the world's tallest building until the completion of the Empire State Building the following year. The Empire State Building rises 1,250 feet (381 m) and contains 102 stories. Raskob's

A worker bolts beams during the construction of the Empire State Building in New York City. Finished in 1931, the skyscraper displaced the recently completed Chrysler Building *(right)* as the city's—and the world's—tallest building. *(Lewis Hine/United States Federal Government)*

architect, William Lamb, used materials preassembled in factories to speed construction, and on average the workers completed about four and a half floors per week. Approximately 60,000 tons of steel were transported from Pennsylvania to New York City for completion of the building. Located at the corner of Fifth Avenue and 34th Street—some 10 blocks south of the Chrysler Building—the Empire State Building occupies a central spot in the New York City skyline and remains one of the world's most distinctive skyscrapers.

Federal Farm Board   Created by the AGRICULTURAL MARKETING ACT of 1929, the Federal Farm Board reflected President Hoover's desire to balance the needs of government, industry, and agriculture. The legislation creating the Farm Board appropriated $500 million for its operations. It was the most powerful federal agricultural agency up to that point in history, but it relied on farmer voluntarism for its success. Hoover used the Farm Board for political purposes;

he made sure that the new chair, Alexander Legge, and all of his appointees to the board opposed the various export-debenture plans to raise domestic farm income via the provision of debenture certificates to exporters for use against the customs on imported goods. The plans were popular with insurgent lawmakers from farm states in the Midwest and West.

Hoover instructed the board to organize marketing cooperatives according to the various crops produced in the country. In addition to funding new cooperatives, the board could also loan money to existing cooperatives. He did not want the board to manage the agricultural economy via government purchasing of these commodities. At his behest, the Federal Farm Board initiated its operations in the Midwest, working with wheat production. Additionally, the Farm Board arranged provisions for regional conferences, marketing facilities for crops, and educational campaigns about the benefits of cooperatives. The Farm Board assisted

Federal Farm Board, July 1929 *(Library of Congress)*

cooperatives in purchasing agricultural supplies—equipment and fertilizer, for example—in bulk to reduce production costs for those farmers who were members. Similarly, Hoover hoped the cooperatives could help farmers bargain for a better return on their crops than would be available to individual farmers. Crop stabilization corporations received loans from the Farm Board to facilitate this process. These corporations bought agricultural produce and kept it off the market until a more favorable price could be obtained. These moves made the Farm Board and the government competitors with private industry, but Hoover refused to acknowledge this reality, arguing that it preserved economic freedom.

Once the GREAT DEPRESSION set in, the Federal Farm Board played a role in Hoover's economic recovery strategies. Soon after the crash, Legge arranged loans to the cooperatives, specifically those focused on cotton and wheat, to guard against falling agricultural prices. Little attention or notice was given to the role of the federal government in this price-fixing experiment, but Hoover did receive sufficient criticism to cause him to question the actions of the Farm Board. Legge responded that its purchases guarded against not only excessively low prices but also excessively high prices. When Legge and other administration officials encouraged farmers to scale back production as another means of price stabilization, their arguments were met with much disapproval from farmers. The falling price of wheat, from 10-year record lows of $1.01 a bushel in February 1930 to $0.36 a bushel in the summer of 1931, provided an accurate measure of the difficulties Hoover and his Farm Board faced once the depression worsened. The operations of the Federal Farm Board reflected Hoover's belief in CORPORATISM and gave evidence of the weaknesses inherent within his philosophy of government. From its inception in 1929 through 1931, the Farm Board lost $345 million in loans to cooperatives.

Federal Home Loan Bank Act (1932)   Long a believer in home ownership, the spate of depression-induced mortgage foreclosures propelled President Hoover to demand congressional action on this problem. The Federal Home Loan Bank Act of 1932 provided for a Federal Home Loan Bank Board made up of five members. This board supervised a nationwide network of discount banks with an initial capitalization of $125 million. From this structure funds would then be made available to local lending institutions in the home mortgage business. Various types of financial institutions in business, including savings banks, insurance companies, and building and loan associations, were eligible for membership. The legislation helped forestall the rate of foreclosures, and it contributed to generating new jobs in the home construction industry. However, it did nothing for families that had already lost their homes. The legislation demonstrated the potential of activist government programs to assuage the effects of the depression.

Great Depression   Sparked by the STOCK MARKET CRASH of October 1929, the Great Depression of the 1930s was the greatest economic collapse in American history. To understand the origins of the Great Depression, one must also grasp the significance of the large systemic changes that the American economy underwent in the early 20th century. The nation had moved away from small, independently owned businesses and toward large-scale corporate ownership. In fact, by 1929, just 200 corporations controlled almost half of all industry in the United States. Without thousands and thousands of small businesses dominating the economy, market equilibrium was much harder to maintain.

Although the background context is simple enough, scholarly agreement on causes has never materialized. Too often politics have been interwoven in academic studies of the depression. Scholars have also divided over whether there was a single or more than one cause, whether the depression's origins were domestic or international, whether supply-side or demand-side interpretations should dominate, and whether the collapse was inevitable. Monetarists argue that there simply was not enough currency in circulation.

Titled *Migrant Mother,* this photograph taken by Dorothea Lange shows a destitute pea picker and her children in Nipomo, California, during the Great Depression. *(Library of Congress)*

Throughout his presidency, which began just months before the stock market crash, Hoover contended that the depression originated in Europe, and certainly shifts in the worldwide balance of economic power had been important. No longer was Great Britain the economic superpower it had been in the 19th century. The United States and Germany (temporarily set back by its loss in World War I) were both vying for preeminence. Additionally, worldwide agricultural overproduction in the 1920s had a deleterious effect on American farmers and the American economy.

The prevailing view of the causes of the depression concentrates on the decline in spending, consumption, and investment, but equally important was the uneven distribution of income in the United States. According to a Brookings Institution study, 0.1 percent of the richest American families earned incomes equal to that of the bottom 42 percent. Disparity in wealth was even greater. The stock market boom and bust also played a role in triggering, if not causing, the Great Depression. During the Hoover administration (1929–33), a variety of economic statistics tell a poignant and painful story of the country's decline from the Coolidge prosperity of the mid-1920s. Unemployment hovered at 3.3 percent throughout the 1920s, but it soared to 8.9 percent in 1930. Economic investment plummeted 35 percent, and bank failures doubled from 659 in 1929 to 1,352 in 1930. In 1932, economic investment fell 88 percent. The deflation rate went from 2.6 percent in 1930 to 18 percent in 1933.

By 1933, after Hoover was defeated for reelection, unemployment rates neared 25 percent, the highest in American history. Furthermore, the public perception that Herbert Hoover cared little for the suffering of the people caused his name to be used in various negative ways to characterize the changed circumstances in which people lived their lives. For example, shantytowns became Hoovervilles and discarded newspapers became Hoover blankets. The Great Depression continued into the Franklin D. Roosevelt administration (1933–45) and did not fully abate until World War II.

Individualism   Notions of individualism and a belief in the survival of the fittest had spread widely through the United States in the late 19th century with the application of Charles Darwin's theory of evolution to human beings in the form of Social Darwinism. President Hoover's concepts of individualism differed significantly from the ruthless, unadulterated application of Social Darwinism to human existence, which posited that only the strong would survive and that assistance to the poor or needy would only perpetuate "weaker" people. For Hoover, responsibility for society at large was as important as individual identity. In many ways, his philosophy balanced or tempered individualism with communitarian responsibility.

In 1922, six years before he was elected president, Hoover published the book *American Individualism*. He had been thinking intensively about the ideas that permeated this text since the late 1910s, and, as some scholars and biographers have argued, his perspective on individualism dates to his rural childhood and to his Quaker faith. Specifically, Hoover respected the socially responsible individualism that permeated Quakerism. He saw these values as essential to the success of community in America. For Hoover, voluntary community cooperation required that each individual contribute from his or her own talents and abilities to the larger benefit of the community to which they belonged.

That few Americans, even Hoover, could achieve and maintain this balance mattered less to the future president than did the optimistic, and perhaps unrealistic, goal of infusing political and economic policy with the Hooverian notions of individualism. Adoption of his philosophy suffered because he used uninteresting words to describe what he meant and because the word *individualism* already carried a meaning very different from the one that Hoover sought to apply. His concept of individualism played a significant role in his approach to the GREAT DEPRESSION during his presidency. While president, Hoover attempted to balance his belief in individualism with collectivist tendencies. Any presidential effort to save the U.S. economic system for the American people, Hoover believed, was wrong-headed and dangerous to American individualism. Instead, the American people needed to save themselves by adopting policies that applied the balanced approach he advocated between individualism and collectivism.

Lindbergh Baby Kidnapping (1932)   On March 1, 1932, 20-month-old Charles A. Lindbergh, Jr. was kidnapped from his family home in Hopewell, New Jersey. His father, Charles A. Lindbergh, Sr., was the most famous aviator in the world, having been the first pilot to fly across the Atlantic Ocean from New York to Paris in 1927. Because of his father's fame and because of the extensive search for the kidnappers, the case and ensuing trial attracted massive public attention. Lindbergh insisted to authorities that he be allowed to negotiate with the kidnappers without police interference. No arrests were initially made, and, on May 12, 1932, the baby's body was found. After a lengthy investigation and trial, Bruno Hauptmann was found guilty in 1935 based on circumstantial evidence. He was executed for the crime the following year. Uncertainties have lingered about the accuracy of this verdict. The case also had legislative ramifications. In 1932, Congress enacted legislation that made kidnapping a federal felony when state lines were crossed. The Department of Justice's Division of Investigation (later the Federal Bureau of Investigation) gained jurisdiction and established an impressive record of recovery in its first years of responsibility for these crimes.

One of the most sensational cases in American history involved the kidnapping and murder of the baby of Charles and Anne Morrow Lindbergh. Above, Charles Lindbergh testifies at the trial in Flemington, New Jersey. *(Library of Congress)*

London Naval Conference (1930)   The five largest naval powers in the world—the United States, Great Britain, Japan, France, and Italy—met in London from January to April 1930. Despite American efforts to encourage reduction of each country's navy, few substantial gains resulted beyond an across-the-board limitation on the size of navies. Because world affairs remained relatively peaceful, the delegates had little incentive to demobilize their nation's navies. The lawyers and experts who advised the various national delegations disputed the equity of using tonnage to establish and maintain ratios of ships the nations could retain in their navies, arguing instead that age, speed, armor, and fighting value should also be calculated.

France left the conference when it became apparent that neither the Americans nor the British were interested in a collective security agreement. Italy also left the conference because of tension with the French, leading Secretary of State Henry L. Stimson to settle for a three-power treaty among Great Britain, Japan, and the United States. Japanese demands to increase its navy brought further haggling, which resulted

in a slight benefit to Japan (in practical terms the ratio came closer to 10:10:7 than the negotiated 10:10:6, meaning that for every 10 capital ships in the U.S. and British navies, the Japanese could have seven), but many people in Japan nonetheless felt disgraced by the terms. Other terms of the agreement included a moratorium on capital ship construction until 1936; permission for the United States to surpass the ratio if other nations had already done so; and maintenance of the 10:10:7 tonnage ratios until 1936. After much debate, the Senate ratified the agreements, which many in and out of the government termed a failure despite the very real limitations put in place on all classifications of ships.

***Look Homeward, Angel,* by Thomas Wolfe (1929)**   This 1929 autobiographical novel by Thomas Wolfe tells the coming-of-age story of Eugene Gant, a native of rural North Carolina who moves to Boston to study at Harvard University. The novel provides a thorough recounting of small town life and the pain of leaving it. The novel has fallen out of favor with critics because of its verbose prose and outdated, stereotyped depictions of race and gender. Nonetheless, *Look Homeward, Angel* received wide critical praise when it was published, and Wolfe was regarded as a writer whose talent equaled that of Ernest Hemingway, F. Scott Fitzgerald, and William Faulkner.

Moratorium on Reparations and War Debts (1931)   In June 1931, President Hoover announced a one-year moratorium on all World War I–era debts. The action resulted from his belief that the GREAT DEPRESSION had as its source the economic problems in Europe. Throughout the 1920s, Germany had relied heavily on American loans to repay its World War I reparations debts to Britain and France, but the availability of credit declined with the onset of the Great Depression. In fact, with Germany close to defaulting on its existing loans, numerous bank runs occurred in the United States. To deal with their homefront economic problems, Germany and Austria reduced foreign imports, and France responded by withholding funds from German and Austrian banks. In May 1931, Credit Anstalt, the Austrian central bank, failed. In the aftermath, governments and creditors questioned whether Austria could remain on the gold standard while foreigners withdrew heavily from the institution. To remedy the situation, the Austrian government imposed rigid controls over transactions involving gold and foreign currencies. Soon Hungary and Germany followed suit.

Hoover hoped that his moratorium plan would halt the international run on European banks. Even as he took this action, his advisers, most notably Secretary of State Henry L. Stimson, noted that the moratorium would also mean a halt in repayment of war reparations from Germany to Britain and France. Hoover, though, incorrectly viewed the problems as separate. To make the plan work, Hoover had to win over Congress and the American people, neither of whom were eager to forgive the Allied debt, along with the French government, which viewed German reparations in more emotional terms as necessary because of the damage inflicted in northern parts of the country occupied by Germany from 1914 to 1918. Stimson negotiated French compliance with the deal, and Hoover effectively lobbied Congress to gain world approval. Immediately after its approval, observers credited the moratorium with preventing an economic and political crisis in Germany. Such views were premature for the moratorium only forestalled the collapse in Germany, a disaster that contributed to the rise of Adolf Hitler in the 1930s.

Museum of Modern Art Opens (1929)   In response to the concerns and actions of three leading art patrons—Lillie P. Bliss, Mary Sullivan, and Abby Aldrich Rockefeller—a museum dedicated to the preservation and study of modern art opened in New York City in 1929. The public eagerly flocked to the museum, which featured, among others, the works of famed European artists Paul Cézanne, Paul Gauguin,

Georges Seurat, and Vincent van Gogh and included departments of painting and sculpture, architecture and design, film and video, and photography. Multiple renovations have expanded the popular midtown Manhattan landmark, and its massive collection of modern works has made it one of the major art museums in the world.

National Credit Corporation   *See* RECONSTRUCTION FINANCE CORPORATION ACT (1932)

National Institute of Health Act (1930)   The National Institutes of Health can trace its origins to the 1887 founding of a single laboratory within the Marine Hospital Service, a precursor to the Public Health Service. Health care problems during World War I with regard to contaminated equipment, the spread of tetanus spores, and the influenza pandemic caused great concern in the military. Under the National Institute of Health Act of 1930, also known as the Ransdell Act after its sponsor Senator Joseph Ransdell (D-LA), the Hygienic Laboratory was renamed the National Institute of Health and funds for research fellowships were made available for the study of basic biological and medical problems. While funding amounts were limited due to the realities of the depression, its passage marked a significant turning point toward publicly funded medical research. A companion bill, the Parker Act, charted the actions of the Public Health Service through the early 1970s. President Hoover supported both pieces of legislation. In 1948 the agency's name was changed to the National Institutes of Health to reflect the agency's expanded mission.

***Near v. Minnesota* (1931)**   Argued in January 1930 and decided by the Supreme Court in June 1931, *Near v. Minnesota* dealt with the question of whether or not a Minnesota "gag law" restricted the First Amendment's protections for freedom of the press. The *Saturday Press,* a Minneapolis newspaper edited by Jay Near, routinely assailed local politicians in charging that they were affiliated with gangsters. Minnesota officials used an injunction to stop Near from printing further accusations, relying on state law that banned regular publication of obscene, malicious, and defamatory material. The Supreme Court found the law unconstitutional in its application against Near because the law functioned as a prior restraint against publications that had not yet occurred. The ruling did not deter authorities from seeking criminal charges or other means of redress after the fact of publication, though.

Norris-LaGuardia Act (1932)   As secretary of commerce in 1922, Herbert Hoover had fought for recognition of the eight-hour day in the steel industry and against the use of the injunction to break strikes. After his election to the presidency in 1928, Hoover had the opportunity to sign legislation outlawing the injunction as a strike-breaking device, but the authors of the legislation questioned whether the president, in fact, supported the measure or whether he signed the bill because he had no other choice. Documents in the Hoover Presidential Library give some credence to these doubts. Hoover's congressional liaison disliked the more liberal components of the bill, especially provisions with regard to strikers' violence, boycotts, demonstrations, and picketing. The Norris-LaGuardia Act of 1932, named for its sponsors, Senator George W. Norris (R-NE) and Representative Fiorello LaGuardia (R-NY), granted workers the right to join labor unions, limited the federal injunction against strikers, eradicated the use of "yellow dog" contracts, and allowed for the removal of biased judges in contempt cases. This measure served as an important precedent for stronger guarantees of labor rights enacted in the New Deal.

Pecora Wall Street Investigation (1932–1934)

The Senate Banking Committee directed its chief counsel, Ferdinand Pecora, to run an investigation into the practices of Wall Street bankers as they related to the onset of the GREAT DEPRESSION. The leading bankers in the country were called as witnesses, and in one well-publicized moment a circus performer climbed onto J. P. Morgan, Jr.'s lap and posed for pictures. The hearings, which ran from 1932 to 1934, revealed significant misconduct, including lists of preferred customers who were able to purchase the initial public offering of stocks at bargain basement prices. Charles E. Mitchell, the president of National City Bank, admitted to substantial stock speculations through his own bank with the bank's money. Faced with a mounting tax bill for 1929, Mitchell sold some of this stock to his wife for a significant paper loss, which eliminated his income tax debt. Greed within the banking community resulted in still other misdeeds, including manipulated stock prices, trading the stocks of one's own bank, unstable holding companies, "loans" to bank officials, and tax evasion. Passage of several key New Deal measures, including banking reform, securities reform, and holding company reform, marked the most important legacy of the Pecora investigation.

President's Emergency Committee for Employment

In October 1930, President Hoover created a cabinet committee on unemployment, the President's Emergency Committee for Employment (PECE). He named Colonel Arthur Woods, a colleague from World War I, chairman of PECE. The name of the organization reflected Hoover's overall approach to the nation's economic crisis. It also stressed positive thinking about the GREAT DEPRESSION. The words *emergency* and *employment* were used so as to make the crisis seem temporary and to avoid drawing attention to the unemployment rate. The new entity consisted of eight divisions that coordinated their efforts with those of the executive departments, state and local officials, industry, social welfare organizations,

Circus performer Lya Graf jumped into J. P. Morgan, Jr.'s lap during the Pecora Wall Street investigation in 1933. *(Associated Press)*

public works departments, statistical organizations, women's groups, and public agencies.

Hoover used his administrative experiences in World War I as a model for determining the structure and organization of PECE, which he hoped would bring centralized coordination to the multitude of scattered entities involved with relief work. He did not want to centralize or federalize the overall relief process but instead to create a clearinghouse to facilitate better functioning of the local efforts. One critic of the agency noted that it focused too much on positive, anecdotal examples of relief and too little on either the collection of unemployment statistics or data about available relief funds. Woods realized that, with factory unemployment on the rise, the mandate of his agency was not sufficient to meet the problems confronting the American people. He suggested that Hoover ask Congress to create a $375 million program for public employment, but the president ignored this advice and Woods resigned his post in April 1931 without any fanfare. Four months later, Hoover disbanded PECE and replaced it with the PRESIDENT'S ORGANIZATION ON UNEMPLOYMENT RELIEF.

President's Mountain School   When the Hoovers visited the site that would ultimately house CAMP RAPIDAN, the presidential retreat in the Blue Ridge Mountains of Virginia, President Hoover used the occasion to do some fishing. In August 1929, five months after he became president, Hoover struck up a conversation with a local boy, who had sought him out to present the president with a birthday gift—a 15-pound possum. Hoover inquired where the boy attended school, and upon learning that no school was located in the vicinity, Herbert and first lady LOU HENRY HOOVER set about building, equipping, and staffing a school for the area children, drawing on their own funds as well as other private gifts. Lou Henry Hoover was especially involved in the project.

The President's Mountain School, as it was called, also served as a community center for adults. The teacher used pragmatic techniques, such as the Sears-Roebuck catalog,

President Hoover fly fishing at Camp Rapidan in the Blue Ridge Mountains of Virginia, where he and first lady Lou Henry Hoover built the President's Mountain School. *(National Park Service)*

to teach reading and arithmetic. Students were encouraged to read about products of value to them and their families, while they practiced basic mathematic calculations in filling out order blanks. The school, which served 32 students at the peak of its operations, operated between February 1930 and May 1933, when area residents moved away to make room for the opening of the Shenandoah National Park. The Hoovers' involvement in this project exemplified their belief in private philanthropy and their conviction that charitable works should be done for altruistic, not self-serving, motives. As such, the Hoovers never publicized the contributions they made in establishing the President's Mountain School.

President's Organization on Unemployment Relief (1931)
In August 1931, the President's Organization on Unemployment Relief (POUR) replaced the PRESIDENT'S EMERGENCY COMMITTEE FOR EMPLOYMENT (PECE). President Hoover appointed Walter Gifford, the president of the American Telephone and Telegraph Company, as the chair of POUR. Fred C. Croxton, a lieutenant in PECE who had worked closely with PECE chairman Arthur Woods, oversaw the day-to-day operations of POUR. POUR differed from PECE in that it contained five national committees with oversight responsibility for resource mobilization, relief administration, employment plan advisement, suggestions for federal public works, and coordination of national entities.

Because Hoover's sentiments were well known, POUR never called for a direct federal program of relief. Instead, POUR functioned largely as an advertising agency for Hooverian optimism about depression relief. One POUR advertisement pictured an unemployed worker declaring that he would rather have a job than a handout and stating his allegiance to the United States as the greatest country in the world. Soon after the reorganization of PECE into POUR, editors with the *Kiplinger Washington Letter,* a financial newsletter, observed that if POUR could not significantly increase the charitable funds available for relief, the Hoover administration would face serious challenges from Congress. Furthermore, the editors at the *Kiplinger Washington Letter* commented that Hoover found himself on the divide between two diametrically opposed theories of social organization, one that advocated private business responsibility with the smallest amount of government involvement possible and another that promoted a combination of social business responsibility with government activism.

As unemployment rose precipitously in the fall of 1931, POUR's efforts seemed much too meagre given the magnitude of the national crisis. Calls for reinvigorated consumer product consumption, maintenance of community morale, neighborliness toward the unemployed, and assistance to students proved popular but ineffective, and critics charged they were akin to using a band-aid to treat a severed limb.

More troubling was Gifford's apparent ignorance as to the depth of the unemployment problem; he told the president in the fall of 1931 that the states could handle any relief problems they faced during the upcoming winter. In its defense, POUR constituted but one component of the Hoover relief strategy, and its purpose was to forestall congressional calls for a more activist government strategy. Nonetheless, when Gifford appeared before a Senate subcommittee in January 1932, one lawmaker chastised him for the hopefulness he continued to espouse in face of the dire economic realities. POUR ended with the Hoover administration.

Press Relations   Throughout his presidency, Herbert Hoover failed miserably to establish an effective working relationship with the press. His inability to do so resulted in part because he never understood the importance of creating and maintaining a personal relationship with the public and in part because of the role of the media in the 1928 presidential election. Disdainful of crowds, Hoover never enjoyed mixing with large numbers of people; still, prior to 1929 he had effectively managed the press. From his World War I days with the Committee for the Relief of Belgium through his tenure as secretary of commerce from 1921 to 1929, Hoover had been the beneficiary of good press notices. Soon after his election, Hoover indicated that he would meet with the press twice a week and that he would permit direct quotations of his statements as opposed to requiring journalists to draw from the statements of intermediaries.

His announcement pleased reporters, but they were not happy for long. Three weeks into his presidency, Hoover required that journalists submit their questions in advance for approval and he often replied with written statements. Without adequate questions, Hoover regularly told the press corps that he had nothing to say. That Hoover favored a few reporters over others only worsened the situation. Hoover never mastered the art of communicating with the general public through the radio or the newsreels, both of which were becoming immensely popular during this period. He did not understand the importance of human interest stories and avoided any and all press coverage of his family life. Politics also played a role in Hoover's problems with the press. During the 1928 campaign, both Hoover and his Democratic rival, Al Smith, had been built up by the press as larger than life personalities. High-ranking Democratic partisans, frustrated at the loss, reasoned that the same media responsible for the Hoover victory could be used to discredit the president. Indeed, the Democratic Party generated much negative coverage of Hoover, including both mistakes that he clearly made and policies that he only grudgingly supported.

Reconstruction Finance Corporation Act (1932)   On December 7, 1931, President Hoover asked Congress to pass legislation creating the Reconstruction Finance Cor-

poration after the short-lived National Credit Corporation (NCC) failed. Created in October 1931, the NCC attempted to impose voluntary cooperation on the banking industry so that stronger banks would shore up struggling ones. Stronger banks, however, had little incentive to help their competitors, and this recovery plan proved ineffective. The NCC spent only $10 million of the $500 million available to it, worrying that an aggressive strategy of saving those banks in trouble would destroy the corporation by requiring more funds than were available to be dispersed. Writing later in his published memoirs, Hoover chastised the National Credit Corporation as too conservative.

To replace it, Hoover called on Congress to create the Reconstruction Finance Corporation (RFC), which he modeled after the World War I agency, the War Finance Corporation. Using a wartime reference suggested that Hoover both realized the severity of the depression and also intended the RFC to play a temporary role in the American economy. This request was part of the president's State of the Union address, but Congress postponed action for about a month. While lawmakers easily approved the bill, questions were nonetheless raised by liberals and progressives, who distrusted the banking community's support for the bill. The bill, which passed in January 1932, appropriated $500 million in funds and provided for another $1.5 billion in bonds and debenture or unsecured notes as security for federal loans to specific industries suffering during the depression, including banks, railroads, and selected agricultural organizations.

The purpose of the RFC was to rescue the financial services industry, which consisted of commercial and savings banks, credit unions, insurance companies, and trust companies. Later the RFC was expanded to provide loans for railroads facing bankruptcy, but only after the Interstate Commerce Commission gave its approval. This configuration of assistance led liberals and progressives to view the measure as nothing more than relief for the already suspect banking industry. Nothing in the bill provided aid to cities and towns or to individual Americans suffering the ill-effects of the depression. Those same congressional critics had no competing plan, however, so their complaints carried little weight.

In terms of its scale and scope of activism, the Reconstruction Finance Corporation was an unprecedented organization. Never before had a president called for an executive agency to be given such independent authority over the economy. The RFC put primary emphasis on business confidence and credit as solutions to the depression. This private sector, financial approach ignored the human side of the depression. Provision of government credit to banks, Hoover believed, would make credit more available to individuals throughout the country. Enlarging the credit supply was not a solution in and of itself because it did not automatically create new demands for goods and services. What the RFC did manage to accomplish during the Hoover administration was a temporary restoration of the American banking industry. The Reconstruction Finance Corporation became even more important during the presidency of Franklin D. Roosevelt (1933–45) when it served as a funding conduit for both New Deal and World War II expenditures.

St. Valentine's Day Massacre (1929)   With enactment of Prohibition after World War I, organized crime became a significant problem in American society. In their efforts to control the illegal "bootleg" alcohol trade, Johnny Torrio and Al Capone became the dominant mobsters in Chicago in the 1920s and their operations proved a model for criminals throughout the country. It took the Torrio-Capone gang almost the entire decade to take over their leading competitors and to assume their preeminent role in underworld operations. During the first half of the 1920s more than 200 gang-related murders occurred in Chicago, the result of the Torrio-Capone struggle for dominance against other mobsters.

The St. Valentine's Day Massacre of 1929 ended the contest for control of the Chicago underworld. On February 14, 1929, four men claiming to be police officers pretended to conduct a raid on the warehouse that George "Bugs" Moran and his gang used to store bootleg liquor. Six members of an opposing gang and one other individual were lined up

and executed with machine guns. Al Capone was the leading suspect but was never tried for the crime. Nonetheless, Moran's North Side gang was Capone's most significant rival and had wreaked havoc on Capone's operations. The massacre shocked the public and became a symbol not only of gang violence but also of the Chicago underworld. It also marked the Torrio-Capone Gang as the leaders of the underworld with annual earnings of approximately $70 million.

Scottsboro Case   On March 25, 1931, nine African-American teenagers and two young white females were riding on the Southern Railroad's freight train between Chattanooga and Memphis, Tennessee. Two young white males accompanied the females, and there were a dozen or so unemployed white youths on the train. All were victims of the Great Depression and were following rumors of job availability elsewhere. An interracial scuffle ensued when one of the white male youths stepped on the hand of one of the African-American teenagers. The African-American teenagers forced all but one of the white teenagers off the train, and they then complained to authorities of a gang attack. Local whites formed a posse and met the train at its next stop. The nine captured blacks, dubbed the "Scottsboro Boys" because the first trials took place in Scottsboro, Alabama, were also accused of rape when two mill workers from Huntsville, Alabama—Victoria Price and Ruby Bates—met the posse and identified the captured

In 1937, NAACP worker Juanita E. Jackson *(fourth from left)*, accompanied by another woman, visits the Scottsboro defendants, nine young African-American boys and men convicted of raping two white women on a freight train in 1931. Despite flimsy evidence and contradictory testimony, the defendants remained in jail for many years. *(Library of Congress)*

African Americans as their supposed attackers. The accused African-American youths denied the allegations, and local whites planned to lynch the boys that evening. The Alabama governor thwarted the pending lynching when he called out the National Guard to protect the youths.

The first of what would be four trials began quickly with defense attorneys who were later deemed to be incompetent (the prosecution wanted separate cases to protect against a reversible error in a single case that would void a guilty verdict). On the flimsiest of evidence, an all-white jury found eight of the nine black defendants guilty and sentenced them to death. The jury hung on the question of death for the youngest of the accused—13 year-old Roy Wright.

Fear that defending against rape allegations, a touchy subject in the South, would harm its overall agenda led the National Association for the Advancement of Colored People (NAACP) to sit on the sidelines, but the Communist Party was less circumspect, stepping in to defend the youths via their International Labor Defense (ILD) operation. The NAACP decided too late that the youths were innocent and that it should defend them. Under ILD direction, the case of the Scottsboro defendants was appealed to the Alabama Supreme Court, which upheld all but one of the convictions. Further appeal to the U.S. Supreme Court, in the case of *Powell v. Alabama,* resulted in a reversal and order for new trials. The Supreme Court ruled that the defendants had been denied right to counsel as guaranteed under the Fourteenth Amendment's due process clause.

New trials followed in 1933. Ruby Bates recanted her testimony, claiming she had lied and that she had never been raped or assaulted. Nonetheless, an all-white jury again found the defendants guilty. Those convictions were also appealed to the U.S. Supreme Court in 1935 in the case of *Norris v. Alabama,* which found the Alabama jury selection system unconstitutional because it had barred virtually all African Americans from serving. Still undeterred, Alabama pursued yet another round of trials with five of the defendants found guilty and all charges dropped against the other four. A hoped-for pardon in 1938 never materialized. Via paroles and escapes by 1950, all of the Scottsboro defendants had left Alabama. The repeated miscarriages of justice in the local courts illustrated the profound and pervasive racism of the Jim Crow era.

Smoot-Hawley Tariff (1930)   Soon after becoming president in 1929, Hoover planned to call a special session of Congress to address the economic problems that beset the nation's farmers. While U.S. farmers had enjoyed historically high earnings during World War I, the postwar period had proved calamitous with the expansion of worldwide agricultural productivity and a dangerous cycle of overproduction to compensate. As a result, farm prices fell in the second half of the decade. It was this problem that Hoover aimed to solve and which ultimately resulted in the Smoot-Hawley Tariff.

The president believed that an increased tariff on agricultural imports would provide the necessary relief.

During the legislative battles over the tariff, Hoover fought intensively with Senator William E. Borah, an insurgent Republican from Idaho. The two men disagreed over Hoover's call for flexibility in the legislation. The idea of granting the Tariff Commission power to study tariffs, contrast them with realities of the domestic and global economies, and make recommendations to the president troubled Borah because the result would be increased power for the president. Further complicating the fate of the tariff bill was Hoover's belief that Congress should act independently from the White House. As such, he provided little guidance in the drafting of, and the subsequent deliberations on, the tariff bill, opening the door for substantial "pork barrel" politics. Members of Congress took the occasion to protect narrow interests as opposed to national interests. The legislation ballooned to include protections for the industrial sector as well.

Tariff politics in the 1920s revealed the partisan cleavages between Democrats and Republicans. The former typically criticized high protective tariffs without making many substantive arguments about the proposals while the latter believed them necessary to protect American manufacturing interests. Insurgent Republicans, though, also fought the industrial protections. Lawmakers debated this tariff legislation for over six months, fighting about whether or not to include export debentures (the presumed panacea of the farm bloc, namely, the use of debentures, or certificates, to encourage more agricultural exports via a reduction of duties for imported goods) in the plan and whether or not to grant the Tariff Commission flexibility to adjust tariff schedules. Hoover opposed the debentures and supported the more flexible approach—both of which ultimately passed. In all, the legislation, sponsored by Senator Reed Smoot (R-UT) and Representative Willis Hawley (R-OR), addressed 3,293 items subject to the tariff. During the course of their deliberations, lawmakers increased rates on 887 of those items and decreased rates on another 235.

On June 17, 1930, Hoover signed the Smoot-Hawley Tariff, which increased rates on agricultural imports from almost 40 percent to almost 50 percent. Scholars who have studied the Smoot-Hawley Tariff have discounted the importance of the flexibility provision, which Hoover had hoped would have a beneficial impact on the domestic economy. Scholars have also doubted that the tariff revisions had any real impact on either domestic manufacturing or agricultural protection, the former already well protected from foreign competition and the latter struggling against almost insurmountable surpluses, such that the lessening of foreign competition would have no meaning. Indeed, the tariff satisfied none but the most conservative Republicans; in fact, it became a rallying cry for Democrats ready to attack the administration at every juncture. It also worsened the GREAT DEPRESSION by inciting retaliatory measures from foreign governments, thus ensuring a reduction of foreign trade. U.S. imports from Europe stood at $1.3 billion in 1929 but dropped to $390 million in 1932; U.S. exports also declined precipitously, from $2.3 billion in 1929 to $784 million in 1932. Between 1929 and 1934, world trade fell 66 percent.

The Sound and the Fury, by William Faulkner (1929)

Prolific author William Faulkner preferred *The Sound and the Fury* over his many other novels. Critics have agreed, terming it his first masterpiece. Published in 1929, *The Sound and the Fury* tells the story of the Compson family's decline from its position among the southern aristocracy. The four parts of the novel present different perspectives on Caddy Compson's story written in a stream-of-consciousness style. Critics have examined the novel's many themes, including its tragic story line and the role of order, honor, and religion in southern life.

South American Trip (1928–1929)

After his victory in the 1928 presidential election, Herbert Hoover was the recipient of significant media attention. Concerned that his continued presence in Washington, D.C., might prove detrimental to the ability of CALVIN COOLIDGE to govern during the remaining days of is presidency, Hoover arranged for a tour of South America. Motivated even more than by a wish to

After winning the presidency in November 1928, Hoover set off on a good-will tour of South America but, as this cartoon suggests, kept informed of political developments in Washington. *(Library of Congress)*

escape national politics, the new president saw the trip as an opportunity to begin his good neighbor foreign policy with the region. Hoover and Coolidge disagreed on the proper mode of transportation. Hoover wanted to take battleships so there would be sufficient space for his traveling party—his wife LOU HENRY HOOVER, various diplomatic advisers, and the traveling press corps—but Coolidge wanted Hoover to take cruisers, a less expensive option. In the end, Hoover and his party traveled to South America on the battleship the USS *Maryland.*

They departed on November 19, 1928, and returned on the battleship the USS *Utah* on January 6, 1929. During the trip, the press became disenchanted with the censorship the president's staff imposed on their work. Regardless, Hoover forged favorable relationships with the national leaders he visited in Honduras, El Salvador, Nicaragua, Costa Rica, Ecuador, Peru, Chile, Argentina, and Brazil. Protests against the "Colossus of the North" paled in comparison with favorable reaction to Hoover's calls for increased contact between the United States and the nations of Central and South America, an American role in fostering economic development and prosperity in the region, and U.S. support for freedom and democracy throughout the hemisphere. Hoover hoped a policy of nonintervention in the region would cement the new partnerships he sought.

Stimson Doctrine (1932) Historians have regarded the Stimson Doctrine, enunciated in 1932, as the most significant foreign policy development of the Hoover presidency (1929–33). It resulted from Japan's expansionist policies in the late 1920s and early 1930s, specifically its use of the Kwangtung Army in China, which was wracked at the time by civil war. Wanting to annex the Chinese province of Manchuria, the Japanese precipitated a conflict in the region and then escalated the hostilities. Secretary of State Henry L. Stimson characterized the action as a breach both of international law and of treaties to which Japan was a signatory power. Because Hoover refused economic sanctions as punishment for the Japanese hostilities, Stimson called for a policy of nonrecognition of any and all territorial changes resulting from Japan's military actions in Manchuria. The League of Nations used the Stimson Doctrine to draft its own nonrecognition policy. Because there were no effective enforcement measures, short of war, available to the world community, Japan ignored both the Stimson Doctrine and the League resolution, making Manchuria a puppet state under its control. The eventual outbreak of war between China and Japan in 1937 demonstrated the weakness of the Stimson Doctrine.

Stock Market Crash (1929) The stock market crash of 1929 ushered in the GREAT DEPRESSION, the worst economic slowdown in American history. While the immediate crisis unfolded over several days, the crash was rooted in the unhealthy speculative fervor of the decade of the 1920s. Many middle-class Americans adopted the tenet that everyone should be rich and that one path to prosperity was to invest in the stock market. The Democratic National Committee chairman even penned an article for *Ladies Home Journal,* a leading women's magazine, making that argument in 1929. The Florida real estate boom of the mid-1920s, though, previewed the dangers of this get-rich-quick mentality. Mild weather, railroads, and the automobile made Florida a popular destination for the wealthy and a target for land speculators. The overwhelming majority of Florida land bought and sold in the 1920s was never intended for the personal use of the purchaser but for investment and resale purposes. As such, much of the land traded was not desirable beachfront property but rather interior swampland. By 1926, values deflated and investors sought to get out and recoup as much of their investments as possible. Two hurricanes that summer helped close the season on the Florida boom.

Much the same process of "boom mentality" investment was underway on the stock market. Unlike the Florida example, however, stock market purchases of the 1920s resulted from very real technological innovations, such as automobiles and radios, that warranted investor excitement. The reality of who did and did not invest in the stock market bears consideration. Although many people claimed that almost everyone traded on the market, in reality only about 4 million Americans out of a population of 120 million owned stocks, and of that number only 1.5 million had portfolios sufficient to require the services of a stockbroker. Statistics about dividend distribution reveals the excessive concentration of stock market ownership: approximately three-quarters of all dividends went to less than 600,000 people.

So what caused the speculative boom? The Federal Reserve Board's 1927 decision to lower interest rates made for cheaper money and encouraged both investment and spending. More important, views changed as to why stocks should be purchased. Traditional investors believed that stocks were purchased to secure stable long-term earnings from the dividends, but the pursuit of instant riches in the 1920s led this perspective to give way to a new view, namely, that stocks should be seen as an investment to be bought when values were low and then quickly sold when values were high. Earnings from the stock's dividends—actual or potential—mattered little. Nor did the quality of the stock. For example, stock in RCA, or more formally the Radio Corporation of America, rose from $85 to $420 without paying a single dividend. This process was repeated over and over so much that the Dow Jones average—an index of the price of major securities—increased 100 percent between early 1928 and September 1929. Margin buying—purchasing stocks on borrowed money—helped fuel much of this increase. Customers who opted for this approach paid a small percentage down, typically 10 percent, and used the stock as collateral for a loan to cover the rest of the purchase price. The startling profits that traders accumulated were called leverage, but the process worked in reverse as well. Just as traders could gamble on the prospects of 3,400 percent gains on margin buying so also could traders experience equally staggering losses. A stock bought on the margins at a price that then plummeted left the purchaser with a huge debt and no collateral to cover it. Prior to the crash, though, the leverage process gave rise to investment trusts and pyramids, which existed only to sell and own stock.

The bubble burst slowly, over about an eight-week period of time between mid-September 1929 and mid-November 1929. Earlier downturns in December 1928 and March 1929 had been short-lived because confidence in the market remained high. During the long, slow spiral downward in the fall of 1929, investors pulled away from the market in record numbers. The process began on September 3, when the long bull market of the 1920s reached its apex. On September 5, market prices fell, but investors dismissed the results as nothing more than a brief correction. In reality, prices continued to drop throughout the month and into October even as investors remained confident because there were brief upswings in the trading. By October 21, all signs indicated that the bubble had definitively burst. So many stocks were sold that the ticker could not keep pace with the traders. Fear of falling stock values was exacerbated by lack of knowledge about how far the decline had gone. The result was even more frenzied selling off against additional losses. Some scholars have argued that October 23 was the key day of the market crash because the Dow Jones lost 21 points in an hour. Greater losses came later, but this proved to be a decline from which there was no return. On "Black Thursday," October 24, the bottom fell out of the market. That afternoon saw a brief ray of hope when bankers such as Thomas W. Lamont of J. P. Morgan bought up falling stocks in record numbers. The market stabilized over the weekend, but the new week saw another freefall made worse by the bankers' realization that they lacked the power to halt the trend. On "Black Tuesday," October 29, 16.4 million shares were sold (when buyers could be found). Almost 40 years passed before the volume of shares traded surpassed this record. A brief recovery followed the next day, but the larger downward trend continued into November. As prices dropped and stocks lost value, investments were wiped out, sending companies and individuals into bankruptcy and ushering in the Great Depression.

Supreme Court Appointments   President Hoover generated much controversy in and out of Congress with his initial appointments to the Supreme Court. His first appointment to the Court stemmed from Chief Justice WILLIAM HOWARD TAFT's resignation in February 1930. Liberals in and out of the government hoped that Hoover would elevate his good friend and former cabinet colleague, Associate Justice Harlan Fiske Stone, to serve as the new chief justice. Stone and Hoover shared similar backgrounds and temperaments, both preferring intellectual conversation to the Washington social scene, for example. As a sitting member of the Court, though, Stone could not make his ambition to secure the post of chief justice known to the president when Hoover polled him about potential nominees. Hoover ultimately named Charles Evans Hughes to the position (Hughes had been an associate justice between 1910 and 1916, when he resigned to run for the presidency). Conservatives applauded the appointment as a signal that Hoover hoped the Supreme Court would continue much in the vein that Taft had established during the 1920s, and the Senate confirmed him by a vote of 52 to 26 on March 13, 1930.

When Associate Justice Edward T. Sanford died that same month, Hoover was compelled to make a second Supreme Court appointment, which resulted in even more rancorous political maneuvering within the Senate. Hoover nominated John J. Parker, a member of the Fourth Circuit Court of Appeals in Richmond, Virginia, to the post. Despite a thorough White House vetting of Parker, Republican insurgents in the Senate undertook their own investigation of Parker. Working with the American Federation of Labor, the National Association for the Advancement of Colored People, and *The New Republic,* a progressive journal, these Republican insurgents and Hoover opponents attacked Parker for his decision in a labor union injunction case and for charges that he opposed rights for African Americans. While neither charge was clear-cut, opponents of the Parker nomination assembled sufficient information to block Senate confirmation by a vote of 41 to 39.

After this imbroglio, Hoover quickly named Owen Roberts to the Court, a choice that met with Senate approval. A former law professor at the University of Pennsylvania and one of the prosecutors in the Teapot Dome case, Roberts received a unanimous vote in the Senate Judiciary Committee, and the full Senate did likewise without even a roll-call vote. The whole affair was completed in less than a minute.

Hoover's final Supreme Court appointment, liberal Benjamin Cardozo, had spent almost two decades on the Court of Appeals. Cardozo was tapped to fill the vacancy created by the resignation of Oliver Wendell Holmes, Jr., in February 1932. Cardozo enjoyed an easy confirmation process, winning a unanimous vote in the Senate.

Swope Plan (1931)   Gerard Swope, the president of General Electric and a supporter of President Hoover, developed a plan in September 1931 for compulsory economic and welfare planning. Swope's success, combined with his political connections to the president, gave him the luxury to suggest his views on industry's social and economic responsibilities to the nation. His observations became the basis for a depression recovery plan, which provided benefits for both workers and consumers. Under the Swope Plan, workers would have received social welfare protections in the form of old-age pensions, life insurance, and unemployment insurance. For the consuming public, the Swope Plan proposed greater federal regulation of business practices and public membership on all trade association boards. Business would also have benefited from the Swope Plan. While membership in the requisite trade association would have been mandatory, business would have gained price-fixing authority, production controls, and regulation of trade practices.

Because the Swope Plan resulted from the statist approach to CORPORATISM, not the decentralized approach Hoover preferred, the president opposed it. By the fall of 1931, Hoover argued that the depression stemmed from international, not domestic, economic problems. As such, he believed that domestic tinkering such as that proposed in the Swope Plan was unnecessary and unlikely to bring much relief. Hoover contended that the additional bureaucracy inherent within the Swope Plan constituted an unconstitutional extension of executive power. He argued that it would be coercive and dehumanizing, and he even went so far as to suggest that it was rooted in Stalin's Five Year Plan for the Soviet Union. Most important, the president believed that adoption of the Swope Plan, or anything else like it, would have been an admission of failure. Because he was not inclined to admit mistakes, Hoover was not willing to embrace a new policy such as the Swope Plan. This plan nonetheless helped influence one of the early policy proposals of FRANKLIN D. ROOSEVELT's New Deal in 1933, namely, the National Industrial Recovery Act.

Veterans Administration Created (1930)   Although the BONUS MARCH of 1932 sullied President Hoover's reputation among the nation's veterans, Hoover had played an instrumental role in establishing the Veterans Administration, a federal agency created in 1930 to assist soldiers and former soldiers. The Veterans Administration combined the work of three distinct federal agencies—the Veterans Bureau, the Bureau of Pensions of the Interior Department, and the National Home for Disabled Volunteer Soldiers—with oversight responsibility for disability compensation, insurance for both active duty soldiers and veterans, and vocational rehabilitation for disabled soldiers. During the Hoover administration (1929–33), more than $675 million was spent on various veterans' programs, including housing, hospitalization, and disability services. In 1988, the Veterans Administration was elevated to cabinet-level status as the Department of Veterans Affairs.

White House Conference on Child Health and Welfare (1930)   Held in 1930, the White House Conference on Child Health and Welfare was the first important conference of the Hoover administration. President Hoover raised $500,000 of private money to fund the conference. Approximately 2,500 delegates attended. These men and women were professionals well familiar with the problems under discussion. Attendees analyzed the status of child care and protection throughout the United States, and they made recommendations for a variety of child welfare services that could be provided through the aegis of the federal, state, and local governments. The Children's Charter that was drafted included 19 issues, among which were education, child labor, vocational training, recreation, family welfare, health, and child growth and development. Perhaps the most notable component of the charter was the first Bill of Rights for the Handicapped Child. The resulting report totaled 35 volumes. The conference led to significant private initiatives. W. K. Kellogg, the breakfast cereal entrepreneur, founded the W. K. Kellogg Foundation to benefit the interests of children. More important, the ground-breaking conference resulted in numerous improvements at the state and local levels but far less in the way of national reform.

Wickersham Commission on Law Enforcement (1929–1931)   President Hoover charged the Wickersham Commission with an expansive mandate, which included the examination, reorganization, and simplification of the entire federal justice system, jury selection reform, and improvement of federal investigations and prosecutions. Hoover appointed the commission in May 1929. In addition to these issues, Hoover also hoped the commission would pay particular attention to Prohibition. Commission members included leading political experts in the field of criminal justice. The chair of the commission, George W. Wickersham, had served as attorney general from 1909 to 1913 during WILLIAM HOWARD TAFT's presidency. Other notable commission members included former secretary of war Newton D. Baker, U.S. circuit judge William S. Kenyon, and Harvard Law School dean Roscoe Pound. Well qualified though these men were, leading prohibitionist organizations, including the Anti-Saloon League of America and the Women's Christian Temperance Union, complained that they had been ignored. The slight was purposeful; Hoover did not believe that the social activists would provide quality recommendations. The president was nonetheless committed to Prohibition, not so much for reasons of personal conviction as for reasons of constitutional responsibility.

Wickersham complicated the work of his commission when he acknowledged a basic truth about Prohibition enforcement: to be done right, the states needed to play an active role because the job was beyond the ability of the federal government. Wickersham argued the federal government should concentrate on the importation, shipment, and manufacture of alcohol in interstate commerce while the states should work to prevent the sale of alcoholic beverages. Wickersham's statement angered prohibitionists, who saw it as weak, and satisfied anti-prohibitionists, who saw it as forthright. When it came time for the Wickersham Commission to issue its report, seven of the 11 members called for revisions to the Eighteenth Amendment, ratified in 1919, which authorized Prohibition. The report was submitted in June 1931, when the commission disbanded. Hoover sent this report to Congress with a slight prevarication; he contended that the commission recommended against repeal and that Prohibition enforcement had improved when it had not. Furthermore, the commission said little if anything about the other issues it was charged with considering.

World Disarmament Conference (1932) The World Disarmament Conference, formally known as the Conference for the Reduction and Limitation of Armaments, occurred concurrently with the debate about the debt moratorium plan to relieve Great Britain and France from paying their World War I obligations to the United States while also forgiving German reparations for a year. The subject of disarmament had been in vogue since World War I. While world leaders were skeptical that effective multilateral disarmament could be achieved, nongovernmental organizations, especially the Women's International League for Peace and Freedom (WILPF), had lobbied hard for the reform. Jane Addams, the founder of the social settlement Hull-House in Chicago, served as the president of the WILPF, and the organization delivered to conference delegates a petition with six million signatures demanding disarmament. Furthermore, President Hoover supported disarmament largely for economic reasons.

The World Disarmament Conference convened in Geneva in early 1932. Attendees included every nation in the world except Ecuador, Nicaragua, Paraguay, and El Salvador. Whereas world leaders had long expected such a conference would be held, none took the meeting seriously. Conflicting aims of various nations hamstrung the effectiveness of the negotiations. The French wanted guarantees against future German attacks, specifically calling for an international police force and a collective security agreement with Britain and the United States. Hoover advocated across-the-board reductions in armaments, which Secretary of State Henry L. Stimson viewed as a fanciful product of Hoover's Quaker faith. In fact, Stimson believed the United States should not play a leadership role at the conference because it had already reduced its armaments. He believed that the Atlantic Ocean provided sufficient protection from any future European hostilities.

Little came of the various arms limitations proposals. By October 1933, Adolf Hitler had arranged for Germany's withdrawal from the ongoing conference as well as from the League of Nations. Nevertheless, Stimson cited two positive results from the conference: It brought world leaders together and it gave the United States the occasion to push its nonrecognition policy, which posited that the United States would not recognize territorial changes in the Far East that occurred in violation of American treaty rights. Stim-

son's assertions notwithstanding, little of substance resulted from the World Disarmament Conference, which finally disbanded in failure in 1934.

Nancy Beck Young

Further reading

Agricola, Georg. *De Re Metallica.* Translated and annotated from the first Latin edition of 1556, by Herbert Clark Hoover and Lou Henry Hoover. New York: Dover, 1950.

Barber, William J. *From New Era to New Deal: Herbert Hoover, the Economists, and American Economic Policy, 1921–1933.* New York: Cambridge University Press, 1985.

Best, Gary Dean. *Herbert Hoover: The Postpresidential Years, 1933–1964.* 2 vols. Palo Alto, Calif.: Hoover Institution Press, 1983.

———. *The Politics of American Individualism: Herbert Hoover in Transition, 1918–1921.* Westport, Conn.: Greenwood Press, 1975.

Burner, David. *Herbert Hoover, a Public Life.* New York: Knopf, 1978.

Clements, Kendrick A. *Hoover, Conservation, and Consumerism: Engineering the Good Life.* Lawrence: University Press of Kansas, 2000.

Fausold, Martin L. *The Presidency of Herbert C. Hoover.* Lawrence: University Press of Kansas, 1985.

Hamilton, David E. *From New Day to New Deal: American Farm Policy from Hoover to Roosevelt, 1928–1933.* Chapel Hill: University of North Carolina Press, 1991.

Hawley, Ellis W. *The Great War and the Search for Modern Order: A History of the American People and Their Institutions, 1917–1933.* New York: St. Martin's Press, 1979.

Hoover, Herbert. *Addresses Delivered during the Visit of Herbert Hoover, President-Elect of the United States, to Central and South America, November–December, 1928.* Washington, D.C.: Pan American Union, 1929.

———. *Addresses upon the American Road.* 8 vols. New York: Scribner, 1938–1946.

———. *Addresses upon the American Road. 1945–1948.* New York: Van Nostrand, 1949.

———. *Addresses upon the American Road, 1948–1950.* Palo Alto, Calif.: Stanford University Press, 1951.

———. *Addresses upon the American Road, 1950–1955.* Palo Alto, Calif.: Stanford University Press, 1955.

———. *Addresses upon the American Road, 1955–1960.* Caldwell, Idaho: Caxton Printers, 1961.

———. *America's First Crusade.* New York: C. Scribner's Sons, 1942.

———. *An American Epic.* 4 vols. Chicago: H. Regnery, 1959–1964.

———. *American Ideals versus the New Deal.* New York: Scribner, 1936.

———. *American Individualism.* Garden City, N.Y.: Doubleday, Page, 1922.

———. *A Boyhood in Iowa.* New York: Aventine, 1931.

———. *Campaign Speeches of 1932, by President Hoover and Ex-president Coolidge.* Garden City, N.Y.: Doubleday, Doran, 1933.

———. *The Challenge to Liberty.* New York: C. Scribner's Sons, 1934.

———. *40 Key Questions about Our Foreign Policy, Answered in Important Addresses and Statements Delivered between 1941 and 1952.* Scarsdale, N.Y.: Updegraff, 1952.

———. *Further Addresses upon the American Road, 1938–1940.* New York: C. Scribner's Sons, 1940.

———. *The Hoover-Wilson Wartime Correspondence, September 24, 1914, to November 11, 1918,* edited by Francis William O'Brien. Ames: Iowa State University Press, 1974.

———. *Memoirs.* Vol. 1, *Years of Adventure, 1874–1920;* Vol. 2, *The Cabinet and the Presidency, 1920–1933;* Vol. 3, *The Great Depression, 1929–1941.* New York: Macmillan, 1951–1952.

———. *The New Day; Campaign Speeches of Herbert Hoover, 1928.* Palo Alto, Calif.: Stanford University Press, 1928.

———. *The Ordeal of Woodrow Wilson.* New York: McGraw-Hill, 1958.

———. *Public Papers of the Presidents of the United States, Herbert Hoover, Containing the Public Messages, Speeches, and Statements of the President, 1929–1933.* 4 vols. Washington, D.C.: U.S. Government Printing Office, 1974–1977.

———. *The State Papers and Other Public Writings of Herbert Hoover.* 2 vols. Edited by William Starr Myers. Garden City, N.Y.: Doubleday, Doran, 1934.

———. *Two Peacemakers in Paris: The Hoover-Wilson Post-armistice Letters, 1918–1920,* edited by Francis William O'Brien. College Station: Texas A&M University Press, 1978.

———, and Hugh Gibson. *The Basis of Lasting Peace.* New York: D. Van Nostrand, 1945.

———, and Hugh Gibson. *The Problems of Lasting Peace.* Garden City, N.Y.: Doubleday, Doran, 1942.

Irwin, Will. *Herbert Hoover: A Reminiscent Biography.* New York and London: Century, 1928.

Joslin, Theodore G. *Hoover Off the Record.* Garden City, N.Y.: Doubleday, Doran, 1934.

Lisio, Donald J. *The President and Protest: Hoover, Conspiracy, and the Bonus Riot.* Columbia: University of Missouri Press, 1974.

Lyons, Eugene. *Herbert Hoover, a Biography.* Garden City, N.Y.: Doubleday, 1964.

Mayer, Dale C., ed. *Lou Henry Hoover: Essays on a Busy Life.* Worland, Wyo.: High Plains Publishing, 1994.

Nash, George H. *The Life of Herbert Hoover.* Vol. 1, *The Engineer, 1874–1914;* Vol. 2, *The Humanitarian, 1914–1917;* Vol. 3, *Master of Emergencies, 1917–1918;* Volume 4, *Imperfect Visionary, 1918–1928.* New York: W.W. Norton, 1983– .

Olson, James Stuart. *Herbert Hoover and the Reconstruction Finance Corporation, 1931–1933.* Ames: Iowa State University Press, 1977.

Romasco, Albert U. *The Poverty of Abundance: Hoover, the Nation, the Depression.* New York: Oxford University Press, 1965.

Schwarz, Jordan A. *The Interregnum of Despair: Hoover, Congress, and the Depression.* Urbana: University of Illinois Press, 1970.

Smith, Gene. *The Shattered Dream: Herbert Hoover and the Great Depression.* New York: Morrow, 1970.

Smith, Richard Norton. *An Uncommon Man: The Triumph of Herbert Hoover.* New York: Simon and Schuster, 1984.

Sobel, Robert. *Herbert Hoover at the Onset of the Great Depression, 1929–1930.* Philadelphia: Lippincott, 1975.

Unrau, William E. *Mixed-Bloods and Tribal Dissolution: Charles Curtis and the Quest for Indian Identity.* Lawrence: University Press of Kansas, 1989.

Walch, Timothy, ed. *Uncommon Americans: The Lives and Legacies of Herbert and Lou Henry Hoover.* Westport, Conn.: Praeger, 2003.

Weissman, Benjamin M. *Herbert Hoover and Famine Relief to Soviet Russia, 1921–1923.* Palo Alto, Calif.: Hoover Institution Press, 1974.

Wilson, Joan Hoff. *Herbert Hoover, Forgotten Progressive.* Boston: Little, Brown, 1975.

Young, Nancy Beck. *Lou Henry Hoover: Activist First Lady.* Lawrence: University Press of Kansas, 2004.

DOCUMENTS

—⟋⟋⟋—

Document One: President Herbert Hoover, Inaugural Address, March 4, 1929

President Hoover expressed great optimism about the strength and security of the United States and its economy in his inaugural address on March 4, 1929. He also laid out an ambitious reform agenda, but less than eight months later the stock market crashed, ushering in the Great Depression and transforming these words into a cruel taunt.

. . . If we survey the situation of our nation both at home and abroad, we find many satisfactions; we find some causes for concern. We have emerged from the losses of the Great War and the reconstruction following it with increased virility and strength. From this strength we have contributed to the recovery and progress of the world. What America has done has given renewed hope and courage to all who have faith in government by the people. In the large view, we have reached a higher degree of comfort and security than ever existed before in the history of the world. Through liberation from wide-spread poverty we have reached a higher degree of individual freedom than ever before. The devotion to and concern for our institutions are deep and sincere. We are steadily building a new race—a new civilization great in its own attainments. The influence and high purposes of our nation are respected among the peoples of the world. We aspire to distinction in the world, but to a distinction based upon confidence in our sense of justice as well as our accomplishments within our own borders and in our own lives. For wise guidance in this great period of recovery the nation is deeply indebted to Calvin Coolidge.

But all this majestic advance should not obscure the constant dangers from which self-government must be safeguarded. The strong man must at all times be alert to the attack of insidious disease.

THE FAILURE OF OUR SYSTEM OF CRIMINAL JUSTICE

The most malign of all these dangers today is disregard and disobedience of law. Crime is increasing. Confidence in rigid and speedy justice is decreasing. I am not prepared to believe that this indicates any decay in the moral fibre of the American people. I am not prepared to believe that it indicates an impotence of the Federal Government to enforce its laws.

It is only in part due to the additional burdens imposed upon our judicial system by the 18th Amendment. The problem is much wider than that. Many influences have increasingly complicated and weakened our law enforcement organization long before the adoption of the 18th Amendment.

To re-establish the vigor and effectiveness of law enforcement we must critically consider the entire federal machinery of justice, the redistribution of its functions, the simplification of its procedure, the provision of additional special tribunals, the better selection of juries, and the more effective organization of our agencies of investigation and prosecution that justice may be sure and that it may be swift. While the authority of the Federal government extends to but part of our vast system of national, state and local justice, yet the standards which the Federal Government establishes have the most profound influence upon the whole structure. . . .

A NATIONAL INVESTIGATION

I propose to appoint a national commission for a searching investigation of the whole structure of our federal system of jurisprudence, to include the method of enforcement of the 18th Amendment and the causes of abuse under it. Its purpose will be to make such recommendations for re-organization of the administration of Federal laws and court procedure as may be found desirable. In the meantime it is essential that a large part of the enforcement activities be transferred from the Treasury Department to the Department of Justice as a beginning of more effective organization.

THE RELATION OF GOVERNMENT TO BUSINESS

The election has again confirmed the determination of the American people that regulation of private enterprise and not Government ownership or operation is the course rightly to be pursued in our relation to business. In recent years we have established a differentiation in the whole method of business regulation between the industries which produce and distribute commodities on the one hand, and public utilities on the other. In the former, our laws insist upon effective competition; in the latter, because we substantially confer a monopoly by limiting competition, we must regulate their services and rates. The rigid enforcement of the laws applicable to both groups is the very base of equal opportunity and freedom from domination for all our people, and it is just as essential for the stability and prosperity of business itself as for the protection of the public at large. Such regulations should be extended by the Federal Government within the limitations of the constitution and only when the individual States are without power to protect their citizens through their own authority. On the other hand, we should be fearless when the authority rests only in the Federal Government.

COOPERATION BY THE GOVERNMENT

The larger purpose of our economic thought should be to establish more firmly stability and security of business and employment and thereby remove poverty still further from our borders. Our people have in recent years developed a newfound capacity for co-operation among themselves to effect high purposes in public welfare. It is an advance toward the highest conception of self-government. Self-government does not and should not imply the use of political agencies alone. Progress is born of co-operation in the community— not from governmental restraints. The Government should assist and encourage these movements of collective self help by itself co-operating with them. Business has by co-operation made great progress in the advancement of service, in stability, in regularity of employment and in the correction of its own abuses.

Such progress, however, can continue only so long as business manifests its respect for law.

There is an equally important field of co-operation by the Federal Government with the multitude of agencies, state, municipal and private, in the systematic development of those processes which directly affect public health, recreation, education and the home. We have need further to perfect the means by which Government can be adapted to human service. . . .

WORLD PEACE

The United States fully accepts the profound truth that our own progress, prosperity and peace are interlocked with the progress, prosperity and peace of all humanity. The whole world is at peace. The dangers to a continuation of this peace today are largely the fear and suspicion which still haunts the world. No suspicion or fear can be rightly directed toward our country.

Those who have a true understanding of America know that we have no desire for territorial expansion, for economic or other domination of other peoples. Such purposes are repugnant to our ideals of human freedom. Our form of government is ill adapted to the responsibilities which inevitably follow permanent limitation of the independence of other peoples. . . .

The recent treaty for the renunciation of war as an instrument of national policy sets an advanced standard in our conception of the relations of nations. Its acceptance should pave the way to greater limitation of armament, the offer of which we sincerely extend to the world. But its full realization also implies a greater and greater perfection in the instrumentalities for pacific settlement of controversies between nations. In the creation and use of these instrumentalities we should support every sound method of conciliation, arbitration and judicial settlement. . . .

Our people have determined that we should make no political engagements such as membership in the League of Nations, which may commit us in advance as a nation to become involved in the settlements of controversies between other countries. They adhere to the belief that the independence of America from such obligations increases its ability and availability for service in all fields of human progress. . . .

SPECIAL SESSION OF THE CONGRESS

Action upon some of the proposals upon which the Republican Party was returned to power, particularly further agricultural relief and limited changes in the tariff, cannot in justice to our farmers, our labor and our manufacturers be postponed. I shall therefore request a special session of Congress for the consideration of these two questions. I shall deal with each of them upon the assembly of the Congress.

OTHER MANDATES FROM THE ELECTION

It appears to me that the more important further mandates from the recent election were the maintenance of the integrity of the Constitution; the vigorous enforcement of the laws; the continuance of the economy in public expenditure; the continued regulation of business to prevent domination in the community; the denial of ownership or operation of business by the government in competition with its citizens; the avoidance of policies which would involve us in the controversies of foreign nations; the more effective reorganization of the Departments of the Federal Government; the expansion of public works; and the promotion of welfare activities affecting education and the home. . . .

CONCLUSION

This is not the time and place for extended discussion. The questions before our country are problems of progress to higher standards; they are not the problems of degeneration. They demand thought and they serve to quicken the conscience and enlist our sense of responsibility for their settlement. And that responsibility rests upon you, my countrymen, as much as upon those of us who have been selected for office.

Ours is a land rich in resources; stimulating in its glorious beauty; filled with millions of happy homes; blessed with comfort and opportunity. In no nation are the institutions of progress more advanced. In no nation are the fruits of accomplishment more secure. In no nation is the government more worthy of respect. No country is more loved by its people. I have an abiding faith in their capacity, integrity and high purpose. I have no fears for the future of our country. It is bright with hope.

Source: Public Papers of the Presidents of the United States, Herbert Hoover, Containing the Public Messages, Speeches, and Statements of the President, 1929 (Washington, D.C.: U.S. Government Printing Office, 1974), 1–12.

Document Two: President Hoover, Statement on Public Works and Unemployment, January 3, 1930

In early 1930, President Hoover called for an extensive program of public works to address the problems of the Great Depression.

Our drive for increase in construction and improvement work to take up unemployment is showing most encouraging results, and it looks as if the work undertaken will be larger for 1930 than for 1929.

The Department of Commerce now has complete returns from the Governors of 16 States covering public works to be undertaken in 1930 by the State, municipal, and county authorities. They have partial returns from 13 more States. The total so far reported, and including the Federal Government is about $1,550 million, and in nearly all cases larger than for 1929. The surveys are coming in daily, and should be completed by mid-January.

The preliminary estimate of the railways for construction and betterments for 1930 was $1,050 million, and for the public utilities $2,100 million, including the telephones. The total of these items so far is $4,700 million. This does not include the balance of the State, municipal, and county work, nor the building construction, nor the industrial and factory improvements, which latter are now under survey by the special business committee.

The steel companies inform me this morning that the effect of the drive is already showing in their orders, which are beyond their expectations.

Source: Public Papers of the Presidents of the United States, Herbert Hoover, Containing the Public Messages, Speeches, and Statements of the President, 1930 (Washington, D.C.: U.S. Government Printing Office, 1976), 5.

Document Three: President Hoover, Veto of the Muscle Shoals Resolution, March 3, 1931

In 1931, President Hoover vetoed legislation to provide for the conversion of Muscle Shoals into a government-run power plant and fertilizer manufacturer. This same facility would later become the nexus of the Tennessee Valley Authority during the Franklin D. Roosevelt administration.

To the Senate:

I return herewith, without my approval, Senate Joint Resolution 49, "To provide for the national defense by the creation of a corporation for the operation of the Government properties at and near Muscle Shoals in the State of Alabama; to authorize the letting of the Muscle Shoals properties under certain conditions; and for other purposes."

This bill proposes the transformation of the war plant at Muscle Shoals, together with important expansions, into a permanently operated Government institution for the production and distribution of power and the manufacture of fertilizers. . . .

The plants at Muscle Shoals were originally built for a production of nitrates for use in war explosives. I am advised by the War Department that the very large development in the United States by private enterprise in the manufacture of synthetic nitrogen now affords an ample supply covering any possible requirements of war. It is therefore unnecessary to maintain this plant for any such purposes.

This bill provides that the President for a period of 12 months may negotiate a lease of the nitrate plants for fertilizer manufacture under detailed limitations, but in failure to make such a lease the bill makes it mandatory upon the Government to manufacture nitrogen fertilizers at Muscle Shoals by the employment of existing facilities or by modernizing existing plants or by any other process. . . .

I am firmly opposed to the Government entering into any business the major purpose of which is competition with our citizens. There are national emergencies which require that the Government should temporarily enter the field of business, but they must be emergency actions and in matters where the cost of the project is secondary to much higher considerations. There are many localities where the Federal Government is justified in the construction of great dams and reservoirs, where navigation, flood control, reclamation or stream regulation are of dominant importance, and where they are beyond the capacity or purpose of private or local government capital to construct. In these cases power is often a by-product and should be disposed of by contract or lease. But for the Federal Government deliberately to go out to build up and expand such an occasion to the major purpose of a power and manufacturing business is to break down the initiative and enterprise of the American people; it is destruction of equality of opportunity amongst our people; it is the negation of the ideals upon which our civilization has been based.

This bill raises one of the important issues confronting our people. That is squarely the issue of Federal Government ownership and operation of power and manufacturing business not as a minor by-product but as a major purpose. Involved in this question is the agitation against the conduct of the power industry. The power problem is not to be solved by the Federal Government going into the power business, nor is it to be solved by the project in this bill. The remedy for abuses in the conduct of that industry lies in regulation and not by the Federal Government entering upon the business itself. I have recommended to the Congress on various occasions that action should be taken to establish Federal regulation of interstate power in cooperation with State authorities. This bill would launch the Federal Government upon a policy of ownership and operation of power utilities upon a basis of competition instead of by the proper Government function of regulation for the protection of all the people. I hesitate to contemplate the future of our institutions, of our Government, and of our country if the preoccupation of its officials is to be no longer the promotion of justice and equal opportunity but is to be devoted to barter in the markets. That is not liberalism, it is degeneration.

This proposal can be effectively opposed upon other and perhaps narrower grounds. The establishment of a Federal-operated power business and fertilizer factory in the Tennessee Valley means Federal control from Washington with all the vicissitudes of national politics and the tyrannies of remote bureaucracy imposed upon the people of that valley without voice by them in their own resources, the overriding of State and local government, the undermining of State and local responsibility. The very history of this project over the past 10 years should be a complete demonstration of the ineptness of the Federal Government to administer such enterprise and of the penalties which the local community suffers under it.

This bill distinctly proposes to enter the field of powers reserved to the States. It would deprive the adjacent States of the right to control rates for this power and would deprive them of taxes on property within their borders and would invade and weaken the authority of local government. . . .

The real development of the resources and the industries of the Tennessee Valley can only be accomplished by the people in that valley themselves. Muscle Shoals can only be administered by the people upon the ground, responsible to their own communities, directing them solely for the benefit of their communities and not for purposes of pursuit of social theories or national politics. Any other course deprives them of liberty. . . .

HERBERT HOOVER

Source: Public Papers of the Presidents of the United States, Herbert Hoover, Containing the Public Messages, Speeches, and Statements of the President, 1931 (Washington, D.C.: U.S. Government Printing Office, 1976), 120–129.

Document Four: President Hoover, Statement about Signing the Reconstruction Finance Corporation Act, January 22, 1932

In forming the Reconstruction Finance Corporation in 1932, President Hoover demonstrated his belief that depression relief should be pursued by saving banks, railroads, and industry and not by means of a dole.

I have signed the Reconstruction Finance Corporation Act.

It brings into being a powerful organization with adequate resources, able to strengthen weaknesses that may develop in our credit, banking, and railway structure, in order to permit business and industry to carry on normal activities free from the fear of unexpected shocks and retarding influences.

Its purpose is to stop deflation in agriculture and industry and thus to increase employment by the restoration of men to their normal jobs. It is not created for the aid of big industries or big banks. Such institutions are amply able to take care of themselves. It is created for the support of the smaller banks and financial institutions, and through rendering their resources liquid to give renewed support to business, industry, and agriculture. It should give opportunity to mobilize the gigantic strength of our country for recovery.

In attaching my signature to this extremely important legislation, I wish to pay tribute to the patriotism of the men in both Houses of Congress who have given proof of their devotion to the welfare of their country irrespective of political affiliation.

Source: Public Papers of the Presidents of the United States, Herbert Hoover, Containing the Public Messages, Speeches, and Statements of the President, 1932–1933 (Washington, D.C.: U.S. Government Printing Office, 1977), 29–30.

Franklin D. Roosevelt

January 30, 1882–April 12, 1945

Thirty-second President of the United States
March 4, 1933–April 12, 1945

FRANKLIN D. ROOSEVELT

Place of Birth: Hyde Park, New York

Date of Birth: January 30, 1882

Place of Residence: New York

Class Background: elite

Father's Career: landed gentleman

Mother's Career: homemaker

Number of Siblings: one

Religion: Episcopalian

Education: graduated Harvard College, 1904; attended Columbia Law School

Political Party: Democrat

Military Service: none

Spouse: Eleanor Roosevelt

Spouse's Education: Allenswood School in England

Spouse's Career: investigator with the National Consumer's League, settlement house worker, homemaker, reform politician, writer, co-owner of Val-Kill Industries, co-owner of Todhunter School for Girls, radio commentator, delegate to the United Nations, head of U.N. Commission on Human Rights

Number of Children: six

Sports and Hobbies: sailing, stamp collecting, swimming

Career Prior to the Presidency: lawyer, state senator, assistant secretary of the navy, governor of New York

Age upon Entering the White House: 51 years, 33 days

Reason for Leaving the White House: died in office

Date of Death: April 12, 1945

Cause of Death: cerebral hemorrhage

Last Words: "I have a terrific headache."

Burial Site: Hyde Park, New York

Value of Estate at Time of Death: $1,085,500

Preceding page: Franklin D. Roosevelt *(Library of Congress)*

BIOGRAPHY OF ROOSEVELT

Franklin Delano Roosevelt has been called the savior of capitalism for his efforts to combat the Great Depression and the savior of democracy for his efforts to beat back totalitarianism during World War II. Roosevelt himself recognized this dual struggle, saying in 1943, after 10 years in office, that the time for "Dr. New Deal" had ended and that "Dr. Win-the-War" had taken his place. During his years in the White House, Roosevelt amassed and used a vast array of presidential powers often at the expense of the legislative branch, and his critics—Democrats and Republicans alike—charged him with being a dictator. His unprecedented four terms as president, spanning just over 12 years, were among the most momentous in American history.

Roosevelt's childhood is most important for anyone hoping to understand his presidency. Born on January 30, 1882, Franklin was the only child of Sara Delano and James Roosevelt. The family lived along the Hudson River in Dutchess County, New York, where James Roosevelt played at a business career while enjoying his status as a member of the landed gentry. As much as possible the Roosevelts copied the mores of the English aristocracy, meaning that Franklin had a childhood unlike most American boys in the late 19th century. His parents doted on him, with James striving to model for his son how to be a proper landowner and gentleman and Sara making him the center of her life. A health crisis left a major impact on the development of Franklin's personality. His father suffered a heart attack in 1891, and when his health deteriorated in the years that followed, Franklin compensated by adopting a tranquil, but also jovial disposition that hid from both his father and, later, the world any anxieties or concerns that troubled him. This demeanor would play an important role in Roosevelt's political success as an adult.

Young Franklin had few interactions with other children. His early education came from Swiss tutors and from regular travel abroad. As such, his parents' decision to send him to boarding school in 1896 proved traumatic. As a 15-year-old student at Groton, an elite Massachusetts institution founded in 1884 to prepare young men for "the active work of life," Roosevelt never made a niche for himself. His previous existence in an almost exclusively adult world left him little prepared for interaction with other adolescents. He had few friends at Groton, nor did he excel at athletics, which was the centerpiece of life at the school.

Four years later upon his matriculation at Harvard College, Roosevelt adopted a different persona and actively sought to become a campus leader. His friendships were wide-ranging across campus, and he was elected editor of the *Crimson*, the student newspaper. Because his collegiate years coincided with his cousin THEODORE ROOSEVELT's presidency, young Franklin purposefully borrowed those phrases most frequently associated with the 26th president—"delighted" and "bully." These efforts were not sufficient to win Roosevelt a place in the exclusive Porcellian Club, though. Nor did Roosevelt excel in his studies. He took the "gentleman's C" for his largely mediocre work.

During his Harvard years (1900–04), Roosevelt lost his father. Additionally, Sara Roosevelt moved to Boston so that she could be closer to her son. While he appreciated her love and devotion, he also longed for the personal freedom that accompanied attendance at college for many young men his age. Roosevelt coped by hiding significant elements of his personal life from his mother, most important of which was his budding romance and eventual engagement to his distant cousin ELEANOR ROOSEVELT, a niece of Theodore Roosevelt. Eleanor and Franklin were as different as two people could be—she was introspective and intellectual and he was amiable and attractive—but they forged a meaningful bond soon after their courtship began in 1902. Two years later, they con-

Franklin D. Roosevelt, 1897 *(Franklin D. Roosevelt Library)*

ELEANOR ROOSEVELT

(1884–1962) *first lady of the United States, March 4, 1933–April 12, 1945*

Born on October 11, 1884, Anna Eleanor Roosevelt grew up in a wealthy New York family but she did not have a happy childhood. Her parents were emotionally distant. Young Eleanor's mother, Anna Hall Roosevelt, constantly criticized her daughter's appearance. She died when her daughter was eight. Eleanor's father, Elliott Roosevelt, was the younger brother of Theodore Roosevelt but suffered from alcoholism so serious that he was kept from his daughter for periods of time. He died when Eleanor was 10. Relatives of Eleanor's mother cared for her and her brother Hall, but this was not necessarily a positive change for the children were more a duty and less a joy to their guardians. From these experiences, Eleanor Roosevelt developed a negative self-image as being unattractive and unworthy of love and unable to depend on others.

After finishing her education abroad, Eleanor, imbued with a passion for social justice, began working with the National Consumer's League and taught immigrant children in a New York City settlement house. She became romantically linked with her distant cousin, Franklin D. Roosevelt, in November 1902. He viewed her as intelligent and compassionate, and she responded to his outgoing demeanor. Eleanor did not think their relationship would last because of his good looks. Nonetheless, the couple married in 1905. Six children were born to the union—Anna Eleanor (1906–75), James (1907–91), Franklin Delano, Jr. (1909), Elliott (1910–90), Franklin Delano, Jr. (1914–88), and John Aspinwall (1916–81).

The marriage suffered from frequent intrusions by Franklin's mother, Sara Delano Roosevelt, who overruled Eleanor's desire to continue her settlement house work for fear she would transmit disease to her children. Additionally, Sara Roosevelt paid the bills for her son and his family. She directed the household staff and the work of rearing their children. Initially, Eleanor welcomed the assistance, but with time she became frustrated with the interference.

Franklin's entry into politics had the unintended consequence of providing Eleanor a means of reentering public life, through voluntary activism and later her own political causes. For example, during World War I when Franklin served as assistant secretary of the navy, she worked with navy relief and the Red Cross. During these years when she was first discovering her public voice, Eleanor Roosevelt received another push outward in the form of her husband's adultery with Lucy Mercer. She offered to divorce him, but Franklin refused out of concern for what would

Eleanor Roosevelt *(Library of Congress)*

spired to marry, and despite Sara Roosevelt's objections, the couple married in March 1905. Six children were born to the union: Anna Eleanor (1906–75), James (1907–91), Franklin Delano, Jr. (1909), Elliott (1910–90), Franklin Delano, Jr. (1914–88), and John Aspinwall (1916–81).

After his graduation from Harvard in 1904, Roosevelt matriculated law school at Columbia University. He did not graduate, but he did pass the bar exam and practice law for a few years in New York City. He worked first for a large firm as a clerk where he did routine work on petty cases, wills, and claims in municipal courts. Next, he opened a firm with two others. One of his partners said he never specialized in anything. Unhappy with his work, Roosevelt welcomed the opportunity to run as a Democrat for the New York State Senate in 1910. (The Hudson River valley Roosevelts, from which Franklin Roosevelt came, had always been Democrats, whereas the Oyster Bay Roosevelts, from which Theodore Roosevelt came, had always been Republicans.) The Dutchess County seat was typically a Republican stronghold, but divisions in the party helped make possible a Roosevelt win. Reform Republicans called his opponent "a stench in the nostrils of the people." Furthermore, Roosevelt charged that his opponent had blocked the reforms of Progressive-Republican governor Charles Evans Hughes. Roosevelt spent the five-week campaign in a rented Maxwell car traveling all over the counties of Dutchess, Putnam, and Columbia. Roosevelt clinched his victory with his attacks on the political bosses. Once elected, Roosevelt continued in this happen to his political career and what his mother would do. Instead, he vowed to sever all ties with Mercer (a pledge he broke in the war years). The unfortunate incident hardened Eleanor, made her more independent, and confirmed her fears about her looks. For the remainder of her life, Eleanor became a public figure devoted to social betterment and improving the lot of the unfortunate.

In the 1920s, after her husband's polio was diagnosed, Eleanor became increasingly active politically, using his infirmity to justify her behavior, but she was more than just his "legs and eyes" as she then explained. She became a leader in the League of Women Voters, the Women's Trade Union League, the Women's City Club, and the Women's Division of the New York State Democratic Committee. At the time, she was most interested in efforts to limit the work week to five days, abolish child labor, and strengthen the League of Nations. In the process, Roosevelt built an important network with other women who shared her views. She merged her activism with the new personal support networks she crafted to replace the void left in her marriage. Eleanor Roosevelt feared that her husband's reentry into politics, as governor of New York, would limit her own activism. She was even less excited about becoming first lady in 1933.

Eleanor misjudged what powerful executive posts for her husband would mean for her life. Her years in Albany and even more in Washington, D.C., made her a national and international leader for human rights. In the 1930s, she worked to increase the number of women in federal government service, she lobbied for civil rights for African Americans, and she pushed antipoverty and education and training programs such as the National Youth Administration. During her years as first lady Eleanor Roosevelt wrote a sometimes controversial newspaper column, "My Day," numerous magazine articles, and six books, all while maintaining an extensive speaking schedule across the country. Because she lobbied her husband on behalf of liberal causes, he talked about

the difficulty he had in controlling the "Missus." No first lady in American history had ever been so politically active, and like her husband she became a familiar, larger-than-life figure to many Americans. Her ongoing activism as first lady irked Republican critics, who, opposing Franklin's reelection in 1940, adopted the slogan "We Don't Want Eleanor Either." During that year's presidential election, she helped convince the Democratic National Convention to accept Henry Wallace as the vice-presidential nominee. Eleanor Roosevelt remained active during the war years, but she wielded less clout in Washington.

Eleanor was shocked by both her husband's death on April 12, 1945, and the circumstances surrounding it, especially Lucy Mercer Rutherfurd's presence by Franklin's side. In the remaining years of her life Eleanor became even more important on the national and international stage. She worked on behalf of progressive Democratic politics, supporting the founding of Americans for Democratic Action and two-time Democratic presidential candidate Adlai E. Stevenson. Additionally, Roosevelt became a vocal critic of Senator Joseph McCarthy (R-WI) and the prominent role he played in the postwar Red Scare. In 1946, Roosevelt accepted an appointment from President Harry Truman to become a delegate to the newly founded United Nations. In that capacity, she chaired the United Nations Human Rights Commission and championed the United Nations Declaration of Human Rights as enacted by the General Assembly in 1948. Her last major public appointment was as chair of President John F. Kennedy's Commission on the Status of Women. Until the end of her life she actively crusaded for African-American equality.

Eleanor Roosevelt died in New York City on November 7, 1962, of bone-marrow tuberculosis. She was an important, tough politician in her own right, and she revealed the vast power that activist first ladies could wield. Some scholars of the Roosevelt years have called her the most influential American woman of the 20th century.

vein, defending the state's agricultural interests against Tammany Hall, the Democratic Party machine in New York City. In his 1912 reelection campaign, Roosevelt forged an alliance with a journalist, Louis M. Howe, who would remain an important adviser into the 1930s. Under Howe's tutelage Roosevelt abandoned his patrician behaviors and broadened his political base.

In 1913, Roosevelt followed in the footsteps of his cousin Theodore Roosevelt when President WOODROW WILSON appointed him to to post of assistant secretary of the navy. Roosevelt had been a strong supporter of Wilson in the 1912 presidential campaign. Moving to Washington, D.C., he enjoyed the political and social whirl of the nation's capital. Roosevelt proved himself a capable administrator even if

he did challenge Josephus Daniels, the secretary of the navy and his boss, too frequently. His post in Washington did not lead to a diminished interest in New York politics. Roosevelt failed in his bid to gain election to the U.S. Senate in 1914. His anti-Tammany stance played well in Dutchess County but not in the remainder of the state, and he lost his bid in the Democratic primary. In response to his defeat, Roosevelt tempered his criticism of Tammany Hall, and he developed a working relationship with the New York City machine.

During his years as assistant secretary of the navy from 1913 to 1920 Roosevelt was a strong proponent of military preparedness prior to the outbreak of World War I, and once the hostilities commenced in 1914, he supported U.S. involvement in the war. During the war, he played a significant role

Franklin Roosevelt, assistant secretary of the Navy, 1913 *(Library of Congress)*

Republicans came into power, they tried to use the scandal to embarrass Roosevelt. A Senate investigation ensued in 1921. Its report, written by Republicans, blasted Daniels and Roosevelt, but it included little damaging information.

Franklin and Eleanor's marriage underwent significant strains during their years in Washington, D.C. She disliked the social circuit so important for politicians on the rise, but he enjoyed the conviviality of such events. This personality difference contributed to Roosevelt's affair with Lucy Mercer, the woman Eleanor Roosevelt had hired to be her social secretary. Mercer was young, beautiful, outgoing, and graceful. Eleanor Roosevelt discovered the affair in 1918, and she offered her husband a divorce, which he refused. Instead, he promised to end the affair with Mercer. He did, but he resumed the relationship in the 1940s, and Mercer was with him at Warm Springs, Georgia, when he died in 1945. Although the affair in 1918 did not end the Roosevelt marriage, it did forever change the nature of their union. Because the betrayal hurt her deeply, Eleanor began to develop her own life apart from Franklin. Their marriage became little more than a public prop. Romantic, intimate love between the two was replaced with a relationship based on fondness and respect.

Service as assistant secretary of the navy brought Roosevelt to the attention of Democratic Party leaders. Because of his work in the Navy Department and his famous family name, he gained the vice-presidential nomination in 1920 on the ticket with James M. Cox, the governor of Ohio. Roosevelt

in naval policy and in strategic and tactical debates, the latter a precedent for assistant secretaries. Specifically, Roosevelt advocated the use of antisubmarine mines in the North Sea and the construction of small ships designed for defending the U.S. coastline. During the war years, public concern grew about moral issues confronting the American troops, especially from progressives who had been fighting for Prohibition for years. Once large numbers of troops were stationed at confined bases, many progressives campaigned against prostitution and homosexuality. As a part of his duties, Roosevelt played a role in an effort to address these conditions outside the naval station at Newport, Rhode Island, where 25,000 sailors were stationed. Roosevelt asked the Justice Department to investigate the charges, but they were too busy chasing supposed radicals during the Red Scare. When the Navy Department started its own investigation Roosevelt distanced himself from it other than issuing an authorization inquiry into the behavior of the sailors and events in the Newport community. These efforts to entrap supposed homosexuals, including a well-known Protestant preacher, became public in 1919, and a Providence newspaper publisher went on a crusade attacking Roosevelt despite the lack of evidence of his culpability. As a result, a scandal erupted, and, once the

Eleanor Roosevelt *(Photo by Fotosearch/Getty Images)*

BIOGRAPHICAL TIME LINE

1882
January 30 Franklin Delano Roosevelt is born.

1896
Roosevelt's parents enroll him at Groton Preparatory School in Massachusetts.

1904
Roosevelt graduates from Harvard College.

1905
March 17 Franklin marries his distant cousin Eleanor Roosevelt, a niece of Theodore Roosevelt.

1910
Roosevelt is elected to the New York State Senate.

1913
President Woodrow Wilson appoints Roosevelt to the post of assistant secretary of the Navy.

1918
Eleanor Roosevelt discovers her social secretary and her husband had an affair. Roosevelt ends the affair.

1920
Roosevelt runs for vice president on the Democratic ticket.

1921
Roosevelt contracts polio while vacationing at his summer home on Campobello Island in Canada.

1928
Roosevelt is elected governor of New York State.

1930
Roosevelt easily wins reelection as governor of New York.

1932
November 8 Roosevelt is elected president of the United States in a landslide.

1933
March 4 Roosevelt takes the oath of office of the president of the United States.

1936
November 3 Roosevelt is reelected president in a decisive victory.

1937
January 20 Roosevelt is inaugurated as president for a second term in office. With passage of the Twentieth Amendment to the Constitution, he is the first president inaugurated on January 20.

1940
November 5 Breaking the third term precedent, Roosevelt is elected to a third term as president.

1941
January 20 Roosevelt is inaugurated as president for a third term in office.

1944
November 7 Roosevelt is elected to an unprecedented fourth term as president.

1945
January 20 Roosevelt is inaugurated as president for a fourth term in office, but because of war conditions the ceremony is held at the White House.

April 12 While resting at Warm Springs, Georgia, Roosevelt suffers a stroke and dies.

---

was an aggressive though not always consistent campaigner, giving as many as seven speeches a day and sometimes contradicting himself from place to place. Specifically, he stressed the importance of the League of Nations even though Americans were turning away from involvement in European affairs. Roosevelt even claimed falsely that because he had been responsible for the new Haitian constitution (he had visited Haiti only in 1917 on a junket), he would be able to control the nation's vote in the League. These blunders did not hurt Roosevelt's reputation with Democratic leaders. Cox and Roosevelt were nonetheless soundly trounced in 1920 by WARREN HARDING and his running mate, CALVIN COOLIDGE.

A far greater challenge came in 1921. After his defeat for national office, Roosevelt accepted the vice presidency of a bonding company and joined a New York law practice. He planned to reenter politics at the first opportunity, but a major health crisis that summer doomed such hopes. While vacationing with his family at their summer home on Campobello Island in Canada, he contracted polio, an infectious viral disease of the central nervous system that triggered paralysis. Roosevelt's case was severe. Days after the initial attack, Roosevelt's legs became paralyzed and he was in terrible pain. The medical experts agreed that he would never regain use of his lower limbs.

Stubborn and determined, Roosevelt refused to give in to the diagnosis. For much of the 1920s, he devoted significant time and money to find a cure for his malady. While he experimented with many different therapies, he became convinced of the efficacy of spa-baths. As such, he purchased a resort hotel in Warm Springs, Georgia, and oversaw its conversion into a polio treatment center. He returned to Warm Springs many times over the course of his lifetime. Despite his strenuous efforts to rehabilitate his limbs, Roosevelt would never stand or walk unaided again.

Nor did Roosevelt want the public to see him as disabled, fearing that it would hurt his political career. He mastered the difficult art of hiding his condition from unknowing observers. He wore heavy leg braces to support his body when he needed to appear erect. To compensate for his inability to walk, he carried a cane and relied on the support of a companion. He learned to move his paralyzed legs forward by swinging his hips. A much less obtrusive press than that of the late 20th and early 21st centuries saw no need to report the reality of Roosevelt's health, so most Americans never knew that he was wheelchair bound for much of the remainder of his life.

Roosevelt did not discuss what the disease meant to him, but his biographers agree that his struggle with polio constituted a significant turning point in his life. Coping with polio helped Roosevelt relate to the suffering of others while it also sharpened his intentions to reenter the political arena. He was as determined to recover from the malady as he was to hide from the public its physical ravages. As such, polio exacerbated Roosevelt's tendencies toward obfuscation and evasion. These traits were balanced with an outgoing demeanor and so they were not apparent to the public.

Roosevelt's family disagreed about how he should handle his condition. His mother, who remained a strong presence in his life, tried to insist that her son retreat from the public sphere entirely. She wanted him to return to Hyde Park where he could rest. However, Eleanor agreed with her husband, who was determined to return to political life. She and Louis M. Howe helped him maintain a presence in New York politics. They did so through correspondence with other political leaders in the state. Roosevelt even forged a political union with Al Smith, the governor of New York and an ally of

President Roosevelt holds his black Scottie, Fala, while talking to Ruthie Bie, granddaughter of the caretakers of the Hill Top Cottage at his Hyde Park, New York, home in February 1941. This is one of two known photographs of Roosevelt in a wheelchair. *(M.L. Suckley/FDR Library/Associated Press)*

Tammany Hall. Smith was the leader of one of the two most significant factions in the Democratic Party, namely, urban, immigrant, Catholic, eastern voters. At the same time Roosevelt was courting Smith he also strengthened his ties with southern, western, rural, and Protestant Democrats nationwide, the other major factions within the party.

By 1924, Roosevelt was ready to reenter the political fray. He made his debut at the Democratic National Convention, where party leaders tapped him to give the speech nominating Al Smith for president. Roosevelt ended the speech with a quote from William Wordsworth, "This is the Happy Warrior; this is he That every man in arms should wish to be." Although Smith failed to gain the Democratic nomination, the speech revived Roosevelt's political career and the designation of Smith as the "Happy Warrior" stayed with him for the remainder of his life. Making the speech, though, taxed Roosevelt's strength. He was able to mount the podium only with the aid of crutches. He spent the next several years continuing his recuperation while at the same time maintaining his political correspondence.

In 1928, Roosevelt again nominated Smith for the presidency; this time the New York governor gained the nomination, but he would lose the race to HERBERT HOOVER. Roosevelt appeared in better health, walking with the aid of a cane and supported by his son. He seemed ready for the rigors of politics. Later that year he became a candidate for the New York governorship. Party insiders, especially Smith advisers, believed Roosevelt had several assets as a candidate: His name and regional identification in the state would attract Republicans, he had a reputation for opposing Tammany even though he had actually strengthened his ties with the urban machine, he had very few political enemies, and, as a Protestant, he would likely help the Catholic Smith in New

York. In the general election, Roosevelt won a narrow victory even though Smith did not carry New York in his losing race against Hoover.

Roosevelt's years in Albany coincided with the onset of the Great Depression. He became an activist governor, arguing that government must play a significant role in economic recovery. He championed programs for public as opposed to private electrical power, utility rate reform, tax reduction for farmers, and state unemployment relief. With so many Americans out of work, Roosevelt also called on the federal government to address the problems of joblessness and he advocated national unemployment insurance. In addition to these appeals, he urged President Hoover to balance the

Candidate Franklin Roosevelt waves his hat as he campaigns in Detroit on October 3, 1932. Seated in front of him is Mayor Frank Murphy and beside him are local Democratic politician Horatio Abbott and the candidate's wife, Eleanor Roosevelt. *(Associated Press)*

federal budget and end government meddling in the economy. Read after the fact, this plea sounds ironic, but prior to March of 1933, Hoover had taken a more activist stance in addressing the nation's economic misery than had any previous president facing economic panic. As governor of New York, Roosevelt was simply reflecting orthodox views when he criticized Hoover's activism.

A popular governor, in the nation's most populous state, Roosevelt easily won reelection in 1930, making him a leading presidential contender for 1932. As such, he shifted into the role of rival to Al Smith, who had been his political benefactor during his recovery from polio and hoped to run again for president. Roosevelt's principal advisers were Howe and James A. Farley, with whom he had worked on his gubernatorial campaigns. Farley helped Roosevelt gain support in the South and the West where Smith—still identified with the urban, immigrant, Catholic elements of the party—was weak. Speaker of the House JOHN NANCE GARNER, a moderate Texas Democrat, was another rival for the nomination when Democrats gathered in Chicago on June 27, 1932, for their convention. Smith and Garner had both won several important presidential primaries, and between them they had enough delegates to prevent Roosevelt from gaining the nomination on the first ballot. The convention remained deadlocked through three rounds of voting, but prior to the fourth ballot the Garner camp and the Roosevelt camp struck a deal whereby the Texan released his delegates to Roosevelt in exchange for the vice presidency. On the fourth ballot, Roosevelt won the nomination, 942 to 201½ (in doing so, he forever severed his friendship with Smith). Upon hearing of his nomination, Roosevelt broke precedent and attended the Democratic National Convention in Chicago to accept the nomination in person. In his speech, he declared that were he elected to the presidency he would ensure "a new deal for the American people." This catchphrase became the theme for his campaign and for his first eight years in the White House.

The fall campaign pitted an optimistic Roosevelt against a dour Herbert Hoover, who told Americans not to complain because the depression could be much worse. Roosevelt successfully convinced a majority of voters that they should link the depression with Hoover. The incumbent president had several liabilities, including his inability to show his compassion for those in misery, his lack of personal warmth, and his increasing defensiveness about his record, all of which soured voters toward his reelection bid. Furthermore, the Bonus March incident in the summer of 1932 in which Hoover approved the use of federal troops to remove World War I veterans from vacant office buildings in downtown Washington, D.C., where they had camped out while lobbying Congress for relief from the depression, proved to be the final straw. Roosevelt defeated Hoover handily in the election wining by more than 7 million popular votes and by 472 to 59 in the Electoral College. In addition, he demonstrated

substantial strength down the ballot. Democrats swept into the House of Representatives and the Senate, increasing their control of the former and taking a majority in the latter. Depression relief policy in the interregnum between the election and Roosevelt's inauguration the following March suffered from the heated rhetoric of the campaign trail. For example, Roosevelt and Hoover were unable to agree on a method to stop any further bank closures.

At his inauguration on March 4, 1933, Roosevelt told the American people, "the only thing we have to fear is fear itself." Roosevelt followed the speech by calling Congress into a special session, since dubbed the first "hundred days," in which lawmakers enacted numerous measures to combat the depression. Major laws included initiatives to protect bank deposits, farmers, industry, homeowners, and stock investors from financial ruin. Additional laws put the jobless back to work and provided temporary relief to the destitute. So popular was the New Deal that, contrary to historical trends, the Democratic Party increased its strength in Congress during the 1934 midterm elections.

Early in his presidency Roosevelt achieved an unprecedented status with the American people. Individuals were so taken with the president that they clipped his pictures from the newspapers and pinned them to their walls. Others even believed him to possess godlike qualities. Because of his successful use of the media, through the fireside chats on radio and regular press conferences, Roosevelt allowed the American people to develop an artificial sense of familiarity. The White House received over 5,000 letters a day from well-wishers and aid-seekers. The replies were carefully crafted so that correspondents would believe the president had read and attended to their concerns. This practice furthered the personal connection between average people and the president. As such, Americans savored every human interest story available about Roosevelt and his family. Careful readers of the press knew when FDR, as the president frequently became known, went to bed at night and what he liked to read. They did not know much about his paralysis, though, for the press did not report it. These details belie a more important development: the increased security concerns for the president in the modern age meant that Roosevelt was much more removed from the people than any 19th-century chief executive had been. ABRAHAM LINCOLN, according to one private secretary, spent 75 percent of his time meeting with people.

Nor did the American people know about the problems in the Roosevelt marriage. The legacy of Roosevelt's affair with Lucy Mercer remained so strong that Eleanor Roosevelt, very active in public policy advocacy and politics, mostly used memoranda to communicate with her husband. Instead, Missy LeHand, Roosevelt's personal secretary, gradually assumed the role of surrogate wife, although likely not in a romantic way, during the White House years. In addition to LeHand, Roosevelt drew companionship from his children, several of whom lived off and on in the White House.

In 1935, the New Deal faced several serious challenges. The Supreme Court declared two laws from the First Hundred Days unconstitutional, one pertaining to agricultural relief and the other to industrial relief. Combined with criticisms of the president from the right for going too far and from the left for not going far enough, the challenge by the Court led the president to adopt an even more liberal agenda. In 1935, an impressive list of reform measures became law, including banking reform, restrictions on holding companies, tax reform, the SOCIAL SECURITY ACT, and labor reform.

Despite or perhaps because of Roosevelt's successes with Congress in 1933 and 1935, concern grew about his reelection: Conservative business and financial interests worried that he had gone too far with some of the New Deal economic reforms while many on the left looked to the New Deal as nothing more than a prop for a capitalist system that needed to be eliminated. His most vocal critics included Louisiana senator and demagogue Huey P. Long, who might well have challenged Roosevelt for the Democratic nomination had he not been assassinated in 1935. Father Charles E. Coughlin, a Detroit radio priest, and Dr. Francis Townsend, an advocate for federally funded old-age pensions, helped form the Union Party, which nominated Representative William Lemke of North Dakota, but ultimately it was not a factor in the race. Despite these critics, Roosevelt remained hugely popular with voters. The Republicans struggled to find a candidate. They needed someone who was not tied to Herbert Hoover but who possessed national stature and would appeal to the party's various ideological wings. They settled on Kansas governor Alfred Landon. A *Liberty Digest* poll suggested Roosevelt would lose the race, but the poll was flawed in that it only surveyed voters with telephones (not yet common in working-class and poor people's homes). While he did not formally begin campaigning for reelection until September 1936, he and his advisers began working behind the scenes in the fall of 1935. Roosevelt won a decisive victory in the popular vote, carrying more than 60 percent, and he swept the Electoral College, 523-8.

So vast was his margin of victory that Roosevelt overreached in his second term. He believed his most important priority was to protect the 1935 reform legislation from a conservative Supreme Court. His first mistake was to push for the SUPREME COURT REORGANIZATION PLAN to reform the Court by adding additional justices for each member over the age of 70. He also wanted the reform applied to the entire federal court system. Considered by many a threat to judicial independence, the "court-packing" plan generated much conflict and went down to defeat. (A change in ideological direction on the Court combined with the death and retirement of several justices rendered Roosevelt's concerns moot.) Roosevelt compounded his error regarding the Court by spending much of 1938 attempting to purge conserva-

tives from the Democratic Party. His efforts to unseat certain members of Congress who were critical of the New Deal failed miserably. Furthermore, the economic RECESSION OF 1937 added to the president's woes. Despite these setbacks, Congress passed many critical New Deal laws sought by Roosevelt, including the National Housing Act of 1937 and the FAIR LABOR STANDARDS ACT (FLSA) of 1938.

Still, by 1940, Roosevelt's presidency was in trouble. World War II, which was then raging in Europe and in Asia, provided the opportunity for FDR to remake himself. He feared that no Democrat or Republican had the credentials to lead the United States through the war. As such, he devised a movement within the Democratic Party to draft him to run for an unprecedented third term. Since GEORGE WASHINGTON had stepped down after two terms in 1797, no president had ever run for a third consecutive term. Roosevelt's sitting vice president, John Nance Garner, believed this a danger to the Constitution, and with supporters waged a brief, unsuccessful challenge. Roosevelt was renominated and he replaced Garner on the ticket with HENRY A. WAL-

In this 1941 Herblock cartoon, captioned "Where seldom is heard a discouraging word," a somber John Nance Garner sits on his ranch in Texas. After serving two terms as Roosevelt's vice president, Garner hoped to succeed him as president but was blocked when FDR ran for a third term in 1940. The title refers to a line from "Home on the Range," reportedly Roosevelt's favorite song. *(A Herblock Cartoon, copyright by the Herb Block Foundation)*

LACE, secretary of agriculture. In part for political reasons but largely because of national defense concerns regarding the war, Roosevelt delayed active campaigning until a few weeks before the election. He wanted to show the nation a busy president working to keep the country safe. Still, the rhetoric grew ugly as Republicans searched for any means to defeat the incumbent president. When Roosevelt promised in late October that he would not send U.S. troops into a foreign war (a refrain he had articulated many times since hostilities broke out in Europe), he omitted the phrase "except in the case of an attack." He defeated Wendell Willkie, a liberal, internationalist Republican that fall. There was a 5 million vote spread in the popular balloting, but the Electoral College was much more decisive: 449 to 82.

Roosevelt spent the overwhelming majority of his remaining years in the White House working on war-related issues—some domestic, some foreign. Between his third inaugural on January 20, 1941, and the attack on PEARL HARBOR on December 7, 1941, Roosevelt used every available means to funnel aid to the British in their fight against Germany. He also tried to negotiate with the Japanese to prevent the widening of hostilities in Asia. Through it all, Roosevelt believed that war would come to the United States; he wrongly believed that Germany would be the aggressor.

After Pearl Harbor and the American declaration of war on December 8, 1941, Roosevelt spent most of his time attending to grand strategy. He left the majority of military decisions to his generals while he negotiated with British prime minister Winston Churchill and Soviet leader Joseph Stalin about when and where to go about attacking Germany and Italy. The various wartime conferences that these men held—Casablanca (January 1943), Cairo (November 1943), Teheran (November to December 1943), and Yalta (February 1945)—set the trend for summit diplomacy that would last well into the Cold War years. On the home front, politics remained a constant with conservatives looking for every opportunity to thwart the advances of the New Deal. As such, the 1942 midterm elections and the 1944 presidential election suggested a decline in support for the range of programs passed in the 1930s.

Despite these challenges, politics on the home front remained productive, due in large part to the ability of Roosevelt to work with the congressional leadership. Lawmakers made sound, if sometimes unpopular, wartime decisions about taxation, rationing, and price controls. A Senate investigation of defense contractors won tremendous praise in the popular press and paved the way for Missouri senator HARRY S. TRUMAN's* vice-presidential

nomination in 1944. Less sound decisions were made about wartime labor strikes and about INTERNMENT OF JAPANESE AMERICANS.

The events of the war dominated the 1944 presidential campaign and election. Victories at D-Day and at the BATTLE OF LEYTE GULF cemented FDR's argument that he was a successful wartime leader. Roosevelt wanted a fourth term not because he was afraid the United States would otherwise lose the war but because he did not trust any other political leader to win the peace, so important to him was creation of and membership in what became the United Nations. No public discussion of Roosevelt's reelection plans took place until after May 1944. Nor was there a chance that the Democrats would deny FDR the nomination once he made his intentions known, and he easily gained renomination at the Democratic National Convention. Much more tenuous was the contest for the vice-presidential nomination. Henry Wallace had lost favor with many moderates and conservatives in the party, and he was ultimately replaced with Senator Truman, who had made a name for himself by chairing a major Senate investigation into national defense contractors. The Republican Party was not unified in 1944 and it had difficulty forming a strategy. New York governor Thomas E. Dewey ultimately gained the nomination, and he ran a campaign that argued the Democrats had been in power too long. The argument was not persuasive with voters, who accepted the Democratic Party contention that FDR was "indispensable." Roosevelt ultimately won a relatively easy victory in a closely fought contest.

As Roosevelt began his unprecedented fourth term on January 20, 1945, he looked a shadow of the man who first became president in 1933. His health had grown fragile in proportion to the demands of his office. Despite this, he traveled to Yalta in February, where he discussed postwar plans with Churchill and Stalin. Two months later, on April 12, 1945, Roosevelt died of a stroke. He left one of the most important political legacies of any individual to ever sit in the White House. In 12 years and 39 days as president, he shepherded the nation through not one but two major crises: the Great Depression and World War II. He refashioned the Democratic Party into a much broader coalition of southern Democrats, urban workers, northern African Americans, westerners, big city bosses, and ethnic immigrants. His New Deal established a more activist federal government, and his wartime foreign policy ensured that the United States would become a superpower and major world leader in the second half of the 20th century. One of the century's towering figures, he is often ranked with Lincoln and Washington among the nation's greatest leaders, and presidents who followed him in office have been judged by the standards Roosevelt set.

---

*For more information on Harry Truman, Franklin D. Roosevelt's third vice president, see the chapter on Truman, who was president from 1945 to 1953.

Roosevelt's funeral procession along Pennsylvania Avenue in Washington, D.C., on April 14, 1945 *(Library of Congress)*

PRESIDENTIAL ELECTION OF 1932

The severity of the Great Depression imbued the presidential election of 1932 between Republican president HERBERT C. HOOVER and his Democrat challenger, Governor Franklin Delano Roosevelt of New York, with a significance not seen since the election of ABRAHAM LINCOLN in 1860, or at least the election of WILLIAM McKINLEY in 1896. Americans everywhere realized the gravity of the economic issues and the divide between the two parties. More recently, scholars have noted precedents for Roosevelt's New Deal within the Hoover administration and that Hoover's activism outstripped all previous presidents who had dealt with financial panics, but these findings do not diminish the vastly differing views of the two parties at the time of this pivotal election. Despite the economic misery of the nation, which saw unem-

ployment soar to more than 13 million by 1932—a number approaching 25 percent of the nation's workforce—the Republican Party did not seek a replacement candidate for Herbert Hoover, who had a lock on his party's nomination. Tradition prevented any challenge to the sitting president, however low his popular support had fallen.

While most observers believed 1932 would be a Democratic year, little consensus existed as to which Democrat would claim the prize. In addition, concern was widespread that the party would self-destruct as it had in 1924 when it took more than 100 ballots to select a nominee. The party was divided along ideological and regional lines. It also had suffered from the big issue that shaped politics in the 1920s, namely, Prohibition. After the 1928 presidential election, conservatives took charge of the machinery of the Democratic Party. John Jakob Raskob, a New York financier, actively recruited conservatives to make the race. He believed the party platform should be one

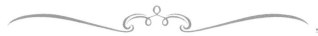

JOHN NANCE GARNER

(1868–1967) *vice president of the United States, March 4, 1933– January 20, 1941*

Known as a shrewd, whiskey-drinking, card-playing politician, John Nance "Cactus Jack" Garner had been a member of the U.S. House of Representatives from Uvalde, Texas, since 1903 and served as Speaker of the House of Representatives between 1931 and 1933. He was born to John Nance Garner III and Sarah Guest, both farmers, in Blossom Prairie, Texas, on November 22, 1868. Young Garner studied briefly at Vanderbilt University before returning to Clarksville, Texas, where he read law and entered the bar in 1890. A bout with tuberculosis caused him to move to Uvalde, Texas, in 1893. Two years later, he married Mariette Rheiner; they had one child. In addition to legal work in Uvalde, Garner also published a newspaper, provided banking services, was elected county judge, and invested in land. After two terms in the state legislature, Garner won a seat in Congress in 1902.

During his first campaign for the House, Garner stressed progressive issues such as the graduated income tax. Over the course of his career, he rarely participated in floor debates, nor did he introduce much legislation. He rose quickly in his new position, gaining election as Democratic whip in 1911 and a seat on the all important Ways and Means Committee in 1913. Garner used his power in Washington to bring economic development projects to his district, including a deep-water port for Corpus Christi. During World War I, Garner helped move President Woodrow Wilson's legislative package through Congress.

Garner became frustrated with the Republican takeover of Congress in the postwar era, but he remained in the House to fight the Ku Klux Klan. While many members of the Texas congressional delegation tried to avoid a position on the Klan in the 1922 midterm elections, Garner openly criticized the organization. After 1922, the Klan faded as a force in Texas politics. In retrospect, he viewed his congressional service in the 1920s as the pinnacle of his political career. During the 1920s, Garner became the ranking Democrat on the Ways and Means Committee; he fashioned working relationships with Republican presidents Warren G. Harding, Calvin Coolidge, and Herbert Hoover; and he practiced the politics of back-room compromise, not demagogic obstruction. A hideaway Capitol office dubbed the Bureau of Education jointly operated with House Speaker Nicholas Longworth served as the location for many of these private discussions. His views on tariffs and taxation are a case in point. Garner disagreed with the majority of both parties, disliking the Republican tendency to favor the wealthy and the Democratic advocacy of free trade. It was not uncommon for Garner to display such political individualism. Longworth even called him a "one man cabal."

John Nance Garner   *(Library of Congress)*

that advocated states' rights, balanced budgets, free enterprise, and repeal of Prohibition. In fact, Democratic Party leaders criticized Hoover for his extravagant spending. Conservative Democrats in Congress had even pushed unsuccessfully for a national sales tax to balance the federal budget. This issue led progressives and liberals in the party to work together to find a candidate strong enough to win the White House and purge the party of its conservative wing.

Progressive Democrats thought Governor Franklin D. Roosevelt of New York more than anyone else in the party could unseat the president, and the 1930 gubernatorial election in the Empire State became, in the words of one Roosevelt biographer, a trial run for the 1932 campaign for the White House. Republicans understood this point, and three of Hoover's cabinet secretaries went to New York to campaign against FDR. (Like his distant cousin THEODORE ROOSEVELT, who was the first president known by his initials—TR—Franklin D. Roosevelt was commonly called FDR.) Hoover's allies tried unsuccessfully to make the 1930 race a referendum on corrupt politics in New York City. This effort only increased the media attention on the race, which Roosevelt savored.

Roosevelt's reelection as governor in 1930 sharpened the contest for the Democratic nomination. He accom-

Following the 1930 midterm elections, the Democrats retook control of Congress, and Garner became Speaker of the House of Representatives. He had long coveted the post, but his two years in power were not satisfying. Even though his fellow lawmakers held him in high esteem, they resisted his tendencies toward economic conservatism as counterproductive to ameliorating the Great Depression. They also disliked his iron-fisted rule over the Democrats; he brooked no dissent within his party. Garner's willingness to cooperate with the Hoover administration early on resulted in several key accomplishments, including creation of the Reconstruction Finance Corporation, strengthening of the Federal Land Banks and the Federal Reserve System, additional public works projects, and agricultural relief. Most troubling to Democrats and progressive Republicans was his support of the Hoover administration's request for a national sales tax. Garner endorsed the measure because he believed it would help maintain a balanced budget, but it was defeated nonetheless.

This fight coincided with Garner's efforts to make a run for the White House in 1932. He enjoyed the backing of the Hearst newspapers around the country, and he went into the Democratic National Convention both with favorite-son status from Texas and with a victory in the California presidential primary. Even though he had approximately 100 delegates, Garner worried that the convention would deadlock. To prevent another Democratic debacle such as the one that had occurred in 1924, he released his delegates after the third ballot. That move assured the nomination for Franklin D. Roosevelt, and it brought Garner the vice-presidential nomination.

The Roosevelt-Garner ticket swept to victory in 1932. For the next eight years, Garner held the vice presidency, but he did not much enjoy it, once remarking that the office was not "worth a pitcher of warm piss." Still, Garner worked hard as vice president. He presided over the Senate with utmost fairness. He ensured that new members of the Senate learned parliamentary procedure. He proved himself to be an important adviser to the president, and he fought for inclusion of the Federal Deposit Insurance Corporation in the New Deal banking reforms. Most important for understanding the remainder of Garner's career, though, was his growing frustration with the New Deal. Garner was never as liberal as Roosevelt, but during their first term together, Garner tried to support the president, disagreeing with FDR only on a few issues such as the decision to recognize the Soviet Union. His support for early New Deal domestic policy was a function of party loyalty, not ideological commitment to the reform measures.

After his reelection in 1936, Garner grew more restive with Roosevelt's politics. He disliked the increased reliance on deficit spending, and he opposed on principle the president's 1937 plan to add additional members to the federal courts, including the Supreme Court. Once the Supreme Court reform plan went down to defeat, Garner did, however, push through legislation reforming the lower courts. Roosevelt, though, was displeased, believing his vice president should have done more for the initial reform package. The following year brought more tension to the Roosevelt-Garner relationship as the president sought to have uncooperative, conservative Democrats defeated in their reelection bids. Nor did Garner approve of Roosevelt's third term bid. He himself tried for the nomination but could not even muster meaningful support in his home state of Texas, where the pro-Roosevelt faction dominated the state convention.

In 1941, Garner retired to Uvalde. He stayed out of national politics for the remainder of his life, but he noted that had he remained Speaker of the House he might have been able to better serve the nation than he did as vice president. From that powerful post, Garner reasoned, he could have more easily restrained some of the excesses of the New Deal. Unfairly dubbed in 1940 "a poker-playing, whiskey-drinking, labor-baiting, evil old man" by labor union activist John L. Lewis, John Nance Garner was a moderate Democrat whose integrity was beyond dispute. He died on November 7, 1967.

plished several important tasks in his successful gubernatorial reelection bid: He remained ambiguous about the troubling and divisive Prohibition issue in his speeches, he focused on economics, and he castigated the Hoover administration for its failure to ameliorate the depression. Not only did Roosevelt win by a landslide, but he captured a significant number of Republican votes while also reconciling the factions within the Democratic Party. The day after New Yorkers reelected Roosevelt as governor, the humorist Will Rogers noted: "The Democrats nominated their president yesterday." National newspapers agreed, dubbing him the likely nominee for the Democrats. As a result, the Roosevelt camp became overly confident about their chances in 1932.

Al Smith, however, the former governor of New York and the Democratic nominee in 1928, wanted another shot at the White House. Because Roosevelt's victory in New York—the nation's most populous state—surpassed that of any previous governor of the state, it triggered a break between the former allies (Roosevelt had nominated Smith for the presidency in 1924 and 1928, and Smith had played a role in FDR's return to politics following his bout with polio). Few political prognosticators gave Smith much of a chance in 1932. His 1928 race had stirred so much acrimony that, with the stakes so high, Democrats realized the risk of a repeat performance. Instead, Smith's real chance lay in dividing the Democratic National Convention and forcing a compromise candidate.

The fight for the nomination was protracted especially since other Democrats also sought the prize. They included internationalist and economic conservative Newton D. Baker, the former secretary of war during the WOODROW WILSON administration; populist JOHN NANCE GARNER, the crusty Texan and Speaker of the House of Representatives; William Gibbs McAdoo, the secretary of the treasury under Wilson and a vehement opponent of Smith; and Smith him-

self. Smith and McAdoo both believed they had a greater claim to the nomination than Roosevelt because of their past accomplishments. Early on, Smith provided the most serious challenge to Roosevelt. He already had the backing of the urban political machines and the conservative East Coast Democrats. Roosevelt, despite his northeastern regional identification, sought and won support from southern and western Democrats.

The Roosevelt and Smith factions waged several battles within the Democratic National Committee, all of which Roosevelt won. Roosevelt's challenge in the period before

In this Clifford Kennedy Berryman cartoon titled "All Set for the Campaign!" the Democratic Tammany Tiger sits with a Roosevelt/Garner poster and a "whoopee" sign, already visibly fatigued by the 1932 election. *(Library of Congress)*

the Democratic National Convention in 1932 was to avoid an irreparable divide in the party. To defeat Hoover, the support of all Democrats, including the urban machines, would be necessary. On the issues, Roosevelt crafted an unassailable record in Albany as governor of New York: He supported important reforms in agriculture, conservation, public power, social welfare, and unemployment relief, in what some have described as a preview of the New Deal. The only vexing domestic issue was the political corruption of Tammany Hall, the Democratic political machine in New York City, and the only potential foreign policy issue was the League of Nations, specifically, whether Roosevelt supported admission to the League. Roosevelt, though, avoided any discussion of issues prior to the convention for fear that a stated position might cause him to lose delegate support. Walter Lippmann, a leading journalist and public intellectual, castigated him for this preconvention stance. "[Roosevelt is] an amiable man with many philanthropic impulses, but he is not the dangerous enemy of anything," Lippmann wrote. "He is too eager to please. Franklin D. Roosevelt is no crusader. He is no tribune of the people. He is no enemy of entrenched privilege. He is a pleasant man who, without any important qualifications for the office, would very much like to be President."

Anti-Roosevelt Democrats welcomed this critique, which embodied the weaknesses of Roosevelt. Lippmann continued to lambaste Roosevelt, and in so doing, he also hinted at his support for Baker's candidacy. Baker hoped that the two front-runners going into 1932—Roosevelt and Smith—would verbally spar enough that they would cancel each other out at the convention later that year. He positioned himself as a compromise candidate when the Democrats met in Chicago, but he did not use the Lippmann analysis as much or as effectively as the Smith camp.

To maintain Roosevelt's seeming advantage, Jim Farley, FDR's leading strategist, announced soon after the gubernatorial election that Roosevelt would capture the nomination in 1932 with ease. More important, Roosevelt and his allies, Farley and Louis M. Howe, began the arduous work of lining up the support of the state delegations that would ultimately decide the nomination at the Democratic National Convention in 1932. Governor Roosevelt wrote numerous letters to local and state Democratic leaders throughout the nation. The campaign also reached out to Roosevelt's colleagues from his days with the Woodrow Wilson administration when he served as assistant secretary of the navy. The most significant challenge would be gaining enough support to surmount the century-old requirement, in effect since the era of ANDREW JACKSON in the 1830s, that Democratic nominees secure two-thirds of the delegates to win the nomination. The two-thirds rule gave the South its power within the Democratic Party because delegates from that region acting in concert could block any nominee not to their liking.

The next step for the Roosevelt campaign was to assemblace a team of academic advisers, dubbed the "BRAIN TRUST" by newspaper writers. Howe recruited professors from Columbia University to assist Roosevelt on policy questions. Doing so mattered at the time because FDR wanted to run a campaign that focused on issues, not personality. Ironically enough it was personality that became one of Roosevelt's most potent political weapons. Those who were brought into the Roosevelt fold included economist Rexford G. Tugwell, who dealt with agricultural issues, and Adolf A. Berle, Jr., who concentrated on the credit problem and corporations. Tugwell and Berle were the most important members of the Brain Trust, which operated under Raymond Moley, a Barnard College professor who had worked in the gubernatorial administration, and Samuel I. Rosenman, a speechwriter for Roosevelt. The Brain Trust schooled Roosevelt on economic and social policy questions about which he was ignorant and on which the 1932 campaign would turn. Tugwell found Roosevelt to be a good student, able to grasp new information after just five minutes of instruction and then explain it to another person with emotion.

The issue of the League of Nations became central to the fight for the Democratic nomination when New York newspaper publisher William Randolph Hearst began favoring John Nance Garner. On January 1, 1932, Hearst declared that the next president must put "America first" and reject Wilsonian internationalism. He then threw his support to Garner, suggesting that the Texan was the ideal candidate to lead the Democratic Party and the nation. Hearst's editorial policy was a blow to Roosevelt, who had hoped to avoid discussion of foreign policy and who had endorsed the League while a member of the Wilson administration and while a candidate for the vice presidency in 1920. Roosevelt handled this problem by attacking the League for having departed from Wilson's goal of an international peace-keeping body in having devolved into a debating society focused on European problems, which had no effect on the United States. The statement troubled Wilsonian Democrats—one of whom quipped FDR "ought to be spanked"—but it ensured that Roosevelt remained a viable candidate for the Democratic nomination.

In the first half of 1932, Roosevelt followed a middle-ground strategy: He rejected the increasingly outmoded pose of waiting for the nomination to be presented to him, but he did not undertake an aggressive modern campaign for the White House. Roosevelt delivered several speeches and radio addresses in which he avoided making specific promises at the same time that he claimed the progressive mantle for his candidacy. On April 7, 1932, he attacked Hoover for not solving the problems of the Great Depression, especially as it affected the "forgotten men" of the middle and lower classes. Roosevelt said that the government must do more to help farmers and homeowners avoid foreclosure. This statement

Thousands turned out to hear Roosevelt speak in Omaha, Nebraska, on September 29, 1932. *(Associated Press)*

frightened conservatives in the party, and Smith exploited the comment, arguing that class demagoguery was out of place. Not content to let the commotion settle, Roosevelt gave yet another speech in which he argued, "the country needs, and unless I mistake its temper, the country demands bold, persistent experimentation."

The race for delegates ensued. Roosevelt secured huge leads in the South and the West. Prior to the convention, Roosevelt secured delegates from 12 of the 16 southern and border states. He also garnered most of the midwestern and western state delegations. At the same time, he suffered several major losses. Smith trounced him three to one in the Massachusetts primary. After McAdoo abandoned his own presidential dreams, he worked with Hearst, and they secured a win in California for Garner, who also took Texas as a favorite-son candidate. Roosevelt's critics worried about suspect personality traits, including an overarching opti-

mism, political opportunism, and a tendency toward political vacillation.

Against this backdrop the Republicans gathered in Chicago on June 14 to nominate their candidate for the presidency. Some observers described the Republican National Convention as a funeral, so uninspired were the delegates. President Herbert Hoover dominated every aspect of the proceedings, including the selection of the convention chair and the writing of the platform. That document, which was celebratory of the Hoover record, talked at length about how best to repair the damage of the Great Depression, but the convention delegates only wanted to debate Prohibition. Hoover insisted on maintaining the Eighteenth Amendment, but most Republicans—and most Americans as well—wanted to revise or repeal it. Secretary of the Treasury Ogden Mills and Secretary of State Henry L. Stimson finally convinced Hoover to accept a plank that called for the repeal of Prohibition but that also permitted states that wished to remain dry to do so. The convention never discussed the depression in a meaningful way, although the platform included planks in favor of state and local, not federal, relief programs, a balanced budget, banking reform to protect depositors, and tariff protection for agriculture. That Hoover would be renominated for a second term was never in doubt. Hoover would have liked to replace Vice President Charles Curtis, a mediocre politician more interested in the Washington social scene than in matters of governance, on the ticket, but without a viable alternative, Curtis was renominated as well.

On the eve of the Democratic convention, Roosevelt had a simple majority of the delegates, but he lacked the two-thirds necessary for nomination on the first ballot. His delegate strength made his nomination probable but not definite. It also allowed him to claim control of the machinery of the convention, which opened in Chicago on June 27 and adjourned on July 2. This victory proved important regarding the selection of the convention's permanent chair. Jouett Shouse, who was the chair of the Democratic National Committee and a Smith backer, wanted the post, which he could then use to derail Roosevelt's quest for the nomination. The Roosevelt forces defeated Shouse by claiming that the convention's arrangements committee had only commended him, not recommended him. Smith's backers claimed bad faith when Senator Thomas J. Walsh of Montana was selected as the permanent chair.

The convention also debated retention of the two-thirds rule for presidential nominations. Backers of Roosevelt had considered challenging the outmoded requirement, especially after the debacle of 1924 in which over 100 ballots were necessary to select a nominee and in which the original majority choice of the convention was thwarted. Senator Huey P. Long of Louisiana pushed for eliminating the rule, but he acted before the delegates had been primed for such a move. His effort failed, and Roosevelt abandoned the idea. The "stop Roosevelt movement," which was dubbed the "Allies," took this vote as a signal that they might prevail. However, the Allies were not united behind a particular candidate. Smith, Garner, and Baker all wanted the nomination. This divide helped the Roosevelt camp, which negotiated with all three for their delegates. Similarly, the Allies tried to win over wavering Roosevelt delegations, specifically those from Mississippi, Iowa, Michigan, and Maine. Smith contended that loyalty to Roosevelt was thin and that his delegates would abandon him after the first ballot.

Once the convention turned its attention to balloting for the presidential nomination, the tension thickened. As was the custom, Roosevelt was not in Chicago with the Democrats. Back in Albany, he followed the drama through the night of June 30, 1932. In the early hours of the morning on July 1, with the delegates leaning toward Roosevelt, he called for a vote to show his strength. The front-runner amassed 666¼ votes to 201¾ for Smith and 90¼ for Garner. Seven other candidates divided the remaining votes. Despite his overwhelming lead, Roosevelt needed 100 more votes to capture the nomination. With two more ballots, Roosevelt increased his lead incrementally, but nowhere near enough to capture the votes he needed to surmount the two-thirds required for nomination. Roosevelt strategists understood that if the convention went to a fifth ballot, the door would be open for Baker as a compromise candidate to block the New York governor.

To prevent Baker from taking the nomination away from Roosevelt, negotiations began in earnest with Garner's key advisers, specifically Congressman Sam Rayburn of Texas. The knowledge that several delegations pledged to Roosevelt were on the verge of defecting added to the tensions surrounding the negotiations. Mississippi was the most vulnerable state, and if it dropped Roosevelt, then Arkansas would follow suit. As such, Farley and Howe concentrated on securing Texas. They talked at length with Rayburn, who told them, "we'll see what can be done." Simultaneously Wall Street financier Joseph P. Kennedy (father of future president JOHN F. KENNEDY) tried to bring California, which backed Garner, into the Roosevelt column. Hearst loathed Baker, who was the dark horse candidate most likely to claim the nomination if the convention deadlocked. Joe Kennedy told Hearst it would be Baker unless he supported FDR. To do so required a conversation with Garner. The Texan had already refused calls from Smith, who also coveted the California delegates. Kennedy worked through Hearst, who detested Smith and dreaded Baker, to try to bring the state's votes to FDR. Rayburn and Garner discussed the matter, and Garner leaned toward releasing his delegates to Roosevelt for several reasons: He believed that a divided convention would produce a weak candidate and he believed Roosevelt held positions closer to his own than either Smith or Baker. After their conversation, Rayburn told the Roosevelt camp that California would vote for Roosevelt, but Texas would remain with Garner unless the Speaker was made the vice-presidential nominee. Garner himself was not eager for the post, but he sardonically quipped, "Hell, I'll do anything to see the Democrats win one more national election."

When the convention voted its fourth ballot for the presidential nomination on June 30, William Gibbs McAdoo declared California wanted to nominate a president, not divide the party. The bystanders in the gallery, packed with stop-Roosevelt partisans, protested, but a bandwagon effect followed with all but the most loyal Smith delegations throwing their support to Roosevelt. Roosevelt gained the nomination. Some scholars have attributed Roosevelt's triumph solely to the deal-making with Garner, but long-term tensions between urban and rural factions within the Democratic Party were just as important. Smith and McAdoo personified these factions, and because they were unable to

After rushing to Chicago upon receiving the Democratic nomination for president, Roosevelt became the first candidate to deliver his acceptance speech in person. It was in this speech on July 2, 1932, that Roosevelt pledged "a new deal for the American people." *(Associated Press)*

agree on a compromise candidate, Roosevelt, who had positioned himself appropriately, took advantage of the situation.

The acrimony over the nomination was short-lived, reasonably contained, and did not spill over to the party as a whole. The Democrats rallied behind Roosevelt with ease. The newly minted nominee facilitated the process by breaking with tradition and traveling to Chicago to accept the nomination in person. Arriving on July 2, he told the cheering delegates: "I pledge you, I pledge myself, to a new deal for the American people. . . . Give me your help, not to win votes alone, but to win in this crusade to restore America to its own people." Although not intended, the "new deal" would become the phrase embodying Roosevelt's programs when he became president the following year.

Commentators at the time were not convinced that Roosevelt had the ability to defeat Hoover. One even quipped that he was the weakest Democratic nominee since FRANK-LIN PIERCE. Another contended that Garner, not Roosevelt,

was the stronger person on the ticket. Party insiders even advised Roosevelt to stay at home, arguing that campaigns don't win elections.

The Roosevelt campaign that followed was both strategic and anticlimactic. Roosevelt took every opportunity to turn the election into a referendum on the depression. Political considerations shaped both the policies and the ideology that he advocated. Because his base was in the South and the West, Roosevelt talked of refashioning the Democratic Party along progressive lines, but he was cautious. Roosevelt understood that the progressives in the party were good at fighting for issues but were bad at cooperation, so he did not want to move too far too fast. Furthermore, Hoover's celebration of American individualism, a conservative posture, encouraged Roosevelt to talk about things such as national economic planning.

FDR knew that he would lose a purely partisan contest simply because more than two-thirds of the nation's registered voters were Republican. He thus hoped to gain disaffected Republicans. Despite concern about his health and his intellectual depth, Roosevelt staged a vigorous campaign. He traveled by train to the West and to the South, where not a single electoral vote was in jeopardy. His "whistle stop" tour of the country involved brief, polite remarks to well-wishers at each destination. He would visit with the congressional leadership and launch initial conversations about his legislative agenda for his new administration should he prove victorious in November.

Roosevelt's campaign speeches were pitched in positive terms and reflected a progressive tone. He avoided all specific details whenever possible, and he offered targeted policy generalities to each of his audiences. When in farm country he spoke of subsidy programs that would increase the earnings of farmers who then generally supported inflationist policies, but when addressing urban, middle-class consumers he talked of maintaining a balanced budget. At no time did he suggest the need for inflation. With one issue, though, Roosevelt did make specific promises: hydroelectric power development. He contended that only the federal government could provide equal access to electrical power, and he promised he would address the issue in his administration.

The campaign that fall proved a study in contrasts. While there were many similarities and indeed much affection between Hoover and Roosevelt in the early days of their political careers—the two men both began public life as progressives and admirers of Theodore Roosevelt and both served in Wilson's administration—by 1932, they had become political opposites, certainly with regard to personality. Hoover appeared lifeless and monotone on the campaign trail. He became increasingly defensive of his record, and he remained steadfast in his belief that the federal government should not engage in a program of direct relief payments to the needy. Ironically, on that point Roosevelt agreed. He shared Hoover's view that relief should flow from the state and local levels, but during the early years of the depression, as governor, FDR had talked openly about the need for more (state) government involvement in relief. On the other hand, Hoover had stressed the importance of a hands-off (federal) government policy regarding direct relief payments. The public missed the nuanced agreement between the two men.

Ironically, the two party platforms were similar in tone and emphasis. Roosevelt had made sure that the Democratic platform contained little that could be controversial. Democratic senator Key Pittman of Nevada complained that "the platform has the merit of being short, and the demerit of being cold. There is not a word in it with regard to the 'forgotten man.'" Both platforms covered the well-worn arguments of the past that had divided the two parties, but the Democrats were slightly more ambitious with regard to social welfare policies.

Compared with his predecessors who had served during periods of financial panic, most notably MARTIN VAN BUREN in the late 1830s and GROVER CLEVELAND in the 1890s, Hoover proved himself an activist in his response to the Great Depression. He created the RECONSTRUCTION FINANCE CORPORATION, called for an expansion of public works, extended the power of Farm Loan banks, and initiated a moratorium on German debt repayment. Despite those efforts, however, only one in four Americans who needed relief was receiving it in 1932. As such, by 1932 few Americans cared much about Hoover's record prior to his presidency of facilitating disaster relief during the Belgian crisis in World War I and during the Mississippi River flooding of 1927. So negative was public opinion of Hoover that his name had become synonymous with that of misery, with the term *Hoovervilles* being applied to shantytowns and makeshift settlements.

Meanwhile, the Hoover camp pinned its hopes on the perception of Roosevelt as a weak candidate and on the chance that a dramatic return to prosperity would ensue. Regarding the former, Roosevelt answered back by finally taking bold steps under New York State law to remove the corrupt mayor of New York City, Jimmy Walker, from his post. Walker resigned his office on September 1, 1932, after detailed hearings into his ethical violations. Regarding the latter, the Republicans touted figures from the "Weekly Index

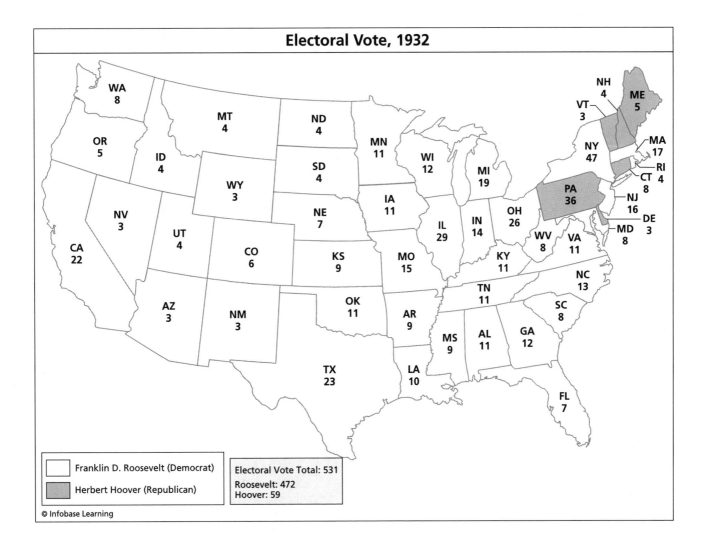

© Infobase Learning

1932 Election Statistics

State	Number of Electors	Total Popular Vote	Elec Vote D	Elec Vote R	Pop Vote D	Pop Vote R	Pop Vote S	Margin of Victory Votes	Margin of Victory % Total Vote
Alabama	11	245,354	11		1	2	3	173,235	70.61%
Arizona	3	118,251	3		1	2	3	43,160	36.50%
Arkansas	9	216,787	9		1	2	3	159,364	73.51%
California	22	2,267,966	22		1	2	3	476,255	21.00%
Colorado	6	457,696	6		1	2	3	61,260	13.38%
Connecticut	8	594,183		8	2	1	3	6,788	1.14%
Delaware	3	112,901		3	2	1	3	2,754	2.44%
Florida	7	276,252	7		1	2	3	137,137	49.64%
Georgia	12	255,590	12		1	2	4	214,255	83.83%
Idaho	4	186,625	4		1	2	4	38,062	20.39%
Illinois	29	3,407,926	29		1	2	3	449,548	13.19%
Indiana	14	1,576,927	14		1	2	3	184,870	11.72%
Iowa	11	1,036,687	11		1	2	3	183,586	17.71%
Kansas	9	791,978	9		1	2	3	74,706	9.43%
Kentucky	11	983,063	11		1	2	3	185,858	18.91%
Louisiana	10	268,804	10		1	2	-	230,565	85.77%
Maine	5	298,444		5	2	1	3	37,724	12.64%
Maryland	8	511,054	8		1	2	3	130,130	25.46%
Massachusetts	17	1,580,114	17		1	2	3	63,189	4.00%
Michigan	19	1,664,765	19		1	2	3	131,806	7.92%
Minnesota	11	1,002,843	11		1	2	3	236,847	23.62%
Mississippi	9	146,034	9		1	2	3	134,988	92.44%
Missouri	15	1,609,894	15		1	2	3	460,693	28.62%
Montana	4	216,479	4		1	2	3	49,208	22.73%
Nebraska	7	570,137	7		1	2	3	157,905	27.70%
Nevada	3	41,430	3		1	2	-	16,082	38.82%
New Hampshire	4	205,520		4	2	1	3	2,949	1.43%
New Jersey	16	1,629,507	16		1	2	3	30,988	1.90%
New Mexico	3	151,606	3		1	2	3	40,872	26.96%
New York	47	4,688,614	47		1	2	3	596,996	12.73%
North Carolina	13	711,501	13		1	2	3	289,222	40.65%
North Dakota	4	256,290	4		1	2	3	106,578	41.58%
Ohio	26	2,609,728	26		1	2	3	74,376	2.85%
Oklahoma	11	704,633	11		1	2	-	328,303	46.59%
Oregon	5	368,808	5		1	2	3	77,852	21.11%
Pennsylvania	36	2,859,177		36	2	1	3	157,592	5.51%
Rhode Island	4	266,170	4		1	2	3	31,338	11.77%
South Carolina	8	104,407	8		1	2	3	100,369	96.13%
South Dakota	4	288,438	4		1	2	4	84,303	29.23%
Tennessee	11	390,256	11		1	2	4	132,721	34.01%
Texas	23	874,446	23		1	2	3	672,891	76.95%
Utah	4	206,578	4		1	2	3	31,955	15.47%
Vermont	3	136,980		3	2	1	3	22,718	16.58%
Virginia	11	297,942	11		1	2	3	114,342	38.38%
Washington	8	614,814	8		1	2	4	144,615	23.52%
West Virginia	8	743,774	8		1	2	3	74,393	10.00%
Wisconsin	12	1,114,808	12		1	2	3	359,669	32.26%
Wyoming	3	96,962	3		1	2	3	14,787	15.25%
Total	531	39,759,143	472	59	1	2	3	7,068,754	17.78%

Roosevelt Democratic		Hoover Republican		Thomas Socialist		Others	
207,910	84.74%	34,675	14.13%	2,030	0.83%	739	0.30%
79,264	67.03%	36,104	30.53%	2,618	2.21%	265	0.22%
186,829	86.18%	27,465	12.67%	1,269	0.59%	1,224	0.56%
1,324,157	58.39%	847,902	37.39%	63,299	2.79%	32,608	1.44%
250,877	54.81%	189,617	41.43%	13,591	2.97%	3,611	0.79%
281,632	47.40%	288,420	48.54%	20,480	3.45%	3,651	0.61%
54,319	48.11%	57,073	50.55%	1,376	1.22%	133	0.12%
206,307	74.68%	69,170	25.04%	775	0.28%	0	0.00%
234,118	91.60%	19,863	7.77%	461	0.18%	1,148	0.45%
109,479	58.66%	71,417	38.27%	526	0.28%	5,203	2.79%
1,882,304	55.23%	1,432,756	42.04%	67,258	1.97%	25,608	0.75%
862,054	54.67%	677,184	42.94%	21,388	1.36%	16,301	1.03%
598,019	57.69%	414,433	39.98%	20,467	1.97%	3,768	0.36%
424,204	53.56%	349,498	44.13%	18,276	2.31%	0	0.00%
580,574	59.06%	394,716	40.15%	3,853	0.39%	3,920	0.40%
249,418	92.79%	18,853	7.01%	0	0.00%	533	0.20%
128,907	43.19%	166,631	55.83%	2,489	0.83%	417	0.14%
314,314	61.50%	184,184	36.04%	10,489	2.05%	2,067	0.40%
800,148	50.64%	736,959	46.64%	34,305	2.17%	8,702	0.55%
871,700	52.36%	739,894	44.44%	39,205	2.35%	13,966	0.84%
600,806	59.91%	363,959	36.29%	25,476	2.54%	12,602	1.26%
140,168	95.98%	5,180	3.55%	686	0.47%	0	0.00%
1,025,406	63.69%	564,713	35.08%	16,374	1.02%	3,401	0.21%
127,286	58.80%	78,078	36.07%	7,891	3.65%	3,224	1.49%
359,082	62.98%	201,177	35.29%	9,876	1.73%	2	0.00%
28,756	69.41%	12,674	30.59%	0	0.00%	0	0.00%
100,680	48.99%	103,629	50.42%	947	0.46%	264	0.13%
806,394	49.49%	775,406	47.59%	42,988	2.64%	4,719	0.29%
95,089	62.72%	54,217	35.76%	1,776	1.17%	524	0.35%
2,534,959	54.07%	1,937,963	41.33%	177,397	3.78%	38,295	0.82%
497,566	69.93%	208,344	29.28%	5,591	0.79%	0	0.00%
178,350	69.59%	71,772	28.00%	3,521	1.37%	2,647	1.03%
1,301,695	49.88%	1,227,319	47.03%	64,094	2.46%	16,620	0.64%
516,468	73.30%	188,165	26.70%	0	0.00%	0	0.00%
213,871	57.99%	136,019	36.88%	15,450	4.19%	3,468	0.94%
1,295,948	45.33%	1,453,540	50.84%	91,223	3.19%	18,466	0.65%
146,604	55.08%	115,266	43.31%	3,138	1.18%	1,162	0.44%
102,347	98.03%	1,978	1.89%	82	0.08%	0	0.00%
183,515	63.62%	99,212	34.40%	1,551	0.54%	4,160	1.44%
259,473	66.49%	126,752	32.48%	1,796	0.46%	2,235	0.57%
771,109	88.18%	98,218	11.23%	4,450	0.51%	669	0.08%
116,750	56.52%	84,795	41.05%	4,087	1.98%	946	0.46%
56,266	41.08%	78,984	57.66%	1,533	1.12%	197	0.14%
203,979	68.46%	89,637	30.09%	2,382	0.80%	1,944	0.65%
353,260	57.46%	208,645	33.94%	17,080	2.78%	35,829	5.83%
405,124	54.47%	330,731	44.47%	5,133	0.69%	2,786	0.37%
707,410	63.46%	347,741	31.19%	53,379	4.79%	6,278	0.56%
54,370	56.07%	39,583	40.82%	2,829	2.92%	180	0.19%
22,829,265	57.42%	15,760,511	39.64%	884,885	2.23%	284,482	0.72%

of Business Activity," that ran in the *New York Times*. Beginning on August 6, 1932, the column suggested evidence existed of heightened levels of business activity. Any economic rebound in the steel, electric power, and automobile industries, however, had limited immediate impact on the poorest of Americans and on those hardest hit by the depression. Agriculture remained stagnant.

More troubling for Hoover and the Republicans, though, was the president's handling of the ill-fated BONUS MARCH. Approximately 20,000 veterans of World War I and their families had begun gathering in Washington, D.C., in the early months of 1932 to lobby Congress for enactment of legislation providing for early payment of a "bonus" promised to them in 1924 for their military service. Congress had authorized such payment to be made in 1945, but with worsened economic conditions veterans demanded immediate payment of this much-needed money. Despite their best efforts, the measure failed to gain sufficient support in the Senate. The majority of the "Bonus Army" went home disappointed, but a core group remained in the nation's capital, occupying vacant downtown buildings and campgrounds near the Anacostia River. On July 28, 1932, Hoover gave the order for the U.S. Army to dislodge the Bonus Army from the abandoned buildings. The skirmish that resulted shocked the American people, who saw newsreel footage of the army's use of brute force—four cavalry troops with drawn sabers, six tanks, and an infantry column with fixed bayonets—against destitute veterans and their families. The action severely hurt Hoover's chances for reelection, and Roosevelt's partisans saw little prospect that Hoover could recover from such a debacle.

Nor did Hoover frame his campaign in positive terms. His speeches and his body language conveyed a dour image to the voters. The president told audiences that were it not for the programs of his administration the depression would be even worse. More important, Hoover avowed that Roosevelt threatened the very foundations of the republic. He argued that the race was not simply a contest between Democrats and Republicans but a referendum on what philosophy of government should dominate in the nation.

Hoover and Roosevelt differed also on what they believed to be the source of the Great Depression. Hoover argued that the nation's financial miseries were international in origin, beyond the scope of the federal government to ameliorate. Roosevelt disagreed, arguing that it was a domestic failure. In doing so, he placed little emphasis on international affairs, dismissing the key foreign policy issues of the day—the tariff and the League of Nations—from any prominent mention in his campaign. Furthermore, by suggesting that the depression was a domestic problem, Roosevelt placed himself in a position to blame Hoover for it. Roosevelt then developed a justification for policies that can best be described as economic nationalism, encompassing a combination of social and economic planning with both government thrift and a balanced budget. That those aims were contradictory—with the former requiring a large, activist federal government intimately involved in the workings of the economy and the latter relying on a small federal government that played but a scant role in domestic social and economic matters—mattered little. Because his speeches were so vague, the voters were often not aware of this discrepancy.

When voters went to the polls on November 8, 1932, Roosevelt won in a landslide. He captured 42 states, 472 electoral votes, and 57.4 percent of the popular vote. Hoover, on the other hand, won just six states—all in the Northeast—and 59 electoral votes wile garnering just 39.6 percent of the popular vote. The popular vote divided 22,829,265 for Roosevelt and 15,760,511 for Hoover. His defeat was the worst to date for a Republican except for 1912 when the party was divided. Upon learning of his victory, Roosevelt declared, "This is the greatest night in my life." *The New Republic* cut closer to the truth, though, when it wrote that "all informed observers agree that the country did not vote for Roosevelt; it voted against Hoover."

PRESIDENTIAL ELECTION OF 1936

—m—

During the second half of President Franklin Roosevelt's first administration in the mid-1930s the coalition he formed of southern and western progressives, urban bosses, eastern conservatives, workers, and consumers began to show cracks. Discontent was most apparent on the left and right extremes. Financiers and the business community came to distrust what they believed to be the unorthodox economics of New Deal policy. Just as strong was the outcry from the left. Some liberals, along with a host of fringe groups, believed that Roosevelt had not gone far enough in punishing the capitalists for their misdeeds and protecting the poor and disfranchised. Senator Huey P. Long (D-LA) was perhaps the most serious challenger to Roosevelt for the Democratic presidential nomination in 1936. He had touted a scheme whereby every American would receive a guaranteed income. However, Long's untimely death by an assassin's bullet on September 10, 1935, left Roosevelt with an open path to renomination.

The incumbent president staged a stealth campaign starting in the fall of 1935. Roosevelt did not adopt a formal campaign pose until late September 1936. Instead, he showed himself busy with the people's business of running the country. In the intervening year, he made frequent trips around the United States, where he met with state and local political leaders, tested campaign ideas, and examined PUBLIC WORKS ADMINISTRATION projects. For two reasons, Roosevelt did not want to institute formal campaigning until the fall. First, he did not want to have the enthusiasm for his reelection peak too soon. Second, he did not want to preview his strategy and thus provide a potential benefit for the Republicans. He told one of his leading political advisers, James A. Farley, "Of course, there won't be anything political about . . . inspection trips."

When it came time to deliver his annual message to Congress in January 1936, Roosevelt journeyed to Capitol Hill, appeared before a special evening session of Congress, and he made his address over a live radio broadcast. This appearance foreshadowed what would become the norm in the age of television a generation later. As to the coming presidential election, Roosevelt did reveal one important card. After defending the American policy of neutrality regarding possible hostilities in Europe, Roosevelt argued that his administration had rightfully "earned the hatred of entrenched greed." His unabashed attacks on big business corruption signaled that his leftward shift in 1935 would remain in effect.

The only indication that Roosevelt might face a difficult campaign came from a horribly flawed poll run by *Liberty Digest.* The magazine solicited the views of almost 1 million telephone subscribers and car owners, and the results revealed a 62 percent opposition to Roosevelt's reelection. The president did not worry overly much about these numbers because he knew *Liberty Digest* had overlooked the group where most of his votes were found—the poor and the working classes, most of whom did not have telephone service or own automobiles in 1936. As final testament to *Liberty Digest*'s blunder, the magazine went bankrupt soon after. Other, more scientific polls—just beginning to be used in the 1930s—revealed the depth of support for FDR.

Republicans faced a challenge in their search for a credible candidate in 1936. Because the Democratic triumph had been so great in 1932 and again in the 1934 midterm congressional elections, few Republicans with national stature were available and interested in making the race for the presidency. Furthermore, the party needed a candidate who was not in any way associated with the administration of HERBERT HOOVER and the depression. Finally, the party faced the question of whether to draft a candidate from the party's insurgent left, a moderate from the center, or a conservative. Democratic strategists hoped for the latter.

Republicans who ultimately sought their party's nomination included Senator William E. Borah (ID), Senator Lester Dickinson (IA), Chicago newspaper publisher Frank Knox, Governor Alfred Landon (KS), and Senator Arthur H. Vandenberg (MI). The Republicans held their convention in June in Cleveland, and everyone who was watching the political contest realized that Landon enjoyed overwhelming delegate strength, so much so that the managers for his closest opponents, Borah and Knox, chose to do nothing that would prevent Landon from securing the nomination. Landon was a moderate with a strong record of leading Kansas through the depression. Landon was the only Republican governor to win

election in 1934, he had no links to the discredited Hoover, and he was seen as a moderate in the party. The convention named Knox as his running mate.

The Landon-Knox ticket adopted a strategy that surprised no one. They separated themselves and their party as best as possible from old guard, conservative Republicans. They agreed with the stated purpose of the New Deal, but they criticized Roosevelt's administration of it, contending the result had been, "Twenty-five billion dollars spent. Thirteen billion dollars added to the public debt. Eleven million unemployed left." Landon contended that the federal government should operate its relief programs more efficiently, but he failed to explain how. While Roosevelt constituted the central issue in the campaign, Landon did not level nasty charges against the incumbent president until the very end.

There were several intriguing points of comparison between the two candidates. While editorial writers tended to prefer Landon, newspaper reporters overwhelmingly sympathized with Roosevelt. Ironically, the Republicans had an easier time of it on the fundraising trail. The Democratic money sources of 1932—bankers and brokers—were not forthcoming in 1936. Labor proved the most important contributor to Democratic coffers, but party managers did not publicize the fact for fear that Republicans would make a campaign issue out of that alliance. As a result, the Republicans outspent the

Republican nominee Alfred Landon *(Library of Congress)*

1936 Election Statistics

State	Number of Electors	Total Popular Vote	Elec Vote		Pop Vote			Margin of Victory	
			D	R	D	R	U	Votes	% Total Vote
Alabama	11	275,744	11		1	2	5	202,838	73.56%
Arizona	3	124,163	3		1	2	3	53,289	42.92%
Arkansas	9	179,423	9		1	2	5	114,726	63.94%
California	22	2,638,882	22		1	2	-	930,405	35.26%
Colorado	6	488,684	6		1	2	3	113,754	23.28%
Connecticut	8	690,723	8		1	2	3	103,444	14.98%
Delaware	3	127,603	3		1	2	3	12,466	9.77%
Florida	7	327,365	7		1	2	-	170,869	52.20%
Georgia	12	293,175	12		1	2	4	218,422	74.50%
Idaho	4	199,617	4		1	2	3	59,427	29.77%
Illinois	29	3,956,522	29		1	2	3	712,606	18.01%
Indiana	14	1,650,897	14		1	2	3	243,404	14.74%
Iowa	11	1,142,733	11		1	2	3	133,779	11.71%
Kansas	9	865,514	9		1	2	4	66,793	7.72%
Kentucky	11	926,206	11		1	2	3	172,242	18.60%
Louisiana	10	329,778	10		1	2	-	256,103	77.66%
Maine	5	304,240		5	2	1	3	42,490	13.97%
Maryland	8	624,896	8		1	2	-	158,177	25.31%
Massachusetts	17	1,840,357	17		1	2	3	174,103	9.46%
Michigan	19	1,805,098	19		1	2	3	317,061	17.56%
Minnesota	11	1,129,975	11		1	2	3	348,350	30.83%
Mississippi	9	162,142	9		1	2	-	152,866	94.28%
Missouri	15	1,828,635	15		1	2	3	413,152	22.59%
Montana	4	230,512	4		1	2	3	96,092	41.69%
Nebraska	7	608,023	7		1	2	3	99,714	16.40%
Nevada	3	43,848	3		1	2	-	20,002	45.62%
New Hampshire	4	218,114	4		1	2	3	3,818	1.75%
New Jersey	16	1,819,127	16		1	2	3	364,128	20.02%
New Mexico	3	169,136	3		1	2	3	44,310	26.20%
New York	47	5,596,398	47		1	2	-	1,112,552	19.88%
North Carolina	13	839,464	13		1	2	6	392,858	46.80%
North Dakota	4	273,716	4		1	2	3	90,397	33.03%
Ohio	26	3,012,589	26		1	2	3	619,285	20.56%
Oklahoma	11	749,740	11		1	2	-	255,947	34.14%
Oregon	5	414,021	5		1	2	3	144,027	34.79%
Pennsylvania	36	4,138,426	36		1	2	3	663,787	16.04%
Rhode Island	4	311,178	4		1	2	3	40,207	12.92%
South Carolina	8	115,437	8		1	2	-	112,145	97.15%
South Dakota	4	296,452	4		1	2	3	34,160	11.52%
Tennessee	11	475,538	11		1	2	6	180,563	37.97%
Texas	23	849,736	23		1	2	3	635,291	74.76%
Utah	4	216,677	4		1	2	3	85,691	39.55%
Vermont	3	143,689		3	2	1	-	18,899	13.15%
Virginia	11	334,590	11		1	2	5	136,644	40.84%
Washington	8	692,338	8		1	2	3	252,687	36.50%
West Virginia	8	829,945	8		1	2	-	177,224	21.35%
Wisconsin	12	1,258,560	12		1	2	3	422,156	33.54%
Wyoming	3	103,382	3		1	2	3	23,885	23.10%
Total	531	45,653,008	523	8	1	2	3	11,074,457	24.26%

Roosevelt Democratic		Landon Republican		Lemke Union		Others	
238,196	86.38%	35,358	12.82%	551	0.20%	1,639	0.59%
86,722	69.85%	33,433	26.93%	3,307	2.66%	701	0.56%
146,765	81.80%	32,039	17.86%	4	0.00%	615	0.34%
1,766,836	66.95%	836,431	31.70%	0	0.00%	35,615	1.35%
295,021	60.37%	181,267	37.09%	9,962	2.04%	2,434	0.50%
382,129	55.32%	278,685	40.35%	21,805	3.16%	8,104	1.17%
69,702	54.62%	57,236	44.85%	442	0.35%	223	0.17%
249,117	76.10%	78,248	23.90%	0	0.00%	0	0.00%
255,364	87.10%	36,942	12.60%	141	0.05%	728	0.25%
125,683	62.96%	66,256	33.19%	7,678	3.85%	0	0.00%
2,282,999	57.70%	1,570,393	39.69%	89,439	2.26%	13,691	0.35%
934,974	56.63%	691,570	41.89%	19,407	1.18%	4,946	0.30%
621,756	54.41%	487,977	42.70%	29,687	2.60%	3,313	0.29%
464,520	53.67%	397,727	45.95%	497	0.06%	2,770	0.32%
541,944	58.51%	369,702	39.92%	12,501	1.35%	2,059	0.22%
292,894	88.82%	36,791	11.16%	0	0.00%	93	0.03%
126,333	41.52%	168,823	55.49%	7,581	2.49%	1,503	0.49%
389,612	62.35%	231,435	37.04%	0	0.00%	3,849	0.62%
942,716	51.22%	768,613	41.76%	118,639	6.45%	10,389	0.56%
1,016,794	56.33%	699,733	38.76%	75,795	4.20%	12,776	0.71%
698,811	61.84%	350,461	31.01%	74,296	6.58%	6,407	0.57%
157,333	97.03%	4,467	2.75%	0	0.00%	342	0.21%
1,111,043	60.76%	697,891	38.16%	14,630	0.80%	5,071	0.28%
159,690	69.28%	63,598	27.59%	5,549	2.41%	1,675	0.73%
347,445	57.14%	247,731	40.74%	12,847	2.11%	0	0.00%
31,925	72.81%	11,923	27.19%	0	0.00%	0	0.00%
108,460	49.73%	104,642	47.98%	4,819	2.21%	193	0.09%
1,083,549	59.56%	719,421	39.55%	9,405	0.52%	6,752	0.37%
106,037	62.69%	61,727	36.50%	924	0.55%	448	0.26%
3,293,222	58.85%	2,180,670	38.97%	0	0.00%	122,506	2.19%
616,141	73.40%	223,283	26.60%	2	0.00%	38	0.00%
163,148	59.60%	72,751	26.58%	36,708	13.41%	1,109	0.41%
1,747,140	57.99%	1,127,855	37.44%	132,212	4.39%	5,382	0.18%
501,069	66.83%	245,122	32.69%	0	0.00%	3,549	0.47%
266,733	64.42%	122,706	29.64%	21,831	5.27%	2,751	0.66%
2,353,987	56.88%	1,690,200	40.84%	67,468	1.63%	26,771	0.65%
165,238	53.10%	125,031	40.18%	19,569	6.29%	1,340	0.43%
113,791	98.57%	1,646	1.43%	0	0.00%	0	0.00%
160,137	54.02%	125,977	42.49%	10,338	3.49%	0	0.00%
327,083	68.78%	146,520	30.81%	296	0.06%	1,639	0.34%
739,952	87.08%	104,661	12.32%	3,281	0.39%	1,842	0.22%
150,246	69.34%	64,555	29.79%	1,121	0.52%	755	0.35%
62,124	43.24%	81,023	56.39%	0	0.00%	542	0.38%
234,980	70.23%	98,336	29.39%	233	0.07%	1,041	0.31%
459,579	66.38%	206,892	29.88%	17,463	2.52%	8,404	1.21%
502,582	60.56%	325,358	39.20%	0	0.00%	2,005	0.24%
802,984	63.80%	380,828	30.26%	60,297	4.79%	14,451	1.15%
62,624	60.58%	38,739	37.47%	1,653	1.60%	366	0.35%
27,757,130	60.80%	16,682,673	36.54%	892,378	1.95%	320,827	0.70%

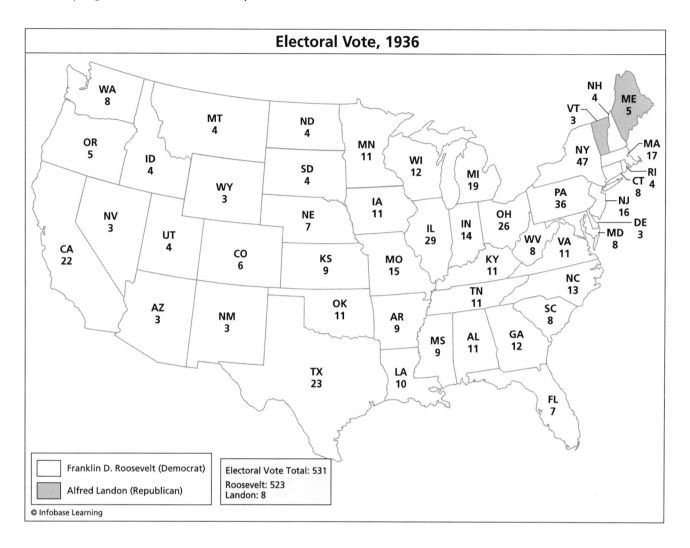

Electoral Vote, 1936

Franklin D. Roosevelt (Democrat)

Alfred Landon (Republican)

Electoral Vote Total: 531
Roosevelt: 523
Landon: 8

© Infobase Learning

Democrats $14 million to $9 million. Furthermore, both parties issued brief, perfunctory platforms.

The Democratic National Convention in Philadelphia was a virtual coronation ceremony for President Roosevelt and Vice President JOHN NANCE GARNER. In his acceptance speech, Roosevelt delivered a line that has since come to embody much of his presidency: "There is a mysterious cycle in human events. To some generations much is given. Of other generations much is expected. This generation of Americans has a rendezvous with destiny." Roosevelt and Garner were renominated by acclamation.

A third party challenge did ultimately materialize but it was inconsequential to the outcome of the race. Two depression-era demagogues, Father Charles E. Coughlin, a Catholic radio priest based out of Detroit and known for his attacks on Wall Street financiers and international bankers as treasonous enemies of democracy, and Dr. Francis Townsend, a proponent of old-age pensions, backed the formation of the Union Party. The Union Party nominated for president Representative William Lemke of North Dakota, a leader in the

Non-Partisan League, but neither Lemke nor the party drew much support.

Roosevelt opened his formal campaign on September 29 at the New York State Democratic convention. He told his audience a parable that he hoped would explain away the Republican criticism of the New Deal for destroying the privileges of the wealthy: "In the summer of 1933, a nice old gentleman wearing a silk hat fell off the end of a pier. He was unable to swim. A friend ran down the pier, dived overboard and pulled him out; but the silk hat floated off with the tide. After the old gentleman had been revived, he was effusive in his thanks. He praised his friend for saving his life. Today, three years later, the old gentleman is berating his friend because his silk hat was lost." For the remainder of the campaign, Roosevelt stressed the importance of the New Deal. He tolerated the vituperative rhetoric from Landon and his surrogates—even the normally moderate Landon charged that FDR aspired to be a dictator at one point in the campaign.

When election day came, no one doubted that Roosevelt would be the victor; the only question was by how large a margin. Even the president was shocked by his margin over Landon. Roosevelt won by more than 9 million in the popular vote, prevailing 27,757,130 to 16,682,673. Roosevelt also overwhelmed Landon in the Electoral College by 523 to 8, winning every state but Maine and Vermont. Lemke polled a mere 892,378 votes. Roosevelt came away from this victory with an inflated sense of his popularity, which would create political problems during his second term as he misspent his political capital. The Democratic Party was an even bigger victor. It assembled a governing coalition of farmers from the South and the West, the poor and the unemployed, northern African Americans, the urban working classes, old school progressives, and newly fashioned liberals that would remain in place until 1968.

PRESIDENTIAL ELECTION OF 1940

The war in Europe and Asia dominated the presidential campaign and election of 1940. While isolationists in the United States wanted to avoid any involvement in the war, other Americans feared a coming fight against fascism was inevitable. The onset of World War II and a belief in his indispensability to the nation ultimately led President Franklin D. Roosevelt to back away from a statement he had made in 1939 to his long-time political adviser and postmaster general, James A. Farley, that he would not seek reelection in 1940. No president had ever run before for a third consecutive term, and Roosevelt remained noncommittal in the early months of 1940. Big city bosses and administration insiders pushed Roosevelt into the race. First lady Eleanor Roosevelt acknowledged years later that, in 1940, she did not know what her husband intended to do.

The president gave some signs that he would retire gracefully on January 21, 1941. He even agreed to become a contributing editor for *Collier's* magazine. His political actions, though, helped ensure his race for a third term. He never unequivocally declared himself out of the race. Nor did he groom a Democratic successor. Instead, he criticized all those who wanted the job. He dismissed Vice President JOHN NANCE GARNER as too conservative, Secretary of State Cordell Hull as too old, RECONSTRUCTION FINANCE CORPORATION chairman Jesse Jones as too ill, Secretary of Agriculture HENRY WALLACE as too weak, and Senator Burton Wheeler as too unacceptable (so much so that FDR said he would rather vote Republican than support Wheeler).

Given the changed world circumstances, FDR did not wish to relinquish the presidency, nor did he want to campaign outwardly for the nomination of his party, breaking the two-term tradition that GEORGE WASHINGTON had established in the 1790s. He did not consider any Republican or any other Democrat capable of leading the United States

in these perilous times. Yet, Roosevelt faced a delicate challenge. Were he to gain the nomination, he planned to use the war to justify his candidacy. For the isolationists in both parties, however, such logic strained credulity for they believed that another Roosevelt presidency would ensure U.S. participation in the war.

A number of Republicans were interested in the presidency in 1940. Thirty-eight-year-old Thomas E. Dewey, a popular antiracketeering district attorney in New York, performed well in the Republican primaries. Republicans liked Dewey, but they believed him to be too young and inexperienced to compete in 1940. Some even dubbed him the diminutive "Buster." Given the isolationist strength of the Republican Party, Senator Robert A. Taft of Ohio, the son of former president WILLIAM HOWARD TAFT, held the advantage as late as June 1940. The other noteworthy contender was Wendell Willkie, a former Democrat. Willkie had voted for FDR in 1932 and had become a Republican only in 1939. As the president of Commonwealth and Southern Utility Company, Willkie had long been a critic of Roosevelt's New Deal, especially the TENNESSEE VALLEY AUTHORITY, but he supported the president's efforts to aid Britain against Germany. His position within the private power industry would not make vote gathering easy. Nor was his lack of name identification an asset. Eastern, internationalist Republicans had begun a quiet campaign on behalf of Willkie in February 1939. As evidence of how unlikely Willkie's nomination was, just two months before the convention he had not yet garnered a single delegate. Still, he had some advantages: Willkie presented an eloquent and effective challenge to the New Deal; he had better odds to beat FDR than any other candidate; he had a folksy charm; finally, his rise with Commonwealth Southern gave him credentials in the business world.

On the brink of the Republican National Convention in early June 1940, Roosevelt performed a master stroke: He named two Republicans to his cabinet, former vice-presidential candidate Frank Knox as secretary of the navy and Henry L. Stimson, the former secretary of war for William Howard Taft and former secretary of state for HERBERT HOOVER, as secretary of war. Knox and Stimson were strong advocates of U.S. participation in the war. The appointments served both political and military ends. The move not only angered Republican operatives, but it also provided the president with seasoned advisers at the moment when the country was moving to intensify its support for the British.

News from abroad shaped the outcome of the Republican National Convention. Headlines detailing the fall of France provided enough of a boom for Willkie to take the prize from Dewey and Taft. Eastern Republicans, political amateurs enamored with Willkie's credentials, and professional politicians secured the Willkie nomination. Between the professionals who ensured that the delegates were inundated on a daily basis with pro-Willkie telegrams and the

Former Democrat Wendell Willkie surprised everyone and gained the Republican nomination for president in 1940. *(Library of Congress)*

amateurs who screamed "We Want Willkie" at every gathering during the convention, it was hard for Republicans to escape the bandwagon.

When the balloting began on June 27, Dewey won a plurality on the first ballot: 360 to 189 for Taft and 105 for Willkie. Support for Dewey was not deep, however, and Willkie supporters were actively lobbying for Dewey delegates. Indeed, Dewey lost delegates after the first ballot while Willkie continued to gain those delegates as well as the various favorite-son delegates. On the second ballot, Willkie remained in third

place, but his total increased to 171 votes. By the third ballot, he moved into second place with 259 votes. On the fourth and fifth ballots, Willkie continued to gain at Dewey's expense while Taft stalled. Willkie finally persevered on the sixth ballot. The party never fully unified behind Willkie as exemplified both by its choice for the vice-presidential nomination of isolationist senator Charles McNary of Oregon and by its platform, which vacillated on the important foreign policy questions before the country. Journalist H. L. Mencken described it as "fit[ting] both the triumph of democracy and the collapse of democracy, and approv[ing] both sending arms to England or only sending flowers."

The Democratic National Convention met in July in Chicago, with several candidates seeking nomination. None of the most noteworthy challengers were isolationists; instead, they hoped to moderate the domestic course Roosevelt had taken over the last eight years and they objected to breaking the two-term tradition. The most prominent challengers included Hull, Garner, Farley, and Paul V. McNutt, a former governor of Indiana and the director of the Federal Security Agency.

The Democratic Party's powerbrokers believed that their only choice was to nominate Roosevelt for they understood that none of the other aspirants could defeat Willkie. Although Roosevelt shared that assessment, he still played coy about his intentions, instructing the chairman of the convention to tell delegates: "The President has never had and has not today any desire or purpose to continue in the office of the President, to be a candidate for that office or to be nominated by the convention for that office. He wishes in all earnestness and sincerity to make it clear to all that

this convention is free to vote for any candidate." The most important words were the last two: "any candidate" included Roosevelt.

Roosevelt hoped this strategy would induce the delegates to "draft" him for a third term. When the big hoped-for demonstration failed to erupt, pro-Roosevelt convention managers arranged for a booming voice to fill the loudspeakers: "Illinois wants Roosevelt. . . . New York wants Roosevelt. . . . America wants Roosevelt. . . . The world wants Roosevelt." While this outburst finally generated an enthusiastic pro-FDR demonstration, critics later learned that the announcer had been Chicago's superintendent of sewers, revealing the close ties that Roosevelt had made with the urban political bosses. This relationship was cemented when FDR unified the various factions in the Democratic Party over his two terms in the White House. It also reflected the fact that the convention was held in Chicago, the government of which was controlled by the Democratic machine of Ed Kelly. Roosevelt gained the nomination on the first ballot by a vote of 946 for the president to 72 for Farley and 61 for Garner.

Addressing the Democratic National Convention on July 19, 1940, Eleanor Roosevelt became the first of the country's first ladies to speak at a national nominating convention. (© Bettmann/CORBIS)

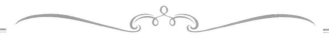

HENRY A. WALLACE

(1888–1965) *vice president of the United States, January 20, 1941–January 20, 1945*

Henry Agard Wallace served as secretary of agriculture from 1933 to 1941 and as vice president during Franklin Roosevelt's third term (1941–45). He later served as secretary of commerce and ran for president in 1948. Wallace was born into a family of agricultural leaders in rural Iowa on October 7, 1888. His parents were Henry Cantwell Wallace, secretary of agriculture during the Warren G. Harding and Calvin Coolidge administrations, and Carrie May Brodhead. After receiving a bachelor's degree in animal husbandry from Iowa State College in 1910, Wallace began a career in agriculture. He studied how hog farmers might increase their earnings and how to produce hybrid corn commercially. The latter endeavor led him to form the Hi-Bred Corn Company in 1926, a most profitable business. Since college, he had also worked on the family newspaper, *Wallace's Farmer,* which had been started by his grandfather, Henry "Uncle Henry" Wallace. Young Wallace married Ilo Browne on May 20, 1914, and they had three children.

The agricultural depression of the 1920s became a consuming passion for Henry A. Wallace. He viewed overproduction as the problem, and he initially advised farmers to restrict their production voluntarily. When that failed, Wallace became an advocate of the McNary-Haugen plan for exporting surplus agricultural produce abroad. A lifelong Republican, he broke with the party over Calvin Coolidge's veto of the bill in 1928. Ultimately, Wallace came to support worldwide tariff reduction and government subsidies to agriculture to address the woes of farmers.

After backing Franklin D. Roosevelt's bid for the presidency in 1932, Wallace was appointed secretary of agriculture, a post that he held for almost eight years until his entry into the race for the vice presidency in 1940. He was a strong supporter of the New Deal agricultural program, which enhanced the role of the federal government in the activities of American farmers. His efforts in the summer of 1933 to implement agricultural reform proved controversial. The Agricultural Adjustment Act (AAA) did not pass until after the cotton crop had been planted and the sows on the nation's hog farms had been bred. Wallace approved a plan to pay farmers to plow up 10 million acres of cotton and to slaughter 6 million pigs. Such measures were unthinkable in the midst of a depression, but Wallace survived in his position.

Wallace believed that the AAA production cutbacks were not sufficient to address the depression. Through the Commodity Credit Corporation, which he oversaw, farmers who abided by AAA crop allotments were eligible to receive loans for produce stored in government warehouses. Additionally, he endorsed Secretary of State Cordell Hull's work for reciprocal trade agreements to increase world trade in agricultural commodities. In addition to agricultural issues, Wallace was interested in mysticism. Less successful were his efforts to generate a

Henry A. Wallace *(Library of Congress)*

The Democratic Party's platform proved just as ambiguous as the Republican platform. The only noteworthy statement included a declaration on the war: "We will not send our armed forces to fight in lands across the sea." Roosevelt convinced the convention to add "except in case of attack." That clarification became important as the campaign against Willkie intensified.

After selecting Roosevelt, the issue for Democrats became the vice-presidential nomination, made much more complicated by virtue of Garner's break with Roosevelt over his decision to seek a third term. Roosevelt used this vacancy to deflect the animus of his isolationist critics in the party, suggesting he might support them for the number two spot. The president wanted someone else, though, spiritual revival and encourage a rejection of "pagan nationalism" among the American people. His agriculture department, though, won other important victories, including soil conservation initiatives, the development of a food stamp program and a school lunch program, and aid for tenant farmers through the Farm Security Administration.

Wallace became Roosevelt's choice for the vice presidency in 1940, when Roosevelt's split with Vice President John Nance Garner widened. This turn of events set a precedent in that previous presidents and presidential candidates had not directly selected their running mates, leaving that decision to party leaders. While Wallace, as a midwesterner, provided the traditional geographic balance for the Democrats, his selection did not please party insiders. It took a convention floor fight to approve his nomination. As a wartime vice president, though, Wallace was most visible. He traveled the world on behalf of the administration, and he took a greater role in public and foreign policy questions than had previous vice presidents. Wallace went to Mexico in 1940, and he made a sweep through Latin America in 1943. The following year he went to the Soviet Union and China.

Wallace held several bureaucratic posts during his years as vice president. He chaired the Board of Economic Warfare, the Economic Defense Board, and the Supply Priorities and Allocations Board. In these capacities, Wallace helped direct the nation's transition from a peacetime to a wartime economy. His position on the Board of Economic Warfare brought him into conflict with Jesse Jones, the secretary of commerce, and Cordell Hull, the secretary of state. He spoke harsh words against Jones and Hull in violation of an order from the president that members of the administration should not criticize one another in public. When it became impossible for Wallace and Jones to compromise, FDR disbanded the Board of Economic Warfare. This episode exemplifies Wallace's shortcomings as vice president.

Nor did Wallace get along well with members of the Senate, the body over which he presided. For example, he turned the vice president's Capitol Hill office into a dry area, no longer serving drinks to his colleagues as his predecessor, John Nance Garner, had so freely done. He disliked the free and open debate of the Senate, a vaunted tradition in the upper chamber, and

when he attempted to participate in the deliberations he was dismissed.

As the 1944 presidential election neared, Wallace came in for heightened criticism from party regulars who did not understand or appreciate the vice president's philosophical bent toward liberalism. Wallace spoke routinely of the "century of the common man," emphasizing that the United States must help increase the standard of living throughout the world even as it sought international economic and spiritual unity. His critics dismissed him, saying Wallace wanted to give "a quart of milk to every Hottentot." Wallace countered that they were "American fascists."

As the Democratic National Convention drew near in 1944, FDR assured Wallace he would still be on the ticket, but the president suggested to party insiders that he would welcome other vice-presidential candidates such as Supreme Court Justice William O. Douglas or Senator Harry S. Truman. This strategy signaled to the convention that the president would not fight for Wallace, so Truman easily gained nomination for the number two spot on the ticket. Despite this betrayal, Wallace worked hard for the Democratic ticket that fall and was rewarded with an appointment as secretary of commerce.

Wallace continued his controversial style in this new role and he remained as secretary of commerce under President Truman. He called for more open dialogue with the Soviet Union, suggesting that the United States should share its atomic information with the Russians. In July 1946, he urged Truman to adopt a more understanding attitude toward the Soviet perspective regarding international security concerns. Such thinking was contrary to the views of American policy makers in the early years of the Cold War. When Wallace gave a public speech making the same argument in September 1946, Truman fired him.

Wallace ended his career as the editor of *The New Republic,* where he continued his support for cooperative policies with the Soviets. In 1948, he made an ill-fated race for the presidency on the Progressive Party ticket. Dismissed as a communist dupe, he received more than 1 million votes but had little impact on the outcome. In retirement, Wallace returned to his agrarian roots in undertaking the study of plant genetics. He died in Danbury, Connecticut, on November 18, 1965.

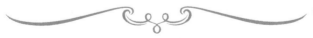

and he exerted heavy pressure on Cordell Hull to accept the position. Hull refused because he opposed FDR's decision to seek a third term and because of the many times the president had slighted him in his role as secretary of state. After several fruitless days, Roosevelt then considered and rejected Senator James F. Byrnes, a conservative South Carolinian who supported FDR's foreign policy. The only concern was

Byrnes's birth as a Catholic, which it was feared would lead many Protestant voters not to support him. Because of his rejection of Farley as both a potential successor and a vice-presidential nominee, also a Catholic, Roosevelt worried about a repeat of 1928 (when Catholic Al Smith went down to defeat) even though Byrnes had long since converted to the Episcopalian faith. Roosevelt finally settled on Henry A.

Wallace. Party insiders fumed about the president's choice. Wallace was viewed as too liberal and out of touch with party regulars (he had not even registered as a Democrat until 1936 despite the fact that he had been Roosevelt's secretary of agriculture since 1933). Roosevelt opted for Wallace in the end to secure the progressive Republican vote, which had been important in the past and would be again given the Republicans' nomination of Willkie.

The delegates to the Democratic National Convention were almost as disdainful of Wallace as were the party insiders. Their irritation was heightened because Roosevelt aides had wrongly suggested that the vice-presidential nominee would be chosen by the delegates, not the president. When the delegates showed signs of balking at Wallace, Roosevelt began drafting a speech rejecting the presidential nomination. To sell the convention on Wallace, Eleanor Roosevelt gave a speech endorsing his candidacy, but when the nomination speeches began, delegates gave long celebrations for the candidates other than Wallace. Byrnes was more pointed in his remarks to the convention: "For God's sake" he asked, "do you want a President or a Vice President?" Wallace bested his nearest competitor, Speaker of the House William B. Bankhead, by a vote of 628 to 329, but he did not deliver a speech to the convention, so heated had been the opposition to his candidacy.

When Roosevelt accepted his party's nomination he made the expected remarks about the New Deal, but he emphasized collective security above all else. He knew the issues that fall would center on his views on national defense and the war in Europe. After the convention Roosevelt set about trying to prove why he should remain in the White House; he went to work on defense matters and ignored the campaign trail. While necessity forced this decision, Roosevelt knew there was political advantage in it as well. He believed that Willkie would rise and fall in the minds of voters if no active debate took place until weeks before the election. Willkie's attacks on FDR seemed without merit: The imminent wartime economic boom countered complaints about the continuation of the depression, the upsurge of war plant employment belied criticisms that FDR had not ended unemployment, and the parade of businessmen to Washington to volunteer their services in the production of armaments diminished charges that the president had not built up the nation's defenses.

Politics intersected with the war when Roosevelt negotiated an arrangement with Britain whereby the United States agreed to exchange U.S. destroyers for access to British air and naval bases in the North Atlantic. The deal reflected Britain's desperation for additional weapons against Nazi Germany. Willkie was irate when he learned of the deal, calling it the most arbitrary and dictatorial

action ever taken by any president in the history of the United States." Supporters pressured Willkie not to exploit the arrangement for political benefit because it would only focus attention on Roosevelt's greatest strength and his own greatest weakness in the campaign: the war issue. Out of deference to the isolationists, Roosevelt had not pushed as hard as he believed necessary on another defense issue: a peacetime draft. Willkie even led in the Gallup poll in early August with regard to the Electoral College but not the popular vote.

The campaign grew nasty as November neared. Roosevelt tried to suggest he was above the fray, even as attacks hit close to home. Republicans charged that Roosevelt's sons had obtained commissions as officers. "I want to be a captain too" became the GOP refrain. Moreover, suggestions that Wallace, who Roosevelt had chosen to placate liberals, was not rational carried the potential to derail the Democratic campaign. At issue was the emergence of some "dear guru" letters that Wallace had written to a mystic, suggesting the chasm that separated his belief system from those of ordinary Americans. To keep the letters out of circulation, Democrats threatened to discuss Willkie's extramarital affair (no one considered the hypocrisy here). Finally, Willkie contended that Roosevelt had himself appeased fascism by doing nothing to stop Hitler from taking Czechoslovakia at the Munich Conference in 1938. Willkie then made promises to stay out of the foreign war. By mid-October 1940, Roosevelt knew he needed to begin campaigning in earnest. On October 18, he announced that he would give five campaign speeches during the next two weeks in which he would rebut the Republican charges against him.

While Roosevelt and Willkie both endorsed collective security, both tried to convince voters they would not go to war while their opponent would. So isolationist had Willkie's rhetoric become that one observer noted he had come to oppose himself as much as he had Roosevelt. Roosevelt was more consistent in his speeches. He regularly attacked isolationist congressmen Joseph W. Martin, Bruce Barton, and Hamilton Fish as emblematic of the isolationist opposition to aiding the allies. The chant of "Martin, Barton, and Fish" became standard at Democratic rallies. In the closing days of the campaign, Roosevelt suggested that his reelection was necessary to prevent the "unholy alliance" of reactionaries and radicals from taking over the country with their "hate" for "democracy and Christianity." So nasty was the campaign and so desperate were the candidates to win the election that Roosevelt even abandoned his escape clause, telling voters on October 30, "I have said this before, but I shall say it again and again and again: 'Your boys are not going to be sent into foreign wars.'" When an aide queried him about the missing disclaimer ("except in case of attack"), Roosevelt responded that an attack on U.S. soil meant the war could no longer be considered foreign.

This political calculation by the president was enough to capture the peace vote, but not that of the hard-core isolationists. In Cleveland, Ohio, on November 2, he clinched his reelection by giving a rousing speech about the domestic causes he hoped to pursue in the future, including an end to poverty, old-age security, natural resource conservation, protection of small business, improved educational opportunities, and a renewed commitment to tolerance and diversity. The speech proved sufficient to hold together the core of FDR's constituency. To ensure victory, though, Roosevelt made a determined effort to win the African-American vote, a first in his political career. Inserted in the Democratic Party platform was a plank that read, "We shall continue to strive for complete legislative safeguards against discrimination in government service and benefits,

and in national defenses forces." Roosevelt also met for the first time with key black leaders. Polling on the eve of the election predicted a victory for Roosevelt. The president feared a narrow margin, and while Willkie was more popular with the electorate than either Herbert Hoover in 1932 or Alf Landon in 1936 had been, the margin was comfortable. Roosevelt won 27,314,045 popular votes to 22,347,744 for Willkie, and he won the Electoral College 449 to 82. Roosevelt's greatest strengths were in urban, poor districts. After gaining reelection, Roosevelt noted, "We seem to have avoided a Putsch." Soon after, Willkie called on Americans to give their loyalty to the president and in 1941, when isolationists upped their attacks on Roosevelt in the months before the attack on Pearl Harbor, Willkie became again an ardent supporter of aid to Britain. On January 20, 1941, Roosevelt became the first and only president to be inaugurated a third time.

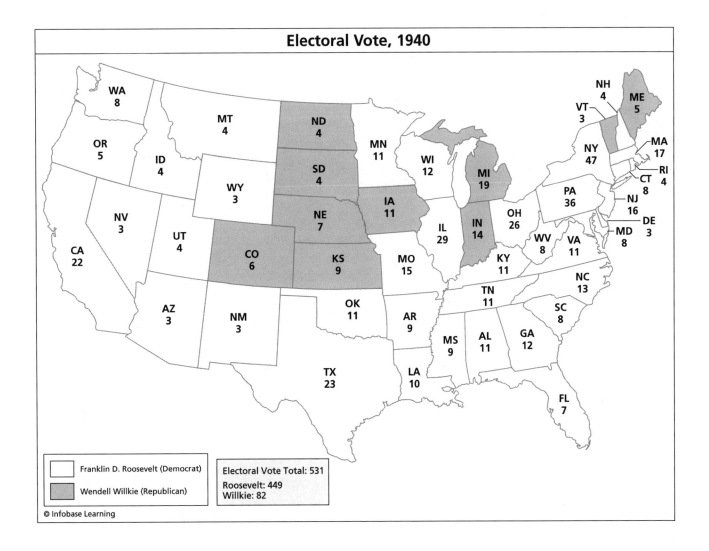

Electoral Vote, 1940

Franklin D. Roosevelt (Democrat)
Wendell Willkie (Republican)

Electoral Vote Total: 531
Roosevelt: 449
Willkie: 82

© Infobase Learning

1940 Election Statistics

State	Number of Electors	Total Popular Vote	Elec Vote		Pop Vote		Margin of Victory	
			D	R	D	R	Votes	% Total Vote
Alabama	11	294,219	11		1	2	208,542	70.88%
Arizona	3	150,039	3		1	2	41,237	27.48%
Arkansas	9	200,743	9		1	2	116,501	58.03%
California	22	3,268,791	22		1	2	526,199	16.10%
Colorado	6	549,004		6	2	1	14,022	2.55%
Connecticut	8	781,502	8		1	2	55,802	7.14%
Delaware	3	136,374	3		1	2	13,159	9.65%
Florida	7	485,492	7		1	2	233,176	48.03%
Georgia	12	312,551	12		1	2	218,834	70.02%
Idaho	4	235,168	4		1	2	21,289	9.05%
Illinois	29	4,217,935	29		1	2	102,694	2.43%
Indiana	14	1,782,747		14	2	1	25,403	1.42%
Iowa	11	1,215,430		11	2	1	53,570	4.41%
Kansas	9	860,297		9	2	1	124,444	14.47%
Kentucky	11	970,163	11		1	2	146,938	15.15%
Louisiana	10	372,305	10		1	2	267,305	71.80%
Maine	5	320,840		5	2	1	7,473	2.33%
Maryland	8	660,117	8		1	2	115,012	17.42%
Massachusetts	17	2,026,993	17		1	2	136,822	6.75%
Michigan	19	2,085,929		19	2	1	6,926	0.33%
Minnesota	11	1,251,188	11		1	2	47,922	3.83%
Mississippi	9	175,824	9		1	2	160,903	91.51%
Missouri	15	1,833,729	15		1	2	87,467	4.77%
Montana	4	247,873	4		1	2	46,119	18.61%
Nebraska	7	615,878		7	2	1	88,524	14.37%
Nevada	3	53,174	3		1	2	10,716	20.15%
New Hampshire	4	235,419	4		1	2	15,165	6.44%
New Jersey	16	1,974,214	16		1	2	71,528	3.62%
New Mexico	3	183,258	3		1	2	24,384	13.31%
New York	47	6,313,897	47		1	2	224,440	3.55%
North Carolina	13	822,648	13		1	2	395,382	48.06%
North Dakota	4	280,775		4	2	1	30,554	10.88%
Ohio	26	3,319,912	26		1	2	146,366	4.41%
Oklahoma	11	826,212	11		1	2	125,441	15.18%
Oregon	5	481,240	5		1	2	38,860	8.07%
Pennsylvania	36	4,078,714	36		1	2	281,187	6.89%
Rhode Island	4	321,148	4		1	2	43,529	13.55%
South Carolina	8	99,832	8		1	2	91,110	91.26%
South Dakota	4	308,427		4	2	1	45,703	14.82%
Tennessee	11	522,823	11		1	2	182,448	34.90%
Texas	23	1,124,531	23		1	2	697,282	62.01%
Utah	4	247,819	4		1	2	61,126	24.67%
Vermont	3	143,062		3	2	1	14,102	9.86%
Virginia	11	346,607	11		1	2	126,598	36.52%
Washington	8	793,833	8		1	2	140,022	17.64%
West Virginia	8	868,076	8		1	2	123,248	14.20%
Wisconsin	12	1,405,522	12		1	2	25,615	1.82%
Wyoming	3	112,240	3		1	2	6,654	5.93%
Total	531	49,914,514	449	82	1	2	4,966,301	9.95%

Roosevelt Democratic		Willkie Republican		Others	
250,726	85.22%	42,184	14.34%	1,309	0.44%
95,267	63.49%	54,030	36.01%	742	0.49%
158,622	79.02%	42,121	20.98%	0	0.00%
1,877,618	57.44%	1,351,419	41.34%	39,754	1.22%
265,554	48.37%	279,576	50.92%	3,874	0.71%
417,621	53.44%	361,819	46.30%	2,062	0.26%
74,599	54.70%	61,440	45.05%	335	0.25%
359,334	74.01%	126,158	25.99%	0	0.00%
265,194	84.85%	46,360	14.83%	997	0.32%
127,842	54.36%	106,553	45.31%	773	0.33%
2,149,934	50.97%	2,047,240	48.54%	20,761	0.49%
874,063	49.03%	899,466	50.45%	9,218	0.52%
578,800	47.62%	632,370	52.03%	4,260	0.35%
364,725	42.40%	489,169	56.86%	6,403	0.74%
557,322	57.45%	410,384	42.30%	2,457	0.25%
319,751	85.88%	52,446	14.09%	108	0.03%
156,478	48.77%	163,951	51.10%	411	0.13%
384,546	58.25%	269,534	40.83%	6,037	0.91%
1,076,522	53.11%	939,700	46.36%	10,771	0.53%
1,032,991	49.52%	1,039,917	49.85%	13,021	0.62%
644,196	51.49%	596,274	47.66%	10,718	0.86%
168,267	95.70%	7,364	4.19%	193	0.11%
958,476	52.27%	871,009	47.50%	4,244	0.23%
145,698	58.78%	99,579	40.17%	2,596	1.05%
263,677	42.81%	352,201	57.19%	0	0.00%
31,945	60.08%	21,229	39.92%	0	0.00%
125,292	53.22%	110,127	46.78%	0	0.00%
1,016,404	51.48%	944,876	47.86%	12,934	0.66%
103,699	56.59%	79,315	43.28%	244	0.13%
3,251,918	51.50%	3,027,478	47.95%	34,501	0.55%
609,015	74.03%	213,633	25.97%	0	0.00%
124,036	44.18%	154,590	55.06%	2,149	0.77%
1,733,139	52.20%	1,586,773	47.80%	0	0.00%
474,313	57.41%	348,872	42.23%	3,027	0.37%
258,415	53.70%	219,555	45.62%	3,270	0.68%
2,171,035	53.23%	1,889,848	46.33%	17,831	0.44%
182,182	56.73%	138,653	43.17%	313	0.10%
95,470	95.63%	4,360	4.37%	2	0.00%
131,362	42.59%	177,065	57.41%	0	0.00%
351,601	67.25%	169,153	32.35%	2,069	0.40%
909,974	80.92%	212,692	18.91%	1,865	0.17%
154,277	62.25%	93,151	37.59%	391	0.16%
64,269	44.92%	78,371	54.78%	422	0.29%
235,961	68.08%	109,363	31.55%	1,283	0.37%
462,145	58.22%	322,123	40.58%	9,565	1.20%
495,662	57.10%	372,414	42.90%	0	0.00%
704,821	50.15%	679,206	48.32%	21,495	1.53%
59,287	52.82%	52,633	46.89%	320	0.29%
27,314,045	54.72%	22,347,744	44.77%	252,725	0.51%

PRESIDENTIAL ELECTION OF 1944

—◦◦◦—

World War II dominated the presidential campaign of 1944. As testament to both the importance of democracy to American life and the necessity of partisan politics for successful governance, no move was made to abandon elections for the duration of the war as had been done in Britain. The successful D-Day landing at Normandy in June 1944 and General Douglas MacArthur's victory at the Battle of Leyte Gulf later that fall provided sufficient positive headlines that the United States was winning the war and gave few voters reason to question President Franklin Delano Roosevelt's leadership. Nonetheless, Roosevelt's race for a fourth term was unprecedented. Roosevelt, though, viewed his race as even more important for winning the peace. Hindsight suggests the inevitability of the United Nations and the United States as an internationally engaged superpower in the postwar period, but at the time, substantial doubt existed as to what the postwar period would bring. In addition to uncertainty about the world after the war, the potential for voter apathy proved worrisome. Roosevelt believed it to be an even more powerful opponent than any Republican nominee.

Early on, Roosevelt seemingly took little interest in the campaign. As late as May 1944, few outside Roosevelt's innermost circle knew his intentions. Some Democrats in Congress predicted that, if he did not run, Senator Harry F. Byrd of Virginia would be the nominee. However, others questioned this prediction because Byrd's vehement opposition to the New Deal appealed only to conservatives. There was never any doubt that Roosevelt would receive the nomination of his party for a fourth term if he wanted it. Leading Democrats knew that no other member of their party could win against the Republicans. In fact, when the Democrats met in Chicago that summer the vote on the first ballot was 1,086 for Roosevelt and 89 for Byrd. If anything, the votes for Byrd foreshadowed the Dixiecrat revolt of 1948 and the brewing tensions over race in the party.

In 1944, the biggest drama involved the question of whether Roosevelt would retain Henry Wallace as his vice president. To many observers Wallace looked like a strong running mate. He shared Roosevelt's liberal vision for the postwar world at home and abroad, was loyal to the administration, and had the support of several important constituencies within the Democratic Party—northern urban liberals, African Americans, and organized labor. Just as fervent, though, was conservative discontent with Wallace. Nor was he popular with wartime bureaucrats or lawmakers, especially in the Senate, where he was the presiding officer. Both groups believed him to lack political substance and a pragmatic appreciation of how the government worked. Furthermore, the election of 1944 promised to be a close one, and polls and political analysts alike predicted that Wallace might take anywhere from 1 to 3 million votes away from Roosevelt if he remained on the ticket.

As early as 1943 a quiet but intense race for the vice-presidential nomination began. The contenders included Senator John H. Bankhead (D-AL), Senate Majority Leader Alben Barkley (D-KY), Supreme Court justice William O. Douglas, former senator and Supreme Court justice and current czar of wartime production James Byrnes, Senator Scott Lucas (D-IL), Speaker of the House Sam Rayburn (D-TX), and Senator Harry S. Truman (D-MO). Regarding the large number of vice-presidential aspirants, Roosevelt quipped, "the more the merrier." The most serious contenders were Douglas, Byrnes, Rayburn, and Truman. Roosevelt held the advantage. Even if he preferred to appear distant from the process, insiders knew that Roosevelt would have the final say in selecting his running mate. The result was a drama that made Roosevelt appear to be one of those political bosses against which he had run early in his New York political career more than 30 years before.

Roosevelt did not want to dismiss Wallace publicly from the ticket and thereby alienate the vice president's supporters. To keep Wallace occupied during the runup to the convention, Roosevelt sent him abroad to China and the Soviet Union. Rayburn was the first vice-presidential contender to fall out of favor through actions largely beyond his control. When the conservative-dominated Texas Democratic convention met in Austin on May 23, it refused to endorse either Roosevelt or Rayburn, charged the president with harboring communists, and called for an official policy of white supremacy. Rayburn's candidacy became untenable. Furthermore, while Roosevelt never completely ruled Byrnes out, his residency in South Carolina, a southern state with a poll tax that kept most African Americans from voting, eliminated him from consideration for all practical purposes, but no one shared this point with Byrnes. Douglas, who had not heard of Roosevelt's interest in his candidacy, elected to wait for 1948. Instead of attending the convention in 1944, he went camping in the West. These circumstances, combined with Truman's solid senatorial record, meant that the Missourian would likely get the nomination. Truman was a supporter of most of the administration's legislation, had gained favorable public opinion for his investigation into the defense industry, was from a border state, and got along well with the southern barons in the Senate.

Roosevelt met with several key Democratic strategists about a week before the convention, and he agreed to support Truman for the vice presidency. Roosevelt wrote a postdated letter to the chairman of the Democratic National Committee, Robert Hannegan, to provide political cover for his behind-the-scenes machinations: "You have written me about Harry Truman and Bill Douglas. I should, of course, be very glad to run with either of them and believe that either one of them would bring real strength to the ticket." The letter conveyed the view that Roosevelt had not offered an endorsement and that he had not chosen a particular nominee but had assented to two possible candidates.

Once Wallace returned from Asia, Roosevelt tried to get subordinates to tell Wallace he was off the ticket, but Wallace knowingly avoided all political talk. Nor could the president bring himself to give Wallace the bad news. Days before the convention, FDR even whispered to Wallace, "while I cannot put it just that way in public, I hope it will be the same old team." Roosevelt conveyed a different message to convention delegates: "I would vote for his renomination if I were a delegate to the convention."

Byrnes and Wallace both went to the convention actively seeking the nomination. Truman knew that party insiders were working for his nomination, but he denied his interest. Byrnes also knew that others were being pushed for the nomination, so he sagely recruited his former Senate colleague, Truman, to back him in his quest. Truman agreed. To most political pundits Byrnes appeared to have a lock on the nomination, but complex machinations involving organized labor stalled the vote and confused the delegates. Before Roosevelt's advisers signaled the convention, FDR told them they had to "clear it with Sidney" Hillman, the head of the CIO Political Action Committee and one of the nation's most influential labor leaders. Hillman indicated that Wallace was the president's first choice and Truman his second choice. Hillman rejected Byrnes who had little support among union members. A modified version of this information was communicated to Truman. Given these signals, Truman asked Byrnes to be released from his promise to offer a nominating speech, but since Truman never heard directly from the president regarding his views he continued to support Byrnes. Roosevelt worked with Hannegan to determine if Truman had agreed to take a spot on the ticket. Finally, Roosevelt reached Hannegan while he was with Truman. Hannegan held the phone so that Truman could hear the president: "Well, tell the Senator that if he wants to break up the Democratic party by staying out, he can; but he knows as well as I what that might mean at this dangerous time in the world." Truman replied, "Jesus Christ! But why the hell didn't he tell me in the first place?" The rest was anticlimactic. Wallace carried the first ballot, as expected by the party insiders, 429½ to 319½ for Truman, which was not a majority of the delegates. Truman won the nomination on the second ballot, 1,031 to 105 for Wallace, again as expected by the party insiders who had engineered the vice-presidential balloting. Truman campaigned vigorously that fall.

Roosevelt worried more about the logistics of the election. The demographics of Roosevelt's support caused the president concern. His popularity was strongest with younger Americans, but many of them were in military service. The soldier voting laws were complicated. Nor was it easy for war workers who had moved across state lines to register and vote in their new state of residence. For example, Maryland law required that new residents declare a year in advance their intent to register. Labor leaders, specifically Hillman, worked hard to ensure a high voter turnout that November.

The Republican campaign in 1944 never developed a coherent strategy. Part of the problem resulted from internal divisions and part from the unwritten rules of proper political decorum, which prevented a substantive discussion of Roosevelt's health and of his handling of military policy in the midst of the war. A number of Republicans initially sought their party's nomination or at least had their names on the ballots in primary states. The contenders included 1940 Republican nominee Wendell Willkie, New York governor Thomas E. Dewey, and former Minnesota governor Harold Stassen, who was making the first of his many tries for the White House. These three men were all internationalists, but other contenders held isolationist sentiments, including Ohio governor John W. Bricker, who was the choice of Robert A. Taft, one of the leading opponents of Roosevelt in the Senate. Another potential Republican challenger, General Douglas MacArthur, was a conservative but not an isolationist. He had long complained that Roosevelt had given preference to the needs of the European Theater of Operations over the Pacific Theater of Operations.

When Willkie was trounced in the Wisconsin primary, running behind Dewey, Stassen, and MacArthur, he dropped out of the race. Liberals and Democrats were the most troubled by the outcome, because they viewed Willkie as an easy candidate to defeat. Willkie's decision did not mean that the party was trending isolationist, rather, it reflected pragmatic politics. Willkie understood that staying in the race might well result in a convention divided between his supporters and those of Dewey and lead to the nomination of a weak, compromise candidate. His decision meant that Dewey had a clear path to the nomination. The other possibilities, such as Senators Arthur Vandenberg and Robert Taft, had strong isolationist records from the 1930s that did not look good while the nation was at war. A tough contender in 1940, Dewey entered the race within a reputation as a clean, honest politician.

The Republican convention was held in Chicago. California Republican governor Earl Warren gave a keynote address in which he declared, "the New Deal came to power with a song on its lips: 'Happy Days are Here Again.' That song is ended. Even the melody does not linger on. Now we are being conditioned for a new song: 'Don't Change Horses in the Middle of a Stream.' For eleven long years we have been in the middle of a stream. We are not amphibious. We want to get across. We want to feel dry and solid ground under our feet again." The speech cheered an otherwise lifeless convention that was witness to the frustrations felt by Republican governors over the inordinate power that congressional Republicans from Washington exerted over the party. The governors contended that the revival of the party was occurring at the state-level and that state-level leaders

On November 4, 1944, three days before the election, Republican candidate Thomas E. Dewey addresses a crowd at Madison Square Garden in New York City. He is surrounded by his wife, Frances Dewey, baseball slugger Babe Ruth, and Ruth's wife, Claire. *(Associated Press)*

should be given more of a role in charting the party's future. Despite these frustrations, the convention quickly accepted the platform, in 20 seconds to be exact, without change. The document called in a general way for U.S. participation in postwar international governance, and it was full of promises designed to appeal to various interest groups. It also attacked the centralization of the New Deal years.

The Republicans balanced their ticket by pairing a conservative with Dewey. Bricker assumed the number two spot on the ticket. The Republican campaign made less of an issue of Roosevelt's leadership of the country during the war and instead suggested that the Democrats had been in power for too long, that their ideas were stale, and that the president's health was fragile. Dewey did not push this latter point very

hard, though. To do so in 1944 would have been considered rude and inappropriate. There was, though, substantial reason to worry. Roosevelt had been diagnosed with hypertension, hypertensive heart disease, congestive heart failure, and bronchitis. His doctors had not given him the full diagnosis, and he had not inquired. Nor did Dewey raise questions—as some had in Congress—as to whether Roosevelt had known in advance of the Japanese attack on Pearl Harbor but ignored them to bring a speedy U.S. entry into the war. (In seven decades no evidence has surfaced indicating Roosevelt had prior knowledge.)

The Democratic strategy in the fall of 1944 was to stress the "indispensability" of the president to the winning of the war and the peace that would follow. As such, Roosevelt appeared the elder statesman upon whom the safety of the world depended. He also withstood brutally harsh winter weather to campaign in the last few weeks of the election, a feat that showed his strength to voters.

Many observers, from *Time* magazine to his own daughter, had questioned his vitality. Roosevelt delivered his first major political speech of the campaign on September 23, 1944, to the Teamsters' Union in Washington, D.C. His daughter was worried that he was not up to the task. The editors of *Time* magazine asked a similar question, but FDR wowed his audience both in person and over the radio. He dismissed the various charges Republicans had made that the depression would return when the war ended and that the soldiers would be retained in the military as a result. Moreover, Roosevelt captivated his audience when he discussed Republican charges against his family. Their specific complaint had been the use of tax dollars to send a destroyer to the Aleutian Islands to retrieve Roosevelt's dog, Fala, which

had been left behind while the president was on a trip to the Pacific theater: "These Republican leaders have not been content with attacks on me, or my wife, or on my sons. No, not content with that, they now include my little dog, Fala. Well, of course, I don't resent attacks, and my family doesn't resent attacks, but Fala *does* resent them."

The speech conveyed the impression that Roosevelt was his old self, strong and vigorous. It was also unfair in that it implied that Dewey was responsible for the attacks on Fala, thus associating Dewey with the most reactionary of Republican views even though the Republican contender held moderate to liberal views not dissimilar from those of the president. In response, Dewey adopted a more aggressive stance. For example, he charged that FDR's speech before the Teamsters was akin to the methods employed by Hitler and his propaganda minister, Joseph Goebbels. Such arguments were nothing more than political propaganda designed to inflame his audience. He also implied that the ranks of the

President Roosevelt's last inauguration, January 20, 1945 *(Library of Congress)*

1944 Election Statistics

State	Number of Electors	Total Popular Vote	Elec Vote D	Elec Vote R	Pop Vote D	Pop Vote R	Margin of Victory Votes	Margin of Victory % Total Vote
Alabama	11	244,743	11		1	2	154,378	63.08%
Arizona	4	137,634	4		1	2	24,639	17.90%
Arkansas	9	212,954	9		1	2	85,414	40.11%
California	25	3,520,875	25		1	2	475,599	13.51%
Colorado	6	505,039		6	2	1	34,400	6.81%
Connecticut	8	831,990	8		1	2	44,619	5.36%
Delaware	3	125,361	3		1	2	11,419	9.11%
Florida	8	482,592	8		1	2	196,162	40.65%
Georgia	12	328,109	12		1	2	208,307	63.49%
Idaho	4	208,321	4		1	2	7,262	3.49%
Illinois	28	4,036,061	28		1	2	140,165	3.47%
Indiana	13	1,672,091		13	2	1	94,488	5.65%
Iowa	10	1,052,599		10	2	1	47,391	4.50%
Kansas	8	733,776		8	2	1	154,638	21.07%
Kentucky	11	867,921	11		1	2	80,141	9.23%
Louisiana	10	349,383	10		1	2	213,814	61.20%
Maine	5	296,400		5	2	1	14,803	4.99%
Maryland	8	608,439	8		1	2	22,541	3.70%
Massachusetts	16	1,960,665	16		1	2	113,946	5.81%
Michigan	19	2,205,223	19		1	2	22,476	1.02%
Minnesota	11	1,125,529	11		1	2	62,448	5.55%
Mississippi	9	180,080	9		1	2	156,878	87.12%
Missouri	15	1,572,474	15		1	2	46,280	2.94%
Montana	4	207,355	4		1	2	19,393	9.35%
Nebraska	6	563,126		6	2	1	96,634	17.16%
Nevada	3	54,234	3		1	2	5,012	9.24%
New Hampshire	4	229,625	4		1	2	9,747	4.24%
New Jersey	16	1,963,761	16		1	2	26,539	1.35%
New Mexico	4	152,225	4		1	2	10,701	7.03%
New York	47	6,316,817	47		1	2	316,591	5.01%
North Carolina	14	790,554	14		1	2	264,244	33.43%
North Dakota	4	220,171		4	2	1	18,391	8.35%
Ohio	25	3,153,056		25	2	1	11,530	0.37%
Oklahoma	10	722,636	10		1	2	82,125	11.36%
Oregon	6	480,147	6		1	2	23,270	4.85%
Pennsylvania	35	3,794,793	35		1	2	105,425	2.78%
Rhode Island	4	299,276	4		1	2	51,869	17.33%
South Carolina	8	103,375	8		1	3	85,991	83.18%
South Dakota	4	232,076		4	2	1	38,654	16.66%
Tennessee	12	510,692	12		1	2	108,396	21.23%
Texas	23	1,150,331	23		1	2	630,180	54.78%
Utah	4	248,319	4		1	2	52,197	21.02%
Vermont	3	125,361		3	2	1	17,707	14.12%
Virginia	11	388,485	11		1	2	97,033	24.98%
Washington	8	856,328	8		1	2	125,085	14.61%
West Virginia	8	715,596	8		1	2	69,958	9.78%
Wisconsin	12	1,339,152		12	2	1	24,119	1.80%
Wyoming	3	101,340		3	2	1	2,502	2.47%
Total	531	47,977,090	432	99	1	2	3,594,987	7.49%

Roosevelt Democratic		Dewey Republican		Others	
198,918	81.28%	44,540	18.20%	1,285	0.53%
80,926	58.80%	56,287	40.90%	421	0.31%
148,965	69.95%	63,551	29.84%	438	0.21%
1,988,564	56.48%	1,512,965	42.97%	19,346	0.55%
234,331	46.40%	268,731	53.21%	1,977	0.39%
435,146	52.30%	390,527	46.94%	6,317	0.76%
68,166	54.38%	56,747	45.27%	448	0.36%
339,377	70.32%	143,215	29.68%	0	0.00%
268,187	81.74%	59,880	18.25%	42	0.01%
107,399	51.55%	100,137	48.07%	785	0.38%
2,079,479	51.52%	1,939,314	48.05%	17,268	0.43%
781,403	46.73%	875,891	52.38%	14,797	0.88%
499,876	47.49%	547,267	51.99%	5,456	0.52%
287,458	39.18%	442,096	60.25%	4,222	0.58%
472,589	54.45%	392,448	45.22%	2,884	0.33%
281,564	80.59%	67,750	19.39%	69	0.02%
140,631	47.45%	155,434	52.44%	335	0.11%
315,490	51.85%	292,949	48.15%	0	0.00%
1,035,296	52.80%	921,350	46.99%	4,019	0.20%
1,106,899	50.19%	1,084,423	49.18%	13,901	0.63%
589,864	52.41%	527,416	46.86%	8,249	0.73%
168,479	93.56%	11,601	6.44%	0	0.00%
807,804	51.37%	761,524	48.43%	3,146	0.20%
112,556	54.28%	93,163	44.93%	1,636	0.79%
233,246	41.42%	329,880	58.58%	0	0.00%
29,623	54.62%	24,611	45.38%	0	0.00%
119,663	52.11%	109,916	47.87%	46	0.02%
987,874	50.31%	961,335	48.95%	14,552	0.74%
81,389	53.47%	70,688	46.44%	148	0.10%
3,304,238	52.31%	2,987,647	47.30%	24,932	0.39%
527,399	66.71%	263,155	33.29%	0	0.00%
100,144	45.48%	118,535	53.84%	1,492	0.68%
1,570,763	49.82%	1,582,293	50.18%	0	0.00%
401,549	55.57%	319,424	44.20%	1,663	0.23%
248,635	51.78%	225,365	46.94%	6,147	1.28%
1,940,479	51.14%	1,835,054	48.36%	19,260	0.51%
175,356	58.59%	123,487	41.26%	433	0.14%
90,601	87.64%	4,610	4.46%	8,164	7.90%
96,711	41.67%	135,365	58.33%	0	0.00%
308,707	60.45%	200,311	39.22%	1,674	0.33%
821,605	71.42%	191,425	16.64%	137,301	11.94%
150,088	60.44%	97,891	39.42%	340	0.14%
53,820	42.93%	71,527	57.06%	14	0.01%
242,276	62.36%	145,243	37.39%	966	0.25%
486,774	56.84%	361,689	42.24%	7,865	0.92%
392,777	54.89%	322,819	45.11%	0	0.00%
650,413	48.57%	674,532	50.37%	14,207	1.06%
49,419	48.77%	51,921	51.23%	0	0.00%
25,612,916	53.39%	22,017,929	45.89%	346,245	0.72%

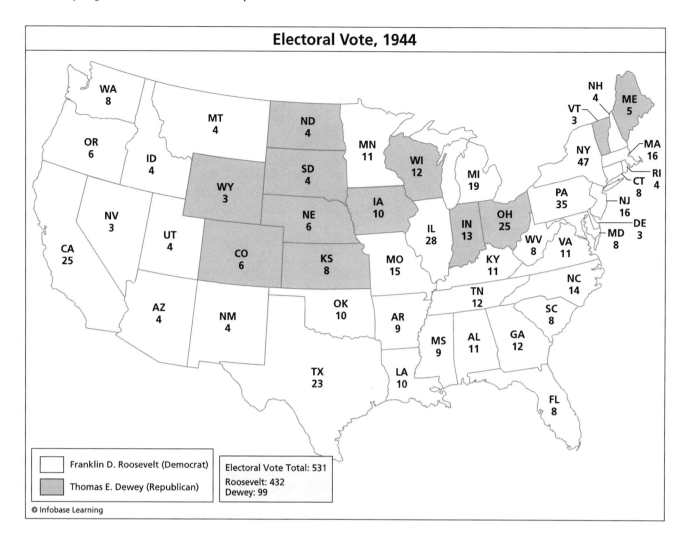

Electoral Vote, 1944

Franklin D. Roosevelt (Democrat)

Thomas E. Dewey (Republican)

Electoral Vote Total: 531
Roosevelt: 432
Dewey: 99

© Infobase Learning

Roosevelt administration were filled with communists and communist sympathizers. His speeches grew increasingly strident and belligerent.

Since Dewey elected not to offer any substantive policy differences from those of the president, adopting such a tone was his only real choice. Roosevelt parodied the Republican campaign in his speeches to voters: "'those incompetent blunderers and bunglers in Washington have passed a lot of excellent laws about social security and labor and farm relief and soil conservation—and many others—and we promise that if elected we will not change any of them.' And they go on to say, 'Those same quarrelsome, tired old men—they have built the greatest military machine the world has ever known, which is fighting its way to victory; and,' they say, 'if you elect us, we promise not to change any of that, either.' 'Therefore,' say these Republican orators, 'it is time for a change.'"

The 1944 election gave rise to two important developments in the history of presidential electioneering. First was the increased reliance on political polling to help the candidates plan their strategies. Roosevelt contended that one should never argue with the results of a Gallup poll. While

political polling was a relatively new phenomenon in American politics, Gallup had predicted FDR would win in 1936 when everyone else thought he would lose. The other significant development was the use of radio together with celebrity endorsements. On the day before the election the Democratic National Committee aired an hour-long program in which prominent movie actors offered their praise of Roosevelt, interspersed with equally positive commentary from average Americans.

Roosevelt prevailed on election day, winning an unprecedented fourth term as president. He garnered 53.4 percent of the vote to Dewey's 45.9 percent, the narrowest margin since 1916. The divide in the Electoral College was much wider: 432 to 99. The low turnout proved more damaging to Roosevelt than to Dewey for the group least likely to vote that year was poor Americans, usually a solid vote for Roosevelt. They were absent from the polls because they had moved to take wartime factory jobs and failed to register in new places. The vote can best be described as a mandate for Roosevelt's prosecution of the war and for his plans for active U.S. participation in the postwar world. Along with the president's reelection, American voters also defeated most of the congressional isolationists on the ballot. Despite his loss, the youthful Dewey remained a popular politician. He began considering another run for the White House in 1948. The most significant feature of the campaign had been the decision to replace Wallace with Truman. Less than three months after his inauguration in January 1945, FDR would be dead and Truman would be president. The differences between Wallace and Truman were extensive, but so were the differences between Roosevelt and Truman, which the latter's presidency would reveal.

ROOSEVELT ADMINISTRATION (1933–1945)

The "forgotten men" of the Great Depression lionized Franklin D. Roosevelt, who became president in 1933, whereas wealthy Americans sneered at "that man" for being a traitor to his class. Indeed, passions ran high about the 32nd president of the United States, who held the office for 12 years, longer than anyone else in American history. Debates among scholars and others have proliferated about his presidency. Historian William Leuchtenberg has written of the "shadow" that FDR cast over the presidencies that followed. Many have championed Roosevelt for originating, or at least perfecting, the modern presidency in making it a more centralized institution whereby the president became the popular center of the federal government, not the Congress and not the political parties of past generations. Others have debated the degree of radicalism present in the New Deal—the programs initiated to combat the depression—and its meaning in shaping attitudes toward governance in the years that followed. Still others have fixated on Roosevelt's less flattering traits in noting the confidence infused with egomania, duplicity, secretiveness, and desire for control that he displayed. Finally, scholars have tried to understand how Roosevelt, first as "Dr. New Deal" and then as "Dr. Win the War," led the country through the two great crises of the 20th century, the depression and World War II.

The Interregnum

In the four months between the general election in November 1932 and the presidential inauguration in March 1933, foolish pride and substantive differences about how the federal government should work prevented any meaningful cooperation between Roosevelt and HERBERT HOOVER. These reasons provided little comfort to the swelling number of unemployed Americans, from 12 million in 1932 to 15 million at the inauguration, or about a quarter of the workforce. The United States had weathered depressions in the past, but none so devastated the country as that of the early 1930s. By all measures, the American economy was deteriorating to the point that some wondered whether capitalism could be saved. One writer even spoke of smelling the depression in the air. A bountiful plenty of agricultural produce and of commercial output surrounded a desperate want of nameless, faceless poverty. As inauguration day approached the governments of 38 states, including Illinois and New York, had closed all their banks, and in the other 10 states only limited banking services could be had. The New York Stock Exchange closed its doors on inauguration day. By the time Roosevelt assumed the presidency, 5,000 banks had gone under and, with them, 9 million savings accounts had been obliterated. Indeed, bankers assumed villainous status for their supposed role in fomenting the depression. Senators lambasted bankers with ease. For example, Senator Burton K. Wheeler of Montana likened bankers to the notorious gangster Al Capone in suggesting that they receive comparable treatment, which meant lengthy jail terms.

In the midst of this economic calamity, Congress met in a lame duck session between December 1932 and February 1933. Leading progressive lawmakers complained that their colleagues were interested only in trivial matters. No one could muster a majority to debate, let alone pass, significant

During the Great Depression bankers became so unpopular that bank robbers, such as Bonnie and Clyde (*above*), became folk heroes. *(Library of Congress)*

ROOSEVELT, THE FIRESIDE CHATS, AND THE RISE OF RADIO

Between the mid-1910s and the early 1920s, radio ceased serving as the domain of the tinkerers and hobbyists in being transformed into a big business with the entry of corporations such as American Telephone & Telegraph, Westinghouse, and General Electric into the field. More important, a new company, the Radio Corporation of America, appeared to exploit the potential. In the process, radio became a significant venue for entertainment and popular culture. During the 1920s, radio stations were established and a range of programming proliferated. While Franklin D. Roosevelt was not the first American politician to use the radio, he was the first to demonstrate its full potential for blending politics and celebrity.

The myth of Roosevelt has him sitting in a rocking chair by a fireplace recording regular radio broadcasts for the American people in a conversational style as if he were a guest in someone's home. The reality is more complex. During his 12 years as president, Roosevelt recorded and delivered 27 fireside chats. But they were not casual, conversational, almost accidental, utterances. Instead, a team of advisers helped Roosevelt craft each message, as was the case with all of his public speeches. Furthermore, in order to broadcast the talks, Roosevelt sat at a desk before an immense bank of microphones. Approximately 20 to 30 members of his staff sat and listened to his performances. Frances Perkins, his secretary of labor, recalled that he often forgot his surroundings and assumed a posture as if he were visiting in the home of a neighbor.

The fireside chat became an important political tool for Roosevelt because commercial radio emerged as a viable new technology during his presidency. At the beginning of the 1930s less than 50 percent of American homes were equipped to receive radio broadcasts, but by the end of the decade 80 percent of the people in the country owned a radio. So valuable was the radio that destitute Americans prized it over more necessary items such as bedding and furniture and they refused to let their radios be repossessed.

Furthermore, Roosevelt was uniquely talented to manipulate the radio. A good public speaker, he mixed an agreeable baritone voice with his authoritative patrician accent. He employed simple and direct phrasing, making it easier for Americans to relate to his words. His conversational style made it sound as if he was chatting rather than orating, enabling him to come across in his fireside chats as a wise friend or neighbor who had the answer to problems created by the depression.

The fireside chats were aired in prime time on Sunday evenings, usually between the hours of nine and 11. They ranged between 12 and 45 minutes in duration. Roosevelt's first fireside chat was devoted to the banking crisis. It was aired on March 12, 1933, just eight days after his inauguration. He explained to his audience the reasons for the bank holiday that he had proclaimed earlier in the week and he thanked them for their cooperation through this difficult period. Roosevelt gave Americans a basic lesson on economics in describing how banks function and why the majority of deposits are not kept in bank vaults but rather are invested. "We had a bad banking situation," Roosevelt explained in reassuring words. "Some of our bankers had shown themselves either incompetent or dishonest in their handling of the people's funds. . . . It was the Government's job to straighten out this situation and do it as quickly as possible—and the job is being performed."

This first talk set the tone for the fireside chats that would follow. During the next 12 years President Roosevelt addressed the nation in this forum on a variety of topics, including economic recovery, drought and the dust bowl, proposed reforms of the Supreme Court, and various war and defense issues. Taken collectively, these talks demonstrated an important new trend in American politics, namely the use of a mass communications medium devoted largely to entertainment for decidedly political purposes. Through the new medium of radio, Roosevelt's voice became a familiar presence in people's homes and contributed to making the president not just the nation's leader but also a celebrity.

---

economic legislation. Huey Long, the popular but demagogic senator from Louisiana, consumed valuable floor time with a filibuster. President Hoover preferred that the lawmakers go home and business leaders concurred, so bad was the reputation of Congress for positive action.

The tensions that developed between Hoover and Roosevelt during the election spilled over into deliberation of two economic issues during the interregnum, first, the international debt crisis and, second, the domestic bank crisis. In early November 1932, soon after the election, British and French officials asked the Hoover administration to forgive the World War I debt payments due the following month.

Hoover asked Roosevelt to participate in drafting a solution to the crisis, but the two men were bound to disagree because Hoover believed the depression to be an international problem and Roosevelt believed that its origins were domestic. As a result, Roosevelt rejected Hoover's efforts to address the problem by reintroducing the gold standard for international trade. Roosevelt believed that tackling the debt issue would bring significant political problems and that its resolution mattered little for the economic recovery of the country. Nor were the two able to cooperate in dealing with the escalating banking crisis. In principle, Roosevelt agreed that a joint request from the president and the president-elect might be useful in preventing further bank closures, but he refused to agree to any of the stipulations Hoover wanted to impose. Roosevelt realized the problems that could result for his administration, not yet officially begun, if he agreed to policies laid down by the Hoover administration. As examples, Roosevelt ignored requests from Hoover that he pledge to balance the budget and adopt sound money policies throughout his administration. Doing so, he believed, would limit his flexibility in the White House.

"The Only Thing We Have to Fear": Inaugurating a New President

Political insiders said of the new administration, "come at once to Washington, great things are happening." Six months into the New Deal, Representative Wright Patman (D-TX) declared that the "revolution is here now. . . . We're changing laws and business. The changes are so radical it's almost impossible to describe them. A hundred years from now historians will describe them as a revolution." These positive views of governance stemmed in large part from the tone Roosevelt set for his administration during his inaugural. This speech gave Americans an adrenalin boost, and it helped to establish Roosevelt as a larger-than-life figure.

On March 4, 1933, Roosevelt delivered his first of four inaugural addresses and what would become one of the most important speeches in American political history. He used reassuring words to comfort those individuals suffering the worst effects of the depression. "This great Nation will endure as it has endured, will revive and will prosper. So, first of all, let me assert my firm belief that the only thing we have to fear is fear itself—nameless, unreasoning, unjustified terror which paralyzes needed efforts to convert retreat into advance." The comfort derived from these words stemmed more from Roosevelt's tone of delivery and from the confidence he expressed that the nation's economic infrastructure could be saved than from any actual truths. In reality, there was plenty for the unemployed and underemployed to fear, including starvation, disease, and lack of shelter.

Just as important as Roosevelt's words of comfort were Roosevelt's words of contempt for those he blamed for the depression. "The money changers have fled from their high seats in the temple of our civilization. We may now restore that temple to the ancient truths. The measure of the restoration lies in the extent to which we apply social values more noble than mere monetary profit. Happiness lies not in the mere possession of money; it lies in the joy of achievement, in the thrill of creative effort. The joy and moral stimulation of work no longer must be forgotten in the mad chase of evanescent profits. These dark days will be worth all they cost us if they teach us that our true destiny is not to be ministered unto but to minister to ourselves and to our fellow men." This attempt to speak to the nation's hope and ideals was only partially successful, for by the end of the Roosevelt presidency

the war-induced prosperity generated a tremendous postwar economic frenzy of consumption.

Most important in the inauguration address of 1933 was Roosevelt's use of war imagery. In lines that drew the most applause from his audience, the new president declared: "It is to be hoped that the normal balance of executive and legislative authority may be wholly adequate to meet the unprecedented task before us. But it may be that an unprecedented demand and need for undelayed action may call for temporary departure from that normal balance of public procedure. I am prepared under my constitutional duty to recommend the measures that a stricken nation in the midst of a stricken world may require. These measures, or such other measures as the Congress may build out of its experience and wisdom, I shall seek, within my constitutional authority, to bring to speedy adoption. But in the event that the Congress shall fail to take one of these two courses, and in the event that the national emergency is still critical, I shall not evade the clear course of duty that will then confront me. I shall ask the Congress for the one remaining instrument to meet the crisis—broad Executive power to wage a war against the emergency, as great as the power that would be given to me if we were in fact invaded by a foreign foe."

This passage helps provide context for understanding what might very well be the most important organizational development of Roosevelt's presidency: the proliferation of the executive branch of the federal government and its emergence as the focus of national politics. Historians have long debated who was the first "modern" president—a vigorous leader who consistently spearheaded policy and dominated the government—with arguments put forward for GROVER CLEVELAND, WILLIAM MCKINLEY, THEODORE ROOSEVELT, WOODROW WILSON, and Franklin D. Roosevelt. During his tenure in office FDR took advantage of the precedents established in these previous administrations. The combination of policy changes, public expectations, and national and international conditions ensured that organizational developments during the 1930s and 1940s became entrenched. These changes, though, resulted from larger systemic shifts, namely, the industrial revolution and the concentration of economic power that it brought. The myriad of depression relief and war production agencies that Roosevelt advocated and oversaw were central to the emergence of a new social contract. This social contract was based on countervailing powers in which the burgeoning federal government along with newly empowered labor unions checked the excesses of big business on behalf of average working people. Under Roosevelt, then, the concept of "rugged individualism" gave way to government protections against economic insecurity. These sometimes controversial changes unfolded slowly and were rooted in the dual crises of depression and war.

(continues on page 106)

ADMINISTRATION TIME LINE

1933

March 4 Roosevelt is inaugurated president.

March 6 Roosevelt declares a "bank holiday," closing all banks in the country until they proved their solvency.

March 9 A special session of Congress is convened, lasting until June 16. It was later dubbed the "hundred days" because of the volume of legislation passed during these months.

The Emergency Banking Relief Act of 1933 is passed, providing legislative authorization for the bank holiday Roosevelt had declared days earlier.

March 12 Roosevelt delivers his first "fireside chat."

March 20 The Economy Act is passed.

Congress passes the Beer-Wine Revenue Act, legalizing and taxing beer and wine.

April 5 Roosevelt issues an executive order creating the Civilian Conservation Corps, following passage of congressional legislation authorizing the program.

April 20 The president takes the nation off the gold standard.

May 12 The Agricultural Adjustment Act is passed by Congress.

The Federal Emergency Relief Administration is created when Congress passes authorizing legislation, distributing $500 million for depression relief through state and local agencies.

May 18 Roosevelt signs the Tennessee Valley Authority into law.

May 27 The Federal Securities Act is passed.

June 13 The Home Owners' Loan Act is passed, providing protection for existing mortgages, mortgage insurance for new home purchases, and public housing construction.

June 16 Congress passes the Banking Act, also known as the Glass-Steagall Act, a measure that separated commercial and investment banking as well as instituting a host of other banking reforms, including the Federal Deposit Insurance Corporation.

The National Industrial Recovery Act is signed into law, creating the National Recovery Administration and the Public Works Administration.

The Farm Credit Act is passed.

November 8 The Civil Works Administration is created to employ unemployed Americans in infrastructure-building programs.

November 16 Roosevelt opens diplomatic relations with the Soviet Union.

December 5 The Twenty-first Amendment is ratified, ending Prohibition in the United States.

1934

April 12 The Nye Committee is created to investigate charges that the munitions industry conspired to lead the United States into World War I.

June 6 Roosevelt signs the Securities Exchange Act into law, creating the Securities and Exchange Commission.

June 12 The Reciprocal Trade Agreements Act is passed, providing for bilateral negotiations to reduce tariff rates.

June 18 The Indian Reorganization Act is passed, giving Indian tribes authority over their lands and strengthening tribal government.

June 19 The Communications Act is passed, creating the Federal Communications Commission.

June 28 Roosevelt signs the National Housing Act into law, creating the Federal Housing Authority to insure private mortgages for Americans.

1935

January 29 The Senate rejects a treaty providing for U.S. membership in the World Court.

May 1 Roosevelt issues an executive order creating the Resettlement Administration to address the problems of rural poverty.

May 6 The Works Progress Administration is created by executive order.

May 11 Roosevelt signs an executive order creating the Rural Electrification Administration.

May 27 The Supreme Court rules in *Schechter Poultry Corp. v. United States* that the National Recovery Administration is unconstitutional, overturning the New Deal's industrial recovery program.

June 26 The National Youth Administration is created when Roosevelt signs an executive order. The program provides work and school assistance for youth struggling in the depression.

July 5 Roosevelt signs the National Labor Relations Act into law.

August 14 Congress passes, and Roosevelt signs, the Social Security Act, providing a minimum welfare state to protect workers in retirement through a pension program.

August 23 Roosevelt signs the Banking Act of 1935, centralizing the operations of the Federal Reserve in Washington, D.C.

August 25 Congress passes the Public Utilities Holding Company Act, an attempt to break apart the large utility holding companies.

August 30 The Wealth Tax Act is signed into law.

The Guffey-Snyder Act is passed, attempting to regulate the coal industry.

August 31 Roosevelt signs the Neutrality Act of 1935 into law, requiring the president to declare when a state of war existed between two countries and to implement an embargo on all trade with belligerents.

September 8 Senator Huey P. Long is assassinated, dying two days later.

1936
January The magazine *Literary Digest* publishes a poll indicating Roosevelt would not be reelected that fall.

January 6 The Supreme Court declares the Agricultural Adjustment Act unconstitutional in *United States v. Butler*.

February 29 The Neutrality Act of 1936 is signed into law, banning loans or credit to belligerent nations.

March 2 Roosevelt signs the Soil Conservation and Domestic Allotment Act, providing for a soil erosion protection program in the wake of the Dust Bowl.

November 3 Roosevelt defeats Alf Landon to win reelection as president.

December 21 The Supreme Court rules in *United States v. Curtiss-Wright Export Corporation* that the president has more power for independent action in foreign policy than in domestic policy, including unilateral authority to reach executive agreements with other nations.

December 30 Sit-down strikes begin in the Detroit auto industry.

1937
January 6 The first Neutrality Act of 1937 is passed, applying the earlier neutrality laws to the Spanish Civil War.

January 11 The so-called Battle of the Running Bulls begins as part of the sit-down strikes in Detroit. The National Guard is brought in the following day to maintain order.

January 20 Roosevelt is inaugurated for a second term as president.

February 5 Roosevelt introduces the Supreme Court Reorganization Plan, dubbed "court packing" by its critics. Congress refuses to pass the legislation providing for an expansion of the federal judiciary for judges over the age of 70.

February 11 An agreement is signed between General Motors and the United Auto Workers, recognizing that union as the only representative for auto workers. The sit-down strikes end.

March 29 In *West Coast Hotel Co. v. Parrish* the Supreme Court upholds a minimum wage law for women. It signals that it might be more supportive of federal regulatory law as it found no discussion of freedom of contract in the Constitution and as

(continues)

ADMINISTRATION TIME LINE *(continued)*

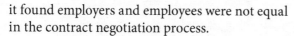

it found employers and employees were not equal in the contract negotiation process.

April 12 In *NLRB v. Jones & Laughlin Steel Corporation,* the Supreme Court upholds the constitutionality of the National Labor Relations Act.

April 26 The Bituminous Coal Act is passed in the wake of a Supreme Court decision overturning the Guffey-Snyder Act, which attempted to regulate the coal industry.

May 1 Congress renews the neutrality laws, making them permanent. Included are mandatory embargoes against nations at war and bans against travel on belligerent ships. The new law did permit "cash-and-carry" trade of nonmilitary goods.

July 22 The Bankhead-Jones Farm Tenancy Act is passed, creating the Farm Security Administration.

August The recession of 1937 begins, with the stock market down 58 percent and unemployment up to 28 percent.

August 20 Roosevelt signs legislation authorizing construction of Bonneville Dam.

September 2 The Wagner-Steagall Act is passed, creating the U.S. Housing Authority and funding new public housing projects.

October 5 Following Japanese attacks against China, Roosevelt delivers his "quarantine" speech, warning that the world community had a responsibility to isolate aggressor nations such as Japan.

December 12 Japan sinks the *Panay,* a U.S. gunboat then anchored in the Yangtze channel in China.

1938

February 16 The Agricultural Adjustment Act of 1938 is signed into law.

April The Temporary National Economic Committee is created.

June 21 The Natural Gas Act is passed, the first ever federal regulation of the natural gas industry.

June 23 Roosevelt signs the Civil Aeronautics Act into law, creating a new regulatory structure for federal civil aviation.

June 25 Roosevelt signs the Fair Labor Standards Act into law, providing for a minimum wage and maximum hours.

1939

June Roosevelt forbids any of the Jewish refugees aboard the German liner *St. Louis* from entering the United States.

August 2 The Hatch Act is passed, reflecting conservative criticism of the New Deal because it banned federal employees from political advocacy.

August 23 Joseph Stalin and Adolf Hitler sign a nonaggression pact.

September 1 Germany invades Poland and World War II begins in Europe.

November 4 Roosevelt signs a new Neutrality Act, lifting the arms embargo but retaining the cash-and-carry requirements.

1940

June U.S. involvement in the Battle of the Atlantic begins when President Roosevelt proposes to Navy secretary Frank Knox that orders for two destroyer escorts be placed with a shipbuilding company. The battle ends in May 1943 following a period of intense activity by German U-boats during which it seemed the Allies would not prevail.

June 20 Roosevelt names Republicans Frank Knox and Henry L. Stimson to his cabinet as secretary of the navy and secretary of war, respectively.

June 29 The Alien Registration Act is passed, requiring the registration of the 5 million noncitizens living in the United States.

July 18 Henry Wallace is named Roosevelt's running mate as vice president at the Democratic National Convention.

September 3 The destroyer for bases deal is negotiated with the British.

September 16 The Burke-Wadsworth Selective Service Training Act is signed into law, providing for the first peacetime draft in American history.

November 5 Roosevelt defeats Wendell Willkie to win a third term as president.

1941

January 7 Roosevelt issues an executive order to create the Office of Production Management to address the needs of a wartime economy.

January 20 Roosevelt is inaugurated for a third term as president.

March 11 Roosevelt signs the Lend-Lease Act into law.

April 11 The Office of Price Administration and Civilian Supply is created to stabilize prices and rents. The agency is later renamed the Office of Price Administration.

June 25 The Fair Employment Practices Committee is created via Executive Order 8802 to forestall a protest march against discrimination in employment.

July 30 The Board of Economic Warfare is established by presidential order to oversee foreign trade, war production, and the domestic economy. It was eliminated on July 15, 1943, with the transfer of its authority to the Office of Economic Warfare in the Office for Emergency Management.

August 14 Roosevelt and British prime minister Winston Churchill sign the Atlantic Charter during their meeting off the coast of Newfoundland, Canada.

November 24 In *Edwards v. California,* the Supreme Court overturns a California law that made it a misdemeanor to help indigent persons enter the state. The law had been passed to try to prevent further migration to the state by Dust Bowl refugees.

December 7 Japan attacks Pearl Harbor.

December 8 Roosevelt delivers his "Day of Infamy" speech, asking Congress for a declaration of war against Japan, which was approved by a near unanimous vote that same day.

December 11 Germany and Italy declare war on the United States, and that same day Congress declares war on Germany and Italy.

1942

January 12 Roosevelt creates the National War Labor Board, authorizing it to prevent wartime labor stoppages.

January 13 The Office of War Information is created as a wartime propaganda agency.

January 16 Roosevelt creates the War Production Board to ease the conversion to a wartime economy, limit unnecessary civilian economic activity, and harmonize the supply of raw materials for wartime production.

January 19 Roosevelt approves research to produce an atomic bomb, launching what became the Manhattan Project.

February 19 Roosevelt signs an executive order implementing internment of Japanese Americans.

March 12 U.S. forces begin their retreat, following defeat in the Battle of Java Sea, which began February 27.

April The General Maximum Price Regulation, nicknamed "General Max," is issued and generates significant criticism for its price control programs.

April 10 The Bataan Death March begins.

April 18 Roosevelt creates the War Manpower Commission to oversee labor recruitment for both war and essential civilian industries.

May 3–8 The United States wins a victory in the Battle of the Coral Sea.

May 6 The United States surrenders after losing the Battle of Corregidor to Japan.

June 4 The Battle of Midway ends in victory for the United States.

August 7 The Battle of Guadalcanal begins. It ends in an American victory in February 1943 following a long siege.

November 8 Operation Torch, the invasion of North Africa, begins.

(continues)

ADMINISTRATION TIME LINE (continued)

1943

January 14–24 Roosevelt meets with Winston Churchill at the Casablanca Conference, which produces no clear battle plans for invading Germany. Roosevelt asserts that nothing less than unconditional surrender would be required to end the war.

April The Bermuda Conference is held to address the problem of war refugees, but no adequate solution is found, especially for the Jewish refugee crisis.

May 13 The North Africa campaign ends with the Allies triumphant.

May 27 Roosevelt creates the Office of War Mobilization, giving it wide-ranging authority over manpower and material mobilization.

June 3–10 Zoot suit riots occur in Los Angeles.

June 9 The Ruml Plan is enacted into law, providing for income tax withholding.

June 20–21 The Detroit race riot takes place, spurred by tensions related to wartime economic and social dislocation.

June 21 In *Hirabayashi v. United States,* the Supreme Court upholds the decision of the federal government to intern Japanese Americans.

June 25 The Smith-Connally Antistrike Act is passed over Roosevelt's veto.

July 6 The Barden-LaFollette Act is passed, providing for the rehabilitation of physically handicapped Americans.

July 10 Allied troops invade Sicily.

November 22–26 Roosevelt, Winston Churchill, and Jiang Jieshi (Chiang Kai-shek) meet at the Cairo Conference in preparation for the Teheran Conference.

November 28–December 1 Roosevelt, Churchill, and Joseph Stalin meet at the Teheran Conference and develop plans for D-Day and the opening of a second front in Europe.

December 17 The Chinese Exclusion Act is repealed as a war measure to appease the Chinese government.

1944

January Roosevelt creates the War Refugee Board to assist the resettlement of Jewish refugees.

April 3 In *Smith v. Allwright,* the Supreme Court rules unconstitutional the white primary in Texas.

June 4 German resistance in Italy ends.

(continued from page 101)

Students and scholars alike have struggled for years to discern the most analytically potent method for understanding the activism of the Roosevelt years. The demarcation between the depression of the 1930s and the war years of the early 1940s has been reasonably clear, and even the president noted it, saying early in the war that he needed to switch from his "Dr. New Deal Hat" to his "Dr. Win the War Hat." Sorting out the two periods, especially the New Deal years, has proven more challenging. Some historians have grouped the policies of the 1930s into a first and a second and sometimes a third New Deal (even though there was no comparable spate of reform to match the output of 1933 and 1935 in the second term). Others have attempted to categorize the policies according to whether they were primarily intended to promote relief, recovery, or reform. Still others have grouped New Deal programs according to social and economic categories, such as agricultural policy, banking policy, labor policy, and the like. The problem with the latter two approaches is the overlap within programs. The clearest way, then, to study the Roosevelt presidency is as follows: first New Deal (1933–34), second New Deal (1935–36), second term failures (1937–41), from neutrality to war (1933–41), the grand strategy (1940–45), and war and the American home front (1939–45).

The First New Deal

Just about every aspect of the nation's economy was in crisis when Roosevelt became president in 1933: agriculture, banking, industry, and the investment sector. Lawmakers in Congress had been working during the Hoover administration (1929–33) on various proposals to remedy aspects of the cri-

June 6 Allied forces are successful in the D-Day landing on the beaches at Normandy, France.

June 19–20 The Battle of Philippine Sea ends in victory for the United States, the most decisive carrier battle of the war.

June 22 Roosevelt signs legislation creating the GI Bill of Rights.

July 21 Harry S. Truman is named as Roosevelt's running mate at the Democratic National Convention.

July 22 The Bretton Woods Agreement is signed at the Bretton Woods Conference, which met to deliberate global monetary affairs for the postwar era, resulting in the creation of the International Monetary Fund.

August 21–October 7 The Dumbarton Oaks Conference meets to draw up plans for creating a postwar United Nations.

October 23–25 The United States wins the Battle of Leyte Gulf.

November 7 Roosevelt defeats Thomas E. Dewey to win a fourth term as president.

December 16 The Battle of the Bulge begins as a German attack on the U.S. and Allied positions in the Ardennes Forest in Belgium.

December 18 The Supreme Court rules in *Korematsu v. United States* that military necessity was an appropriate justification for the internment of the Japanese Americans.

1945

January 20 Roosevelt is inaugurated for a fourth term as president.

February 4–11 The Yalta Conference is held, resulting in agreements about Germany, Soviet entry into the war against Japan, and the postwar United Nations.

February 19 The Battle of Iwo Jima begins, ending approximately a month later as a victory for the United States.

March 9–19 The Tokyo air raids result in the death of 90,000 people and mark the opening of an extended series of air strikes against Japan that include air raids against 66 cities and kill 900,000 people.

April 1 The Battle of Okinawa begins, lasting until June 22, two months after Roosevelt's death. A victory for the United States, it is the last major battle in World War II.

April 12 Roosevelt dies at Warm Springs, Georgia.

---

sis. The failure to accomplish much stemmed from too many competing proposals, the lack of leadership able to provide a grand vision for reform, and no consensus about the causes of the depression. While the New Deal alone did not bring a complete economic recovery, it nonetheless achieved important accomplishments. Foremost, those most in danger received life-sustaining assistance from the federal government. Furthermore, the New Deal repaired the infrastructure of American capitalism, including some of the causes of the depression. Finally, the New Deal restored the political faith of millions of Americans in democracy at a time when citizens across the Western world were losing faith in democratic governments.

Because the banking crisis was paramount, Roosevelt made it the first matter for consideration, declaring a "bank holiday" two days into his presidency. All banks in the country were required to close until they could prove their fiscal soundness. Days later, Roosevelt called Congress into a special session, which lasted from March 9 to June 16 and that was later dubbed the "hundred days." The output of this legislative session (and Congress generally during the Roosevelt years) is testament to the talent and wisdom of lawmakers in Congress, lobbyists for interest groups, presidential assistants, government bureaucrats, and Roosevelt himself. Collaboration and a desire to work for the public interest motivated the principal actors. During the hundred days, Congress passed, and the president signed, 15 major laws dealing with the various economic and social problems of the depression.

The AGRICULTURAL ADJUSTMENT ACT provided relief for farmers, by providing price supports and acreage reductions. The leading farm organizations helped shape the law. To remedy the problems of industrial production and

President Roosevelt was responsible for a multitude of depression relief agencies. One such agency was the Works Progress Administration, which oversaw the Federal Art Project. More than 200,000 works of art were created by the Federal Art Project, including this 1940 poster. *(Library of Congress)*

of workers, Congress crafted the NATIONAL INDUSTRIAL RECOVERY ACT (NIRA) with the help of the U.S. Chamber of Commerce. Roosevelt supported the measure in part to stave off an initiative from Senator Hugo Black (D-AL) providing for a 30-hour work week. To address the needs of the destitute, the FEDERAL EMERGENCY RELIEF ADMINISTRATION pumped money into the economy to enable people to obtain food, shelter, and clothing. Lawmakers appropriated $500 million for this successful program, which traced its origins to the efforts of social workers who recruited members of Congress to initiate such a measure during the Hoover years. One critical goal of the New Deal was to provide jobs programs for the unemployed. The PUBLIC WORKS ADMINISTRATION hired people out of work to build airports, dams, aircraft carriers, schools, hospitals, public buildings, and bridges, and the CIVILIAN CONSERVATION CORPS (CCC) hired young people to fight land erosion and work at reforestation flood control. The New Deal also embraced massive local projects, such as the TENNESSEE VALLEY AUTHORITY (TVA). The TVA had long been the brainchild of Senator George W. Norris (R-NE), but Roosevelt expanded the flood control and public power project to include regional planning and development.

Middle-class Americans benefited from banking reforms, most notably the FEDERAL DEPOSIT INSURANCE CORPORATION (which protected savings accounts), stock market regulations, and mortgage protections. Roosevelt only had a hand in the drafting of two laws during the hundred days, the CCC and the ECONOMY ACT, a measure designed to trim federal spending and fulfill his campaign promises.

Ironically, given this and subsequent legislative advances, Roosevelt envisioned himself more as a "preaching president" focused on moral leadership than as a legislative president concerned with the details of drafting policy. He believed the latter could not be accomplished if the public was not educated to the need for change. His rhetoric was filled with appeals for the Americans to deepen their religious faith. He believed that heightened spirituality would help bring the country out of economic misery. Roosevelt's brand of religious faith drew from New Testament calls for social activism, not unlike the social gospel movement prominent during the Progressive Era. He used the Old Testament as well, telling one audience: "This is a history and a sermon on the subject of water power, and I preach from the Old Testament. The text is 'Thou shalt not steal.'" The president envisioned a Christian commonwealth governed by the Golden Rule. He did not think that all people would be equal; instead, he believed that talent, class, and racial differences would remain but that people would be more respectful of their fellow citizens.

Roosevelt used the spoken and written word to educate the public about governance of the country. He routinely made himself available for press conferences twice a week. His press availability compared favorably with his recent predecessors, who either did not have the intellectual ability, in the case of WARREN G. HARDING, the verbal fluidity, in the case of CALVIN COOLIDGE, or the temperament, in the case of Herbert Hoover, to respond well to the media. Reporters appreciated Roosevelt's openness and availability, and they shared in a "gentlemen's agreement" not to photograph or discuss the physical handicap that prevented him from walking unaided. In speeches, messages to Congress, and "fireside chats"—radio addresses delivered directly to the American people—Roosevelt explained often complex public policy problems in simple, easy to grasp terms. While he shared similar economic goals with his predecessor, Herbert Hoover, Roosevelt's statement that he wanted relief, recovery, and reform struck a chord with the American people and made the New Deal seem a vast improvement over the Hoover era.

Roosevelt benefited throughout his presidency from outstanding advisers. Louis M. Howe, who had been with Roosevelt since his New York days in the 1910s, remained an important political strategist until his death in 1936. Roosevelt's team included the "BRAIN TRUST" of academic experts organized during the 1932 presidential campaign, including Adolf A. Berle, Jr., Raymond Moley, and Rexford G. Tugwell. Key cabinet officials during the New Deal years included

Thousands of people wait in line outside the New York State Labor Bureau building in New York City on November 24, 1933, hoping to register for a federal relief job. *(Associated Press)*

James A. Farley, postmaster general; Harold L. Ickes, secretary of the interior; Henry Morgenthau, Jr., secretary of the treasury; Frances Perkins, secretary of labor; and HENRY A. WALLACE, secretary of agriculture. Roosevelt had other capable advisers, including Harry L. Hopkins, a key White House official; Hugh S. Johnson of the National Recovery Administration; and Jesse H. Jones of the RECONSTRUCTION FINANCE CORPORATION. Perhaps most important of all was his wife ELEANOR ROOSEVELT, one of the most active first ladies in American history. She was more liberal than her husband, pushing him to do more for the poorest Americans and to pay attention to gender and racial discrimination.

Roosevelt had hoped that the legislative package assembled during the hundred days would be sufficient to pull the nation out of the depression save only for minor adjustments. As such, he was not enthusiastic to undertake additional reforms when Congress met in regular session in 1934. The president discouraged lawmakers from pursuing a host of initiatives, including a plan for national unemployment

insurance, a federal antilynching bill, and a labor relations bill to provide protections for unions. Roosevelt did support the creation of the SECURITIES AND EXCHANGE COMMISSION to regulate the stock market. A few other noteworthy congressional accomplishments included the RECIPROCAL TRADE AGREEMENTS ACT, devaluation of the dollar, and home loan protections. Most significant, Roosevelt participated in eliminating the CIVIL WORKS ADMINISTRATION (CWA), a resoundingly successful relief program created in the fall of 1933 to address privation in the winter months in providing jobs to the poor to build roads, schools, and other infrastructure needs. Although Roosevelt had spoken during his campaign about the need to experiment with and support innovative new programs, he fell victim to conservative complaints that the CWA would encourage a permanent class of aid seekers. The business community was troubled by the efficiency and success demonstrated by the CWA in infrastructure construction compared with the lackluster performance of private-sector initiatives.

Despite the mixed results from Congress in 1934, the American people registered overwhelming approval of Roosevelt and the New Deal in the midterm elections that year. Typically, the party in power loses seats in a midterm election, but not in 1934. Democrats picked up 10 Senate seats, giving them a total of 69 to 25 Republicans, 1 Progressive, and 1 Farmer-Laborite. Democrats also gained 9 House seats, up to 322, with just 103 Republicans, 7 Progressives, and 3 Farmer Laborites. When election returns streamed into the White House, Harry Hopkins noted, "boys, this is our hour!"

The Second New Deal

Roosevelt did not face the smooth sailing suggested by the 1934 election when Congress assembled in 1935. Instead, pressure came from the right and from the left, both dissatisfied with the direction of the New Deal, and it was exacerbated by actions from the Supreme Court. Senator Huey P. Long (D-LA), Dr. Francis Townsend of California, radio priest Father Charles Coughlin, novelist Upton Sinclair, and leaders of various third-party movements all questioned Roosevelt's commitment to relieving poverty. Long advocated the "Share Our Wealth" program whereby large fortunes would be confiscated and redistributed. His greatest popularity was in his native South. Townsend pushed for old-age pensions, and Coughlin, with an audience of over 40 million working-class Americans, castigated bankers and financiers. Sinclair, the author of *The Jungle,* ran for governor of California in 1934, campaigning for state ownership of industry. The third-party movements, most prevalent in the Midwest, challenged the existence of the two-party system. These movements, all critical of capitalism, also tapped a societal concern about modernization.

Meanwhile, elements in the business community grew increasingly skeptical of the New Deal. Most troubling was the failure of Roosevelt to balance the budget. Other complaints included the decision to move the United States off the gold standard. Nor were business owners happy with protections for workers, especially the support for labor unions contained within the NIRA. The massive increase in the number of government regulatory initiatives generated complaints from business. Roosevelt never completely understood or accepted these criticisms because the New Deal had included substantial government largesse for business. The National Recovery Administration, created by the NIRA, permitted businesses to write their own regulations. No tax increases had been levied on corporate wealth. Finally, the Reconstruction Finance Corporation had loaned as much money to banks and businesses as had been paid out in relief for unemployment. The final challenge to the New Deal came from the Supreme Court, which overturned key provisions of the first New Deal, including the NIRA, in the summer of 1935.

These various pressures combined to encourage a leftward shift in New Deal legislation, prompting some scholars to categorize the major reform initiatives of 1935 as a second New Deal. Again, most of the initiatives came from a Congress that wanted to go even farther than the president. Not only did lawmakers approve Roosevelt's call for a new $5 billion public works program, the WORKS PROGRESS ADMINISTRATION (WPA), it tried but failed to require that WPA workers receive the prevailing wage, which would have put the government in direct competition with private industry.

It took Roosevelt until June 1935 to decide to work with Congress for new legislation. With pressure from the left mounting, he asked lawmakers to postpone their planned summer vacation until they passed measures controlling holding companies, reforming banking practices, protecting labor unions and industrial workers, enacting Social Security, and reforming tax policy. The NATIONAL LABOR RELATIONS ACT, also known as the Wagner Act, replaced the NIRA and guaranteed labor the right to organize and bargain collectively. The BANKING ACT of 1935 modernized the nation's banking system and shifted power to the Federal Reserve Board in Washington, D.C. The PUBLIC UTILITIES HOLDING COMPANY ACT of 1935 proved powerful enough to force the dissolution of most holding companies within three years.

Roosevelt's call for tax reform, including the inheritance taxes he believed necessary to forestall the accumulation of great fortunes, produced scant results in comparison with his morally charged rhetoric. The WEALTH TAX ACT of 1935 increased rates and made the code more progressive, but it did not accomplish the promised redistribution of wealth. Roosevelt was not concerned with these results because he was more interested in deflating Huey Long as a political rival than in actually changing the distribution of wealth in the country. His other goal, sending a warning to the owners of great fortunes about what might befall them if they overreached, failed too because the legislation only managed to heighten the opposition of the wealthy to FDR.

Likewise concerning Social Security Roosevelt talked of an expansive program while ensuring that the result was more modest. In private conversations he acknowledged the need for a "cradle to grave" system of social welfare, including national health insurance, but he feared that Congress would not support such a plan. As a result, Roosevelt sought much less from lawmakers. He also backed off on calls to fund the proposed Social Security program with income taxes, arguing that a payroll tax deduction would give workers a legal right to benefits upon retirement. Furthermore, he added, "with those taxes in there, no damn politician can ever scrap my social security program." The SOCIAL SECURITY ACT of 1935 remains one of the most enduring legacies of the New Deal.

In comparison to what had been sought by liberal and progressive lawmakers and by some of the demagogues, the results of the second New Deal were modest. Roosevelt himself was less interested in policy changes, in the case of tax reform, than in rhetorical flourish. Even so, the New Deal was revolutionary. It helped transform the federal government into an active and positive force in the lives of the American people, and it included protections against some of the systemic problems that had led to the Great Depression, specifically those in the banking industry and the stock market. Critics and students alike have been baffled by its lack of ideological consistency, but pragmatism was crucial to its success. Another feature both vital to its success and worthy of criticism was the amount of money that went to banks and businesses instead of to the unemployed and the needy. In combating the farming crisis, wealthy landowners benefited more than impoverished tenant farmers from the New Deal agricultural initiatives. These realities have led critics to lament that the New Deal ensured the survival of capitalism, but it also changed the rules: Organized labor became a significant player in the economy and a host of federal regulations forced the business community to play by the rules and account for their actions.

Second-Term Failures

The contrast between Roosevelt's overwhelming reelection victory in 1936 and the failures of his second term is vast. When the Republicans nominated Kansas governor Alfred M. "Alf" Landon for the presidency in 1936, they opted for a moderate candidate who had no major complaints about the New Deal. The campaign offered few surprises; because the majority of Americans supported the New Deal, Roosevelt won over 60 percent of the popular vote and lost in only two states: Maine and Vermont.

The attitude of the U.S. Supreme Court to New Deal legislation quickly became the foremost problem, according to the president, during his second term. In 1936, the Supreme Court had ruled the AGRICULTURAL ADJUSTMENT ACT unconstitutional, finding that it aimed to regulate agriculture, a power reserved to the states. The decision struck a blow at Roosevelt's program for farm recovery. Even though Congress was considering farm tenancy legislation and had also passed the SOIL CONSERVATION AND DOMESTIC ALLOTMENT ACT in 1936 and would pass another Agriculture Adjustment Act in 1938, administration insiders worried. They did not want to be in a position of passing legislation, having it overturned by the Court, and having to go back to Congress for more legislation. Another concern was that since much of the New Deal legislation was regulatory in nature it might meet with a similar fate. These fears drove the president to consider a program for reforming the nation's federal courts.

Less than a month after his second inaugural (moved by the Twentieth Amendment from the traditional March 4 date to January 20, where it has since remained), Roosevelt called for a major reform of the judicial code, the SUPREME COURT REORGANIZATION PLAN. The president sought authority to appoint additional justices to both the Supreme Court and the lower federal courts for each member past the age of 70. While the number of justices on the Supreme Court was not fixed either by statute or by terms of the Constitution, it had remained at nine for many years. Critics of the plan saw the Roosevelt initiative as political manipulation of the federal

"You can't have everything" is the original caption of this Herblock cartoon, drawn after Congress blocked President Roosevelt's "court-packing" plan in 1937. *(A Herblock Cartoon, copyright by the Herb Block Foundation)*

system of divided powers. Accusing the president of seeking too much executive power at the expense of the judiciary, they dubbed the measure "court packing," the name by which it has since been known. Democrats joined with Republicans to hand the president a resounding defeat from which he never fully recovered in his second term. However, the Supreme Court did begin to rule favorably on New Deal laws.

Roosevelt's agenda for his second term also included a plan for EXECUTIVE REORGANIZATION. Acting out of concern for the demands of governing in the modern era, Roosevelt put forward a plan that would concentrate additional power in the executive branch. Conservative critics lambasted the bill as evidence of FDR's ambition to become a dictator. Not until 1939 did anything come of this proposal. The result was a modest effort at modernization but not centralization. Like the effort at court reform, this initiative did more harm than good for Roosevelt's relationship with Congress.

The economy provided the president with severe challenges in his second term. In August 1937 a serious recession set in, ruining the economic recovery of the past four years. Liberal economists blamed Roosevelt's spending cuts from earlier that year. The recession surprised and befuddled New Dealers, who thought that the depression was over. The downturn caused the president and his team to reevaluate their strategy, and two important initiatives resulted. First, the attack on monopolies ceased being simply a rhetorical device when the administration created the Temporary National Economic Committee, which studied the problem for three years. Because its report came out after World War II had begun, little resulted from it. There were no major antimonopoly legislative programs introduced or implemented. Additionally, the Justice Department increased its antitrust prosecutions until the war forced an abandonment of the policy. The second initiative involved a revised approach toward government spending. Roosevelt abandoned his belief in balanced budgets and turned purposefully toward deficit spending, or the use of fiscal policy, to manage the economy. He drew on the thinking of economists such as John Maynard Keynes in convincing Congress to enact a $5 billion spending program for additional relief and public works initiatives.

The following year saw passage of the FAIR LABOR STANDARDS ACT, a landmark law that included establishing a minimum wage and a maximum 40-hour work week as well as abolishing child labor. Along with the Social Security Act and National Labor Relations Act, this law provided essential benefits for working people and the poor. Also important was Roosevelt's disastrous efforts to remake the Democratic Party. He had long hoped that the Republicans and Democrats could more neatly divide according to ideology, with the former serving as the party of the conservatives and the latter the party of the liberals. He was angry with conservative Democrats for scuttling his efforts to reorganize the courts and the executive branch. In 1938, he campaigned against 10 conservative Democrats; still all but one were reelected. Furthermore, political purists complained that WPA workers had actively campaigned for Democratic liberals in several states, suggesting a political quid pro quo for depression relief benefits. That fall, the divide between Democrats and Republicans in the House and the Senate narrowed with Republicans gaining new seats for the first time in a decade: there were 81 new Republicans in the House and seven in the Senate. Conservatives increased their power in Congress, and a coalition of southern Democrats and Republicans was able to block liberal initiatives.

With the New Deal effectively over by the late 1930s, Roosevelt's presidency looked as if it might receive mixed reviews. The country had never returned to prosperity levels in place before the crash, and the economy would not fully recover until World War II. Indeed, Roosevelt's handling of the war saved his presidency from the failures of his second term.

From Neutrality to War

During the early weeks of his presidency in 1933, Roosevelt had met with European, Asian, and Latin American foreign dignitaries at the White House at a conference to deliberate on issues regarding the worldwide depression and to discuss arms controls. The meeting suggested that Roosevelt might embrace again the internationalism of the Woodrow Wilson era, but the conference suffered from an inability to compromise and from U.S. domestic policy decisions at odds with the stated goals. Roosevelt did employ his personal approach to diplomacy, meeting privately with the various diplomats. World leaders came away from the conference with a perception that the new American president could not be trusted. He appeared to say one thing in his diplomatic meetings and then his government enacted contradictory legislation, specifically regarding monetary stabilization and fixed currency exchange ratios.

Another key foreign policy decision early in the Roosevelt presidency involved Latin America, where he worked for improved trade and diplomatic relations. The efforts were dubbed the "Good Neighbor Policy" and they sought to overcome the negative views of the United States in the region resulting from U.S. policies toward Mexico and the Caribbean region in the 19th and early 20th centuries.

The country and Congress by and large had adopted isolationist attitudes in the years after World War I. Roosevelt, who during the 1932 campaign had tried to distance himself from his earlier advocacy of Wilsonian internationalism, spent the first five years of his presidency carefully balancing demands for isolation and neutrality with a heightened presence in world politics. As such, Congress played an important role in determining foreign policy in the 1930s. For example, in 1935, the Senate rejected a treaty that Roosevelt wanted providing for U.S. membership in the World Court, an auxiliary agency of the League of Nations.

Investigative and legislative initiatives from Congress stymied a return to internationalism. Against the backdrop of legislative hearings into whether or not munitions makers had conspired to bring the nation into World War I, five major NEUTRALITY ACTS were passed between 1935 and 1939 that made illegal the conditions believed responsible for U.S. entry into the war, including trade with belligerent nations and travel in war zones. Roosevelt supported these legislative initiatives as long as the laws remained flexible.

In 1937, when Japanese military incursions into China intensified, Roosevelt gave an important speech in which he called for the world community to "quarantine" "aggressor" nations such as Japan. Both the press and the public criticized the president for his strong position, and again he retreated. The following year, Roosevelt, like other Western leaders, accepted Hitler's promise that the acquisition of the Sudetenland region of Czechoslovakia at the Munich Conference would bring peace. FDR wired Prime Minister Neville Chamberlain of Great Britain his congratulations for defusing tensions in Europe.

World War II began in Europe in September 1939, when Germany invaded Poland. In 1940, the war shifted to the western part of the continent when Germany conquered France, Denmark, Norway, Belgium, the Netherlands, and Luxembourg. Throughout this early period of the war Roosevelt continued to respect the political clout of the isolationists. He was, though, more realistic in his response than

President Woodrow Wilson had been in 1917. "This nation will remain a neutral nation," contended Roosevelt, "but I cannot ask that every American remain neutral in thought as well." More important, he began channeling as much aid as possible to the British, who now remained the sole opponent of Nazi Germany. In the process, Roosevelt developed a crucial diplomatic relationship with Winston Churchill, the wartime prime minister of Britain.

The president used a combination of executive maneuvers and legislative actions to enable the United States to support the British in fighting fascism overseas. Repeal of the Neutrality Acts began in 1940, permitting the United States to sell weapons to the British. The U.S. military became involved in the Battle of the Atlantic in 1940 when submarines and naval convoys were used against German U-boat attacks on the shipping lanes to Europe. Pressure to create a peacetime draft came not from the president but from internationalists in and out of Congress. In September 1940, the Burke-Wadsworth Selective Service Training Act was passed, providing for a one-year draft. The legislation was just barely renewed in 1941. Other key initiatives in the efforts to aid Great Britain included a deal, concluded in September 1940, whereby the United States sent 50 World War I destroyers to the British in exchange for access to British air and naval bases.

Against this backdrop, Roosevelt won an unprecedented third term as president. In his campaign against businessman Wendell Willkie, Roosevelt both promised to keep the country out of "foreign wars" and suggested he was the only politician who could protect the country in such perilous times.

Passage of the Lend-Lease Act, which provided another means of provisioning a financially starved Britain, followed early in 1941. An August 1941 meeting off the coast of Newfoundland, Canada, cemented the Churchill-Roosevelt relationship with the signing of the Atlantic Charter, a document clarifying the war aims for the defeat of totalitarianism. After Hitler invaded Russia in June 1941 and the United States entered the war in December 1941, the "Big Three," including Roosevelt, Churchill, and Soviet leader Joseph Stalin, led the Allied powers.

For Roosevelt, the biggest question was how to shape U.S. foreign policy regarding the war, make the country ready for war, and at the same time protect his administration from

Two English women, members of the Auxiliary Territorial Service, carry recently arrived rifles from the United States, following passage of the Lend-Lease Act. *(National Archives)*

the wrath of the isolationists. Political and military insiders understood that the United States could not avoid World War II entirely. The question was not if the country would become a combatant but when and how. Most military minds of the day believed the war would originate with Germany as a result of American aid initiatives to Europe.

On December 7, 1941, life in the United States changed. A dawn attack by the Japanese on Pearl Harbor in the Hawaiian Islands plunged the country immediately into World War II. Diplomatic relations between the United States and the Japanese had been deteriorating for months. When the United States placed an embargo on Japan and froze its American assets in retaliation for its aggression in China, Japan waged war to claim the oil-rich British and Dutch colonies in the Pacific. While the United States had cracked Japanese codes and knew that the island nation planned a major Pacific attack, none knew that Pearl Harbor was the

target. Outrage and anger dominated the national mood, and a declaration of war against Japan sailed through the Congress on December 8. When Germany and Italy declared war on the United States three days later, the American government responded in kind, and the United States was officially fighting a multifront war. In the European and North African theaters, the United States was allied with the British and the Soviets, but in the Pacific theater, only the British fought with the United States against Japan.

The Grand Strategy

The U.S. effort to defeat the Axis powers of Germany, Italy, and Japan in World War II was a bipartisan effort. In 1940, Roosevelt had made two significant changes in his cabinet. He named Henry Stimson as his secretary of war and Frank Knox as his secretary of the navy. Stimson and Knox were both prominent Republicans, the former having served in

President Roosevelt shakes hands with Henry L. Stimson after the Senate confirmed his nomination as secretary of war, July 10, 1940. (© Bettmann/CORBIS)

both the WILLIAM HOWARD TAFT and the Herbert Hoover administrations as secretary of war and secretary of state, respectively, and the latter was an influential publisher from Chicago with a strong commitment to internationalism. Just as important, avowed New Dealers found their presence less secure in the war years, and some left the government. Once the war came, Roosevelt made it a practice to defer to his generals and his leading advisers regarding daily war operations. His detached style permitted him to concentrate on wartime diplomacy and grand strategy. Roosevelt viewed Europe, not Japan, as the primary target because Hitler seemed the greater threat, and, in the early years of the war, the Pacific theater received just 20 percent of the total resources that the United States devoted to defeating the Axis powers.

Almost immediately significant disagreements emerged among the Big Three leaders—Roosevelt, Churchill, and Stalin—about how to proceed against Germany and Italy. Stalin, besieged by German troops invading deep into the Soviet Union, begged for the immediate opening of a second front in western Europe by invading across the English Channel. Roosevelt initially agreed, but he succumbed to pressure from Churchill. The British prime minister feared that taking the war directly to the Nazis through France would result in another quagmire like the trench warfare of World War I. Instead, he pushed for a strategy of chipping away at the periphery.

Churchill contended that a NORTH AFRICAN CAMPAIGN followed by an ITALIAN CAMPAIGN would do the greatest damage by attacking Hitler in his weakest spots. The results were mixed. The fighting, especially in Italy, took precious time and the ensuing delay in opening a full-fledged second front created much ill-will with Stalin and the Soviets, who came to distrust the motives of Churchill and Roosevelt. For the Americans, these campaigns provided valuable time for expanding the size of the army and ensuring that U.S. troops and weapons systems were ready for the much more intensive demands of a cross-channel invasion.

The war in the Pacific continued unabated even as Roosevelt was preoccupied with the conflict between Churchill and Stalin over the timing of a second front in Europe. U.S. territorial losses in the Pacific were very great in the months immediately after the attack on Pearl Harbor, forcing the United States to cede all U.S.-held islands west of Hawaii to Japan. Following the surprise attack, Americans lost to the Japanese in the BATTLE OF CORREGIDOR, which also forced the U.S. evacuation of the Philippines and the horrifically brutal BATAAN DEATH MARCH. The island hopping strategy commenced in the spring of 1942, and two U.S. victories at the BATTLE OF THE CORAL SEA and the BATTLE OF MIDWAY set the tone for much of the rest of the Pacific theater combat. Especially after Midway, a much more decisive victory, the United States took the offensive against Japan in the Pacific, attacking its position in the Solomon Islands located off the

northern coast of Australia. The BATTLE OF GUADALCANAL (1942–43) revealed the full force of barbarity on both sides, even if American newspaper coverage depicted U.S. soldiers as heroes, and previewed what would be required to defeat Japan on its home islands, a lesson that was repeated at the BATTLE OF IWO JIMA in 1945.

Roosevelt spent much of 1943 either meeting with Churchill and Stalin or preparing for meetings with these leaders. The topic that dominated these gatherings was the timing and strategy for opening a second front in western Europe. The CASABLANCA CONFERENCE held in Morocco in January was the first gathering of the year, but only Churchill and Roosevelt attended. Churchill dominated the meeting, and no firm plans were made for a channel invasion of the German position in France. To appease the Soviets and to prove American military prowess, Roosevelt promised to require an unconditional surrender from Hitler.

In 1943, a shift in the balance of power within the Big Three took place. At the start of the year, Churchill was the senior partner, but Roosevelt sought to dominate decisions on strategy. As such, he wanted the TEHERAN CONFERENCE, scheduled for late in the year, to exclude Churchill. It would be his first opportunity to meet with Stalin in person and he wanted no distractions. Churchill disagreed and not only did he insist on attending the Teheran Conference but also he convinced Roosevelt to attend a preliminary meeting in Cairo in November. At the CAIRO CONFERENCE, Roosevelt limited the deliberations to the war in Asia. At Teheran a few days later, the topic changed to consideration of Operation Overlord and planning for D-DAY AND THE BATTLE FOR NORTHWEST EUROPE. Additionally, Stalin, who held the upper hand against Hitler on the eastern front, agreed that, once Germany was defeated, he would declare war on Japan.

The Allied landings at Normandy on D-Day, June 6, 1944, marked an important turning point in the war. As American and British troops secured a beachhead and began pushing east, the world witnessed the unfolding might of the Allied powers over the remaining months of the year; this display strengthened Roosevelt's call for the Allies to maintain their teamwork in the postwar era. To cement this cooperation, 26 nations signed the United Nations Declaration, and two important conferences occurred in 1944. The Bretton Woods meeting in New Hampshire in July focused on global monetary affairs, leading to formation of the International Monetary Fund, while at the DUMBARTON OAKS CONFERENCE, delegates developed plans for creating the United Nations.

Perhaps Roosevelt's most significant contribution to the grand strategy of the war came with his military decision to secretly fund research into atomic weaponry. The MANHATTAN PROJECT was launched in 1942, and the results were not known until three months after Roosevelt's death, but the atomic bombs developed during the war and dropped on Japan in August 1945 forever changed the history of the world.

The Yalta Conference in February 1945 was Roosevelt's last major opportunity to participate in formulating the grand strategy of the war. With the end of combat in Europe in sight, the meeting focused on postwar planning, and agreements were reached regarding Germany, Soviet entry into the war against Japan, and the formation of the United Nations. The participants noted Roosevelt's deteriorating health from arteriosclerosis, which left him a near invalid, and the president's critics argued that his sickness contributed to his decisions to give in to too many Soviet demands. The record indicates that Roosevelt was a vigorous and competent negotiator at Yalta. Careful consideration of the military realities in February 1945, though, suggests that Roosevelt could not have gotten different results at Yalta. By the time of the president's death in April 1945, the Allies were nearing victory in both Europe and Japan. VE-Day (for victory in Europe) would come on May 8, 1945, and VJ-Day (victory in Japan) followed on August 15, 1945.

War and the American Home Front

Efforts to ready the home front for war began well before the attack on Pearl Harbor in 1941. The war in Europe and Asia prompted Congress and President Roosevelt to consider changes to taxation policy and to implement rationing and price controls. The demands raised by efforts to provision the Allies meant that defense contractors became much more prominent in the political economy. Some questioned the predominant reliance on big business for such work and others sought to root out corruption in the national defense industries. Efforts were begun to ensure fair hiring practices among the contractors. Questions about labor generally changed from a depression-era context to a wartime context. Lawmakers and the president alike ignored other war-related policy concerns, specifically the immigration problems related to the Jewish refugee crisis in Nazi Germany. Soon after the United States became a combatant, plans were developed for the internment of Japanese Americans. In sum, the war years both narrowed the values of the New Deal and redefined liberalism, with the enactment of a G.I. Bill of Rights in 1944 embodying this home front political transformation.

The economy was perhaps the president's biggest domestic wartime concern. Weaknesses lingering from the depression meant little room existed for error. Furthermore, government revenue needs would be massive. A tax policy unfolded that saw upper rates for the highest earners reaching the 90th percentile. For the first time in the country's history, middle-and low-income Americans were brought into the income tax system as their earnings soared as a result of the war. The Ruml Plan, implemented in 1943, provided for payroll tax deductions and made the payment of income taxes less painful than the previous method whereby taxes were collected annually in one lump sum. The adoption of price and wage controls along with rationing policies proved most challenging as these decisions were fraught with politi-

As defense jobs became plentiful during World War II and the United States approached full employment, many women entered the workforce. Above, a worker at the Vultee plant in Nashville, Tennessee, helps construct a bomber, 1943. *(Library of Congress)*

cal considerations. In dealing with both, Roosevelt tried to balance the demands of the war with his earlier commitments to progressive governance. More nettlesome were the congressional efforts to outlaw wartime strikes. The real target of this effort was the labor reforms of the 1930s, such as the National Labor Relations Act, and Roosevelt tried hard to thwart union opponents. Passage of antistrike legislation in 1943 over Roosevelt's veto resulted from a shift in Congress (the 1942 midterm elections had produced a decidedly more conservative Congress). Here, more than anywhere else, Roosevelt tried to sustain elements of the New Deal by fighting, not always successfully, lawmakers who wanted more conservative labor, tax, and rationing policies.

Both a strength and a weakness of Roosevelt's leadership of the home front economy stemmed from the proliferation of executive branch agencies created to manage the various components of military mobilization. Multiple, conflicting jurisdictions with unclear organizational powers were characteristic of the wartime administrative apparatus. This technique served an important political purpose: It defused congressional criticisms of the war and it allowed Roosevelt room to maneuver if he believed changes were in order. For example, at least half a dozen agencies dealt directly or indirectly with the issues of price control and rationing during the war.

To run the new war agencies, Roosevelt tapped leading business and political figures. The prominence of executives most at home in corporate boardrooms troubled the more liberal New Dealers, but there was little to prevent capitalists from dominating the economic mobilization. More worrisome was the near abandonment of the New Deal ethos during the war. No major reform initiatives were proposed or passed as wartime legislation. Instead, conservatives in

(continues on page 120)

WESTERN DEFENSE COMMAND AND FOURTH ARMY
WARTIME CIVIL CONTROL ADMINISTRATION
Presidio of San Francisco, California
April 1, 1942

INSTRUCTIONS
TO ALL PERSONS OF
JAPANESE
ANCESTRY
Living in the Following Area:

All that portion of the City and County of San Francisco, State of California, lying generally west of the north-south line established by Junipero Serra Boulevard, Worchester Avenue, and Nineteenth Avenue, and lying generally north of the east-west line established by California Street, to the intersection of Market Street, and thence on Market Street to San Francisco Bay.

All Japanese persons, both alien and non-alien, will be evacuated from the above designated area by 12:00 o'clock noon Tuesday, April 7, 1942.

No Japanese person will be permitted to enter or leave the above described area after 8:00 a. m., Thursday, April 2, 1942, without obtaining special permission from the Provost Marshal at the Civil Control Station located at:

1701 Van Ness Avenue
San Francisco, California

The Civil Control Station is equipped to assist the Japanese population affected by this evacuation in the following ways:

1. Give advice and instructions on the evacuation.

2. Provide services with respect to the management, leasing, sale, storage or other disposition of most kinds of property including: real estate, business and professional equipment, buildings, household goods, boats, automobiles, livestock, etc.

3. Provide temporary residence elsewhere for all Japanese in family groups.

4. Transport persons and a limited amount of clothing and equipment to their new residence, as specified below.

The Following Instructions Must Be Observed:

1. A responsible member of each family, preferably the head of the family, or the person in whose name most of the property is held, and each individual living alone, will report to the Civil Control Station to receive further instructions. This must be done between 8:00 a. m. and 5:00 p. m., Thursday, April 2, 1942, or between 8:00 a. m. and 5:00 p. m., Friday, April 3, 1942.

2. Evacuees must carry with them on departure for the Reception Center, the following property:

(a) Bedding and linens (no mattress) for each member of the family;

(b) Toilet articles for each member of the family;

(c) Extra clothing for each member of the family;

(d) Sufficient knives, forks, spoons, plates, bowls and cups for each member of the family;

(e) Essential personal effects for each member of the family.

All items carried will be securely packaged, tied and plainly marked with the name of the owner and numbered in accordance with instructions received at the Civil Control Station.

The size and number of packages is limited to that which can be carried by the individual or family group.

No contraband items as described in paragraph 6, Public Proclamation No. 3, Headquarters Western Defense Command and Fourth Army, dated March 24, 1942, will be carried.

3. The United States Government through its agencies will provide for the storage at the sole risk of the owner of the more substantial household items, such as iceboxes, washing machines, pianos and other heavy furniture. Cooking utensils and other small items will be accepted if crated, packed and plainly marked with the name and address of the owner. Only one name and address will be used by a given family.

4. Each family, and individual living alone, will be furnished transportation to the Reception Center. Private means of transportation will not be utilized. All instructions pertaining to the movement will be obtained at the Civil Control Station.

Go to the Civil Control Station at 1701 Van Ness Avenue, San Francisco, California, between 8:00 a. m. and 5:00 p. m., Thursday, April 2, 1942, or between 8:00 a. m. and 5:00 p. m., Friday, April 3, 1942, to receive further instructions.

J. L. DeWITT
Lieutenant General, U. S. Army
Commanding

SEE CIVILIAN EXCLUSION ORDER NO. 5

This poster instructing all people of Japanese ancestry living in a particular area of San Francisco, California, to be prepared for evacuation was created by the Western Defense Command and Fourth Army Wartime Civil Control Administration. Following President Roosevelt's issuing of Executive Order 9066 in February 1942, the U.S. government placed some 120,000 Americans of Japanese descent into internment camps for the duration of the war. *(Instructions for all persons of Japanese ancestry from the Western Defense Command and Fourth Army Wartime Civil Control Administrations. April 1, 1942. Unknown Maker. Poster. Collections of the Oakland Museum of California)*

CABINET, COURT, AND CONGRESS

Cabinet Members

Secretary of State
Cordell Hull, 1933–44
Edward R. Stettinius, Jr., 1944–45

Secretary of War
George H. Dern, 1933–36
Harry H. Woodring, 1936–40
Henry L. Stimson, 1940–45

Secretary of the Treasury
William H. Woodin, 1933
Henry Morgenthau, Jr., 1934–45

Postmaster General
James A. Farley, 1933–40
Frank C. Walker, 1940–45

Attorney General
Homer S. Cummings, 1933–39
Frank Murphy, 1939–40
Robert H. Jackson, 1940–41
Francis B. Biddle, 1941–45

Secretary of the Interior
Harold L. Ickes, 1933–45

Secretary of Agriculture
Henry A. Wallace, 1933–40
Claude R. Wickard, 1940–45

Secretary of the Navy
Claude A. Swanson, 1933–39
Charles Edison, 1940
Frank Knox, 1940–44
James V. Forrestal, 1944–45

Secretary of Commerce
Daniel C. Roper, 1933–38
Harry L. Hopkins, 1938–40
Jesse H. Jones, 1940–45
Henry A. Wallace, 1945

Secretary of Labor
Frances Perkins, 1933–45

Supreme Court Appointments

*(Nominated for Chief Justice)

Name	Confirmation Vote	Dates of Service
Hugo Black	63–16, Confirmed	1937–71
Stanley Reed	Voice Vote, Confirmed	1938–57
Felix Frankfurter	Voice Vote, Confirmed	1939–62
William O. Douglas	62–4, Confirmed	1939–75
Frank Murphy	Voice Vote, Confirmed	1940–49
*Harlan Stone	Voice Vote, Confirmed	1941–46
James F. Byrnes	Voice Vote, Confirmed	1941–42
Robert Jackson	Voice Vote, Confirmed	1941–54
Wiley Rutledge	Voice Vote, Confirmed	1943–49

Legislative Leaders

Congress	Speaker of the House	State	Party
73rd Congress (1933–35)	Henry T. Rainey	Illinois	Democrat
74th Congress (1935–36)	Joseph W. Byrns	Tennessee	Democrat
74th Congress (1936–37)	William B. Bankhead	Alabama	Democrat
75th Congress (1937–39)	William B. Bankhead	Alabama	Democrat
76th Congress (1939–40)	William B. Bankhead	Alabama	Democrat
76th Congress (1940–41)	Sam Rayburn	Texas	Democrat
77th Congress (1941–43)	Sam Rayburn	Texas	Democrat
78th Congress (1943–45)	Sam Rayburn	Texas	Democrat
79th Congress (1945)	Sam Rayburn	Texas	Democrat

CABINET, COURT, AND CONGRESS

Congress	House Majority Leader	State	Party
73rd Congress (1933–35)	Joseph W. Byrns	Tennessee	Democrat
74th Congress (1935–37)	William B. Bankhead	Alabama	Democrat
75th Congress (1937–39)	Sam Rayburn	Texas	Democrat
76th Congress (1939–40)	Sam Rayburn	Texas	Democrat
76th Congress (1940–41)	John W. McCormack	Massachusetts	Democrat
77th Congress (1941–43)	John W. McCormack	Massachusetts	Democrat
78th Congress (1943–45)	John W. McCormack	Massachusetts	Democrat
79th Congress (1945)	John W. McCormack	Massachusetts	Democrat

Congress	House Minority Leader	State	Party
73rd Congress (1933–35)	Bertrand H. Snell	New York	Republican
74th Congress (1935–37)	Bertrand H. Snell	New York	Republican
75th Congress (1937–39)	Bertrand H. Snell	New York	Republican
76th Congress (1939–41)	Joseph W. Martin, Jr.	Massachusetts	Republican
77th Congress (1941–43)	Joseph W. Martin, Jr.	Massachusetts	Republican
78th Congress (1943–45)	Joseph W. Martin, Jr.	Massachusetts	Republican
79th Congress (1945)	Joseph W. Martin, Jr.	Massachusetts	Republican

Congress	House Democratic Whip	State	Party
73rd Congress (1933–35)	Arthur H. Greenwood	Indiana	Democrat
74th Congress (1935–37)	Patrick J. Boland	Pennsylvania	Democrat
75th Congress (1937–39)	Patrick J. Boland	Pennsylvania	Democrat
76th Congress (1939–41)	Patrick J. Boland	Pennsylvania	Democrat
77th Congress (1941–42)	Patrick J. Boland	Pennsylvania	Democrat
77th Congress (1942–43)	Robert Ramspeck	Georgia	Democrat
78th Congress (1943–45)	Robert Ramspeck	Georgia	Democrat
79th Congress (1945)	Robert Ramspeck	Georgia	Democrat

Congress	House Republican Whip	State	Party
73rd Congress (1933–35)	Harry L. Englebright	California	Republican
74th Congress (1935–37)	Harry L. Englebright	California	Republican
75th Congress (1937–39)	Harry L. Englebright	California	Republican
76th Congress (1939–41)	Harry L. Englebright	California	Republican
77th Congress (1941–43)	Harry L. Englebright	California	Republican
78th Congress (1943–45)	Leslie C. Arends	Illinois	Republican
79th Congress (1945)	Leslie C. Arends	Illinois	Republican

Congress	Senate Majority Leader	State	Party
73rd Congress (1933–35)	Joseph T. Robinson	Arkansas	Democrat
74th Congress (1935–37)	Joseph T. Robinson	Arkansas	Democrat
75th Congress (1937)	Joseph T. Robinson	Arkansas	Democrat
75th Congress (1937–39)	Alben Barkley	Kentucky	Democrat

(continues)

CABINET, COURT, AND CONGRESS *(continued)*

Congress	Senate Majority Leader	State	Party
76th Congress (1939–41)	Alben Barkley	Kentucky	Democrat
77th Congress (1941–43)	Alben Barkley	Kentucky	Democrat
78th Congress (1943–45)	Alben Barkley	Kentucky	Democrat
79th Congress (1945)	Alben Barkley	Kentucky	Democrat
Congress	**Senate Minority Leader**	**State**	**Party**
73rd Congress (1933–35)	Charles L. McNary	Oregon	Republican
74th Congress (1935–37)	Charles L. McNary	Oregon	Republican
75th Congress (1937–39)	Charles L. McNary	Oregon	Republican
76th Congress (1939–41)	Charles L. McNary	Oregon	Republican
77th Congress (1941–43)	Charles L. McNary	Oregon	Republican
78th Congress (1943–45)	Wallace H. White, Jr.	Maine	Republican
79th Congress (1945)	Wallace H. White, Jr.	Maine	Republican

(continued from page 116)
Congress used the war to justify the dismantling, or at least the scaling back, of New Deal agencies, specifically the Works Progress Administration, the NATIONAL YOUTH ADMINISTRATION, and the Civilian Conservation Corps.

Liberals, including many African Americans, hoped to use the nation's war rhetoric against Nazi racism to end longstanding discrimination in the United States. When union leader A. Philip Randolph, head of the Brotherhood of Sleeping Car Porters, threatened a march on Washington, D.C., in 1941, Roosevelt, fearing the march's impact on war mobilization efforts at home and the image of the United States abroad, signed an executive order to create the FAIR EMPLOYMENT PRACTICES COMMITTEE in 1941.

Other examples of American dissonance between justice and discrimination can be cited. Most notable was internment of Japanese Americans. In response to the bombing of Pearl Harbor, the U.S. government forced approximately 120,000 Japanese Americans living on the mainland of the United States into internment camps. While arguments were put forward about national security and loyalty, both racism and greed for the property and businesses accumulated by the Japanese Americans were the underlying motivators. Just as troubling was the failure of the U.S. government to help Jewish refugees seeking asylum from Hitler's Germany in the late 1930s. The reality of the war in the 1940s, though, made any solution, short of defeating the Nazis, impossible.

Even before the war ended, Roosevelt and Congress turned their attention to government policies for the soldiers who would be veterans once victory was achieved. No one wanted a repeat of the debacles following past wars whereby veterans' pensions were politicized and poorly managed. In 1944, Congress enacted the SERVICEMEN'S READJUSTMENT ACT, more commonly known as the GI Bill of Rights. This law followed on the logic of the New Deal in that it stipulated a powerful federal government interested in protecting the welfare of its citizens. The housing and educational benefits provided under the act constituted another variant of government welfare and they served as forerunners for programs characteristic of postwar liberalism.

With the war approaching its end but still not won in 1944, Roosevelt ran for an unpredicted fourth term as president. In this contest he was most concerned about leadership of the postwar world. He spent little time on the campaign trail, and he defeated his Republican challenger, Thomas E. Dewey of New York, with 53 percent of the vote. The decision to replace Vice President Henry Wallace on the Democratic ticket with Missouri senator HARRY S. TRUMAN was the most significant act of the campaign.

Signs of Roosevelt's declining health were apparent to close observers in the fall election. Further concerns were raised when he attended the conference of the Big Three at Yalta in February 1945. Roosevelt had lived an increasingly isolated life during the war years. He lost his mother, Sara Roosevelt, with whom he had been close, in 1941. His sons were in the military overseas. Eleanor Roosevelt had become even more active with progressive causes during the war years and spent less time with her husband. His personal secretary, Missy LeHand, had a stroke in 1941, and she died in 1944. Daughter Anna Roosevelt, unmarried cousins, and various women provided the president with companionship. More important, Roosevelt resumed his illicit relationship with Lucy Mercer, with whom he had had an affair during World War I. Mercer had since married and been widowed. She was visiting with the president at Warm Springs, Georgia, on April 12, 1945, when Roosevelt, who was suffering from arteriosclerosis, complained of a terrible headache. He collapsed from a stroke and died within hours.

For Americans who came of age during the depression and war years, often referred to as the "Greatest Generation," the only president they had ever known was dead. For more than 12 years Roosevelt had been a larger-than-life figure in U.S. politics. He is commonly credited with saving the country from two of the biggest challenges it has ever faced: the Great Depression and World War II. Ideas about and expectations of the federal government changed significantly during the years Roosevelt was in office. The federal government increased its responsibilities and its power over the lives of average people, and most viewed these changes as good. A nascent welfare state took shape in the 1930s, with the federal government balancing the competing interests of capital and labor in the interest of the people. With the defeat of Germany, Japan, and Italy, the threat of fascism was obliterated in the 1940s, and the postwar years witnessed the expansion of democracy around the globe. Just as important was the shifting of foreign policy onto pragmatic terrain. The notion of collective security continued to dominate for the remainder of the 20th century. In both domestic and foreign affairs, Roosevelt changed the direction of the United States and the federal government, helping to establish the parameters that would mark political debate into the early 21st century.

MAJOR EVENTS AND ISSUES

Agricultural Adjustment Act (1933)   Because he viewed the farm crisis as the key to depression recovery, President Franklin D. Roosevelt wanted the Agricultural Adjustment Act, which was passed on May 12, 1933, to have the backing of all the major farm leaders. The administration courted the conservatives in the agricultural community, trusting that liberal farm groups had no choice but to support the legislation. Provisions of the legislation included price supports for farmers, reduced agricultural production, a processing tax, and measures for currency inflation.

To oversee the law, the act created the Agricultural Adjustment Administration (AAA). In its first year of operation, 10 million acres of cotton were plowed under. The government purchased 8 million pigs and hogs, with 6 million pigs sent to slaughter. The 2 million hogs were processed to feed people on relief, but 90 percent of the salt pork was inedible. These decisions, which helped increase farm income by 10 percent, nonetheless generated much criticism over the destruction of foodstuffs against the backdrop of significant poverty and hunger. In June 1933, Congress also passed leg-

islation providing bankruptcy relief for agrarian landowners. A major problem with the AAA program was the manner in which southern landowners almost universally froze out their tenant farmers and sharecroppers from receiving benefits. Thus, poor whites and blacks in the region received no benefits from this attempt at agricultural reform.

In the 1936 case of *United States v. Butler,* the Supreme Court declared the processing tax unconstitutional because its purpose was regulation and control of agricultural production, a right reserved to the states. Farm prices fell after the decision. Congress then wrote a new Agricultural Adjustment Act of 1938, which provided for storing surplus crops, soil conservation programs, crop loans, crop insurance for wheat farmers, and a program of acreage allotments and subsidies for growers of staple crops. While New Deal farm subsidies and crop reductions helped landowners, the net result was an increase in production, which glutted the market. Only the onset of World War II provided a solution through increased demand for farm products.

Air War in Europe (1942–1943)   The Allied air assault on Germany began in earnest after the CASABLANCA CONFERENCE in January 1943, but it had been a component of the war against Germany the previous year. Proponents of the air war viewed it as a potential second front against Germany and an opportunity to prove the superiority of aerial fighting. The air war disproved the old adage that generals always fight the last war and demonstrated a decided preference to avoid another war of stalemate and attrition, such as had been the case during World War I. It reflected American thinking about how to fight: An air war meant fewer American casualties and little disruption of the American home front, and American technological and industrial superiority could dominate strategic thinking. Within the air force (a division of the army throughout World War II) leaders privileged high-value economic targets over more general civilian targets prior to American entry into the war.

The British, though, had come to realize the impossibility of the former, and by 1942 had shifted toward a strategy of massive nighttime bombing runs against the Germans. Less for moral reasons than out of concern for limited resources and for the impact that civilian bombing would have on U.S. public opinion, the Americans pushed for strategic bombing runs and they saw limited action in France. American flyers had never entered German airspace.

After President Roosevelt and British prime minister Winston Churchill met in Casablanca in 1943, however, the Americans and the British began bombing Germany around the clock, each using its own preferred strategy. General Hap Arnold, who was in charge of this mission, had identified 60 targets that would require 2,700 heavy bombers and 800 medium bombers (the United States possessed less than half that in inventory). Two air raids against the ball-bearing works at Schweinfurt, one against the German oil refineries at Ploesti in Romania, and one against a fighter aircraft plant at Regensburg all failed to produce results. These raids suffered because the long-range bombing runs surpassed the distance fighter escorts could cover, thus leaving the bombers vulnerable.

Alien Registration Act (1940)   Also known as the Smith Act after its sponsor, Representative Howard Worth Smith (D-VA), the Alien Registration Act, which was passed on June 29, 1940, required the 5 million aliens living within the United States to register. The Department of Justice was charged with undertaking this work. Proponents of the law believed that the global unrest resulting from World War II made it necessary, but critics charged that the Smith Act would serve to create discord among citizens and noncitizens. When President Franklin D. Roosevelt signed this measure into law, he declared that it "should be interpreted and administered as a program designed not only for the protection of the country but also for the protection of the loyal aliens who are its guests." Roosevelt contended that the majority of aliens in the United States who were loyal and law-abiding individuals should not be harassed by the enforcement of Smith Act regulations. He also insisted that the states should not try to duplicate the federal effort. He closed with an assertion that disloyal aliens would be dealt with "vigorously" by the federal government. The Smith Act also imposed criminal penalties, including a maximum fine of $10,000 or 10 years of jail time, on those aliens who advocated the violent overthrow of the U.S. government. This portion of the law targeted Communist Party organizers, and it was used in 1949 to secure the convictions of 11 Communist Party leaders in New York.

Antimonopoly Policies   In the earliest days of the New Deal President Roosevelt's advisers were divided between those who advocated pursuit of antitrust measures and those who supported regulatory control measures. The NATIONAL INDUSTRIAL RECOVERY ACT of 1933 was a compromise measure, but because of Supreme Court intervention, it was short-lived. In the second half of the 1930s, Roosevelt and his advisers sought other ways to deal with monopolies. The Temporary National Economic Committee (TNEC) constituted the president's answer in April 1938 to this lingering problem. Roosevelt directed TNEC to launch a joint legislative-executive investigation into the issue. He named Thurman Arnold of the Justice Department's Anti-Trust Division to chair TNEC. In his position at Justice, Arnold had enlarged his staff and intensified antitrust prosecution efforts, not so much to break up all monopolies as to notify the business community of government dominance in directing antitrust actions.

TNEC never satisfied the ambitions of those opposed to trusts. Instead, Roosevelt and his leading New Deal advisers were departing from the Progressive Era vision of antitrust as a central tenet of progressivism and were replacing it with Keynesian economic theory. Even the few examples of antitrust legislation during the 1930s—the Robinson-Patman Act in 1936, which attempted to protect small "mom and pop" stores from the purchasing advantages of chain stores, and the Miller-Tydings Act of 1937, which provided for price stabilization of nationally branded merchandise—stemmed from congressional and not executive origins. Furthermore, while these new laws enhanced the clout to the Federal Trade Commission, they did not halt the trend toward the establishment of large corporations in American business.

Anzio   *See* ITALIAN CAMPAIGN (1943–1945)

***Appalachian Spring,* by Aaron Copland (1944)**   The composer Aaron Copland wanted to create a distinctly American style of classical music and his 1944 ballet, *Appalachian Spring,* was one of his most important works. It resulted from collaboration with dancer and choreographer Martha Graham and won the Pulitzer Prize for music in 1945. Set in the Appalachian Mountains of Pennsylvania and using simple Shaker melodies, the work tells of a bride and groom immediately after their wedding. It reveals the bride's anxiety as it tells of her relationship as a pioneer wife, with her husband, a revivalist preacher. Written during World War II, Copland

Composer Aaron Copland leaning against his piano at his home in Ossining, New York *(Associated Press)*

and Graham used *Appalachian Spring* to warn of the threat that Nazism posed to American democracy.

Assassination of Huey Long (1935)

Huey Long, who was shot on September 8, 1935, and died on September 10, was a popular, if sometimes demagogic, governor of Louisiana (1928–32) and U.S. senator (1932–35). Though he had been elected to the Senate in 1930, he did not assume his new office until after his successor in Louisiana was selected in 1932. He sympathized with the populist political traditions of Winn Parish, where he was born and raised. As governor, he upgraded the state's infrastructure, including overseeing improvements to roads, hospitals, and schools, notably Louisiana State University, while increasing taxes on corporations and well-to-do individuals. As a U.S. senator, he advocated wealth redistribution, and he broke with President Franklin D. Roosevelt, whom he believed to be insufficiently committed to such reforms. A gifted speechmaker, Long presented himself as a savior of the "common people," first in Louisiana and then in the nation.

Because he hungered after power and was ruthless in his methods, however, Long amassed an extensive list of critics. Many called him a demagogue and believed he harbored dictatorial tendencies. Long's program for recovery from the Great Depression, the Share Our Wealth Plan, was conceived more as a means by which to increase his national following than to actually ameliorate the causes of the nation's economic woes. The new taxes on incomes and inheritances as called for in his plan were insufficient to fulfill his promised "homestead" allotment of $5,000 to every family in America along with his promised annual income of $2,500.

Still, many among the public liked what Long had to say because he highlighted the problems of maldistribution of wealth. By 1935, it was obvious that Long either would himself be a candidate for the presidency in 1936 or would support a third-party challenge to Roosevelt. His popularity was such that his entry into the race threatened to weaken the Democrats and make possible the election of a Republican president. Roosevelt heeded the challenge, and the legislative initiatives he proposed to Congress in 1935—for tax reform, Social Security, and increased public works spending—were designed to deflate Long's political sails.

Long was assassinated by Carl Austin Weiss, a New Orleans physician, while lobbying the Louisiana state legislature. The reason for the assassination remains unknown because the senator's bodyguards killed Weiss almost immediately after he shot Long. The assassination of Huey Long ended the movement he was forging to challenge Roosevelt the following year. The ghost of Huey Long, though, haunted Louisiana politics into the 1960s. On the national level, his efforts revealed both the popularity of populist ideas and the fear of too much power held by the federal government.

A potential challenger to Roosevelt in 1936, Louisiana senator Huey Long was shot to death in 1935. *(State of Louisiana)*

Atlantic Charter (1941)

In the summer of 1941, President Franklin D. Roosevelt and British prime minister Winston Churchill held their first meeting as leaders of their respective countries. This secret strategy session took place in August in the North Atlantic aboard ship. Churchill arrived on the HMS *Prince of Wales* and Roosevelt on the U.S. cruiser *Augusta*. The specific site was in Placentia Bay just offshore from an obsolete mining camp in Argentia, Newfoundland, Canada.

The two men had clear but not necessarily mutually agreeable goals for the meeting. Britain had been fighting Germany for almost two years, but the United States had not yet formally entered World War II. Churchill sought a U.S. declaration of war on Germany. He remarked that he would rather have a war declaration than twice the volume of supplies that Americans were currently providing Britain. Roosevelt, on the other hand, sought to negotiate terms for postwar diplomacy. The president worried that the alliance by the British with the Russians against the Germans would prove harmful to democracy. As such, he reached agreement with Churchill on a document that became the Atlantic Charter.

The two world leaders signed this accord on August 14. The Atlantic Charter stipulated that national self-determination, free trade, nonaggression, and freedom of the seas would be the principles on which the postwar peace settlements would be based. The Atlantic Charter also contained rather vague language about continuing the wartime alliance of nations after the war for the purpose of preserving the peace. Roosevelt and Churchill also promised aid to Soviet premier Joseph Stalin, and they indicated that diplomatic negotiations among the three should begin soon.

Bankhead-Jones Farm Tenancy Act (1937)   *See* FARM SECURITY ADMINISTRATION

Banking Act (1933)   Also known as the Glass-Steagall Act, after its sponsors Senator Carter Glass (D-VA) and Representative Henry Steagall (D-AL), the Banking Act of 1933 differed from the EMERGENCY BANKING RELIEF ACT of 1933 in that it attempted to put in place reforms of the American banking system. It was passed by Congress on June 16. Changes to the Federal Reserve System included the use of government securities instead of gold to support Federal Reserve bank notes, Federal Reserve authority over open market operations, and Federal Reserve examinations of bank holding companies. Based on the findings of the Pecora Committee's investigation of Wall Street irregularities, this legislation called for the separation of commercial and investment banking. Over President Franklin D. Roosevelt's objections, Senator Arthur Vandenberg (R-MI) and Representative Henry Steagall (D-AL) drafted an amendment creating the Federal Deposit Insurance Corporation. They hoped to protect middle-class bank customers, the currency in circulation, and small banks. As a result of this provision fewer banks failed in the remaining years of the 1930s than at any point in the 1920s.

Banking Act (1935)   The genesis of the Banking Act of 1935 came from President Roosevelt's newly appointed Federal Reserve Board (Fed) chairman Marriner Eccles, who wanted significant reform of his agency. He called for White House control of the Fed, reduced authority for private bankers, and increased power of the Fed over monetary policy. While the House of Representatives passed the legislation without making any substantive changes, Senator Carter Glass (D-VA) vehemently opposed the centralization of banking.

Because Roosevelt had not endorsed Eccles's recommendations, the Fed chairman was the only administration figure lobbying for the bill. Others in the administration, most notably RECONSTRUCTION FINANCE CORPORATION chairman Jesse Jones, worked against the bill. By June 1935, Roosevelt had come out in favor of the bill, but its passage had more to do with Eccles's lobbying and Glass's rewriting of the bill.

As passed on August 23, the Banking Act of 1935 still provided for centralization of the Federal Reserve Board's operations in Washington, D.C. The president gained power to appoint members of the Fed's seven Board of Governors for 14-year terms. The Board of Governors controlled the regional banks in the Federal Reserve System. The legislation also required that state banks join the Federal Reserve System. This legislation further modernized banking in the United States.

Barden-LaFollette Act (1943)   Cosponsored by Representative Graham Barden (D-NC) and Senator Robert M. LaFollette, Jr. (R-WI), the Barden-LaFollette Act, which was passed on July 6, 1943, provided for the rehabilitation of physically handicapped Americans and was alternatively known as the Vocational Rehabilitation Amendments. It sought to address weaknesses in the extant law—the Vocational Rehabilitation Act of 1920 and the SOCIAL SECURITY ACT of 1935. The World War II manpower shortage provided additional impetus for action on behalf of disabled Americans, as lawmakers believed that the disabled might be able to play a greater role in national defense. Proponents contended that it was wise public policy to rehabilitate the disabled so that they could gain wider opportunities for employment and thus become taxpayers. The legislation also provided for psychiatric care for the mentally handicapped and the cognitively disabled. Those with visual impairments, war-disabled civilians, and government employees injured while at work benefited from special provisions under the law. The U.S. Veterans Administration provided similar services to veterans. The law removed existing ceilings on expenditures for vocational rehabilitation.

Bataan Death March (1942)   Following the surrender of U.S. troops to invading Japanese forces at Corregidor on Manila Bay, Philippines, on May 6, 1942, one of the most cruel episodes of the war in the Pacific ensued. The Bataan Death March of 1942 highlighted the horrific brutality in what was a dehumanizing war in all theaters. It constituted the means chosen by Japanese commanders of dealing with too many prisoners and too few resources to manage them. The early end to hostilities at the BATTLE OF CORREGIDOR left the Japanese with a logistical problem. They had planned on taking approximately 40,000 prisoners, but the numbers far exceeded this estimate; that spring they found themselves burdened with 70,000 Americans and Filipinos. The captives included 10,000 Americans, many of whom suffered from malnutrition and physical injuries incurred during the hostilities. The Bataan Death March also exemplified a cultural clash in that the Japanese viewed their charges with contempt simply because they had surrendered.

The march began on April 10, and it took a little over a week for the prisoners to reach Camp O'Donnell at San Fernando, Pampanga. During the 80-mile forced march along the Bataan Peninsula prisoners were denied water, and they were beaten and stabbed for failing to keep pace. The death toll was high; approximately 600 Americans and 10,000 Filipinos perished on the march. Those who did not perish were sent to a prisoner of war camp, Cabanatuan, where many more died. Over the course of the war, 9,000 U.S. POWs

Prisoners, hands tied behind their backs, on the Bataan Death March, 1942 *(National Archives)*

were lodged there. Others were sent via so-called Hell Ships to slave labor camps in Asia. News of the march leaked out a year afterward only because three Americans escaped and managed to get to Australia.

Battle of the Atlantic (1940–1943) American participation in the Battle of the Atlantic predated the 1941 Japanese attack on Pearl Harbor and official U.S. entry into World War II by almost two years. The Battle of the Atlantic belied the possibility of American isolation in the face of the worldwide fascist threat to democracy. It commenced early in 1940 when the United States stepped up its efforts to supply the British with the weapons and supplies they needed to fight the Germans and the Italians. At its core, the Battle of the Atlantic was fought to gain control of the ocean shipping lanes between the United States and Great Britain. Passage of the LEND-LEASE ACT in early 1941 bolstered the British military and led the Germans to intensify their attacks on Allied shipping. Nazi leader Adolf Hitler authorized German U-boats to operate east as far as the east coast of Greenland.

The burgeoning size of the German submarine fleet allowed for a dangerous new strategy, the "wolf-pack attack," by which multiple U-boats attacked shipping convoys, drew off the escort vessels, and pilloried the merchant ships. U.S. law prohibited a response to these attacks. Public opinion in the United States was divided between isolationists and interventionists and about aid to Britain. Ultimately, President Roosevelt adopted a policy of patrolling, not escorting, the convoys. He also extended the eastern coastal security zone to include the western third of Hitler's Atlantic combat zone. Patrols meant that U.S. ships would provide only

reconnoitering services for the British; they would not shoot at German ships.

On April 10, 1941, Roosevelt announced that the United States would take possession of Greenland to prevent a German occupation of the Danish colony (Denmark had fallen to the Nazis). This action brought Greenland under the protection of the Monroe Doctrine, which disallowed invasion by European powers. By June, Roosevelt had taken charge of Iceland in a similar fashion, declaring it also to be within the North American Protection zone. These geographic allowances were necessary to allow the president to station troops at these outposts (the Selective Service Act prohibited the military from serving outside the Western Hemisphere). Isolationists criticized these actions as nudging the nation toward war.

In the fall of 1941, Franklin Delano Roosevelt used the incident involving the USS *Greer* as an excuse to do what he had planned to do: send armed escorts with shoot-on-sight orders to protect American merchant ships. The *Greer* had been on a mail delivery run to Iceland when it spotted a U-boat. It tracked the German ship and reported its movements to the British air force. When the British shot at the German submarine, the U-boat mistakenly attributed the assault to the *Greer* and launched an attack. The *Greer* returned fire. None of these attacks was successful.

After the United States formally entered the war in December 1941, General DWIGHT D. EISENHOWER termed protection of the shipping lanes as the highest U.S. goal in the European theater of operations. Hitler knew this, and after his declaration of war against the United States he removed all restrictions on his submarine forces, the most sophisticated of which could reach the U.S. shoreline. Within three months, Germany had sunk 216 ships between Newfoundland and Bermuda, costing the Allies 1.25 million tons of shipping capacity. The glow of the coastal city lights emanated 10 miles out to sea and lit up the targets for the German U-boats. One U-boat sank eight ships in 12 hours. American coastal cities, including New York, Atlantic City, and Miami, nonetheless remained lighted for the benefit of tourists. German efforts to use the U-boats to land saboteurs on American soil were less successful, but because U.S. naval resources were divided between the Pacific and the Atlantic Oceans the Germans still held the upper hand. Furthermore, U.S. antisubmarine forces were antiquated, many of them dating to World War I.

By the summer of 1942, the interlocking convoy system protected coastal shipping lanes from Brazil to Newfoundland. The convoys consisted of 10 columns of 60 merchant ships each, protected by about 12 warships. The merchant ships were American and the warships were British or Canadian. Allied loss rates plummeted, and Germany withdrew the U-boats from North American waters. The action on the eastern sea frontier slowed American mobilization and hampered American shipping, but it did not prove disastrous beyond the point of recovery to the Allied cause.

The Battle of the Atlantic shifted in 1942 to the middle of the ocean. The German command hoped to sink 700,000 tons a month, which they believed would be enough to win the war. The convoys were most vulnerable when they were out of range of air cover, and that is where the U-boats concentrated their attacks. Most of the attacks occurred in the Norwegian Sea en route to Murmansk and Archangel in the Soviet Union and in mid-ocean southeast of Greenland, through which all convoys passed. By early 1943, the Allies were in jeopardy of losing the war to Germany, so heavy were the shipping losses.

The CASABLANCA CONFERENCE opened in early 1943 with news of a successful German attack against a convoy of oil tankers that were en route from Trinidad to supply troops in North Africa. As such, Roosevelt and Churchill were even more determined to win the Battle of the Atlantic. Two developments helped make this possible. British code breakers successfully broke the previously indecipherable German code machine Enigma, which was used to send messages about locations of the convoys in helping to direct the U-boat attacks. More important, the production of U.S. escort vessels increased, which led to the destruction of greater numbers of U-boats. All meaningful U-boat action on the North Atlantic ceased in late May 1943, the Allies having proved victorious after three years of intense fighting.

Battle of the Bulge (1944–1945)   *See* D-DAY AND THE BATTLE FOR NORTHWEST EUROPE

Battle of the Coral Sea (1942)   The Battle of the Coral Sea in World War II stemmed from Japan's strategy to occupy all territory between Burma (now Myanmar) and the Dutch East Indies and to establish an oceanic defensive perimeter against the United States and its use of Australia as a staging area. U.S. intelligence learned of Japanese plans to take Port Moresby on the island of New Guinea. The consequence was the Battle of the Coral Sea, which took place between May 3 and May 8, 1942, across hundreds of miles of ocean in the Coral Sea between New Guinea and Australia. This was the first naval battle in which both sides relied exclusively on carrier-based aircraft. The naval action that resulted was indirect; the U.S. and Japanese warships did not fire on each other at close range. Japanese airplanes mistakenly tried to land on a U.S. carrier, and they reported incorrectly as having sunk two U.S. carriers, the *Yorktown* and the *Saratoga* (the U.S. Navy did lose the *Lexington;* the ship was scuttled because of the strikes it received in the battle).

At the end of the five-day battle, Japan withdrew its forces poised to land at Port Moresby, and forswore occupying that outpost. For this reason, some have considered the Battle of the Coral Sea as a victory for the United States. In other ways, the Coral Sea was a setback, especially when the loss of the *Lexington* is calculated against the overall weakness of the U.S. carrier fleet in comparison with Japanese naval strength. Furthermore, the Japanese were able to land their forces at Tulagi, an island in the Solomon Islands a few miles removed from Guadalcanal.

Battle of Corregidor (1941–1942)   The Battle of Corregidor occurred in the Philippines on the main island of Luzon. General Douglas MacArthur, who had been stationed in Manila when Pearl Harbor was attacked on December 7, 1941, did not launch an invasion force from the Philippines to attack Japanese positions on Taiwan (Formosa). As a result, when the Japanese attacked Manila 10 hours later (across the international date line) on December 8, MacArthur lost all the B-17 bombers under his command and hundreds of other aircraft. It was on the strength of that arsenal that he had bragged he could defend the Philippines on the beaches. By late December, MacArthur decided that a retreat to the fortress of Corregidor Island was in order.

The speed with which this maneuver occurred left many of the troops woefully undersupplied and thousands stranded on the Bataan Peninsula. President Roosevelt, who had been frustrated by MacArthur's failure to attack after Pearl Harbor, ordered the general to evacuate to Australia. When MacArthur left the Philippines, famously declaring, "I shall return," General Jonathan Wainwright gained the island command. However, his mission was doomed given constant Japanese aerial and artillery bombardment ongoing since early April. Still, he fought steadily until May 6, 1942, when he finally surrendered. The number of U.S. and Filipino casualties in the Battle of Corregidor is estimated at 16,000. General DWIGHT D. EISENHOWER noted in his diary that Wainwright "did the fighting," but he was much more sarcastic in his assessment of MacArthur, who he noted received "such glory as the public could find. . . . [H]e's a hero! Yah."

Battle of Guadalcanal (1942–1943)   The Battle of Guadalcanal in the Solomon Islands occurred because the United States and the Japanese reversed strategies following the BATTLE OF MIDWAY. The United States went on the offensive in the aftermath of that victory in the Pacific, and Japan increasingly took a defensive posture. The Japanese had landed on Guadalcanal immediately after their defeat at Midway with the intention of building an airstrip. The United States was unwilling to cede that territory without a fight because a Japanese presence in the Solomons could prove a menace to American shipping lanes to Australia.

The army and the navy disagreed about strategy. This divided command shaped the events at Guadalcanal, which constituted an exercise in improvisation and inadequate funding. (The simultaneous NORTH AFRICAN CAMPAIGN received a higher priority in the distribution of American resources.) The First Marine Division consisted largely of men who had enlisted after Pearl Harbor and it was not scheduled for action until 1943, nonetheless it was sent to Guadalcanal with insufficient provisions and ammunition in early August 1942. On August 7, the marines quickly took control of the Japanese airstrip, renaming it Henderson Field after an American killed at Midway.

The battle against the main encampment of Japanese on nearby Tulagi that same day made it clear to Americans that they were battling a determined foe unwilling to ever surrender. This skirmish reflected a statistical trend that defined the nearly four years of fighting against Japan: a 10 to one death ratio of Japanese to Americans. The landing of American marines at Guadalcanal was compromised by an unwise strategic decision. Admiral Frank Jack Fletcher was unwilling to leave the three aircraft carriers under his command off the coast of Guadalcanal for more than three days even though the marines insisted it would take at least five days to complete the landing. He was concerned that losses to the carrier group would be dangerous to the overall U.S. efforts in the Pacific, but his caution can also be read as cowardliness.

Next came the fighting for Savo Island on August 8 and 9, 1942. This encounter proved to be the worst U.S. naval defeat ever on the high seas, and American casualties numbered 2,000. What the Japanese did not do was to prevent the marine landing of troops and supplies, leaving the Battle of Savo Island a victory without consequence. Given the lack of air cover, the U.S. forces decided to abort the remainder of the landing on August 9, and the 17,000 marines already on Tulagi and Guadalcanal were left to fend for themselves in what became a six-month siege that lasted until early February 1943.

Six major naval battles and three significant land battles followed in this pivotal standoff. Unlike in the remainder of the Pacific war, U.S. forces were undersupplied and were defending rather than attacking an island position. Even with these disadvantages, Japan underestimated American will and American strength. The biggest problem for the Americans at this point was the strategic indecision about Guadalcanal: Was this battle simply about protecting shipping to Australia, or was it about positioning U.S. forces for an attack on the Japanese in Rabaul to the north, a much more complicated undertaking? When the Japanese finally evacuated in January and February 1943, the American military had experienced a clash replete with barbarism on both sides. The fighting at Guadalcanal had been vicious and bloody, but the few journalists who reported from the frontlines conveyed a fabled story of American heroism that ignored the brutality of U.S. forces toward the Japanese.

Battle of Iwo Jima (1945)   U.S. bombing missions to Japan with the new B-29 Superfortresses started flying in November 1944 from the Marianas. The island of Iwo Jima, located halfway between Saipan and Tokyo, gained immense strategic importance to both sides. The United States wanted

The Iwo Jima Memorial in Arlington, Virginia, dedicated to the U.S. Marines *(Michael G. Smith/Shutterstock)*

control of the island to make the raids on Japan easier (an airfield and radio station on Iwo Jima made the U.S. flight plan less challenging), and Japan wanted Iwo Jima for the advantage it held in defending the home islands. The U.S. Marines who attempted to take the island faced not only a well-entrenched foe who was well armed but also a difficult terrain that included a muddy combination of quicksand and volcanic ash along the beaches.

Americans had the advantage of Navaho "code-talkers," specially trained soldiers who, for example, used their native language, unknown to all but a few non-Navaho people, as an open code to report to their American commanders the taking of Mount Suribachi in a bloody battle on February 22, 1945. When several marines raised the U.S. flag on Suribachi—with the battle still raging—a photograph was taken. That scene, later reenacted for the media, has become one of the most famous of World War II, but the success at Suribachi did not end the Battle of Iwo Jima.

The fighting did not cease until one month later, when the casualties were high on both sides: 20,000 Japanese and 6,000 Americans died. Of the Japanese who perished, many were burned alive by flamethrowers who targeted their bunkers. Success at Iwo Jima required, according to U.S. Admiral Chester Nimitz, the "uncommon valor" that was "a common virtue" on the island.

Battle of the Java Sea (1942)   The World War II Battle of the Java Sea, which began on February 27, followed a Japanese invasion of the Dutch East Indies in late February 1942. Japan coveted the region's oil resources to fuel its military ambitions in the Pacific. The United States fought in conjunction with the British, the Dutch, and the Australians, but their efforts were woefully inadequate. American losses were the most severe since Pearl Harbor, and the defeat rendered the Allied coalition ineffective against Japan in that part of the Pacific. The United States lost three cruisers and several destroyers. An Allied retreat occurred on March 12. Many of the Indonesian people welcomed the Japanese as liberators who would free them from Dutch colonial rule.

Battle of Leyte Gulf (1944)   In September 1944, an American pilot conducting air strikes against the Philippines was shot down over the island of Leyte. His discovery that Leyte was void of Japanese forces hastened the U.S. invasion of the Philippines. American convoys carrying none other than General Douglas MacArthur landed on Leyte on October 20, 1944. MacArthur, forced to leave the Philippines in the 1942 after the BATTLE OF CORREGIDOR, declared, "People of the Philippines, I have returned." He asked that they "rally to me." The battle that resulted, lasting three days, was the biggest in naval history. The fighting ranged over 100,000 square miles of ocean and involved almost 300 ships and 200,000 personnel. Near the end of this battle, the Japanese unleashed a new weapon that testified to both the extent of their desperation and the strength of their will to continue fighting: suicide attacks from kamikaze pilots. Despite heavy Japanese losses at Leyte Gulf—four carriers, three battleships, nine cruisers, 12 destroyers, several hundred airplanes, and thousands of lives—the Americans did not secure the island until December and the Philippines until late March 1945. The latter came after the Battle of Manila, a struggle that took place in the streets similar to the actions in Berlin and Warsaw. The battle claimed more than 100,000 Filipino casualties.

Battle of Midway (1942)   A significant conflict within the Japanese military about whether to continue with the successful southern Pacific Ocean strategy or to build on the victory at Pearl Harbor with an attack on Midway Island, located 1,100 miles west of Hawaii, precipitated the Battle of Midway. Success at Midway, the Japanese believed, would either bring leverage against the United States for a negotiated settlement or would force a major sea battle between the two nations, which the Japanese believed they would win. Furthermore, the Japanese believed that success at Midway would provide them with a defensive perimeter throughout the Pacific Ocean, would jeopardize the U.S. positions in the Philippines and Guam, and would even threaten Hawaii and Australia.

U.S. strategy for a war against the Japanese, developed early in the 20th century, followed a similar premise. The problem in 1942 was lack of sufficient resources. To counter this problem, the U.S. Navy undertook a series of air raids against both outlying islands in Japan's possession and the main island of Japan. The latter, known as the Doolittle Raids in being named for the leader of the operations, Lieutenant Colonel James H. Doolittle, made little military impact on Japan but were psychologically decisive. Doolittle commanded 16 B-25 bombers from the USS *Hornet*, which had managed to approach within 650 miles of Tokyo. While the planes were not built for use with an aircraft carrier, they nonetheless were used to bomb Tokyo and other Japanese cities on April 18, 1942. Because these raids pushed the planes beyond their limit, the pilots were forced to crash land in China. Of the captured pilots, one died in prison and three were executed following highly publicized trials. The Japanese government, though, never acknowledged the attacks.

The most significant result of the Doolittle Raids was the proof they offered of the Japanese island's exposure to attack from Midway. This realization pushed the Japanese military to pursue the U.S. position at Midway. As Japanese naval officers planned their attack on Midway, American cryptologists worked on a project called "Magic" to decode secret Japanese messages. Their efforts helped to ensure American success at Midway and to eliminate the possibility of another Japanese surprise attack such as the one at Pearl Harbor.

Knowing the Japanese planned to attack, Admiral Chester Nimitz, the U.S. commander of the Pacific Fleet, used this information to set a trap for the Japanese at Midway. When the battle unfolded on the morning of June 4, 1942, U.S. forces were prepared: Japan lost four of its six aircraft carriers while the United States lost only one carrier. Five minutes of American dive-bombing against the Japanese fleet gave the United States naval superiority in the Pacific and turned the tide in the war against Japan.

Midway proved what had been tested at the BATTLE OF THE CORAL SEA, namely, the advent of the aircraft carrier meant that naval battles would never again be fought with ships facing off in sight of one another. The efficacy of naval air power was unmatched. Finally, Midway meant that the war between the United States and Japan would not end quickly. In a long war, the United States enjoyed a significant advantage in production over the much smaller Japanese economy. By 1944, the United States had built 17 new fleet carriers to just six for Japan. In the same two-year time period, the Americans also constructed 10 medium-sized carriers and another 86 escort carriers.

Battle of Okinawa (1945)   Located just 350 miles south of Japan's home islands, Okinawa was an important prize for the United States in its efforts to win World War II. Possession of it would vastly improve the success of an amphibious invasion of Japan, projected for the fall of 1945. It would also make air strikes against Japan much easier. Japanese defenders at Okinawa had an impossible task—slow down the advancing Americans, who everyone believed would prevail, long enough to permit increased fortifications on the home islands of Japan. Japanese strategists hoped the fighting would be so brutal that the Americans would seek a compromise peace instead of unconditional surrender.

The Battle of Okinawa lasted from April 1 through June 22, 1945. After meeting relatively little resistance on landing, U.S. forces faced stiff resistance when they reached the 250-foot-high cliffs. At the same time, U.S. forces offshore suffered countless kamikaze raids. Upon President Franklin D. Roosevelt's death on April 12, Japanese troops celebrated, but their glee was short-lived. The U.S. troops used napalm to burn the Japanese who were using caves as garrisons. To avoid such a horrific death and to escape being taken prisoners, many Japanese forces committed suicide. Only 7,000 of the 77,000 Japanese forces on Okinawa were alive when the fighting ended. American casualties were less severe, 7,613 killed or missing and more than 30,000 wounded out of more than 182,000 making the assault. The death rates at Okinawa and earlier at Iwo Jima foretold for American military strategists what U.S. forces could expect in an invasion of the home islands.

On June 18, President HARRY S. TRUMAN met with his military advisers to discuss plans for an attack on Japan in the fall. Accounts of the meeting vary as to the estimates of American casualties that were projected in carrying out Olympic, the code name for the planned attack. Sources dispute whether General George C. Marshall predicted 31,000 or more than 63,000 U.S. deaths. Ambassador William D. Leahy guessed as high as 268,000. Assistant Secretary of War John J. McCloy cautioned that the president should consider either amending the call for an unconditional surrender or warning the Japanese about the as yet untested atomic bomb. Truman approved Olympic, but he ended the meeting with hopes that some other way could be found to end the war with Japan. The dropping of two atomic bombs in August led Japan to surrender. The Battle of Okinawa was the last major battle of World War II.

Battle of the Philippine Sea (1944) The Battle of the Philippine Sea was fought in mid-June 1944. The battle ensued when U.S. rear admiral Raymond A. Spruance deviated from the protective role his forces had played in the Battle of Saipan, a bloody conflict for control of the strategically important Mariana Islands that resulted in an American victory and made possible effective U.S. air strikes against Japan. Spruance had learned that the Japanese navy was headed for the Marianas, and he believed that he could stop the enemy in a naval battle on the open waters of the Philippine Sea. The resultant aerial battle pitted the experienced and well-equipped Americans against Japanese pilots with little training. U.S. forces shot down over 300 planes and lost only 30. Three Japanese carriers

were sunk. Dubbed the "Great Marianas Turkey Shoot," this conflict was the most decisive carrier battle in the war. It left the Japanese unable to continue naval air operations, but it was not the decisive naval battle that both sides sought. Because Spruance had kept one eye on Saipan he had not been able to destroy as many Japanese ships as American military planners had hoped. However, the BATTLE OF LEYTE GULF, just a few weeks later, provided that opportunity.

Berlin Olympics (1936) The 1936 Summer Olympics in Berlin gave German dictator Adolf Hitler an opportunity to hide from the world the reality of his racist, anti-Semitic, militaristic, and expansionistic Nazi ideology. They offered an opportunity for Germany to win world approval of its regime, newly installed three years before. Debates in the United States and elsewhere in the West took place about whether to boycott the games. The United States came closer to boycotting the games than did any other nation, with Judge Jeremiah Mahoney of the Amateur Athletic Union contending that official German policies of racial and religious discrimination made Germany unfit for hosting the games. But Avery Brundage, the president of the American Olympic Committee, argued that the Olympic movement should be free of the influence of politics and so the games went on as scheduled. President Franklin D. Roosevelt stayed out of the debate, even though foreign policy experts cautioned that the Berlin Olympics would become a propaganda tool for Hitler.

Some national newspapers supported a boycott, but the *Chicago Defender*, a leading African-American newspaper, noted that black athletes, including track standout Jesse Owens, supported attendance at the Berlin games. Owens and others believed that their participation in the games would expose Nazism's intellectual bankruptcy. The black community in the United States found the views of boycott activists to be hypocritical given their failure to attack similar forms of racism in the United States. A total of 18 black athletes competed on the U.S. team in the 1936 summer games, up from six in the 1932 Los Angeles Olympics.

Athletes from 49 nations participated in the Berlin games. Germany had the largest team and the United States had the second largest team. The track-and-field events, dominated by black athletes from the United States, challenged Hitler's theories of Aryan supremacy. Jesse Owens won four gold medals in the 100-meter dash, 200-meter dash, long jump, and 4 × 100 meter relay. His 100-meter sprint performance tied the world record, and he set, or helped to set, world records in his other events. Other African Americans to medal at the games included John Woodruff, who earned a gold medal in the 800-meter race; high jumpers Cornelius Johnson, David Albritton, and Delos Thurber, who swept the medals in that event; Matthew "Mack" Robinson, the older brother of future baseball star Jackie Robinson, who won the silver medal in the 200-meter dash; Archie Williams, who

Jesse Owens during the 200-meter race at the 1936 Olympics in Berlin, where he won four gold medals *(Library of Congress)*

won the 400 meters; James LuValle, who won the 400-meter bronze medal; Ralph Metcalfe, who earned gold in the 4 × 100 meter relay and silver in the 100-meter dash; Frederick Pollard, Jr., who earned a bronze in the 100-meter hurdles; and Jack Wilson, who won a silver medal in bantamweight boxing. These 14 medals won by black athletes represented 25 percent of the U.S. total medal count of 56. Despite orders from Nazi leaders to eliminate racist language from the German press, Nazi journalists were disdainful of the African-American victories.

The other significant story of race at the Berlin games involved the treatment of Jewish athletes. Germany banned all Jews from its team except for Helene Mayer, a fencer who was half-Jewish. When she won a silver medal for individual foil, she gave the Nazi salute on the podium as did other German winners. When it came to the running of the 4 × 100 meter relay, the U.S. coach replaced two Jewish Americans, Marty Glickman and Sam Stoller, with African-Americans Jesse Owens and Ralph Metcalfe, who were the fastest U.S. sprinters. The logic for the change was never made clear, with some hypothesizing that the move was strategic given the greater speed of Owens and Metcalfe, and others suggesting that it was made to placate anti-Semitism. According to this

view, Avery Brundage wanted to avoid embarrassing Hitler with a victory by Jewish American athletes. Stoller discounted this assertion, but he was nonetheless humiliated by the move. Despite Owens's exceptional performance, Germany surpassed the United States and all other nations in the medal count, and it gained international goodwill, which Hitler drew upon as he proceeded on his quest for world conquest.

Bituminous Coal Act (1937)   *See* GUFFEY-SNYDER ACT (1935)

Board of Economic Warfare   President Franklin D. Roosevelt established the Board of Economic Warfare on July 30, 1941, to oversee foreign trade, war production, and the domestic economy. Vice President HENRY A. WALLACE was placed in charge of the agency. The Board of Economic Warfare was subdivided into three smaller agencies: the Office of Exports, the Office of Imports, and the Office of Economic Warfare Analysis. A presidential reshuffling of wartime administrative responsibilities led to increased power for the Board of Economic Warfare in the spring of 1942. Wallace was given a place in Roosevelt's "war cabinet" along with the army, the navy, and the WAR PRODUCTION BOARD. The concern then was that Jesse H. Jones, the secretary of commerce, was too slow in stockpiling resources. As a result, the Board of Economic Warfare gained power over importing rubber and copper, blocking Axis powers from foreign markets, determining industrial targets for Allied bombing campaigns, and engaging in trade and aid with Allied nations.

Unlike the Axis Powers, whose officials drew no divisions between diplomacy and economics, Wallace struggled to balance the competing priorities within the U.S. government and society. His endeavors won for him the hostility of Secretary of State Cordell Hull, who viewed this new power for the Board of Economic Warfare as an intrusion into the diplomatic sphere, the purview of his department. The following year, Jones feuded with Wallace over the purchasing of strategic raw materials, and the Board of Economic Warfare fell into disfavor within the administration. The president eliminated it with an executive order on July 15, 1943. The responsibilities of the Board of Economic Warfare were transferred to the Office of Economic Warfare, which was a division of the Office for Emergency Management.

Bonneville Dam   In the 1932 presidential campaign, Franklin D. Roosevelt promised to bring hydroelectric power to the Pacific Northwest. Residents there were as interested in public power development as were the supporters of the TENNESSEE VALLEY AUTHORITY (TVA) in the South. With the advent of electrical household appliances during the 1920s and 1930s, much debate occurred about the corruption and exorbitant pricing for electricity derived from private, for-

Built along the Columbia River by the U.S. government, Bonneville Dam provided electrical power to the Pacific Northwest. Above, workers pose on a turbine before its installation in the dam. *(Library of Congress)*

profit companies. Reformers argued that electrical power should be a public resource available to consumers at cost.

Construction of the dam in Bonneville, Washington, raised numerous issues. Democrats advocated a TVA-style program for the entire region. They provoked bureaucratic squabbles, with the Army Corps of Engineers and the Bureau of Reclamation competing for control of the power project. While the enacting legislation, which President Roosevelt signed on August 20, 1937, was modeled after that of the TVA, the project ultimately resulted in nothing more than a vehicle for publicly generated electrical power. The revolutionary features that addressed social, class, and economic relationships in the region were eliminated. Secretary of the Interior Harold Ickes had been a leading opponent of the more expansive goals. The onset of World War II further reduced the dam's mission when the WAR PRODUCTION BOARD directed all public and private power projects to be united in a single grid.

Bonneville marked the Roosevelt administration's final effort at delivering power through a public system. His desire to create a national public power system was never realized. Roosevelt himself opted not to back Senator George Norris's legislative proposal for a national system of regional power authorities. He also never articulated a clear strategy for achieving energy reform, leaving its fate to be debated among lawmakers and various administrative entities. The results of the Bonneville debate reflect the diversity of views in the Roosevelt administration. For example, Roosevelt oversaw various strategies for achieving public power, and he insisted on local control to ensure that this reform remained in place beyond his tenure in office. The dam's significance, then, lies in its role in conjunction with other such projects, which together established the precedent for public power if not for its perfect implementation.

Bracero Program   The demands of raising an army combined with the need to increase the civilian workforce, especially in defense production, created a significant manpower shortage as early as 1942. To help relieve this shortage, the United States created the *bracero* program, which provided for the temporary migration of Mexican workers into the United States. The idea for this program came from a similar endeavor during World War I. Because Mexican workers had been treated poorly in Texas during that war, the Texas Proviso initially blocked implementation of the program in Texas. Ultimately, however, El Paso, Texas, became a very important recruitment destination for the migrant workers because demand for agricultural workers was high in the state. *Bracero* workers performed a host of jobs: railroad work in the Southwest, potato harvesting in Idaho, migrant agricultural labor in California, and apple and wheat harvesting in Washington. Under the *bracero* program, more than 200,000 Mexicans came to work in the United States during the war years

and approximately 4.5 million came over the course of the program, which lasted until 1964. The rise of illegal immigration along with the increasing mechanization of agriculture brought an end to the *bracero* program. The program played an important role in the southwestern agricultural boom, and it also facilitated a circular migration pattern wherein Mexicans came to the United States, returned to Mexico, and came back to the United States in search of work.

Brain Trust   During his first campaign for the presidency in 1932, Franklin D. Roosevelt brought together a collection of university professors to serve as his advisers. Dubbed the "Brain Trust," this group included scholars from Columbia University and Barnard College. Samuel Rosenman, FDR's attorney, helped recruit these individuals. Raymond Moley, a professor of public law and a longtime urban reformer, was a key figure in the Brain Trust. Economics professor Rexford Guy Tugwell advised the president on agricultural policy and economic planning while Adolph A. Berle, a law professor, addressed finance questions and corporate concerns. Others on whom FDR relied came from business and political circles. Bernard Baruch, a Wall Street financier who had served in the U.S. government during World War I, touted his own expertise on government financial policy. Democratic senators James Byrnes of South Carolina and Key Pittman of Nevada also proved to be important informal advisers to the president.

Functioning as a think tank of sorts, Brain Trust members presented ideas to the president who then determined their utility. FDR encouraged consensus among his Brain Trust, and he wanted their conclusions to reflect the complexity of the various issues before the country. In the months leading up to the 1932 Democratic National Convention, the Brain Trust argued economic policy with Roosevelt. The Brain Trusters all believed in maintaining a cooperative relationship between business and government but they disagreed as to whether business or government should be granted the favored position. Some argued that large business interests should predominate, while others favored broad national planning to address the economic problems engendered by the Great Depression. While the group officially broke apart after the election, Roosevelt continued to rely on individual members of the group. Never, though, did the president allow himself to be trapped by any particular ideological perspective as advanced by the Brain Trust. For example, when Moley presented FDR with two competing tariff policies, Roosevelt instructed him to craft a policy that merged the two conflicting proposals.

Bretton Woods Agreement (1944)   The Bretton Woods Agreement was signed on July 22, 1944, following meetings held during the first three weeks of July. It accomplished the same purpose for international trade as the United Nations did for international relations. The United States was crucial to the success of both. The Bretton Woods Agreement aimed to promote global trade and stabilize national currencies, which nations had heretofore freely manipulated to help control imports and exports. Currency was no longer to be a free medium of exchange. These strident, remedial measures were necessary to prevent a postwar, international economic crisis.

Chief architects of the plan were economist John Maynard Keynes of Great Britain and Harry Dexter White of the U.S. Treasury Department. Bretton Woods did not prove sufficient to restore worldwide free trade, but it helped to create conditions that predisposed nations to favor free enterprise and tariff reduction. Specifically, Bretton Woods mandated creation of the International Monetary Fund and the World Bank. Participating nations contributed to both institutions according to a proportional formula of national economic power. Similar proportionality was used to determine governance of the new institutions. The United States contributed more than twice the amount of any other nation.

The International Monetary Fund was intended to correct short-term trade inequities. It also was tasked with pegging national currencies against one another and against the U.S. dollar to establish par values. International trade was to be determined from these values. National currency valuations could fluctuate no more than 10 percent without approval from the International Monetary Fund.

The World Bank, planned as an international RECONSTRUCTION FINANCE CORPORATION, was responsible for assuaging long-term trade imbalances. It guaranteed private foreign loans intended to strengthen the economy of creditor nations. Direct loans from the bank were used to supplement the U.S. Export-Import Bank.

Significant support from the American business community deflated the neo-isolationist critics of Bretton Woods. The stable and adjustable exchange rates created under Bretton Woods remained in effect for 25 years, until this system collapsed in 1971. A system of floating exchange rates took its place. The Bretton Woods system was significant because participation in it required surrender of national sovereignty over exchange rates. It also eliminated the need for nations with balance of payments deficits to deflate their domestic economies. The adjustable peg meant that even though currencies were convertible into gold, there was no fixed gold exchange standard.

Burke-Wadsworth Selective Service Training Act (1940)

Also known as the Selective Service Act, the Burke-Wadsworth Selective Service Training Act of 1940 constituted a bipartisan effort to expand the nation's military force on the eve of World War II. It was signed into law on September 16. The legislation provided for the first peacetime draft in American history. The troops raised under this measure would serve for one year and would not be deployed outside the Western Hemisphere. The measure did not satisfy the top military generals, who wanted comprehensive mobilization. President Franklin D. Roosevelt was not a strong supporter of the measure initially because he feared that it would wreak havoc on the Democratic Party in the fall elections, but when Republican presidential candidate Wendell Willkie refused to attack the bill, it passed easily in mid-September 1940. Sixteen million men aged 21 to 35 registered for the draft in the month that followed, and approximately 900,000 were mustered into service. Once the military was expanded and geopolitical conditions deteriorated in the North Atlantic, Roosevelt stretched the definition of the Western Hemisphere in authorizing the stationing of troops in Iceland. In the summer of 1941, Congress debated, and narrowly passed, an amendment extending the draft for 18 months. Had the measure failed (it carried by only one vote in the House) virtually no army would have been in existence when Pearl Harbor was attacked later that year.

Cairo Conference (1943)

President Roosevelt had wanted the TEHERAN CONFERENCE, his first meeting with Soviet premier Joseph Stalin, to be limited to the two statesmen, but British prime minister Winston Churchill felt miffed at being left out. Not only did Churchill insist on attending the Teheran Conference in Iran, but he also convinced Roosevelt to meet with him in Egypt at Cairo on the way to Teheran. Roosevelt was annoyed with both demands, so he invited to Cairo both Stalin and Jiang Jieshi (Chiang Kaishek), the leader of China. Stalin declined to attend this preliminary meeting out of concern for provoking the Japanese, with whom the Soviet Union was not at war. Nonetheless, Roosevelt used the Chinese leader's attendance at Cairo to avoid Churchill. The president also kept the focus of the Cairo meetings on the Asian war, where there was considerable disagreement between the Americans and the British. Churchill viewed winning the war in Asia as essential in retaining the British Empire, but Roosevelt understood the rising importance of the decolonization movement. Furthermore, Roosevelt wanted China to become an important regional, if not global, power. He believed the Chinese could counter a resurgent Japan and an expansionist Soviet Union in postwar Asia. The late November 1943 meetings at Cairo resulted in American promises to increase Lend-Lease aid to the Chinese, to provide additional military assistance and step up attacks in the CHINA-BURMA-INDIA THEATER, and to create the inter-Allied Southeast Asia Command.

Casablanca Conference (1943)

The Soviet victory at the Battle of Stalingrad provided the background for the conference between President Franklin D. Roosevelt and British prime minister Winston Churchill. Their meeting in Casablanca, Morocco, in January 1943 was the first time that Roosevelt had ever traveled outside the Americas while president. George C. Marshall, the chief of staff of the army, had advised the president previous to his departure to push for an attack across the English Channel instead of concentrating Anglo-American operations against Germany in the Mediterranean, which he believed to be an area peripheral to the war. Continued fighting in the Mediterranean brought the possibility of incurring major shipping losses whereas an invasion across the English Channel threatened to produce large numbers of human casualties. Marshall contended that the troops were expendable while shipping was not.

At this meeting, Churchill dominated Roosevelt, who was not yet strong enough to control strategy sessions between the two. Churchill brought with him a larger retinue of staff. When the conference concluded, Churchill

For two days in early January 1943, President Franklin D. Roosevelt, Prime Minister Winston Churchill, and top advisers met in Casablanca, Morocco, to strategize their next moves during World War II. Here, Roosevelt and Third Army general George Patton award the Congressional Medal of Honor to Brigadier General William H. Wilbur. General George C. Marshall presides as well. *(Library of Congress)*

and Roosevelt issued a joint communiqué reflecting the aims sought by the British. The two leaders agreed to continue waging war against the German U-boats in the North Atlantic, to complete the Lend-Lease shipments to the Soviet Union, to instigate a 24-hour bombing campaign against Germany, to intensify actions in the Pacific theater, and to remain in the Mediterranean once the NORTH AFRICAN CAMPAIGN was completed. Both Marshall and the Soviets were displeased with these decisions, which comported perfectly with Churchill's wishes.

The final and perhaps most significant result of the Casablanca Conference was Roosevelt's statement to the press that an "unconditional surrender" would be demanded of Germany, Italy, and Japan. This statement, not part of the official agreement, reflected not American strength but American weakness. Because the United States could not convince the British to adhere to its strategy recommendations and because the United States could not yet impose its will on postwar peace planning, Roosevelt used the language of unconditional surrender to demonstrate a nonexistent military might that did not have to be tested immediately but could be forestalled until the end of the war. In the years that followed, however, the idea of unconditional surrender gained widespread support.

China-Burma-India Theater (1942–1945)   The China-Burma-India theater, typically referred to as the CBI theater, was never a major area of fighting during World War II. Action in it reflected the differing American and British views of what the war in Asia was really about. For British prime minister Winston Churchill and the British people, the Asian war was about retaining the colonies. On the other hand, the Americans advocated decolonization and the development of China as a counterweight to both future Japanese and Soviet aggression in the region.

From a military perspective the primary goals in the CBI theater were to acquire Chinese air bases that could be used to attack Japan and to ensure that supply routes to China remained open. By March 1942, the Japanese had chased the British army out of Burma and had closed down the Burma Road, the last available land route for the resupply of China. U.S. lieutenant general Joseph W. Stilwell was sent to China in early 1942. Stilwell turned his attention to recapturing Burma and the construction of another road from India through Burma to China, the Ledo Road. Until its completion, the only way to get supplies into China was by means of flights from India over a section of the Himalayan Mountains, a route known as "the Hump." Stilwell's forces were unsuccessful in their Burmese mission in no small part because the Chinese troops fighting under his command disobeyed his orders in favor of directions from China's leader Jiang Jieshi (Chiang Kai-shek), who wanted to avoid as much as possible fighting the Japanese so as to stockpile his resources in a

resumption of the civil war against China's communist leader Mao Zedong.

Stilwell groused that stepped-up efforts undertaken by the Allied Southeast Asian Campaign (SEAC), agreed to in late 1943, would tax his scant resources. The CBI was given the lowest priority by the Americans. To Stilwell's men, SEAC meant "Save England's Asiatic Colonies" and CBI meant "Confused Bastards in India." Chinese developments in 1944 did not change these impressions; instead, less attention was given to the CBI theater following Japan's capture of the Chinese air bases and U.S. capture of bases in the Marianas. When World War II ended in 1945, China was already mired in a civil war and its forces played no major role in the defeat of Japan.

Civil Aeronautics Act (1938)   The Civil Aeronautics Act of 1938 was part of the new regulatory edifice created during Roosevelt's presidency. It was signed into law on June 23, and it established the Civil Aeronautics Authority, a new regulatory agency that gained oversight responsibility for federal civil aviation, which had previously been vested with the Department of Commerce. New responsibilities included airfare regulation and authority to determine which routes airlines would serve. Two years later Roosevelt divided the agency into the Civil Aeronautics Administration and the Civil Aeronautics Board. The former controlled air traffic, certified machinery and personnel, enforced safety regulations, and aided airport development. The latter wrote safety regulations, investigated accidents, and provided economic regulation of the industry. The Department of Commerce oversaw both organizations, with the Civil Aeronautics Board enjoying more independence. Prior to the 1938 legislation, the only statutory regulations for the airline industry were found in the various airmail acts. Because there was no oversight agency the industry suffered from price wars and injurious competition while flying routes that were not permanent. The 1938 legislation was significant because it provided a strong and effective regulatory structure for an emerging industry that would prove crucial to American transportation and commerce.

Civil Works Administration   Because the FEDERAL EMERGENCY RELIEF ADMINISTRATION (FERA) had not done enough to ameliorate poverty and suffering by the fall of 1933, the Roosevelt Administration created the Civil Works Administration (CWA) on November 8, 1933, to help prevent starvation in the coming winter months. The goal of the Civil Works Administration was to hire the unemployed to improve the nation's infrastructure. Unlike the FERA, the CWA was entirely a federal operation, with 50 percent of the employees coming from the relief rolls. Numbering more than 4 million, those workers earned a minimum wage, not a stipend, for their jobs, many of which CWA director Harry Hopkins had invented solely for the purpose of this program. CWA projects centered on building and restoring the country's infrastructure; workers constructed or repaired over 500,000 miles of roads, 40,000 schools, 3,500 playgrounds, and 1,000 airports. Additionally, 50,000 CWA teachers worked in rural schools and with urban adult education. Altogether this program generated an additional billion dollars of spending power for the nation's economy. Because it was an expensive program for the federal government, the president eliminated it in the spring of 1934. He did not want the beneficiaries to become permanently dependent on the federal government for employment. Unfinished projects fell to the FERA for completion, which paid less than half of CWA wages.

Civilian Conservation Corps (1933–1942)   Created by Congress in eight days and enacted on April 5, 1933, the Civilian Conservation Corps (CCC) employed young people in reforestation, flood control, and beautification work. Over its lifetime more than 3 million young men participated in this program. Living away from home in military-style barracks, CCC workers earned $30 a month, $25 of which was sent home to their families. Under the program 4 million acres of forests were thinned, a billion fish were stocked in American waterways, battlefields from the American Revolution and Civil War were refurbished, 30,000 wildlife shelters were constructed, and countless ditches and canals were dug. Among its fire protection work, the CCC built lookout towers and firebreaks to help beat back wildfires in the national forests. Numerous improvements were made to the national park system, including campground, trail, and museum construction. The CCC's most important work, though, was in planting trees in areas that had previously been burned out, eroded, or otherwise destroyed. The labor movement initially criticized the program as overly regimented and as tak-

The Civilian Conservation Corps (CCC) was founded in 1933 as part of the first wave of President Roosevelt's New Deal programs. Its primary objectives were twofold: to provide employment and on-the-job training for millions of young men, and conserve and improve the nation's environment. Here CCC director James J. McEntee looks on, while enrollees James Crotts of Salem, Virginia, and Fred Steele of Christiansburg, Virginia, receive direction from instructor L. W. Overstreet for assembling a crank shaft and connecting rods at a repair shop. *(Library of Congress)*

ing jobs away from union workers. Quickly, though, the CCC became the most popular of the New Deal programs. After nine years in existence, the CCC was terminated in 1942 when labor demands stemming from World War II made unemployment relief unnecessary.

Communications Act (1934) The Communications Act of 1934 created the Federal Communications Commission and provided regulatory structures for all wired and wireless communications industries, including radio, telephones, telegraph, and later television. The law contained the "fairness doctrine," requiring broadcasters to air information important to the public interest and to provide equal time for opposing political candidates. The legislation received little criticism and passed Congress without difficulty. Legislative amendments in 1967 dealt with the creation of public television and in 1984 and again in 1992 with the emergence of cable television.

Coral Sea *See* BATTLE OF THE CORAL SEA (1942)

Corregidor *See* BATTLE OF CORREGIDOR (1941–1942)

"Court-packing" *See* SUPREME COURT REORGANIZATION PLAN (1937)

D-Day and the Battle for Northwest Europe (1944–1945)
On D-Day, June 6, 1944, approximately 160,000 Allied forces began crossing the English Channel to liberate France and push the Germans eastward in opening a second front in northwest Europe. But even before a single landing craft hit the beaches at Normandy, General DWIGHT D. EISENHOWER, the supreme allied commander, faced a major challenge from the weather in preparing for the D-Day landing. For the invasion to work, Eisenhower needed a nighttime sky with at least a half moon shining for the troops to be able to see the landing zones and a low tide to negotiate the German defensive perimeter. He had a window of opportunity between June 5 and June 7, 1944, and would have no other chance until June 19, too late to satisfy the Soviets who were skeptical that Great Britain and the United States would ever open a second front. Bad weather aborted the June 5 choice, but when Eisenhower learned there would be a break in the weather the following day, he gave the order to go. The Germans under the command of General Erwin Rommel believed the weather would force a longer Allied delay and so were not prepared.

The British attacked from the east and the Americans from the west. The airborne assault of paratroopers was nothing if not chaotic, but this confusion aided the Allied cause because it proved even more confusing to the Germans. Breaks in the German command structure and belief that this was a decoy maneuver for a larger invasion at Pas de Calais to the east further limited the German response to D-Day. The air war on D-Day tilted heavily in favor of the

Allies, who flew 15,000 sorties that day against only 319 for the Germans. Furthermore, Allied warships fired mercilessly at the German positions from just offshore. When British and Canadian forces landed at Sword, Juno, and Gold beaches (all code names), they did not meet heavy resistance. U.S. forces landing at Utah beach faced but scant resistance while those landing at Omaha beach faced an unrelenting assault from German gunnery posts in the cliffs above. The infantrymen who were coming ashore had already fought a battle with seasickness and fear as they made their way across the channel. The Allied death toll of 2,000 at Omaha nearly forced an abandonment of that beach, but the constant influx of new troops pushed those who were not killed forward to the interior. Total Allied losses during the operation amounted to approximately 10,000 killed or missing in action.

Determined to avoid the mistakes of Anzio in the ITALIAN CAMPAIGN—when U.S. forces tried to control the beachhead rather than pushing inland, a mistake that trapped them there for four months of bloody fighting—commanders of the D-Day mission forced the fighting to the interior of France as quickly as possible. However, this proved difficult. British forces under the command of General Bernard Montgomery were unable to take Caen on June 6, fighting instead for that strategic location throughout the month of June. The terrain in northern France provided additional hazards for the Allied forces. Centuries earlier Norman farmers had constructed elaborate hedgerows, or earthen barriers dividing fields. These hedgerows were often five feet high and 10 feet wide, and they slowed the advance of the troops. The Germans also enjoyed more sophisticated heavy weaponry, especially tanks. Montgomery's victory at Caen on July 10, though, paved the way for the American advance at St. Lo. Behind a massive air attack, U.S. forces broke through the German defensive perimeter and reached the southwestern border of Normandy in just five days. The Third Army under the command of General George S. Patton moved quickly through Brittany toward the Loire River.

The Allies faced setbacks, though, in that they were unable to take the seaports along either the channel or the Atlantic coast. This failure had less bearing on the battle for northwest Europe than it did on events later in the war. Even though there was little chance of German victory in France, few were willing to challenge Hitler, who was unwilling to cede the territory. The remaining Allied forces scored an important victory at Falaise in August, securing the remainder of Normandy.

The swelling number of Allied forces in France—20 U.S. divisions, 12 British divisions, three Canadian divisions, one French division, and one Polish division—contrasted with significant German losses: more than 225,000 dead or wounded and an equally high number taken prisoner. Many of the remaining Germans escaped along the Seine River. The liberation of Paris followed on August 25. The speed of the advance when juxtaposed against the memory of trench

An LCVP (Landing Craft, Vehicle, Personnel) from the U.S. Coast Guard–manned USS *Samuel Chase* disembarks troops of the U.S. Army's First Division on the morning on June 6, 1944, D-Day, at Omaha Beach, in Normandy, France. *(Chief Photographer's Mate Robert F. Sargent, U.S. Coast Guard)*

warfare in World War I brought jubilation to Allied commanders, some of whom even predicted victory over the Germans before the end of the year.

This tremendous success following the initial difficulties at D-Day meant that the Allies had reached the German border approximately eight months ahead of schedule. Equally important, both Montgomery and Patton were eager to move eastward into Germany to the Ruhr and the Saar regions, respectively. Eisenhower took care to handle this situation with delicacy, knowing that no one nation could be in the position of claiming credit for the defeat of the Germans. Given the proximity to Antwerp, Belgium, and the ease of resupply along with the importance of the Ruhr, Eisenhower ultimately approved Montgomery's request to move forward. The operation was code-named Market-Garden and it resulted in a failure.

In response, the Germans tried to retake Antwerp by launching a last stand on the western front that culminated in the Battle of the Bulge in the Ardennes Forest of Belgium. Even though Hitler had initially attacked France through the Ardennes, Eisenhower gambled that the terrain was too densely forested to mount either an attack or a counterattack. As such, he concentrated Allied troop strength north and south of that location. The German offensive that began on the morning of December 16 took the Allies by surprise—10,000 troops surrendered almost immediately. However, at Bastogne, Belgium, a critical U.S. garrison, the American commander replied "Nuts!" when asked to surrender. Eisenhower was initially unsure of the German objective, but given its strategic location, the supreme commander knew that Antwerp was the only logical goal. Eisenhower directed Patton's forces to pivot northward from their eastern position and defend Bastogne. By the middle of January 1945, Hitler had withdrawn most of his forces from what by how had become a losing effort. Though casualty estimates vary, sources agree that the Battle of the Bulge was very deadly.

Approximately 81,000 Americans were killed, wounded, captured, or missing in action. The U.S. deaths were between 6,700 (Eisenhower's estimate at the time) and 1,900 (the U.S. Army historian's estimate after the fact).

These victories enabled the Allies to launch an overwhelming air assault against Germany. Bombing campaigns in the battle in northwest Europe halted more than 30 percent of German tank and aircraft production. A terror bombing campaign against Berlin and other cities, notably Dresden, on February 13–15, 1945, brought much criticism for the high civilian casualties: 25,000 in the first instance and 35,000 in the second. Dresden was even more problematic because the bombs ignited a firestorm in which the victims burned and suffocated. Meanwhile, Eisenhower and his forces fought their way into Germany, reaching the Elbe River by April 11. They stopped at the river because that was the line that had been agreed would mark the division between what would become the Western and the Soviet zones of occupation. The Soviet Union ultimately triumphed in bloody street fighting in Berlin. V-E Day followed on May 8, 1945.

Detroit Race Riot (1943)   The automobile industry had made Detroit a natural hub for defense production during World War II. One result was a massive influx of black and white migrants—many from the South—seeking greater economic opportunity. Labor recruiters helped encourage the migrations. Since 1940, 50,000 blacks and 200,000 whites had moved to the area, putting a strain on housing and social services. Blacks faced racial discrimination practically everywhere. Only one public housing complex was open to them, and most African Americans ended up living in structures without indoor plumbing and at rents two and three times higher than what whites paid. Numerous incidents of racial violence occurred on the factory floor, typically with whites refusing to work alongside blacks. The Ku Klux Klan, a terrorist hate group, was prominent in the white working-class community.

Blacks in Detroit grew restive in the face of this prejudice and violence, and a "bumping" campaign ensued in which African Americans would purposefully bump into whites when passing on the street. Tensions rose in the city in the early months of 1943, and on Sunday, June 20, some African-American teenagers, unhappy that they had been dismissed from Eastwood Park the previous week, gathered at the Belle Isle municipal park. White teenagers challenged them and the two groups fought. Conditions deteriorated quickly, and rumors circulated in both the black and the white communities. According to one account, a white mob had thrown a black woman and her baby off the Belle Isle bridge. A crowd of 500 blacks began rioting in response. In a working-class community populated by white southern migrants, a rumor circulated that African Americans had

During the deadly Detroit race riot of 1943, a white mob overturns a car owned by a black man. *(© Bettmann/CORBIS)*

raped and murdered a white woman on the Belle Isle bridge, prompting the formation of another mob. Violence erupted with street fighting.

Before the situation was brought under control six Detroit police officers were shot and another 75 were injured. The riot lasted for 36 hours, and 34 people were killed, including 25 blacks and 9 whites. Another 1,800, mostly African Americans, were arrested for looting or other crimes related to the riot. Civil rights leaders sharply criticized the Detroit police for punishing the crimes of black rioters and ignoring the crimes of white rioters. The riot proved so violent that CBS radio aired an open letter on race hatred and the dangers that it posed for a country at war against totalitarianism.

Doolittle Raids   *See* Battle of Midway (1942)

Dumbarton Oaks Conference (1944)   In the fall of 1944, representatives from the United States, China, Great Britain, and the Soviet Union met at Dumbarton Oaks, a private mansion in Washington, D.C., to begin deliberations concerning the creation of a postwar international peacekeeping agency. The four nations involved in these talks submitted their proposals for a world organization to all the Allied nations of World War II. The proposal called for the creation of a United Nations with four divisions: a General Assembly of all member nations; a Security Council of 11 members, including five permanent members (the United States, the Soviet Union, Great Britain, China, and France) and six rotating members selected by the General Assembly for two-year terms; an International Court of Justice; and a secretariat. Included in the General Assembly would be an Economic and Social Council charged with adjudicating human rights issues. The Security Council was charged with preventing future wars, while the General Assembly was to foster international cooperation, deliberate peace and security issues, and oversee disarmament. The General Assembly was blocked from arbitrating matters before the Security Council. Another institutional element of the United Nations was a provision requesting members to contribute armed forces for preventing war and suppressing aggression. The Dumbarton Oaks Conference did not address the issue of how the Security Council would vote (those discussions ensued at the Yalta Conference the following February). Dumbarton Oaks became the working document for the San Francisco Conference, held in the spring of 1945, and the charter for what became the United Nations. The Dumbarton Oaks proposals sought to avoid future war by putting in place an international organization that would keep the peace.

Dust Bowl   The early and mid-1930s witnessed the advent of the "Dust Bowl," a significant ecological and human disaster in the southern Great Plains affecting 97 million acres of land. A combination of mechanized farming, especially plowing, and a multiyear drought caused much of the topsoil in the panhandles of Oklahoma and Texas along with regions of New Mexico, Colorado, Kansas, and Nebraska to be blown away. Constant plowing to plant more acreage decimated what was a very thin layer of topsoil.

A drought that began in 1930 and lasted until the middle of the decade meant that in much of the region no discernable moisture could be detected for at least a depth of three feet. A mass of blowing dust resulted that carried away with it any remaining nutrient rich soil. The dust clouds were actually 8,000 feet waves of destruction that rendered the region uninhabitable. This disaster cannot be blamed solely on natural forces, however. Human greed also played a key role, as the inhabitants, in an effort to cultivate additional acreage, engaged in unwise farming tactics.

More than 300,000 refugees, nicknamed "Okies," left Oklahoma and the other affected states across the Midwest. Most of the Okies headed west and resettled in California. By 1933, conditions were so bad that farmers who elected to remain behind asked the federal government for help. The issue was handled by the Forest Service, which devised the Shelterbelt Project. The plan called for planting a swath of trees 100 miles wide from Bismarck, North Dakota, to Amarillo, Texas, to control the winds and end or at least lessen the dust storms. In 1935, the western boundary of the Shelterbelt Project was moved eastward and ran between Devil's Lake, North Dakota, and Mangum, Oklahoma, to take advantage of higher annual precipitation rates. The project was discontinued in 1942 after having planted 18,600 miles of shelterbelts. A majority of the trees that were planted survived.

Other federal government remedies included soil conservation demonstration projects, which taught farmers about terracing, contour plowing, and farming drought-resistant crops. The Resettlement Administration, and its successor agency the Farm Security Administration, purchased the lands most eroded by the storms and reseeded the areas with native grasses. After 1960, several of these projects were designated as national grasslands. Monies extended by the Agricultural Adjustment Administration to farmers for not planting certain crops such as cotton and wheat saved many from bankruptcy (the storms would have prevented cultivation with or without the New Deal program in effect). Additionally, the poorest farmers who were not able to receive conventional financing from a bank obtained loans from the Resettlement Administration, which they used to purchase seeds and supplies. This intervention was not enough to save all the affected farmers, especially when property values dropped by as much as 90 percent because of the drought and the storms. By the early 1940s, weather conditions returned to normal and the area began to recover from the disasters of the 1930s.

Farm equipment and machinery lie buried in Dallas, South Dakota, during the Dust Bowl, an agricultural, ecological, and economic disaster that struck the Great Plains region in the 1930s. *(United States Department of Agriculture)*

Economy Act (1933)   During the 1932 presidential campaign, Franklin D. Roosevelt had called for a balanced federal budget. He made enactment of this promise one of his priorities in his new administration. President Roosevelt wanted to reduce veterans benefits by $400 million and the federal payroll by $100 million, two of the larger drains on the budget. Director of the Budget Lewis Douglas encouraged Roosevelt to adopt the Economy Act of 1933 out of concern that the administration of HERBERT HOOVER had spent money too easily. Its introduction brought vociferous protests from Democrats in Congress. Liberals contended that the bill was written for the benefit of bankers and to the detriment of federal workers and the indigent. Were it not for the depression, these arguments would likely have held sway. President Roosevelt, though, commanded much authority and lawmakers ultimately ceded to his wishes. One conservative Democrat told his fellow House members that they should think carefully about whether or not they wanted to be recorded in opposition to the president. When the vote was taken, over 90 Democrats broke with the president in the House, but the Economy Act passed without great difficulty on March 20, giving the administration a victory in its efforts to adhere to fiscal orthodoxy.

***Edwards v. California* (1941)**   Because California became a popular destination for impoverished Americans fleeing the depressed economies of states affected by the DUST BOWL, that state passed legislation popularly referred to as the "Okie law" making it a misdemeanor to help the indigent enter the state. When a California man named Edwards traveled to Texas in December 1939 and brought his impoverished brother-in-law home with him on January 5, 1940, he was charged with violation of this statute and given a six-month suspended jail sentence. In 1941, the Supreme Court ruled in *Edwards v. California* that the California statute violated the Constitution's commerce clause in excluding indigents from entering the state.

Emergency Banking Relief Act (1933)   During the transition period between the election of 1932 and the inauguration of Franklin D. Roosevelt as president of the United States in March 1933, the nation's banks underwent a serious crisis. The decision to keep the U.S. dollar on the gold standard worsened the situation because the worldwide trend was to abandon gold as a means of currency support. Investors were hoarding gold in anticipation of price increases once the gold standard was eliminated. Meanwhile, shaky banks that held worthless securities could no longer pay depositors. As long as the gold standard remained in effect, a bank's gold reserves could not be used and depositors could not be paid. This situation precipitated a run on the banks with depositors lining up to close out their accounts before the banks closed their doors for good.

The early 1933 bank runs forced many teetering banks over the edge into insolvency. To address the problem at the state level many governors declared bank "holidays," closing the banks until they could prove their liquidity. No comparable federal action, though, could occur unless the outgoing and the incoming presidents could reach an agreement to cooperate. While President HERBERT HOOVER made overtures to President-elect Roosevelt, neither man was willing to meet the conditions of the other. Not until after Roosevelt's inauguration and passage of the Emergency Banking Relief Act on March 9, 1933, was action taken.

This legislation provided for the closure of all banks under a program dubbed the bank holiday. Banks would not be permitted to reopen until their books had been examined and their soundness authenticated. Other banks were to be reorganized. Additional provisions of the legislation included presidential control of gold movements, penalties for hoarding gold, and the issuance of Federal Reserve bank notes. Lawmakers were surprised at the overall conservative tone of the legislation, expecting a much more radical proposal from the new president.

Private bankers and Hoover administration Treasury Department officials had drafted this legislation. It passed Congress in record time. House members never even received a printed copy of the bill but nonetheless passed it unanimously. Only seven senators dissented. This legislation saved the nation from a haphazard system of dependence on company scrip and foreign currencies and from even more bank failures.

Executive Reorganization   In 1937, at the same time that he was lobbying for his SUPREME COURT REORGANIZATION PLAN, President Roosevelt asked Congress to consider legislation overhauling the executive branch of the federal government. The proliferation of executive branch agencies early in the New Deal made some effort at achieving order imperative. Roosevelt's proposals had as their origin the advice from independent experts who counseled the importance of modernizing the federal bureaucracy in accord with the latest principles of organizational management. In addition to modernizing and centralizing the work of the executive, the legislative proposal gave the president more budgetary power as well as additional oversight over personnel and administration. The measure also contained mechanisms for greater national economic planning and resource management.

Critics charged that the proposals would turn the presidency into a dictatorship and would render the other two branches of the government powerless. Congress refused to act on this measure until 1939, when it passed a much weaker bill than the president had advocated. Roosevelt did what he could to improve the functioning of his office even though he was dissatisfied with the legislative offering. He issued an executive order creating the Executive Office of the President, giving a bureaucratic structure to the White House and to the various executive agencies operating independently of any overarching structure. A significant component of this decision was the placement of all defense agencies under the aegis of the Executive Office of the President, an important precedent given the wartime proliferation of such entities.

Fair Employment Practices Committee   As the nation moved onto a war footing in 1940, the issue of segregation became a significant problem in terms of both military expansion and civilian wartime production. Military leaders made it known that the new troops mustered into service would be organized into segregated units. Furthermore, defense contractors stated explicitly that they did not intend to hire African-American workers.

A. Philip Randolph, the leader of the Brotherhood of Sleeping Car Porters, became outraged when President Roosevelt refused to address this problem. He began discussions with other African-American leaders to consider holding a march on Washington of 100,000 blacks demanding equality in the workplace and the military. This provocative proposal met with indifference in much of the black community as other civil rights activists feared a backlash.

Roosevelt opposed the march and asked that his wife, ELEANOR ROOSEVELT, and those among his advisers who enjoyed good relations with the African-American community try to forestall the protest. When these entreaties failed, Roosevelt met with Randolph at the White House on June 18, 1941, just two weeks before the scheduled march. The president began by inquiring when Randolph had graduated from Harvard, the president's alma mater. Randolph tersely replied he had not attended Harvard. When Roosevelt asked Randolph what he wanted, the union leader replied that he sought an executive order desegregating defense industry employment. Roosevelt refused to issue the order as long as the march was scheduled, and Randolph refused to call off the march unless an order was issued.

Fiorello LaGuardia, the mayor of New York City, also attended the meeting, and he convinced both Roosevelt and Randolph to compromise. They agreed to draft Executive Order 8802, which read, "There shall be no discrimination in the employment of workers in defense industries or government because of race, creed, color, or national origin." This order, issued on June 25, 1941, also provided for the creation of a Fair Employment Practices Committee to adjudicate complaints. The order did not address military segregation, which continued throughout World War II. Nor was the order alone sufficient to address defense plant segregation. In 1943, the president increased the budget for the Fair

Employment Practices Committee to $500,000 and shifted the agency from part-time to full-time management.

Still the agency remained unpopular in Congress with many southerners and conservatives attacking it at every opportunity. As a result of the Fair Employment Practices Committee, African-American employment rates in the defense industry grew from 3 percent to 8 percent. The number of blacks working for the federal government tripled, but government and defense jobs often tended to be menial ones. When the war ended, efforts to abolish the agency intensified. The agency was eliminated in 1946, but congressional supporters tried unsuccessfully for the remainder of the decade to restore and make permanent the Fair Employment Practices Committee.

Fair Labor Standards Act (1938)   First proposed by President Roosevelt in May 1937, the wages and hours legislation that became the Fair Labor Standards Act was the last of the New Deal style reforms enacted in the 1930s. The aim of the bill was to create a minimum wage and a standard workweek for laborers nationwide. It was one of the most acrimoniously fought bills in Congress. Business interests did not like the concept because of its impact on operating budgets and southerners opposed it because it would mean the end of a wage differential that helped attract industry to the low-wage South. Additionally, conservatives believed the momentum was with them since they had successfully deflected the president's court reform legislation (popularly known as the court-packing bill).

Nonetheless, labor humanitarians and liberal activists saw the bill through the Senate, which approved it 56 to 28 on July 31, 1937. The bill faced an entirely different fate in the House. Conservative Democrats teamed up with Republicans to block the bill from reaching the floor for debate. Arcane parliamentary measures were required to bring the bill to the floor. One of the main reasons that the bill took so long to become law was the complex cast of external proponents and opponents—conservatives versus liberals, northern versus southern industrialists, intralabor movement squabbles, and southern conservatives versus southern liberals. The House approved the measure 314 to 97 on May 24, 1938, and President Roosevelt signed it into law on June 25.

The Fair Labor Standards Act constituted little more than a symbolic victory at the time, because so many categories of workers were exempted from it, but it nonetheless had a long-term, far-reaching impact for society; it provided for a forty-cent minimum wage and a forty-hour workweek by 1940. The law also contained a provision banning child labor in interstate commerce. In addition to the problem of numerous exemptions, the law failed to address the regional wage differential. One lawmaker quipped that someone should be appointed to study whether anyone was subject to the law. Other members of Congress worked to exempt the prominent industries in their districts. In the 1941 case of *United States v. Darby*, the Supreme Court unanimously upheld this legislation.

Farm Security Administration (1937–1946)   Created by the Bankhead-Jones Farm Tenancy Act, which was enacted on July 22, 1937, the Farm Security Administration (FSA) assumed the responsibilities of the defunct RESETTLEMENT ADMINISTRATION. Its primary mission was threefold: the FSA made rehabilitation loans to farmers, loaned money to tenant farmers so they could buy their own farms, and operated migrant labor camps. Other FSA projects included helping cooperatives buy grain elevators and providing health care services for farmers. Of the various New Deal relief programs for agriculture, this agency was the only one that specifically targeted tenant farmers and sharecroppers. The billion dollars it spent included a large number of loans that would be repaid. In fact, the FSA bragged of its high loan repayment rate. This measure of success, though, does not mean the FSA solved the problem of rural tenancy. Instead, the majority of FSA clients were effectively disfranchised as a result of their economic privation. As such, Congress never adequately funded the agency, and the FSA never achieved its promise. By 1943, Congress had so significantly scaled back its appropriations that the FSA never again played an active role in public life. It was officially disbanded in 1946.

Federal Deposit Insurance Corporation   *See* BANKING ACT (1933)

Federal Emergency Relief Administration   Created on May 12, 1933, the Federal Emergency Relief Administration (FERA) aimed to provide funds to the poor and unemployed. It was meant as a temporary relief program to ease the hardship stemming from the Great Depression. In its first several months, FERA distributed $500 million to the needy through state and local agencies. President Roosevelt named Harry Hopkins, a social worker from Iowa who had directed the New York State relief efforts during Roosevelt's tenure as governor, to run the agency. He eventually became the most powerful official working for the president. In his first two hours as FERA director, Hopkins commandeered a desk in the hall of the RECONSTRUCTION FINANCE CORPORATION building and dispersed $5 million in relief.

When the FERA did not make enough progress in securing economic relief, a new agency, the CIVIL WORKS ADMINISTRATION (CWA), was created in the fall of 1933 to address the problem of poverty during the coming winter months. Roosevelt abolished the CWA in the following spring, and the FERA resumed relief responsibility, picking up the projects the CWA had not completed. The majority of FERA work projects involved public infrastructure construction, but Hopkins also tried to find appropriate work for unemployed white-collar workers. Those on FERA work relief projects earned just $6.50 a week while those on the CWA, during its lifetime, had earned $15.04 a week. Nonetheless, the FERA became a target for New Deal critics, who complained of "boondoggles." The white-collar relief projects attracted the most criticism, and they proved politically dangerous to the future of the FERA. The agency was already under fire in 1934 for its parsimonious pay scale in comparison to the moribund CWA and for the degrading process required of individuals to prove financial need.

The need for relief agencies had not abated by the end of 1934, and Roosevelt grew weary with the lack of progress. More than $2 billion had been spent on relief by FERA, but new people were added to the rolls every day. Approximately 20 million individuals were dependent on public largesse. The FERA was important not because it assuaged the problems of the depression but because it revealed the depth of the Roosevelt administration's commitment to relief and its willingness to experiment with various strategies to implement that pledge.

Flood Control Act (1936)   In the late 1920s and the early 1930s several destructive floods occurred in the United States, propelling Congress to pass legislation granting the federal government authority for flood control. The Flood Control Act of 1936 provided for the construction of many upstream storage reservoirs as a major tool of flood control. This method replaced levy construction as the primary flood prevention strategy. Policymakers in the 1930s saw flood damage avoidance as an important key to economic prosperity.

GI Bill of Rights   *See* SERVICEMEN'S READJUSTMENT ACT (1944)

Guadalcanal   *See* BATTLE OF GUADALCANAL (1942–1943)

Guffey-Snyder Act (1935)   During the New Deal, Congress legislated regulations governing the usage of coal. The Guffey-Snyder Act, which passed on August 30, 1935, and was named for its sponsors Senator Joseph F. Guffey (D-PA) and Representative John Buell Snyder (D-PA), drew from the legacy of the National Recovery Administration after it had been dismantled as a result of the *Schechter* case. It reinstated the old bituminous coal code. Impetus for the legislation came from the threat issued by United Mine Workers leader John L. Lewis to take his union out on strike unless the coal industry were again regulated. The Guffey-Snyder Act included guaranteed collective bargaining, wage and hour protections, and price fixing and production controls. It required that nonproductive mines be closed, and it instituted a production tax that would fund miner rehabilitation projects. The law was declared unconstitutional in 1936, leading Congress to pass the Guffey-Vinson Act of 1937. This legislation contained the same provisions as those found in Guffey-Snyder with the exception of wage and hour protections.

Hatch Act (1939)   Charges of improper partisanship within the WORKS PROGRESS ADMINISTRATION ultimately resulted in congressional debate and passage of the Hatch Act, an omnibus law passed on August 2, 1939, that banned all federal employees from engaging in political work. Initially, the purpose of the Hatch Act, named for its sponsor Senator Carl Hatch (D-NM), had been narrower—protection of relief recipients from political manipulation—but it gained a wider mandate as it worked through the legislative process. The law hit the Democratic Party hard because the party controlled both the executive and the legislative branches and thus dominated patronage. Instead, multiple interests would now contest for patronage power, including labor unions, rural conservatives in the state legislatures, and local elites.

Home Owners' Loan Act (1933)   New Deal era housing legislation dealt with three major areas: existing mortgage protections, mortgage insurance for new home purchases, and public housing construction. Because the home foreclosure rate had soared during the Great Depression—250,000 people lost their homes in 1932 and, for the first six months of 1933, approximately 1,000 foreclosures took place per day—Congress passed the Home Owners' Loan Act on June 13, which provided for mortgagors to trade defaulted loans for government bonds without any discount to the initial debt. Liberal critics charged the bill did more for the financial services industry than it did for debtors. Nonetheless, the Home Owners Loan Corporation, created by this act, helped 20 percent of all mortgage holders to refinance their loans, providing a benefit to consumers as well as industry.

Urban housing reform never captured President Roosevelt's attention. His preference for rural life caused him to overlook the housing problems of impoverished urban workers. The president more often saw housing policy as a way to assist the recovery of the building trades. Furthermore, he preferred private housing to public housing projects.

The main proponent of the housing reform initiatives of the 1930s was Senator Robert F. Wagner (D-NY). The National Housing Act of 1934 created a new agency, the Federal Housing Authority, which was empowered to insure private mortgages for middle-class Americans. Wagner continued fighting for additional housing legislation, including a bill that would provide for public housing. The Wagner-Steagall Act, also known as the U.S. Housing Act of 1937, authorized creation of the U.S. Housing Authority. The law provided for $500 million in public housing loans, and by 1940, 350 public housing projects were under construction.

Indian Reorganization Act (1934)   Called the "Indian New Deal," the Indian Reorganization Act of 1934 reversed 50 years of federal government policy toward Native Americans. Since the mid-19th century, forced assimilation and the elimination of Indian control of tribal land and assets had been the preferred method of dealing with Native Americans. In the 1930s, policymakers reexamined the relationship of

Secretary of the Interior Harold Ickes hands the first constitution issued under the Indian Reorganization Act to delegates of the Confederated Tribes of the Flathead Indian Reservation in 1935. *(Library of Congress)*

American Indians to the U.S. government and society. Under the Indian Reorganization Act, Native Americans regained authority over their lands and strengthened tribal self-government. Forced assimilation policies were replaced with gradual assimilation, and tribes were encouraged to preserve their heritage and culture. However, not all Indians approved these policies, viewing them as part of an effort to turn their peoples into museum objects. World War II brought an end to the federal government's active commitment to the legislation.

Internment of Japanese Americans   In 1942, some 120,000 Japanese Americans were deemed security threats and forced into internment camps for the duration of World War II. The story of Japanese-American internment is one of massive civil liberties violations, injustice, and indignity for a population that was almost universally loyal to the United States. The Japanese-American population of the

United States at the time of Japan's attack on Pearl Harbor in 1941 stood at more than 300,000, with 120,000 living on the mainland, primarily on the West Coast, and the remainder in Hawaii. The latter group contained approximately 40,000 Issei, or alien Japanese immigrants ineligible for American citizenship according to U.S. law, and 80,000 Nisei, or Japanese Americans who were American citizens by virtue of their birth in the United States.

Immediately after Pearl Harbor no immediate calls by the public for reprisals against Japanese Americans were made. Based on FBI surveillance initiatives dating back to 1935, 2,000 Japanese and Japanese Americans identified as security risks were quickly arrested and detained as were 14,000 German and Italian Americans. Attorney General Francis Biddle even stated publicly his desire to avoid the government-induced discrimination that had pervaded the home front during World War I. His hopes were quashed as anti-Japanese sentiment spread on the West Coast.

A now discredited investigation chaired by U.S. chief justice Owen J. Roberts incited further calls for action following its finding that the PEARL HARBOR ATTACK had been made possible by the work of Japanese spies in Hawaii, including American citizens of Japanese descent. The investigation fueled an outcry among the public against Japanese Americans in citing these individuals as a security threat, and calls for internment rose. Later a War Department report, *Final Report, Japanese Evacuation from the West Coast, 1942,* cited skewed evidence, such as the recovery of 60,000 rounds of ammunition (actually from a sporting goods store).

The argument was made that "military necessity" justified internment, but several government agencies denied these claims. FBI director J. Edgar Hoover even issued an unqualified denial that Japanese espionage had occurred on the West Coast. Similarly, the Federal Communications Commission (FCC) contended no evidence could be found of illicit radio transmissions between Japanese Americans and the Japanese government. However, comments from Hoover and the FCC were ignored, and the racist, xenophobic calls for internment intensified. As a representative of the California Grower-Shipper Vegetable Association remarked: "We're charged with wanting to get rid of the Japs for selfish reasons. We might as well be honest. We do. It's a question of whether the white man lives on the Pacific Coast or the brown man."

While racism and greed drove the internment process on the mainland, the Japanese Americans living in Hawaii were left alone. There, persons of Japanese ancestry made up approximately half of the population and they were well integrated into the mainstream of economic, cultural, and political life on the islands. But since Japanese Americans totaled less than 1 percent of the population on the mainland, it was much easier to marginalize, discriminate, and scapegoat them here. General John L. DeWitt, the chairman of the Western Defense Command for the U.S. Army, had first opposed any move toward internment, but after hearing the growing rumors, he disregarded the intelligence reports from the FBI, and he reversed his position on internment in February 1942.

After much wrangling within the administration, President Franklin D. Roosevelt signed Executive Order 9066 on February 19, 1942, which provided for the wholesale internment of the Issei and the Nisei living in the United States, the overwhelming majority of them living on the mainland. The order from the president authorized the War Department to exclude "any and all persons" from military zones. The War Relocation Authority was created to oversee the process. Initially, 15,000 Japanese voluntarily left the Pacific coastal zone, but by late March DeWitt called for an end to voluntary withdrawal in large part because officials in interior states objected to a mass influx of Issei and Nisei. In its place the government set up a network of 10 internment camps in Arizona, Arkansas, California, Colorado, Idaho, Utah, and Wyoming.

The Japanese Americans were ordered first to gather at temporary "assembly centers," including horse barns at area racetracks, and later they were sent to permanent "relocation centers." The relocation process took several weeks. Approximately 120,000 Japanese Americans were relocated, losing approximately $400 million in property in the process. The camps were equipped with layers of barbed wire fencing, guard towers, searchlights, and machine-gun installations. To replicate as best as possible the functioning of normal community life, internees published camp newspapers, formed schools, established markets, and organized fire and police protection services. Families lived in cramped one-room wooden barracks and took their meals communally. They used communal toilets and showers. Furniture and accessories consisted of army cots and light bulbs hanging from the ceiling.

Provisions were made for internees to leave the camps for day work in the area of their confinement. After being questioned and having denied loyalty to the emperor of Japan and expressed a willingness to serve in the U.S. military, internees of military age joined the armed services and were dispatched to the European theater in segregated units. One of them, the 442nd Regimental Combat Team, served heroically in Italy and was the most decorated in the army. Those who proved uncooperative were sent to a special internment camp for the disloyal.

In 1943, the War Relocation Authority introduced a process by which internees could leave the camps. Those who wished to depart the camps had to show proof of employment in the interior of the United States and proof of loyalty to the country. They had to demonstrate that they would be welcome in the communities where they planned to settle, and that they would keep the War Relocation Authority apprised of any address changes. In 1943, 17,000 people left the camps under these terms, and in 1944, approximately 18,000 departed. Even though policymakers were leaning toward the release of all loyal detainees, fear of political repercussions in the 1944 elections led to a delay. By January 1945, most of the detainees had been released from the camps. No evidence of disloyalty was ever found.

Japanese Americans challenged internment in the courts, arguing that as American citizens internment violated their constitutional rights. In *Hirabayashi v. United States* (1943), a unanimous Court found in favor of the government, but only on a technicality. The 1943 decision included a strong warning. Associate Justice Frank Murphy wrote that internment bore "a melancholy resemblance to the treatment accorded to members of the Jewish race in Germany and in other parts of Europe."

A second case, *Korematsu v. United States,* generated a heated conflict between the War Department and the Justice Department over the question of whether military necessity justified internment. The Justice Department contended that War Department justifications for internment were a lie, but the War Department successfully suppressed evidence from the former. Had the unedited Justice Department brief gone to the Court, the justices would likely have found against the government. In a 6-3 decision the Supreme Court ruled against Fred Korematsu in upholding the argument of military necessity. Associate Justice Hugo Black's majority opinion, though, revealed discomfort with the government's actions. He affirmed that "all legal restrictions which curtail the civil rights of a single racial group are immediately suspect."

Efforts to compensate Japanese Americans have been minimal: a 1948 law provided only $37 million in reparations while a measure approved in the late 1980s gave each internee $20,000. President RONALD REAGAN issued an apology in 1988: "Yes, the nation was then at war, struggling for its survival. And it's not for us today to pass judgment upon those who may have made mistakes while engaged in that great struggle. Yet we must recognize that the internment of Japanese-Americans was just that, a mistake." As another act of governmental contrition, President BILL CLINTON honored Fred Korematsu with the Presidential Medal of Freedom in 1998.

Italian Campaign (1943–1945)   In 1943 at the conclusion of the NORTH AFRICAN CAMPAIGN, the British and the United States continued to delay opening a second front against Germany, this time by beginning a campaign against Italy, first with fighting for control of Sicily and then for the Italian Peninsula proper. The campaigns in Sicily and Italy were undertaken at British prime minister Winston Churchill's insistence and over the objections of military leaders in the United States. In fact, American military planners hoped the Sicilian campaign would mark the end of operations in the Mediterranean.

The Sicilian campaign involved British troops under the control of General Bernard Montgomery and U.S. troops under General George S. Patton, who had a subsidiary assignment to protect Montgomery in the battle for Messina. Because two German divisions slowed Montgomery's troops, Patton ordered his troops on to Messina at the northern tip of Sicily, the holding of which also controlled access to the Italian Peninsula. Neither Patton nor Montgomery were able to prevent the evacuation of the mass of German and Italian troops from the island, making the campaign of dubious importance. The Sicilian campaign was further marred by high casualty rates among Patton's troops, by the general's unsuccessful efforts to cover up U.S. brutality that included the murder of German prisoners of war and unarmed Italians, and by Patton's verbal and physical abuse of U.S. soldiers. During the Sicilian campaign, Italian leader Benito Mussolini was removed from power and negotiations by Italy for an unconditional surrender began.

At this juncture, Churchill argued that Italy should be invaded. Because the invasion of France across the English Channel could not be launched before the spring of 1944, Churchill contended that U.S. troops must be kept battle-tested through additional fighting. President Roosevelt ultimately agreed, but he also countered that no additional American resources would be used for fighting in Italy. Instead, additional American troops and resources would be shipped to Britain for the invasion across the English Channel.

The Italian campaign faced several challenges: It was not the subject of careful military planning, comparatively scant resources were devoted to it, and there was no strategic benefit to capturing the peninsula. The military challenge grew when Hitler dispatched 16 divisions to Italy. No longer did the British and the Americans engage in a residual operation against a country pursuing a peace treaty; rather, they found themselves fighting a German army occupying Italy. The American landing at Salerno proved difficult and nearly had to be abandoned on September 12, 1943.

A war of attrition ensued during the following 18 months. U.S. troops found themselves pinned down at Monte Cassino. To compensate, Churchill proposed another amphibious landing, this time at Anzio to the north and west. After considerable discussions, Churchill convinced Roosevelt to go along with the plan. The assault at Anzio began in late January 1944. An error by the American general in command, John P. Lucas, meant that the U.S. forces were not able to capitalize on their relatively easy landing. Instead of pushing inland immediately, Lucas had mistakenly tried to control the beachhead, allowing the Germans to trap his men on the blood-soaked sand for four months. Even after French Moroccan and Polish troops rescued the U.S. units at Monte Cassino and Anzio, the German forces managed to escape. They were able to do so because the Americans put too much stock in the capture of Rome, which carried no military significance. Retreating to the north, the Germans burned all the bridges, except the historic Ponte Vecchio, in Florence, preventing further Allied advance. In the end, the Italian campaign of 1943 to 1945 brought huge Allied casualties: 188,000 for the Americans and 123,000 for the British while it failed to divert few Germans away from the eastern front.

Iwo Jima   *See* BATTLE OF IWO JIMA (1945)

Java Sea   *See* BATTLE OF THE JAVA SEA (1942)

Jewish Refugee Crisis   Anti-Semitic policies instituted by the Nazi regime of dictator Adolf Hitler that included measures to ensure racial purity led more than 340,000 Jews to leave Germany and Austria between 1933 and 1945. Approximately 100,000 relocated to countries that were captured by the Germans. In the prewar period, some 85,000 came to the United States, and many more hoped to take refuge in America. In the years preceding the attack on Pearl Harbor in 1941, however, the U.S. government refused to alter national immigration laws to permit asylum to Jews fleeing from persecution in Germany and eastern Europe. Congress failed to pass legislation permitting unrestricted immigration of Jewish children, and, in June 1939, the U.S. government barred admission of the 930 Jewish refugees aboard the German ocean liner MS *St. Louis.* This prewar approach of ignoring the problems Jews faced in Europe provided the context for U.S. deliberation of the Jewish refugee crisis at the conclusion of World War II.

As such, Jews sought refuge elsewhere. The Haavara (Transfer) Agreement of 1935 permitted approximately 50,000 German Jews to enter Palestine. Palestine became a less feasible destination in 1939 when the British parliament, which then controlled the region, limited Jewish immigration. Shanghai, China was one of the few locations where Jews were welcome without restrictions.

In August 1942, officials with the World Jewish Congress informed the Americans of the mass murders of Jews in German-controlled territory, but U.S. officials suspected that this report was nothing more than a vicious rumor. By the end of the year, additional intelligence revealed the truth of these reports, and the question became one of how to rescue the Jews from the death camps. Given that no American troops were yet fighting on the European continent, the challenge was all the more difficult, but President Roosevelt did win agreement from British prime minister Winston Churchill and Soviet premier Joseph Stalin that war crimes trials would be held at the conclusion of hostilities.

FDR hoped that an April 1943 conference on war refugees in Bermuda might draft a solution, but when the British resisted authorizing Palestine as a destination place nothing of substance was accomplished. A Romanian proposal to release 70,000 Jews in its territory met opposition from the State Department out of concern that they would be sent to Palestine. Officials in the Treasury Department were irate, and they drafted a report for the secretary, Henry Morgenthau, who was Jewish, on January 13, 1944, titled "Report to

Jews captured by the Germans during the Warsaw Ghetto uprising in 1944. The original German caption reads: "Forcibly pulled out of dug-outs." *(unknown Stroop Report photographer/United States Holocaust Memorial Museum)*

Starving prisoners in Mauthausen Concentration Camp liberated on May 5, 1945. The Nazis killed some 6 million Jews during the Holocaust. Hundreds of thousands became refugees. *(National Archives)*

the Secretary on the Acquiescence by This Government in the Murder of the Jews." Less than two weeks after receiving the report, Morgenthau convinced Roosevelt to establish the War Refugee Board to assist in the resettlement of Jewish refugees. By the fall of 1943 the War Refugee Board (WRB) had rescued only 923 Jews and brought them to the United States. Better results were achieved in Hungary, where 200,000 Jews were saved from the death camps by WRB efforts. U.S. officials debated, but rejected, a proposal to bomb Auschwitz, the largest concentration camp where Jews were being murdered. A tacit decision was reached to save the Jews by defeating Hitler, not by bombing the camps, which, it was affirmed, would result in the death of innocent victims.

The question then became what would happen to the Jews upon liberation. Zionists argued that Palestine should be opened for any and all Jewish refugees. Following the YALTA CONFERENCE in February 1945, President Roosevelt met with three Middle Eastern and African kings, Ibn Saud of Saudi

Arabia, Farouk of Egypt, and Haile Selassie of Ethiopia. The meeting took place aboard ship in the Suez Canal, and Ibn Saud made clear that he would not approve the additional immigration of Jewish refugees into Palestine. At the end of the war, hundreds of thousands of Jewish refugees in Europe were homeless and impoverished. When the Soviets liberated Auschwitz in January 1945, they discovered 7,000 prisoners that the Germans had left in place. They had previously taken three camps in the summer of 1944—Belzec, Sobibor, and Treblinka—but all the Jewish prisoners there had been shot or relocated as the Germans tried to hide the evidence of their crimes against humanity. U.S. forces made similar discoveries as they liberated Buchenwald, Dachau, and Mauthausen, all major concentration camps, as well as countless subcamps.

After all the camps had been liberated, the Allies discovered well over 100,000 Jewish prisoners and other victims of Hitler's race purification policies. Many of these men, women, and children died from starvation and illness soon after they had obtained their freedom. Most scholars include more than just the camp inmates in their studies of Holocaust survivors. They include all those displaced by the war, thus elevating the number of Hitler's victims significantly. After the liberation of the concentration camps and the end of the war in Europe, wartime Jewish refugees and other displaced persons (DPs) were placed in Allied-run camps throughout Italy and western Europe, but many of the concentration camp victims were detained in their wartime camps, while they awaited decisions on where they would be allowed to go.

The United States viewed the operation of the DP camps and the concentration camps under their control initially as a humanitarian issue, but by 1947 a shift in policy took place with the DPs viewed as a political problem that needed to be resolved. Great Britain wanted a repatriation program based on the nationality, not the ethnicity or religion, of the detainees. Furthermore, the British argued against Palestine as a solution. President HARRY TRUMAN did not want to force repatriation of DPs to their countries of origin nor did he want to stop the flow of illegal immigration to Palestine. The Soviet Union and the countries of Eastern Europe wanted to be rid of as many of the Jewish refugees who had flooded into their countries as possible.

Because much of the world was economically unable to receive the refugees, because restrictive U.S. immigration laws remained in place, and because of British and Arab hostility to opening Palestine, few options were available to the Jews. Many of those who tried to enter Palestine illegally were placed in British-run internment camps on Cyprus. Nonetheless, approximately 100,000 Jews escaped to Palestine between 1945 and 1948. In 1945, revisions to U.S. law made possible the entry of 400,000 DPs; of that number approximately 80,000 to 90,000 were Holocaust survivors. The creation of the state of Israel in what had been Palestine in May 1948 opened that country to additional Jewish refugees.

Korematsu v. United States (1944)   *See* INTERNMENT OF JAPANESE AMERICANS

Lend-Lease Act (1941)   On January 6, 1941, President Franklin D. Roosevelt asked Congress to consider a Lend-Lease bill providing for $7 billion in aid to Great Britain and the Allies in the war against Germany. The words *lend* and *lease* were used to win support from isolationists, who opposed any involvement in the war, because this chosen vocabulary suggested that Britain and the Allies would be granted only temporary assistance, or, as Roosevelt put it, the whole situation was akin to loaning a garden hose not in use to a neighbor fighting a house fire.

Unlike previous executive actions to assist the Allied cause during World War II, Roosevelt moved this measure through Congress because of the appropriations requirements. In his message to Congress, dubbed the Four Free-

doms speech, Roosevelt explained that the Lend-Lease aid would protect freedom of speech, freedom of religion, freedom from want, and freedom from fear. These ideals later played a major role in setting forth the goals of World War II for the American people. Artist Norman Rockwell even captured these sentiments in four paintings.

The debate about Lend-Lease that ensued was strenuous, loud, and principled. The bill was symbolically introduced in Congress as H.R. 1776, and hearings began four days after the president's address. In an effort to deflect isolationist fears that this aid package was but a prelude to full-scale American intervention in the war, British prime minister Winston Churchill stressed that American troops were not needed to stop German aggression but that American war materials were. Isolationists did not accept this logic, but they also did not have the numbers to defeat the legislation. Their rhetoric was nonetheless biting. One senator, Burton K. Wheeler (D-MT), charged that Lend-Lease would "plow under every fourth American boy" just as New Deal agricultural legislation had required the destruction of crops.

To qualify for aid under the Lend-Lease program, Roosevelt argued, the British would have to expend all their capital resources and the Americans would compel the sale of British assets in the United States. This display helped ease congressional passage of Lend-Lease. Isolationists did force an amendment preventing U.S. Navy convoys from aiding in the transportation of supplies to Britain. Roosevelt agreed, probably because he and his war counsel acknowledged that presidential power as commander in chief superceded the amendment. Roosevelt signed the bill into law on March 11, 1941. During the course of the war, American aid to the Allies under the Lend-Lease program approached $50 billion.

Leyte Gulf   *See* BATTLE OF LEYTE GULF (1944)

Life Magazine First Published by Henry Luce (1936)
Henry Luce, the creator of *Time* magazine, which debuted in 1923, was the preeminent magazine publisher in the United States by the late 1930s. His work was especially popular with journalists and middle-class Americans. First introduced on November 23, 1936, *Life* mirrored the strategy that had succeeded so well for *Time*. It used pictures to summarize and simplify the newsworthy events of the week. By 1940, *Life* had become the most popular magazine in Luce's publishing empire. *Life* not only dealt with traditional news items, but also celebrity culture. Favorable coverage in *Life* could secure box office success for newly released motion pictures much more so than items in traditional newspapers. *Life,* like *Time* and *Fortune,* the business monthly that Luce published, possessed a seemingly all-knowing and at times overly shrewd view of the world. The influence of Time Inc. was so widespread that Luce replaced William Randolph Hearst as the nation's most significant media mogul by the

early 1940s. *Life* magazine ceased weekly publication on December 29, 1972.

Long, Huey   *See* ASSASSINATION OF HUEY LONG (1935)

Manhattan Project   The Manhattan Project was the name given the U.S. effort to build an atomic weapon during World War II. Although work was done throughout the country—in Los Alamos, New Mexico; Oak Ridge, Tennessee; Hanford, Washington; and other places—much of the theoretical work was done at Columbia University in Manhattan, and thus it was called the Manhattan Project. The Manhattan project came to fruition due to major developments in science, starting with the discovery of radioactivity in the 1890s. From that base, scientists postulated about what sort of energy might be emitted from a purposeful effort to split the atom and release

its forces all at once instead of naturally over time. The discovery of the neutron in 1932 and the process of fission seven years later gave the scientific community the knowledge base necessary to build a nuclear weapon.

Most of the principal researchers were German and Italian refugee scientists who had relocated to the United States in the 1930s after the rise of Hitler and Mussolini to power. The governments of Germany, Great Britain, the Soviet Union, and Japan launched programs to develop nuclear weapons. It took much pressure from the refugee scientists to convince U.S. officials of the need to do likewise. Soon after reading a plea for action from Albert Einstein, who was already well known for his theory of relativity, President Franklin Roosevelt established the Advisory Committee on Uranium on October 21, 1939. The three questions that these and other scientists explored were how the radioactive

Operators at their calutron control panels at the Y-12 plant in Oak Ridge, Tennessee, during World War II. During the Manhattan Project effort to construct an atomic bomb, employees worked in secrecy, with no idea what they were working to create. Gladys Owens, the woman seated in the foreground, did not know what she had been working on until seeing this photograph in a public tour of the facility 50 years later. *(Ed Wescott/US Army/Manhattan Engineering District)*

bomb-making material should be collected, how much material was necessary to cause a chain reaction, and how quickly could an atomic bomb be constructed. Because of the seeming difficulty of the task, early U.S. efforts concentrated more on proving the impossibility of the bomb rather than on trying to build one.

Roosevelt's June 28, 1941, appointment of Vannevar Bush, a leading scientist, to head the Office of Scientific Research and Development marked an important step toward the construction of the atomic bomb. Bush encouraged a three-pronged approach to research on nuclear weaponry, which necessitated the cooperation of the government, big business, and major research universities. After British researchers proved that significantly less radioactive material was needed than had previously been assumed, Bush convinced Roosevelt to support the bomb-making program. In the fall of 1941, FDR named a top policy group consisting of Vice President HENRY WALLACE, Secretary of War Henry Stimson, Army Chief of Staff George C. Marshall, Bush, and James Bryant Conant, the president of Harvard University, to direct the effort.

Meanwhile, University of California at Berkeley physicist Robert Oppenheimer convinced a number of his colleagues to join him in Los Alamos, New Mexico, where they could work together on bomb research. The isolated site, high atop a mesa, was surrounded with razor wire and a steel fence. In the fall of 1942, Oppenheimer's group was placed under the jurisdiction of the War Department. General Leslie Groves commanded the initiative.

During the course of the war, the Manhattan Project cost the government over $2 billion and employed more than 150,000 people. Ironically, this project, which had originated with fear of a German atomic bomb, proved successful whereas Germany abandoned the effort and Japan never made it a priority. Both Axis nations believed that the development of a bomb could not occur in time to influence World War II. Roosevelt never shared with Soviet premier Stalin information about the Manhattan Project; nor did he tell HARRY TRUMAN when the latter became his vice president in 1945. Atomic bombs were used successfully against Japan at Hiroshima on August 6, 1945, and at Nagasaki on August 9, 1945, thus ending the war.

Midway   *See* BATTLE OF MIDWAY (1942)

Miller-Tydings Act (1937)   *See* ANTIMONOPOLY POLICIES

National Housing Act   *See* HOME OWNERS' LOAN ACT (1933)

National Industrial Recovery Act (1933)   Senate passage of a 30-hour workweek in early April 1933 pressured the Roosevelt administration into formulating an industrial recovery policy to rejuvenate American business during the

Great Depression. President Roosevelt instructed a number of people to develop legislative proposals, including Gerard Swope of General Electric and Henry I. Harriman of the U.S. Chamber of Commerce, who drafted what became the preferred plan for industrial recovery. It included industrywide planning through trade associations and a suspension of antitrust laws to make the former possible.

The War Industries Board that had helped organize the U.S. industrial mobilization during World War I served as an important precedent for drafting the National Industrial Recovery Act. New Dealers liked this model because it permitted maximum government intervention while preserving capitalism. Key union leaders went along with this otherwise business friendly plan out of fear that the industries in which their members worked were on the verge of collapse and out of a contention that the industrial recovery legislation would be more likely to benefit union-friendly employers than those that paid very low wages. However, champions of workers' rights in Congress refused to consider the bill until it included protections for collective bargaining.

The National Industrial Recovery Act contained different provisions for different constituencies. Employers were happy to see provisions for constructing industrywide codes of competition paired with antitrust exemptions. Government planners appreciated the federal oversight of business behavior. Labor leaders welcomed the protections for collective bargaining and the provisions for a minimum wage and maximum hours. Finally, for victims of the depression, the bill contained $3.3 billion for public works projects, which was realized in the PUBLIC WORKS ADMINISTRATION. While the House passed the bill with very little opposition on May 26, 1933, various factions in the Senate fought against the measure: antitrusters, supporters of the 30-hour workweek, inflationists who believed currency expansion was the path to recovery, and conservatives who disliked the labor reforms and the government activism. The Senate ultimately approved the bill by a seven-vote margin and Roosevelt signed it on June 16, 1933.

To oversee this complex legislation, Congress created the National Recovery Administration (NRA) under the directorship of General Hugh Johnson, a retired army officer who had worked with the War Industries Board in World War I and who had experience in dealing with supply and procurement. Johnson contended the odds of success were slim, but he nonetheless directed his new agency to begin negotiations on industry codes. While economic projections improved soon after the legislation passed, the failure of the most significant industries in the county to arrive at satisfactory codes resulted in little long-term economic improvement. To address this problem, the New Dealers undertook a massive publicity campaign to encourage compliance with the NRA. The slogan, "We Do Our Part," was featured on posters with the symbol of a blue eagle. This symbol was proudly displayed by businesses and industries that had embraced the NRA experiment. By early August, the shipbuilding, woolens, electrical, and garment industries had all negotiated codes, and by the end of the month, Johnson had brought the other major industries on board, including oil, steel, lumber, automobiles, and soft coal. Patriotism and social pressure, not legal threats, became Johnson's primary enforcement tools.

Less than a year after its inception, the NRA had amassed numerous critics: Consumers disliked high prices, business owners and conservative Democrats opposed government intervention, workers were upset because labor reforms remained incomplete, progressives pointed to the negative impact on small business, and some New Dealers worried the NRA codes would retard recovery. Roosevelt himself found fault with the NRA. He disliked the proliferation of codes to cover insignificant industries and the price policies of the NRA. To fix the problems, he encouraged Johnson to resign and he named Donald Richberg to become director. Once new leadership was in place, contemporary critics judged the NRA a failure. The complaints were excessive. The price policies were not as damaging as believed. Industrial concentration was not the fault of the NRA. The NRA did not damage small business as many believed. In fact, many small business owners disliked the NRA because of its curtailment of labor exploitation, not its monopolistic features.

NRA accomplishments included jobs for 2 million people, a halt to the deflationary spiral, improved corporate ethics, the creation of a pattern for wages and hours, and the curtailment of child labor. However, this positive legacy was not offset completely by the agency's failings. The NRA's record on depression recovery was mixed, neither improving nor worsening the situation. Its power to act was linked to the crisis conditions. Large businesses used the codes to retard competition within individual industries.

The NRA experiment ended with a court case that resulted from private business frustrations with the agency and its codes. In the 1935 case of *Schechter Poultry Corp. v. United States* the Supreme Court contended that when Congress passed the National Industrial Recovery Act and empowered the executive branch to draft codes of industrial conduct, it authorized an unconstitutional delegation of legislative power to the presidency. The Court thus ended this New Deal program.

National Labor Relations Act (1935)   Following the Supreme Court's decision declaring the National Industrial Recovery Act unconstitutional in 1935, Congress and President Roosevelt sought a new legislative strategy to address problems faced by American workers. Senator Robert F. Wagner (D-NY) had long advocated such a measure, but the National Labor Relations Act did not gain legislative traction until the president reversed his opposition to it and gave his support. The Wagner Act, as it was often called, cre-

ated the National Labor Relations Board (NLRB), an independent agency given authority over union elections and oversight of unfair labor practices by businesses. The labor practices defined as unfair included employer failure to bargain with employees, dismissal of union workers, and formation of company unions. Despite the law's revolutionary provisions—government protection for collective bargaining and requirements that businesses accept without protest worker unionization efforts—the legislation, which placed no restrictions on workers' behavior, faced very little opposition in either chamber of Congress. Roosevelt signed the bill on July 5, 1935.

In *NLRB v. Jones & Laughlin Steel Corporation* (1937) the Supreme Court upheld the National Labor Relations Act as a narrowly and properly constructed regulation of industrial behavior with regard to union activities. The Wagner Act proved one of the most significant labor laws in American history. It spurred union organization nationwide. The most important development stemming from the NLRA was creation of the Committee for Industrial Organization (renamed the Congress of Industrial Organizations [CIO] in 1938), which targeted industrial rather than craft workers.

National War Labor Board   Created by presidential decree in 1942, the National War Labor Board (NWLB) was charged with preventing wartime work stoppages. Wartime patriotism, which reduced the tendency of workers to strike, helped simplify its mission. During its existence from 1942 to 1946, the NWLB intervened in 20,000 wage disputes involving 20 million workers. It endorsed 415,000 wartime wage agreements. It also played a role in the government takeover of those few plants, just over 20, where strikes could not be resolved. For the benefit of workers, the NWLB helped increase union membership, which grew approximately 67 percent during the war years, and it helped improve wages and working conditions. The phenomenal upsurge in union membership came because of the board's "maintenance-of-membership" rule, which provided that all new employees in union shops would automatically be enrolled in the union unless they asked to be excluded. Such requests had to be made within 15 days of employment.

The NWLB faired well in the face of two threats to its authority. The first came from United Mine Workers leader John L. Lewis, who opposed President Roosevelt and this example of government intervention in union affairs (the mine workers already enjoyed a closed shop). Lewis took his mine workers out on strike in 1943; protracted negotiations were not settled until the following year. While Lewis won his wage concessions, he lost the public's goodwill and he failed to weaken the NWLB.

The NWLB persevered in another widely publicized showdown, this one with Sewell L. Avery of Montgomery Ward. When Avery tried to block the maintenance-of-membership rule in his company, U.S. attorney general Francis Biddle used the U.S. Army to take control of Avery's company. The image of troops taking Avery out of his office became fodder for conservative critics of the administration, but it also proved to the labor movement the government's commitment to labor as a vital participant in the war effort. The NWLB faded from existence in 1946 after its duties were transferred to the National Labor Relations Board, which had been created in 1935 by the NATIONAL LABOR RELATIONS ACT.

National Youth Administration (1935–1943)   President Roosevelt created the National Youth Administration (NYA) by executive order on June 26, 1935, after first lady ELEANOR ROOSEVELT, who had a long-term commitment to the problems of impoverished youth, suggested establishing an aid program for young people to Harry Hopkins, director of the FEDERAL EMERGENCY RELIEF ADMINISTRATION. The depression had all but obliterated employment opportunities for the generation that came of age in the late 1920s and early 1930s. Aubrey Williams, a social worker from Alabama, was tapped to direct the NYA. During its existence the NYA employed more than 600,000 college students and 1.5 million high school students in part-time jobs. In contrast, the CIVILIAN CONSERVATION CORPS targeted unemployed youth not in school.

Even though most of the NYA jobs were clerical, project directors tried to match student interest to the available positions. These student aid programs alleviated unemployment by helping many students remain in school. An additional 2.6 million unemployed young people who were not in school gained NYA job relief, building a range of structures from tuberculosis isolation huts in Arizona to a cattle barn at Texas A&M University and tennis courts in Topeka, Kansas.

While NYA officials hoped that these building projects would provide job training, the dual goals never achieved the hopes of NYA planners. Thus, in 1937, the NYA reorganized its programs for young people not in school to focus more directly on vocational training. That year the NYA also launched a program specifically for African-American

Two posters (one with a misspelling) for the Illinois branch of the National Youth Administration promoting educational opportunities for young women and young men seeking training for employment *(Library of Congress)*

youth under the direction of Mary McLeod Bethune, a noted educator and the founder of Bethune-Cookman College. In 1939, the NYA redirected its priorities to merge job training with war readiness. Despite the success achieved by the agency in educating young people in war industries, Congress abolished the NYA in 1943.

Native Son, by Richard Wright (1940)

Born in Mississippi in 1908, Richard Wright moved to Chicago in 1927 to avoid the oppression of Jim Crow racism. He later settled in New York City, where he worked as an editor on the *Daily Worker,* a Communist Party newspaper, and other periodicals. He published *Uncle Tom's Children,* a collection of short stories, in 1938. Two years later he published *Native Son,* which earned for him the status as the first African American to write a bestselling novel and a Book-of-the-Month Club selection. *Native Son* was unyielding in its argument of national guilt for the racial problems of the United States. Wright wanted the book to jar white readers and force them to question both themselves and their country.

Bigger Thomas, the 19-year-old protagonist of the novel, was already a criminal on Chicago's south side when the novel opens. Bigger nonetheless gains a job as a chauffeur for an elite white family. There he developed sexual feelings toward Mary, the daughter of his employer. (These passages were removed from the 1940 edition of the novel and were not restored until 1993.) Events unfold quickly in the novel, and Bigger ends up accidentally murdering Mary after a night of drunken excess. Earlier in the evening, Bigger had driven Mary and her communist lover to a South Chicago eatery that catered to African Americans. The evening ends with Bigger taking a drunken Mary to bed, where he kissed her. Fearful of discovery, he smothers Mary with a pillow as her blind mother enters the room. To hide the murder, he burns the body in the furnace, hoping that her family would make racial assumptions that he was too ignorant to commit the crime.

Wright uses snowfall and a blizzard to symbolize how Bigger was encased by the white world after Mary's death. Even though he returns to his mother's tenement house proud of his actions, he is trapped by his guilt, which leads him to purposefully and violently murder Bessie, his girlfriend. Eventually captured and tried for his crimes, he is found guilty only of Mary's assumed rape, which was viewed as a more serious offense than her murder. Ultimately, a lawyer for the Communist Party defends Bigger but never discerns what had motivated him. Wright used this to demonstrate the failure of the Communist Party—despite its efforts to fight segregation—to understand and to adequately address the plight of black America.

After the publication of *Native Son,* the African-American community celebrated Wright's success while also questioning why he had highlighted such a negative stereotype of black men. Wright saw the situation differently; he believed Bigger's type to be the progeny of American racism, and equally important, he believed that until the nation ended its segrationist policies and attitudes there would be more Biggers created.

Natural Gas Act (1938)

The Natural Gas Act of 1938 marked the first time that Congress or the federal government directly regulated the natural gas industry. The impetus for the legislation came from interstate pipeline companies and their power over the gas market. The Natural Gas Act provided the Federal Power Commission with the authority to establish rates for the transmission and sale of natural gas in interstate commerce. Additionally, the Federal Power Commission gained oversight responsibility for the construction and operation of interstate gas pipelines as well as for the termination of pipeline facilities. The oil and gas executives grew to dislike both this federal regulatory power and this legislation.

Neutrality Acts (1935–1939)

The 1934 hearings conducted by Senator Gerald P. Nye (R-ND) into whether or not munitions makers had conspired to bring the United States into World War I combined with the failure of the United States to join the World Court provided the context for passage of neutrality legislation from 1935 to 1939. President Roosevelt correctly feared that isolationism would soon hold sway over American foreign policy at a moment when fascist dictators threatened world peace. Nonetheless, he also supported flexible neutrality legislation, and he called on Congress to act accordingly.

Lawmakers drafted, and the president signed, the first of five major Neutrality Acts in 1935. The 1935 legislation required the president to declare when a state of war existed between two nations and to impose an embargo on all trade with the belligerents. The president had no latitude to determine which nation was the aggressor and which nation was the victim. Additionally, the legislation stated that American citizens who traveled on ships registered to belligerent powers did so at their own risk. The intent was to avoid putting the United States in circumstances similar to those that had led to entry into World War I. Italy's efforts to build an empire in Africa, specifically Ethiopia, proved the futility of the neutrality legislation. The League of Nations tried to impose an oil embargo on Italy, but U.S. cooperation was necessary for it to succeed since half of the world's oil came from the United States. Roosevelt was able to call only for an unenforceable moral embargo since oil was not enumerated in the goods subject to embargo by the Neutrality Act of 1935.

In February 1936, Congress extended the Neutrality Act in banning the loan of money or the provision of credit to belligerent nations. The first of two Neutrality Acts in 1937 applied provisions of the law to the Spanish civil war, which had started the previous year, and to civil wars generally. With this legislation about to expire, Congress again renewed the Neutrality Act in 1937, this time making it permanent. The mandatory embargo against warring nations was retained; travel on belligerent vessels was made illegal; and trade in nonmilitary goods such as oil was limited to a "cash-and-carry" basis, whereby purchasing nations were required to pay in cash and use their own shipping to transport the material. However, this legislation did nothing to address the hostilities between China and Japan because a formal declaration of war had not been made by these two powers. Roosevelt chose not to impose the act because he wanted to provide military aid to China and because Japan would still be able to purchase what it most needed from the United States—oil and scrap iron—under the cash-and-carry provisions.

By 1939, Roosevelt realized that the threat to world peace was so severe that the neutrality legislation had to be revised. Once Germany invaded Poland and World War II began in Europe in September, FDR was forced by the Neutrality Acts to declare an embargo against all the warring powers. This move alarmed the British, who were dependent on the American arsenal of production. Roosevelt knew this, and he called Congress back into session to consider revisions to the Neutrality Acts. He scored only a partial victory: While the arms embargo requirement was eliminated, isolationists revived the cash-and-carry provisions so that there could be no loans or credits issued to the Allied powers under the terms of this law. Between the passage of this legislation in 1939 and the attack on Pearl Harbor in 1941 Roosevelt found himself negotiating around the Neutrality Acts to provide maximum support to Great Britain.

NLRB v. Jones & Laughlin Steel Corporation (1937)   *See* National Labor Relations Act (1935)

North African Campaign (1942–1943)   The origins of the North African campaign stem from a strategic miscalculation by the Allies and a disagreement between President Roosevelt and British prime minister Winston Churchill about how to defeat Germany. The Americans favored an invasion across the English Channel to France at the earliest possible date, which they believed would lead to a decisive defeat of the Nazis. The British feared that such an approach would spell disaster, but Churchill communicated his views indirectly through the Soviets instead of challenging Roosevelt directly. Instead, Churchill wanted to concentrate on the fighting in North Africa, where the British were battling eight Italian divisions and three German divisions.

When the understandably impatient Soviets, who were fighting the Germans alone on the eastern front, approached the Americans, Roosevelt promised several times to open a second front within the calendar year 1942 at a cost of reduced Lend-Lease aid to Russia. In response, Churchill worked hard to sway Roosevelt to accept his strategic approach, namely, to

use a blockade and a bombing campaign to isolate Germany on the Continent, gain control of the Mediterranean and the Middle Eastern oilfields, and encourage the resistance movement on the Continent. The danger was that Germany would defeat Russia before Churchill's approach made headway. Churchill's major advantage lay with American unreadiness for military action.

The two Allied leaders met at Hyde Park, New York, in June 1942. During the sessions, Churchill learned of a major British loss in North Africa, which gave the Axis powers access to Egypt and the Middle Eastern oilfields. Churchill used this development to push Roosevelt to commit to a troop buildup in North Africa, suggesting this campaign was in fact the necessary second front. American generals disagreed, however, stressing instead that North Africa was on the fringes of the war. Churchill nonetheless prevailed, and Operation Torch, as the North African campaign was called, was born.

Roosevelt was not without his own reasons for agreeing to proceed. He understood that the American people were impatient to fight, and North Africa provided a good setting for warfare while the nation's factories revved up the war machine on the home front. Soviet leader Joseph Stalin was irate, but he had little leverage. To facilitate Operation Torch, the North Atlantic convoys were redirected to support action in Africa.

The strategy for defeating the Italians and the Germans called on a British-American force to pressure the Axis from the west while British general Bernard Montgomery fought from the east. The American landing point, French Morocco and Algeria, were under the control of the Vichy French, who were collaborating with Hitler. Roosevelt's efforts to maintain good relations with Vichy leader Marshal Henri Phillipe Pétain were for naught. Dwight D. Eisenhower was made the commander of this operation to try to convince the French of the fiction that the North African campaign was a U.S.—rather than a British—initiative. Furthermore, American and British troops were to land separately so that the French would not attack the former. Pétain did not follow through as the Allies had hoped. As a result, the first two days of the U.S. landing operation were met by heavy French fire. Eisenhower was ultimately able to negotiate a cease-fire. The Darlan deal, as it was known, generated much criticism because the French official with whom Eisenhower dealt was a Nazi collaborator.

A British victory at El Alamein in early November 1942 forced German general Erwin Rommel's forces to push westward toward Eisenhower's position. A major battle ensued at Kasserine Pass in Tunisia in February 1943. There the Germans handily defeated the Allies under Eisenhower's command. The combination of a British naval blockade, Rommel's failing health, and an attack by U.S. general George S. Patton were enough for Montgomery to prevail. By May 13, 1943, the Axis forces had surrendered in North Africa.

Office of Price Administration (1941–1947)   First created on April 11, 1941, as the Office of Price Administration and Civilian Supply, this federal agency became the Office of Price Administration (OPA) in August 1941. Charged with stabilizing prices and rents nationwide by establishing maximum commodity prices (except for agricultural produce pricing that was controlled by the secretary of agriculture) and maximum rents in defense areas, the OPA became an independent agency in January 1942, one month after the United States entered World War II. Regulations issued in April 1942, the General Maximum Price Regulation, or "General Max," provoked heated criticism.

The OPA also oversaw a rationing program and determined which commodities would be given production subsidies. With many basic products and reserves needed for the war, the OPA rationed meat, butter, coffee, tires, and gasoline. The OPA generated substantial political controversy as members of Congress used it as much to promote economic redress for their districts as to achieve a wartime command economy. Most egregious was the artificially high price ceiling placed on agricultural commodities by farm bloc lawmakers. By attempting to maintain the economic status quo, the OPA differed markedly from the New Deal era when the focus had been on economic redistribution. The OPA was disbanded in March 1947.

Office of Production Management   In May 1940, President Franklin D. Roosevelt was compelled to confront the problems of containing and regulating an economy expanding to meet the possibility of war. To prevent inflation and to ensure efficient mobilization in preparation for war, the president first relied on the World War I–era National Defense Advisory Commission, but that agency had never exerted much power over the economy. By January 1941, its weaknesses were apparent and so Roosevelt created the Office of Production Management on January 7, 1941, by an executive order. This agency too failed to operate effectively. To address the conflict between capital and labor, Roosevelt appointed co-directors for the Office of Production Management, William Knudsen of General Motors and Sidney Hillman of the Amalgamated Clothing Workers. However, he failed to give the office sufficient power to address the serious production problems of the nation. Weeks later, Roosevelt created other agencies to deal with price control and war resources. As the war progressed, Roosevelt created still more agencies whose responsibilities overlapped with those of the Office of Production Management. This development reflected what would become the Roosevelt management style during the war years—agency proliferation. The strategy allowed the president to avoid giving too much power over the economy to businesses but it made for organizational chaos. As a result, wartime economic power remained with the president.

Office of War Information (1942–1945)   Formed on January 13, 1942, as a government propaganda agency, the Office of War Information worked in a wide range of areas, including movies, magazines, photographs, information coordination within the federal government, censorship, manpower mobilization, and propaganda posters. Elmer Davis, a respected radio broadcaster for CBS News, was named director of the agency. President Roosevelt wanted to ensure that this agency avoided the dangerous propaganda excesses of the World War I–era Committee on Public Information, which exacerbated ethnic tensions. The photography program documented extensively the mobilization of the home front. The movie industry cooperated with the Office of War Information to produce films that celebrated American diversity and American wartime unity. However, by late 1943 Congress had grown weary of the Office of War Information's identification with liberalism, and it cut funds for the domestic programs of the agency. The Office of War Information completely disbanded in 1945.

Office of War Mobilization   On May 27, 1943, President Franklin D. Roosevelt created the Office of War Mobilization, one of the very few wartime agencies with wide-ranging responsibilities over both manpower and material mobilization together with the power to enforce its regulators. The president acted because he was dissatisfied with the record of the WAR PRODUCTION BOARD. The Office of War Mobilization evolved from the Office of Economic Stability and it was charged with responsibilities dealing with domestic and foreign concerns from matters as trivial as tavern closing times to those as consequential as rationing. To run the Office of War Mobilization, Roosevelt appointed the Office of Economic Stabilization director James F. Byrnes, a former Democratic senator from South Carolina and a former member of the U.S. Supreme Court. Byrnes amassed so much power and authority over domestic affairs that some referred to him as the "assistant president" while others called him a czar. Among FDR's advisers, Byrnes became more powerful than Vice President HENRY WALLACE and War Production Board chairman Donald Nelson. When the war began to wind down, the name and the mission of Byrnes's agency changed to the Office of War Mobilization and Reconversion.

Okinawa   *See* BATTLE OF OKINAWA (1945)

Panay   *See* SINKING OF THE *PANAY* (1937)

Pearl Harbor Attack (1941)   In a surprise attack on December 7, 1941, Japan bombed the U.S. naval base at Pearl Harbor in Hawaii. The United States declared war on Japan the next day, beginning direct American involvement in World War II. U.S.-Japanese relations in the months prior to Pearl Harbor played an important role in the Japanese decision to launch the surprise attack. In late July 1941, the Roosevelt administration decided to freeze Japanese assets in the United States. This move was less severe than what the hard-liners preferred—an oil embargo as a weapon to halt Japanese aggression in China and the Pacific. Trade between the two nations could continue if the U.S. government approved. This move together with succeeding diplomatic negotiations with Japan was not intended to provoke war but to prevent it. Nonetheless, relations between the two nations steadily deteriorated, and by the end of the summer the freeze on assets had become a total trade embargo. As a result, Japan calculated that its available oil supply would last no more than two years. That realization had a major impact on the island nation's leaders. Japan wanted the West to cede China to Japanese domination and it wanted renewed trade with the United States.

The Americans were not willing to appease Japan, even though Roosevelt's focus was not on Asia but rather on Europe in assisting the British in countering the Nazi threat. The United States feared that if China fell Japan might attack the Soviet Union next, making the defeat of Germany far more difficult. On November 26, 1941, Secretary of State Cordell Hull had presented the Japanese with a 10-point list of demands that included Chinese independence and Japanese departure from Southeast Asia. That same day, the commander in chief of the Japanese navy, Admiral Isoroku Yamamoto, ordered an attack on the U.S. Pacific Fleet, which was based at Pearl Harbor. The fleet was directed to return to base should negotiations between Japan and the United States over scrap iron and oil sales be resolved (the Americans hoped that trade embargoes would halt Japanese aggression, but the Japanese contended that the United States had no right to criticize Japanese policies in the Pacific). By early December the chances for peace had all but disappeared. The attack on the Hawaiian Islands was planned in conjunction with Japan's Southern Operation, which involved targeted

The Japanese attack on the U.S. naval base at Pearl Harbor on December 7, 1941, brought the United States into World War II. *(U.S. Army/National Archives)*

assaults on the Philippines, Malaya, and the oil-producing Dutch East Indies. Yamamoto knew that a surprise attack and a quick victory were essential to achieving Japanese success against the United States.

On the morning of December 6 (December 7 in the United States), Yamamoto's forces began their attack. Approximately 350 aircraft, comprising two attack waves, went aloft. When the carriers were positioning themselves for the aircraft to launch, General George C. Marshall received a lengthy decoded response to Hull's demands, which the United States had intercepted from Tokyo. The message was intended for Kichisaburo Nomura, the Japanese ambassador to the United States. It instructed him to break off relations with the United States. Attached to it was a codicil stating that he must act by 1 p.m. Washington, D.C., time on December 7. Marshall viewed the codicil with considerable foreboding, and he alerted U.S. bases in the Pacific of this diplomatic development.

Bad weather conditions prevented speedy delivery of the warning to Hawaii, so Marshall immediately sent a telegram, the next fastest means of communication available at the time. The telegram was en route to U.S. headquarters when the attack commenced. Other missed opportunities to thwart the Japanese surprise attack included the spotting of a Japanese submarine by a U.S. destroyer on the same day as the attack (the incident was termed inconclusive and marked for further research) and an army radar operator's detection of a mass of incoming aircraft. His commanding officer dismissed the report, insisting that the blips on the radar screen were U.S. B-17 Flying Fortresses en route to the Philippines.

The pilot in the lead Japanese plane broke radio silence at 7:53 a.m. Hawaii time, yelling into his mouthpiece, "Tora! Tora! Tora!" The attack was on. An hour later, 18 U.S. ships had been destroyed, including eight battleships. Additional destruction included 180 aircraft beyond repair and another 120 aircraft in need of restoration. The death toll numbered 2,403. Of that number, 1,103 died when the USS *Arizona* was sunk. Injuries totaled 1,178. Significantly, however, all the U.S. aircraft carriers, the repair shops for the U.S. military, and the fuel-oil tank farm had escaped destruction. The Japanese commanders rejected suggestions that they launch a second attack, having lost only 29 aircraft in the attack.

Politically and diplomatically, Pearl Harbor did not prove beneficial to the Japanese. Instead of encouraging the Americans to negotiate a settlement, the attack brought an end to isolationist sentiment and launched a war that became for many a bloodthirsty quest for revenge. On December 8, the United States declared war on Japan. Nor did Pearl Harbor give the Japanese a strategic advantage. Following Pearl Harbor, German dictator Adolf Hitler and Italian dictator Benito Mussolini declared war on the United States. In response, Roosevelt asked for, and Congress quickly provided, war declarations against Germany and Italy on December 11. Hitler's decision made it possible for Roosevelt and the Allied powers to proceed with the strategy they favored—a preference to fight Germany first.

In the search for explanations about how Japan was able to launch such a successful attack, some Americans latched onto conspiracy theories, none of which have withstood scholarly analysis. Most severe were charges that Roosevelt purposefully maneuvered the attack. Careful study of official Washington's attitude toward Japan undercuts this argument. Prior to Pearl Harbor Roosevelt and his advisers viewed Japan as a nuisance that stood in the way of the real target—Germany. Furthermore, U.S. analysts did not believe Japan capable of the attack. Some scholars have instead questioned why Roosevelt did not place greater emphasis on negotiating with Japan, blaming him not for complicity in the attack but for short sightedness in failing to appreciate the threat from the Pacific.

Philippine Sea   *See* BATTLE OF THE PHILIPPINE SEA (1944)

***Porgy and Bess,* by George Gershwin (1935)**   Composer George Gershwin worked with white novelist DuBose Heyward and his brother lyricist Ira Gershwin to write the opera *Porgy and Bess.* Heyward had previously published a novel, *Porgy,* and a Broadway play with the same name (the latter was coauthored by his wife Dorothy Heyward). This opera is the only American produced work in the genre to gain international and popular acclaim. The music from *Porgy and Bess* is now considered a jazz classic.

Premiering in New York City on October 10, 1935, the opera tells the story of struggling African Americans at the turn of the 20th century. Porgy was a beggar, and Bess suffered from a sullied reputation. The story takes place at Catfish Row in Charleston, South Carolina. In the opening scene, Porgy tries to join a craps game while Bess and a drunken boyfriend named Crown walk toward the scene. The men stop their play to yell insults at Bess, and Porgy defends her. Meanwhile, Crown joins the game, loses, and kills a man. Bess then searches for someone to help her. No one in the town other than Porgy will. He takes her in, but the townspeople disapprove. Eventually Porgy finds and kills Crown. While he is being questioned, Bess leaves for New York with another man. Porgy is determined to find her.

African American critics have charged that the opera does not so much portray black life in the late 19th and early 20th centuries as it depicts the way whites wanted black life to be. Nonetheless, Hitler banned the opera during World War II and it was the first American work performed in the Soviet Union in the postwar years (this performance was part of a larger tour of the opera through Europe, the Middle East, South America, and Mexico). Heyward's novel serves as an example of primitivism, a movement that celebrated the "noble savage," whose innocence trumped the technological progress of Western civilization.

Public Utility Holding Company Act (1935)   Also known as the Wheeler-Rayburn Act after its sponsors Senator Burton K. Wheeler (D-MT) and Representative Sam Rayburn (D-TX), the Public Utility Holding Company Act, was enacted on August 26, 1935. The perspective offered by Supreme Court justice Louis Brandeis, who had warned against the dangers of "bigness" in the economy since early in the 20th century, helped shape the new law. Holding companies, defined as businesses that purchased a controlling interest in other enterprises, had garnered a bad reputation for cheating consumers, corrupting lawmakers, and avoiding the regulatory codes in existence. Roosevelt aides Thomas Corcoran and Benjamin Cohen helped draft the bill for Wheeler and Rayburn.

The most controversial feature of the bill, the so-called death sentence, authorized the SECURITIES AND EXCHANGE COMMISSION (SEC) to dismantle all holding companies that could not justify their reason for existing as of January 1, 1940. The utility companies spent over 1 million dollars in lobbying against the bill, which was popular in the West but not in the East. While the Senate passed the bill as written, the House removed the death sentence. Critics attacked this move, but the House bill did not constitute a weak substitute. It required the SEC to justify its orders to break apart any holding company. However, the administration and congressional supporters did not agree with this perspective. Instead, the fight for the death sentence continued.

Opponents prevailed and President Roosevelt had to accept a compromise. As passed, the Public Utility Holding Company Act eliminated utility holding companies with more than two layers of ownership separation from the operating companies. Furthermore, companies not in the public interest and beyond one layer of ownership separation were to be eradicated. As a result, most of the holding company empires disappeared within three years.

Public Works Administration   Despite the fact that President Roosevelt disavowed the role of public works projects in combating the depression, he moved forward with the Public Works Administration (PWA), a component of the NATIONAL INDUSTRIAL RECOVERY ACT of 1933, a government program that employed people on public works projects. The president asked Secretary of the Interior Harold Ickes to run the PWA. Because Ickes followed a muted strategy the PWA achieved few results with regard to stimulating the economy. His caution stemmed from recollections of the Teapot Dome scandal during the WARREN G. HARDING administration (1921–23) and his concern that local politicians would abuse the program. In 1933, Ickes authorized only $110 million, leading one assistant to complain that his boss spent too much time micromanaging the PWA. Ickes's failure to spend aggressively destroyed any chance the PWA would have to bring economic recovery.

In time, Ickes oversaw an impressive record of construction, including roads, schools, courthouses, and hospitals. Several projects that became significant features in the national landscape were part of this construction boom, including the Triborough Bridge, Lincoln Tunnel, and LaGuardia Airport in New York City; Skyline Drive in Virginia; the Overseas Highway in Florida; and the San Francisco–Oakland Bay Bridge in California. PWA projects also included a number to meet military needs, among which were aircraft carriers and light cruisers. Between July 1933 and March 1939, the PWA funded the construction of more than 34,000 projects. With a budget of $3.3 billion, it was also responsible for 70 percent of the new schools and one-third of the hospitals built during that time.

Recession of 1937   The year 1937 began with much economic promise. Output surpassed 1929 levels by the spring, but by August leading economic indicators told a different story, one of recession, a stock market that had fallen by 58 percent, and unemployment that had risen to 28 percent. The downturn should have surprised no one. Significant problems from early in the decade had not been resolved. Instead, deficit spending had been the source of the 1937 recovery. When President Roosevelt worried that inflation was likely, he cut spending for both the WORKS PROGRESS ADMINISTRATION and the PUBLIC WORKS ADMINISTRATION, leaving countless relief recipients jobless and halting work on infrastructure improvements. Furthermore, the initial collection of Social Security taxes removed money from circulation.

Administration officials disagreed vehemently over the proper strategy. While some moderates and conservatives argued for additional budget balancing measures, liberals noted that those were the policies that had initially triggered the recession. They wanted to adopt policies formulated by the leading British economist John Maynard Keynes, who advocated significant government spending in recessions and depressions so as to stimulate the private economy. In times of prosperity Keynes had called for heavy, progressive taxation to prevent the economy from overheating. Additionally, liberals believed monopolies served as a roadblock to recovery because their price structures were inflexible.

After Roosevelt initially listened to the budget balancers, liberals undertook a publicity campaign blaming monopolists for the recession. The search for a correct solution reflected the president's own doubts about how best to address the problem. Yet, by early 1938 the threat of starvation increased for those who had lost their relief payments. Journalists discussing the "Roosevelt recession" directed the brunt of their criticism at the president. He lost his authority with Congress, and, as a result, the consensus for any further New Deal reforms evaporated. The only exception was the FAIR LABOR STANDARDS ACT, which was enacted in 1938.

Reciprocal Trade Agreements Act (1934)   The depression and the domestic problems that resulted from it did not entirely eliminate President Franklin D. Roosevelt's commitment to internationalism. Secretary of State Cordell Hull was a former representative and senator from Tennessee who believed in free trade. Hull advocated enactment of the Reciprocal Trade Agreements Act to help lower tariffs and foster free trade, and Roosevelt agreed with the policy. Adopted on June 12, 1934, the Reciprocal Trade Agreements Act provided for bilateral negotiations to reduce tariff rates. On a related note, Hull negotiated reciprocity treaties with other countries on a most-favored-nation basis. A significant departure from the protective tariff rationale of the Smoot-Hawley Tariff of 1930, this policy ultimately led to the postwar General Agreement on Tariffs and Trade and the World Trade Organization.

Reconstruction Finance Corporation   When he became president in 1933, Franklin D. Roosevelt inherited the Reconstruction Finance Corporation (RFC) from the HERBERT HOOVER administration, and the new president quickly set about putting his own stamp on the agency. Hoover had wanted the agency, created on January 22, 1932, to provide loans to large businesses such as banks and railroads. He believed this action would shore up the rest of the economy. The appointment of Texas banker Jesse H. Jones to direct the agency signaled that Roosevelt preferred to encourage the aggressive business entrepreneurship characteristic of the Southwest over the established industries of the East Coast.

Jones brought a skepticism of Wall Street to his post that was common in the 1930s. Gone was the Hoover strategy of making loans to banks. In its place, Jones directed the RFC to purchase bank-preferred stock to increase banking capital, not banking debt, as had been the result of the loans to banks made under Hoover. Jones's strategy converted the RFC into the largest bank and the largest investor in the country. The RFC also spawned numerous subsidiary agencies, which worked in the fields of home mortgages, the commodity market, electricity development, and foreign trade. By the late 1930s, the RFC was engaged in direct federal lending to businesses, and Jones exerted much influence over the management of businesses that received largesse from the RFC.

Congressional appropriations for the RFC exceeded $13 billion by 1939. Jones infused the RFC with his values: personal loyalty, a borrower's perspective, and a fixation on profit. Even though Jones gave up his chairmanship of the RFC in 1939 he retained considerable influence until he left government service altogether in 1945. The RFC expanded significantly during World War II, providing many loans to businesses converting to wartime production. It was gradually dismembered in the 1950s, with its functions taken over by the Small Business Administration during the DWIGHT D. EISENHOWER administration.

Resettlement Administration   Created by Congress in May 1935, the Resettlement Administration (RA) was tasked with responsibility to address rural poverty needs. President Roosevelt appointed Rexford Tugwell, an agrarian reformer, to direct the agency. The RA continued the rural rehabilitation programs that Harry Hopkins had drafted during his tenure with the FEDERAL EMERGENCY RELIEF ADMINISTRATION. It also gained responsibility for subsistence homestead projects even though Tugwell opposed such experiments, which he considered were outdated. Instead, Tugwell favored the construction of "greenbelt communities," and three entirely new towns were built outside Washington, D.C., Cincinnati, and Milwaukee. Those suburban communities balanced proximity to urban employment with closeness to the rural countryside. However, Tugwell's primary responsibility was to oversee the movement of farm families from marginal, unproductive land to rich, fertile ground where a decent living could be had. This task fell victim to an inadequate budget. Instead of moving the planned half million families, the RA relocated less than 4,500. Because this program provided

Resettlement Administration poster *(Library of Congress)*

little to benefit tenant farmers and sharecroppers, the RA was ultimately replaced with a new agency, the FARM SECURITY ADMINISTRATION, in 1937.

Robinson-Patman Act (1936)   *See* ANTIMONOPOLY POLICIES

Ruml Plan (1943)   Designed by Beardsley Ruml, the chairman of the New York Federal Reserve Bank and the treasurer of R. H. Macy and Company, the Ruml Plan of 1943 aimed to assuage problems related to the expansion of the income tax to take in more citizens as taxpayers. For several years, Ruml had been interested in a tax reform that would move the country to a system whereby tax collection was kept current with workers' earnings. This plan created the system of income tax withholding, and its passage was linked to the context of the wartime tax revolution. The Revenue Act of 1942 had provided for $7 billion in new taxes, which almost doubled the previous year's tax collections. Before the attack on Pearl Harbor in 1941, only 4 million Americans paid income taxes out of a population that exceeded 130 million people. The median annual wage in 1939 was $1,231 and those with incomes under $1,500 a year paid no income tax. Those with incomes between $1,500 and $4,000 paid but a nominal tax. The Revenue Act of 1942 lowered the threshold to $624 for personal exemptions and brought an additional 13 million Americans into the tax system. Expanding wartime employment and higher wages turned millions more into taxpayers. By 1945, more than 42 million Americans were paying income taxes at rates ranging between 6 and 94 percent.

In 1943, lawmakers debated a system of employer withholding of estimated income tax payments for the following tax year to solve the problem of tax payments constantly being in arrears (in other words, Americans did not pay their 1941 taxes until 1942). The financial shock of the 1942 legislation combined with calls for additional tax legislation in 1943 led taxpayers to balk at the idea of paying the past year's taxes while at the same time having money deducted from their paychecks for the current year's taxes, which were not due until the following year.

The Ruml Plan offered a compromise. It proposed that the majority of taxes due for 1942 be forgiven, meaning that they would not have to be paid. All tax bills under $50 were forgiven and 75 percent of tax bills over $50 were forgiven. Roosevelt did not like the Ruml Plan, calling it a boon for the wealthy who would no longer be required to make a meaningful sacrifice for the war effort and who would dodge their wartime responsibility. He also disapproved of the loss of revenue for the government, but Congress passed the plan anyway, and Roosevelt signed it on June 9, 1943. Ruml contended that the plan would do nothing more than "move the tax clock forward, and cost the Treasury nothing until Judg-

ment Day" when everyone would be dead, and, according to one politician, "no one will give a damn."

Rural Electrification Administration (1935–1994)   More than any other component of the New Deal, the Rural Electrification Administration transformed the way people lived in the United States. It came closer to reducing social and economic inequality than did legislation designed for that purpose. Previous to its 1935 inception, 90 percent of American farms were without electricity, resulting in a stark divide between rural and urban citizens. The overwhelming majority of the latter enjoyed electricity. The Rural Electrification Administration stepped in where private companies had refused to provide electricity. Because of the heavy expenses and low profits expected, the latter had been unwilling to erect utility lines even when offered low-cost government loans. To counter this refusal, the Rural Electrification Administration fostered a nonprofit electric cooperative movement that quickly spanned the country. Over 400 rural electrical cooperatives serving almost 300,000 households were established in the first four years of the Rural Electrification Administration's operation. By 1941, 40 percent of farms were served with electricity and by 1950 that figure had increased to 90 percent. The Rural Electrification Administration was abolished in 1994.

Schechter Poultry Corp. v. United States (1935)   *See* NATIONAL INDUSTRIAL RECOVERY ACT (1933)

Securities and Exchange Commission   Created by the Securities Exchange Act of 1934, which Congress passed overwhelmingly, the Securities and Exchange Commission (SEC) proved to be one of the most important regulatory agencies in the U.S. government. Representative Sam Rayburn (D-TX) debated whether it "passed so readily because it was so damned good or so damned incomprehensible." The legislation and the regulatory body that was created targeted eliminating the monopoly of reliable information about the stock market then held by investment bankers. Financier Joseph P. Kennedy (and the father of future president JOHN F. KENNEDY) became the first chairman of the SEC. The SEC oversaw mandated disclosure of financial information about the companies traded on the stock market and independent auditing of this data. As a result, businesses were compelled to meet stringent reporting requirements and accountants became much more important in the business world. Instead of jeopardizing free-market capitalism, the SEC strengthened the financial markets by protecting them from dangerous downswings. Furthermore, the Chandler Act of 1938 gave the SEC authority to work with the federal judiciary in cases involving corporate reorganization. The SEC remains one of the most enduring agencies created during the New Deal.

Selective Service Act (1940)   *See* BURKE-WADSWORTH
SELECTIVE SERVICE TRAINING ACT

Servicemen's Readjustment Act (1944)   More popularly
known as the GI Bill of Rights, the Servicemen's Readjustment Act received near universal support in Congress and in
the country. Lawmakers and President Roosevelt acted out of
concern that failure to provide adequate social, educational,
and economic services to veterans returning from World
War II would prove disastrous for the postwar economy.
This worry was linked to the larger fear that the end of the
war might bring a return of the Great Depression. Veterans
groups, specifically the American Legion, lobbied for the GI
Bill, Congress passed it unanimously, and Roosevelt signed
the measure into law on June 22, 1944.

The GI Bill offered former soldiers a choice to pursue
vocational training or to obtain scholarships for college. The
purpose was twofold: to prevent a massive influx of new veterans into the workforce, which the economy could not handle,
and to help increase the standard of living for veterans on a
long-term basis. Those veterans attending school were eligible
for additional housing and medical benefits. Because so many
veterans took advantage of the program, the nation's colleges
and universities began a shift from existing as bastions for the
privileged few into serving as conduits for middle-class status,
a transformation that continued for the remainder of the 20th
century. The GI Bill also provided for low-interest home and
business startup loans. The former helped turn the United
States into a nation of homeowners and propelled the massive
postwar suburbanization movement.

The only real cry of protest against the GI Bill came from
the country's elite colleges and universities. The president of
the University of Chicago complained that the GI Bill would
produce "educational hobo jungles" with the veterans as
"educational hobos." This view, however, proved to be wrong,
as the millions of veterans who attended college in the years
immediately after World War II were good students interested in learning.

The Servicemen's Readjustment Act of 1944 was of
incalculable importance for spurring the nation's postwar
economic boom. Within seven years, approximately 8 million veterans received educational benefits. Over 2 million
attended colleges and universities, while the remainder
completed high school and gained on-the-job training. The
original GI Bill expired in 1956. During its lifetime, $14.5 billion had been awarded to veterans for educational purposes.
Another $33 billion had gone to home loans, which numbered 4.3 million and accounted for 20 percent of all new
homes built after the war.

Sinking of the *Panay* (1937)   The Sino-Japanese War
broke out in July 1937 after a brief skirmish near the Chinese
city of Beijing. China was then fighting a civil war between
nationalist and communist forces. Because Japan wanted
war, it moved aggressively against China with a brutal attack
against Nanjing, which was the Nationalist Chinese capital.
From December 1937 to March 1938 between 200,000 and
300,000 Chinese civilians were murdered in what became
known as the Rape of Nanjing. Significant American sympathy for China developed, but there was no accompanying
support for military action. On December 12, 1937, Japanese
pilots fired upon the *Panay*, a U.S. gunboat anchored in the
Yangtze channel. The *Panay* sank, killing two people and
injuring 30 more. Even though the ship was clearly marked
as an American vessel Japan claimed that the Japanese pilots
were too high to see the American flags. Evidence from an
accompanying film crew disproved Japanese claims. Despite
the sinking, American public opinion remained isolationist.
The attack intensified a push for both a U.S. exodus from
China and passage of a constitutional amendment requiring a
national referendum to determine U.S. entry into war (unless
the nation suffered a direct attack). The measure failed in the
House of Representatives by only 21 votes in January 1938.

Sit-down Strikes (1936–1937)   The American automobile
industry in the 1930s stirred with pent-up resentment against
the oligarchic practices of the three big automakers: General
Motors (GM), Ford, and Chrysler. Their profit margins came
not from increased prices for the cars they sold but through
squeezing the labor costs and discouraging union membership, often with violent, illegal tactics. The result was that the
traditional mass action strike proved impossible to implement. Instead, GM workers in Flint, Michigan, employed the
sit-down strike. Careful planning within the United Automobile Workers (UAW) union, which the auto manufacturers
did not recognize, and among communist labor activists was
necessary to make a success of this strike, which began on
December 30, 1936. The methodology of the strike involved
halting production at a plant critical to the overall health of
the automobile industry.

The strike started in Fisher Body Plant Number One,
which was partially responsible for production of the vehicle
bodies for GM's 1937 line, including Pontiacs, Oldsmobiles,
Buicks, and Cadillacs. After one worker noted railroad cars
on the loading dock, the signal went out for the strike to
commence during the swing shift at 8:00 p.m. After the meal
break, the workers filed back into the plant and sat down.
When the starting whistle blew no one returned to work. By
sitting down and refusing to work, strikers effectively shut
the factory, halting all production and shipping from Fisher
One. Rather than protesting outside or refusing to enter the
factory, standard practices during strikes, workers had seized
the plant and forced it to close.

The workers' demands were for recognition of the
UAW as their only bargaining representative with management, implementation of a grievance procedure, shorter

General Motors workers staging a sit-down strike in Flint, Michigan (©*Bettmann/CORBIS*)

workweeks, and a minimum wage scale. But sit-down strikes spread as the UAW undertook similar actions across Flint: Workers at Fisher Body Plant Number Two went on strike on December 30, 1936, and workers at Chevrolet Number Four went out on February 1. Officials at GM were irate; they called the strike an unlawful trespass and gained a court injunction to force the workers out of the plant. Strike leaders required that the strikers remain disciplined during the sit-down. According to one historian of the CIO, the UAW's parent union, this strike reflected both worker anger and union restraint. The strike benefited from a cohesive union culture that involved wives of strikers bringing in food on a daily basis and other examples of community solidarity.

The so-called Battle of the Running Bulls began on January 11, 1937, a day when the temperature measured 16 degrees. GM officials turned off the heat immediately after

noon and blocked the evening delivery of food into Fisher Body Plant Number Two, the weakest held of the striking plants. Several dozen police gathered outside the plant, and they later threw tear gas inside. Pickets outside the plant fought back, heaving makeshift weapons ranging from door hinges to chunks of pavement at the police and forcing their retreat. Thirteen of the 16 wounded strikers, sympathizers, and spectators were hit by police gunfire. Ten law enforcement officials were injured. A gas bomb hit a restaurant where journalists and workers had gathered.

At 5:00 A.M. on January 12, Michigan governor Frank Murphy, a Democrat and loyal New Dealer, ordered in the National Guard to maintain order. He opposed both the strike and the intervention by the court. He also authorized the state to make relief payments to the families of strikers. President Franklin D. Roosevelt pushed GM executives to recognize the union at the same time that Murphy worked with union officials, specifically John L. Lewis, to lessen some of their demands. Because the strike was successful in halting GM's production, the company wanted a speedy resolution (Ford and Chrysler were profiting from the strike).

On February 11, 1937, Lewis signed an agreement with GM making the UAW the sole representative of workers at the striking plant, but no deal was struck regarding the other demands. Still, the strike had ended, and the main issue, the right of industrial unions to bargain collectively, had been won. The workers left the plants, viewed as heroes to working-class union members throughout the country. The example of worker economic power that the strike offered had an impact in other major industries where strike talk was rampant. On March 2, 1937, U.S. Steel recognized the Steel Workers Organizing Committee, authorized a pay increase, implemented the eight-hour workday and the 40-hour workweek, and approved overtime pay at the rate of time and a half. Throughout this process, the newly organized National Labor Relations Board did nothing substantive to end the strike. However, its creation under the Wagner Act proved sufficient to help make possible the new terrain of labor-management relations. In the aftermath of the sit-down strikes, industrial union membership soared from 88,000 to 200,000 in the UAW and to 300,000 among steelworkers.

Smith v. Allwright (1944)

Among the devices white southerners employed to limit the impact of the Fifteenth Amendment that enfranchised black men was the white primary, implemented by Texas state law and copied throughout the region. Because the Republican Party had little prominence in the South, the Democratic Party was the only viable political organ, and its primary elections—when voters selected candidates—were much more significant for determining local and state officeholders than were general elections. The Texas law provided that since primary elections were private, the political parties could restrict membership and limit participation in their contests.

Lonnie E. Smith, an African-American dentist and National Association for the Advancement of Colored People (NAACP) activist in Houston, Texas, paid his poll tax, which was standard, and he tried unsuccessfully to vote in the 1940 Texas Democratic primary. Election officials barred him from voting because he was black, and Smith sued precinct election judge, S. E. Allwright. NAACP lawyers Thurgood Marshall and William Hastie defended Smith in a case heard by the Supreme Court. Marshall and Hastie contended that payment of the poll tax enabled Smith to vote in the primary election and that the Texas law violated the Fifteenth Amendment. The Court agreed in its 1944 ruling, overturning the white primary as unconstitutional. The voluntary status of Democratic Party membership did not mitigate against the fact that its contests were governed by statute and were thus public affairs. The *Smith v. Allwright* decision marked a major victory in the emerging Civil Rights movement and helped begin the process of securing voting rights for African Americans.

Social Security Act (1935)

Passed on August 14, 1935, the Social Security Act proved to be the most far-reaching legislation enacted under the New Deal. President Franklin D. Roosevelt began the year with a request that Congress begin work on Social Security legislation. While conservatives opposed the legislation, the more significant opposition came from liberals who viewed the bill as too mild. The Social Security Act passed Congress in the summer of 1935. It established a national pension system in which most workers were required to participate, and it established 65 as the retirement age. Workers would draw monthly pensions financed by worker and employer payroll taxes. The benefit checks were linked to worker earnings. The law also provided for the care of destitute elderly persons who were not otherwise beneficiaries of the program. Funding for these benefits derived equally from federal and state contributions. Limited unemployment insurance, aid for dependent mothers and children, assistance for the disabled, and a public health services program rounded out the provisions of the law. Never before had the U.S. government assumed such responsibilities.

Because the welfare provisions for impoverished senior citizens came from payroll tax deductions and not the general revenue fund, the law reflected the conservative tendencies inherent within the American political system. The massive outlay of capital required to implement the program strained the government's resources. The Social Security program did not cover everyone, particularly some of the most needy workers, namely, farm laborers and domestic servants. Nor did it make any provision for sickness, the typical cause of unemployment for otherwise healthy workers in a normally functioning economy. Finally, the act overlooked both a national system of unemployment compensation and the writing of national standards for unemployment policy.

Despite these limitations, the Social Security Act marked an important reform in the relationship between the federal government and the American people. Aged Americans, then the poorest demographic in the country, went from being a burden on their families to having money for their support. The law established a social safety net on the federal level. Conservative in comparison with the welfare systems in the rest of the industrialized world, the United States Social Security system was nonetheless a milestone, a sign to many Americans that the federal government had a responsibility to protect the social rights of the individual. Finally, the provisions of the law were carefully written to avoid a court challenge and to stand the test of time.

The regressive taxes were a purposeful choice to ensure that no future politician could eliminate the program without facing substantial voter outcry. The strategy worked. Roosevelt succeeded in his goal to create a program that would achieve enduring popularity. He realized that if the taxes that paid for the program came from payroll deductions, a regressive feature that disadvantaged the poor and working classes, then "no damn politician can ever scrap my Social Security program."

Soil Conservation and Domestic Allotment Act (1935)

In part a response to the DUST BOWL and in part a reflection of larger concerns about the nationwide problem of soil erosion, Congress passed the Soil Conservation and Domestic Allotment Act in 1935. The law created the Soil Conservation Service as a division of the Department of Agriculture. The new agency was charged with researching land usage and devising policy to prevent future soil erosion. Federal government compensation to farmers and businesses for limiting erosion was the preferred method for addressing this conservation problem.

Strange Fruit, by Lillian Smith (1944)

Florida-born and Georgia-based white writer Lillian Smith published *Strange Fruit* in 1944. The novel depicts a love affair between two

Lillian Smith, author of *Strange Fruit,* published in 1944
(Library of Congress)

young southerners, a white well-to-do man just home from military service in World War I, Tracy Deen, and a light-skinned African-American woman, Nonnie Anderson, against the backdrop of a fundamentalist religious revival. When Nonnie gets pregnant, Tracy tries to get her to have an abortion or marry another African American. Criticized for being obscene, the bestselling novel was banned by the U.S. Postal Service. Smith's follow-up denunciation of racism, *Killers of the Dream,* was published in 1949. As such, Smith became one of the first notable white southern writers to challenge racism and segregation. Her efforts won for her criticism from both southern moderates, who believed she had gone too far, and African-American intellectuals, who found her work patronizing because college-educated Nonnie fell for Tracy despite his poor treatment of her. A reviewer for the *Atlanta Constitution* even called the book a waste of paper at a time when resources were scarce, suggesting that Smith's story created much discomfort for white southerners.

Supreme Court Reorganization Plan (1937)

Following the election of 1936, President Franklin Roosevelt hoped to solidify and expand the New Deal. He believed that existing legislation was not safe from a conservative judiciary that had overturned key New Deal laws in declaring them to be unconstitutional. On February 5, 1937, the president presented Congress with the Supreme Court Reorganization Plan to reform the federal court system. Quickly dubbed the "court-packing plan," Roosevelt sought the power to appoint up to six additional justices for every member of the Supreme Court over the age of 70 who elected not to retire. The president's legislative request applied to the lower courts as well, where he proposed up to 44 new appointments. Roosevelt argued that crowded court dockets made the reform necessary.

The proposal quickly provoked opposition, not because there was historical significance in having nine justices on the Supreme Court (in the 19th century the number had fluctuated between five and 10) but because he had no substantive evidence of a clogged court system and because his veiled references to senility among the justices was deemed inappropriate. Roosevelt's real targets were James C. McReynolds, George Sutherland, Willis Van Devanter, and Pierce Butler, the four conservative Supreme Court justices who had consistently ruled against New Deal legislation. Ironically, they were younger than the Court's three liberal justices: Louis Brandeis, Benjamin Cardozo, and Harlan Fiske Stone. Chief Justice Charles Evans Hughes and Owen J. Roberts were the swing votes. Roosevelt's proposal faced immediate political criticism for being, in the words of the *New York World-Telegram,* "too clever, too damned clever."

Roosevelt did have justifiable concerns: After four years in office he had yet to make a single appointment to the Court (the first president since ANDREW JOHNSON to be in that position) and the Court had opposed virtually everything attempted in the New Deal. Since THEODORE ROOSEVELT'S presidency a generation earlier, liberal reformers decried conservative judicial activism for overturning federal and state legislation as unconstitutional. Recent examples from the 1920s included rulings rejecting a ban on child labor and a minimum wage for female workers. In 1935, the Court had unanimously declared the NATIONAL INDUSTRIAL RECOVERY ACT unconstitutional, and in 1936 it disallowed the AGRICULTURAL ADJUSTMENT ACT, the GUFFEY-SNYDER ACT'S bituminous coal code, and a New York State minimum wage law. That same year Congress considered over 100 pieces of legislation that proposed adjustments to the balance of power between the legislative and the judicial branches of the federal government.

Given the long-standing concern about judicial activism, Roosevelt's plan was startling only in that it was relatively weak. It failed because of public opinion and because the president mishandled the strategy of securing its adoption. Perhaps his strongest, most important opposition came from within the Democratic Party's congressional leadership. In the Senate, Majority Leader Alben Barkley (D-KY) complained that no advance discussion of the idea had been offered, and Representative Hatton Sumners (D-TX), the chairman of the House Judiciary Committee, broke with the New Deal over this legislation, remarking, "boys, here's where I cash in." Vice President JOHN NANCE GARNER was equally disdainful of the measure. Conservative southern Democrats, liberals, and progressives in the party all opposed the president in part for political reasons but more out of concern that the president was grabbing power at the expense of the judiciary.

So loud was the chorus of opposition that the president changed tactics, calling for the reform out of concern over judicial philosophy. But this backfired; charges that Roosevelt was seeking dictatorial powers that would upset the relationships between the three branches of the federal government intensified. On March 29, 1937, the Supreme Court ended the standoff between the president and his party in Congress in its landmark decision, *WEST COAST HOTEL CO. v. PARRISH*. This case upheld a Washington State minimum wage law, signaling Court deference to legislatures on questions of economics. Roberts was the justice who changed his mind. He explained that in the 1936 minimum wage case involving the 1923 Supreme Court case of *Adkins v. Children's Hospital*, the attorneys had not asked for that case to be overturned, but that the attorneys in *Parrish* had. Some Court watchers termed his vote the "switch in time that saved nine" from the president's court reform package. Soon thereafter the Court upheld the Wagner Act, using its broader interpretation of the commerce power as developed in the *Parrish* case.

Equally important, Roosevelt finally gained opportunities to appoint justices to the Supreme Court. In the next six years, Roosevelt approved eight new justices to the Supreme Court: Hugo Black (1937) replaced Willis Van Devanter; Stanley F. Reed (1938) replaced George Sutherland; Felix Frankfurter (1939) replaced Benjamin N. Cardozo; William O. Douglas (1939) replaced Louis D. Brandeis; Frank W. Murphy (1940) replaced Pierce Butler; James F. Byrnes (1941) replaced James C. McReynolds; Robert H. Jackson (1941) replaced Harlan Fiske Stone; and Wiley B. Rutledge (1943) replaced Byrnes. The court-packing plan was one of Roosevelt's strategic blunders. It weakened his presidency and made it unlikely that he would oversee more domestic reform comparable to what had been accomplished in his first term.

Teheran Conference (1943)   Discussions among the Big Three—President Roosevelt, British prime minister Winston Churchill, and Soviet premier Joseph Stalin—at the Teheran Conference in Iran in 1943 were much more substantive than those at the recently completed CAIRO CONFERENCE and were focused on waging the war in Europe, specifically devising strategy for what would become Operation Overlord, or the opening of the long-delayed second front against Germany.

Roosevelt arrived distrustful of Stalin. He had recently received reports from his advisers in Moscow that the Soviets no longer sought a cross-channel invasion of continental Europe, instead preferring the Americans and the British to fight in Italy and the Balkans. Roosevelt did not know if this was an accurate report, but for the United States, the invasion of France was central to the eventual defeat of Germany. The president did not relish a Soviet change of heart on this important issue of strategy, especially because it would mean two of the Big Three opposed the plan. Churchill had long opposed an invasion across the English Channel, fearing it would lead to slaughter such as that which took place in the trench warfare of World War I and believing that Stalin could better be controlled if the three Allies jointly approached Germany through the Balkans. Upon arriving in Teheran, Roosevelt met privately with Stalin but he failed to make a personal connection.

In the plenary sessions, Roosevelt, Stalin, and Churchill discussed Overlord, Poland's postwar boundaries, the future of Germany in the postwar period, the war in Asia, and the concept of a United Nations to succeed the League of Nations. Roosevelt intimated that he understood Soviet goals to achieve a preponderance of influence in Poland and in Latvia, Lithuania, and Estonia. Agreement was general that Germany would be dismembered into a collection of smaller states, but no specific plans were formulated.

These matters aside, Overlord dominated the meetings. During an early conversation about the plan for invading France, Roosevelt introduced controversy into the conversa-

The Big Three—Franklin Roosevelt *(center)*, Joseph Stalin *(left)*, and Winston Churchill—sit on the portico of the Russian Embassy in Teheran, Iran, during the 1943 conference. *(Library of Congress)*

tion. He queried his counterparts about a major attack on Germany launched from the Mediterranean region. Knowing Churchill's views all too well, Roosevelt hoped to learn Stalin's current thinking. Stalin began by suggesting he would enter the Asian war upon Germany's defeat. Next, he contended that the second front should be opened in France, not in Italy, which was cut off from the heart of Europe by the Alps, and not in the Balkans, which were also far removed from Germany. Churchill argued that Overlord should not detract from continued Italian operations, and Stalin agreed.

Stalin pressed for a decision about who would command Overlord and on what date it would begin. The British and the Americans declined to answer the first question, but Roosevelt indicated that May 1, 1944, was the target date for the invasion. The Teheran Conference ended with little but the Overlord campaign decided. Postwar concerns had been discussed but potential for disagreement remained and issues would be addressed at the YALTA CONFERENCE and the Potsdam Conference, both held in 1945.

Temporary National Economic Committee   *See* ANTIMONOPOLY POLICIES

Tennessee Valley Authority   On April 10, 1933, President Franklin D. Roosevelt asked Congress to authorize a hydroelectric development project at Muscle Shoals, Alabama, in the Tennessee River valley. His request expanded on proposals advocated for many years by Senator George W. Norris (R-NE). Roosevelt wanted a publicly owned company known as the Tennessee Valley Authority (TVA) to generate and distribute electricity along with the construction of dams to control flooding and to generate even more electricity; fertilizer production; a program countering soil erosion; efforts to

prevent deforestation; construction of a 650-mile waterway between Knoxville, Tennessee, and Paducah, Kentucky; new health and education programs in the region; the construction of recreational facilities; and efforts to entice industry to the area.

Roosevelt understood that the TVA would operate on the basis of no specific philosophy, but he hoped that it would become the model for developing other regions of the country. He even told Norris that it was "neither fish nor fowl, but, whatever it is, it will taste awfully good to the people of the Tennessee Valley." Republican Progressives and southern Democrats alike celebrated the measure for the modernizing reforms it would bring to the seven southern states within the Tennessee River valley.

Still, when it came time to establish the TVA and develop a specific program, no clear guidelines existed. The TVA nonetheless amassed a number of significant accomplishments: Dam construction provided flood control, eased river navigation, and provided affordable public power; its administration from the Tennessee Valley, not Washington, D.C., marked an important experiment in citizen participation in the government; and its nonpartisan employment program was combined with community outreach, job training, education programs, and community and economic development. As one historian has argued, this measure helped ensure the transformation of the region known as the Cotton Belt into the Sun Belt.

Tokyo Air Raids (1945)   Air Force general Curtis LeMay took command of the 21st Bomber Command on January 7, 1945. His mission was to undertake a sustained aerial attack on Japan. LeMay's beliefs about war, specifically that civilians should not be immune from attack, positioned him well for what would ensue. He used modern technology—the M-69 projectile bomb that spewed gelatinized gasoline and the long-range B-29 intercontinental bomber—to rain havoc first over Tokyo and then over major Japanese cities for five months beginning on March 9, 1945. That night, LeMay commanded 334 B-29 Superfortresses in a methodical strike on Tokyo. The pilots unleashed their firebombs in such a way as to create an unyielding inferno that left 1 million people homeless and that killed approximately 90,000 in the most horrific of fashions: Some perished from the burning gasoline from the bombs that adhered to human flesh and could not be extinguished by conventional means while others boiled to death in superheated canals and streams. The ongoing air raids targeted 66 cities in Japan, obliterated more than 40 percent of structures in these cities, left 8 million people homeless, killed 900,000 individuals, and wounded 1.3 million civilians.

Twenty-first Amendment (1933)   Even before Franklin Roosevelt was inaugurated president on March 4, 1933, Congress acted on one of his campaign promises: a new constitutional amendment to repeal the Eighteenth Amendment, which provided for Prohibition. On February 20, 1933, Congress approved the Twenty-first Amendment and sent it to the states for ratification. The necessary three-quarters of the states endorsed repeal by December 5, 1933. The Twenty-first Amendment was then incorporated into the U.S. Constitution, thus ending America's experiment with Prohibition. Earlier, on March 20, 1933, Congress had passed the Beer-Wine Revenue Act in preparation for the repeal of Prohibition. This legislation legalized, and authorized taxes on, beer and wine.

United States v. Curtiss-Wright Export Corporation (1936)

This case involved a plan to sell 15 machine guns to Bolivia by the Curtiss-Wright Export Corporation. In 1934, Congress had passed a joint resolution authorizing the president to prohibit the sale of arms to Bolivia for use in its conflict with Paraguay over the Chaco region, arguing that this ban would help bring peace to the area. Roosevelt implemented the resolution as soon as Congress approved it. The Supreme Court was left to decide whether the resolution involved an unconstitutional delegation of legislative power to the president. In 1936, the Court ruled in *United States v. Curtiss-Wright Export Corporation* that it did not because the issue involved foreign and not domestic affairs. In the conduct of foreign policy, argued Justice George Sutherland, the president wielded much more power for independent action than in the conduct of domestic affairs. Put simply, the president possessed the unilateral authority to reach executive agreements with other nations without seeking the approval of the Senate as required of treaties.

United States v. Darby (1941) *See* FAIR LABOR STANDARDS ACT (1938)

U.S.A., by John Dos Passos (1930s)

In *U.S.A.*, a trilogy of three novels published in the 1930s—*The 42nd Parallel, 1919,* and *The Big Money*—John Dos Passos conveyed the American democratic ideal as it had unfolded in the first three decades of the 20th century. Like many writers of his generation, Dos Passos was a radical who was concerned with what he believed were undesirable and dangerous developments stemming from modernity, which was leading to the disintegration of American values. He critiqued the consumer culture for its deleterious effects on workers and farmers. Dos Passos used modernist techniques to tell what was essentially a naturalist's story. This work by one of the greatest American writers marked an attempt to answer timeless questions about identity, belonging, and allegiance. The three novels were subdivided into four parts: "newsreels," which dealt with popular culture; "camera eyes," which included 51 stream-of-consciousness, autobiographical ruminations about topics in the novels; biographies of leading historical figures from the early 20th century; and descriptions of the major and minor characters in the novel. The myriad of topics Dos Passos described included advertising and public relations, popular films, credit, and the stock market. He argued that *U.S.A.* was "the speech of the people." He tried to capture both the successes and the failures of average people. By the 1940s, though, Dos Passos abandoned his radicalism out of a growing suspicion of mass movements and he became increasingly reactionary.

Wagner Act (1935) *See* NATIONAL LABOR RELATIONS ACT (1935)

War Manpower Commission (1942-1945)

On April 18, 1942, President Franklin D. Roosevelt created by executive order the War Manpower Commission (WMC) as a component of the Office for Emergency Management. The federal security administrator was given the chairmanship of the WMC, which included representatives from the War Department, the Agriculture Department, the Labor Department, the Navy Department, the WAR PRODUCTION BOARD, the Selective Service System, the Civil Service Commission, and the Federal Security Agency. The WMC replaced the functions of several other war agencies, including the Natural Resources Planning Board and the OFFICE OF PRODUCTION

War Manpower Commission poster *(Library of Congress)*

MANAGEMENT. Its responsibilities included labor recruitment for war and essential civilian industries, job training, analysis of manpower utilization, and labor market record keeping. Between the middle of 1942 and the middle of 1943, the WMC oversaw the work of the FAIR EMPLOYMENT PRACTICES COMMITTEE (the latter became an independent agency in May 1943).

Despite the extensive definition of its responsibilities, the WMC had no real authority over the size of the military, civilian workforce priorities, labor relations, or occupational deferments. President Roosevelt tried to fix this problem in late 1942 when he gave Paul McNutt, the director of the WMC, authority over the Selective Service System. McNutt immediately used his new power to issue a "work-or-fight" order that ended deferments for fathers, arguing that occupational status and not family status should determine whether a person entered the military. These policy recommendations earned McNutt the immediate hostility of Congress, organized labor, and those operating the Selective Service System, and they were not implemented on McNutt's terms (fathers were later subjected to the draft, but only after the Selective Service Commission freed itself from McNutt's oversight). The War Manpower Commission lost its authority over manpower policy with the creation of the OFFICE OF WAR MOBILIZATION in 1943, and it was abolished in September 1945.

War of the Worlds, Radio Broadcast by Orson Welles (1938)

On October 30, 1938, panic struck among some Americans who tuned in for the radio broadcast of an adaptation by Orson Welles of a science fiction novel, *The War of the Worlds,* published in 1898 by H. G. Wells. Science fiction was a very popular genre with readers and listeners in the 1930s. Actors with Welles's Mercury Theater group described a meteorite falling on a New Jersey farm and a Martian attack on New York City. In Welles's version, the play replicated an actual news broadcast that had interrupted the regularly scheduled programming. As a consequence, some listeners believed the attack to be real, and they called the media and the police for emergency assistance. Even though the program had begun with a statement that the following broadcast was based on a play written by Wells, many listeners never heard the opening notice because they were tuned to a very popular program on a different radio network that featured the ventriloquist Edgar Bergen and his dummy Charlie McCarthy.

The tenor of the programming mimicked broadcasts of the Munich Conference in September 1938 at which Great Britain and France had agreed to Hitler's demands to acquire for Germany the Sudetenland from Czechoslovakia. The broadcast contributed to the sense of alarm Americans were beginning to feel about their security. It also played a role in the emerging battle for audiences between the venerable newspaper industry and the fledgling radio business. Newspapers, annoyed that radio had scooped them with coverage of the Munich Conference, overstated the hysteria that resulted from the program. *The War of the Worlds* succeeded because Welles understood how to play with the imagination of the audience, revealing the persuasive power of mass communications.

War Production Board (1942-1945)

On January 16, 1942, one month after the United States entered World War II, President Roosevelt created the War Production Board, with the goal of ensuring a smooth conversion to a wartime economy, limiting unnecessary civilian economic activity, and harmonizing the supply of raw materials with production priorities. He appointed Donald Nelson, an executive with Sears, Roebuck, and Company, to run the War Production Board, which was modeled on the World War I–era War Industries Board.

However, the War Production Board was never as powerful in practice as it had been in design, and despite the gravity of its task, Nelson never had enough power to accomplish his mission. In areas of the economy where supply was most critical, such as rubber and petroleum, control was taken from Nelson and given to independent "czars." Nor did Nelson have any authority over prices or labor mobilization. Furthermore, he enjoyed no effective enforcement mechanisms regarding business expansion and conversion. Contract letting was not rationalized according to available facilities and labor sources; instead, the military and Congress used wartime contracts as prizes for favored constituencies. Additional complications came from critics who

The U.S. War Production Board seal of an eagle clutching a missile *(United States Federal Government)*

charged Nelson with favoring big business over small business. Congress responded by creating the Smaller War Plants Corporation, which achieved few meaningful results.

When the War Production Board failed to remedy the shortages in steel, copper, and aluminum, the Roosevelt administration drafted the Controlled Materials Plan in 1943 to grant the military authority over wartime production contracts and Nelson responsibility for material allocation and production schedules. The solution improved the situation but it was not permanent. That year, Roosevelt also created the OFFICE OF WAR MOBILIZATION and gave its director, James F. Byrnes, wide latitude over the wartime economy. The War Production Board remained as a powerless agency until the fall of 1945 when it was abolished.

Wealth Tax Act (1935)   In June 1935, President Roosevelt asked Congress to consider a revolutionary tax bill that provided for wealth and power redistribution. Specifically, the president sought to introduce higher inheritance taxes, gift taxes, higher graduated taxes on the wealthiest American incomes, and a corporate income tax rate proportional to corporate income. The president's request was based on multiple motivations. He was annoyed at the constant criticism of his administration's policies from the business community. He worried about the political impact of the radical populist senator Huey P. Long (D-LA), who had presidential aspirations for 1936. Finally, he heeded the advice of administration insiders, including Treasury Department officials and future Supreme Court justice Felix Frankfurter, a critic of business concentration.

Much media criticism ensued from this proposal, and some questioned whether Roosevelt really wanted a bill as strong as the one he had outlined to Congress. His actions following his message to lawmakers did not suggest a strong interest in the bill's passage, just its discussion. Progressive senator Robert M. LaFollette, Jr. (R-WI) took advantage of the situation. Along with 20 other senators he issued a document declaring that they would force the upper chamber to remain in session until the president's package of legislation, which included Social Security, labor legislation, public utility legislation, and banking reform as well as the tax bill, passed. This forced the president and his legislative leaders to step up their efforts.

Congressional critics, who termed the bill class legislation, removed the inheritance tax, minimized the corporate income tax, and eliminated all traces of wealth redistribution. As passed, the Wealth Tax Act of 1935 provided for estate, gift, capital, stock, surtax and excess profits taxes. The law ultimately failed to raise much revenue for the government, and ironically the new taxes were regressive not progressive. Additional regressive taxation, namely, the sales tax, was levied at the state level. Not until World War II did wealthy Americans see their tax bills increase.

***West Coast Hotel Co. v. Parrish* (1937)**   This Supreme Court case involved the question of minimum wage payments to female workers. Elsie Parrish worked for the West Coast Hotel Company in Wenatchee, Washington, and despite a state minimum wage law she was paid at a rate below the minimum wage. The question for the Court was whether the law violated the liberty of contract provisions of the Fifth Amendment and its application to the states by the Fourteenth Amendment.

In 1937, the Supreme Court rendered a 5-4 decision in *West Coast Hotel Co. v. Parrish* that upheld the minimum wage for women. In a major reversal of previous New Deal decisions, the Court avowed that there was no explicit discussion of the freedom of contract in the Constitution. Furthermore it found that due process provided restraints on liberty, noting that employers and employees were not equal in the contract negotiation process. Workers, argued the Court, were much less powerful than employers. This decision overruled the 1923 decision in *Adkins v. Children's Hospital,* which had overturned a minimum wage law as an improper extension of the state's police power. Before the Court adopted this new interpretation of the Constitution in the *Parrish* case, it had overturned a number of New Deal laws in citing their effect in blocking the freedom of businesses to contract with its workers. Such a position had prevented a legislative remedy for economic disparity. This decision provided for legislative superiority over the judiciary with regard to reasonable economic regulations and ensured further protections for workers.

Works Progress Administration   After the overwhelming Democratic sweep of Congress in the 1934 midterm elections, President Roosevelt discussed with several of his key advisers, including Harry Hopkins, Harold Ickes, and Henry Morgenthau, his desire for a major new program to address unemployment. Once the new Congress was sworn in the administration pushed through a $4.8 billion appropriation for unemployment relief in creating the Works Progress Administration, renamed the Work Projects Administration in 1939 (WPA). During the course of its existence, the WPA spent more than $11 million in unemployment relief. Based on his experience with the FEDERAL EMERGENCY RELIEF ADMINISTRATION and the CIVIL WORKS ADMINISTRATION, Hopkins was appointed to direct the WPA. Ickes was not pleased—he wanted to maintain his status as Roosevelt's leading administrator of depression relief—but his focus on large-scale construction projects with the PUBLIC WORKS ADMINISTRATION all but ruled him out of consideration. He nonetheless criticized Hopkins's decentralized administration of the program, contending that the lack of centralized direction would lead to waste and corruption.

Under Hopkins's direction, local entities proposed projects, state boards determined approval, and funding came from the federal level. The WPA required that 90 percent of the workers come from the relief rolls. Monthly pay initially ranged from $60 to $100, figures that were above the poverty level but below what could be earned in the private sector. In southern states, WPA pay was much lower. The WPA remained in existence until 1943 when conservatives in Congress were able to eliminate it as a war economy measure. During its years in operation the WPA employed approximately 8 million people or 20 percent of the workforce. It also earned significant criticism as a make work program. The tendency of lawmakers to use the WPA for political patronage purposes did not help to counter this claim. The majority of WPA jobs involved manual labor, such as paving roads, building drainage systems, erecting public buildings, and constructing parks and recreational facilities.

Several important WPA projects were also geared toward unemployed artists and entertainers: the Federal Writers Project, the Federal Art Project, the Federal Theater Project, and the Federal Music Project. The Writers Project compiled the American Guide Series, which consisted of informative state and city guidebooks complete with information on local history and popular culture. The Arts Project worked in a variety of media but it was best known for employing artists to paint murals in public buildings throughout the country. These murals drew from the talents of both leading artists, such as Thomas Hart Benton and Jackson Pollock, and individuals of only modest ability. The Theater Project introduced many Americans to live stage performances and

exemplified the social and cultural pluralism that permeated all the arts projects. The best example was the performance of *It Can't Happen Here,* a cautionary tale about the dangers of dictatorship performed simultaneously in 21 theaters and 17 states. The cultural components of the WPA provided an important precedent for a permanent federal government commitment to the arts and humanities, realized a generation later during the Great Society of LYNDON B. JOHNSON with the creation of the National Endowment for the Arts and the National Endowment for the Humanities.

Overall assessments of the WPA have proved difficult. While the program met long-held recommendations of social workers for work relief as opposed to a charitable dole, it never benefited more than one-third of unemployed Americans. Its concentration on wages meant that the WPA had a negligible impact on economic recovery. Even the high level of spending associated with the WPA proved insufficient to counter the damage done to business and industry by the Great Depression. Its partisanship was borne out by the fact that 80 percent of its beneficiaries were Democratic voters. Although it relied on heavy deficit spending, the WPA transcended these difficulties and transformed the federal approach to unemployment. The WPA became one of the major New Deal programs, employing over 8.5 million people in both public construction projects and arts projects. The WPA was responsible for constructing 572,000 miles of roads, 2,500 hospitals, 1,000 airports, 5,900 schools, and 85,000 public buildings. Of its arts projects displayed in pub-

Established in 1935 to provide employment, the WPA lasted until 1943. This poster, created by the WPA's Federal Art Project during World War II for New York City's Department of Water Supply, Gas and Electricity, urged water conservation. *(Library of Congress)*

lic buildings, 2,566 murals were painted and 17,744 sculptures were completed.

Yalta Conference (1945) In early February 1945, the Big Three—President Franklin Roosevelt, Soviet premier Joseph Stalin, and British prime minister Winston Churchill—met at Yalta, a Black Sea resort on the Crimean Peninsula. With World War II almost over, the three leaders hoped to resolve four major areas of disagreement: how nations would join and vote in the new United Nations, the political and economic future of Poland and the remainder of eastern Europe, Germany's future, and whether the Soviet Union would declare war on Japan. In a private session with Stalin before the first general meeting of the Big Three, Roosevelt signaled his approval of the brutal treatment being meted out to captured German officers by the Russians. The president also criticized the weakness of France, and he made disparaging remarks about the British.

Stalin's military advantage in Europe—the Red Army was but a few miles from Berlin while U.S. and British troops had not yet crossed the Rhine River—perhaps underlay the arrogant behavior he displayed at the time of the conference. Stalin insisted that each country should have veto power on the United Nations Security Council. He also wanted the Ukraine and White Russia to occupy seats as voting members of the General Assembly. Roosevelt assented to both requests even though the latter was opposed by nations in western Europe.

Negotiations concerning Poland, which the Soviet Union wanted to dominate, were more intractable. At the time of the Yalta Conference two rival governments stood ready to rule in Poland: The London Poles operated a government in exile that enjoyed the patronage of British financial interests and the Lublin Poles ran a communist government located in the eastern Polish city of that name. To advance the validity of that government over the London Poles, Stalin had approved the massacre of Polish army officers in the Katyn Forest in 1940 and had not acted to prevent the German suppression of the Warsaw uprising in 1944. The solution to the Polish question agreed to at Yalta was the Declaration on Liberated Europe, which called for free elections in liberated countries. The ideals of the document, however, competed with the realities of the Red Army, and Roosevelt knew it. He could do no more toward ensuring democracy in eastern Europe short of fighting the Red Army.

Regarding Germany, Stalin argued for dismemberment and reparations. He was unaware that a major debate about Germany had been underway both within the United States and between the United States and Great Britain. Consideration of those debates is necessary for a full understanding of the Yalta Conference. Treasury secretary Henry Morgenthau had advocated deindustrializing the Ruhr and the Saar and dividing Germany into several nations shorn of industry and largely agriculture based. Secretary of State Cordell Hull had disagreed, arguing that the Morgenthau Plan would wreck the entire European economy. Secretary of War Henry Stimson concurred. Churchill had at first opposed the Morgenthau Plan, but when he learned that postwar American aid might be tied to the fate of Germany he revised his views. At the Quebec Conference in September 1944, Roosevelt and Churchill had agreed to the Morgenthau Plan, but Hull and Stimson refused to go along. The pressure they exerted on the president was such that FDR ultimately backed away from the Morgenthau Plan, leaving him without a position on Germany at the start of the Yalta Conference. The best Roosevelt could do was to focus the conversation on zones of occupation for Germany, not permanent partition. Roosevelt also agreed to the principle of reparations—Stalin wanted $10 billion from Germany's industrial production centers—knowing that the heavily industrialized Saar and Ruhr regions would be located in a western zone of occupation.

On the topic of Japan, Roosevelt coaxed from the Soviets an agreement to declare war against the island nation. He hoped that Soviet participation in the defeat of Japan would shorten the overall course of the war, prevent the need for an invasion of the Japanese islands, permit the United States to use Siberian air bases for attacks against Japan, and hinder Stalin from creating problems in Europe. Stalin exacted a heavy price: annexation of the Kurile Islands, southern Sakhalin Island, and the ports of Darien and Port Arthur, and control of two railroads in Manchuria. China opposed these actions, but neither the British nor the Chinese learned of this particular agreement in a timely fashion. While Roosevelt and Stalin held these conversations bilaterally and while no public announcement of these terms was issued immediately after the Yalta Conference, a secret, sinister motivation lay behind them.

Back in the United States, Roosevelt talked only of how the agreements reached at Yalta would mean the spread of democracy at the conclusion of the war. Nonetheless, news of the deal giving the Soviets additional representation at the United Nations General Assembly helped spread rumors of an ill president who had been duped by Stalin. Roosevelt's actions at the Yalta Conference came under criticism from conservatives who believed he should have been more forceful in standing up to the Soviets. Others argued that there was little else that the United States could have done at Yalta, that the agreements made were in keeping with the trajectory of Big Three diplomacy throughout the war and reflected the military realities of February 1945. Roosevelt himself said of Yalta, "I didn't say the result was good, I said it was the best I could do."

Zoot Suit Riots (1943) The worst race riots in Los Angeles's history to date occurred during the first two weeks of June 1943. The conflict took place between white American sailors and youthful Mexican American *pachucos* sporting the rebellious "zoot suit" made up of long-tailed jackets and pants baggy through the legs but fitted at the ankles. The zoot suit style, which was associated with jazz culture, was also popular with African-American youths, and a few blacks were involved in the riots as well.

The sailors took it as their mission to remove the offending garments from the bodies of the Mexican youths, often leaving their victims bloody and beaten. In one typical incident, sailors found two *pachucos* in a movie theater. They dragged them to the stage, forcefully stripped them naked, and urinated on the garments. Some of the victims were as young as 12, and only half were wearing the zoot suit. At the end of the riots, several dozen people were hospitalized. Hundreds suffered beatings, 132 of which were significant, but no one was killed. Even though white sailors started the rioting, 94 Mexican Americans were arrested compared with 20 military personnel and 30 non-Hispanic citizens. There was little property damage.

The riots occurred within the larger context of recent large-scale migration to Los Angeles of Mexicans, who were drawn to the city's surging wartime economy, a high number of sailors and soldiers waiting to be shipped to the Pacific theater, and a Mexican-American population increasingly unwilling to accept subordination and prejudice. Whites viewed the zoot suiters as lawless youth, even though there was no proof for such claims. Furthermore, during the war years teenagers were increasingly left to their own devices in the afternoon and evenings as their parents were occupied with either war work or military service. As a result, a social outcry grew about rising juvenile delinquency rates. This development provided further context for the Los Angeles riots. Underlying racial and social differences along with conflicting views of patriotism helped spark the zoot suit riots. For example, the abundant fabric used to make the zoot suit violated the edicts of wartime rationing, which required that men's suits be made with less fabric than had been true several years previously. Competition for the affections of young women also contributed to the violent conflicts.

Media coverage emphasized the riots as proof that Mexicans and African Americans of draft age were avoiding military service and were simply causing trouble. The press did not discuss the failure of the authorities to prevent the attacks, which originated with the actions of the white sailors. Nor did it mention the Mexican-American servicemen, who refused to behave violently toward the *pachuco* gangs. California politicians worried that the riots would threaten friendly relations between the United States and Mexico and would impede the BRACERO PROGRAM for bringing Mexican workers into the United States.

Local officials looked to stricter enforcement mechanisms against Mexican- and African-American youths to prevent further riots. California governor Earl Warren formed a commission to study the riots, which noted the depressed economic conditions prevalent among the approximately 250,000 Mexican Americans in Los Angeles County. President Roosevelt made only a general statement condemning the violence, which did little to prevent similar outbreaks elsewhere that summer. Indeed, the violent encounters spread throughout southern California and to other southwestern states, including Texas and Arizona, and to other major cities, including Detroit, New York, and Philadelphia.

Nancy Beck Young

Further Reading

Alter, Jonathan. *The Defining Moment: FDR's Hundred Days and the Triumph of Hope.* New York: Simon and Schuster, 2006.

Badger, Anthony J. *The New Deal: The Depression Years, 1933–40.* Chicago: Ivan R. Dee, 2002.

Bailey, Thomas A., and Paul B. Ryan. *Hitler vs. Roosevelt: The Undeclared Naval War.* New York: Free Press, 1979.

Barber, William J. *Designs within Disorder: Franklin D. Roosevelt, the Economists, and the Shaping of American Economic Policy, 1933–1945.* New York: Cambridge University Press, 1996.

Bellush, Bernard. *Franklin D. Roosevelt as Governor of New York.* New York: Columbia University Press, 1955.

Best, Gary Dean. *Pride, Prejudice, and Politics: Roosevelt versus Recovery, 1933–1938.* New York: Praeger, 1991.

Blum, John Morton. *V Was for Victory: Politics and American Culture during World War II.* New York: Harcourt Brace Jovanovich, 1976.

Brinkley, Alan. *The End of Reform: New Deal Liberalism in Recession and War.* New York: Knopf, 1995.

Burns, James MacGregor. *Roosevelt: The Lion and the Fox.* New York: Harcourt, Brace, 1956.

———. *Roosevelt: The Soldier of Freedom.* New York: Harcourt, 1970.

Cashman, Sean Dennis. *America in the Twenties and Thirties: The Olympian Age of Franklin Delano Roosevelt.* New York: New York University Press, 1989.

———. *America, Roosevelt, and World War II.* New York: New York University Press, 1989.

Churchill, Winston. *Churchill & Roosevelt: The Complete Correspondence.* 3 vols. Edited by Warren F. Kimball. Princeton, N.J.: Princeton University Press, 1984.

Cohen, Robert. *Dear Mrs. Roosevelt: Letters from Children of the Great Depression.* Chapel Hill: University of North Carolina Press, 2002.

Cole, Wayne S. *Roosevelt & the Isolationists, 1932–45.* Lincoln: University of Nebraska Press, 1983.

Conkin, Paul K. *The New Deal.* Wheeling, Ill.: Harlan Davidson, 1992.

Dallek, Robert. *Franklin D. Roosevelt and American Foreign Policy, 1932–1945.* New York: Oxford University Press, 1979.

Davis, Kenneth S. *FDR: The Beckoning of Destiny, 1882–1928; A History.* New York: Putnam, 1972.

———. *FDR, into the Storm, 1937–1940: A History.* New York: Random House, 1993.

———. *FDR, the New Deal Years, 1933–1937: A History.* New York: Random House, 1986.

———. *F.D.R., the New York Years, 1928–1933.* New York: Random House, 1985.

———. *FDR, the War President, 1940–1943: A History.* New York: Random House, 2000.

Dickinson, Matthew J. *Bitter Harvest: FDR, Presidential Power, and the Growth of the Presidential Branch.* New York: Cambridge University Press, 1997.

Divine, Robert A. *Roosevelt and World War II.* Baltimore: Johns Hopkins University Press, 1969.

Donahoe, Bernard F. *Private Plans and Public Dangers: The Story of FDR's Third Nomination.* Notre Dame, Ind.: University of Notre Dame Press, 1965.

Farnham, Barbara Rearden. *Roosevelt and the Munich Crisis: A Study of Political Decision-Making.* Princeton, N.J.: Princeton University Press, 1997.

Fraser, Steve, and Gary Gerstle, eds. *The Rise and Fall of the New Deal Order, 1930–1980.* Princeton, N.J.: Princeton University Press, 1989.

Freidel, Frank. *F.D.R. and the South.* Baton Rouge: Louisiana State University Press, 1965.

———. *Franklin D. Roosevelt.* 4 vols. Boston: Little, Brown, 1952–1973.

———. *Franklin D. Roosevelt: A Rendezvous with Destiny.* Boston: Little, Brown, 1990.

Glantz, Mary E. *FDR and the Soviet Union: The President's Battles over Foreign Policy.* Lawrence: University Press of Kansas, 2005.

Goodwin, Doris Kearns. *No Ordinary Time: Franklin and Eleanor Roosevelt: The Home Front in World War II.* New York: Simon and Schuster, 1994.

Gordon, Colin. *New Deals: Business, Labor, and Politics in America, 1920–1935.* New York: Cambridge University Press, 1994.

Hamby, Alonzo L. *For the Survival of Democracy: Franklin Roosevelt and the World Crisis of the 1930s.* New York: Free Press, 2004.

Harper, John Lamberton. *American Visions of Europe: Franklin D. Roosevelt, George F. Kennan, and Dean G. Acheson.* New York: Cambridge University Press, 1994.

Hawley, Ellis W. *The New Deal and the Problem of Monopoly: A Study in Economic Ambivalence.* Princeton, N.J.: Princeton University Press, 1966.

Heinrichs, Waldo. *Threshold of War: Franklin D. Roosevelt and American Entry into World War II.* New York: Oxford University Press, 1988.

Hoopes, Townsend, and Douglas Brinkley. *FDR and the Creation of the U.N.* New Haven, Conn.: Yale University Press, 1997.

Houck, Davis W., and Amos Kiewe. *FDR's Body Politics: The Rhetoric of Disability.* College Station: Texas A&M University Press, 2003.

Kennedy, David M. *Freedom from Fear: The American People in Depression and War, 1929–1945.* New York: Oxford University Press, 1999.

Kimball, Warren F. *Forged in War: Roosevelt, Churchill, and the Second World War.* New York: William Morrow, 1997.

———. *The Juggler: Franklin Roosevelt as Wartime Statesman.* Princeton, N.J.: Princeton University Press, 1991.

Lash, Joseph P. *Eleanor and Franklin: The Story of Their Relationship, Based on Eleanor Roosevelt's Private Papers.* New York: Norton, 1971.

Leuchtenburg, William E. *The FDR Years: On Roosevelt and His Legacy.* New York: Columbia University Press, 1995.

———. *Franklin D. Roosevelt and the New Deal, 1932–1940.* New York: Harper & Row, 1963.

———. *In the Shadow of FDR: From Harry Truman to George W. Bush.* 3d ed. Ithaca, N.Y.: Cornell University Press, 2001.

———. *The Supreme Court Reborn: The Constitutional Revolution in the Age of Roosevelt.* New York: Oxford University Press, 1995.

———. *The White House Looks South: Franklin D. Roosevelt, Harry S. Truman, Lyndon B. Johnson.* Baton Rouge: Louisiana State University Press, 2005.

Maney, Patrick J. *The Roosevelt Presence: A Biography of Franklin Delano Roosevelt.* New York: Twayne, 1992.

McJimsey, George. *The Presidency of Franklin Delano Roosevelt.* Lawrence: University Press of Kansas, 2000.

———, ed. *The Documentary History of the Franklin D. Roosevelt Presidency.* 47 vols. Bethesda, Md.: University Publications of America, 2001– .

Milkis, Sidney M. *The President and the Parties: The Transformation of the American Party System since the New Deal.* New York: Oxford University Press, 1993.

Morgan, Ted. *FDR: A Biography.* New York: Simon and Schuster, 1985.

Neal, Steve. *Happy Days Are Here Again: The 1932 Democratic Convention, the Emergence of FDR—and How America Was Changed Forever.* New York: William Morrow, 2004.

Parmet, Herbert S., and Marie B. Hecht. *Never Again; A President Runs for a Third Term.* New York: Macmillan, 1968.

Patterson, James T. *Congressional Conservatism and the New Deal: The Growth of the Conservative Coalition in Congress.* Lexington: University of Kentucky Press, 1967.

Perlmutter, Amos. *FDR & Stalin: A Not So Grand Alliance, 1943–1945.* Columbia: University of Missouri Press, 1993.

Persico, Joseph E. *Roosevelt's Secret War: FDR and World War II Espionage.* New York: Random House, 2001.

Polenberg, Richard. *Reorganizing Roosevelt's Government, 1933–1939.* Cambridge, Mass.: Harvard University Press, 1966.

———. *War and Society: The United States, 1941–1945.* Philadelphia: Lippincott, 1972.

Ritchie, Donald A. *Electing FDR: The New Deal Campaign of 1932.* Lawrence: University Press of Kansas, 2007.

Robinson, Greg. *By Order of the President: FDR and the Internment of Japanese Americans.* Cambridge, Mass.: Harvard University Press, 2001.

Romasco, Albert U. *The Politics of Recovery: Roosevelt's New Deal.* New York: Oxford University Press, 1983.

Roosevelt, Eleanor. *This I Remember.* New York: Harper, 1949.

Roosevelt, Franklin D. *Complete Presidential Press Conferences of Franklin D. Roosevelt.* 25 vols. New York: Da Capo Press, 1972– .

———. *F.D.R., Columnist: The Uncollected Columns of Franklin D. Roosevelt.* Edited by Donald Scott Carmichael. Chicago: Pellegrini and Cudahy, 1947.

———. *F.D.R.: His Personal Letters.* 4 vols. Edited by Elliott Roosevelt. New York: Duell, Sloan and Pearce, 1947–1950.

———. *FDR's Fireside Chats.* Edited by Russell D. Buhite and David W. Levy. New York: Penguin, 1992.

———. *Franklin D. Roosevelt and Conservation, 1911–1945.* 2 vols. Edited by Edgar B. Nixon. Hyde Park, N.Y.: General Services Administration, National Archives and Records Service, Franklin D. Roosevelt Library, 1957.

———. *Franklin D. Roosevelt and Foreign Affairs.* 3 vols. Edited by Edgar B. Nixon. Cambridge, Mass.: Belknap Press of Harvard University Press, 1969– .

———. *Franklin D. Roosevelt and Foreign Affairs, January 1937–August 1939.* 10 vols. Edited by Donald B. Schewe. New York: Garland, 1979– .

———. *Government—Not Politics.* New York: Covici-Friede, 1932.

———. *The Happy Warrior, Alfred E. Smith; A Study of a Public Servant.* Boston: Houghton Mifflin, 1928.

———. *Looking Forward.* New York: John Day, 1933.

———. *My Dear Mr. Stalin: The Complete Correspondence between Franklin D. Roosevelt and Joseph V. Stalin.* Edited by Susan Butler. New Haven, Conn.: Yale University Press, 2005.

———. *On Our Way.* New York: John Day, 1934.

———. *The Public Papers and Addresses of Franklin D. Roosevelt.* 13 vols. New York: Random House, 1938–1950.

———. *Public Papers of Franklin D. Roosevelt, Forty-Eighth Governor of the State of New York, 1929–1932.* 4 vols. Albany: J. B. Lyon, 1930–1939.

———. *Rendezvous with Destiny; Addresses and Opinions of Franklin Delano Roosevelt.* Edited by J. B. S. Hardman. New York: Dryden, 1944.

———. *Roosevelt and Frankfurter: Their Correspondence, 1928–1945.* Edited by Max Freedman. Boston: Little, Brown, 1967.

———. *Wartime Correspondence between President Roosevelt and Pope Pius XII.* Edited by Myron C. Taylor. New York: Macmillan, 1947.

Rosen, Elliot A. *Hoover, Roosevelt, and the Brains Trust: From Depression to New Deal.* New York: Columbia University Press, 1977.

———. *Roosevelt, the Great Depression, and the Economics of Recovery.* Charlottesville: University of Virginia Press, 2005.

Savage, Sean J. *Roosevelt, the Party Leader, 1932–1945.* Lexington: University Press of Kentucky, 1991.

Schlesinger, Arthur M., Jr. *The Age of Roosevelt.* 3 vols. Boston: Houghton Mifflin, 1957–1960.

Schwarz, Jordan A. *The New Dealers: Power Politics in the Age of Roosevelt.* New York: Knopf, 1993.

Shesol, Jeff. *Supreme Power: Franklin Roosevelt vs. the Supreme Court.* New York: W. W. Norton, 2010.

Shogan, Robert. *Backlash: The Killing of the New Deal.* Chicago: Ivan R. Dee, 2006.

Sparrow, Bartholomew H. *From the Outside In: World War II and the American State.* Princeton, N.J.: Princeton University Press, 1996.

Stoler, Mark A. *Allies in War: Britain and America against the Axis Powers, 1940–1945.* New York: Oxford University Press, 2005.

Ward, Geoffrey C. *Before the Trumpet: Young Franklin Roosevelt, 1882–1905.* New York: Harper and Row, 1985.

———. *A First-Class Temperament: The Emergence of Franklin Roosevelt.* New York: Harper and Row, 1989.

———, ed. *Closest Companion: The Unknown Story of the Intimate Friendship between Franklin Roosevelt and Margaret Suckley.* Boston: Houghton Mifflin, 1995.

Winfield, Betty Houchin. *FDR and the News Media.* Urbana: University of Illinois Press, 1990.

DOCUMENTS

—⁂—

Document One: President Franklin D. Roosevelt, Inaugural Address, March 4, 1933

When Franklin D. Roosevelt was inaugurated president on March 4, 1933, the country was mired in the Great Depression. The new president spoke in bold but general terms about how he would handle the nation's economic problems.

This is a day of national consecration, and I am certain that my fellow Americans expect that on my induction into the Presidency I will address them with a candor and a decision which the present situation of our Nation impels.

This is preeminently the time to speak the truth, the whole truth, frankly and boldly. Nor need we shrink from honestly facing conditions in our country today. This great Nation will endure as it has endured, will revive and will prosper.

So, first of all, let me assert my firm belief that the only thing we have to fear is fear itself—nameless, unreasoning, unjustified terror which paralyzes needed efforts to convert retreat into advance.

In every dark hour of our national life a leadership of frankness and vigor has met with that understanding and support of the people themselves which is essential to victory. I am convinced that you will again give that support to leadership in these critical days.

In such a spirit on my part and on yours we face our common difficulties. They concern, thank God, only material things. Values have shrunken to fantastic levels; taxes have risen; our ability to pay has fallen; government of all kinds is faced by serious curtailment of income; the means of exchange are frozen in the currents of trade; the withered leaves of industrial enterprise lie on every side; farmers find no markets for their produce; the savings of many years in thousands of families are gone.

More important, a host of unemployed citizens face the grim problem of existence, and an equally great number toil with little return. Only a foolish optimist can deny the dark realities of the moment.

Yet our distress comes from no failure of substance. We are stricken by no plague of locusts. Compared with the perils which our forefathers conquered because they believed and were not afraid, we have still much to be thankful for. Nature still offers her bounty and human efforts have multiplied it. Plenty is at our doorstep, but a generous use of it languishes in the very sight of the supply.

Primarily this is because rulers of the exchange of mankind's goods have failed through their own stubbornness and their own incompetence, have admitted their failure, and have abdicated. Practices of the unscrupulous money changers stand indicted in the court of public opinion, rejected by the hearts and minds of men.

True they have tried, but their efforts have been cast in the pattern of an outworn tradition. Faced by failure of credit they have proposed only the lending of more money.

Stripped of the lure of profit by which to induce our people to follow their false leadership, they have resorted to exhortations, pleading tearfully for restored confidence. They know only the rules of a generation of self-seekers.

They have no vision, and when there is no vision the people perish.

The money changers have fled from their high seats in the temple of our civilization. We may now restore that temple to the ancient truths.

The measure of the restoration lies in the extent to which we apply social values more noble than mere monetary profit.

Happiness lies not in the mere possession of money; it lies in the joy of achievement, in the thrill of creative effort.

The joy and moral stimulation of work no longer must be forgotten in the mad chase of evanescent profits. These dark days will be worth all they cost us if they teach us that our true destiny is not to be ministered unto but to minister to ourselves and to our fellow men.

Recognition of the falsity of material wealth as the standard of success goes hand in hand with the abandonment of the false belief that public office and high political position are to be valued only by the standards of pride of place and personal profit; and there must be an end to a conduct in banking and in business which too often has given to a sacred trust the likeness of callous and selfish wrongdoing.

Small wonder that confidence languishes, for it thrives only on honesty, on honor, on the sacredness of obligations, on faithful protection, on unselfish performance; without them it cannot live.

Restoration calls, however, not for changes in ethics alone. This Nation asks for action, and action now.

Our greatest primary task is to put people to work. This is no unsolvable problem if we face it wisely and courageously.

It can be accomplished in part by direct recruiting by the Government itself, treating the task as we would treat the emergency of a war, but at the same time, through this employment, accomplishing greatly needed projects to stimulate and reorganize the use of our natural resources.

Hand in hand with this we must frankly recognize the overbalance of population in our industrial centers and, by engaging on a national scale in a redistribution, endeavor to provide a better use of the land for those best fitted for the land.

The task can be helped by definite efforts to raise the values of agricultural products and with this the power to purchase the output of our cities.

It can be helped by preventing realistically the tragedy of the growing loss through foreclosure of our small homes and our farms.

It can be helped by insistence that the Federal, State, and local governments act forthwith on the demand that their cost be drastically reduced.

It can be helped by the unifying of relief activities which today are often scattered, uneconomical, and unequal. It can be helped by national planning for and supervision of all forms of transportation and of communications and other utilities which have a definitely public character.

There are many ways in which it can be helped, but it can never be helped merely by talking about it. We must act and act quickly.

Finally, in our progress toward a resumption of work we require two safeguards against a return of the evils of the old order: there must be a strict supervision of all banking and credits and investments, so that there will be an end to speculation with other people's money; and there must be provision for an adequate but sound currency.

These are the lines of attack. I shall presently urge upon a new Congress, in special session, detailed measures for their fulfillment, and I shall seek the immediate assistance of the several States.

Through this program of action we address ourselves to putting our own national house in order and making income balance outgo.

Our international trade relations, though vastly important, are in point of time and necessity secondary to the establishment of a sound national economy.

I favor as a practical policy the putting of first things first. I shall spare no effort to restore world trade by international economic readjustment, but the emergency at home cannot wait on that accomplishment.

The basic thought that guides these specific means of national recovery is not narrowly nationalistic.

It is the insistence, as a first considerations, upon the interdependence of the various elements in and parts of the United States—a recognition of the old and permanently important manifestation of the American spirit of the pioneer.

It is the way to recovery. It is the immediate way. It is the strongest assurance that the recovery will endure.

In the field of world policy I would dedicate this Nation to the policy of the good neighbor—the neighbor who resolutely respects himself and, because he does so, respects the rights of others—the neighbor who respects his obligations and respects the sanctity of his agreements in and with a world of neighbors.

If I read the temper of our people correctly, we now realize as we have never realized before our interdependence on each other; that we cannot merely take but we must give as well; that if we are to go forward, we must move as a trained and loyal army willing to sacrifice for the good of a common discipline, because without such discipline no progress is made, no leadership becomes effective.

We are, I know, ready and willing to submit our lives and property to such discipline, because it makes possible a leadership which aims at a larger good.

This I propose to offer, pledging that the larger purposes will bind upon us all as a sacred obligation with a unity of duty hitherto evoked only in time of armed strife.

With this pledge taken, I assume unhesitatingly the leadership of this great army of our people dedicated to a disciplined attack upon our common problems.

Action in this image and to this end is feasible under the form of government which we have inherited from our ancestors.

Our Constitution is so simple and practical that it is possible always to meet extraordinary needs by changes in emphasis and arrangement without loss of essential form.

That is why our constitutional system has proved itself the most superbly enduring political mechanism the modern world has produced. It has met every stress of vast expansion of territory, of foreign wars, of bitter internal strife, of world relations.

It is to be hoped that the normal balance of Executive and legislative authority may be wholly adequate to meet the unprecedented task before us. But it may be that an unprecedented demand and need for undelayed action may call for temporary departure from that normal balance of public procedure.

I am prepared under my constitutional duty to recommend the measures that a stricken Nation in the midst of a stricken world may require.

These measures, or such other measures as the Congress may build out of its experience and wisdom, I shall seek, within my constitutional authority, to bring to speedy adoption.

But in the event that the Congress shall fail to take one of these two courses, and in the event that the national emergency is still critical, I shall not evade the clear course of duty that will then confront me.

I shall ask the Congress for the one remaining instrument to meet the crisis—broad Executive power to wage a war against the emergency, as great as the power that would be given to me if we were in fact invaded by a foreign foe.

For the trust reposed in me I will return the courage and the devotion that befit the time. I can do no less.

We face the arduous days that lie before us in the warm courage of national unity; with the clear consciousness of seeking old and precious moral values; with the clean satisfaction that comes from the stern performance of duty by old and young alike.

We aim at the assurance of a rounded and permanent national life.

We do not distrust the future of essential democracy. The people of the United States have not failed. In their need they have registered a mandate that they want direct, vigorous action.

They have asked for discipline and direction under leadership. They have made me the present instrument of their wishes. In the spirit of the gift I take it.

In this dedication of a Nation we humbly ask the blessing of God. May He protect each and every one of us. May He guide me in the days to come.

⬦

Source: Henry Steele Commager and Milton Cantor, eds., *Documents of American History*, Vol. 2, *Since 1898*, 10th ed. (Englewood Cliffs, N.J.: Prentice Hall, 1988), 239–242.

Document Two: President Roosevelt, Fireside Chat on Banking, March 12, 1933

President Roosevelt used the fairly new medium of radio throughout his presidency to communicate in a more informal manner with the American people in what became known as "fireside chats." The first such fireside chat occurred just eight days into his presidency on the subject of the banking crisis.

I want to talk for a few minutes with the people of the United States about banking—with the comparatively few who understand the mechanics of banking but more particularly with the overwhelming majority who use banks for the making of deposits and the drawing of checks. I want to tell you what has been done in the last few days, why it was done, and what the next steps are going to be. I recognize that the many proclamations from State capitols and from Washington, the legislation, the Treasury regulations, etc., couched for the most part in banking and legal terms, should be explained for the benefit of the average citizen. I owe this in particular because of the fortitude and good temper with which everybody has accepted the inconvenience and hardships of the banking holiday. I know that when you understand what we in Washington have been about I shall continue to have your cooperation as fully as I have had your sympathy and help during the past week.

First of all, let me state the simple fact that when you deposit money in a bank the bank does not put the money into a safe deposit vault. It invests your money in many different forms of credit—bonds, commercial paper, mortgages and many other kinds of loans. In other words, the bank puts your money to work to keep the wheels of industry and of agriculture turning around. A comparatively small part of the money you put into the bank is kept in currency—an amount which in normal times is wholly sufficient to cover the cash needs of the average citizen. In other words, the total amount of all the currency in the country is only a small fraction of the total deposits in all of the banks.

What, then, happened during the last few days of February and the first few days of March? Because of undermined confidence on the part of the public, there was a general rush by a large portion of our population to turn bank deposits into currency or gold—a rush so great that the soundest banks could not get enough currency to meet the demand. The reason for this was that on the spur of the moment it was, of course, impossible to sell perfectly sound assets of a bank and convert them into cash except at panic prices far below their real value.

By the afternoon of March 3d scarcely a bank in the country was open to do business. Proclamations temporarily closing them in whole or in part had been issued by the Governors in almost all the States.

It was then that I issued the proclamation providing for the nationwide bank holiday, and this was the first step in the Government's reconstruction of our financial and economic fabric.

The second step was the legislation promptly and patriotically passed by the Congress confirming my proclamation and broadening my powers so that it became possible in view of the requirement of time to extend the holiday and lift the ban of that holiday gradually. This law also gave authority to develop a program of rehabilitation of our banking facilities. I want to tell our citizens in every part of the Nation that the national Congress—Republicans and Democrats alike—showed by this action a devotion to public welfare and a realization of the emergency and the necessity for speed that it is difficult to match in our history.

The third stage has been the series of regulations permitting the banks to continue their functions to take care of the distribution of food and household necessities and the payment of payrolls.

This bank holiday, while resulting in many cases in great inconvenience, is affording us the opportunity to supply the currency necessary to meet the situation. No sound bank is a dollar worse off than it was when it closed its doors last Monday. Neither is any bank which may turn out not to be in a position for immediate opening. The new law allows the twelve Federal Reserve Banks to issue additional currency on good assets and thus the banks which reopen will be able to meet every legitimate call. The new currency is being sent out by the Bureau of Engraving and Printing in large volume to every part of the country. It is sound currency because it is backed by actual, good assets.

A question you will ask is this: why are all the banks not to be reopened at the same time? The answer is simple. Your Government does not intend that the history of the past few years shall be repeated. We do not want and will not have another epidemic of bank failures.

As a result, we start tomorrow, Monday, with the opening of banks in the twelve Federal Reserve Bank cities—those banks which on first examination by the Treasury have already been found to be all right. This will be followed on Tuesday by the resumption of all their functions by banks already found to be sound in cities where there are recognized clearing houses. That means about 250 cities of the United States.

On Wednesday and succeeding days banks in smaller places all through the country will resume business, subject, of course, to the Government's physical ability to complete its survey. It is necessary that the reopening of banks be extended over a period in order to permit the banks to make applications for necessary loans, to obtain currency needed to meet their requirements and to enable the Government to make common sense checkups.

Let me make it clear to you that if your bank does not open the first day you are by no means justified in believing that it will not open. A bank that opens on one of the subsequent days is in exactly the same status as the bank that opens tomorrow.

I know that many people are worrying about State banks not members of the Federal Reserve System. These banks can and will receive assistance from member banks and from the Reconstruction Finance Corporation. These State banks are following the same course as the National banks except that they get their licenses to resume business from the State authorities, and these authorities have been asked by the Secretary of the Treasury to permit their good banks to open up on the same schedule as the national banks. I am confident that the State Banking Departments will be as careful as the national Government in the policy relating to the opening of banks and will follow the same broad policy.

It is possible that when the banks resume a very few people who have not recovered from their fear may again begin withdrawals. Let me make it clear that the banks will take care of all needs—and it is my belief that hoarding during the past week has become an exceedingly unfashionable pastime. It needs no prophet to tell you that when the people find that they can get their money—that they can get it when they want it for all legitimate purposes—the phantom of fear will soon be laid. People will again be glad to have their money where it will be safely taken care of and where they can use it conveniently at any time. I can assure you that it is safer to keep your money in a reopened bank than under the mattress.

The success of our whole great national program depends, of course, upon the cooperation of the public—on its intelligent support and use of a reliable system.

Remember that the essential accomplishment of the new legislation is that it makes it possible for banks more readily to convert their assets into cash than was the case before. More liberal provision has been made for banks to borrow on these assets at the Reserve Banks and more liberal provision has also been made for issuing currency on the security of these good assets. This currency is not fiat currency. It is issued only on adequate security, and every good bank has an abundance of such security.

One more point before I close. There will be, of course, some banks unable to reopen without being reorganized. The new law allows the Government to assist in making these reorganizations quickly and effectively and even allows the Government to subscribe to at least a part of new capital which may be required.

I hope you can see from this elemental recital of what your Government is doing that there is nothing complex, or radical, in the process.

We had a bad banking situation. Some of our bankers had shown themselves either incompetent or dishonest in their handling of the people's funds. They had used the money entrusted to them in speculations and unwise loans. This was, of course, not true in the vast majority of our banks, but it was true in enough of them to shock the people for a time into a sense of insecurity and to put them into a frame of mind where they did not differentiate, but seemed to assume that the acts of a comparative few had tainted them all. It was the Government's job to straighten out this situation and do it as quickly as possible. And the job is being performed.

I do not promise you that every bank will be reopened or that individual losses will not be suffered, but there will be no losses that possibly could be avoided; and there would have been more and greater losses had we continued to drift. I can even promise you salvation for some at least of the sorely pressed banks. We shall be engaged not merely in reopening sound banks but in the creation of sound banks through reorganization.

It has been wonderful to me to catch the note of confidence from all over the country. I can never be sufficiently grateful to the people for the loyal support they have given me in their acceptance of the judgment that has dictated our course, even though all our processes may not have seemed clear to them.

After all, there is an element in the readjustment of our financial system more important than currency, more important than gold, and that is the confidence of the people. Confidence and courage are the essentials of success in carrying out our plan. You people must have faith; you must not be stampeded by rumors or guesses. Let us unite in banishing fear. We have provided the machinery to restore our financial system; it is up to you to support and make it work.

It is your problem no less than it is mine. Together we cannot fail.

Source: Samuel I. Rosenman, ed., *The Public Papers and Addresses of Franklin D. Roosevelt*, Vol. 2, *The Year of Crisis, 1933* (New York: Random House, 1938), 61–66.

Document Three: President Roosevelt, Press Conference [about *Schechter Poultry Corp. v. United States*], May 31, 1935

In this press conference on May 31, 1935, President Roosevelt discussed the Supreme Court decision Schechter Poultry Corp. v. United States, *which declared the National Industrial Recovery Act unconstitutional, and the case's impact on economic recovery policies.*

. . . Q. Do you care to comment any on the N.R.A.?

THE PRESIDENT: Well, Steve, if you insist. That's an awful thing to put up to a fellow at this hour of the morning just out of bed. Suppose we make this background and take some time because it is an awfully big subject to cover, and it is just possible that one or two of you may not have read the whole twenty-eight or twenty-nine pages of the Supreme Court decision.

I have been a good deal impressed by—what shall I call it?—the rather pathetic appeals that I have had from all around the country to do something. They are very sincere as showing faith in the Government. They are so sincere that you feel in reading them—and so far there have been somewhere between two and three thousand by letter and telegram and I haven't seen this morning's mail yet—so sincere that you feel the country is beginning to realize that something in the long run has to be done. And they are all hoping that something will be done right away.

I think probably the best way to illustrate it is to read you just a few telegrams that came out of this huge pile. They are all from business men, every one. I took out only the telegrams from business men. And they illustrate pretty well that the information that they have received since Monday through the press and through the radio has failed to explain to them the implications of the Supreme Court's decision. In other words, they

are groping, and they have not yet had information from either the press or the radio or from me, which would put this situation in plain, lay language.

Well, for instance, here is one from Indiana. A State association of small—well, they are drug-store people. They start off:

"We commend you for what you have done to protect the small business man from ruthless destructive trade practices. We hope you will continue your sincere efforts to the end that Constitutional legislation be enacted that will save the small business man from eventual extinction." In other words, "Mr. President, do please get some constitutional legislation that will save us." . . .

Here is another firm:

"All good citizens are looking to you to exercise whatever power is at your command to prevent business chaos which seems inevitable following Supreme Court decision. Already [and then mentioning the name of a very large store] and many smaller people are rashly cutting prices." . . .

I suppose there are several thousand along the same line, mainly from business men.

Now, coming down to the decision itself. What are the implications? For the benefit of those of you who haven't read it through I think I can put it this way: the implications of this decision are much more important than almost certainly any decision of my lifetime or yours, more important than any decision probably since the Dred Scott case. . . .

Now we come down to this big thing. The implication of the provisions as applied to intrastate transactions. Why is it—let me put it this way—why is it that so many of these telegrams are futile? Why is it that so many of these letters and telegrams show that the senders do not realize what the rest of this decision means?

Let's put the decision in plain lay language in regard to at least the dictum of the Court and never mind this particular sick chicken or whatever they call it. That was a question of fact, but of course the Court in ruling on the question of fact about these particular chickens said they were killed in New York and sold and probably eaten in New York, and therefore it was probably intrastate commerce. But of course the Court does not stop there. In fact the Court in this decision, at least by dictum—and remember that dictum is not always followed in the future—has gone back to the old Knight case in 1885, which in fact limited any application of interstate commerce to goods in transit—nothing else! . . .

Well, what does it do? It seems to me it brings— oh, I suppose you will want to say an issue. I accept the word "issue" on one condition; and that is that you make it very clear that it is not a partisan issue. It is infinitely deeper than any partisan issue; it is a national issue. Yes, and the issue is this—going back to these telegrams that I have been reading to you: Is the United States going to decide, are the people of this country going to decide that their Federal Government shall in the future have no right under any implied power or any court-approved power to enter into a solution of a national economic problem, but that that national economic problem must be decided only by the States?

The other part of it is this: Shall we view our social problems—and in that I include employment of all kinds—shall we view them from the same point of view or not; that the Federal Government has no right under this or following opinions to take any part in trying to better national social conditions? Now that is flat and that is simple!

If we accept the point of view that under no interpretation of the Constitution can the Federal Government deal with construction matters, mining matters (which means everything that comes out of the ground), manufacturing matters or agricultural matters, but that they must be left wholly to the States, the Federal Government must abandon any legislation. Thus we go back automatically to the fact that there will be not merely thirteen Governments as there were in 1789 at a time where none of these questions existed in the country—but we will go back to a Government of forty-eight States.

Or we can go ahead with every possible effort to make national decisions based on the fact that forty-eight sovereignties cannot agree quickly enough or practically enough on any solution for a national economic problem or a national social problem. . . .

You and I know human nature. Fundamentally it comes down to this. In the long run can voluntary processes on the part of business bring about the same practical results that were attained under N.R.A.? I mean the good results. Of course there have been some bad ones. But I mean the good results. Can it be done by voluntary action on the part of business? Can we go ahead as a Nation with the beautiful theory, let us say, of some of the press, "At last the rule of Christ is restored. Business can do anything it wants and business is going to live up to the golden rule so marvelously that all of our troubles are ended." It is a school of thought that is so delightful in its naivete.

And so we are facing a very, very great national non-partisan issue. We have got to decide one way or the other. I don't mean this summer or winter or next fall, but over a period, perhaps, of five years or ten years we have got to decide: whether we are going to

relegate to the forty-eight States practically all control over economic conditions—not only State economic conditions but national economic conditions; and along with that whether we are going to relegate to the States all control over social and working conditions throughout the country regardless of whether those conditions have a very definite significance and effect in other States outside of the individual States. That is one side of the picture. The other side of the picture is whether in some way we are going to turn over or restore to—whichever way you choose to put it—turn over or restore to the Federal Government the powers which exist in the national Governments of every other Nation in the world to enact and administer laws that have a bearing on, and general control over, national economic problems and national social problems.

That actually is the biggest question that has come before this country outside of time of war, and it has to be decided. And, as I say, it may take five years or ten years.

This N.R.A. decision—if you accept the obiter dicta and all the phraseology of it—seems to be squarely on the side of restoring to the States forty-eight different controls over national economic and social problems. This is not a criticism of the Supreme Court's decision; it is merely pointing out the implications of it.

In some ways it may be the best thing that has happened to this country for a long time that such a decision has come from the Supreme Court, because it clarifies the issue. If the press and the radio of this country can make that issue perfectly clear, it will be doing a very great service. The telegrams that I have been reading to you, suggesting every kind of method of overcoming the decision, will not continue to come in, because all except a very few of them suggest remedies which are wholly outside of the opinion of the Supreme Court. In other words, they are in violation of that opinion—nine suggested remedies out of ten are in violation of the strict interpretation of that opinion.

I think it is perfectly proper to say further that the implications of this decision could, if carried to their logical conclusion, strip the Federal Government of a great many other powers. . . . We have forty-eight Nations from now on under a strict interpretation of this decision—forty-eight Nations, each of which will prescribe a different standard for its own liquor, and will be completely powerless to prevent liquor from the next-door State, or ten States away, from coming into its borders.

It is a perfectly ridiculous and impossible situation. But it is a very good example of what forty-eight-independent-Nation control means. . . .

You see the implications of the decision. That is why I say it is one of the most important decisions ever rendered in this country. And the issue is not going to be a partisan issue for a minute. The issue is going to be whether we go one way or the other. Don't call it right or left; that is just first-year high-school language, just about. It is not right or left—it is a question for national decision on a very important problem of Government. We are the only Nation in the world that has not solved that problem. We thought we were solving it, and now it has been thrown right straight in our faces. We have been relegated to the horse-and-buggy definition of interstate commerce.

Now, as to the way out—I suppose you will want to know something about what I am going to do. I am going to tell you very, very little on that.

❖

Source: Samuel I. Rosenman, ed., *The Public Papers and Addresses of Franklin D. Roosevelt*, Vol. 4, *The Court Disapproves, 1935* (New York: Random House, 1938), 200–222.

Document Four: President Roosevelt, Address at Barnesville, Georgia, August 11, 1938

During the 1938 midterm elections, President Roosevelt tried and failed to purge the Democratic Party in Congress of some of its more conservative members by campaigning for moderate and liberal Democrats. This August 11, 1938, speech is one such example of Roosevelt's efforts to shape local political decisions.

Governor Rivers, Senator George, Senator Russell, and my neighbors of Georgia:

Fourteen years ago a democratic Yankee, a comparatively young man, came to a neighboring county in the State of Georgia, in search of a pool of warm water wherein he might swim his way back to health; and he found it. The place—Warm Springs—was at that time a rather dilapidated small summer resort. His new neighbors there extended to him the hand of genuine hospitality, welcomed him to their firesides and made him feel so much at home that he built himself a house, bought himself a farm, and has been coming back ever since. And he proposes to keep to that good custom. I intend coming back very often.

There was only one discordant note in that first stay of mine at Warm Springs. When the first of the month bill came in for electric light for my little cottage, I found that the charge was eighteen cents per kilowatt hour—about four times as much as I was paying in another community, Hyde Park, New York. That light bill started my long study of proper public utility charges for electric current, started in my mind the whole subject of getting electricity into farm homes throughout the United States.

So, my friends, it can be said with a good deal of truth that a little cottage at Warm Springs, Georgia, was the birthplace of the Rural Electrification Administration. Six years ago, in 1932, there was much talk about the more widespread and cheaper use of electricity; but it is only since March 4, 1933, that your Government has reduced that talk to practical results. Electricity is a modern necessity of life, not a luxury. That necessity ought to be found in every village, in every home and on every farm in every part of the United States. The dedication of this Rural Electrification Administration project in Georgia today is a symbol of the progress we are making—and we are not going to stop. . . .

bout a month ago, I invited a group of distinguished, broad-minded Southerners to meet in Washington to discuss the economic conditions and problems of the South. When they met, I said to them:

"My intimate interest in all that concerns the South is, I believe, known to all of you; but this interest is far more than a sentimental attachment born of a considerable residence in your section and of close personal friendship with so many of your people. It proceeds even more from my feeling of responsibility toward the whole Nation. It is my conviction that the South presents right now the Nation's No. 1 economic problem—the Nation's problem, not merely the South's. For we have an economic unbalance in the Nation as a whole, due to this very condition in the South itself.

"It is an unbalance that can and must be righted for the sake of the South and of the Nation."

The day before yesterday when I landed in Florida I received the report and the recommendations based on the advice of this distinguished commission. This report and the recommendations will be made public in the course of the next day or two; and I hope you will read it.

It is well said that this report "presents in only a small degree the manifold assets and advantages possessed by the South" because the report is concerned primarily not with boasting about what the South has, but in telling what the South needs. It is a short report divided into fifteen short sections; and it covers in a broad way subjects of vital importance, such as economic resources, soil, water, population, private and public income, education, health, housing, labor, ownership and use of land, credit, use of natural resources, industry and purchasing power.

I am listing those fifteen headings with a definite purpose in mind. The very fact that it is necessary to divide the economic needs of the South into fifteen important groups—each one a problem in itself—proves to you and to me that if you and I are to cover the ground effectively, there is no one single simple answer. It is true that many obvious needs ought to be attained quickly—such as the reduction of discriminatory freight rates, such as putting a definite floor under industrial wages, such as continuing to raise the purchasing power of the farm population. But no one of these things alone, no combination of a few of them, will meet the whole of the problem. Talking in fighting terms, we cannot capture one hill and claim to have won the battle, because the battlefront extends over thousands of miles and we must push forward along the whole front at the same time. . . .

The task of meeting the economic and social needs of the South, on the broad front that is absolutely necessary, calls for public servants whose hearts are sound, whose heads are sane-whose hands are strong, striving everlastingly to better the lot of their fellowmen. . . .

It is not an attack on state sovereignty to point out that this national aspect of all these problems requires action by the Federal Government in Washington. I do not hesitate to say from long experience that during the past five years there has been a closer and more effective peacetime cooperation between the Governors of the forty-eight states and the President of the United States than at any other time in our whole national history. . . .

Translating that into more intimate terms, it means that if the people of the State of Georgia want definite action in the Congress of the United States, they must send to that Congress Senators and Representatives who are willing to stand up and fight night and day for Federal statutes drawn to meet actual needs. . . .

You, the people of Georgia, in the coming Senatorial primary, for example, have a perfect right to choose any candidate you wish. I do not seek to impair that right, and I am not going to impair that right of the people of this State; but because Georgia has been good enough to call me her adopted son and because for many long years I have regarded Georgia as my "other state," I feel no hesitation in telling you what I would do if I could vote here next month. . . .

Let me preface my statement by saying that I have personally known three of the candidates for the United States Senate for many years. All of them have had legislative or executive experience as Government servants. We may therefore justly consider their records and their public utterances—and we can justly, also, seek to determine for ourselves what is their inward point of view in relationship to present and future problems of government. . . .

Here in Georgia . . . my old friend [Walter George], the senior Senator from this State, cannot possibly in my judgment be classified as belonging to the liberal school of thought—and, therefore, the argument that he has long served in the Senate falls by the wayside. . . .

To carry out my responsibility as President, it is clear that if there is to be success in our Government there ought to be cooperation between members of my own party and myself—cooperation, in other words, within the majority party, between one branch of Government, the Legislative branch, and the head of the other branch, the Executive. That is one of the essentials of a party form of government. It has been going on in this country for nearly a century and a half. The test is not measured, in the case of an individual, by his every vote on every bill—of course not. The test lies rather in the answer to two questions: first, has the record of the candidate shown, while differing perhaps in details, a constant active fighting attitude in favor of the broad objectives of the party and of the Government as they are constituted today; and, secondly, does the candidate really, in his heart, deep down in his heart, believe in those objectives? I regret that in the case of my friend, Senator George, I cannot honestly answer either of these questions in the affirmative.

In the case of another candidate in the State of Georgia for the United States Senate—former Governor Talmadge—I have known him for many years. His attitude toward me and toward other members of the Government in 1935 and in 1936 concerns me not at all. But, in those years and in this year I have read so many of his proposals, so many of his promises, so many of his panaceas, that I am very certain in my own mind that his election would contribute very little to practical progress in government. That is all I can say about him.

The third candidate that I would speak of, United States Attorney Lawrence Camp, I have also known for many years. He has had experience in the State Legislature; he has served as Attorney General of Georgia and for four years; he has made a distinguished record in the United States District Court, his office ranking among the first two in the whole of the United States in the expedition of Federal cases in that Court. I regard him not only as a public servant with successful experience but as a man who honestly believes that many things must be done and done now to improve the economic and social conditions of the country, a man who is willing to fight for these objectives. Fighting ability is of the utmost importance.

Therefore, answering the requests that have come to me from many leading citizens of Georgia that I make my position clear, I have no hesitation in saying that if I were able to vote in the September primaries in this State, I most assuredly should cast my ballot for Lawrence Camp.

In dedicating this important project today, I want to express once more my abiding faith that we as a nation are moving steadily and surely toward a better way of living for all of our people. This electrification project is a symbol of our determination to attain that objective. But it is only one symbol; it is one hill out of ten thousand which must be captured. You and I will never be satisfied until all our economic inequalities are corrected, until every one of us, North, East, West and South has the opportunity so to live, that his education, his job and his home will be secure.

In many countries democracy is under attack by those who charge that democracy fails to provide its people with the needs of modern civilization. I do not, you do not, subscribe to that charge. You and I, we, the people of this State and the people of all the states, believe that democracy today is succeeding, but that an absolute necessity for its future success is the fighting spirit of the American people—their insistence that we go forward and not back.

Source: Samuel I. Rosenman, ed., *The Public Papers and Addresses of Franklin D. Roosevelt,* Vol. 7, *The Continuing Struggle for Liberalism, 1938* (New York: Macmillan, 1938).

Document Five: President Roosevelt, State of the Union Address [regarding the "Four Freedoms"], January 6, 1941

Even though the United States was not yet at war, President Roosevelt used the State of the Union address in 1941 to articulate what would become the nation's war aims, including what he called the "four freedoms": freedom of speech and expression, freedom of religion, freedom from fear, and freedom from want.

I address you, the Members of the Seventy-seventh Congress, at a moment unprecedented in the history of the Union. I use the word "unprecedented," because at no previous time has American security been as seriously threatened from without as it is today. . . .

It is true that prior to 1914 the United States often had been disturbed by events in other Continents. We had even engaged in two wars with European nations and in a number of undeclared wars in the West Indies, in the Mediterranean and in the Pacific for the maintenance of American rights and for the principles of peaceful commerce. But in no case had a serious threat been raised against our national safety or our continued independence.

What I seek to convey is the historic truth that the United States as a nation has at all times maintained clear, definite opposition, to any attempt to lock us in behind an ancient Chinese wall while the procession of civilization went past. Today, thinking of our children and of their children, we oppose enforced isolation for ourselves or for any other part of the Americas. . . .

Every realist knows that the democratic way of life is at this moment being directly assailed in every part of the world—assailed either by arms, or by secret spreading of poisonous propaganda by those who seek to destroy unity and promote discord in nations that are still at peace. During sixteen long months this assault has blotted out the whole pattern of democratic life in an appalling number of independent nations, great and small. The assailants are still on the march, threatening other nations, great and small.

Therefore, as your President, performing my constitutional duty to "give to the Congress information of the state of the Union," I find it, unhappily, necessary to report that the future and the safety of our country and of our democracy are overwhelmingly involved in events far beyond our borders. . . .

The need of the moment is that our actions and our policy should be devoted primarily—almost exclusively—to meeting this foreign peril. For all our domestic problems are now a part of the great emergency. Just as our national policy in internal affairs has been based upon a decent respect for the rights and the dignity of all our fellow men within our gates, so our national policy in foreign affairs has been based on a decent respect for the rights and dignity of all nations, large and small. And the justice of morality must and will win in the end.

Our national policy is this:

First, by an impressive expression of the public will and without regard to partisanship, we are committed to all-inclusive national defense.

Second, by an impressive expression of the public will and without regard to partisanship, we are committed to full support of all those resolute peoples, everywhere, who are resisting aggression and are thereby keeping war away from our Hemisphere. By this support, we express our determination that the democratic cause shall prevail; and we strengthen the defense and the security of our own nation.

Third, by an impressive expression of the public will and without regard to partisanship, we are committed to the proposition that principles of morality and considerations for our own security will never permit us to acquiesce in a peace dictated by aggressors and sponsored by appeasers. We know that enduring peace cannot be bought at the cost of other people's freedom.

In the recent national election there was no substantial difference between the two great parties in respect to that national policy. No issue was fought out on this line before the American electorate. Today it is abundantly evident that American citizens everywhere are demanding and supporting speedy and complete action in recognition of obvious danger. Therefore, the immediate need is a swift and driving increase in our armament production. . . .

Our most useful and immediate role is to act as an arsenal for them as well as for ourselves. They do not need man power, but they do need billions of dollars worth of the weapons of defense. . . .

Let us say to the democracies: "We Americans are vitally concerned in your defense of freedom. We are putting forth our energies, our resources and our organizing powers to give you the strength to regain and maintain a free world. We shall send you, in ever-increasing numbers, ships, planes, tanks, guns. This is our purpose and our pledge." In fulfillment of this purpose we will not be intimidated by the threats of dictators that they will regard as a breach of international law or as an act of war our aid to the democracies which dare to resist their aggression. Such aid is not an act of war, even if a dictator should unilaterally proclaim it so to be. When the dictators, if the dictators, are ready to make war upon us, they will not wait for an act of war on our part. They did not wait for Norway or Belgium or the Netherlands to commit an act of war. Their only interest is in a new one-way international law, which lacks mutuality in its observance, and, therefore, becomes an instrument of oppression.

The happiness of future generations of Americans may well depend upon how effective and how immediate we can make our aid felt. No one can tell the exact character of the emergency situations that we may be called upon to meet. The Nation's hands must not be tied when the Nation's life is in danger. We must all prepare to make the sacrifices that the emergency— almost as serious as war itself—demands. Whatever stands in the way of speed and efficiency in defense preparations must give way to the national need.

A free nation has the right to expect full cooperation from all groups. A free nation has the right to look to the leaders of business, of labor, and of agriculture to take the lead in stimulating effort, not among other groups but within their own groups. The best way of dealing with the few slackers or trouble makers in our midst is, first, to shame them by patriotic example, and, if that fails, to use the sovereignty of Government to save Government.

As men do not live by bread alone, they do not fight by armaments alone. Those who man our defenses, and those behind them who build our defenses, must have the stamina and the courage which come from unshakable belief in the manner of life which they are defending. The mighty action that we are calling for cannot be based on a disregard of all things worth fighting for.

The Nation takes great satisfaction and much strength from the things which have been done to make its people conscious of their individual stake in the preservation of democratic life in America. Those things have toughened the fibre of our people, have renewed their faith and strengthened their devotion to the institutions we make ready to protect. Certainly this is no time for any of us to stop thinking about the social and economic problems which are the root cause of the social revolution which is today a supreme factor in the world.

There is nothing mysterious about the foundations of a healthy and strong democracy. The basic things expected by our people of their political and economic systems are simple. They are: Equality of opportunity for youth and for others. Jobs for those who can work. Security for those who need it. The ending of special privilege for the few. The preservation of civil liberties for all. The enjoyment of the fruits of scientific progress in a wider and constantly rising standard of living.

These are the simple, basic things that must never be lost sight of in the turmoil and unbelievable complexity of our modern world. The inner and abiding strength of our economic and political systems is dependent upon the degree to which they fulfill these expectations.

Many subjects connected with our social economy call for immediate improvement.

As examples: We should bring more citizens under the coverage of old-age pensions and unemployment insurance. We should widen the opportunities for adequate medical care. We should plan a better system by which persons deserving or needing gainful employment may obtain it.

I have called for personal sacrifice. I am assured of the willingness of almost all Americans to respond to that call. . . .

In the future days, which we seek to make secure, we look forward to a world founded upon four essential human freedoms.

The first is freedom of speech and expression— everywhere in the world.

The second is freedom of every person to worship God in his own way—everywhere in the world.

The third is freedom from want—which, translated into world terms, means economic understandings which will secure to every nation a healthy peacetime life for its inhabitants—everywhere in the world.

The fourth is freedom from fear—which, translated into world terms, means a world-wide reduction of armaments to such a point and in such a thorough fashion that no nation will be in a position to commit an act of physical aggression against any neighbor—anywhere in the world.

That is no vision of a distant millennium. It is a definite basis for a kind of world attainable in our own time and generation. That kind of world is the very antithesis of the so-called new order of tyranny which the dictators seek to create with the crash of a bomb.

To that new order we oppose the greater conception—the moral order. A good society is able to face schemes of world domination and foreign revolutions alike without fear.

Since the beginning of our American history, we have been engaged in change—in a perpetual peaceful revolution—a revolution which goes on steadily, quietly adjusting itself to changing conditions—without the concentration camp or the quick-lime in the ditch. The world order which we seek is the cooperation of free countries, working together in a friendly, civilized society.

This nation has placed its destiny in the hands and heads and hearts of its millions of free men and women; and its faith in freedom under the guidance of God. Freedom means the supremacy of human rights everywhere. Our support goes to those who struggle to gain those rights or keep them. Our strength is our unity of purpose. To that high concept there can be no end save victory.

Source: Henry Steele Commager and Milton Cantor, eds., *Documents of American History,* Vol. 2, *Since 1898,* 10th ed. (Englewood Cliffs, N.J.: Prentice Hall, 1988), 446–449.

Document Six: President Roosevelt, Address to Congress Requesting a Declaration of War with Japan, December 8, 1941

On December 8, 1941, the day after the Japanese attack at Pearl Harbor, President Roosevelt gave this powerful speech to a joint session of Congress. Lawmakers replied with a near unanimous vote to wage war against Japan.

Yesterday, December 7, 1941—a date which will live in infamy—the United States of America was suddenly and deliberately attacked by naval and air forces of the Empire of Japan.

The United States was at peace with that Nation and, at the solicitation of Japan, was still in conversation with its Government and its Emperor looking toward the maintenance of peace in the Pacific. Indeed, one hour after Japanese air squadrons had commenced bombing in the American Island of Oahu, the Japanese Ambassador to the United States and his colleague delivered to our Secretary of State a formal reply to a recent American message. And while this reply stated that it seemed useless to continue the existing diplomatic negotiations, it contained no threat or hint of war or of armed attack.

It will be recorded that the distance of Hawaii from Japan makes it obvious that the attack was deliberately planned many days or even weeks ago. During the intervening time the Japanese Government has deliberately sought to deceive the United States by false statements and expressions of hope for continued peace.

The attack yesterday on the Hawaiian Islands has caused severe damage to American naval and military forces. I regret to tell you that very many American lives have been lost. In addition American ships have been reported torpedoed on the high seas between San Francisco and Honolulu.

Yesterday the Japanese Government also launched an attack against Malaya. Last night Japanese forces attacked Hong Kong. Last night Japanese forces attacked Guam. Last night Japanese forces attacked the Philippine Islands. Last night the Japanese attacked Wake Island. And this morning the Japanese attacked Midway Island.

Japan has, therefore, undertaken a surprise offensive extending throughout the Pacific area. The facts of yesterday and today speak for themselves. The people of the United States have already formed their opinions and well understand the implications to the very life and safety of our Nation.

As Commander in Chief of the Army and Navy I have directed that all measures be taken for our defense.

Always will we remember the character of the onslaught against us.

No matter how long it may take us to overcome this premeditated invasion, the American people in their righteous might will win through to absolute victory.

I believe that I interpret the will of the Congress and of the people when I assert that we will not only defend ourselves to the uttermost but will make it very certain that this form of treachery shall never endanger us again.

Hostilities exist. There is no blinking at the fact that our people, our territory, and our interests are in grave danger.

With confidence in our armed forces—with the unbounding determination of our people—we will gain the inevitable triumph—so help us God.

I ask that the Congress declare that since the unprovoked and dastardly attack by Japan on Sunday, December 7, 1941, a state of war has existed between the United States and the Japanese Empire.

Source: Henry Steele Commager and Milton Cantor, eds., *Documents of American History*, Vol. 2, *Since 1898*, 10th ed. (Englewood Cliffs, N.J.: Prentice Hall, 1988), 451–452.

Document Seven: President Roosevelt, Excerpts from the Press Conference on D-Day, June 6, 1944

President Roosevelt was jubilant in his press conference when discussing the success of the D-Day landings on June 6, 1944.

. . . THE PRESIDENT: Well, I think this is a very happy conference today. Looking at the rows of you coming in, you have the same expressions as the anonymous and silent people this side of the desk who came in just before you—all smiles!

I have very little more news that I can tell you than what you all got in your offices.

I think it's all right to use this, which has not been published yet. It came in a dispatch from Eisenhower on the progress of the operations, as of about 12 o'clock today. The American naval losses were two destroyers and one L.S.T. And the losses incident to the air landing were relatively light—about one percent.

Q. That's the air-borne troops, sir?

THE PRESIDENT: Well, air losses as a whole.

And, of course, there are a great deal of reports coming in all the time, and it's being given out over there just as fast as it possibly can. I think the arrangements seem to be going all right. I think that's all that I have over here. You are getting it just as fast as we are.

Q. Mr. President, how do you feel about the progress of the invasion?

THE PRESIDENT: Up to schedule. And, as the Prime Minister said, "That's a mouthful." (Laughter)

Q. Mr. President, could you now tell us how closely held this secret was, or how many people were in on the actual "know"?

THE PRESIDENT: I don't know. You would have to ask in London. Over here, there were relatively few. When

I say relatively few, of course, a great many people in both the War Department and the Navy Department knew that we were sending very large forces over to the other side. A very small number knew the actual timing.

Q. That is what I refer to.

THE PRESIDENT: Yes—very few.

Q. On the fingers of your hand, sir?

THE PRESIDENT: No, I wouldn't say that. It must have been more than that, but not very much more.

Q. Mr. President, how long have you known that this was the date?

THE PRESIDENT: I have known since—(pausing)—I am trying to think back—I would say Teheran, which was last December, that the approximate date would be the end of May or the very first few days of June. And I have known the exact date just within the past few days.

And I knew last night, when I was doing that broadcast on Rome, that the troops were actually in the vessels, on the way across.

Q. I was wondering if you could explain what were the elements entering into the consideration as far back as Teheran that would lead military leaders to be able to choose a date which seems to be quite far ahead?

THE PRESIDENT: Did you ever cross the English Channel?

Q. Never been across the English Channel.

THE PRESIDENT: You're very lucky.

Q. Tide? Is it largely a question of—

THE PRESIDENT: (interposing) Roughness in the English Channel, which has always been considered by passengers one of the greatest trials of life, to have to cross the English Channel. And, of course, they have a record of the wind and the sea in the English Channel; and one of the greatly desirable and absolutely essential things is to have relatively small-boat weather, as we call it, to get people actually onto the beach. And such weather doesn't begin much before May. . . .

Q. Mr. President, was it timed to come after the fall of Rome?

THE PRESIDENT: No, because we didn't know when Rome was going to fall.

Q. Mr. President, you said only one day after the time—was it postponed one day?

THE PRESIDENT: Yes, yes.

Q. That was the weather consideration again?

THE PRESIDENT: That was the consideration. But, of course, you have all seen—and you will see increasingly—the reasons why we didn't institute, at the behest of politicians and others, a second front a year ago when they began clamoring for it; because their plea for an immediate second front last year reminds me a good deal of that famous editor and statesman who said years ago, before most of you were born, during the Wilson administration, "I am not worried about the defense of America. If we are threatened, a million men will spring to arms overnight." And, of course, somebody said, "What kind of arms? If you can't arm them, then what's the good of their springing to something that 'ain't' there?"

Well, it will be shown that the preparations for this particular operation were far bigger and far more difficult than anybody except the military could possibly determine beforehand. We have done it just as fast as we possibly could. The thing came up—of course, it enters into the general, the highest strategy of the war—oh, back the first time that we held a conference of the combined staffs, which was in late December, 1941, and early January, 1942. Why, we took up the question of a second front—of course we did. And we have been taking it up at every conference in the meantime. But there were so many other things that had to be done, and so little in the way of trained troops and munitions to do it with, we have had to wait to do it the very first chance we got. Well, this particular operation goes all the way back to December, 1941, and it came to a head—the final determination—in Cairo and Teheran. I think it is safe to say that. . . .

Q. Mr. President, can you tell us anything about the impact of this invasion on the home front—the population here?

THE PRESIDENT: No. It has all been coming across the ocean. I haven't heard anything except that the whole country is tremendously thrilled; and I would say on that that I think that it is a very reasonable thrill, but that I hope very much that there will not be again too much overconfidence, because overconfidence destroys the war effort.

A fellow came in some time ago whom I have known for quite a while—near home—and he had come—oh, this was several months ago, at the time we took Sicily—and he had had a mighty good job out on the Pacific coast. I don't know what he was—a welder or something like that.

I said, "What are you doing back home?"

"Oh," he said, "the war's over. I am going to try and get a permanent job before everybody quits working on munitions."

He just walked out, quit his job—and he was a good man, he was a munitions worker—because when we took Sicily he said to himself the war's over.

Now, that's the thing we have got to avoid in this country. The war isn't over by any means. This opera-

tion isn't over. You don't just land on a beach and walk through—if you land successfully without breaking your leg—walk through to Berlin. And the quicker this country understands it the better. Again, a question of learning a little geography.

Source: Samuel I. Rosenman, ed., *The Public Papers and Addresses of Franklin D. Roosevelt,* Vol. 13, *Victory and the Threshold of Peace, 1944–45* (New York: Harper, 1950).

Document Eight: Joint Statement of Roosevelt, Churchill, and Stalin at the Yalta Conference, February 11, 1945

This joint statement from the Yalta Conference indicated the planning of the Big Three—President Roosevelt, British prime minister Winston Churchill, and Soviet premier Joseph Stalin—for securing the peace once the war in Europe was concluded. Later, much controversy ensued in the United States over the provisions for Poland emanating from the Yalta Conference.

. . . We have agreed on common policies and plans for enforcing the unconditional surrender terms which we shall impose together on Nazi Germany after German armed resistance has been finally crushed. These terms will not be made known until the final defeat of Germany has been accomplished. Under the agreed plan, the forces of the three powers will each occupy a separate zone of Germany. Coordinated administration and control has been provided for under the plan through a central control commission consisting of the Supreme Commanders of the three powers with headquarters in Berlin. It has been agreed that France should be invited by the three powers, if she should so desire, to take over a zone of occupation, and to participate as a fourth member of the control commission. The limits of the French zone will be agreed by the four Governments concerned through their representatives on the European Advisory Commission.

It is our inflexible purpose to destroy German militarism and Nazism and to ensure that Germany will never again be able to disturb the peace of the world. We are determined to disarm and disband all German armed forces; break up for all time the German General Staff that has repeatedly contrived the resurgence of German militarism; remove or destroy all German military equipment; eliminate or control all German industry that could be used for military production; bring all war criminals to just and swift punishment and exact reparation in kind for the destruction wrought by the

Germans; wipe out the Nazi Party, Nazi laws, organizations and institutions, remove all Nazi and militarist influences from public office and from the cultural and economic life of the German people; and take in harmony such other measures in Germany as may be necessary to the future peace and safety of the world. It is not our purpose to destroy the people of Germany, but only when Nazism and militarism have been extirpated will there be hope for a decent life for Germans, and a place for them in the comity of Nations. . . .

We are resolved upon the earliest possible establishment with our allies of a general international organization to maintain peace and security. We believe that this is essential, both to prevent aggression and to remove the political, economic, and social causes of war through the close and continuing collaboration of all peace-loving peoples.

The foundations were laid at Dumbarton Oaks. On the important question of voting procedure, however, agreement was not there reached. The present Conference has been able to resolve this difficulty.

We have agreed that a conference of United Nations should be called to meet at San Francisco in the United States on April 25, 1945, to prepare the charter of such an organization, along the lines proposed in the informal conversations at Dumbarton Oaks.

The Government of China and the Provisional Government of France will be immediately consulted and invited to sponsor invitations to the conference jointly with the Governments of the United States, Great Britain, and the Union of Soviet Socialist Republics. As soon as the consultation with China and France has been completed, the text of the proposals on voting procedure will be made public. . . .

A new situation has been created in Poland as a result of her complete liberation by the Red Army. This calls for the establishment of a Polish provisional government which can be more broadly based than was possible before the recent liberation of western Poland. The provisional government which is now functioning in Poland should therefore be reorganized on a broader democratic basis with the inclusion of democratic leaders from Poland itself and from Poles

abroad. This new government should then be called the Polish Provisional Government of National Unity.

M. Molotov, Mr. Harriman, and Sir A. Clark Kerr are authorized as a commission to consult in the first instance in Moscow with members of the present provisional government and with other Polish democratic leaders from within Poland and from abroad, with a view to the reorganization of the present government along the above lines. This Polish Provisional Government of National Unity shall be pledged to the holding of free and unfettered elections as soon as possible on the basis of universal suffrage and secret ballot. In these elections all democratic and anti-Nazi parties shall have the right to take part and to put forward candidates.

When a Polish Provisional Government of National Unity has been properly formed in conformity with the above, the Government of the U.S.S.R., which now maintains diplomatic relations with the present provisional government of Poland, and the Government of the United Kingdom and the Government of the U.S.A. will establish diplomatic relations with the new Polish Provisional Government of National Unity, and will exchange ambassadors by whose reports the respective Governments will be kept informed about the situation in Poland.

The three heads of government consider that the eastern frontier of Poland should follow the Curzon line with digressions from it in some regions of five to eight kilometers in favor of Poland. They recognized that Poland must receive substantial accessions of territory in the North and West. They feel that the opinion of the new Polish Provisional Government of National Unity should be sought in due course on the extent of these accessions and that the final delimitation of the western frontier of Poland should thereafter await the peace conference. . . .

❧

Source: Samuel I. Rosenman, ed., *The Public Papers and Addresses of Franklin D. Roosevelt,* Vol. 13, *Victory and the Threshold of Peace, 1944–45* (New York: Harper, 1950).

Harry S. Truman

May 8, 1884–December 26, 1972

Thirty-third President of the United States
April 12, 1945–January 20, 1953

HARRY S. TRUMAN

Place of Birth: Lamar, Missouri

Date of Birth: May 8, 1884

Place of Residence: Missouri

Class Background: modest

Father's Career: farmer and livestock trader

Mother's Career: homemaker

Number of Siblings: two

Religion: Baptist

Education: attended night classes at Kansas City School of Law

Political Party: Democrat

Military Service: World War I: Captain, National Guard, 1917–19

Spouse: Bess Wallace Truman

Spouse's Education: Miss Barstow's Finishing School for Girls

Spouse's Career: homemaker and secretary for Senator Truman

Number of Children: one

Sports and Hobbies: piano, poker, swimming, walking

Career Prior to the Presidency: bank and mailroom clerk, farmer, National Guard officer in World War I, haberdasher, county administrative judge, U.S. senator, vice president

Age upon Entering the White House: 60 years, 339 days

Reason for Leaving the White House: decided not to seek another term in 1952

Career after the Presidency: writer, public speaker, planned his presidential library

Date of Death: December 26, 1972

Cause of Death: minor lung congestion, complexity of organ failures, collapse of cardiovascular system

Last Words: unknown

Burial Site: Independence, Missouri

Value of Estate at Time of Death: unknown

Preceding page: Harry S. Truman *(Library of Congress)*

BIOGRAPHY OF TRUMAN

Harry Truman felt both great adoration and great contempt from the American people during his tenure as president of the United States from 1945 to 1953. The joke, "to err is Truman," coexisted with the chant, "Give 'Em Hell Harry!" Because he acceded to the presidency upon the death of FRANKLIN D. ROOSEVELT, he had to prove himself equal to the demands of his new office. Most immediate was a successful end to World War II, which involved a complex calculus of diplomatic, military, and domestic policy considerations. A necessary component of this work involved gaining and maintaining public confidence, a proposition made tricky by Roosevelt's 12 years in office. One entire generation, later dubbed the "greatest generation," had known no other president.

The thick-skinned Missourian was more than up to the task, as an in-depth review of his life history reveals. Born to Martha E. Young and John A. Truman on May 8, 1884, in Lamar, Missouri, young Harry lived with his parents and his brother, John Vivian, and his sister, Mary Jane, in Jackson County, Missouri. His father was a farmer and livestock dealer and his mother was a homemaker. He spent much of his youth on his maternal grandmother's farm in Grandview, where Harry and his siblings gained extensive experience in agriculture. Between 1890 and 1906, the family lived in Independence and Kansas City, Missouri, where the children attended school. Young Harry, who suffered from poor vision throughout his life, never acquired a taste for sports. He did, though, develop into a bookish sort, a habit he retained throughout his life. He met and became enchanted with young Elizabeth Virginia (Bess) Wallace while a boy in Independence.

After his high school graduation in 1901, Harry worked a variety of jobs, specifically, railroad construction timekeeper, newspaper wrapper, clerk, and assistant to a bank vice president. When he and his family returned to Grandview, Harry gained additional responsibility managing the financial records for the farm but not necessarily more income. After his father's death in 1914, Harry gradually moved away from farm work, activity that he really did not like. He filled his time reading history and playing the piano, two of his favorite pastimes. He joined the Masonic lodge and participated in several other fraternal organizations. He broadened his civic involvement when he returned home from World War I in 1919, joining the Reserve Officers Association, the American Legion, and a downtown Kansas City improvement association.

Despite his age and occupation—he was 33 and a farmer—Truman volunteered for military service in 1917 when the United States entered World War I. He had been a member of the National Guard between 1905 and 1911. He helped organize the 129th Artillery Regiment and was elected a first lieutenant. He was promoted to captain when he went to Europe in 1918. There he commanded Battery D, which had a reputation for undisciplined behavior, of the 129th Artillery Regiment. Captain Truman provided the necessary discipline, and led his men in the Meuse-Argonne offensive in France. Military service benefited Truman in important ways. He gained a much more sophisticated understanding of the world, and he developed important leadership skills. Years earlier, he had gotten his first taste of politics from his father, who had taken him to the Democratic National Convention in 1900. William Jennings Bryan, the Democratic nominee for president that year, became one of Truman's heroes. Later, when he began his Jackson County political career, Truman enjoyed the loyal support of his military comrades.

Upon his return from wartime military service Truman formed two important unions. First, he entered into a business relationship with Edward Jacobson, a former sergeant who had served in the same field artillery unit, thus avoiding a return to the farm, which his brother Vivian had taken responsibility for. The two men opened a haberdashery, which, despite early success, failed to turn a profit in large part because of the recession of 1920–21. His more successful postwar partnership resulted from his marriage to Bess

Young Harry S. Truman *(Library of Congress)*

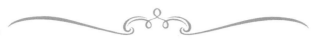

BESS TRUMAN

(1885–1982) *first lady of the United States, April 12, 1945–January 20, 1953*

Elizabeth "Bess" Virginia Wallace was born on February 13, 1885, to David Willock Wallace and Margaret "Madge" Gates Wallace in the small town of Independence, Missouri. She had three younger brothers. Her parents were of upper-class status because of Madge Wallace's wealthy parents. David Wallace had been elected treasurer of Jackson County twice, in 1888 and 1890, as well as receiving an appointment as customs surveyor in Kansas City. Interspersed with these local political posts were periods of unemployment replete with unhappiness and alcoholism. A happy, confident, and athletic child who excelled in school, Bess was close to both her parents. When her father committed suicide in 1903, Bess gained additional responsibilities: care of her younger brothers and her emotionally fragile mother. Bess's grandparents made sure that she attended finishing school in Kansas City.

In 1910, Bess became reacquainted with a childhood friend, Harry S. Truman. The two had first met at the First Presbyterian Church in Independence when Bess was five and Harry six. Harry Truman recalled later in life that he had loved Bess from that moment onward, but Bess was less enamored of Harry. As young adults, Bess and Harry slowly nurtured their friendship. They became engaged three and a half years later. The outbreak of World War I and Harry's enlistment in the army delayed their wedding until June 28, 1919. The young couple struggled in their first years together because Truman's haberdashery business

Bess Truman *(Library of Congress)*

Wallace on June 28, 1919. When he had first proposed to Bess in 1911, she rejected him. Harry nonetheless remained confident, pursuing Bess for the next eight years. Five years after their marriage, the couple had a daughter, Mary Margaret, in 1924. While Bess tended toward the more traditional roles of wife and mother, she and Harry were equal intellectual partners, and she proved to be among his most important advisers and confidantes over the long course of his public career.

The year 1922 saw the end of Truman's business partnership and the beginning of his political career. A military contact helped with the latter. James Pendergast introduced Truman to Thomas J. Pendergast, the boss of the Democratic political machine in Kansas City. Truman ran for and was elected county judge, or, in effect, the county commissioner for eastern Jackson County. While Truman did have business and managerial experience, Pendergast chose Truman because of his electability. He served alongside the judge for the western part of the county, including Kansas City, and as a presiding judge, elected countywide. Defeated for reelection in 1924 on the wave of an anti-Pendergast vote,

Truman won election in 1926 and 1930 as presiding judge. In this post he learned to balance the parochial interests of the eastern and western judges with the implementation of a public works program. Furthermore, he had to accomplish the latter while avoiding corruption in the bidding process. This proved a difficult proposition because a major component of Boss Pendergast's wealth came from his interests in the local construction industry. Truman nonetheless only let contracts to the low bidders. He oversaw the construction of county roads and courthouses for Independence and Kansas City, building a positive, progressive record with the voters throughout Missouri and retaining his relationship with Pendergast. Both were necessary for Truman's next step—a successful race for the U.S. Senate in 1934. Truman bested his opponents Jacob (Tuck) Milligan and John J. Cochran in a difficult Democratic primary when charges of corruption were leveled on all sides of the campaign. Once he had the Democratic nomination he easily beat his Republican opponent, incumbent Roscoe Conkling Patterson.

As a new senator, Truman proved himself a loyal Democrat in the New Deal coalition, supporting President Franklin failed. They also suffered personal loss when Bess Truman had two miscarriages. Their daughter and only child, Mary Margaret, was born in 1924.

Harry Truman found his purpose when he entered politics, first earning a spot as county judge in Jackson County and then election to the U.S. Senate in 1934. Bess Truman worried that the move to Washington, D.C., would not be to her liking, but she found the capital's southern lifestyle pleasing, and regular trips back to Missouri eased the transition. She was not enamored of politics, but she became her husband's most important asset, calming his temper, editing his speeches, and offering political advice. She worked in her husband's Senate office in 1941, then a typical course of action for congressional spouses.

Just three months after her husband became vice president in 1945, Franklin D. Roosevelt died. Because Bess Truman did not enjoy the public spotlight she had no intention of approaching her new post as had Eleanor Roosevelt. At the time many assumed that Bess Truman felt inadequate in comparison with the popular and outgoing first lady. However, her real concern was: how to preserve her own identity. She solved this problem by compartmentalizing her life into her formal, public obligations as first lady, which she met on her limited terms, and her private life and relationship with her husband. Early in her husband's presidency, she became upset when he used atomic weapons to end World War II without consulting her, so accustomed had she become to their regular debates about policy matters. They resolved their differences, and Bess resumed her informal advisory role in her husband's administra-

tion. Correspondence with her husband suggests that this responsibility was much more significant to the nation than her hostess duties, but Americans in the 1940s knew and judged her by the latter. Media relations challenged the first lady. She had initially agreed to let Eleanor Roosevelt introduce her to the journalists who had covered her weekly press conferences. Truman had agreed from a sense of duty, but when she learned she was not required to hold briefings she channeled her communication with the media through her secretaries. Public criticism of her choices and her family troubled Bess Truman greatly. When invited to attend a tea in her honor given by the Daughters of the American Revolution (DAR) at Constitution Hall, the first lady accepted. Controversy ensued when African-American congressman Adam Clayton Powell (D-NY) dubbed her the "Last Lady." His statement reflected his anger at the DAR, which had denied his wife, who was a pianist, the opportunity to play in Constitution Hall, much as the organization had denied the African-American opera singer Marian Anderson from appearing there in 1939. Bess Truman responded to this criticism by resolving to conduct her duties as she defined them, not as other interpreted them. More troubling was occasional press criticism of her daughter, Margaret. Bess Truman reinstituted the formal White House social calendar, including afternoon teas, state receptions, and musicales. Overall, Bess Truman received little criticism, the public admired her integrity, and the entire press corps in Washington came to respect her. She returned to Independence, Missouri, with Harry Truman when his presidency ended in 1953, where she lived until her death on October 18, 1982.

D. Roosevelt on most of the significant votes. The junior senator from Missouri disagreed with Roosevelt over the issue of early payment for the soldier's bonus (Truman supported it while Roosevelt vetoed it only to be overridden by Congress in 1936) and packing the Supreme Court in 1937 (here, Truman voted with the president despite his reservations). Even though the White House administered patronage for Missouri through the senior senator, Bennett Champ Clark, Truman did yeoman labor for constituents who needed help from the federal government. Initially intimidated by his colleagues and his surroundings, Truman eventually found himself unimpressed by many senators, whom he considered nothing more than loud, boastful politicians. He learned that the work of the Senate was done largely in committee and that the way to become a success in Washington was through hard work. As such, he made it his mission to be well schooled on all legislation that came before the committees of which he was a member.

As a member of the Interstate and Foreign Commerce Committee, Truman made issues regarding transportation, especially on the national level, his legislative priority. He

was a sponsor of the Civil Aeronautics Act of 1938, a measure that regulated the airline industry until the 1970s. Additionally, he worked closely with the chair of the Commerce Committee, Burton K. Wheeler (D-MT), to investigate the nation's transportation system. Truman gained significant media attention for the publicity he won in calling attention to the financial collusion among railroad executives, lawyers, and bankers who worked on railroad reorganization in the mid- and late 1930s. Ultimately, Truman and Wheeler sought guarantees for fair competition among the railroad, barge, and trucking industries. The ensuing legislation, enacted in 1940, stemmed from Truman's hard work in committee and provided an important regulatory apparatus for the transportation industry.

That same year, Truman faced a difficult campaign for reelection. His position was complicated because of the collapse of the Pendergast machine in Missouri. After Tom Pendergast was found guilty of income tax evasion in 1939, the 50,000 or so fraudulent votes that typically went to machine candidates were eliminated from the electoral process. While the U.S. attorney was investigating Pendergast, Truman delivered a speech condemning the prosecutor and President Roosevelt for unfairly attacking his benefactor. Both the U.S. attorney and the governor of Missouri declared against Truman in the primary election and attempted to taint him with the corruption of the Pendergast machine despite the fact that Truman's integrity was beyond reproach. Even though the antimachine vote was divided, Truman's chances remained in doubt until election day. Truman retained his popularity with the state's rural voters, but it was votes from the political machine in St. Louis that guaranteed his victory in the primary. Without meaningful Republican opposition, Truman prevailed in the general election as well.

Truman became a national figure during his second term in the Senate. With the onset of World War II in Europe, he had learned of the financial corruption involved in the construction of military bases. Worried about the potential for this problem, left unchecked, to hinder the national military buildup, Truman made a 10,000-mile tour of the nation's military bases in 1941. He learned that contractors earned guaranteed profits despite the lack of efficiency among their workers, and that eastern corporations received a disproportionate share of the military construction. As a result he

Harry S. Truman *(front, center)* and Bess Wallace *(right)* were married on June 28, 1919. The bridesmaid on the left is Louise Wells and on the right is Bess's cousin, Helen Wallace. In the back row are the best man, Ted Marks, and Bess's brother, Frank, who "gave her away." *(Truman Family/Associated Press)*

pushed for the creation of the Special Senate Committee to Investigate the National Defense Program. Military leaders opposed the formation of the committee, worrying it would replicate the harm done to the Union army during the Civil War by the Joint Committee on the Conduct of the War. The Democratic leadership in the Senate approved the committee on March 1, 1941, however, believing that Truman would be congenial to the president and reasoning that he could do little with a budget of just $15,000. Indeed, Truman had no intention of publicly squabbling with the president, but he did want to make a significant impact on national defense policy. To maintain a positive relationship with the White House, Truman made sure Roosevelt knew of any pending report before its publication so that the president could avoid negative publicity.

Under Truman's leadership from 1941 until his election as vice president three years later, the Special Senate Committee to Investigate the National Defense Program amassed a positive record and forced numerous cost-saving measures on the military, preventing graft and fraud from hampering the war effort. The committee sought as one of its goals a better working relationship among business, labor, and government. The Truman Committee, as it became known, also publicized poor equipment choices by military procurement authorities and labor union abuses. It helped develop policy to deal with the rubber shortage. It called for a stronger civilian role in wartime economics, denouncing the excessive military production demands. It pushed for greater participation of small business in the war effort. Finally it called for planning for the eventual postwar ECONOMIC RECONVERSION.

The senators who served with Truman were more interested in accomplishments than grandstanding. Most of the work was done through the subcommittee process, and all committee reports were unanimous. Preliminary drafts were circulated among the military, businesses, or unions discussed in the findings. Factual errors—but not interpretive conclusions—were open to revision before the final drafts were printed. Because the Truman Committee enjoyed such a favorable reputation in government circles and among the public, even the threat of an investigation could compel the needed reforms. Truman's effective leadership drew wide praise and elevated his public profile.

As the presidential election of 1944 approached, Roosevelt, who had already served an unprecedented three terms in office, announced he would run for a fourth term. Dissatisfaction with Henry Wallace, the sitting but unpredictable vice president, was widespread with all factions of the Democratic Party except liberals, leading Roosevelt and his advisers to seek a replacement. Contenders included Senate Majority Leader ALBEN BARKLEY of Kentucky and James Byrnes of South Carolina. Barkley's public fight with the president over tax policy earlier in the year, though, disqualified him from serious consideration. Byrnes, a former senator and Supreme

BIOGRAPHICAL TIME LINE

1884
May 8 Harry Truman is born.

1901
Truman graduates from high school.

1917
Truman volunteers for military service with U.S. entry into World War I.

1919
June 28 Truman marries Bess Wallace.

November Truman opens a haberdashery business with Edward Jacobson, a friend from the same field artillery unit.

1922
The haberdashery fails because of the economic recession.

Truman runs for and is elected county judge, or, in effect, the county commissioner for eastern Jackson County.

1924
Truman loses reelection as county judge.

1926
Truman wins election as county judge.

1930
Truman wins election as presiding judge.

1934
Truman wins election to the U.S. Senate.

1940
Truman wins reelection to the U.S. Senate.

1941
Truman is put in charge of the Special Senate Committee to Investigate the National Defense Program.

1944
Truman is elected vice president of the United States.

1945
January 20 Truman becomes vice president.

April 12 Upon the death of Franklin D. Roosevelt, Truman is sworn in as president.

1948
Truman is elected president in an upset election.

1949
January 20 Truman is inaugurated president.

1952
Truman announces that he will not seek reelection.

1953
January 20 Truman's last day as president.

1972
December 26 Truman dies.

Court justice who then worked in the administration, was close to the president but was tainted by his segregationist record and his conversion from Catholicism. Other names that were mentioned included Supreme Court justice William O. Douglas and Speaker of the House Sam Rayburn, but neither seemed suitable. Harry Truman's name was another that the president and party insiders considered.

Truman, though, was initially uninterested in running for vice president, satisfied as he was with his job in the Senate. He went to the Democratic National Convention in Chicago with plans to nominate Byrnes. Bob Hannegan,

a Democratic leader from St. Louis, helped swing support for Truman, but in the runup to the convention, Roosevelt remained coy as to his preferences. Hannegan and party chieftains Edwin Pauley of California, Postmaster General Edwin Walker, Edward J. Flynn of New York, and Mayor Edward J. Kelley of Chicago steered Roosevelt to Truman. Roosevelt chose Truman because of the honest reputation he had gained in chairing the Truman Committee, because he had the least amount of negatives compared to other potential candidates, and because the party leaders favored him. The president finally made his intentions known to Truman

Harry S. Truman campaigning *(Library of Congress)*

via a telephone call during the convention. Truman was in a hotel room meeting with party heavyweights, all of whom were pushing Truman to run for the vice presidency. When Roosevelt called to see what the problem was, Hannegan suggested Truman was as stubborn as a mule. The president then told Truman that if he did not fight for the nomination he would be responsible for destroying the Democratic Party in the midst of the war. That argument persuaded Truman, and it took only two convention ballots to sway the delegates to vote for Truman over Wallace. Party insiders recognized that Roosevelt would not likely live to the end of another term; this closely guarded knowledge was not shared with the American people.

The campaign that fall featured some criticism of Truman, from liberal Democrats who felt Wallace had been betrayed, from Republicans who belittled Truman's stature, and from the media, which incorrectly charged that Truman had been a member of the Ku Klux Klan (he had fought the Klan while a Jackson County official). Even Eleanor Roosevelt was lukewarm on Truman. A friend of Wallace, she said that while she did not know Truman she had heard he was a good man. But voters did not much care about who was running for vice president. It was the top of the ticket that mattered, and they wanted the stability and continuity that Roosevelt would bring to the conclusion of the war. Roosevelt and Truman were elected that fall, and Truman became vice president on January 20, 1945.

Truman's 82 days as vice president were spent presiding over the Senate. Little changed regarding the rhythm of Truman's life. He kept his same apartment and his same Capitol

Hill office. Never close to Roosevelt, he met with the president only a few times. He knew little of the White House plans that were being made for the postwar world. His most important work on behalf of the administration was to help gain confirmation for Roosevelt's appointment of Wallace as secretary of commerce, a conciliation prize for losing the vice presidency (the following year when he was president in his own right, Truman dismissed Wallace from the cabinet). He tried unsuccessfully to patch the growing rift between the legislative and the executive branches of government. Members of Congress had chafed at the often heavy-handed manner in which Roosevelt had comported himself since he arrived in Washington in 1933. Truman received negative press for attending Tom Pendergast's funeral in January 1945. Truman made the decision to attend as a gesture of respect for a friend who had helped launch his political career and who had never asked him to break the law. Critics took the move as proof of Truman's poor judgment and his parochialism. Truman opponents shuddered a few weeks later when he played the piano for soldiers at a stage show held at Washington's Press Club. One of the entertainers in attendance was actress Lauren Bacall, who was hoisted up on the piano in a striking pose while a smiling Truman continued to play.

Truman plays the piano as movie star Lauren Bacall, perched on top, looks on. *(Associated Press)*

The date of Thursday, April 12, 1945, found Truman presiding over the Senate. Unimpressed with the speeches and debates of the day, he wrote letters to his mother and his sister back in Missouri. Six hundred miles away in Warm Springs, Georgia, President Roosevelt's health failed him, and he suffered a fatal cerebral hemorrhage. Not yet aware of this life-changing event, Truman adjourned the Senate and joined some of his closest friends in House Speaker Sam Rayburn's hideaway office where they routinely drank and debated the political situation. Truman arrived without his secret service agent, which was not uncommon since his protection detail, the first for a vice president, was scattered at best. Rayburn gave him a message to call the White House immediately. Truman did so and received instructions to come at once and to say nothing about the call. When Truman arrived, he was ushered into the family quarters where he learned of the president's death. At first unable to speak, Harry Truman offered his condolences and prayers for the first lady, but Eleanor Roosevelt responded that she was ready to help Truman, however necessary, for he was the one as she said "in trouble now."

Truman took over as president at a crucial time in U.S. history, and yet in many ways he was unprepared for the office. Roosevelt had met with him only several times since the election and had failed to inform Truman on key postwar issues. Within his first month as president the war in Europe came to an end on May 8, 1945. Truman was learning fast the challenges he faced. In July, the POTSDAM CONFERENCE with Soviet premier Joseph Stalin and British prime ministers Winston Churchill and Clement Atlee, was held to plan for the future of Germany. At the same time, planning for the end of the war in the Pacific was ongoing. Truman only learned of the atomic bomb program after being sworn in as president. News of the successful atomic bomb test in the New Mexico desert reached Truman while he was at the Potsdam Conference. The president chose to use the new atomic weapon as a means to hasten the end of the war in the Pacific. It was perhaps the most significant decision of his presidency.

As president, Truman oversaw the transformation of American peacetime foreign policy. He applied the lessons of the war era to the new global, superpower responsibilities of the nation. The activist, interventionist strategies that were born of war became a permanent feature of the postwar era as the United States entered into what would become a cold war with the Soviet Union that spanned 50 years. Truman did make a few key shifts from the Roosevelt era, most notably instituting a more bipartisan approach to foreign policy considerations. While isolationists carped about this new role for the United States, they were such a minority in the government that their concerns received scant attention. Conservatives in both parties worried about the costs of the cold war, but the biggest cause for criticism of Truman's foreign policy

In his first speech as president, Harry Truman addresses a joint session of Congress on April 16, 1945. *(Library of Congress)*

came with the KOREAN WAR in 1950. Because Truman tried to fight a limited war under the aegis of the United Nations, extreme nationalists worried about the future of American sovereignty in a world they feared would be dominated by the new international organization.

Truman's domestic policy proved much more problematic. Neither the people nor the Congress supported expansion of the experimental liberalism of the New Deal era. As such, Truman's domestic reform policies, dubbed the FAIR DEAL, met with mixed success. Growth of popular programs such as Social Security was possible but the creation of new programs, specifically national health insurance, which Truman favored, failed to achieve the consensus needed for passage. In the increasingly important area of civil rights, Truman understood he could act only through executive orders, knowing that Congress was unwilling to legislate on this matter. Perhaps his boldest move came in 1948 when he issued an executive order providing for the DESEGREGATION OF THE MILITARY. The biggest flaw in Truman's domestic agenda was the degree to which he abetted the burgeoning anticommunist paranoia with his LOYALTY SECURITY

PROGRAM, which ultimately became associated with the unsavory tactics of Senator Joseph McCarthy (R-WI).

The 1948 presidential campaign and election proved an important turning point for Truman's presidency. The issues and the attitudes of American voters suggested that 1948 should have been a Republican year. Truman's popularity was quite low, and he enjoyed little confidence among the American people. The Democratic Party appeared hopelessly divided in 1948: Liberals remained unhappy that Henry Wallace had been removed as vice president in 1944 and replaced by Truman, and they ultimately formed the Progressive Party with Wallace as the standard-bearer to challenge for the White House; likewise, conservative white southerners opposed to civil rights formed the States Rights Party, alternatively known as the Dixiecrat Party, and they tapped the segregationist South Carolina governor J. Strom Thurmond as their nominee. The Republicans nominated New York governor Thomas Dewey, who had been the party's candidate in 1944. The party adopted a liberal platform in sync with Dewey's views. These choices gave Truman the opening he needed. After the Republican convention, he called the 80th Congress, led by conservative Republicans, into special session in late July, essentially daring it not to pass the Republican platform. The Congress failed to act, as Truman expected would be the case, and he made the "do-nothing 80th Congress" an issue in the fall elections. Truman ignored both the Wallace and the Thurmond candidacies, and, despite the predictions of the *Chicago Tribune* in its infamous headline "Dewey Defeats Truman" printed on election night before the returns from the West Coast were in, Truman was elected president in his own right with 303 electoral college votes to 189 for Dewey, 39 for Thurmond, and none for Wallace. Truman also captured the popular vote: 24,179,347 to 21,991,292 for Dewey, 1,175,946 for Thurmond, and 1,157,328 for Wallace.

During his presidency Truman remained very close with and protective of his family, even trying to eat lunch with his wife every day. The most well-known manifestation of the latter involved his daughter, Margaret, who aspired to a career as a musician. While she possessed a degree of talent, she also received a number of negative reviews. When the music critic for the *Washington Post* gave a harsh review of her singing performance in December 1950, Truman dashed off a note to the critic threatening various types of bodily harm should they ever meet. The critic published the letter and a public controversy ensued. Truman tried to deflect the situation by saying he was just a father looking out for his daughter. He maintained a distinct daily routine while president. Waking early in the morning, he took a brisk walk every day, had a massage, a drink of bourbon, and breakfast. After lunch he swam in the White House pool and napped for a short period. Most evenings were spent with BESS TRUMAN, but he did play poker with friends on a regular basis. Vacations were usually spent cruising on the presidential yacht or in Key West, Florida.

Exempt from the recently ratified TWENTY-SECOND AMENDMENT to the Constitution, which limited presidents to two terms in office, Truman nonetheless opted not to run for another term as president in 1952. Instead, Harry and Bess Truman retired to their home in Independence, Missouri, where they lived for the remainder of their lives. He undertook several actions to preserve the memory of his presidency. Foremost was the construction of his presidential library and museum in Independence. Located near his home, the library opened in 1957. Truman maintained an office and worked out of the library on a regular basis. The former president also wrote his memoirs, consisting of two volumes on his presidency. One volume covered his first year in office while the other volume treated the last seven years of his presidency. He remained active in Democratic politics and spoke out on matters of public concern.

He died in Kansas City on December 26, 1972. Instead of having an elaborate state funeral, Episcopal Church services were held at the Truman Library in Independence. Overseeing the proceedings were a Baptist minister and the Grand Masonic leader of Missouri. Truman's grave, located in the courtyard of his library, was marked with a simple stone. The former president wrote his epitaph, which merely noted his birth and death dates, his daughter's birth, and his public offices.

When Truman left office in 1953, his public approval rating was extremely low—just over 30 percent and it had been as low as 22 percent—but by the time of his death he had become something of a folk hero. Politicians of both parties made appeals to his memory and legacy. Scholarly evaluation of Truman has undergone similar fluctuations. While typically ranked as above average by most scholars, some leftist historians have attacked his role in bringing on the cold war, have questioned his liberal credentials, and have suggested he was unfit to be president. Later events in American history, though, such as the Vietnam War and the Watergate scandal, led observers to praise Truman for his honesty, forthrightness, and personal responsibility as a leader. While Truman also had a reputation for being impetuous, in reality he rarely made hasty decisions in the White House, applying instead a cool and rational intelligence to the problems that crossed his desk. Two anecdotes reveal not only Truman's personality, but also the reasons for his success in the White House. A sign that he kept on his desk in the Oval Office, which read "the buck stops here" served to let it be known that he was the one in charge, responsible for decisions. And at a meeting between Truman and Soviet foreign minister V. M. Molotov, the Soviet diplomat complained that he had never been spoken to in the gruff manner Truman had used. Truman replied that it would not happen again as long as Molotov kept his promises.

PRESIDENTIAL ELECTION OF 1948

—⟋⟍⟍—

Upset of the century—these words are not too strong a description of the 1948 presidential contest. On paper Harry Truman appeared to be destined to lose. A December 1946 public opinion poll ranked his popularity at a dismal 35 percent. His liabilities included a poor speaking style, an unstatesmanlike bearing, a vastly fluctuating public approval rating, and little credit for his accomplishments. The Republican sweep of the midterm elections in 1946 suggested a possible change in the nation's political compass. The likely Republican nominee was New York governor Thomas E. Dewey. Though he was the failed Republican candidate in 1944, he wanted another shot at the White House and he accepted many of the New Deal reforms of the 1930s. However, for a number of reasons Harry Truman remained competitive. More Americans described themselves as Democrats than as Republicans; Truman had a large army of volunteers in and out of the unified Democratic National Committee ready to do whatever it took to ensure his victory; and the Republican Party was divided between the conservatives, who held power in Congress, and the more moderate Dewey.

Once the election was concluded, Truman won just under 50 percent of the popular the vote, but a clear majority of the electoral votes. The complex landscape of postwar American politics helps explain this narrow win for the president. In November 1947, Jim Rowe, who had worked in the White House under FRANKLIN D. ROOSEVELT, prepared a detailed memorandum that Clark Clifford, special counsel to the president, presented to Truman on the political situation in 1948. Clifford proved a talented prognosticator for he correctly contended that Dewey would gain the Republican nomination. He also predicted that Henry Wallace, the former vice president who had been replaced on the Democratic ticket in 1944 by Truman, would run in a third-party bid. The only candidate that Clifford did not predict was South Carolina governor J. Strom Thurmond, who ran on the States' Rights Party ticket in opposition to Truman's CIVIL RIGHTS PROGRAM.

The burgeoning Cold War with the Soviet Union shaped Truman's thinking about whether or not to run for president in 1948. While he believed he had devised a solid strategy for waging the Cold War, he also assumed that not everyone who might run for the presidency was up to the challenge of dealing with the issues. Nonetheless, he was not overjoyed with his position. The job had been frustrating for him. Since becoming president upon Roosevelt's death on April 12, 1945, he had spoken harshly about a host of groups—foreign leaders, Republicans, uncooperative Democrats, union bosses, business leaders, Congress, and the media—that would vex whomever was in the White House. Crowds, scrutiny of his family life, and life in the White House also bothered him. In February 1948, he wrote in his diary: "it's hell to be the Chief of State!" Not running for election in his own right, though, was not an option for Truman. He had multiple motivations for entering the fray in 1948, the most important of which were his unfinished foreign and domestic initiatives, his sense of duty to the Democratic Party, his desire to best his political foes, his distrust of those who might succeed him, and his ambition to win the office in his own right. Nonetheless he did not discuss his plans until well into 1948.

Early in 1947 Clark Clifford had assembled an informal committee to advise the president about political strategy. Membership came from the ranks of the administration, tilted toward pragmatic politics, and omitted most of those advisers who had been in Roosevelt's and Henry Wallace's inner circles. This group identified issues ripe for political manipulation and advised Truman on policy questions that could frame the election, among which were integration of the military, veto of the TAFT-HARTLEY ACT, and RECOGNITION OF ISRAEL. Additionally, officials with the Democratic National Committee sagely cautioned Truman to avoid speaking as a partisan candidate until after the Democratic National Convention, instead addressing the country as its national leader.

By late 1947, Truman telescoped his intentions for the following year. He named Senator J. Howard McGrath (D-RI) as chair of the Democratic National Committee, and McGrath went so far as to tell the press he was working for Truman's reelection. McGrath attempted to retract the statement, saying he only had a hunch about the pending election, but the president hinted in a February 5, 1948, press conference that McGrath had a good hunch. The following month, on March 8, McGrath announced Truman's candidacy.

Perhaps Truman's biggest election hurdle came from within his own party. Liberal and moderate Democrats who had enjoyed being in power since the early 1930s had never trusted Truman. They resented the manner in which President Roosevelt had selected Truman to replace their hero, Henry Wallace, on the Democratic ticket in 1944. Furthermore, they viewed Truman as a corrupt political hack from Missouri who lacked Roosevelt's grand vision and intelligence. Truman's reliance on middling, conservative advisers was the coup de grâce for them. The formation of two Democratic groups after the 1946 election debacle—Republicans gained control of both the Senate and the House of Representatives—threatened to destabilize the party in 1948. Liberals who organized the new Progressive Citizens of America would ultimately work for Wallace while the more moderate Americans for Democratic Action courted DWIGHT D. EISENHOWER as a replacement candidate for Truman.

When Wallace declared his candidacy on December 29, 1947, these intraparty divisions became a reality. He tapped Idaho senator Glen Taylor, a Democrat, to serve as his running mate on the Progressive Party ticket. Wallace's ambition was less to secure a victory, which would have been nearly impossible, than it was to shift the public policy debate leftward. The issues he believed most important for the country's future included a more cooperative relationship with the Soviet Union. Wallace feared that nothing good could come of the CONTAINMENT POLICY emerging from the Truman administration. When he had made his views on this subject public in a September 12, 1946, speech, Truman later asked for and received his resignation from his position as secretary of commerce. Along with cooperation with the Soviets, Wallace advocated racial justice, a massive expansion of social welfare programs, and an elimination of monopolies through their nationalization. He hoped his candidacy would block Truman's election because he believed, as did his leftist supporters, that a Republican administration would lead the American people to seek a return to rule by liberal Democrats at the next election. Beyond his splashy entry into the race, though, the Wallace campaign never amounted to much.

In one key way, however, the Wallace campaign made indirect trouble for Truman. By emphasizing civil rights, the Wallace camp forced Truman to become more supportive on the issue. This move drew opposition from the white power-base in the South and ultimately led to the formation of the States' Rights Party under the leadership and candidacy of South Carolina governor J. Strom Thurmond. Thurmond and four other southern governors wrote to McGrath in telling the Democratic National Committee leader not to count on white southern votes that fall. Thurmond's candidacy threatened Truman's strategy of using civil rights to appeal to liberals and blacks and using party loyalty to retain the white South.

The last important figure in the drama leading up to the Democratic National Convention was Dwight D. Eisenhower, the popular general from World War II. The Americans for Democratic Action hoped that Eisenhower could unify the disparate factions in the Democratic Party in a way that they believed Truman could not. Other Democratic constituencies courted Eisenhower, including southern whites, union officials, and urban politicos. This outpouring of support was strange considering that the popular general had never made his political affiliations known and that he had never voted. Truman viewed these efforts as traitorous, but he benefited from the draft Eisenhower movement. Because the general never outwardly declined these entreaties, no time remained for another candidate to challenge Truman before the Democratic National Convention and prevent his nomination. Additionally, Truman had made a nationwide speaking tour before the convention in which he previewed the extemporaneous speaking style he would use that fall in the general election contest. By "being Harry" instead of giving a dry policy speech he captivated the voters' attention.

The Republican National Convention was held first, in Philadelphia in June. Based on their success in 1946 and on the more conservative trend of the electorate, Republican regulars believed they would recapture the White House in 1948. The only way they believed the Democrats could hold on would be if Eisenhower ran on that party's ticket, and they doubted that scenario would transpire. As such, the contest for the Republican nomination was fierce. In addition to Governor Dewey, the other front-runners were Senator Robert Taft of Ohio, a conservative, and former Minnesota governor Harold E. Stassen, a moderate and an internationalist. Taft had emerged as an influential Republican senator during World War II, and his politics were largely in tune with congressional Republicans, termed by Truman as the worst Congress ever for its conservatism. Stassen did well in four presidential primaries (not all states used primaries to select convention delegates), and he had bested Truman in some public opinion polls. (Stassen would unsuccessfully seek the Republican nomination eight more times, in 1952, 1956, 1960, 1964, 1968, 1972, 1976, and 1988.)

As part of his preconvention strategy, Stassen believed that a victory in the Oregon primary would make him the leading candidate for the Republican nomination. Alarmed, Dewey campaigned hard in Oregon. Dewey and Stassen debated on a nationwide radio broadcast in which Dewey's previous work as district attorney, in which he had honed his speaking skills, paid off handsomely; he won the Oregon primary in beating Stassen handily. That victory together with the support of most state Republican organizations gave Dewey the lead heading into the convention. Dewey's biggest liability was his personality. Described as aloof, arrogant, secretive, and humorless, one Republican official's wife said, "You have to know Mr. Dewey very well in order to dislike him." His stiffness hurt his ability to connect with the American voters, but such concerns were not enough to stop Republicans from nominating him.

Dewey prevailed on the third ballot. His party's platform was liberal in substance and he made few overt criticisms of the Truman administration. He accepted the goals of the New Deal, questioning only the methods of implementation. This placed his candidacy in direct opposition to the 80th Congress, which was almost strident in its resistance to Truman and the Democrats. Truman and the Democrats immediately recognized this dichotomy and sought to exploit it. He told the press that he liked Earl Warren, the Republican governor of California who was the vice-presidential nominee, and had nothing against Dewey. Were he to get his party's nomination at its July convention, Truman hinted he would make the 80th Congress the target of his invective.

Also meeting in Philadelphia, the Democratic National Convention easily nominated Truman after failed blocking moves from disgruntled liberals and southerners. The former had tried unsuccessfully to recruit another candidate while the latter made a show of pushing the candidacy of Georgia senator Richard B. Russsell, leader of the segregationist forces on Capitol Hill. Truman had garnered well over the required votes for the nomination by the second day of the convention, but the southerners refused to make his nomination unanimous. The Mississippi delegation and half of the Alabama delegation went so far as to walk out of the convention. The other southern delegates remained just so they could vote against Truman. They were unhappy that they had lost both the nomination fight and the battle over the civil rights plank in the party platform. While the Truman White House had written the platform, Minneapolis mayor and Minnesota senatorial candidate Hubert Humphrey forced the convention to strengthen the civil rights plank with a stirring address to the convention. He had the backing of the Americans for Democratic Action. Truman did not mind too much, since he favored the changes.

With the platform changes approved, Truman moved on to the selection of a running mate. He had given little thought to the question of the vice presidency. After first approaching Supreme Court justice William O. Douglas, who said running for office from his position would be unseemly, Truman settled on Kentucky senator ALBEN BARKLEY, who was popular with his colleagues.

When Truman gave his acceptance speech few believed he had much of a chance that fall. The sitting president used that speech to preview his strategy of attacking the Republicans in Congress, not Dewey. He announced a special session of Congress in which he would give the Republican majority a chance to enact its platform promises, knowing that the conservative lawmakers would have nothing to do with the liberal platform. The two-week session starting on July 26, lived up—or down—to Truman's expectations, passing nothing of significance other than a loan for the construction of the United Nations building in New York City. Truman agreed with a reporter's characterization of the Congress as "do-nothing" and the description became a Democratic theme for the rest of the campaign.

Days after the conclusion of the Democratic convention the States Rights Party held its convention in Birmingham, Alabama. J. Strom Thurmond received the presidential nomination and Fielding Wright, the governor of Mississippi, the vice-presidential nomination. They did not, however, attract as many voters away from the Democratic Party's right flank as they had hoped. Likewise, Henry Wallace's attack on the Democratic left flank was losing steam. Postconvention polling revealed that neither Dewey nor Truman had received a bounce in the polls; both held at their preconvention percentages: 48 percent for Dewey and 37 percent for Truman. Given that both the right and the left wings of the Democratic Party had been peeled away, though, Truman's constant poll numbers were a good sign. Furthermore, the elimination of southern whites from the party, at least in a formal sense, made it politically tenable for Truman to issue the

long-promised executive orders to desegregate the military, strengthening his civil rights credentials.

As his electioneering strategy unfolded, Truman made no mention of Wallace or Thurmond. Their extremist candidacies had rendered them insignificant to the fall elections. Thurmond was too racist, even for many white southerners, and Wallace attracted few voters with his civil rights appeals and left-wing proposals. Furthermore, his reputation for favoring Stalin hurt him with voters. Traversing the country by train in September and October, Truman made multiple impromptu speeches a day from the rear of his private car, the "Ferdinand Magellan." Crowds in the 28 states he visited during his "whistle-stop" campaign were enthusiastic, often chanting, "Give 'em hell, Harry." He spent most of his time in the Midwest, specifically Ohio. He spoke against what he believed were the two key threats to the United States: domestic special interests and foreign authoritarianism. He advocated on behalf of a long list of issues: universal military training, foreign aid, support for Israel, anticommunism, inflation control, housing reform, federal aid to education, health care, minimum wage increases, expansions to the Social Security program, flood control, public utilities, civil rights, labor law reform, the environment, agricultural subsidy reform, and business regulation. Collectively, this agenda was designed to leaven out the distribution of resources in

Harry Truman winks on the back of a train during his whistle-stop campaign, 1948. *(Library of Congress)*

ALBEN BARKLEY

(1877–1956) *vice president of the United States, January 20, 1949–January 20, 1953*

Alben William Barkley lived the American dream. Born the son of Kentucky tenant farmers Electra Smith and John Wilson Barkley on November 24, 1877, Alben Barkley achieved the second-highest office in the land. Barkley entered Marvin College without benefit of a high school degree. After his 1897 graduation, he matriculated to Emory College in Oxford, Georgia (now Emory University in Atlanta, Georgia), where he studied law for one year. Young Barkley was unable to afford further study so he moved to Paducah, Kentucky, where he read the law with seasoned attorneys. In 1901, he was admitted to the Kentucky bar, and in 1902, he studied law for an additional summer term at the University of Virginia. Marriage to Dorothy Brower followed in 1903. The couple had three children.

Public oratory and politics provided Barkley his path to national prominence. In the first decade of the 20th century he ran for, and won, two posts in western Kentucky, first as county attorney and second as county judge. In 1912, he gained election to the U.S. House of Representatives as a Democrat. He held that post until his election to the U.S. Senate in 1926.

The national political mood of Barkley's early House years could not have better matched his own political temperament. The Kentuckian's upbringing inculcated in him an innate agrarian liberalism from which he never deviated. As such, Barkley eagerly supported President Woodrow Wilson's New Freedom legislation. Since Wilson and Barkley arrived in Washington at the same time, the two developed a close working relationship. Their similar backgrounds facilitated this cooperation, and the president became something of a mentor for the new congressman, teaching Barkley the importance of viewing political issues from a national, not a local or regional perspective. At the end of his career, Barkley contended that of the seven presidents under whom he had served Wilson was the best.

The Republican politics of the 1920s frustrated Barkley so much so that he considered leaving Washington to run for governor of Kentucky. His unsuccessful bid for his state's highest executive office in 1923, though, solidified his legislative career in Washington. Because his seat was considered safe, Barkley bought a house in the nation's capital.

Franklin D. Roosevelt's election to the presidency in 1932 energized Barkley and other liberal Democrats in Congress. Barkley became a significant power in both national Democratic politics—functioning as the keynote speaker at the 1932 Democratic National Convention—and in Senate politics—working as a leader for the New Deal legislation Roosevelt wanted enacted. In 1937, when Majority Leader Joseph T. Robinson (D-AR) died, Barkley gained election to the post by one vote. Conservative Democrats dismissed him as a lackey for the Roosevelt administration. Barkley tried to lead the Senate by following a strategy of consensus building as opposed to one in which he exerted his will over what has been described as the most exclusive club in the United States whose membership rarely acknowledged superiors.

Alben Barkley *(Library of Congress)*

World War II affected Barkley's career in several key ways. First, he had hoped that he could gain the Democratic nomination for the presidency in 1940, but the onset of the war in Europe led Roosevelt to seek a third term, thwarting Barkley's national ambitions for the first of three times. Second, during the war, Barkley served as the pivotal figure in a showdown between the legislative and the executive branches. In 1944, Roosevelt vetoed the tax legislation that Congress had passed, calling it a relief measure for the wealthy. Because Barkley believed that Roosevelt's veto message contained an attack on the integrity of the Senate, he resigned his post as majority leader. Lawmakers overrode the veto, Roosevelt apologized, and the Democrats unanimously reelected Barkley. Later that year Roosevelt passed over Barkley (in favor of Senator Harry S. Truman) when he sought a new running mate, concerned that the Kentuckian was too old for the vice presidency.

Truman felt differently in 1948, and Barkley proved himself an indefatigable campaigner that year, flying 150,000 miles and making 250 speeches. As vice president, or the "Veep" as his grandson dubbed him, Barkley made as much of the post as possible. He relished his role as presiding officer in the Senate, and he actively supported Truman's domestic and foreign legislative agenda. After his wife died in 1947, he married Jane Rucker Hadley in 1949, a woman almost half his age. As the Truman presidency approached its end, Barkley ran unsuccessfully as a candidate for the Democratic nomination in 1952. Retiring to Kentucky, he sought and won a Senate seat in 1956. He returned to Washington stripped of his seniority, but he was happy to be back in the political game. He died on April 30, 1956, immediately after giving a speech at Washington and Lee University.

the country. Economic expansion, Truman argued, made these reforms possible. Nevertheless, these appeals were not enough for some Democrats, who were convinced Truman would lose the election.

During this whistle-stop campaign, Truman painted himself as a hard worker with vast political experience while the Republicans in comparison appeared either bland, in the case of Dewey, or reactionary, in the case of Congress. Eventually, Truman's combative, feisty, take-no-prisoners attitude won him converts. He threatened that the Republicans would even repeal the New Deal. He was not afraid to speak negatively about voters who opted for the Republicans. In early September, he told a Detroit audience: "Remember that the reactionary of today is a shrewd man. He is a man with a calculating machine where his heart ought to be." He also suggested that since the Republicans were lying to Americans, he was the only person who would tell the truth.

Dewey's campaign strategy compounded the picture Truman had painted. As the front-runner, Dewey opted to speak in generalities. He described himself as talented and fit for the job, promising Americans that once he was elected he would fix the country's problems. Dapper and good-looking but dull and uninspiring, Dewey was a weak candidate. He made choices that further hampered his campaign, especially when he had poll-tested controversial topics, he spoke only in generalities. Dewey gained a reputation as "the little man on the wedding cake" in the words of Alice Roosevelt Longworth, daughter of Theodore Roosevelt and a longtime observer of national politics. Dewey believed that by not making controversial, confrontational statements about specific issues he would preserve his lead in the polls and his favorable image with the media. Furthermore, he wanted to avoid giving offense to Democratic and independent voters. Another factor guiding the Dewey camp was fear of further dividing the Republican Party. He did not want to repeat the mistake he believed he had made in his 1944 race when he had been much more belligerent in his attacks on Franklin D. Roosevelt and the Democrats. In 1948, Dewey gave few speeches; instead, he made promises that his administration would be different from, and better than, the current one.

As the election drew nearer, Truman gained in strength, even if the polls did not reflect it. A Gallup poll taken in the middle of October and published the day before the election registered 49.5 percent for Dewey and 44.5 percent for Truman. Truman nonetheless reached out to those constituencies he believed would be most affected by the campaign: the working class, farmers, and African Americans. He returned to Independence with his family to vote on November 2. He enjoyed lunch with friends, and he waited out the results of the election in a local hotel. Truman went to bed around 9:00 p.m. with the first East Coast returns coming in. He told his secret service agent not to wake him unless it was important. Near midnight he awoke, listened to the radio for a bit, then

went back to bed. While he was leading by over 1 million votes at midnight, NBC news reported that Dewey would make up the difference and win the election. Secret service agents awakened Truman at 4 A.M. to tell him to turn on the radio. His lead had increased to 2 million votes and was not expected to change. Dewey conceded by the middle of the next day.

Truman's victory stunned most Americans, especially the editors at the *Chicago Tribune*. That paper published its story of the election before all the returns came in and ran as its headline: "Dewey Defeats Truman." (Later editions of the paper retracted the headline.) A smiling Truman held up a copy of this paper two days after the election. The results of the election vindicated his decision to ignore the media and concentrate on reaching voters directly. While only 15 percent of the nation's newspapers endorsed Truman, he won 24,179,347 popular votes to 21,991,292 for Dewey. Thurmond and Wallace garnered just over 1 million votes each, with 1,175,946 for the Dixiecrat candidate and 1,157,328 for the Progressive Party standard-bearer. The Electoral College margin was not even close: Truman won 303 votes, Dewey gained 189, and Thurmond, his support concentrated in the South, collected the remaining 39. Truman carried with him Democratic candidates down the ballot as his party won back control of the House and the Senate. While the president benefited from an impressive Democratic coalition forged by Roosevelt during the 1930s, Truman bears significant credit for his win. Had he not campaigned vigorously and had he

In one of the greatest photographs in American political history, a smiling president Truman holds up a mistakenly headlined edition of the *Chicago Daily Tribune* after his stunning come-from-behind victory in 1948. *(Library of Congress)*

1948 Election Statistics

State	Number of Electors	Total Popular Vote	Elec Vote D	Elec Vote R	Elec Vote SR	Pop Vote D	Pop Vote R	Pop Vote SR	Margin of Victory Votes	Margin of Victory % Total Vote
Alabama	11	214,980			11	9	2	1	130,513	60.71%
Arizona	4	177,065	4			1	2	-	17,654	9.97%
Arkansas	9	242,475	9			1	2	3	98,700	40.71%
California	25	4,021,538	25			1	2	6	17,865	0.44%
Colorado	6	515,237	6			1	2	-	27,574	5.35%
Connecticut	8	883,518		8		2	1	-	14,457	1.64%
Delaware	3	139,073		3		2	1	-	1,775	1.28%
Florida	8	577,643	8			1	2	3	87,708	15.18%
Georgia	12	418,764	12			1	3	2	169,591	40.50%
Idaho	4	214,816	4			1	2	-	5,856	2.73%
Illinois	28	3,984,046	28			1	2	-	33,612	0.84%
Indiana	13	1,656,214		13		2	1	-	13,246	0.80%
Iowa	10	1,038,272	10			1	2	-	28,362	2.73%
Kansas	8	788,819		8		2	1	-	71,137	9.02%
Kentucky	11	822,658	11			1	2	3	125,546	15.26%
Louisiana	10	416,336			10	2	3	1	67,946	16.32%
Maine	5	264,789		5		2	1	-	38,318	14.47%
Maryland	8	596,735		8		2	1	5	8,293	1.39%
Massachusetts	16	2,107,146	16			1	2	-	242,418	11.50%
Michigan	19	2,109,609		19		2	1	-	35,147	1.67%
Minnesota	11	1,212,226	11			1	2	-	209,349	17.27%
Mississippi	9	192,190			9	2	3	1	148,154	77.09%
Missouri	15	1,578,628	15			1	2	5	262,276	16.61%
Montana	4	224,278	4			1	2	-	22,301	9.94%
Nebraska	6	488,940		6		2	1	-	40,609	8.31%
Nevada	3	62,117	3			1	2	-	1,934	3.11%
New Hampshire	4	231,440		4		2	1	6	13,304	5.75%
New Jersey	16	1,949,555		16		2	1	-	85,669	4.39%
New Mexico	4	187,063	4			1	2	-	25,161	13.45%
New York	47	6,178,502		47		2	1	8	60,959	0.99%
North Carolina	14	791,209	14			1	2	3	200,498	25.34%
North Dakota	4	220,716		4		2	1	5	19,327	8.76%
Ohio	25	2,936,071	25	0		1	2	-	7,107	0.24%
Oklahoma	10	721,599	10			1	2	-	183,965	25.49%
Oregon	6	524,080		6		2	1	-	17,757	3.39%
Pennsylvania	35	3,735,148		35		2	1	-	149,771	4.01%
Rhode Island	4	327,702	4			1	2	-	52,949	16.16%
South Carolina	8	142,571			8	2	3	1	68,184	47.82%
South Dakota	4	250,105		4		2	1	-	11,998	4.80%
Tennessee	12	550,283	11		1	1	2	3	67,488	12.26%
Texas	23	1,249,577	23			1	2	3	520,768	41.68%
Utah	4	276,305	4			1	2	-	24,749	8.96%
Vermont	3	123,382		3		2	1	-	30,369	24.61%
Virginia	11	419,256	11			1	2	3	28,716	6.85%
Washington	8	905,059	8			1	2	-	89,850	9.93%
West Virginia	8	748,750	8			1	2	-	112,937	15.08%
Wisconsin	12	1,276,800	12			1	2	-	56,351	4.41%
Wyoming	3	101,425	3			1	2	-	4,407	4.35%
Total	531	48,794,710	303	189	39	1	2	3	2,188,055	4.48%

Truman Democratic		Dewey Republican		Thurmond States' Rights		Wallace Progressive		Others	
0	0.00%	40,930	19.04%	171,443	79.75%	1,522	0.71%	1,085	0.50%
95,251	53.79%	77,597	43.82%	0	0.00%	3,310	1.87%	907	0.51%
149,659	61.72%	50,959	21.02%	40,068	16.52%	751	0.31%	1,038	0.43%
1,913,134	47.57%	1,895,269	47.13%	1,228	0.03%	190,381	4.73%	21,526	0.54%
267,288	51.88%	239,714	46.52%	0	0.00%	6,115	1.19%	2,120	0.41%
423,297	47.91%	437,754	49.55%	0	0.00%	13,713	1.55%	8,754	0.99%
67,813	48.76%	69,588	50.04%	0	0.00%	1,050	0.75%	622	0.45%
281,988	48.82%	194,280	33.63%	89,755	15.54%	11,620	2.01%	0	0.00%
254,646	60.81%	76,691	18.31%	85,055	20.31%	1,636	0.39%	736	0.18%
107,370	49.98%	101,514	47.26%	0	0.00%	4,972	2.31%	960	0.45%
1,994,715	50.07%	1,961,103	49.22%	0	0.00%	0	0.00%	28,228	0.71%
807,833	48.78%	821,079	49.58%	0	0.00%	9,649	0.58%	17,653	1.07%
522,380	50.31%	494,018	47.58%	0	0.00%	12,125	1.17%	9,749	0.94%
351,902	44.61%	423,039	53.63%	0	0.00%	4,603	0.58%	9,275	1.18%
466,756	56.74%	341,210	41.48%	10,411	1.27%	1,567	0.19%	2,714	0.33%
136,344	32.75%	72,657	17.45%	204,290	49.07%	3,035	0.73%	10	0.00%
111,916	42.27%	150,234	56.74%	0	0.00%	1,884	0.71%	755	0.29%
286,521	48.01%	294,814	49.40%	2,476	0.41%	9,983	1.67%	2,941	0.49%
1,151,788	54.66%	909,370	43.16%	0	0.00%	38,157	1.81%	7,831	0.37%
1,003,448	47.57%	1,038,595	49.23%	0	0.00%	46,515	2.20%	21,051	1.00%
692,966	57.16%	483,617	39.89%	0	0.00%	27,866	2.30%	7,777	0.64%
19,384	10.09%	5,043	2.62%	167,538	87.17%	225	0.12%	0	0.00%
917,315	58.11%	655,039	41.49%	42	0.00%	3,998	0.25%	2,234	0.14%
119,071	53.09%	96,770	43.15%	0	0.00%	7,313	3.26%	1,124	0.50%
224,165	45.85%	264,774	54.15%	0	0.00%	0	0.00%	1	0.00%
31,291	50.37%	29,357	47.26%	0	0.00%	1,469	2.36%	0	0.00%
107,995	46.66%	121,299	52.41%	7	0.00%	1,970	0.85%	169	0.07%
895,455	45.93%	981,124	50.33%	0	0.00%	42,683	2.19%	30,293	1.55%
105,464	56.38%	80,303	42.93%	0	0.00%	1,037	0.55%	259	0.14%
2,780,204	45.00%	2,841,163	45.98%	16	0.00%	509,559	8.25%	47,560	0.77%
459,070	58.02%	258,572	32.68%	69,652	8.80%	3,915	0.49%	0	0.00%
95,812	43.41%	115,139	52.17%	374	0.17%	8,391	3.80%	1,000	0.45%
1,452,791	49.48%	1,445,684	49.24%	0	0.00%	37,596	1.28%	0	0.00%
452,782	62.75%	268,817	37.25%	0	0.00%	0	0.00%	0	0.00%
243,147	46.40%	260,904	49.78%	0	0.00%	14,978	2.86%	5,051	0.96%
1,752,426	46.92%	1,902,197	50.93%	0	0.00%	55,161	1.48%	25,364	0.68%
188,736	57.59%	135,787	41.44%	0	0.00%	2,619	0.80%	560	0.17%
34,423	24.14%	5,386	3.78%	102,607	71.97%	154	0.11%	1	0.00%
117,653	47.04%	129,651	51.84%	0	0.00%	2,801	1.12%	0	0.00%
270,402	49.14%	202,914	36.87%	73,815	13.41%	1,864	0.34%	1,288	0.23%
824,235	65.96%	303,467	24.29%	113,776	9.11%	3,920	0.31%	4,179	0.33%
149,151	53.98%	124,402	45.02%	0	0.00%	2,679	0.97%	73	0.03%
45,557	36.92%	75,926	61.54%	0	0.00%	1,279	1.04%	620	0.50%
200,786	47.89%	172,070	41.04%	43,393	10.35%	2,047	0.49%	960	0.23%
476,165	52.61%	386,315	42.68%	0	0.00%	31,692	3.50%	10,887	1.20%
429,188	57.32%	316,251	42.24%	0	0.00%	3,311	0.44%	0	0.00%
647,310	50.70%	590,959	46.28%	0	0.00%	25,282	1.98%	13,249	1.04%
52,354	51.62%	47,947	47.27%	0	0.00%	931	0.92%	193	0.19%
24,179,347	49.55%	21,991,292	45.07%	1,175,946	2.41%	1,157,328	2.37%	290,797	0.60%

Electoral Vote, 1948

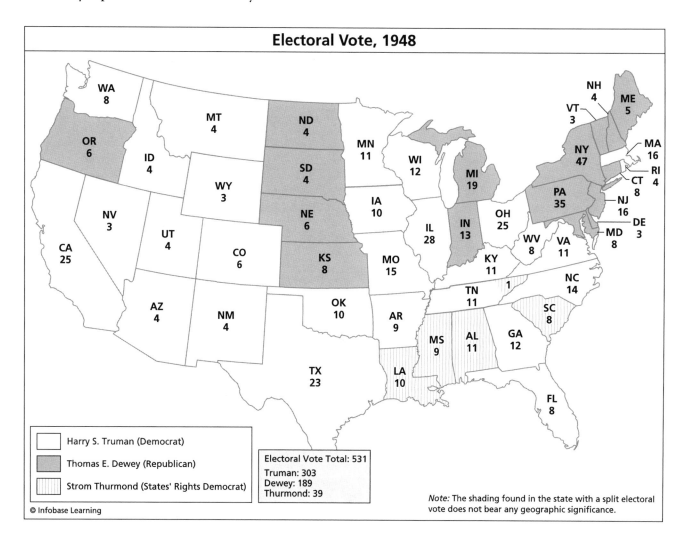

Harry S. Truman (Democrat)

Thomas E. Dewey (Republican)

Strom Thurmond (States' Rights Democrat)

Electoral Vote Total: 531
Truman: 303
Dewey: 189
Thurmond: 39

Note: The shading found in the state with a split electoral vote does not bear any geographic significance.

© Infobase Learning

accepted Republican prognostications, the results in 1948 would likely have been very different. Because it was driven by personality more than by ideology, the victory, however, failed to provide Truman with a mandate for the reforms he had discussed during the campaign. Nevertheless, his unexpected victory remains one of the great upsets in presidential history.

TRUMAN ADMINISTRATION (1945–1953)

Perhaps no man entered the White House with more at stake than Harry S. Truman. When he became president following FRANKLIN D. ROOSEVELT's death on April 12, 1945, he inherited responsibility for ending World War II in Europe and in Asia. Once the hostilities ceased, Truman would need to launch an intensive diplomatic effort to sustain the peace in the postwar world. He would struggle with a contentious home front, where few plans had been developed for postwar

ECONOMIC RECONVERSION and where the population was eager to be free from wartime restrictions. Finally, he would grapple with political turmoil, with Republicans restive for a greater say in national governance and Democrats divided into competing factions. Questions of how the postwar economy would function and what would become of New Deal liberalism dominated domestic considerations while issues in foreign affairs dealt with questions about how active the United States would be in international politics.

Complicating these demands, Truman lacked knowledge about the Roosevelt administration's policies for war and peace. Truman had been vice president for only 82 days, and had had little contact with Roosevelt during that period. Furthermore, he had had little involvement with foreign policy concerns in his political career. Perhaps most significant of all was the inevitable comparison between Roosevelt and Truman. President for more than 12 years, longer than any person in U.S. history, Roosevelt had redefined both the image and the responsibilities of the chief executive. Because he had been a larger-than-life figure inspiring either great love, among the overwhelming majority of Americans, or

TRUMAN, HOUSING POLICY, AND THE RISE OF LEVITTOWN

Housing policy was a predominate social issue during the Truman administration in the late 1940s and early 1950s. There were three concerns—what to do about the immediate needs of returning veterans from World War II, what to do about the plight of the poor, and what to do about the middle-class aspirations for home ownership. Emergency legislation passed in 1945 helped assuage the housing crisis as it affected veterans. Administration efforts to increase the number of public housing units were only moderately successful. Most significant was the role played by the GI Bill of Rights, legislation from late in the Roosevelt administration, for fostering home ownership. The low-interest home loans made it possible for returning veterans to purchase homes for their families. One observer commented that the GI Bill did more than any other program to prevent the advent of radicalism within the American government. In other words, maintaining a home took up too much time for Americans to pursue radical ideologies.

The rapid expansion of home ownership in the United States, though, had as much to do with private enterprise as it did federal law. William J. Levitt, a real estate developer, figured prominently in this development. He essentially turned the construction of single-family homes into an assembly-line process instead of the custom construction that was then standard. Working from one basic floor plan for an 800-square-foot home, Levitt relied on prefabricated materials and on specially trained workers who did just one job moving from construction site to construction site. Popular news magazines told of a painter whose only job was to paint window sills. He moved from site to site to ply his trade. These tactics allowed Levitt's company to construct as many as 36 houses a day, in the process erecting instantaneous suburbs. They also meant that union labor could be avoided and that worker turnover would not be a problem. Additionally, Levitt's company enjoyed a vertical monopoly in that it owned or controlled every phase of home construction from the lumberyards to the real estate sales offices.

Levitt constructed his first suburb—called Levittown—on Long Island between 1947 and 1951. It filled 7.3 square miles. The 17,500 Cape Cod–style homes included as symbolic homage to the New England past split rail fences and chimneys in the middle of the homes. The design also allowed for low-cost construction. Built on concrete slabs, the houses were uniform in appearance until owners personalized their property. The plumbing was less expensive to install because the kitchen and the bathroom were on one side of the floor plan. Because the kitchen and the living room were located on the front of the house plan, the underlying assumption was that the street would trump the backyard as a place of play for the children. The floor plans also made possible conversion of the homes from single-story two-bedroom houses to three- or four-bedroom homes by finishing the attic as additional living space. Plain but affordable, the houses sold for just under $8,000. Most veterans were able to purchase this style of housing for no money down and monthly payments under $100.

So profitable and popular was the Levittown concept that builders around the country mimicked the method. The expansion of freeways helped facilitate this suburban boom, which revolutionized where and how middle-class Americans lived. Because of highway growth middle-class workers could live farther from their jobs and away from city centers. Newly developed suburban shopping centers came to replace the downtown department stores. Suburban life took on negative aspects with frequent reliance on restrictive covenants in housing sales to prevent African Americans and Jews from purchasing homes in the newly constructed neighborhoods. Folk singer Malvina Reynolds later satirized suburban conformity in her song, "Little Boxes." The suburban revolution launched during the Truman years ushered in a major transformation in where and how Americans lived and played a key role in stabilizing American attitudes about postwar liberalism. Homeowners favored a political economy that encouraged growth and discouraged significant changes to the status quo.

---

great hatred, among a vocal minority, the challenges before Truman were all the more daunting.

Born to a different regional culture and in different socioeconomic circumstances, Truman lacked Roosevelt's patrician bearing. Not tall and not short, Truman looked too average to many Americans. Indeed, while many believed that Roosevelt fought for the "common man," many Americans believed that Truman *was* the "common man." His flat midwestern accent and his colloquial manner of speaking sounded very different, and less presidential, from Roosevelt's aristocratic speech. In his favor, Truman was hardworking, honest, and willing to take responsibility for his

actions. He appreciated the various components of American pluralism.

Upon becoming president, Truman strived for as much continuity with the Roosevelt administration as possible. He retained the cabinet and other key figures in the executive branch. This decision was perhaps unwise because Truman did not feel comfortable in dealing with Roosevelt partisans in high-ranking government positions. Within a year, Truman had replaced those officials. Lacking the distinction common among Roosevelt's advisers, Truman's nominees did not serve him well. Attorney General J. Howard McGrath was most known for scandal. Truman brought in dependable allies for the most important staff jobs, but he was very hands-on in the operation of his administration, functioning almost as his own chief of staff.

On May 7, 1945, less than a month into his presidency, Germany surrendered, ending World War II in Europe. The end of the war in the Pacific theater, however, was not immi-

Atomic bombing of Nagasaki, August 9, 1945 *(National Archives)*

nent. It appeared that the total victory in Asia that Americans wanted would require substantial bombing and an invasion of the island nation. Military planners believed this battle plan would take a year to execute and would involve 200,000 American casualties. Only after becoming president did Truman learn of the atomic weapons development program in Los Alamos, New Mexico, known as the Manhattan Project. In July 1945, American scientists exploded the first atomic bomb and informed President Truman that the devastating nuclear weapon was available. In the most fateful decision of his presidency, Truman ordered the detonation of the atomic bomb over Hiroshima on August 6 and another one over Nagasaki three days later. Following the BOMBING OF HIROSHIMA AND NAGASAKI, Japan surrendered, ending World War II. The vast death toll stunned Truman, and he hoped to avoid using atomic weaponry again. He maintained, though, that even more Japanese and American lives would have been lost had the United States invaded Japan.

This cataclysmic end to World War II proved to be but a prelude to the dramatic events that would follow. The significant events in foreign affairs during the Truman presidency included the end of World War II and the dawn of both the cold war and the atomic age. Interventionist in its focus, Truman's foreign policy became the template for much of the remainder of the 20th century. Scholars have given the Truman presidency high marks for international relations. As such, attention to the personnel and the infrastructure of Truman's foreign policy is needed. Truman was served by four secretaries of state—Edward Stettinius, who had been in the Roosevelt administration; James F. Byrnes, who did not work well with Truman; George C. Marshall, who had been the army chief of staff during the war; and Dean Acheson, who had been an undersecretary of state. Marshall and Acheson were important figures in Truman's foreign policy team. Passage of the NATIONAL SECURITY ACT of 1947 unified the separate branches of the military, created the Department of Defense, and established the Central Intelligence Agency and the National Security Council. One of Truman's first efforts in the foreign policy arena proved of central importance: He worked to make the United Nations a success. He relied on negotiations to ensure Soviet participation in this international peacekeeping organization established in 1945.

Scholars have long debated when the cold war began. For the purposes of understanding the Truman presidency and foreign policy, though, it is important to know that tensions with the Soviet Union became a much more significant matter as the war-imposed alliance abated and was replaced with a postwar contest for the ideological fealty of the nations of the world. The Yalta Conference, which occurred in February 1945 when Roosevelt was still president, marked an important turning point in the relationship between the United States and the Soviet Union. Little of substance was accomplished at Yalta, but conservative critics still blamed Roosevelt for not preventing Stalin from advancing his ambitions in Poland and Eastern Europe, though doing so was an impossibility given the military realities of World War II. Truman knew little of the accords reached at Yalta when he became president. Disagreements about how Poland would be governed were central to the problem. Ultimately, the Soviet Union ignored agreements that free elections would be held in Poland, instead establishing a communist government there and elsewhere in Eastern Europe to insure a protective buffer with the West.

Truman nonetheless wanted to preserve a friendly alliance with the Soviets, believing that hard-hitting negotiations and a willingness to compromise would preserve the relationship, but the president's advisers warned that the strategy would likely fail. The POTSDAM CONFERENCE, held in July 1945, gave Truman the opportunity to meet in person with Soviet premier Joseph Stalin and British prime minister Winston Churchill (and later Prime Minister Clement Atlee, who replaced Churchill following a British election) but few substantive agreements were reached. While Truman left the conference convinced he could work with Stalin, the events that followed ultimately changed his mind. In late 1945 and early 1946 the Soviet Union exerted greater authority over Eastern Europe and made advances on Iran and Turkey. A combination of American military force and diplomacy thwarted the latter, but Stalin nonetheless spoke publicly of the coming conflict with capitalism.

Foreign policy experts and political leaders who evaluated the Soviet Union painted a grim portrait in 1946. George Kennan, the chargé d'affaires with the State Department in Moscow, sent the "LONG TELEGRAM" to officials in Washington, arguing that Soviet expansionist tendencies must be contained. The views outlined in this telegram proved to be integral to the development of Truman's foreign policy of containment toward the Soviet Union. Weeks later Winston Churchill told a Fulton, Missouri, audience that the Soviets were responsible for erecting an "iron curtain" across Europe and that the West should resist Soviet expansionist moves. During 1946 American policymakers developed a more active strategy of opposition that involved financial investment, military troops, and ideological coherence. A $3.75 billion loan to Great Britain demonstrated the American commitment to European recovery as did promises to keep troops in Germany. Furthermore, when Secretary of Commerce Henry Wallace called for a more friendly, cooperative relationship with Moscow, Truman fired him.

While there has been much debate then and since about whether the United States did enough to prevent the advance of communism in Asia, the Truman administration did not ignore the region. Reconstruction of Japan's government in the American image proved successful and helped launch that country's dramatic economic growth. A civil war

(continues on page 215)

ADMINISTRATION TIME LINE

1945

April 12 Harry S. Truman takes the oath of office as president in the White House upon learning of Franklin Roosevelt's death.

April 25 The San Francisco Conference opens, and during these meetings the charter to the United Nations is agreed upon, establishing the international body.

May 7 Germany surrenders, ending World War II in Europe.

July 16 American scientists explode the first atomic bomb in New Mexico.

July 17–August 2 The Potsdam Conference is held by the leaders of Great Britain, the Soviet Union, and the United States.

August 6 American forces drop an atomic bomb over Hiroshima, Japan.

August 9 Another atomic bomb is dropped over Nagasaki, Japan.

August 14 Japan surrenders, ending World War II.

1946

February 20 The Employment Act is signed into law, declaring it the policy of the federal government to encourage "maximum employment," providing for an annual presidential report to Congress detailing the economic conditions of the nation and suggesting any necessary legislation to implement the goals of the Employment Act, and creating the Council of Economic Advisors.

February 22 George F. Kennan, the chargé d'affaires with the State Department in Moscow, writes what has become known as the "Long Telegram" stating the reasons for Soviet actions and articulating the containment policy of U.S. foreign policy.

July 3 Truman signs legislation to create a National Institute of Mental Health, which was formally established in 1949.

August The Hospital Survey and Construction Act, also known as the Hill-Burton Act, is signed into law, authorizing federal funding for hospital construction. It created a shared local, state, and federal funding partnership for hospital construction.

August 1 Truman signs the Atomic Energy Act into law, creating the U.S. Atomic Energy Commission, which would govern atomic research and development and be placed under civilian control.

August 2 Truman signs the Legislative Reorganization Act into law, reducing the number of House committees from 48 to 19, and the number of Senate committees from 33 to 15. Among other reforms the legislation provided for professional, enlarged congressional committee staffs.

August 14 Truman signs the Farmers Home Administration Act into law, consolidating various existing agencies—the Farm Security Administration and the Emergency Crop and Feed Loan Division—into the Farmers Home Administration, which insured loans made to farmers by other lenders and made direct loans using government funds.

September 20 Eight days after Secretary of Commerce Henry Wallace gives a speech criticizing U.S. foreign policy, Truman asks for his resignation.

November Truman creates a temporary loyalty program.

November 5 The Republican Party gains control of Congress in the midterm congressional elections.

December 5 Truman creates the President's Committee on Civil Rights.

1947

March 12 Truman delivers an address to Congress calling for aid to Greece and Turkey, reflecting a major shift in American foreign policy away from appeasing the Soviet Union and toward containment of communism.

March 21 Truman issues Executive Order 9835, making the Federal Employee Loyalty Program permanent.

May 22 Truman signs legislation appropriating the funds for Greece and Turkey articulated in the Truman Doctrine.

June 5 Secretary of State George C. Marshall gives the commencement address at Harvard University in which he details plans to help rebuild war-devastated Europe.

June 20 Truman vetoes the Taft-Hartley Act, which Congress overrides three days later.

July 26 Truman signs the National Security Act into law, unifying the separate branches of the military, creating the Department of Defense, and establishing the Central Intelligence Agency and the National Security Council.

October The President's Committee on Civil Rights issues *To Secure These Rights,* a report containing 35 recommendations for reform at the local, state, and federal levels.

1948

March Czechoslovakia, previously an independent democracy, falls to communism.

March 8 Democratic National Committee chairman J. Howard McGrath announces that Truman will run for the presidency in his own right.

April 3 Truman signs the European Recovery Act into law.

May 3 In *Shelley v. Kraemer,* the Supreme Court declares that a restrictive covenant in residential housing was contrary to the Fourteenth Amendment.

May 14 The United States recognizes the new state of Israel.

June The Selective Service Act, the first postwar draft in the United States, becomes law.

June 24 The Soviet Union blocks all ground traffic by the Western powers in and out of the city of Berlin, initiating the Berlin blockade that would continue into 1949. Two days later, Truman orders the airlift that would keep West Berlin supplied until the blockade was lifted.

June 25 Truman signs the Displaced Persons Act, providing for the United States to take a leading roll in the relief and resettlement of displaced persons.

July 26 The two-week special session of Congress opens.

Truman signs an executive order desegregating the military.

August Whittaker Chambers, an editor for *Time* magazine and a former communist, accuses Alger Hiss, former State Department worker and head of the Carnegie Endowment for International Peace, of being a communist.

September 6 Truman begins his formal campaign for the presidency, running against the "do-nothing" Congress.

November 2 Truman wins election in the greatest upset in presidential history.

1949

January 20 President Truman delivers his State of the Union address calling his legislative agenda the Fair Deal.

March 30 Truman signs legislation to maintain rent controls until the postwar housing shortage eased.

April 4 The NATO treaty is signed by 12 Western European and North American nations.

May 12 The Soviet Union lifts the Berlin blockade.

July 15 Truman signs the Housing Act, establishing a postwar housing policy.

September 23 Truman announces that the Soviet Union has detonated an atomic bomb.

(continues)

ADMINISTRATION TIME LINE (continued)

October 1 Mao Zedong comes to power in China.

1950

January 31 Truman announces plans to develop the hydrogen bomb.

February 9 Speaking to a Republican women's group in Wheeling, West Virginia, Senator Joseph McCarthy makes his first charge that 205 communists are employed in the federal government. In subsequent speeches the number would change.

April 7 The National Security Council issues its report, National Security Council Document 68 (NSC-68), that argued that the West must expand both its nuclear and its conventional arsenal until its troop strength and its weaponry surpassed that of the Soviets.

May The Kefauver Crime Committee investigations begin, the first ever-televised congressional hearings.

June 5 In *Sweatt v. Painter,* the Supreme Court strikes down an attempt by the state of Texas to create a separate but equal law school for Heman Sweatt.

June 25 North Korea invades South Korea, initiating the Korean War.

September The Defense Production Act is passed, giving businesses incentives to increase production, make war orders a priority over other production needs, place limits on civilian production, and provide for wage and price stabilization.

September 23 Congress overrides Truman's veto of the McCarran Internal Security Act, which outlawed Communist Party activity, mandated the registration of communist organizations with the federal government, and discouraged communist sympathizers.

October 15 Truman and General Douglas MacArthur meet on Wake Island to discuss U.S. policy in the Far East.

December 16 Truman implements wage and price controls.

1951

February 27 The Twenty-second Amendment is ratified limiting presidents to two terms.

April 5 Douglas MacArthur's letter to House minority leader Joseph Martin is published, reflecting the general's disregard of civilian control of the military by ignoring the president's orders and publicly criticizing him.

Julius and Ethel Rosenberg are found guilty of spying for the Soviet Union and sentenced to death.

April 11 President Truman fires General MacArthur for insubordination.

June 4 In *Dennis v. United States,* the Supreme Court upholds the lower court rulings that Eugene Dennis and other leaders of the Communist Party of America conspired to teach and advocate the overthrow or destruction of the U.S. government.

July 10 Truce talks to end the fighting in Korea begin.

1952

March 29 Truman announces he will not seek another term as president.

April 8 Truman issues an executive order authorizing the steel mills to be seized by the federal government to prevent a strike.

June 2 In *Youngstown Sheet and Tube Company v. Sawyer,* the Supreme Court rules that no congressional statute gave the president authority to seize the mills and that presidential authority as commander in chief provided no such remedy over strikes.

June 25 Truman vetoes the McCarran-Walter Immigration Act, providing that all immigrants be checked at the border to determine whether they were subversive and repealing the provision in the Naturalization Act of 1790 that barred non-white immigrants from gaining U.S. citizenship. Congress overrides the veto days later.

November 1 The United States detonates a hydrogen bomb, the first ever.

1953

January 20 Truman spends his last day as president.

(continued from page 211)

in China between the nationalists under the leadership of Chiang Kai-shek (now Jiang Jieshi) and the communists under the leadership of Mao Zedong complicated U.S. efforts to shape the direction of that country. Jiang's corruption helped pave the way for Mao's victory in 1949. So frustrated was Truman with Jiang that he expressed a willingness to work with Mao, that is, before Mao allied with the Soviet Union and articulated an anti-American stance. With the formation of the People's Republic of China in October 1949 came Chiang's retreat to Formosa—the island now known as Taiwan—where he dug in, claiming to be the rightful leader of China. The United States recognized his government and not the People's Republic as the legitimate government of China. Truman was criticized for "losing" China, but he could have done nothing short of war to prevent Mao's victory. These international developments were not without impact on American domestic politics, helping to fuel the Red Scare.

In fall 1945, Truman clarified his approach to New Deal liberalism. He hoped to maintain the major reforms of the 1930s and expand on those he believed were most significant to ensuring economic growth in the postwar period. His articulation of these needs, though, lacked zeal. The new president gave Congress a list of 21 reforms, including new public works programs, guarantees for full employment, an increased minimum wage, a permanent Fair Employment Practices Committee, expansions of Social Security, and enactment of national health insurance. Additionally, Truman wanted military demobilization to proceed apace. To prevent sharp, dangerous economic fluctuations during the reconversion process, Truman called for a continuation of wartime economic controls on prices and wages. Despite its Democratic majority, Congress proved uninterested in debating and enacting these measures. The crisis rationale for the New Deal reforms was gone, and the vast economic productivity of the war years suggested additional reform was unnecessary. For example, full-employment legislation, which promised employment guarantees, as enacted in the EMPLOYMENT ACT of 1946 lacked any such guarantees.

Truman's efforts at reconversion were equally dissatisfying. With the war over, labor unions were eager for an improvement in wages and working conditions. While Truman wanted to maintain PRICE CONTROLS, he ultimately supported the removal of wage controls because of public pressure. As a result, numerous strikes were staged with unions demanding higher pay than employers were willing to grant. The industries affected included steel, coal, automobiles, and railroads. Because the strikes meant fewer consumer goods were for sale and because reconversion was slowed, Truman called for mediation and arbitration, threatening even to draft striking railroad workers into the military. The federal government even sued the United

Mine Workers. Ultimately, the strikes were settled, and workers gained many of their demands, although they did so at the price of straining the president's relationship with the labor movement, a key constituency within the Democratic Party.

The struggle over price controls became more and more problematic until the middle of 1946 when the Office of Price Administration, renewed and neutered by Congress, began removing all controls. Those consumer goods that had been most highly sought by Americans who had sacrificed during the war increased dramatically in price when they became available. Meat, for example, doubled in price in just two weeks, prompting a renewal of controls and enraging meat producers who stopped selling. Anger boiled over during the midterm congressional elections in 1946. Just 32 percent of Americans rated Truman's performance favorably in September of that year. Democrats suffered as a result in the elections, and Republicans gained control of both the House and the Senate. The questions became what could Truman do to govern for the next two years and how could he hope to gain election in 1948.

The cold war continued to be a major issue for Truman. Drawing on theories and language articulated by charge d'affaires George Kennan in his Long Telegram that communism and the Soviet Union must be contained, Truman and his administration developed a foreign policy in 1947 known as containment. Fear that nations in Western Europe might elect communist leaders drove the actions in Washington. Also important was Great Britain's decision to pull back from its involvement in the eastern Mediterranean. Because it was believed that Moscow sought to extend its influence in Greece and Turkey, the British move was problematic for the United States. To fill that void, the president announced the TRUMAN DOCTRINE, a $400-million program of precedent-setting financial AID TO GREECE AND TURKEY. He declared it would be the official U.S. policy to aid "free peoples" who were facing "subjugation by armed minorities or by outside pressures." The MARSHALL PLAN, a vast aid package for war-ravaged Europe that aimed to encourage both political and economic security in the region, was announced in the summer of 1947. While the United States included the Soviet Union in its initial planning, Stalin's government rejected the offer. Congressional approval for the Marshall Plan followed in 1948. More than anything else, it was these actions that remade the American role in the postwar world. For the duration of the cold war, the policy of the United States became one of using its financial and military resources to encourage democracy, or to at least thwart communism, throughout the world. Actions in the remainder of the Truman administration would further entrench this strategy.

The problem of Palestine also plagued Truman's administration. It did not fit easily into the emerging cold war

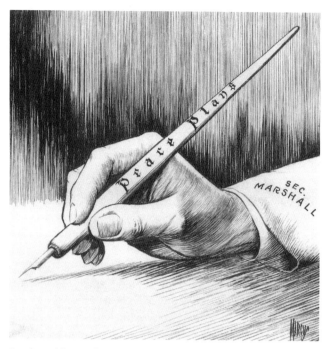

Captioned "May His Pen Be as Mighty as His Sword," this Edwin Marcus cartoon shows the hand of Secretary of State George C. Marshall holding a pen labeled "Peace Plans." Marshall, a former general, proposed the massive economic aid program credited with rescuing the Western European nations after World War II that become known as the Marshall Plan. *(By Permission of the Marcus Family)*

rubrics; rather, it foreshadowed the post–cold war international relations of the late 20th and early 21st centuries. Great Britain held a responsibility for Palestine that began with a League of Nations mandate implemented at the end of World War I and it had been unable to solve the conflict between Arabs and Jews. In 1947, the British announced they would leave the administration of Palestine to the United Nations, which announced that it would partition Palestine into two countries. This decision resulted in a guerrilla war between Arab and Jewish forces. Initially Truman was unsure how to respond. While the Jewish vote was important to the Democratic Party, the State Department contended that access to oil should govern American policy in the Middle East. Truman ultimately decided to support the partition plan, but events overtook him. After the Jewish forces defeated the Arabs in Palestine, they declared independence. The United States recognized the new state of Israel on May 14, 1948, just minutes after its creation.

On the domestic front, the new Republican-controlled 80th Congress gave Truman a target for his invective. Whereas political problems had arisen in arguing policy with congressional Democrats, who had not been enthusiastic about Truman's legislative agenda, no such restraints existed after the 1946 elections. Additionally, the Republicans had to prove themselves to the American people by doing

something with their new majority status. Truman crafted a potent strategy. First, he used his State of the Union address in 1947 to emphasize the major problem before the nation—labor strife—without proposing a solution. He asked for a special panel to study the labor question, and he stressed he would approve no legislation that attacked workers' rights. The Republican response, the TAFT-HARTLEY ACT of 1947, became the major issue of contention for organized labor. It restricted the freedom of unions to engage in political activism, endorsed "right to work" laws, and provided for "cooling-off" periods. Truman vetoed the bill, and Congress overrode the president. When inflation continued to beset the domestic economy, especially food prices, Truman called for new PRICE CONTROLS, knowing that Republicans would balk. The resulting legislation was ineffective, reflecting poorly on the Republicans. Additionally, Truman retained his liberal appeal with advocacy of low-income housing projects and federal assistance for education. He opposed Republican tax bills that would have benefited the wealthy. This record helped Truman regain the trust of the Democratic Party faithful.

Truman staked out civil rights as another important issue for national attention in 1947. Building on his 1945 support for a permanent Fair Employment Practices Committee, he took several important steps toward making the Democratic Party the proponent of civil rights. He spoke openly before the National Association for the Advancement of Colored People about the need for civil rights, the first president to do so. His commission on civil rights published its report, *To Secure These Rights,* calling for reform legislation. Given the controversial nature of this issue and the importance of the white South to the Democratic Party—at the time most southern blacks were disfranchised—Truman sent several bills to Congress, but he did not make them a priority. He did issue executive orders to desegregate the military and the civil service. He included appeals on behalf of civil rights in his 1948 State of the Union address and in speeches during his presidential campaign that year.

The 1948 presidential election was a divided and dramatic affair. The Democratic Party split according to ideology. After Truman gained his party's nomination, liberals, who distrusted the president, bolted to form the Progressive Party and nominated former vice president and cabinet member Henry Wallace. White southerners who were dominated by racist political motivations and economic conservatism formed the States' Rights Party, also known as the Dixiecrats, and they nominated Strom Thurmond for president. With Democrats split into three separate parties, most observers predicted an easy Republican victory in November. The Republicans chose New York governor Thomas Dewey as their candidate, who had been their candidate in 1944 as well. Truman used a "whistle-stop" strategy to great effect. His impromptu speeches from the rear of his train were informal and widely popular with voters, who came to view the pragmatic and tough president as a strong leader. He used these and other speeches to lambaste the "do-nothing" 80th Congress. Truman went so far as to call a special session of Congress, arguing that if the Republican platform was so important for the country it should be enacted immediately. This strategy was most effective because the Republicans on Capitol Hill were much more conservative than their party's candidate for the White House. When nothing of substance resulted from the special session, Truman gained more momentum going into the November election, but pundits still expected a Dewey victory. The *Chicago Tribune* was so confident that the Republicans would persevere that it printed the front-page headline for its postelection edition, "Dewey Defeats Truman," before all the West Coast returns were counted. But Truman won, and after his successful election, a grinning Truman held up a copy emblazoned with the erroneous headline. The Democrats prevailed in the congressional elections that year as well, regaining control of both houses of Congress with wide majorities.

After his election, Truman articulated the FAIR DEAL, his legislative program for his next term in office. He had taken his 1948 victory to mean substantial voter support existed for a sweeping liberal reform agenda. However, the vote in 1948 had been more a referendum on Truman than it had been on his politics. In addition to measures he had unsuccessfully advocated for the past four years, the proposals he included expanded on the New Deal programs and were very popular with liberal Democrats. The comprehensive catalogue of Fair Deal initiatives included agricultural reform, economic planning legislation, a raise in the minimum wage, expansion of Social Security, housing reform, national health insurance, repeal of the Taft-Hartley Act, regional waterway development programs, immigration reform, and civil rights legislation. Opposition from Republicans and conservative Democrats was steep, however, and few of these measures passed Congress. Most heated was the lobbying effort against the health care reforms. Public housing legislation, a minimum wage increase, Social Security reform, and a whittled-down agriculture bill were the only measures to be enacted into law. Truman misread both public opinion, which favored a continuation and not an expansion of the New Deal, and congressional sentiment, which opposed an expanded welfare state. By the summer of 1950 when the KOREAN WAR started any remaining support for domestic reform legislation had evaporated.

Economic concerns also weakened support for the Fair Deal reforms. Unemployment and inflation were serious problems in the first half of 1949, causing many to worry that the postwar boom had ended. While Truman had wanted to balance the budget with continued high taxes and reduced spending, the economic woes of 1949 led him to retreat from this agenda and instead push for business tax breaks. This strategy worked, and the economy rebounded in 1950. By making economic growth his major priority Truman established an important precedent for the presidents who followed him.

During 1948 and 1949 the cold war intensified in important ways. First, in February 1948, Czechoslovakia, previously an independent democracy, fell to communism. Later that year, the process of splitting Germany into two nations intensified. The United States, Britain, and France unified the administration of their zones of occupation in Germany. The Soviet Union opposed the move and retaliated by instituting a blockade around Berlin, the capital, which was located entirely within the Soviet zone but was occupied by all four powers. Truman refused to accept the Soviet move, and he determined to solve the crisis without resorting to the use of force. A year-long airlift of basic supplies proved successful not only in supplying the needs of West Berliners, but also in gaining favorable world opinion. However, upon successful completion of the BERLIN BLOCKADE AND AIRLIFT Stalin refused to permit the Soviet zone in Germany to be merged with the British, French, and American zones to reunite the country. The result was a permanent division of Germany into two nations—East Germany and West Germany. Not until the end of the cold war in 1990 would Germany be unified. The most important legacy of the Berlin airlift was the creation of the NORTH ATLANTIC TREATY ORGANIZATION, a regional security pact that included the United States, Canada, and the major and many of the minor nations of Western Europe. The political, economic, military, and ideological divisions in Europe were hardening.

Even more important to the worsening of the cold war in 1949 was the Soviet detonation of an atomic bomb, making it the second nation to possess nuclear weapons. To ensure national security Truman made two important decisions. First, he authorized the construction of the hydrogen bomb, leading to an accelerated arms race with the Soviets. Second, he ultimately endorsed the National Security Council report, known as NATIONAL SECURITY COUNCIL DOCUMENT 68 (NSC-68), which called for a redirection of American military strategy. Not fully implemented until after the outbreak of the Korean War, NSC-68 called for a vast expansion of American weaponry—conventional and nuclear. This growing reliance on an arms race to defeat the Soviet Union had significant budgetary implications for the United States and it helped to advance the militarization of much of the economy. In other words, American economic growth became intrinsically linked to defense spending.

The Korean Peninsula proved to be the most significant danger zone for American foreign policy during the Truman presidency. Artificially divided at the 38th parallel following World War II into two zones—communist North Korea

German children watch a U.S. plane laden with supplies preparing to land during the Berlin airlift in 1948. *(Library of Congress)*

led by dictator Kim Il Sung and noncommunist South Korea led by elected president Syngman Rhee—the peninsula became the first significant client state for cold war hostilities. A surprise invasion by North Korea on June 25, 1950, of South Korea led the United States to defend Syngman Rhee's government. Truman and his advisers wrongly believed the Soviet Union was responsible for the attack. Actually, North Korean leader Kim Il Sung plotted the attack. The Soviets had forsworn any military participation (but they did later provide air support). Following the North Korean invasion of South Korea, Truman relied on the United Nations to support American military action. The UN Security Council denounced Kim Il Sung's government and sent UN forces to defend the South, making the U.S. efforts there part of a multilateral force. A likely Soviet veto would have forestalled UN action, but the Soviet Union was boycotting the Security Council over the UN decision not to seat delegates from the People's Republic of China.

The initial American military action against the North Koreans proved futile, and U.S. troops were pushed deep into South Korean territory. Not until General Douglas MacArthur's amphibious assault at Inchon did the course of the war turn. After pushing the North Koreans back beyond the 38th parallel, MacArthur gained permission to take the war into North Korea. Truman agreed because he hoped that Korea could be unified under one government. Nonetheless, this strategy risked drawing the Soviets and the Chinese into the fighting given their close proximity to North Korea. When the Chinese did subsequently enter the fray, the UN forces were pushed south of the 38th parallel. By the spring of 1951, the action was stalemated. Truman reformulated his objectives, hoping to preserve the boundary at the 38th parallel. MacArthur publicly criticized this plan, and Truman fired him, unleashing a domestic political firestorm. Truman's unpopular decision was important, nonetheless, because it secured the civilian preeminence over the military. It took two years for peace talks to formalize the stalemate that still endures in Korea. The Truman administration's handling of the Korean War was significant for several reasons: It signaled American commitment to fighting communism in Asia as well as in Europe; it regularized the expanded defense spending called for in NSC-68; and it brought increased American financial support for French efforts to prevent a communist advance in Indochina. Put simply, the cold war was militarized and it expanded as a result of the conflict in Korea.

The outbreak of the Korean War in 1950 had economic repercussions in the United States. Fresh from the successful experiments with managed economies during World War II, Truman gained congressional approval for the Defense Production Act and used an executive order to create the Office of Defense Mobilization. Even though unemployment and inflation were relatively low during the Korean War, credit controls proved bothersome to a majority of Americans. The biggest wartime economic ordeal for Truman was the threatened work stoppage in the steel industry. When government mediation of the contract negotiations proved unsuccessful, Truman took over the steel industry. A Supreme Court case ensued, and the presidential seizure of the private industry was declared unconstitutional in the summer of 1952. With the return of private management came a strike that lasted for nearly two months before a new contract could be secured. This episode did nothing to improve the image of the Truman administration with the public.

Convicted of conspiracy to commit espionage in 1951, Ethel and Julius Rosenberg were executed two years later. *(Library of Congress)*

Charges of corruption marred the Truman presidency. The sources were Truman's history with the Pendergast machine in Missouri, Republican partisanship, and, most important, the charge that individuals in the administration engaged in questionable, and perhaps illegal, activities. In 1950, Senator J. William Fulbright (D-AR) investigated Truman's military aide, Harry Vaughan, who was known for granting government access to friends and businessmen.

CABINET, COURT AND CONGRESS

Cabinet Members

Secretary of State
Edward R. Stettinius Jr., 1945
James Byrnes, 1945–47
George C. Marshall, 1947–49
Dean G. Acheson, 1949–53

Secretary of War
Henry L. Stimson, 1945
Robert P. Patterson, 1945–47
Kenneth C. Royall, 1947

Secretary of Defense
James V. Forrestal, 1947–49
Louis Johnson, 1949–50
George C. Marshall, 1950–51
Robert Lovett, 1951–53

Secretary of the Treasury
Henry Morgenthau, Jr., 1945

Frederick M. Vinson, 1945–46
John W. Snyder, 1946–53

Postmaster General
Frank C. Walker, 1945
Robert E. Hannegan, 1945–47
Jesse M. Donaldson, 1947–53

Attorney General
Francis B. Biddle, 1945
Thomas C. Clark, 1945–49
J. Howard McGrath, 1949–52
James P. McGranery, 1952–53

Secretary of the Interior
Harold L. Ickes, 1945–46
Julius A. Krug, 1946–49
Oscar L. Chapman, 1949–53

Secretary of Agriculture
Claude R. Wickard, 1945
Clinton P. Anderson, 1945–48
Charles F. Brannan, 1948–53

Secretary of the Navy
James V. Forrestal, 1945–47

Secretary of Commerce
Henry A. Wallace, 1945–46
William Averell Harriman, 1946–48
Charles Sawyer, 1948–53

Secretary of Labor
Frances Perkins, 1945
Lewis B. Schwellenbach, 1945–48
Maurice J. Tobin, 1948–53

Supreme Court Appointments

*(Nominated for Chief Justice)

Name	Confirmation Vote	Dates of Service
Harold Burton	Voice Vote, Confirmed	1945–58
*Fred Vinson	Voice Vote, Confirmed	1946–53
Tom Clark	73–8, Confirmed	1949–67
Sherman Minton	48–16, Confirmed	1949–56

Legislative Leaders

Congress	Speaker of the House	State	Party
79th Congress (1945–47)	Sam Rayburn	Texas	Democrat
80th Congress (1947–49)	Joseph W. Martin, Jr.	Massachusetts	Republican
81st Congress (1949–51)	Sam Rayburn	Texas	Democrat
82nd Congress (1951–53)	Sam Rayburn	Texas	Democrat

Fulbright's committee found Vaughan guilty of minor legal and ethical infractions. The corruption Fulbright uncovered in the Reconstruction Finance Corporation involved questionable loans and kickbacks but investigators did not reach far into the Truman administration. Administration critics savored these charges, and they used Truman's defense of his friend Vaughan as proof of the president's culpability. More serious problems in the Internal Revenue Service forced

Congress	House Majority Leader	State	Party
79th Congress (1945–47)	John W. McCormack	Massachusetts	Democrat
80th Congress (1947–49)	Charles A. Halleck	Indiana	Republican
81st Congress (1949–51)	John W. McCormack	Massachusetts	Democrat
82nd Congress (1951–53)	John W. McCormack	Massachusetts	Democrat

Congress	House Minority Leader	State	Party
79th Congress (1945–47)	Joseph W. Martin, Jr.	Massachusetts	Republican
80th Congress (1947–49)	Sam Rayburn	Texas	Democrat
81st Congress (1949–51)	Joseph W. Martin, Jr.	Massachusetts	Republican
82nd Congress (1951–53)	Joseph W. Martin, Jr.	Massachusetts	Republican

Congress	House Democratic Whip	State	Party
79th Congress (1945)	Robert Ramspeck	Georgia	Democrat
79th Congress (1945–47)	John J. Sparkman	Alabama	Democrat
80th Congress (1947–49)	John W. McCormack	Massachusetts	Democrat
81st Congress (1949–51)	J. Percy Priest	Tennessee	Democrat
82nd Congress (1951–53)	J. Percy Priest	Tennessee	Democrat

Congress	House Republican Whip	State	Party
79th Congress (1945–47)	Leslie C. Arends	Illinois	Republican
80th Congress (1947–49)	Leslie C. Arends	Illinois	Republican
81st Congress (1949–51)	Leslie C. Arends	Illinois	Republican
82nd Congress (1951–53)	Leslie C. Arends	Illinois	Republican

Congress	Senate Majority Leader	State	Party
79th Congress (1945–47)	Alben Barkley	Kentucky	Democrat
80th Congress (1947–49)	Wallace H. White, Jr.	Maine	Republican
81st Congress (1949–51)	Scott W. Lucas	Illinois	Democrat
82nd Congress (1951–53)	Ernest W. McFarland	Arizona	Democrat

Congress	Senate Minority Leader	State	Party
79th Congress (1945–47)	Wallace H. White, Jr.	Maine	Republican
80th Congress (1947–49)	Alben Barkley	Kentucky	Democrat
81st Congress (1949–51)	Kenneth S. Wherry	Nebraska	Republican
82nd Congress (1951)	Kenneth S. Wherry	Nebraska	Republican
82nd Congress (1952–53)	Styles Bridges	New Hampshire	Republican

Truman to demand the resignation of Attorney General J. Howard McGrath, who had poorly handled his investigation of the agency.

The politics of anticommunism as practiced by Senator Joseph McCarthy (R-WI) constituted the biggest domestic issue during the Truman administration. McCarthy famously but erroneously charged that the federal government, specifically the State Department and the U.S. Army, was riddled with communists. Because McCarthy was so strongly associated with this issue in the public mind, the term McCarthyism became a shorthand reference for the wide-ranging efforts to both defame people without evidence and rid the body politic of leftists and supposed subversives. The emerging cold war with the Soviet Union provided the international backdrop for McCarthyism, but just as important was conservative frustration with the dominance of liberal and moderate Democrats, who had held power ever since the early 1930s. Truman himself helped advance fears of communist infiltration of the federal government with his creation of a loyalty security program, first as a temporary measure in November 1946 and then as a permanent entity the following year. Congress had its own committee responsible for investigating communist subversion, the House Committee on Un-American Activities (HUAC). Created in 1938 to ferret out Nazism in the government, HUAC turned its attention to communism during the war years. Headlines about spy cases intensified the anticommunist fervor, especially after the Soviet Union successfully detonated a nuclear bomb in 1949. Alger Hiss, a high-ranking government official during the 1930s and 1940s, was ultimately convicted of perjury while the British government convicted Klaus Fuchs, a scientist on the Manhattan Project, of spying. Among Fuchs's supposed contacts were two New York radicals, Julius and Ethel Rosenberg; although no proof could be found of Ethel's guilt, both were convicted of conspiracy to commit espionage in 1951 and executed in 1953.

As McCarthyism reached extreme levels in the early 1950s, Truman tried unsuccessfully to deflate its power. Congressional Republicans quietly encouraged McCarthy, believing partisan benefit could be had from charges against a Democratic administration. Furthermore, lawmakers from both parties introduced bills that legislated against communism. Senator Patrick McCarran (D-NV) authored the McCarran Internal Security Act of 1950, which limited the political rights of communists. Calling the measure a violation of civil liberties and a duplication of existing legislation, Truman vetoed the bill, and Congress overrode the president. In 1952, McCarran introduced immigration legislation that was also anticommunist in intent. The trajectory of this bill followed that of the previous McCarran effort, with a Truman veto and a congressional override. Truman's efforts to halt the anticommunist hysteria were met with charges that the administration was "soft on communism." International events—the Soviet development of atomic weapons, the fall of China to communism, and the Korean War—seemingly supported these claims, or at least made them plausible to many Americans.

In 1950, Truman had privately indicated that he would not seek reelection two years later out of respect for the two-term tradition that George Washington had established, but he told no one of his intentions. The events of the intervening years—domestic and foreign—caused Truman's standing to fall in the public opinion polls and make a race for the presidency all the more difficult. Truman tried to recruit a successor, but both Fred Vinson, the chief justice of the United States, and General Dwight D. Eisenhower turned him down. The eventual Democratic nominee, Illinois governor Adlai Stevenson, was a weak candidate. In late March 1952, Truman announced that he would not run and would retire from public life at the end of his term. Truman's campaigning for Stevenson proved futile. The popular Eisenhower easily prevailed on the Republican ticket in 1952.

Truman left office one of the most unpopular presidents in history. His reputation had suffered from the Korean War, charges of wrongdoing by his associates, and the politics of McCarthyism. Americans changed their minds quickly, though, and soon turned Truman into something of a folk hero during his retirement. The substance of his policies, especially in foreign affairs, proved crucial to this turnaround. Truman identified and responded effectively to the Soviet threat. The containment policies—political, diplomatic, military, and economic—that Truman and his administration deployed established important precedents for fighting the cold war rather than starting a third world war. The creation of the North Atlantic Treaty Organization (better known as NATO) revealed just how important regional security organizations could be to American policy in the cold war. The relationships that Truman built with Israel and South Korea extended beyond the end of the cold war and they remained important to American foreign policy into the 21st century.

Truman's domestic record was also significant. During his presidency, the American economy was successfully converted from wartime to peacetime production, and the postwar economic juggernaut began. Key aspects of the New Deal, such as Social Security, were strengthened, and the overall concept of federal responsibility for the social welfare of the country became routinized. His commitment to civil rights, marked by his desegregation of the armed forces, helped pave the way for even more significant reforms a generation later. Academic critics have argued that Truman was unwise to listen to General MacArthur, that he should have communicated with the public more fully the realities of the Chinese civil war and especially the problems with Jiang Jieshi, that he did not do enough to stop the advent of McCarthyism or help the Civil Rights movement, and that he overreached in advocating domestic reforms. These criticisms ignore the reality of political divisions within the Democratic Party and between Democrats and Republicans. Given this context any progress would have been noteworthy; that Truman achieved so much in both foreign and domestic affairs during a tumultuous period of international ferment and crisis makes his administration all the more commendable.

MAJOR EVENTS AND ISSUES

80th Congress *See* ELECTION OF 1946

Aid to Greece and Turkey   In the immediate post–World War II period Communist Party politicians made bids for governmental control in both Greece and Turkey. The Greek situation traced back to 1944 when, upon Germany's departure from that nation, an attempt was made to restore the monarchy. Communists and left-wing politicos fought back. They encountered little resistance because the other political interests were divided. As such, the British called on the United States for help. The Americans provided economic aid and extended advice on holding free elections, in which the left took no part. The monarchist victory triggered violence with the communists, causing U.S. observers to worry about excessive Soviet influence in the region and the potential for additional difficulties in the Middle East. Concurrently, American policy makers worried about potential Soviet incursions into Turkey, which, if successful, would further ease Soviet access to the Middle East. By early 1947, the turmoil in Greece escalated into a civil war. American officials tried to engineer a change in the Greek government.

The situation deteriorated further when the British announced they could no longer provide the wherewithal to help either Greece or Turkey. Cabinet officials, including Secretary of State George C. Marshall, Secretary of War Robert P. Patterson, and Secretary of Navy James V. Forrestal, conferred with President Truman about how best to handle the situation. They rejected proposals to seek United Nations assistance, relying instead on George Kennan's policy of containment as an operating philosophy. Next, administration officials lobbied Congress for support, arguing that Soviet success in Greece and Turkey would mean a communist advance into not only the Middle East, but also Western Europe and Africa. Truman actively sought and gained Republican as well as Democratic support for this initiative.

On March 12, 1947, Truman delivered an address to Congress calling for aid to Greece and Turkey. The president argued, "it must be the policy of the United States to support free peoples who are resisting attempted subjugation by armed minorities or by outside pressure." He called for $400 million in appropriations for aid to Greece and Turkey along with the deployment of American civilian and military per-

sonnel to oversee training and reconstruction. The speech set forth what quickly became known as the Truman Doctrine, and it reflected a major shift in American foreign policy away from appeasing the Soviet Union and toward containment of communism where it already existed and preventing its further spread. The Truman Doctrine also established a precedent for significant American economic intervention in other nations. This new American forcefulness became the dominant foreign policy for the next 40 years. Truman arranged for a bipartisan administration of the Truman Doctrine, and by 1950 officials believed that Greece and Turkey had been secured as important fellow allies in the anticommunist struggle.

Atomic Energy Act (1946)   By the fall of 1945, President Truman had moved from dealing with the international issues that the atomic bomb had raised to considering its domestic implications. In early October, Truman called for the creation of the U.S. Atomic Energy Commission, which would govern atomic research and development. The most significant conflict that the legislation introduced was whether the new agency should be under civilian or military control. Because Truman handed off the drafting of the legislation to the War Department, the resulting bill skewed control of the U.S. Atomic Energy Commission to the military. The president would not even have appointment power for the atomic energy administrator. Doubts were raised about giving so much control to a military clique, and a competing bill was introduced, which gave the president significant power over a civilian commission. Truman much preferred this version of the Atomic Energy Act, and when his secretaries of navy and war advocated for the military control bill, he ordered them to stop. The legislation that passed Congress in August 1946 followed the civilian governance plan, with an amendment to create a military liaison committee and a general advisory committee of nuclear scientists.

Berlin Blockade and Airlift (1948–1949)   At the end of World War II, Germany was divided into four zones of occupation, and one of the victorious World War II Allies oversaw each zone: the Soviets, the British, the French, and the Americans. By early 1948, the British, the French, and the Americans had begun talks to unite their three zones into one centralized administrative unit for the western areas of Germany. These deliberations drew objections from the Soviet Union, which responded with new limits on travel in and out of Berlin, the capital, located entirely within the Soviet zone but divided into four sectors.

The Berlin blockade was a purposeful strategy to divide the Western powers and prevent the emergence of a West German state with power comparable to the East German state operating as a Soviet satellite. On June 24, the Soviet Union blocked all ground traffic to and from the West in and out of the city. The Berlin blockade initially flummoxed the West, whose right of access to Berlin was not clearly established. A military confrontation with the Soviet Union including use of ground troops, which could provoke war, was not an attractive option, but neither was abandoning West Berlin to Soviet occupation. No branch of the U.S. government—the Pentagon, the Central Intelligence Agency, or the National Security Council—could construct a likely scenario for victory. Four days after the Soviets implemented the blockade, Truman announced his intentions for the United States to remain in Berlin.

Ultimately, modern technology and superior organizational planning and not military might or diplomatic strategizing solved the dilemma. Secretary of State George C. Marshall announced a plan for the aerial resupply of West Berlin on June 30. The Western powers coordinated several other tactics with the airlift: negotiations with the Soviets, increased American troop strength in Europe, enhanced defenses in Western Europe, and Western support for Yugoslavia in its quarrels with the Soviet Union. The Soviets achieved none of their objectives in Berlin. The airlift, which averaged hundreds of flights a day with one plane landing every three minutes, provided over 8,000 tons of supplies a day at its peak until September 1949 (the Soviets lifted the blockade on May 12, 1949). The image of American pilots dropping life-sustaining materials along with candy for the children over a city that had been bombed nearly beyond recognition just a few years earlier proved powerful. In addition to losing the war for public opinion, the Soviet blockade of Berlin strengthened the Western alliance against the Soviets, ensured the creation of the West German government in 1949, and pushed the United States to increase its troop commitment by almost 200,000 to more than 1.6 million by June 1949. Most important, the sustained cooperation by the Western powers to defeat the Berlin blockade helped pave the way for creation of the NORTH ATLANTIC TREATY ORGANIZATION.

Bombing of Hiroshima and Nagasaki (1945)   After his first cabinet meeting as president of the United States on April 12, 1945, Harry S. Truman learned from Secretary of War Henry L. Stimson of a new weapon more destructive than any previously known to mankind. Not until April 25 did Truman learn the details of the atomic bomb and the top-secret Manhattan Project under which the work had been carried out since the early 1940s. An interim committee was formed to determine the conditions appropriate for using the bomb. This committee recommended that no warning be given to Japan prior to the bomb's use, that the target be military and not civilian, and that the bomb be used in such a way as to maximize the psychological impact on the Japanese people. President Truman, though, believed the Japanese should be warned prior to the bombing.

While there has been much debate over whether the bombing of Hiroshima and later Nagasaki was undertaken at least in part to send a message of American power and American nuclear superiority to the Soviets, the best evidence suggests that a desire to end the war with Japan was the primary motive. Not until the POTSDAM CONFERENCE in July did Truman learn the extent of the power behind the atomic bomb following its first successful detonation in a test conducted in the New Mexico desert. This secret news gave the president what he believed was extra leverage against the Japanese. Soon decisions were made to use the bomb by the 10th of August against a military target in Japan and to issue a joint ultimatum together with the British and the Chinese about the bomb's destructive capabilities. This ultimatum was so vaguely worded that no real hint was given the Japanese as to what awaited them should they fail to give the Allies an unconditional surrender. Truman rejected calls for an international demonstration of the bomb's power prior to its military use.

Soon speed became the overriding concern for Truman. He wanted to end the war quickly to save as many American lives as possible, and he hoped to minimize the Soviet involvement in the Pacific theater. Given these priorities, Truman moved away from his plan to warn the Japanese and was less convinced of the need for a military target. That the United States did not provide sufficient time for the Japanese to react to the ultimatum, that the targets were not purely military, that a sufficiently clear warning was not given about the bomb's capabilities, and that no provisions were offered for Japanese retention of their emperor all combined to weaken the moral position of the United States. With regard to the Soviet Union, Truman failed completely in his goal of intimidation because the Russians, through espionage, already knew of the atomic bomb. In U.S.-Soviet relations, the development of the bomb intensified mistrust and raised the stakes of intelligence gathering.

Because the Japanese had not met the Sino-British-American ultimatum with an unconditional surrender, Truman ordered the dropping of an atomic bomb on the city of Hiroshima on August 6. The *Enola Gay*, piloted by Colonel Paul Tibbets, dropped its payload over an unsuspecting city. The resulting immediate deaths numbered between 70,000 and 130,000. In the aftermath of the bombing, Truman worried about the deaths of innocent children and about the meaning of atomic warfare for the future of the world, but he also declared the bomb to be the greatest development in history. Americans almost universally agreed. In a poll taken two days after the bombing, 85 percent of the populace registered their support for the president's decision. Three days after the attack on Hiroshima and one day after the Soviets entered the war against Japan, the United States dropped a second atomic bomb on Japan. This time the target was the city of Nagasaki. Approximately 45,000 people were killed immediately. Even before this bomb was dropped, forces in Japan had begun to discuss seriously the possibility of surrender. News of the second bomb interrupted these discussions. While the military leaders of Japan were not willing to surrender, Emperor Hirohito prevailed.

News of a Japanese surrender, conditional upon retention of the emperor, was announced on August 10. The Americans and the other Allies accepted these terms with the caveat that the emperor would be subject to the authority of the supreme Allied commander for Japan. Perhaps no president ever faced a more fateful choice than Truman in making the decision or to drop the atomic bomb, but Truman himself never doubted his action.

The Catcher in the Rye, by J. D. Salinger (1951)

This postwar coming-of-age novel published in 1951 identified an important generation gap between teenagers and their parents that would only widen as the baby boomers entered puberty in the 1950s and 1960s. Holden Caulfield, the teenaged antihero of *The Catcher in the Rye,* summed up the attitude of many young people when he described older people as phonies. The book, narrated by the 16-year-old Caulfield, tells of the days after he was expelled from prep school and portrays his alienation from friends and society. Its taut tone

J. D. Salinger, author of *The Catcher in the Rye,* published in 1951 (© *Pictorial Press, Ltd./Alamy*)

and controversial subject matter have caused some school districts and libraries to ban the book.

Civil Rights Program

With regard to civil rights, President Truman believed in legal equality even if his Missouri upbringing made it difficult for him to accept calls for social equality. An intensification of violence against African Americans led Truman in 1946 to create the President's Committee on Civil Rights. In October 1947, the committee issued a report, *To Secure These Rights,* which contained 35 recommendations for reform at the local, state, and federal levels. The reforms suggested included equal rights legislation and an end to mob violence. Truman asked Congress to consider antilynching legislation, the creation of a permanent Fair Employment Practices Committee, antipoll tax legislation, and action to end discrimination in interstate transportation. The lawmakers rejected all these initiatives. He issued executive orders desegregating the military and the civil service.

Not until the Democratic National Convention in July 1948 did Truman move forward with support for civil rights. Pushed by liberals in the party, Truman accepted placing a forceful civil rights plank in the Democratic Party platform, but he moved slowly to implement it. Truman's caution resulted both from the deep divisions within the Democratic Party with regard to race and from his concerns for the fall election. Elected president in his own right, Truman contended that he would move his civil rights agenda through Congress in 1949. The power wielded by the conservative coalition of southern Democrats and Republicans led to his failure to do so. Truman did use his appointment power to name African Americans to government posts, most notably William H. Hastie as judge on the Third Circuit Court of Appeals. Modest in terms of accomplishments, Truman's civil rights program was nonetheless revolutionary if only because he spoke openly in favor of this reform legislation and because he used his executive authority to implement changes, something previous presidents had not done.

Common Sense Baby and Child Care, by Benjamin Spock (1946)

Published at the dawn of the baby boom in 1946, *Common Sense Baby and Child Care* became an immensely popular advice book for new parents. It sold approximately 1 million copies a year in the late 1940s and the 1950s. This book replaced the informal system of baby advice that women from previous generations had used. Prior to the postwar suburbanization of America, new parents were much more likely to live in close proximity to their parents, siblings, or other family members. As such, they were able to draw on the wealth of parenting wisdom that these relatives possessed. But as Americans moved to new homes in rapidly developing suburbs, they often lived far from relatives. This book by Dr. Benjamin Spock helped fill this void. The book also reflected the increased importance that Americans at midcentury placed on expert advice. Conservatives wrongly criticized the book for its permissive approach to parenting, especially discipline. In reality, Dr. Spock's book conveyed a traditional, conservative message about parenting. He argued that mothers should provide the primary care for their children at least until they reached the age of three. Furthermore, he contended that fathers were much less important to the parenting process than were mothers.

Containment Policy   With the end of World War II in 1945, tensions between the United States and the Soviet Union increased. As the Truman administration responded in an ad hoc fashion to various instances of Soviet aggression against other nations, specifically in Eastern Europe, a U.S. policy of containment ultimately emerged. Based in large part on the theoretical perspectives developed by George Kennan, the chargé d'affaires with the State Department in Moscow, the doctrine of containment posited that Soviet communism should be tolerated where it already existed but that the full force of U.S. economic, political, diplomatic, and military power should be used to prevent the spread of Soviet communism to nations or regions where it did not exist. Examples of the containment policy in action included the Truman Doctrine, the MARSHALL PLAN, and the Berlin airlift. This strategy proved effective for the United States because of American economic superiority at the end of World War II and because the Soviets did not want a direct military confrontation with the West.

Arthur Miller, author of *Death of a Salesman,* published in 1949 *(Library of Congress)*

***Death of a Salesman,* by Arthur Miller (1949)**   Arthur Miller, along with Tennessee Williams and William Inge, was one of the leading playwrights in postwar America. Written in just six weeks in 1949 and perhaps his greatest play, *Death of a Salesman* reflected the influence of the Great Depression and World War II and the frustration and turmoil that these crises produced. The main character, Willy Loman, is a failed businessman searching for meaning in his life. He never achieved the success in business and as a father that he wanted, and both his employers and his sons reject his efforts. He kills himself to provide the insurance settlement to his family. Some critics have compared this tragedy with characters from Shakespeare. Key themes in the play include loyalty, sacrifice, success, and failure. The play won the Pulitzer Prize, enjoyed a successful run, and made Miller a millionaire.

Defense Production Act (1950)   In the summer of 1950, President Truman sought from Congress legislation to boost war production. The Defense Production Act, which was passed in September, gave businesses incentives to increase production, made war orders a priority over other production needs, placed limits on civilian production, and provided for wage and price stabilization. Because Truman viewed

this legislation as the domestic cornerstone of his KOREAN WAR policies, he made a radio and television address to the nation about the Defense Production Act soon after its passage. He explained that the law's provisions would ensure a doubling of defense spending to $30 billion per year. Truman told Americans that the law would also require payment of higher taxes, and they would have to work harder, have fewer consumer goods available for purchase, endure wage and PRICE CONTROLS, and face restrictions on consumer credit. Furthermore, fewer resources would be available for social programs. Benefits would accrue for certain workers with new jobs created in the defense industry. The following year, Truman had difficulty getting Congress to improve the terms of the legislation. Lawmakers would provide only production incentives; they balked at economic controls, government financing for defense plants, and increased protections for farm parity. The impasse resulted because Congress did not view the threat of inflation to be as serious as Truman suggested. Nor did lawmakers accept presidential arguments that production targets were in jeopardy of being filled.

***Dennis v. United States* (1951)**   The Supreme Court rendered its decision in this case on June 4, 1951. *Dennis v. United States* resulted from the arrest of Eugene Dennis and other leaders of the Communist Party of America. These individuals were charged with violating the Smith Act, a 1946 law that outlawed conspiracy to teach and advocate the overthrow or destruction of the U.S. government. The guilty verdict had been upheld in the lower courts. The high court deliberated whether or not the Smith Act violated the First Amendment to the Constitution and the justices upheld the lower court decision by a 6-2 vote. The Supreme Court distinguished between the simple teaching of communism and the purposeful advocacy of it. The latter posed a "clear and present danger" independent of whether communism as an ideology might prove successful.

Desegregation of the Military In 1948, President Truman began to move slowly on the issue of civil rights. He knew that the chance to pass legislation was slim given the power of southern Democrats in Congress. To counter this problem, he promised early in the year to issue executive orders addressing discrimination in the armed services and in the civil service. Truman did not act on this promise until after the Democratic National Convention in July 1948. His order governing the civil service did not address segregation, only discrimination, and was of limited impact. His order governing the military proved revolutionary in the long term,

General Douglas MacArthur pins the Distinguished Service Cross on Sergeant Curtis Pugh for heroism shown in Korea, February 13, 1951. *(Jim Pringle/Associated Press)*

although, at the time the impact of the order was limited. Military leaders did not welcome Truman's efforts at what critics termed "social engineering" and were unwilling to cooperate. The generals worried that an integrated military would lack discipline, that whites would not accept orders from blacks, that it would reduce the comradely spirit among the troops. The outbreak of the KOREAN WAR in 1950 accelerated desegregation of the military. Complete equality among the races in the military, though, was not achieved. African American soldiers had not gained majority status in any unit, nor were a significant number of blacks promoted through the chain of command. With time, military service became an avenue toward a middle-class life for many African Americans, in part as a result of Truman's executive order. Furthermore, the peaceful integration of the armed services provided an example of how this change could be enacted throughout the country.

Displaced Persons Act (1948) The issue of displaced persons arose after World War II ended in 1945. The biggest problem in providing for persons with no safe place to go at the end of the war was the reluctance of any nation, including the United States, to provide safe haven for these individuals. Race and ethnicity played a role in how governments reacted to displaced persons. No one did much of anything for the displaced persons in Asia. European Jews composed the largest group of displaced persons, and President Truman viewed the British protectorate of Palestine as an appropriate destination for them. Furthermore, at Truman's behest, the United Nations formed the International Refugee Organization in 1946 to assist the resettlement of displaced persons. The Displaced Persons Act passed by Congress in 1948 provided for the United States to take a leading role in the relief and resettlement of displaced persons. By 1952, more than 1 million displaced individuals had been resettled, 400,000 of them in the United States.

Economic Reconversion As the fighting in World War II wound down, attention to the domestic economy became one of the most important issues for the Truman administration. The primary concerns were what would be the long-term status of New Deal–era reforms and how to prevent both postwar economic disruptions and a return to the problems of the Great Depression. The wartime failure to plan a postwar economic reconversion policy made that task all the more difficult for the Truman administration. President FRANKLIN D. ROOSEVELT had wanted the National Resources Planning Board to fill that role, but Congress eliminated the agency in 1943. What remained were a multiplicity of agencies, committees, and interest groups interested in the issue in whole or in part. These groups made no concerted effort to work in harmony. As such, few if any of their recommendations were implemented before the war ended in 1945.

How exactly to convert from wartime military production to peacetime civilian production led to an extension of agricultural price supports for two years beyond the war, plans for the sale of surplus war property, and discussions about how to achieve orderly termination of government contracts. None of these measures addressed how to shift production priorities. As a result, no real discussion took place about how to avoid postwar inflation, and the termination of PRICE CONTROLS occurred in a most unsatisfactory fashion. Nor had any attention been given to the inevitable disputes between labor and management once wartime controls on wages were eliminated. To achieve a peaceful reconversion, President Truman called for a one-year extension of wage and price controls. He believed this step necessary to prevent inflation, but once the hostilities ended voters demanded an end to these controls and Congress refused to meet Truman's request.

When Truman presented his legislative agenda to Congress in the fall of 1945 he asked for a wide range of laws and reforms, further complicating the reconversion process. This 21-point program for reconversion sent to Congress in September touched on wage policy, employment policy, farm policy, government support and cooperation with scientific research, tax policy, public works, foreign aid, atomic policy, military policy, small business assistance, waterway development, air transportation policy, housing policy, medical care, and education. Lawmakers viewed this list with a jaundiced eye, seeing it as partisan fodder for the 1946 midterm elections. Truman fared poorly at steering the items that constituted a continuation of the New Deal through Congress, but he achieved much success with measures that encouraged business production.

Acting independently of Congress, the Truman administration cancelled numerous wartime government contracts, developed demobilization plans for nine of the 12 million military personnel, removed manpower controls, and cut back on the rationing program. Maintaining employment levels was the most important goal of the administration. To achieve that end, removal of production controls became paramount. Other strategies included the preserving low-interest rates, reducing income taxes, removing export and import controls, and encouraging Americans to spend their savings. Legislation from Congress that fall was limited to surplus property disposal, a reduction of federal expenditures, a mechanism for executive branch reorganization that included the elimination of wartime agencies, a six-month extension of price controls, and tax reduction. Despite the uncoordinated and clumsy efforts at reconversion, over 90 percent of industrial facilities were ready to undertake civilian production by the end of 1945.

Election of 1946   The 1946 midterm congressional elections revealed the extent of voter frustrations with President Truman, the lingering issues of the war, and the difficulty of achieving postwar ECONOMIC RECONVERSION. At the start of the year, Truman enjoyed an approval rating of over 80 percent, but by June his favorable rating had fallen to just over 50 percent. Inflation and foreign policy problems intensified dislike for the president that summer. Furthermore, Truman and the Democrats took for granted two of their most important constituencies—organized labor and farmers.

However, Republicans were ready to exploit frustrations with the status quo. The saying "to err is Truman" encapsulated the general mood of the people in 1946, and the Republican slogan—"Had Enough? Vote Republican"—resonated with a majority of voters. In the midterm elections of 1946, Republicans gained control of both the House and the Senate. Their majority in the lower chamber was 245-188 and in the Senate 51-45. These results produced the first Republican Congress since the HERBERT HOOVER administration 15 years earlier.

The newly empowered Republicans were eager to roll back the social and economic reforms enacted by Democrats during the 1930s. The 80th Congress, which was seated in January 1947, disagreed with much of the FAIR DEAL legislation Truman proposed, and it served as a constant irritant to the president on questions of domestic policy. In terms of foreign policy, though, the 80th Congress supported the significant programs Truman initiated, such as AID TO GREECE AND TURKEY and the MARSHALL PLAN. As such, the legacy of the election of 1946 proved more complicated than partisans on either side of the electoral divide were willing to admit.

Employment Act (1946)   Economic planning for future stability constituted a significant component of the liberal, Democratic Party agenda during the New Deal and World War II years. Liberals in and out of Congress began drafting legislation to guarantee full employment even before the war ended. The full employment bill proposed a comprehensive reform package, which included a stated government commitment to full employment and mandated public spending to achieve this goal. The bill, though, was destined to fail. When the House of Representatives considered the measure, it was stripped of its strongest provisions. The legislation as passed in 1946 declared it the policy of the federal government to encourage "maximum employment." The weakened measure provided for an annual presidential report to Congress detailing the economic conditions of the nation and suggesting any necessary legislation to implement the goals of the Employment Act. It also created the Council of Economic Advisors, a three-person panel of economic experts to advise the president, and the Joint Committee on the Economic Report, a combined House and Senate committee to consider related legislative concerns. The legislation sailed through the two chambers in its weakened form and passed in February. No one could predict with any certainty whether it would actually do any good, but it also carried little risk of economic harm. As such, a vote for the Employment Act was not controversial.

Fair Deal   In President Truman's January 1949 State of the Union address he put forward a reform agenda termed the Fair Deal. Political heir to the New Deal of President Roosevelt, Truman's Fair Deal depended on the goodwill of the newly elected Democratic Congress. A 54-42 majority in the Senate and a 263-171 majority in the House of Representatives were not sufficient to overcome the decline of liberalism associated with postwar prosperity. Nonetheless, Truman called for the repeal of the TAFT-HARTLEY ACT, a more progressive income tax system, an increase in the minimum wage, agricultural reform, increased federal commitment to both resource development and public power, an expansion of Social Security to include more workers, national medical insurance, federal aid to education, civil rights, and an enlarged federal housing program. By 1950, Congress had passed legislation reforming public housing, the minimum wage, and Social Security. The conservative coalition in Congress blocked consideration of civil rights legislation while special-interest groups stymied Fair Deal reforms for labor, agriculture, education, and health insurance. Finally, the outbreak of the KOREAN WAR and the heightened cold war climate put an end to any other movement to enact measures proposed under the Fair Deal during the Truman administration. Still, the Fair Deal marked an important statement of postwar liberal reform. Measures contained in it would remain as staple Democratic Party policy proposals for much of the remainder of the 20th century and into the 21st century.

Farmers Home Administration Act (1946)   Rooted in New Deal–era legislation to reform agricultural operations in the United States, the Farmers Home Administration Act of 1946 also reflected postwar realities, specifically the return of World War II veterans who wished to farm but had insufficient funds to acquire land. In addition to consolidating various existing agencies—the Farm Security Administration and the Emergency Crop and Feed Loan Division—the Farmers Home Administration insured loans made to farmers by other lenders and made direct loans using government funds.

Federal Airport Act (1946)   This legislation further enhanced the responsibility of the federal government for the construction of domestic airports, a role that dated as far back as the 1920s. Under the Federal Airport Act of 1946, Congress provided $3 million to develop the new airport construction plans and $500 million worth of grants for construction projects to be paid out over the next seven years. The legislation capped individual grants at half the specified

project's cost with the remainder to be funded through local bond initiatives. Furthermore, the legislation made compliance with Civil Aeronautics Association requirements for airport construction and safety a condition for obtaining the money. Finally, the legislation required that tax revenue generated by airports be retained for airport operations and maintenance. The larger purpose of the legislation was to help develop an integrated system of public airports congenial with the increased volume of air travel.

Federal Rent Control Act (1949)   President Truman had asked for a continuation and strengthening of rent controls in his 1948 State of the Union address. The following year, on March 30, 1949, Truman signed legislation extending authority for federal rent control. At the signing ceremony, Truman lambasted the real estate lobby for its efforts to kill the bill. He argued that, with passage of the Federal Rent Control Act, Congress had committed itself to protecting renters until the postwar housing shortage was eliminated.

Firing of General MacArthur (1951)   Public opinion about the Truman presidency had deteriorated concurrently with the unfolding of the KOREAN WAR in 1950 and 1951. After early U.S. victories, American troops had been stopped, the war was viewed as a stalemate, and General Douglas MacArthur, the commanding officer of U.S. and United Nations forces in Korea, wanted to invade or at least bomb China. Not wanting to expand the war, Truman opposed MacArthur's plan. Furthermore, the limited nature of this U.S. police action, as Truman had described it to the American people, was especially troubling to many Americans.

When Truman fired MacArthur, the public controversy that resulted encapsulated the debate about Truman's war policies. MacArthur, though, had certainly exacerbated the situation. Throughout his military career, he had never demonstrated a deep respect for the president as commander in chief of the military. He had been insubordinate as far back as the HERBERT HOOVER administration. Because of this record, MacArthur's views were not routinely consulted in the plotting of strategy for the Korean War. This angered the general, who grew increasingly impatient with Truman.

Partisan politics also played a role in bringing on the controversy between the president and the general. Representative Joseph W. Martin Jr. (R-MA), the Republican leader in the House of Representatives, had been vocal in his criticisms of the Korean War. He wanted to bring Chiang Kai-shek (now Jiang Jieshi) and his Nationalist Chinese forces into the war and expand the fighting from the Korean Peninsula into mainland China. He doubted whether the administration even wanted to win the war, suggesting that any other strategy was nothing more than license to murder the American troops in Korea. Martin disregarded the wisdom of Truman's limited war strategy, which according to the president was designed to force China and North Korea to negotiate a peaceful settlement and avoid World War III.

To better his argumentative position, Martin wrote to MacArthur to secure his frank assessment of the president's strategy. In a March 1951 letter, MacArthur offered a damning evaluation of the Truman war strategy and foreign policy in general. Martin held the letter in confidence until two Democratic congressional leaders publicly disagreed with the administration about the possibility of World War III with the Soviet Union. The letter displayed MacArthur's disregard for the principle of civilian control of the military by ignoring the president's orders and publicly criticizing him. The letter challenged the cherished system under which clear lines of civilian control were maintained over the military. Truman reacted harshly to the April 5 publication of MacArthur's letter, terming it a political act by the general and insubordination of the worst kind.

The president spoke with key military and foreign policy advisers, including Dean Acheson, the secretary of state;

George C. Marshall, the former secretary of state; and Omar Bradley, the chairman of the Joint Chiefs of Staff. After two days of meetings a unanimous agreement was reached that MacArthur should be relieved of his command, and the orders were transmitted on April 9. Truman took this drastic step not only out of anger over MacArthur's overt partisanship, but also because his behavior threatened the potential for cease-fire talks in Korea.

After the firing, Martin invited MacArthur to address a joint session of Congress. Congressional Democrats reluctantly concurred, but Truman did not criticize the invitation. The president's decisive behavior had helped significantly with his public approval ratings, and he had little to fear from the general's congressional appearance. Mail to the White House initially revealed an almost two to one ratio of approval for the president. Even before MacArthur returned to the United States and made his congressional appearance, the public attitude shifted. Gallup poll figures showed a 66 percent disapproval rating for the president. This sea change

Two weeks after being fired by President Truman for insubordination, Douglas MacArthur addresses an audience of 50,000 at Soldier's Field in Chicago, on April 25, 1951. *(United States Federal Government)*

occurred because the public viewed the controversy as a contest between a strong and decisive general and a weak president unable to thwart communist expansion in Asia. While the White House tried to move beyond the controversy by ignoring it, Republican congressional critics used the issue to challenge the balance of power between the executive and legislative branches and to gain an electoral advantage for 1952.

Foreign Assistance Act   *See* MARSHALL PLAN

Fulbright Act (1946)   In 1946, Senator J. William Fulbright (D-AR) sponsored legislation to create a merit-based exchange scholarship program for graduate students, teachers, and scholars. No restrictions were placed as to fields of study, recipients came from throughout the United States, and qualified veterans were given preference in the application process. The legislation came in the form of an amendment to the Surplus Property Act of 1944. Fulbright's amendment authorized the secretary of state to negotiate with foreign governments to finance educational exchanges. Individuals from the United States who earned Fulbright scholarships would be eligible to study and teach abroad, while foreign scholars, teachers, and students would come to America. The program sought to increase international understanding among the peoples of the world and reduce global misunderstandings. The legislation, known as the Fulbright Act, passed through the Senate without debate, and it was signed by Truman on August 1, 1946. Fulbright believed the program would assist in preparing well-qualified leaders for the future and would contribute to world peace by encouraging understanding among nations.

Hiss Case (1948–1950)   Between the summer of 1948 and January 1950, the most notable case of the Red Scare unfolded. It involved Alger Hiss, a former State Department worker, and Whittaker Chambers, an editor for *Time* magazine and a former communist, who accused Hiss of being a communist. Hiss's troubles began in August 1948 with hearings before the House Committee on Un-American Activities (HUAC), which aimed to root out subversion in government agencies. At that time, several former communists had appeared before HUAC and given names of other communists. Whittaker Chambers, a communist until his 1938 disavowal of the party, named Hiss among others as former communist associates. Sloppy in appearance and mentally unbalanced, Chambers was a less than ideal witness despite his vitriolic condemnations of communism. The accusation tested credulity for many Washington insiders. Chambers testified that Hiss was a member of the communist underground and by implication a spy.

Hiss had compiled an impressive résumé. Educated at Johns Hopkins University and Harvard Law School, he had

Alger Hiss testifying before the House Committee on Un-American Activities in Washington, D.C., 1948 *(file/Associated Press)*

clerked for Supreme Court justice Oliver Wendell Holmes, worked for various New Deal agencies, and attended a number of wartime international conferences, including Yalta as a State Department employee. At the time of Chambers's testimony, Hiss served as head of the Carnegie Endowment for International Peace. Furthermore, he was physically attractive and erudite in his speech. For those who considered the plausibility of Chambers's charges, the possibility of Hiss's communist past suggested that no limit existed as to how far communist infiltration of the American government could reach. In other words, if Alger Hiss, with his impeccable credentials, was a communist then anyone in the federal employ could be a communist. Hiss insisted on appearing before HUAC, where he denied all of Chambers's accusations. Furthermore, Hiss challenged Chambers to level his charges outside of the HUAC hearings and without congressional immunity. When Chambers did so, Hiss sued him for libel. Even President Truman believed Hiss; the president attacked the HUAC investigations as lacking substance.

Representative RICHARD NIXON (R-CA), a leading HUAC protagonist, believed Chambers and continued to pursue Hiss. The FBI aided Nixon by providing him with evidence allegedly implicating Hiss. The next move belonged to Chambers. Chambers led some HUAC staff members to his farm, where he produced microfilmed evidence that supposedly proved Hiss had transferred confidential government documents to the Soviet Union. To heighten the drama, Chambers revealed that he had hidden the microfilm in a hollowed-out pumpkin. The microfilm revealed a 65-page typed document with annotations in Hiss's handwriting that summarized or copied State Department cables from 1938.

As a result of these declarations, the Hiss case moved to a grand jury. Because the statute of limitations had expired for leveling any charges of espionage, Hiss was charged with perjury in lying to HUAC. His first trial ended in a hung jury, but at a second trial Hiss was found guilty. Throughout it all, Hiss maintained his innocence. The debate over whether or not Hiss was in fact innocent continued for much of the remainder of the 20th century. The end of the cold war and the opening of Soviet archives to the West provided strong evidence of Hiss's guilt, though Hiss's defenders have challenged this.

Hospital Survey and Construction Act (1946)   Also known as the Hill-Burton Act, after its sponsors Senators Lister Hill (D-AL) and Harold Burton (R-OH), the 1946 Hospital Survey and Construction Act constituted a conservative alternative to Truman's proposal for a system of national health insurance and received the backing of the American Medical Association. Truman wanted a system of national health insurance. Under his plan, a federal tax of 4 percent on the first $3,600 of personal income would have funded health insurance for all Americans. Coverage for the poor would come from general revenues. The plan never had much chance of passage. The American Medical Association called the plan socialistic, and congressional conservatives defeated the measure. Instead, lawmakers gravitated to a health care bill that benefited hospitals. This legislation authorized federal funding for hospital construction. It created a shared local, state, and federal funding partnership for the building of hospitals. It did not address the larger questions of who received medical care and how that medical care would be paid for. As such, both doctors and the construction industry heartily approved the measure. Approximately $4 billion was spent on hospital construction between 1946 and 1975. By the mid-1980s, over 9,000 health care facilities received funding through this legislation, which required hospitals constructed with funds from this program to provide a certain percentage of free or reduced cost care to poor and indigent patients. The beneficiaries of the Hospital Survey and Construction Act included physicians, hospital administrators, and insurance companies.

Housing Act (1949)   For President Truman, provision of public housing was an integral part of his FAIR DEAL program. He wanted to expand significantly on the number of public housing units that had been made available under New Deal–era legislation passed in 1937, which had provided for 170,000 units. Relying on Republican and southern Democratic support, Truman called for congressional approval of 810,000 additional public housing units, to be constructed over a six-year period. The real estate lobby vehemently objected to this legislative reform.

The administration blundered in its handling of the bill's introduction in Congress. Senator Robert Taft (R-OH), an influential conservative lawmaker, had been willing to work with Truman on public housing, but he had received the bill only an hour before its introduction. He replied by author-

ing a competing proposal, but ultimately Truman and Taft resolved their differences. With Taft's support, the bill faced little difficulty in the Senate. The fighting was much more intense in the House of Representatives, where opponents used racial prejudice to defeat the measure. Specifically, an amendment banning racial discrimination in public housing was offered, not with the intent of improving conditions for African Americans but to divide northern and southern supporters of the bill. Opponents of the bill understood that the southern supporters would not vote for it with this provision. Lawmakers recognized the ruse for what it was and passed the Housing Act without the amendment in 1949.

The legislation, as enacted, proved far less successful than Truman had hoped. Within three years, just 156,000 units had been started and, by 1964, completed units totaled only 356,000. Furthermore, the housing was poorly built. Nor did planners think about the environmental context, building housing units that were unattractive and uniform in style. Community formation initiatives were nonexistent. The legacy of Truman's public housing initiatives was mixed at best.

Integration of the Brooklyn Dodgers (1947)   In 1945, Branch Rickey, the general manager of the Brooklyn Dodgers, signed Jackie Robinson, an African-American ball player, to a minor league contract with the hope that he would possess talent sufficient to break the color barrier in major league baseball. Two years later, in 1947, Robinson became the first black ball player in the major leagues since the 19th century. Rickey's decision did not stem from any long-standing commitment to civil rights but from what he believed was best for

Brooklyn Dodgers star Jackie Robinson became the first black baseball player in the major leagues in the 20th century. *(Library of Congress)*

his team and for the game of baseball. Robinson was the perfect candidate to integrate major league ball. He had attended the University of California, Los Angeles, and had served in the army during World War II. That he did not drink or smoke further boosted Robinson's credentials as did his intelligence, his courage, and his competitiveness. Robinson debuted on April 15, 1947. While Robinson faced hostility from his teammates as well as opposing ball players, he deflected their racist behavior with his talent and skills. He went on to win the Rookie of the Year Award and helped lead the Dodgers to the National League pennant. Robinson's experience in major league baseball suggested that, despite opposition, a peaceful transition to integration could take place smoothly and without incident. A combination of aggressive confrontation, economic pressure, and moral influence helped explain the success of the Robinson experiment.

Israel   *See* RECOGNITION OF ISRAEL (1948)

Kefauver Crime Committee (1950–1951)   Senator Estes Kefauver (D-TN) chaired the Special Committee on Organized Crime in Interstate Commerce, popularly known as the Kefauver Committee. In 1950, he began hearings into organized crime and corruption in America. Republicans cooperated in this effort. Often Kefauver's targets were political machine bosses in the big cities with affiliations to the Democratic Party. St. Louis and Kansas City, Missouri, were among the cities Kefauver investigated. This Missouri connection did nothing to gain the favor of President Truman, who came from Missouri. Because the hearings brought significant criticism to the Democratic Party, Truman looked upon Kefauver as a traitor. Kefauver gained much public prominence from these hearings because the media gave them extensive coverage and because they were televised—a first for a congressional investigation. More than 30 million Americans tuned in to these hearings. The hearings were more significant for the publicity they generated than for any convictions. In fact, few of Kefauver's targets were found guilty. At best, the Kefauver hearings made possible future investigations and anticrime legislation. Even more important were the political implications of the hearings. Kefauver tried unsuccessfully to convert his media recognition into a race for the presidency in 1952. Not surprisingly, Republicans were the chief beneficiaries of the hearings. They gained a salient issue for the 1952 elections even while Democrats found themselves on the defensive. In 1956 Kefauver was the Democratic vice-presidential candidate.

Korean War (1950–1953)   Fought between June 1950 and July 1953, the Korean War proved an important point of departure in cold war policy. It shifted the American efforts to beat back communism from Europe to Asia. While ultimately ending in a stalemate, policymakers at the time feared the conflict on the remote Korean Peninsula would lead to World War III. By the time a cease-fire was reached Americans had met only a portion of their objectives—prevention of a communist North Korean takeover of South Korea—while failing to reunite the two Korean states into one government friendly to the West. The conflict resulted in almost 4 million casualties, more than 50 percent of whom were civilians. More than 36,000 Americans died in the Korean War.

Since Japan had played a role in Korea since the mid 19th century and had technically colonized the peninsula in the 1910s, the defeat of Japan in World War II left Korea "open" for conflict over what type of government should be established there. The roots of this war can be traced to the conclusion of World War II when military officials in the United States made an arbitrary decision to divide the Korean Peninsula at the 38th parallel for purposes of occupation with the Soviet Union overseeing the North and the United States the South. This temporary division became permanent with the escalation of the cold war. The North Korean government, under the leadership of communist dictator Kim Il Sung, and the South Korean government, under the leadership of American-educated president Syngman Rhee, had been fighting since 1945. North Korean forces swept into South Korea on June 25, 1950, thus expanding the conflict immediately. Soviet-supplied weaponry was used in the onslaught, but no Soviet soldiers took part. The North Koreans made quick work of pushing back their adversaries, capturing Seoul, the capital of South Korea, and pushing farther southward toward the Korea Strait.

Upon learning of the attack, President Truman sought and gained a United Nations resolution calling for an end of the hostilities and a North Korean withdrawal above the 38th parallel. On June 30, Truman ordered the military into action without seeking a congressional declaration of war but after consultation with congressional leaders. Truman justified this intervention based on what had happened after the appeasement of Nazi leader Adolf Hitler in the late 1930s. Initially, American troops seemed unready for battle given postwar demobilization. In late 1950, General Douglas MacArthur halted the North Korean advance southward, and he managed to launch a successful, amphibious assault on the communists at Inchon. This action paved the way for retaking Seoul and ultimately resulted in the decimation of North Korean troops in South Korea.

These quick victories encouraged Truman to call for an expansion of the war aims, from simply pushing the North Koreans back beyond the 38th parallel to reunification of the two Koreas as long as the additional fighting would not engage the Soviets or the Chinese Communists. MacArthur relished the new orders, believing that the threat of communist expansion in Asia was much more serious than in Europe. China opposed this turn of strategy and announced that it would join with the North Koreans in the fight if the

Residents from Pyongyang, North Korea, and elsewhere crawl over shattered girders of the city's bridge as they flee south across the Taedong River to escape the advance of Chinese troops, December 4, 1950. *(Maz Desfor, File/Associated Press)*

United States crossed the 38th parallel. Truman and MacArthur had a very public meeting on Wake Island to determine the next move. Because MacArthur was certain victory could be had by Christmas 1950, plans for an invasion of North Korea continued. However, MacArthur's foray into the north failed miserably in large part because the Chinese entered the fighting.

In response, Truman placed further limits on what MacArthur could do, precipitating the conflict that resulted in the president's decision to fire the general on April 11, 1951. The event that triggered the FIRING OF DOUGLAS MACARTHUR was publication on April 5 of a letter the general had written in March to Joseph Martin, the minority leader in the U.S. House of Representatives. In this letter, MacArthur criticized Truman's strategy in fighting the war.

By this point, the situation in Korea had reached a stalemate. The sides began discussing a truce on July 10, 1951. Not until late November was agreement reached that the armistice line should be located at the battle line and not at the 38th parallel. The Americans and the North Koreans also disagreed on the issue of prisoner repatriation, with the Koreans wanting automatic repatriation and the Americans opposing forced repatriation. The UN forces made no appreciable progress in the fall of 1951. Military action against the North Koreans was limited to air strikes. It appeared that Kim wanted the war over in the spring of 1952, but the Chinese and the Soviets both opposed concessions regarding Chinese prisoners of war.

The war became an issue in the 1952 presidential election, prompting Republican candidate and World War II general DWIGHT D. EISENHOWER to promise that he would go to Korea to resolve the crisis. After winning victory and becoming president, he did so. After three days at the front in December 1952, Eisenhower concluded that the hostilities had to be ended. On July 27, 1953, five months after he became president, a cease-fire took effect, but a formal conclusion to the hostilities was never reached.

The casualties in the Korean War were staggering. The Koreans suffered approximately 1 million military casualties in the war and another 2 million civilian casualties. The estimates of Chinese casualties varies widely from Chinese sources, which put the number at 382,000, to American sources, which put the number at 1 to 1.5 million. There were 142,000 U.S. casualties in the war. All parties discouraged Rhee from resuming hostilities out of concern that further warfare in Korea would spread beyond the region. The conflict led to an arms buildup in the United States and in Western Europe. The war proved a boon to the American economy, but it heightened the domestic Red Scare. More than 50 years after the cease-fire, South Korea and North Korea remain separate nations.

Legislative Reorganization Act (1946)   World War II exposed significant weaknesses in congressional practices, some of which lawmakers were willing to address at the end of the war in 1945. The staffs of both individual lawmakers and congressional committees were too small and often too parochial to be able always to deal effectively with the many wartime concerns before Congress. In 1945, responsibility for revising congressional procedures was given to the Joint Committee on the Organization of Congress. Its findings provided the fodder for the Legislative Reorganization Act of 1946. The number of House committees was reduced from 48 to 19, and the number of Senate committees was reduced from 33 to 15. The legislation provided for professional, enlarged congressional and committee staffs, established a fixed meeting schedule for committees, mandated the retention of committee records, required public committee meetings, and compelled committee chairs to administer legislation according to established procedures. Furthermore, it created the Joint Budget Committee and the Congressional Research Service, a division of the Library of Congress.

Other congressional weaknesses were ignored by the reform measure, specifically the antidemocratic functioning of the seniority system and the autocratic operations of the House Rules Committee, which retained the power to block legislation from the floor. Even with Republican control of Congress after the 1946 midterm elections, the beneficiaries of seniority, potential and actual, were unwilling to change the system in such a way that their powers might be weakened. Thus, the era of committee government remained largely as it had been. Significant changes to the governance of Congress did not come until the 1970s.

Long Telegram (1946)   On February 9, 1946, Soviet premier Joseph Stalin gave a speech that the West termed inflammatory. Stalin argued that world peace was impossible as long as capitalists governed the noncommunist nations. He blamed capitalism for the onset of World War II, and he explained that the Soviet Union, to protect itself, would expand its defense production. George F. Kennan, the chargé d'affaires with the State Department in Moscow, wrote what has become known as the "Long Telegram" on February 22. This document provided a rational analysis of Stalin's intentions and outlined what the author considered the best foreign policy options for the United States.

Kennan argued that Stalin's speech reflected Soviet insecurity about its place in the world. That insecurity led the Soviet Union to adopt a heightened defensive posture and to maintain a dictatorship at home. Kennan concluded that this approach toward the world meant that negotiation with the Soviet Union was fruitless. The Long Telegram marked one of the first efforts by U.S. officials to articulate what would become the doctrine of containment. Because Navy secretary James Forrestal distributed the telegram among leading policy makers, Kennan enhanced his influence within the Truman administration.

Perhaps the most important, if unstated, reason for the telegram's positive reception was that it told policymakers what they wanted to hear, namely, that the ideological and totalitarian imperatives that drove Soviet policy explained Stalin's behavior. When Kennan later anonymously published a longer version of the telegram in *Foreign Affairs* in July 1947, identifying himself as Mr. X, the article had a similar impact on the American public. While it is hard to pinpoint when the general public learned that Mr. X was Kennan, State Department staff knew the identity of the author shortly after publication of the article.

Loyalty Security Program   When World War II ended in 1945, the Truman administration intensified its loyalty programs despite the brief easing of tensions in the world prior to the escalation of the cold war. Many of the wartime security initiatives were retained, including a reorganized and strengthened wiretapping program. Its legality, though, was dubious. The 1946 congressional elections triggered an expansion in the number of loyalty programs. Republicans charged that Democrats were sympathetic to the communist agenda. In response, President Truman first created the Temporary Commission on Employee Loyalty and then a permanent loyalty program for civil servants. The program banned individuals who exhibited doubtful loyalties from gaining employment with the federal government. All known communist organizations were placed on a list, and individuals who had any affiliation with these groups were automatically blocked from being hired. Some of the officials responsible for following the program's guidelines proved to be fanatics in blocking communists or suspected communists and thus they wreaked havoc in the lives of countless innocent people. This loyalty security program proved an important first step toward institutionalizing the postwar Red Scare.

Marshall Plan   Ultimately implemented by the Foreign Assistance Act in 1948, the Marshall Plan was first proposed in June 1947 when Secretary of State George C. Marshall gave the commencement address at Harvard University. One historian of the Truman administration has termed the Marshall Plan a sequel to the Truman Doctrine. At Harvard, Marshall spoke of the importance of large-scale American economic aid to Europe to redress the hunger, poverty, and chaos stemming from World War II. Marshall contended that the aid would be available to all nations of Europe, and that the recipients would have to be coequal partners in the implementation of the program.

European powers were not uniformly enthused about the proposal. The Soviets termed it a tool of American imperialism, avowing that they would not participate. Thus, the plan showed that the United States was willing to cooperate with the Soviet Union, whereas the Russians proved unwilling to act in concert for the betterment of postwar Europe. As such, public opinion in the United States and in Europe ran heavily in favor of the Americans and against the Soviets. Still, had the Soviets participated in receipt of Marshall Plan aid, the implementation of the program very well might have failed.

On July 12, 1947, 16 national delegations representing Austria, Belgium, Denmark, France, Great Britain, Greece, Iceland, Ireland, Italy, Luxembourg, the Netherlands, Norway, Portugal, Sweden, Switzerland, and Turkey met in Paris to deliberate the needs of the participating countries assembled in the Committee of European Economic Cooperation. This committee was responsible for drafting proposals for European reconstruction and submitting them to the U.S. government. In response, the Soviets formed the Molotov Plan for the Soviet Union's satellite nations.

The Truman administration developed and sold the plan as a bipartisan initiative. In December 1947 Truman asked Congress to pass the implementing legislation. The Foreign Assistance Act easily passed both chambers of Congress and provided for $17 billion in aid over four years. American motivations for the Marshall Plan included concerns for meeting humanitarian needs, addressing the long-term impact of war-torn European conditions on the American economy, building a European market for trade with the United States, and preventing the spread of communism in the democratic governments of Europe.

McCarran Internal Security Act (1950)   The KOREAN WAR provided a backdrop for conservatives to push for heightened domestic security measures. Conservatives had first talked of such a bill during the 80th Congress, which met from 1947 to 1949. The proposed legislation outlawed Communist Party activity, mandated the registration of communist organizations with the federal government, and discouraged communist sympathizers. Truman, who disdained this legislation, tried but failed to get the Senate majority leader, Democrat Scott Lucas of Illinois, to block the measure from consideration on the floor of the Senate. Further complicating matters for the president were the actions of leading Senate liberals, who introduced their own internal security bill. This measure provided compulsory detention of suspects in times of emergency while also including habeas corpus protections. The Senate defeated this bill, but Senator Patrick McCarran (D-NV), who had authored the more conservative measure, added the detention provision, without habeas corpus protections, to his bill.

Truman argued that the McCarran measure was unnecessary; existing laws already provided ample protection against subversive behavior. He suggested the following revisions to existing laws as an alternative: stricter espionage enforcement, foreign agent registration, heightened security at military facilities, and detention of deportable aliens. Truman's tactics failed, and lawmakers easily passed the McCarran bill, fearing that a no vote would result in a label of communist sympathizer attached to their names. Truman delivered a strong veto message, but Congress overrode the veto on September 23, 1950. The McCarran Internal Security Act was, as Truman predicted, difficult to enforce. The courts declared much of it unconstitutional. It did achieve some of its goals in that its passage helped quiet dissent in the country for a number of years.

McCarran-Walter Immigration Act (1952)   Sponsored by Senator Pat McCarran (D-NV) and Representative Francis Walter (D-PA), the McCarran-Walter Immigration Act of 1952, also known as the Immigration and Nationality Act, overhauled U.S. immigration, naturalization, and nationality policy. Specifically, it provided that all immigrants be checked at the border to determine whether they were subversives. It also repealed the provision in the Naturalization Act of 1790 that barred nonwhite immigrants from gaining U.S. citizenship. The context for this provision was recognition of the service of Japanese Americans in the U.S. military during World War II. A third provision of the McCarran-Walter legislation provided for a slight increase in the quota of Asian immigrants permitted to enter the United States in any given year. This legislation reflected the xenophobic and anti-communist sentiments of conservatives in Congress. When President Truman vetoed the bill, he acknowledged that its merits—elimination of national and racial barriers to naturalization—did not outweigh its deficiencies—retention of the discriminatory national origin quota system for immigration and severe reduction in the percentage of peoples allowed to immigrate from countries that did not share American democratic values. In the debates over whether to override the presidential veto, critics of the bill made arguments in citing the Declaration of Independence and biblical quotations, and they expressed concerns for offending allies and harming the standing of the United States in the eyes of the world that passage might provoke. The fear of communism and of immigrants proved more powerful; both the Senate and the House voted to override Truman's veto. These immigration restrictions remained in effect until 1965, when, under immigration reform legislation, the quota system was removed.

McCarthyism   McCarthyism is the term generally given to describe the second major Red Scare, which unfolded in the decade after World War II (the first major Red Scare took place after World War I). Named for Senator Joseph R. McCarthy (R-WI), this movement, undertaken to preserve American values, actually undercut many American values and traditions. On February 9, 1950, McCarthy delivered a speech in Wheeling, West Virginia, claiming, without evidence, that communists had infiltrated the U.S. government. Although the origins of McCarthyism predated this speech, the address catapulted him into the forefront of the movement. Furthermore, McCarthyism had both Democratic and Republican architects. For Republicans, McCarthyism became a means to attack the Democratic Party, which they believed had been in power for too long and had become subject to corruption. For Democrats, McCarthyism offered an opportunity to adopt a defensive strategy to thwart accusations of being soft on communism. Truman's LOYALTY SECURITY PROGRAM of 1947 constituted an early example of the latter tendency.

The characteristics of McCarthyism included overblown rhetoric, a lack of consideration regarding who was being attacked, the preeminence of demagoguery over ideology, and a scatter-shot approach to victim selection. It included attacking people without evidence, smearing them for their political beliefs, and charging them with guilt by association. As a result, many people lost their jobs and were blacklisted. Some even committed suicide. McCarthyism reflected both regional and class divides in the country in that it embodied antiestablishment, anti–East Coast, and anti-elitist attitudes. The most significant factors in sustaining McCarthyism, though, were political elites and related interest groups who feared communism together with partisan Republicans who viewed McCarthyism as a path back to majoritarian status. Political polls of voters reveal that only once in 1954 did a majority of the people indicate their support for McCarthy. The irony, then, is that McCarthyism, a movement that relied on antielite appeals, needed elites to sustain its existence.

During the Truman era, Democrats tried to deflect McCarthy by debunking his charges. Senator Millard Tydings (D-MD) chaired a special subcommittee of the Senate Foreign Relations Committee, which, in its majority report, argued that McCarthy's falsehoods and exaggerations were nothing more than a con against the American people. To counter the committee charges, McCarthy and his allies dismissed the Maryland senator as a partisan hack and a communist sympathizer. Ultimately McCarthy's charges against him helped bring about Tydings's defeat for reelection in 1950. McCarthy even went to Maryland to campaign against him. During the Truman era, most Republicans were unwilling to challenge McCarthy even though they typically disliked him and his methods. Maine senator Margaret Chase Smith's declaration of conscience speech before the Senate constituted an exception to the rule. Senator Robert A. Taft (R-OH) knew that his presidential ambitions for 1952 would benefit from allowing McCarthy to continue his accusations so he did nothing to quiet the Wisconsin senator.

When Republicans were returned to political power in the 1952 elections, Democrats made McCarthyism a problem that the new majority party would have to solve for itself. For example, LYNDON B. JOHNSON (D-TX), the minority leader of the U.S. Senate, stressed his party could never be the one to publicly challenge McCarthy. He said doing so would be like having a high school debate over the topic of whether or not communism was good for the United States with the

"You Mean I'm Supposed To Stand On That?"

In this Herblock cartoon, conservative Republican senators Kenneth S. Wherry, Robert A. Taft, and Styles Bridges and Republican national chairman Guy Gabrielson push a reluctant GOP elephant to mount the rickety and unsavory platform. Printed on March 29, 1950, this was the first use of the word "McCarthyism." *(A Herblock Cartoon, copyright by the Herb Block Foundation)*

Democrats taking the affirmative. Indeed, Republicans were compelled to act when McCarthy's tactics threatened the ability of Republicans to govern. That bridge was crossed in 1954 when McCarthy implied that the president, DWIGHT D. EISENHOWER, was soft on communism. The Senate voted to censure McCarthy later that year. He drank heavily and died in 1957. After the censure vote, the issue of McCarthyism lost its political power but not before countless careers—both among the elite and the nonelite—were ruined.

McCarthy's Speech in Wheeling, West Virginia (1950) On February 9, 1950, Senator Joseph R. McCarthy (R-WI), gave a controversial speech before a Republican women's group in Wheeling, West Virginia. He charged that 205 known communists were working in the State Department. Reporters pounced on the story, and skeptics asked to see the list of names McCarthy had referenced in his speech. The senator never provided the list, and when he made additional speeches on the topic, he changed the number to 57. McCarthy likely drew the numbers from FBI investigations of State Department employees, but, if so, most of those individuals no longer worked for the federal government. Put simply, McCarthy's evidence did not hold up to external scrutiny. When he made essentially the same speech in the Senate, he again changed the number, this time to 81. His critics were not able to rebut him because McCarthy adroitly questioned the motives and the allegiances of all who challenged him. For McCarthy, these speeches served the purpose of generating publicity for his political career. Previous to his Wheeling address, he had tried unsuccessfully to gain public acclaim with several other issues. Anticommunism became his signature issue, and he used it to generate publicity and support. Over the next few years McCarthy accused numerous individuals, organizations, and government entities of having communist ties, but he never produced evidence. McCarthy's speech in Wheeling, West Virginia, played into growing fears that communists and Soviet spies were undermining the United States.

National Mental Health Act (1946) President Truman signed the National Mental Health Act on July 3, 1946. It provided for the creation of a National Institute of Mental Health, which was formally established in 1949. The legislation also provided for federally funded research into mental health questions, the mind, the brain, and behavior. It helped pave the way for a dramatic increase in knowledge about mental health and mental illness.

National School Lunch Act (1946) In 1946, President Truman signed the National School Lunch Act, which created the National School Lunch Program. The National School Lunch Program provided federal assistance for food services in public schools, nonprofit private schools, and residential child care institutions. The meals were nutritionally balanced and were available either free or at low cost, depending on the income of the family.

National Security Act (1947) One of Truman's goals for his presidency was to improve the efficiency of the nation's military forces. The proposed changes resulted from observations of the military's effectiveness during World War II. In mid-January 1947, the secretaries of war and of the navy announced a proposal for unifying the armed forces into a single cabinet-level Department of Defense. Legislation to that end went to Congress in February 1947 and was enacted in July. The new organizational structure eliminated cabinet-level positions for the secretaries of war and of the navy. These positions were replaced by the new secretary of defense, who oversaw all branches of the service, which was divided into Departments of the Army, the Navy, and the Air Force. Each department had a secretary who reported to the secretary of defense. The legislation also created the Joint Chiefs of Staff, the members of which included the uniformed heads of each service. Other new agencies resulting from the National Security Act of 1947 included the National Security Council, a presidential advisory body that dealt with issues of strategy; the National Security Resources Board, which had responsibility for supply questions; and the Central Intelligence Agency (CIA), which was responsible for foreign intelligence concerns.

In 1949, the entire apparatus was reorganized. The defense secretary gained additional powers. While the National Security Resources Board never functioned as well as it had been hoped, the National Security Council's usefulness depended on its membership. Nonetheless, the National Security Council did improve communications between the White House and the various military and executive branch entities involved with foreign policy. The CIA proved the most controversial of the new agencies created. Critics doubted its effectiveness. Furthermore, the agency often disregarded its limits and used its secrecy to avoid congressional oversight. Most historians agree that the National Security Act and the new organizational structure it created greatly increased the power of the presidency vis-á-vis Congress.

National Security Council Document 68 (1950) In 1950, the National Security Council issued a report, National Security Council Document 68 (NSC-68), which marked a significant departure in American foreign policy. The architects of NSC-68 worried excessively about the Soviet Union's successful explosion of an atomic bomb in 1949 and about the fall of mainland China to communism also in 1949. They contended (incorrectly as it turned out) that, by 1954, the Soviets would have 100 nuclear bombs to use against the United States. Rejecting the theory that the Soviets could be contained by means of economic, military, political, and psychological tactics, the authors of NSC-68 argued that the Soviets sought world domination. They affirmed that to address this problem, the United States and its allies had to expand both their nuclear and their conventional arsenal until both troop strength and weaponry surpassed that of the Soviets. The report used absolute language, comparing freedoms enjoyed by the democratic peoples in the West to the enslaved communist-ruled peoples of the Soviet Union and its satellite states. It also contended that the economic power of the United States was such that the country could undertake this military buildup without requiring any sacrifice by citizens on the home front.

NSC-68 presented a worst-case scenario, overlooking competing tendencies toward caution within Soviet foreign policy. Furthermore, it posited American strategy not in terms of American strategic interests but in terms of potential Soviet actions. NSC-68 overlooked the overwhelmingly defensive nature of Soviet military action. When President Truman received the report, he neither endorsed nor rejected it. Instead, he sent it along for economic impact studies. The outbreak of the KOREAN WAR in 1950 more than anything else ensured that NSC-68 would be implemented and that the militarization of American foreign policy would intensify.

North Atlantic Treaty Organization   The North Atlantic Treaty Organization (NATO) is a collective security alliance created in 1949 in the aftermath of the BERLIN BLOCKADE AND AIRLIFT. The 12 signatory nations included Belgium, Canada, Denmark, France, Iceland, Italy, Luxembourg, the Netherlands, Norway, Portugal, the United Kingdom, and the United States. Even before the Soviet Union blocked access by the Western powers to West Berlin, the United States Senate had deliberated about the possibility of forming a permanent, regional security alliance with Western Europe. Sponsored by Senator Arthur Vandenberg (R-MI), the Vandenberg Resolution was designed to thwart the threat of a Soviet veto on the United Nations Security Council. Vandenberg worried the Soviets would use the veto to halt any UN peacekeeping efforts. Senators eagerly voted to enact the resolution after a proposal for military aid was removed. The public endorsed the legislative action as borne out by a series of Gallup polls taken in the spring, summer, and fall of 1948.

President Truman began talks with other nations in July 1948, but the fall elections produced a postponement to the negotiations. The delay did little harm; the participants in the talks had already agreed to the idea of a North Atlantic treaty when the negotiations resumed in December 1948. The Americans and Western Europeans shared the same motives in drafting a treaty: fear of standing alone against the Soviets and heightened cold war tensions. All parties to the negotiations agreed that a collective security arrangement would forestall Soviet aggression westward. The most significant

components of the treaty included a provision that stated that an attack on any one of the 12 members equaled an attack on all 12 nations. When the treaty came to the Senate for ratification in July, lawmakers approved it by a vote of 82-13. U.S. participation in NATO marked the first time the country joined in a peacetime military alliance. Even more significant, in the early years of NATO Truman worked to increase the military prowess of the organization. Indeed, NATO and the commitment to regional security alliances became an important component of the government's cold war strategy under the Truman administration.

Potsdam Conference (1945)   In July 1945, President Truman attended the Potsdam Conference of the Big Three—the three main victors of World War II—held in a wealthy suburb of Berlin that had been relatively unscathed by the war. As chair of the sessions with British prime minister Winston Churchill, who was later replaced by Clement Atlee as a result of British elections held in the midst of the conference, and Soviet premier Joseph Stalin, Truman maintained a steady workflow. The goal of the conference was to plan for the occupation and control of Germany, the defeat of Japan, and other problems stemming from the war.

Truman held a positive outlook throughout the meetings, in large part because he learned midway through the discussions that American scientists had successfully detonated the atomic bomb. Consultations within the American delegation about when and how to use the bomb against Japan was, according to one historian, the most important component of the Potsdam Conference. The negotiations at Potsdam led Truman and Stalin to develop a mutual respect for one another.

Regarding postwar issues, the leaders of the Big Three decided that no trace of Nazism would be allowed to remain

Winston Churchill *(left)*, Harry S. Truman *(center)*, and Joseph Stalin *(right)* shake hands at the Potsdam Conference in Germany, July 23, 1945. *(FLS/Associated Press)*

in Germany; democratic elections would be held in the countries of Eastern Europe (this point was not implemented to the satisfaction of the West); there would be guarantees for freedom of speech, the press, and religion; and Germany would be treated as a single country in terms of economic questions (the four zones of occupation worked in practice to make this point moot). Occupying powers in Germany were granted the right to take reparations from their zones. The Big Three agreed to divide among themselves the remaining German munitions. The Soviets asked for access to the Black Sea through Turkey, and the Big Three agreed that negotiations to that effect could move forward with the Turkish government. Decisions about the Polish border, the fate of Italy's colonies, the Soviet desire to control Tangier, and Western requests that the Allies withdraw quickly from Iran were postponed.

Truman believed that the Potsdam Conference had been a success because he thought its terms fair to all competing interests. Truman was happy that agreements about reparations did not require the United States to fund Soviet desires for punishing Germany. More important, the language adopted called for the Allies to continue to work together for the maintenance of peace in the postwar world through the creation of a Council of Foreign Ministers (composed of British, French, Soviet, American, and Chinese officials) that would address lingering wartime issues. After the Potsdam Conference was over, though, Truman became pessimistic about whether the agreements reached there would be carried out and whether the Soviets could be counted upon as allies for peace. His fears were borne out, and, as a result, Truman never participated in another such conference. The mixed results of this conference ultimately led to heightened distrust between the Americans and the Soviets, and they helped to initiate the cold war.

Price Controls   On May 1, 1945, President Truman declared his satisfaction with the work of the Office of Price Administration (OPA), arguing that the agency and the price controls it enforced should remain in effect for at least a year. While price controls provided a check on inflation, consumers benefited from the cost protections but they suffered from the restrictions on available goods. With each month that passed after the war ended, consumer frustration with price controls increased. Furthermore, price controls retarded industrial reconversion by making the return to full production difficult. Congress did not welcome this announcement and resisted action to implement Truman's request. Officials with the National War Labor Board and the Office of Economic Stabilization suggested that wages be held constant or be permitted to rise. War Production Board (WPB) officials wanted to end production controls as soon as possible, but the OPA dissented, recognizing it could not maintain price controls if WPB controls were terminated.

When Truman tried to have it both ways—removal of WPB controls to boost civilian production and retention of OPA controls to prevent inflation—he faced difficulties. Inflation concerns troubled Truman and by the end of 1945 he sought stronger anti-inflation controls through the OPA. The reimposition of construction controls along with new OPA ceilings for cotton prices resulted in much political fallout. Difficulties within the agricultural sector and with labor-management negotiations threatened the effectiveness of controls. In fact, to ease these latter tensions often involved rolling back some controls.

An effective program of price controls also suffered from tensions between the OPA and the Office of War Mobilization and Reconversion. Leadership of the latter organization distrusted the New Deal and viewed controls as a wartime necessity but as an improper means to control business decisions in peacetime. Chester Bowles, the director of the OPA, was a New Deal idealist who drafted policy that would benefit labor concerns. The spring of 1946 saw Congress embroiled in an ideological debate about the future of the OPA. Liberals blamed business interests for the problems arising from price controls while conservatives targeted bureaucrats with unrealistic expectations. Likewise liberals advocated on behalf of consumers and conservatives for business operators.

The resultant legislation provided for a toothless OPA, stripped of all its powers. While liberals blamed the president for this outcome, the fault rested with the business lobby on Capitol Hill and with the lawmakers who acceded to these demands. Never did lawmakers or the administration debate the merits of price controls, whether the program worked and whether it benefited or harmed reconversion. Truman opted to veto this unworkable bill. The ensuing increase in prices forced Congress to produce another bill, not much better than the one Truman vetoed. This time Truman signed it because he knew he would never get anything better from the rural and small town–oriented lawmakers. The president, though, shares a significant portion of the blame for the failure of price controls. His leadership was inconsistent on this issue. The public outcry against Truman and the price control debacle caused one journalist to remark that the president could not even gain reelection in Missouri, so bad were his public approval ratings.

Recognition of Israel (1948)   The question of what to do about Palestine proved a vexing one for President Truman in the immediate postwar era. Because there were numerous constituencies with strong views on how the territory's future should be resolved, Truman hoped that the United Nations would handle the problem, relieving the United States from angering various groups, including Arabs, Jews, the British, and the Soviets. Assessment of the importance of each constituency along with its likely responses guided Truman. He knew that a conflict over Palestine would not end the alliance with Britain. He also believed that the Soviet Union favored relief for Jews, and would likely intervene only if the United States failed to act. He did not mind provoking Arab hostility. Finally, he knew of the strong support given by American Jews for the creation of a Jewish state. The other significant current influencing Truman's decisions on this matter was his own support for a Jewish national homeland, which resonated from his Judeo-Christian moral compass, a perspective that many Americans shared.

The path of Palestine from British mandate to the creation of the state of Israel was tumultuous. In the fall of 1947, the United Nations General Assembly approved the concept of dividing Palestine into Jewish and Arab areas. The potential for success of this plan diminished with the announcement by Britain that it would leave Palestine on May 15, 1948. Further complications resulted from the actions of Jews and Arabs in Palestine, who both sought to claim the better territory, and from the UN's unwillingness to provide troops to ensure a peaceful partition. Divisions within the U.S. government did nothing to improve matters. Truman had already promised Zionist leaders he would support the UN resolution, but the Departments of State and Defense had other ideas. Officials there worried about the Arab reaction and the potential for civil war. Acting without authorization from Truman, the U.S. ambassador to the United Nations called for a different course of action in Palestine—the temporary joint trusteeship of the area by the United States, Britain, and France.

When Truman read about this declaration in the newspapers, he became irate because the trusteeship proposal made him out to be a hypocrite given his public support for the UN partition. To salvage the situation, Truman declared the trusteeship would not replace the partition plan but would function as a bridge between the mandate and the partition. Events in Palestine superseded these machinations.

On May 14, Zionists proclaimed the formation of a Jewish state in Palestine. Truman immediately recognized Israeli statehood. His motives involved both his genuine support for Israel and his concern that the Soviets would act first. An Arab invasion of Israel followed the next day, leading the American government to offer aid to Israel. A United Nations negotiated truce barely held for the remainder of the year before it was broken. The role of the United States in the creation of Israel had a significant impact on U.S. foreign policy for the remainder of the 20th century and into the 21st century. American Jews welcomed Truman's courage and rewarded him politically in the 1948 presidential election. Arabs in the Middle East resented U.S. support for Israel, and American relations with the Arabs deteriorated with each Israeli border conflict. While the formation of Israel solved one generation's problem—the creation of a Jewish homeland for European refugees from the Holocaust—it created new problems for another generation—Arab-Israeli tensions over who should rightfully control Palestine.

Rosenberg Case (1950–1953)   The Rosenberg case resulted indirectly from the Soviet Union's explosion of an atomic bomb in 1949. Americans refused to believe that the Soviets had developed a nuclear weapon on their own just four years after the United States had detonated the world's first atomic bomb, leading many to posit that the Soviets had infiltrated the U.S. government and stolen the information through a massive spy network. Both the FBI and military officials had suspected that Soviet spies had been among the scientists involved with the Manhattan Project that developed the bomb during World War II.

In February 1950 British authorities arrested physicist Klaus Fuchs, who acknowledged spying for the Soviet Union. As its next step the FBI searched for Fuchs's American contact. Julius Rosenberg, a leftist and a junior engineer with the U.S. Army Signal Corps during World War II, became the target. He was arrested on July 17, 1950, and charged with conspiracy to commit espionage but said nothing to authorities. The detention of his wife Ethel Rosenberg, a homemaker, in August did nothing to coax a confession. Neither Rosenberg said a word; they would not even acknowledge membership in the Communist Party.

Their trial nonetheless followed in 1951 and coincided with the height of the KOREAN WAR. The only witness against the Rosenbergs was David Greenglass, Ethel's brother. During the trial, Greenglass, a low-level functionary at Los Alamos, admitted passing a sketch on to the Soviets. He also contended that Julius Rosenberg had recruited him for spy work. The Rosenbergs denied these charges, but they did not object to the government's demand that the sketch be kept secret for the purpose of national security. Their attorney made mistakes in the trial: His cross-examination of David Greenglass was inept, and he did not cross-examine other witnesses. Evidence uncovered decades later indicated that there is little doubt that Julius Rosenberg was involved with Soviet spying; it remains unclear, however, what he told them or whether the material he gave them was of any use. However, Ethel was, by all measures, innocent, and no evidence has surfaced to connect her to spying. Her arrest and involvement in the case involved nothing more than a failed FBI tactic to try to force a confession from Julius.

Nonetheless both Rosenbergs were found guilty and sentenced to execution. While the government had not initially wanted to impose the death sentence—it was another tool used to try to force a confession and uncover further evidence about Soviet spying in the United States—Julius and Ethel remained silent. Despite international appeals to spare their lives, they were executed on June 19, 1953. Hundreds of thousands of people around the world protested this event as a miscarriage of justice. The case has had many meanings over the years. To conservatives it has been viewed as proof of the internal communist threat to American national security. At the time, liberals and radicals in the United States viewed the case as a miscarriage of justice and evidence of oppressive government action.

San Francisco Conference (1945) Scheduled to begin on April 25, 1945, less than two weeks after President FRANKLIN D. ROOSEVELT's death, the San Francisco Conference had as its purpose the drafting of a charter for the United Nations. The four nations sponsoring the conference included the United States, Great Britain, China, and the Soviet Union. The delegation heads for these four nations rotated the chairmanship responsibilities for the sessions. In all, the 45 nations that had declared war on Germany and Japan and had accepted the United Nations Declaration regarding the war were invited to participate.

Once the conference convened, 50 national delegations were in attendance. The Polish government did not attend because the composition of its government had not been decided in time, but Poland was an original signatory power to the charter. The nations added to the conference included Syria, Lebanon, the Byelorussian Soviet Socialist Republic, the Ukrainian Soviet Socialist Republic, Denmark, and Argentina. The national delegates, numbering 850 in all, represented over 80 percent of the world's population. With support staff and journalists included, more than 6,000 people were in San Francisco for the conference. Delegates worked from the Dumbarton Oaks proposals outlined at a meeting near Washington, D.C., in 1944, to draft a charter for a United Nations organization dedicated to the preservation of world peace.

The majority of the work in San Francisco was done outside the plenary sessions where final votes were taken. The success of this preliminary work can be measured by the fact that each part of the charter was approved by the required two-thirds vote. Equally important to the success and the speed of the conference—meetings lasted for just two months—was the Steering Committee of delegation heads. This Steering Committee deliberated all substantive questions before the conference. A smaller Executive Committee of 14 prioritized the work of the 50-member Steering Committee. Four commissions examined at the four main parts of the proposed charter and prepared reports. This hierarchical structure simplified the meeting structure and helped bring consensus regarding the charter.

Controversies involved the relationship between regional security organizations and the proposed United Nations. Ultimately, the delegates recognized the necessity of these arrangements and provided mechanisms for cooperation with the United Nations. Another controversy involved whether territories placed in trusteeship to the United Nations should be prepared for independence or self-government. The delegates decided that either independence or self-governance should be the goal. Disagreement about power of decisions taken by the International Court of Justice led to a decision that its jurisdiction would be voluntary.

The most controversial debate involved whether or not the five permanent members of the Security Council would have veto power over decisions in that body. Small powers contended that the veto would mean that an aggressive big power would render the Security Council meaningless given its veto threat. Big powers countered that since they would bear the largest burden for maintaining world peace they needed the veto. While this quarrel threatened to break up the conference, ultimately the small powers relented. A shared determination to create the best possible international organization caused each delegation to compromise when necessary to ensure a successful conference.

On June 25, 1945, the delegates voted to approve the charter not by the customary show of hands but by standing. Every delegation member and every audience member ultimately stood together; the unanimous approval was met with a thundering ovation. The following day, each delegate signed the Charter of the United Nations and the Statute of the International Court of Justice. Approval of the charter was left to the individual governments of the signatory powers who had to ratify it. By October 24, 1945, the five permanent members of the Security Council—China, France, Great Britain, the Soviet Union, and the United States—along with a majority of the signatory nations had ratified the charter, and the United Nations thus became a reality.

Selective Service Act (1948) From the beginning of his presidency in 1945, Truman had advocated an end to the draft. He wanted to replace the selective service system with a program of universal military training. One of his biographers has argued that Truman's affinity for universal military training stemmed from his preference for citizen soldiers over a professional military. As a young man, he had served in the National Guard and as president he continued to believe in this approach to military service. Liberals and moderates had fought for universal military training during the war years, but they had never succeeded in gaining its passage. His view of the military under this program included small standing services (army, navy, and air force), a National Guard of organized reserves, and a general reserve of individuals who had received universal training. Truman's proposal called for all able-bodied young men to undertake one year of military training along with additional education. Truman hoped that this measure, if passed, would minimize any tendencies toward militarism by ensuring a small standing military. Critics argued that the ultimate result was still conscription and that militarism could not be avoided given the connections between universal training and the standing military. Additionally, critics contended that the one year of training was not sufficient for the specialization that would be required if the recruits were needed for active duty in one of the services.

While universal military training had little likelihood of passage, the reinstitution of the draft in 1948 seemingly spelled the end of Truman's visionary program. Truman had not pushed for the continuation of the draft in 1947, viewing its elimination as an economy measure, but the worsening of world conditions in 1948 led him to call for the reintroduction of the draft. Czechoslovakia had already gone communist. The Soviets had intensified their outward aggressiveness in reaction to the Truman Doctrine with forays into France, Italy, the Far East, and the Middle East. Furthermore, the warfare in Greece had increased, and Finland was on the verge of falling to communists. These realities meant Truman wanted a stronger military available for deployment abroad. Passage of the Selective Service Act of 1948 established the first postwar draft in the United States. It reflected the militarization of the American state. The legislation authorized local draft boards and state directors to carry out the program. Men between the ages of 19 and 26 were subject to the draft; terms of service lasted for 12 months. In 1951, Congress passed the Universal Military Training and Service Act, which lowered the draft age to 18 and lengthened the term of service to two years. Congress also approved the notion of universal military training, but it never implemented the program.

Sexual Behavior in the Human Male, by Alfred Kinsey (1948)

Trained as an entomologist, Dr. Alfred Kinsey was a professor at Indiana University when he began a massive research project in the 1930s into the nature of American sexuality. The jargon-laden text of *Sexual Behavior in the Human Male*, which was replete with charts and graphs, made its way onto the bestseller list when it was published in 1948. Kinsey's companion study, *Sexual Behavior in the Human Female*, published in 1953, also created controversy. The statistics Kinsey included in these books surprised many Americans. Kinsey argued that from 68 to 90 percent of American men had been sexually active prior to marriage as had 50 percent of women. Kinsey reported that 92 percent of men and 62 percent of women had masturbated. Fifty percent of men and 26 percent of women had committed adultery prior to the age of 40, wrote Kinsey. His statistics on homosexuality were the most provocative; according to the two books, 37 percent of men and 13 percent of women had had at least one homosexual experience. These findings raised controversy and provoked a significant backlash. One critic even argued that Kinsey had helped facilitate the advance of communism in the United States. Most significant, though, was the controversy over whether Kinsey's data was accurate. While some of his numbers may not have been entirely accurate, Kinsey publicized important social trends, particularly the increase in premarital sex and the incidence of homosexuality. Furthermore, no better research data from others was available in the late 1940s and early 1950s. Kinsey's greatest contribution to American society was to explain the varieties of sex to his readers.

Shelley v. Kraemer (1948)

The Supreme Court decided the case of *Shelley v. Kraemer* in 1948. The case resulted from a suit the Kraemers, a white couple from St. Louis, Missouri, brought when the Shelleys, a black couple, bought a home in the Kraemers' neighborhood. The Kraemers contended that a restrictive covenant, a legal agreement restricting what owners could do with their homes including to whom they could and could not sell their property, applied to the housing in their neighborhood. While restrictive covenants in real estate can apply to a host of issues, in the first half of the 20th century they typically were used to prevent African Americans and members of other groups from buying property in white neighborhoods. The question before the Supreme Court was whether the racially restrictive covenant violated the equal protection clause of the Fourteenth Amendment to the Constitution. The Court found that in and of themselves restrictive covenants were not unconstitutional, but that when state courts issued injunctions to enforce such agreements that action was contrary to the Fourteenth Amendment. The Supreme Court decision marked an important initial step in eliminating housing discrimination in America.

Steel Seizure Case   See YOUNGSTOWN SHEET AND TUBE COMPANY V. SAWYER (1952)

Sweatt v. Painter (1950)

The Supreme Court decided the *Sweatt v. Painter* case in 1950. It involved law school admissions for African Americans at the University of Texas. Heman Marion Sweatt had applied for admission to the University of Texas law school in 1946, but state law provided for a segregated admissions policy at the university. Sweatt took the university to court, naming University of Texas president Theophilus S. Painter as defendant. To thwart Sweatt, the state attempted to create a separate but equal law school—the School of Law of the Texas State University for Negroes. The Supreme Court deliberated whether this arrangement violated the equal protection clause of the Fourteenth Amendment. It ruled unanimously that Sweatt must be admitted to the university. The newly created law school, contended the justices, was unequal in terms of faculty, course offerings, library resources, opportunities for legal writing, and reputation in the community at large. As such, students who attended the makeshift law school would be at a major disadvantage in their careers. The justices did not find the doctrine of separate but equal unconstitutional but made it easier for such a decision in the future. The case meant that African Americans in Texas would be able to pursue graduate and professional studies at the University of Texas but would still be relegated to Prairie View A&M University or Texas Southern University for any degree programs offered at either of those two black universities. Sweat and several other African Americans enrolled at the law school of the University of Texas for the 1950–51 school year.

Taft-Hartley Act (1947)   Conservative Democrats and Republicans had chafed at the protections enacted under the New Deal for organized labor from the moment they had been passed. During World War II, this coalition passed antistrike legislation, and with the end of the war they hoped to roll back the collective bargaining process at the first available opportunity. Following Republican victories in the election of 1946, Representative Fred A. Hartley, Jr. (R-NJ), the chairman of the House Labor and Education Committee, sponsored the more extreme bill, while Senator Robert A. Taft (R-OH), the chairman of the Senate Labor and Public Welfare Committee, introduced a more moderate bill. The Hartley bill provided for using antitrust laws to control labor unions. It outlawed large-scale picketing, eliminated most industry-wide collective bargaining, and banned bargaining for fringe benefits. The Senate refused to pass this extreme bill, and legislators put forward the Taft offering instead. It took a conference committee to resolve the differences between the two chambers. The legislation that resulted provided for union liability for contract violations, annual union financial reports to the members and to the Department of Labor, a ban on union and corporate campaign contributions, a requirement that union leaders declare annually that they were not communists, a presidentially appointed fact-finding board when a strike threatened the national interest, and a presidentially obtained injunction to halt such strikes for an 80-day settlement period. Additionally, it outlawed secondary boycotts and jurisdictional strikes.

When Congress passed the legislation that emerged from the conference committee in June 1947, Truman faced a difficult decision whether to sign or veto the bill. Labor and liberal groups advocated a veto while business and conservative groups urged him to sign. The fight over the Taft-Hartley bill dominated newspaper headlines and captured significant public attention. Democratic Party insiders told Truman he should veto the bill while the majority of the cabinet advised signing it.

Truman ultimately vetoed the bill, calling it unfeasible, conflict-ridden, inequitable, and a threat to democracy. Congress overrode the veto, and the Taft-Hartley Act became law. In doing so, it became a cause célèbre for liberal politicians who worked hard for its repeal. Liberals and labor activists focused on the discriminatory, divisive features of the law while overlooking the additional power it granted to the government to regulate union activity. These changes did little damage to the union movement. When Truman and the presidents who served after him resorted to the Taft-Hartley

Act, they did so to reinforce the results of collective bargaining and to ensure industrial peace. Some historians have argued that Taft-Hartley was the most significant domestic legislation of the Truman presidency.

Truman Doctrine   *See* AID TO GREECE AND TURKEY

Truman Era Scandals   When Harry Truman became president in 1945, he enjoyed something of a dual reputation. He had garnered much positive public acclaim for his honesty and integrity as chairman of the Senate's Special Committee to Investigate the National Defense Program. In that role he and his Senate colleagues had ferreted out much waste in government and military contracts related to the war effort. His entire political career, though, had been subject to questioning for his early associations with the Pendergast Machine, which played a significant role in Kansas City politics. Historian Andrew J. Dunar has argued that "a strict Baptist morality" tempered his roots in machine politics.

This tension was tested throughout the Truman presidency in a series of scandals, some almost comic by more modern standards. Upon becoming president, Truman's appointments received much scrutiny. While some were meritorious and the individuals performed admirably in their posts, other appointments, and Truman's later defense of their failings, smacked of the cronyism usually associated with machine politics. Perhaps the most significant example was General Harry Vaughan, Truman's longtime friend whom Truman appointed as his White House military aide in 1945. Washington journalists who made their careers searching out scandal identified Vaughan's weaknesses and wrote articles designed to embarrass both Vaughan and the president, including Vaughan's receipt of an award from the Argentine dictatorship. Vaughan endured even more scrutiny in the scandal of the "five percenters." In 1949, he found himself as the leading witness in a congressional probe of Washington influence peddling. For a down payment of $1,000, fees of $500 a month for expenses, and a commission of 5 percent, government contracts could be had without the troubles necessitated by the competitive bidding process.

Truman dismissed the allegations against Vaughan as nothing more than a continuation of the press attacks against his aide and friend. As such, he overlooked the parallels between this investigation and the one he had chaired as a war-time senator. Cooperation with the congressional investigators could have resulted in significant reform of the government procurement system. Members of Congress involved with the investigation also share blame for the incomplete results. The partisan efforts to attack Vaughan and the president by proxy ensured Truman's enmity and the failure to achieve meaningful reform.

Another scandal that affected the Truman administration involved the Reconstruction Finance Corporation

(RFC). This government agency, created during the HERBERT HOOVER administration, had performed well during the depression and the war, but by the time Truman became president it had outlived its usefulness. However, Truman did not cause the problems at the RFC, which included charges of an influence ring and preferential treatment for favored businesses. Senate Democrats held hearings in 1951, which resulted in little substantive change. Even the fate of the RFC was unchanged. Not until the DWIGHT D. EISENHOWER administration in the 1950s was the RFC terminated in favor of the new Small Business Administration.

While the five percenter scandal and the RFC investigation suggested the need for accountability in the spending of public funds, difficulties with the Internal Revenue Service called into question the collection of tax funds. Problems included patronage appointments, which resulted in conflict between tax collectors and civil service bureaucrats.

Truman's biggest weakness, according to the leading student of these scandals, was not his unremitting loyalty to friends but rather his tendency to view people in stark terms as either good or evil. This unwillingness to recognize complexity limited Truman's effectiveness and responsiveness to the challenges that beset his administration.

In 1952, a final scandal involving his attorney general, J. Howard McGrath, reached its climax. McGrath had turned a deaf ear to the problem of organized crime and graft as revealed by Senator Estes Kefauver's Special Committee on Organized Crime in Interstate Commerce in 1950 and 1952. An independent investigator was appointed in 1952, but McGrath fired him. The situation became so bad that Truman fired McGrath in April. By the end of his presidency, Truman had shifted from a belief that the charges of corruption were either political or media-driven and he recognized the real problems that they posed but he was unable to effect real change.

Twenty-second Amendment (1951)   In 1947, the newly elected Republican Congress proposed a constitutional amendment to limit presidents to two terms. While it exempted President Truman, the measure also very much reflected Republican and conservative Democratic animosity toward FRANKLIN D. ROOSEVELT, who had been elected to four terms as president. A sufficient number of states ratified the amendment, which took effect in 1951.

***Youngstown Sheet and Tube Company v. Sawyer* (1952)**
This Supreme Court case resulted from President Truman's seizure of the steel industry in April 1952, and it revealed the limits to presidential power. Truman ordered the secretary of commerce, Charles Sawyer, to seize and operate the steel mills to prevent the United Steelworkers of America from going on strike. The steelworkers had argued for sig-

nificant wage increases, which would have jeopardized the president's anti-inflation program. The government's Wage Stabilization Board found in favor of the steelworkers, but managers of the steel mills were staunchly opposed to the recommendations. Truman's advisers were divided over what he should do next.

Truman argued that a strike would disrupt American progress in the KOREAN WAR. He took this action instead of implementing an 80-day cooling-off period as prescribed by the TAFT-HARTLEY ACT. Truman wanted no part of the Taft-Hartley mechanism because he had vetoed the bill in 1947, which Congress overrode. Nor did he want to go to Congress to secure special legislation governing the steel industry. He used his emergency war powers as commander in chief to take control of the companies in which strikes were threatened. Truman made numerous public appeals for support. He blamed management for the impasse. A general shouting match resulted in Congress with demands for Truman's impeachment and for limiting the federal funds available to run the mills.

More important, the steel mills sought legal redress to combat what they believed to be presidential abuse of power. In their suit against the government the steel companies did not deny the power of the government to take over an industry in an emergency but they argued that such power rested with Congress, not the president. They claimed that Truman had violated the separation of powers, and six members of the Supreme Court agreed. Justice Hugo Black wrote a majority opinion that contended presidents must obey the law even in wartime.

Youngstown Sheet and Tube Company v. Sawyer proved significant in that it attempted to restore a degree of balance to the division of power among the president, Congress, and the courts. Critics had contended that the presidency had grown too powerful in the 1930s and 1940s during the depression, World War II, and the early years of the Cold War. Arguing that no congressional statute gave the president authority to seize the mills and that presidential authority as commander in chief provided no such remedy over strikes, the Court concluded that the executive had no authority to make law, which was the de facto result of the seizure action. While Truman complained that the Supreme Court and Congress exhibited antiquated thinking as regards the case, he nonetheless acceded to the ruling and relinquished control of the steel mills. The labor crisis, though, did not abate. After additional negotiations with management failed, Truman sought congressional authority to seize the mills again but he was rebuffed. By late July 1952, the labor dispute was settled. Steel industry wages and prices increased as did inflation. The steel seizure episode, thus, revealed the limits of presidential power.

Nancy Beck Young

Further Reading

Bell, Jonathan. *The Liberal State on Trial: The Cold War and American Politics in the Truman Years.* New York: Columbia University Press, 2004.

Berman, William C. *The Politics of Civil Rights in the Truman Administration.* Columbus: Ohio State University Press, 1970.

Bernstein, Barton J., and Allan J. Matusow, eds. *The Truman Administration: A Documentary History.* New York: Harper and Row, 1966.

Beschloss, Michael. *The Conquerors: Roosevelt, Truman and the Destruction of Hitler's Germany, 1941–1945.* New York: Simon and Schuster, 2002.

Caute, David. *The Great Fear: The Anti-communist Purge under Truman and Eisenhower.* New York: Simon and Schuster, 1978.

Culver, John C., and John Hyde. *American Dreamer: The Life and Times of Henry A. Wallace.* New York: Norton, 2000.

Davies, Richard O. *Housing Reform during the Truman Administration.* Columbia: University of Missouri Press, 1966.

Davis, Polly Ann. *Alben W. Barkley, Senate Majority Leader and Vice President.* New York: Garland, 1979.

Documentary History of the Truman Presidency. 20 vols. Edited by Dennis Merrill. Bethesda, Md.: University Publications of America, 1995– .

Donaldson, Gary A. *Truman Defeats Dewey.* Lexington: University Press of Kentucky, 1999.

Donovan, Robert J. *Conflict and Crisis: The Presidency of Harry S. Truman, 1945–1948.* New York: Norton, 1977.

———. *Tumultuous Years: The Presidency of Harry S. Truman, 1949–1953.* New York: Norton, 1982.

Dunar, Andrew J. *The Truman Scandals and the Politics of Morality.* Columbia: University of Missouri Press, 1984.

Elsey, George McKee. *An Unplanned Life: A Memoir.* Columbia: University of Missouri Press, 2005.

Ferrell, Robert H. *Choosing Truman: The Democratic Convention of 1944.* Columbia: University of Missouri Press, 1994.

———. *Harry S. Truman: A Life.* Columbia: University of Missouri Press, 1994.

———. *Harry S. Truman and the Cold War Revisionists.* Columbia: University of Missouri Press, 2006.

———. *Harry S. Truman and the Modern American Presidency.* Boston: Little, Brown, 1983.

Ferrell, Robert H., ed. *Truman in the White House: The Diary of Eben A. Ayers.* Columbia: University of Missouri Press, 1991.

Fordham, Benjamin O. *Building the Cold War Consensus: The Political Economy of U.S. National Security Policy, 1949–51.* Ann Arbor: University of Michigan Press, 1998.

Freeland, Richard M. *The Truman Doctrine and the Origins of McCarthyism: Foreign Policy, Domestic Politics, and Internal Security, 1946–1948.* New York: Knopf, 1971.

Goldzwig, Steven R. *Truman's Whistle-Stop Campaign.* College Station: Texas A&M University Press, 2008.

Gullan, Harold I. *The Upset That Wasn't: Harry S. Truman and the Crucial Election of 1948.* Chicago: Ivan R. Dee, 1998.

Hamby, Alonzo L. *Beyond the New Deal: Harry S. Truman and American Liberalism.* New York: Columbia University Press, 1973.

———. *Man of the People: A Life of Harry S. Truman.* New York: Oxford University Press, 1995.

Hartmann, Susan M. *Truman and the 80th Congress.* Columbia: University of Missouri Press, 1971.

Haynes, Richard F. *The Awesome Power, Harry S. Truman as Commander in Chief.* Baton Rouge: Louisiana State University Press, 1973.

Hechler, Ken. *Working with Truman: A Personal Memoir of the White House Years.* New York: Putnam, 1982.

Heller, Francis H., ed. *The Truman White House: The Administration of the Presidency, 1945–1953.* Lawrence: University Press of Kansas, 1980.

Hess, Gary R. *Presidential Decisions for War: Korea, Vietnam, and the Persian Gulf.* Baltimore: Johns Hopkins University Press, 2001.

Hogan, Michael J. *A Cross of Iron: Harry S. Truman and the Origins of the National Security State, 1945–1954.* New York: Cambridge University Press, 1998.

Kaufman, Burton I. *The Korean War: Challenges in Crisis, Credibility, and Command.* Philadelphia: Temple University Press, 1986.

Kirkendall, Richard S., ed. *Harry's Farewell: Interpreting and Teaching the Truman Presidency.* Columbia: University of Missouri Press, 2004.

Kutler, Stanley I. *The American Inquisition: Justice and Injustice in the Cold War.* New York: Hill and Wang, 1982.

Lee, R. Alton. *Truman and Taft-Hartley: A Question of Mandate.* Lexington: University of Kentucky Press, 1966.

Leuchtenburg, William E. *The White House Looks South: Franklin D. Roosevelt, Harry S. Truman, Lyndon B. Johnson.* Baton Rouge: Louisiana State University Press, 2005.

Marcus, Maeva. *Truman and the Steel Seizure Case: The Limits of Presidential Power.* New York: Columbia University Press, 1977.

Markowitz, Norman D. *The Rise and Fall of the People's Century: Henry A. Wallace and American Liberalism, 1941–1948.* New York: Free Press, 1973.

Matusow, Allen J. *Farm Policies and Politics in the Truman Years.* Cambridge, Mass.: Harvard University Press, 1967.

McCoy, Donald R. *The Presidency of Harry S. Truman.* Lawrence: University Press of Kansas, 1984.

McCoy, Donald R., and Richard T. Ruetten. *Quest and Response: Minority Rights and the Truman Administration.* Lawrence: University Press of Kansas, 1973.

McCullough, David. *Truman.* New York: Simon and Schuster, 1992.

McFarland, Keith D., and David L. Roll. *Louis Johnson and the Arming of America: The Roosevelt and Truman Years.* Bloomington: Indiana University Press, 2005.

Merrill, Dennis, ed. *The Documentary History of the Harry S. Truman Presidency.* 35 vols. Bethesda, Md.: University Publications of America, 1995–   .

Messer, Robert L. *The End of an Alliance: James F. Byrnes, Roosevelt, Truman, and the Origins of the Cold War.* Chapel Hill: University of North Carolina Press, 1982.

Mitchell, Franklin D. *Harry S. Truman and the News Media: Contentious Relations, Belated Respect.* Columbia: University of Missouri Press, 1998.

Neal, Steve. *Harry and Ike: The Partnership That Remade the Postwar World.* New York: Scribner, 2001.

Offner, Arnold A. *Another Such Victory: President Truman and the Cold War, 1945–1953.* Palo Alto, Calif.: Stanford University Press, 2002.

Pemberton, William E. *Harry S. Truman: Fair Dealer and Cold Warrior.* Boston: Twayne Publishers, 1989.

Perret, Geoffrey. *Commander in Chief: How Truman, Johnson, and Bush Turned a Presidential Power into a Threat to America's Future.* New York: Farrar, Straus and Giroux, 2007.

Peterson, F. Ross. *Prophet without Honor: Glen H. Taylor and the Fight for American Liberalism.* Lexington: University Press of Kentucky, 1974.

Pierpaoli, Paul G., Jr. *Truman and Korea: The Political Culture of the Early Cold War.* Columbia: University of Missouri Press, 1999.

Poen, Monte M. *Harry S. Truman versus the Medical Lobby: The Genesis of Medicare.* Columbia: University of Missouri Press, 1979.

Public Papers of the Presidents of the United States, Harry S. Truman, Containing the Public Messages, Speeches, and Statements of the President, 1945–1953. 8 vols. Washington, D.C.: U.S. Government Printing Office, 1961–1966.

Reichard, Gary W. *Politics as Usual: The Age of Truman and Eisenhower.* Arlington Heights, Ill.: Harlan Davidson, 1988.

Roosevelt, Eleanor. *Eleanor and Harry: The Correspondence of Eleanor Roosevelt and Harry S. Truman.* Edited by Steve Neal. New York: Scribner, 2002.

Savage, Sean J. *Truman and the Democratic Party.* Lexington: University Press of Kentucky, 1997.

Schapsmeier, Edward L., and Frederick H. Schapsmeier. *Prophet in Politics: Henry A. Wallace and the War Years, 1940–1965.* Ames: Iowa State University Press, 1970.

Schmidt, Karl M. *Henry A. Wallace: Quixotic Crusade, 1948.* Syracuse, N.Y.: Syracuse University Press, 1960.

Schrecker, Ellen. *Many Are the Crimes: McCarthyism in America.* Boston: Little, Brown, 1998.

Smith, Richard Norton. *Thomas E. Dewey and His Times.* New York: Simon and Schuster, 1982.

Snetsinger, John. *Truman, the Jewish Vote, and the Creation of Israel.* Palo Alto, Calif.: Hoover Institution Press, 1974.

Spalding, Elizabeth Edwards. *The First Cold Warrior: Harry Truman, Containment, and the Remaking of Liberal Internationalism.* Lexington: University Press of Kentucky, 2006.

Stone, I. F. *The Truman Era.* New York: Random House, 1972.

Stueck, William Whitney, Jr. *The Road to Confrontation: American Policy toward China and Korea, 1947–1950.* Chapel Hill: University of North Carolina Press, 1981.

Theoharis, Athan G. *Seeds of Repression: Harry S. Truman and the Origins of McCarthyism.* Chicago: Quadrangle Books, 1971.

———. *The Yalta Myths: An Issue in U.S. Politics, 1945–1955.* Columbia: University of Missouri Press, 1970.

Truman, Harry S. *The Autobiography of Harry S. Truman.* Edited by Robert H. Ferrell. Boulder: Colorado Associated University Press, 1980.

———. *Dear Bess: The Letters of Harry to Bess Truman, 1910–1959.* Edited by Robert H. Ferrell. New York: Norton, 1983.

———. *Defending the West: The Truman-Churchill Correspondence, 1945–1960.* Edited by G. W. Sand. Westport, Conn.: Praeger, 2004.

———. *Letters Home by Harry Truman.* Edited by Monte M. Poen. New York: Putnam, 1983.

———. *Memoirs.* 2 vols. Garden City, N.Y.: Doubleday, 1955–1956.

———. *Miracle of '48: Harry Truman's Major Campaign Speeches and Selected Whistle-Stops.* Edited by Steve Neal. Carbondale: Southern Illinois University Press, 2003.

———. *Mr. Citizen.* New York: Bernard Geis Associates, 1960.

———. *Mr. President.* New York: Farrar, Straus and Young, 1952.

———. *Off the Record: The Private Papers of Harry S. Truman.* Edited by Robert H. Ferrell. New York: Harper and Row, 1980.

———. *Strictly Personal and Confidential: The Unmailed Letters of Harry Truman.* Edited by Monte M. Poen. Boston: Little, Brown, 1982.

———. *Where the Buck Stops: Personal and Private Writings of Harry S. Truman.* Edited by Margaret Truman. New York: Warner Books, 1989.

Truman, Margaret. *Harry S. Truman.* New York: Morrow, 1972.

Truman, Margaret, ed. *Letters from Father: The Truman Family's Personal Correspondence.* New York: Arbor House, 1981.

Walker, J. Samuel. *Prompt and Utter Destruction: Truman and the Use of Atomic Bombs against Japan.* Chapel Hill: University of North Carolina Press, 1997.

Walton, Richard J. *Henry Wallace, Harry Truman, and the Cold War.* New York: Viking, 1976.

White, Graham, and John Maze. *Henry A. Wallace: His Search for a New World Order.* Chapel Hill: University of North Carolina Press, 1995.

DOCUMENTS

—͡ຓ—

Document One: President Harry S. Truman, Statement Announcing the Use of the Atomic Bomb at Hiroshima, August 6, 1945

On August 6, 1945, the United States dropped the first atomic bomb on the Japanese city of Hiroshima. Later that day, President Truman explained and justified the use of the weapon against the Japanese during World War II.

SIXTEEN HOURS AGO an American airplane dropped one bomb on Hiroshima, an important Japanese Army base. That bomb had more power than 20,000 tons of T.N.T. It had more than two thousand times the blast power of the British "Grand Slam" which is the largest bomb ever yet used in the history of warfare.

The Japanese began the war from the air at Pearl Harbor. They have been repaid many fold. And the end is not yet. With this bomb we have now added a new and revolutionary increase in destruction to supplement the growing power of our armed forces. In their present form these bombs are now in production and even more powerful forms are in development.

It is an atomic bomb. It is a harnessing of the basic power of the universe. The force from which the sun draws its power has been loosed against those who brought war to the Far East.

Before 1939, it was the accepted belief of scientists that it was theoretically possible to release atomic energy. But no one knew any practical method of doing it. By 1942, however, we knew that the Germans were working feverishly to find a way to add atomic energy to the other engines of war with which they hoped to enslave the world. But they failed. We may be grateful to Providence that the Germans got the V-1's and V-2's late and in limited quantities and even more grateful that they did not get the atomic bomb at all.

The battle of the laboratories held fateful risks for us as well as the battles of the air, land and sea, and we have now won the battle of the laboratories as we have won the other battles.

Beginning in 1940, before Pearl Harbor, scientific knowledge useful in war was pooled between the United States and Great Britain, and many priceless helps to our victories have come from that arrangement. Under that general policy the research on the atomic bomb was begun. With American and British scientists working together we entered the race of discovery against the Germans.

The United States had available the large number of scientists of distinction in the many needed areas of knowledge. It had the tremendous industrial and financial resources necessary for the project and they could be devoted to it without undue impairment of other vital war work. In the United States the laboratory work and the production plants, on which a substantial start had already been made, would be out of reach of enemy bombing, while at that time Britain was exposed to constant air attack and was still threatened with the possibility of invasion. For these reasons Prime Minister Churchill and President Roosevelt agreed that it was wise to carry on the project here. We now have two great plants and many lesser works devoted to the production of atomic power. Employment during peak construction numbered 125,000 and over 65,000 individuals are even now engaged in operating the plants. Many have worked there for two and a half years. Few know what they have been producing. They see great quantities of material going in and they see nothing coming out of these plants, for the physical size of the explosive charge is exceedingly small. We have spent two billion dollars on the greatest scientific gamble in history—and won.

But the greatest marvel is not the size of the enterprise, its secrecy, nor its cost, but the achievement of scientific brains in putting together infinitely complex pieces of knowledge held by many men in different fields of science into a workable plan. And hardly less marvelous has been the capacity of industry to design, and of labor to operate, the machines and methods to do things never done before so that the brain child of many minds came forth in physical shape and performed as it was supposed to do. Both science and industry worked under the direction of the United States Army, which achieved a unique success in managing so diverse a problem in the advancement of knowledge in an amazingly short time. It is doubtful if such another combination could be got together in the world. What has been done is the greatest achievement of organized science in history. It was done under high pressure and without failure.

We are now prepared to obliterate more rapidly and completely every productive enterprise the Japanese have above ground in any city. We shall destroy their docks, their factories, and their communications. Let there be no mistake; we shall completely destroy Japan's power to make war.

It was to spare the Japanese people from utter destruction that the ultimatum of July 26 was issued at Potsdam. Their leaders promptly rejected that ultimatum. If they do not now accept our terms they may expect a rain of ruin from the air, the like of which has never been seen on this earth. Behind this air attack will follow sea and land forces in such numbers and power as they have not yet seen and with the fighting skill of which they are already well aware. . . .

The fact that we can release atomic energy ushers in a new era in man's understanding of nature's forces. Atomic energy may in the future supplement the power that now comes from coal, oil, and falling water, but at present it cannot be produced on a basis to compete with them commercially. Before that comes there must be a long period of intensive research.

It has never been the habit of the scientists of this country or the policy of this Government to withhold from the world scientific knowledge. Normally, therefore, everything about the work with atomic energy would be made public.

But under present circumstances it is not intended to divulge the technical processes of production or all the military applications, pending further examination of possible methods of protecting us and the rest of the world from the danger of sudden destruction.

I shall recommend that the Congress of the United States consider promptly the establishment of an appropriate commission to control the production and use of atomic power within the United States. I shall give further consideration and make further recommendations to the Congress as to how atomic power can become a powerful and forceful influence towards the maintenance of world peace.

Source: Public Papers of the Presidents of the United States, Harry S. Truman, Containing the Public Messages, Speeches, and Statements of the President, 1945 (Washington, D.C.: U.S. Government Printing Office, 1961), 197–200.

Document Two: White House Statement Concerning Controls Over the Price and Distribution of Meat, May 3, 1946

With World War II over for more than eight months, demand for the removal of price controls intensified in the United States. In the following statement issued on May 3, 1946, President Truman explained his position.

DURING the last few days there has been a series of unfortunate misinterpretations of the Government's intentions with regard to price and distribution controls on meat. This misunderstanding has apparently resulted from a confusion of terms.

The President wishes it clearly understood that as long as there are dangerous upward pressures on meat prices and as long as the Government has the authority to deal with them, price controls on livestock and meat will be firmly maintained.

Both Secretary of Agriculture Anderson and Economic Stabilization Director Bowles concur in this view.

The confusion on this question has apparently risen from misunderstanding of the term "meat controls" as it was used at the President's press conference on Thursday, May 2, and at a hearing of the Senate Banking and Currency Committee on May 1 at which Secretary Anderson testified. Both the President and Secretary Anderson took the term to mean, not price controls, but rather the slaughter controls which were reinstituted on April 28 by the Office of Price Administration and the Department of Agriculture.

These controls are designed to direct the nation's livestock supplies back into established, legitimate channels and to reduce the operations of slaughterers who have increased their production to such an extent that they have upset normal meat distribution and have made it difficult to enforce price ceilings.

As Secretary Anderson pointed out in his Senate Committee testimony, this slaughter quota program brought the black market in livestock and meat under control after it was put into effect in April, 1945. It was dropped after V-J Day when meat supplies seemed ample.

There is every reason to believe that the slaughter control plan will work effectively again. But if for any reason it does not appear to be producing the desired results, other additional measures will be used to whatever extent seems necessary.

However, neither the President nor Secretary Anderson suggested that livestock and meat price controls could be abandoned with the demand for meat at its present extremely high level in relation to supply.

Source: Public Papers of the Presidents of the United States, Harry S. Truman, Containing the Public Messages, Speeches, and Statements of the President, 1946 (Washington, D.C.: U.S. Government Printing Office, 1962), 231.

Document Three: President Truman, Special Message to Congress on Greece and Turkey: The Truman Doctrine, March 12, 1947

With the articulation of the Truman Doctrine on March 12, 1947, the president applied the theory of containment to the practical workings of U.S. foreign policy, establishing the precedent of using foreign aid to achieve results favorable to the United States in the cold war.

Mr. President, Mr. Speaker, Members of the Congress of the United States:

The gravity of the situation which confronts the world today necessitates my appearance before a joint session of the Congress. The foreign policy and the national security of this country are involved.

One aspect of the present situation, which I present to you at this time for your consideration and decision, concerns Greece and Turkey.

The United States has received from the Greek Government an urgent appeal for financial and economic assistance. Preliminary reports from the American Economic Mission now in Greece and reports from the American Ambassador in Greece corroborate the statement of the Greek Government that assistance is imperative if Greece is to survive as a free nation.

I do not believe that the American people and the Congress wish to turn a deaf ear to the appeal of the Greek Government. . . .

The very existence of the Greek state is today threatened by the terrorist activities of several thousand armed men, led by Communists, who defy the government's authority at a number of points, particularly along the northern boundaries. A Commission appointed by the United Nations Security Council is at present investigating disturbed conditions in northern Greece and alleged border violations along the frontier between Greece on the one hand and Albania, Bulgaria, and Yugoslavia on the other.

Meanwhile, the Greek Government is unable to cope with the situation. The Greek army is small and poorly equipped. It needs supplies and equipment if it is to restore authority to the government throughout Greek territory.

Greece must have assistance if it is to become a self-supporting and self-respecting democracy. The United States must supply this assistance. We have already extended to Greece certain types of relief and economic aid but these are inadequate. There is no other country to which democratic Greece can turn. No other nation is willing and able to provide the necessary support for a democratic Greek government.

The British Government, which has been helping Greece, can give no further financial or economic aid after March 31. Great Britain finds itself under the necessity of reducing or liquidating its commitments in several parts of the world, including Greece.

We have considered how the United Nations might assist in this crisis. But the situation is an urgent one requiring immediate action, and the United Nations and its related organizations are not in a position to extend help of the kind that is required. . . .

Greece's neighbor, Turkey, also deserves our attention. The future of Turkey as an independent and economically sound state is clearly no less important to the freedom-loving peoples of the world than the future of Greece. The circumstances in which Turkey finds itself today are considerably different from those of Greece. Turkey has been spared the disasters that have beset Greece. And during the war, the United States and Great Britain furnished Turkey with material aid. Nevertheless, Turkey now needs our support.

Since the war Turkey has sought additional financial assistance from Great Britain and the United States for the purpose of effecting that modernization necessary for the maintenance of its national integrity. That integrity is essential to the preservation of order in the Middle East.

The British Government has informed us that, owing to its own difficulties, it can no longer extend financial or economic aid to Turkey. As in the case of Greece, if Turkey is to have the assistance it needs, the United States must supply it. We are the only country able to provide that help. . . .

At the present moment in world history nearly every nation must choose between alternative ways of life. The choice is too often not a free one.

One way of life is based upon the will of the majority, and is distinguished by free institutions, representative government, free elections, guarantees of individual liberty, freedom of speech and religion, and freedom from political oppression.

The second way of life is based upon the will of a minority forcibly imposed upon the majority. It relies upon terror and oppression, a controlled press and radio, fixed elections, and the suppression of personal freedoms.

I believe that it must be the policy of the United States to support free peoples who are resisting attempted subjugation by armed minorities or by outside pressures.

I believe that we must assist free peoples to work out their own destinies in their own way.

I believe that our help should be primarily through economic and financial aid which is essential to economic stability and orderly political processes.

The world is not static, and the status quo is not sacred. But we cannot allow changes in the status quo in violation of the Charter of the United Nations by such methods as coercion, or by such subterfuges as political infiltration. In helping free and independent nations to maintain their freedom, the United States will be giving effect to the principles of the Charter of the United Nations.

It is necessary only to glance at a map to realize that the survival and integrity of the Greek nation are of grave importance in a much wider situation. If Greece should fall under the control of an armed minority, the effect upon its neighbor, Turkey, would be immediate and serious. Confusion and disorder might well spread throughout the entire Middle East.

Moreover, the disappearance of Greece as an independent state would have a profound effect upon those countries in Europe whose peoples are struggling against great difficulties to maintain their freedoms and their independence while they repair the damages of war.

It would be an unspeakable tragedy if these countries, which have struggled so long against overwhelming odds, should lose that victory for which they sacrificed so much. Collapse of free institutions and loss of independence would be disastrous not only for them but for the world. Discouragement and possibly failure would quickly be the lot of neighboring peoples striving to maintain their freedom and independence.

Should we fail to aid Greece and Turkey in this fateful hour, the effect will be far reaching to the West as well as to the East. We must take immediate and resolute action.

I therefore ask the Congress to provide authority for assistance to Greece and Turkey in the amount of $400,000,000 for the period ending June 30, 1948. . . .

The seeds of totalitarian regimes are nurtured by misery and want. They spread and grow in the evil soil of poverty and strife. They reach their full growth when the hope of a people for a better life has died. We must keep that hope alive. The free peoples of the world look to us for support in maintaining their freedoms.

If we falter in our leadership, we may endanger the peace of the world—and we shall surely endanger the welfare of this Nation.

Great responsibilities have been placed upon us by the swift movement of events. I am confident that the Congress will face these responsibilities squarely.

Source: Public Papers of the Presidents of the United States, Harry S. Truman, Containing the Public Messages, Speeches, and Statements of the President, 1947 (Washington, D.C.: U.S. Government Printing Office, 1963), 176–180.

Document Four: President Truman, Radio Address to the American People on the Veto of the Taft-Hartley Bill, June 20, 1947

Republicans and conservatives had long chafed at the National Labor Relations Act, the 1935 law that guaranteed workers and unions the right to collective bargaining. After gaining control of Congress in the 1946 midterm elections, Republicans passed the Taft-Hartley bill, trimming the rights of organized labor. In this stinging veto, President Truman won back support from labor unions, who had initially questioned his credentials as a liberal Democrat. A few days later, however, Congress overrode the veto and enacted Taft-Hartley into law.

My fellow countrymen:

At noon today I sent to Congress a message vetoing the Taft-Hartley labor bill. I vetoed this bill because I am convinced it is a bad bill. It is bad for labor, bad for management, and bad for the country.

I had hoped that the Congress would send me a labor bill I could sign.

I have said before, and I say it now, that we need legislation to correct abuses in the field of labor relations.

Last January I made specific recommendations to the Congress as to the kind of labor legislation we should have immediately. I urged that the Congress provide for a commission, to be made up of representatives of the Congress, the public, labor and management, to study the entire field of labor management relations and to suggest what additional laws we should have.

I believe that my proposals were accepted by the great majority of our people as fair and just.

If the Congress had accepted those recommendations, we would have today the basis for improved labor-management relations. I would gladly have signed a labor bill if it had taken us in the right direction of stable, peaceful labor relations—even though it might not have been drawn up exactly as I wished.

I would have signed a bill with some doubtful features if, taken as a whole, it had been a good bill.

But the Taft-Hartley bill is a shocking piece of legislation.

It is unfair to the working people of this country. It clearly abuses the right, which millions of our citizens now enjoy, to join together and bargain with their employers for fair wages and fair working conditions.

Under no circumstances could I have signed this bill.

The restrictions that this bill places on our workers go far beyond what our people have been led to believe. This is no innocent bill.

It is interesting to note that on June 4, Congressman Hartley on the floor of the House of Representatives, made the following statement, and I quote: "You are going to find there is more in this bill than may meet the eye."

That is a revealing description of this bill by one of its authors.

There is so much more in it than the people have been led to believe, that I am sure that very few understand what the Taft-Hartley bill would do if it should become law.

That is why I am speaking to you tonight. I want you to know the real meaning of this bill.

We have all been told, by its proponents, that this is a "moderate" bill. We have been told that the bill was "harsh" and "drastic" when it was first passed by the House of Representatives, but that the Senate had persuaded the House to drop out the harsh provisions and that the final bill-the bill sent to me-was "mild" and "moderate."

But I found no truth in the claims that the bill sent to me was mild or moderate. I found that the basic purpose and much of the language of the original House of Representatives bill were still in the final bill. In fact, the final bill follows the provisions of the original House bill in at least 36 separate places.

We have all been told that the Taft-Hartley bill is favorable to the wage earners of this country. It has been claimed that workers need to be saved from their own folly and that this bill would provide the means of salvation. Some people have called this bill the "workers' bill of rights."

Let us see what this bill really would do to our workingmen.

The bill is deliberately designed to weaken labor unions. When the sponsors of the bill claim that by weakening unions, they are giving rights back to individual workingmen, they ignore the basic reason why unions are important in our democracy. Unions exist so that laboring men can bargain with their employers on a basis of equality. Because of unions, the living standards of our working people have increased steadily until they are today the highest in the world.

A bill which would weaken unions would undermine our national policy of collective bargaining. The Taft-Hartley bill would do just that. It would take us back in the direction of the old evils of individual bargaining. It would take the bargaining power away from the workers and give more power to management.

This bill would even take away from our workingmen some bargaining fights which they enjoyed before the Wagner Act was passed 12 years ago.

If we weaken our system of collective bargaining, we weaken the position of every workingman in the country.

This bill would again expose workers to the abuses of labor injunctions.

It would make unions liable for damage suits for actions which have long been considered lawful.

This bill would treat all unions alike. Unions which have fine records, with long years of peaceful relations with management, would be hurt by this bill just as much as the few troublemakers. . . .

Another defect is that in trying to correct labor abuses the Taft-Hartley bill goes so far that it would threaten fundamental democratic freedoms. One provision undertakes to prevent political contributions and expenditures by labor organizations and corporations. This provision would forbid a union newspaper from commenting on candidates in national elections. It might well prevent an incorporated radio network from spending any money in connection with the national convention of a political party. It might even prevent the League of Women Voters—which is incorporated-from using its funds to inform its members about the record of a political candidate.

I regard this provision of the Taft-Hartley bill as a dangerous challenge to free speech and our free press.

Source: Public Papers of the Presidents of the United States, Harry S. Truman, Containing the Public Messages, Speeches, and Statements of the President, 1947 (Washington, D.C.: U.S. Government Printing Office, 1963), 298–301.

Document Five: President Truman, Statement Announcing Recognition of the State of Israel, May 14, 1948

After intense lobbying, President Truman decided to recognize the state of Israel, a decision that has had momentous consequences for U.S. relations with the Middle East. He issued a brief statement on May 14, 1948, to that effect.

THIS GOVERNMENT has been informed that a Jewish state has been proclaimed in Palestine, and recognition has been requested by the provisional government thereof.

The United States recognizes the provisional government as the de facto authority of the new State of Israel.

Source: Public Papers of the Presidents of the United States, Harry S. Truman, Containing the Public Messages, Speeches, and Statements of the President, 1948 (Washington, D.C.: U.S. Government Printing Office, 1964), 258.

Document Six: President Truman, Address to the American People on the Situation in Korea, July 19, 1950

In this speech delivered on July 19, 1950, President Truman explained the origins of the U.S. intervention in Korea, a decision that revealed new assertions of presidential power to wage war and the primacy of Asian concerns in the cold war.

. . . Korea is a small country, thousands of miles away, but what is happening there is important to every American.

On Sunday, June 25th, Communist forces attacked the Republic of Korea.

This attack has made it clear, beyond all doubt, that the international Communist movement is willing to use armed invasion to conquer independent nations. An act of aggression such as this creates a very real danger to the security of all free nations.

The attack upon Korea was an outright breach of the peace and a violation of the Charter of the United Nations. By their actions in Korea, Communist leaders have demonstrated their contempt for the basic moral principles on which the United Nations is founded. This is a direct challenge to the efforts of the free nations to build the kind of world in which men can live in freedom and peace.

This challenge has been presented squarely. We must meet it squarely. . . .

In December 1948, the Soviet Union stated that it had withdrawn its troops from northern Korea and that a local government had been established there. However, the Communist authorities never have permitted the United Nations observers to visit northern Korea to see what was going on behind that part of the Iron Curtain.

It was from that area, where the Communist authorities have been unwilling to let the outside world see what was going on, that the attack was launched against the Republic of Korea on June 25th. That attack came without provocation and without warning. It was an act of raw aggression, without a shadow of justification.

I repeat that it was an act of raw aggression. It had no justification whatever.

The Communist invasion was launched in great force, with planes, tanks, and artillery. The size of the attack, and the speed with which it was followed up, make it perfectly plain that it had been plotted long in advance.

As soon as word of the attack was received, Secretary of State Acheson called me at Independence, Mo., and informed me that, with my approval, he would ask for an immediate meeting of the United Nations Security Council. The Security Council met just 24 hours after the Communist invasion began.

One of the main reasons the Security Council was set up was to act in such cases as this—to stop outbreaks of aggression in a hurry before they develop into general conflicts. In this case the Council passed a resolution which called for the invaders of Korea to stop fighting, and to withdraw. The Council called on all members of the United Nations to help carry out this resolution. . . .

The Security Council then met again. It recommended that members of the United Nations help the Republic of Korea repel the attack and help restore peace and security in that area.

Fifty-two of the 59 countries which are members of the United Nations have given their support to the action taken by the Security Council to restore peace in Korea.

These actions by the United Nations and its members are of great importance. The free nations have now made it clear that lawless aggression will be met with force. The free nations have learned the fateful lesson of the 1930's. That lesson is that aggression must be met firmly. Appeasement leads only to further aggression and ultimately to war. . . .

Source: Public Papers of the Presidents of the United States, Harry S. Truman, Containing the Public Messages, Speeches, and Statements of the President, 1950 (Washington, D.C.: U.S. Government Printing Office, 1965), 537–542.

Dwight D. Eisenhower

October 14, 1890–March 28, 1969

Thirty-fourth President of the United States
January 20, 1953–January 20, 1961

◈◈ DWIGHT D. EISENHOWER ◈◈

Place of Birth: Denison, Texas

Date of Birth: October 14, 1890

Places of Residence: Texas, Kansas, New York

Class Background: modest

Father's Career: shopkeeper and laborer

Mother's Career: homemaker

Number of Siblings: six

Religion: Presbyterian

Education: graduated West Point, 1915

Political Party: Republican

Military Service: World War I, World War II, Korean War: General of the Army, 1915–48, 1951–52

Spouse: Mary "Mamie" Geneva Doud Eisenhower

Spouse's Education: Miss Woolcott's Finishing School

Spouse's Career: homemaker

Number of Children: two

Sports and Hobbies: bridge, fishing, football, golf, hunting, painting

Career Prior to the Presidency: professional soldier, U.S. Army general in World War II, president of Columbia University, Supreme Allied Commander of the North Atlantic Treaty Organization

Age upon Entering the White House: 62 years, 98 days

Reason for Leaving the White House: completed two terms; was ineligible for a third term by virtue of the Twenty-second amendment to the Constitution

Career after the Presidency: writer, public speaker, planned his presidential library

Date of Death: March 28, 1969

Cause of Death: heart disease

Last Words: "I've always loved my wife. I've always loved my children. I've always loved my grandchildren. And I have always loved my country."

Burial Site: Abilene, Kansas

Value of Estate at Time of Death: unknown

BIOGRAPHY OF EISENHOWER

—⁓—

David Dwight Eisenhower was born on October 14, 1890, in Denison, Texas, to David Jacob Eisenhower and Ida Elizabeth Stover Eisenhower. The third of seven sons, his mother always called him Dwight and later switched the order of his given names to avoid the confusion of having two Davids in the house. To friends and neighbors, Eisenhower was known as "Little Ike" (his older brother Edgar was "Big Ike"), and later just "Ike," a nickname that stuck. When he first ran for president in 1952, "I like Ike" became one of the catchiest, most popular slogans in American presidential history.

The Eisenhowers were of German Mennonite ancestry, belonging to a branch of the group known as the River Brethren. The first Eisenhowers had settled in Pennsylvania in the 1740s. In 1878, young David Eisenhower moved from Pennsylvania with his parents to homestead in Dickinson County, Kansas. He trained as an engineer at Lane University in LeCompton, Kansas, where he met Ida Stover, who came from a similar German Mennonite background, and they married in 1885. David initially opened a small country store

EDGAR NEWTON EISENHOWER

♣

"Big Ike" is the greatest football player of the class. Also on his head there is a depression due to non-development of the conscious and over-development of the subconscious brain. Football teams '07, '08, '09.

DAVID DWIGHT EISENHOWER

♣

"Little Ike," now a couple inches taller than "big Ike," is our best historian and mathematician. President of Athletic Association, '09; Football, '07, '08; Baseball '08, '09.

David Dwight Eisenhower *(right)*—his mother later switched the order of his first and middle names—pictured in his high school yearbook next to his brother, 1909 *(Associated Press)*

MAMIE EISENHOWER
(1896–1979) *first lady of the United States, January 20, 1953–January 20, 1961*

Mary "Mamie" Geneva Doud was born on November 14, 1896, in Boone, Iowa, to John Sheldon Doud and Elvira Carlson "Minnie" Doud. She was the second of four daughters. Her father was a successful meatpacker who moved the family to Denver, Colorado, in 1905 to accommodate the frail health of her elder sister, Eleanor. Beginning in 1910, the family wintered at a second home in San Antonio, Texas. "Mamie," as she was called, therefore split her schooling between Denver and San Antonio before attending Miss Wolcott's prestigious finishing school in Denver in 1914–15. Although Mamie had little interest in academics and grew up in relative comfort, her father taught her finance and budgeting skills that would later serve her well as a military spouse.

Mamie and Dwight Eisenhower first met through a mutual friend at Fort Sam Houston, Texas, in October 1915, and the two formed an immediate mutual attraction. The slight, popular, "vivacious and attractive" 18-year-old Mamie later recalled that the dashing second lieutenant was "just about the handsomest man" she had ever seen. The next day, Eisenhower pressed her for a date and a whirlwind courtship followed. Eisenhower quickly won over the entire Doud family. The two became engaged on Valentine's Day 1916, and they married at the Douds' Denver home on July 1. They honeymooned in Colorado and Abilene, Kansas, where Mamie charmed Eisenhower's parents and brothers, before taking up the peripatetic life of a military family.

Eisenhower devoted her life to her husband and his military career. Over the next 37 years, she moved 33 times, rarely complaining, even though several postings took a toll on her sometimes fragile health. She excelled as a hostess. Wherever the Eisenhowers were posted, fellow officers and their wives gravitated to "club Eisenhower," as the pair's quarters were usually

Mamie Eisenhower *(Library of Congress)*

in Hope, Kansas, but he went bankrupt and had to move to Texas where he found work cleaning train locomotives for the Missouri-Texas-Kansas Railroad. The sojourn in Texas, where Eisenhower was born in 1890, proved to be brief. In 1891, David moved the family back to Abilene, Kansas, to accept his brother-in-law's offer of a job as a mechanic at the River Brethren's newly opened Belle Spring Creamery, where he would work for the rest of his life.

Dwight Eisenhower's upbringing in small-town Kansas instilled values that would remain with him for life. From a young age, the Eisenhower boys learned the importance of religion, hard work, thrift, and education. They lived modestly in a two-story, white frame house, rising at five o'clock every morning to supplement their father's income by holding odd jobs, raising most of their own food and selling any surplus locally. David was a strict disciplinarian, while Ida tempered her lessons with love and tenderness. Stressing the importance of self-discipline, she helped the young Dwight begin to master his ferocious temper, which he shared with his father. At the insistence of their parents, all of the Eisenhower boys attended high school. Dwight proved to be a popular student. He excelled at mathematics and history, but he was much more interested in athletics, particularly football. Although he graduated high school with his brother Edgar in 1909, tight family finances precluded both boys from attending college at the same time so Dwight took a job at the creamery to help support his brother's education until Edgar could return the favor.

Eisenhower's entry into the military came rather fortuitously when his close friend, Everett "Swede" Hazlett, suggested that he sit the competitive examinations for the service academies as a way of obtaining a free college education. Although the River Brethren were pacifists, his parents supported their son's decision because they recognized the dubbed, for food, singing, cards, and companionship. Eisenhower's finishing school training also rubbed off on her husband as she helped to instill in him social graces that would prove valuable as he reached the upper echelons of the army.

Mamie Eisenhower bore two sons. Doud Dwight ("Icky") was born on September 24, 1917, but he tragically succumbed to scarlet fever in January 1921. Both parents sank into a deep depression and the loss strained the marriage, but just as Fox Conner took Ike under his wing and helped the young officer focus on his military career, Virginia Conner befriended Eisenhower and helped her pull through her despair and rebuild her relationship with her husband. A second son, John Sheldon Doud, was born in Denver on August 3, 1922. Understandably, she became extremely protective of him, obsessing over his health and later admitting that she never stopped worrying about him until after he had married and had children of his own.

World War II was particularly hard on Mamie Eisenhower. While her husband masterminded the Allied strategy in Europe, she spent most of the war alone in Washington, D.C., not seeing him for three years. Not only did she worry about the physical danger he faced and the intense stress he endured, but she also had to deal with unsubstantiated rumors that he was having an affair with his driver, Kay Summersby. Eisenhower battled anxiety and depression by submerging herself in personally answering thousands of letters from all over the world, volunteering as a waitress in an army canteen, and supporting other wartime charitable work. Despite the physical distance between them, Mamie and Ike corresponded almost daily throughout the war years.

Eisenhower's hopes for a quiet postwar retirement were dashed when her husband again responded to the call to serve, first as supreme commander of the North Atlantic Treaty Organization and then as president of the United States, but she stood loyally by him despite her own frequent health problems. As first lady, Mamie Eisenhower epitomized the 1950s ideal of American womanhood: charming, stylish, a gracious hostess, a frugal manager of the household, but apparently retiring on political issues. In fact, the president frequently sounded her out informally on policy matters and respected her as a shrewd judge of character. During his serious illnesses, Mamie Eisenhower took charge of the president's business, carefully regulating visitors and shielding him from the burdens of office while he recuperated. Ike's 1955 heart attack also led Mamie to become actively involved in the battle against heart disease, assuming the chairmanship of the American Heart Association's fundraising activities. A hugely popular first lady, Eisenhower continued to appear on "Most Admired Women" lists long after she vacated the White House.

The Eisenhowers spent their retirement at the Gettysburg farmhouse they had purchased in 1950, the only home they ever owned. After Ike died in 1969, Mamie made an annual pilgrimage to his grave and that of Icky in Abilene. To counter scurrilous stories about Ike's alleged wartime affair, she arranged for the publication of their intimate wartime correspondence. Eisenhower established friendships with all successive first families, and she felt a special bond with the Nixons, whose daughter Julie married her grandson David. In late 1979, Mamie Eisenhower suffered a stroke and was hospitalized at Walter Reed Army Hospital. On October 31, she told her granddaughter Mary that she would die the next day. She passed away in her sleep on November 1, 1979, and she was laid to rest beside her beloved husband and Icky in Abilene.

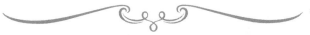

importance of higher education and a stable career. Eisenhower placed second and won a place at the U.S. Military Academy at West Point in 1911. There, he was a middling student but excelled on the football field until a serious knee injury curtailed his playing career. Thereafter, he took up coaching the junior varsity team and cheerleading and he proved to be a natural leader. Despite his modest academic accomplishments, West Point instilled in Eisenhower the values of selflessness, honor, duty, patriotism, and teamwork. He graduated in 1915 ranked 61 out of 164 cadets in a class that would later boast 59 generals.

The next three years brought mixed fortunes for Eisenhower. His first posting was to Fort Sam Houston, Texas, where he met Mary ("Mamie") Geneva Doud, the daughter of an affluent businessman from Denver whose family migrated to the warmth of San Antonio for the winter season. The couple married on July 1, 1916, and their first child, Doud Dwight ("Icky"), was born in September the following year. Despite his new domestic obligations, when the United States declared war on Germany on April 6, 1917, and entered World War I, Eisenhower, like most of his fellow junior officers, itched to get into combat. Instead, his commanding officers recognized Eisenhower's exceptional training abilities and, to his utter frustration, he spent the war stateside teaching troops about the new technology of tank warfare. Although his exceptional service led to the award of the Distinguished Service Medal, he worried that his future military career would be impeded by his failure to secure active duty in Europe.

In the immediate postwar years, Eisenhower endured professional setbacks and personal tragedy. As the army demobilized and fell on relatively hard times, Eisenhower reverted from his temporary wartime rank of lieutenant colonel to major, a rank he would maintain for the next 16 years. As an instructor at the Infantry Tank School at Camp Meade, Maryland, Eisenhower and his new friend, George S. Patton, began to contemplate employing faster-moving armored vehicles in a new concept of mobile warfare, but his superiors remained dyed-in-the-wool infantry officers who rejected such nonconformist views and eventually ordered the two innovators not to waste their time. Worse, the Eisenhowers' beloved son Icky, not yet four years old, succumbed to scarlet fever and died in January 1921. Both parents were devastated, Eisenhower later calling it "the greatest disappointment and disaster" of his life.

Eisenhower's professional fortunes quickly improved when he was befriended by Brigadier General Fox Conner, who had been impressed by Eisenhower's ideas about tank warfare during a visit to Fort Meade, and who became a mentor to the young officer. As a friend of U.S. Army chief of staff General John J. Pershing, Conner secured Eisenhower's appointment as his executive officer to the 20th Infantry Brigade at Camp Gaillard in the Panama Canal Zone in 1922. For the next two and one-half years, under Conner's tutelage, Eisenhower became a serious student of military history and tactics and gained important experience drafting orders for the command. Conner encouraged Eisenhower to prepare himself for the next war, predicting that the Treaty of Versailles was a flawed peace that made another world war inevitable and that the United States would have to fight with a coalition of allies. Conner also imbued in Eisenhower two clichés that he would recite continually: "All generalities are false, including this one"; and "always take your job seriously, never yourself." Eisenhower blossomed under Conner's mentorship, and the birth of his second son John in 1922, added to his happiness. In 1925, Conner's influence secured Eisenhower a place at the prestigious Army Command and General Staff School at Fort Leavenworth, Kansas. At the school, Eisenhower eagerly applied the lessons learned under Conner and graduated first in his class. Next, he graduated first in his class at the Army War College. These distinctions marked Eisenhower as a prime candidate for a future high leadership position.

After drafting a guidebook on American battlefields in Europe for the American Battle Monuments Commission, which included spending a year in Paris, France, Eisenhower moved to Washington, D.C., in 1929 to work in the War Department and undertake the next phase of his military education. He took up an appointment in the office of the assistant secretary for war, preparing plans for industrial mobilization in the event of war. When Douglas MacArthur became U.S. Army chief of staff in 1930, he took a keen interest in the project and was impressed with Eisenhower's attention to detail and clear writing style. After the change in administration in 1933, MacArthur appointed Eisenhower as his personal assistant and relied heavily on him to prepare speeches and reports and brief members of Congress on army budgetary matters. Eisenhower admired MacArthur's self-assurance, his rigorous mind, and his command of an argument, but he disliked his chief's outspokenness on controversial subjects and his dabbling in partisan politics. In 1932, when MacArthur controversially used military force to disperse the so-called Bonus Army from the streets of Washington, D.C., Eisenhower dutifully accompanied his boss but privately questioned his assertion that the unemployed throng were dangerous revolutionaries on the brink of insurrection. Nevertheless, MacArthur considered Eisenhower an indispensable staff officer and insisted that he accompany him to the Philippines when his tour as chief ended in 1935 and he took up a new appointment as military adviser to Philippine president Manuel Quezon. In Manila, Eisenhower drafted a defense plan for the islands for officials to implement after the country secured complete independence from the United States, scheduled for 1946, and he also polished his diplomatic skills as liaison between the general and Quezon. Although Eisenhower was promoted to

Mamie and Dwight D. Eisenhower in 1916, the year they were married *(Library of Congress)*

lieutenant colonel in 1936, his relationship with the egotistical MacArthur began to sour, Mamie grew weary of life in the tropics, and with the outbreak of World War II in Europe in September 1939, Eisenhower returned to the United States.

For the next two years, as the world situation deteriorated and the United States prepared for war, Eisenhower held a series of positions preparing recruits and junior officers for wartime responsibilities in the rapidly expanding

BIOGRAPHICAL TIME LINE

1890
October 14 Dwight Eisenhower is born in Denison, Texas.

1891
The Eisenhower family moves to Abilene, Kansas.

1911
Eisenhower matriculates the U.S. Military Academy at West Point.

1915
Eisenhower graduates in 1915, ranking 61 out of 164 cadets in a class that would later boast 59 generals.

1916
July 1 Eisenhower marries Mary ("Mamie") Geneva Doud.

1922
Eisenhower is posted to Camp Gaillard in the Panama Canal Zone.

1925
Eisenhower enters the Army Command and General Staff School at Fort Leavenworth, Kansas.

1933
U.S. Army chief of staff Douglas MacArthur appoints Eisenhower as his personal assistant.

1941
U.S. Army chief of staff George Marshall summons Eisenhower to his General Staff in Washington, D.C.

1942
June Marshall appoints Eisenhower commander in chief, European theater.

November Eisenhower is named commander in chief, Allied Forces, North Africa for Operation

Torch, the Anglo-American offensive against German forces.

1943
Eisenhower is named supreme commander, Allied Expeditionary Forces.

1944
June 6 Eisenhower leads the D-Day landing of Allied forces in Normandy, France.

1945
May 7 Eisenhower receives the unconditional surrender of German forces.

1948
Eisenhower retires from the army and becomes president of Columbia University.

1950
Eisenhower is appointed the first supreme allied commander of the newly organized North Atlantic Treaty Organization (NATO).

1952
November 4 Eisenhower is elected president.

1953
January 20 Eisenhower is inaugurated president.

1956
November 6 Eisenhower is reelected president.

1957
January 20 Eisenhower is inaugurated to his second term as president.

1961
January 20 Eisenhower's last day as president. He retires to Gettysburg, Pennsylvania.

1969
March 28 Eisenhower dies.

As a general during World War II, Eisenhower valued efficient organization and was committed to duty and public service. He is shown here with other U.S. Army officers in 1945. Standing in the back, from left to right, are Generals Ralph F. Stearley, Hoyt Vandenberg, Walter Bedell Smith, Otto P. Weyland, and Richard E. Nugent. Seated in the front, from left to right, are Generals William H. Simpson, George S. Patton, Carl A. Spaatz, Eisenhower, Omar Bradley, Courtney H. Hodges, and Leonard T. Gerow. *(National Archives)*

army. These activities culminated in his appointment as chief of staff to General Walter Krueger's Third Army, where he was instrumental in devising the successful plan of battle against the Second Army in major maneuvers in Louisiana in September 1941. His achievements brought high praise from Krueger and promotion to temporary brigadier general, attracted attention from the national press, and, more significantly, convinced U.S. Army chief of staff George Marshall that Eisenhower had exceptional planning and leadership abilities. When Japan attacked Pearl Harbor on December 7, 1941, drawing the United States into World War II, Marshall summoned Eisenhower to his General Staff in Washington, D.C., quickly elevating him to head the newly established Operations Division.

Marshall appreciated Eisenhower's abilities and assigned him ever increasing levels of responsibility. At first, in Washington, Eisenhower was intimately involved in fashioning the general strategy that the United States and the Allies would pursue throughout the war. As Germany was the most dangerous enemy, a "Germany first" plan was adopted, envisioning an Anglo-American attack on Germany through northern France, using Britain as a base, and supplying Lend-Lease aid to the Soviet Union to keep that country in the war pending the assault in the west. The Pacific war would be of secondary importance. In June 1942, Marshall passed over numerous senior officers and dispatched Eisenhower to London as commander in chief, European theater, with responsibility for working with the British to implement the strategy. When President FRANKLIN D. ROOSEVELT decided that American troops had to enter the ground war against Germany before the end of the year, Eisenhower was named commander in chief, Allied Forces, North Africa for Operation Torch, the Anglo-American offensive against German forces there. Drawing on his lessons learned under Fox Conner on coalition warfare, his political skills refined during his years in Washington, and his own talents in mastering detail, together with his unpretentiousness and willingness to make hard decisions, Eisenhower forged a solid working relationship with the British and conducted a successful military campaign. Most important, he developed a personal rapport with British prime minister Winston Churchill, which helped reduce Anglo-American differences over strategy. In 1943, Eisenhower commanded the Allied invasions of Sicily and Italy, leading to Italy's surrender, and he earned promotion to major general.

Marshall had expected to command Operation Overlord, the invasion of France across the English Channel and the drive into the heart of Germany, but when Roosevelt insisted that he needed him in Washington, Eisenhower was named supreme commander, Allied Expeditionary Forces in late 1943. Eisenhower built a truly combined staff, resolved numerous inter-Allied and interservice differences over strategy and tactics, supervised the necessary logistical preparations, and took the time to mix frequently with regular troops to boost their morale and instill confidence in his leadership. Although poor weather conditions forced a nerve-wracking 24-hour delay, Eisenhower took a calculated risk and ordered the landings to go ahead on D-Day, June 6, 1944. The gamble paid off handsomely as the Allies secured their beachheads in France and landed over 1 million men within a matter of weeks. While following the general outlines of the strategic plan, Eisenhower nevertheless maintained sufficient flexibility to exploit contingencies at the tactical level, focusing on destroying enemy forces rather than occupying terrain. Although the German counterattack at the Battle of the Bulge in December 1944 caught the Allies by surprise, Eisenhower quickly reorganized his commands and seized the opportunity to destroy German reserves. By this time, Eisenhower had been promoted to five-star General of the Army. On May 7, 1945, Eisenhower received the unconditional surrender of German forces.

When Eisenhower returned to the United States a war hero, speculation began almost immediately about a possible political career. Despite Eisenhower's protestations that he had no presidential ambitions, the leaders of both major political parties were enthralled by the prospect of an Eisenhower candidacy in the 1948 election. Even President HARRY S. TRUMAN confidentially pledged to support Eisenhower should he run for the presidency. Eisenhower repeatedly cooled such talk. Nevertheless, when Eisenhower succeeded Marshall as army chief of staff (1945–48), he became increasingly frustrated with the intensely political atmosphere in Washington and the Truman administration's lack of a coherent, long-term strategy for containing the increasingly menacing Soviet communist threat to Western interests.

When Eisenhower retired from the military in 1948 to take up the presidency of Columbia University and write his wartime memoirs, he cultivated friendships and associations with some of the nation's wealthiest business leaders, most of whom were moderate, internationalist Republicans. He

General Eisenhower speaks with U.S. paratroopers of the 502d Parachute Infantry Regiment, 101st Airborne Division, on the evening of D-Day, June 6, 1944. *(Library of Congress)*

found that he shared their views about the dangers that big government, high taxes, and bureaucratic regulation posed to the economic health of the nation and to individual liberties. Thus, when his friend, New York governor Thomas E. Dewey, unexpectedly lost the 1948 election to Truman, Eisenhower began to position himself to be drafted by the Republicans in the next election if no suitable alternative appeared.

In the meantime, after the Soviets developed their own atomic bomb in 1949 and the Korean War broke out in 1950, Eisenhower accepted President Truman's request to return to active duty as the first supreme allied commander of the newly organized North Atlantic Treaty Organization (NATO). Eisenhower's immense prestige bolstered European confidence in the alliance and also helped to sell the notion of a long-term U.S. military commitment to Western European defense to the American public. But as the Korean War evolved into a stalemate, and isolationist Senate minority leader Robert A. Taft (R-OH) emerged as the front-runner for the Republican presidential nomination, Eisenhower allowed his powerful friends at home to persuade him that he had a duty to enter the presidential race, both to safeguard the collective security system which he considered essential to winning the cold war and to prevent another Republican defeat. Thus, in mid-1952, Eisenhower resigned his position and returned to the United States to campaign for the Republican nomination, securing a narrow victory over Taft at the Republican convention.

Eisenhower rode his popularity to victory in the general election. Although he and his young running mate, Senator RICHARD M. NIXON* (R-CA), berated Truman and the Dem-

---

*For more information on Richard Nixon, Dwight Eisenhower's vice president, see the chapter on Nixon, who was president from 1969 to 1974.

ocrats for losing China to the Communists, failing to win the Korean War, and allowing communist subversion in the federal government, campaign organizers focused primarily on Eisenhower's status as a war hero, portraying him as a statesman who stood above partisan politics. Even a minor scandal over allegations that Nixon had received gifts in return for political favors and an embarrassing moment in Wisconsin during which Eisenhower followed the advice of Republican strategists and refrained from criticizing red-baiting senator Joseph McCarthy's attack on the character of Eisenhower's mentor, George Marshall, could not derail the momentum for the general. His announcement that, if elected, he would "go to Korea," suggesting that he would end the unpopular war, helped to cement his victory. On election day, Eisenhower defeated Illinois governor Adlai E. Stevenson by 6 million popular votes, becoming the first Republican since HERBERT C. HOOVER in 1928 to win the presidency.

Inaugurated on March 4, 1953, as the nation's 34th president, Eisenhower drew on his extensive military and diplomatic experience. He appointed a strong chief of staff to manage the daily operations of the White House, brought in loyal subordinates to run the major government departments, and focused his own attention on the major strategic and policy decisions. Contemporary critics charged that Eisenhower delegated too much responsibility and did not know what was going on within his administration. In fact, Eisenhower deliberately employed a "hidden-hand" leadership style, making the major policy decisions himself, often in small meetings, and then letting his subordinates implement those policies and explain them to the public. This approach mirrored his military leadership style. It had the added advantage of deflecting criticism of his administration's policies from Eisenhower personally and enabling him to sustain his image as a leader who was above partisan politics. In international affairs, Eisenhower focused on maintaining the peace, often enjoying the advantage of working with world leaders whom he knew personally from the war years. At home, he supported traditional Republican positions in advocating lowering taxes, reducing government spending, and balancing the budget, but he also supported some modest expansions of the welfare state to provide economic security for the disadvantaged.

The most serious obstacle to Eisenhower's success as president was ill health. First elected president at age 62, an age when many people might be considering retirement, the ravages of high-pressure leadership positions and heavy smoking—he smoked cigarettes until 1949—had taken their toll. Eisenhower had a history of heart and stomach problems and initially expected to be a one-term president. He suffered a major heart attack on September 24, 1955, and was hospitalized for six weeks. Although he made a strong recovery, the next June he suffered an attack of ileitis, a painful swelling of the lower intestine, which required surgery. Although

these episodes turned his thoughts to possible successors, he reluctantly concluded that none of his preferred candidates had the necessary party or popular support to win. He therefore allowed himself to be persuaded once again that he had a duty to run.

The 1956 election constituted a rematch of the 1952 contest between Eisenhower and Stevenson, and the popular incumbent increased his margin of victory. A healthy economy and generally successful foreign policy translated into strong public approval for Eisenhower's first-term performance. Stevenson's effort to challenge Eisenhower's expertise in national security affairs by calling for a ban on atmospheric nuclear tests backfired when Soviet premier Nikolai Bulganin endorsed the idea, allowing Eisenhower to denounce foreign interference in an American election and portray Stevenson as a dupe of the Soviets. Foreign policy crises in Poland, Hungary, and Egypt in the runup to the election further played to Eisenhower's strength as a wise elder statesman who could best safeguard the nation's security in an increasingly dangerous world. On election day, Eisenhower almost doubled his margin of victory in the popular vote and carried 41 states. His only disappointment was that his great personal popularity did not translate into congressional gains for the Republican Party.

Eisenhower's health problems continued into his second term. On November 25, 1957, he suffered a stroke, temporarily rendering him unable to speak. He made a sufficiently swift recovery to travel to Europe to meet with NATO leaders the following month, but his ongoing chronic health problems necessitated some reduction of his ceremonial duties and made him increasingly irritable. Only in 1959 did Eisenhower seem to return to full health. Overall, these medical setbacks had little impact on the functioning of the administration, but they were sufficiently serious for Mamie to insist that Eisenhower not be asked to undertake extensive campaigning for his vice president and Republican candidate Richard Nixon in the 1960 presidential election.

After leaving office in 1961, Eisenhower devoted his retirement years to writing his memoirs, playing golf, painting, and living the life of a gentleman farmer in a modest farmhouse in Gettysburg, Pennsylvania, the first house he and Mamie had ever owned. As a respected elder statesman, however, he frequently received distinguished visitors and responded to periodic calls from Presidents JOHN F. KENNEDY and LYNDON B. JOHNSON for advice on foreign affairs until his health began to fail. From 1965 onward, Eisenhower suffered a series of heart attacks, and he spent the final year of his life at Walter Reed Army Hospital. He died on March 28, 1969, and was laid to rest next to his son, Icky, in the Chapel of Memories on the grounds of the Eisenhower Library and Museum in Abilene, Kansas.

Eisenhower's considerable achievements in both wartime and peacetime established his reputation as one of the

Funeral services for Eisenhower, March 31, 1969 *(Oliver F. Atkins/National Archives)*

great American statesmen of the 20th century. His leadership skills and personality were vital to the success of the Anglo-American coalition in World War II. As president, he negotiated an armistice in Korea, established the long-term strategy of containment that would contribute to the eventual demise of the Soviet empire, and presided over seven years of relative prosperity. Although critics decried his failure to tackle the excesses of Senator Joseph McCarthy head-on and his lack of leadership on the issue of African-American civil rights, Eisenhower maintained the dignity of the presidency by working behind the scenes to thwart McCarthy, and his administration pushed through the first significant, if limited, civil rights acts since Reconstruction. Significantly, Eisenhower left office with his popularity intact. His leadership qualities and accomplishments have also stood the test of time. Recent assessments of presiden-

tial leadership by historians rank Eisenhower among the top 10 U.S. presidents.

PRESIDENTIAL ELECTION OF 1952

The 1952 election took place at the height of the cold war. With the United States embroiled in an increasingly frustrating and unpopular war in Korea (which had begun in 1950), the Soviet Union apparently closing the gap in the atomic arms race, and the nation captivated by the sensational allegations of Senator Joseph R. McCarthy (R-WI) of communist subversives in government, incumbent Democratic president HARRY S. TRUMAN's approval ratings sank to record lows. When Truman decided not to seek reelection, his party eventually nominated Illinois governor Adlai E. Stevenson for the presidency. The Republicans countered with popular World War II hero Dwight D. "Ike" Eisenhower. On election day, Eisenhower won a smashing victory, becoming the first Republican to win the presidency since HERBERT HOOVER in 1928 and helping the Republicans gain a narrow majority in Congress.

Despite his personal unpopularity, Truman was widely expected to seek reelection in 1952. The recently passed Twenty-second Amendment to the Constitution, limiting presidents to two terms, specifically did not apply to the incumbent Truman and the president was expected to vigorously defend his administration against Senator McCarthy's charges that it was riddled with communist fellow-travelers. The bloody stalemate in Korea, however, and revelations of corruption within Truman's inner circle seriously damaged the president's prospects for reelection. The final straw was the New Hampshire primary early in 1952, where Senator Estes Kefauver (D-TN), who had developed a reputation as a good government reformer by taking on organized crime and corrupt politicians, surprisingly beat the president and secured that state's delegates for the Democratic National Convention. Shortly thereafter, Truman formally withdrew from the race, throwing the Democratic field wide open.

Although Truman's withdrawal left Kefauver as the immediate front-runner, the Democratic Party establishment generally disliked the reforming senator. His well-publicized investigations into urban corruption had led to embarrassing revelations about ties between organized crime and some Democratic political machines in the nation's large cities. Kefauver proceeded to win most of the primary elections,

Eisenhower campaigns for president in Baltimore, September 1952 (Library of Congress)

but Truman and the party bosses searched for an alternative candidate who could outmaneuver the Tennessean at the Democratic National Convention in Chicago, where the nomination would be decided. Ultimately, nine challengers took on Kefauver at the convention. Although Kefauver won the most votes of any candidate on the first round of balloting, he failed to achieve the clear majority needed to attain the nomination. Gradually, Illinois governor Adlai E. Stevenson II emerged as the choice of the anti-Kefauver party bosses. The scion of a distinguished Illinois family—his grandfather had served as vice president under GROVER CLEVELAND—an eloquent orator, an intellectual and a political moderate, Stevenson won the nomination on the third ballot with strong support from delegates from the Midwest and the Northeast. The convention then balanced the ticket by selecting the southern segregationist Senator John Sparkman (D-AL) for vice president.

The battle for the Republican Party nomination pitted Senator Robert A. Taft (R-OH), son of former President WILLIAM HOWARD TAFT, against Dwight D. Eisenhower and several other candidates. Taft was the Senate minority leader and represented the more conservative, isolationist wing of the party. A staunch opponent of the New Deal, he hoped to dismantle many of the Democrats' social welfare programs. He had also opposed the Marshall Plan and the North Atlantic Treaty Organization (NATO) on the grounds that they were too costly and would drag the United States into unnecessary European conflicts and deflect attention from the communist danger in Asia. Eisenhower, meanwhile, enjoyed the backing of eastern internationalists in the Republican Party, led by New York governor and former presidential candidate Thomas E. Dewey, who accepted the necessity for a minimal welfare state and believed that the United States had to play the leading role in rallying the free world behind containment of communism. Indeed, Taft's emergence as the Republican front-runner by 1952 convinced Eisenhower, at that time the first NATO supreme commander, to enter the race, both to safeguard the collective security system he deemed vital to winning the cold war and to prevent yet another Republican defeat in the general election and the possible collapse of the two-party system. Truman's decision not to seek reelection made Eisenhower's entry into the presidential race somewhat easier as he would not now have to run against his former commander in chief.

Although Eisenhower did not begin formal campaigning until resigning his NATO post in mid-1952, the two leading Republican candidates arrived at the Republican National Convention holding a virtual tie among committed delegates. Several contested southern delegations held the key to victory. In an area with few Republicans—the Solid South was then heavily Democratic—Taft party loyalists controlled most of the delegates, but "Eisenhower Republicans," many of whom had switched party allegiance from the Democrats because of Eisenhower, argued that they

With the night session of the Republican convention in Chicago about to begin on July 8, 1952, "Ike" straw hats cover the seats of New York delegates. *(Associated Press)*

minority party, he had to secure not only the traditional base of Republican voters, but also a substantial number of independents and disaffected Democrats. Eisenhower papered over significant differences between Republicans by hammering home the themes of "Korea, Communism, and Corruption," referring to the Truman administration's failure to secure victory in Korea, the allegations of communist subversion in the federal government, and the charges of corruption against several prominent members of Truman's inner circle. He also played down his own role in participating in Truman's major foreign policy initiatives, such as NATO, and he embraced the aggressive foreign policy platform drafted by John Foster Dulles that criticized containment as "negative" and "immoral" and instead advocated "liberation" of the "captive peoples" under the Soviet yoke. For the most part, however, Eisenhower capitalized on his image as a war hero and statesman above petty party politics. He turned to surrogates such as Nixon and McCarthy to deliver the harshest attacks on the Democrats. On the positive side, Eisenhower proposed lowering taxes, halting the expansion of the federal government, and balancing the budget while expanding the safety net provided by Social Security.

The Stevenson campaign, faced with the considerable obstacle of Eisenhower's personal popularity, focused on

had been unfairly shut out of the delegations from Georgia and Texas. Eisenhower's campaign manager, Senator Henry Cabot Lodge (R-MA), therefore introduced a "fair play" resolution at the convention calling for the "stolen" delegates not to be seated and for the convention, not the party bosses in the Republican National Committee, to determine whom to seat. When the resolution passed and Taft lost the disputed delegates, Eisenhower's victory was assured. He was nominated on the first ballot. Eisenhower then immediately tried to repair relations with the Taft conservatives by magnanimously meeting with the defeated senator, embracing a party platform drafted by Taft's supporters, and selecting Senator RICHARD M. NIXON (D-CA) as his running mate. Despite his own conservative credentials, Nixon was convinced that Eisenhower stood a better chance of victory in the national election than Taft, and he had worked hard behind the scenes on the California delegation at the convention to support the "fair play" resolution. Nixon's strong anticommunist credentials, his political acumen, his ability to bridge the gap between the conservatives and moderates in the party, his western origins, and his relative youth—he was just 39—made him an ideal running mate for the 61-year-old Eisenhower.

During the 1952 general election, Eisenhower performed a delicate balancing act. As the candidate of the

Nixon the family man: In this image from the cover of a 1952 campaign pamphlet, the vice-presidential candidate appears with his wife and two daughters. *(Richard Nixon Presidential Library and Museum)*

1952 Election Statistics

State	Number of Electors	Total Popular Vote	Elec Vote R	Elec Vote D	Pop Vote R	Pop Vote D	Margin of Victory Votes	Margin of Victory % Total Vote
Alabama	11	426,120		11	2	1	125,844	29.53%
Arizona	4	260,570	4		1	2	43,514	16.70%
Arkansas	8	404,800		8	2	1	49,145	12.14%
California	32	5,341,603	32		1	2	777,941	14.56%
Colorado	6	630,103	6		1	2	134,278	21.31%
Connecticut	8	1,096,911	8		1	2	129,363	11.79%
Delaware	3	174,025	3		1	2	6,744	3.88%
Florida	10	989,337	10		1	2	99,086	10.02%
Georgia	12	655,803		12	2	1	257,844	39.32%
Idaho	4	276,231	4		1	2	85,626	31.00%
Illinois	27	4,481,058	27		1	2	443,407	9.90%
Indiana	13	1,955,325	13		1	2	334,729	17.12%
Iowa	10	1,268,773	10		1	2	357,393	28.17%
Kansas	8	896,166	8		1	2	343,006	38.27%
Kentucky	10	993,148		10	2	1	700	0.07%
Louisiana	10	651,952		10	2	1	38,102	5.84%
Maine	5	351,786	5		1	2	113,547	32.28%
Maryland	9	902,074	9		1	2	104,087	11.54%
Massachusetts	16	2,383,398	16		1	2	208,800	8.76%
Michigan	20	2,798,592	20		1	2	320,872	11.47%
Minnesota	11	1,379,483	11		1	2	154,753	11.22%
Mississippi	8	285,532		8	2	1	59,600	20.87%
Missouri	13	1,892,062	13		1	2	29,599	1.56%
Montana	4	265,037	4		1	2	51,181	19.31%
Nebraska	6	609,660	6		1	2	233,546	38.31%
Nevada	3	82,190	3		1	2	18,814	22.89%
New Hampshire	4	272,950	4		1	2	59,624	21.84%
New Jersey	16	2,419,554	16		1	2	358,711	14.83%
New Mexico	4	238,608	4		1	2	26,509	11.11%
New York	45	7,128,241	45		1	2	848,214	11.90%
North Carolina	14	1,210,910		14	2	1	94,696	7.82%
North Dakota	4	270,127	4		1	2	115,018	42.58%
Ohio	25	3,700,758	25		1	2	500,024	13.51%
Oklahoma	8	948,984	8		1	2	87,106	9.18%
Oregon	6	695,059	6		1	2	150,236	21.61%
Pennsylvania	32	4,580,969	32		1	2	269,520	5.88%
Rhode Island	4	414,498	4		1	2	7,642	1.84%
South Carolina	8	341,086		8	2	1	4,922	1.44%
South Dakota	4	294,283	4		1	2	113,431	38.54%
Tennessee	11	892,553	11		1	2	2,437	0.27%
Texas	24	2,075,946	24		1	2	133,650	6.44%
Utah	4	329,554	4		1	2	58,826	17.85%
Vermont	3	153,557	3		1	2	66,362	43.22%
Virginia	12	619,689	12		1	2	80,360	12.97%
Washington	9	1,102,708	9		1	2	106,262	9.64%
West Virginia	8	873,548		8	2	1	33,608	3.85%
Wisconsin	12	1,607,370	12		1	2	357,569	22.25%
Wyoming	3	129,251	3		1	2	33,113	25.62%
Total	531	61,751,942	442	89	1	2	6,700,439	10.85%

Eisenhower Republican		Stevenson Democratic		Others	
149,231	35.02%	275,075	64.55%	1,814	0.43%
152,042	58.35%	108,528	41.65%	0	0.00%
177,155	43.76%	226,300	55.90%	1,345	0.33%
3,035,587	56.83%	2,257,646	42.27%	48,370	0.91%
379,782	60.27%	245,504	38.96%	4,817	0.76%
611,012	55.70%	481,649	43.91%	4,250	0.39%
90,059	51.75%	83,315	47.88%	651	0.37%
544,036	54.99%	444,950	44.97%	351	0.04%
198,979	30.34%	456,823	69.66%	1	0.00%
180,707	65.42%	95,081	34.42%	443	0.16%
2,457,327	54.84%	2,013,920	44.94%	9,811	0.22%
1,136,259	58.11%	801,530	40.99%	17,536	0.90%
808,906	63.75%	451,513	35.59%	8,354	0.66%
616,302	68.77%	273,296	30.50%	6,568	0.73%
495,029	49.84%	495,729	49.91%	2,390	0.24%
306,925	47.08%	345,027	52.92%	0	0.00%
232,353	66.05%	118,806	33.77%	627	0.18%
499,424	55.36%	395,337	43.83%	7,313	0.81%
1,292,325	54.22%	1,083,525	45.46%	7,548	0.32%
1,551,529	55.44%	1,230,657	43.97%	16,406	0.59%
763,211	55.33%	608,458	44.11%	7,814	0.57%
112,966	39.56%	172,566	60.44%	0	0.00%
959,429	50.71%	929,830	49.14%	2,803	0.15%
157,394	59.39%	106,213	40.07%	1,430	0.54%
421,603	69.15%	188,057	30.85%	0	0.00%
50,502	61.45%	31,688	38.55%	0	0.00%
166,287	60.92%	106,663	39.08%	0	0.00%
1,374,613	56.81%	1,015,902	41.99%	29,039	1.20%
132,170	55.39%	105,661	44.28%	777	0.33%
3,952,815	55.45%	3,104,601	43.55%	70,825	0.99%
558,107	46.09%	652,803	53.91%	0	0.00%
191,712	70.97%	76,694	28.39%	1,721	0.64%
2,100,391	56.76%	1,600,367	43.24%	0	0.00%
518,045	54.59%	430,939	45.41%	0	0.00%
420,815	60.54%	270,579	38.93%	3,665	0.53%
2,415,789	52.74%	2,146,269	46.85%	18,911	0.41%
210,935	50.89%	203,293	49.05%	270	0.07%
168,082	49.28%	173,004	50.72%	0	0.00%
203,857	69.27%	90,426	30.73%	0	0.00%
446,147	49.99%	443,710	49.71%	2,696	0.30%
1,102,878	53.13%	969,228	46.69%	3,840	0.18%
194,190	58.93%	135,364	41.07%	0	0.00%
109,717	71.45%	43,355	28.23%	485	0.32%
349,037	56.32%	268,677	43.36%	1,975	0.32%
599,107	54.33%	492,845	44.69%	10,756	0.98%
419,970	48.08%	453,578	51.92%	0	0.00%
979,744	60.95%	622,175	38.71%	5,451	0.34%
81,047	62.71%	47,934	37.09%	270	0.21%
34,075,529	55.18%	27,375,090	44.33%	301,323	0.49%

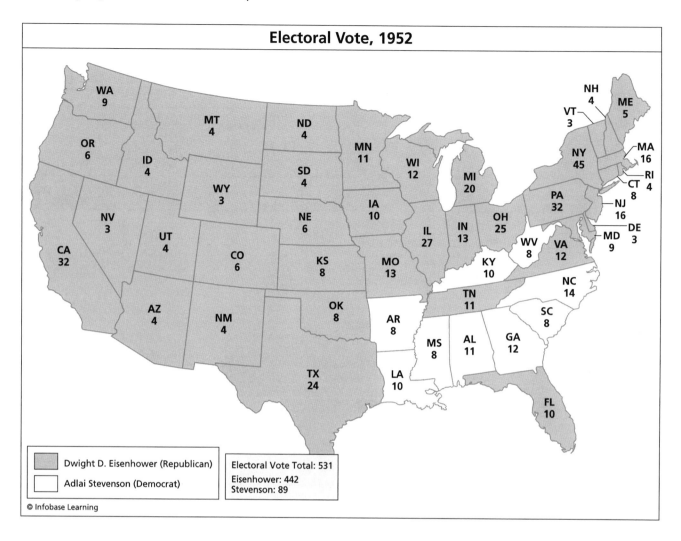

Electoral Vote, 1952

WA 9
MT 4
ND 4
MN 11
NH 4
VT 3
ME 5
NY 45
MA 16
RI 4
CT 8
OR 6
ID 4
SD 4
WI 12
MI 20
PA 32
NJ 16
DE 3
WY 3
IA 10
OH 25
MD 9
NV 3
UT 4
NE 6
IL 27
IN 13
WV 8
VA 12
CA 32
CO 6
KS 8
MO 13
KY 10
NC 14
AZ 4
NM 4
OK 8
AR 8
TN 11
SC 8
TX 24
LA 10
MS 8
AL 11
GA 12
FL 10

Dwight D. Eisenhower (Republican)
Adlai Stevenson (Democrat)

Electoral Vote Total: 531
Eisenhower: 442
Stevenson: 89

© Infobase Learning

traditional Democratic issues in an attempt to hold together the New Deal coalition that had dominated American presidential elections since the Great Depression. Stevenson called for further expansion of the popular New Deal and Fair Deal reforms of his Democratic predecessors, reminded voters of the unprecedented prosperity since World War II in contrast to the dark days of the last Republican administration under Herbert Hoover (1929–33), vigorously condemned the smear campaign launched by McCarthy and his allies against Democrats, and insisted that the aggressive and isolationist foreign policy advocated by the Taft Republicans was a recipe for disaster. Rather than being above politics, the Stevenson campaign tried to suggest that Eisenhower was actually the puppet of Republican extremists such as Taft and McCarthy.

The election campaign itself blended traditional and modern techniques. Both candidates took to the stump, but the 61-year-old Eisenhower's whistle-stop, eight-week campaign by rail, covering over 50,000 miles, 45 states, and speeches in 232 communities, eclipsed the younger Stevenson's efforts. The campaigns also turned to the rela-

tively new technology of television. Stevenson purchased half-hour blocs of airtime in the evenings in which he delivered substantive talks on a variety of issues designed to capitalize on his eloquence and demonstrate his experience in governing in contrast to the political novice Eisenhower. The broadcasts further cemented his reputation as an intellectual, which played into Republican depictions of him as an elitist out of touch with the American people. The Eisenhower campaign instead exploited their candidate's personal popularity, running short, 20-second spots before and after popular primetime programming in which "ordinary" Americans asked candidate Eisenhower a question and he responded with folksy, commonsense answers. The Eisenhower campaign also commissioned Irving Berlin to pen a catchy ditty, "I Like Ike," which was set to a short cartoon for television depicting Americans rallying to the war hero. After the election, pollsters found that many voters obtained most of their information about the candidates from television rather than radio, newspapers, or magazines, making the 1952 campaign the first one in which television played a central role.

A day after Richard Nixon *(right)* delivered his "Checkers Speech" that saved his candidacy for vice president, he and Eisenhower appeared at a rally in Wheeling, West Virginia, on September 24, 1952. *(Stf/Associated Press)*

Television also played a role in the most serious challenge to Eisenhower's election, the allegation that Nixon had received $18,000 from wealthy Republicans for undisclosed purposes. Although the amount was small and the practice of gift-giving to government officials was widespread, the charges resonated because Nixon had lambasted his Democratic opponents for precisely this type of corruption. Nixon decided to contest the allegations in a live, half-hour television broadcast on September 23, 1952, claiming that he had used all donations appropriately and that the only gift he had received was a small dog, "Checkers." He detailed his personal finances while challenging the other candidates to do the same. Nixon's performance in the "Checkers Speech," as it came to be called, not only saved his candidacy, but also set a precedent, forcing future candidates for high office to disclose their finances.

To the consternation of his political managers, Eisenhower insisted on campaigning in the South, a traditional Democratic stronghold, because he believed that his per-

sonal popularity and growing regional disenchantment with the national Democratic Party leadership provided an opportunity to cut into his opponents' base of support. During his visit, Eisenhower courted white conservatives by stressing such themes as balancing the budget, limiting the size of the federal government, and deferring to the states on the controversial issue of civil rights. Despite the presence of Sparkman on the Democratic ticket, the Eisenhower campaign exploited white southerners' anxieties over Stevenson's position on civil rights.

Throughout the election campaign, polls suggested that Eisenhower enjoyed a significant lead. The darkest moment for Eisenhower came during a campaign stop in Milwaukee, Wisconsin, in October, where he had planned to issue a strong defense of his mentor and former secretary of state, George C. Marshall, whose loyalty had been questioned by Senator McCarthy. In deference to the wishes of Wisconsin Republicans, however, he omitted the passage but advance copies of the speech had already been distributed to the press. To many observers, it appeared as though the principled Eisenhower had capitulated to the demagogues in order to win the election. The whole episode embarrassed Eisenhower, but he maintained his lead in the polls and cemented that lead later in the month when he promised that, if elected, he would "go to Korea" and end the war. Stevenson had contemplated doing just that should he be elected but had decided not to make a public announcement for fear of appearing to be grandstanding. Eisenhower's impeccable national security credentials, however, gave his announcement the air of statesmanship. It was precisely what the voters wanted to hear. The military hero Eisenhower would find a way to end the stalemated Korean War. His victory was assured.

On election day, November 4, Eisenhower defeated Stevenson by more than 6 million popular votes, carrying all but nine states. Eisenhower's insistence on campaigning in the South was vindicated when he became the first Republican in a generation to capture the traditionally Democratic states of Texas, Virginia, Tennessee, and Florida, marking the beginning of the end of the Democratic Solid South. Eisenhower won 55 percent of the popular vote to Stevenson's 44 percent, and he carried the electoral vote by a margin of 442 to 89. Significantly, Eisenhower's broad personal popularity enabled the Republicans to win both houses of Congress by a narrow majority: 221 to 214 in the House of Representatives, and a 48 to 48 tie in the Senate, allowing Vice President Nixon to cast the deciding vote for Republican control. For the first time in six elections—almost a quarter century—a Republican was elected to the White House.

PRESIDENTIAL ELECTION OF 1956

The 1956 presidential election involved a rematch of the 1952 contest. The popular incumbent, Dwight D. Eisenhower, again faced former governor of Illinois Adlai E. Stevenson II. Running on his record, and aided by international crises on the eve of the election, Eisenhower increased his margin of victory over Stevenson to secure a second term as president.

By early 1956, the prospects for Eisenhower's reelection seemed to be good. Despite the controversy over public school desegregation following the Supreme Court's historic BROWN V. BOARD OF EDUCATION OF TOPEKA, KANSAS ruling in 1954, Eisenhower's personal popularity remained robust. A healthy economy and low inflation coupled with a generally successful foreign policy that had ended the Korean War in 1953 also augured well. The biggest question was whether Eisenhower would actually seek another term.

Early in his presidency, Eisenhower had confided to close friends his intention of being a one-term president. He

had run in 1952, he claimed, to reinvigorate the Republican Party and save the nation from the "mess" in Washington but he expected to step aside in 1956 in favor of a younger Republican candidate who would continue his "progressive moderate" policies. Eisenhower's heart attack in September 1955 added a complicating factor to his thinking about whether to seek reelection. During his convalescence, the president contemplated his political future and mulled over several possible Republican presidential candidates who shared his philosophy and might become legitimate contenders. One by one, however, he found reasons to rule them out and he eventually came to the conclusion that only he commanded the necessary public support and could ensure the required party unity to secure victory over the Democrats and preserve his legislative accomplishments. After receiving a clean bill of health, Eisenhower finally ended the speculation over his intentions by announcing his candidacy at the end of February 1956.

Having determined upon his own candidacy, Eisenhower dallied over the choice of his running mate. He had never developed a close relationship with Vice President RICHARD M. NIXON but he admired his loyalty and sterling efforts on behalf of Republican candidates around the nation. Privately, however, he worried that Nixon had not matured, remained too partisan, and lacked strong support beyond the ranks of Republican voters. In late 1955, Eisenhower mortified Nixon by offering him any post in the cabinet, except secretary of state, suggesting that this would broaden his administrative experience and improve his presidential prospects in 1960. Nixon disagreed with Eisenhower's analysis but loyally offered to do whatever Eisenhower ordered him to do. In effect, Nixon challenged Eisenhower to fire him. Ultimately, Eisenhower could not identify a suitable alternative to Nixon, and the vice president quietly accumulated enough commitments from delegates to the Republican National Convention to make the matter moot. After Eisenhower's belated endorsement, the convention selected Nixon with only one dissenting vote.

On the Democratic side, Stevenson and populist senator Estes Kefauver (D-TN) engaged in a hard-fought primary contest as most leading Democrats stood aside in the expectation that the popular Eisenhower would be reelected. As in 1952, the reformer Kefauver alarmed party bosses by capturing several primary victories. On the eve of the Florida primary, Stevenson and his campaign advisers decided to capitalize on their candidate's oratorical skills by debating Kefauver on live television, the first televised presidential debate. After a solid performance, Stevenson went on to secure a narrow victory in Florida and then achieved a landslide in California as Kefauver's camp ran out of funds and suspended campaigning. A last-minute effort to derail Stevenson's nomination at the Democratic National Convention by New York governor W. Averill Harriman, backed by

Democratic candidate Adlai E. Stevenson addresses a crowd in Paterson, New Jersey, 1956 *(Library of Congress)*

former President HARRY S. TRUMAN, fell short and Stevenson took the nomination on the first ballot.

Stevenson then energized the convention by throwing the selection of his running mate to the delegates. Kefauver enjoyed an initial advantage because of the backing of his primary delegates, but Senator JOHN F. KENNEDY (D-MA) commanded surprisingly strong support and almost won the nomination on the second ballot. As numerous "favorite son" candidates dropped out of the running, Kefauver gradually picked up the votes he needed to secure the nomination. In a generous concession speech, Kennedy cemented his credentials as a potential presidential candidate of the future.

Compared with the drama surrounding the nominating conventions, the presidential election campaign was rather anticlimactic. The Eisenhower campaign basked in the glow of peace and prosperity, and although Eisenhower could point to solid legislative accomplishments, the campaign stressed its major asset, the war hero's undiminished

personal popularity. Stevenson, meanwhile, campaigned much more aggressively than in 1952 and worked tirelessly to energize the base of traditional Democratic voters that would suffice to defeat Eisenhower. He even attempted to challenge Eisenhower's previously unimpeachable record on foreign policy by suggesting that the United States should ban atmospheric nuclear tests as a way of avoiding further radioactive contamination and jump-starting serious disarmament talks. Nixon quickly branded Stevenson an appeaser while the Eisenhower campaign pointed out the inconsistency in Stevenson's logic. If he were serious about abolishing the draft and moving toward a smaller, all-volunteer military, another of his campaign themes, then the United States would have to continue testing and deploying nuclear weapons to offset the Soviet bloc's numerical advantage in conventional forces. Stevenson was also embarrassed when Soviet leader Nikolai Bulganin endorsed his position on nuclear testing, allowing the Eisenhower team to con-

1956 Election Statistics

State	Number of Electors	Total Popular Vote	Elec Vote			Pop Vote		Margin of Victory	
			R	D	O*	R	D	Votes	% Total Vote
Alabama	11	496,871		10	1	2	1	85,150	17.14%
Arizona	4	290,173	4			1	2	64,110	22.09%
Arkansas	8	406,572		8		2	1	26,990	6.64%
California	32	5,466,355	32			1	2	607,533	11.11%
Colorado	6	663,074	6			1	2	130,482	19.68%
Connecticut	8	1,117,121	8			1	2	306,758	27.46%
Delaware	3	177,988	3			1	2	18,636	10.47%
Florida	10	1,124,220	10			1	2	163,478	14.54%
Georgia	12	663,480		12		2	1	224,442	33.83%
Idaho	4	272,989	4			1	2	61,111	22.39%
Illinois	27	4,407,407	27			1	2	847,645	19.23%
Indiana	13	1,974,607	13			1	2	398,903	20.20%
Iowa	10	1,234,564	10			1	2	227,329	18.41%
Kansas	8	866,243	8			1	2	270,561	31.23%
Kentucky	10	1,053,805	10			1	2	95,739	9.09%
Louisiana	10	617,544	10			1	2	85,070	13.78%
Maine	5	351,706	5			1	2	146,770	41.73%
Maryland	9	932,351	9			1	2	187,125	20.07%
Massachusetts	16	2,348,506	16			1	2	445,007	18.95%
Michigan	20	3,080,468	20			1	2	353,749	11.48%
Minnesota	11	1,340,005	11			1	2	101,777	7.60%
Mississippi	8	248,149		8		2	1	83,813	33.78%
Missouri	13	1,832,562		13		2	1	3,984	0.22%
Montana	4	271,171	4			1	2	38,695	14.27%
Nebraska	6	577,137	6			1	2	179,079	31.03%
Nevada	3	96,689	3			1	2	15,409	15.94%
New Hampshire	4	266,994	4			1	2	86,155	32.27%
New Jersey	16	2,484,312	16			1	2	756,605	30.46%
New Mexico	4	253,926	4			1	2	40,690	16.02%
New York	45	7,093,336	45			1	2	1,589,571	22.41%
North Carolina	14	1,165,592		14		2	1	15,468	1.33%
North Dakota	4	253,991	4			1	2	60,024	23.63%
Ohio	25	3,702,265	25			1	2	822,955	22.23%
Oklahoma	8	859,350	8			1	2	88,188	10.26%
Oregon	6	735,597	6			1	2	77,189	10.49%
Pennsylvania	32	4,576,503	32			1	2	603,483	13.19%
Rhode Island	4	387,611	4			1	2	64,029	16.52%
South Carolina	8	300,583		8		3	1	47,861	15.92%
South Dakota	4	293,857	4			1	2	49,281	16.77%
Tennessee	11	939,404	11			1	2	5,781	0.62%
Texas	24	1,955,545	24			1	2	220,661	11.28%
Utah	4	333,995	4			1	2	97,267	29.12%
Vermont	3	152,978	3			1	2	67,841	44.35%
Virginia	12	697,978	12			1	2	118,699	17.01%
Washington	9	1,150,889	9			1	2	97,428	8.47%
West Virginia	8	830,831	8			1	2	67,763	8.16%
Wisconsin	12	1,550,558	12			1	2	368,076	23.74%
Wyoming	3	124,127	3			1	2	25,019	20.16%
Total	531	62,021,979	457	73	1	1	2	9,551,152	15.40%

* One elector voted for Walter B. Jones for president.

Eisenhower Republican		Stevenson Democratic		Others	
195,694	39.39%	280,844	56.52%	20,333	4.09%
176,990	60.99%	112,880	38.90%	303	0.10%
186,287	45.82%	213,277	52.46%	7,008	1.72%
3,027,668	55.39%	2,420,135	44.27%	18,552	0.34%
394,479	59.49%	263,997	39.81%	4,598	0.69%
711,837	63.72%	405,079	36.26%	205	0.02%
98,057	55.09%	79,421	44.62%	510	0.29%
643,849	57.27%	480,371	42.73%	0	0.00%
216,652	32.65%	441,094	66.48%	5,734	0.86%
166,979	61.17%	105,868	38.78%	142	0.05%
2,623,327	59.52%	1,775,682	40.29%	8,398	0.19%
1,182,811	59.90%	783,908	39.70%	7,888	0.40%
729,187	59.06%	501,858	40.65%	3,519	0.29%
566,878	65.44%	296,317	34.21%	3,048	0.35%
572,192	54.30%	476,453	45.21%	5,160	0.49%
329,047	53.28%	243,977	39.51%	44,520	7.21%
249,238	70.87%	102,468	29.13%	0	0.00%
559,738	60.04%	372,613	39.96%	0	0.00%
1,393,197	59.32%	948,190	40.37%	7,119	0.30%
1,713,647	55.63%	1,359,898	44.15%	6,923	0.22%
719,302	53.68%	617,525	46.08%	3,178	0.24%
60,685	24.46%	144,498	58.23%	42,966	17.31%
914,289	49.89%	918,273	50.11%	0	0.00%
154,933	57.13%	116,238	42.87%	0	0.00%
378,108	65.51%	199,029	34.49%	0	0.00%
56,049	57.97%	40,640	42.03%	0	0.00%
176,519	66.11%	90,364	33.84%	111	0.04%
1,606,942	64.68%	850,337	34.23%	27,033	1.09%
146,788	57.81%	106,098	41.78%	1,040	0.41%
4,340,340	61.19%	2,750,769	38.78%	2,227	0.03%
575,062	49.34%	590,530	50.66%	0	0.00%
156,766	61.72%	96,742	38.09%	483	0.19%
2,262,610	61.11%	1,439,655	38.89%	0	0.00%
473,769	55.13%	385,581	44.87%	0	0.00%
406,393	55.25%	329,204	44.75%	0	0.00%
2,585,252	56.49%	1,981,769	43.30%	9,482	0.21%
225,819	58.26%	161,790	41.74%	2	0.00%
75,700	25.18%	136,372	45.37%	88,511	29.45%
171,569	58.39%	122,288	41.61%	0	0.00%
462,288	49.21%	456,507	48.60%	20,609	2.19%
1,080,619	55.26%	859,958	43.98%	14,968	0.77%
215,631	64.56%	118,364	35.44%	0	0.00%
110,390	72.16%	42,549	27.81%	39	0.03%
386,459	55.37%	267,760	38.36%	43,759	6.27%
620,430	53.91%	523,002	45.44%	7,457	0.65%
449,297	54.08%	381,534	45.92%	0	0.00%
954,844	61.58%	586,768	37.84%	8,946	0.58%
74,573	60.08%	49,554	39.92%	0	0.00%
35,579,180	57.37%	26,028,028	41.97%	414,771	0.67%

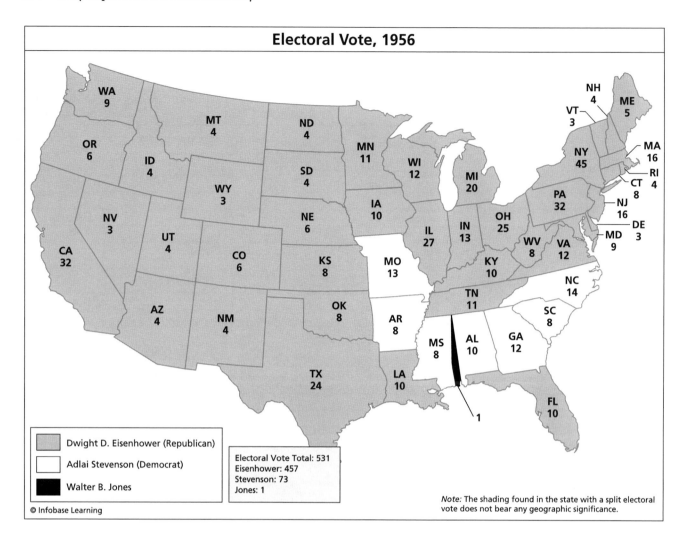

Electoral Vote, 1956

Dwight D. Eisenhower (Republican)

Adlai Stevenson (Democrat)

Walter B. Jones

Electoral Vote Total: 531
Eisenhower: 457
Stevenson: 73
Jones: 1

Note: The shading found in the state with a split electoral vote does not bear any geographic significance.

© Infobase Learning

demn foreign meddling in an American election and paint Stevenson as a dupe of the Soviets.

As in 1952, television figured prominently in both campaigns but the Republicans again employed it far more effectively. As an incumbent president, Eisenhower had to continue to conduct the nation's business and he lacked the time to travel as extensively as he had done in his first election. More important, his continuing health problems, particularly a bout of ileitis in mid-1956 that required surgery, persuaded the president that he would not have the stamina to conduct a whistle-stop campaign. He therefore embraced the new technology as a way to reach millions of Americans he could not otherwise address. Stevenson, however, preferred grass-roots campaigning and always viewed television as a necessary evil, scoffing that serious discussion of public policy could not be done in five-minute spots that sold presidential candidates like soap.

Although he mirrored his opponent's television advertising, he suffered from the fact that the major Madison Avenue advertising agencies refused to work for a Democrat out of fear of losing their wealthy Republican business clients.

Consequently, Stevenson's spots lacked the polish of Eisenhower's. Also, whereas Eisenhower welcomed professional acting advice, Stevenson never mastered the medium, resulting in such problems as mistakes while reading from a teleprompter and occasionally overrunning his allotted time so that the screen faded to black with the candidate in mid-sentence. Although the impact of television on voters' behavior remains unclear, the use of television enabled Eisenhower to spend only 13 days on the road, compared with Stevenson's 42 days, while still blanketing the nation with his message.

In the final days of the campaign, foreign policy crises flared up that played to Eisenhower's strength. In October, riots in Poland led to a change in government and similar disturbances in Hungary briefly saw the emergence of a reformist government until the Hungarians threatened to leave the Warsaw Pact and their movement was ruthlessly crushed by Soviet troops. At the same time, an Anglo-French-Israeli invasion of Egypt that attempted to seize the Suez Canal and topple Egyptian president Gamal Abdel Nasser produced a crisis in the Western alliance. Eisenhower condemned the Soviets' repression in Hungary but he wisely refused to be drawn into the conflict within the Soviet bloc. In the Middle East, meanwhile, he opposed his allies' resort to military force and led efforts by the United Nations to achieve a cease-fire. The events reminded American voters of the dangers of the cold war and probably reinforced their sense that the nation's security was already in experienced, reliable hands.

On election day, November 6, 1956, Eisenhower won a sweeping personal mandate. His almost 10 million-vote margin of victory far exceeded his 1952 plurality, and he prevailed in the popular vote by 57 percent to 42 percent. He carried 41 of 48 states, and made further inroads into the formerly Democratic South by picking up Louisiana, the first Republican president to carry the state since 1876. He also added Kentucky and West Virginia to the Republican column, with only Missouri switching over to Stevenson from Eisenhower. The only blemish for Eisenhower was that his great personal popularity failed to translate into a congressional victory for the Republicans. Democrats had reclaimed Congress in the 1954 midterm elections. As in 1952, he ran well ahead of his party, which lost two seats in the House of Representatives and one in the Senate. Eisenhower therefore began his second term with a resounding vote of personal support but constrained by Democratic majorities in both houses of Congress.

EISENHOWER ADMINISTRATION (1953–1961)

Eisenhower's Philosophy

Dwight D. Eisenhower came to the presidency with a set of deeply held beliefs about the proper role of the national government in the modern age and the ideal society, and these shaped his approach to government throughout his two terms as president from 1953 to 1961. As a former military man who had led Allied forces to victory in World War II, he had a keen appreciation for efficient organization, a general dislike for politics and politicians, a suspicion of popular democracy, and a profound commitment to duty and public service. His philosophy has been described by historian Robert Griffith as "the corporate commonwealth." He hoped to resolve the contradictions of modern capitalism by fostering a harmonious society, stressing the mutual interdependence of all classes and economic interests. Ideally, he wanted to encourage all interest groups to work together cooperatively for the common good to achieve order, stability, and progress.

The key to achieving this "corporate commonwealth" was to seek balance, what Eisenhower called a "middle way," between labor and capital, liberalism and conservatism, and the federal government and the private sector. Like the more conservative Republicans, Eisenhower wanted to halt the expansion of the federal government's role in the nation's affairs, but unlike them he was willing to concede a limited role for the state in the political economy. For example, he believed that the government had a responsibility to prevent or correct abuses stemming from unregulated capitalism. The government might also bring competing interests together to encourage social harmony and blend the individual and the public good. Eisenhower often repeated the dictum attributed to ABRAHAM LINCOLN that: "The legitimate object of government is to do for a community of people whatever they need to have done but cannot do at all or cannot do so well. In all that the people can individually do . . . for themselves Government ought not to interfere."

Eisenhower's distaste for politicians, whom he believed pandered to an uneducated public opinion, encouraged him to seek the help of like-minded public-spirited leaders from the private sector who would exercise disinterested judgment on the pressing issues of the day. Indeed, many progressive-minded business leaders shared Eisenhower's vision of the corporate commonwealth and had backed his candidacy. Naturally, as president, Eisenhower turned to some of these same people to provide the expert leadership he sought.

Economic Policy in the First Term

Eisenhower's "middle way" philosophy manifested itself in his administration's major economic policies. On the one hand, Eisenhower agreed with conservatives about eliminating unpopular Korean War price controls, balancing the budget, and reforming the New Deal system of agricultural price supports. On the other hand, while generally seeking to limit the size of the government, he recognized the necessity for a modest expansion of the welfare state in certain areas.

Eisenhower came to office determined to cut federal spending, reduce taxes, and move toward a balanced budget. Like most Republicans, he worried that the 20 years of deficit spending under the Democrats had fueled price inflation, weakened the value of the dollar, and undermined private initiative. Only by restoring fiscal discipline, he believed, could the national government create conditions conducive to long-term economic growth. Influenced by the thinking of his chief economic adviser, Columbia University economist Arthur F. Burns, Eisenhower moved his administration toward the notion of a stabilizing budget. Under this idea, the budget would be balanced over the course of the business cycle rather than every fiscal year. Thus, during periods of economic downturn, when government revenues declined and unemployment payments increased, compensatory budget deficits would be tolerated in the expectation that they would be offset by surpluses during more prosperous times.

Eisenhower's economic ideas faced their first real challenge in the economic downturn of 1953–54. Cutbacks in military spending following the armistice in Korea, tight

IKE LOVES LUCY: EISENHOWER AND THE RISE OF TELEVISION

Television manufacturer RCA ran full-page advertisements in late 1952 championing the fact that "television has brought their government back to the people!" This claim was based on the fact that so much of the campaign that year between Republican Dwight D. Eisenhower and Democrat Adlai Stevenson was broadcast through television, and certainly politics is one vehicle that can be used to study the rise of television, but it is not necessarily the only or best one for that purpose. Instead, students interested in the rise and impact of television while the medium was still in its infancy would be well advised to examine the interface between entertainment programming and politics to understand how broadcasting might evolve.

I Love Lucy (1951–57), starring real-life wife and husband Lucille Ball and Desi Arnaz as Lucy and Ricky Ricardo, was a phenomenally popular television program in the 1950s, counting Dwight and Mamie Eisenhower among its many fans. Arnaz's insistence that the program use three fixed cameras and be taped revolutionized the genre and created a second life for the program in syndication. In key ways, it intersected and paralleled the popularity of President Eisenhower while also reflecting the importance television would come to play in American politics and popular culture for the rest of the 20th century.

Ball was charged with being a communist in 1953, but her immense popularity insulated her from the sort of mudslinging that ruined the careers of others in show business. On September 6, 1953, Walter Winchell, the celebrity gossip columnist, wrote that Ball was a communist. The year earlier she had admitted before the House Committee on Un-American Activities (HUAC) to briefly registering with the Communist Party out of deference to her grandfather's wishes in 1936. HUAC cleared her of any wrongdoing and her career did not suffer as a result. On Friday, September 11, 1953, the evening that the first live episode of the new season was to be filmed, Arnaz spoke to the audience: "Lucy has never been a Communist. Not now and never will be. I was kicked out of Cuba because of Communism. We despise everything about it. Lucy is as American as Barney Baruch and Ike Eisenhower. By the way, we both voted for Eisenhower." The audience roared its approval, and when a teary-eyed Ball came on stage her husband declared, "And now I want you to meet my favorite wife—my favorite redhead—in fact, that's the only thing red about her, and even *that's* not legitimate."

Earlier that year, when her character gave birth to television son Little Ricky, the episode, which aired on January 19, 1953, garnered more viewers that Eisenhower's inauguration the following day. In all, 44 million Americans—more than one-quarter of the U.S. population—tuned in to see Ricky Ricardo in the waiting room, far more than the 29 million who watched the inauguration. This episode marked the culmination of Ball's real-life pregnancy, which was filmed on television as a major component of the story line that season, the first time a pregnant woman was depicted on television or in a film. The episodes depicting Lucy Ricardo's pregnancy were shot out of order, and in real life Lucille Ball gave birth to Desiderio Alberto Arnaz IV at 8 a.m. on January 19, 1953. One scholar has argued that Lucy's triumph over Ike in the ratings wars reflected the prominence of domesticity over politics and public life in the 1950s. Certainly, the double birth of Little Ricky on television and young Desi in real life garnered more viewers than Eisenhower's inauguration, but a better explanation of the confluence of the Lucy and the Ike phenomenon is to view it in the larger confluence of politics with entertainment. Here television played a major role as politicians found new ways to exploit the medium.

Eisenhower was the first televised president. He and his campaign advisers realized the power of television used wisely for politicking. Just as Arnaz revolutionized the production of situation comedies, Eisenhower was the first candidate for the White House to make effective use of the short advertising spot. His opponent in 1952, Adlai Stevenson, paid for 30-minute blocks of time, and even then talked longer than the time permitted, but Eisenhower ran short commercials during and after popular television programs such as *I Love Lucy*. Unfortunately for Stevenson, one of his 30-minute paid blocks of time on television preempted an episode of *I Love Lucy*, angering countless fans and prompting one voter to write the Democratic hopeful: "I love Lucy, I like Ike, drop dead." That threatening letter conveyed more than perhaps its author intended: If politicians could not learn how to coexist and manipulate television they would not survive in the late 20th century.

money policies at the Federal Reserve to curtail anticipated postwar inflation, falling farm prices and a natural downturn in the business cycle pushed the economy into recession by late 1953. The Eisenhower administration responded with a conservative variant of Keynesian economics. The president authorized accelerated outlays for government projects already funded, liberalized the terms for federally insured home mortgages to stimulate home construction, and privately encouraged bankers to lower interest rates. Additionally, the administration agreed to reduce Korean War excise taxes and corporate taxes even at the cost of running a budget deficit. This combination of actions seemed to work and the economy revived in late 1954. By 1956, Eisenhower had succeeded in achieving a balanced budget.

To the surprise of some fellow Republicans, Eisenhower's middle way philosophy led him to seek a modest expansion of the welfare state. In such areas as Social Security, health insurance, and public housing, he believed that the government had a responsibility to establish "a floor that covers the pit of disaster" for American workers. In 1954, he persuaded Congress to expand Social Security coverage to an additional 10.5 million workers and raise monthly benefits. He failed, however, to expand private health insurance to the 63 million Americans without coverage by having a federal fund underwrite the risks of health insurance carriers who extended coverage to high-risk consumers. Staunch opposition from the American Medical Association and many insurance companies killed the health reinsurance plan in Congress. Eisenhower's public housing program was only modestly successful. His comprehensive housing bill proposed building 140,000 public housing units per year, but opposition from fellow Republicans resulted in a final law that limited the number of units built in any given year to the number of units demolished through urban renewal programs.

In agriculture and natural resource development, Eisenhower sought to reduce the role of the federal government. In conjunction with Secretary of Agriculture Ezra Taft Benson, the president attempted to replace the depression-era system of farm subsidies, which had become the single most expensive domestic program but had failed to solve the fundamental problem of agricultural surpluses and declining farm incomes, with a more market-oriented solution. In 1954, Congress enacted more flexible price supports, supposedly allowing the secretary of agriculture to adjust them according to market conditions, and two years later Congress approved Eisenhower's Soil Bank scheme that paid farmers to take land out of production. Neither approach had much impact on the persistent farm problem. With regard to natural resource development, Eisenhower determined to check any further expansion of the Tennessee Valley Authority (TVA), a government corporation created in 1933 to provide flood control and electrical power to a seven-state region in the South. Viewed as a shining centerpiece of the New Deal by liberal Democrats, Eisenhower publicly referred to it as an example of "creeping socialism" that competed unfairly with private enterprise. Although he was not willing to sell off the TVA, as favored by some Republicans, he curtailed new federal power contracts with the agency and appointed a director dedicated to putting it on a self-sustaining basis.

Perhaps the domestic economic program that best epitomized Eisenhower's public-private approach, and its inherent flaws, was the 1956 NATIONAL INTERSTATE AND DEFENSE HIGHWAYS ACT. This was an area in which Eisenhower considered federal activism essential. Despite the rapidly increasing number of automobiles, the nation lacked urban expressways and four-lane highways connecting major cities because for years no consensus had emerged on how to administer or fund a federal highway program. For Eisenhower, modernizing the nation's roads was vital both for economic development and for national defense, and only the national government had the necessary wherewithal to direct such a major undertaking. He delegated the task of developing the national highway program to a blue-ribbon advisory commission made up of experts whose recommendations formed the basis of legislation submitted to Congress in 1955. The administration's plan envisioned a 41,000-mile system of interstate highways linking the major cities and funded primarily through a Highway Trust Fund that would keep most of the program off budget. Enacted in 1956, funding came from pay-as-you-go federal taxes on gasoline, tires, and trucks. On the surface, the program appeared to epitomize Eisenhower's faith in expert leadership and public-private cooperation. Critics would later note, however, that the final measure paid little attention to the long-term impact on the urban landscape and ignored environmental issues such as air quality and inefficient energy consumption.

Anticommunism

One of the most troubling political problems confronting Eisenhower when he took office in 1953 was Senator Joseph R. McCarthy (R-WI) and his self-aggrandizing crusade to purge the government of communists and fellow-travelers. The junior Republican senator from Wisconsin had exploded onto the national scene in 1950 with spectacular allegations that America's reversals in the Cold War were the result of communist subversion in the federal government. These assaults on prominent Democrats had helped secure the Republican victory in 1952, but McCarthy's actions now caused difficulties for the new administration. First, he held up Senate confirmation of several of Eisenhower's nominees for top diplomatic posts while he investigated unfounded allegations about their loyalty. Later, he launched investigations into the Voice of America and U.S. Information Agency, institutions now run by the Republican administration.

Eisenhower had cynically used McCarthy during the election campaign to discredit the Democrats, but initially he was unsure how to handle him as president. Eisenhower personally loathed the senator, his tactics, and his demagoguery but he was reluctant to speak out against his excesses. Direct confrontation went against Eisenhower's preference for building consensus, especially as McCarthy seemed to command broad popularity. In addition, McCarthy craved publicity and a public spat with the president would play into his hands and demean the presidency. Finally, Eisenhower agreed with McCarthy's critique of communist subversion, although he preferred to handle such problems quietly through established administrative and judicial procedures rather than in the court of public opinion. His own internal security policies resulted in the firing of over 500 State Department employees and he had no hesitation about

The interstate highway system remains one of the enduring legacies of Eisenhower's presidency. *(Caitlin Mirra/Shutterstock)*

stripping J. Robert Oppenheimer, arguably the most famous American scientist who had earned celebrity for his wartime work on the atomic bomb, of his security clearances because of his Communist Party connections. Eisenhower's approach to McCarthy was to deal with him indirectly, in effect giving him enough rope to hang himself. Only when McCarthy launched an investigation into alleged communist penetration of Eisenhower's beloved army did he openly break with the senator. During several weeks of televised hearings in the spring of 1954, the infamous ARMY-MCCARTHY HEARINGS, Eisenhower worked with Vice President RICHARD NIXON and Republican surrogates in the Senate to undermine the demagogue. At the end of the year, the full Senate censured McCarthy, finally breaking his power. As historian Richard Fried has observed, however, giving McCarthy enough rope "enabled him to hang others before hanging himself."

Civil Rights in the First Term

The most pressing moral issue confronting the nation when Eisenhower entered office was the African-American struggle for civil and political rights, but in this area his philosophy and leadership style were found wanting. Like many leaders of his generation, Eisenhower held conservative views on civil rights. Born and raised in a racially segregated society and professionalized in a segregated military, Eisenhower accepted the status quo in race relations. As a candidate in 1952, he courted conservative white southerners. He believed that real progress in race relations could be achieved only by changing long-held attitudes and rejected federal compunction on the grounds that it would promote the expansion of federal authority and provoke defiance and disorder. As president, he repeatedly counselled African Americans to exercise patience and restraint and to adopt gradualist tactics.

Eisenhower's ambivalence over civil rights surfaced in his handling of the public school desegregation cases before the Supreme Court collectively known as *BROWN V. BOARD OF EDUCATION OF TOPEKA, KANSAS*. He only reluctantly allowed the Justice Department to present a brief advocating a gradual transition to integrated schools, privately suggested to Chief Justice Earl Warren—whom he had appointed—that the status quo in southern schools should be preserved, and refused to issue any public endorsement when the Court

A man going into the "colored" entrance of a movie house on a Saturday afternoon in Belzoni, Mississippi *(Library of Congress)*

issued its landmark 1954 ruling declaring "separate but equal" educational facilities "inherently unequal." Eisenhower personally believed the ruling a mistake that would threaten white support for public schools in the South and possibly create a backlash by white segregationists that would further set back the cause of racial equality.

When the Court later heard arguments regarding implementation of the ruling, Eisenhower helped to draft a brief counselling a gradualist approach that would allow white southerners time to adjust to the new reality. Although the justices declared that desegregation should proceed "with all deliberate speed," they failed to establish a timetable for compliance and Eisenhower ensured that his Justice Department would not take the initiative. Eisenhower's lack of leadership in support of the Court's ruling allowed southern white resistance to mobilize and thwart the Court's intent. Significantly, during the 1956 election campaign, Eisenhower vetoed a statement in the Republican Party platform crediting his administration with the *Brown* decision.

The "New Look"

Foreign policy had been the key issue in Eisenhower's decision to run for the presidency in 1952, but despite the Republicans' criticism of President HARRY S. TRUMAN's strategy of containment as too negative and their promise to "liberate" the captive peoples of Eastern Europe and Asia from the Sino-Soviet communist yoke, Eisenhower's thinking had much in common with his predecessor. Unlike many isolationists in his own party, Eisenhower strongly supported collective security and containment. Where the Truman administration had erred, he believed, was in its failure to develop a coherent strategic concept that balanced the nation's international commitments with its limited resources. Real national security entailed defending a "way of life" rather than just territory, and he therefore set out to devise a strategy of containment that would be sustainable indefinitely. In effect, he sought a "middle way" between isolationism and unrestrained globalism. The result was the "NEW LOOK," designed to deliver "security with solvency" over the long haul that would form the basis of Eisenhower's national security policy for the remainder of his presidency.

In late 1953, following extensive discussions within the National Security Council, the Eisenhower administration codified its New Look strategy in National Security Council Paper 162/2. The strategy was designed to meet the Soviet threat without "seriously weakening the U.S. economy" or undermining the nation's "fundamental values and institutions." It advocated a capital-intensive approach that emphasized the massive retaliatory power of nuclear weapons to deter general war with the Sino-Soviet bloc and a readiness to employ such weapons should deterrence fail. It also reiterated the importance of collective security, stressing the necessity of overseas air bases and the military and economic

resources of the major industrialized states for the free world cause. To the dismay of Republican isolationists, American troops would have to remain deployed overseas for the foreseeable future because they symbolized America's commitment to its friends and allies. Stimulating international trade and encouraging global economic growth and prosperity, however, would eventually enable these allies to assume complete responsibility for their own defense. The administration expected that increased reliance on cost-efficient air-atomic power, coupled with reductions in relatively expensive conventional forces, would stabilize peacetime defense spending at around $34 billion annually, significantly less than the $50 billion Truman's advisers had advocated. Although critics in the armed forces, Congress, and even his own administration would periodically challenge what they saw as a dangerous overreliance on weapons of mass destruction and an unwise obsession with budget ceilings, the New Look remained the core of Eisenhower's grand strategy throughout his presidency.

Eisenhower's secretary of state, John Foster Dulles, publicly articulated this asymmetrical strategy of deterrence. Henceforth, the United States would prevent communist aggression by shoring up local defenses and building up its own "massive retaliatory power." Potential aggressors would no longer be free to "pick the time, place, and method of warfare" because the United States would develop "a great capacity to retaliate, instantly, by means and at places of our choosing." The United States would not necessarily revert to all-out nuclear warfare to meet every contingency but would develop the flexibility to employ various responses, including tactical nuclear weapons. To make this asymmetrical deterrence credible, moreover, Eisenhower and Dulles asserted their resolve to go to war and employ nuclear weapons if necessary. The key for policymakers, as Dulles described it, was to be prepared to go "to the brink" of nuclear war without getting into one, a policy that came to be known as "brinkmanship."

Crises in Asia

Upon taking office, Eisenhower and Dulles employed the art of nuclear brinkmanship toward the ongoing war in Korea and the deadlocked armistice talks. Terminating the war satisfactorily would reduce the burden on American resources, thereby effecting the savings anticipated in the New Look, and restore faith in the credibility of the United States to contain communist aggression. In May 1953, Eisenhower approved contingency plans to expand the war with a new ground offensive accompanied by tactical nuclear air strikes against Chinese air bases and Dulles signalled to the Chinese that the United States was willing to resort to nuclear war if negotiations collapsed. The threats seemed to work. The Chinese and North Koreans accepted Western demands on the voluntary repatriation of prisoners of war, paving the way for an armistice in July. Eisenhower and Dulles believed that nuclear brinkmanship had prevailed, although scholars would later suggest that Chinese and North Korean war weariness and a focus on domestic economic and political problems by the new government in the Soviet Union following Joseph Stalin's death weighed more heavily in the decision by these governments to seek a negotiated settlement.

The collapse of French colonial rule in Indochina provided a second test for massive retaliation and brinkmanship. Following World War II, France had fought a war in the region to try to regain its colonial empire, but in 1954, following defeat at the BATTLE OF DIEN BIEN PHU, France abandoned its ambitions in Southeast Asia. Eisenhower worried that the imminent defeat of French forces at the hands of the communist-led Viet Minh threatened the stability of all Southeast Asia and might undermine American efforts to contain communism by building up Japan as a regional bulwark. As international negotiations commenced at Geneva to determine Indochina's future, the United States hinted at direct military intervention if no satisfactory agreements were reached. Neither the Soviet Union nor China wanted a wider war and both powers pressed Vietnamese leader Ho Chi Minh to accept a settlement short of total victory. The GENEVA ACCORDS temporarily divided Vietnam at the 17th parallel, leaving Ho in control of the North and a noncommunist regime in the South pending nationwide elections scheduled for 1956. The United States pledged "not to disturb" the agreements but quickly threw its support to strongman Ngo Dinh Diem in the South and encouraged him not to allow elections to take place, which Washington feared would entail a communist victory. In this case, Eisenhower's diplomacy succeeded in limiting territorial losses to communism but the growing commitment to noncommunist South Vietnam created future difficulties.

Almost immediately, a third challenge to massive retaliation and brinkmanship appeared in September 1954, when the People's Republic of China (PRC) began shelling the small islands of Quemoy (now Jinmen) and Matsu (now Mazu) off the Chinese coast that were still occupied by Chinese Nationalists loyal to Chiang Kai-shek (now Jiang Jieshi) on Taiwan. In 1949 communist Mao Zedong had defeated Chiang's forces in the Chinese Revolution and established the PRC on mainland China. An American ally in World War II who had close ties to prominent Republicans, Chiang had ambitions to recover the mainland from Mao's Communists and had been using the islands to stage raids. The United States tried to deter any move against the islands by negotiating a mutual defense treaty with Chiang, committing the United States to the defense of Taiwan and the Pescadores (now Penghu) islands, an archipelago just off the west coast of Taiwan, and "such other territories as may be determined by mutual agreement." This attempt at deterrence through ambiguity failed when Mao's forces seized another National-

ist-held island chain, the Tachens, early in 1955 and shelling of the other offshore islands continued sporadically. Eisenhower therefore decided to "draw the line" unambiguously in the Taiwan Strait, assuring Chiang that the United States would defend Quemoy and Matsu and seeking congressional preapproval for possible military action. Again, American contingency planning contemplated the use of tactical nuclear weapons and Eisenhower hinted at the use of such weapons. Having attained his immediate objective in the Tachens and under Soviet pressure to ease tensions, Mao ceased the bombardment. The threat of massive retaliation apparently helped to resolve the crisis but American actions strained relations with European allies who saw no logical reason to risk a global nuclear war over several small islands lacking clear strategic value.

Third World Problems in the First Term

As the various Asian crises demonstrated, Eisenhower entered office at a time of political ferment in the so-called third world, a term that referred to underdeveloped nations unaligned with either the communist or the noncommunist bloc. As the old European empires gave way to newly independent states, Eisenhower faced a difficult dilemma. The United States had to maintain sound relations with key European allies, such as Britain and France, but the nation needed also to convince peoples in developing countries that their long-term interests would best be served by aligning themselves with the free world in the cold war struggle. Moreover, the vast manpower and essential raw materials in these areas were vital to the continued prosperity and strength of the free world and their loss to communism might decisively alter the world balance of power. In practice, Eisenhower's avowed intention to encourage "slower and more orderly" change in developing nations ran up against cold war perceptions and geopolitics, and the administration tended to back the pro-Western status quo in a way that frustrated popular nationalist movements.

Where Western interests appeared to be directly challenged by misguided nationalist leaders who were opening the door to communist influence, Eisenhower acted ruthlessly. Thus, in Iran, the Central Intelligence Agency (CIA) collaborated with the pro-Western elements of the Iranian military to oust nationalist prime minister Mohammed Mossadegh, who had nationalized the holdings of the Anglo-Iranian Oil Company and was on the verge of inviting Soviet technicians to run the nation's oil industry. In the aftermath, Shah Mohammed Reza Pahlavi emerged with enhanced powers and his government gratefully signed a new oil agreement that opened Iran's lucrative oil market to American companies. Similarly, the CIA conspired with Guatemalan dissidents against democratically elected president Jacobo Arbenz Guzmán, whose populist land redistribu-

(continues on page 286)

ADMINISTRATION TIME LINE

1953

January 20 Dwight Eisenhower is inaugurated president.

February 11 President Eisenhower denies petitions for clemency for Julius and Ethel Rosenberg, and the couple are executed on June 19.

March 5 Joseph Stalin's death is announced by the Soviet Union.

April 1 Congress authorizes the creation of the Department of Health, Education and Welfare.

May 22 Eisenhower signs the Submerged Lands Act.

July 26 Eisenhower announces that an armistice has been reached in the Korean War.

August 19 CIA operation AJAX overthrows Iranian prime minister Mohammed Mossadegh.

September 30 Eisenhower nominates Earl Warren to be chief justice of the United States.

October Eisenhower's "New Look" solution to achieving security with solvency is formally codified in National Security Council Paper 162/2.

October 8 Eisenhower announces that a hydrogen bomb was tested in the Soviet Union.

December 8 At the United Nations General Assembly, Eisenhower calls on the other nuclear powers—Great Britain and the Soviet Union—to join the United States in donating a set amount of fissionable material from their weapons stockpiles to peaceful purposes under international auspices, known as "Atoms for Peace."

1954

April 7 At a press conference Eisenhower speaks about the "falling domino" principle, more popularly known as the domino theory.

April 22 The Army-McCarthy hearings begin.

April 26 The Geneva Conference convenes with the foreign ministers of the United States, the Soviet Union, France, and Great Britain in attendance to seek peace in Korea and Indochina.

May 7 Dien Bien Phu, the French garrison in Vietnam, falls, terminating French colonial rule and assuring U.S. involvement in Indochina.

May 17 The Supreme Court announces its unanimous decision in *Brown v. Board of Education of Topeka, Kansas,* removing the most important constitutional obstacle to equal educational opportunities for African-American school children.

May 27 The Atomic Energy Commission's Personnel Security Board finds J. Robert Oppenheimer to be loyal but nonetheless deems him a security risk and recommends that his security clearance be revoked.

June 16 Eisenhower orders the Atomic Energy Commission to issue a contract to Dixon-Yates, a private firm, instead of to the public TVA.

June 18 Jacobo Arbenz Guzmán, elected president of Guatemala, is overthrown in a CIA-backed coup.

July 21 The Geneva Accords are signed, providing a temporary partition in Vietnam.

August 24 The Communist Control Act is passed by Congress.

September 3 The People's Republic of China begins shelling the small islands of Quemoy (Jinmen) and Matsu (Mazu) off the Chinese coast that were still occupied by Chinese Nationalists loyal to Jiang Jieshi (Chiang Kai-shek) on Taiwan.

September 8 The United States, Britain, France, Australia, New Zealand, Thailand, the Philippines, and Pakistan sign the Manila Pact, establishing SEATO, the Southeast Asia Treaty Organization, a regional collective security system.

December 2 The full Senate votes 67–22 to censure McCarthy for bringing "dishonor and disrepute" to the Senate.

1955

January 28 Congress passes the Formosa (Taiwan) Resolution, giving Eisenhower a blank check to wage war in defense of Taiwan.

March 16 Eisenhower issues a statement supporting the use of nuclear weapons in the event of a war with China.

July After much controversy, Eisenhower orders the cancellation of the Dixon-Yates contract.

July 21 At the 1955 Geneva summit, Eisenhower introduces the "Open Skies" concept, calling for the United States and the Soviet Union to exchange blueprints of military installations and permit mutual aerial surveillance.

September 24 Eisenhower suffers a heart attack.

October 10 The Supreme Court orders the integration of the University of Alabama.

November 15 Adlai Stevenson announces that he will again seek the Democratic presidential nomination.

November 25 Segregation on interstate train and bus travel is banned by the Interstate Commerce Commission.

December 1 Rosa Parks is arrested for refusing to give up her seat to a white man on a Montgomery, Alabama, bus.

December 26 Eisenhower talks with Vice President Richard Nixon about taking a cabinet post instead of running for reelection in 1956.

1956
February 29 Eisenhower announces that he will be a candidate for reelection.

March 12 The Southern Manifesto is signed by 19 senators and 81 members of the House of Representatives.

April 25 After a second failed attempt to persuade Nixon to move from the vice presidency to the cabinet, Eisenhower announces that Nixon will remain on the ticket with him in 1956.

May 28 Eisenhower signs into law the Soil Bank Act, an attempt to conserve soil and water and to address the problem of persistent agricultural surpluses.

May 31 Eisenhower authorizes the use of U-2 planes to spy on the Soviet Union.

June 29 Eisenhower signs the National Interstate and Defense Highways Act, laying the basis for the modern interstate highway system in the United States.

July 26 The Suez Canal is nationalized.

October 29 The 1956 Suez crisis, also known as the Suez-Sinai War, starts with Britain, France, and Israel secretly engaging in a joint effort to reclaim the Suez Canal. President Eisenhower opposes such action.

November 6 Eisenhower wins a sweeping reelection victory by a vote margin of almost 10 million.

1957
January 5 The Eisenhower Doctrine for the Middle East, offering economic and military assistance to friendly regimes and promising military support to any nation threatened by "international communism," is announced.

January 20 Eisenhower is inaugurated to a second term as president.

March 9 Eisenhower signs legislation implementing the Eisenhower Doctrine.

September 9 Eisenhower signs the first civil rights bill into law since the 19th century.

September 24 Eisenhower dispatches 1,000 paratroopers and federalizes the Arkansas Guard to protect the nine African-American students integrating Central High School in Little Rock, Arkansas.

October 4 The Soviet Union launches the first earth satellite, *Sputnik.*

1958
April 2 Eisenhower recommends the creation of the National Aeronautic and Space Administration (NASA) as a civilian agency to plan for and oversee space exploration.

April 27 Vice President Nixon leaves for a tour of Latin America. His car is attacked on May 8 in Peru and on May 13 in Venezuela.

(continues)

ADMINISTRATION TIME LINE *(continued)*

July 15 Eisenhower orders 14,000 marines and army personnel into Beirut, Lebanon, after President Camille Chamoun indicated that he feared a coup and claimed it was communist inspired.

July 29 Eisenhower signs legislation creating NASA.

August 6 The Defense Reorganization Act of 1958 is passed, creating greater unification of the armed forces and establishing the management structure over the military that would remain in effect for a generation.

August 23 The Chinese Communist forces renew a bombing campaign against Quemoy and Matsu.

September 2 Eisenhower signs the National Defense Education Act providing federal funds to improve scientific education.

1959

January 1 Fidel Castro comes to power in Cuba.

July 24 The "kitchen debate" between Vice President Nixon and Soviet premier Nikita Khrushchev takes place in Moscow.

September 14 Eisenhower signs the Landrum-Griffin Act into law, providing more oversight and controls on labor unions.

September 15–27 Khrushchev is the first Soviet leader to visit the United States.

1960

January 9 Vice President Nixon announces he will be running for president that fall, and four days later Eisenhower states his support for Nixon.

March 17 Eisenhower approves a CIA covert plan to replace Castro's government by isolating Cuba internationally, waging economic warfare against the regime, beaming anti-Castro radio broadcasts at the island, and training a paramilitary force of Cuban exiles to lead the armed struggle and, possibly, assassinate Castro.

May 5 The Soviet Union announces it has shot down an American U-2 spy plane in Soviet airspace, embarrassing the United States and dashing the prospects for any significant détente in East-West relations for the remainder of the Eisenhower presidency.

May 6 Eisenhower signs the Civil Rights Act of 1960.

May 16 Nine days after he acknowledged the U-2 flights over the Soviet Union, Eisenhower refuses to apologize, ending the summit held in Paris with the Soviet Union.

1961

January 17 Eisenhower delivers his farewell address, warning the nation against the dangers of the "military-industrial complex."

January 20 Eisenhower spends his last day in office.

(continued from page 283)
tion program threatened the holdings of the nation's largest landowner, the American-owned United Fruit Company, and whose administration contained several communists. After Arbenz's ouster, the new U.S.-backed regime staged a counterrevolution that restored lands to the previous owners and broke up peasant and labor unions. In both instances, containing communism took precedence over progressive nationalist reform and economic development.

In Egypt, Eisenhower initially seemed to find the sort of charismatic nationalist leader who might be effectively courted, only to be rudely disabused. President Gamal Abdel Nasser had overthrown the pro-Western monarchy and harbored ambitious plans to modernize Egypt, eliminate old-style imperialism, and unite the Arab world. At first, Eisenhower tried to accommodate Nasser as a potential regional ally, persuading the British to give up their Egyptian military bases around the Suez Canal, the traditional lifeline of the British Empire. Nasser, however, remained adamantly independent, seeking military and economic support from both East and West. In 1956, when the Eisenhower administration clumsily tried to use economic aid to tie Nasser to the West, the Egyptian president nationalized the Anglo-French Suez Canal Company, provoking a sharp split among the Western allies. The Eisenhower administration urged restraint and warned that colonial-style military interven-

Egyptian president Gamal Abdel Nasser is cheered in Cairo after issuing his order nationalizing the Suez Canal Company, August 1, 1956. *(Central Intelligence Agency/United States Federal Government)*

tion would inflame the entire Arab world against the West and open the door to Soviet influence, but the advice fell on deaf ears. A farcical Anglo-French-Israeli invasion to topple Nasser and recover the canal ended ignominiously. The Eisenhower administration led condemnation of the aggressors in the United Nations and used economic pressure to force the three powers to withdraw. In the aftermath of that debacle, the British decided to tie themselves more closely to the United States and France moved toward a more independent stance. Nasser emerged as a hero of the Arab world and defiantly turned to the Soviet Union for massive economic assistance.

European Settlement in the First Term

By the time Eisenhower entered office in 1953, Europe was divided into Western and Soviet spheres of influence, and at its heart lay a divided Germany. Neither the United States nor the Soviet Union was willing to accept German reunification on the other's terms. But Stalin's death in March 1953, rising concern about the accelerating nuclear arms race, and growing sentiment among the Europeans for negotiations between East and West seemed to hold out the prospect for an easing of tensions and a possible diplomatic settlement. Ultimately, continuing mistrust between East and West, alliance politics, and resistance to arms control within the Eisenhower administration prevented any dramatic breakthroughs in détente (relaxing tensions) or ending the cold war.

Although the new Soviet leadership began to speak of "peaceful coexistence," the Eisenhower administration concluded that the Soviet "peace offensive" constituted little more than a tactical ploy to undermine Western European unity and possible German rearmament. American strategists believed that German manpower, even if only from the western part of Germany, was essential for the long-term security of Western Europe. Thus, the Eisenhower administration resisted comprehensive disarmament proposals and European demands for summit talks with the Soviets until a satisfactory German solution had been found. After several false starts, in late 1954 the Western allies agreed to restore West German sovereignty and incorporate German military forces into the North Atlantic Treaty Organization (NATO). In turn, Germany agreed not to develop weapons of mass destruction nor seek forcible German reunification. When the Federal Republic of Germany formally entered NATO in 1955, the Soviets countered with their own defensive alliance of Eastern European satellite nations, the Warsaw Pact.

With the resolution of West German rearmament and the Soviets' surprising accession in 1955 to an Austrian peace treaty, which included agreement on neutralization of that country, a skeptical Eisenhower agreed to a summit meeting with the Soviets in Geneva. He expected to make no agreements but hoped the summit would "create a new spirit" that might ease cold war tensions and make future agreements possible. In fact, Eisenhower believed that time was working against the Soviets, as evidenced by their economic troubles and signs of discontent within the Eastern bloc, and so the West could hold out for complete Soviet capitulation to Western demands. He also saw an opportunity to wrest the "peace offensive" from the Soviets by dramatically announcing "OPEN SKIES," a plan for mutual aerial inspection of military facilities that would provide reassurance that neither side was preparing for war. As expected, Nikita Khrushchev, who became the leader of the Soviet Union after Stalin's death, denounced the "bald espionage plot." The summit produced no agreements but briefly led to more cordial East-West relations.

The "spirit of Geneva" quickly dissipated as Khrushchev's reforms unleashed centrifugal forces in Eastern Europe and American psychological warfare against the Soviets encouraged internal dissent. Khrushchev's denunciation of Stalin's crimes and advocacy of local variations of communism fostered popular unrest in Poland and Hungary, fueled by American radio broadcasts encouraging "captive peoples" to throw off the Soviet yoke. In late 1956, when the Hungarian reformers threatened to abandon the Warsaw Pact, Khrushchev exposed the hollowness of the American strategy of "peaceful liberation" in a ruthless military crackdown in which more than 20,000 Hungarians perished. Eisenhower had neither the military means nor the will to liberate Hungary by force of arms. Detaching a satellite from the Soviet bloc was not worth a global war. Thus, by 1956, the cold war seemed as dangerous as ever. The crisis in Hungary coupled with the simultaneous crisis over the Suez Canal, however, probably convinced the American electorate that Eisenhower's experienced leadership was more important than ever and helped to secure his overwhelming reelection victory in 1956.

Holding the Line during the Second Term

Eisenhower's resounding reelection in 1956 represented a solid vote of confidence in his leadership. The so-called Eisenhower prosperity, rising expectations about advancing the "Geneva spirit" in superpower relations, and Eisenhower's sure handling of the Hungarian and Suez crises raised his approval ratings to unprecedented heights. Yet within months a series of domestic and international episodes dealt the Eisenhower administration serious blows from which it was never quite able to recover. The Eisenhower prosperity slipped into the Eisenhower recession; white defiance of school integration forced the president to employ military force at Little Rock, Arkansas; the Soviets punctured the comfortable assumption of American technological superiority by launching the first earth satellite, SPUTNIK; and Eisenhower's Republican Party suffered dramatic midterm election losses. Eisenhower found his economic and national security policies under assault from ever more vocal critics, and he spent much of his second term attempting to hold the line against the increasingly ambitious spending and reform programs of his opponents.

Eisenhower endured a damaging personal defeat in his battle with the Democratic-controlled Congress over the 1958 budget. Early in 1957, the Eisenhower administration reluctantly submitted a $71.8 billion spending proposal, the largest peacetime budget ever. Rising defense costs brought on by price inflation and faster than anticipated deliveries forced the administration to abandon its original New Look $34 billion military budget ceiling, but even then the armed services and Democratic critics alleged that the administration was not doing enough to maintain the lead in the strategic arms race. Some $3.8 billion for foreign aid to promote development and contain Soviet economic penetration of developing nations and rising domestic spending also added to the total. Eisenhower and Treasury Secretary George M. Humphrey, however, feared that Democrats in Congress would seek even greater expenditures, worsening inflationary pressures in the economy and further delaying prospects for a major reduction in corporate taxes. Humphrey therefore issued a stern warning that irresponsible spending and indefinite postponement of tax cuts would unleash "a depression that will curl your hair." Eisenhower even invited Congress to find savings in the administration's budget. The result was a political disaster for the president as Republicans eager for a balanced budget and tax cuts broke ranks and joined with Democrats looking to embarrass the president to slash spending by $4 billion. The whole affair cast doubt on Eisenhower's political astuteness and handling of the economy.

Civil Rights Revisited

President Eisenhower also ran into difficulties with congressional Democrats as he struggled to maintain his "middle way" on race relations. He believed that his 1956 reelection, in which he made gains among both black and white voters, vindicated his moderate approach to civil rights. He therefore submitted a civil rights bill, crafted by Attorney General Herbert S. Brownell, to protect African-American voting rights, reasoning that enfranchised black voters would have more power to protect their interests and would therefore be less likely to seek direct relief from the federal government. The bill also attempted to remove a potentially divisive issue from politics by creating a nonpartisan Civil Rights Commission to investigate race relations and issue recommendations for reform. Eisenhower's lack of commitment to the bill, however, allowed Senate majority leader LYNDON B. JOHNSON (D-TX) to attach a series of amendments that seriously watered down the provisions to protect African-American voting rights. Johnson did so because otherwise a southern filibuster would have defeated the bill. Despite its weaknesses, the CIVIL RIGHTS ACT was the first civil rights legislation passed since Reconstruction.

Eisenhower's hopes of maintaining a "middle way" on race relations were dashed when Arkansas governor Orval Faubus manipulated school integration for political gain. In September 1957 Faubus defied a federal court order by preventing the integration of Central High School in Little Rock by nine African-American children. Eisenhower's efforts to broker a compromise with Faubus failed and when the governor withdrew the Arkansas National Guard from the building and left the children at the hands of an angry mob, the president believed he had no choice other than to dispatch federal troops to maintain order. Under protection of federal troops, the black children entered the school. Although Eisenhower insisted that he was simply upholding the authority of a federal court and had no personal commitment to school integration, white segregationists across the South denounced the "invasion" by federal troops. Faubus had the last word, winning reelection in 1958 and then closing the public schools the next school year rather than comply with integration, and he reopened them as all-white private institutions.

For the remainder of his presidency, Eisenhower tried to avoid overt intervention in civil rights issues other than voting rights. He would not use the Justice Department to pursue legal action against states that circumvented school integration, nor would he employ the Federal Bureau of Investigation (FBI) to investigate white southern resistance, and he refused civil rights leaders' requests for a strong presidential statement endorsing desegregation as a moral issue. In light of evidence accumulated by the new Civil Rights Commission of continuing systematic disfranchisement, Eisenhower did undertake a second round of civil rights legislation in 1960 allowing for court-appointed referees to supervise voting procedures in counties where discriminatory practices had prevented blacks from voting, but Eisenhower used the new powers only twice, resulting in the addition of fewer than 100 new voters. In part, Eisenhower's preference for gradualism and his philosophy of limited government militated against greater activism in civil rights, but his personal sympathies seemed to be entirely with white southerners.

Sputnik Crisis

The third major crisis to afflict the Eisenhower administration in 1957 was the Soviet Union's launch of the first earth satellite, *Sputnik I* in October. The Soviet space achievement dealt a psychological blow to most Americans' faith in the superiority of U.S. science and technology, and Soviet leader Nikita Khrushchev seized on the propaganda victory to tout the superiority of socialism over capitalism. Democrats in Congress then criticized the administration's defense policies, the one area where Eisenhower's expertise and leadership had previously been unassailable. Similarly, the military services saw an opportunity to break free of the administration's New Look budgetary ceilings and courted allies in Congress and the private sector for increased defense outlays. After *Sputnik*, Eisenhower found himself increasingly on the defensive, seeking to preserve his "security with solvency" approach to national security from rising demands for expensive crash programs to close various alleged "gaps" with the Soviet Union.

Sputnik was not a complete surprise to the Eisenhower administration as both the United States and the Soviet Union had undertaken to launch a space satellite as part of an international cooperative scientific endeavor called the International Geophysical Year, but critical alarm among the American people toward *Sputnik* surprised the president. Eisenhower had deliberately separated the civilian American scientific satellite project from military programs because he wanted to convince world opinion of the peaceful nature of the U.S. space program and establish the principle of "freedom of outer space" for later military reconnaissance satellites. Thus, the American satellite was never assigned the same priority as the military missile and satellite programs, unlike the Soviet project, which involved placing a satellite on a large military rocket. Eisenhower's efforts to make this distinction clear to the American people and reassure them about the overall strength of American deterrent forces had little effect. Public confidence was further eroded by a second, larger *Sputnik* and a top secret report by a group of civilian consultants under H. Rowan Gaither warning of the increasing vulnerability of manned bombers to a surprise Soviet missile strike. The Gaither panel recommended a major overhaul of defense policies, including accelerated missile programs, greater dispersal and protection of the bomber fleet, speedy development of an intercontinental ballistic missile (ICBM) warning system, and fallout shelters to protect the civilian population in the event of nuclear attack. Eisenhower found the report to be unduly pessimistic

Soviet postage stamp depicting *Sputnik I*. The caption translates to: The world's first Soviet artificial satellite of the Earth. *(Russian Federation)*

although he took some measures to improve the security of the strategic deterrent. However, when portions of the report were leaked to the press it further fueled criticisms that Eisenhower was sacrificing the nation's security to outmoded fiscal considerations. Senator Lyndon Johnson's highly publicized hearings into the space and missile programs provided a forum for the administration's critics to claim that the Soviets had opened a "missile gap" with the United States.

The National Security State

Eisenhower confessed that he had underestimated the psychological impact of *Sputnik* on American and world opinion, but he remained convinced of the essential wisdom of the New Look and undertook a three-pronged strategy to preserve its essentials. First, he accepted modest increases in defense spending and a reallocation of resources to ensure the adequacy of the strategic deterrent. He provided additional funds to accelerate the existing long-range missile programs, disperse B-52 bombers, and improve force readiness. Second, Eisenhower responded to concerns about the state of the nation's educational system and the growing disparity between the number of scientists and engineers produced in the United States and the Soviet Union by supporting a limited package of federal aid for education. He dramatically increased the National Science Foundation's budget to bolster science education initiatives and he supported legislation to fund student loans and encourage the teaching of science, mathematics, and foreign languages in the schools. Commentators criticized the limited nature of the measures but Eisenhower reluctantly set a precedent of greater federal involvement in education.

The third aspect of Eisenhower's strategy entailed an overhaul of the national security bureaucracy. Long an advocate of greater unification of the armed forces to rationalize management in the Pentagon, reduce interservice rivalry, and eliminate wasteful duplication, Eisenhower pushed through the 1958 DEFENSE REORGANIZATION ACT. The law reduced the powers of the three service secretaries by eliminating them from the chain of command, encouraged the Joint Chiefs of Staff to take a corporate view of national defense matters by reducing their service responsibilities and augmenting their staff, and centralizing military research and development in the Pentagon rather than the separate services. Additionally, Eisenhower supported legislation to establish a civilian space agency, the National Aeronautics and Space Administration (NASA), recognizing that space science and exploration were now national priorities and part of the larger cold war struggle with the Soviet Union for international prestige. While publicly disclaiming the notion of a "space race" with the Soviets, his administration adopted a space policy designed to "achieve and demonstrate overall U.S. superiority in outer space without necessarily requiring U.S. superiority in every phase of space activities." Thus, despite his oft-stated desire to avoid a "garrison state" at home, Eisenhower's responses to the *Sputnik* crisis acknowledged the cold war significance of education and space science and nudged the United States farther down that road.

Recession and Retrenchment in the Second Term

In addition to public anxiety over national security, growing dissatisfaction with the administration's overall economic policies also dogged Eisenhower for the remainder of his presidency. A slowing economy exacerbated the president's difficulties. As with the issue raised by *Sputnik,* Eisenhower remained determined to hold the line against unwise spending programs, and to a large extent he succeeded, but his Republican Party paid a high political price.

As the economy slipped into recession in late summer 1957, fundamental philosophical differences emerged between the administration, congressional Democrats, and even some Republicans. Eisenhower's overriding concern was to hold down creeping inflation and he therefore resisted

demands to increase spending, which he believed would worsen the budget deficit and add to inflationary pressures. Democrats, however, wanted to increase public works to stimulate employment. Eisenhower vetoed their proposals. Fellow Republicans, meanwhile, were divided between those who supported the administration and those who advocated new corporate tax cuts to stimulate investment coupled with targeted tax cuts to boost demand. Vice President Nixon, with an eye to the upcoming 1958 elections and the 1960 presidential race, urged such cuts. Eisenhower remained unmoved, convinced that inflation was the chief danger facing the economy, and he also vetoed a farm bill favored by some Republicans that would have provided high price supports to help farmers through the recession. Although the worst of the recession was over by mid-1958, lingering concern about the economy and criticism of the administration's response loomed large in that year's congressional elections. The Republicans suffered their worst defeat since the 1930s as Democrats emerged with majorities of 64 to 34 in the Senate and 282 to 154 in the House.

The electoral setback renewed Eisenhower's determination to hold the line on federal spending, and for the remainder of his presidency he waged an effective battle by cultivating a conservative coalition of Republicans and southern Democrats dedicated to fiscal discipline. In 1959, the president slashed domestic spending on housing and farm programs, vetoed numerous Democratic spending proposals, and was able to achieve a small budget surplus. The following year, despite political grandstanding on the defense budget by several Democratic senators with presidential aspirations, Eisenhower again achieved a budget surplus. Similarly, Eisenhower worked closely with the conservative coalition to enact a new labor law curtailing the powers of labor unions by outlawing secondary boycotts, restricting picketing, and extending federal oversight of internal union affairs. Ironically, Eisenhower's effectiveness in balancing the budget, retiring debt, curbing inflation, and restoring foreign confidence in the dollar probably worked against the Republicans in 1960. When another mild recession hit in mid-1960 and unemployment spiked, Eisenhower refused to undertake short-term spending measures for the sake of political expediency, vetoing an area redevelopment bill that Nixon and other Republicans supported. Getting the economy "moving again" became a mainstay of the Democrats' 1960 campaign.

Eisenhower Doctrine

Just as Eisenhower experienced mounting domestic difficulties during his second term, so too did his administration encounter increasing international problems, particularly in the Middle East. The SUEZ CRISIS not only strained relations among the Western allies but also opened the door to the expansion of Soviet influence. The Eisenhower administration's efforts to contain communism in the region, however, seemed to conflate Arab nationalism with communism.

Eisenhower and Secretary of State Dulles believed that the Anglo-French setback at Suez created a power vacuum that the United States had to fill both to check Soviet expansion and to bolster pro-Western Arab regimes under assault from Egyptian president Nasser's radical brand of pan-Arab nationalism. In January 1957, the administration unveiled the Eisenhower Doctrine for the Middle East, offering economic and military assistance to friendly regimes and promising military support to any nation threatened by "international communism." In reality, Nasserism represented the most pressing threat to Western interests. The administration quickly dispatched aid to assist King Hussein of Jordan to preserve his crown against Nasserites, but he was unable to prevent the union of Syria and Egypt under Nasser's leadership as the United Arab Republic (UAR). In July 1958, after a republican palace coup in Iraq, the Eisenhower administration landed 16,000 marines in neighboring Lebanon to forestall a similar move by pro-Nasser forces against President Camille Chamoun. Although the communist threat was nonexistent, Eisenhower reasoned that American credibility necessitated military action to support a friendly regime and maintain Western interests in a region whose loss would be "far worse than the loss of China, because of the strategic position and resources of the Middle East." A political settlement in Lebanon soon allowed for the withdrawal of American forces without incident, but the episode aroused further popular Arab antagonism toward the West and encouraged closer ties between the UAR, Iraq, and the Soviet Union. Belatedly, the Eisenhower administration recognized that military intervention merely inflamed Arab nationalism and played into the Soviets' hands. During his final years in office, Eisenhower therefore undertook a new policy of seeking an accommodation with the aspirations of the Arab people and normalizing relations with Nasser.

Second Offshore Islands Crisis

Even before American troops departed Lebanon, a second crisis erupted in the Taiwan Strait in August 1958, when Chinese Communist forces initiated a new bombardment and blockade of Quemoy, an archipelago off the Chinese coast controlled by Nationalist China. Again, Eisenhower determined that American credibility as a friend and ally of Taiwan required a forceful response, including the possibility of direct military intervention using nuclear weapons should the People's Republic of China (PRC) attempt an invasion. He authorized the U.S. Navy to escort supply ships to the islands, reinforced American air forces in the Taiwan area, and delivered stern warnings to the PRC while holding out the prospects for diplomatic negotiations to settle the status of Taiwan peacefully. The tough stance unnerved European allies, who still did not consider the islands worth a nuclear war, and also the Soviets, who pressed PRC leader Mao Zedong to exercise restraint. By October the crisis abated as Mao recognized that the islands could not be intimidated into surrender, Sino-American diplomatic talks commenced, and Nationalist leader Chiang Kai-shek gave vague assurances that he would not use force to retake the mainland.

The second offshore islands crisis revealed tensions in both the American and Soviet alliance systems and raised questions about the credibility of Eisenhower's nuclear strategy. Mao criticized Khrushchev's inadequate support of wars of national liberation and espousal of "peaceful coexistence" while Khrushchev viewed Mao as unnecessarily provocative and dangerous, which eventually led him to renege on an earlier pledge to assist the PRC in developing nuclear weapons. For the Europeans, Eisenhower's nuclear threats seemed reckless. At home, meanwhile, critics questioned whether massive retaliation was still a credible strategy in light of improved Soviet nuclear capabilities.

Soviet-American Relations and the Failed Summit

In November 1958, the Western allies faced an even more dangerous situation when Khrushchev initiated a crisis over Berlin, announcing that the Soviet Union would sign a separate peace treaty with the German Democratic Republic and terminate Western transit and occupation rights in West Berlin in six months. Eisenhower and Dulles believed that Khrushchev would back down in the face of a firm NATO response and they persuaded the allies to develop military contingency plans to keep access routes to Berlin open but also offered negotiations at Geneva on the whole German question timed to coincide with Khrushchev's deadline. British prime minister Harold Macmillan visited Khrushchev and persuaded him to accept talks to be followed by a summit meeting. Although the Geneva talks stalled, Khrushchev's deadline passed without incident and Eisenhower invited Khrushchev to visit the United States "to soften up the Soviet leader." At Camp David in September 1959, both leaders reaffirmed their commitment to peace and agreed to hold a summit conference on outstanding European issues in Paris the following spring.

Eisenhower and Khrushchev also intended to use the summit to advance disarmament, specifically a ban on nuclear testing. Adverse world reaction to the dangerous radioactive fallout created by the atmospheric testing of nuclear weapons and assurances from his science adviser that a verifiable test ban would both freeze an American advantage in nuclear weapons and open up the previously closed Soviet Union to inspection convinced Eisenhower to pursue a test ban. In early 1958, both the Soviets and the Americans suspended further nuclear tests, and by the end of the year a conference of technical experts had designed an inspection regime that promised to detect most future tests.

CABINET, COURT, AND CONGRESS

Cabinet Members

Secretary of State
John Foster Dulles, 1953–59
Christian A. Herter, 1959–61

Secretary of Defense
Charles E. Wilson, 1953–57
Neil H. McElroy, 1957–59
Thomas S. Gates, Jr., 1959–61

Secretary of the Treasury
George M. Humphrey, 1953–57
Robert B. Anderson, 1957–61

Postmaster General
Arthur E. Summerfield, 1953–61

Attorney General
Herbert Brownell, Jr., 1953–57
William P. Rogers, 1957–61

Secretary of the Interior
Douglas J. McKay, 1953–56
Frederick A. Seaton, 1956–61

Secretary of Agriculture
Ezra Taft Benson, 1953–61

Secretary of Commerce
Sinclair Weeks, 1953–58
Lewis Strauss, 1958–59
Frederick H. Mueller, 1959–61

Secretary of Labor
Martin P. Durkin, 1953
James P. Mitchell, 1953–61

Secretary of Health, Education and Welfare
Oveta Culp Hobby, 1953–55
Marion B. Folsom, 1955–58
Arthur Flemming, 1958–61

Supreme Court Appointments

*(Nominated for Chief Justice)

Name	Confirmation Vote	Dates of Service
*Earl Warren	Voice Vote, Confirmed	1953–69
John Marshall Harlan	No action	
John Marshall Harlan	71–11 Confirmed	1955–71
William Brennan, Jr.	Voice Vote, Confirmed	1956–90
Charles Whittaker	Voice Vote, Confirmed	1957–62
Potter Stewart	70–17, Confirmed	1958–81

Legislative Leaders

Congress	Speaker of the House	State	Party
83rd Congress (1953–55)	Joseph W. Martin, Jr.	Massachusetts	Republican
84th Congress (1955–57)	Sam Rayburn	Texas	Democrat
85th Congress (1957–59)	Sam Rayburn	Texas	Democrat
86th Congress (1959–61)	Sam Rayburn	Texas	Democrat

Although new data cast doubt on the efficacy of the so-called Geneva System, the United States developed a proposal to ban all atmospheric and underwater tests, accompanied by a suspension of underground tests above a certain threshold, which the Soviets accepted on condition that the Western powers also agreed not to resume tests below that threshold for five years. Over opposition from his own military and nuclear weapons developers, Eisenhower intended to iron out the details of a test ban agreement at the Paris summit.

The high expectations for the May 1960 Paris summit were dashed when the Soviets shot down an American U-2 spy plane on May 5. Since 1956, Eisenhower had authorized such flights to gather data on the Soviet nuclear and missile programs and prevent a nuclear Pearl Harbor. The Eisen-

CABINET, COURT, AND CONGRESS

Congress	House Majority Leader	State	Party
83rd Congress (1953–55)	Charles A. Halleck	Indiana	Republican
84th Congress (1955–57)	John W. McCormack	Massachusetts	Democrat
85th Congress (1957–59)	John W. McCormack	Massachusetts	Democrat
86th Congress (1959–61)	John W. McCormack	Massachusetts	Democrat

Congress	House Minority Leader	State	Party
83rd Congress (1953–55)	Sam Rayburn	Texas	Democrat
84th Congress (1955–57)	Joseph W. Martin, Jr.	Massachusetts	Republican
85th Congress (1957–59)	Joseph W. Martin, Jr.	Massachusetts	Republican
86th Congress (1959–61)	Charles A. Halleck	Indiana	Republican

Congress	House Democratic Whip	State	Party
83rd Congress (1953–55)	John W. McCormack	Massachusetts	Democrat
84th Congress (1955–57)	Carl Albert	Oklahoma	Democrat
85th Congress (1957–59)	Carl Albert	Oklahoma	Democrat
86th Congress (1959–61)	Carl Albert	Oklahoma	Democrat

Congress	House Republican Whip	State	Party
83rd Congress (1953–55)	Leslie C. Arends	Illinois	Republican
84th Congress (1955–57)	Leslie C. Arends	Illinois	Republican
85th Congress (1957–59)	Leslie C. Arends	Illinois	Republican
86th Congress (1959–61)	Leslie C. Arends	Illinois	Republican

Congress	Senate Majority Leader	State	Party
83rd Congress (1953)	Robert A. Taft	Ohio	Republican
83rd Congress (1953–55)	William F. Knowland	California	Republican
84th Congress (1955–57)	Lyndon B. Johnson	Texas	Democrat
85th Congress (1957–59)	Lyndon B. Johnson	Texas	Democrat
86th Congress (1959–61)	Lyndon B. Johnson	Texas	Democrat

Congress	Senate Minority Leader	State	Party
83rd Congress (1953–55)	Lyndon B. Johnson	Texas	Democrat
84th Congress (1955–57)	William F. Knowland	California	Republican
85th Congress (1957–59)	William F. Knowland	California	Republican
86th Congress (1959–61)	Everett McKinley Dirksen	Illinois	Republican

hower administration's clumsy efforts to cover up the nature of the flight backfired when the captured CIA pilot was put on display in Moscow, and Khrushchev, under mounting pressure from Mao and hard-liners at home, arrived in Paris just long enough to denounce the United States, demand an apology, and storm out. The failed summit prevented any prospect of an agreement on the German question and the nuclear test ban and thwarted Eisenhower's hopes for a thaw in East-West relations before the end of his administration.

Containing Castro's Cuba

In the final two years of the Eisenhower administration, Latin America again became a major focus in the struggle to contain communism. The extent of popular resentment in the region toward the administration's support for anticommunist but repressive regimes and for its neglect of economic development became vividly apparent when Vice President Nixon was assailed by angry crowds during his 1958 South American "goodwill" visit. Shortly after, the administration attempted to signal its preference for democratically elected leaders, entered commodity agreements to stabilize the price of Latin American exports, and established a regional development bank to promote modernization projects.

Fidel Castro's 1959 revolutionary triumph in Cuba over long-time, pro-American strongman Fulgencio Batista led the Eisenhower administration to face a conundrum. Castro headed a broad popular movement, but his repressive actions against political opponents and expropriations of foreign-owned property alienated Eisenhower. After Castro concluded a trade and aid deal with the Soviets in 1960, Eisenhower decided that he, like Arbenz before him, would have to go. In March 1960, the president approved a CIA covert plan to replace Castro's government by isolating Cuba internationally, waging economic warfare against the regime, beaming anti-Castro radio broadcasts at the island, training a paramilitary force of Cuban exiles to lead the armed struggle and, possibly, assassinate Castro. Under pressure from the United States, Castro moved closer to the Soviets, and his defiance became an embarrassment for Nixon during the 1960 presidential election campaign. After JOHN F. KENNEDY's victory in November, Eisenhower advised the president-elect to step up the training of the anti-Castro guerrilla forces and do whatever was necessary to topple the Cuban leader.

The "Military-Industrial Complex"

Eisenhower found his last months in office to be increasingly frustrating. His hopes for a thaw in East-West relations had been dashed, communism seemed to be on the rise among developing countries, and Castro's upstart regime was even challenging U.S. hegemony in the Western Hemisphere. Worse, Eisenhower considered the election of John F. Kennedy to be a repudiation of his philosophy of limited government and sound fiscal policies. Eisenhower addressed the heightened dangers of the cold war in his final speech to the American people, but he also took the opportunity to issue one more warning about the dangers of a militarized garrison state at home. The "conjunction of an immense military establishment and a large arms industry" in peacetime represented a new departure for the United States, and he urged "an alert and knowledgeable citizenry" to maintain its guard against the "unwarranted influence" of "the military-industrial complex." Ironically, Eisenhower's New Look strategy, with its emphasis on high-technology strategic weapons systems, had done more than any previous administration to contribute to the growth of that very complex.

MAJOR EVENTS AND ISSUES

—⁓—

Army-McCarthy Hearings (1954)   The Army-McCarthy hearings of 1954 marked the final break between President Dwight D. Eisenhower and Senator Joseph R. McCarthy (R-WI). Republican leaders, including Eisenhower, had cynically tolerated and even encouraged McCarthy's allegations of communist subversives in the federal government to embarrass Democrats and achieve an electoral victory in 1952. After the election, however, McCarthy continued his anticommunist crusade and launched investigations of federal agencies now controlled by a Republican administration. At first, Eisenhower was reluctant to challenge McCarthy directly for fear of splitting his party and giving the senator even more publicity, but when McCarthy targeted Eisenhower's beloved army the president acted.

After failing to prove charges of a radar spy ring at the army's Fort Monmouth research facility in New Jersey, McCarthy and his aides, Roy Cohn and G. David Schine, concentrated their efforts on the case of Irving Peress, a draftee dentist who had refused to answer routine screening questions about past political affiliations and had been promoted before being honorably discharged. Early in 1954, McCarthy hauled Peress's commanding officer, General Ralph Zwicker, before his Senate Permanent Investigating Committee and browbeat the decorated war hero. Secretary of the Army Robert T. Stevens then met with McCarthy and several Republican leaders to ensure that future army witnesses would be treated with dignity, but McCarthy portrayed the meeting as a complete capitulation by the administration to the senator. Eisenhower responded by delivering a stirring public tribute to Zwicker's patriotism, and he retaliated by releasing a chronology detailing efforts by McCarthy and Cohn to secure preferential treatment for their associate, Schine, who had recently been inducted into the army. McCarthy then accused the army of trying to use Schine to blackmail the senator into halting his investigations.

Throughout the spring of 1954, several weeks of inconclusive televised hearings into charges and countercharges gave the American public its first prolonged exposure to McCarthy's undignified badgering of witnesses and to diversionary tactics that he employed. At one key point in the hearings, Special Counsel for the Army Joseph N. Welch queried McCarthy, "Let us not assassinate this lad further, Senator. You have done enough. Have you no sense of decency sir, at long last? Have you left no sense of decency?" Opinion polls began to indicate that, for the first time, McCarthy's support was slipping. When McCarthy tried to expand his inquiry into the activities of White House staffers, Eisenhower asserted the right of "executive privilege" and frustrated the senator by refusing to let his aides testify. As the hearings

THE
ADMINISTRATION

M^cCARTHY

"EISENHOWER IS BOSS!"

B. GREEN

Not One to Turn Your Back On

This political cartoon titled "Not One to Turn Your Back On" shows President Eisenhower as a lion tamer, trying to hold Senator Joseph McCarthy at bay. *(Library of Congress)*

wound down, moderate Republicans worried that McCarthy was alienating voters before the upcoming elections, and in July Senator Ralph Flanders (R-VT) introduced a censure resolution. In December, the full Senate voted 67–22 to censure McCarthy for bringing "dishonor and disrepute" to the Senate. McCarthy's power was effectively broken.

Atomic Energy Act (1954)   Early in 1954, the Eisenhower administration sought significant revisions to the 1946 Atomic Energy Act in order to allow for the sharing of nuclear weapons information with allies envisioned under the NEW LOOK, the pooling of nuclear data and materials under an international agency as proposed in the president's "ATOMS FOR PEACE" initiative, and the encouragement of private-sector development of commercial nuclear power facili-

ties. The first two general provisions elicited little debate in Congress but a heated dispute erupted between advocates of public power and those favoring a free-market approach. The former argued that the massive federal investment in atomic energy research and development to date should not be given away to for-profit corporations. Rather, the federal government should develop its own commercial nuclear power plants to provide abundant, cheap electricity for the nation. The private electrical industry, supported by the Eisenhower administration, contended that the free enterprise system would provide the best guarantee of efficient nuclear power facilities and that government expansion into commercial activities should be halted.

Although advocates of public power succeeded in attaching some measures to protect the public interest, such as regulating nuclear power rates through the Federal Power Commission and federal licensing of commercial nuclear power plants, the final measure represented a victory for the private electric power industry and the administration by limiting the commercial production and sale of nuclear power solely to private corporations. The final law also allowed the president to exchange data and nuclear materials with another nation for peaceful uses and authorized the Defense Department to transfer certain restricted data, but not information on weapons design, to allies for military planning purposes. Despite the opposition of most House Democrats, the new bill became law on August 30, 1954.

Atoms for Peace   By 1953, mounting international concern about the escalating nuclear arms race and about the advent of a new generation of thermonuclear weapons a thousand times more powerful than the atomic bombs used in World War II together with anxiety over whether the fear of global nuclear war might undermine allied resolve to contain the Soviet bloc, convinced President Dwight D. Eisenhower to seek progress toward nuclear arms control. Early in his administration, a panel of distinguished consultants, headed by physicist J. Robert Oppenheimer, warned of the unprecedented destructive power being accumulated by both sides in the cold war, urged renewed efforts at arms control, and proposed that the government undertake a policy of candor to educate American public opinion to the grim realities of the nuclear arms race and facilitate the formulation of an informed national security policy. Eisenhower's advisers were skeptical about the ability of ordinary Americans to comprehend the realities of the arms race without becoming unduly alarmed, but he personally embraced the idea of nuclear arms control.

In September 1953, a month after the Soviets detonated a thermonuclear device, Eisenhower hit upon the idea of pursuing arms control by gradual stages designed to build a degree of mutual trust and pave the way for more comprehensive measures later. At the United Nations General Assembly in December, Eisenhower called on the nuclear powers, Great Britain and the Soviet Union, to join the United States in donating a set amount of fissionable material from their weapons stockpiles to peaceful purposes under international auspices. Under "Atoms for Peace," Eisenhower envisaged both slowing down the nuclear arms race and encouraging the application of atomic energy to medical research, power generation, and other productive purposes. The plan received a warm reception at the United Nations but it was dismissed by the Soviet Union. Soviet leaders argued that Atoms for Peace would neither limit the use of nuclear weapons nor halt the arms race. They also understood that the scheme was actually a clever ploy to prolong American nuclear superiority by diverting fissionable material from the much smaller Soviet stockpile. Although the

United States eventually modified its atomic energy laws to provide for the sharing of nuclear information and materials with other countries on a limited basis, and several years of negotiations resulted in the establishment of the International Atomic Energy Agency in 1957, Atoms for Peace was primarily a propaganda victory for the United States and it failed to check the nuclear arms race.

Battle of Dien Bien Phu (1954)   The Battle of Dien Bien Phu marked the climactic engagement of the Indochina war (1945–54) between the Vietnamese nationalists, or Viet Minh, and French colonial forces. Since 1945, Ho Chi Minh's communist and nationalist movement had been battling for independence while France had desperately sought to restore its hold over Indochina after being driven out by the Japanese during World War II. The siege of Dien Bien Phu stemmed from the French strategy of seeking to draw the Viet Minh into a conventional pitched battle during which superior French firepower and discipline were expected to decimate the insurgents. General Henri Navarre, the French commander in Indochina, placed a strong garrison at Dien Bien Phu, deep in the heart of Viet Minh territory in northwest Vietnam, because of its strategic location astride the route to Laos, where the Viet Minh had been aiding Laotian communists against the French-backed monarchy. It proved to be a poor choice for an advanced base, however, as the Viet Minh occupied the surrounding high ground and, unbeknownst to the French, amassed hundreds of artillery and anti-aircraft pieces with help from Communist Chinese advisers.

As anticipated, the Viet Minh launched a major offensive against the garrison in March 1954, outnumbering the French colonial troops by as much as five-to-one. Within a few days, the sole landing strip became virtually unusable, forcing resupply operations to be done by parachute drop. Relentless Viet Minh ground assaults and heavy artillery and antiaircraft fire gradually choked off resupply and reinforcements for the beleaguered garrison. As the position of the defenders deteriorated, the French sounded out the United States about direct military intervention and Admiral Arthur Radford, the chairman of the American Joint Chiefs of Staff, even contemplated employing nuclear weapons against the Viet Minh. Officials within Congress and the Eisenhower administration, however, expressed no enthusiasm for a last-minute direct military intervention. The remaining French garrison of more than 11,000 men surrendered on May 7, 1954, the day before the Indochina phase of the GENEVA CONFERENCE convened to reach a peace settlement. The battle effectively marked the end of French efforts to preserve their empire in Indochina and the start of assumption by the United States of increasing responsibility for containing the spread of communism in the region.

French paratroopers land near a blockhouse to help defend the Vietnamese city of Dien Bien Phu, March 23, 1954. *(Associated Press)*

Berlin Crisis In November 1958, Soviet leader Nikita Khrushchev set off an international crisis over the status of Berlin when he announced his intention to sign a separate peace treaty with East Germany, known formally as the German Democratic Republic (GDR), which would terminate the transit and occupation rights of the United States, Britain, and France in West Berlin, and gave the Western allies six months to withdraw their military forces from the city. Like Germany as a whole, the World War II Allies had divided Berlin, the former German capital, into two parts after World War II: a pro-Soviet East Berlin and a pro-Western West Berlin. Located deep in the heart of communist East Germany, the increasingly prosperous capitalist West Berlin represented both an embarrassment and a security problem for the Soviet bloc. Streams of highly skilled East German workers took advantage of the freedom of movement in Berlin to flee to better economic opportunities in West Germany while the presence of Western military forces threatened the GDR's security.

Khrushchev apparently initiated the crisis to force the Western allies to reopen discussions on the larger German issue, bolster his credentials as the leader of the international socialist movement, and possibly exploit divisions among the Western allies. Under American and West German pressure, the North Atlantic Treaty Organization (NATO) insisted on maintaining Western access rights, denounced Khrushchev's ultimatum, and initiated military contingency planning to break any communist blockade of the city. The NATO allies also offered Khrushchev a face-saving way out by suggesting diplomatic talks scheduled to coincide with the expiration of the six-month ultimatum. Khrushchev accepted the proposal, and although foreign ministers' talks at Geneva and then a summit meeting between President Dwight D. Eisenhower and Khrushchev failed to reach a final agreement on Germany, the ultimatum expired without incident and the immediate crisis abated. In 1961, Khrushchev again pressed the new U.S. president, JOHN F. KENNEDY, to resolve the status of Berlin. In August, the East Germans stemmed the flow of émigrés by erecting the Berlin Wall to close off access between East and West Berlin.

Bricker Amendment The Bricker Amendment was actually a series of constitutional amendments introduced by Senator John W. Bricker (R-OH) to limit the president's conduct of foreign affairs and safeguard the constitutional prerogatives of Congress by imposing restrictions on treaties and executive agreements between heads of state. First introduced in 1951, Bricker sought to prevent the negotiation of any treaty that abridged any individual rights or freedoms under the Constitution or affected any other matters "within the domestic jurisdiction" of the United States and prohibit executive agreements that required no congressional vote. Bricker and like-minded conservative nationalists feared that liberal reformers in the United Nations could subvert

domestic American institutions for their own ends, and they were particularly troubled by extensive social welfare guarantees incorporated into the draft United Nations Covenant on Human Rights.

President Dwight D. Eisenhower privately opposed the amendment's restrictions on the executive's conduct of foreign affairs but, anxious not to alienate a major segment of his own party, he worked behind the scenes to kill it. In 1954, Eisenhower encouraged Senator Walter F. George (D-GA) to introduce an alternative measure to draw conservative Democratic support from Bricker's proposal. After the Senate voted down Bricker's version, George's amendment failed by one vote. Despite his defeat, Bricker persisted in offering new versions of his amendment for three years, although none ever came to a vote. Eisenhower attempted to address conservative nationalists' concerns by promising not to sign the Covenant on Human Rights and seeking congressional resolutions for the possible use of force in Formosa in 1955 and for the EISENHOWER DOCTRINE in 1957. The Supreme Court, meanwhile, reassured conservatives with its 1957 ruling in *Reid v. Covert* that the United States could not abrogate the rights guaranteed to citizens in the Bill of Rights through international agreements.

Brown v. Board of Education of Topeka, Kansas (1954)

One of the most momentous Supreme Court decisions of the 20th century, *Brown v. Board of Education of Topeka, Kansas* (1954) removed the most important constitutional obstacle to equal educational opportunities for African-American school children. The case originated when Oliver Brown brought suit against the public school system in Topeka, Kansas, on behalf of his young daughter, Linda, who had been barred from attending a nearby white school because of her race. Since 1896, the Supreme Court had validated racially segregated education under the doctrine of "separate but equal," which was articulated in the case of *Plessy v. Ferguson*. During the 1930s and 1940s, the Legal Defense Fund of the National Association for the Advancement of Colored People (NAACP) won a series of challenges to segregated law schools and graduate schools, setting the stage for an assault on segregated grade schools in a series of cases from South Carolina, Virginia, Delaware, Washington, D.C., and Kansas that were grouped together as *Brown v. Board of Education of Topeka, Kansas*.

Although the case reached the Supreme Court in late 1952, the potentially momentous decision divided the justices until President Dwight D. Eisenhower appointed Earl Warren as chief justice to replace the late Fred M. Vinson in 1953 and the Court heard additional arguments. Under Warren's diplomatic guidance, the Court reached a unanimous decision in May 1954. The Court declared that, "in the field of education the doctrine of 'separate but equal' has no place." The children in the four affected states and the District of Columbia had been deprived of the equal protection of the laws guaran-

Brown v. Board of Education of Topeka, which outlawed school segregation, was one of the most significant 20th-century Supreme Court decisions regarding civil rights. In the photograph above, Nathaniel Stewart, a black student at the Saint-Dominique school in Washington D.C., stands and reads as his fellow students, both black and white, look on. The school applied the decision for the first time on May 21, 1954, the day this photo was taken. *(Staff/AFP/Getty Images)*

teed under the Fourteenth Amendment. Separate educational facilities were ruled to be "inherently unequal." Eisenhower privately considered the decision a mistake and he refused to make any public comment endorsing the finding beyond affirming that as president he was bound to honor it. The following year, the justices ruled that school desegregation should proceed "with all deliberate speed." Eisenhower interpreted this to mean that school integration should be done gradually rather than immediately and he refused to use the Justice Department to pursue school integration suits. Despite the Court's ruling, executive branch inaction and massive white resistance in the South effectively postponed school integration for more than a decade. *Brown v. Board of Education* provided a key spark for the Civil Rights movement.

CIA Intervention in Guatemala (1954) The Central Intelligence Agency's (CIA) intervention in Guatemala cannot be understood apart from the precedent of Operation AJAX, a successful CIA INTERVENTION IN IRAN, which encouraged President Eisenhower to resort to similar methods to depose another troublesome foreign leader in 1954. Jacobo Arbenz Guzmán, elected president of Guatemala in 1950, sought to modernize his Central American country by encouraging economic diversification, expanding the franchise, and enacting land reform. In 1952, the Guatemalan National Assembly unanimously approved his agrarian reform plan, which called for the seizure and redistribution of uncultivated tracts on the large estates that accounted for 70 percent of the nation's arable land. Landowners would be compensated with government bonds in the amount that they had declared the land to be worth for tax purposes.

The American-owned United Fruit Company, Guatemala's largest landowner, resisted the land reform program, which threatened its privileged position in the Guatemalan economy and lobbied the incoming Eisenhower administration about the growing communist menace in Guatemala.

Although the Guatemalan Communist Party had only a few thousand members, Arbenz had recently legalized the party and appointed several communists to positions in his land and labor reform programs. By August 1953, the Eisenhower administration concluded that Arbenz's left-leaning regime threatened the national security interests of the United States.

The president approved Operation PBSUCCESS, a CIA plan to remove Arbenz through a combination of psychological, economic, diplomatic, and paramilitary actions. The CIA broadcast "black propaganda" into Guatemala to stir up opposition to Arbenz, the United States cut off economic assistance and restricted trade, American diplomats worked to isolate Guatemala in the international community, and the CIA provided weapons and training for a small invasion force of Guatemalan exiles in Honduras led by Colonel Carlos Castillo Armas, who had led an unsuccessful coup in 1950. When Arbenz attempted to defend his regime by purchasing a shipment of arms from Czechoslovakia, the Eisenhower administration pointed to the deal as proof that Arbenz was beholden to the Soviet bloc and intent on fomenting communist revolution.

In May 1954, the United States instituted a naval blockade of Guatemala and, on June 18, Castillo Armas's 50-man army invaded. The Guatemalan army quickly defected, forcing Arbenz to resign and flee into exile. In what the Eisenhower administration considered an unalloyed success, Castillo Armas soon became the new president and reversed Arbenz's reforms. In consequence, however, Guatemala's short-lived experiment with democracy was destroyed and the country was plagued by autocratic regimes and periodic civil war for the next four decades.

CIA Intervention in Iran (1953)

In 1953, President Dwight D. Eisenhower authorized a covert Central Intelligence Agency (CIA) operation to overthrow Iranian prime minister Mohammed Mossadegh. The immediate origins of the Iranian crisis dated back to 1951, when the Iranian parliament nationalized the British-owned Anglo-Iranian Oil Company (AIOC) that monopolized Iran's oil industry. The British responded by organizing an international boycott of Iranian oil and Mossadegh severed diplomatic relations with Britain. Iran's economy deteriorated rapidly from the loss of oil revenues, and Mossadegh appealed to newly elected president Eisenhower for assistance. Eisenhower, however, worried that nationalization set a dangerous precedent that might jeopardize American oil companies in the region. Moreover, Mossadegh seemed to be moving closer to the Tudeh (Iranian Communists) and preparing to consolidate his own power at the expense of the pro-Western head of state, Shah Mohammed Reza Pahlavi.

When Mossadegh opened trade negotiations with the Soviets, Eisenhower approved Operation AJAX, a covert CIA operation developed in conjunction with the British, to engineer a coup against the prime minister by sympathetic elements in the Iranian military. In August 1953, American agents, led by Kermit Roosevelt, cultivated the support of military officers loyal to the shah and organized street demonstrations against Mossadegh. Although Mossadegh thwarted the first attempt to remove him and the shah initially fled to Italy, several days of street fighting resulted in Mossadegh's capitulation, his replacement by a general, and the shah's triumphant return.

Immediately, the United States extended economic aid to the new regime. In the following months, the new government restored diplomatic relations with Britain and reopened negotiations on the oil dispute. Iran eventually agreed to pay AIOC $25 million compensation for the assets seized three years earlier and accepted an American-brokered agreement for a new international oil consortium to develop Iran's oil industry, which broke the British monopoly. Under the new arrangements, AIOC and American oil companies each received a 40 percent stake in Iranian oil and the consortium accepted a fifty-fifty profit-sharing arrangement with the Iranian government but retained control of production levels. Eisenhower believed that covert action had effectively secured U.S. interests by turning back the danger of communist expansion and opening up new opportunities for American oil corporations. In the longer term, continuing United States support for the shah greatly circumscribed nationalist and democratic forces in Iran and generated considerable anti-American sentiment.

Civil Rights Act (1957)

The 1957 Civil Rights Act was the first federal civil rights legislation since 1875, but opponents ensured that it fell far short of the sweeping reforms sought by African-American activists and their allies. Within the Eisenhower administration, Attorney General Herbert P. Brownell led the push for civil rights legislation, both because of a genuine conviction that more had to be done to protect black voting rights and because he recognized an opportunity to exploit the North-South split in the Democratic Party for political purposes. The emphasis on voting rights appealed to President Dwight D. Eisenhower's sensibilities because, if African Americans could secure the franchise, they would be able to mobilize at the state and local levels to protect their interests and would not need federal intervention.

Early in 1956, the administration submitted a bill providing for the creation of a nonpartisan Civil Rights Commission to investigate the state of black-white relations, a new Civil Rights Division in the Justice Department, and revisions of the federal code increasing voting rights protections and granting the attorney general authority to seek injunctive relief. Senate majority leader LYNDON B. JOHNSON killed the legislation in committee to prevent an embarrassing split in Democratic ranks before the 1956 elections. After his electoral triumph, in which he had made significant gains among black voters, Eisenhower resubmitted the bill in 1957. This time, Johnson saw an opportunity to boost his presidential ambitions by drafting a compromise bill.

The final legislation retained the Civil Rights Commission, which Eisenhower hoped would take the divisive civil rights issue out of politics, but Johnson's efforts greatly watered down the voting rights protections by eliminating the provisions for the attorney general to seek injunctive relief and permitting, among other things, all-white juries to adjudicate voting rights cases. This change was made to ensure that the bill could survive a southern filibuster and become law. Although some civil rights advocates urged the president not to sign the final bill, Eisenhower agreed with Martin Luther King, Jr., leader of the MONTGOMERY BUS BOYCOTT, that the compromise bill was better than no bill at all and he signed it into law on September 9, 1957.

Civil Rights Act (1960)   The continuing violence against African Americans in the South and the systematic disfranchisement documented by the new Civil Rights Commission led the Eisenhower administration to seek a second installment of civil rights legislation in 1959. President Dwight D. Eisenhower emphasized the need for additional voting rights protections, but the bill also included measures to curb mob violence by making it a federal crime both to interfere with a federal court desegregation order and to cross state lines

for purposes of avoiding prosecution for the destruction of a public school. Southern Democrats and a handful of conservative Republicans wary of any enhancement of federal power opposed further civil rights legislation, while a minority of liberal Democrats and Republicans wanted the administration to seek even stronger measures to protect civil rights. Failure to achieve consensus prevented passage of any bill in 1959, but the following year more moderate forces in both parties secured approval of the Civil Rights Act of 1960. The measure retained the criminal provisions for obstructing a federal court desegregation order and crossing state lines to evade prosecution for damaging a public school. It also strengthened the voting rights protections of the 1957 act by allowing court-appointed referees to supervise voting procedures in counties where discrimination had prevented blacks from voting. Finally, the Civil Rights Commission, due to expire in 1960, was extended for two additional years. The additional voting rights protections had little immediate effect. The Eisenhower administration implemented them only twice, resulting in the addition of fewer than 100 black voters.

Communist Control Act (1954)   As the crusade for internal security against communist subversives reached its peak in 1954, both political parties vied to establish their anticommunist credentials. Senator Joseph R. McCarthy (R-WI) stepped up his Senate subcommittee investigations while

The Information Division of the U.S. Army issued this anticommunist poster in 1956. *(©National Archives, Washington, D.C./The Art Archive at Art Resource, NY)*

congressional Democrats moved to enact new legislation. One of the results was the Communist Control Act. Building on the 1940 Smith Act, which made membership in organizations that advocated the violent overthrow of the U.S. government a crime, and the 1950 Internal Security Act, which required communist-front organizations to register with the attorney general and barred communists from obtaining or using passports, the new law took restrictions one step further by requiring "Communist-infiltrated" organizations and Communist Party members to register with the attorney general. The former provision was directed primarily against labor unions, with the Subversive Activities Control Board established under the 1950 legislation assuming responsibility for defining which groups were "Communist-infiltrated." Additional features prohibited Communist Party members from holding union office or representing employers before the National Labor Relations Board. Some members of Congress, notably Senator Hubert H. Humphrey (D-MN), wanted to go even further and criminalize membership in the Communist Party, but the final wording fudged the issue by stating ambiguously that the Communist Party "should be outlawed." Passed unanimously in the Senate and by a margin of 265–2 in the House, President Dwight D. Eisenhower signed the measure into law on August 19, 1954.

Defense Reorganization Act (1958)　President Dwight D. Eisenhower had long been an advocate of greater unification of the armed forces, and when the launch of the Soviet satellite SPUTNIK in late 1957 prompted calls for an overhaul of the Defense Department, Eisenhower pushed through legislation to that end. The National Security Act of 1947 had provided for a single National Military Establishment, later named the Department of Defense, but the measure was essentially a compromise that retained separate military departments and the Joint Chiefs of Staff (JCS). In Eisenhower's view, the military services retained too much autonomy, resulting in unnecessary waste and duplication. He wanted to augment the power of the Office of the Secretary of Defense by removing the service secretaries from the chain of command, encourage the JCS to take a corporate view of national defense by relieving them of some of their service responsibilities and expanding their Joint Staff, and centralize coordination of all research and development in the Pentagon under a highly qualified scientist. Reflecting his increasing difficulties in keeping the services in line on the defense budget, he also sought to have all defense appropriations made directly to the secretary of defense rather than the individual services.

Congressional resistance to surrendering the power of the purse over the armed services forced Eisenhower to abandon his latter provision. Congress also reserved the right to veto the transfer of any major combat functions among the services and protected the right of the service secretaries

and military chiefs to present dissenting views before Congress, dubbed "legalized insubordination" by Eisenhower. Nevertheless, the Defense Reorganization Act of 1958, signed into law on August 6, provided most of what Eisenhower requested and established the management structure over the military that would remain in effect for a generation.

Dien Bien Phu　*See* BATTLE OF DIEN BIEN PHU (1954)

Dixon-Yates Scandal　The Dixon–Yates scandal grew out of Republican efforts to halt further expansion of the Tennessee Valley Authority (TVA), the depression-era government corporation established in 1933 to provide flood control and electrical power to a seven-state region in the Southeast. While some Republicans viewed the TVA as a prime example of "creeping socialism" that had to be eliminated, President Dwight D. Eisenhower preferred instead to curtail its further growth. When the Atomic Energy Commission (AEC) sought additional power for its nuclear facility in Paducah, Kentucky, the administration ordered the AEC to contract with a private utility combine, Dixon-Yates, which would construct a new plant near Memphis, Tennessee, rather than allowing TVA to build additional capacity. In effect, AEC would pay for power that the Dixon-Yates facility would supply to the Memphis metropolitan area, freeing TVA power for the AEC facility in Paducah.

The Eisenhower administration believed that the complicated Dixon-Yates contract would both save the federal government money, by avoiding additional TVA construction costs, and rein in the TVA. Advocates of public power, however, strongly opposed the arrangement and their supporters in Congress almost derailed passage of the 1954 ATOMIC ENERGY ACT over the controversy. Congressional investigations into the contract also revealed that it had been negotiated by the Bureau of the Budget (BOB) and AEC chairman Lewis L. Strauss without the knowledge of the other AEC commissioners. Subsequent congressional investigations in 1955 revealed that the contract was tainted by a conflict-of-interest scandal. Adolphe Wrenzell, a BOB financial adviser, was a vice president of First Boston Corporation, the investment bank chosen by Dixon-Yates to secure financing for the proposed plant. Eventually, the city of Memphis decided to construct its own municipal power plant, enabling the government to cancel the Dixon-Yates contract in November 1955. Dixon-Yates sued for $1.8 million in damages, but the U.S. Supreme Court threw out the case in 1961 because of the conflict of interest violation.

Domino Theory　The "falling domino" principle, more popularly known as the domino theory, was coined by President Dwight D. Eisenhower at a press conference in April 1954 in explaining the strategic importance of Indochina to the United States. Eisenhower likened the nations of Southeast Asia to a row of dominoes stood on end. If the first domino fell to communism, then inevitably all the remaining dominoes would fall in sequence. A similar analogy had been used by Undersecretary of State Dean G. Acheson in 1947 to explain the need for American military and economic assistance to Greece and Turkey to stem the expansion of communism in the eastern Mediterranean when he referred to an entire barrel of good apples being infected by one rotten one.

Eisenhower believed the loss of Indochina to communism could have immediate and dire consequences for Burma (present-day Myanmar), Thailand, Malaya, and Indonesia. Not only might the Communist bloc secure the human resources of this vast area, but Japan might potentially lose one of its biggest markets and sources of raw materials, forcing that nation to gravitate toward the Soviet orbit and thereby imperiling the entire strategic position of the United States and its allies in the Pacific. The domino theory therefore justified increased American aid to friends and allies in Southeast Asia to contain communism, particularly the French colonial forces in Indochina and, subsequently, noncommunist South Vietnam. Although the domino theory glossed over significant differences between the nations of Southeast Asia and indigenous communist movements in each, the analogy was later employed to justify direct American military intervention in Vietnam in the 1960s.

Eisenhower Doctrine (1957)   Following the 1956 SUEZ CRISIS, President Dwight D. Eisenhower and Secretary of State John Foster Dulles concluded that the impending demise of British and French influence in the Middle East was creating a power vacuum that the Soviets might exploit. With Egyptian leader Gamal Abdel Nasser's brand of radical Arab nationalism apparently on the rise and tension between Israel and its Arab neighbors threatening to erupt into a regional war at any moment, Eisenhower and Dulles believed that only the United States had the necessary military and economic resources to contain communism in the region, reassure friendly pro-Western Arab regimes of continuing support, and extinguish any sparks that might ignite the whole powder keg. In January 1957, they unveiled the American Doctrine, soon dubbed the Eisenhower Doctrine, for the Middle East.

Building on the precedents of the 1947 Truman Doctrine and the 1955 FORMOSA (TAIWAN) RESOLUTION, Eisenhower requested congressional approval for $200 million in military and economic assistance over the next two years to preserve the independence and integrity of nations in the region. He also sought approval to send American troops to any nation that requested assistance when threatened with overt armed aggression "by any country controlled by international communism." Eisenhower insisted that such an American commitment was necessary because the Soviet Union was actively seeking to extend its influence in the region and the creation of Soviet satellite states in the Middle

East might threaten vital sea lanes and the supply of oil to the West. A strong indication of U.S. resolve would bolster the confidence of pro-Western regimes in the area and deter communist encroachment. Although Eisenhower's request met with skepticism in some quarters, and some congressional leaders balked at granting the president a blank check to deploy military forces, the Middle East Resolution passed both houses of Congress with only minor amendment and was signed into law on March 9, 1957. The Eisenhower Doctrine effectively extended the American policy of containment to the Middle East.

Farewell Address (1961)   On the evening of January 17, 1961, in his brief farewell radio and television address to the nation three days before he left office, President Eisenhower reiterated several of the themes that had preoccupied him during his two terms as president and offered guidance for his successors. Reflecting the pessimism surrounding the demise of the 1960 Paris summit, he reminded his audience of the overarching reality of the cold war and the "hostile ideology" that would confront the United States indefinitely. He also delivered a final warning about the dangers of the garrison state, emphasizing the need for a balanced response to the Soviet threat that would not jeopardize the American way of life. In the most memorable portion of the speech, he noted the unprecedented creation of "an immense [peacetime] military establishment and a large arms industry," and he called on Americans to remain alert to "guard against the acquisition of unwarranted influence, whether sought or unsought, by the military-industrial complex." Military security, he argued, should not come at the expense of individual liberty, national solvency, and democratic institutions. The speech, however, struck a powerful note of irony. The Eisenhower administration's NEW LOOK national security policies, with an emphasis on science, technology, and advanced weaponry, had done more than any other peacetime administration to foster the growth of the vast "military-industrial complex" he now cautioned against.

Formosa (Taiwan) Resolution (1955)   The Formosa (Taiwan) Resolution was enacted by the U.S. Congress on January 29, 1955, in the midst of the first of the TAIWAN STRAIT CRISES. The United States and the Republic of China on Taiwan had signed a Mutual Defense Treaty in 1954, shortly after the Communist People's Republic of China (PRC) had begun shelling the Nationalist-held offshore islands of Quemoy (Jinmen) and Matsu (Mazu). As the shelling continued and PRC forces attacked the Tachen (Dachen) islands, 200 miles northwest of Taiwan, President Dwight D. Eisenhower sought congressional approval to employ American military forces to defend Taiwan, the Pescadores (Penghu) islands just of the west coast of Taiwan, and "related positions and territories of that area now in friendly hands." The resolution easily passed the House of Representatives and Senate by votes of 409 to 3 and 85 to 3, respectively.

In effect, the legislation gave Eisenhower a blank check to wage war if necessary until such time as he determined that "the peace and security of the area is reasonably assured." Although the Formosa Resolution did not mention Quemoy and Matsu specifically, the PRC denounced the congressional authorization to use military force as a war message and vowed to defend its interests. By communicating American resolve to fight, however, the resolution probably contributed to Soviet pressure on the PRC to find a diplomatic solution to the crisis. In the 1958 Taiwan Strait crisis, the Eisenhower administration relied on the authority of the Formosa Resolution to make military contingency plans to defend the offshore islands. Opponents of the Formosa Resolution, though few in number, criticized Congress for giving the president advance authorization to wage war. Later, the Formosa Resolution provided the model for the 1964 Gulf of Tonkin Resolution, which granted President Lyndon B. Johnson advance authority to wage war in Vietnam.

Geneva Accords (1954)   The Geneva Accords were signed by the Soviet Union, the People's Republic of China, France, and Great Britain at the 1954 Geneva Conference on Korea and Indochina in an effort to establish a lasting peace in Indochina. After the French defeat at the Battle of Dien Bien Phu, the Eisenhower administration hinted at American or multilateral military intervention to assist the noncommunist state of Vietnam should no acceptable agreement be reached. Having just terminated hostilities in Korea, neither the Soviets nor the Chinese wanted U.S. military intervention and a wider war, so they pressed Viet Minh leader Ho Chi Minh to make concessions despite his recent military triumph. The Soviets also hoped that conciliatory gestures at Geneva might weaken French support for German rearmament in Europe. Ho, meanwhile, wanted to forestall direct U.S. military intervention that might prolong the independence struggle and therefore agreed to accept terms that might pave the way for the eventual reunification of Vietnam by peaceful political means.

Under the Geneva Accords, Cambodia and Laos gained their independence and the Viet Minh agreed to withdraw

Following their victory over the French and the signing of the Geneva Accords, Viet Minh soldiers march through the streets of Hanoi on October 9, 1954. *(Associated Press)*

their forces from both countries. Vietnam was temporarily divided at the 17th parallel, with the Viet Minh withdrawing to the North and French troops to the South pending the outcome of national reunification elections to be held in 1956 under an international control commission made up of India, Poland, and Canada. In the interim, neither party was to introduce new forces or equipment into the area, allow the establishment of foreign military bases, or join a military alliance.

Although the Eisenhower administration believed that the accords represented about the best deal possible under the circumstances, the United States was not a signatory to the agreements and only pledged "not to disturb" them. In practice, the Eisenhower administration quickly threw its support to President Ngo Dinh Diem who established the Republic of Vietnam in the South and refused to allow the scheduled elections. For the United States, a divided Vietnam with a noncommunist government in the South was preferable to a unified Vietnam under Ho Chi Minh. Later, as Diem consolidated his rule, Ho's supporters in South Vietnam formed the National Liberation Front, dubbed the Vietcong (Vietnamese Communists) by Diem, and they launched an insurrection to overthrow the Republic of Vietnam and force national reunification.

Geneva Conference (1954)   At the suggestion of the foreign ministers of the United States, the Soviet Union, France, and Britain, the Geneva Conference convened in April 1954 to seek peace in Korea and Indochina. The first phase of the conference addressed the divided Korean Peninsula, where an armistice had been arranged the previous year, but no peace agreement could be reached between the Republic of Korea (ROK) in the South and the Democratic People's Republic of Korea in the North. Although the European allies and British Commonwealth nations that had fought to defend South Korea alongside the United States under the United Nations (UN) banner wanted to ease international tensions and establish working relations with the Communist bloc countries, neither South Korea nor the United States was anxious to reach any agreement that might reunify Korea at the expense of ROK president Syngman Rhee's noncommunist regime. Rhee insisted that reunification could only be achieved after the complete withdrawal of Chinese Communist troops, followed by elections supervised by the United Nations in the North for delegates to the existing ROK National Assembly. On the communist side, the Soviets, Chinese and North Koreans wanted a peace settlement that would ease tensions and free resources for their own economic modernization and reconstruction programs, but they rejected any role for the UN in Korean reunification because the UN had been a belligerent and insisted that new elections should be held throughout the entire peninsula.

After the BATTLE OF DIEN BIEN PHU in May, the United States became even more adamantly opposed to concessions toward the communist side as it sought to bolster anticommunist allies in Asia and U.S. military bases in South Korea suddenly assumed increased strategic importance. Thus, while the conference adopted a series of agreements, known as the GENEVA ACCORDS, providing for the temporary division of Vietnam, the United States did not sign the accords and persuaded its allies to terminate the Geneva Conference in June without reaching a permanent settlement on Korea. In effect, the major powers agreed to maintain the status quo of a divided Korean Peninsula and hold their respective proxies in check.

Guatemala   *See* CIA INTERVENTION IN GUATEMALA (1954)

Iran   *See* CIA INTERVENTION IN IRAN (1953)

Khrushchev Visit (1959)   In September 1959, Communist Party secretary general Nikita Khrushchev became the first Soviet leader to visit the United States. Secretary of State John Foster Dulles had always opposed a summit meeting with Soviet leaders, but his death in April 1959 coupled with pressure from prominent allies persuaded President Dwight D. Eisenhower to extend an invitation. Eisenhower intended that the visit would be contingent upon satisfactory progress on the German question and the BERLIN CRISIS at the Geneva foreign ministers' meeting, but a mix-up between the White House and the State Department led to the issuing of an invitation without any precondition. Khrushchev, who sought to bolster his standing at home and abroad as the leader of the Communist bloc, quickly accepted before the oversight could be corrected. Eisenhower hoped that his personal diplomacy might "soften up" Khrushchev and pave the way for an easing of international tensions. Khrushchev arrived amid much publicity, visiting Hollywood and an Iowa corn farm before conducting two days of talks with Eisenhower at the presidential retreat at Camp David, Maryland.

No substantive agreements were reached, but Eisenhower conceded that the allied position in Berlin was "an anomaly" and the United States had no desire to remain there indefinitely and Khrushchev reciprocated by dropping the idea of a separate Soviet peace treaty with East Germany and agreeing to negotiate a mutually satisfactory Berlin settlement without the pressure of any deadline. The two leaders also agreed to hold a summit in Paris the following spring and Eisenhower accepted an invitation to visit the Soviet Union. Overall, the visit eased tensions over Berlin and provided a brief thaw in Soviet-American relations, but the U-2 CRISIS the following year when American pilot Francis Gary Powers was shot down over Soviet air space and the failure of the Paris summit destroyed the prospect of achieving any significant détente in East-West relations before the end of Eisenhower's presidency.

Landrum-Griffin Act (1959)

President Dwight D. Eisenhower entered office in 1953 seeking modest reforms in labor laws that reflected his "middle way" philosophy of ensuring a voice for workers in their affairs. Specifically, he sought to scale back some of the provisions of the controversial 1947 Taft-Hartley Act, enacted by the conservative 80th Congress and depicted by organized labor as an antiunion measure, such as restrictions on the ability of workers to freely elect their own representatives and the requirement for all union officers to swear that they were not members of the Communist Party. Eisenhower's efforts to find common ground for reform came to nothing until 1958, when a Senate investigation by John McClellan (D-AR) uncovered serious abuses in the conduct of union affairs by a handful of labor leaders. Congress quickly enacted the Welfare and Pensions Act to provide greater federal supervision of welfare and pension plans, but additional anticorruption and labor reforms died in the House of Representatives in 1958.

The following year, Eisenhower called for legislation to safeguard workers' union contributions, ensure secret ballots in union elections, and protect the public interest during labor disputes. He eventually threw his support behind a measure drafted by Representatives Phil Landrum (D-GA) and Robert Griffin (R-MI) that was backed by most Republicans and conservative Democrats and became law on September 14, 1959. The legislation outlawed secondary boycotts, restricted picketing, and extended federal supervision over internal union affairs. To the president's delight, it also included elimination of the anticommunist affidavit for union officials and allowed striking workers the right to vote in union representation elections, two of his original labor reform ideas. Eisenhower therefore achieved most of what he had originally sought, but the changed political climate stemming from the McClellan Committee findings resulted in a far more stringent law than unions had wanted.

Lebanon, Intervention in

Although the 1957 EISENHOWER DOCTRINE stressed the menace of external communist aggression, President Dwight D. Eisenhower recognized that the most pressing threat to Western interests in the Middle East was the rise of radical Arab nationalism under the leadership of Egyptian president Gamal Abdel Nasser. In Lebanon, Christian president Camille Chamoun had aligned his nation closely with the United States in the cold war and he vocally supported the Eisenhower Doctrine. His country was sharply divided, however, between Christians and Muslims. Chamoun's political ambitions threatened to plunge his nation into civil war when he tried to amend the constitution to secure a second successive term and rigged parliamentary elections. Muslim opponents demanded new elections and

looked to Nasser for support while Chamoun accused his critics of communist sympathies and appealed to the United States for help under the auspices of the Eisenhower Doctrine.

Eisenhower and Dulles privately admitted that Chamoun's difficulties were caused by internal problems rather than by international communism, but the president felt compelled to send military forces to Lebanon if Chamoun formally requested them in order to maintain American credibility. On July 14, 1958, a military coup by pro-Nasser forces in Baghdad suddenly overthrew the Iraqi monarchy and, fearing for his own regime, a panicked Chamoun immediately appealed for U.S. help. The following day, the first of some 14,000 marines and army personnel went ashore in Beirut and Eisenhower informed the American people that the intervention was necessary to thwart communist aggression and prevent a wider conflict. A quick political settlement, whereby Chamoun agreed to step down in favor of a general, stabilized the situation and allowed for the withdrawal of all American forces within a few weeks. The intervention had been bloodless and succeeded in propping up a pro-Western ally in the region, but it also aroused popular Arab antagonism against the West and encouraged the closer ties between the Soviet Union, Nasser, and Iraq that the Eisenhower Doctrine was supposed to prevent. After the Lebanon intervention, the Eisenhower administration attempted to craft a new approach to the region that sought to win support among adherents of more moderate variants of Arab nationalism.

Little Rock Crisis (1957)

In September 1957, Arkansas governor Orval Faubus sought to capitalize on widespread white southern opposition to the Supreme Court's 1954 BROWN V. BOARD OF EDUCATION OF TOPEKA, KANSAS ruling requiring the desegregation of public schools to mobilize voters behind his bid to win an unprecedented third term as governor. Although Faubus had previously presided over the quiet integration of state colleges, he departed from his moderate stance on race relations and he tried to solidify the segregationist vote in the upcoming 1958 election by joining forces with private citizens in Little Rock, the state capital, who had secured a state court injunction to block the planned integration of Central High School by nine black schoolchildren. When the local school board obtained a federal injunction against all those seeking to interfere with the integration process, Faubus cited the prospect of violent resistance to the school's integration and he ordered units of the Arkansas National Guard to maintain law and order by preventing the admission of the black children.

President Dwight D. Eisenhower had little desire to intervene in the matter, but Faubus requested a meeting with the president to work out an accommodation. At their September 14 meeting, Eisenhower believed that Faubus had agreed to comply with the federal court order requiring integration and would save face by simply changing his orders to

Soldiers from the 101st Airborne Division escort the Little Rock Nine students into the all-white Central High School in Little Rock, Arkansas, in September 1957. *(National Archives)*

the guardsmen to allow the black children to enter the school under their protection. Instead, Faubus continued to use his troops to prevent desegregation and he failed to attend the legal hearing on the matter. When the federal judge barred Faubus and the Arkansas Guard from taking any further actions to block school integration, Faubus withdrew the troops and disclaimed any further responsibility for upholding law and order in the city.

On Monday, September 23, an angry white mob milled around Central High School as the black students entered the building and the school board later decided to send the children home early to avoid violence. The next day, as an increasingly menacing mob assembled, Eisenhower responded to the mayor's plea for help by dispatching a force of 1,000 paratroopers to Little Rock and federalizing the Arkansas Guard. That evening, the president addressed the nation. He appealed for calm, noted the harm that mob violence was causing to the nation's image abroad, and insisted that as president he had no choice but to uphold a federal court order. For the next month, troops escorted the "Little Rock Nine" to school and between classes. As passions abated, Eisenhower reduced the army presence and gradually de-federalized the guard units. Faubus remained defiant.

In September 1958, after the U.S. Supreme Court upheld the federal integration order, Arkansas closed its public schools and reopened them as private, all-white institutions. Only in 1959 did Central High School reopen on an integrated basis.

Modern Republicanism   The term *Modern Republicanism* was employed extensively by President Dwight D. Eisenhower and speechwriter Arthur Larson during the 1956 presidential election to distinguish Eisenhower's philosophy from that of so-called Old Guard Republicans. Sometimes also dubbed "the middle way," "Liberal Republicanism," or "Eisenhower Republicanism," this philosophy recognized that in a modern industrial society, the federal government had a positive, if limited role to play. Whereas conservative Republicans hoped to overturn much of the New Deal and Fair Deal legislation of the 1930s and 1940s, which had dramatically expanded the role and power of the national government, Modern Republicanism accepted the need for a limited welfare state to provide "a floor over the pit of personal disaster" for ordinary Americans. Similarly, while conservative Republicans exhibited deep suspicions of an internationalist foreign policy, opposed American involvement in international organizations and alliances, and tended to be protectionists, Modern Republicanism accepted the need to contain communism on a global scale, pursue a multilateral foreign policy, and encourage the liberalization of international trade. Eisenhower believed that the long-term viability of the Republican Party rested on its willingness to discard old-style conservatism and embrace Modern Republicanism, but he was ineffective in achieving any such transformation.

Montgomery Bus Boycott (1955–1956)   The Montgomery, Alabama, bus boycott was a year-long African-American protest against racially segregated seating on the city's buses that helped to energize the modern Civil Rights movement and resulted in the desegregation of all public buses. The protest stemmed from the arrest of Rosa Parks on December 1, 1955, for refusing to give up her seat to a white man as the bus filled with passengers. Her action had been planned, and she was involved in local black politics. The local Women's Political Council initially organized a day-long boycott of the city's buses by African Americans, who made up a majority of the ridership, to coincide with Parks's court appearance on December 5, while the local chapter of the National Association for the Advancement of Colored People (NAACP) used the case to mount a legal challenge to segregated seating on the buses.

On the evening after Parks's conviction, a mass meeting of several thousand African Americans organized the Montgomery Improvement Association (MIA), headed by local black church leaders, to sustain the boycott until segregated seating was eliminated. The charismatic 26-year-old Martin Luther King, Jr., was elected president of the MIA, which coordinated the protest and organized alternative forms of transportation for black residents, and he used his position to articulate his philosophy of nonviolent direct action. Despite attempts to intimidate the MIA and black residents by means of police harassment, legal challenges, and violence, the boycott persisted. Having failed to negotiate a satisfactory compromise with city leaders, in February 1956 the MIA filed a federal suit against the bus segregation ordinances.

In June, a three-judge federal panel ruled that the statutes requiring segregated seating violated the due process and equal protection clauses of the Fourteenth Amendment and in November the U.S. Supreme Court upheld the lower court's decision in *Gayle v. Browder,* effectively overturning the 1896 ruling in *Plessy v. Ferguson* that had sanctioned "separate but equal" accommodations in public transportation.

Following the year-long bus boycott, Rosa Parks sits near the front of the bus, in Montgomery, Alabama, 1956. *(Library of Congress)*

On December 21, 1956, the day when the Court's ruling took effect, the leaders of the boycott rode Montgomery's buses in triumph. King emerged from the boycott as a national leader in the Civil Rights movement and his newly organized Southern Christian Leadership Conference sought to sustain the momentum for other acts of nonviolent direct action.

National Aeronautics and Space Act (1958)   In the aftermath of the launch by the Soviet Union of *Sputnik* in late 1957, President Dwight D. Eisenhower reluctantly concluded that a new federal agency was required to manage the nation's emerging space program. He initially favored centralizing all space programs in the Department of Defense, where numerous military missile projects were already well underway, but he eventually bowed to the preferences of his science advisers for a civilian space agency. He accepted their views that a civilian agency would be best suited to conducting space research that had no immediate military utility, would ensure the participation of the nation's leading scientists who generally disliked working under military management, and would cultivate a positive image of the United States as a nation dedicated to peaceful space science and exploration rather than military applications.

The administration therefore proposed reconstituting the existing National Advisory Committee for Aeronautics, which had been supporting aeronautical research since 1915 and had established a reputation for technical competence and good working relations with the military services, as the new space agency. The Pentagon would retain control of military space activities while the new National Aeronautics and Space Administration (NASA) would plan, direct, and conduct civilian space activities, including developing plans for international cooperation in space. A military liaison committee would ensure coordination of the military and civilian space programs. At the insistence of Senator LYNDON B. JOHNSON (D-TX), Eisenhower accepted the inclusion of a Space Council, composed of cabinet members and chaired by the president, to ensure that space received high-level consideration. The new agency would be headed by an administrator appointed by the president. Eisenhower signed the National Aeronautics and Space Act into law on July 29, 1958, and NASA commenced operations on October 1, 1958, almost a year to the day after the first Soviet *Sputnik* was launched.

National Defense Education Act (1958)   The launch of the Soviet *Sputnik* reopened a longstanding debate over the state of the nation's schools and the growing disparity between the number of scientists and engineers produced in the Soviet Union compared with the United States. At the urging of his science advisers and the Department of Health, Education and Welfare, President Dwight D. Eisenhower proposed legislation to improve scientific education by means of short-term federal aid. Eisenhower personally disliked the notion of federal involvement in public education, a view shared by many in Congress and across the nation, but the temporary national emergency seemed to make a limited intervention necessary for national security reasons.

As finally enacted, the National Defense Education Act (NDEA) authorized a $295 million loan fund for student loans, with preference given to superior students in science, mathematics, engineering, or foreign languages. Loan recipients who became teachers in elementary or secondary schools could have up to 50 percent of their loans forgiven after five years of teaching. The legislation also provided matching grants to the states and loans to private schools for the purchase of equipment essential for the teaching of mathematics, science, and foreign languages, funded various college and university institutes to improve teacher training in foreign languages, and supported research into modern teaching methods using new technology, such as television. Finally, the NDEA encouraged the development of new graduate centers by providing almost $60 million for three-year graduate fellowships for students attending such schools and colleges. The most controversial aspect of the legislation was a requirement that all NDEA loan recipients swear a loyalty oath to the United States. Eisenhower signed the NDEA into law on September 2, 1958, predicting that it would greatly strengthen American education and improve national security. As he had feared, however, his legislation established a precedent for greater federal involvement in education and the act was extended and amended by his successors in the 1960s.

National Interstate and Defense Highways Act (1956)   The National Interstate and Defense Highways Act of 1956 laid the basis for the modern interstate highway system in the United States. The origins of such a system dated back to the late 1930s, but by the time President Dwight D. Eisenhower entered office little progress had been made toward construction of the 40,000-mile system envisioned in legislation that had been passed in 1944. Eisenhower took a keen interest in the program, having participated in the army's first transcontinental convoy in 1919 and witnessed firsthand the German autobahns in World War II. In 1954, Eisenhower urged federal action, both to spur economic growth and to facilitate the movement of men and materiel in the event of a national security emergency.

Given the lack of consensus over how to fund and administer a comprehensive highway program, Eisenhower turned the matter over to a commission of experts headed by former general Lucius D. Clay. In 1955, the commission recommended construction of a 41,000-mile system of interstate highways linking the major cities, with a federal Highway Trust Fund covering 90 percent of the construction costs through the issue of 30-year revenue bonds funded through a gasoline tax and other user fees and taxes. The legislation stalled in Congress for a year as Democrats pressed for

NASA scientist Wernher von Braun *(left)* shows President Eisenhower the front of a *Saturn I* vehicle at the Marshall Space Flight Center in Huntsville, Alabama, on September 8, 1960. *(NASA)*

funding on a pay-as-you-go basis. Eventually, Eisenhower agreed to a compromise measure that retained the trust fund but provided funding through pay-as-you-go taxes and authorized $25 billion for the next 12 years. Eisenhower signed the legislation into law on June 29, 1956. He considered it the landmark domestic legislation of his presidency, predicting that it would "change the face of America."

New Look   President Dwight D. Eisenhower entered office determined to devise a rational national security strategy that could contain the Sino-Soviet bloc over the long haul without adversely affecting the American economy. As he frequently reminded his military advisers, the United States was defending a way of life, not just territory. His solution to achieving security with solvency was dubbed the New Look. Formally codified in October 1953 as National Security Council Paper 162/2, the New Look advocated a capital-intensive approach predicated on American superiority in military technology and weapons of mass destruction while reducing the size of relatively more expensive conventional forces.

The strategy emphasized the massive retaliatory power of nuclear weapons to deter general war with the Soviet Union and a readiness to employ such weapons should deterrence fail. It also reiterated the importance of collective security, stressing the need for overseas bases for American strategic forces and the importance of the military, manpower, and economic resources of the major industrialized states to the free world cause. American mutual security and foreign aid programs would further this strategy by building up the economic and military capabilities of the free world and allowing for the gradual reduction of American forces deployed overseas. Finally, the New Look envisaged using cost-effective "political, economic, propaganda and covert measures" to create and exploit problems for the Sino-Soviet bloc.

In practical terms, the New Look allowed the Eisenhower administration to stabilize the defense budget at around $40 billion per year, considerably less than the $50 billion per year envisaged by the outgoing HARRY TRUMAN administration but significantly higher than the $13 billion pre–Korean War budget. The Eisenhower administration achieved the savings primarily by reducing the size of the army, allowing a modest increase in the air force, and integrating nuclear weapons into the arsenal for both strategic and tactical purposes. Despite criticisms about overreliance on nuclear weapons, the increased danger of global nuclear war, and the rising costs of modern weapons systems such as missiles, Eisenhower retained the essentials of the New Look throughout his presidency and was able to achieve three balanced budgets.

Open Skies   As both the United States and Soviet Union built up their nuclear arsenals and modified their long-range delivery systems, President Dwight D. Eisenhower sought a way to safeguard against the danger of surprise attack and establish a degree of mutual confidence. At the July 1955 summit in Geneva, Eisenhower introduced the "Open Skies" concept, calling for the United States and the Soviet Union to exchange blueprints of military installations and permit mutual aerial surveillance. The proposal would redound to the advantage of the Western allies by penetrating the Iron Curtain, and Soviet leader Nikita Khrushchev quickly denounced it as "a bald espionage plot." Eisenhower, however, moved ahead with plans to implement Open Skies unilaterally using the high-flying U-2 spy plane and, later, reconnaissance satellites. Much later, as the cold war was drawing to a close, President GEORGE H. W. BUSH revived Eisenhower's idea, and, in 1992, the North Atlantic Treaty Organization and Warsaw Pact powers signed the Open Skies Treaty in Helsinki, Finland. The treaty went into effect in 2002.

Oppenheimer Case (1954)   In 1954, the most well-known American scientist, physicist J. Robert Oppenheimer, widely regarded as the "father of the atomic bomb" for his role in the Manhattan Project in World War II, fell victim to the heightened concerns over internal security and communist subversion. In late 1953, Federal Bureau of Investigation (FBI) director J. Edgar Hoover passed on to the Eisenhower administration derogatory information about Oppenheimer. Since the war, Oppenheimer had been an important consultant on atomic energy matters. His past associations with communists among his friends and family members in the late 1930s and early 1940s were already well known to security officers who had nevertheless cleared him to work on the nuclear weapons program.

The principal new allegations against him actually concerned differences of opinion over nuclear weapons policy. Fellow physicist Edward Teller and allies in the air force alleged that Oppenheimer, who had advised against development of the hydrogen bomb in 1949 on moral and technical grounds, had hindered timely development of the weapon by influencing other prominent scientists not to work on the project. Atomic Energy Commission (AEC) chairman Lewis L. Strauss also held a personal grudge against the scientist who had embarrassed him before a congressional hearing by demolishing Strauss's flawed technical arguments against exporting certain radioactive isotopes to other countries. President Eisenhower did not personally share the suspicions of Teller and Strauss about Oppenheimer's loyalty, but he had already decided to freeze Oppenheimer out of his advisory positions because of the influence he wielded over his colleagues.

The new allegations forced Eisenhower's hand, however, because Senator Joseph R. McCarthy (R-WI) was ready to pounce on them to embarrass the administration and possibly launch further investigations into the loyalty of the nation's scientists. The administration quickly suspended Oppenheimer's security clearances and asked the physicist to resign from his advisory positions. When Oppenheimer refused and requested a hearing by the AEC's Personnel Security Board, Strauss ensured that the board was composed of members who could be expected to rule against the scientist, denied Oppenheimer's lawyer access to classified documents that were to be used to incriminate his client, and bugged Oppenheimer's conversations with his defense team. In May 1954, the board found Oppenheimer to be loyal but deemed him a security risk and recommended that he be denied clearance, a decision ratified by the AEC commissioners. Oppenheimer was thus forced out of government service. In 1963, President JOHN F. KENNEDY would make a gesture of atonement for what was widely perceived to have been an injustice by awarding Oppenheimer the prestigious Enrico Fermi Award.

SEATO Established (1954)   The Southeast Asia Treaty Organization (SEATO) stemmed from efforts by U.S. secretary of state John Foster Dulles to erect a regional collective security system to replace French power and contain communism in Southeast Asia. Dulles initially attempted to organize multilateral military intervention, dubbed United Action, against the Viet Minh during the BATTLE OF DIEN BIEN PHU, but he ran into resistance from the British, who considered the French colonial regime in Vietnam a lost cause. In September 1954, however, the United States, Britain, France, Australia, New Zealand, Thailand, the Philippines, and Pakistan signed the Manila Pact, establishing SEATO and agreeing to consult in the event of a common danger. Although the GENEVA ACCORDS prohibited Cambodia, Laos, and South Vietnam from joining a military alliance, a special protocol stated that the allies would regard any threat to those areas as a danger to their "peace and security." Thus, SEATO violated the spirit, if not the letter, of the Geneva Accords by extending a degree of recognition to South Vietnam. Headquartered in Bangkok, Thailand, SEATO differed significantly from the North Atlantic Treaty Organization in that it had no dedicated military forces of its own and an attack on one member was not necessarily considered an attack on all members. The alliance also required unanimity for any joint action. Thus, the United States failed to secure multilateral military intervention to shore up noncommunist South Vietnam under SEATO auspices because of French and British opposition. After the end of the Vietnam War, the major purpose for SEATO disappeared and various members left. The alliance formally dissolved in 1977.

Soil Bank Act (1956)   President Dwight D. Eisenhower conceived of the Soil Bank in 1955 as a mechanism both to conserve soil and water and to address the problem of persistent agricultural surpluses and low commodity prices by paying farmers to take land out of production. The Soil Bank became the main feature of the administration's farm legislation for 1956. The Acreage Reserve would provide a short-term reduction of the crops in greatest surplus by paying participating farmers to take land out of production for three to four years. The Conservation Reserve took a long-range approach by helping defray the cost to farmers of permanently converting farmland to the production of forage or trees or for the construction of ponds or reservoirs. Together, these measures could possibly take 50 million acres out of production. The bill fell victim to election-year politics as farm state congressmen incorporated their own preferences for a return to rigid high price supports, which effectively contradicted the intent of the Soil Bank. Eisenhower defied his own farm-state Republicans and angrily vetoed what he called "the jumbled-up, election year monstrosity" on April 16, 1956. Two days later, the House of Representatives fell well short of the necessary votes to override the president's veto. Realizing that time was running out to pass a farm bill before the November elections, Eisenhower's opponents relented and enacted the Soil Bank without the objectionable price supports. Eisenhower signed the measure into law on May 28, 1956.

Southeast Asia Treaty Organization   *See* SEATO ESTABLISHED (1954)

Southern Manifesto (1956)   The Southern Manifesto expressed white southern congressional opposition to the Supreme Court's historic 1954 *BROWN V. BOARD OF EDUCATION* ruling striking down the constitutionality of racially segregated public schools and the related ruling requiring desegregation to be conducted "with all deliberate speed." Drafted in February 1956 by several senior southern Democrats, including Senators Strom Thurmond (D-SC), Richard Russell (D-GA), and J. William Fulbright (D-AR), and eventually signed by 101 representatives and senators from nine southern states, the petition was partly designed to rally wavering or moderate southern politicians behind a united regional front for maintaining segregation.

The Southern Manifesto accused the Supreme Court of a "clear abuse of judicial power." The document claimed that the Court's rulings had no basis in law or legal precedent, arguing that neither the Constitution nor any amendment referred to education and thus the matter should remain the preserve of the states. According to the manifesto, the same Congress that had enacted the Fourteenth Amendment, which the Court had cited as the basis for overturning the doctrine of "separate but equal" educational facilities, had also provided for segregated public schools in Washington, D.C., and so the original intent of the legislature was clearly not to dismantle segregated schools. The Court's "unwarranted exercise of power" was therefore "contrary to the

Constitution" and was allegedly destroying the previously harmonious relations between the races in the affected states.

The signatories declared their support for those states that had announced their intention to resist forced integration and pledged to employ "all lawful means" to reverse the Court's decision. When asked about the manifesto, President Dwight D. Eisenhower conceded that it would take a long time to change people's thinking on segregated educational facilities but he welcomed what he identified as the moderate tone of the document and the authors' commitment to peaceful and orderly resistance. In fact, Eisenhower's reluctance to take the lead on school desegregation and the extent of white southern opposition to the Court's decision in *Brown* evident in the Southern Manifesto encouraged "massive resistance" campaigns at the state and local levels that thwarted school desegregation for well over a decade.

Sputnik (1957)   On October 4, 1957, the Soviet Union launched the first artificial earth satellite, *Sputnik*, ushering in the beginning of the space age and the "space race" between the United States and the Soviet Union. Both the Soviets and the Americans had announced their intention to launch such a satellite as part of the International Geophysical Year (IGY), an international cooperative scientific endeavor, but the American public reacted to *Sputnik* with shock and alarm. Although the satellite itself was a modest device, an aluminum sphere 22 inches in diameter weighing approximately 184 pounds and carrying a radio transmitter, the Soviet achievement challenged Americans' comfortable assumptions about the superiority of American science and technology and, more generally, the advantages of the free market system over Soviet communism. President Dwight D.

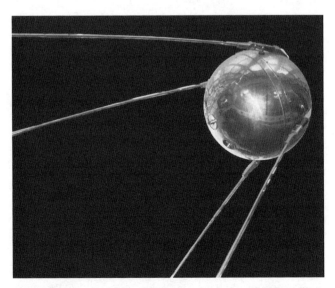

The Soviet launch of *Sputnik (above)*—the first artificial satellite and about the size of a beach ball—on October 4, 1957, led Congress to create NASA, the National Aeronautics and Space Administration, the following year. *(NASA)*

Eisenhower had not paid much attention to the psychological aspects of being the first in space, partly because the administration hoped that the IGY satellites would establish the principle of the freedom of outer space and smooth the way for the reconnaissance satellites already under development.

Eisenhower was confident about the overwhelming strength of the nation's defenses and downplayed the national security significance of *Sputnik,* but the November 3 launch of the 1,200-pound *Sputnik II,* which carried a live dog and remained in orbit for 200 days, undermined his reassurances. Senate majority leader LYNDON B. JOHNSON (D-TX) exploited the administration's discomfiture and boosted his presidential prospects for 1960 by holding lengthy hearings into the nation's missile and satellite programs that provided military and scientific experts a forum in which to demand increased funding for their pet projects. The first attempts to launch Project Vanguard, the American IGY satellite, failed spectacularly, but the army successfully launched the first American satellite, *Explorer I,* on January 31, 1958. Belatedly, Eisenhower approved plans for the creation of a new National Aeronautics and Space Administration (NASA) to oversee the civilian space program and approved a national space policy that acknowledged the international prestige and psychological value of space exploration. *Sputnik* also provided the impetus for organizational reforms in the Pentagon's research and development programs and federal support for scientific and technical education through the NATIONAL DEFENSE EDUCATION ACT.

Submerged Lands Act (1953)   The Submerged Lands Act settled a longstanding dispute between several coastal states and the federal government known as the tidelands controversy. The conflict concerned whether individual states or the federal government held title and the right to develop offshore natural resources, particularly oil. In 1945, President HARRY S. TRUMAN had issued an executive order affirming exclusive federal ownership of all mineral rights in the continental shelf within state boundaries, and the Supreme Court upheld his claim in *United States v. California* in 1947. In 1952, Truman vetoed legislation transferring title to the states. The Republican platform that year vowed to restore the tidelands to the states, a position supported by conservatives of both parties who championed states' rights and oil companies that preferred state over federal regulation. After the election, President Dwight D. Eisenhower and the new Republican majority in Congress, with support from conservative Democrats, pushed through the Submerged Lands Act of 1953. The legislation confirmed and established the titles of coastal states to submerged lands and natural resources within their historical boundaries within three miles of the coastline, or their boundaries prior to entry into the Union or previously approved by Congress. If the Supreme Court subsequently determined that title belonged to the nation, the law provided for the states' right to license development of the resources anyway. The following year, the Supreme Court upheld the act in *Alabama v. Texas.*

Suez Crisis (1956)   The 1956 Suez crisis, also known as the Suez-Sinai War, marked the low point in Anglo-American relations in the 1950s. The crisis stemmed from Egyptian president Gamal Abdel Nasser's efforts to modernize Egypt and break free of the vestiges of European colonialism and British, French, and Israeli fears for their interests in the face of rising Arab nationalism under Nasser's leadership. The Eisenhower administration initially hoped to lure Nasser to the Western camp in the cold war and co-opt him in a regional Arab-Israeli peace process, but Nasser remained stubbornly independent in the East-West conflict and irreconcilably hostile to Israel. After Nasser signed an arms deal with the Soviet bloc in 1955 and recognized the People's Republic of China in 1956, the United States and Britain withdrew offers of economic and technical assistance for Nasser's Aswan Dam project. Nasser responded by nationalizing the Anglo-French Suez Canal Company in July 1956.

While the United States urged its allies to find a diplomatic solution, Britain, France and Israel laid secret plans for military action. On October 29, 1956, Israel attacked Egypt in the Sinai Peninsula and the next day Britain and France issued the prearranged ultimatum calling on both sides to pull back from the Suez Canal and allow Anglo-French forces to secure it. When Nasser refused, Anglo-French aircraft began bombing Egyptian bases and a combined fleet began an invasion. Before the canal could be secured, Nasser sank dozens of ships to block it and his allies in Syria cut the oil pipeline from Iraq to the Mediterranean.

President Dwight D. Eisenhower was outraged at his allies' actions, which inflamed Arab opinion against Western imperialism and allowed the Soviet Union to pose as the friend of Arab peoples. He therefore led efforts in the United Nations to arrange a cease-fire and exerted economic and financial pressure on the British to undertake a prompt withdrawal. Within a week, the British accepted a cease-fire and France and Israel reluctantly followed suit. Anglo-American forces withdrew at the end of December, and Israel gave up the Sinai Peninsula the following March. The episode led to the downfall of British prime minister Anthony Eden and an understanding that, in the future, Britain's interests would best be protected by maintaining close relations with the United States. The French government drew the opposite lesson, namely, that it could not rely on the Anglo-Americans to safeguard its vital interests. Nasser, meanwhile, emerged from the crisis with greatly enhanced standing throughout the Arab world. The Suez Canal reopened to shipping in April 1958.

Taiwan Strait Crises (1954–1955 and 1958)   The unresolved Chinese civil war between Mao Zedong's Communist People's Republic of China (PRC) and Chiang Kai-shek's (Jiang Jieshi) Nationalist Republic of China (ROC) led to military clashes over a series of islands in the Taiwan Strait. Chiang had been driven from the mainland and established his government on Taiwan but his forces still held dozens of small offshore islands adjacent to the mainland. For Chiang, whose regime was still recognized by the United States as the legitimate government of China, the islands both symbolized his resolve to recover the mainland and provided staging areas for raids against the PRC. In September 1954, the PRC commenced bombardment of Quemoy (Jinmen) just two miles from the port of Xiamen, both to deter the United States from signing a mutual security treaty with the ROC and to divert attention from a planned invasion of the Tachens, another Nationalist-held island chain farther north.

The Eisenhower administration considered the action a test of American resolve to defend friendly regimes in the area and reacted by signing the defense treaty with Chiang, which committed the United States to defend Taiwan and "other territories," while Chiang pledged not to initiate war by invading the mainland. The crisis escalated in January 1955 when Mao's forces invaded the Tachens. The United States publicly pledged to defend Quemoy and Matsu (Mazu), Congress passed the FORMOSA (TAIWAN) RESOLUTION granting the president the authority to employ American forces for the defense of the ROC, and Chiang agreed to withdraw his remaining forces from the indefensible Tachens. As the shelling continued, Eisenhower hinted at the use of nuclear weapons to defend the Nationalist-held islands. Having achieved his immediate territorial objectives in the Tachens, Mao bowed to Soviet pressure to avoid further escalation and ceased the bombardment in April, announcing his willingness to open talks with the United States.

The PRC briefly resumed the shelling of Quemoy in August 1958 to inhibit Chiang's continuing military buildup on the islands, protest American refusal to recognize the PRC, and demonstrate support for the Arabs' anti-imperialist struggle against the United States in Lebanon. Again, the United States hinted that a PRC assault on the islands would bring an American military response and U.S. warships began escorting Nationalist supply ships through international waters. Having conveyed a diplomatic point, the PRC gradually lifted the bombardment and resumed diplomatic talks with the United States.

U-2 Crisis (1960)   On May 1, 1960, Soviet air defenses shot down an American U-2 spy plane in Soviet airspace, embarrassing the United States and dashing the prospects for any significant détente in East-West relations for the remainder of the presidency of Dwight D. Eisenhower. As both the United States and the Soviet Union built up their nuclear arsenals and modernized their strategic delivery systems in the 1950s, Eisenhower had authorized the U-2 program to gather strategic intelligence and reduce the threat of a devastating nuclear surprise attack. The unarmed U-2 flew at 70,000 feet, originally thought to be above the altitude at which it could be detected by Soviet ground radar, and it carried high-powered cameras able to photograph swaths of territory up to 25 miles wide. The Central Intelligence Agency (CIA) began operational flights in mid-1956 but Soviet radar picked up the very first flight. Nevertheless, Soviet air defense systems could not initially reach the aircraft and so the flights continued unmolested. Given the sensitivity of the operations, however, Eisenhower insisted on personally authorizing each series of overflights.

On May 1, 1960, just two weeks before the scheduled East-West summit in Paris, the Soviets finally brought down a U-2 flown by CIA pilot Francis Gary Powers near Sverdlovsk. After Soviet leader Nikita Khrushchev announced the shoot down, Eisenhower, believing the pilot killed, authorized a cover story about the accidental loss of a weather plane. When Khrushchev revealed that the pilot had survived and espionage equipment had been recovered, he caught the Eisenhower administration in a lie. On May 11, Eisenhower acknowledged full responsibility for the U-2 flights and defended them as a prudent defensive measure. Khrushchev demanded an apology and a halt to any further flights, and when Eisenhower refused he stormed out of the Paris summit on May 16. The collapse of the summit destroyed any prospect for an early nuclear test ban agreement or a German peace treaty. Powers, meanwhile, was tried and convicted of espionage and remained in a Soviet prison until he was exchanged for a Soviet spy in February 1962. The U-2 itself was soon superseded by reconnaissance satellites.

Richard Damms

Further Reading

Accinelli, Robert. *Crisis and Commitment: United States Policy toward Taiwan, 1950–1955.* Chapel Hill: University of North Carolina Press, 1996.

Alexander, Charles C. *Holding the Line: The Eisenhower Era, 1952–1961.* Bloomington: Indiana University Press, 1975.

Ambrose, Stephen E. *Eisenhower: Soldier, General of the Army, President-Elect, 1890–1952.* New York: Simon and Schuster, 1983.

———. *Eisenhower: The President.* New York: Simon and Schuster, 1984.

Anderson, David L. *Trapped by Success: The Eisenhower Administration and Vietnam, 1953–1961.* New York: Columbia University Press, 1991.

Balogh, Brian. *Chain Reaction: Expert Debate and Public Participation in American Commercial Nuclear Power, 1945–1975.* New York: Cambridge University Press, 1991.

Bartley, Numan V. *The Rise of Massive Resistance: Race and Politics in the South during the 1950s.* Baton Rouge: Louisiana State University Press, 1999.

Bates, Daisy. *The Long Shadow of Little Rock: A Memoir.* Fayetteville: University of Arkansas Press, 1998.

Benson, Ezra Taft. *Cross Fire: The Eight Years with Eisenhower.* Garden City, N.Y.: Doubleday, 1962.

Bill, James A. *The Eagle and the Lion: The Tragedy of Iranian-American Relations.* New Haven, Conn.: Yale University Press, 1989.

Billings-Yun, Melanie. *Decision against War: Eisenhower and Dien Bien Phu, 1954.* New York: Columbia University Press, 1988.

Bischof, Gunter, and Saki Dockrill, eds. *Cold War Respite: The Geneva Summit of 1955.* Baton Rouge: Louisiana State University Press, 2000.

Bowie, Robert R., and Richard H. Immerman. *Waging Peace: How Eisenhower Shaped an Enduring Cold War Strategy.* New York: Oxford University Press, 1998.

Boyle, Peter G. *Eisenhower.* London: Longman, 2005.

Broadwater, Jeff. *Adlai Stevenson and American Politics: The Odyssey of a Cold War Liberal.* New York: Twayne, 1994.

———. *Eisenhower and the Anti-communist Crusade.* Chapel Hill: University of North Carolina Press, 1992.

Burk, Robert F. *The Eisenhower Administration and Black Civil Rights.* Knoxville: University of Tennessee Press, 1984.

Caute, David M. *The Great Fear: The Anti-communist Purge under Truman and Eisenhower.* New York: Simon and Schuster, 1978.

Chen, Jian. *Mao's China and the Cold War.* Chapel Hill: University of North Carolina Press, 2001.

Christiansen, Thomas J. *Useful Adversaries: Grand Strategy, Domestic Mobilization, and Sino-American Conflict, 1947–1958.* Princeton, N.J.: Princeton University Press, 1996.

Churchill, Winston. *The Churchill-Eisenhower Correspondence, 1953–1955.* Edited by Peter G. Boyle. Chapel Hill: University of North Carolina Press, 1990.

Clarfield, Gary. *Security with Solvency: Dwight D. Eisenhower and the Shaping of the American Military Establishment.* Westport, Conn.: Praeger, 1999.

Clowse, Barbara B. *Brainpower for the Cold War: The Sputnik Crisis and the National Defense Education Act of 1958.* Westport, Conn.: Greenwood, 1981.

Congress and the Nation, 1945–1964: A Review of Government and Politics in the Postwar Years. Washington, D.C.: Congressional Quarterly Service, 1965.

Cullather, Nick. *Secret History: The CIA's Classified Account of Its Operations in Guatemala, 1952–1954.* Palo Alto, Calif.: Stanford University Press, 1999.

Damms, Richard V. *The Eisenhower Presidency, 1953–1961.* London: Longman, 2002.

Divine, Robert A. *The Sputnik Challenge: Eisenhower's Response to the Soviet Satellite.* New York: Oxford University Press, 2003.

Dockrill, Saki. *Eisenhower's New Look National Security Policy, 1953–1961.* New York: St. Martin's Press, 1996.

DuBofsky, Melvyn. *The State and Labor in Modern America.* Chapel Hill: University of North Carolina Press, 1994.

Duram, James C. *A Moderate among Extremists: Dwight D. Eisenhower and the School Desegregation Crisis.* Chicago: Nelson-Hall, 1981.

Eden, Anthony, Earl of Avon. *The Eden-Eisenhower Correspondence, 1955–1957.* Edited by Peter G. Boyle. Chapel Hill: University of North Carolina Press, 2005.

Eisenhower, Dwight D. *At Ease: Stories I Tell to Friends.* New York: Doubleday, 1967.

———. *Crusade in Europe.* Garden City, N.Y.: Doubleday, 1948.

———. *Dear General; Eisenhower's Wartime Letters to Marshall.* Edited by Joseph Patrick Hobbs. Baltimore: Johns Hopkins University Press, 1971.

———. *The Eisenhower Diaries.* Edited by Robert H. Ferrell. New York: Norton, 1981.

———. *Eisenhower: The Prewar Diaries and Selected Papers, 1905–1941.* Edited by Daniel D. Holt, et al. Baltimore: Johns Hopkins University Press, 1998.

———. *Eisenhower Speaks; Dwight D. Eisenhower in His Messages and Speeches.* Edited by Rudolph L. Treuenfels. New York: Farrar, Straus, 1948.

———. *Ike's Letters to a Friend, 1941–1958.* Edited by Robert Griffith. Lawrence: University Press of Kansas, 1984.

———. *Letters to Mamie.* Edited by John S. D. Eisenhower. Garden City, N.Y.: Doubleday, 1978.

———. *The Papers of Dwight David Eisenhower.* 21 vols. Edited by Alfred D. Chandler, Jr., et al. Baltimore: Johns Hopkins University Press, 1970–1978.

———. *The White House Years: Mandate for Change, 1953–1956.* Garden City, N.Y.: Doubleday, 1963.

———. *The White House Years: Waging Peace, 1956–1961.* Garden City, N.Y.: Doubleday, 1965.

Eisenhower, John S. D. *General Ike: A Personal Reminiscence.* New York: Simon and Schuster, 2003.

Eisenhower, Susan. *Mrs. Ike: Portrait of a Marriage.* New York: Farrar, Straus and Giroux, 1996.

Fall, Bernard. *Hell in a Very Small Place: The Siege of Dien Bien Phu.* New York: DaCapo Press, 2002.

Freiberger, Steven Z. *Dawn over Suez: The Rise of American Power in the Middle East, 1953–1957.* Chicago: Ivan R. Dee, 1992.

Fried, Richard M. *Nightmare in Red: The McCarthy Years in Perspective.* New York: Oxford University Press, 1990.

Gardner, Lloyd C. *Approaching Vietnam: From World War II through Dien Bien Phu.* New York: Norton, 1988.

Garrow, David J. *Bearing the Cross: Martin Luther King, Jr., and the Southern Christian Leadership Conference.* New York: HarperCollins, 2004.

Gendzier, Irene L. *Notes from the Minefield: United States Intervention in Lebanon and the Middle East, 1945–1958.* New York: Columbia University Press, 1996.

Gleijeses, Piero. *Shattered Hope: The Guatemalan Revolution and the United States, 1944–1954.* Princeton, N.J.: Princeton University Press, 1991.

Greenstein, Fred I. *The Hidden-Hand Presidency: Eisenhower as Leader.* New York: Basic Books, 1982.

Griffith, Robert. "Dwight D. Eisenhower and the Corporate Commonwealth." *American Historical Review* 87 (1982): 87–122.

———. *The Politics of Fear: Joseph R. McCarthy and the Senate.* Lexington: University of Kentucky Press, 1971.

Hahn, Peter L. *Crisis and Crossfire: The United States and the Middle East since 1945.* Washington, D.C.: Potomac Books, 2005.

Haynes, John Earl. *Red Scare or Red Menace? American Communism and Anticommunism in the Cold War Era.* Chicago: Ivan R. Dee, 1998.

Heiss, Mary Anne. *Empire and Nationhood: The United States, Great Britain, and Iranian Oil.* New York: Columbia University Press, 1994.

Herken, Gregg. *Brotherhood of the Bomb: The Tangled Lives and Loyalties of Robert Oppenheimer, Ernest Lawrence, and Edward Teller.* New York: Henry Holt, 2002.

Hewlett, Richard G., and Jack M. Holl. *Atoms for Peace and War, 1953–1961: Eisenhower and the Atomic Energy Commission.* Berkeley: University of California Press, 1989.

Holt, Marilyn Irvin. *Mamie Doud Eisenhower: The General's First Lady.* Lawrence: University Press of Kansas, 2007.

Hughes, Emmet J. *The Ordeal of Power: A Political Memoir of the Eisenhower Years.* New York: Atheneum, 1963.

Immerman, Richard H. *The CIA in Guatemala: The Foreign Policy of Intervention.* Austin: University of Texas Press, 1982.

Kingseed, Cole C. *Eisenhower and the Suez Crisis of 1956.* Baton Rouge: Louisiana State University Press, 1995.

Kinnard, Douglas. *Eisenhower: Soldier-Statesman of the American Century.* Washington, D.C.: Brassey's, 2002.

Kinzer, Stephen. *All the Shah's Men: An American Coup and the Roots of Middle East Terror.* New York: Wiley, 2003.

Khrushchev, Sergei N. *Nikita Khrushchev and the Creation of a Superpower.* University Park: Penn State University Press, 2000.

Kluger, Richard. *Simple Justice: The History of* Brown v. Board of Education *and Black America's Struggle for Equality.* New York: Knopf, 1975.

Kunz, Diane B. *The Economic Diplomacy of the Suez Crisis.* Chapel Hill: University of North Carolina Press, 1991.

Kyle, Keith. *Suez.* New York: St. Martin's Press, 1991.

Lee, R. Alton. *Eisenhower and Landrum-Griffin: A Study in Labor Management Politics.* Lexington: University of Kentucky Press, 1990.

Lee, Stephen Hugh. *The Korean War.* London: Longman, 2001.

Lewis, Catherine M. *"Don't Ask What I Shot": How Eisenhower's Love of Golf Helped Shape 1950s America.* New York: McGraw-Hill, 2007.

Little, Douglas. *American Orientalism: The United States and the Middle East since 1945.* 3d ed. Chapel Hill: University of North Carolina Press, 2008.

Lyon, Peter. *Eisenhower: Portrait of the Hero.* Boston: Little, Brown, 1974.

McDougall, Walter A. *The Heavens and the Earth: A Political History of the Space Age.* New York: Basic Books, 1985.

McMillan, Priscilla J. *The Ruin of J. Robert Oppenheimer and the Birth of the Modern Arms Race.* New York: Viking, 2005.

Nichols, David A. *A Matter of Justice: Eisenhower and the Beginning of the Civil Rights Revolution.* New York: Simon and Schuster, 2007.

Oshinsky, David M. *A Conspiracy so Immense: The World of Joe McCarthy.* New York: Oxford University Press, 2005.

Pach, Chester, Jr., and Elmo Richardson. *The Presidency of Dwight D. Eisenhower.* Rev. ed. Lawrence: University Press of Kansas, 1991.

Patterson, James T. *Brown v. Board of Education: A Civil Rights Milestone and Its Troubled Legacy.* New York: Oxford University Press, 2001.

Perret, Geoffrey. *Eisenhower.* New York: Random House, 1999.

Pickett, William B. *Eisenhower Decides to Run: Presidential Politics and Cold War Strategy.* Chicago: Ivan R. Dee, 2000.

Pilate, Joseph F., Robert E. Pendley, and Charles K. Ebinger, eds. *Atoms for Peace: An Analysis after Thirty Years.* Boulder, Colo.: Westview, 1985.

Public Papers of the Presidents of the United States, Dwight D. Eisenhower, Containing the Public Messages, Speeches, and Statements of the President, 1953–1961. 8 vols. Washington, D.C.: U.S. Government Printing Office, 1958–1961.

Rae, Nichol C. *The Decline and Fall of the Liberal Republicans from 1952 to the Present.* New York: Oxford University Press, 1989.

Reichard, Gary W. *The Reaffirmation of Republicanism: Eisenhower and the Eighty-Third Congress.* Knoxville: University of Tennessee Press, 1973.

Robinson, Jo Ann Gibson. *The Montgomery Bus Boycott and the Women Who Started It: The Memoir of Jo Ann Gibson Robinson.* Knoxville: University of Tennessee Press, 1987.

Roman, Peter J. *Eisenhower and the Missile Gap.* Ithaca, N.Y.: Cornell University Press, 1995.

Roosevelt, Kermit. *Countercoup: The Struggle for Control of Iran.* New York: McGraw-Hill, 1979.

Rose, Mark H. *Interstate: Express Highway Politics, 1941–1989.* Knoxville: University of Tennessee Press, 1990.

Rostow, W. W. *Open Skies: Eisenhower's Proposal of July 21, 1955.* Austin: University of Texas Press, 1982.

Schapsmeier, E. L., and F. H Schapsmeier. *Ezra Taft Benson and the Politics of Agriculture.* Danville, Ill.: Interstate Press, 1975.

Schlesinger, Stephen, and Stephen Kinzer. *Bitter Fruit: The Untold Story of the American Coup in Guatemala.* Garden City, N.Y.: Doubleday, 1982.

Schrecker, Ellen. *Many Are the Crimes: McCarthyism in America.* Boston: Little, Brown, 1998.

Seely, Bruce E. *Building the American Highway System: Engineers as Policy Makers.* Philadelphia: Temple University Press, 1987.

Statler, Kathryn C. *Replacing France: The Origins of American Intervention in Vietnam.* Lexington: University Press of Kentucky, 2007.

Tananbaum, Duane. *The Bricker Amendment Controversy: A Test of Eisenhower's Political Leadership.* New York: Cornell University Press, 1988.

Taubman, William. *Khrushchev: The Man and His Era.* New York: Free Press, 2004.

Trachtenberg, Marc. *A Constructed Peace: The Making of the European Settlement, 1945–1963.* Princeton, N.J.: Princeton University Press, 1999.

Wagner, Steven. *Eisenhower Republicanism: Pursuing the Middle Way.* DeKalb: Northern Illinois University Press, 2006.

Watson, Robert J. *History of the Office of the Secretary of Defense.* Vol. 4. *Into the Missile Age.* Washington, D.C.: Historical Office of the Office of the Secretary of Defense, 1997.

Wildavsky, Aaron. *Dixon-Yates: A Study in Power Politics.* New Haven, Conn.: Yale University Press, 1962.

Wright, Roberta Hughes. *The Birth of the Montgomery Bus Boycott.* Southfield, Mich.: Charro Press, 1991.

Young, Marilyn B. *The Vietnam Wars, 1945–1990.* New York: HarperCollins, 1991.

Young, Nancy Beck, ed. *The Documentary History of the Dwight D. Eisenhower Presidency.* 13 vols. Bethesda, Md.: Lexis-Nexis, 2005–   .

Zhang, S. G. *Deterrence and Strategic Culture: Chinese-American Confrontations, 1949–1958.* Ithaca, N.Y.: Cornell University Press, 1993.

Zubok, Vladislav M., and Constantine Pleshakov. *Inside the Kremlin's Cold War: From Stalin to Khrushchev.* Cambridge, Mass.: Harvard University Press, 1996.

DOCUMENTS

—◊◊◊—

Document One: President Dwight D. Eisenhower, Statement upon Signing the Submerged Lands Act, May 22, 1953

The question of whether the states or the federal government controlled the mineral-rich tidelands demanded much attention early in Eisenhower's presidency, and he released a statement on the subject on May 22, 1953.

I AM PLEASED to sign this measure into law recognizing the ancient rights of the States in the submerged lands within their historic boundaries. As I have said many times I deplore and I will always resist federal encroachment upon rights and affairs of the States. Recognizing the States' claim to these lands is in keeping with basic principles of honesty and fair play.

This measure also recognizes the interests of the Federal Government in the submerged lands outside of the historic boundaries of the States. Such lands should be administered by the Federal Government and income therefrom should go into the Federal Treasury.

Source: Public Papers of the Presidents of the United States, Dwight D. Eisenhower, Containing the Public Messages, Speeches, and Statements of the President, 1953 (Washington, D.C.: U.S. Government Printing Office, 1960), 326–327.

Document Two: President Eisenhower, Letter to the Shah of Iran Concerning the Settlement of the Oil Problem, released August 5, 1954; dated August 4, 1954

A year following the CIA-assisted coup in Iran, which removed the democratically elected Mohammad Mossadegh, President Eisenhower wrote to the shah of Iran on August 4, 1954, about U.S. access to Iranian oil.

Your Imperial Majesty:

The important news that your Government, in negotiation with the British, French, Dutch and United States oil companies, has reached, in principle, a fair and equitable settlement to the difficult oil problem is indeed gratifying.

Your Majesty must take great satisfaction at the success of this significant phase in the negotiations to which you personally have made a valuable contribution. I am confident that implementation of this agreement, under Your Majesty's leadership, will mark the beginning of a new era of economic progress and stability for your country.

Like myself, all Americans have a deep concern for the well-being of Iran. With them I have watched closely your courageous efforts, your steadfastness over the past difficult years, and with them I too have hoped that you might achieve the goals you so earnestly desire. The attainment of an oil settlement along the lines which have been announced should be a significant step in the direction of the realization of your aspirations for your people.

There is concrete evidence of the friendship that exists between our two countries and of our desire that Iran prosper independently in the family of free nations. We have endeavored to be helpful in the form of economic and technical assistance and we are happy to have helped in finding a solution to the oil problem.

I can assure Your Majesty of the continued friendly interest of the United States in the welfare and progress of Iran, and of the admiration of the American people for your enlightened leadership.

With sincere best wishes for the health and happiness of Your Majesty and the people of Iran,
Sincerely,
DWIGHT D. EISENHOWER

Source: Public Papers of the Presidents of the United States, Dwight D. Eisenhower, Containing the Public Messages, Speeches, and Statements of the President, 1954 (Washington, D.C.: U.S. Government Printing Office, 1960), 688–689.

Document Three: President Eisenhower, Statement Upon Signing the Communist Control Act, August 24, 1954

On August 24, 1954, President Eisenhower issued the following statement upon signing the Communist Control Act, a legislative attempt to deal with concerns during the cold war about communist subversion in the United States.

I HAVE TODAY signed S. 3706, An Act to make illegal the Communist Party and to prohibit members of Communist organizations from serving in certain representative capacities.

The American people are determined to protect themselves and their institutions against any organization in their midst which, purporting to be a political party within the normally accepted meaning, is actually a conspiracy dedicated to the violent overthrow of our entire form of government. The American people, likewise, are determined to accomplish this in strict conformity with the requirements of justice, fair play and the Constitution of the United States. They realize that employment of any other means would react unfavorably against the innocent as well as the guilty, and, in the long run, would distort and damage the judicial procedures of our country. The whole series of bills that the Administration has sponsored in this field have been designed in just this spirit and with just these purposes.

The new law which I am signing today includes one of the many recommendations made by this

Administration to support existing statutes in defeating the Communist conspiracy in this country. Administratively, we have in the past 19 months stepped up enforcement of laws against subversives. As a result, 41 top Communist leaders have been convicted, 35 more are indicted and scheduled for trial, and 105 subversive aliens have been deported.

The new laws enacted in this session of the Congress provide to the FBI and the Department of Justice much more effective weapons to help destroy the Communist menace. . . .

[T]he bill which I have signed today further carries out an important part of the recommendations made by this Administration. It creates within the framework of the Internal Security Act of 1950 a new category entitled, "Communist-Infiltrated Organizations." This provision will enable the Administration to assist members of those few labor organizations which are dominated by Communists, to rid themselves of the Communist control under which they have been forced to operate.

In the final days of the session, the Congress added to this measure certain clauses denying to Communists all rights, privileges and immunities which they have under the Federal Government. These provisions also subject members of the Communist Party or its front organizations, having knowledge of their revolutionary aims and objectives, to the provisions and penalties of the Internal Security Act. The full impact of these clauses upon the enforcement of the laws by which we are now fighting the Communist conspiracy in this country will require further careful study. I am satisfied, however, that they were not intended to impair or abrogate any portion of the Internal Security Act or the criminal statutes under which the leaders of the Communist Party are now being prosecuted and that they may prove helpful in several respects.

The Congress has thus enacted a substantial portion of the Administration's recommendations to strengthen our internal security laws.

In order to provide aggressive administration and enforcement of the foregoing measures, I have already strengthened the mechanism for carrying out more effectively our entire anti-Communist program by the creation of the Division of Internal Security in the Department of Justice.

We have made great progress in the past year and a half in prosecuting the leadership of the Communist conspiracy. I am proud that in this battle against the subversive elements in this country we have been able to preserve the rights of the accused in accordance with our traditions and the Bill of Rights. The 83d Congress has added effective new legal weapons to assist us in our fight to destroy communism in this country.

⌘

Source: Public Papers of the Presidents of the United States, Dwight D. Eisenhower, Containing the Public Messages, Speeches, and Statements of the President, 1954 (Washington, D.C.: U.S. Government Printing Office, 1960), 756–759.

Document Four: President Eisenhower, Telegram to Senator Russell of Georgia Regarding the Use of Federal Troops at Little Rock, September 27, 1957

On September 27, 1957, President Eisenhower sent a telegram to Georgia senator Richard Russell, a staunch segregationist, about the use of federal troops to uphold order and assist the integration of Central High School in Little Rock, Arkansas. A copy of the telegram was released to the media the following day

The Honorable Richard B. Russell
United States Senate
Washington, D.C.

Few times in my life have I felt as saddened as when the obligations of my office required me to order the use of force within a state to carry out the decisions of a Federal Court. My conviction is that had the police powers of the State of Arkansas been utilized not to frustrate the orders of the Court but to support them, the ensuing violence and open disrespect for the law and the Federal Judiciary would never have occurred. The Arkansas National Guard could have handled the situation with ease had it been instructed to do so. As a matter of fact, had the integration of Central High School been permitted to take place without the intervention of the National Guard, there is little doubt that the process would have gone along quite as smoothly and quietly as it has in other Arkansas communities. When a State, by seeking to frustrate the orders of a Federal Court, encourages mobs of extremists to flout the orders of a Federal Court, and when a State refuses to utilize its police powers to protect against mobs persons who are peaceably exercising their right under the Constitution as defined in such Court orders, the oath of office of the President requires that he take action to give that protection. Failure to act in such a case would be tantamount to acquiescence in anarchy and the dissolution of the union.

I must say that I completely fail to comprehend your comparison of our troops to Hitler's storm troopers. In one case military power was used to further the ambitions and purposes of a ruthless dictator; in the other to preserve the institutions of free government.

You allege certain wrong-doings on the part of individual soldiers at Little Rock. The Secretary of the Army will assemble the facts and report them directly to you. . . .

◈

Source: Public Papers of the Presidents of the United States, Dwight D. Eisenhower, Containing the Public Messages, Speeches, and Statements of the President, 1957 (Washington, D.C.: U.S. Government Printing Office, 1958), 695–696.

Document Five: President Eisenhower, News Conference Regarding *Sputnik*, October 9, 1957

In this October 9, 1957, press conference, President Eisenhower talked with reporters about the Soviet Union's launch of a satellite, Sputnik, *into outer space.*

Q. Merriman Smith, United Press: Mr. President, Russia has launched an earth satellite. They also claim to have had a successful firing of an intercontinental ballistics missile, none of which this country has done. I ask you, sir, what are we going to do about it?

THE PRESIDENT. Well, let's take, first, the earth satellite, as opposed to the missile, because they are related only indirectly in the physical sense, and in our case not at all.

The first mention that was made of an earth satellite that I know of, was about the spring of 1955—I mean the first mention to me—following upon a conference in Rome where plans were being laid for the working out of the things to be done in the International Geophysical Year.

Our people came back, studying a recommendation of that conference that we now undertake, the world undertake, the launching of a small earth satellite; and somewhere in I think May or June of 1955 it was recommended to me, by the Committee for the International Geophysical Year and through the National Science Foundation, that we undertake this project with a satellite to be launched somewhere during the Geophysical Year, which was from June 1957 until December 1958.

The sum asked for to launch a missile was $22 million and it was approved. . . .

Now, every scientist that I have talked to since this occurred—I recalled some of them and asked them—every one of them has spoken in most congratulatory terms about the capabilities of the Russian scientists in putting this in the air.

They expressed themselves as pleased rather than chagrined because at least the Soviets have proved the first part of it, that this thing will successfully orbit. But there are a lot of other things in the scientific inquiry that are not yet answered, and which we are pushing ahead to answer.

Now that is the story on the satellite. . . .

As to their firing of an intercontinental missile, we have not been told anything about the details of that firing. They have proved again and, indeed, this launching of the satellite proves, that they can hurl an object a considerable distance. They also said, as I recall that announcement, that it landed in the target area, which could be anywhere, because you can make target areas the size you please; and they also said it was a successful re-entry into the atmosphere, and landing at or near the target.

Now, that is a great accomplishment, if done. I have talked to you in the past about our own development in this regard as far as security considerations permit, and I can say this: the ICBM, the IRBM, we call them, are still going ahead—those projects—on the top priority within the Government, incidentally a priority which was never accorded to the satellite program. . . .

Q. Charles S. von Fremd, CBS News: Mr. President, Khrushchev claims we are now entering a period when conventional planes, bombers, and fighters will be confined to museums because they are outmoded by the missiles which Russia claims she has now perfected; and Khrushchev's remarks would seem to indicate he wants us to believe that our Strategic Air Command is now outmoded. Do you think that SAC is outmoded?

THE PRESIDENT. No. I believe it would be dangerous to predict what science is going to do in the next twenty years, but it is going to be a very considerable time in this realm just as in any other before the old is completely replaced by the new, and even then it will be a question of comparative costs and accuracy of methods of delivery.

It is going to be a long term. It is not a revolutionary process that will take place in the reequipping of defense forces, it will be an evolutionary.

Q. Robert E. Clark, International News Service: Mr. President, do you think our scientists made a mistake in not recognizing that we were, in effect in a race with Russia in launching this satellite, and not asking you for top priority and more money to speed up the program?

THE PRESIDENT. Well, no, I don't, because even yet, let's remember this: the value of that satellite going around the earth is still problematical, and you must remember the evolution that our people went through and the evolution that the others went through.

From 1945, when the Russians captured all of the German scientists in Peenemunde, which was their great laboratory and experimental grounds for the production of the ballistic missiles they used in World War II, they have centered their attention on the ballistic missile.

Originally, our people seemed to be more interested in the aerodynamic missile. We have a history of going back for quite a ways in modest research in the intercontinental ballistic missile, but until there were very great developments in the atomic bomb, it did not look profitable and economical to pursue that course very much, and our people did not go into it very earnestly until somewhere along about 1953, I think.

Now, so far as this satellite itself is concerned, if we were doing it for science, and not for security, which we were doing, I don't know of any reasons why the scientists should have come in and urged that we do this before anybody else could do it.

Now, quite naturally, you will say, "Well, the Soviets gained a great psychological advantage throughout the world," and I think in the political sense that is possibly true; but in the scientific sense it is not true except for the proof of the one thing, that they have got the propellants and the projectors that will put these things in the air. . . .

Q. Mrs. May Craig, Portland (Maine) Press Herald: Mr. President, you have spoken of the scientific aspects of the satellite. Do you not think that it has immense significance, the satellite, immense significance in surveillance of other countries, and leading to space platforms which could be used for rockets?

THE PRESIDENT. Not at this time, no. There is no—suddenly all America seems to become scientists, and I am hearing many, many ideas. [Laughter] And I think that, given time, satellites will be able to transmit to the earth some kind of information with respect to what they see on the earth or what they find on the earth.

But I think that that period is a long ways off when you stop to consider that even now the Russians, under a dictatorial society where they had some of the finest scientists in the world who have for many years been working on this, apparently from what they say they have put one small ball in the air.

I wouldn't believe that at this moment you have to fear the intelligence aspects of this. . . .

Q. Chalmers M. Roberts, Washington Post: Is it a correct interpretation of what you have said about your satisfaction with the missile program as separate from the satellite program that you have no plans to take any steps to combine the various government units which are involved in this program, and which give certainly the public appearance of a great deal of service rivalry, with some reason to feel that this is why we seem to be lagging behind the Soviets?

THE PRESIDENT. Well now, Mr. Roberts, there seem to be certain facts that are obvious. First of all, I didn't say I was satisfied. I said I didn't know what we could have done better.

The cost of these duplicating, or seemingly duplicating, programs is quite enormous, and I would like to save it. But even now, where two in the IRBM class seem to have gone far enough that we should have some basis of comparison, at my direction there was set up a committee of experts to decide which way we should go; and they have decided—or did the last time, just certainly a few days ago—that they didn't have quite yet the basis of fact on which they could determine which was the best direction to go.

Now, in almost every field that I know of, air-to-air, ground-to-air, air-to-ground, ground-to-ground, ballistic missiles, aerodynamic, there are some of these programs that are overlapping all the time.

As I think I told you before, the last estimate I had on armed military research and development, the money we spend yearly without putting a single weapon in our arsenal is $5,200,000,000. Now that isn't any weak, pusillanimous effort; that is a lot of money. . . .

***

Source: Public Papers of the Presidents of the United States, Dwight D. Eisenhower, Containing the Public Messages, Speeches, and Statements of the President, 1957 (Washington, D.C.: U.S. Government Printing Office, 1958), 719–732.

Document Six: President Eisenhower, Farewell Address to the American People, January 17, 1961

Three days before leaving office, President Eisenhower delivered a potent farewell address on January 17, 1961, in which he cautioned against the danger the "military-industrial complex" posed to the health of American democracy.

My fellow Americans:

Three days from now, after half a century in the service of our country, I shall lay down the responsibilities of office as, in traditional and solemn ceremony, the authority of the Presidency is vested in my successor. . . .

We now stand ten years past the midpoint of a century that has witnessed four major wars among great nations. Three of these involved our own country. Despite these holocausts America is today the strongest, the most influential and most productive nation in the world. Understandably proud of this pre-eminence, we yet realize that America's leadership and prestige depend, not merely upon our unmatched material progress, riches and military strength, but on how we use our power in the interests of world peace and human betterment.

Throughout America's adventure in free government, our basic purposes have been to keep the peace; to foster progress in human achievement, and to enhance liberty, dignity and integrity among people and among nations. To strive for less would be unworthy of a free and religious people. Any failure traceable to arrogance, or our lack of comprehension or readiness to sacrifice would inflict upon us grievous hurt both at home and abroad.

Progress toward these noble goals is persistently threatened by the conflict now engulfing the world. It commands our whole attention, absorbs our very beings. We face a hostile ideology—global in scope, atheistic in character, ruthless in purpose, and insidious in method. Unhappily the danger it poses promises to be of indefinite duration. To meet it successfully, there is called for, not so much the emotional and transitory sacrifices of crisis, but rather those which enable us to carry forward steadily, surely, and without complaint the burdens of a prolonged and complex struggle—with liberty the stake. Only thus shall we remain, despite every provocation, on our charted course toward permanent peace and human betterment. . . .

A vital element in keeping the peace is our military establishment. Our arms must be mighty, ready for instant action, so that no potential aggressor may be tempted to risk his own destruction.

Our military organization today bears little relation to that known by any of my predecessors in peacetime, or indeed by the fighting men of World War II or Korea.

Until the latest of our world conflicts, the United States had no armaments industry. American makers of plowshares could, with time and as required, make swords as well. But now we can no longer risk emergency improvisation of national defense; we have been compelled to create a permanent armaments industry of vast proportions. Added to this, three and a half million men and women are directly engaged in the defense establishment. We annually spend on military security more than the net income of all United States corporations.

This conjunction of an immense military establishment and a large arms industry is new in the American experience. The total influence—economic, political, even spiritual—is felt in every city, every State house, every office of the Federal government. We recognize the imperative need for this development. Yet we must not fail to comprehend its grave implications. Our toil, resources and livelihood are all involved; so is the very structure of our society.

In the councils of government, we must guard against the acquisition of unwarranted influence, whether sought or unsought, by the military-industrial complex. The potential for the disastrous rise of misplaced power exists and will persist.

We must never let the weight of this combination endanger our liberties or democratic processes. We should take nothing for granted. Only an alert and knowledgeable citizenry can compel the proper meshing of the huge industrial and military machinery of defense with our peaceful methods and goals, so that security and liberty may prosper together.

Akin to, and largely responsible for the sweeping changes in our industrial-military posture, has been the technological revolution during recent decades.

In this revolution, research has become central; it also becomes more formalized, complex, and costly. A steadily increasing share is conducted for, by, or at the direction of, the Federal government. . . .

The prospect of domination of the nation's scholars by Federal employment, project allocations, and the power of money is ever present—and is gravely to be regarded.

Yet, in holding scientific research and discovery in respect, as we should, we must also be alert to the equal and opposite danger that public policy could itself become the captive of a scientific-technological elite.

It is the task of statesmanship to mold, to balance, and to integrate these and other forces, new and old, within the principles of our democratic system—ever aiming toward the supreme goals of our free society.

Another factor in maintaining balance involves the element of time. As we peer into society's future, we—you and I, and our government—must avoid the impulse to live only for today, plundering, for our own ease and convenience, the precious resources of tomorrow. We cannot mortgage the material assets of our grandchildren without risking the loss also of their political and spiritual heritage. We want democracy to survive for all generations to come, not to become the insolvent phantom of tomorrow.

Down the long lane of the history yet to be written America knows that this world of ours, ever growing smaller, must avoid becoming a community of dreadful fear and hate, and be, instead, a proud confederation of mutual trust and respect.

Such a confederation must be one of equals. The weakest must come to the conference table with the same confidence as do we, protected as we are by our moral, economic, and military strength. That table, though scarred by many past frustrations, cannot be abandoned for the certain agony of the battlefield.

Disarmament, with mutual honor and confidence, is a continuing imperative. Together we must learn how to compose differences, not with arms, but with intellect and decent purpose. Because this need is so sharp and apparent I confess that I lay down my official responsibilities in this field with a definite sense of disappointment. As one who has witnessed the horror and the lingering sadness of war—as one who knows that another war could utterly destroy this civilization which has been so slowly and painfully built over thou-

sands of years—I wish I could say tonight that a lasting peace is in sight.

Happily, I can say that war has been avoided. Steady progress toward our ultimate goal has been made. But, so much remains to be done. As a private citizen, I shall never cease to do what little I can to help the world advance along that road.

Source: Public Papers of the Presidents of the United States, Dwight D. Eisenhower, Containing the Public Messages, Speeches, and Statements of the President, 1960–1961 (Washington, D.C.: U.S. Government Printing Office, 1961), 1,035–1,040.

John F. Kennedy

May 29, 1917–November 22, 1963

Thirty-fifth President of the United States
January 20, 1961–November 22, 1963

≈ JOHN F. KENNEDY ≈

Place of Birth: Brookline, Massachusetts

Date of Birth: May 29, 1917

Place of Residence: Massachusetts

Class Background: wealthy

Father's Career: millionaire businessman and public official

Mother's Career: homemaker

Number of Siblings: eight

Religion: Roman Catholic

Education: graduated Harvard College, 1940

Political Party: Democrat

Military Service: World War II: Lieutenant, U.S. Naval Reserve, 1941–45

Spouse: Jacqueline Bouvier Kennedy

Spouse's Education: attended Vassar College and the Sorbonne; graduated from George Washington University, 1951

Spouse's Career: photographer, *Washington Times-Herald;* homemaker; editor at Doubleday and Company

Number of Children: three

Sports and Hobbies: sailing, swimming, touch football

Career Prior to the Presidency: World War II naval officer, journalist, U.S. representative, U.S. senator

Age upon Entering White House: 43 years, 236 days

Reason for Leaving the White House: assassinated in office

Date of Death: November 22, 1963

Cause of Death: assassination

Last Words: "My God, I've been hit." (some sources say Kennedy said nothing after being shot)

Burial Site: Arlington National Cemetery, Virginia

Value of Estate at Time of Death: unknown, in the millions

Preceding page: John F. Kennedy *(John F. Kennedy Library)*

BIOGRAPHY OF KENNEDY

The 35th president of the United States, John Fitzgerald Kennedy, was the first American president born in the 20th century and became an iconic symbol of his generation. Born in Brookline, Massachusetts, on May 29, 1917, to a wealthy third-generation Irish Catholic family, Kennedy epitomized white ethnic America's social mobility. Similar to other Irish families, the Kennedy clan had originally emigrated to America during the potato famine of the 1840s. It was Patrick Kennedy who originally left County Wexford, Ireland, for Boston. After settling in Irish-dominated East Boston, Kennedy took a job as a barrel maker and married Bridget Murphy. The marriage produced three daughters and one son—Patrick Joseph "P. J." Kennedy, a saloonkeeper who became John Kennedy's paternal grandfather. After marrying Mary Hickey, P. J. Kennedy parlayed his single saloon into a wholesale liquor distributorship and a seat in the Massachusetts state senate.

In 1888, P. J. Kennedy's son Joseph Patrick Kennedy was born. From an early age, young Joseph P. Kennedy combined his father's competitive spirit and nose for business with the family's newfound social connections. Fueled by his desire to "become a millionaire," Kennedy engineered a takeover of the Columbia Trust Company and in the process became the nation's youngest bank president at age 25. In 1914, Kennedy married Rose Fitzgerald, who was the daughter of Boston mayor John "Honey Fitz" Fitzgerald. Joseph Kennedy's marriage elevated his social standing. In addition, Kennedy's investments in the motion picture industry and stock market reaped millions in profits.

With Rose playing the role of the proper Victorian wife and mother, the couple had four children within the first five years of marriage. Starting in the summer of 1915, Rose bore Joe, Jr., and over the next 17 years John, Rosemary, Kathleen, Eunice, Patricia, Robert, Jean, and Edward (Ted) were born. With Joseph absorbed in his various business ventures it was Rose who closely supervised her children's activities. As one biographer noted about the roles John F. Kennedy's parents played, "Joe provided the fire in the family, but Rose provided the steel." With an estimated fortune of $400 million, Joseph Kennedy intended that his wealth would help make one of his four son's president of the United States.

While the Kennedys presented an idealized image to the outside world all was not what it seemed. The patriarch, Joseph, was well known for his womanizing. The oldest Kennedy daughter, Rosemary, suffered from severe mental retardation and was eventually institutionalized. In addition, John—the future president—was a sickly child who suffered from illnesses ranging from scarlet fever to whooping cough. Young John Kennedy's greatest malady was his unstable back, which afflicted him throughout his life. As a child, Kennedy was a regular patient at the Mayo Clinic. Despite his illnesses, John Kennedy threw himself into the family's legendary touch football games and always projected an image of fitness and physicality.

As a youth, John Kennedy, or Jack as he was known to family and friends, was shaped by his illnesses and his sibling rivalry with his older brother Joe, Jr. Despite their rivalry, family and friends claim that John idolized Joe. Unlike Joe who excelled in his studies and athletics, John's talents lay in winning friends and wooing young women. Blessed with a fun-loving spirit and fond of pranks, Kennedy was a natural social butterfly. Despite his indifference to academics, John's senior thesis, *Why England Slept*, allowed him to graduate from Harvard College with honors in 1940 and revealed his abiding interest in current events. With considerable help from his father and Henry Luce, publisher and cofounder of *Time-Life* and one of the most influential press barons of the time, Kennedy published his senior thesis as a book and attracted considerable attention. *Why England Slept* examined the British appeasement policy at the Munich crisis in 1938 prior to World War II. In the book, Kennedy argued that since Britain had not increased its defense expenditures in the 1930s, Britain had no other alternative but to seek appeasement with German dictator Adolf Hitler.

Just back from Europe, a 21-year-old John F. Kennedy reads the *Daily Mirror* on January 1, 1939. *(Associated Press)*

JACQUELINE KENNEDY

(1929–1994) *first lady of the United States, January 20, 1961–November 22, 1963*

Born on July 28, 1929, in Southampton, New York, Jacqueline Lee Bouvier was the daughter of John Vernon Bouvier III and Janet Norton Lee. Like her husband, John F. Kennedy, Jacqueline Bouvier was reared in an environment of privilege. Indeed even more than Kennedy, Jacqueline was the product of an American aristocracy. Because of her sense of style, cultural sensibilities, and her husband's tragic death, she became an iconic symbol of her generation.

Bouvier attended elite schools and was educated in the fine arts. In addition to ballet, painting and poetry, she was a well-trained equestrienne, a skill for which she won numerous awards in her early life. While Jacqueline's world might have appeared perfect, her family life was tumultuous. Three months after her birth, her father, a Wall Street stock speculator, lost much of his wealth in the 1929 stock market crash. In addition to these financial losses, the Bouviers' marriage was a rocky one and John was known as a womanizer. Indeed, Jackie, as she was often called, vividly recounted the one time her parents bid her goodnight before they headed out for an evening of dancing because it was such a rare moment of relative marital bliss.

Never close to her mother, Jacqueline developed a close relationship with her father despite his womanizing ways. With her brunette hair, full lips, and dark eyes, she resembled her father, who was nicknamed "Black Jack" for his perpetual tan and dark hair. When Jackie was seven, her parents divorced. Soon after, her mother married a wealthy banker, Hugh Auchincloss, and Jackie moved into her stepfather's estate in McLean, Virginia.

After attending boarding school, Bouvier enrolled at Vassar College in Poughkeepsie, New York. At Vassar, she continued to study art and French and lived one year in Paris, perfecting her language skills. After spending a year abroad, Poughkeepsie held little charm, so she finished her studies at George Washington University in Washington, D.C. After graduating in 1951, she landed a job with the *Washington Times-Herald* as the "Inquiring Camera Girl." In this position she posed provocative questions to an array of Washingtonians ranging from housewives to congressmen and snapped their photos, which ran above their answers.

Soon after taking this job, Bouvier met and began dating John F. Kennedy, a young congressman from Massachusetts. On the surface, Kennedy and Bouvier were well-matched. Both were Catholic, products of wealthy and powerful families, well traveled, and highly educated. There were significant differ-

Jacqueline Kennedy *(Library of Congress)*

ences, though, which would place enormous pressures upon their relationship and marriage. For one, Bouvier was 12 years younger than Kennedy and she was quite unused to the world of politics.

In June 1953, the year Kennedy entered the Senate, the Kennedy-Bouvier engagement was officially announced. The stylish young senator's impending marriage attracted considerable attention including a feature story in *Life* magazine. Jacqueline settled into her new role, as a senator's wife, with some distress, forced to deal with her husband's demanding schedule, philandering, and his considerable health issues.

After suffering two miscarriages, Kennedy gave birth to Caroline Bouvier Kennedy in 1957. With a photogenic family and his shrewd wife in tow, Senator Kennedy began a campaign for the presidency in which Jackie Kennedy played an indispensable role. Kennedy's advisers, such as John Kenneth Galbraith and Arthur Schlesinger, Jr., both appreciated her acute political sense and keen ability to judge of character. Her campaign schedule was halted by another pregnancy, and two weeks after Kennedy was elected president, Jackie Kennedy gave birth to John Kennedy, Jr., in November 1960.

Just 31 years old, Jacqueline Kennedy was one of the youngest first ladies in American history. Despite her role as first lady, Kennedy was most concerned with providing her children with a normal childhood. In pursuit of this goal, she established a play group, nursery school, and kindergarten in the White House. Located in the White House Solarium, the "school" allowed Caroline to avoid the media glare. Kennedy sought to avoid media attention as well and even shunned press conferences, though she did allow the occasional televised interview.

While Kennedy participated in the official business of the White House, she refused to accompany the president on most political trips so that she could tend to Caroline and John, Jr. Her extended absences enabled the president to continue his prodigious womanizing of which the first lady was aware. With a veil drawn around her private life, the press focused on Jackie's public activities, which included restoring the White House, promoting the arts, and entertaining foreign dignitaries. Her fashion savvy shaped the tastes of American women in the 1960s as she popularized such apparel as the pillbox hat. As had several first ladies before her, notably Lou Henry Hoover and Mamie Eisenhower, Jackie Kennedy routinely invited leading artists to perform at the White House, including Pablo Casals, Igor Stravinsky, Aaron Copland, Isaac Stern, and Tennessee Williams.

Jackie Kennedy was an extraordinary asset during her husband's trips abroad. Well schooled in manners and charm, the first lady wooed the famously dour French president Charles de Gaulle and even thawed the belligerent Nikita Khrushchev. So thoroughly did she capture the affections of these leaders that President Kennedy remarked of his trip to France in 1961 that he was "the man who accompanied Jacqueline Kennedy to Paris." Aside from these successes, Jackie's most publicized role was her restoration of the White House. With keen managerial skills combined with unrelenting effort, Jackie oversaw an expensive and wide-ranging restoration and personally searched through government warehouses in search of forgotten White House antiques. This work was funded in part through the sale of the first White House guidebook, which Jackie Kennedy wrote.

The first lady's efforts resulted in the nationally televised *A Tour of the White House with Mrs. John F. Kennedy* on February 14, 1962. Shown on all three networks and viewed by three of every four Americans, the hour-long broadcast was a hit and Jackie's most lasting contributions of White House preservation and remodeling in a sophisticated, historically accurate fashion was made secure. Equally important, she ensured that the White House was listed in the National Register of Historic Places.

In August 1963, tragedy struck as Kennedy's prematurely born son Patrick Bouvier Kennedy died when he was less than two days old. According to observers, the crisis brought the couple closer together than they had ever been before. Jackie

Kennedy returned to the White House in October and gradually began attending and overseeing White House social events.

In November, Jackie Kennedy, who seldom accompanied her husband on political trips, shocked the White House staff by agreeing to travel on such a trip to Dallas, Texas. Observers noted that she finally seemed to enjoy her role as a politician's wife. On November 22, 1963, she was seated by her husband during a seven-mile motorcade route through the city, lined by enthusiastic crowds. At the end of the route, the president was shot and the right side of his skull was shattered. As Jackie Kennedy cradled her dead husband in her lap, she repeated "Jack. Jack. Jack, can you hear me? I love you, Jack." Two hours later she stood beside Lyndon Johnson when he took the oath of office aboard Air Force One as a gesture of support for his presidency, but she refused to change from the clothes that were stained with her husband's blood. She noted, "I want them to see what they've done."

The president's sudden death shocked the nation and devastated the entire Kennedy family. Despite her grief, Kennedy managed to choreograph and manage her husband's funeral. One week after the president's death, she convinced the journalist Theodore White to write the Kennedy administration's epitaph in *Life* magazine. Borrowing a line from a popular Broadway musical about King Arthur, she compared the administration's 1,000-day reign to "the one brief shining moment that was known as Camelot." White's article and evocation of Camelot caught the public's fancy and "Camelot" became a common label for describing the Kennedy era.

After leaving the White House, the former first lady focused on raising her children and protecting her husband's legacy. In addition to public appeals for the establishment of Kennedy's Presidential Library, she lobbied her husband's associates to delete offensive private and personal anecdotes from memoirs and books that were written in the years that followed.

In 1968, Jackie married her longtime friend Aristotle Onassis, a wealthy Greek shipping magnate. Onassis died in 1975, leaving Jackie independently wealthy and twice widowed at the young age of 46. She nonetheless took a job as an editor at Doubleday and Co. She forsook the public limelight in favor of raising her two children, who both earned law degrees and avoided the difficulties that plagued much of the extended Kennedy family. Nonetheless, the press hounded her for any tidbit of information or photograph that could be had. In the final decade of her life, Jackie Onassis and Maurice Templesman shared a committed relationship. On May 19, 1994, Jackie succumbed to lymphoma at the age of 64. With Templesman by her side, Jackie Kennedy Onassis died in her home in New York City.

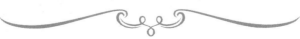

BIOGRAPHICAL TIME LINE

1917
May 29 John F. Kennedy is born in Brookline, Massachusetts.

1940
Kennedy graduates from Harvard College.

1943
While serving in the South Pacific during World War II Kennedy rescues his crew when a Japanese destroyer rammed his boat, the PT-109.

1946
At the age of 29 Kennedy is elected to the U.S. House of Representatives from Massachusetts.

1952
Kennedy is elected to the U.S. Senate.

1953
Kennedy marries Jacqueline Bouvier.

1957
Kennedy's book *Profiles in Courage* wins the Pulitzer Prize.

1958
Kennedy wins reelection to the Senate by a record margin.

1960
November 8 Kennedy is elected president of the United States.

1961
January 20 John F. Kennedy is sworn in as president.

1963
November 22 President Kennedy is assassinated while riding in a motorcade in Dallas, Texas.

Despite Kennedy's spotty medical record, his father used his clout and won his son the command of a patrol torpedo, or PT, boat in the Pacific during World War II. As a naval officer, Kennedy rescued his crew when his boat, the PT-109, was rammed by a Japanese destroyer in 1943. After John Hershey published an account of the incident in *The New Yorker,*

Joe Kennedy had the story reprinted in the *Reader's Digest.* John's heroism pushed his older brother Joe, Jr. to volunteer for a dangerous bombing mission over Germany in 1944—a mission from which he never returned. The death of Joe, Jr. shook the Kennedy family. Tall, athletic, and handsome with an engaging personality, Joe, Jr. was viewed as the Kennedy son who would enter politics and eventually seek the presidency. This expectation now shifted to Jack; the ambassador would now promote his second son for a political career after the war.

After discharge from the navy, Kennedy worked as a reporter for the Hearst newspapers covering the inaugural United Nations Conference in San Francisco and early postwar developments in Europe. In 1946, the 29-year-old Kennedy ran for a seat in the U.S. House of Representatives in Massachusetts's 11th congressional district. The campaign is memorable for the influence Joe Kennedy used to assure his son's victory. The senior Kennedy spent large amounts of money, the campaign had some of the best Boston politicos on its payroll, and the family hosted numerous teas and meet the candidate get-togethers. Kennedy was victorious in the contest. Soon after his election to the House of Representatives, Kennedy was diagnosed with the life-threatening Addison's disease. Indeed, immediately prior to his diagnosis, Kennedy had become so ill that a priest gave him last rites. Caused by a dearth of cortisol hormones that fight infection and regulate the body's metabolism, Addison's disease is typically fatal and Kennedy expected that he would die in his early forties. With the advent of cortisone, he was able to lead a relatively normal life but since stress was believed to produce an "addisonian crisis" even a simple tooth extraction was cause for significant concern.

Although he also suffered severe back pain, which he blamed on injuries he sustained during the PT-109 sinking in World War II, the exact roots of his "failed back syndrome" are unknown. Kennedy did undergo several surgeries including "double-fusion" spinal surgery. Rather than solving the underlying issues, the operations produced chronic and constant pain. During his presidency, his back pain became so acute Kennedy was forced to walk on crutches at times.

Starting in 1960, the year he ran for president, Kennedy began to see a New York doctor named Max Jacobson. Despite lacking hospital privileges, Jacobson regularly treated prominent figures such as the author Truman Capote. Jacobson's favored remedy was an injection "cocktail" that was comprised of amphetamines, steroids, vitamins, enzymes, and calcium. Although this combination of drugs was legal, it was also addictive and the president's associates convinced him to cut ties with Jacobson in 1962.

As if Addison's and failed-back syndrome were not enough, Kennedy also suffered from irritable bowel syndrome, which caused severe abdominal cramps and diarrhea on a daily basis. With his variety of medical ailments and nagging allergies, Kennedy took at least seven prescrip-

President Kennedy often suffered from back pain, forcing him to use crutches. Here he is with White House associate press secretary Andrew T. Hatcher in June 1961. *(Library of Congress)*

the entire Kennedy family devote its collective energy to secure John's victory. Running against a popular incumbent in what was a Republican year—Democrats lost the White House for the first time in 20 years—would have derailed most campaigns but with Joe Kennedy's deep pockets and an extraordinarily dedicated campaign staff, headed by his brother Robert Kennedy, John Kennedy eked out a victory over Lodge.

With his stunning underdog triumph, Kennedy became the most significant Democrat in Massachusetts and a national figure. After taking office in 1953, Kennedy made two fateful decisions—he married Jacqueline Bouvier and hired Theodore Sorensen to be his administrative assistant. Sorenson developed into an indispensable aide and speechwriter, and he was even dubbed Kennedy's "intellectual blood bank." Writing articles under Kennedy's name for leading publications such as the *New Republic* and *The Atlantic*, Sorensen buttressed the senator's image as a scholar-statesman and emerging star in the party.

Kennedy's marriage not only rendered his national aspirations realistic, but also Bouvier's aesthetic sense and beauty added much to the Kennedy mystique. Like her husband, Bouvier was reared in an environment of privilege. As a senator's wife, however, Jackie, as she was often called, struggled in dealing with her husband's crowded work schedule and philandering. Nonetheless, JACKIE KENNEDY was indispensable in her husband's blossoming political career. The Kennedys had three children, a daughter Caroline born in 1957; a son John, Jr. born days after his father won the presidency in 1960 (who later died in an airplane crash in 1999); and another son Patrick, who died two days after his birth in 1962.

While Kennedy never became an active, hands-on legislator, moving up to the Senate forced him to mature. During his initial Senate years, Kennedy struggled to define himself politically. While the senator had begun his career as a moderate conservative with liberal tendencies, he soon surrounded himself with liberals. Nonetheless, Kennedy's early conservatism and pragmatic voting record made most liberals wary of him. No issue highlighted Kennedy's ambiguous relationship with conventional liberals more than the censure of Senator Joseph McCarthy, a Wisconsin senator whose communist "witch hunt" led to gross violations of civil liberties and whose name was used to coin the phrase *McCarthyism* to describe such actions. When the Senate voted to censure McCarthy in the fall of 1954, Kennedy abstained and earned the animus of party liberals, such as Eleanor Roosevelt, for years to come. Several factors help explain his decision. McCarthy's charges were popular with many different ethnic and religious groups, including Catholics who made up a large portion of the Massachusetts population. Conservative business interests including Joe Kennedy and people truly fearful of a possible communist takeover of the United States also admired McCarthy. At the time of the censure vote Kennedy was convalescing from back surgery and absent

tions on a daily basis. Ironically, on the eve of his death in 1963 Kennedy might have been in the best health of his life. Because he was following an exercise regimen and avoiding questionable physicians, such as Jacobson, Kennedy had finally gained some control over his tenuous health.

Despite his health problems, the young congressman settled into his new career in the late 1940s. Kennedy backed minimum wage increases, the extension of Social Security benefits, and low-income housing; he also supported President HARRY TRUMAN's Marshall Plan and entry into the North Atlantic Treaty Organization. Kennedy was easily reelected to Congress in 1948; he had no opponent that year and, in 1950, he had only a token Republican opponent. The House of Representatives, however, was always a way station for Kennedy, who had the Senate in his sights from the time he took his first oath of office in 1947.

Without the aid of a distinguished record in the House, Kennedy nevertheless decided to challenge Republican senator Henry Cabot Lodge, Jr. for his Senate seat in 1952. As a member of one of New England's prominent WASP families, Lodge was a formidable opponent and the race required that

President John F. Kennedy walks with his son John F. Kennedy, Jr., at the White House, 1963. *(Cecil Stoughton/John F. Kennedy Presidential Library)*

from the Senate. However, observers note that he could have given his vote by proxy or paired his vote with another senator to have his vote on record.

With Kennedy's reputation with party liberals in tatters, the senator spent his time convalescing from major back surgery by pondering issues of moral and political courage. Prompted by his conversations with Jackie regarding political boldness and idealism, Kennedy produced a collective biography called *Profiles in Courage*. Published in 1956, the work recounted the careers of eight senators who risked their political careers for the sake of the national interest. While it was Sorensen and historian Jules Davids who wrote and researched much of the work, Kennedy won the 1957 Pulitzer Prize for the biography, which further catapulted him into the national political spotlight.

Following up on the heels of his wildly successful book, Kennedy turned his attention to securing the 1956 Democratic nomination for vice president. At the 1956 Democratic

National Convention in Chicago, Kennedy narrated a film about FRANKLIN D. ROOSEVELT and officially placed Adlai Stevenson's name in nomination for the presidency. Even though he narrowly lost the second spot on the ticket to Tennessee senator Estes Kefauver, Kennedy, just 39 years old, emerged from the convention as a shining star.

After he easily won reelection to the Senate in 1958, defeating Vincent J. Celeste by a record margin, Kennedy turned his attention to the presidency and announced his candidacy on January 2, 1960, 10 months before election day (which at the time was extremely early). Brandishing his youth and vigor, the senator claimed he would get "America moving again" and that a Kennedy administration would bring "a more vital life for our people." With most of his potential Democratic rivals sitting out the primaries, such as Senate majority leader LYNDON B. JOHNSON* of Texas, former Democratic candidate Adlai Stevenson of Illinois, and Senator Stuart Symington of Missouri, Kennedy's main opponent was Minnesota senator Hubert H. Humphrey. He also had to confront anti-Catholic bigotry. No Catholic had ever been elected president and in 1928 Democratic presidential candidate Alfred E. Smith lost in large part due to a strong anti-Catholic vote. Many Protestant voters were fearful that a Catholic president would freely take instructions from the pope or defer to Vatican viewpoints in U.S. foreign and domestic policy. Kennedy confronted the issue head-on in the primary in the predominantly Protestant state of West Virginia, where he triumphed over Humphrey, smoothing his path to the nomination. The final vestiges of the anti-Catholic issue were put away when Kennedy addressed the Greater Houston Ministerial Association about his Catholic faith and his belief in the separation of church and state.

At the Democratic presidential convention in Los Angeles, Kennedy encountered a late challenge from Texas senator Lyndon Johnson and his supporters. Other individuals at the convention offered themselves in case of a deadlocked convention (including Adlai Stevenson and Stuart Symington). Kennedy, however, prevailed, receiving 806 votes on the first ballot and securing the nomination for president. Kennedy tapped Senator Johnson to be his vice president and unveiled his campaign theme "the NEW FRONTIER."

While the rhetoric might suggest otherwise, Kennedy and his opponent, Vice President RICHARD NIXON, differed very little on the issues as both supported Roosevelt's New Deal welfare state policies and Truman's containment policy in foreign affairs. Kennedy's primary task was to convince voters that he was experienced enough for the job. For the

---

*For more information on Lyndon B. Johnson, John F. Kennedy's vice president, see the chapter on Johnson, who was president from 1963 to 1969.

first time in American history, the two candidates agreed to hold presidential debates, which were televised nationally. Reflecting the new and little understood power of television, the debates showed a handsome, tanned, and relaxed Kennedy compared to Nixon, who had a beard stubble, beady eyes, and perspiration that was noticeable in part by his refusal to wear makeup. Of the three televised debates the first one was the most highly watched and polling indicated that viewers thought Kennedy won. Radio listeners, who composed a much smaller audience, thought Nixon won. Johnson campaigned in the South almost exclusively to try to hold that region for the Democratic nominee. Civil rights was a much larger issue than in previous campaigns. In the final week of the campaign, Kennedy telephoned Coretta Scott King after her husband, Martin Luther King, Jr. had been arrested and offered his support. Publicized in the black community, the call helped gain him significant support among African-American voters. The election proved to be one of the closest presidential elections in U.S. history. Kennedy won by a mere 118,574 votes (out of more than 68 million cast), but he carried the electoral vote, 303 to 219.

John F. Kennedy took the oath of office on January 20, 1961. In his inaugural address, considered among the most notable in U.S. history, he declared, "Let the word go forth from this time and place, to friend and foe alike, that the torch has been passed to a new generation of Americans." He closed by challenging Americans to "ask not what your country can do for you, ask what you can do for your country." In office, the president was committed to reviving an activist executive branch. In that regard, Kennedy and his staff worked tirelessly to place the president in the middle of significant legislative and political battles. Despite the administration's desire, the "conservative coalition" of Republicans and mostly southern Democrats complicated the political environment, and early in his presidency, Kennedy once complained "[I] couldn't get a Mother's Day Resolution through the goddamn Congress."

Kennedy's legislative victories were few. They included a bill to raise the minimum wage 25 cents an hour to $1.25 an hour. Additionally Kennedy moved through Congress legislation providing for more affordable housing construction. Legislation to increase presidential authority over trade and tariffs passed in 1962, but little of what Kennedy called for in his New Frontier became law. Nor was he much more successful with civil rights. Because he realized the composition of Congress would all but prevent passage of civil rights legislation, the majority of Kennedy's work with that issue came in the form of executive orders. Even there, he failed to use presidential orders to ban housing discrimination in federally funded facilities until 1962. Toward the end of his first term events such as the integration of the University of Mississippi in 1962 and the protests in Bir-

mingham in 1963 caused him to grow more interested in pushing civil rights legislation through Congress.

While Kennedy's domestic record was mixed and marked with inaction, his foreign policy record, also mixed, was much more activist. The 1961 effort to overthrow the Castro regime in Cuba with the BAY OF PIGS invasion resulted in disaster and helped contribute to the most dangerous international moment in the Kennedy presidency, the CUBAN MISSILE CRISIS in October 1962. The risk of nuclear war was averted, and Kennedy learned valuable lessons about the importance of negotiation. He faced off against Soviet premier Nikita Khrushchev over the issue of the Berlin wall, which was constructed in 1962. Most important, Kennedy escalated the VIETNAM WAR, increasing the number of U.S. military personnel in that country from several hundred to nearly 17,000 at the time of his death in November 1963. The Kennedy administration's decision to support the coup that removed Ngo Dinh Diem from power in South Vietnam resulted in a power vacuum there and an intensification of the war.

During Kennedy's tenure in the White House, his wife, Jackie, proved to be a valuable asset on trips abroad. Well schooled in manners and charm, the first lady wooed the famously dour French president Charles de Gaulle and even thawed the belligerent Soviet premier Nikita Khrushchev. Aside from these behind-the-scenes successes, Jackie was well known for restoring and redecorating the White House. With managerial skill and unrelenting effort, Jackie oversaw an expensive and wide-ranging restoration and personally searched through government warehouses for forgotten White House antiques.

Despite the fear of many Kennedy officials that Jackie's expensive restoration would damage the president, the first lady's efforts resulted in a bonanza of positive media coverage. Foremost among this coverage was the nationally televised *A Tour of the White House with Mrs. John F. Kennedy.* Shown on all three networks and viewed by an estimated three of every four Americans, the hour-long broadcast was a hit. Jackie's most lasting contribution in preserving the White House, making it more sophisticated, and emphasizing its history was made secure.

While Jackie participated in the official business of the White House, she refused to accompany her husband on domestic political trips. She devoted most of her attention and time raising Caroline and John, Jr. Jackie's extended absences from the president enabled him to continue his prodigious womanizing, of which the first lady was aware. In August 1963, tragedy struck as the Kennedys' son Patrick Bouvier Kennedy was born prematurely and died when he was less than two days old. According to observers, the death of their son brought the couple closer together than they had ever been before.

In November, Jackie shocked the White House staff by agreeing to travel to Texas with the president on a political

President and Mrs. Kennedy watching the America's Cup race onboard the USS *Joseph P. Kennedy, Jr.* (a ship named after the president's brother), September 1962 *(Robert Knudsen, Office of the Naval Aide to the President/White House Photographs)*

trip to raise money and mend political fences. Though she told friends that she was surprised by her decision, Jackie declared that she was looking forward to the campaign trail. Observers noted that for the first time, Jackie seemed to enjoy being a politician's wife.

Even though Kennedy's advisers had been worried about violent protesters, the president was ambivalent about the possible danger. While traveling in a motorcade through Dallas on November 22, 1963, President Kennedy was assassinated while sitting beside his wife. Assassin Lee Harvey Oswald fired three shots from a sixth floor window of the Texas School Book Depository. He hit the president in the

back and fatally wounded him with a shot to the head. Doctors at Parkland Memorial Hospital in Dallas pronounced Kennedy dead at 1 P.M. Central Standard Time.

Oswald was arrested later that day for the crime. Two days later, when Oswald was being moved from the city jail to the county jail, Dallas nightclub owner Jack Ruby shot and killed him. This murder was broadcast live on television, adding to the national trauma of the Kennedy assassination. This event caused some to question whether a conspiracy had been formed to kill President Kennedy. The Warren Commission, named by President Lyndon B. Johnson to investigate the Kennedy assassination and led by Chief Jus-

President and Mrs. Kennedy during their motorcade in Dallas, November 22, 1963, moments before the assassination. In front are Texas governor John Connally and his wife, Nellie Connally. *(Library of Congress)*

tice Early Warren, found in September 1964 that no credible evidence existed that "Jack Ruby was part of any conspiracy, foreign or domestic." Furthermore, the Warren Commission found that Oswald had acted alone. While conspiracy theorists have pointed to contradictions in the case, no arguments that they have raised have proved satisfactory either. The best available evidence supports the Warren Commission findings. Instead, the attraction of the conspiracy theories can best be understood as an outgrowth of the grief over Kennedy's tragic death.

PRESIDENTIAL ELECTION OF 1960

The 1960 presidential election gave both parties, Republicans and Democrats, strong reason to hope for victory. For Republicans, Vice President RICHARD M. NIXON seemed

the likely successor for President DWIGHT D. EISENHOWER. Eisenhower's tenure in the 1950s had been characterized by peace and prosperity. Still, Democrats believed with equal vigor that they could manipulate Eisenhower's age by calling for a new generation of leadership. Also working against the Republicans was a minor economic recession and the Soviet Union's launch of *Sputnik* in 1957, which suggested to some Americans that the United States was falling behind the Soviets in science and technology. Just as important was the chasm between Eisenhower's personal popularity and the lesser regard Americans had for the Republican Party in general.

Armed with his family's fortune and his father's dream that a Kennedy would become the nation's first Roman Catholic president, John F. Kennedy had his eye upon the White House from the moment he was first elected to Congress in 1946 from Massachusetts. Kennedy was the first Catholic candidate for the presidency since Democrat Al Smith challenged HERBERT HOOVER in 1928. Smith lost in a race that featured considerable prejudice and bigotry, problems which Kennedy knew he had to overcome if he hoped to secure the nomination and win the presidency.

Kennedy had made his first bid for national office in 1956 when he sought his party's nomination for the vice presidency. Even though Kennedy failed to capture the vice-presidential nomination that year, he emerged from the Democratic convention as a shining star, untarnished by the lackluster campaign of Democratic candidate Adlai Stevenson. In early 1957, Kennedy's national image was burnished by the Pulitzer Prize he won for his book *Profiles in Courage.* Consequently, the senator became a highly sought after speaker, receiving 2,500 speaking invitations in 1957 alone. With an expressed intent on becoming "a total politician" who dealt with the party bosses and the voters, Kennedy courted all the disparate Democratic interest groups in the years leading up to 1960. Realizing that the presidential nomination was potentially his, Kennedy maintained a relentless travel and speaking schedule. Between 1957 and 1960, Kennedy visited 47 states and spoke to tens of thousands of Democratic voters and activists.

Slowly formulating his own political creed, Kennedy calibrated a moderate liberalism that would appeal to liberals in the Northeast and the more conservative South. With an eye toward winning union support, he used his chairmanship of the Senate labor subcommittee to draft a bill favorable to organized labor in 1958. That legislation also marked the first time that the senator had made a steadfast effort to pass significant legislation. While he wooed labor on the one hand, Kennedy soothed southerners by soft-pedaling civil rights legislation. The senator's primary interest, however, continued to be foreign affairs and with his seat on the Senate's Foreign Relations Committee, Kennedy was free to develop a coherent anticommunist policy that differed significantly from his Republican counterparts. Kennedy was both an internationalist and a committed cold war warrior but he favored distinctly different tools—the development of counterinsurgency forces to respond quickly to crises and the creation of a PEACE CORPS—than those employed by the Eisenhower administration. Also, during the campaign Kennedy argued that the United States was suffering from a "missile gap" with the Soviet Union. However, once he became president he learned the country was much better off in this regard, and the missile issue quickly faded.

Even as Kennedy was crafting his political philosophy he was also carefully orchestrating a media campaign that sold the Kennedy image. Appearing in the pages of *Redbook*

Senator Kennedy greets supporters in Wisconsin during the presidential campaign, November 1959. *(Time & Life Pictures/Getty Images)*

and *Life* with his wife, Jacqueline, the smiling and attractive images of John and Jacqueline Kennedy were designed to appeal to an increasingly affluent, middle-class electorate. While this "soft" media offensive was undoubtedly effective to some degree, it did little to sway liberals who distrusted Kennedy, believing him to be shallow and untested. Leading the charge against the senator was the matriarch of the Democratic Party, former first lady Eleanor Roosevelt. Fearing that Kennedy was too young and immature for the White House, Roosevelt publicly attacked the senator in print and on television. Specifically, Roosevelt was angry about the senator's silence regarding Senator Joseph McCarthy (R-WI).

When the Senate voted to censure McCarthy in 1954, Kennedy had abstained—a controversial and self-serving decision that hounded him for years. In reaction to Eleanor Roosevelt's attacks, Kennedy wisely refused to spar with the former first lady and courted party liberals in other ways. Claiming that liberalism needed to be "rethought and renewed," Kennedy sought to update the Democratic Party's program to meet the exigencies of an affluent age. While the senator remained most interested in foreign policy and the cold war, he attracted several advisers who aided him in developing a domestic agenda to attract liberals. Primarily, it was the historian and political activist Arthur Schlesinger, Jr. who helped Kennedy define his "new liberalism" and refine his quest for the presidency.

After he won reelection to the Senate in 1958, Kennedy turned his attention to the presidency and announced his candidacy on January 2, 1960. Contrasting his youth and vigor and the promise of an activist White House against the supposed "somnolent" Eisenhower, Kennedy, who was a generation younger than Eisenhower, pledged to "get America moving again." Reflecting Schlesinger's Rooseveltian model of presidential leadership, Kennedy promised a new era of "progressivism and forward movement." While he was promising a new type of liberalism, Kennedy's campaign platform featured much of the standard liberalism of the New Deal, including minimum wage increases, increased funding for public housing, and assistance to the elderly.

Armed with a palatable rhetorical strategy and a clear vision of presidential leadership, Kennedy built an effective campaign staff. The senator's inner circle consisted of his brother Robert Kennedy, who managed the presidential campaign, and his brother-in-law Steve Smith. In addition to his family, Arthur Schlesinger, Jr., Theodore Sorensen, and the "Irish Mafia"—longtime aides Lawrence O'Brien, Kenneth O'Donnell, and David Francis Powers, who shared Kennedy's ethnic Irish background—rounded out his campaign staff.

After relinquishing his job as a Capitol Hill staffer in 1959 to write a book about his work in the Senate, Robert Kennedy managed his brother's campaign with bulldog intensity. At one of the campaign staff's first meetings, Robert dressed down his brother for the operation's lack of preparation, "Jack, how do you expect to run a successful campaign if you don't get started . . . [i]t's ridiculous that more work hasn't been done already." With his brother in charge, there was always one person who gave frank advice.

Kennedy's team focused on 16 state primaries. With most of his Democratic rivals—Texas senator LYNDON B. JOHNSON, former Democratic candidate Adlai Stevenson, and Missouri senator Stuart Symington—sitting out the primaries, Kennedy's main opponent was liberal Minnesota senator Hubert H. Humphrey. Humphrey, like Kennedy, hoped that a string of primary victories would give his candidacy enough momentum to win the nomination. In attempting to do so, Humphrey faced a huge challenge: for as well funded as the Kennedy campaign was, Humphrey faced serious financial shortfalls. This problem limited the number of primaries in which Humphrey could realistically compete. Kennedy, as a result, never believed that Humphrey would actually get the nomination. Rather, the senator feared that the Minnesotan's candidacy would throw the nomination to either Stevenson or Symington.

The other Democratic contenders believed they had good reasons for waiting until the convention to challenge for the presidential nomination. Stevenson viewed himself as the elder statesman of the party, having run twice against Eisenhower in the 1950s. As such, he believed the nomination should be given to him rather than he should have to seek the prize. Meanwhile, Johnson and Symington sat out the primaries in favor of a convention-based strategy. Both were hoping that neither Kennedy nor Humphrey would attract much attention and would be deadlocked when the Democrats met to nominate a president. Furthermore, Johnson relied on his leadership position in the Senate to translate into presidential votes while Symington believed former president HARRY S. TRUMAN's endorsement would carry him through. Indeed, Kennedy believed that it was Senator Symington of Missouri who posed the greatest threat to his nomination. As a former secretary of the air force, Symington's border state credentials, liberal voting record, and military experience rendered him acceptable to all sectors of the party.

Other than defeating Humphrey in the primaries so that he could go into the Democratic National Convention as the favored candidate, Kennedy's central task was to prove that he could win Protestant votes. Until Kennedy showed that he could appeal to non-Catholics, the "religious issue" would remain his most formidable roadblock to the nomination. As a New England native, Kennedy's landslide victory in the New Hampshire primary in March was expected and he ran unopposed in both Indiana and Nebraska. Kennedy secured deals with Ohio governor Mike DiSalle and California governor Pat Brown whereby the two governors would win their primaries on May 3 and June 7, respectively, but they would support Kennedy at the convention. Winning uncontested primaries did little to quiet fears that a Catholic could not win Protestant votes, though. Despite Kennedy's string of victories, his path to the nomination depended on winning Wisconsin because this was the first primary in which Kennedy and Humphrey faced each other directly.

The Badger State proved a formidable challenge for Kennedy. Indeed, Humphrey was called the "third senator from Wisconsin" due to his close relationship with the neighboring state's farmers and liberals. Despite Humphrey's advantage, Kennedy had the backing of Wisconsin governor Patrick Lucey, and Madison, Wisconsin, mayor Ivan Nestige. Realizing that Wisconsin was key, Humphrey and Kennedy campaigned frenetically in February, March, and April, stumping across the state for six weeks. Kennedy benefited from the large Catholic population in Wisconsin and from conservative Republicans who crossed party lines to vote for him. On April 5, Kennedy won handily with 56.5 percent of the vote, but he failed to capture a majority of Protestant votes, which made the Wisconsin primary a draw to many observers.

Consequently, the West Virginia primary in May became a crucial test for Kennedy's Protestant appeal. With a population that was 96 percent Protestant and overwhelmingly rural, the Kennedy team saw West Virginia as an opportunity to finally "bury the religious issue." In his first day of campaigning in West Virginia, Kennedy confronted the issue head-on. Responding to a question about his faith, Kennedy rhetorically asked the crowd "I'm able to serve in Congress and my brother [Joe] was able to give his life [in World War II], but we [Catholics] can't be president?" Thereafter, Kennedy continually reminded West Virginians of his family's military service, which insulated him from charges that a Catholic president owed fealty to the pope rather than to the Constitution.

In West Virginia, Humphrey backers made a blatant appeal to latent religious bigotry with his campaign song "I'm Gonna Vote for Hubert Humphrey," sung to the very familiar spiritual "Give Me That Old-Time Religion," but Kennedy's intense two-week campaign proved effective. Traveling to little-known mining towns and "hills-and-hollers" such as, Slab Fork, West Virginia, Kennedy revealed

his talent for retail politics, which helped him transcend the "religious issue." In addition to his travels, he gave a 30-minute television address on religion. The Kennedy family fortune also played a significant role in West Virginia because bribery was an ingrained part of the state's political culture. The Kennedy campaign paid thousands of dollars to cover "printing costs" but in actuality the funds went to county political bosses who delivered votes for the senator. Even though Humphrey's backers cried foul about this form of bribery, several investigations into the matter turned up no technical wrongdoing. Due to Kennedy's campaigning and the backing of county political bosses, Kennedy defeated Humphrey 60.8 percent to 39.2 percent on May 10. This triumph forced Humphrey out of the race on May 11, and Kennedy swept to victory in the final primaries in Maryland and Oregon later in the month.

With a string of seven primary victories in a row, Kennedy not only had dispatched Humphrey and proved he could win Protestant votes, but also his path to the nomination seemed secure. On the eve of the Democratic National Convention, Johnson and Speaker of the House Sam Rayburn, playing on their bipartisan friendship with Dwight Eisenhower, met with the president at the White House and begged him to "say something publicly" to help them stop Kennedy. Eisenhower recalled the two arguing that Kennedy was "a mediocrity in the Senate, as a nobody who had a rich father." The president further remembered them pleading "for the good of the country, you cannot let that man become elected President. Now, he might get the nomination out there, he probably will, but he's a dangerous man." Rather than blocking the senator's nomination, Johnson earned the lasting hatred of Robert Kennedy, who learned of the meeting and never forgave the Texan.

Once Democrats convened in Los Angeles to officially nominate a president, Robert Kennedy worked tirelessly to ensure his brother's victory. Though Kennedy had performed well in the primaries, most of the states did not yet use a presidential primary to indicate a presidential preference, instead relying on the state party machinery. Exuding the image of

Democratic National Convention, Los Angeles, California, July 1960 *(Library of Congress)*

a campaign that was sweeping to inevitable victory, Robert worked behind the scenes to keep the Kennedy delegates in line so they would claim the 761 delegate votes needed to win on the first ballot. Despite their tireless work, it was not until Wyoming cast its 15 votes that Kennedy secured the nomination with 765 votes. Following Wyoming, several states with favorite-son candidates switched to Kennedy to increase his totals. Kennedy thus claimed the nomination on the first ballot by a vote of 806 to 409 for Johnson, with Symington and Stevenson claiming 86 and 79½, respectively. A handful of favorite-son candidates took the remaining votes.

After securing the nomination, Kennedy was faced with the most significant decision of the entire campaign—the selection of a running mate. In addition to Johnson, Humphrey, Stevenson, and Symington, Washington senator Henry Jackson and Minnesota governor Orville Freeman were on the short-list of potential vice-presidential nominees. With Kennedy still angry with the liberal establishment for opposing his candidacy, there was little chance he would tap one of their own, such as Freeman or Stevenson. In addition, Symington and Jackson were considered too young to be paired with the youthful Kennedy, which left one logical choice—Lyndon Johnson.

Despite significant liberal opposition to Johnson and the personal animus between Robert Kennedy and the Senate majority leader, the political calculus was clear at least to Jack Kennedy. The candidate wanted Johnson because he respected the Texas senator's legislative talents and the strength he would bring to the ticket, especially in the South. Robert Kennedy, though, had promised party liberals that Johnson, often known by his initials LBJ, would not be on the ticket, so any move toward the Texan proved embarrassing to him. Robert's views proved irrelevant. In fact, Jack Kennedy had known for some time, at least a month before the convention, from key Johnson intimates that the Texan would accept the vice presidency if it were offered. When Kennedy was again assured during the convention that LBJ would take the nomination, he replied, "Of course I want Lyndon Johnson. . . . The only thing is I would never want to offer it and have him turn me down; I would be terrifically embarrassed. He's the natural. If I can ever get him on the ticket, no way we can lose." After Kennedy won the nomination, Johnson telegrammed his congratulations: "LBJ now means Let's Back Jack." With Johnson as a running mate, Kennedy could win Texas and compete in the South, which was essential for a Democratic victory.

Once Kennedy selected Johnson to be his running mate, he was free to begin his campaign for the presidency under the banner "the NEW FRONTIER." The New Frontier reflected the candidate's sense that the 1960s were the dawn of a new era, and it was designed to delight liberals who wanted a revival of the New Deal and Fair Deal traditions. Moreover,

Kennedy repaired his relationship with party liberals by publicly securing the support of Adlai Stevenson, Eleanor Roosevelt, and Harry Truman. Truman captured the sentiment of many establishment Democrats regarding Kennedy's candidacy, "I never liked Kennedy. I hate his father . . . [h]owever, that no good son-of-a-bitch Dick Nixon called me a communist and I'll do anything to beat him."

Vice President Richard Nixon enjoyed a much easier path to his party's nomination. He faced no significant challenger during the primaries, but wealthy New York governor Nelson Rockefeller, who had earlier toyed with entering the primaries, quietly encouraged a "draft" movement at the convention. To aid his cause, Rockefeller made several pointed, public criticisms of the Eisenhower-Nixon foreign policy on the eve of the convention. He claimed more than 1 million supporters. To avoid a brokered convention, Nixon arranged a meeting with Rockefeller, who was really more interested in shaping the Republican platform. The New York governor used the threat of a presidential bid from the convention floor to win a number of important platform concessions from Nixon: support for civil rights, health care, and education funding.

When the Republicans met in Chicago in late July, Nixon tapped UN ambassador Henry Cabot Lodge, a northeastern, liberal Republican with a long history of family involvement in politics to serve as his running mate. A former senator from Massachusetts—Kennedy had narrowly defeated him in 1952—Lodge was well known to Americans because UN sessions were televised in the 1950s, and he seemed to be a foreign policy expert to many, helping the Republican ticket in the process. Nixon stole his own show when he delivered his acceptance speech. Stressing a renewed commitment to the spread of freedom, Nixon issued a direct challenge to the Soviet Union: "When Mr. Khrushchev says our grandchildren will live under communism, let us say his grandchildren will live in freedom." Republicans left their convention with a slight lead over Kennedy and the Democrats.

Kennedy planned to win by targeting big states with large numbers of electoral votes plus relying on Johnson to bring the South solidly into the Democratic column. The Democrats also relied on their large corps of youthful volunteers to boost Democratic voter registration. Nixon meanwhile visited all 50 states, and he stressed his experience and the positive record of the Eisenhower years. Kennedy was not able to begin his campaign as aggressively because the Senate was in session, a move on Johnson's part to show off the Democratic agenda and help Democratic congressional candidates achieve victory. Both candidates relied heavily on television advertising, with the Republicans spending more money but devising less effective uses for it. For example, in the last week of the campaign, Nixon made nightly 15-minute appeals to voters. Also his campaign purchased a $400,000

1960 Election Statistics

State	Number of Electors	Total Popular Vote	Elec Vote			Pop Vote			Margin of Victory	
			D	R	I	D	R	I	Votes	% Total Vote
Alabama	11	564,473	5		6	1	2	-	80,322	14.23%
Alaska	3	60,762		3		2	1	-	1,144	1.88%
Arizona	4	398,491		4		2	1	-	44,460	11.16%
Arkansas	8	428,509	8			1	2	-	30,541	7.13%
California	32	6,506,578		32		2	1	-	35,623	0.55%
Colorado	6	736,246		6		2	1	-	71,613	9.73%
Connecticut	8	1,222,883	8			1	2	-	91,242	7.46%
Delaware	3	196,683	3			1	2	-	3,217	1.64%
Florida	10	1,544,176		10		2	1	-	46,776	3.03%
Georgia	12	733,349	12			1	2	-	184,166	25.11%
Hawaii	3	184,705	3			1	2	-	115	0.06%
Idaho	4	300,450		4		2	1	-	22,744	7.57%
Illinois	27	4,757,409	27			1	2	-	8,858	0.19%
Indiana	13	2,135,360		13		2	1	-	222,762	10.43%
Iowa	10	1,273,810		10		2	1	-	171,816	13.49%
Kansas	8	928,825		8		2	1	-	198,261	21.35%
Kentucky	10	1,124,462		10		2	1	-	80,752	7.18%
Louisiana	10	807,891	10			1	2	3	176,359	21.83%
Maine	5	421,773		5		2	1	-	59,449	14.10%
Maryland	9	1,055,349	9			1	2	-	76,270	7.23%
Massachusetts	16	2,469,480	16			1	2	-	510,424	20.67%
Michigan	20	3,318,097	20			1	2	7	66,841	2.01%
Minnesota	11	1,541,887	11			1	2	-	22,018	1.43%
Mississippi	8	298,171			8	2	3	1	7,886	2.64%
Missouri	13	1,934,422	13			1	2	-	9,980	0.52%
Montana	4	277,579		4		2	1	-	6,950	2.50%
Nebraska	6	613,095		6		2	1	-	148,011	24.14%
Nevada	3	107,267	3			1	2	-	2,493	2.32%
New Hampshire	4	295,761		4		2	1	-	20,217	6.84%
New Jersey	16	2,773,111	16			1	2	-	22,091	0.80%
New Mexico	4	311,107	4			1	2	-	2,294	0.74%
New York	45	7,291,079	45			1	2	-	383,666	5.26%
North Carolina	14	1,368,556	14			1	2	-	57,716	4.22%
North Dakota	4	278,431		4		2	1	-	30,347	10.90%
Ohio	25	4,161,859		25		2	1	-	273,363	6.57%
Oklahoma	8	903,150		7	1	2	1	-	162,928	18.04%
Oregon	6	776,421		6		2	1	-	40,658	5.24%
Pennsylvania	32	5,006,541	32			1	2	-	116,326	2.32%
Rhode Island	4	405,535	4			1	2	-	110,530	27.26%
South Carolina	8	386,688	8			1	2	-	9,571	2.48%
South Dakota	4	306,487		4		2	1	-	50,347	16.43%
Tennessee	11	1,051,792		11		2	1	-	75,124	7.14%
Texas	24	2,311,084	24			1	2	-	46,257	2.00%
Utah	4	374,709		4		2	1	-	36,113	9.64%
Vermont	3	167,324		3		2	1	-	28,945	17.30%
Virginia	12	771,449		12		2	1	-	42,194	5.47%
Washington	9	1,241,572		9		2	1	-	29,975	2.41%
West Virginia	8	837,781	8			1	2	-	45,791	5.47%
Wisconsin	12	1,729,082		12		2	1	-	64,370	3.72%
Wyoming	3	140,782		3		2	1	-	14,120	10.03%
Total	537	68,832,483	303	219	15	1	2	-	112,827	0.16%

* Note: Unpledged electors won in Mississippi with 116,248 votes. These eight electors along with six unpledged electors in Alabama and one rogue Nixon elector in Oklahoma voted for Harry Byrd.

Kennedy Democratic		Nixon Republican		Others	
318,303	56.39%	237,981	42.16%	8,189	1.45%
29,809	49.06%	30,953	50.94%	0	0.00%
176,781	44.36%	221,241	55.52%	469	0.12%
215,049	50.19%	184,508	43.06%	28,952	6.76%
3,224,099	49.55%	3,259,722	50.10%	22,757	0.35%
330,629	44.91%	402,242	54.63%	3,375	0.46%
657,055	53.73%	565,813	46.27%	15	0.00%
99,590	50.63%	96,373	49.00%	720	0.37%
748,700	48.49%	795,476	51.51%	0	0.00%
458,638	62.54%	274,472	37.43%	239	0.03%
92,410	50.03%	92,295	49.97%	0	0.00%
138,853	46.22%	161,597	53.78%	0	0.00%
2,377,846	49.98%	2,368,988	49.80%	10,575	0.22%
952,358	44.60%	1,175,120	55.03%	7,882	0.37%
550,565	43.22%	722,381	56.71%	864	0.07%
363,213	39.10%	561,474	60.45%	4,138	0.45%
521,855	46.41%	602,607	53.59%	0	0.00%
407,339	50.42%	230,980	28.59%	169,572	20.99%
181,159	42.95%	240,608	57.05%	6	0.00%
565,808	53.61%	489,538	46.39%	3	0.00%
1,487,174	60.22%	976,750	39.55%	5,556	0.22%
1,687,269	50.85%	1,620,428	48.84%	10,400	0.31%
779,933	50.58%	757,915	49.16%	4,039	0.26%
108,362	36.34%	73,561	24.67%	116,248	38.99%
972,201	50.26%	962,221	49.74%	0	0.00%
134,891	48.60%	141,841	51.10%	847	0.31%
232,542	37.93%	380,553	62.07%	0	0.00%
54,880	51.16%	52,387	48.84%	0	0.00%
137,772	46.58%	157,989	53.42%	0	0.00%
1,385,415	49.96%	1,363,324	49.16%	24,372	0.88%
156,027	50.15%	153,733	49.41%	1,347	0.43%
3,830,085	52.53%	3,446,419	47.27%	14,575	0.20%
713,136	52.11%	655,420	47.89%	0	0.00%
123,963	44.52%	154,310	55.42%	158	0.06%
1,944,248	46.72%	2,217,611	53.28%	0	0.00%
370,111	40.98%	533,039	59.02%	0	0.00%
367,402	47.32%	408,060	52.56%	959	0.12%
2,556,282	51.06%	2,439,956	48.74%	10,303	0.21%
258,032	63.63%	147,502	36.37%	1	0.00%
198,129	51.24%	188,558	48.76%	1	0.00%
128,070	41.79%	178,417	58.21%	0	0.00%
481,453	45.77%	556,577	52.92%	13,762	1.31%
1,167,567	50.52%	1,121,310	48.52%	22,207	0.96%
169,248	45.17%	205,361	54.81%	100	0.03%
69,186	41.35%	98,131	58.65%	7	0.00%
362,327	46.97%	404,521	52.44%	4,601	0.60%
599,298	48.27%	629,273	50.68%	13,001	1.05%
441,786	52.73%	395,995	47.27%	0	0.00%
830,805	48.05%	895,175	51.77%	3,102	0.18%
63,331	44.99%	77,451	55.01%	0	0.00%
34,220,984	49.72%	34,108,157	49.55%	503,342	0.73%

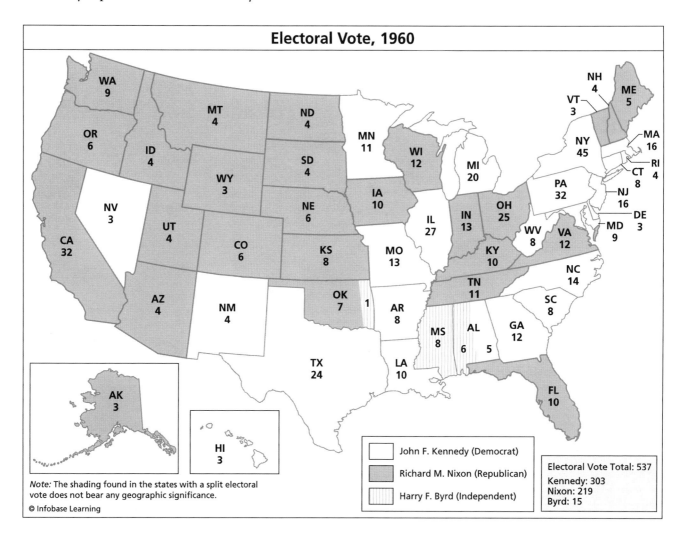

Electoral Vote, 1960

Note: The shading found in the states with a split electoral vote does not bear any geographic significance.
© Infobase Learning

John F. Kennedy (Democrat)
Richard M. Nixon (Republican)
Harry F. Byrd (Independent)

Electoral Vote Total: 537
Kennedy: 303
Nixon: 219
Byrd: 15

four-hour afternoon telethon on the day before the election, which was combined with an hour-long appeal in primetime and with late-night programming featuring celebrity pitches for the Republican Party.

When the general election campaign began in earnest after Labor Day, polls indicated a dead heat between the two candidates, prompting Kennedy to once again confront the religious issue. In a televised speech to several hundred conservative Protestant ministers in Houston, Texas, Kennedy declared: "I believe in an America that is officially neither Catholic, Protestant nor Jewish—where no public official either requests or accepts instructions on public policy from the Pope, the National Council of Churches or any other ecclesiastical source—where no religious body seeks to impose its will directly or indirectly upon the general populace or the public acts of its officials—and where religious liberty is so indivisible that an act against one church is treated as an act against all." He handled himself with such aplomb that Speaker Sam Rayburn exclaimed afterwards, "He's eating them blood raw. This young feller will be a great President!"

After temporarily dispensing with the religious issue, Kennedy was free to attack the Eisenhower administration for the sluggish rate of economic growth and its failures to keep pace with Soviet advances in technology and education. Indeed, one of Kennedy's most effective broadsides against the Eisenhower administration was that it had allowed a "missile gap" between the Soviet and American arsenals to emerge, which placed the United States in a poor strategic position.

While the rhetoric might suggest otherwise, Nixon and Kennedy differed very little on the issues. Locked in a dead heat and lacking substantial policy or ideological differences, the election was decided by the candidate's contrasting images, which were cast in the nation's first-ever presidential debates and broadcast on television to a national audience. The first of the four debates proved decisive as Kennedy looked to be more than Nixon's equal. Before an audience of more than 70 million, Kennedy appeared calm and cool while the vice president, who had refused makeup, sweated profusely and looked frightened as he glowered at the camera. Nixon had been ill before the

AND AWAY THEY GO!

This Gib Crockett cartoon shows Republican Richard Nixon and Democrat John F. Kennedy cruising to victory in their respective parties' primary election in New Hampshire on March 8, 1960. *(Library of Congress)*

debate, but still the radio audiences gave the Republican the edge, believing his responses to have been more substantive on the issues. Kennedy's success on screen, however, signaled the growing importance that television would come to play in American politics.

To prove his important role as vice president, a necessary move to sustain his argument of superior experience, Nixon contended he had been responsible for much of substance that came from the Eisenhower White House. Reporters then went to the president, asking for examples of what the vice president had done. Eisenhower, who had never particularly liked or promoted his vice president, quipped to a reporter that "if you give me a week, I might think of one" key contribution Nixon provided to his administration.

Race also factored into the outcome in 1960 in several important ways. Lodge had indicated that if Nixon were elected he would name an African American to the cabinet. While this promise helped the Republican Party with urban black voters it harmed the party with southern whites, and Nixon retracted the promise. More important was the way Nixon and Kennedy responded to the arrest of civil rights leader Martin Luther King, Jr. that fall. When stopped for a minor traffic violation, King was sentenced to four months in jail in part because he was already on probation for his civil disobedience in various civil rights protests. While Nixon

sympathized with King, he did nothing. The Kennedys on the other hand were proactive. Robert Kennedy negotiated for a suspended sentence, gaining favorable reviews from African-American voters. King's father, an important Atlanta preacher, black leader, and lifelong Republican, announced publicly, "I've got a suitcase full of votes, and I'm going to take them to Mr. Kennedy."

These campaign incidents combined with Kennedy's youthful appeal and promise to "get the country moving again," spelled the difference in an election that proved one of the closest in American history. Out of more than 68 million popular votes cast, Kennedy prevailed over Nixon by a mere 112,827 votes, or 49.72 percent to Nixon's 49.55 percent. Undoubtedly, the religious issue cost Kennedy Protestant votes in the South and Midwest but it aided him in the Electoral College as Catholics swung key industrial states in the North and Midwest into Kennedy's column. There were also incidents of voting irregularities, or fraud, in the race. Charges were raised that in Chicago, Cook County, Illinois, votes were registered from cemeteries while Texas Democrats had allegedly discarded votes for Nixon. These rumors lacked an evidentiary foundation, but Republicans still urged a recount. Nixon declined, telling the media, "The country can't afford the agony of a constitutional crisis, and I will not be party to creating one, just to become president." While Kennedy's Electoral College margin, 303 to 219, was substantial, his razor-thin margin in the popular vote and allegations of voter fraud in Chicago robbed him of any claim to a "mandate."

KENNEDY ADMINISTRATION (1961–1963)

As the president-elect, Kennedy began assembling an ideologically diverse, young, and experienced staff. Working with his brother Robert and brother-in-law Sargent Shriver, Kennedy appointed Republicans Robert McNamara and Douglas Dillon to serve as his secretaries of defense and treasury, respectively, and liberals Stewart Udall and Orville Freeman to serve as the secretaries of interior and agriculture. The most controversial of all of his cabinet appointments was his nomination of his brother Robert Kennedy to be the nation's attorney general. Kennedy's advisers were termed "the best and the brightest." Most of them had enjoyed elite educations. Lost in the shuffle of Kennedy's inner circle was the vice president—LYNDON JOHNSON. Despite Kennedy's best efforts to treat Johnson with dignity and respect, the vice president was on the outside looking in and he brooded throughout his tenure in that office.

On the cold, sunny, and snow-covered day of January 20, 1961, John F. Kennedy took the oath of office as the 35th president of the United States and delivered a memorable inaugural address. Evoking the sense of mission that millions of Americans had come to associate with activist Democratic presidents, the youthful president declared that "the torch has been passed to a new generation," and he imbued his audience with a new sense of service when he declared: "my fellow Americans: ask not what your country can do for you, ask what you can do for your country." Kennedy focused exclusively upon foreign affairs and pledged "let every nation know, whether it wishes us well or ill, that we shall pay any price, bear any burden, meet any hardship, support any friend, oppose any foe to assure the survival and the success of liberty."

Kennedy wanted an activist White House. To achieve that end, he worked carefully with his staff to be sure that he was always in the middle of key legislative and political fights.

Kennedy had five legislative goals that he hoped to achieve during his administration: federal aid for education, medical care for the elderly, improved mass transit, establishment of a Department of Urban Affairs, and economic assistance for the impoverished Appalachian region of the country. Kennedy's goal to be a strong legislative president ran into serious opposition from the "conservative coalition" of Republicans and mostly southern Democrats. In the Senate there were 64 Democrats and 36 Republicans. Nineteen of the Democrats were from the South and routinely cooperated with the Republican Party. In the House there were 263 Democrats and 174 Republicans. Just over 100 of the Democrats in the House, though, were from the South and given to participate in the conservative coalition. These numbers complicated the political environment for the Kennedy agenda. Early in

President Kennedy delivers his inaugural address, January 20, 1961. Among those seated in the front row are first lady Jacqueline Kennedy, former president Dwight D. Eisenhower, Vice President Lyndon B. Johnson, and former vice president Richard Nixon. *(U.S. Army Signal Corps photograph in the John F. Kennedy Presidential Library and Museum, Boston)*

THE KENNEDYS AND THE BABY BOOM

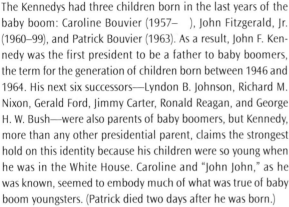

The Kennedys had three children born in the last years of the baby boom: Caroline Bouvier (1957–), John Fitzgerald, Jr. (1960–99), and Patrick Bouvier (1963). As a result, John F. Kennedy was the first president to be a father to baby boomers, the term for the generation of children born between 1946 and 1964. His next six successors—Lyndon B. Johnson, Richard M. Nixon, Gerald Ford, Jimmy Carter, Ronald Reagan, and George H. W. Bush—were also parents of baby boomers, but Kennedy, more than any other presidential parent, claims the strongest hold on this identity because his children were so young when he was in the White House. Caroline and "John John," as he was known, seemed to embody much of what was true of baby boom youngsters. (Patrick died two days after he was born.)

Depression and war in the 1930s and 1940s had a significant impact on marriage and birth patterns in the United States. First the straightened economic times of the Great Depression era meant that fewer babies were born because families could not afford the additional children. The war produced similar results for different reasons: The service of the so-called Greatest Generation, the term used to describe the men and women who came of age in the depression and war years, in the military further delayed family formation. The war did not delay marriage, though. Between the years 1939 and 1942, U.S. marriage rates rose by 25 percent. Proportionately, more people married during the war than ever before. There was also a baby boomlet during the early years of the war, prefiguring what would occur once hostilities ended. More important, but too often ignored in histories of the baby boom, was the 20 percent increase in the birthrate between 1939 and 1943. These marriages and births can be explained relatively easily in conjunction with the history of the war. Many of the marriages resulted very quickly between couples who were about to be separated by the war, and many of the babies born during these years can be attributed to the passion and emotion of military induced farewells. The wartime boomlet tended to follow approximately nine months after several key dates: the creation of a peacetime draft in 1940, the extension of that draft in the summer of 1941, and the bombing of Pearl Harbor in December 1941, which brought the United States into the war. Taken together these trends anticipated the demographic explosion of the postwar era, but wartime demographers missed all these signs, predicting that the postwar years would see a shrinking of the population.

The end of the war coincided with a strong economy in the United States. These two factors, along with government policies, specifically the GI Bill of Rights for World War II veterans, made it very easy for members of the Greatest Generation to start or expand their families because veterans received loans to buy homes, start businesses, and attend college and professional school. The baby boom, during which approximately 80 million Americans were born, was on. The postwar birthrate soared dramatically and consistently until it peaked in 1957—the year Kennedy's first child was born—with an average birthrate of 3.8 children per woman. This statistic was almost unprecedented in an industrialized economy. By 1964, the latest year associated with the baby boom, the average birthrate had fallen to 3.2 children per woman, and in the second half of the decade the birthrate fell to 2.6. By the early 1970s, the birthrate had dropped to 2.0, a rate lower than during the Great Depression.

As children, the baby boomers lived more luxurious lives than their parents. They came of age with television, and their teenage years were marked by the advent of rock and roll. As college students in the 1960s and 1970s, the baby boomers became renowned for their leadership roles in a host of political and protest movements, including civil rights, antiwar, feminism, environmentalism, and gay rights. John F. Kennedy's presidency helped motivate much of this activism for at least the first wave of the baby boom, those born in the late 1940s and the early 1950s. The tone that Kennedy struck in his inaugural address with his assertion, "Ask not what your country can do for you—ask what you can do for your country," inspired altruism among many baby boomers. Kennedy was their president. They identified with his youthful vigor, and when he was murdered in 1963, so too was much of their idealism about politics and government service.

his presidency, Kennedy once complained "[I] couldn't get a Mother's Day Resolution through the goddamn Congress."

Kennedy's domestic record is a matter for debate among scholars. From 1961 to 1963, Congress passed 108 of his legislative initiatives, albeit often in weakened form. Constrained by Congress, Kennedy reached out directly to the public. At the urging of his press secretary, Pierre Salinger, Kennedy became the first president to hold live press conferences on television. With an engaging wit and ready reply, the president's press conferences were an immediate sensation. Kennedy proved much more effective rallying public support for his agenda than he did securing congressional backing.

The president had identified housing legislation, a minimum wage increase, federal aid to public schools, medical insurance for the elderly, and aid to economically depressed areas as his primary domestic priorities. Many of these key initiatives, however, were stymied or substantially gutted by the time of their passage. With his domestic agenda neutered, Kennedy turned to foreign policy.

Kennedy convinced Congress to raise defense spending by 15 percent, increase the number of special forces and combat-ready units, and expand the nation's nuclear capability. With an eye on the nonaligned world, the president focused his energies on Cuba with disastrous results. When Kennedy entered office, CIA director Allen Dulles convinced the president to approve an American-backed invasion of the island at the BAY OF PIGS intended to remove the communist dictator Fidel Castro from power. Termed "the perfect failure" by scholars, the Bay of Pigs invasion in 1961 was a disaster from the start. Poorly planned and executed, the invasion never had a chance to succeed. After issuing a press release in which the president accepted full responsibility for the incident, Kennedy learned key lessons from the fiasco.

Compounding the Bay of Pigs disaster was the BERLIN CRISIS, which featured heightening tensions with the Soviets over the status of that city. Located 100 miles within Soviet-backed East Germany, the city of Berlin had been divided

between the Western powers and the Soviet Union in the aftermath of World War II. West Berlin remained part of U.S.-backed West Germany and a thorn in the side of the Soviets. These tensions came to the surface during the June 1961 VIENNA SUMMIT between Kennedy and Soviet premier Nikita Khrushchev. At the summit, Khrushchev threatened to sign a treaty with East Germany that would sever Western access and rights to Berlin. Khrushchev conducted most of his foreign policy in this bullying manner. For example, he had previously taken his shoe off while attending a session of the United Nations and preceded to bang it on the desk in the General Assembly.

Kennedy's dealings with Khrushchev left him worried that the Soviet premier had few qualms about starting a war over the status of Berlin. In 1961, the Soviets constructed a 13-foot-high wall 96 miles long that physically divided the city. Kennedy saw construction of the Berlin wall as a godsend because it constituted a peaceful resolution to a thorny issue. Nonetheless, the president believed that the Soviets threatened to surround America and its allies with hostile

President Kennedy addresses a crowd of more than 300,000 people in West Berlin on June 26, 1963. *(Associated Press)*

states, and he felt it absolutely necessary to resist this expansionism. During a visit to West Berlin on June 26, 1963, Kennedy drew loud cheers when he declared, "Ich bin ein Berliner," or "I am a Berliner" in English.

One of Kennedy's most consistent criticisms of the DWIGHT EISENHOWER administration had been its overreliance on developing nuclear weapons. To deter communist expansion, Kennedy advocated a number of innovative programs that were part foreign aid and part public diplomacy. Three programs—Food-for-Peace, which was a renamed program more than 50 years old that had been created to increase agricultural exports for the purpose of peace; the ALLIANCE FOR PROGRESS, a program to increase economic and social standing in Latin American countries; and the PEACE CORPS, created in 1961 to send young American volunteers to impoverished countries to help improve social and economic conditions in the developing countries—underlined the new multipronged strategy the administration employed to combat communist expansion in the Third World. Of these programs, the Peace Corps is recognized as one of the most enduring legacies of Kennedy's presidency.

While foreign policy dominated much of his agenda, the president realized that his reelection hinged upon his administration's ability to jump-start the nation's economy and avoid a forecasted recession for 1964. With the stock market tumbling earlier in summer 1962 and unemployment spiking to nearly 6 percent that August, Kennedy proposed a 40 percent reduction in corporate tax rates and an overhaul of the tax code. Even though opinion polls showed that 72 percent of Americans opposed his TAX CUT PROPOSALS if they increased the nation's debt load, the president pressed for quick and urgent action. Despite a vigorous offensive, Kennedy's tax cuts, like much of his legislative agenda, were passed posthumously.

Even as Kennedy calmed a domestic political storm, the most profound foreign policy crisis of his administration, the CUBAN MISSILE CRISIS, emerged. In October 1962, U-2 surveillance flights discovered evidence of Soviet medium-range ballistic missiles in Cuba, and Kennedy was given a briefing about these findings on the morning of October 15, 1962. As a result, he called a meeting of national security officials termed the Executive Committee of the National Security Council—or Ex Comm for short—to discern the best method of securing the removal of the missiles.

Sparked by Soviet and Cuban fears of an imminent American invasion if the Soviets refused to remove the missiles, the nuclear face-off brought the world to the brink of annihilation, but the heightened tensions led the president and Khrushchev to rethink their bellicosity. While the crisis marked a high-water mark of Kennedy's presidency, the administration bears much of the blame for sparking it in the first place. A mere seven months after the Bay of Pigs fiasco,

Kennedy approved the CIA-sponsored Operation Mongoose, which was a "secret war" designed to undermine the Cuban regime and assassinate Castro. Indeed, both the president and the attorney general became obsessed with Castro. Republicans, who promised to make Cuba "the dominant issue" in the 1962 midterm elections, further fueled their preoccupation.

In reaction to American provocations in Cuba, Khrushchev sought to protect a key ally and compensate for the Soviets' profound missile gap by deploying 24 medium-range R-12 missiles and 16 intermediate R-14 missiles. Unlike the Soviet missiles deployed in Europe, the weapons in Cuba threatened the continental United States. Conscious of his weakened domestic political situation in the Soviet Union and anxious to buttress his revolutionary credentials, Khrushchev believed that he could sneak the missiles into Cuba without American detection and use them as bargaining chips in negotiations.

The 13 days during which the Cuban missile crisis transpired were agonizingly difficult, causing even Kennedy to become angry. These tensions were hidden as best as possible from the press. The options before the president included a preemptive military strike, negotiation, and a naval blockade of Cuba combined with a demand for the removal of all Soviet missiles from the island. Kennedy opted for the latter, announcing his plan to Congress and the American people on October 22. Several days later, Khrushchev countered with a proposal for the United States to remove its Jupiter missiles from Turkey and a promise to not invade Cuba. Khrushchev also sent a contradictory and much more angry message. The White House elected to ignore the latter and make a deal based on the former.

On the domestic front, Kennedy's CIVIL RIGHTS POLICIES bear close consideration. Indeed, the Civil Rights movement had become increasingly important in 1961 and 1962. The president, however, remained ambiguous on civil rights as he struggled to balance his party's sectional divide between segregationists in the South and integrationists in the North. While Kennedy undoubtedly opposed segregation, the political calculus of reelection—he counted on winning the South in 1964—and his detached demeanor prevented him from fully backing civil rights until events forced him to do so.

The Civil Rights movement was the dominant domestic issue of his administration. In spite of Kennedy's reluctance, Martin Luther King, Jr., prodded by African-American student leaders, forced the president to act on their movement's behalf. Indeed, the Civil Rights movement approached its apex during the Kennedy years and commanded mainstream support and approval. Upon taking office, the president did make a number of significant and symbolic gestures such as integrating the U.S. Coast Guard, creating the President's Committee on Equal Employment Opportunity, appointing 40 African Americans to key administrative posts, and inviting more blacks to the White House than any previous president.

In spite of these advances, more militant civil rights organizations than the National Association for the Advancement of Colored People (NAACP), such as the Congress of Racial Equality (CORE), the Student Non-Violent Coordinating Committee (SNCC), and King's Southern Christian Leadership Conference (SCLC), were creating a broad-based mass movement calling for immediate federal action in ending segregation. Led by young

ADMINISTRATION TIME LINE

1961

January 20 John F. Kennedy is sworn in as president.

March 1 By executive order Kennedy creates the Peace Corps to develop a different type of post-colonial relationship with the developing world, sending recent college graduates to live and work in the developing world.

March 13 Kennedy advocates the Alliance for Progress in Latin America.

April 17 The Bay of Pigs, a CIA-sponsored invasion of Cuban exiles to overthrow the Fidel Castro regime, fails miserably.

May 4 The Freedom Rides, an effort to force integration of the interstate bus system in the South, begins.

May 5 Alan Shepard of NASA's Mercury project becomes the first American launched beyond the earth's atmosphere into outer space.

Kennedy signs legislation increasing the minimum wage from $1.00 to $1.25 per hour but excluding many laborers.

May 25 Kennedy delivers a speech to Congress pledging to land a man on the moon within the decade.

June Kennedy signs the Housing Act, a measure that required a 3 percent down payment in return for a low-interest 35-year mortgage.

June 4–5 President Kennedy and Soviet premier Nikita Khrushchev meet at a summit conference in Vienna, Austria, to talk about cold war issues but fail to come to any meaningful conclusion.

June 19 The Supreme Court in *Mapp v. Ohio* decides that the exclusionary rule did apply to state criminal courts and that evidence seized without a search warrant or probable cause for the warrant was inadmissible.

August 13 East Germany and the Soviet Union begin construction of the Berlin wall to stem the tide of defectors to the West.

September 26 Kennedy signs the Arms Control and Disarmament Act, establishing the Arms Control and Disarmament Agency.

December 14 Kennedy appoints the President's Commission on the Status of Women to examine the problem of discrimination based on gender and make recommendations.

1962

March 15 Kennedy signs the Manpower Development and Training Act, which was designed to retrain workers whose skills had been rendered obsolete by automation.

March 26 The Supreme Court rules in *Baker v. Carr* that Tennessee's apportionment of state legislative seats was "arbitrary and capricious."

April 11 To forestall inflation, Kennedy forces the chairman of US Steel not to raise steel prices higher than the administration wished. He had already secured a union agreement to a smaller than desired wage increase.

June 25 The U.S. Supreme Court reverses precedent in *Engel v. Vitale*, ruling against state-sponsored prayer in the public schools.

August 31 Kennedy signs the Communications Satellite Act, creating the Communications Satellite Corporation (COMSAT) and launching a number of satellites that ushered in a new era of international communication.

September 30 Riots break out on the campus of Ole Miss (the University of Mississippi) when Mississippi governor Ross Barnett encouraged large-scale resistance to the entry of African-American student James Meredith.

African-American student leaders such as John Lewis and Gloria Johnson-Powell, CORE and SNCC employed King's direct action tactics in forcing SCLC and the NAACP to pressure the administration to take action against segregation and discrimination. High on CORE's and SNCC's agenda was an immediate end to segregation in interstate buses and facilities. CORE sponsored the FREEDOM RIDES, in which college-aged blacks and whites rode together on buses across the South to force the integration of the interstate bus system.

October 10 Kennedy signs the Kefauver-Harris Drug Amendments, which derived from the Thalidomide drug scare and required drugs to be safe and effective and drug advertising in medical journals to list the risks as well as the benefits of a product.

October 11 Kennedy signs the Trade Expansion Act, allowing the president to slash tariffs by 50 percent, eradicate some tariffs altogether, and negotiate the elimination of "unreasonable" trade policies.

October 16–28 During the course of 13 days the United States and the Soviet Union take the world to the brink of nuclear annihilation when Soviet nuclear missiles were discovered in Cuba. The episode becomes known as the Cuban missile crisis.

October 22 Kennedy speaks to the American people about the missiles in Cuba.

1963

January 3 The Battle of Ap Bac exposes the fallacy that South Vietnamese forces were prepared to engage the Vietcong. This encouraged Washington to think that it would take a heavy American presence for South Vietnam to win.

February 18 In a 5-4 decision, the Supreme Court rules in *Kennedy v. Mendoza-Martinez* that Americans could not be stripped of their citizenship for draft evasion alone.

March 18 In *Gideon v. Wainwright,* the Supreme Court rules that the right to counsel was a fundamental right.

April 12 Martin Luther King, Jr. is arrested during protests in Birmingham.

June 10 Kennedy signs the Equal Pay Act, which declared that men and women must receive equal pay for equal work.

June 11 Kennedy speaks on television about the Civil Rights movement.

Thich Quang Duc, a 73-year-old Buddhist monk, sets himself on fire in Saigon to protest South Vietnamese president Ngo Dinh Diem's anti-Buddhist policies.

June 17 The Supreme Court rules in *Abington School District v. Schempp* that required religious exercises led by state-paid teachers were unconstitutional.

June 26 Kennedy visits Berlin and declares, "Ich bin ein Berliner"—"I am a Berliner" in English.

August 28 Martin Luther King, Jr. gives his "I Have a Dream" speech at the March on Washington for Jobs and Freedom.

September 15 Segregationists bomb the Sixteenth Street Baptist Church in Birmingham, Alabama, killing four young African-American girls.

September 24 Kennedy signs the Health Professions Educational Assistance Act, which channeled federal money into the construction of educational facilities for the medical profession and provided direct aid to needy students.

October 7 Kennedy signs the Limited Test Ban Treaty prohibiting the testing of nuclear weapons in the atmosphere.

October 31 Kennedy signs the Community Mental Health Centers Act providing for the deinstitutionalization of the mentally ill and for "troubled" patients to receive treatment at "community-based" facilities.

November 2 South Vietnamese president Ngo Dinh Diem is overthrown in a military coup with tacit Kennedy administration approval. Not part of the administration's plan was the assassination of Diem and his brother in the military takeover.

November 22 President Kennedy is assassinated in Dallas, Texas.

When civil rights leaders turned away from the direct action of the Freedom Riders in favor of promoting voter registration in the South, the administration reacted with glee. Believing that the ballot box was the route toward changing segregationist attitudes in the South, the administration unveiled legislation in 1962 to eliminate the poll tax and the literacy test and facilitate black voter registration.

The Kennedy administration wanted the Civil Rights movement removed from the front pages of America's newspapers, but the UNIVERSITY OF MISSISSIPPI INTEGRATION CRISIS in the fall of 1962 ensured that the demand for racial equality would intensify. James Meredith, the grandson of a slave, tried to enroll at the University of Mississippi, but he was rejected because of his race. With the help of the NAACP, he took his case to the federal court system, which ordered his admission. After a long standoff and a presidential decision to send federal troops, Meredith was admitted.

The integration of the University of Mississippi marked a watershed in Kennedy's approach to civil rights. Forced to confront the ugly realities of white southern racism and segregation, Kennedy's civil rights stance changed markedly. Despite the success in Mississippi, King continued to press the issue and spawned a new phase in the civil rights struggle—the desegregation of entire communities. After failing to win a battle for desegregation in Albany, Georgia, King chose Birmingham, Alabama, as the location for the next phase of the movement. The choice of Birmingham was not by accident. Called the "Johannesburg" of the South—an allusion to the system of apartheid in South Africa—Birmingham had been long considered the most segregated city in the region and the most hostile to civil rights for its black citizens. In the first week of April 1963, King and his supporters implemented their Project-C campaign, which caused massive disruptions throughout downtown Birmingham, by marching and staging sit-ins throughout the downtown area.

When he was jailed for violating a court's injunction against demonstrating, King wrote his eloquent "Letter from a Birmingham Jail," which buttressed the movement's moral position for equality and justice while also gaining international media attention. Once King was released from prison he unleashed a new tactic in his direct action campaign—children. Mobilizing more than 1,000 black school children to march in a direct action campaign, King challenged Birmingham police chief Eugene "Bull" Connor to direct his aggressive and violent tactics, including the use of German shepherd police dogs and fire hoses, against school children. As the violence and protests in Birmingham escalated and received widespread publicity, Kennedy publicly backed the compromise settlement that effectively desegregated downtown Birmingham. In a televised May 12 address to the nation, the president praised the compromise agreement and "recognized the fundamental right of all citizens to be accorded equal treatment."

Even as King and the administration worked to permanently desegregate Birmingham, another controversy was brewing just down the road in Tuscaloosa, Alabama, that threatened to shatter the fragile compromise and spread racial strife across the South. Following James Meredith's lead, two black students planned to enroll for the summer term at the University of Alabama. In reaction, Governor George Wallace, who had famously promised in his gubernatorial inauguration address "segregation now, segregation tomorrow, segregation forever," planned to stand in the doorway of the registration building to symbolically block the black students' integration of the university.

After Wallace delivered his prepared remarks he refused to step aside until the Alabama National Guard was federalized and federal officials prepared to enforce the court order militarily. That night, June 11, Kennedy placed himself firmly behind the Civil Rights movement in an eloquent and nationally televised address that he delivered to the nation. More significantly, Kennedy was finally persuaded to draft comprehensive civil rights legislation to compel desegregation of all public accommodations. While Kennedy did not live to see the passage of his legislation, the 1964 Civil Rights Act is recognized as one of the most significant legislative commitments to racial equality in the 20th century.

The summer of 1963 proved to be a dramatic turning point in the Civil Rights movement. In the months following Kennedy's embrace of integration and black equality, civil rights leaders planned the MARCH ON WASHINGTON FOR JOBS AND FREEDOM, which was originally intended as a crusade against racial discrimination in employment. Kennedy and his advisers were originally skeptical about King's plans, but they changed their minds when they became convinced the march could be used to benefit the campaign for an omnibus civil rights bill. As a result, the administration began helping with plans for the march.

While President Kennedy was wary that the march would erupt into violence, the demonstration became an iconic event of the 1960s and of American history. However, it did little to help move the civil rights bill through Congress, where the legislation remained stalled. The August 28, 1963, demonstration brought 250,000 marchers to Washington, D.C. Staged against the backdrop of the Lincoln Memorial, the march featured civil rights luminaries such as SNCC's John Lewis and folk singer Bob Dylan, but it was King's "I Have a Dream Speech" that endures as the day's most remembered moment.

In Kennedy's term in office, he was confronted with a series of domestic and international controversies that

U.S. deputy attorney general Nicholas Katzenbach *(right)* confronts Alabama governor George Wallace, who is attempting to block integration at the University of Alabama, on June 11, 1963. *(Library of Congress)*

shaped and sharply limited the latitude with which he could act. No particular issue was guided by events more than his VIETNAM WAR policy. After dealing with the fallout from the Bay of Pigs, Khrushchev's bullying at the Vienna summit, and construction of the Berlin wall, Kennedy felt he had to "stand tough" in Vietnam. By the summer of 1963, however, it was clear to Kennedy that his administration's policy in Vietnam had failed.

Even though the Cuban missile crisis had convinced Kennedy to strike a more conciliatory tone with the Soviets, the president remained a cold war warrior committed to safeguarding South Vietnam. The Vietnam War was rooted in

the early cold war. The conflict in Southeast Asia had begun almost as soon as World War II ended with French attempts to regain its Indonesian colonies. Once the French pulled out of Indochina in 1954, the conflict became a civil war between the communist North and the anticommunist South. In addition, he understood the domestic political consequences of communist expansion. He was mindful of the political fallout that so damaged the HARRY TRUMAN administration when opponents claimed it had "lost" China. Fearing that the "loss" of South Vietnam would signal American weakness, Kennedy opted to support Ngo Dinh Diem's oppressive but anticommunist government in South Vietnam. Prior to late

Some 250,000 people gathered for the March on Washington for Jobs and Freedom on August 28, 1963, where Martin Luther King, Jr., delivered his "I Have a Dream" speech. *(Getty Images)*

1963, the United States helped support a 250,000-man South Vietnamese army and it committed American military advisers and equipment. During the Kennedy administration the number of U.S. military advisers in Vietnam grew from 700 in 1960 to 16,575 in December 1963.

By the summer of 1963 it was clear to American military advisers that Diem and his government were a lost cause and that the administration's policy in Vietnam had failed. In August, Kennedy and his staff began rethinking the administration's policy in considering options ranging from backing a COUP AGAINST NGO DINH DIEM to withdrawal of American troops. In November after the administration signaled that a coup would not lead to cessation of U.S. military aid, Diem was deposed and murdered. The coup sparked much debate within the administration over what to do next in Vietnam, but Kennedy was assassinated before he could make a final decision.

In autumn 1963, President Kennedy made a trip to Texas to raise money for the 1964 presidential election and to help build enthusiasm among Democrats there. On November 22, 1963, Kennedy's motorcade traveled through downtown Dallas. The president insisted on keeping the top off the car so that he could be seen easily by the crowds lining the streets. From the sixth floor window of the Texas School Book Depository, communist sympathizer and loner Lee Harvey Oswald fired three shots at the motorcade. One fatally wounded the president, who was pronounced dead at nearby Parkland Memorial Hospital at 1 p.m. Central Standard Time. Vice President LYNDON B. JOHNSON was sworn in as the nation's 36th president later that afternoon aboard Air Force One. Kennedy was the fourth president to be assassinated and the eighth to die in office.

Kennedy's presidential record is ambiguous, but his legacy is clear. Constrained by a recalcitrant Congress and lacking an electoral mandate, Kennedy's domestic agenda was doomed from the start. In fact, the president did well to pass the domestic legislation that he did. Like other presidents before and since, Kennedy was freer to act in foreign affairs and in that realm his record of accomplishments are less opaque. As a staunch cold war warrior, Kennedy came into office prepared to battle the Soviets, but he soon realized the dangers of escalation and the necessity for negotiation. While his administration is best remembered for the Cuban missile crisis, Kennedy's most enduring foreign policy legacy remains innovative public diplomacy programs such as the Peace Corps and Food for Peace.

Kennedy came to office seeking to revive the Rooseveltian model of the presidency. Exuding vigor and confidence, he articulated a liberal agenda but was much more moderate in terms of results. His ability to communicate effectively on television would serve as a model for President RONALD REAGAN in the 1980s and President BILL CLINTON in the 1990s. Whether it was seeking the "best and the brightest" to staff the cabinet or holding live press conferences, Kennedy's legacy and imprint upon the office has outstripped his administration's 1,000 days in power.

Holding the hands of her children, Caroline *(left)* and John *(right)*, Jacqueline Kennedy leaves the Capitol after the funeral service for her slain husband. Behind her are the former president's brother, Attorney General Robert F. Kennedy, sister Jean Kennedy Smith, and brother-in-law Peter Lawford *(far left)*. *(Abbie Roew/White House Photographs)*

CABINET, COURT, AND CONGRESS

Cabinet Members

Secretary of State
Dean Rusk, 1961–63

Secretary of Defense
Robert S. McNamara, 1961–63

Secretary of the Treasury
C. Douglas Dillon, 1961–63

Postmaster General
J. Edward Day, 1961–63
John A. Gronouski, 1963

Attorney General
Robert F. Kennedy, 1961–63

Secretary of the Interior
Stewart Udall, 1961–63

Secretary of Agriculture
Orville L. Freeman, 1961–63

Secretary of Commerce
Luther Hodges, 1961–63

Secretary of Labor
Arthur J. Goldberg, 1961–62
W. Willard Wirtz, 1962–63

Secretary of Health, Education and Welfare
Abraham Ribicoff, 1961–62
Anthony J. Celebrezze, 1962–63

Supreme Court Appointments

Name	Confirmation Vote	Dates of Service
Byron White	Voice Vote, Confirmed	1962–93
Arthur Goldberg	Voice Vote, Confirmed	1962–65

Legislative Leaders

Congress	Speaker of the House	State	Party
87th Congress (1961)	Sam Rayburn	Texas	Democrat
87th Congress (1961–63)	John W. McCormack	Massachusetts	Democrat
88th Congress (1963)	John W. McCormack	Massachusetts	Democrat

MAJOR EVENTS AND ISSUES

Abington School District v. Schempp (1963) On the heels of the Supreme Court's controversial 1962 ENGEL V. VITALE decision, which declared prayers written by government bodies unconstitutional, *Abington School District v. Schempp* tested the constitutionality of school prayer that was free of "official authorship." Stemming from a case set in Abington, Pennsylvania, and popularly referred to as the decision that "kicked God and prayer out of the schools," this 1963 Supreme Court ruling placed significant restrictions on prayer and Bible readings in public schools. In this series of Warren Court rulings on Bible-reading and prayer cases in the public schools, the Court did not strike down voluntary religious exercise. Rather, in Associate Justice Tom C. Clark's opinion, the Court ruled that required religious exercises led by state-paid teachers were unconstitutional.

The *Abington* case resulted from a 1949 law passed by the Pennsylvania state legislature that mandated daily Bible readings of at least 10 verses followed by the recitation of the Lord's Prayer. Teachers who refused to lead these exercises were threatened with termination. With the aid of the American Civil Liberties Union, Edward and Sidney Schempp, the parents of three children enrolled in the Abington Township's public schools, challenged the state law in claiming that it violated their religious freedom, which was protected under the First and Fourteenth Amendments.

In the interim between the suit and the Court's ruling, the state changed the statute by allowing students to be excused from the exercise, but this compromise proved to be of no avail. The Supreme Court ruled 8 to 1 that school-sponsored religious exercises were unconstitutional. In his concurring opinion, Clark claimed that the religious activities violated the establishment clause of the First Amendment because the readings constituted a "religious ceremony." Moreover, mak-

CABINET, COURT, AND CONGRESS

Congress	House Majority Leader	State	Party
87th Congress (1961)	John W. McCormack	Massachusetts	Democrat
87th Congress (1961–63)	Carl B. Albert	Oklahoma	Democrat
88th Congress (1963)	Carl B. Albert	Oklahoma	Democrat

Congress	House Minority Leader	State	Party
87th Congress (1961–63)	Charles A. Halleck	Indiana	Republican
88th Congress (1963)	Charles A. Halleck	Indiana	Republican

Congress	House Democratic Whip	State	Party
87th Congress (1961)	Carl B. Albert	Oklahoma	Democrat
87th Congress (1961–63)	Hale Boggs	Louisiana	Democrat
88th Congress (1963)	Hale Boggs	Louisiana	Democrat

Congress	House Republican Whip	State	Party
87th Congress (1961–1963)	Leslie C. Arends	Illinois	Republican
88th Congress (1963)	Leslie C. Arends	Illinois	Republican

Congress	Senate Majority Leader	State	Party
87th Congress (1961–63)	Mike Mansfield	Montana	Democrat
88th Congress (1963)	Mike Mansfield	Montana	Democrat

Congress	Senate Minority Leader	State	Party
87th Congress (1961–63)	Everett McKinley Dirksen	Illinois	Republican
88th Congress (1963)	Everett McKinley Dirksen	Illinois	Republican

ing the activity "voluntary" did not satisfy the Court since the very act of school-sponsored religious exercises violated the establishment clause.

Alliance for Progress As a presidential candidate in 1960, Kennedy criticized the DWIGHT D. EISENHOWER administration for its overreliance on nuclear deterrence in the struggle against communist expansion. As president, Kennedy formulated a number of innovative programs that were designed to deter the attraction of communism to those living in the developing world. Part foreign aid and part public diplomacy, three programs were emblematic of the administration's new strategy: Food for Peace, the Alliance for Progress, and the PEACE CORPS. It was the Alliance for Progress that was central to the administration's strategy in Latin America. When he announced the program, Kennedy promised he would spend $20 billion. Seeking to overhaul America's imperialist image, the Alliance for Progress was launched as a "Marshall Plan" for Latin America. Inspired by President FRANKLIN D. ROOSEVELT's Good Neighbor Policy, Kennedy's program promised economic aid and political democratization for the region.

With the Castro regime firmly entrenched in Cuba and committed to exporting revolution throughout the hemisphere, the administration was forced to try to change its public image in the region. The program featured three primary parts: democratization, land and tax reform, and economic assistance. Placing the administration firmly behind a trend that had toppled 10 dictatorships in the region from 1956 to 1960, Kennedy tried to offer Latin America an alternative to Castroism and socialism.

Social and economic reforms constituted the most successful portion of the program. In this regard, the administration funded the construction of hospitals, roads, and electric power plants, which offered tangible improvements in people's lives. The program, however, failed to deliver effective economic assistance partly because the aid came in the form of loans rather than grants as were offered under the Marshall Plan. Indeed, the Alliance for Progress never lived up to its initial promise. It was stymied by the administration's obsession with Castro and overreliance on military aid to halt communist insurgencies.

Ap Bac   *See* Battle of Ap Bac (1963)

Arms Control and Disarmament Act (1961)   While Kennedy came into office as a cold war warrior who was primarily interested in international affairs, his foreign policy differed significantly from that advocated by conservatives. Rejecting what he called the false choice between "holocaust and humiliation," Kennedy sought a balanced policy that gave foreign policymakers options that would avert war. As president, Kennedy was a pragmatist who emphasized that international issues were not "solved" so much as they were "managed."

As a consequence, his foreign policy is not easily categorized. While he agreed with many conservatives about the nature of the communist threat and the necessity of a strong defense posture in resisting expansion, he believed that military power would not determine the cold war. To him, the realities of nuclear war had rendered "massive retaliation" or "preemptive first strikes" obsolete. Indeed, the nuclear age made the cold war "unwinnable" in the traditional sense. To Kennedy, the cold war was a problem that had to be managed and thus made negotiation with the Soviets inevitable.

With a firm belief that the ambition of communist nations could and had to be controlled by negotiation rather than war, Kennedy focused on policies of disarmament and peace in addition to defense buildup. What began as a campaign pledge—a call for a central government agency working on issues of arms control and disarmament—became the Arms Control and Disarmament Act of 1961, which authorized establishment of the Arms Control and Disarmament Agency. The most notable achievement during the Kennedy administration was passage of the 1963 Limited Test Ban Treaty. The treaty signed on October 7, 1963, prohibited the testing of nuclear weapons in the atmosphere and was signed by the United States, Great Britain, and the Soviet Union. The agency was responsible for developing American arms control policy and its director became the primary adviser on arms control and disarmament policy to the president and secretary of state. Kennedy's choice as director of the agency, William Chapman Foster, remained in his post through Lyndon Johnson's term in office.

Assassination of President Kennedy (1963)   Seeking to mend political fences and raise money for his reelection bid in 1964, President John F. Kennedy planned a trip to Dallas in November 1963. Kennedy deemed the trip so significant that he convinced his wife, first lady Jacqueline Kennedy,

to accompany him—the first such time she had ventured on a purely political trip during his presidency. Even though Kennedy's advisers had been worried about violent protesters, the president was ambivalent about the danger. After showing Jackie a particularly ugly anti-Kennedy advertisement in the *Dallas Morning News* he cautioned her: "if somebody wants to shoot me from a window with a rifle, nobody can stop it, so why worry about it?"

In Dallas, the FBI had been so worried about extreme right-wing protesters that they ignored Lee Harvey Oswald. The 24-year-old Oswald was a communist sympathizer who had lived in Russia and who worked at the Texas School Book Depository, which overlooked the path of the Kennedy motorcade. As the motorcade passed by on the afternoon of November 22, President Kennedy and the first lady sat beside each other, behind Texas governor John Connally and his wife. Around 12:30, Oswald fired three shots from a sixth-floor window. The bullets hit the president in the back and fatally wounded him in the head. At 1 p.m. Central Standard Time, physicians at Dallas's Parkland Memorial Hospital announced Kennedy's death. Later that afternoon, Vice President Lyndon B. Johnson took the oath of office and became the nation's 36th president. Like the previous assassinations of presidents Abraham Lincoln in 1865, James Garfield in 1881, and William McKinley in 1901, Kennedy's murder shocked the country and the entire world. Two days later, as Oswald was being transferred to the county jail, nightclub owner Jack Ruby shot and murdered him.

The investigation into the Kennedy assassination has sparked as much (if not more) popular and scholarly attention than has Kennedy's presidency. President Johnson appointed Chief Justice Earl Warren to chair a commission to investigate the assassination. Filled with political heavyweights, including former CIA director Allen Dulles and House minority leader (and future president) Gerald Ford, the Warren Commission was designed to put conspiracy theories surrounding Kennedy's death to rest. The commission ruled that Oswald acted alone in assassinating the president and that Ruby, in killing Oswald, had acted to save the Kennedy family from further grief.

From the start, the 900-page *Warren Commission Report*, released in 1964, was subjected to exhaustive criticism. Critics pointed to Ruby's close ties to organized crime, Oswald's mysterious past, eyewitnesses who heard additional gun shots from behind a nearby "grassy knoll," and the implausibility of a single "magic bullet," which (according to the commission) inflicted several serious wounds on Kennedy and Governor Connally. The Warren Commission's refusal to investigate all leads whether legitimate or not has led to a proliferation of questions and the rise of conspiracy theories surrounding Kennedy's death. Indeed, the controversy surrounding the Kennedy assassination and the fact that it

Two days after he assassinated President Kennedy, Lee Harvey Oswald, handcuffed to detective James Leavelle, is shot by Jack Ruby, November 24, 1963. *(Library of Congress)*

predated a tumultuous era of social strife help explain why many Americans remember the Kennedy presidency with a romantic aura.

Baker v. Carr (1962)   In the years preceding this landmark case, the Supreme Court had consistently refused to interfere in how and when states redistricted state legislative seats. In 1946, for example, Justice Felix Frankfurter claimed that apportionment cases lacked "justiciability" because apportionment was essentially a "political question."

By the 1960s, however, the Supreme Court, and even Frankfurter himself, changed positions on the justiciability of apportionment cases. Decided in 1962, *Baker v. Carr* stemmed from a legal challenge to Tennessee's system of apportionment. At issue was the state legislature's failure to redraw its boundaries despite the state's changing demographics as more and more residents moved from rural to urban areas. The state legislature, dominated by conserva-

tives, had refused to reapportion its districts because Tennessee's urban and minority population had swelled, thus creating an imbalanced ratio with rural districts and so maintaining disproportionate representation in the legislature. Consequently, the electoral influence of rural, white voters remained what it had been in the early 20th century, while that of urban, minority voters was undermined. Charles W. Baker, a Republican resident of Shelby County, filed the lawsuit to increase the county's representation. Joe C. Carr, the Tennessee secretary of state, defended the current system. At issue was who held political power in the state: urban, largely minority voters or rural, largely white voters.

In its 6 to 2 decision, the Supreme Court, with Frankfurter joining the majority, ruled that Tennessee's apportionment was "arbitrary and capricious." Claiming that apportionment cases were justiciable when state apportionment schemes negatively affected the civil rights of its citizens, the Court opened the door for legal challenges to southern apportionment and voting patterns. While the Court did not offer a ready remedy, civil rights leaders were emboldened and successfully challenged apportionment patterns that discriminated against African American voters.

Battle of Ap Bac (1963)　In late 1962, the Kennedy administration was confronted with a spate of bad news in South Vietnam, which was fighting a civil war with North Vietnam. In reaction, the president asked Mike Mansfield (D-MT), the Senate majority leader and that body's resident expert on Asian affairs, to lead a bipartisan group of senators on a fact-finding mission to Southeast Asia. After reporting on the South Vietnamese government's continued failure to quell the National Liberation Front, North Vietnam's military force, also known as the Vietcong, Mansfield warned Kennedy against "Americanizing" the war by deploying U.S. soldiers.

On the heels of Mansfield's sobering report, the Battle of Ap Bac took place on January 3, 1963. In the months prior to this battle, U.S. military advisers had reported greater success in the field due to direct American support of the South Vietnamese army. Through the use of armored personnel carriers and helicopters, American military advisers believed that they were turning the tide in the war.

After radio intercepts revealed a Vietcong force was located in Ap Bac, in the heart of the Mekong Delta near Saigon, a South Vietnamese force was sent to capture it. American adviser John Paul Vann encouraged the South Vietnamese leader to attack the Vietcong forces. Instead, the South Vietnamese leader did nothing for a day, allowing the Vietcong to learn of the presence of South Vietnamese troops. When the South began a three-pronged attack and met resistance, some units allowed enemy forces to escape, and some units refused to engage in combat. In a battle in which the South had overwhelming superiority, it lost more than 60 men while the Vietcong lost just three. The Vietcong used new tactics that neutralized the technological advantages enjoyed by their adversaries. Moreover, South Vietnamese commanders refused to take significant losses in the field. This strategy allowed Vietcong units to inflict heavy damage upon their opponents and, in so doing, elude capture. South Vietnam's poor performance at the Battle of Ap Bac attracted media attention and revealed the country's inability to defeat the Vietcong. This encouraged Washington to think that it would take a heavy American presence for the South to win.

Bay of Pigs (1961)　When Kennedy assumed the presidency in 1961, he was immediately confronted with the decision to approve a CIA-sponsored covert invasion of Cuba to topple dictator Fidel Castro. Termed "Operation Bumpy Road," Central Intelligence Agency director Allen Dulles's plan called for several thousand Cuban exiles (the Cuban Brigade) to lead an invasion of the island, which would spark a popular revolt against the Castro regime. The combination of the administration's inexperience and advocacy of the plan by the Joint Chiefs of Staff and former president Dwight Eisenhower convinced Kennedy to approve the invasion.

Poorly planned and executed, the operation never had a chance to succeed. In the days and weeks leading up to the mid-April attack, word of it leaked out to the press. During an April 12, 1961, news conference, one reporter asked Kennedy to what extent would the United States participate in an "invasion of Cuba." The president replied: "Well, first I want to say that there will not be, under any conditions, be an intervention in Cuba by United States armed forces, and this government will do everything it possibly can, and I think it can meet its responsibilities, to make sure that there are no Americans involved in any actions inside Cuba."

When a squadron of B-26s attacked the island on April 15, Castro realized that an invasion was imminent and he mobilized his military to thwart the threat. The Cuban Brigade finally arrived off the Cuban coast at the Bay of Pigs on April 17, but it lacked the element of surprise. Within one day it was clear that the invasion had failed spectacularly. Of the 1,400 men in the Cuban Brigade as many as 1,200 were killed or taken captive.

Termed "the perfect failure" by scholars, the Bay of Pigs invasion was a diplomatic disaster for the infant administration. Kennedy, however, deftly acted to keep the episode from becoming a political nightmare. The president issued a press release in which he accepted full responsibility for the incident by declaring that "I'm the responsible officer of the Government." More important, Kennedy learned that advice from the Joint Chiefs of Staff had to be accepted cautiously. With cold war tensions mounting, Kennedy realized he would be tested again, and he was ready.

Berlin Crisis　Armed with lessons learned from the Bay of Pigs fiasco of April 1961, President Kennedy and the Soviets wrangled over the status of Berlin, the former German capital partitioned into four occupation zones: West Berlin, dominated by the United States, and East Berlin, dominated by the Soviet Union. Located 100 miles within East Germany, West Berlin remained part of U.S.-backed West Germany and it proved to be a thorn in the sides of the Soviets. The partition of the city marked one of the last unsolved dilemmas of World War II. Indeed, the Soviets had sponsored blockades of the city in 1948 and 1958. The economic revival of West Berlin and its transformation into a modern, vibrant city only highlighted the failure of the communist East German regime. In the late 1950s it is estimated that it was through West Berlin that thousands of Germans escaped to the West. Many of these individuals were highly educated; thus, the East was suffering a "brain drain." Numbers continued to grow, with more than 200,000 people migrating to West Berlin in the first seven months of 1961. Tensions over Berlin

President Kennedy *(right)* meets with Soviet premier Nikita Khrushchev in Vienna, June 3, 1961. *(Library of Congress)*

surfaced again during the Vienna summit meeting between President Kennedy and Soviet premier Nikita Khrushchev in June 1961.

Determined to change the status of Berlin, Khrushchev termed the current arrangement "intolerable" and he threatened to sign a treaty with East Germany that would sever Western access to Berlin. After the Soviet premier threatened war over Berlin, Kennedy coolly responded, "it will be a cold winter." Though the president tried to project an image of confidence, he was shaken by Khrushchev's belligerent threats.

Kennedy's dealings with Khrushchev left him worried that the Soviet premier had few qualms about starting a war over the status of Berlin. Indeed, when the Soviets oversaw the building of the Berlin wall in 1962, Kennedy viewed its construction as a godsend because it marked a peaceful resolution to a thorny issue. The president's interpretation of the event was borne out when Khrushchev called for a resumption of negotiations.

Birmingham Church Bombings (1963)   Following two of the Civil Rights movement's greatest successes to date—the desegregation of public facilities in Birmingham in the spring of 1963 and the March on Washington for Jobs and Freedom in the summer of 1963—racist opponents of civil rights struck back. On September 15, 1963, segregationists bombed the Sixteenth Street Baptist Church in Birmingham, Alabama, killing four young African-American girls: Denise McNair, aged 11; Addie Mae Collins, aged 14; Carole Robertson, aged 14; and Cynthia Wesley, aged 14. Once again, Birmingham, which had earned the nickname "Bombingham," was rocked by racial violence.

In the week immediately preceding the bombing, Alabama governor George Wallace had been stoking the fire of white racism. Wallace told the *New York Times* that the state

could use a "few first-class funerals" to stymie integration of its public schools. In the hours immediately following the bombing, though, many white Alabamans expressed considerable sympathy for the victims and even shock at the horrific act. Within days, however, racial animus returned and the Birmingham police barricaded blacks in their neighborhoods to keep the tenuous situation from exploding into a race war.

While Martin Luther King, Jr. unsuccessfully lobbied President Kennedy for federal action, civil rights activists John Lewis and Diane Nash responded to the heinous act with a plan to register Alabama's black citizens to vote. This movement, which was centered in Selma, Alabama, eventually resulted in the passage of the landmark 1965 Voting Rights Act.

Meanwhile, white southern officials did little to prosecute and convict the perpetrators of the bombing. After an eyewitness identified Robert Chambliss, a member of the Ku Klux Klan, as the man who had placed the bomb underneath the steps of the church, authorities arrested him, but he was quickly acquitted of murder and given a $100 fine and six-month prison sentence for possession of dynamite. In November 1977, Chambliss was tried again, found guilty, and sentenced to life in prison. In 2000, the FBI announced that a splinter group from the Ku Klux Klan, the Cahaba Boys, was responsible for the bombing. In addition to Chambliss, Herman Cash, Thomas Blanton, and Bobby Cherry were named as codefendants and assailants. Cash had died in 1994, but Blanton was indicted in 2000, found guilty of murder in 2001, and sentenced to life in prison. Cherry was convicted of murder in 2002 after several relatives came forward and stated that he had bragged about his participation in the bombing. He was sentenced to life in prison.

Birmingham Riots (1963)   In 1963, Birmingham was rocked by race riots as the city's African-American citizens took their frustrations to the streets. These episodes were sparked by a series of bombings that were directed against black leaders, black-owned businesses, and churches.

On Saturday night, May 11, 1963, Ku Klux Klan–inspired terrorists bombed the home of A. D. King, the brother of Martin Luther King, Jr. This bombing took place in the aftermath of Martin Luther King's successful Project-C Campaign. King had used this campaign to challenge the segregation that was rampant throughout downtown Birmingham. His arrest had produced one of the most potent statements of the American creed, the "Letter from Birmingham Jail." The Project-C Campaign ended after the local police, led by Sheriff Eugene "Bull" Connor, and officials of the Birmingham Fire Department used fire hoses and police dogs against the children who led the peaceful marches.

As a result of this springtime confrontation, emotions remained raw among Birmingham's blacks as they and

Walter Gadsden, a 17-year-old high school student demonstrating for civil rights, is attacked by a police dog in Birmingham, Alabama, March 3, 1963. *(Associated Press/Bill Hudson)*

their neighbors were the ones who directly experienced the wrath of Bull Connor and his police department. After a second bomb ripped through the Gaston Motel in downtown Birmingham the same day that A. D. King's home was bombed, African Americans left the bars and dance halls for Kelly Ingram Park, where they threw rocks and bricks at the police and set stores on fire.

In September of the same year, riots broke out after the Sixteenth Street Church bombing killed four African-American girls (see BIRMINGHAM CHURCH BOMBINGS). In both instances, the race riots did not cease until authorities restored order through force. The Birmingham riots marked the dawn of a new era. Throughout the remainder of the 1960s, most major American cities witnessed at least one race riot. Moreover, the threat of disturbances loomed every summer throughout the 1960s. Because the Birmingham riots occurred on the heels of some the Civil Rights movement's greatest moments, they signaled the practical limits of King's nonviolent movement.

Buddhist Uprising in Vietnam (1963)   In May and June 1963, American policy in South Vietnam took a fateful turn

when Buddhist monks staged a series of demonstrations against the South Vietnamese government. The president of the Republic of South Vietnam, Ngo Dinh Diem, was a Roman Catholic who had little tolerance for Buddhists, the country's religious majority, and his hapless handling of the Buddhist uprising proved to be his final undoing.

The uprising began on May 7, 1963, the day celebrated as the Buddha's birthday. To commemorate the event, Buddhists in Vietnam's old imperial capital, Hue, unfurled flags as part of the celebration. In reaction, the deputy province chief enforced a law that prohibited the display of religious flags. The next day, thousands of Buddhists gathered in the streets of Hue to protest the government's actions. As tensions mounted, troops fired upon protesters, killing nine and wounding 14. Even after this bloodletting, Diem refused to apologize, and he refused to acquiesce to protesters' demands for religious equality.

The crisis took a dramatic turn on June 11, when Thich Quang Duc, a 73-year-old Buddhist monk, set himself on fire in front of the Cambodian embassy in Saigon to protest Diem's anti-Buddhist policies. With the gripping image of the Buddhist monk setting himself aflame appearing on front pages of newspapers across the world, Diem faced a major public relations crisis.

Despite President Kennedy's pleas that he compromise, Diem refused to concede to Buddhist demands and he placed South Vietnam under martial law. The Buddhist uprising forced Kennedy to change policy in Vietnam. The president tacitly approved a coup that removed Diem from power in November and installed a military junta.

Civil Rights Policies   Early in his administration, President Kennedy's civil rights policies were ambiguous. He had promised during the 1960 campaign to end housing discrimination by signing an executive order, but he hesitated so long that civil rights groups sent him thousands of pens to facilitate the reform. Upon assuming office in 1961, Kennedy believed that the president's real power lay in the realm of foreign rather than domestic policy. Moreover, he realized that key congressional committee chairs were held by white southerners opposed to integration, which meant that passage of civil rights legislation would be difficult. Using his executive powers, the president appointed an African American, Robert C. Weaver, to head the Housing and Home Finance Agency and he established the Committee on Equal Employment Opportunity to ban racial discrimination in the employment practices of the federal government.

Aside from careful executive action, Kennedy stood on the sidelines as civil rights activists pressed for a vigorous federal role in securing rights for black citizens. Portraying himself as a nationalist who was primarily concerned with fighting the cold war, Kennedy promised gradual action on integration as part of the fight against the Soviet Union.

Although Kennedy began his presidency holding one set of ideas, events on the ground slowly changed his attitudes. After wrangling with Governors Ross Barnett of Mississippi and George Wallace of Alabama over issues of school integration and the safety of the FREEDOM RIDERS, Kennedy no longer saw civil rights simply as a political issue to be managed. Rather, civil rights became a moral issue for the president. In the summer of 1963, Kennedy delivered an impassioned, nationally televised address in which he claimed that the moral issues surrounding the Civil Rights movement were "as old as the scriptures and is as clear as the American Constitution."

Thereafter, Kennedy became convinced of the necessity of a civil rights bill. With Vice President LYNDON JOHNSON wooing southern supporters and Attorney General Robert Kennedy helping to write the bill, the president backed what would ultimately become the most ambitious civil rights legislation of the 20th century. Realizing that he lacked the votes of southern Democrats to end debate in the Senate, Kennedy pursued the support of Republicans, such as House minority leader Charles Halleck (IN) and Senate minority leader Everett Dirksen (IL). While Kennedy's actions on behalf of civil rights never won the unqualified approval of black leaders, he successfully pushed the civil rights agenda forward and he did so without causing a political revolt from the South.

Clean Air Act (1963)   The 1963 Clean Air Act marked the federal government's first attempt at crafting a national "clean air policy." While the law's policy oversight was groundbreaking, the Clean Air Act itself constituted a compromise that merely offered federal aid for the development of state environmental control agencies and called on federal agencies to help regulate interstate pollution issues.

The 1963 Clean Air Act did not give the federal government the power to create and enforce clean air standards. This was accomplished through a 1965 amendment to the original legislation and the Clean Air Act of 1970. These acts gave the federal government the power to regulate and enforce environmental standards.

The 1963 legislation was a product of efforts undertaken by the nascent environmental movement, which was sparked by Rachel Carson's 1962 bestseller *Silent Spring*. In her book, Carson argued that insecticides and other pollutants threatened both natural and human environments. In addition, Kennedy's secretary of the interior, Stewart Udall, was a staunch environmentalist who consistently pushed for a stronger federal role in regulating and enforcing national standards.

Communications Satellite Act (1962)   In the years following the Soviet Union's 1957 launch of *Sputnik* the United States initiated its own SPACE PROGRAM. In 1958, President DWIGHT EISENHOWER proposed the creation of the National Aeronautics and Space Administration (NASA). While NASA worked to develop its own satellite system, private industry and Congress vied over control of the commercial uses of space technology.

Eisenhower had believed that private industry should develop satellite communication technologies, but President Kennedy understood the international political significance of the "space race" and the potential propaganda boon the administration could reap from sharing this technology. In 1961–62, Congress found itself engaged in a heated debate over which sector, the public or private, should control satellite communications. Backed by the administration, Senators Wayne Morse (D-OR) and Estes Kefauver (D-TN) advocated legislation to create a "government corporation" that worked as a private business yet acted in the public interest.

The 1962 Communications Satellite Act created the Communications Satellite Corporation (COMSAT). In short order, COMSAT launched a number of satellites that ushered in a new era of international communication. More important, the United States shared usage of its satellites with the governments of its allies and with those of friendly developing nations. In doing so, the Communications Satellite Act revealed the NEW FRONTIER's nondoctrinaire approach to the cold war.

Community Mental Health Centers Act (1963)

The 1963 Community Mental Health Centers Act is one of the least recognized pieces of domestic legislation enacted during the Kennedy presidency. The legislation constituted a watershed in federal policy toward the mentally ill. Prior to 1963, many Americans with mental illness were housed in state hospitals. Under the supervision of the state, patients were fed, drugged, and kept out of public view. The 1963 legislation called for alternatives to institutionalization and the establishment of community-based facilities. Kennedy's first-hand experience in having a sister with mental disabilities is generally regarded as an important reason why he pushed for this bill.

Prior to the Kennedy administration, the federal government had been debating changes in its mental health policy since World War II. The National Institute of Mental Health was formally established in 1949, and the 1955 Mental Health Study Act established the Joint Commission on Mental Illness and Mental Health. The latter proposed many of the policies contained in the 1963 Community Mental Health Centers Act.

The 1963 law called for the deinstitutionalization of the mentally ill and for "troubled" patients to receive treatment at "community-based" facilities. When states began shuttering mental institutions and patients were "deinstitutionalized," most communities could not adequately meet the increased demands for mental health services. As a result, states shifted the meager funds that were spent on mental institutions to other priorities and they refused to spend on community mental health centers. Consequently, some among the mentally ill moved to out-of-state institutions but many were forced to live on the streets. Paradoxically, Kennedy's well-intentioned legislation is cited as a cause for the proliferation in the number of homeless that has occurred since the 1960s.

Coup Against Ngo Dinh Diem (1963)

As South Vietnam's president from 1954 through November 1963, Ngo Dinh Diem ruled during a key juncture in Vietnam's history. Diem was president when the communist Vietcong gained the upper hand in the South. Hailing from a well-connected Catholic family, Diem was a key member of the government of Emperor Bao Dai, which preceded his own administration, and his brother, Ngo Dinh Thuc, was Roman Catholic archbishop of Vietnam.

By the time of Kennedy's inauguration in 1961, Diem's regime was mired in political and social turmoil. In the mid-1950s, Diem had started down a course which led to his eventual undoing. After Diem implemented an anticommunist purge and failed to bring about land reform, Vietnamese communists successfully appealed to peasants in making promises of thoroughgoing reforms. Diem's repressive policies so antagonized noncommunists in the South that senior military officers staged an unsuccessful coup in 1960. Buoyed by Diem's ineptitude, Ho Chi Minh and his North Vietnamese government created the National Liberation Front whose military wing, the People's Liberation Army (the Vietcong), operated as a guerrilla force within South Vietnam.

Despite the growing strength of the Vietcong and Diem's poor leadership, Kennedy increased American military and economic aid to South Vietnam. In the spring of 1963, Diem further isolated himself politically through his inept handling of the BUDDHIST UPRISING IN VIETNAM. Diem's bloody repression of Buddhists sparked widespread protest and revealed to Kennedy that the regime was lost. Kennedy's newly appointed ambassador to Vietnam, Henry Cabot Lodge, reported that several high-level officers sought Kennedy's tacit support for a coup. After weeks of agonizing internal debate the administration approved the coup. Despite warnings from the Kennedy administration that his life was in danger, Diem refused to seek asylum and instead was assassinated on November 2, 1963. A junta led by General Duong Van Minh took control of South Vietnam's government.

Cuban Missile Crisis (1962)

The Cuban missile crisis is widely regarded as one of the Kennedy administration's greatest triumphs. Occurring over 13 days in October 1962 (October 16–28), the crisis was sparked by Soviet and Cuban fears of an imminent American invasion. The face-off not only brought the world to the brink of nuclear annihilation, but it also led President Kennedy and Soviet premier Nikita Khrushchev to rethink their bellicosity.

While the diplomatic impasse marked a high-water mark of his presidency, the administration bears much of the blame for sparking it in the first place. A mere seven months after the BAY OF PIGS fiasco in 1961, in which Cuba defeated a poorly planned American invasion of the island, Kennedy approved Operation Mongoose, which empowered the CIA to launch a "secret war" designed to undermine or assassinate Cuban dictator Fidel Castro. Indeed, both the president and his brother, Attorney General Robert Kennedy, became obsessed with Castro. Because Republicans promised to make Cuba the dominant issue in the 1962 midterm elections, the Kennedy preoccupation intensified with time.

Alarmed by rumors of another American invasion, Khrushchev acted to protect Castro, a key ally. In addition to aiding Cuba, Khrushchev sought to compensate for the Soviets' global strategic disadvantage by deploying 24 medium-range R-12 missiles and 16 intermediate R-14 missiles. When American U-2 surveillance flights over Cuba discovered that the Soviets were building medium-range ballistic missile sites that had the capability of reaching American cities, the administration was forced to react.

Speaking on television from the Oval Office of the White House on October 22, 1962, President Kennedy announces a naval quarantine of Cuba. *(©Archive Photos)*

On the morning of October 15, 1962, Kennedy was briefed on the discoveries, prompting him to call for a meeting of national security officials termed the Executive Committee of the Nation Security Council, or Ex Comm. In relative short order, the president decided that "we weren't going to [allow the missiles]" to remain in Cuba and it became Ex Comm's task to secure the missiles' removal.

Over the course of the next 13 days, Ex Comm, guided by Robert Kennedy and Secretary of Defense Robert McNamara, met and deliberated on how to remove the missiles. Ex Comm committee members recalled those days as excruciatingly tense times that even pushed the famously "cool" president to lose his temper. Navigating between the Joint Chiefs of Staff, who advocated a preemptive military strike, and those who called for negotiation, Kennedy opted for a third approach, one that was favored by McNamara, namely, a naval blockade of Cuba and a demand for the removal of all Soviet missiles from the island.

On Monday October 22, after five days of intense deliberations, the president told congressional leaders of his plan to blockade Cuba and had European leaders and the Soviet ambassador to the United States informed of his policy. At 7 P.M. the president delivered a 17-minute televised national address to nearly 100 million viewers in which he called for the unconditional removal of the missiles. Kennedy told the American people that "unmistakable evidence" existed that the Soviets had installed nuclear weapon sites in Cuba. He announced a "strict quarantine on all offensive military equipment." Furthermore, Kennedy declared that the United States would consider "any nuclear missile launched from Cuba against any nation in the Western Hemisphere as an attack by the Soviet Union on the United States, requiring a full retaliatory response against the Soviet Union."

With the world poised on the brink of a nuclear confrontation, Kennedy personally supervised the situation. As tensions mounted, communiqués went back and forth between the Kremlin and the White House. Khrushchev instructed Soviet naval forces to ignore the blockade and proceed to Cuba. As the Soviet navy approached the blockade zone, Khrushchev reversed the order on October 24. On October 26, the premier sent a rambling and seemingly personal letter to the president offering to remove the missiles if the

United States dismantled its Jupiter missiles in Turkey and pledged never to invade Cuba. Khrushchev wrote in part: "I propose: we, for our part, will declare that our ships bound for Cuba are not carrying any armaments. You will declare that the United States will not invade Cuba with its troops and will not support any other forces which might intend to invade Cuba. Then the necessity of the presence of our military specialists in Cuba will disappear." Soon after that letter arrived another more belligerent message from the premier was received, which contradicted the first message.

Replying to the more conciliatory letter, Kennedy agreed to Khrushchev's noninvasion proviso. Simultaneously, the president sent Robert Kennedy to confer with Anatoly Dobrynin, the Soviet ambassador to the United States. In his meeting with Dobrynin, Kennedy agreed to discreetly remove the Jupiter missiles in the near future but to keep the matter quiet. On October 27, the threat of war loomed even larger when a U.S. U-2 pilot flew over Soviet air space. He escaped with no shots fired, but when Defense Secretary McNamara learned of the incident, he yelled, "this means war with the Soviet Union." Kennedy was calmer, laughing that someone did not "get the word." That day, a U-2 plane was shot down over Cuba. Also that day, the Kremlin accepted Kennedy's demands and the superpowers stepped back from the brink of war. Even though the Joint Chiefs of Staff continued to call for air strikes, the president ignored their advice and accepted the compromise. Khrushchev announced on Radio Moscow on October 28, "the Soviet government, in addition to previously issued instructions on the cessation of further work at the building sites for the weapons, has issued a new order on the dismantling of the weapons which you describe as 'offensive,' and their crating and return to the Soviet Union." Kennedy replied that Khrushchev had made "an important and constructive contribution to peace." The Cuban missile crisis had ended.

Education Legislation   Among the domestic issues confronting the Kennedy administration was whether Congress would pass the president's call for federal aid to public schools (primary and secondary education). In crafting a liberal agenda to meet the challenges of an age of affluence, Kennedy had included federal aid to public education as one of his five "must" pieces of domestic legislation (the others were medical care for the aged, mass transit, creation of a Department of Urban Affairs, and economic assistance to the impoverished Appalachian region).

To Kennedy and his policymakers, many states and localities simply lacked the resources to provide an adequate public education. Despite this, Catholic parochial schools and race were the major obstacles blocking federal funding of public schools prior to the 1960s. Indeed, after the Supreme Court had ruled in 1947 that parochial schools could receive public monies, Catholic politicians worked tirelessly to bring federal aid to church-supported schools. However, conservatives and many southern Democrats remained opposed to federal funding of public schools due to fiscal concerns and religious bigotry.

To counteract concerns about aid to Catholic schools, Kennedy's $2.3 billion education bill was intended for public schools only. Rather than rendering the bill more palatable to its opponents, Kennedy's exemption of parochial schools from the legislation merely added Catholic members of Congress to the bill's list of opponents. Civil rights activist and Representative Adam Clayton Powell, Jr. (D-NY) posed another threat to the Kennedy-backed legislation. As chairman of the House Committee on Education, Powell attached to any piece of legislation that passed through his committee "the Powell Amendment," which forbade the disbursement of federal funds to segregated schools.

In the face of these considerable obstacles, Kennedy's education bill remained stalled in the House for the duration of his presidency. After his death, President LYNDON JOHNSON took Kennedy's education bill and transformed it into the landmark 1965 Elementary and Secondary Education Act, which fundamentally changed the relationship between the federal government and public schools.

***Engel v. Vitale* (1962)**   While most legal scholars point to *Brown v. Board of Education* (1954) or *Miranda v. Arizona* (1966) as the Warren Court's seminal decisions, few Supreme Court cases have had such profound political implications as *Engel v. Vitale* (1962). The *Engel* case was the first of a series of church-state decisions in which the Warren Court reversed precedent and ruled against state-sponsored prayer in the public schools.

At issue in *Engel* was the constitutionality of a nondenominational prayer that the New York State Board of Regents had prepared for students in the public schools. The New York Regents had so acted to save the local school boards from a potential controversial issue. A number of local school boards had adopted the prayer and mandated that it be recited before the school day commenced. Recital of the prayer was strictly voluntary and any comment on a student's unwillingness to participate was prohibited. When Steven Engel, a Jewish father, saw one of his children saying the prayer, he and four other parents, Lawrence Roth, David Lichtenstein, Monroe Lerner, and Leonore Lyons, ultimately brought suit on behalf of their children. Some of the parents and their children were atheists, some Unitarians, and some were members of the New York Society for Ethical Culture. The suit was brought against the local school district board, and it named the president of the board, William J. Vitale, Jr., as the defendant.

Previous to the Warren Court, the justices relied upon the free exercise clause of the First Amendment to the Constitution, interpreting the amendment to mean that Congress cannot coerce any particular religious belief. The Warren Court, however, relied almost exclusively upon the Amendment's establishment clause, which bars Congress from establishing any religion. Declaring the regent's prayer unconstitutional, Justice Hugo Black ruled that the establishment clause meant that the government could not compose official prayers for public ceremonies even if they were nondenominational and participation was voluntary. This ruling not only unleashed a torrent of popular protest, but it also led to other church-state cases in which the Court further refined the limits of prayer and other religious exercises in public.

Equal Pay Act (1963)   Passed by Congress in 1963, the Equal Pay Act declared that men and women must receive equal pay for equal work. Prior to this legislation, it was legal for newspaper classified ads to list employment opportunities under the subheading of "Help Wanted Male" and "Help Wanted Female." Often the same position would be listed under each subheading but the advertised pay for the male was significantly higher. Indeed, scholars estimate that in the years from 1950 to 1960 women earned about 59 to 64 percent of what their male counterparts earned from employment both in general and when working the same job.

In the weeks following Kennedy's election in 1960, he sought to broker a compromise between liberals, who sought an Equal Rights Amendment, and organized labor, which was far less interested in gender equity issues. He benefited in this pursuit from the presence of Esther Peterson as the director of the Women's Bureau within the Department of Labor and who also served as an assistant secretary of labor. Additionally she was a former AFL-CIO lobbyist. Peterson was able to bridge the gap within a historically divided women's movement, which had disputed the need for an Equal Rights Amendment since the 1920s, and between feminists and labor activists. Peterson played an important role in passing the Equal Pay Act. The legislative proposal also gained traction from the recommendations of the PRESIDENT'S COMMISSION ON THE STATUS OF WOMEN, which endorsed equal pay legislation. The bill as passed did not end the problem of pay inequity because it provided no administrative enforcement and it granted exceptions for issues such as seniority, merit pay, pay hikes based on quantity and quality of production, and any other measurement that did not use sex as a category.

Farm Policy   Although President Kennedy's home state of Massachusetts boasted a low number of commercial farmers, the farm issue loomed large in 1960. Throughout the 1950s, the American agricultural sector had been hit hard by sluggish commodity prices. As a result, farm income and living standards fell even further behind that of urban and suburban America. Despite federal agricultural subsidies that were intended to boost farm income, overproduction combined with the DWIGHT D. EISENHOWER administration's "flexible

farm supports" caused over 3 million Americans to leave their family farms in the course of the decade. Throughout the Eisenhower era, farm income dropped by 35 percent even while federal farm subsidies were boosted by an average of $4 billion annually from 1953 to 1960. During the 1960 campaign, Kennedy blamed Eisenhower's secretary of agriculture, Ezra Taft Benson, for the plight of America's family farmers. The farm issue was ripe for the Democrats. To reap the farm vote, Kennedy called for more stringent production controls and price supports.

Despite Kennedy's pursuit of the farm vote, he did poorly with farmers in 1960. As president, however, he had a significant agenda for the agricultural sector. Starting with his appointment of Orville Freeman as secretary of agriculture, the president invested talent, time, and energy into formulating and passing farm legislation. In April 1961, the administration sent a comprehensive farm bill to Congress, which, like so much of his proposed legislation, remained bottled up in committee. While the administration's efforts to contend with overproduction and underconsumption generally failed, Kennedy fared better when he turned to foreign policy and agriculture. Using America's surplus food supply as a "carrot" to draw the support of nonaligned developing nations, the administration instituted the Food for Peace program. Kennedy believed that supplying these countries with American food surplus would not only win allies but would also help solve the problems of overproduction and actually boost farm prices. Despite his efforts, the president's farm policy failed to significantly raise farm income or reduce federal spending on farm supports.

***The Feminine Mystique*, by Betty Friedan (1963)**   Considered by many feminists to be the progenitor of the modern women's movement, Betty Friedan burst onto the national scene with the publication of *The Feminine Mystique* in 1963. Born to an immigrant, Jewish family in Peoria, Illinois, Friedan studied at Smith College and undertook graduate work at the University of California-Berkeley. After marrying and moving to New York City to write for a labor newspaper, Friedan was fired from her job when her boss learned she was pregnant.

She worked subsequently as a free lance writer for an assortment of women's magazines and was deeply involved in the leftist-labor politics of the 1940s. Indeed, Friedan, a delegate to the 1948 Progressive Party Convention, had presciently warned: "Men, there's a revolution brewing in the American kitchen."

Friedan's "revolution"—the women's movement of the 1960s and 1970s—stemmed directly from her political activity in the 1940s. In preparation for a reunion of her 1942 Smith College class, Friedan sent out questionnaires to gauge her classmate's satisfaction with their postgraduate lives. The results revealed that many of her classmates were acutely

Betty Friedan, author of *The Feminine Mystique,* published in 1963 *(The Bridgeman Art Library)*

dissatisfied with their lives. The questionnaire also crystallized many issues for Friedan. Calling this sense of malaise "the problem that has no name," Friedan described the frustrations experienced by educated, stay-at-home women in *The Feminine Mystique,* which became a bestseller.

To Friedan, women experienced frustration and depression because they were financially, intellectually, and emotionally dependent upon their husbands. In her book, Friedan directly confronted cultural norms that required women to find identity and meaning through their husband and children. *The Feminine Mystique* became a national phenomenon and helped spark what is commonly termed "Second Wave Feminism." In contrast to the earlier brand of feminism that focused on issues of education and job opportunities, Second Wave feminists focused on reproductive rights and sexuality and sought to change the domestic and private lives of women.

First U.S. Space Flight (1961)   On May 5, 1961, Alan Shepard became the first American launched beyond the earth's atmosphere into outer space. Not only was this a significant achievement for NASA's Mercury project, but it also convinced President Kennedy that the United States could successfully compete with the Soviet Union in space. Since the Soviet's launch of *Sputnik* in 1957, space had become the newest arena in which the two superpowers competed in

touting the relative merits of the capitalist and communist systems.

In the late 1950s, the Soviet Union's space program was more advanced than its American counterpart. Indeed, *Sputnik* had become a symbol of how the United States had "fallen behind" during DWIGHT D. EISENHOWER's presidency and was one sphere in which Kennedy had promised to "get the country moving again." Seeking to make good on his campaign promises, Kennedy closely monitored the Mercury program. When Shepard's mission was successful, the president had his space committee and NASA study the practicalities of a manned mission to the moon.

Weeks after Shepard's mission, Kennedy unveiled his plan for a manned lunar landing. Telling Congress "[t]his nation should commit itself to achieving the goal, before this decade is out, of landing a man on the moon," Kennedy used the SPACE PROGRAM to capture the world's imagination and leapfrog the Soviets. Using the drama of a lunar landing as his hook, Kennedy convinced Congress to appropriate monies for the Apollo program, which became inextricably linked to his presidency and which culminated in successfully landing a man on the moon on July 20, 1969.

Freedom Rides (1961)   In the first months of Kennedy's term in office in 1961, the administration faced a domestic political issue that threatened to consume the president's agenda—integration and civil rights. Fueled by the Supreme Court's 1960 *Boynton v. Virginia* decision, which declared segregated interstate transportation unconstitutional, civil rights activists sought to integrate interstate buses and bus terminal facilities. In the summer of 1961, the Congress of Racial Equality (CORE) sponsored "Freedom Rides" in which black and white activists traveled across the South in integrated buses to force the integration of the interstate bus system. This was not the first time CORE had attempted such a strategy to integrate interstate bus travel. In 1947, following a Supreme Court ruling that segregated interstate bus service was illegal, CORE and another civil rights group, the Fellowship of Reconciliation, staged integrated bus rides in the upper South. This effort attracted little attention and few positive results ensued.

Joining CORE in its sponsorship of the Freedom Rides in 1961 were the Student Non-Violent Coordinating Committee (SNCC) and Dr. Martin Luther King, Jr.'s Southern Christian Leadership Conference (SCLC). They hoped to spark a broad-based movement that would elicit federal action on behalf of civil rights. One significant challenge they faced was a less than ideal working relationship between the students and King, who wondered whether the freedom rides were a wise strategy for tackling segregation.

Departing from Washington, D.C. on May 4, 1961, on a Greyhound bus and a Trailways bus, seven African Americans and six whites directly confronted the South's system of racial segregation. When the buses stopped in Virginia, minor resistance, some violence, and a few arrests occurred. The riders faced the first real problems in Rockhill, South Carolina. Two riders were beaten there, and one was arrested for using the white restroom. The press covered these incidents. When the Freedom Riders arrived in Atlanta, Georgia, they had dinner with King, who told a reporter, "You will never make it through Alabama." On May 14, the travelers went to Anniston, Alabama, where riders met a racist mob who slashed the tires and threw stones at the bus. Local Anniston officials had told the local Ku Klux Klan that they could do what they wanted to the riders without fear of arrest. When the bus pulled into Anniston, the driver told the white protesters at the station, "Well, boys, here they are. I brought you some niggers and nigger-lovers." Outside of Anniston the bus was firebombed. When the buses arrived in Birmingham, Alabama, the riders, upon departing the bus, were attacked and beaten. This violence led to the end of the CORE-sponsored Freedom Rides.

At this juncture, SNCC sponsored a new round of Freedom Rides, which included many of the original participants. Embarking from Nashville on May 17, the Freedom Riders returned to Birmingham, where the riders were arrested for violating the segregation laws. No driver could be found to continue the journey, and the riders were stranded in Birmingham. Through the efforts of Attorney General Robert Kennedy a new bus driver was found. When the Freedom Riders departed Birmingham, they left under a police escort. They lost that protection in the Alabama capital of Montgomery, their next stop, and as a result they were beaten severely. The police, after failing to provide the protection that the Justice Department had requested, served the riders with an injunction to prevent them from continuing their protest in Alabama.

When King learned of the situation, he returned to Alabama from a speaking engagement in Chicago and began lending the movement his public, vocal support. Some in the movement, though, were critical that King did not join the riders. Instead, it was Robert Kennedy who helped negotiate an end to the crisis. The Kennedy administration announced on May 29 that the Interstate Commerce Commission had been ordered to end segregation in all interstate bus facilities. Still, the Freedom Rides went on, with more and more college students joining the movement, riding the buses, and getting arrested in Mississippi. The heightened level of activity brought more media attention and an ultimate resolution to the crisis. Careful to tread a course so as not to overly offend northern liberals or southern segregationists, Robert Kennedy managed the crisis and oversaw the de facto desegregation of interstate bus travel by the fall of 1961.

Gideon v. Wainwright (1963)

Whether it was church-state relations or the apportionment of state legislative seats, the Warren Court steadily expanded the purview of the Supreme Court in the 1950s and 1960s. In *Gideon v. Wainwright,* the Court further injected itself into the administration of local-level criminal justice issues.

Reversing the 1942 *Betts v. Brady* decision, the Court ruled in *Gideon v. Wainwright* in 1963 that indigent defendants had to be provided counsel free of charge in state and federal courts. Prior to this ruling, the Court had mandated that states must provide an attorney for capital murder trials or in a felony case involving "exceptional circumstances." When Clarence Earl Gideon was charged with a misdemeanor count of breaking and entering, he was denied counsel because his crime was neither a capital offense nor an exceptional felony. Forced to defend himself at trial, Gideon was convicted of burglary and sentenced to five years in prison. He brought suit against Louie L. Wainwright, the secretary of the Florida Division of Corrections. In a unanimous decision, the Court ruled that the right to counsel constituted a fundamental legal right.

Health Professions Education Assistance Act (1963)

The 1963 Health Professions Education Assistance Act allocated federal money for the construction of educational facilities for the medical profession and provided direct aid to needy students. Part and parcel of a federal effort to increase the number of Americans gaining a postsecondary education, this legislation was the first congressional act that was designed to directly increase the numbers of doctors, dentists, and surgeons.

Indeed, prior to this legislation, studies revealed that a shortage of health care workers existed and Congress responded. After President Kennedy's death in 1963, his successor, LYNDON JOHNSON, built upon this legislation by signing a law that offered direct grants to medical students (rather than loans), funded the construction of even more facilities, and made the federal government a partner in secondary and higher education to a degree unlike any before.

Housing Act (1961)

While much of Kennedy's major domestic legislation floundered in Congress, the president's far-reaching housing legislation was passed in June 1961. Following in the tradition of HARRY TRUMAN's housing policy, the Housing Act provided financial assistance and public housing for the elderly and chronically poor. In addition, the law offered aid to middle-income earners who failed to qualify for public housing but nonetheless struggled to purchase a home.

The law marked the federal government's first foray in crafting a middle-class housing program. The legislation required a 3 percent down payment in return for a low-interest 35-year mortgage. While the $4.88 billion omnibus housing bill represented a rare victory for the administration, Congress refused to give the administration all that it wanted.

Kennedy had hoped to elevate the Department of Urban Affairs and Housing into a cabinet-level agency and had even chosen Robert Weaver to serve as its head. Because Weaver would have become the first African-American cabinet official, many southern members of Congress refused to support the administration's proposal. Kennedy's housing program, along with his wrangling with Congress over Weaver's appointment, served as a microcosm of his relations with the Congress in enacting his domestic agenda. (When Congress finally established the Department of Housing and Urban Development under President Lyndon Johnson, Weaver was appointed secretary and served from 1966 to 1968.)

Kefauver-Harris Drug Amendments (1962)   During the late 1950s and early 1960s, doctors in Western Europe routinely prescribed Thalidomide for morning sickness and as

In August 1962, President John F. Kennedy presented the President's Award for Distinguished Federal Civilian Service to Dr. Frances Kelsey for her role in averting devastating birth defects across the United States by refusing to approve the drug Thalidomide. (© *Alliance Images/Alamy*)

a sleep aid for pregnant women. Because the side effects of Thalidomide were poorly studied, approximately 10,000 children with severe birth defects and deformities were born to mothers who had taken the medication.

Luckily, for Americans, Dr. Frances Oldham Kelsey, a pharmacologist who worked for the Food and Drug Administration (FDA), had refused to approve Thalidomide for the U.S. market. Instead, Kelsey had insisted that Thalidomide be "fully tested" prior to its approval. Once the birth defects caused by Thalidomide became widely known and the drug was proven to be dangerous, Kelsey was hailed as a hero and her ideas pertaining to drug safety shaped the congressional response to the issue. The Kefauver-Harris Drug Amendments, or the Drug Efficacy Amendment, of 1962 fundamentally changed the way in which the FDA approved drugs for the American market.

Prior to the Kefauver-Harris Drug Amendments, U.S. drug companies merely had to show that products were "safe." The new law stipulated that no drug was "safe" unless it was also effective. Moreover, effectiveness had to be proven before the drug could be sold to consumers. In addition, the law mandated that pharmaceutical firms send reaction reports to the FDA, and drug advertising in medical journals list the risks as well as the benefits of a product. Named for its sponsors, Senator Estes Kefauver (D-TN) and Representative Oren Harris (D-AR), the Kefauver-Harris Drug Amendments of 1962 significantly improved the safety of the drugs available to the American consumer.

***Kennedy v. Mendoza-Martinez* (1963)**   In a closely contested and controversial 5–4 decision, the Supreme Court ruled in *Kennedy v. Mendoza-Martinez* in 1963 that Congress must adhere to due process and procedural safeguards even during times of war and a national crisis. At issue was Francisco Mendoza-Martinez's American citizenship, which was revoked under the authority of the 1940 Selective Training and Service Act. Born in the United States, Martinez was a dual citizen of the United States and Mexico but he fled to the latter in 1942 to avoid military service.

Upon returning to the United States, Martinez was arrested, pled guilty to avoiding the draft, and served more than one year in prison. Under the provisions of the Selective Training and Service Act, draft dodgers were to be divested of their American citizenship. With this provision in mind, Martinez was deported upon his release from prison. He challenged this decision, bringing suit against U.S. attorney general Robert F. Kennedy. Upon appeal, the Court ruled that in deporting Martinez his rights to due process and procedural safeguards, such as incremental penal structures, were violated.

Essentially, the Court claimed that Americans could not be stripped of their citizenship for draft evasion alone. Writing for the majority, Justice Arthur Goldberg argued, "the imperative necessity for safeguarding these rights to procedural due process under the gravest of emergencies has existed throughout our constitutional history." In the Martinez case, the Court placed limits on government power in times of national emergencies and war.

Laotian Crisis The 1954 Geneva Peace Accords not only ended 100 years of French imperialism in Indochina, but they also ended hostilities in Laos. Bordering North Vietnam and China, Laos was a landlocked nation that nonetheless occupied a strategic position in the region. In particular, a major north-south resupply route, which connected South Vietnam to China, went through the heart of Laos.

Even though the Geneva Accords called for the establishment of neutral governments, the United States rejected the agreement and helped oust Prince Souvanna Phouma's nonaligned Laotian government. As a result, Phoui Sananikone established a pro-Western administration in 1958 and purged the communist Pathet Lao from his regime, sparking a civil war. Due to the civil war, Sananikone's government fell and was followed by a pro-American general, Phouami Nosavan, who received the backing of the DWIGHT EISENHOWER administration.

In the first months of the Kennedy administration in the spring of 1961, the possible overthrow of an American-backed government by communist-supported forces emerged as a real threat. In his meetings prior to his inauguration Kennedy and President Eisenhower discussed the problem of Laos more than any other issue. Once in office, Kennedy intended to reverse Eisenhower's policy toward Laos and replace it with a more subtle and nuanced position that was equally anticommunist yet was calibrated to help neutral governments ward off communist insurgencies. Believing that the communists were gaining momentum in Laos, Kennedy considered sending military troops but he rejected the Joint Chiefs of Staff's advice. Rather than sending troops to Laos, the administration negotiated and secured the Geneva Protocol in which 19 nations agreed to respect the neutrality of Laos. The agreement proved satisfactory to the Kennedy administration. During the presidential campaign staffers had pushed for an activist agenda especially in foreign policy. But it would not be Laos but rather in Vietnam where they would pursue that objective.

Limited Test Ban Treaty (1963) In the aftermath of the CUBAN MISSILE CRISIS, both President Kennedy and Soviet premier Nikita Khrushchev pursued better relations. In addition to installing a "hot line" teletype link between the White House and the Kremlin, Khrushchev ceased pressuring Kennedy on the status of West Berlin. Both leaders pursued the 1963 Limited Test Ban Treaty as part of this emerging détente.

Surrounded by members of Congress, President Kennedy signs the Limited Test Ban Treaty, October 7, 1963. *(Associated Press)*

The treaty itself represented a moderate breakthrough, as it constituted an agreement among the United States, the Soviet Union, and Great Britain to prohibit nuclear testing in the atmosphere, outer space, and underwater. It did, however, allow for limited underground nuclear testing, as long as no radioactive debris escaped the "outside territorial limits" of the testing site.

The treaty further revealed the failure of Kennedy's and Khrushchev's early policies, which had featured nuclear buildups, increased tensions, and a near nuclear showdown over Cuba. The treaty negotiations exposed the limits of détente. Kennedy, for example, never trusted the Kremlin, and negotiators consistently deadlocked over the number of annual onsite inspections allowed as the Americans pushed for eight to 10 visits while the Soviets wanted no more than three.

While Kennedy was concerned with the environmental impact of nuclear testing and easing cold war tensions, he was most uneasy about the proliferation of nuclear weapons. In particular, both the Soviets and the Americans worried about China's nuclear program. In the years following the treaty's negotiation and approval, 116 countries signed it. France and China were two notable exceptions. The

Chinese later acquired nuclear weapons, antagonizing the burgeoning rift between China and the Soviet Union. Thus, the treaty significantly curtailed nuclear proliferation and helped undermine the Soviet Union's relationship with a key ally.

Manpower Development and Training Act (1962)   This legislation was designed to provide assistance in retraining workers whose skills had been rendered obsolete by automation. While it benefited more than 12,000 workers by the end of 1962 alone, critics rightly claimed that the training made workers eligible only for low-wage jobs. The legislation reveals how potent the memory of the Great Depression remained in American political life.

Even though Kennedy's NEW FRONTIER was designed to update liberalism for an age of affluence, the president still heeded the legacy of FRANKLIN D. ROOSEVELT and the New Deal. In particular, it was Roosevelt's Economic Bill of Rights that provided a roadmap for postwar liberalism. High on this list was the right to "a useful and remunerative job."

Using Roosevelt's Economic Bill of Rights as his guide, President HARRY S. TRUMAN signed the 1946 Employment Act into law, which created the president's Council of Economic Advisers and enshrined "full employment" as the goal of federal policymakers. Following in the footsteps of Roosevelt's New Deal, Kennedy championed the 1962 Manpower Development and Training Act as yet another tool in the quest for full employment.

Mapp v. Ohio **(1961)**   In May 1957, Cleveland, Ohio, police officers forcibly entered Dollree Mapp's home without a search warrant, claiming they were looking for a suspect. After the police lied to Mapp about a search warrant they conducted a thorough search of the residence and discovered "obscene" materials in a basement trunk, which led to Mapp's arrest and conviction in an Ohio state court.

Arguing that the Fourth Amendment protected Mapp against unreasonable search and seizure, Mapp's attorney called for her conviction to be overturned. He claimed that the "federal exclusionary rule" forbids the use of unlawfully obtained evidence from being used against his client. In the 1912 *Weeks v. United States* case, the Supreme Court had originally adopted the "federal exclusionary rule," which banned illegally obtained evidence from use in court. In 1949, however, in *Wolf v. Colorado,* the Court ruled that the exclusionary rule applied only to the federal courts.

In the 5–4 *Mapp* decision, the Supreme Court ruled that the exclusionary rule did apply to state criminal courts and that evidence seized without a search warrant or probable cause for the warrant was inadmissible. This 1961 ruling marked the Court's initial and most significant step in asserting itself as the administrator of criminal justice at the state level.

March on Washington for Jobs and Freedom (1963)   Long considered the high watermark of the Civil Rights movement and Martin Luther King, Jr.'s public career, the March on Washington for Jobs and Freedom remains an iconic event of the 1960s. The August 28, 1963, event drew 250,000 supporters to Washington, D.C., and was staged against the backdrop of the Lincoln Memorial. The march featured civil rights luminaries such as the Student Non-violent Coordinating Committee's John Lewis and recording artist Bob Dylan, but it was King and his "I Have a Dream Speech" that remains the best remembered moment of the day. United Auto Workers president Walter Reuther spoke on behalf of labor, and members of the Jewish, Catholic, and Protestant faiths also spoke.

The march was organized by Bayard Rustin, a civil rights veteran; A. Philip Randolph, a senior civil rights veteran and president of the Brotherhood of Sleeping Car Porters; James Farmer, president of the Congress of Racial Equality; John Lewis of the Student Non-Violent Coordinating Committee; Roy Wilkins, the president of the National Association for the Advancement of Colored People; Whitney Young, the president of the Urban League; and King, the president of the Southern Christian Leadership Conference. It was originally intended as a means by which to advocate an end to racial discrimination in employment. In the months preceding the march, the Kennedy administration remained wary of the project. Once the president was convinced that the protest could become a demonstration of support for his omnibus civil rights bill, the administration not only endorsed it, but also Kennedy became personally involved. In addition to its blessing, the administration convinced the organizers to move the program from the Capitol to the Lincoln Memorial and recruited the participation of white church leaders and organized labor so that the march would become an interracial event. Attorney General Robert Kennedy delegated a member of his staff with responsibility for providing food, water, and public toilets for the crowd. In this way, the Kennedy administration helped transform the March on Washington into an interracial, highly publicized event.

The March on Washington was covered by the television networks. During his speech, King declared, "In a sense we've come to our nation's capital to cash a check. When the architects of our republic wrote the magnificent words of the Constitution and the Declaration of Independence, they were signing a promissory note to which every American was to fall heir. This note was a promise that all men, yes, black men as well as white men, would be guaranteed the 'unalienable Rights' of 'Life, Liberty and the pursuit of Happiness.' It is obvious today that America has defaulted on this promissory note, insofar as her citizens of color are concerned. Instead of honoring this sacred obligation, America has given the Negro people a bad check, a check which has come back marked 'insufficient funds.'" In the speech King also remarked that "the fierce urgency of Now" demanded immediate action. "This is

March on Washington for Jobs and Freedom, August 28, 1963 *(Library of Congress)*

March organizers Bayard Rustin *(left)* and Cleveland Robinson flank a "March on Washington for Jobs and Freedom" sign in front of their headquarters in New York City. *(Library of Congress)*

no time to engage in the luxury of cooling off or to take the tranquilizing drug of gradualism. Now is the time to make real the promises of democracy." Perhaps the most famous part of the speech was his declaration, "I have a dream that one day this nation will rise up and live out the true meaning of its creed: 'We hold these truths to be self-evident, that all men are created equal.' I have a dream that one day on the red hills of Georgia, the sons of former slaves and the sons of former slave owners will be able to sit down together at the table of brotherhood. I have a dream that one day even the state of Mississippi, a state sweltering with the heat of injustice, sweltering with the heat of oppression, will be transformed into an oasis of freedom and justice. I have a dream that my four little children will one day live in a nation where they will not be judged by the color of their skin but by the content of their character." Despite the march's success, Kennedy's civil rights bill remained mired in Congress, and southern whites continued to resist integration. Only in 1964, after Kennedy's assassination, did Congress pass the Civil Rights Act.

Mercury Project   *See* First U.S. Space Flight (1961)

Minimum Wage Legislation (1961)   In President Kennedy's initial months in office in 1961 he unveiled an expansive domestic agenda that Congress ignored or watered down considerably. The president wanted to stimulate a sluggish economy by increasing the minimum hourly wage from $1.15 to $1.25 and extending the coverage of federal wage law to an additional 4.3 million workers, including laundry laborers and truck drivers.

Kennedy's legislation made its way to the House floor relatively quickly but it floundered because southern Democrats opposed the wage increase for laundry workers who were usually African-American women. Even though Kennedy gave in to this southern demand, his minimum wage bill failed to pass the House. His legislation did pass the Senate and a conference committee eventually hammered out a compromise bill that raised the minimum wage from $1.00 to $1.25. Nonetheless, the president's minimum wage law excluded laundry workers and an additional 350,000 other laborers, which the bill had covered in its original form. The president's inability to pass a more extensive minimum wage bill revealed the difficulty his administration would have in working with Congress to pass his agenda.

Mutual Educational and Cultural Exchange Act (1961)
Sponsored by Senator J. William Fulbright (D-AR), the Mutual Educational and Cultural Exchange Act (MECEA) of 1961 reflected the Kennedy administration's innovative approach to the cold war and the shockwave of fear that the Soviet launch of *Sputnik* sent through American society. An expansion of the better-known Fulbright Program (founded in 1946), MECEA targeted domestic policy and education.

Following the tradition of the 1958 National Defense Education Act, the Fulbright-Hays Act, as it was also called, constituted a response to the Soviet Union's perceived lead in the study of science, technology, and foreign languages. In this way, the MECEA was not a program of public diplomacy so much as it was aimed at buttressing foreign language and area studies expertise among Americans. Indeed, it reflected the administration's desire to lead the Soviets in science, technology, foreign languages, and area studies.

New Frontier   Following in the tradition of Woodrow Wilson (New Freedom), Franklin D. Roosevelt (New Deal), and Harry S. Truman (Fair Deal), Kennedy coined a short-hand term for his legislative program while running for the presidency. The New Frontier, as he called it, was designed to attract liberals who wanted a revival of the New Deal and Fair Deal traditions, and it reflected the candidate's sense that the 1960s represented a new era in American life. Moreover, the New Frontier was an attempt to update liberalism to meet the challenges of the cold war and an age of affluence.

Kennedy unveiled his New Frontier at the 1960 Democratic National Convention in Los Angeles when he became his party's nominee for president. Using the heroism of western settlers as his metaphor, Kennedy urged voters to take up the challenges of the cold war similar to their forbearers. To Kennedy and many intellectuals, the 1950s had been a decade of complacency and the mass affluence in progress in America threatened to undermine the country's will to resist totalitarianism. Thus, Kennedy's New Frontier not only promised to build upon the New Deal, but it also responded to the exigencies of the period.

Once Kennedy became president in 1961, his New Frontier proposals included several liberal goals, such as MINIMUM WAGE LEGISLATION, federal aid to education, health care for the elderly, urban renewal, civil rights, and poverty relief, but there were several significant points of departure, namely his call for a major tax cut. To Kennedy, the New Frontier differed from past liberal programs because it challenged Americans rather than merely offering government assistance. In particular, Kennedy's PEACE CORPS was an innovative program that asked young Americans to sacrifice for their country by working abroad to improve the lives of the impoverished and the destitute. Despite these departures from the liberalism of the past, much of Kennedy's legislative agenda remained moored in the New Deal–Fair Deal tradition, and it ran into resistance in Congress, which was dominated by a conservative coalition of southern Democrats and Republicans. Little of the New Frontier was enacted into law during Kennedy's presidency.

Peace Corps   Originally designed as one part of a multipronged public diplomacy strategy to combat the lure of communism in developing countries in Asia, Africa, and Latin America, the Peace Corps has become one of President Kennedy's most enduring legacies and an iconic symbol of his administration. Seeking to develop a different type of postcolonial relationship with the developing world, the Peace Corps sent recent college graduates to live and work in the developing world. In the process, volunteers provided concrete and tangible benefits for their host country and, at the same time, served as ambassadors for the American way of life.

Kennedy did not promote the policy until the final weeks of the 1960 presidential campaign, telling an audience of college students at the University of Michigan about the importance of public service abroad. Once president, Kennedy signed an executive order on March 1, 1961, creating the Peace Corps. Later Congress voted its approval of the new federal agency to be housed within the State Department. He had his brother-in-law, Sargent Shriver, direct the program. Indeed, it was Shriver, more than Kennedy, who was responsible for building congressional support for the Peace Corps. Since its inception, the Peace Corps has sent thousands of Americans to scores of countries and the goodwill the program has produced has helped the United States to build cooperative relationships with developing countries.

President Kennedy greets Peace Corps volunteers, 1962. *(© Bettmann/CORBIS)*

While the Peace Corps's concrete achievements in the developing world were uneven, the program enhanced America's image abroad and changed the lives of tens of thousands of the volunteers, many of whom returned to the United States recommitted to achieving reform and social justice at home.

Pop Art Movement   The pop art movement of the 1960s constituted a reaction against European modes of artistic expression. Pop art pioneers such as Roy Lichtenstein used well-known commercial images and cartoons in their art to both mock high art and critique mass culture. The movement's most famous figure, Andy Warhol, was trained as a commercial artist and worked as an illustrator at *Vogue* and *Harper's Bazaar*. Warhol is best known for his paintings of mass-produced products such as Coke bottles and Campbell soup cans.

Pop artists critiqued the mass affluence of the 1950s. Splashy, colorful, and often provocative, the pop art movement gained wide attention and reflected distinctive American sensibilities. It was democratic and it rejected the hierarchical continuum that separated "low" and "high" art. In this way, pop artists were trying to destroy the boundaries that separated mass media from art. They were successful in a variety of ways. For example, music album covers became a primary venue for pop artists to both express themselves and popularize their work. While this movement was confined to Great Britain and the United States, it foreshadowed many of the vast cultural changes that occurred throughout the West in the 1960s. Although critics assailed the movement for being corrupted by commercialism, it was hugely popular and shaped the "look" of the decade.

President's Commission on the Status of Women   In 1961, Kennedy appointed the President's Commission on the Status of Women (PCSW). In so doing, he at least implicitly recognized that the problem of discrimination based on gender existed. The more common forms of discrimination in the United States included laws and customs preventing women from serving on juries, permitting husbands control of their wives' property and income, barring women from certain professions, denying women the right to own property, ensuring women were paid lower wages, and limiting female opportunities for advancement in the business world. Not all feminists endorsed the PCSW, and some even viewed it as a mechanism to prevent the adoption of the Equal Rights Amendment, a constitutional amendment that had divided feminists since the 1920s. Chaired by former first lady Eleanor Roosevelt until her death in 1962, the PCSW reflected the Kennedy administration's dedication to women's's issues. Indeed, the president appointed several cabinet members to the committee, including Attorney General Robert Ken-

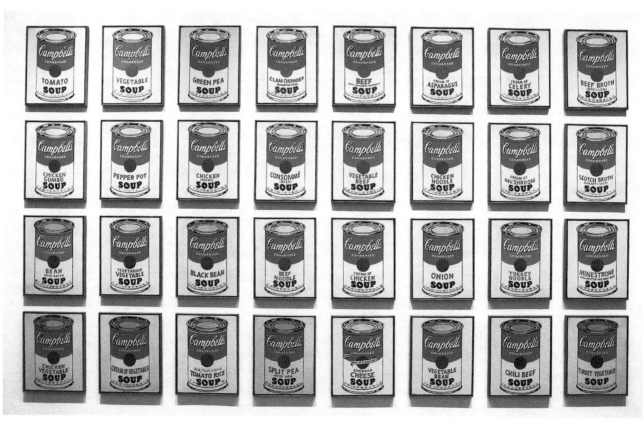

Campbell's Soup Cans by Andy Warhol, at the Museum of Modern Art in New York City, 1962 *(© Nik Barak/Alamy)*

nedy, his brother. In the commission's final report, members severely criticized the social and legal status of American women and recommended eliminating the social mores that made being female a handicap for gaining social, economic, and political equality; protecting the right of women to work for pay; eliminating wage inequities between men and women; ensuring that women could pursue continuing education; guaranteeing gender neutral employment policies; providing paid maternity leaves and equal benefits for widows; and eliminating legal discrimination against women found to be in violation of the Fifth and Fourteenth Amendments of the Constitution. Notably, the commission did not endorse the Equal Rights Amendment. It did encourage the institutional growth of feminism in the 1960s, with the establishment of state-level commissions on the status of women. Furthermore, several key PCSW figures took a leading role in founding the National Organization of Women in 1966.

Rules Committee Fight (1961) Without an electoral mandate from the voters in 1960 or the respect of congressional leaders, President Kennedy's legislative agenda was endangered from the start. Indeed, Kennedy had to fight for every legislative victory despite the Democrats commanding congressional majorities. Rather than enjoying the traditional "honeymoon" with Congress, Kennedy's relations with southern Democrats and conservatives were strained from the beginning. Ever since the 1938 midterm election, a coalition of conservative Republicans and southern Democrats had stymied much liberal legislation. This coalition benefited from the fact that many of its members held important committee chairs as a result of the seniority system. Southerners were less likely to vote out an incumbent, especially one who represented their values and brought home sufficient federal projects, than were voters in the rest of the country. The absence of a viable Republican Party in that region made it even less likely that there would be meaningful turnover of officeholders.

The House Rules Committee was perhaps the most significant tool of obstruction available to the conservative coalition. Members of that committee determined what legislation would go to the House floor and what rules would be applied to the debate about that legislation. If the Rules Committee membership disliked a particular bill it could prevent the full House from considering it even though the jurisdictional committee (i.e., the House Committee on Education and Labor) had voted in favor of the measure and even though a majority of the full House would likely support the bill.

The 1960 election produced Democratic majorities but the same conservative coalition that had blocked reform initiatives from FRANKLIN D. ROOSEVELT and HARRY S. TRUMAN also promised to undermine Kennedy's NEW FRONTIER. Compounding the president's dilemma was the failing health of Speaker of the House Sam Rayburn (who died in late 1961). Without an effective ally and leader in the Senate, such as former Senate majority leader LYNDON JOHNSON who was now vice president, Kennedy feared that his agenda was likely to founder on the shoals of the conservative coalition. To prevent that outcome, Rayburn led a fight in the last year of his life to expand the number of members who sat on the powerful House Rules Committee. With a 12-member committee comprised of eight Democrats and four Republicans, chairman Howard Worth Smith, an arch-conservative Democrat from Virginia, needed only one other southern Democrat to side with him and the Republicans to stymie any piece of legislation.

In choosing to fight to expand the Rules Committee by three members, Rayburn and Kennedy were taking a chance. The White House threatened to turn many House members against the administration because it was violating a long-held principle of congressional autonomy. Though Rayburn and the administration narrowly won the fight and expanded the Rules Committee, by a vote of 217–212, the contentiousness of the fight and the razor-thin margin of victory revealed the difficulty the president would have in passing his agenda.

***Silent Spring*, by Rachel Carson (1962)** A marine biologist by trade, Rachel Carson revealed to the mass reading public that insecticides and other pollutants threatened both natural and human environments. Carson's publication of *Silent Spring* in 1962 constituted a significant literary event and it is credited with helping to launch the modern environmental movement.

Carson is notable because she helped popularize ecology, which held that all creatures are part of a complex web of life. Indeed, even Carson's early works celebrated the interconnectedness of nature. Prior to 1962, Carson was a well-regarded writer whose 1952 book *The Sea Around Us* garnered the National Book Award and remained on the *New York Times* bestseller list for 86 weeks.

After spending years writing about ocean ecology, Carson became aware of the harmful side effects of the pesticide DDT. Developed during the early years of World War II, DDT was used to destroy the malaria-causing mosquito in the South Pacific. In 1945, DDT was approved for civilian use and it was sprayed indiscriminately throughout the United States. Unlike other pesticides, DDT did not merely kill one type of pest—it destroyed hundreds of insects and animals at once.

In response to the government's wanton use of DDT, Carson began writing a book detailing the dangers of DDT and other pesticides. In *Silent Spring*, she described how DDT entered the food chain and could (in sufficient amounts) cause cancer and genetic damage to humans. Using her literary credentials, Carson convinced Simon and Schuster to publish *Silent Spring* despite the threat of lawsuits by chemical companies. When Kennedy's Science Advisory Commit-

Marine biologist and nature writer Rachel Carson at her home in 1962. Her book *Silent Spring* changed many people's attitudes toward DDT and helped launch the modern environmental movement. *(Time & Life Pictures/Getty Images)*

tee vindicated *Silent Spring,* the warnings contained in the book of the potential environmental pitfalls stemming from technological advances received mainstream acceptance.

Space Program   Unlike his predecessor DWIGHT D. EISENHOWER, President Kennedy was unambiguously committed to an ambitious space program. The president, like most Americans, had rarely shown much interest in space prior to the Soviets' successful launch of *Sputnik* in 1957. Once Kennedy became convinced of the space program's utility in winning the cold war, he placed the prestige of his presidency behind the program. Less than four months after he became president, NASA sent the first American astronaut into space.

Realizing that many opposed the space program due to its cost, Kennedy tied the program to victory in the cold war and publicly proclaimed that the country would send a man to the moon before 1970. President Kennedy and his successors successfully built public support for the Apollo program, which proceeded to carry out a manned lunar landing in 1969.

Steel Crisis (1962)   In early 1962, President Kennedy was struggling to formulate an economic policy that was friendly to both corporate interests and traditional Democratic constituencies such as organized labor. Occurring from April 10 to 12, the steel crisis reemphasized the difficulty the president faced in cultivating a working relationship with big business while remaining faithful to a traditional Democratic agenda.

Kennedy was most concerned with jump-starting the nation's economy while restraining inflation. The president's advisers told him that rising steel prices had caused 40 percent of price hikes in the 1950s. To prevent inflation, Kennedy strongly urged the steelworkers union, the United Steel Workers of America, to seek responsible wage increases so that the steel companies would not be forced to raise prices, an act which would ripple through the economy. Kennedy's secretary of labor, Arthur Goldberg, helped negotiate a small wage increase to stop this cycle of wage and price increases, which undermined stable economic growth, and prevent a strike. Kennedy convinced steel workers to negotiate a noninflationary agreement with steel executives. Despite this agreement, on April 10, 1962, Roger Blough, the chairman of US Steel, informed Kennedy that steel companies intended to raise prices by 3.5 percent. This made the administration look like it had been duped and it also made US Steel look greedy.

In reaction, the administration unleashed a public relations and legal campaign designed to reverse the steel price hike. In short order, the Defense Department purchased steel only from companies that had not raised prices, and the attorney general began investigating steel executives for evidence of price collusion. With public sentiment on the president's side and the pressure mounting, the steel companies reversed the price hikes by April 12. Despite his balanced budget and tax cut policies, Kennedy's relations with big business remained cool for the remainder of his presidency.

Strategic Hamlet Program   In the spring and early summer of 1961, South Vietnam president Ngo Dinh Diem introduced the Strategic Hamlet Program, which was designed to limit communist subversion by North Vietnam and control the rural population. Similar to an earlier scheme, Diem's strategy was designed to separate the peasants from the communist National Liberation Front, North Vietnam's fighting force known as the Vietcong. The plan called for existing rural communities to live within fortifications that would be secured by South Vietnam's army until the local populace was trained for self-defense against communist infiltration.

Reasoning that land reform and security from "communist terror" would win the rural populace over to the side of the government, Diem planned to place all 16,000 of the country's hamlets into this program. According to the plan, once the populace supported the government and the communists had no place to hide, the Vietcong would be forced to fight in the open against the superior firepower of the South. Even though Diem designed and began implementing the plan without consulting the Kennedy administration, Secretary of Defense Robert McNamara and other key officials quickly embraced the policy. With American aid flowing in, the Diem government moved more than 4.3 million peasants into 3,225 hamlets by September 1962 and by July 1963, more than 8.5 million people had been settled into 7,205 hamlets.

As with most other plans aimed at countering the Vietcong, this scheme quickly antagonized rural peasants and it served as a propaganda boon for the communists. Indeed, Vietnamese peasants were loyal to their home territories and believed that to abandon their lands was tantamount to spiting their ancestors. Even though Diem claimed that fewer than 5 percent of all peasants would be forced to vacate their land this was not the case. Moreover, once the peasants were made to leave (oftentimes at gunpoint) they were rarely compensated. Nor were they supplied with building materials for their new hamlets. Unfortunately, South Vietnamese officials embezzled tens of thousands of dollars in foreign aid that was intended to offset the costs of constructing the strategic hamlets. Due to these massive failures, the strategic hamlet program collapsed in late 1963 after the assassination of Diem.

Tax Cut Proposals   With an eye cast toward his 1964 reelection campaign, President Kennedy proposed wide-ranging tax cuts to jump-start economic growth and lower unemployment. In 1962, the president was concerned with unemployment because it had spiked to nearly 6 percent and the stock market had tumbled in the summer of the same year. Convinced that the tax system constituted a drain on the economy and that deficit spending would lead to economic growth and lower deficits, the president proposed a 40 percent reduction in corporate tax rates and the overhaul of the tax system.

To gain congressional support for tax cuts, Kennedy worked to alter the conventional wisdom that governed fiscal policy. In particular, most members of Congress and the business community remained resolutely opposed to deficit spending of any sort. To undermine the prevalent myth that balanced budgets were always best, Kennedy and members of his administration embarked on a series of luncheons, dinners, and meetings with business leaders to persuade them of the efficacy of tax cuts and deficit spending.

Despite the opposition of many leading liberals in Congress to budget deficits, the House passed the tax cut bill in September 1963 and it was slated to clear the Senate in early 1964. As with so much of Kennedy's agenda, it was President Johnson who passed the 1964 Revenue Act. The legislation had a significant effect on the nation's economy. By 1965, the unemployment rate dropped to 4.1 percent and the rate of economic growth rose more than 6 percent.

Trade Expansion Act (1962)   The Kennedy administration's 1962 Trade Expansion Act marked one of the president's few significant legislative victories and it reflected Kennedy's concern with balance of payments and trade deficits. Since the United States maintained a substantial trade deficit with its European allies, Kennedy feared that if America's trading partners exercised their right to convert dollars into gold the American economy would be destabilized.

Kennedy's concern with the balance of payments issue highlighted an ironic choice for the administration. On the one hand, the president's efforts to spur economic growth would inevitably raise the nation's trade deficit with Europe. On the other hand, most policies designed to depress trade deficits would also undermine economic growth. Faced with this dilemma, Kennedy opted for economic growth and promotion of expanded exports to Europe. Thus, the 1962 Trade Expansion Act was designed to counter the balance of payments deficit and promote domestic economic growth.

The legislation gave Kennedy the power to slash tariffs by 50 percent, eradicate some tariffs altogether, and negotiate the elimination of "unreasonable" trade policies. In the short term, American exports to Europe increased and the balance of payments deficit was cut. In the long term, America's trade deficit with Europe continued to grow despite Kennedy's initiative.

University of Mississippi Integration Crisis (1962)

In the early days of the Kennedy administration, officials hoped that the legislative process and voter registration would preempt the direct action that civil rights activists were demanding. The attempted integration of the University of Mississippi in the fall of 1962, however, dashed these hopes.

Ironically, it was Kennedy's inaugural address that served to inspire James Meredith, an African American, to enroll at the all-white university in Oxford, Mississippi. He applied for transfer admission on January 31, 1961. He was already a student at the all-black Jackson State University. On February 4, Meredith's application was denied. After Meredith enlisted the support of the National Association for the Advancement of Colored People, the federal courts ordered the university to admit Meredith in 1962, which made Attorney General Robert Kennedy, the president's brother, and the Justice Department responsible for implementing the judiciary's decision.

The attorney general's initial dealings with Mississippi governor Ross Barnett had led him to believe that implementation of integration of the university would be a relatively calm and peaceful affair. Kennedy was misinformed. Barnett observed that before he permitted the admission of "that boy" to Ole Miss, as the university was known, the governor would go to jail for violating the court order. Barnett was an odd admixture, combining traits of the genteel southern planter with those of the bombastic southern populist.

After the governor reneged on several accords, the Kennedy administration found itself in a difficult position. It could not arrest Barnett because doing so would only boost Barnett's popularity with white Mississippians. Nor could the administration allow Barnett to get his way. Above all, the administration wanted to avoid a situation such as the one that unfolded in Little Rock, Arkansas, in 1957 when President DWIGHT D. EISENHOWER sent federal troops to protect black students seeking to attend a white high school. As a result, the Kennedys worked as much as possible behind the scenes and with the courts to gain admission for Meredith.

Accompanied by U.S. marshals, James Meredith walks to class at the University of Mississippi on October 1, 1962. *(Library of Congress)*

The Kennedys also used the media when appropriate, and they calmly carried on negotiations with Barnett.

Ultimately, the incident had international implications. American policymakers learned they could not effectively fight the cold war when such blatantly racist actions received massive publicity worldwide. The murder of a foreign reporter by the white mob protesting Meredith drew international criticism. Moreover, the episode harmed efforts to negotiate with unaligned African nations. This diplomacy was rooted in the cold war competition with the Soviet Union. One African diplomat remarked, "We are waiting to see what President Kennedy will do in Mississippi. . . . Action by the President will be welcomed by Africans. It will strongly demonstrate whether his use of the words 'free world' is merely a propaganda phrase." Moreover, the Soviet newspaper *Pravda* ran a headline, "Washington Surrenders to Racist Onslaughts," when it appeared Barnett and Mississippi would get their way.

On September 10, the Supreme Court ordered Ole Miss to admit Meredith, but Barnett still refused. On September 30, riots broke out on the campus, and President Kennedy sent 500 federal marshals to ensure that Meredith could enroll. With Barnett and the state police encouraging massive resistance to integration, thousands of whites stormed the campus and threatened both Meredith and the federal marshals. Because of the threat to the federal marshals, the president was forced to send troops into Oxford to restore order. Integration of the University of Mississippi proceeded, and Meredith attended his first class on October 1.

Because the president had managed the crisis with relative aplomb and had appeased both moderate southerners, who opposed the firebrand tactics of the segregationists and African Americans, the episode marked a watershed in Kennedy's approach to civil rights. With a new and more profound understanding of southern racism, Kennedy's civil rights stance changed markedly in that he became more sympathetic to demands for civil rights legislation.

Vienna Summit (1961)   On June 4 and 5, 1961, President Kennedy and Soviet premier Nikita Khrushchev met at a summit conference in Vienna, Austria. It was the first time the two leaders met. Occurring just after the BAY OF PIGS fiasco in Cuba in April and with U.S.-Soviet tensions simmering, Kennedy arrived at the summit politically weak. Kennedy, aged 44, and Khrushchev, 67, confronted a plethora of issues from Laos to Berlin over which the two superpowers differed profoundly. Realizing that the Soviet economy was lagging hopelessly behind that of the United States and that America retained decisive strategic advantages, Khrushchev tried to bully the young president—a tactic that effectively torpedoed the summit and further heightened cold war tensions.

Whether it was a formal conversation or an informal stroll, Khrushchev remained combative throughout the summit. When the president admitted to making a "miscalculation in Cuba," Khrushchev seized upon this and berated his foe for continually siding against revolutions of national liberation. Aside from Cuba, the status of Berlin dominated Khrushchev's attention. Since the end of World War II Germany and the city of Berlin had each been partitioned into four occupation areas: British, French, American, and Soviet. The British, French, and U.S. zones had merged to form West Germany and the city of West Berlin, while the Soviet zone formed East Germany and East Berlin The success of the Berlin airlift in 1948–49 kept the city divided between the eastern and western zones. For more than a decade thousands of East Germans fled to West Berlin. Because the number of refugees kept growing the East German government faced severe economic disruption. Promising to sign a separate treaty with East Germany, Khrushchev threatened the West's access to Berlin, which posed a risk to the peace in Europe.

Despite Kennedy's pleadings that a separate peace with East Germany would increase the likelihood of war, Khrushchev refused to yield any ground. At the final meeting of the two-day summit, the premier claimed that the United States was trying to humiliate the Soviets by maintaining rather than resolving the situation in Berlin. After the premier angrily told the president: "The decision to sign a peace treaty is firm and irrevocable," Kennedy responded: "Then, Mr. Chairman, there will be a war. It will be a cold winter." In August the Soviets and East Germans began building the Berlin wall, a physical barrier to prevent East Germans from fleeing to West Berlin. Kennedy considered the summit at Vienna a failure and his memory of Khrushchev's tempestuous nature shaped their encounter during the CUBAN MISSILE CRISIS the following year.

Vietnam War   Lasting from 1946 through April 30, 1975, the Vietnam War pitted the communist forces of North Vietnam (the Democratic Republic of Vietnam) and the Vietcong (the National Front for the Liberation of South Vietnam) against the anticommunist Republic of Vietnam (South Vietnam) and its Southeast Asia Treaty Organization (SEATO) allies. While Australia, New Zealand, South Korea, and Thailand contributed a small number of forces to SEATO, the United States ultimately supplied hundreds of thousands of troops. Both Presidents HARRY S. TRUMAN and DWIGHT D. EISENHOWER had made decisions that increased the U.S. commitment to South Vietnam, Truman by funding the unsuccessful French quest to retain its empire in Indochina in the early 1950s and Eisenhower by blocking the 1956 elections to unify North and South Vietnam.

In contrast to President LYNDON JOHNSON who would escalate the American involvement and commitment to fighting communism in Southeast Asia in the mid-1960s, the Kennedy administration's Vietnam policy was more ambiguous and noncommittal. From the start, Kennedy never believed that Southeast Asia constituted a significant front in the cold war and, as a consequence, his Vietnam policy was shaped by other events. Nonetheless, because Kennedy was confronted with the BAY OF PIGS, the LAOTIAN CRISIS, and the construction of the Berlin wall in his first 10 months in office, he felt he had to "stand tough" in Vietnam. In addition, the president was influenced by the political tumult that had enveloped the Truman administration when opponents accused it of having "lost" China to the communists.

Fearing that his refusal to staunchly back the anticommunist South Vietnamese government would signal American weakness to Moscow, Kennedy opted to support Ngo Dinh Diem's government, as had Eisenhower. Prior to late 1963, the administration financed a 250,000-man South Vietnamese army and committed military advisers and helicopters. Furthermore, Kennedy escalated the American presence in Vietnam. When he became president in 1961 approximately 650 American military personnel were stationed in the country, and by the time of his assassination in November 1963 that number had risen to 16,700.

It was not until the summer of 1963, however, that the president spent much appreciable time on Vietnam. Prior to 1963, the president's primary goal was to avoid a politically embarrassing defeat in Southeast Asia so he conspicuously avoided any calls for a negotiated settlement. By the summer of 1963, it was clear to Kennedy that Diem and his government were a lost cause and that the administration's policy in Vietnam had failed. In August, Kennedy and his staff began rethinking the administration's policy and considered options ranging from backing a coup against Diem to withdrawal of American troops. In November 1963, the administration signaled to Diem opponents that a coup would not lead to the cessation of U.S. military aid, and Diem was deposed and murdered.

The coup sparked much debate within the administration over its policy in Vietnam. The president was assassinated, however, before he could make a decision. Scholars have long debated whether Kennedy's policy would have differed from that of his successor, Lyndon Johnson. Ultimately, these debates engage hypothetical questions that can never be fully answered. The facts are that Johnson committed 500,000 combat troops, and he did so in consultation with the foreign policy team that Kennedy had assembled. Furthermore, the Kennedy administration never had a long-term contingency plan for Vietnam. Finally, Kennedy's decision to support the coup against Diem further tied the United States to the fate of South Vietnam, and doing so helped create conditions that led to Johnson's escalation of the war in 1965.

Vocational Education Act (1963) The 1963 Vocational Education Act funded the construction of vocational education facilities, provided part-time work for unemployed youths, changed the conception of what constituted "education for work," and created a presidential advisory committee on vocational education. While federal support of vocational education dated back to the 1862 Morrill Act, both the GI Bill of Rights of 1944 and the Vocational Education Act of 1963 reaffirmed the government's commitment.

In the 1960 presidential campaign, Kennedy had promised a thoroughgoing program of federal aid to state and local schools, but, like so much of his domestic program, the vocational education bill remained mired in Congress during his presidency. Indeed, the legislation was passed posthumously in December 1963. Unlike Kennedy, President Johnson, who signed the new law, had an expansive vision for his domestic agenda and believed that EDUCATION LEGISLATION would be the linchpin for his "War on Poverty."

Jeffrey H. Bloodworth

Further Reading
Bass, Warren. *Support Any Friend: Kennedy's Middle East and the Making of the U.S.-Israel Alliance.* New York: Oxford University Press, 2003.

Benson, Thomas W. *Writing JFK: Presidential Rhetoric and the Press in the Bay of Pigs Crisis.* College Station: Texas A&M University Press, 2004.

Bernstein, Irving. *Promises Kept: John F. Kennedy's New Frontier.* New York: Oxford University Press, 1991.

Beschloss, Michael R. *The Crisis Years: Kennedy and Khrushchev, 1960–1963.* New York: Edward Burlingame Books, 1991.

Brauer, Carl M. *John F. Kennedy and the Second Reconstruction.* New York: Columbia University Press, 1977.

Brinkley, Douglas, and Richard T. Griffiths, eds. *John F. Kennedy and Europe.* Baton Rouge: Louisiana State University Press, 1999.

Bryant, Nick. *The Bystander: John F. Kennedy and the Struggle for Black Equality.* New York: Basic Books, 2006.

Burner, David. *John F. Kennedy and a New Generation.* 2d ed. New York: Pearson/Longman, 2005.

Carty, Thomas J. *A Catholic in the White House? Religion, Politics, and John F. Kennedy's Presidential Campaign.* New York: Palgrave Macmillan, 2004.

Dallek, Robert. *An Unfinished Life: John F. Kennedy, 1917–1963.* Boston: Little, Brown, 2003.

Freedman, Lawrence. *Kennedy's Wars: Berlin, Cuba, Laos, and Vietnam.* New York: Oxford University Press, 2002.

Gifford, Laura Jane. *The Center Cannot Hold: The 1960 Presidential Election and the Rise of Modern Conservatism.* DeKalb: Northern Illinois University Press, 2009.

Giglio, James N. *The Presidency of John F. Kennedy.* 2d ed. Lawrence: University Press of Kansas, 2006.

Gould, Lewis L., ed. *The Documentary History of the John F. Kennedy Presidency.* 18 vols. Bethesda, Md.: LexisNexis, 2005– .

Hellmann, John. *The Kennedy Obsession: The American Myth of JFK.* New York: Columbia University Press, 1997.

Hersh, Seymour M. *The Dark Side of Camelot*. Boston: Little, Brown, 1997.

Kaiser, David. *American Tragedy: Kennedy, Johnson, and the Origins of the Vietnam War*. Cambridge, Mass.: Belknap Press of Harvard University Press, 2000.

Kennedy, John F. *The Burden and the Glory*. Edited by Allan Nevins. New York, Harper and Row, 1964.

———. *JFK Wants to Know: Memos from the President's Office, 1961–1963*. Edited by Edward B. Claflin. New York: Morrow, 1991.

———. *Kennedy and the Press; The News Conferences*. Edited by Harold W. Chase and Allen H. Lerman. New York: Crowell, 1965.

———. *Prelude to Leadership: The European Diary of John F. Kennedy, Summer 1945*. Washington, D.C.: Regnery, 1995.

———. *Profiles in Courage*. New York: Harper, 1956.

———. *Why England Slept*. New York: W. Funk, 1940.

Leaming, Barbara. *Jack Kennedy: The Education of a Statesman*. New York: W.W. Norton, 2006.

Lubin, David M. *Shooting Kennedy: JFK and the Culture of Images*. Berkeley: University of California Press, 2003.

Manchester, William. *The Death of a President, November 20–November 25, 1963*. New York: Harper and Row, 1967.

Matthews, Christopher. *Kennedy & Nixon: The Rivalry That Shaped Postwar America*. New York: Simon and Schuster, 1997.

May, Ernest R., and Philip D. Zelikow. *The Kennedy Tapes: Inside the White House during the Cuban Missile Crisis*. Cambridge, Mass.: Belknap Press of Harvard University Press, 1997.

Mayer, Frank A. *Adenauer and Kennedy: A Study in German-American Relations, 1961–1963*. New York: St. Martin's Press, 1996.

Naftali, Timothy J., ed. *The Presidential Recordings: John F. Kennedy, July 30–August 1962*. New York: Norton, 2001.

———. *The Presidential Recordings: John F. Kennedy, September–October 21, 1962*. New York: Norton, 2001.

Naftali, Timothy J., Philip Zelikow, and Ernest R. May, eds. *John F. Kennedy: The Great Crises*. New York: Norton, 2001.

Perret, Geoffrey. *Jack: A Life Like No Other*. New York: Random House, 2001.

Perry, Barbara A. *Jacqueline Kennedy: First Lady of the New Frontier*. Lawrence: University Press of Kansas, 2004.

Porter, Gareth. *Perils of Dominance: Imbalance of Power and the Road to War in Vietnam*. Berkeley: University of California Press, 2005.

Prados, John, ed. *The White House Tapes: Eavesdropping on the President*. New York: New Press, 2003.

Public Papers of the Presidents of the United States, John F. Kennedy, Containing the Public Messages, Speeches, and Statements of the President, 1961–1963. 3 vols. Washington, D.C.: U.S. Government Printing Office, 1962–1964.

Rabe, Stephen G. *The Most Dangerous Area in the World: John F. Kennedy Confronts Communist Revolution in Latin America*. Chapel Hill: University of North Carolina Press, 1999.

Reeves, Richard. *President Kennedy: Profile of Power*. New York: Simon and Schuster, 1993.

———. *A Question of Character: A Life of John F. Kennedy*. New York: Free Press, 1991.

Rorabaugh, W. J. *Kennedy and the Promise of the Sixties*. New York: Cambridge University Press, 2002.

———. *The Real Making of the President: Kennedy, Nixon, and the 1960 Election*. Lawrence: University Press of Kansas, 2009.

Rosenberg, Jonathan, and Zachary Karabell. *Kennedy, Johnson, and the Quest for Justice: The Civil Rights Tapes*. New York: W.W. Norton, 2003.

Savage, Sean J. *JFK, LBJ, and the Democratic Party*. Albany: State University of New York Press, 2004.

Schlesinger, Arthur M., Jr. *A Thousand Days: John F. Kennedy in the White House*. Boston: Houghton Mifflin, 1965.

Sorensen, Theodore C. *Kennedy*. New York: Harper and Row, 1965.

Stern, Mark. *Calculating Visions: Kennedy, Johnson, and Civil Rights*. New Brunswick, N.J.: Rutgers University Press, 1992.

Stern, Sheldon M. *The Week the World Stood Still: Inside the Secret Cuban Missile Crisis*. Palo Alto, Calif.: Stanford University Press, 2005.

Talbot, David. *Brothers: The Hidden History of the Kennedy Years*. New York: Free Press, 2007.

Weisbrot, Robert. *Maximum Danger: Kennedy, the Missiles, and the Crisis of American Confidence*. Chicago: Ivan R. Dee, 2001.

White, Theodore H. *The Making of the President, 1960*. New York: Pocket Books, 1961.

Wicker, Tom. *JFK and LBJ: The Influence of Personality upon Politics*. Chicago: Ivan R. Dee, 1991.

DOCUMENTS

—⁓—

Document One: President John F. Kennedy, Inaugural Address, January 20, 1961

President Kennedy delivered an inaugural address on January 20, 1961, that inspired the baby boom generation. The president spoke of the importance of public service, while also articulating a hawkish agenda for U.S. foreign policy.

Vice President Johnson, Mr. Speaker, Mr. Chief Justice, President Eisenhower, Vice president Nixon, President Truman, Reverend Clergy, fellow citizens:

We observe today not a victory of party but a celebration of freedom—symbolizing an end as well as a beginning—signifying renewal as well as change. For I have sworn before you and Almighty God the same solemn oath our forebears prescribed nearly a century and three quarters ago.

The world is very different now. For man holds in his mortal hands the power to abolish all forms of human poverty and all forms of human life. And yet the same revolutionary beliefs for which our forebears fought are still at issue around the globe—the belief that the rights of man come not from the generosity of the state but from the hand of God.

We dare not forget today that we are the heirs of that first revolution. Let the word go forth from this time and place, to friend and foe alike, that the torch has been passed to a new generation of Americans—born in this century, tempered by war, disciplined by a hard and bitter peace, proud of our ancient heritage—and unwilling to witness or permit the slow undoing of those human rights to which this nation has always been committed, and to which we are committed today at home and around the world.

Let every nation know, whether it wishes us well or ill, that we shall pay any price, bear any burden, meet any hardship, support any friend, oppose any foe to assure the survival and the success of liberty.

This much we pledge—and more.

To those old allies whose cultural and spiritual origins we share, we pledge the loyalty of faithful friends. United, there is little we cannot do in a host of cooperative ventures. Divided, there is little we can do—for we dare not meet a powerful challenge at odds and split asunder.

To those new states whom we welcome to the ranks of the free, we pledge our word that one form of colonial control shall not have passed away merely to be replaced by a far more iron tyranny. We shall not always expect to find them supporting our view. But we shall always hope to find them strongly supporting their own freedom—and to remember that, in the past, those who foolishly sought power by riding the back of the tiger ended up inside.

To those peoples in the huts and villages of half the globe struggling to break the bonds of mass misery, we pledge our best efforts to help them help themselves, for whatever period is required—not because the communists may be doing it, not because we seek their votes, but because it is right. If a free society cannot help the many who are poor, it cannot save the few who are rich.

To our sister republics south of our border, we offer a special pledge—to convert our good words into good deeds—in a new alliance for progress—to assist free men and free governments in casting off the chains of poverty. But this peaceful revolution of hope cannot become the prey of hostile powers. Let all our neighbors know that we shall join with them to oppose aggression or subversion anywhere in the Americas. And let every other power know that this Hemisphere intends to remain the master of its own house.

To that world assembly of sovereign states, the United Nations, our last best hope in an age where the instruments of war have far outpaced the instruments of peace, we renew our pledge of support—to prevent it from becoming merely a forum for invective—to strengthen its shield of the new and the weak—and to enlarge the area in which its writ may run.

Finally, to those nations who would make themselves our adversary, we offer not a pledge but a request: that both sides begin anew the quest for peace, before the dark powers of destruction unleashed by science engulf all humanity in planned or accidental self-destruction.

We dare not tempt them with weakness. For only when our arms are sufficient beyond doubt can we be certain beyond doubt that they will never be employed.

But neither can two great and powerful groups of nations take comfort from our present course—both sides overburdened by the cost of modern weapons, both rightly alarmed by the steady spread of the deadly atom, yet both racing to alter that uncertain balance of terror that stays the hand of mankind's final war.

So let us begin anew—remembering on both sides that civility is not a sign of weakness, and sincerity is always subject to proof. Let us never negotiate out of fear. But let us never fear to negotiate.

Let both sides explore what problems unite us instead of belaboring those problems which divide us.

Let both sides, for the first time, formulate serious and precise proposals for the inspection and control of arms—and bring the absolute power to destroy other nations under the absolute control of all nations.

Let both sides seek to invoke the wonders of science instead of its terrors. Together let us explore the stars, conquer the deserts, eradicate disease, tap the ocean depths and encourage the arts and commerce.

Let both sides unite to heed in all corners of the earth the command of Isaiah—to "undo the heavy burdens . . . (and) let the oppressed go free."

And if a beach-head of cooperation may push back the jungle of suspicion, let both sides join in creating a new endeavor, not a new balance of power, but a new world of law, where the strong are just and the weak secure and the peace preserved.

All this will not be finished in the first one hundred days. Nor will it be finished in the first one thousand days, nor in the life of this Administration, nor even perhaps in our lifetime on this planet. But let us begin.

In your hands, my fellow citizens, more than mine, will rest the final success or failure of our course. Since this country was founded, each generation of Americans has been summoned to give testimony to its national loyalty. The graves of young Americans who answered the call to service surround the globe.

Now the trumpet summons us again-not as a call to bear arms, though arms we need—not as a call to battle, though embattled we are—but a call to bear the burden of a long twilight struggle, year in and year out, "rejoicing in hope, patient in tribulation"—a struggle against the common enemies of man: tyranny, poverty, disease and war itself.

Can we forge against these enemies a grand and global alliance, North and South, East and West, that can assure a more fruitful life for all mankind? Will you join in that historic effort?

In the long history of the world, only a few generations have been granted the role of defending freedom in its hour of maximum danger. I do not shrink from this responsibility—I welcome it. I do not believe that any of us would exchange places with any other people or any other generation. The energy, the faith, the devotion which we bring to this endeavor will light our country and all who serve it—and the glow from that fire can truly light the world.

And so, my fellow Americans: ask not what your country can do for you—ask what you can do for your country.

My fellow citizens of the world: ask not what America will do for you, but what together we can do for the freedom of man.

Finally, whether you are citizens of America or citizens of the world, ask of us here the same high standards of strength and sacrifice which we ask of you. With a good conscience our only sure reward, with history the final judge of our deeds, let us go forth to lead the land we love, asking His blessing and His help, but knowing that here on earth God's work must truly be our own.

⟨⟩

Source: Public Papers of the Presidents of the United States, John F. Kennedy, Containing the Public Messages, Speeches, and Statements of the President, 1961 (Washington, D.C.: U.S. Government Printing Office, 1962), 1–3.

Document Two: President Kennedy, Statement Concerning Interference with the Freedom Riders in Alabama, May 20, 1961

In response to the violent attacks against the Freedom Riders, who were taking interstate bus routes through the Deep South to force the federal government to enforce integration of interstate bus transportation, President Kennedy issued a brief statement calling for an end to the violence on May 20, 1961.

THE SITUATION which has developed in Alabama is a source of the deepest concern to me as it must be to the vast majority of the citizens of Alabama and other Americans. I have instructed the Justice Department to take all necessary steps based on their investigations and information. I call upon the Governor and other responsible State officials in Alabama as well as the Mayors of Birmingham and Montgomery to exercise their lawful authority to prevent any further outbreaks of violence. I would also hope that any persons, whether a citizen of Alabama or a visitor there, would refrain from any action which would in any way tend to provoke further outbreaks. I hope that state and local officials in Alabama will meet their responsibilities. The United States Government intends to meet its.

⟨⟩

Source: Public Papers of the Presidents of the United States, John F. Kennedy, Containing the Public Messages, Speeches, and Statements of the President, 1961 (Washington, D.C.: U.S. Government Printing Office, 1962), 391.

Document Three: President Kennedy, Radio and Television Report to the American People on the Soviet Arms Buildup in Cuba, October 22, 1962

During the Cuban missile crisis President Kennedy went on national television to address the American people. On October 22, 1962, he informed the nation just how serious conditions were as the nation stood on the brink of a nuclear war with the Soviet Union.

Good evening, my fellow citizens:

This Government, as promised, has maintained the closest surveillance of the Soviet military buildup on the island of Cuba. Within the past week, unmistakable evidence has established the fact that a series of offensive missile sites is now in preparation on that imprisoned island. The purpose of these bases can be none other than to provide a nuclear strike capability against the Western Hemisphere.

Upon receiving the first preliminary hard information of this nature last Tuesday morning at 9 a.m., I directed that our surveillance be stepped up. And having now confirmed and completed our evaluation of the evidence and our decision on a course of action, this Government feels obliged to report this new crisis to you in fullest detail. . . .

This urgent transformation of Cuba into an important strategic base—by the presence of these large, long-range, and clearly offensive weapons of sudden mass destruction—constitutes an explicit threat to the peace and security of all the Americas. . . . This action also contradicts the repeated assurances of Soviet spokesmen, both publicly and privately delivered, that the arms buildup in Cuba would retain its original defensive character, and that the Soviet Union had no need or desire to station strategic missiles on the territory of any other nation. . . .

Neither the United States of America nor the world community of nations can tolerate deliberate deception and offensive threats on the part of any nation, large or small. We no longer live in a world where only the actual firing of weapons represents a sufficient challenge to a nation's security to constitute maximum peril. Nuclear weapons are so destructive and ballistic missiles are so swift, that any substantially increased possibility of their use or any sudden change in their deployment may well be regarded as a definite threat to peace.

For many years, both the Soviet Union and the United States, recognizing this fact, have deployed strategic nuclear weapons with great care, never upsetting the precarious status quo which insured that these weapons would not be used in the absence of some vital challenge. Our own strategic missiles have never been transferred to the territory of any other nation under a cloak of secrecy and deception; and our history—unlike that of the Soviets since the end of World War II—demonstrates that we have no desire to dominate or conquer any other nation or impose our system upon its people. Nevertheless, American citizens have become adjusted to living daily on the bull's-eye of Soviet missiles located inside the U.S.S.R. or in submarines.

In that sense, missiles in Cuba add to an already clear and present danger—although it should be noted the nations of Latin America have never previously been subjected to a potential nuclear threat.

But this secret, swift, and extraordinary buildup of Communist missiles . . . is a deliberately provocative and unjustified change in the status quo which cannot be accepted by this country, if our courage and our commitments are ever to be trusted again by either friend or foe.

The 1930's taught us a clear lesson: aggressive conduct, if allowed to go unchecked and unchallenged, ultimately leads to war. This nation is opposed to war. We are also true to our word. Our unswerving objective, therefore, must be to prevent the use of these missiles against this or any other country, and to secure their withdrawal or elimination from the Western Hemisphere. . . .

Acting, therefore, in the defense of our own security and of the entire Western Hemisphere, and under the authority entrusted to me by the Constitution as endorsed by the resolution of the Congress, I have directed that the following initial steps be taken immediately:

First: To halt this offensive buildup, a strict quarantine on all offensive military equipment under shipment to Cuba is being initiated. All ships of any kind bound for Cuba from whatever nation or port will, if found to contain cargoes of offensive weapons, be turned back. . . .

Second: I have directed the continued and increased close surveillance of Cuba and its military buildup. . . .

Third: It shall be the policy of this Nation to regard any nuclear missile launched from Cuba against any nation in the Western Hemisphere as an attack by the Soviet Union on the United States, requiring a full retaliatory response upon the Soviet Union.

Fourth: As a necessary military precaution, I have reinforced our base at Guantanamo, evacuated today the dependents of our personnel there, and ordered additional military units to be on a standby alert basis.

Fifth: We are calling tonight for an immediate meeting of the Organ of Consultation under the Organization of American States, to consider this threat to hemispheric security and to invoke articles 6 and 8 of the Rio Treaty in support of all necessary action. The United Nations Charter allows for regional security arrangements—and the nations of this hemisphere decided long ago against the military presence of outside powers. Our other allies around the world have also been alerted.

Sixth: Under the Charter of the United Nations, we are asking tonight that an emergency meeting of the Security Council be convoked without delay to take action against this latest Soviet threat to world peace. Our resolution will call for the prompt dismantling and withdrawal of all offensive weapons in Cuba, under the supervision of U.N. observers, before the quarantine can be lifted.

Seventh and finally: I call upon Chairman Khrushchev to halt and eliminate this clandestine, reckless, and provocative threat to world peace and to stable relations between our two nations. I call upon him further to abandon this course of world domination, and to join in an historic effort to end the perilous arms race and to transform the history of man. He has an opportunity now to move the world back from the abyss of destruction—by returning to his government's own words that it had no need to station missiles outside its own territory, and withdrawing these weapons from Cuba by refraining from any action which will widen or deepen the present crisis—and then by participating in a search for peaceful and permanent solutions. . . .

Finally, I want to say a few words to the captive people of Cuba, to whom this speech is being directly carried by special radio facilities. I speak to you as a friend, as one who knows of your deep attachment to your fatherland, as one who shares your aspirations for liberty and justice for all. And I have watched and the American people have watched with deep sorrow how your nationalist revolution was betrayed—and how your fatherland fell under foreign domination. Now your leaders are no longer Cuban leaders inspired by Cuban ideals. They are puppets and agents of an international conspiracy which has turned Cuba against your friends and neighbors in the Americas—and turned it into the first Latin American country to become a target for nuclear war—the first Latin American country to have these weapons on its soil.

These new weapons are not in your interest. They contribute nothing to your peace and well-being. They can only undermine it. But this country has no wish to cause you to suffer or to impose any system upon you. We know that your lives and land are being used as pawns by those who deny your freedom.

Many times in the past, the Cuban people have risen to throw out tyrants who destroyed their liberty. And I have no doubt that most Cubans today look forward to the time when they will be truly free—free from foreign domination, free to choose their own leaders, free to select their own system, free to own their own land, free to speak and write and worship without fear or degradation. And then shall Cuba be welcomed back to the society of free nations and to the associations of this hemisphere.

My fellow citizens: let no one doubt that this is a difficult and dangerous effort on which we have set out. No one can foresee precisely what course it will take or what costs or casualties will be incurred. Many months of sacrifice and self-discipline lie ahead—months in which both our patience and our will be tested—months in which many threats and denunciations will keep us aware of our dangers. But the greatest danger of all would be to do nothing.

The path we have chosen for the present is full of hazards, as all paths are—but it is the one most consistent with our character and courage as a nation and our commitments around the world. The cost of freedom is always high—but Americans have always paid it. And one path we shall never choose, and that is the path of surrender or submission.

Our goal is not the victory of might, but the vindication of right—not peace at the expense of freedom, but both peace and freedom, here in this hemisphere, and, we hope, around the world. God willing, that goal will be achieved.

Thank you and good night.

Source: Public Papers of the Presidents of the United States, John F. Kennedy, Containing the Public Messages, Speeches, and Statements of the President, 1962 (Washington, D.C.: U.S. Government Printing Office, 1963), 806–809.

Document Four: President Kennedy, Commencement Address at American University in Washington, June 10, 1963

In this commencement address at American University on June 10, 1963, President Kennedy discussed the changed world conditions after the Cuban missile crisis. Kennedy called for an end to the cold war in Europe, even as he was increasing U.S. troop commitments in Southeast Asia.

. . . Some say that it is useless to speak of world peace or world law or world disarmament—and that it will be useless until the leaders of the Soviet Union adopt a more enlightened attitude. I hope they do. I believe we can help them do it. But I also believe that we must reexamine our own attitude—as individuals and as a Nation—for our attitude is as essential as theirs. And every graduate of this school, every thoughtful citizen who despairs of war and wishes to bring peace, should begin by looking inward—by examining his own attitude toward the possibilities of peace, toward the Soviet Union, toward the course of the cold war and toward freedom and peace here at home.

First: Let us examine our attitude toward peace itself. Too many of us think it is impossible. Too many think it unreal. But that is a dangerous, defeatist belief. It leads to the conclusion that war is inevitable—that mankind is doomed—that we are gripped by forces we cannot control. . . .

Second: Let us reexamine our attitude toward the Soviet Union. . . .

No government or social system is so evil that its people must be considered as lacking in virtue. As Americans, we find communism profoundly repugnant as a negation of personal freedom and dignity. But we can still hail the Russian people for their many achievements—in science and space, in economic and industrial growth, in culture and in acts of courage.

Among the many traits the peoples of our two countries have in common, none is stronger than our mutual abhorrence of war. Almost unique, among the major world powers, we have never been at war with each other. And no nation in the history of battle ever suffered more than the Soviet Union suffered in the course of the Second World War. At least 20 million lost their lives. Countless millions of homes and farms were burned or sacked. A third of the nation's territory, including nearly two thirds of its industrial base, was turned into a wasteland—a loss equivalent to the devastation of this country east of Chicago.

Today, should total war ever break out again—no matter how—our two countries would become the primary targets. It is an ironic but accurate fact that the two strongest powers are the two in the most danger of devastation. All we have built, all we have worked for, would be destroyed in the first 24 hours. And even in the cold war, which brings burdens and dangers to so many countries, including this Nation's closest allies—our two countries bear the heaviest burdens. For we are both devoting massive sums of money to weapons that could be better devoted to combating ignorance, poverty, and disease. We are both caught up in a vicious and dangerous cycle in which suspicion on one side breeds suspicion on the other, and new weapons beget counter-weapons.

In short, both the United States and its allies, and the Soviet Union and its allies, have a mutually deep interest in a just and genuine peace and in halting the arms race. Agreements to this end are in the interests of the Soviet Union as well as ours—and even the most hostile nations can be relied upon to accept and keep those treaty obligations, and only those treaty obligations, which are in their own interest.

So, let us not be blind to our differences—but let us also direct attention to our common interests and to the means by which those differences can be resolved. And if we cannot end now our differences, at least we can help make the world safe for diversity. For, in the final analysis, our most basic common link is that we all inhabit this small planet. We all breathe the same air. We all cherish our children's future. And we are all mortal.

Third: Let us reexamine our attitude toward the cold war, remembering that we are not engaged in a debate, seeking to pile up debating points. We are not here distributing blame or pointing the finger of judgment. We must deal with the world as it is, and not as it might have been had the history of the last 18 years been different. . . .

The United States will make no deal with the Soviet Union at the expense of other nations and other peoples, not merely because they are our partners, but also because their interests and ours converge.

Our interests converge, however, not only in defending the frontiers of freedom, but in pursuing the paths of peace. It is our hope—and the purpose of allied policies—to convince the Soviet Union that she, too, should let each nation choose its own future, so long as that choice does not interfere with the choices of others. The Communist drive to impose their political and economic system on others is the primary cause of world tension today. For there can be no doubt that, if all nations could refrain from interfering in the self-determination of others, the peace would be much more assured.

This will require a new effort to achieve world law—a new context for world discussions. It will require increased understanding between the Soviets and ourselves. And increased understanding will require increased contact and communication. One step in this direction is the proposed arrangement for a direct line between Moscow and Washington, to avoid on each side the dangerous delays, misunderstandings, and misreadings of the other's actions which might occur at a time of crisis.

We have also been talking in Geneva about other first-step measures of arms control, designed to limit the intensity of the arms race and to reduce the risks of accidental war. Our primary long-range interest in Geneva, however, is general and complete disarmament—designed to take place by stages, permitting parallel political developments to build the new institutions of peace which would take the place of arms. The pursuit of disarmament has been an effort of this Government since the 1920's. It has been urgently sought by the past three administrations. And however dim the prospects may be today, we intend to continue this effort—to continue it in order that all countries, including our own, can better grasp what the problems and possibilities of disarmament are.

The one major area of these negotiations where the end is in sight, yet where a fresh start is badly needed, is in a treaty to outlaw nuclear tests. The conclusion of such a treaty, so near and yet so far, would check the spiraling arms race in one of its most dangerous areas. It would place the nuclear powers in a position to deal more effectively with one of the greatest hazards which man faces in 1963, the further spread of nuclear arms. It would increase our security—it would decrease the prospects of war. Surely this goal is sufficiently important to require our steady pursuit, yielding neither to the temptation to give up the whole effort nor the temptation to give up our insistence on vital and responsible safeguards.

I am taking this opportunity, therefore, to announce two important decisions in this regard.

First: Chairman Khrushchev, Prime Minister Macmillan, and I have agreed that high-level discussions will shortly begin in Moscow looking toward early agreement on a comprehensive test ban treaty. Our hopes must be tempered with the caution of history—but with our hopes go the hopes of all mankind.

Second: To make clear our good faith and solemn convictions on the matter, I now declare that the United States does not propose to conduct nuclear tests in the atmosphere so long as other states do not do so. We will not be the first to resume. Such a declaration is no substitute for a formal binding treaty, but I hope it will help us achieve one. Nor would such a treaty be a substitute for disarmament, but I hope it will help us achieve it. . . .

The United States, as the world knows, will never start a war. We do not want a war. We do not now expect a war. This generation of Americans has already had enough—more than enough—of war and hate and oppression. We shall be prepared if others wish it. We shall be alert to try to stop it. But we shall also do our part to build a world of peace where the weak are safe and the strong are just. We are not helpless before that task or hopeless of its success. Confident and unafraid, we labor on—not toward a strategy of annihilation but toward a strategy of peace.

Source: Public Papers of the Presidents of the United States, John F. Kennedy, Containing the Public Messages, Speeches, and Statements of the President, 1963 (Washington, D.C.: U.S. Government Printing Office, 1964), 459–464.

Document Five: President Kennedy, News Conference [regarding Vietnam], November 14, 1963

In his November 14, 1963, press conference, President Kennedy discussed conditions in South Vietnam following the coup in which Ngo Dinh Diem had been removed from power and executed.

. . . Q. Mr. President, there have been published reports that General Harkins may have lost his usefulness in Viet-Nam because of his identification with the Diem regime and lack of contacts with the new generals running the country. Would you care to comment on that?

THE PRESIDENT. I think it is wholly untrue. I have complete confidence in him. He was just doing his job. I think he said in the interview yesterday he had seen Mr. Nhu, I think, only three times. He had seen President Diem on a number of occasions. That was his job, that is what he was sent for—to work with the government in power—that is what he will do with the new government. I have great confidence in General Harkins. There may be some who would like to see General Harkins go, but I plan to keep him there.

Q. Following up that, sir, would you give us your appraisal of the situation in South Viet-Nam now, since the coup, and the purposes for the Honolulu conference?

THE PRESIDENT. Because we do have a new situation there, and a new government, we hope, an increased effort in the war. The purpose of the meeting at Honolulu—Ambassador Lodge will be there, General Harkins will be there, Secretary McNamara and others, and then, as you know, later Ambassador Lodge will come here—is to attempt to assess the situation: what American policy should be, and what our aid policy should be, how we can intensify the struggle, how we can bring Americans out of there.

Now, that is our object, to bring Americans home, permit the South Vietnamese to maintain themselves as a free and independent country, and permit democratic forces within the country to operate—which they can, of course, much more freely when the assault from the inside, and which is manipulated from the north, is ended. So the purpose of the meeting in Honolulu is how to pursue these objectives.

Q. Mr. President, Madam Nhu has now left the United States, but indicated that she intends to return. Will we renew her tourist visa?

THE PRESIDENT. Yes.

Q. And if she asks for it, will we grant her permanent residence—

THE PRESIDENT. I think we'd certainly permit her to return to the United States, if she wishes to do so. . . .

Q. Mr. President, in view of the changed situation in South Viet-Nam, do you still expect to bring back 1,000 troops before the end of the year, or has that figure been raised or lowered?

THE PRESIDENT. No, we are going to bring back several hundred before the end of the year. But I think on the question of the exact number, I thought we would wait until the meeting of November 20th.

❖

Source: Public Papers of the Presidents of the United States, John F. Kennedy, Containing the Public Messages, Speeches, and Statements of the President, 1963 (Washington, D.C.: U.S. Government Printing Office, 1964), 845–853.

Lyndon B. Johnson

August 27, 1908–January 22, 1973

Thirty-sixth President of the United States
November 22, 1963–January 20, 1969

⚜ LYNDON B. JOHNSON ⚜

Place of Birth: near Stonewall, Texas

Date of Birth: August 27, 1908

Place of Residence: Texas

Class Background: modest

Father's Career: farmer and politician

Mother's Career: teacher and homemaker

Number of Siblings: four

Religion: Disciples of Christ

Education: graduated Southwest Texas State Teachers College (now Texas State University–San Marcos), 1930; attended Georgetown Law School, 1934

Political Party: Democrat

Military Service: World War II: Lieutenant Commander, U.S. Naval Reserve, 1942

Spouse: Claudia Alta Taylor "Lady Bird" Johnson

Spouse's Education: graduated from the University of Texas at Austin, 1934

Spouse's Career: homemaker, secretary for Lyndon Johnson's congressional office, radio and television station owner, environmental activist, member of the University of Texas board of regents, founder of the National Wildflower Research Center

Number of Children: two

Sports and Hobbies: hunting, riding

Career Prior to the Presidency: teacher, secretary to Representative Richard Kleberg (D-TX), Texas state director of the National Youth Administration, World War II Naval aviation officer, member of the U.S. House of Representatives, U.S. senator, vice president, rancher

Age upon Entering the White House: 55 years, 87 days

Reason for Leaving the White House: decided not to seek a second full term

Career after the Presidency: rancher, planned his presidential library

Date of Death: January 22, 1973

Cause of Death: heart failure

Last Words: "Send Mike immediately!" (referring to one of the Secret Service agents)

Burial Site: LBJ Ranch, Texas

Value of Estate at Time of Death: unknown, in the millions

Preceding page: Lyndon B. Johnson *(Arnold Newman, White House Press Office)*

BIOGRAPHY OF JOHNSON

To this day, Lyndon B. Johnson confounds biographers by his tendency in life to make himself all things to all people. Chroniclers of Johnson's life have characterized the man as a mendacious egomaniac bent on power, a self-sacrificing crusader for the common good, a "big daddy" who forged an extended family out of politics, and everything in between. Further confusion arises from his boastfulness and exaggeration that shrouded a deep insecurity, manifesting itself in a overarching ambition and a need to be loved by his constituency, which in his mind consisted of nothing less than the entire electorate, television and newspaper reporters, other politicians, and every interest group imaginable. Like most politicians, Johnson shifted among countless identities, manifesting nearly all of the contradictions of postwar U.S. political culture. At various times—and often simultaneously—Johnson identified as a westerner and a southerner, a New Deal liberal and a Dwight D. Eisenhower conservative, an advocate of tax cuts and tax hikes, a booster of the military-industrial complex and a populist, a staunch anti-communist and a protector of civil liberties, a supporter of civil rights and a paternalist, a friend of the worker and a foe of the union, a fierce party loyalist and a consensus-builder.

Like most successful politicians, Johnson constantly recrafted his image in order to reflect, adapt to, and survive the changing political climate. His ability to navigate politically tumultuous waters better than anyone made him perhaps the biggest political giant of 20th-century U.S. politics. Much of his success resulted from the politician's chameleon-like qualities; thus biographers have found his true nature obscured by self-perpetuated myths as well as legendary animosities and loyalties. Ultimately, however, Lyndon Johnson was a complex but straightforward character. His naked ambition and self-promotion brought him tremendous power and influence, but Johnson tried to use his power to realize all the fundamental American values of justice, freedom, and equality. Thus Johnson's great ambition is inseparable from his great idealism. Lyndon Baines Johnson was born on August 27, 1908, near Stonewall, a mere blip of a community in the midst of the rugged Texas hill country. Johnson's Texas origins would prove both a blessing and a curse throughout his lifetime. The status of Texas as a middle ground between the South and the West allowed Johnson to claim a southern identity when politically expedient, and a western identity when the South's retrograde, even racist, image hampered his national ambitions. His humble Texas origins not only enabled him to identify with the disadvantaged as president, but also made him an easy target of elitist intellectuals.

Lyndon was born to Sam Ealy Johnson, Jr., a successful state politician, and Rebekah Baines, the cultured daughter of a once-wealthy Texas family. The two made for a mismatched and unhappy couple. While Rebekah bemoaned the cultural backwater in which she found herself, Sam quickly made a name for himself as a state legislator popular for his tolerant, populist beliefs.

Lyndon's parents began to instill in him the values they shared with the Hill Country residents: belief in the value of a good education, admiration for self-sacrifice, and esteem for a career in public service. As a child Johnson was bright but needy and spoiled by his mother. As his father turned increasingly to drink, the young boy took on the role of man of the house, overseeing basic domestic chores. In 1913, the family moved to nearby Johnson City. Like many others in town, the Johnsons relied on extended family to get by.

After World War I, Sam Ealy made political waves by taking a risky stand against the Ku Klux Klan. Lyndon took to emulating his father, following him around in order to soak up political gossip and debates. Lyndon's first immersion in politics ended, however, when Sam Ealy's destructive drinking habit, combined with disastrous financial mistakes, resulted in a 1922 implosion when he lost the farm. The family had to move back to Johnson City. Sam Ealy retired from the state legislature soon thereafter. Witnessing his father's decline embedded in young Lyndon a profound insecurity about fate and fortune. Added to his spoiled and indulgent

Lyndon B. Johnson as a little boy at his family home in Johnson City, Texas *(Lyndon B. Johnson Library)*

LADY BIRD JOHNSON

(1912–2007) *first lady of the United States, November 22, 1963–January 20, 1969*

Lady Bird Johnson was born Claudia Alta Taylor on December 22, 1912, in Karnack, Texas. She acquired the nickname "Lady Bird" as a young girl; the name stuck. Her father, Thomas Jefferson Taylor, owned a fortune in land but was domineering; her mother, Minnie Pattillo Taylor, was aloof. She died in 1918. Lady Bird passed a solitary childhood reading and exploring the outdoors. Shy but smart and self-reliant, Lady Bird blossomed when she entered the University of Texas in 1930 at 18 years of age. In Austin she mixed an active academic life with an exciting social life. After receiving a degree in journalism in 1934 Lady Bird returned to her father in Karnack to ponder her future, which she hoped would be in journalism.

In August 1934, Lady Bird Taylor was introduced to Lyndon Johnson, at the time a secretary for a U.S. congressman from Texas. At the end of their first date, Lyndon rashly proposed marriage. Though startled—and by no means lacking for suitors—Lady Bird was intrigued by the charismatic young man's ambition and idealism. For the next few months, he courted her in person as well as long distance from Washington, D.C., via telephone and letters. On November 17, the two married in San Antonio. For both Lyndon and Lady Bird, the marriage had advantages beyond love: Lady Bird's charm, brains, and family wealth would be an asset to an aspiring politician. At the same time, Lyndon offered Lady Bird a chance to escape the dreary isolation of Karnack.

Following mainstream customs of the era, Lady Bird Johnson subordinated any of her own goals to those of her husband, but as a politician's wife she excelled. Indeed, Lady Bird selflessly devoted herself to her husband and his career. She gladly gave $10,000 of her own inheritance to help fund Lyndon's first congressional campaign in 1937. After he won that race, Lady Bird Johnson spent her days in Washington attending to constituents.

During World War II, she ran Lyndon's congressional office while he was on assignment for the navy.

By any measure, the relationship was unequal. Like Lady Bird's father, Lyndon was domineering and brutish. Lyndon thought nothing of being cruel, often berating his wife in public for her appearance. Lyndon took advantage of Lady Bird's loyalty by having many affairs, and his consuming obsession with politics often left her lonely. At the same time, she proved no pushover.

Lady Bird Johnson *(Library of Congress)*

upbringing, this insecurity created in the boy a huge, yet fragile, ego that would last for the rest of his life.

Compared to that of most presidents, Johnson's childhood was indeed modest. But it was not the harsh life of poverty, hardship, and cultural and educational deprivation that he would describe in later years. Sam Ealy Johnson maintained his political contacts, working in state and local campaigns for the remainder of his life. In the mid-1920s, the Texas Highway Department hired him to fill a supervisory post. In the late 1920s, he was named a state bus inspector for the Texas Railroad Commission as a result of his political friendship with Pat Neff, former governor of Texas and new railroad commissioner. By perpetuating a mythical image of hardship overcome, Johnson encouraged a legend that made his achievements seem more impressive. He used that image as anecdotal evidence for his belief that anyone could achieve success in America, if afforded the opportunity.

After Johnson graduated high school in 1924, his parents insisted that he continue his education at college. College tuition was prohibitively expensive for the young man, but after roughly a year of dissembling, Johnson enrolled at Southwest Texas State Teacher's College (SWTS) in San Marcos (now Texas State University). Throughout college, Johnson lived on the verge of destitution, working numerous jobs to support his studies.

She knew that, above all, Lyndon needed her strength, smarts, and honesty. As his only adviser with no ulterior motives, Lyndon knew he could trust Lady Bird's judgment and accordingly she gained influence over his life. Furthermore, the marriage lasted, proof in itself that both parties maintained a degree of mutual affection, respect, and need. When Lyndon suffered a major heart attack in 1955, he turned to his wife for strength, as he often did in times of weakness. "Stay with me Bird," he told her, "I'd rather fight with you beside me."

Most impressive of all, Lady Bird Johnson managed to maintain her own identity while married to a man who usually dominated the will of those around him, including giants of politics and business. A man of legendary ego, Lyndon insisted that when Lady Bird gave birth to daughters in 1944 and 1947 they be given names that would give them the same LBJ initials shared by the entire family—Lynda Bird and Lucy (later Luci) Baines. Nevertheless, Lady Bird Johnson's own accomplishments demonstrate her strong sense of self. In 1943, the Johnsons used Lady Bird's money to purchase KTBC radio in Austin. Lady Bird's own financial skills and hard work quickly turned what had been a small operation into a station reaching 2.5 million listeners by 1945 and earning $500,000 in annual profit by the late 1950s. With Lady Bird running the operations, the Johnsons expanded their radio empire into television and land during the 1950s; by the 1960s they were quite rich.

When Lyndon ascended to the presidency in 1963, Lady Bird continued to be one of the most trusted members of his inner circle. She also acted as a tough but fair critic of her husband's public speaking. After one televised press conference, she told him: "Your looks were splendid. . . . During the statement you were a little breathless and there was too much looking down and I think it was a little too fast. Not enough change of pace. . . . In general, I'd say it was a good B-plus." In 1964, she publicized and popularized the administration's Head Start program of educational aid for the disadvantaged. During the 1964 presidential race, she campaigned on her own by bringing her Lady Bird Special whistle-stop railroad tour to the Deep South—no easy feat since the South was hostile to the administration because of its support for civil rights.

At first Lady Bird Johnson felt uneasy in stepping into the role vacated by her predecessor, the glamorous but reclusive Jackie Kennedy. Johnson quickly took steps to transform the role of first lady, a style that resembled Eleanor Roosevelt more than Jackie Kennedy. Whereas previous first ladies had embraced a single piece of legislation, in 1965 Johnson adopted her own entire agenda: an environmental beautification program. For the rest of the Johnson presidency, she pursued efforts to beautify Washington's tourist areas and its ghettos, pushed for conservation of the nation's natural beauty sites, and lobbied for her own legislative brainchild, the Highway Beautification Act. In another first, she participated in cabinet meetings to help determine the legislative strategy for the beautification bill, and she personally lobbied Congress until the bill passed. Throughout Lyndon's term as president, Lady Bird worried constantly about her husband's health and urged him not to run in 1968. He acceded to her wishes when he announced on March 31, 1968, that he would not seek reelection. By the time she left the White House, Johnson had transformed the role of first lady from that of a celebrity into a distinctly political entity, usually entailing a policy agenda. Because of Johnson's innovations, the office of first lady came to include a staff of speechwriters, aides, and press secretaries.

After Lyndon's death in 1973, Lady Bird Johnson spent more than 30 years on her own, spending time with family, serving on the University of Texas Board of Regents, and, most notably, continuing her pursuit of environmental beautification projects. In Texas she initiated campaigns to plant wildflowers along highways, and she founded the Lady Bird Johnson Wildflower Center in Austin. During the 1990s she received many honors for her environmental work; a stroke in 2002 limited her public appearances. She died on July 11, 2007.

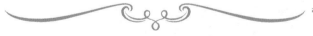

Johnson did not excel at college, but time spent there helped him define himself. No fan of higher learning for its own abstract sake, Johnson saw education as a way to advance in the world. He was not a particularly good student, but when interested in the subject matter he demonstrated a great intellect. In what started a lifelong pattern, Johnson made father figures out of professors and other superiors. Uncomfortable among his peers, he became boastful and phony. His nickname, "Bull" Johnson, indicated that his boasts had yet to become entirely convincing. Instead, Johnson courted his superiors, powerful people such as Cecil Evans, the president of SWTS. His obsequiousness, deference, and loyalty to Evans earned him the president's lifelong friendship and support.

In 1928, a lack of money threatened to derail Johnson's college career. He accordingly put college on pause and took a nine-month teaching job in Cotulla, a small town near the Mexican border. His students were all Mexican American, each neglected and poor outcasts in white society. Johnson had always viewed teaching as a noble profession because education was a way to help Americans of all races and classes to rise in society. In Cotulla, Johnson relentlessly drove his students—and himself—to strive to improve. He drilled in his students the traditional American values of justice and equality, promising them that they had as much right to the American dream as anyone else. By all accounts Johnson proved a great teacher, improving his reputation and the lives of his students. Cotulla was thus the first of many times when helping others also helped Johnson. Far from sinister in his motives, Johnson managed to orchestrate a harmonious synthesis of self-promotion and greater beneficence. His tools were ambition, persuasiveness, and a relentless work ethic; his values were democracy, reform, and equality of opportunity.

During Johnson's remaining time at college, he formulated a nascent political philosophy. Above all, he admired democracy for its advocacy of a common good. Since democracy is a process, creating a common good requires extensive involvement in politics. Johnson thus took it upon himself to become as successful a politician as possible. Politics thus served as a way for Johnson to fulfill his personal ambition as well as meet his higher ideals. He set out to cultivate allies and power, in the process building something of a political machine. Johnson's patient and steady wooing of Cecil Evans won him a job in the president's office, where he eventually acquired enough power to influence the distribution of campus jobs. Johnson also became involved in state politics, giving a speech in support of state senate candidate Welly Hopkins in 1930.

That same year, Johnson graduated from SWTS. Through an uncle he secured a teaching job in Houston. As a teacher of speech, Johnson also supervised the debate team. His unsuspecting students found themselves captive to their teacher's ambition. Heaping praise, scorn, and abuse upon them, and above all exhibiting tireless effort, Johnson whipped the team into a state power. He also managed, in a way that would become typical, to express and encourage love, respect, and loyalty between himself and his pupils. Johnson's ruthless ambition brought out the best in others, encouraging loyalty and building power in the process.

Through his father's political connections, in 1931 Johnson was offered a job as secretary to U.S. congressman Richard Kleberg, a Democrat representing the 14th Texas district. Johnson accepted instantly. As Kleberg's secretary, Johnson again displayed his energy and drive. Somewhere along the way, politics became his all-consuming obsession. Hardly ever would he display any patience whatsoever for any subject besides politics, including art, literature, or sports.

Politics proved the perfect arena for Johnson's temperament. His willingness to learn quickly turned the dreary job into a first-rate political education. As Kleberg was more playboy than politician, Johnson simply ran the office himself. In a familiar pattern, he filled his staff with members of his extended political family, including two members from his Houston debate team. As before, Johnson dominated the younger men, spurring them—and himself—to harder work at increasingly long hours. He engaged in crude actions to enhance his powers. He would, for example, issue orders while urinating (in the White House years he issued orders while defecating), simply to make people feel uncomfortable, giving him a psychological advantage over them. Johnson also spent much of his time making as many connections as possible. He introduced himself to other secretaries, took a job as

Lyndon B. Johnson and his students in 1928 *(© Everett Collection Inc/Alamy)*

BIOGRAPHICAL TIME LINE

1908
August 27 Lyndon Baines Johnson is born in Stonewall, Texas.

1924
Johnson graduates from high school.

1928
Johnson takes a nine-month teaching job in Cotulla, Texas.

1930
Johnson graduates from Southwest Texas State Teachers College.

1931
Johnson accepts the position as secretary for U.S. congressman Richard Kleberg, of the 14th Texas district.

1934
November 17 Johnson marries Claudia Alta Taylor, known as Lady Bird to her friends.

1935
Johnson becomes director of the Texas branch of the National Youth Administration (NYA), a federal agency aimed at helping young people find work.

1937
In a special election Johnson is elected congressman from the 10th Texas district.

1941
Johnson loses in a special U.S. Senate race.

1948
Johnson wins election to the U.S. Senate.

1953
Johnson becomes Senate minority leader.

1955
Johnson is elected Senate majority leader.

Johnson suffers a heart attack.

1957
Johnson helps usher through the Senate the first civil rights bill since the 19th century.

1960
Johnson is elected vice president of the United States.

1961
January 20 Johnson is sworn in as vice president of the United States.

1963
November 22 Johnson is sworn in as president upon the assassination of President John F. Kennedy in Dallas, Texas.

1964
November 3 Johnson wins election as president in his own right in a landslide.

1965
January 20 Johnson is inaugurated president.

1968
March 31 Johnson announces on television that he will not be a candidate for reelection later in the year.

1969
January 20 Johnson spends his last day as president.

1973
January 22 Johnson dies of heart failure.

---

door opener in Congress, and helped revive the Little Congress, a defunct political salon for congressional secretaries.

These early years in Washington deeply influenced Johnson's political beliefs. He found himself awed by the flamboyant senator Huey Long (D-LA); his observation of President Herbert Hoover's intransigence during the Great Depression intensified Johnson's identification with the poor. Like many, he became enthralled with President Franklin D. Roosevelt. Johnson urged Kleberg to support every piece of New Deal legislation, but he was only partially successful.

In 1934, while on business in Austin, Johnson met Claudia Alta Taylor, known as Lady Bird to her friends. Smitten after one date, Johnson impetuously proposed marriage to the young woman. When she ignored his offer, he continued to court her from Washington. Eventually she accepted, and the two were wed later that year. The marriage lasted until Johnson's death nearly 40 years later; throughout it was unequal, as Johnson proved domineering, unfaithful, and—at times—mean spirited. LADY BIRD JOHNSON's strength nevertheless allowed her to maintain her own identity, even if her primary role was that of supporter to her husband.

Johnson left Kleberg's office in 1935 to take a position as director of the Texas branch of the National Youth Administration (NYA), a federal agency tasked with helping young people find work. His job as director entailed providing jobs and relief to students who were unable to afford school because of the depression. Johnson's most famous program put young people to work constructing roadside parks along Texas highways.

At the NYA Johnson was able to pursue his cherished progressive political principles. He believed the New Deal's pragmatic effort to help the needy was the proper function of government. In addition, Johnson saw the NYA as a way to help all Texans, regardless of race. Displaying contempt for the racist sentiment in mainstream Texas culture, Johnson worked behind the scene to see that NYA aid was distributed equally to African Americans. He ensured that these actions were undertaken without publicity.

As he had in Washington, Johnson created an extended family at the NYA, bringing in old friends and expanding his influence. He exerted tireless effort and demanded the same of his staff. His formula once again proved successful, as the Texas branch rapidly developed into one of the leading NYA agencies in the country.

In 1937, Congressman James P. Buchanan, a Democrat representing the 10th Texas district, died unexpectedly. This district included Austin and part of the hill country where Johnson had grown up. Johnson, who had been looking for a way to return to Capitol Hill, immediately announced himself as a candidate. Using $10,000 of his wife's money, he assembled an election team. During the campaign, Johnson ran as an unabashed Roosevelt Democrat, pledging support for the entire New Deal, including the president's controversial court packing plan. In the first instance of another pattern, Johnson nearly worked himself to death during the campaign. Just days before the election, he entered a hospital for an emergency appendectomy. He left the hospital having won the election.

His victory enabled him to meet his hero, President Roosevelt. Johnson would make another father figure out of the patrician president; Johnson's own troubled father passed away in October 1937. As a pet of the president's, Johnson was introduced to many New Deal power brokers in Washington, D.C., including Abe Fortas, James Rowe, and Tom Corcoran. In the House of Representatives, Johnson loyally supported the New Deal, and he also worked to bring Texas into the modern economic mainstream. Because of his seat on the Naval Affairs Committee, Johnson was able to steer substantial public projects to Texas, including naval yard construction contracts awarded to the Brown and Root construction company. For the rest of Johnson's political career, Brown and Root provided Johnson with limitless funding for his election campaigns.

Johnson also cared for his less wealthy constituents. After he met personally with Roosevelt, the president approved a rural electrification program for the Texas hill country, the heart of Johnson's constituency. A massive influx of federal projects would improve the South's economy, enabling the region to catch up economically with the rest of the nation. In the modernization process, Johnson believed, the South would naturally cast off its regressive institutions, especially Jim Crow segregation.

During his years in the House, Lyndon Johnson repeated his usual patterns. He became a disciple of yet another father figure, as he and his wife Lady Bird grew close to Representative Sam Rayburn, the steadfast Texas New Dealer and

Lyndon Johnson poses with his new bride, Lady Bird Johnson, in front of the Capitol in Washington, 1934. *(Lyndon B. Johnson Library)*

eventual Speaker of the House. Johnson also relied upon his ever-expanding coterie of aides, drawn from his years in teaching and at the NYA. Work hardly ever stopped in Johnson's office, as the congressman woke early, skipped meals, and labored away into the late hours; he expected the same dedication from his staff.

Success came easily for Johnson during his years in Congress—so much so that another pattern appeared in his life. Johnson would immerse himself in intense work meeting with immense success. Success would be followed by diminishing returns, however, and he would become withdrawn, yearning for something more. In 1941, already tired of the House, Johnson eyed the U.S. Senate. When a seat opened in 1941 with the death of Democratic senator Morris Sheppard, Johnson decided to run in the 1941 special election even though he faced long odds in a crowded field against the favorite, Texas governor W. Lee "Pappy" O'Daniel.

With backing from the Roosevelt administration, Johnson ran well against O'Daniel, who enjoyed financial support from conservative businessmen. Johnson benefited from massive, unreported funding supplied by Brown and Root, though he hardly differed from other candidates in receiving such financial assistance. Initial voting returns indicated that Johnson would win. In Texas, however, the end of voting merely signaled the start of vote manipulation. Each candidate controlled various precincts; precinct bosses could shift votes around as their preferred candidates needed. When Johnson naively released his vote totals and celebrated victory, the O'Daniel loyalists simply shifted their votes around to compensate. Soon, O'Daniel was declared the winner.

After this gnawing defeat, the Pearl Harbor attack on December 7, 1941, which brought the United States into World War II, came as almost a relief for Johnson. Cognizant of the political value of military service, he immediately requested a naval assignment but he did not resign his seat in Congress. Johnson was subsequently sent to San Francisco to oversee the construction of naval training facilities. With Johnson away from Washington, Lady Bird assumed control of her husband's congressional office. In May and June 1942, Johnson visited the Pacific theater, ostensibly on naval business. Eager to boost his image by experiencing combat, he arranged to join a U.S. flight crew for a bombing run against Japanese targets. After narrowly surviving a dogfight, the plane returned; Johnson received a Silver Star.

The end of the war in 1945 brought a shift in the political winds in Texas in opposition to New Deal liberalism. Johnson consequently took on the characteristics of a chameleon to survive politically in the state. On the surface, he took stands that apparently contradicted his New Deal ideals, for example, he denounced organized labor, anathema to Texas business and oil barons. Yet Johnson maintained his progressive stance by declaring support for the average (that is, nonunion) worker.

Johnson requested a naval assignment immediately after the attack on Pearl Harbor on December 7, 1941. He is shown in this 1942 photograph in his dress blues. *(Lyndon B. Johnson Library)*

The year 1948 presented Johnson with what he saw as his last chance to escape the House of Representatives. O'Daniel had lost interest in the Senate, so Coke Stevenson, the governor of Texas, announced his candidacy, as did Johnson and a host of other hopefuls. On the campaign trail, Johnson trumpeted his record in Congress and attacked Stevenson as the tool of special interests. Stevenson did, in fact, represent the reactionary strain of Texas Democrats. A racist governor who allowed oil and bank interests to run the state, Stevenson was nonetheless a self-made, independent man. Limitless money greased the wheels of both campaigns—Brown and Root for Johnson, oilmen and bankers for Stevenson. When neither man drew a majority in the final tally, election laws required a runoff vote.

The runoff results were extremely close but showed Stevenson with a slight lead. As in 1941, however, shifting votes by both sides after the election determined the outcome. This time, however, Johnson cheated properly. When a pro-Johnson county in South Texas reported previously uncounted (and fraudulent) votes in the congressman's favor, Johnson emerged with a controversial but undeniable 87-vote victory, earning the senator-elect the nickname "Landslide Lyndon."

As with every previous position, Johnson cultivated relationships with powerful mentors in the Senate, Georgia's veteran Democratic senator Richard Russell in particular. Building on this and other relationships, he quickly made himself an influential player in the Senate, mastering its often obscure and opaque culture. Much of Johnson's time in the Senate, however, was spent worrying about Texas politics. Although he hoped to create for himself an image as a progressive, national figure, he had to protect his position at home as Texas drifted to the right. As Johnson told his aide Bobby Baker, "I won by just 87 votes and I ran against a caveman." Johnson therefore resigned himself to fighting civil rights, protecting oil and gas interests, and opposing organized labor. Johnson thus earned a reputation as a conservative among Senate Democrats. Despite these handcuffs, Johnson managed a meteoric rise in the Senate hierarchy. In the waning years of the HARRY S. TRUMAN administration, he was made majority whip. After Republicans took the Senate on Eisenhower's coattails in 1952, Johnson was elected Senate minority leader.

In his new leadership position, Johnson displayed remarkable skill and an insatiable appetite for legislative intelligence. Ravenous for information about the other senators, Johnson gorged on political gossip. When Johnson needed to sway a specific senator, he rapidly processed all the information he could find, including the man's personal feelings and his political philosophy as well as the interests of his constituents. Johnson would then unleash his legendary "JOHNSON TREATMENT," a one-on-one performance that could sway even the most determined political opponent.

Democrats regained the Senate majority in 1954, and Johnson became the Senate majority leader. Conscious of his Texas constituents, he emulated Eisenhower's "modern conservatism," which the president described as "conservative when it comes to economics, and liberal when it comes to human beings." Johnson proved an energetic leader, overseeing minimum wage increases, trade acts, and public housing programs. Johnson knew each bill and each senator inside and out. As before, however, an intense period of work and success was followed by illness. A heart attack in 1955, brought on by excessive smoking and drinking, almost killed the majority leader.

When Johnson returned to the Senate in January 1956, civil rights threatened to tear both the South and the Democratic Party apart. In 1957, Eisenhower presented Congress with a civil rights bill. The southern, segregationist wing of the Democrats threatened to bolt the party over the bill; the liberal northern wing steadfastly supported civil rights. In his most skillful political maneuvering, Johnson guided the bill through the Senate. First, he removed the provisions most odious to segregationists. He then reconfigured the bill as a voting rights bill, drastically weakening it in the process. In classic Johnson style, he believed that a weak bill was better than no bill at all. Though the final bill had hardly any positive effect on civil rights, Johnson's legislative achievement

earned praise from all sides. The Civil Rights Act of 1957 proved a courageous and politically expedient accomplishment for a man looking to transcend a sectional image.

Along with civil rights, the cold war competition between the United States and the Soviet Union shaped the political culture of Johnson's era. In the Senate, Johnson followed the cold war consensus established by President Truman—containment of communism overseas and vigilant anticommunism at home. During the Eisenhower years, Johnson harped on the alleged missile gap with the Soviet Union and he helped jump-start the U.S. SPACE PROGRAM. Johnson also continued to push through liberal measures including housing, highway, and hospital bills. When the launch of the Soviet satellite *Sputnik* in 1957 sparked fears that U.S. intellect and initiative were lagging behind the nation's ideological opponent, Johnson seized the moment to help pass the National Defense Education Act.

Ultimately, Johnson's Senate years exhibited the same pattern of success followed by frustration and apathy. In 1957, his mother Rebekah passed away; in Texas, Johnson grew increasingly unpopular among conservative Democrats. Meanwhile, the 1958 midterm elections brought a large Democratic majority to the Senate. The emboldened Democrats began to chafe under Johnson's dominance.

Facing diminishing returns in the Senate, Johnson set his sights on the presidency. He nonetheless did not jump fully into the race. He had started talking to his money men in the fall of 1959, but his candidacy in 1960 was waged in keeping with the old-fashioned "favorite-son" style. This approach depended on several factors: strong support from the home state delegation, in Johnson's case Texas; the lack of emergence of a consensus candidate ready to claim the nomination on the first ballot; and insider politicking at the Democratic National Convention, whereby Johnson would pick up other state delegations on subsequent rounds of balloting. Johnson himself did not enter the primaries. Instead, he relied on the candidacy of darkhorse senator HUBERT HUMPHREY, a Minnesota liberal, to determine whether or not Massachusetts senator JOHN F. KENNEDY had strength beyond his family's wealth. Some Humphrey supporters viewed their work as primarily a stop-Kennedy effort, while others had great hope for a Humphrey victory. Humphrey dropped out of the race after losing the West Virginia primary in May 1960, where Kennedy family money and mob money had been used to buy votes. Johnson talked with his advisers to see if any other way was possible to stop Kennedy, and even though the chances were slim, Johnson continued his behind-the-scenes race, vacillating about how hard and whether he should fight for the nomination. Finally, on July 5, 1960, Johnson announced publicly that he was running for president. It was too little and too late. The Democratic National Convention opened on July 11, in Los Angeles.

Johnson backers played hardball at the convention. Two intimates of the Texas senator issued a press release suggesting that Kennedy was dying of Addison's disease. Even Johnson recoiled at this truthful discussion of the Massachusetts senator's health. But he was not bashful about leveling charges regarding Kennedy's father, Joseph P. Kennedy, suggesting he had been a Nazi sympathizer in the late 1930s. There was truth to that charge as well. The elder Kennedy in his role as ambassador to the Court of St. James in London from 1938 to 1940 had been cozy with the British upper crust and had approved Neville Chamberlain's policy of appeasement of Adolf Hitler at Munich. Johnson's tactics angered the Kennedys, especially Senator Kennedy's brother Robert F. Kennedy, but they did not matter in the end. Senator Kennedy won a decisive victory on the first ballot.

Although Johnson sought the 1960 Democratic presidential nomination, he could not compete with the money and organization of the ruthless Kennedy political machine. The next issue before the Democratic Party involved the selection of the vice-presidential nominee. Kennedy had nothing on his résumé to appeal to Democrats in the South and the Southwest, and he knew it. Despite promises his brother had made to the liberal establishment that Johnson would not be placed on the ticket as vice president, John Kennedy believed that he needed him and so offered him the position. The Republicans had made gains across Texas and the South during the Eisenhower years. After making the offer, Kennedy was reasonably certain Johnson would accept. (After President Kennedy's death, Robert Kennedy intimated that neither of them had wanted Johnson on the ticket and that they were shocked when he accepted, but the account is not accurate.) Indeed, Johnson knew that he had to accept the offer. The majority leadership in the Senate in the 1960s would not afford the same degree of status and power as it had in the 1950s. If Kennedy won, he would be the leading Democrat in Washington. If his Republican opponent RICHARD M. NIXON won, Johnson might be charged with sinking Kennedy's chances by not running on his ticket. Furthermore, as president Nixon could be expected not to practice the same conciliatory leadership style that had ensured Johnson access to the White House under President Eisenhower. Additionally, Johnson's closest adviser, Speaker of the House Sam Rayburn, detested Nixon from both a political and a personal perspective. Nixon had called Rayburn a traitor, and Rayburn did not want him to be president. Finally, Johnson understood that the vice presidency might very well be his only path to the White House. He calculated that after a successful Kennedy administration, he could run in eight years in his own right and win the presidency. Johnson's mission in the campaign was to help win Texas. On election day, Kennedy and Johnson won by a razor-thin margin that was tarnished by shady results in Illinois and Texas.

Lyndon B. Johnson *(Lyndon B. Johnson Library)*

Johnson became vice president of the United States on January 20, 1961. Bristling in a post that entailed little power, Johnson soon came to loathe the position. Adding to his frustration, the president's coterie of Georgetown intellectuals, Harvard graduates, and liberal reporters frequently ridiculed Johnson as a hick. His pride wounded, the vice president increasingly took his revenge by playing the role of an even more crass country politician than his enemies had imagined. Thus, Johnson's actions, which included lewd stories, raw language, and gross behavior, increased.

Shocking intellectuals with colorful language failed to distract Johnson from his increasing irrelevance, however. Despite his legendary legislative ability, the Kennedy administration rarely sought his assistance. When he could, Johnson continued to encourage efforts to modernize the South. After Kennedy solicited Johnson's help with the space program, Johnson brought high-tech NASA investment to the South, including to Florida and Texas.

Johnson also played a role in the administration's civil rights efforts as chairman of the Committee on Equal Employment Opportunity. This group sought to end discrimination in federal hiring and among contractors working for the federal government. Freed from his reactionary Texas constituency, Johnson thrived as a national civil rights figure. In the spring of 1963, Johnson gave a speech at the Gettysburg battlefield in commemorating the Emancipation Proclamation of 1863 and the address anticipated his future groundbreaking civil rights efforts. "One hundred years ago," he stated, "the slave was freed. One hundred years later, the Negro remains in bondage to the color of his skin." In conclusion, Johnson tied the fate of African Americans to the national destiny: "Until justice is blind to color, until all education is unaware of race, until opportunity is unconcerned with the color of men's skins, emancipation will be a proclamation but emancipation will not be a fact."

When Johnson ascended to the presidency after John F. Kennedy's assassination on November 22, 1963, the new president advocated much reform legislation. Almost immediately, he invoked the memory of Kennedy in order to pass the dead president's civil rights bill that had stalled in Congress. The landmark CIVIL RIGHTS ACT of 1964 barred discrimination in public accommodations and outlawed discrimination in employment based on race, color, religion, sex, or national origin. Johnson used the same legislative strategy to push a tax cut through Congress. The cut created a nearly instantaneous economic boom that benefited the middle class and allowed Johnson to declare a "WAR ON POVERTY," an ambitious effort to uplift the poor and disadvantaged.

As president, Johnson demonstrated the political values that he had honed in a lifetime of politics. He embraced conventional means and refused to take rigid stances. He preached idealism but shied from ideology, and though he feared the label of "appeaser," he preferred peace to confrontation. But Johnson's status as an "accidental president" imprinted a lasting wound to his self-esteem. Hoping to court favor with the Kennedy wing of the Democratic Party, he made the fateful decision to retain his predecessor's entire cabinet. Despite Johnson's efforts, many in the Kennedy court began to idealize the slain president and view Johnson with disdain.

While Johnson pursued a revolutionary reform program at home, he maintained a conventional approach to foreign policy. U.S. policy remained committed to Kennedy's pursuit of negotiation with the Soviet Union and the containment of communism everywhere else. Johnson cared little for foreign affairs, but he remained captive to a fear of domestic anticommunism. In his mind, failure to forcefully confront

communism overseas could lead to his own downfall. As a communist insurgency threatened South Vietnam, Johnson maneuvered the GULF OF TONKIN RESOLUTION through Congress in the summer of 1964. The resolution, popular at the time, authorized the president to use U.S. military power as he saw fit in Vietnam.

In 1964, Johnson won the presidential election in his own right, sweeping every part of the country but the South. With a large mandate supporting him, Johnson unleashed a torrent of reform. For decades Johnson had sought to finish what the New Deal had started—the social and economic uplift of the oppressed, the poor, and the disadvantaged. Through government, Johnson believed, prosperity was possible for all. Johnson's reform program, known as the GREAT SOCIETY, attempted to provide all Americans with equal access to education, health care, and economic opportunity. It offered protection to consumers as well as the environment, and it opened America's doors to millions of immigrants. Just like the New Deal of the 1930s, the Great Society of the 1960s offered something for everyone: even artists and writers received a massive increase in federal funding. The unprecedented economic prosperity of the 1960s, in Johnson's plan, would allow government to help those who could not help themselves, while the U.S. free enterprise system took care of the rest. In this way, Johnson hoped to achieve equality among all Americans without the class conflict that characterized much of the New Deal.

In just slightly more than one term in office, Johnson signed hundreds of pieces of legislation. Not even this master politician, however, was immune to the urgent demands of the tumultuous 1960s. By 1965, Johnson found himself pushed, pulled, and prodded down paths he was not ready to trod. In 1965, the grassroots campaigns of civil rights activists forced Johnson to pursue a federal voting rights act before he thought the South was ready. Even this hasty action was not enough—just days after the signing of the 1965 VOTING RIGHTS ACT, the WATTS RIOT erupted in Los Angeles. The ensuing white backlash foreshadowed the end of Johnson's Great Society a little more than one year after it began.

Events overseas also limited Johnson's options. Although Johnson had delayed action on Vietnam with the Gulf of Tonkin Resolution, the lack of a settlement to the conflict raised calls for involvement of greater U.S. force in 1965. Captive to his own fear of appearing soft on communism, he agreed to an escalation of the war, including a massive bombing campaign. Ultimately unable to broker a settlement, Johnson would eventually become the war's most prominent victim.

Johnson's presidency fell into the pattern of his previous political incarnations. After meeting with brilliant success—this time through his Great Society—Johnson met with increasing frustration. As early as 1966 he found himself hedged in as inflation began to rise, black militants took over

President Johnson speaks with Martin Luther King, Jr., in the Oval Office at the White House, Washington D.C., 1963. *(Yoichi Okamoto/Lyndon B. Johnson Library)*

With former president Harry S. Truman sitting beside him, President Johnson signs the Medicare Bill into law at the Truman Library in Independence, Missouri, on July 30, 1965. Looking on are first lady Lady Bird Johnson, Vice President Hubert Humphrey, and former first lady Bess Truman. *(National Archives)*

part of the Civil Rights movement, and the bombing campaign in Vietnam proved ineffective. The Republicans made impressive gains in the 1966 midterm elections, leading to a major slowdown of the Great Society. In some ways, Johnson was the victim of his own rhetoric. Possessing an enormous ego that craved enormous accomplishments, Johnson had promised more than the Great Society could deliver.

Over time, a "credibility gap" grew between the president and the people. Johnson continued to maintain that victory was assured in Vietnam, but the 1968 Tet offensive revealed the lie behind this claim. Many Americans deemed the president untrustworthy. Other critics claimed the president had concentrated too much power in the executive branch. Indeed on many occasions, Johnson had instructed the FBI to investigate his political enemies, giving credence to charges of an "imperial presidency."

Vietnam proved Johnson's ultimate undoing. Caught between the hawks and the doves, between antiwar liberals and anticommunist conservatives, Johnson never found a way out of his strategic dilemma. He had hoped to escalate the war enough to bully the communists into surrender, yet

he limited the conflict in order to avoid bringing China and possibly the Soviet Union into the war. As the war consumed greater amounts of U.S. dollars, Johnson's Great Society went essentially bankrupt.

Race riots in U.S. cities in 1967 and 1968 made it nearly impossible to achieve any further reforms, and, true to form, Johnson followed his life pattern in withdrawing from the fray. In March 1968 he announced to the nation that he would not seek reelection. As if to underscore his impotence, a wave of violence swept the United States in the ensuing months, most notably including the assassinations of civil rights leader Martin Luther King, Jr. and New York senator Robert F. Kennedy, an antiwar Democratic presidential candidate and brother of former president John F. Kennedy. Bedlam reigned at the 1968 Democratic National Convention as violent demonstrations inside the convention and out protested Johnson's Vietnam War.

Just before leaving office in January 1969, Johnson brokered a bombing halt in Vietnam. The war nevertheless continued well into the 1970s. After leaving the White House, Johnson returned to his Texas ranch. He revived his smoking and drinking habits and mostly stayed out of the public spotlight. His most noteworthy public appearance was at a civil rights conference at the newly opened Lyndon B. Johnson Presidential Library and Museum in Austin, Texas. Prominent civil rights leaders affirmed his legislative successes. He died of heart failure on January 22, 1973, and was buried at the LBJ Ranch on the banks of the Pedernales River.

PRESIDENTIAL ELECTION OF 1964

Observers of the 1964 presidential election witnessed the rarity of a predictable outcome combined with a major, lasting upheaval in U.S. electoral politics. For although Lyndon Johnson's victory became inevitable as soon as the Republicans nominated Barry Goldwater, the shift of the Deep South into the Republican column for the first time signified major transformations within the two parties.

As sitting president, Johnson enjoyed the relative certainty that he would be nominated by the Democrats. But by nature Johnson was anything but confident. Considering himself president only by the fateful accident of John F. Kennedy's assassination, he craved a landslide victory in 1964 both as affirmation and validation for himself and as a mandate for his Great Society reform. In private moments he even dreamed of a victory surpassing the one his hero Franklin D. Roosevelt achieved in 1936.

While the Democrats' nominee was quite certain, the Republican nominee was anything but. The favorites included the 1960 nominee Richard Nixon, New York governor Nelson Rockefeller, and former vice-presidential candidate Henry Cabot Lodge, just back from a stint as U.S. ambassador to South Vietnam. But in the summer of 1964, a number of rank-and-file Republican activists began a grassroots groundswell of support for the ultra-conservative Arizona senator Barry Goldwater. This movement culminated in Goldwater's nomination at the Republican National Convention in San Francisco in July. Astoundingly, the far right fringe of the Republican Party, including members of the John Birch Society, Young Americans for Freedom, and Young Republicans, had triumphed over the more moderate conservatives. Although Old Guard Republicans such as Nixon and Rockefeller remained influential within the party, the Goldwater revolt signaled the growing strength of young conservatives in the GOP as well as the rising of the Republican Party in the South and Southwest. Nixon himself would ride a "southern strategy" to victory in the future elections of 1968 and 1972.

Senator Goldwater had acquired the image of an extreme conservative since beginning his congressional career in 1952. The reputation was well earned indeed. The author of *The Conscience of a Conservative,* Goldwater was

AN AMERICAN TRAGEDY

With Barry Goldwater poised to win the Republican nomination, this Herblock cartoon captioned "An American Tragedy" shows "extremism" drowning the "moderates" in the Republican Party. *(A Herblock Cartoon, copyright by the Herb Block Foundation)*

fond of saying that "Extremism in the defense of liberty is no vice. Moderation in the pursuit of justice is no virtue." The Johnson camp salivated at the thought of running against him. President Johnson had received high approval ratings ever since he succeeded Kennedy, and his aggressive support for civil rights as well as his War on Poverty were popular in all but a few states. During this high tide of liberalism, Goldwater attacked the remaining New Deal programs, promising that he would make Social Security voluntary and privatize the Tennessee Valley Authority. He denounced some of the Democrats' proudest achievements, including the 1963 Limited Test Ban Treaty and the Civil Rights Act of 1964. When critics accused Goldwater of having played no significant role in any legislation, Goldwater proudly declared that he was more interested in repealing laws than passing them. Such a stance alienated many voters at the time but foreshadowed the future growth of a libertarian, antigovernment sentiment among American conservatives.

Senator Goldwater was a hawk on Vietnam and boasted that he would not hesitate to use nuclear weapons against Vietnamese communists to end the conflict. Eager to strike

Attorney General Robert F. Kennedy addresses a crowd outside the Department of Justice in June 1963. After the assassination of his brother, President John F. Kennedy, five months later, he stayed on in President Johnson's cabinet and was considered a possible vice-presidential candidate in 1964. When Johnson chose Hubert Humphrey instead, Kennedy resigned and ran successfully for the U.S. Senate in New York. *(Library of Congress)*

a moderate pose in contrast, President Johnson engineered passage of the GULF OF TONKIN RESOLUTION in early August 1964. At the time, the resolution did little more than help steal some of Goldwater's thunder by boosting the president's approval ratings on Vietnam. But over the next four years, liberals and conservatives alike would point to the resolution as ushering in the "imperial presidency" and trapping the United States in a bloody quagmire in Vietnam.

In some fleeting moments, Johnson considered not running for president in 1964. Always plagued by self-doubt, he wondered if the Democratic Party would actually prefer to run Attorney General Robert F. Kennedy, the brother of the slain president. Furthermore, some of Johnson's closest advisers repeatedly told the president that victory in 1964 was far from assured. Such pessimism was characteristic of Johnson,

but far from discouraging him, it motivated him. And once he dedicated himself to the campaign, he expended the effort of a vast underdog rather than the clear favorite he was.

After the Republicans nominated Goldwater, one of the few remaining mysteries in the campaign involved Johnson's choice of a vice-presidential candidate. Many in the Democratic Party wanted Robert Kennedy for the spot, but aside from a common party affiliation, Kennedy and Johnson shared little but mutual hatred. Both had strong-willed personalities and both distrusted the other. Furthermore, Johnson believed that Bobby Kennedy had never shown him the respect he deserved while Kennedy viewed Johnson as intellectually inferior and a political hack. In July, the president told Kennedy, the sitting attorney general, that the vice-presidential nominee would not come from the current

HUBERT H. HUMPHREY

(1911–1978) *vice president of the United States, January 20, 1965–January 20, 1969*

Hubert H. Humphrey was born on May 27, 1911, to Christine Sannes and Hubert H. Humphrey, Sr. in Wallace, South Dakota. He interrupted his college studies to work in his father's drug store, but he ultimately earned a bachelor's degree from the University of Minnesota in 1939 and a master's degree from Louisiana State University in 1940. He married Muriel Buck in 1936, and they had four children. Humphrey began his political career as the pro-labor, pro–civil rights mayor of Minneapolis, Minnesota. In 1948, he delivered an electrifying speech at the Democratic National Convention that convinced the party to add a vigorous civil rights plank to its platform. Later that year, he won election to the Senate as part of the famous freshman class that included Lyndon B. Johnson (D-TX), Clinton Anderson (D-NM), and Estes Kefauver (D-TN). As senator, Humphrey epitomized the postwar Democratic Party: staunchly anticommunist and supportive of civil rights, labor, health care, education, housing, and tax reform. Loquacious and likeable, Humphrey worked as Johnson's bridge to the liberal wing of the Democratic Party. Humphrey won reelection in 1954 and again in 1960 after a failed run at the Democratic presidential nomination.

In 1964, Johnson, now president, handpicked Humphrey to guide the Civil Rights Act through the Senate. Humphrey's efforts proved critical to the bill's passage, skillfully flattering reluctant senators, including Republican Everett Dirksen of Illinois, to support the bill. Especially crucial were the votes Humphrey amassed for cloture in order to cut off a filibuster by southern Democrats. Humphrey engineered a critical compromise with Dirksen that added a few harmless amendments in exchange for his support on the cloture vote. The successful passage of the law marked the pinnacle of Humphrey's Senate career.

In the presidential election of 1964, Johnson relished the process of choosing a running mate. Most Democrats favored Humphrey, arguing that he would strengthen the ticket in the Midwest and Northeast. Johnson, hoping to create intrigue, complained Humphrey "talks too much to be Vice President." Johnson floated names including Robert Kennedy, Sargent

Hubert H. Humphrey *(Library of Congress)*

cabinet. The decision irked Kennedy, who then ran successfully for the Senate from New York, and further fueled the rivalry between the two men.

With Kennedy out of the picture, nearly everyone expected Johnson to pick Minnesota senator HUBERT H. HUMPHREY. But true to form, Johnson turned his vice-presidential selection into an ego trip. Clearly hoping to milk every last drop of melodrama out of a fairly insignificant process, Johnson temporized. He took particular pleasure in torturing Humphrey by alternately promising him the vice-presidential nomination and then doubting his ability and loyalty. Conversations between the two men usually ended with Johnson making a bald demand of fealty in exchange for the number two spot. As the Democratic National Convention (DNC) began in Atlantic City in August 1964, John-

son had apparently squeezed his melodrama dry. He then proceeded to squeeze even harder. Johnson ordered Humphrey to leave the convention and return to the White House along with Connecticut senator Thomas J. Dodd, hoping to fuel speculation that Dodd might be the president's choice instead. After meeting with Dodd for show, Johnson ushered in the exhausted Humphrey. After pumping him for yet another pledge of loyalty—telling Humphrey "this is like a marriage with no chance of divorce. I need complete and unswerving loyalty"—the president called Humphrey's wife, Muriel, to tell her: "We're going to nominate your boy."

Meanwhile, at the DNC, turmoil over civil rights threatened to upset the proceedings. An interracial, unofficial delegation from Mississippi, calling themselves the Mississippi Freedom Democratic Party (MFDP), contested the official,

---

Shriver, and Robert McNamara, though he probably never seriously considered anyone besides Humphrey. In fact, Johnson hoped to manipulate Humphrey by playing on the senator's presidential ambitions. Again and again Johnson demanded pledges of absolute loyalty from Humphrey, making it clear that the position of vice president depended on subservience. At the 1964 Democratic National Convention in Atlantic City, Johnson forced Humphrey to resolve the Mississippi Freedom Democratic Party (MFDP) dispute as a final test. MFDP activists spurned Humphrey's compromise and abandoned the convention, but the challenge had ended; Johnson was pleased and added him to the ticket.

After the victorious 1964 campaign, Humphrey was Johnson's natural choice as the administration's figurehead on civil rights. At first, Humphrey helped coordinate the numerous civil rights efforts by the many government agencies. But widespread backlash following the 1965 Watts race riot convinced Johnson to turn down the volume on his support for civil rights. He began by removing Humphrey as the administration's civil rights spokesperson. The move was calculated to show that civil rights extremism and violence would make the administration less— not more—cooperative. In 1967, Humphrey chaired a cabinet group charged with preventing the rampant race riots in American cities. When the group urged a major increase in antipoverty funding as well as new job programs, Johnson ignored their recommendations and disbanded the group.

At first, Vice President Humphrey refused to act as Johnson's patsy. When Johnson initiated a bombing campaign against North Vietnam in 1965, Humphrey warned the president against escalating the war. The criticism deeply offended Johnson, who cut off Humphrey from the White House for months. To get back in Johnson's good graces, Humphrey gave

speeches praising the bombing campaign and supporting the president's justification for the war. Welcoming Humphrey back into the fold, Johnson sent the vice president to Asia in 1966 to drum up support for his plan for social and economic reform in Vietnam. Upon his return from Asia, Humphrey delivered the optimistic report that Johnson demanded, claiming the president's plan marked "A historic turning point in American relationships with Asia." One year later, Humphrey visited Saigon and gave Johnson a glowing account of the war in Vietnam, though Humphrey's close friends felt that the vice president, in actuality, believed the complete opposite.

In 1968, when the deteriorating situation in Vietnam and widespread dissatisfaction with his leadership forced Johnson to announce that he would not seek reelection, Humphrey grasped the opportunity to realize his own presidential ambitions. After Humphrey won the Democratic nomination, Democrats pleaded with the candidate to denounce Johnson's Vietnam policy, especially the ineffective and cruel bombing campaign. Johnson consequently wavered in his support of Humphrey during the race. Humphrey, however, remained loyal to the president and would not denounce the bombing campaign. In late September, he finally distanced himself from the president, announcing that he would halt the bombing if elected—his poll numbers surged. Meanwhile, Humphrey's opponent, Republican Richard Nixon, secretly encouraged Saigon to resist participating in peace talks until after the election. Humphrey admirably—but unwisely—refused to reveal these machinations, and failing to do so likely cost himself the election. Although Humphrey continued to gain on Nixon in the closing days of the campaign, he lost a close race. Humphrey returned to the Senate in 1970, where he served until his death from cancer on January 13, 1978.

all-white Mississippi delegation's right to represent their state. Television cameras surrounded the MFDP's Fannie Lou Hamer, who described the violence and fear that kept African Americans in Mississippi from voting. The challenge of the MFDP exposed the hypocrisy of Democratic Party politics in the South, and many Democrats urged Johnson to let the MFDP replace the official Mississippi delegation. But Johnson knew that such a decision would cause most—if not all—of the southern states to bolt the Democratic Party.

The president wanted nothing to mar the convention that he viewed as a coronation. He feared losing support among both African Americans and white southerners, and he ordered Humphrey, just back from the White House, to broker a solution. Working with labor leader Walter Reuther, Humphrey offered the MFDP two at-large convention seats and a promise to improve the situation in Mississippi by 1968. Hamer and her fellow activists rejected the compromise and stormed out. The MFDP challenge signaled a growing disaffection among civil rights activists with the Democratic Party.

With the MFDP confrontation solved relatively peacefully—if not justly—Johnson turned to the convention itself. But he was unable to savor the moment, as Kennedy loyalists had reserved one day for a tribute to John F. Kennedy. The day's keynote speaker was none other than Johnson's nemesis Robert Kennedy. As insecure as ever, Johnson feared that Kennedy's moving tribute might unleash a spasm of pro-Kennedy euphoria, resulting in Robert's nomination for president. Kennedy indeed stole the show with a moving speech about his brother that culminated in a quote from *Romeo and Juliet*. Some Kennedy insiders wondered if the last line was meant as an attack on Johnson: "When he shall die/ Take him and cut him out in little stars/ And he will make the face of heaven so fine/ That all the world will be in love with night,/ And pay no worship to the garish sun."

None of Johnson's fears came to pass. The convention quickly nominated the Johnson-Humphrey ticket. Humphrey gave a rousing speech attacking Goldwater's extremist stance, and Johnson followed with a bland if sufficient speech.

After the conclusion of the Democratic National Convention, all eyes turned to the election. Among Republicans, all but the most diehard Goldwater supporters knew that the cause was lost, but the mere fact that ultra conservatives had succeeded in nominating their candidate foreshadowed the widespread backlash against the Civil Rights movement and the Great Society that flourished during the late 1960s and early 1970s.

Goldwater soldiered on undaunted by his long odds. With New York congressman William Miller as his running mate, Goldwater campaigned against Johnson's reform program. What he lacked in tactical savvy and broad appeal, Goldwater made up for in loyalty to his principles. During

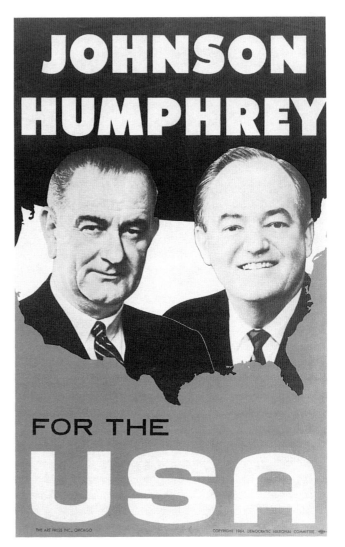

Johnson and Humphrey campaign poster *(Library of Congress)*

the campaign he outlined a clear conservative philosophy that doomed the Republicans in the short term but boosted them to victory in the 1980s and beyond. He vowed to reduce government expenditures, eliminate government bureaucracy, end integration, support states' rights, end welfare, and stifle unions. Noticeably out of touch with the liberal trend in the nation and in the electorate in general—he denounced Social Security in Florida, of all places—Goldwater also erred on foreign policy. He promised to use nuclear weapons in Vietnam, even if doing so brought China into the conflict.

Johnson exploited Goldwater's image as an extremist in a series of television commercials, the most notorious of which featured a young girl picking daisy petals. As an ominous countdown began, the camera zoomed in on the girl's eye, where a nuclear explosion and mushroom cloud were superimposed. As the inferno raged, Johnson's voice declared: "These are the stakes. To make a world in which all of God's children can live, or go on into the dark. We must either love each other, or we must die." Then the announcer came on and said: "Vote for President Johnson on November 3. The stakes are too high for you to stay at home." Public outrage forced the Democrats to pull the ad after one airing, but by then it had already become a news story of its own. Subsequent TV news stories about the commercial replayed the ad countless times.

Part of Johnson's political genius lay in his ability to take all campaigns seriously, exerting all effort and leaving noth-

ing to chance. He had learned this lesson the hard way in 1941 when political naiveté had cost him a U.S. Senate seat. For the rest of his life he campaigned vigorously even when victory was assured, as in 1964. For Johnson knew that victory was not enough—he wanted to win an impressive mandate with which to enact his ambitious Great Society reform program. Consequently Johnson set off to unleash a Democratic landslide. He wanted to represent the entire country, including the South, where white voters fumed over his civil

Lady Bird Johnson aboard the "Lady Bird Special" *(Photo by Frank Muto/Lyndon B. Johnson Library)*

1964 Election Statistics

State	Number of Electors	Total Popular Vote	Elec Vote		Pop Vote		Margin of Victory	
			D	R	D	R	Votes	% Total Vote
Alabama	10	689,817		10	-	1	268,353	38.90%
Alaska	3	67,259	3		1	2	21,399	31.82%
Arizona	5	480,770		5	2	1	4,782	0.99%
Arkansas	6	560,426	6		1	2	70,933	12.66%
California	40	7,057,586	40		1	2	1,292,769	18.32%
Colorado	6	776,986	6		1	2	179,257	23.07%
Connecticut	8	1,218,578	8		1	2	435,273	35.72%
Delaware	3	201,320	3		1	2	44,626	22.17%
District of Columbia	3	198,597	3		1	2	140,995	71.00%
Florida	14	1,854,481	14		1	2	42,599	2.30%
Georgia	12	1,139,336		12	2	1	94,027	8.25%
Hawaii	4	207,271	4		1	2	119,227	57.52%
Idaho	4	292,477	4		1	2	5,363	1.83%
Illinois	26	4,702,841	26		1	2	890,887	18.94%
Indiana	13	2,091,606	13		1	2	259,730	12.42%
Iowa	9	1,184,539	9		1	2	283,882	23.97%
Kansas	7	857,901	7		1	2	77,449	9.03%
Kentucky	9	1,046,105	9		1	2	296,682	28.36%
Louisiana	10	896,293		10	2	1	122,157	13.63%
Maine	4	381,221	4		1	2	143,563	37.66%
Maryland	10	1,116,457	10		1	2	345,417	30.94%
Massachusetts	14	2,344,798	14		1	2	1,236,695	52.74%
Michigan	21	3,203,102	21		1	2	1,076,463	33.61%
Minnesota	10	1,554,462	10		1	2	431,493	27.76%
Mississippi	7	409,146		7	2	1	303,910	74.28%
Missouri	12	1,817,879	12		1	2	510,809	28.10%
Montana	4	278,628	4		1	2	51,214	18.38%
Nebraska	5	584,154	5		1	2	30,460	5.21%
Nevada	3	135,433	3		1	2	23,245	17.16%
New Hampshire	4	288,093	4		1	2	80,035	27.78%
New Jersey	17	2,846,770	17		1	2	903,828	31.75%
New Mexico	4	327,615	4		1	2	62,179	18.98%
New York	43	7,166,015	43		1	2	2,669,597	37.25%
North Carolina	13	1,424,983	13		1	2	175,295	12.30%
North Dakota	4	258,389	4		1	2	41,577	16.09%
Ohio	26	3,969,196	26		1	2	1,027,466	25.89%
Oklahoma	8	932,499	8		1	2	107,169	11.49%
Oregon	6	786,305	6		1	2	218,238	27.75%
Pennsylvania	29	4,822,690	29		1	2	1,457,297	30.22%
Rhode Island	4	390,091	4		1	2	240,848	61.74%
South Carolina	8	524,756		8	2	1	93,348	17.79%
South Dakota	4	293,118	4		1	2	32,902	11.22%
Tennessee	11	1,143,946	11		1	2	125,982	11.01%
Texas	25	2,626,811	25		1	2	704,619	26.82%
Utah	4	400,310	4		1	2	38,946	9.73%
Vermont	3	163,089	3		1	2	53,185	32.61%
Virginia	12	1,042,267	12		1	2	76,704	7.36%
Washington	9	1,258,556	9		1	2	309,515	24.59%
West Virginia	7	792,040	7		1	2	284,134	35.87%
Wisconsin	12	1,691,815	12		1	2	411,929	24.35%
Wyoming	3	142,716	3		1	2	18,720	13.12%
Total	538	70,641,539	486	52	1	2	15,953,286	22.58%

* Note: Other vote in Alabama includes 210,732 votes for unpledged Democratic electors.

Johnson Democratic		Goldwater Republican		Others	
0	0.00%	479,085	69.45%	210,732*	30.55%
44,329	65.91%	22,930	34.09%	0	0.00%
237,753	49.45%	242,535	50.45%	482	0.10%
314,197	56.06%	243,264	43.41%	2,965	0.53%
4,171,877	59.11%	2,879,108	40.79%	6,601	0.09%
476,024	61.27%	296,767	38.19%	4,195	0.54%
826,269	67.81%	390,996	32.09%	1,313	0.11%
122,704	60.95%	78,078	38.78%	538	0.27%
169,796	85.50%	28,801	14.50%	0	0.00%
948,540	51.15%	905,941	48.85%	0	0.00%
522,557	45.87%	616,584	54.12%	195	0.02%
163,249	78.76%	44,022	21.24%	0	0.00%
148,920	50.92%	143,557	49.08%	0	0.00%
2,796,833	59.47%	1,905,946	40.53%	62	0.00%
1,170,848	55.98%	911,118	43.56%	9,640	0.46%
733,030	61.88%	449,148	37.92%	2,361	0.20%
464,028	54.09%	386,579	45.06%	7,294	0.85%
669,659	64.01%	372,977	35.65%	3,469	0.33%
387,068	43.19%	509,225	56.81%	0	0.00%
262,264	68.80%	118,701	31.14%	256	0.07%
730,912	65.47%	385,495	34.53%	50	0.00%
1,786,422	76.19%	549,727	23.44%	8,649	0.37%
2,136,615	66.70%	1,060,152	33.10%	6,335	0.20%
991,117	63.76%	559,624	36.00%	3,721	0.24%
52,618	12.86%	356,528	87.14%	0	0.00%
1,164,344	64.05%	653,535	35.95%	0	0.00%
164,246	58.95%	113,032	40.57%	1,350	0.48%
307,307	52.61%	276,847	47.39%	0	0.00%
79,339	58.58%	56,094	41.42%	0	0.00%
184,064	63.89%	104,029	36.11%	0	0.00%
1,867,671	65.61%	963,843	33.86%	15,256	0.54%
194,017	59.22%	131,838	40.24%	1,760	0.54%
4,913,156	68.56%	2,243,559	31.31%	9,300	0.13%
800,139	56.15%	624,844	43.85%	0	0.00%
149,784	57.97%	108,207	41.88%	398	0.15%
2,498,331	62.94%	1,470,865	37.06%	0	0.00%
519,834	55.75%	412,665	44.25%	0	0.00%
501,017	63.72%	282,779	35.96%	2,509	0.32%
3,130,954	64.92%	1,673,657	34.70%	18,079	0.37%
315,463	80.87%	74,615	19.13%	13	0.00%
215,700	41.10%	309,048	58.89%	8	0.00%
163,010	55.61%	130,108	44.39%	0	0.00%
634,947	55.50%	508,965	44.49%	34	0.00%
1,663,185	63.32%	958,566	36.49%	5,060	0.19%
219,628	54.86%	180,682	45.14%	0	0.00%
108,127	66.30%	54,942	33.69%	20	0.01%
558,038	53.54%	481,334	46.18%	2,895	0.28%
779,881	61.97%	470,366	37.37%	8,309	0.66%
538,087	67.94%	253,953	32.06%	0	0.00%
1,050,424	62.09%	638,495	37.74%	2,896	0.17%
80,718	56.56%	61,998	43.44%	0	0.00%
43,129,040	61.05%	27,175,754	38.47%	336,745	0.48%

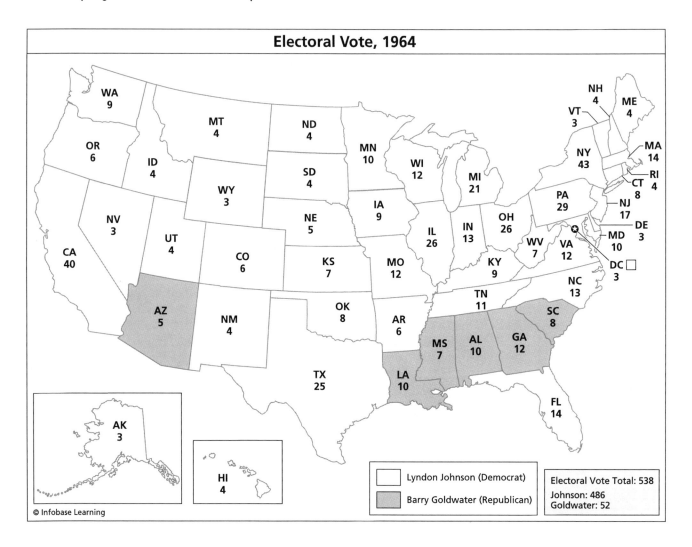

Electoral Vote, 1964

WA 9

MT 4

ND 4

MN 10

OR 6

ID 4

WY 3

SD 4

WI 12

MI 21

NH 4

VT 3

ME 4

NY 43

MA 14

NV 3

UT 4

CO 6

NE 5

IA 9

IL 26

IN 13

OH 26

PA 29

RI 4

CT 8

NJ 17

CA 40

KS 7

MO 12

WV 7

VA 12

MD 10

DE 3

DC 3

KY 9

AZ 5

NM 4

OK 8

AR 6

TN 11

NC 13

SC 8

MS 7

AL 10

GA 12

LA 10

TX 25

FL 14

AK 3

HI 4

Lyndon Johnson (Democrat)

Barry Goldwater (Republican)

Electoral Vote Total: 538
Johnson: 486
Goldwater: 52

© Infobase Learning

rights programs, and the North, where Johnson feared backlash from pro-Kennedy intellectuals. Aside from geography, Johnson also hoped to represent all types of Americans. Campaigning hard among liberal and conservative Democrats alike, Johnson also courted Republicans. Playing off of Goldwater's extremism, Johnson convinced many Eisenhower Republicans to vote for him. He appealed to big business and labor, as well as to every other interest group he could think of, including all religions, races, and classes. Such ambition bordered on hubris, but Johnson believed that only a massive victory would ensure that the country would follow him down the path of reform. As with many other times in Johnson's life, the political giant from Texas fused his aim to achieve for himself personal glory with a genuine desire to improve the common good.

During the campaign, Johnson paid special attention to the South. The Democratic majority in Congress depended heavily on a bloc of southern Democrats who adamantly opposed civil rights. Although Johnson predicted that southerners would bolt the Democratic Party,

he nevertheless tried to keep them on his side. Knowing he might receive a rude reception, he decided to take advantage of the South's tradition of chivalry. Thus, LADY BIRD JOHNSON embarked on a whistle-stop railroad tour of the South in October 1964 campaigning on behalf of her husband the president. Covering 1,700 miles and eight states in four days, Johnson voiced her support for both civil rights and the South. Although confrontational crowds gathered in South Carolina, the "Lady Bird Special" was welcomed by mostly positive crowds and received good press coverage. Johnson campaigned in the South as well, essentially demonstrating that, no matter how it voted, he would not abandon the South.

As election day approached, Johnson's lead over Goldwater continued to grow. Support for Johnson was so overwhelming that the president even decided to campaign in Goldwater's home state of Arizona, where he eventually lost to the senator by only a few thousand votes. Huge crowds turned out to welcome the president in the Northeast. Furthermore, Johnson benefited from a booming economy.

Across the nation, he pledged to fulfill his promise of progress, reform, and containment of communism overseas.

The Johnson campaign proved invincible—even a sex scandal could not damage Johnson's chances. On October 14, Johnson's long-time aide Walter Jenkins was arrested in a YMCA men's room in Washington, D.C., while engaged in a sex act with another male. At first Johnson suspected that Republicans had fabricated the story, but soon he accepted the truth. Mores at the time strictly forbade homosexuality, so Johnson rushed to dissociate himself from Jenkins. Lady Bird Johnson, however, declined to abandon the long-time family friend. She refused to let Johnson fire Jenkins, and then she issued a statement showing support and sympathy for the disgraced aide. Goldwater did not exploit the issue publicly. The scandal was quickly overshadowed later that month when governing circles in the Soviet Union ousted Premier Nikita Khrushchev.

On election day, November 3, 1964, Johnson achieved his wish. The Johnson-Humphrey ticket won the largest landslide ever: 43.1 million Americans voted for him, while just 27.2 million voted for Goldwater, an astounding majority of 61.05 percent. Johnson's electoral votes dwarfed Goldwater, 486–52 (though he did not exceed Roosevelt's electoral majority in 1936). The landslide was not limited to the presidency: Republicans lost 37 seats in the House of Representatives and two in the Senate. Democrats thus controlled the House 295 to 140 and the Senate 68 to 32. The new class of Democratic senators included Robert Kennedy, who won a Senate seat from New York.

The victory provided Johnson with his personal validation and exorcised the ghost of John F. Kennedy. With the nation behind him, he and the Democrats could enact the Great Society and unleash an unprecedented tide of reform. Not surprisingly, however, Johnson demonstrated little pleasure at the result—instead he grumbled that the national press characterized the victory as more of a renunciation of Goldwater than an embrace of President Johnson.

In the end, the victory proved a pyrrhic one for the Democrats. For the first time since the Civil War, the Deep South had supported the party of ABRAHAM LINCOLN. Johnson had of course predicted such an outcome immediately after signing the Civil Rights Act, when he told Texas congressman Jake Pickle (D), "I think we delivered the South to the Republican party for your lifetime and mine." Goldwater swept the Deep South: Alabama, Georgia, Louisiana, Mississippi, and South Carolina all voted Republican (Goldwater also won Arizona). In the following decades, the entire South would increasingly vote Republican. Goldwater Republicans, the young grassroots conservative activists who cut their political teeth on the 1964 campaign, would soon become the heart of the GOP, helping to construct a conservative majority in the 1980s that continued into the 21st century.

JOHNSON ADMINISTRATION (1963–1969)

In terms of legislative achievements, the only presidential record that compares to Lyndon B. Johnson's is that of FRANKLIN D. ROOSEVELT. Johnson's roughly five years in the White House saw an avalanche of reform that, like the New Deal, both liberalized and revolutionized the American state. A master politician with decades of experience in Washington behind him when he took office, this colossus of politicians fared far worse in the foreign policy realm. Johnson's inability to resolve the Vietnam conflict led to his undoing, and in the process ushered in a near civil war in American society during the 1960s. In the aftermath of this divisive conflict, a conservative revolution gained gradual ascendancy in U.S. politics and under which much of Johnson's GREAT SOCIETY was dismantled. The tragedy of Vietnam, with its concurrent conservative shift in American political culture, has in many ways eclipsed Johnson's other accomplishments. That such a monumental record of achievement could be overshadowed at all indicates how large the Vietnam shadow looms.

Johnson assumed the presidency on November 22, 1963, after the assassination of President JOHN F. KENNEDY. On November 27, the president addressed the grieving nation. He called on the country "to do away with uncertainty and doubt," and show the world "that from the brutal loss of our leader we will derive not weakness, but strength; that we can and will act and act now." Kennedy's theme as president had been "let us begin," so, Johnson declared, "Today, in this moment of new resolve, I would say to all my fellow Americans, let us continue." Indeed, the dominant theme of Johnson's presidency would be continuity—both with Kennedy as well as with the presidents who had come before him: DWIGHT D. EISENHOWER, HARRY S. TRUMAN, and Roosevelt. Continuing what these four leaders had started, in affairs both domestic and foreign, would bring Johnson to the zenith, and the nadir, of American politics.

Johnson did continue the Kennedy vision, most concretely by asking the dead president's entire cabinet to remain. Although Johnson came to regret this decision, he deemed it essential to demonstrate continuity to the nation and loyalty to the president's memory. Johnson got along surprisingly well with some of the cabinet, considering his tense relationship with the Kennedy crowd in general. Secretary of the Interior Stuart Udall, for example, managed to work well with Johnson for the most part. Some cabinet members resigned despite Johnson's request. Presidential science adviser Jerome Wiesner, who had been close to Kennedy, resigned in sadness. Johnson replaced him with Princeton scientist Donald Hornig. Although the Kennedy administration had considered removing FBI director J. Edgar Hoover,

Less than two hours after President Kennedy's death on November 22, 1963, Federal District judge Sarah T. Hughes administers the oath of office to Lyndon Johnson in the conference room aboard Air Force One at Love Field, Dallas, Texas. On the left is Johnson's wife, Lady Bird Johnson; on the right is former first lady Jacqueline Kennedy. *(Library of Congress)*

Johnson personally asked the director to remain. Hoover repaid Johnson by providing the president with information about his rivals taken from illegal FBI wiretaps. Of all the Kennedy holdovers, the most significant was Robert F. Kennedy, the former president's brother, who was retained as attorney general. Robert Kennedy came to see Johnson as somehow responsible for his brother's death and he eventually grew to despise the Texan with whom he had never been comfortable; the feeling was mutual.

In most matters, Johnson relied less on the cabinet and more on the intimate circle of friends and cronies with which he surrounded himself. These advisers included staff members Walter Jenkins, Marvin Watson, Horace Busby, Jack Valenti, and Bill Moyers. Particularly essential to Johnson's political career was George Reedy, whose memos on all topics served to focus the president's thoughts and actions on crucial matters. Joseph Califano joined the president's staff later

in the administration, serving as an effective domestic policy adviser. Johnson also retained connections with a number of influential New Dealers, including James Rowe, Tom Corcoran, and, especially, lawyer Abe Fortas. LADY BIRD JOHNSON occupied a unique status among his advisers, as her loyalty to the president was unquestionable. Of all Johnson's intimates, she was the only one who was never accused of harboring ulterior motives.

An examination of Johnson's domestic agenda shows that, although he vowed to continue in the footsteps of John F. Kennedy, Johnson actually saw himself as the spiritual heir of Franklin D. Roosevelt. In fact, Johnson viewed his domestic efforts, cumulatively known as the Great Society, as nothing less than the fulfillment and expansion of the New Deal. In March 1965, Johnson outlined his vision in a speech at the University of Michigan. He stated: "For a century, we labored to settle and to subdue a continent. For half a century we called upon unbounded invention and untiring industry to create an order of plenty of all of our people. The challenge of the next half century is whether we have the wisdom to use that wealth to enrich and elevate our national life, and to advance the quality of our American civilization." America would become a "Great Society," he announced, "a place where men are more concerned with the quality of their goals than the quantity of their goods." He concluded by asking his audience, "Will you join the battle to give every citizen the full equality which God enjoins and the law requires, whatever his belief, or race, or the color of his skin? Will you join in the battle to give every citizen an escape from the crushing weight of poverty? Will you join in the battle to make it possible for all nations to live in enduring peace—as neighbors and not as mortal enemies? Will you join in the battle to build the Great Society?"

Although he appealed to all Americans, Johnson envisioned the Great Society as particularly essential for disadvantaged Americans, the poor and African Americans in particular. Johnson's reference to wealth in the Great Society speech revealed much about his approach. Because of the vast postwar prosperity, Johnson believed that the federal government could afford to fund a massive reform program. He still needed to convince the well-off of the benefit of helping the disadvantaged. For a time Johnson achieved this goal. But Johnson's other rhetorical flourish in his speech is also revealing. By characterizing the Great Society as a "battle," including an ambitious "war" on poverty, Johnson created expectations of victory and triumph. When poverty proved invincible, Americans quickly grew disillusioned with the Great Society.

Beginning with his hasty inauguration aboard Air Force One, Johnson surprised his aides with the urgency with which he approached his task. With uncanny accuracy, Johnson told his advisers that the American public would support reform, but not for very long—at most two years, he guessed. At the same time, Johnson had been stockpiling ideas for reform ever since his first days in Washington during the New Deal. Consequently, he had a laundry list of liberal legislation ready to go as soon as he became president. Pressed by his sense that speed was essential, Johnson took great risks that, at first, produced great rewards. Always conscious of his pledge to continue Kennedy's vision, Johnson first set eyes on two pieces of legislation that Kennedy had introduced and had subsequently stalled in Congress: a tax cut and a civil rights bill.

The first of these called for an $11 billion tax cut. At the time, most liberals supported tax cuts while conservatives opposed them. Always a skillful legislator, Johnson used the moral pulpit of the presidency by frequently invoking the memory of the slain president to rally support for the bill. Johnson's strategy worked—he even managed to get conservatives and business leaders to support the tax cut, which passed the Senate by a wide margin. By February 1964 it was law. The law worked: Consumer demand as well as industrial production increased. The ensuing economic boom benefited the American middle class and provided money to fund the Great Society.

The second piece of stalled Kennedy legislation was far riskier. The 1963 civil rights campaign to desegregate Birmingham, Alabama, which featured the use of fire hoses and police dogs against the marchers, many of whom were children, proved pivotal. The protests were broadcast on television, and the scenes depicted heightened American distaste for the brutalities of the Jim Crow South. In response, Kennedy had introduced a civil rights bill that had made little progress. The prospects of a filibuster by segregationist southern Democrats in the Senate made passage of the bill a long shot. President Johnson, however, had mastered the Senate as majority leader in the 1950s. Again invoking the memory of Kennedy, Johnson skillfully guided the bill through Congress. Working with Minnesota senator HUBERT HUMPHREY, Johnson managed to win a cloture vote to cut off all filibusters. With a filibuster defeated, the bill sped through the Senate; Johnson signed the bill in July. The landmark CIVIL RIGHTS ACT of 1964 outlawed segregation in public places, and it launched the slow death of Jim Crow.

Johnson knew that factors besides Jim Crow held African Americans down, including racism and poverty. Both were notoriously difficult to overcome. Johnson personally appealed to the higher ideals of the United States in order to overcome racism. At Howard University, the president delivered a commencement speech on June 4, 1965. African Americans in the United States, he said, made up "another nation: deprived of freedom, crippled by hatred, the doors of opportunity closed to hope." Emancipation alone was not enough, he continued. "You do not take a person who, for years, has been hobbled by chains and liberate him, bring him up to the starting line of a race and then say, 'you are free to compete with all the others,' and still justly believe that you have been completely fair. Thus it is not enough just to open the gates of opportunity. All our citizens must have the ability to walk through those gates. This is the next and the more profound state of the battle for civil rights. We seek. . . . not just equality as a right and a theory but equality as a fact and equality as a result." The Great Society then, in many ways, acted as one massive civil rights program.

Johnson knew that by outlawing public discrimination, the Civil Rights Act of 1964 had opened the gates of opportunity. He then proceeded to bring the disadvantaged through that gate by the eradication of poverty, which would help the poor of all races realize economic security and equal opportunity. Not surprisingly, Johnson believed that poverty could be eradicated by an avalanche of legislation. In his State of the Union address in 1964, he declared "unconditional war on poverty." What this meant in concrete terms soon took shape.

THE JOHNSONS, BEAUTIFICATION, AND THE NEW ENVIRONMENTALISM

The Johnson presidency began just as American attitudes toward the environment were changing from awareness of conservation to consciousness of environmentalism that questioned the value of industrial development. The change began with the 1962 publication of Rachel Carson's *Silent Spring,* a scientific account of the harm to nature caused by human-industrial systems, in particular the pesticide DDT. Spurred by *Silent Spring,* environmental activism dealt with everything from pollution to nuclear tests to endangered species. Initially fueled by the middle class who valued natural areas for their inherent beauty and utility as vacation sites, the new environmentalism benefited from the booming 1960s economy, which allowed increased spending on the environment.

Both Lyndon and Lady Bird Johnson drew inspiration from the rugged and beautiful Texas landscapes of their childhoods. During their time in the White House, they embraced the new environmentalism by pursuing complementary efforts for environmental protection. Both relied on their particular skills and personal resources: President Johnson enlarged the federal role in environmental regulation through legislation, while Lady Bird Johnson used her status as first lady to promote improvement of the nation's natural beauty, efforts characterized as "beautification."

Believing that the goals of liberal reform and environmental protection were harmonious, Lyndon Johnson gladly included environmental reform with the programs of his Great Society. In one speech, Johnson declared: "We have always prided ourselves on being not only America the strong and America the free, but America the beautiful." By the end of his presidency in 1969, Johnson had signed more legislation on behalf of protecting the environment than all previous presidents, including the Wilderness Act, 1964; Clean Water Act, 1965; Endangered Species Act, 1966; Air Quality Control Act, 1967; and the Wild and Scenic Rivers Act, 1967.

Two specific laws passed during the Johnson administration illustrate the transition from conservation to environmentalism. The Wilderness Act, signed early in Johnson's presidency, protected 9 million acres of land from development. The act reflected conservationists' romantic reverence for the spiritual power of nature, exquisitely stated in the law's definition of wilderness as "an area where the earth and its community of life are untrammeled by man, where man himself is a visitor who does not remain." Though the act embodied the conservation movement's belief in active defense of threatened areas, the successful passage of the bill blazed a trail for the new environmentalism. Grassroots organizations had lobbied heavily for the bill, thus providing a successful political model for environmental groups to follow in the future.

The Clean Water Act reflected the proactive approach of environmentalism, which directly confronted the aspects of modern society that threatened nature. The act empowered the federal government to enforce environmental standards on businesses, cutting pollution at the source rather than downstream. President Johnson hailed the act as a "refusal to be strangled by the wastes of civilization." In future decades, much environmental activism would entail political and legal challenges to polluters.

Environmentalists have criticized Johnson's environmental legislation as weak, and Johnson himself had admitted that more regulation would be needed in later years. But Johnson's efforts set a significant precedent by placing responsibility for protecting the environment squarely within the federal purview. In all, the Johnson administration passed some 300 measures relating to conservation and beautification, reflecting—and encouraging—the growth of environmental activism.

Lady Bird Johnson used her ability to draw publicity as a way to bring attention to the environment. She stated: "I recognize I do have a sort of tool in my hands, by this title I carry, and I want to use it." Although her beautification efforts were often dismissed as merely cosmetic fixes to deep-rooted problems, she embraced a pragmatic approach—shared by her husband—that aimed at achievable goals when fundamental reform proved impossible. Lady Bird Johnson believed that environmental improvements, however small, benefited American society as a whole. As she recorded in her diary, "Getting on the subject of beautification is like picking up a tangled skein of wool—all the threads are interwoven, recreation and pollution and mental health, and the crime rate, and rapid transit, and highway beautification, and the war on poverty, and parks."

Lady Bird Johnson approached beautification through direct efforts, including 200,000 miles of travel to highlight natural areas. She undertook the beautification of Washington, D.C., by coordinating 100 landscape projects, including the planting of hundreds of thousands of bulbs, trees, and plants. In poor, African-American neighborhoods, she initiated cleanup campaigns, flower plantings, school improvements, rat control, trash removal, and playground construction. Though these efforts could hardly expunge the effects of poverty and racism, they suited perfectly the means at her disposal.

Lady Bird Johnson also used her status to shape, promote, and lobby for the Highway Beautification Act of 1965, an effort to halt the deterioration of roadside beauty caused by billboards and junkyards. The resulting bill was weak, primarily because the Johnson administration crafted the law in accordance with the wishes of the Outdoor Advertising Association of America in order to mute industry opposition. Although the law led to the removal of over 1,000 junkyards, hardly any billboards came down. As with her husband's legislation, Lady Bird Johnson's efforts appear, by current standards, imperfect. Still, the idea that the federal government must take an active role in protecting the environment was first given legitimacy by the Johnsons. By the end of the 1960s, membership in the major environmental groups stood at almost eight times the numbers in 1960. Later environmental victories, including the creation of the Environmental Protection Agency, can trace their genesis to the Johnson era.

The ECONOMIC OPPORTUNITY ACT of 1964 created the Office of Economic Opportunity (OEO), an agency empowered to use innovation and voluntarism to eradicate poverty. Sargent Shriver, head of the Peace Corps under Kennedy, was assigned to head the OEO. A colossal and scattered agency, the OEO established education programs, job training, and volunteer agencies; its main innovation was to involve poor people themselves in the WAR ON POVERTY. From the start, funding was a problem for the program. Johnson knew that prosperity could fund reform, but he spread the government's wealth across a vast array of programs. Thus the War on Poverty and the OEO had to compete with other Great Society programs for funding.

Johnson coasted to an overwhelming victory in the 1964 presidential election, but his sense of urgency never ceased. In fact, Johnson was correct that the electorate's support for reform would not last long. He nonetheless erred in his belief that he could integrate America, eradicate poverty, reform health care, and renew the environment in the span of a few years. Overambitious to say the least, Johnson nevertheless made great progress in these and other areas.

The Great Society tackled numerous problems, all orchestrated by Johnson. Reading the temperament of the electorate, the president sent his bills to Congress in a particular order. First on the list was education, a cause always close to Johnson's heart since his days as a school teacher in Cotulla, Texas. The ELEMENTARY AND SECONDARY EDUCATION ACT of 1965 reversed previous presidents' inability to fund U.S. schools with federal dollars. The act sent over $1 billion to schools in nearly every county in the nation. A follow-up bill, the HIGHER EDUCATION ACT, provided needy college students with federal money for financial aid, student loans, and work-study jobs.

Biographers have argued that, as president, Johnson transcended his reputation as a pragmatic compromiser and instead pursued what he thought was right and just. To the contrary, however, many—if not all—of Johnson's policies and bills demonstrate extensive compromises; Johnson remained the consummate pragmatist. Health care offers an example. Reform of the U.S. health care system had eluded previous presidents, especially Harry Truman, who found his efforts paralyzed by the powerful American Medical Association (AMA) lobby that jealously guarded the medicine-for-profit industry. In 1965, Johnson followed his education efforts with a significant overhaul of health care centered around the MEDICARE ACT and the MEDICAID ACT, medical insurance programs for the elderly and poor, respectively. Although these programs overcame AMA resistance—a credit to Johnson's legislative skill—they purposefully omitted cost controls as a concession to the healthcare lobby. Indeed, Johnson always trumpeted his allegiance to the free enterprise system, lest anyone associate his Great Society with socialism. Medicare and Medicaid costs quickly soared; the final result consti-

tuted essentially a compromise between the goal of universal health care and the medical industry's desire for profit.

Johnson loved the idea of consensus—that every American wanted the same thing. His enormous ego convinced him that he could help every man and woman fulfill the American dream. The president took special pride that, like the New Deal, the Great Society provided something for everyone, some type of boon to every interest group in the nation. In this the president did succeed. Hardly a fan of high culture, Johnson nonetheless realized its importance to society and provided funding for the arts and humanities, as well as for public radio and television. Viewing government as the protector of the people, Johnson extended the shield of government to include the environment as well as consumers. The Great Society included protection of wilderness areas and empowered the federal government to set pollution standards and punish polluters. Various pieces of legislation enforced new consumer safety standards on automobiles and medicine, including seat belts and child safety caps. America's major cities, blighted and decaying by the mid-1960s, received urban renewal funding. Hardly any segment of society went unnoticed by the Great Society, including drug addicts who began to be treated according to a medical—rather than a criminal—approach.

One of the least heralded and most influential pieces of Great Society legislation was the IMMIGRATION AND NATIONALITY ACT AMENDMENTS of 1965. This act overturned the racial quotas that had severely restricted nonwhites from immigrating to the United States. The new standards opened American doors to immigrants from Eastern Europe and Latin America as well as Asia. In the process, the act transformed the definition of an "American" from someone of a specific race to someone subscribing to democratic political principles. Of all the Great Society measures, immigration reform had the most profound and lasting effect on American culture and society.

Although the entire Great Society promised the fulfillment of economic and racial equality, Johnson still believed that there were limits to how fast the country was willing to go on civil rights. Johnson thought that, over time, the War on Poverty would improve living conditions for African Americans. As a corollary to the War on Poverty, he pushed for fair housing legislation to enable African Americans to buy homes and speed the integration of neighborhoods, many of which had long been segregated. Urban renewal, including the passage of the DEPARTMENT OF HOUSING AND URBAN DEVELOPMENT ACT, which authorized the creation of the Department of Housing and Urban Development (HUD), was another component of Johnson's strategy. Johnson also appointed African Americans to top leadership positions. Robert C. Weaver, the head of HUD, became the first African-American cabinet member, while Thurgood Marshall became the first African-American Supreme Court

(continues on page 418)

ADMINISTRATION TIME LINE

1963

November 22 After the assassination of President John F. Kennedy in Dallas, Texas, Lyndon Johnson is sworn in as president aboard Air Force One at Dallas Love Field Airport.

November 27 Johnson, in his speech to the nation on the death of Kennedy, states, "Today, in this moment of new resolve, I would say to all my fellow Americans, let us continue."

1964

January 8 In his 1964 State of the Union address Johnson declares: "This administration, today, here and now, declares unconditional war on poverty in America."

February 26 Johnson passes the $11 billion tax cut initially proposed by Kennedy.

March 9 In *New York Times v. Sullivan* the Supreme Court broadens the concept of free speech by protecting people from being held liable for inaccurate statements made about public officials.

May 22 At the University of Michigan, Johnson lays out his ideas on the "Great Society."

June 15 In *Reynolds v. Sims,* an Alabama reapportionment case, the Supreme Court issues the doctrine of one person, one vote, requiring representation in each district to be as mathematically equal as possible and to be updated after every census.

July 2 Johnson signs the Civil Rights Act of 1964 into law. The measure outlawed segregation in public places, such as restaurants, hotels, and museums, as well as racial and sexual discrimination in employment.

July 9 Johnson signs the Urban Mass Transportation Act of 1964, aimed at reducing highway congestion while simultaneously boosting transit networks.

August 2 The USS *Maddox* encounters North Vietnamese torpedo boats while conducting surveillance in the Gulf of Tonkin.

August 4 The USS *Maddox,* along with the *C. Turner Joy,* under stormy skies, report another North Vietnamese attack, though later evidence suggests weather occurrences. Johnson uses these attacks to justify the Gulf of Tonkin Resolution.

August 7 Congress passes the Gulf of Tonkin Resolution, which authorizes the president to use "all necessary measures to repel any armed attacks against the forces of the United States and to prevent further aggression."

August 20 Johnson signs the Economic Opportunity Act, creating the Office of Economic Opportunity (OEO) to direct federal antipoverty policy and a wide-ranging array of antipoverty programs.

August 31 Johnson signs the Food Stamp Act, allowing participants to use their stamps to buy food in stores.

September 3 Johnson signs the Wilderness Act of 1964, setting aside 9 million acres of wilderness under federal government protection and closing the land to development and exploitation.

September 27 The Warren Commission issues its report, concluding that Lee Harvey Oswald acted alone in the assassination of President Kennedy.

November 3 Johnson is elected president in his own right.

December 14 In *Heart of Atlanta Motel v. United States,* one of the first lawsuits to challenge the Civil Rights Act of 1964, the Supreme Court unanimously upholds the act.

In *Katzenbach v. McClung,* the Supreme Court rules against McClung, who refused to serve African Americans at his restaurant.

1965

January 20 Johnson is inaugurated president.

February 21 Malcolm X is assassinated by followers loyal to Elijah Muhammad whose organization Malcolm X had recently left.

March 2 Operation Rolling Thunder begins, a sustained bombing campaign against North Vietnam that continues into the summer in retaliation against the death of American soldiers.

March 7 Known as Bloody Sunday, 600 civil rights marchers approach Selma's Edmund Pettis Bridge, where state troopers, armed with whips, clubs, and tear gas, attack the marchers without warning.

March 8 Two Marine battalions, totaling 1,500 soldiers, arrive in Danang to secure an American air force base, launching the start of large-scale introduction of U.S. combat troops into Vietnam.

March 15 President Johnson announces his voting rights bill.

April 11 Johnson signs the Elementary and Secondary Education Act, providing help in the form of $1.06 billion.

April 28 Johnson sends troops to the Dominican Republic to ensure that the island nation does not fall to leftist groups.

May 18 The Head Start Program begins, providing preschool classes for disadvantaged children, making them less likely to drop out once they enter elementary school.

June 7 In *Griswold v. Connecticut,* the Supreme Court declares unconstitutional an 1879 Connecticut law banning the sale and use of contraceptive devices, including to married couples.

July 15 Johnson signs the Drug Abuse Control Amendments, reorganizing federal drug control authority under the Bureau of Drug Abuse Control within the Food and Drug Administration. This new bureau primarily enforces laws against depressants and stimulants.

July 30 Johnson signs the Medicare Act, establishing federally funded medical insurance for those over the age of 65, and the Medicaid Act, creating a system of federal health insurance for the poor. Medicaid distributes federal matching grants to states; these grants are used to reimburse doctors who treat people on welfare.

August 6 Johnson signs the Voting Rights Act of 1965, empowering the Justice Department to void any restrictions (such as literacy tests) that keeps minorities off voter rolls, as well as sending federal workers to register voters if obstruction continued.

August 11–16 Riots occur in Watts, an African-American neighborhood in Los Angeles, when residents used force in an attempt to prevent the arrest of an African-American man.

September 9 Johnson signs legislation creating the Department of Housing and Urban Development (HUD) to improve city life and substandard housing for poor Americans.

September 29 Johnson signs the National Foundation on the Arts and Humanities Act, creating a National Endowment for the Arts (NEA) as well as a National Endowment for the Humanities.

October 2 Johnson signs the Water Quality Control Act, giving the federal government the power to enforce clean water standards. These new regulations aim at preventing pollution at its source, rather than cleaning it downstream.

October 3 Johnson signs the Immigration Act of 1965, wiping out racial quotas and instead assigning priority to immigrants with family already in the United States, as well as those with valued professional and technical skills.

October 20 Johnson signs the Motor Vehicle Air Pollution Control Act, authorizing the Department of Health, Education and Welfare to set new standards for automobile air pollution.

October 22 Johnson signs the Highway Beautification Act, limiting billboard advertising along interstate highways, mandating the cleanup of junkyards, and improving highway landscaping to make highways less ugly.

November 4 Johnson signs the Food and Agriculture Act, granting direct payments to field crop farmers (including wheat, cotton, and corn producers) who agree to join voluntary acreage reduction programs.

(continues)

ADMINISTRATION TIME LINE *(continued)*

1966

March 21 In *Ginzburg v. United States,* the Supreme Court rules 5-4 that advertisements for pornography were not protected by the First Amendment as free speech.

March 28 In *U.S. v. Price et al.,* the Supreme Court upholds the indictment of the murderers of civil rights workers James Chaney, Andrew Goodman, and Michael Schwerner, arguing that when private individuals cooperate with law enforcement in a lynching, all the participants can be prosecuted.

June 6 In *Sheppard v. Maxwell,* the Supreme Court holds that intrusive publicity prevents a fair trial, setting a precedent that the unrestrained presence of media at a trial can interfere with due process—even if no proof exists that the media's presence has influenced the jury.

June 13 In *Miranda v. Arizona,* the Supreme Court rules 5-4 to protect the rights of suspected criminals to halt police questioning and granting the accused the right to ask for a lawyer.

July 4 Johnson signs the Freedom of Information Act, allowing the public to access the records of the federal government and its agencies.

September 9 Johnson signs the National Traffic and Motor Vehicle Safety Act, creating the National Highway Safety Administration and empowering the federal government to issue and enforce auto safety standards.

October 11 The Child Nutrition Act passes to supply low-income children with nutritious meals.

October 15 Johnson signs the Historic Preservation Act, redefining the concept of "historical" beyond presidential homes and battlefields.

October 16 Johnson signs the Department of Transportation Act, creating the National Transportation Safety Board and a cabinet-level department that encompasses all aspects of transportation, including commerce, public roads, aviation, the Coast Guard, and the Interstate Commerce Commission.

November 3 Johnson signs the Comprehensive Health Planning Act of 1966, which aims to anticipate future needs in the health care industry and allocate resources accordingly.

Johnson signs the Demonstration Cities and Metropolitan Development Act, authorizing the Model Cities program and providing $900 million of federal money to improve inner-city housing, education, health care, crime prevention, and recreation facilities.

November 8 Johnson signs the Narcotic Addict Rehabilitation Act, replacing criminal punishment for drug addicts with treatment through the U.S. Public Health Service.

1967

June 5 Israel launches a preemptive war (the Six-Day War) against Egypt, Jordan, and Syria; just six days later Israel emerges triumphant.

June 13 Johnson appoints the first African American to the Supreme Court, Thurgood Marshall, who had successfully argued the landmark *Brown v. Board of Education* (1954) decision; Marshall had served as a federal judge and solicitor general.

July 13 Rioting begins in Newark, New Jersey.

July 23 The Detroit riots begin a week of violence that shuts down the inner city after police clash with African Americans.

July 27 Johnson appoints the National Advisory Commission on Civil Disorders, also known as the Kerner Commission, to investigate urban rioting.

October 21 More than 100,000 marchers rally at the Pentagon to protest the Vietnam War.

(continued from page 415)

justice. But new bureaucratic agencies and a handful of appointments could not quickly overturn racism. Civil rights activists increasingly urged Johnson to expand civil rights at a quicker pace than he wanted. When activists in Selma, Alabama, launched the SELMA PROTESTS in early 1965, a voting rights campaign that met with violent resistance, Johnson reacted with a voting rights bill. Johnson genuinely wanted

November 7 Johnson signs the Public Broadcasting Act.

November 20 Johnson signs act creating the National Product Safety Commission.

November 21 Johnson signs the Air Quality Control Act, empowering the states to set air quality standards.

December 16 Johnson signs the Age Discrimination in Employment Act to prevent age discrimination and promote the employment of older workers.

1968

January 23 North Korean military forces capture the USS *Pueblo,* an American spy ship stationed in the Sea of Japan.

January 30 The Tet offensive begins when the North Vietnamese and Vietcong forces unleash a massive surprise attack against hundreds of cities, towns, and villages in South Vietnam.

February 29 The National Advisory Commission on Civil Disorders, known as the Kerner Commission, issues its report on the civil unrest in the nation's cities.

March 16 U.S. soldiers enter the village of My Lai searching for enemy Vietcong. When the villagers refuse to cooperate, the enraged soldiers slaughter them; estimates range between 100 and 400 civilian deaths.

March 31 Johnson gives a nationally televised address in which he calls for a bombing halt in North Vietnam and announces he will not run for another term as president.

April 4 Civil rights leader Martin Luther King, Jr. is assassinated in Memphis, Tennessee.

April 11 Johnson signs the Civil Rights Act of 1968 banning discrimination in federally owned housing as well as in apartments with federally insured mortgages.

May The Poor People's March on Washington begins, consisting of a march, large-scale pickets of government agencies, and construction of Resurrection City, a multiethnic shantytown in sight of the U.S. Capitol.

May 20 In *Duncan v. Louisiana,* the Supreme Court affirms a right to a jury trial, guaranteed under the Sixth Amendment.

June 5 Making a brief appearance after winning the California Democratic Party primary, Senator Robert F. Kennedy is assassinated by a Palestinian nationalist named Sirhan Sirhan.

June 10 In *Terry v. Ohio,* the Supreme Court broadens the search powers of police officers.

June 19 Johnson signs the Omnibus Crime Control and Safe Streets Act, including $100 million for law enforcement upgrades, substantially weakening several Supreme Court decisions, allowing local, state, and federal law agencies to wiretap and bug suspects, and removing restrictions on gun ownership.

August 1 Johnson signs the Housing and Urban Development Act of 1968, pledging $5 billion for the construction of 26 million homes and apartments over 10 years, and expanding rent supplements and Model Cities Program funding.

August 28 Chicago police attack protesters at the Democratic National Convention.

October 2 Johnson signs the Wild and Scenic Rivers Act into law.

October 31 All bombing in North Vietnam is halted.

1969

January 20 Johnson spends his last day as president of the United States.

---

to improve voting rights for African Americans; at the same time, he worried that moving too quickly on civil rights would alienate many white southerners from the Democratic Party. Nonetheless, Johnson's VOTING RIGHTS ACT of 1965 generated a significant increase in African-American political participation. The close of the year 1965 marked the highpoint of Johnson's presidency. In just under two years, Lyndon Johnson had instituted the largest government

The protest marches in Selma, Alabama, in March 1965 led directly to passage of the Voting Rights Act, signed by President Johnson in August. *(Library of Congress)*

reform since the New Deal and, in the process, changed the fundamental nature of American society.

President Johnson pursued continuity with his predecessors in foreign policy. Most obviously, Johnson continued the thrust of Kennedy's foreign policy, including a staunch anticommunist line in Latin America and a commitment to support South Vietnam's fight against a communist insurgency. But Johnson's presidency began at a critical juncture in the cold war. Cold war scholars agree that after the Cuban missile crisis ended in October 1962, the focus shifted from direct U.S.-Soviet rivalry to confrontation carried out on the periphery in the developing nations. One of Kennedy's last achievements was securing ratification of the 1963 Limited Test Ban Treaty, an accord that signaled the birth of détente and the policy of coexistence with the Soviet Union. A growing rift between China and the Soviet Union, hardly noticed in Washington, ignited a nascent rivalry between the two communist nations. As the cold war powers focused their attentions increasingly on the developing world, Soviet premier Nikita Khrushchev announced the Soviet Union's intention to support "wars of national liberation" in the former colonies of the West. Although Khrushchev's claim was primarily propaganda aimed at thwarting Chinese expansionist

ambitions, Washington soon saw a communist conspiracy behind every uprising around the globe.

Indeed, the conflation of leftist rebellions and Soviet power can be traced back to the earliest days of the cold war and the launch of the containment policy, when President Truman supported the Greek government against a communist (but non-Soviet) rebellion in 1947. The ensuing Truman Doctrine embraced containment by promising U.S. aid to governments fighting communism anywhere on earth. Eisenhower had also pursued containment, buttressing authoritarian regimes in Latin American and the Middle East to prevent them from going leftist; at the same time, Eisenhower had pursued disarmament—albeit unsuccessfully—with the Soviet Union. In addition to the Test Ban Treaty, Kennedy had launched the Alliance for Progress to fund noncommunist regimes in Latin America, and he had sent the first wave of U.S. military advisers to South Vietnam. Also influencing policy in Southeast Asia was the "domino theory," a belief prevalent since the Eisenhower administration that argued that the fall of Vietnam to communism would inevitably lead, like so many toppled dominoes, to further communist revolutions in Laos, Thailand, Cambodia, Malaysia, and even India. Thus Johnson inherited an utterly consistent but inherently flawed approach to communism and foreign policy.

The domestic politics of anticommunism also shaped Johnson's choices as president. Soon after Johnson had entered the Senate in 1949, Senator Joseph McCarthy (R-WI) began his communist "witch-hunts," in which, despite a lack of evidence, he accused many people of being communists. Aware of McCarthy's fabricated claims, Johnson nevertheless was impressed with the considerable public and political support that the infamous red hunter managed to obtain. Long after Senator McCarthy's crusade ended in disgrace, Johnson retained an instinctive fear that McCarthyism could again be unleashed in the United States. This foreboding often rose to the surface during Johnson's presidency; his fear of being labeled an appeaser of communism led him to commit vast U.S. resources to the pursuit of containment in Vietnam and elsewhere. Johnson also believed that a strong stand against communism abroad would mute opposition to civil rights among conservatives, who frequently accused the Civil Rights movement of having communist origins. At the same time, Johnson showed no similar fear of the Soviet Union itself. In contrast to his Vietnam policy, Johnson's smooth handling of relations with the Soviets, as well as with European allies, has earned praise from historians.

Johnson retained Kennedy's foreign policy cabinet. This group, embracing the so-called best and the brightest of American intellect and industry, included the technocrat Robert S. McNamara as secretary of defense, the quiet and loyal Dean Rusk as secretary of state, and McGeorge Bundy as National Security Advisor. Johnson relied heavily on his foreign policy troika and mostly avoided the conflict that characterized his relationship with the Kennedy holdovers in his domestic cabinet.

The Kennedy administration's attempt to overturn the Castro regime in Cuba, thwarted at the Bay of Pigs in 1961, indicated a general U.S. hostility to communist influence in the Western Hemisphere. Although Kennedy had pledged not to invade Cuba after the Cuban missile crisis the following year, the CIA secretly continued assassination attempts against Cuban leader Fidel Castro. At least officially, Castro had to be tolerated, but Kennedy and then Johnson took pains to ensure that no other Latin American nations would fall to communism. The large-scale U.S. economic investment in Latin America made the region vital to U.S. interests; at the same time, the heavy hand of U.S. influence inevitably inspired leftist opposition across the region. Like his predecessors, Johnson preferred friendly, pro-Western dictators to leftist indigenous leaders.

Johnson did preach an idealism of sorts in foreign relations. He genuinely believed that democratic capitalism of the U.S. model was the best political-economic system. But strict adherence to this belief blinded Johnson (as it had other presidents) to the realities of Latin American affairs. When conflicts broke out in Latin America, Johnson viewed each crisis through the lens of the cold war. Given Johnson's great fear of the political power of domestic anticommunism, Johnson never hesitated to protect U.S. interests in Latin America.

Johnson's earliest foreign policy crisis occurred in January 1964 when Panamanian students started riotous demonstrations against U.S. dominance in Panama. Johnson committed himself to maintaining U.S. interests—specifically the Panama Canal, the prize artery of international trade. But he also perceptively appreciated the Panamanians' desire for more control over their own affairs. Still, Johnson would not cede the upper hand. After he let it be known that he was considering building a second Atlantic-Pacific canal in Nicaragua, Panama quickly agreed to negotiations. Assuring Congress that he would not sacrifice U.S. interests, he began talks, which eventually led to a 1978 accord under President JIMMY CARTER that provided for the return of the Panama Canal by 2000.

Johnson displayed much less flexibility when a revolution erupted in the Dominican Republic in late April 1965. A left-right partisan split in the country's military had broadened into a violent struggle for control of the Caribbean nation. Johnson ordered the immediate dispatch of U.S. Marines to the island; their role, he declared, was to protect American lives threatened by the escalating violence. Meanwhile, U.S. analysts saw Castro's hand at work. The leftist faction, they claimed, included agents of Castro within their leadership. Determined to prevent any leftist regime from taking power, Johnson redefined his troops' role as an offensive one. Eventually more than 20,000 U.S. troops arrived in the Dominican Republic and took control of the fighting. By the early summer U.S. forces had brokered a settlement that brought a moderate noncommunist to power.

Though heavy-handed, U.S. influence had halted the fighting in the Dominican Republic. As an added bonus, democratic elections, ostensibly fair, took place soon after. To achieve his ends, however, Johnson had exaggerated the influence of communists, proving that he appreciated the power of domestic anticommunism as much as he feared it. Johnson hoped he could manage similar results in Vietnam.

In the traditional cold war arena of Europe, Johnson performed quite well. With peace prevailing across the region, some among the Western Europe allies began to chafe under U.S. dominance and demand more of a say in the affairs of NATO, the cold war regional security agency formed during the Truman administration to deter Soviet aggression in Europe. The U.S.-Soviet reconciliation implied by détente gave rise to suspicions among some Western Europeans that the United States would not honor its commitment to NATO in case of an attack. Adding fuel to the fire, a balance of payments deficit, sparked by a European economic boom, troubled U.S. economic policymakers.

The biggest hit to U.S.-European relations occurred in 1966, when French president Charles de Gaulle announced his intent to withdraw from the military command structure of NATO. Johnson recognized the reluctance of the French president, a proud nationalist, to rely for his country's security solely on the U.S. nuclear deterrent. Johnson did not oppose French military withdrawal from NATO, but at the same time he secured an arrangement with President de Gaulle that the French would remain loyal to the NATO treaty itself. Thus he ensured that Article Five, the pledge that an attack on one member is to be considered an attack on all—the very heart of NATO—remained intact.

Apart from policies dealing with Vietnam, Johnson proved a savvy diplomat who demonstrated great restraint and skill in avoiding conflict. When Israel launched the preemptive SIX-DAY WAR in 1967, Johnson—conscious of Soviet interests in the Middle East and sympathetic to American Jews' support for Israel—managed to maintain an effective but unpopular neutrality. The war ended with large-scale territorial gains for Israel, including the West Bank, the Gaza Strip, the Golan Heights, and the Sinai Peninsula.

Johnson proved restrained again during the PUEBLO INCIDENT, when, in 1968, North Korean forces captured the USS *Pueblo*, an American intelligence vessel caught spying on the Koreans. Johnson engaged in patient diplomacy at the United Nations and with the Soviet Union, which eventually secured the release of the captive seamen in 1969.

The pursuit of disarmament and coexistence with the Soviet Union proved a notable, if often overlooked, achievement during these years. Johnson facilitated détente, meeting

President Johnson *(right)* meets with Soviet premier Alexei Kosygin in Glassboro, New Jersey, June 23, 1967. *(Lyndon B. Johnson Library)*

Soviet premier Alexey Kosygin at a summit in Glassboro, New Jersey, in 1967. The president committed the United States to the Nuclear Nonproliferation Treaty that would be ratified during the Nixon years. The president planned a surprise trip in 1968 to the Soviet Union, where he hoped to announce another agreement on arms control and disarmament. When the Soviet Union invaded Czechoslovakia that summer, an exasperated Johnson canceled the summit at the last minute in protest. Above all else, however, Vietnam overwhelmed the president's foreign and domestic accomplishments. In fact, much of the impetus behind the president's outreach to the Soviet Union was his desire for Russian assistance in brokering a peace settlement with North Vietnam.

The war in Vietnam had been ongoing for many years before Lyndon Johnson became president. It resulted from the confluence of several of the most significant geopolitical events of the 20th century: the end of imperialism, the rise of anticolonialism in the developing world, the end of World War II, and the start of the cold war. The Indochinese Peninsula had been a colony of France prior to the start of World War II, but when Germany defeated France in 1940, Japan occupied Indochina. Ho Chi Minh, later the leader of the North Vietnamese, had been allied with the United States during World War II in the fight to defeat Japan. After Japan surrendered on September 2, 1945, ending World War II, Ho Chi Minh declared Vietnam's independence.

The United States supported this effort, but France, seeking to regain its empire, fought a colonial war to hold onto Indochina. That conflict lasted until 1954, and during this period it emerged as a contested region in the intensifying cold war between the United States and the Soviet Union. As such, the United States moved away from support for Ho Chi Minh, who drew on Marxist teachings in support of Vietnamese nationalism. Under President Truman, the Americans gave financial and technical support to the French. By 1952, the United States found itself funding a third of the cost of the war for France, despite evidence that France stood little chance of securing victory. The defeat of French forces at Dien Bien Phu in 1954 led to the inclusion of Vietnam on the agenda in talks at Geneva that year. There a decision was made to temporarily divide Vietnam into northern and southern sections along the 17th parallel. After two years, according to the agreements reached, free elections would be held in Vietnam to unify the country under one government.

The Eisenhower administration initially approved these agreements but reversed course two years later when it became obvious that Ho Chi Minh would win the elections. For the remainder of the Eisenhower presidency, the United States engaged in a project of nation-building in South Vietnam, all the while supporting the civil war between the North and the South in which the North sought to unify the country and the South endeavored to maintain its independence. The leadership structure that the United States supported was not terribly sympathetic to the realities of peasant life in Vietnam or to the Buddhist faith professed by most of the Vietnamese people.

Both the brutality of the South Vietnamese regime and American aid to it increased in the early 1960s during the Kennedy presidency. Finally, a coup in 1963 removed the leadership of South Vietnam from power, and, in so doing, destabilized politics there. Ho Chi Minh and the North Vietnamese used this development to intensify the civil war with the South. Lyndon Johnson inherited this situation when he became president. At the time, few Americans were very much aware of the U.S. commitment to South Vietnam—it was more than two decades old—while policymakers viewed it through the lens of the cold war. Democrats especially were concerned that failure to take a hard line toward Vietnam they might be viewed as being soft on communism after the turmoil of McCarthyism in the 1950s. Furthermore, most American politicians believed in the lesson of World War II that dictators should not be appeased. This was Johnson's frame of reference as he made decisions about Vietnam.

The Gulf of Tonkin Resolution, which gave Johnson authority to use military force in Vietnam, temporarily placated the hawks in Congress. However, eventually the president faced a fateful decision. The South Vietnamese government appeared incapable of defeating the North Vietnamese on its own. Johnson could thus withdraw U.S. advisers, all but guaranteeing a communist takeover of South Vietnam, or he could commit U.S. military might and escalate the war. Viewing the first option as a second Munich and as a capitulation to tyranny, Johnson never seriously considered withdrawal. Politicians such as Johnson who had lived through the years prior to World War II had taken away the lesson that dictators should never be appeased in the manner that European powers had acceded to Nazi leader Adolf Hitler's demands at the Munich Conference in 1938 granting Germany control of the Sudetenland in Czechoslovakia. The decision to escalate the Vietnam War did not come easily, however. In one tortured phone call with his Senate mentor Richard Russell on May 27, 1964, Johnson blanched at the thought of sending U.S. troops into combat. He said to him: "I've got a little old sergeant that works for me over at the house and he's got six children and I just put him up as the United States Army, Air Force, and Navy every time I think about making this decision and think about sending that father of those six kids in there. And what the hell are we going to get out of his doing it? And it just makes the chills run up my back."

On June 11, 1964, Senator Russell accurately predicted that to stay in Vietnam: "It'd take a half million men. They'd be bogged down in there for ten years." When Johnson considered his options, he always argued that the nation's credibility was at stake, especially regarding its treaty commitments. Referring to the Southeast Asia Treaty Organization, Johnson told Russell, "I think that I've got to say that I didn't get you [the United States people] in here, but we're in here by treaty and our national honor's at stake. And if this treaty's no good, none of 'em are any good. Therefore we're there. And being there, we've got to conduct ourselves like men."

Johnson overcame his reluctance after thorough consultation with his foreign policy team and he became committed to escalation. First came the Rolling Thunder bombing campaign in March 1965. Johnson agonized over the bombing, personally selecting targets for U.S. strikes and staying up into the early morning hours to hear the results and casualties taken by American pilots. Johnson also fretted that a stray bomb might hit one of the Soviet or Chinese ships in North Vietnamese harbors, precipitating an international incident. Accordingly, Johnson refused to include the Haiphong harbor area as a U.S. target. Although Haiphong made up the heart of North Vietnamese industrial capacity, many Soviet and Chinese ships harbored there; the destruction of one of these, accidental or not, threatened to spark a world war.

After the start of the bombing campaign came the initial dispatch of U.S. combat troops in March 1965 when 1,500 U.S. MARINES LANDED AT DANANG. At first U.S. troops were used in a defensive manner, but soon their role was expanded to "search-and-destroy" missions. Despite regular

U.S. Marines move through the ruins of the hamlet of Dai Do after several days of intense fighting during the Tet offensive, 1968. *(Schulimson/United States Marine Corps)*

CABINET, COURT, AND CONGRESS

Cabinet Members

Secretary of State
Dean Rusk, 1963–69

Secretary of Defense
Robert S. McNamara, 1963–68
Clark Clifford, 1968–69

Secretary of the Treasury
C. Douglas Dillon, 1963–65
Henry H. Fowler, 1965–68
Joseph Barr, 1968–69

Postmaster General
John A. Gronouski, 1963–65
Lawrence F. O'Brien, 1965–68
W. Marvin Watson, 1968–69

Attorney General
Robert F. Kennedy, 1963–65
Nicholas Katzenbach, 1965–67
Ramsey Clark, 1967–69

Secretary of the Interior
Stewart Udall, 1963–69

Secretary of Agriculture
Orville L. Freeman, 1963–69

Secretary of Commerce
Luther H. Hodges, 1963–65
John T. Connor, 1965–67
Alexander B. Trowbridge, 1967–68
Cyrus R. Smith, 1968–69

Secretary of Labor
W. Willard Wirtz, 1963–69

Secretary of Health, Education and Welfare
Anthony J. Celebrezze, 1963–65
John W. Gardner, 1965–68
Wilbur J. Cohen, 1968–69

Secretary of Housing and Urban Development
Robert C. Weaver, 1966–69
Robert C. Wood, 1969

Secretary of Transportation
Alan S. Boyd, 1967–69

Supreme Court Appointments

*(Nominated for Chief Justice)

Name	Confirmation Vote	Dates of Service
Abe Fortas	Voice Vote, Confirmed	1965–69
Thurgood Marshall	69–11, Confirmed	1967–91
*Abe Fortas	Withdrawn	
Homer Thornberry	No Action	

Legislative Leaders

Congress	Speaker of the House	State	Party
88th Congress (1963–65)	John W. McCormack	Massachusetts	Democrat

escalation of the bombing campaign—eventually U.S. planes dropped more explosives on Vietnam than all sides had used in World War II—and dramatic increases in U.S. troops to more than 500,000 by 1968, the Vietcong and North Vietnamese proved stubbornly resistant to U.S. power. The intractable morass in Vietnam took its toll on Johnson's cabinet. In 1966, McGeorge Bundy resigned as national security advisor when he was named head of the Ford Foundation; the hawkish Walt Rostow, a Kennedy holdover at the State Department, took his place. In late 1967, Robert McNamara announced his resignation as secretary of defense to take over as head of the World Bank; Johnson's longtime adviser Clark Clifford replaced him.

Ultimately Johnson was constrained by two realities. First, the president faced a strategic dilemma. Johnson used the bombing campaign as a way to communicate with North Vietnam. Continued escalation of the bombing campaign demonstrated to North Vietnam that the United States would not let the South fall to communism. At the same time, Johnson had to limit the war so as not to encourage the Chinese, and possibly even the Soviets, from entering the war. In short, Johnson promised limitless escalation to North Vietnam, but

Congress	Speaker of the House	State	Party
89th Congress (1965–67)	John W. McCormack	Massachusetts	Democrat
90th Congress (1967–69)	John W. McCormack	Massachusetts	Democrat

Congress	House Majority Leader	State	Party
88th Congress (1963–65)	Carl B. Albert	Oklahoma	Democrat
89th Congress (1965–67)	Carl B. Albert	Oklahoma	Democrat
90th Congress (1967–69)	Carl B. Albert	Oklahoma	Democrat

Congress	House Minority Leader	State	Party
88th Congress (1963–65)	Charles A. Halleck	Indiana	Republican
89th Congress (1965–67)	Gerald R. Ford	Michigan	Republican
90th Congress (1967–69)	Gerald R. Ford	Michigan	Republican

Congress	House Democratic Whip	State	Party
88th Congress (1963–65)	Hale Boggs	Louisiana	Democrat
89th Congress (1965–67)	Hale Boggs	Louisiana	Democrat
90th Congress (1967–69)	Hale Boggs	Louisiana	Democrat

Congress	House Republican Whip	State	Party
88th Congress (1963–65)	Leslie C. Arends	Illinois	Republican
89th Congress (1965–67)	Leslie C. Arends	Illinois	Republican
90th Congress (1967–69)	Leslie C. Arends	Illinois	Republican

Congress	Senate Majority Leader	State	Party
88th Congress (1963–65)	Mike Mansfield	Montana	Democrat
89th Congress (1965–67)	Mike Mansfield	Montana	Democrat
90th Congress (1967–69)	Mike Mansfield	Montana	Democrat

Congress	Senate Minority Leader	State	Party
88th Congress (1963–65)	Everett McKinley Dirksen	Illinois	Republican
89th Congress (1965–67)	Everett McKinley Dirksen	Illinois	Republican
90th Congress (1967–69)	Everett McKinley Dirksen	Illinois	Republican

a limited war to the Chinese and Soviets. Thus the invasion and occupation of North Vietnam was never an option; nor was the use of nuclear weapons.

The second restraint on Johnson's decision making was his fear of domestic anticommunism. Johnson repeatedly railed that he would not be the first U.S. president to lose a war. Despite his best efforts at conducting a balancing act, Johnson's Vietnam policy pleased no one. Conservatives criticized his inability to defeat the communist insurgency while liberals decried the ever-increasing and wanton destructiveness of the war—especially the bombing campaign that failed to inhibit the enemy but proved wildly successful at devastating the Vietnamese countryside and its civilians. But more than a personal failure of Johnson's, the Vietnam War showed the limits of the containment policy. The cold war consensus that dominated U.S. politics at the beginning of Johnson's presidency failed to account for rivalries among communist powers. Although a few dissident voices pointed out that Vietnam and China had a history of conflict, the containment school saw communism as a monolithic force. By the end of Johnson's presidency in 1969, the cold war consensus had frayed and the doctrine of containment had lost much of its credibility. The Vietnam War continued for another six years, and U.S. presidents after Johnson became reluctant to commit U.S. troops to conflicts overseas.

As early as the summer of 1965, the first stirrings of domestic backlash had foreshadowed the end of Johnson's Great Society, proving that Johnson's sense of urgency was right. When race riots broke out in the Watts neighborhood of Los Angeles in the summer of 1965, Republicans capitalized on the controversy by complaining that Great Society measures simply gave money to radical revolutionaries and lawbreakers. By 1966, Johnson had essentially already lost. Republican gains in midterm elections stemmed the tide of Great Society measures. Meanwhile, the rising cost of the Vietnam War sparked inflation and drained money from Great Society programs, forcing Johnson in 1967 to request a 10 percent income tax surcharge. Yet Johnson continued to inflate the rhetoric and goals of the Great Society, attempting to deflect attention from his increasingly smaller funding requests. As if to mock his attempts to hold the Great Society together, the DETROIT RIOT in 1967 destroyed much of the inner city there.

In 1968, Johnson's presidency fell apart. Although the Johnson administration and other military officials had been promising a quick end to the Vietnam War, the TET OFFENSIVE in January revealed to the public that, far from close, victory remained many years and billions of dollars in the future. The cost of the war, $5 billion in 1965 and $10 billion in 1966, soared to an exorbitant $33 billion by 1968. That year Johnson mentioned the Great Society hardly at all. At the end of March Johnson announced his decision not to run for reelection in order to concentrate all his efforts on a achieving a peace settlement in Vietnam. Still reluctant to give up on the Great Society, Johnson pursued reform when presented with the rare opportunity. After Martin Luther King's assassination on April 4, 1968, he appealed to the memory of the martyred leader in order to pass a housing bill. Congress, however, greatly amended the CIVIL RIGHTS ACT of 1968, transforming it into a bill used to prosecute rioters. Also in 1968, Congress passed a so-called safe streets anticrime bill, but without the tight controls on gun ownership that Johnson desired. Increasingly the streets flooded with antiwar demonstrations and race riots. Eventually the president's own movements were limited by the vociferous and vituperative protests that regularly disrupted his public appearances. Isolated and alone in the White House, Johnson waited out his final days. Just days before the 1968 presidential election, the president announced a bombing halt, though the war would continue well into the 1970s.

Lyndon and Lady Bird Johnson left the White House in 1969, returning to their Texas ranch. In the early 1970s Johnson gave an extended set of interviews in which he bemoaned his plight as president. He blamed Vietnam—"that bitch of a war"—for taking him away from "the woman I really loved—the Great Society." Undoubtedly Johnson genuinely craved securing the equality, justice, and freedom embodied in the Great Society, and he had little interest in foreign policy. But the U.S. role in Vietnam stemmed from Johnson's own decisions, constrained as they were by a rigid American anticommunist tradition. Even without the Vietnam War, the Great Society would have been overambitious. Johnson set out to achieve more than most presidents even attempt in one term; in the end his ambition, bordering on hubris, proved key to his greatest achievements and his biggest failures.

MAJOR EVENTS AND ISSUES

1968 Democratic National Convention   In August 1968, as the Democratic National Convention met in Chicago to nominate a candidate for president, activists from across the antiwar spectrum also gathered to oppose the Vietnam War. President Lyndon Johnson, who had announced in March he would not accept a nomination, secretly hoped the convention might draft him anyway. Johnson's hopes were thwarted, however, as the convention became a sideshow to the chaos outside. Chicago mayor Richard Daley, a Democrat, fiercely opposed to the demonstrators, readied 12,000 police officers in addition to 5,000 National Guard troops and 6,000 federal troops. When 10,000 demonstrators descended on Chicago, Daley refused to allow them permits to march, protest, or sleep in public parks. Most protests were small and conventional, such as the Women Strike for Peace picket, but Daley's confrontational tactics created a volatile mix. The carnivalesque Yippies (Youth International Party) invoked the ire of the police when they nominated a pig named Pigasus for president during a large rally. Violence then broke out in Lincoln Park when demonstrators taunted police. In retaliation, the police attacked, chasing the protesters through the city. Violence even reached Democratic headquarters at the Hilton Hotel, where more angry police beat up demonstrators. Wednesday, August 28, proved the worst day, as a full-scale police riot began. Police attacked marchers with clubs and tear gas indiscriminately—numerous reporters and bystanders were attacked as well. Television cameras captured the violence on film, which was shown to delegates inside the convention and in homes across the country. Observers noticed that many police had obscured or hidden their badge numbers to more freely engage in violence. As violence raged, the Democrats uneventfully nominated HUBERT H. HUMPHREY for president. No one was killed during the riots, but hundreds were injured. Chicago officials later charged eight people with inciting a riot—the so-called Chicago Eight—including Yippies Abbie Hoffman and Jerry Rubin, Students for a Democratic Society leader Tom Hayden, and Black Panther leader Bobby Seale, though in any objective analysis the blame rests with Mayor Daley.

Act to Eliminate the Gold Reserve against Federal Reserve Notes (1968)   In the late 1960s, the U.S. dollar remained tied directly to the gold standard, which meant that, in theory at least, dollars could be redeemed for gold at any time. The price of gold had remained $35 an ounce since 1934, and this price determined currency policy for many nations. In 1968, the reserves of the major gold nations (Belgium, France, Germany, Italy, the Netherlands, the United Kingdom, and the United States) began to dwindle. Soon, only the United States could guarantee the sale of gold at $35 an ounce. Economic officials worried that this policy might deplete U.S. gold reserves and violate the law that required the Federal Reserve to maintain gold reserves worth at least 25 percent of the reserve notes in circulation. The 1968 Act to Eliminate the Gold Reserve against Federal Reserve Notes freed billions of dollars of gold by overturning the Federal Reserve's 25 percent rule. The act reestablished a two-tier market for gold, maintaining $35 an ounce for governments while free market gold traded at its own level. Even this system remained untenable, as the United States abandoned the gold standard entirely in 1971.

Age Discrimination in Employment Act (1967)   The 1960s witnessed the rapid rise of rights-based social movements, including those for civil rights, women's rights, and free speech. Even older Americans engaged in activism, launching the Grey Power movement against age discrimination. In the 1960s, many employers assigned age limits to certain jobs. When workers over 40 lost their jobs, they subsequently found it harder to find new jobs. As a result, unemployment among older Americans was fairly high. In 1967, Congress passed the Age Discrimination in Employment Act to prevent age discrimination and promote the employment of older workers. Section Four, the heart of the act, made it illegal to fire, refuse to hire, or discriminate against a person because of their age. Furthermore, employers were barred from treating an employee differently from other workers because of their age. The act applied the same standards to labor unions. In the ensuing years, the courts interpreted the law to apply to job applicants as well as employees. To enforce the act, the law empowered the Equal Employment Opportunity Commission to investigate and subpoena when necessary. Although the law originally applied to employees between 40 and 64 years old, the classification was eventually broadened to include anyone over 40.

Agent Orange   Over the course of the Vietnam War, the U.S. military sprayed more than 100 million pounds of toxic chemicals on the land and rivers of Vietnam. One of the most notorious of these chemicals was Agent Orange, a defoliant used to strip trees of their leaves so as to uncover the enemy.

Use of Agent Orange began in 1963 during the JOHN F. KENNEDY administration. By the end of the war, Agent Orange had been sprayed upon millions of acres of land, ruining half of the timberlands of South Vietnam. Aside from the widespread destruction of the environment, Agent Orange's toxicity has damaged generations of Vietnamese, and it has been linked to numerous chronic health problems among U.S. veterans of military service in Vietnam.

Air Quality Control Act (1967)   The MOTOR VEHICLE AIR POLLUTION ACT of 1965 together with growing concern over air pollution created an impetus for even more antipollution legislation. In 1966, 60 air pollution bills were introduced in the House of Representatives; a year later the number jumped to 149. The Air Quality Control Act that emerged from these various proposals in 1967 empowered the states to set air quality standards. If states did not set any standards, the federal government retained the right to intervene. In addition, the secretary of the Department of Health, Education and Welfare was given the authority to seek injunctions against companies that violated pollution limits. The act funded research studies of pollution and asserted federal— rather than state—authority to establish automobile exhaust standards. Thus the federal government assumed responsibility for enforcing pollution controls.

Alcoholic Rehabilitation Act (1968)   Until the mid-1960s, Americans had tended to view alcoholism as a personal failing of the drinker stemming from an inability to resist a moral sin. By the late 1960s, however, a "medical model" of alcoholism replaced the previous perception. Congress officially adopted the medical model in 1968 with passage of the Alcoholic Rehabilitation Act. The act redefined alcoholism as a disease that demanded treatment equal to that of other diseases, including early detection, prevention, and rehabilitation.

American Independent Party Emerges (1968)   By 1968, emboldened by the divisive conflicts of race, class, and politics, a conservative backlash began. That year, Alabama governor George Wallace ran for president under the banner of the American Independent Party. Wallace hoped to unify southern racists and capture enough votes to prevent a majority victory in the Electoral College and throw the election to the House of Representatives. Wallace opposed hippies, leftists, feminists, pacifists, and intellectuals, and he appealed to white, working-class Americans in advocating a platform that called for job training, collective bargaining, and an increase in the minimum wage. His promises of "law and order" made clear his stand against Black Power activists and the counterculture in general. While Wallace's greatest support came from residents in the South, he also appealed to white working class inhabitants of the North. Wallace ran a folksy campaign, starting each appearance with country music and prayers. Wallace even encouraged hecklers, upon whom he would unleash a verbal flood of insults. In the election, Wallace won 13.5 percent of the popular vote and 46 electoral votes.

Antiwar March on the Pentagon (1967)   Probably the largest and most cohesive demonstration against the Vietnam War occurred on Saturday, October 21, 1967, in Washington, D.C. After a rally at the Lincoln Memorial, activists marched across the Potomac River to the Pentagon. The march brought together several strains of antiwar activists, from religious pacifists to the counterculture absurdists known as the "Yippies," who promised to levitate and then exorcise the Pentagon. In all, about 100,000 marchers approached the building until they encountered a military barricade. As the marchers surrounded the building, they unleashed a spectacle of passionate politics and psychedelic counterculture, including a surreal moment when hippies placed flowers in the gun barrels of soldiers stationed to preserve order. President Johnson publicly dismissed the protesters, but he privately worried that the march would encourage North Vietnam's war effort. To discourage the marchers, the Johnson administration refused to provide any toilets, first aid, or water for the marchers. The protesters carried on peacefully all the same, as Johnson denounced them as communist subversives. At the end of the day sporadic violence did occur, and 700 demonstrators were arrested.

Antiwar Movement   *See* New Left/Antiwar Movement

Assassination of Malcolm X (1965)   In 1965, Muslim civil rights activist Malcolm X split with Elijah Muhammad and the Nation of Islam to pursue his own vision of black nationalism, which embraced armed self-defense and pan-Africanism. As the mainstream Civil Rights movement began to splinter, younger activists turned to Malcolm, especially following his appearance at an early February civil rights rally in Selma, Alabama. Upon returning to his home base in New York, tensions continued to flare over Malcolm's feud with the Nation of Islam, and several attempts on his life were made. On February 21, 1965, as Malcolm prepared for a speech in Harlem, five assassins from the Nation of Islam infiltrated the audience. When Malcolm took to the stage, the assassins opened up with shotguns, killing him. In martyrdom, Malcolm's message became vastly more popular than it had been during his lifetime.

A demonstrator offers a flower to military police during the antiwar march on the Pentagon, October 21, 1967. *(© Everett Collection Inc/Alamy)*

Assassination of Martin Luther King, Jr. (1968)   Martin Luther King, Jr., spent April 4, 1968, in Memphis, Tennessee, in support of striking African-American sanitation workers. Lodged at a motel at which organizational meetings were held, King took a break on an outdoor balcony around 6 P.M. Just then, a sniper fired a shot that tore through King's jaw, killing the civil rights leader. As word spread of King's assassination, African Americans erupted in rage in more than 100 cities. The worst violence occurred in Washington, D.C., not far from the White House. Days later, Congress passed fair housing legislation in King's honor. King's assassin, James Earl Ray, avoided capture until June. Although King's nonviolent approach to civil rights had begun to show signs of strain, his death put an abrupt end to the movement, and it offered a haunting harbinger of the violence and social disorder of the late 1960s.

Assassination of Robert F. Kennedy (1968)   During the spring of 1968, Robert F. Kennedy, brother of former president JOHN F. KENNEDY, had become the favorite for the Democratic Party presidential nomination. Kennedy had widespread support due to his ability to transcend race and class barriers; his eloquent appeals for racial equality made him especially popular among African Americans. On June 5, Kennedy narrowly won the California primary, making him the front-runner for his party's nomination. Later that night, a Palestinian nationalist named Sirhan Sirhan shot and killed Kennedy in a Los Angeles hotel. Kennedy's death unleashed a massive outpouring of grief among many Americans, who had hoped he could heal a nation riven by war, racism, and violence.

Two months after the assassination of her husband, Martin Luther King, Jr., Coretta Scott King pays her respects at a memorial to the slain senator Robert F. Kennedy, June 8, 1968. *(© Everett Collection Inc/Alamy)*

Battle of Hue (1968)   The city of Hue, located in the northernmost part of South Vietnam, proved a recurrently troublesome hotspot during the Vietnamese civil war. In 1963, Buddhist demonstrations against U.S. influence began in Hue. Three years later, Hue fell to communist fighters but was soon retaken by U.S. forces. During the 1968 TET OFFENSIVE, dozens of cities in South Vietnam fell under attack. Although U.S. troops quickly repelled most of the assaults, Hue remained in enemy hands for over three weeks in early 1968. In a war of small-scale skirmishes waged largely in rural areas, the heavy bombing and sustained urban fighting turned Hue into one of the most bloody and destructive battles of the entire war. In all, the U.S. and South Vietnamese lost 500 soldiers, while the North Vietnamese and Vietcong lost up to 5,000. The damage done to the residents of Hue was far worse, as thousands were killed and tens of thousands were forced to flee the devastated city, adding to a swelling population of homeless refugees.

Beautification Program   The 1960s witnessed a growing concern for the earth's natural environment. In President Lyndon Johnson's view, the beautification of polluted areas and the prevention of air and water pollution fit into the grand vision of the GREAT SOCIETY. The legislative embodiment of this spirit became the Highway Beautification Act of 1965, on behalf of which LADY BIRD JOHNSON exerted great effort. The act limited billboard advertising along interstates, mandated the cleanup of junkyards, and authorized improvements in highway landscaping to make highways less ugly. The new laws were enforced by a threat of revocation of federal highway funds for noncompliance. Beautification never amounted to more than a token effort during the Johnson administration due to the strong influence of the advertising and motor vehicle lobbies on Congress; Johnson himself emphasized that further conservation efforts would be needed in the future. Lady Bird Johnson pursued other efforts to beautify Washington, D.C., as well as protect natural areas across the United States.

Body Counts   Lyndon Johnson's insistence on waging a limited war in Vietnam meant that the United States lacked traditional, identifiable military goals since a conventional invasion of North Vietnam was never an option. In the South, U.S. troops confronted a nearly invisible guerrilla force. Thus military officials could mark progress only by referring to the "body count," or numbers of enemy dead. These figures, however, were notoriously unreliable. No one could accurately count the dead, counters made little attempt to distinguish between civilians and combatants, and U.S. leaders pushed for positive numbers. Eventually, the numbers reported had little or no connection to reality. The U.S. military used these inflated body count numbers as evidence that it was winning the war, but ultimately reliance on the

Flanked by Secretary of the Interior Stewart Udall *(left)* and Laurance Rockefeller *(right)*, Lady Bird Johnson *(center)* points to an architectural model of the Mall area in Washington, D.C., during a "beautification luncheon" on April 27, 1967. *(Photo by Robert Knudsen/Lyndon B. Johnson Library)*

body count was flawed: It succeeded only in emphasizing the escalating violence of the war and made the Johnson administration appear sadistic as the war became increasingly unpopular.

Bruce, Lenny *See* TRIAL OF LENNY BRUCE (1964)

Child Nutrition Act (1966) The educational programs of the GREAT SOCIETY would have been of little use to children not healthy enough to take advantage of them. To provide low-income children with nutritious meals, Congress passed the Child Nutrition Act in 1966. This legislation instituted pilot school breakfast programs at schools in impoverished areas as well as at schools attended by poor children. Under the act, the federal government supplied most of the funding for the food, including $2 million for the 1966–67 school year. The breakfasts served had to meet the nutritional requirements of the Department of Agriculture, and they had to be made available to any student, regardless of his or her ability to purchase the meals.

Cigarette Labeling and Advertising Act *See* FEDERAL CIGARETTE LABELING AND ADVERTISING ACT (1965)

Civil Rights Act (1964) The Civil Rights Act of 1964 marked the culmination of decades of civil rights activism, and it went a long way toward fulfilling the broken promises of Reconstruction. Most important, the law outlawed segregation in public facilities, such as restaurants, hotels, and museums, as well as racial and sexual discrimination in employment. Other sections of the law strengthened protections of voting rights, granted equal access to government facilities and programs, and empowered the Equal Employment Opportunity Commission to enforce the new laws. In one stroke, Lyndon Johnson overturned almost a century of legal oppression and, in so doing, launched a revolutionary change in southern society. Johnson tapped all his political wells to get the bill through Congress, such as when he personally pressed Illinois Republican senator Everett Dirksen to support a cloture vote to cut off the Senate filibuster. Surrounded by Martin Luther King, Jr., and others, President Johnson signed the bill into law on July 2, 1964. The act reflected the Democratic Party's allegiance to African Americans and other minorities, but despite his pride at having brought the law into being, Johnson knew that the act would drive white southerners into the Republican Party.

President Johnson signs the Civil Rights Act as Martin Luther King, Jr. *(directly behind Johnson)* and others look on, July 2, 1964. *(Cecil Stoughton, White House Press Office)*

Civil Rights Act (1968)   After a flurry of urban riots in 1967, President Johnson and civil rights groups unsuccessfully lobbied Congress for a fair housing bill. Preventing discriminatory housing practices would, Johnson believed, help integrate the country. After the ASSASSINATION OF MARTIN LUTHER KING, JR., in April 1968 Congress passed the Civil Rights Act of 1968, in part as a tribute to the slain civil rights leader. The act banned discrimination in federally owned housing as well as in apartments with federally insured mortgages. The law broke down many barriers that had kept countless American neighborhoods segregated. Although the bill ostensibly eased housing conditions in ghettos, it lacked teeth—primarily because it did not create an agency to enforce the new law. The real target of the law turned out to be rioters; an amendment added by the House of Representatives mandated up to five years in prison for crossing state lines to conduct a riot, and a provision defined a riot as threats of violence involving three or more people. H. Rap Brown, the militant African-American leader of the Student Non-violent Coordinating Committee, became the first person prosecuted under the act, which was also used against the antiwar protesters known as the Chicago Eight. The act signaled the end of the civil rights era in U.S. political history.

Comprehensive Health Planning Act (1966)   The Comprehensive Health Planning Act of 1966 was another GREAT SOCIETY attempt to improve the health of all Americans, and especially those who could not afford proper health care. By definition, health planning refers to the federal government's attempt to anticipate future needs in the healthcare industry and allocate resources accordingly. Among the many factors to consider are the supply of doctors and number of hospital beds in particular areas. The 1966 plan specifically coordinated existing efforts by providing grants to local planning boards. These boards used the grants to study the needs of their specific communities and assign priorities to their most pressing issues.

Democratic National Convention (1968)   *See* 1968 DEMOCRATIC NATIONAL CONVENTION

Demonstration Cities and Metropolitan Development Act   *See* MODEL CITIES PROGRAM

Department of Housing and Urban Development Act (1965)   The GREAT SOCIETY's expansive efforts to help the disadvantaged resulted in a vastly enlarged federal government, even at the cabinet level. In 1965, legislation established the Department of Housing and Urban Development (HUD). HUD's mission was to improve city life and substandard housing for poor Americans, especially African Americans. As head of the new department, Lyndon Johnson appointed Robert C. Weaver, who thus became the first African-American member of a presidential cabinet.

Department of Transportation Act (1966)   As president, Lyndon Johnson sought to consolidate control of the nation's transportation network to improve efficiency and safety. Drawing on the federal government's traditional involvement in transportation issues, the president lobbied countless members of the federal bureaucracy and the transportation industry. The Department of Transportation Act of 1966 created a cabinet-level department that encompassed all aspects of transportation, including commerce, public roads, aviation, the U.S. Coast Guard, and the Interstate Commerce Commission, and it authorized creation of the National Transportation Safety Board. Furthermore, the Department of Transportation assumed regulatory authority over local airlines, construction projects, international aviation, and urban transportation. In general, the new organization made roads safer and commerce more efficient and it succeeded in greatly transforming the way Americans traveled.

Detroit Riot (1967)   For a week beginning on July 23, 1967, Detroit was shut down as rioters, looters, arsonists, and snipers controlled the inner city. Like the NEWARK RIOT earlier in the month, the Detroit confrontation began when police clashed with African Americans. The rioters raged against oppression in general, including de facto segregation, a lack of recreational facilities, substandard housing, frequent police brutality, and high unemployment. Knowing that the nonviolent tactics of the Civil Rights movement did not work in northern cities, many residents felt that their only hope lay in massive disruption. In the end, the Detroit riots had to be suppressed by city and state police as well as military troops. Authorities made 7,000 arrests; in addition, 43 people died. In response, Johnson appointed the KERNER COMMISSION to investigate the causes of the riots.

Drug Abuse Control Amendments (1965)   The Drug Abuse Control Amendments of 1965 reorganized federal drug control authority under the Bureau of Drug Abuse Control, within the Food and Drug Administration. This new bureau primarily enforced laws against depressants and stimulants. The new approach originated with a JOHN F. KENNEDY administration committee's recommendation to relax prosecution of small-time drug dealers and users in favor of pursuing drug importers and large-scale distributors.

***Duncan v. Louisiana* (1968)**   The Supreme Court's 1968 decision in *Duncan v. Louisiana* upheld the incorporation doctrine—the concept that under the Fourteenth Amendment, the Bill of Rights applies to the states and not just to federal law. The case centered around Gary Duncan, an African-American resident of Louisiana, who was convicted of misdemeanor battery. Duncan's request for a jury trial was refused because the Louisiana constitution authorized a jury trial only for cases that might result in capital punishment or hard labor sentences. Instead, Duncan received a fine and a 60-day jail sentence. On appeal, Duncan's lawyer claimed that his client's right to a jury trial, guaranteed under the Sixth Amendment, had been denied. The Supreme Court decided 7-2 in favor of Duncan, ruling that the Fourteenth Amendment guarantees the right to jury trial for any "serious offenses." Despite the heavy majority, the Court in future remained divided over the "selective" application of the incorporation doctrine.

Economic Opportunity Act (1964)   Endorsed by Sargent Shriver, the head of the Peace Corps, the Economic Opportunity Act (EOA) of 1964 constituted the legislative embodiment of Lyndon Johnson's WAR ON POVERTY. The law created the Office of Economic Opportunity (OEO) to direct federal antipoverty policy. The EOA also created a wide-ranging array of antipoverty programs, including educational assistance for preschool and college students (HEAD START and Upward Bound); job training for urban youth (Job Corps); and a domestic version of the Peace Corps (Volunteers in Service to America). The EOA also created community action programs (CAPs) to mobilize poor people on local levels. OEO guidelines mandated that CAPs allow the "maximum feasible participation" of poor people in the distribution of federal aid. This mandate angered local city politicians and social workers who traditionally controlled social programs. Maximum feasible participation sometimes turned confrontational, as activists in some cities turned the OEO against itself by using CAP money to train demonstrators in civil disobedience techniques, including leading protests against government offices. Conflicts within the Democratic Party over the CAPs foreshadowed the diminishing support for the EOA and the War on Poverty that took place in the late 1960s.

Economic Opportunity Amendments (1967)   The Office of Economic Opportunity (OEO), the legislative embodiment of the GREAT SOCIETY, came up for renewal in 1967. Many supporters of the Great Society in general and the WAR ON POVERTY in particular feared that the OEO might be eliminated by Republican opposition to radical antipoverty programs and heavy spending policies. A compromise saved the OEO, but resulted in amendments that cut the OEO's most radical provisions. First to go were the Community Action Programs that had mandated the participation of grassroots antipoverty activists as well as poor people themselves.

Elementary and Secondary Education Act (1965)   One of the major objectives of the GREAT SOCIETY was an effort to promote education as a means to help uplift the poor. President Johnson believed that expansion of education would help integrate the poor and other excluded groups into mainstream society, helping to realize the equalitarian goals of the Declaration of Independence. The Elementary and Secondary Education Act of 1965 provided help in the form of $1.06 billion, targeted primarily at low-income schools, though 95 percent of U.S. counties ultimately received money. Aside from direct funds, the act supplied money for libraries, books, and instruction materials; grants for new programs and educational research; and funding for state departments of education. Notably, the act did not allow segregated schools to receive money; in the South, school boards who had resisted desegregation rushed to integrate. To Johnson's dismay, school districts, rather than the federal government, had discretion over how the funds were spent, and the money did not aid poor people nearly as much as he intended. Nevertheless, by all measurements, the act improved a great many lives.

Federal Cigarette Labeling and Advertising Act (1965)   A growing recognition of the dangers of cigarette smoking during the mid-1960s forced tobacco manufacturers to respond to increasingly hostile public opinion. The surgeon general had issued his first report in 1964 detailing the health risks of cigarette smoke. In response to looming federal regulation of tobacco advertisements by the Federal Trade Commission (FTC), the tobacco industry supported passage of the Federal Cigarette Labeling and Advertising Act of 1965. The act, disguised as a health measure, required that a warning be placed on all cigarette labels, though the manufacturer retained discretion as to where to place the warning. The law also approved $2 million for educational campaigns and research on smoking. Cigarette manufacturers, however, saw the law as a victory, as it included provisions that eliminated FTC authority over cigarette advertisements. The law also prevented other agencies (such as the Federal Communications Commission) from mandating warnings, and it blocked state and local laws regulating the sale of cigarettes.

Food and Agriculture Act (1965)   The Food and Agriculture Act of 1965 attempted to aid farmers through the traditional methods of controlling production, reducing the food surplus, and increasing prices for agricultural products. The act granted direct payments to field crop farmers (including wheat, cotton, and corn producers) who agreed to join voluntary acreage reduction programs. The law gave the secretary of agriculture the discretion to alter the program in accordance with changes in the economy. During congressional debate, representatives of urban areas agreed to support the act in exchange for support of a partial repeal of the Taft-Hartley Act of 1947.

Food Stamp Act (1964)   As President Johnson well understood, one of poverty's most crippling side effects is hunger. Part of the GREAT SOCIETY's WAR ON POVERTY took aim at hunger and its concurrent problem, malnutrition. At the same time, agricultural interests hoped to alleviate a food surplus; the easiest way of solving both these problems seemed to be to provide the poor with the surplus food. Food retailers, however, demanded that their interests be protected, too. The Food Stamp Act of 1964 brokered a system to placate all three groups. Food Stamps had first been used during the Great Depression: Participants could trade stamps in for surplus food items. The 1964 plan allowed participants to use their stamps for any item in any store. Households handed over the money they spent on food to a state agency, receiving in return stamps valued at more than the money paid for them. In this way, the retailer received equal value for their commodities, and though participants could not technically save money, they did receive more food for the same amount of money.

Freedom of Information Act (1966)   Passed in 1966, the Freedom of Information Act granted the public access to the records of the federal government and its agencies. Certain records were excluded by an "exemption" and thus were not open, including sensitive information for which revelation might threaten privacy rights, violate confidentiality agreements, or harm national security. Advocates of the act praised the newfound openness of the U.S. government as compared to other, more secretive governments. The act has been a particular boon to journalists and historians, though various presidential administrations have shifted the parameters of the act in adopting a broad interpretation of the exemption powers to keep their actions hidden from the public.

Ginzburg v. United States **(1966)**   During the 1960s, pornography occupied a significant amount of the Supreme Court's time. By 1966, the Court had still failed to establish a clear definition of "obscene," though it had established that judgment depended upon an analysis of the "dominant theme" of the material in question. The 5-4 decision in *Ginzburg v. United States* (1966), however, marked a departure from the idea that the content itself determines obscenity. Ralph Ginzburg, publisher of a sex magazine called *Eros,* had been convicted on obscenity charges not because his publication was itself obscene, but because subscription advertisements for *Eros* emphasized the magazine's erotic nature. Rather than determine whether *Eros* was obscene, the Supreme Court upheld Ginzburg's conviction; the Court argued that the advertisements that promoted *Eros* as arousing clearly identified the publication as obscene. The narrow majority reflected the Court's treatment of issues involving the First Amendment's protection of pornography as free speech.

Great Society   On May 22, 1964, President Lyndon Johnson unveiled the title for his domestic agenda during a speech at the University of Michigan. "In your time," he stated, "we have the opportunity to move not only toward the rich society and the powerful society, but upward to the Great Society. . . . It is a place where men are more concerned with the quality of their goals than the quantity of their goods." The *Great Society* thus became the term that encapsulated Johnson's vision for domestic reform, social justice, and eco-

nomic equality in the United States. Inspired by the liberal activism of FRANKLIN D. ROOSEVELT's New Deal, Johnson believed that his Great Society would lift up the disadvantaged—especially African Americans—who had been left behind by postwar prosperity. Always wary of American opposition to simple welfare measures, Johnson focused many Great Society efforts on providing equality of opportunity rather than direct government handouts. Great Society education measures most concretely embodied this faith in opportunity. Equal access to education, Johnson believed, would open new opportunities for African Americans and the poor. The Great Society went beyond education, into areas including health improvement, housing construction, federal funding for the arts, job training, urban planning, and environmental protection, as well as a noble but ultimately unwinnable WAR ON POVERTY. Though Johnson's landmark civil rights efforts began before he expressed his Great Society vision, his goal of racial equality was essential to the Great Society in general. Overall, the Great Society achieved mixed results. Underfunded and overambitious, the Great Society promised more than it could ever deliver. At its worst, it cre-

Ralph Ginzburg wears handcuffs outside the federal building in Lewisburg, Pennsylvania. He was taken to prison after being convicted on charges of sending obscene literature through the mail. *(Paul Vathis/Associated Press)*

ated a large bureaucracy that moved at a glacial pace; at its best, the Great Society expanded federal protections for the voiceless and the downtrodden.

Griswold v. Connecticut (1965) In *Griswold v. Connecticut* (1965), the Supreme Court declared unconstitutional an 1879 Connecticut law banning the sale and use of contraceptive devices, including to married couples. The case resulted when Estelle Griswold, the executive director of the Planned Parenthood League of Connecticut, and Dr. C. Lee Buxton, the group's medical director, were convicted in state court of violating the 1879 law. The significance of the Supreme Court's 7-2 decision lies not in the fact that the antiquated statute was overturned but in the Court's reasoning that such a law violated the right to privacy. Although not specifically stated in the U.S. Constitution, the Court argued that the right to privacy is implied in several places in the Bill of Rights. The right to privacy first mentioned in the *Griswold* decision later served as the basis for the controversial 1973 *Roe v. Wade* decision, which ruled that abortion was a right protected by the Constitution's guarantee of privacy.

Gulf of Tonkin Resolution (1964) Although hopeful that limited efforts would achieve his objectives in Vietnam, Lyndon Johnson came under increasing pressure from conservatives to escalate the war in 1964. The president also wanted to show North Vietnam that the United States was united behind his Vietnam policy. While engaged in clandestine naval operations off the North Vietnamese coast in the Gulf of Tonkin, the USS *Maddox* entered into a battle with the North Vietnamese on August 2, 1964. In response, Johnson ordered in a second destroyer, the USS *C. Turner Joy*. On August 4, both ships reported they had been attacked. The president ordered air strikes to retaliate even though evidence substantiating the second attack was dubious. The Maddox and *C. Turner Joy* attack in August gave Johnson his opportunity. Glossing over the uncertainty surrounding the incident, Johnson presented Congress with the Gulf of Tonkin Resolution, which granted the president "all necessary measures to repel any armed attacks against the forces of the United States and to prevent further aggression." The president later observed that the resolution was like "Granny's nightgown," in that it "covered everything." Quickly after its introduction, the resolution passed both houses of Congress; the vote was unanimous in the House, and just two senators voted against it. As the war became more unpopular, opponents complained that the resolution sidestepped Congress's responsibility to declare war. At the time, however, the resolution boosted Johnson's approval rating, neutralized conservative criticism, and provided him a blank check for future escalation. In June 1970, as President Richard Nixon continued the war, the Senate overwhelmingly repealed the Gulf of Tonkin Resolution.

Head Start One of the War on Poverty's many educational programs, Head Start was a popular initiative that provided preschool classes for disadvantaged, primarily African American, children. Head Start children improved their academic skills, making them less likely to drop out once they entered elementary school. Started in 1965, more than 500,000 children enrolled in Head Start, many of them, by so doing, receiving their very first educational instruction.

Heart of Atlanta Motel v. United States (1964) The case of *Heart of Atlanta Motel v. United States* (1964) was one of the first lawsuits to challenge the Civil Rights Act of 1964. The white owners of the Heart of Atlanta Motel had barred African Americans from staying at the property. The owners of the motel contested the provisions of Title II of the act, which outlawed discrimination in public accommodations on the basis of the interstate commerce clause of the U.S. Constitution. The Supreme Court unanimously upheld the act, arguing that because the Heart of Atlanta relied heavily on out-of-state business, Congress could outlaw the motel's discriminatory practices. Although several justices believed that the Fourteenth Amendment gave Congress the right to outlaw discrimination, legal validation for the law has rested on the interstate commerce clause.

Higher Education Act (1965) Lyndon Johnson made federal aid to education a core aspect of his Great Society. After approving legislation for elementary and secondary education, Johnson proudly signed the Higher Education Act in 1965. The act authorized millions of dollars in grants for disadvantaged students, provided student loans with deferred interest, and expanded work-study programs. In addition, the act funded college and university community service programs, library improvements, aid to African-American colleges, and federal scholarships. In the years following the act, college enrollment increased dramatically, with the majority of students receiving financial aid in some form from the Higher Education Act.

Historic Preservation Act (1966) Before 1966, historic preservation had been used strictly to protect areas and structures of historic and architectural significance, such as Monticello, the home of President Thomas Jefferson. But by the mid-1960s, many old, urban buildings of cultural—if not national—importance faced demolition by urban redevelopment projects, including the construction of sprawling highways. The 1966 Historic Preservation Act turned preservation into a form of urban conservation in harmony with the ethnic and cultural awakenings of the 1960s and 1970s. The act sought to provide "future generations a genuine opportunity to appreciate and enjoy the rich heritage of our Nation," and pledged the federal government "to expand and accelerate historic preservation programs and activities."

The act broadly redefined the concept of *historic* beyond presidential homes and battlefields. In the process, the act shifted the pace of urban development and the face of the nation's cities.

Ho Chi Minh Trail   North Vietnamese guerrillas forged the Ho Chi Minh trail in 1959, creating an extensive series of paths and dirt roads to supply communist rebels in the South with military equipment. The trail extended 600 miles from North Vietnam into South Vietnam, making occasional detours into Laos and Cambodia. North Vietnam upgraded the trail in 1964, making it capable of handling trucks and transporting troops. The trail played such a crucial role in the war effort that much of the U.S. bombing campaign concentrated on destroying it. The ability of North Vietnamese and Vietcong soldiers to repair and rebuild the trail quickly, however, nullified the bombing campaign. One study found that it took an average of 100 tons of bombs to kill one soldier. At its peak, the trail moved 400 tons of supplies per week and 5,000 soldiers in a month. A public memorial highway commemorates the trail today.

Housing and Urban Development Act (1965)   A bill to improve housing for the poor had been in the works since the John F. Kennedy administration. The Housing and Urban Development Act of 1965 that eventually emerged aimed to provide a new form of public housing. The act created rent supplements that allowed renters who spent one-fourth of their income on rent to receive the remainder from the government. The Johnson administration hoped that the supplements would make building houses for the poor profitable for developers; Republicans, however, dismissed the plan as socialism. The supplements engendered further controversy because they could be applied anywhere, raising white fears of black encroachment in their neighborhoods. Eventually Congress hedged the plan, limiting the supplements only to those already living in public housing. Funding was entirely drained by 1966. And although the act promised construction of 200,000 public housing units, by 1967 only 23,000 were being built annually.

Housing and Urban Development Act (1968)   Despite the efforts of the War on Poverty and such legislation as the Housing and Urban Development Act of 1965, poverty persisted in American cities and among their residents into the late 1960s. President Johnson believed that facilitating home ownership would help alleviate poverty; other, less progressive politicians hoped that home ownership would discourage the rioting that tore apart many cities at the end of the decade. The Housing and Urban Development Act of 1968 pledged $5 billion for the construction of 26 million homes and apartments over 10 years, and it expanded rent supplements and Model Cities program funding. The act

also granted federal subsidies to low-income families for the purchase of homes as well as to developers of new towns and communities. The act, however, did more for special interests than for the poor. Written primarily by the banking lobby, the act did not make homes easier to get; instead, federal subsidies went directly to lenders rather than to the poor themselves.

Immigration and Nationality Act Amendments (1965)
Since the 1920s, U.S. immigration laws had restricted entry based on racial quotas favoring white immigrants over minorities, especially those from Asia. In the mid-1960s, Lyndon Johnson described the racial quota system as "shameful," and he set out to overturn such barriers. The Immigration and Nationality Act Amendments of 1965 eliminated racial quotas, and instead assigned priority to immigrants with family already in the United States as well as to those with valued professional and technical skills. The amendments permitted an annual influx of 120,000 immigrants from the Western Hemisphere (mostly Latin America), and 170,000 from the Eastern Hemisphere (including Asia, Africa, and Europe). Johnson's immigration reform essentially applied his Great Society principle of equal rights to immigration policy. The immigration reforms set in motion a significant relocation of Asian and Latin American immigrants to the United States in thus bringing greater diversity to American society.

"Johnson Treatment"   Lyndon Johnson owed much of his legislative success to what reporters dubbed the "Johnson treatment," a practice he used to cajole, convince, and cower his legislative allies and adversaries. The Johnson treatment was an intense experience—one survivor said that it "ran the gamut of human emotions." The treatment consisted of a three-pronged assault that started on a physical level. Those who endured the treatment recalled Johnson making deep eye contact, grabbing lapels, and draping his arms around their shoulders. Superb at debate and persuasion, Johnson then unleashed rhetorical tactics, showering the victim with facts, statistics, and analogies. Finally, Johnson entered the realm of the psychological, using flattery, threat, aggression, emotional appeals, supplication, or a combination of these, to make his case. But what appeared to be the natural maneuverings and style of a career Texas politician actually proceeded on the basis of careful forethought and skilled preparation. Johnson learned about the strengths, interests, weaknesses, and personal details of his target, and he adjusted his arguments accordingly to apply them to maximum effect.

***Katzenbach v. McClung* (1964)**   The case of *Katzenbach v. McClung* provided an early challenge to the 1964 Civil Rights Act. Ollie McClung, the owner of Ollie's Barbecue in Birmingham, Alabama, refused to serve African Americans at his restaurant. Title II of the act outlawed discrimination in public accommodations under the provisions of the inter-

President Johnson signs the Immigration and Nationality Act Amendments on October 3, 1965, at Liberty Island, New York, as *(from left to right)* Vice President Hubert Humphrey, Lady Bird Johnson, Muriel Humphrey, Senator Edward Kennedy, Senator Robert F. Kennedy, and others look on. *(Lyndon B. Johnson Library)*

state commerce clause of the U.S. Constitution. The owner of Ollie's Barbecue argued in *Katzenbach v. McClung* (1964) that, as a family-owned restaurant located far from any interstates, bus depots, or railroad stations, his business failed to qualify for regulation under the commerce clause. He brought suit against the U.S. government, naming Attorney General Nicholas Katzenbach. The Supreme Court ruled against McClung, affirming that nearly half of the food sold at Ollie's consisted of meat purchased from an out-of-state supplier. Furthermore, the Court ruled that discrimination discourages interstate travel and business in general. The decision upheld the right of Congress to intervene in local matters even when the issue is peripheral to interstate commerce.

Kerner Commission   After massive riots tore apart Newark, Detroit, and other cities in 1967, Lyndon Johnson formed the National Advisory Commission on Civil Disorders, known as the Kerner Commission after its chairman, Illinois governor Otto Kerner. In March 1968, after a year spent investigating the causes of the riots, the commission announced in its report that "Our nation is moving toward two societies,

one black, one white—separate and unequal." The Kerner Report argued that white racism was the fundamental cause of urban unrest as well as the oppression of African Americans in general. The commissioners noted that the rioters were not random agitators looking to stir up trouble, but were instead educated, unemployed, and frustrated individuals. Reasoning that ghetto life created a destructive environment, the commission recommended a massive expansion of government programs to alleviate racism, including funding for jobs, housing, welfare, and education. Johnson balked at the report's recommendations, however, since he knew that the American public was growing increasingly disenchanted with expensive GREAT SOCIETY social programs.

***Maddox* and *C. Turner Joy* Attacks (1964)**   On August 2, 1964, the USS *Maddox* encountered North Vietnamese torpedo boats while conducting surveillance in the Gulf of Tonkin. The *Maddox* repelled the attack, and on the following day, the navy ordered the *Maddox*, along with the *C. Turner Joy,* to return to the area. Late on August 4, under stormy skies, the two ships reported another North Vietnamese attack. As Lyndon Johnson's cabinet prepared a military response, the *Maddox* commander reassessed the situation. Finding no solid evidence of an attack, he admitted that the raging storms might have been mistaken for an attack. But Johnson and other military officials, using unreliable information passed on by intelligence agencies, convinced themselves that an attack had taken place and they ordered swift bombing reprisals. Johnson then placed the GULF OF TONKIN RESOLUTION before Congress, citing the attacks on the *Maddox* as justification. The resolution, which passed overwhelmingly, gave the president unlimited authority to wage war in Vietnam.

Marines Landed at Danang (1965)

In late February 1965, U.S. general William Westmoreland requested that U.S. Marines be called in to protect the Danang airbase in Vietnam. President Johnson had avoided introducing ground troops into Vietnam, but he made the decision to acquiesce to the request. On March 8, two marine battalions, totaling 1,500 soldiers, arrived in Danang. The marines were intended to serve only a defensive role, though this marked an escalation of the advisory role of previous U.S. troops in Vietnam. After the Danang deployment, Johnson's cabinet pushed for more troop increases. By late April, Johnson had agreed to deploy 40,000 ground forces; by summertime, U.S. soldiers were engaged actively in battle.

Media Relations

As president, Lyndon Johnson paid close attention to the news. Press coverage of Johnson was initially positive; Johnson could be affable with reporters, and they supported his progressive policies. Nevertheless, the president worried constantly that the press would turn on him. His fragile ego meant that he always felt slighted by media coverage. Minor errors, for example, became evidence of a smear campaign in Johnson's mind. Johnson could not appreciate the requirement that good journalism demanded balanced coverage; rather, he wanted undivided loyalty. At press conferences Johnson appeared stiff, and he reacted poorly to critical questions. He claimed that television news coverage undermined his Vietnam policies, and he eventually convinced himself of a media conspiracy. Johnson increasingly cloaked his presidency in secrecy to avoid reporters, which only increased his reputation for mendacity. Late in life Johnson blamed reporters for his political ruin. However, in reality, Johnson's love of secrecy had simply clashed with the media's expository responsibilities.

Medicaid Act (1965)

One of the ways in which poverty cripples is by limiting access to proper health care. Hoping to reverse this situation, President Lyndon Johnson signed the Medicaid Act in 1965, which put in place a system of federal health insurance for the poor that mirrored Medicare's insurance for the elderly. Under Medicaid, federal matching grants were distributed to the states; these grants were used to reimburse doctors who treated people on welfare. Medicaid dramatically increased the number of Americans with health coverage, though millions remained uninsured. The funding system depended on state governments to provide money, which the federal government would then match; thus funding varied greatly between states. Recipients also complained that the quality of Medicaid help was low. The bureaucratically cumbersome and fiscally inconsistent Medicaid system undermined the program's antipoverty goals. In the late 1960s, a backlash against welfare recipients led to drastic reductions in Medicaid.

Medicare Act (1965)

President Johnson insisted that access to health care was necessary to achieve the GREAT SOCIETY. In particular, a lack of coverage among the elderly plagued American society; in 1965, half of all senior citizens had no health insurance. For decades the American Medical Association had impeded healthcare reform, but with a heavy Democratic majority in 1965, Johnson maneuvered Medicare through Congress. The Medicare Act established federally funded medical insurance for those over the age of 65. Part A of the plan provided hospitalization insurance while Part B covered various doctors' fees. The plan helped raise many elderly Americans above the poverty line and it received overwhelming public support. Many important costs were not covered, however, including glasses, prescription drugs, and long-term care. To protect the profitability of the medical industry, no cost controls were instituted. Consequently, costs rose rapidly, making health care more expensive and Medicare less effective.

Miranda v. Arizona (1966)

The Supreme Court's 5-4 decision in *Miranda v. Arizona* (1966) aimed to protect the rights of suspected criminals. The case resulted when Ernesto Miranda, who had been convicted of a 1963 kidnapping and rape in Arizona, appealed to the Supreme Court that when he was arrested he had not been advised he was not bound to speak to the police. In particular, the Court expressed concern at the common violation of due process involving interrogation, as well as confessions extracted under duress. Chief Justice Earl Warren argued that the Fifth Amendment's prohibition of self-incrimination dictated that a person under arrest must receive proper warning that he or she has the right to remain silent, that his or her statements can be used as evidence, and that he or she has the right to an attorney. These rights soon became known as "Miranda rights." Essentially, the Supreme Court ruling recognized the right of suspects to halt police questioning by asking for a lawyer.

Mississippi Burning Trial (*United States v. Price et al.*) (1966)

On June 15, 1964, James Chaney, Andrew Goodman, and Michael Schwerner arrived in Mississippi to par-

A stained-glass window in Cornell University's Sage Chapel honoring civil rights workers James Chaney, Andrew Goodman, and Michael Schwerner, who were murdered in Mississippi in 1964. Schwerner had graduated from Cornell in 1961. *(Cornellrockey04)*

ticipate in the Freedom Summer voter registration drive. The next day, local police arrested the three men in Philadelphia, Mississippi. Later that night, a lynching party dragged the men from prison, beat them, and finally shot them. Eventually the sheriff, deputy sheriff, and others were convicted. Prosecutors had been powerless to prosecute lynchings because the Supreme Court narrowly interpreted the U.S. criminal code. Previous courts had argued that the federal government could prosecute only law enforcement officials. In addition, the southern-controlled Senate had blocked a federal antilynching law for decades. In 1966, however, in *United States v. Price et al.,* the Supreme Court upheld the indictment of the murderers of Chaney, Goodman, and Schwerner, arguing that when private individuals cooperate with law enforcement in a lynching, all the participants can be prosecuted.

Model Cities Program   The urban riots of the mid-1960s made evident the need to improve the quality of life in American cities. Originally titled Demonstration Cities, the program was renamed Model Cities because by 1966 the term "demonstration" had become synonymous with urban unrest and counterculture protest. The 1966 Model Cities program provided $900 million of federal money to improve inner-city housing, education, health care, crime prevention, and recreation facilities. Rather than concentrate funds in a few select cities, however, the program distributed funds across the country, resulting in a diluted pool of money. Furthermore, the funds were channeled through the Department of Housing and Urban Development and local mayors' offices, bypassing—and undermining—the Office of Economic Opportunity. Eventually, continued riots eroded congressional support for funding the Model Cities program. As with many WAR ON POVERTY programs, Model Cities helped improve poor communities but failed to address the fundamental causes of poverty.

Motor Vehicle Air Pollution Control Act (1965)   The growing use of cars during the 1950s and 1960s created an increasingly severe smog problem in American cities. The 1963 Clean Air Act had required the surgeon general to conduct a study of automobile air pollution, and the resulting report called for federal control of automobile pollution. The automobile industry actually supported federal legislation, preferring a national standard to countless state and local standards. As public opinion favored increased controls, the Johnson administration voiced its support as well. The Motor Vehicle Air Pollution Control Act of 1965 authorized the Department of Health, Education, and Welfare to set new standards for automobile air pollution.

My Lai Massacre (1968)   In March 1968, U.S. soldiers entered the village of My Lai searching for enemy Vietcong.

When the villagers refused to cooperate, the enraged soldiers began to slaughter them; estimates range between 100 and 400 civilian deaths. The military suppressed all knowledge of the massacre, which went unreported until 1969. In 1971, Lieutenant William Calley, the officer in charge at My Lai, was found guilty of murder and sentenced to life in prison, though his punishment was later reduced. The massacre reflected the growing hostility of U.S. soldiers toward all Vietnamese as well as the escalating brutality brought before the public eye.

Narcotic Addict Rehabilitation Act (1966)   In the mid-1960s, a growing heroin problem menaced American cities; observers noted a direct relationship between drug use and crime in urban areas. The Narcotic Addict Rehabilitation Act (NARA) of 1966 attempted to confront this growing drug abuse problem through a new "civil commitment" method. Instead of criminal punishment, drug addicts received treatment through the U.S. Public Health Service. (Those convicted of federal crimes received treatment through the prison system.) The rehabilitation process involved heavy supervision, monitoring, and testing of addicts, and it provided assistance to addicts with post-addiction issues such as housing and employment. Bureaucratic requirements were handled by the courts, creating a cumbersome process and an administrative avalanche of paperwork that rendered the program less effective than it could have been. On the other hand, NARA provided funding for local treatment, leading to an increase in the number of community-centered drug treatment programs.

National Foundation on the Arts and Humanities Act (1965)   In the 1964 elections, many Democrats swept into Congress on the coattails of Lyndon Johnson's landslide. Many of these newly elected legislators replaced opponents of federal spending on the arts. Furthermore, the expanded role of the state put in motion by the GREAT SOCIETY ended previous opposition to government patronage of the arts. As the new Congress convened, advocates of federal arts and humanities funding joined forces to pass legislation creating a National Foundation on the Arts and Humanities. The act that eventually passed in 1965 led to establishment of a National Endowment for the Arts (NEA) as well as one for the Humanities. The act allocated 20 percent of the funds directly to state arts councils, which, by 1967, existed in each state. The NEA in 1967 received $8 million, but thereafter President Johnson claimed that the cost of the Vietnam War prevented any increased spending on the arts.

National Traffic and Motor Vehicle Safety Act (1966)   The National Traffic and Motor Vehicle Safety Act of 1966 resulted in large part from the uproar sparked by Ralph Nader's UNSAFE AT ANY SPEED, a 1965 book detailing the many hazards of contemporary automobiles. The act authorized creation of the National Highway Safety Administration and empowered the federal government to issue and enforce auto safety standards. The act imposed safety restrictions on automobile manufacturers, rather than on consumers, because adequate safety technology already existed; automakers had simply not bothered to make cars safer. Despite carmakers' predictions to the contrary, safety regulation did not adversely affect the profits of the automobile industry.

Newark Riot (1967)   In early July 1967, in Newark, New Jersey, rumors of police brutality against an African-American taxi driver escalated into widespread violence. Six days of riots followed, resulting in 26 deaths and 1,500 injuries. A raging fire swept the inner city, adding to the millions of dollars in damages. The riots perplexed Lyndon Johnson since he believed that he had been especially attentive to the plight of African Americans, but the disturbances reflected the lack of noticeable improvement in urban areas despite the many GREAT SOCIETY antipoverty measures. As calm was restored in Newark, riots erupted in Detroit, Michigan, on July 23.

New Left/Antiwar Movement   The term *New Left* identified those college students and other radicals of the 1960s who embraced activism in the name of social change. Uneasy with the materialism of the 1950s, the New Left called for an ethical and participatory democracy. The Students for a Democratic Society most clearly articulated this crusading spirit in their "Port Huron Statement," a manifesto written by Tom Hayden and others in Port Huron, Michigan, in 1962. Energized by the Civil Rights movement and the Berkeley Free Speech Movement, the New Left distinguished itself from the "old left" of communists, socialists, labor unions, and mainstream liberals. The escalation of the Vietnam War in 1965 transformed the New Left into a radical antiwar movement. During the late 1960s, New Left activists engaged in countless antiwar protests, including demonstrations, marches, and teach-ins; students even occupied Columbia University in 1968. An ANTIWAR MARCH ON THE PENTAGON in 1967 drew more than 100,000 protesters, and activists tried to block military recruitment centers. Increasingly frustrated with mainstream American politics, the New Left eventually embraced revolutionaries operating in the developing world, including the Vietcong. The New Left, always a vague term, split at the end of the 1960s along racial and gender lines. Despite the end of the New Left, the antiwar movement continued well into the 1970s. The demise of the New Left reflected the increasing divisions within American society, especially between liberals and conservatives and between old and young.

New York City Blackout (1965)   On the evening of November 9, 1965, power grid failures in Canada sent a surge of electricity to power stations in upstate New York. In New York City, emergency shutoffs tripped by the surge left residents without power for 15 hours. The sudden loss of power left people sitting in traffic, stuck in elevators, and stranded in the subway. The blackout was notable for the peaceful, cooperative spirit that emerged across the city, as people poured into the streets to mingle with, and assist, neighbors and strangers alike. The blackout affected residents along

New York City during and after the blackout of November 9, 1965. Much of the Northeast lost electrical power for 15 hours. *(Library of Congress)*

the northeastern seaboard from Buffalo, New York, to the New Hampshire state line, including parts of Canada. Over 30 million people lost power in this blackout. Not so fondly remembered by residents was a second New York blackout in 1977, which was marred by fighting and looting.

New York Times v. Sullivan (1964)

In 1964, four African-American clergymen placed an advertisement in the *New York Times* seeking to raise money for civil rights legal efforts. The ad copy criticized public officials in Alabama, and it contained several factual errors. L. B. Sullivan, a city commissioner in Montgomery, Alabama, sued the *New York Times* for libel. In an attempt to discredit the *Times,* Alabama officials sued the paper and clergymen for libel. A state court in Alabama found both parties guilty, and levied a $500,000 fine. In a unanimous decision in 1964, the Supreme Court reversed the libel verdict. The Court ruled that holding the paper guilty inhibited public discussion; errors, the Court contended, were inevitable in democratic discourse. Since the *Times v. Sullivan* ruling, public figures and officials seeking damages from libel are required to prove that inaccurate statements are the result of "actual malice." The decision broadened the concept of free speech by protecting people from being held liable for inaccurate statements made about public officials.

Nuclear Nonproliferation Treaty (1968–1970)

When China tested nuclear weapons in the late 1960s, the Johnson administration searched for a way to stem the rising tide of nuclear proliferation. The Soviets, also threatened by nuclear parity, shared the desire for a nonproliferation treaty (NPT). Despite this common goal, negotiations dragged on. Many non-nuclear nations complained that a nonproliferation agreement would result simply in a U.S.-Soviet monopoly of these weapons. To placate opponents, Article VI of the treaty required adherents to actively pursue nuclear disarmament. The United Nations approved the NPT in June 1968; the United States ratified the treaty in March 1970. Eventually more than 100 countries adhered to the treaty. Each party vowed not to provide nuclear weapons to other countries and not to develop nuclear weapons if it had not done so already. The treaty did little to encourage disarmament, however. Nuclear powers, including France, Israel, South Africa, China, Pakistan, and India, have refused to sign the treaty. Furthermore, no serious attempt has ever been made by any party to comply with Article VI. Finally, the treaty proved a token measure and a weak deterrent that was easily overcome, as evidenced by North Korea's successful test of a nuclear weapon in 2006.

Omnibus Crime Control and Safe Streets Act (1968)

As the crime rate rose nationwide during the late 1960s, President Lyndon Johnson sought an increase in federal law enforcement funding. Johnson observed that poor people were the most frequent victims of crime, and he hoped that safer neighborhoods would help alleviate poverty. Congress, however, associated the rise in crime with the many Supreme Court decisions strengthening the rights of accused criminals. Thus the Omnibus Crime Control and Safe Streets Act of 1968, although it approved $100 million for law enforcement upgrades, substantially weakened several Supreme Court decisions, including *Miranda v. Arizona.* The law allowed local, state, and federal law enforcement agencies to wiretap and bug suspects, and—thanks to mobilization by the firearms lobby—removed restrictions on gun ownership.

Operation Rolling Thunder (1965–1968)

On February 6, 1965, enemy forces attacked a U.S. base at Pleiku in South Vietnam, killing eight American soldiers and wounding dozens more. After conferring with his advisers, President Lyndon Johnson agreed to retaliate with bombing raids. The retaliation had, by March, become a sustained bombing campaign known as Operation Rolling Thunder. In June alone, U.S. and South Vietnamese pilots flew nearly 5,000 sorties. Johnson hoped that bombing would destroy roads and industry in North Vietnam, reducing the enemy's ability to wage war while simultaneously keeping American casualties low. He also used the bombing campaign as a means by which to convey to North Vietnam that the United States would not hesitate to escalate the war if the North refused a settlement. Still, the United States had to limit the bombing campaign to an extent so as not to bring China or the Soviet Union into the war. Despite nearly three years of almost uninterrupted bombing, Operation Rolling Thunder had little effect on the North's military effort as roads were quickly repaired and supply lines easily diverted. Although Rolling Thunder

U.S. Air Force F-105 Thunderchief pilots drop bombs over Vietnam during Operation Rolling Thunder. *(National Museum of the U.S. Airforce)*

ceased in 1968, Johnson's successor, Richard Nixon, launched his own bombing campaign; by war's end, the United States had deployed three times the amount of bombs used by all sides in World War II.

Poor People's March on Washington (Poor People's Campaign) (1968)

After the ASSASSINATION OF MARTIN LUTHER KING, JR., in April 1968, his followers vowed to proceed with his plan for a Poor People's Campaign in Washington, D.C. Late in his life, King had begun to criticize the pernicious effects of the American capitalist system on African Americans. The Poor People's Campaign, its organizers hoped, would inspire Congress to attack the economic roots of poverty and invest federal dollars in the education, housing, and employment of poor people. Launched in May, the campaign consisted of a march, large-scale pickets of government agencies, and the construction of Resurrection City, a multiethnic shantytown in sight of the U.S. Capitol. Far from eradicating poverty, however, the campaign proved unsuccessful. Instead, activists clashed with each other, often violently. Public opinion, associating civil rights activism with the urban riots of the previous three years, turned against antipoverty initiatives. By June, the few remaining residents of Resurrection City were dispersed by the police.

Pueblo Incident (1968)

On January 23, 1968, North Korean military forces captured the USS *Pueblo,* an American spy ship stationed in the Sea of Japan. Although the ship was carrying no weapons, resistance by the ship's crew resulted in one U.S. fatality; the remaining crew members were taken hostage. In Washington, D.C., Johnson administration officials viewed the capture as part of the TET OFFENSIVE then underway in Vietnam. Although Americans clamored for President Johnson to take action against North Korea, Johnson exercised restraint. Unwilling to plunge into another military confrontation, Johnson engaged in discreet diplomacy in working with the Soviet Union and through United Nations. Eleven months later, in December 1968, North Korea released the hostages.

Reynolds v. Sims (1964)

Under the principle of "one person, one vote," legal activists challenged the nonproportional representation of state legislatures during the 1960s. M. O. Sims, along with David J. Vann and John McConnell, all young attorneys in Jefferson County, Alabama, brought suit in the federal district court for the middle district of Alabama against Judge Bernard A. Reynolds. Electoral districts organized by geography rather than population, they argued, allowed sparsely populated—usually conservative—areas to wield greater influence than densely populated ones. This practice in essence penalized people for where they lived. Citing the equal protection clause of the Fourteenth Amendment, the Supreme Court ruled in *Reynolds v. Sims* (1964)

that both houses of a state legislature must have equal representation for equal numbers of people, thereby affirming the principle of one person, one vote. Thus, representation in each district must be as mathematically equal as possible, and must be updated after every census. Although the *Reynolds* case challenged the representation system in Alabama's state legislature, the 6-3 decision forced states across the country to reorganize their electoral districts. It built on the earlier case of *Baker v. Carr* (1962) that established the principle of "one man, one vote."

Selma Protests (1965)

In 1965, the civil rights revolution spread to Selma, Alabama. Although African Americans made up almost 60 percent of the town's population, less than 1 percent of African Americans of voting age were registered. Activists, including Martin Luther King, Jr., began a voting rights campaign there in January 1965; 3,000 demonstrators were arrested. The campaign then planned a march from Selma to Montgomery, the state capital. On March 7, later known as Bloody Sunday, 600 marchers approached Selma's Edmund Pettis Bridge, where state troopers, armed with whips, clubs, and tear gas, attacked the marchers without warning.

Two days later, 1,500 marchers attempted to defy a federal injunction and cross the Pettis Bridge. But King compromised with federal authorities and turned the march around upon reaching the bridge, angering many demonstrators, who vowed to march again. After substantial delay, President Johnson announced his voting rights bill on March 15. In his televised address, Johnson described the Selma protests as "a turning point in man's unending search for freedom" comparable to Lexington and Concord and Appomattox. Johnson also persuaded Alabama governor George Wallace to allow the march. The march began on March 21, arriving in Montgomery at over 25,000 strong; Johnson signed the VOTING RIGHTS ACT of 1965 in August. Despite this victory, many younger African-American activists began to distance themselves from King's conciliatory approach to civil rights.

Sheppard v. Maxwell (1966)

Under Chief Justice Earl Warren, the Supreme Court demonstrated an increased effort to treat fairly those individuals accused of crimes. In 1954, an Ohio court convicted Dr. Samuel H. Sheppard of murdering his pregnant wife. Before the trial began, however, local newspapers and public opinion predicted Sheppard's guilt. In addition, television and print reporters had unprecedented access to the trial. Over the course of the trial jurors were photographed and witnesses were interviewed. Allowed inside the courtroom, reporters crowded the defendant, inhibiting lawyer-client conversations. Sheppard challenged his conviction based on the argument that media bias had inappropriately affected the verdict. In July 1964, a federal judge released Sheppard from prison on the grounds

On what became known as "Bloody Sunday," police attacked civil rights marchers with tear gas, clubs, and whips in Selma, Alabama, on March 7, 1965. *(Associated Press)*

that the intrusive publicity had prevented a fair trial. Warden E. L. Maxwell of the Ohio State penitentiary challenged this district court order that Sheppard be freed while awaiting a new trial. In *Sheppard v. Maxwell* (1966), the Supreme Court upheld this decision, setting a precedent that the unrestrained presence of media at a trial can interfere with due process—even if no proof exists that the media's presence has affected the jury.

Siege of Khe Sanh (1967–1968)   In late 1967, North Vietnamese and Vietcong forces began an assault on the U.S. Marines base at Khe Sanh, located in South Vietnam near the Laotian border. As the assault continued into early 1968, President Johnson began to fear that the siege of Khe Sanh would end in a repeat of the French defeat at Dien Bien Phu more than a decade earlier. Anxious to protect the garrison and suspicious that the assault marked the start of a major offensive, U.S. generals moved troops north into Khe Sanh. The assault on Khe Sanh was primarily a diversion, however; in late January 1968, North Vietnamese and Vietcong forces launched the Tet offensive

in attacking the vulnerable cities of the South. Nevertheless, the U.S. military eventually succeeded in repulsing the siege of Khe Sanh.

Six-Day War (1967)   In April 1967, Palestinians infiltrated Israel from Syria, Jordan, and Lebanon and carried out terrorist attacks. After Syria fired artillery shells into northern Israel, Israel retaliated by bombing terrorist bases in the Golan Heights and shooting down Syrian planes. On May 22, Egyptian military forces closed the Strait of Tiran, cutting off the Israeli port of Eilat. Meanwhile, in Washington, D.C., Lyndon Johnson, afraid of invoking the ire of the Soviets who had interests in the Middle East, avoided making a response. Jordan and Egypt then signed a mutual defense pact suggesting preparations for war against Israel. On June 5, Israel launched a preemptive war against Egypt, Jordan, and Syria; just six days later Israeli forces emerged triumphant. President Johnson's policy of neutrality during the conflict earned little but criticism from Jews at home and Arabs abroad. A June 10 cease-fire ended the conflict, but Israel's occupation of the Sinai Peninsula, the West Bank,

Israeli paratroopers at the Western Wall during the Six-Day War, June 1967 *(Courtesy Embassy of Israel, Washington, D.C.)*

East Jerusalem, and the Golan Heights set the stage for future decades of instability and violence in the Middle East.

Space Program   As senator and as vice president, Lyndon Johnson had been a driving force behind the American space program. As president, Johnson vowed to fulfill JOHN F. KEN-NEDY's pledge to put a man on the moon before the end of the decade in 1970. For Johnson, this meant increasing NASA's budget from $150 million to over $5 billion and pressing ahead with the Apollo program. Johnson believed that the space program would spur the economy of the nation—especially his native Texas—as well as bolster national pride. By 1967, however, Americans rated space exploration as a low priority even though NASA's budget surpassed spending on education and poverty. Congress began to cut NASA's budget in 1968. The Apollo missions nevertheless proceeded apace, achieving manned orbit of the earth and moon. In 1969, during the Nixon presidency, Apollo successfully put a man on the moon.

Supreme Court Appointments   Lyndon Johnson's two Supreme Court appointments aptly reflect the best and the worst of Johnson's political ideology, namely, groundbreaking social justice on the one hand and unabashed cronyism on the other. When Justice Arthur Goldberg resigned in 1965, Johnson nominated his loyal friend Abe Fortas. Fortas had known Johnson for nearly 30 years; his influence had secured Johnson's disputed 1948 Senate victory. Ever since, Fortas had been one of Johnson's closest advisers. Judicial ethics frown upon close connections between the judicial and executive branches, but during his confirmation hearing, Fortas lied about his ties to the president and was easily approved. On the bench, Fortas performed as expected, supporting GREAT SOCIETY legislation and informing Johnson as to the Court's mood.

As Johnson's term drew to a close, Chief Justice Earl Warren announced his resignation. Fearing for the future safety of civil rights and Great Society legislation, Johnson again rewarded Fortas's loyalty with the chief justice nomination. Johnson then nominated another friend, Homer Thornberry, to fill the vacant seat. This time, the Senate resisted Johnson's scheming. During his confirmation hearings, Fortas continued to lie about his connections to the Oval Office, this time unconvincingly. In addition, Fortas's opponents discovered that he had accepted a university teaching salary paid by wealthy friends and former clients, possibly inviting a conflict of interest. Fortas's nomination for chief justice was defeated, and he resigned from the Court in 1969.

Johnson's second appointment occurred in 1967, when Justice Tom Clark resigned. Hoping to reflect the racial progress of the 1960s, Johnson decided to nominate African-American lawyer Thurgood Marshall to the Court. Johnson also knew that Marshall would protect civil rights and Great Society legislation. All observers agreed that Marshall was a perfect choice. A former NAACP lawyer who had successfully argued the landmark *Brown v. Board of Education* (1954) decision, Marshall had served as a federal judge and solicitor general.

During his confirmation hearings, southern senators challenged Marshall not because of his race, but because of his liberal views, including criminal rights. But nothing could stop the appointment, and Marshall became the first African-American Supreme Court justice. Although he largely served as a liberal dissenter on an increasingly conservative court, Marshall is recognized as a proud champion of the disadvantaged. He resigned from the bench in 1993.

***Terry v. Ohio* (1968)**   While several of the Warren Court's decisions expanded the rights of suspected criminals, *Terry v. Ohio* (1968) broadened the search powers of police officers. The case began when Cleveland police officer Martin McFadden stopped three men he suspected of planning a robbery. After unsatisfactory questioning, a suspicious McFadden frisked them and found a gun in the pockets of one of the men, named John Terry. An Ohio court found Terry guilty of carrying a concealed weapon. The Supreme Court upheld the guilty verdict, arguing that McFadden's search of Terry did not violate the Fourth Amendment because police officers have the right to protect themselves from harm. Warren's opinion in the *Terry* ruling established that if a police officer suspects criminal behavior and thinks the suspect might be armed, he or she can search the outer clothing for weapons after identifying him or herself.

Tet Offensive (1968)   The Tet offensive, launched on January 30, 1968, marked a major turning point in the Vietnam War. Instead of the usual informal cease-fire during Tet, the Vietnamese New Year, North Vietnamese and Vietcong forces unleashed a massive surprise attack against hundreds of cities, towns, and villages in South Vietnam. One assault in Saigon, the capital, nearly succeeded in occupying the U.S. embassy. After two weeks of intense fighting, the U.S. and South Vietnamese military turned back the offensive, inflicting a major defeat on the North. The fighting killed approximately 40,000 North Vietnamese and Vietcong troops, compared to roughly 2,000 South Vietnamese and 1,000 Americans.

The Tet victory proved costly at home, however. Throughout 1967, President Lyndon Johnson had promised that an end to the war was in sight. The widespread carnage of the Tet offensive, however, convinced many Americans that the war was anything but under control. Despite the North's losses, U.S. generals announced that overall victory would require thousands more troops, boosting the ANTIWAR MOVEMENT. Significantly, the mainstream media became far more skeptical of the war. Respected newscaster Walter Cronkite disapprovingly predicted a stalemate; Johnson privately responded, "If I've lost Cronkite, I've lost Middle America." Following the Tet offensive, Johnson's approval ratings plummeted to 36 percent, and the president announced he would not seek reelection.

Trial of Lenny Bruce (1964)   New York comedian Lenny Bruce became famous during the late 1950s and early 1960s for his ribald humor and cutting social criticism. Bruce's routines mixed incisive commentary on sex, politics, race, and religion with graphic imagery and profanity. Notorious by the mid-1960s, Bruce began a string of performances in New York City in March 1964. One night, an undercover policeman sat in the crowd, and heard, among other things, Bruce describe males as so hypersexual that they would willingly perform sexual intercourse with a chicken. Police arrested Bruce for obscenity, and in the ensuing trial Bruce was convicted of "word crimes" and sentenced to four months in prison. The owner of the club where Bruce performed had also been convicted and, though his conviction

had been overturned, Bruce's never was; Bruce died of a drug overdose in 1966. New York governor George Pataki pardoned Bruce posthumously in December 2003. Most observers agree that Bruce's conviction constituted a gross violation of free speech.

***United States v. Price et al.* (1966)**   *See* MISSISSIPPI BURNING TRIAL (*UNITED STATES V. PRICE ET AL.*) (1966)

***Unsafe At Any Speed,* by Ralph Nader (1965)**   By the early 1960s, the automobile industry stood as a driving force behind American economic and labor power. In the mid-1960s, however, the industry came under criticism as the death toll from highway accidents began to rise. In 1965, lawyer Ralph Nader published *Unsafe At Any Speed,* a well-researched exposé of the automobile industry. In the book, Nader argued that defects and design flaws in American automobiles (the Chevrolet Corvair in particular) caused more injuries than the accidents themselves. Because the injuries could be prevented, Nader's argument gave rise to a significant amount of outrage. The publicity surrounding Nader's book resulted in an increase in federally regu-

Ralph Nader, author of *Unsafe At Any Speed,* published in 1965 *(Library of Congress)*

lated safety improvements, including lights, seat belts, and head rests. Nader's successful challenge to the auto industry sparked a consumer rights movement that has endured.

Urban Mass Transportation Act (1964) By the early 1960s, the automobile had come to dominate America's transportation systems. Mass transit was given a status of only minor importance in the urban United States. During the 1960s, however, the Johnson administration attempted to redress the imbalance in funding spent on urban mass transit, which received vastly inferior funding as compared to highways. The Urban Mass Transportation Act of 1964 aimed at reducing highway congestion while simultaneously boosting transit networks used primarily by the urban poor who could not afford cars. The act authorized $375 million in federal funds for transit projects deemed "essential to . . . [an] urban area." Federal funds would pay up to two-thirds of transit projects, and the act cemented the federal government's role in promoting urban transit.

Voting Rights Act (1965) During the 1960s, southern states still used literacy tests, poll taxes, and the naked threat of violence to prevent African Americans from registering to vote. In Mississippi, for example, only 6 percent of voting-age blacks had registered. In February 1965, a voting rights march in Selma, Alabama, ended abruptly when law enforcement officers attacked the marchers. After the SELMA PROTESTS, President Lyndon Johnson immediately introduced a voting rights bill to Congress. Explaining the bill on television, Johnson endorsed the marchers' cause: "It is the effort of American Negroes to secure for themselves the full blessings of American life. Their cause must be our cause too. Because it is not just Negroes, but really it is all of us, who must overcome the crippling legacy of bigotry and injustice." Quoting the anthem of the Civil Rights movement, Johnson added, "And we shall overcome."

Johnson signed the Voting Rights Act on August 6, 1965. One of the landmark civil rights laws of the era, the law targeted areas of the South where less than 50 percent of eligible voters were not registered. The act empowered the Justice Department to void any restrictions (such as literacy tests) that kept minorities off voter rolls, as well as send federal workers to register voters if obstruction continued. By 1967, over 50 percent of voting-age blacks could vote in most of the South. In 1968, even Mississippi had registered 59 percent of its African-American voters. Across the South, African-American voter registration rose to 62 percent.

War on Poverty Lyndon Johnson saw the eradication of poverty as a critical part of his GREAT SOCIETY. In his 1964 State of the Union address, he declared: "This administration, today, here and now, declares unconditional war on poverty in America." Congress quickly passed the ECO-NOMIC OPPORTUNITY ACT (EOA) of 1964, the legislative face of the War on Poverty. The EOA was essentially a grab bag of antipoverty programs, including education assistance for preschool and college students, youth job training, and a domestic version of the Peace Corps. The law created the Office of Economic Opportunity (OEO) to direct federal policy, and it established community action programs on local levels. Later antipoverty efforts included urban redevelopment, health care, and food stamps.

The whirlwind of legislation created a viable safety net for many poor people, but fell short of defeating poverty. Johnson's vision focused on creating opportunity rather than redistributing wealth. Old age, disabilities, racial discrimination, unemployment, and broken families all contributed to poverty in ways that thwarted Johnson's moderate approach. The OEO's initial budget of $1 billion paled in comparison with the multibillion dollar budgets of earlier New Deal programs. Johnson's desire to limit federal expenditures, mixed with the financial drain of the Vietnam War, drained away the War on Poverty's already meager funding, though some programs continued after Johnson's presidency. More than anything else, the declaration of war against an abstract concept created unrealistic expectations of permanent victory.

Warren Commission (1963–1964) Two days after the murder of President JOHN F. KENNEDY on November 22, 1963, Dallas nightclub owner Jack Ruby shot and killed Lee Harvey Oswald, Kennedy's alleged assassin. Oswald's murder fueled rumors about the president's assassination, including allegations of additional gunmen and conspiracies pointing to fringe right-wing groups, Cuba, the Soviet Union, and the Mafia. Other speculation hinted at the involvement of the CIA, the FBI, and Kennedy's successor, Lyndon Johnson.

Hoping to silence the swirling rumors, President Johnson appointed Supreme Court chief justice Earl Warren to head a commission to investigate Kennedy's assassination. The Warren Commission also included Senators Richard Russell (D-GA) and John Sherman Cooper (R-KY), Representatives (and future U.S. president) GERALD FORD (R-MI) and Hale Boggs (D-LA), former CIA director Allen Dulles, and longtime government official John J. McCloy.

The commission's report was released in September 1964, concluding that Oswald acted alone. Oswald, the commission found, had been a troubled loner. After a stint in the marines, he drifted and embraced Marxism as well as communist Cuba and its leader, Fidel Castro. Emotionally unstable and suicidal in nature, Oswald decided to assassinate the president. The report satisfied most of the public as well as most scholars.

Over time, however, limitations in the report surfaced. The commission sealed some evidence for 75 years, encouraging rather than quieting conspiracy theorists. Additionally, the CIA failed to disclose to the committee its attempts to kill

The Warren Commission presents its report on the assassination of President Kennedy to President Johnson in the Cabinet Room of the White House on September 24, 1964. From left to right are John McCloy, J. Lee Rankin, Senator Richard Russell, Representative Gerald Ford, Chief Justice Earl Warren, President Johnson, Allen Dulles, Senator John Sherman Cooper, and Representative Hale Boggs. *(Photo by Cecil Stroughton/Lyndon B. Johnson Library)*

Castro, information that may have given credence to speculation about Cuban involvement. The FBI, embarrassed that it had failed to monitor a dangerous man, refused to divulge Oswald's ties to the Soviet Union. Most significantly, the commission members, as well as Johnson himself, decided at the start to prove that Oswald acted alone. Although Johnson himself suspected Cuban involvement, any link to Soviet or Cuban involvement, Johnson knew, would bring about a geopolitical confrontation.

Water Quality Control Act (1965)   Although not the centerpiece, environmental protection, including such legislation as the 1965 Water Quality Control Act, was one of the more groundbreaking aspects of Lyndon Johnson's GREAT SOCIETY program. The act empowered the federal government to enforce clean water standards. These new regulations aimed at preventing pollution at its source, rather than cleaning it downstream, and thus provided federal grants

to improve sewage treatment plants. States continued to set water standards, but the new law required states to secure the approval of the Department of Health, Education, and Welfare. The 1966 Clean Water Restoration Act approved an additional $3.9 billion in funding; these acts did not noticeably improve water quality, but they did constitute the first steps toward stronger environmental regulation, which would be made in the 1970s.

Watts Riot (1965)   In early August 1965, less than one week after passage of the 1965 VOTING RIGHTS ACT, riots erupted in Watts, an African-American neighborhood in Los Angeles. Violence began when residents used force in an attempt to prevent the arrest of an African-American man. For the next five days, Watts escalated into a maelstrom of armed clashes, sniper attacks, and burning cars, while widespread looting targeted white-owned businesses. Eventually, nearly 14,000 National Guard troops entered Watts to quell the rebellion, but not before the riots caused $35 million in damage. The human costs were 34 dead, 1,000 injured, and 4,000 arrested.

The underlying causes of the Watts riot included unemployment, oppression, and powerlessness. Furthermore, by the mid-1960s, many African Americans had grown frustrated with the slow pace of racial progress as well as the conciliatory approach of the mainstream Civil Rights movement. The Watts riots foreshadowed future uprisings in the late 1960s across the United States. The Johnson administration fearfully predicted—correctly—that the Watts riots would inspire a white backlash, turning mainstream America against federal programs to promote civil rights and reduce poverty.

Wilderness Act (1964)   The Wilderness Act of 1964 set aside 9 million acres of wilderness under federal government protection, closing them to development and exploitation. Eventually, the number of acres protected expanded to 100 million. The law's origins lay in the conservation movement, which had for decades promoted the preservation of natural areas. The bill faced heavy opposition from western industries, including timber, dam, and mining interests. But intense lobbying and educational efforts by conservationists, as well as alliances with other interest groups, ultimately convinced Congress that preserving wilderness as a refuge for Americans would enrich the scientific, educational, and recreational resources of the nation. The act's effectiveness hinged on the definition of wilderness, defined in the act as "an area where the earth and its community of life are untrammeled by man, where man himself is a visitor who does not remain." The act reflected the mainstream approach of the conservation movement, rather than foreshadowing the environmental radicalism of later decades.

Paul Rubinson

Further Reading

Andrew, John A., III. *Lyndon Johnson and the Great Society*. Chicago: Ivan R. Dee, 1998.

Belknap, Michael R. *The Supreme Court under Earl Warren, 1953–1969*. Columbia: University of South Carolina Press, 2005.

Beschloss, Michael, ed. *Reaching for Glory: Lyndon Johnson's Secret White House Tapes, 1964–1965*. New York: Simon and Schuster, 2001.

———. *Taking Charge: The Johnson White House Tapes, 1963–1964*. New York: Simon and Schuster, 1997.

Branch, Taylor. *At Canaan's Edge: America in the King Years, 1965–68*. New York: Simon and Schuster, 2006.

———. *Parting the Waters: America in the King Years, 1954–63*. New York: Simon and Schuster, 1988.

———. *Pillar of Fire: America in the King Years, 1963–65*. New York: Simon and Schuster, 1998.

Caro, Robert A. *The Years of Lyndon Johnson: Master of the Senate*. New York: Vintage, 2002.

———. *The Years of Lyndon Johnson: Means of Ascent*. New York: Vintage, 1990.

———. *The Years of Lyndon Johnson: The Passage of Power*. New York: Knopf, 2012.

———. *The Years of Lyndon Johnson: The Path to Power*. New York: Vintage, 1983.

Conklin, Paul K. *Big Daddy from the Pedernales: Lyndon Baines Johnson*. Boston: Twayne, 1986.

Dallek, Robert. *Flawed Giant: Lyndon Johnson and His Times, 1961–1973*. New York: Oxford University Press, 1998.

———. *Lone Star Rising: Lyndon Johnson and His Times, 1908–1960*. New York: Oxford University Press, 1991.

Divine, Robert A., ed. *Exploring the Johnson Years*. Austin: University of Texas Press, 1981.

———. *The Johnson Years*. Vol. Two: *Vietnam, the Environment, and Science*. Lawrence: University Press of Kansas, 1987.

———. *The Johnson Years*. Vol. Three: *LBJ at Home and Abroad*. Lawrence: University Press of Kansas, 1994.

Gardner, Lloyd C. *Pay Any Price: Lyndon Johnson and the Wars for Vietnam*. Chicago: Ivan R. Dee, 1995.

Gould, Lewis L. *Lady Bird Johnson and the Environment*. Lawrence: University Press of Kansas, 1988.

———. *Lady Bird Johnson: Our Environmental First Lady*. Lawrence: University Press of Kansas, 1999.

Herring, George C. *America's Longest War: The United States and Vietnam, 1950–1975*. 3d ed. New York: McGraw Hill, 1996.

———. *LBJ and Vietnam: A Different Kind of War*. Austin: University of Texas Press, 1994.

Holland, Max, Robert David Johnson, David Shreve, and Kent B. Germany, eds. *Lyndon B. Johnson*. 6 vols. New York: W.W. Norton, 2005–2007.

Isserman, Maurice, and Michael Kazin. *America Divided: The Civil War of the 1960s*. New York: Oxford University Press, 2000.

Johnson, Lady Bird. *A White House Diary*. New York: Holt, Rinehart and Winston, 1970.

Johnson, Lyndon B. *The Choices We Face*. New York: Bantam Books, 1969.

———. *The Johnson Presidential Press Conferences*. 2 vols. New York: E. M. Coleman Enterprises, 1978.

———. *The Kennedy Assassination Tapes*. New York: Alfred A. Knopf, 2004.

———. *Lyndon B. Johnson's Vietnam Papers: A Documentary Collection*. Edited by David M. Barrett. College Station: Texas A&M University Press, 1997.

———. *My Hope for America*. New York: Random House, 1964.

———. *This America*. New York: Random House, 1966.

———. *A Time for Action: A Selection from the Speeches and Writings of Lyndon B. Johnson, 1953–64*. New York: Pocket Books, 1964.

———. *To Heal and To Build; The Programs of Lyndon B. Johnson*. Edited by James MacGregor Burns. New York: McGraw-Hill, 1968.

———. *The Vantage Point; Perspectives of the Presidency, 1963–1969.* New York: Holt, Rinehart and Winston, 1971.

Johnson, Rebekah Baines. *Letters from the Hill Country: The Correspondence between Rebekah and Lyndon Baines Johnson.* Edited by Philip R. Rulon. Austin: Thorp Springs Press, 1982.

Johnson, Robert David. *All the Way with LBJ: The 1964 Presidential Election.* New York: Cambridge University Press, 2009.

Lerner, Mitchell B., ed. *Looking Back at LBJ: White House Politics in a New Light.* Lawrence: University Press of Kansas, 2005.

Middendorf, John William. *A Glorious Disaster: Barry Goldwater's Presidential Campaign and the Origins of the Conservative Movement.* New York: Basic Books, 2006.

Patterson, James T. *Grand Expectations: The United States, 1945–1974.* New York: Oxford University Press, 1996.

Perlstein, Rick. *Before the Storm: Barry Goldwater and the Unmaking of the American Consensus.* New York: Hill and Wang, 2001.

Perret, Geoffrey. *Commander in Chief: How Truman, Johnson, and Bush Turned a Presidential Power into a Threat to America's Future.* New York: Farrar, Straus and Giroux, 2007.

Public Papers of the Presidents of the United States, Lyndon B. Johnson, Containing the Public Messages, Speeches, and Statements of the President, 1963–1969, 10 vols. Washington, D.C.: U.S. Government Printing Office, 1965–1970.

Schulman, Bruce J. *Lyndon B. Johnson and American Liberalism: A Brief Biography with Documents.* 2d ed. Boston: Bedford/St. Martin's, 2007.

Schwartz, Thomas Alan. *Lyndon Johnson and Europe: In the Shadow of Vietnam.* Cambridge, Mass.: Harvard University Press, 2003.

Woods, Randall B. *LBJ: Architect of American Ambition.* New York: Free Press, 2006.

DOCUMENTS

—⁓—

Document One: President Lyndon B. Johnson, Remarks upon Arrival at Andrews Air Force Base, November 22, 1963

Speaking at 6:10 P.M. on November 22, 1963, President Johnson made this short statement upon arrival at Andrews Air Force Base following the assassination of President John F. Kennedy earlier in the day.

THIS is a sad time for all people. We have suffered a loss that cannot be weighed. For me, it is a deep personal tragedy. I know that the world shares the sorrow that Mrs. Kennedy and her family bear. I will do my best. That is all I can do. I ask for your help—and God's.

⸎

Source: *Public Papers of the Presidents of the United States, Lyndon B. Johnson, Containing the Public Messages, Speeches, and Statements of the President,* 1963–1964. Book I—November 22, 1963, to June 30, 1964 (Washington, D.C.: U.S. Government Printing Office, 1965), 1.

Document Two: President Johnson, "Let Us Continue" Address Before a Joint Session of Congress, November 27, 1963

President Johnson addressed a joint session of Congress five days after the Kennedy assassination, delivering a speech entitled "Let Us Continue." By helping turn Kennedy into a martyr, Johnson amassed a broad coalition to pass a host of legislation, including civil rights.

. . . All I have I would have given gladly not to be standing here today.

The greatest leader of our time has been struck down by the foulest deed of our time. Today John Fitzgerald Kennedy lives on in the immortal words and works that he left behind. He lives on in the mind and memories of mankind. He lives on in the hearts of his countrymen. . . .

The dream of conquering the vastness of space—the dream of partnership across the Atlantic—and across the Pacific as well—the dream of a Peace Corps in less developed nations—the dream of education for all of our children—the dream of jobs for all who seek them and need them—the dream of care for our elderly—the dream of an all-out attack on mental illness—and above all, the dream of equal rights for all Americans, whatever their race or color—these and other American dreams have been vitalized by his drive and by his dedication.

And now the ideas and the ideals which he so nobly represented must and will be translated into effective action. . . .

In this age when there can be no losers in peace and no victors in war, we must recognize the obligation to match national strength with national restraint. We must be prepared at one and the same time for both the confrontation of power and the limitation of power. We must be ready to defend the national interest and to negotiate the common interest. This is the path that we shall continue to pursue. Those who test our courage will find it strong, and those who seek our friendship will find it honorable. We will demonstrate anew that the strong can be just in the use of strength; and the just can be strong in the defense of justice.

And let all know we will extend no special privilege and impose no persecution. We will carry on the fight against poverty and misery, and disease and ignorance, in other lands and in our own.

We will serve all the Nation, not one section or one sector, or one group, but all Americans. These are the United States—a united people with a united purpose.

Our American unity does not depend upon unanimity. We have differences; but now, as in the past, we can derive from those differences strength, not weakness, wisdom, not despair. Both as a people and a government, we can unite upon a program, a program which is wise and just, enlightened and constructive. . . .

An assassin's bullet has thrust upon me the awesome burden of the Presidency. I am here today to say I need your help; I cannot bear this burden alone. I need the help of all Americans, and all America. This Nation has experienced a profound shock, and in this critical moment, it is our duty, yours and mine, as the Government of the United States, to do away with uncertainty and doubt and delay, and to show that we are capable of decisive action; that from the brutal loss of our leader we will derive not weakness, but strength; that we can and will act and act now. . . .

On the 20th day of January, in 1961, John F. Kennedy told his countrymen that our national work would not be finished "in the first thousand days, nor in the life of this administration, nor even perhaps in our lifetime on this planet. But," he said, "let us begin."

Today, in this moment of new resolve, I would say to all my fellow Americans, let us continue.

This is our challenge—not to hesitate, not to pause, not to turn about and linger over this evil moment, but to continue on our course so that we may fulfill the destiny that history has set for us. Our most immediate tasks are here on this Hill.

First, no memorial oration or eulogy could more eloquently honor President Kennedy's memory than the earliest possible passage of the civil rights bill for which he fought so long. We have talked long enough in this country about equal rights. We have talked for one hundred years or more. It is time now to write the next chapter, and to write it in the books of law. . . .

And second, no act of ours could more fittingly continue the work of President Kennedy than the early passage of the tax bill for which he fought all this long year. This is a bill designed to increase our national income and Federal revenues, and to provide insurance against recession. That bill, if passed without delay, means more security for those now working, more jobs for those now without them, and more incentive for our economy.

In short, this is no time for delay. It is a time for action—strong, forward-looking action on the pending education bills to help bring the light of learning to every home and hamlet in America—strong, forward-looking action on youth employment opportunities; strong, forward-looking action on the pending foreign aid bill, making clear that we are not forfeiting our responsibilities to this hemisphere or to the world, nor erasing Executive flexibility in the conduct of our foreign affairs—and strong, prompt, and forward-looking action on the remaining appropriation bills. . . .

We meet in grief, but let us also meet in renewed dedication and renewed vigor. Let us meet in action, in tolerance, and in mutual understanding. John Kennedy's death commands what his life conveyed—that America must move forward. The time has come for Americans of all races and creeds and political beliefs to understand and to respect one another. So let us put an end to the teaching and the preaching of hate and evil and violence. Let us turn away from the fanatics of the far left and the far right, from the apostles of bitterness and bigotry, from those defiant of law, and those who pour venom into our Nation's bloodstream.

I profoundly hope that the tragedy and the torment of these terrible days will bind us together in new fellowship, making us one people in our hour of sorrow. So let us here highly resolve that John Fitzgerald Kennedy did not live—or die—in vain. And on this Thanksgiving eve, as we gather together to ask the Lord's blessing, and give Him our thanks, let us unite in those familiar and cherished words:

America, America,
God shed His grace on thee,
And crown thy good
With brotherhood
From sea to shining sea.

Source: Public Papers of the Presidents of the United States, Lyndon B. Johnson, Containing the Public Messages, Speeches, and Statements of the President, 1963-1964. Book I—November 22, 1963 to June 30, 1964 (Washington, D.C.: U.S. States Government Printing Office, 1965), 8-10.

Document Three: President Johnson, Address Following Renewed Aggression in the Gulf of Tonkin, August 4, 1964

Following reports of attacks on U.S. ships in the Gulf of Tonkin, President Johnson delivered the following address on August 4, 1964, asking Congress to pass the Gulf of Tonkin Resolution, authorizing a military response against the North Vietnamese. This resolution later became the legal justification for escalating the Vietnam War.

My fellow Americans:

As President and Commander in Chief, it is my duty to the American people to report that renewed hostile actions against United States ships on the high seas in the Gulf of Tonkin have today required me to order the military forces of the United States to take action in reply.

The initial attack on the destroyer Maddox, on August 2, was repeated today by a number of hostile vessels attacking two U.S. destroyers with torpedoes. The destroyers and supporting aircraft acted at once on the orders I gave after the initial act of aggression. We believe at least two of the attacking boats were sunk. There were no U.S. losses.

The performance of commanders and crews in this engagement is in the highest tradition of the United States Navy. But repeated acts of violence against the Armed Forces of the United States must be met not only with alert defense, but with positive reply. That reply is being given as I speak to you tonight. Air action is now in execution against gunboats and certain supporting facilities in North Viet-Nam which have been used in these hostile operations.

In the larger sense this new act of aggression, aimed directly at our own forces, again brings home to all of us in the United States the importance of the struggle for peace and security in southeast Asia. Aggression by terror against the peaceful villagers of South Viet-Nam has now been joined by open aggression on the high seas against the United States of America.

The determination of all Americans to carry out our full commitment to the people and to the government of South Viet-Nam will be redoubled by this outrage. Yet our response, for the present, will be limited and fitting. We Americans know, although others appear to forget, the risks of spreading conflict. We still seek no wider war.

I have instructed the Secretary of State to make this position totally clear to friends and to adversaries and, indeed, to all. I have instructed Ambassador Stevenson to raise this matter immediately and urgently before the Security Council of the United Nations. Finally, I have today met with the leaders of both parties in the Congress of the United States and I have informed them that I shall immediately request the Congress to pass a resolution making it clear that our Government is united in its determination to take all necessary measures in support of freedom and in defense of peace in southeast Asia.

I have been given encouraging assurance by these leaders of both parties that such a resolution will be promptly introduced, freely and expeditiously debated, and passed with overwhelming support. And just a few minutes ago I was able to reach Senator Goldwater and I am glad to say that he has expressed his support of the statement that I am making to you tonight.

It is a solemn responsibility to have to order even limited military action by forces whose overall strength is as vast and as awesome as those of the United States of America, but it is my considered conviction, shared throughout your Government, that firmness in the right is indispensable today for peace; that firmness will always be measured. Its mission is peace.

———————————————————

Source: Public Papers of the Presidents of the United States, Lyndon B. Johnson, Containing the Public Messages, Speeches, and Statements of the President, 1963–1964. Book II—July 1, 1964 to December 31, 1964 (Washington, D.C.: U.S. Government Printing Office, 1965), 927–928.

Document Four: President Johnson, Special Message to Congress: The American Promise, March 15, 1965

Following the brutal attack on the civil rights marchers in Selma, Alabama, President Johnson went before a joint session of Congress on March 15, 1965, to ask for speedy passage of voting rights legislation.

Mr. Speaker, Mr. President, Members of the Congress:

I speak tonight for the dignity of man and the destiny of democracy. . . .

At times history and fate meet at a single time in a single place to shape a turning point in man's unending search for freedom. So it was at Lexington and Concord. So it was a century ago at Appomattox. So it was last week in Selma, Alabama.

There, long-suffering men and women peacefully protested the denial of their rights as Americans. Many were brutally assaulted. One good man, a man of God, was killed.

There is no cause for pride in what has happened in Selma. There is no cause for self-satisfaction in the long denial of equal rights of millions of Americans. But there is cause for hope and for faith in our democracy in what is happening here tonight. . . .

There is no Negro problem. There is no Southern problem. There is no Northern problem. There is only an American problem. And we are met here tonight as

Americans—not as Democrats or Republicans-we are met here as Americans to solve that problem.

This was the first nation in the history of the world to be founded with a purpose. The great phrases of that purpose still sound in every American heart, North and South: "All men are created equal"—"government by consent of the governed"—"give me liberty or give me death." Well, those are not just clever words, or those are not just empty theories. In their name Americans have fought and died for two centuries, and tonight around the world they stand there as guardians of our liberty, risking their lives.

Those words are a promise to every citizen that he shall share in the dignity of man. This dignity cannot be found in a man's possessions; it cannot be found in his power, or in his position. It really rests on his right to be treated as a man equal in opportunity to all others. It says that he shall share in freedom, he shall choose his leaders, educate his children, and provide for his family according to his ability and his merits as a human being.

To apply any other test—to deny a man his hopes because of his color or race, his religion or the place of his birth—is not only to do injustice, it is to deny America and to dishonor the dead who gave their lives for American freedom. . . .

Many of the issues of civil rights are very complex and most difficult. But about this there can and should be no argument. Every American citizen must have an equal right to vote. There is no reason which can excuse the denial of that right. There is no duty which weighs more heavily on us than the duty we have to ensure that right.

Yet the harsh fact is that in many places in this country men and women are kept from voting simply because they are Negroes.

Every device of which human ingenuity is capable has been used to deny this right. The Negro citizen may go to register only to be told that the day is wrong, or the hour is late, or the official in charge is absent. And if he persists, and if he manages to present himself to the registrar, he may be disqualified because he did not spell out his middle name or because he abbreviated a word on the application.

And if he manages to fill out an application he is given a test. The registrar is the sole judge of whether he passes this test. He may be asked to recite the entire Constitution, or explain the most complex provisions of State law. And even a college degree cannot be used to prove that he can read and write.

For the fact is that the only way to pass these barriers is to show a white skin. . . .

To those who seek to avoid action by their National Government in their own communities; who want to

and who seek to maintain purely local control over elections, the answer is simple:

> Open your polling places to all your people.
> Allow men and women to register and vote whatever the color of their skin.
> Extend the rights of citizenship to every citizen of this land. . . .

But even if we pass this bill, the battle will not be over. What happened in Selma is part of a far larger movement which reaches into every section and State of America. It is the effort of American Negroes to secure for themselves the full blessings of American life.

Their cause must be our cause too. Because it is not just Negroes, but really it is all of us, who must overcome the crippling legacy of bigotry and injustice. And we shall overcome.

As a man whose roots go deeply into Southern soil I know how agonizing racial feelings are. I know how difficult it is to reshape the attitudes and the structure of our society.

But a century has passed, more than a hundred years, since the Negro was freed. And he is not fully free tonight.

It was more than a hundred years ago that Abraham Lincoln, a great President of another party, signed the Emancipation Proclamation, but emancipation is a proclamation and not a fact.

A century has passed, more than a hundred years, since equality was promised. And yet the Negro is not equal.

A century has passed since the day of promise. And the promise is unkept.

The time of justice has now come. I tell you that I believe sincerely that no force can hold it back. It is right in the eyes of man and God that it should come. And when it does, I think that day will brighten the lives of every American.

For Negroes are not the only victims. How many white children have gone uneducated, how many white families have lived in stark poverty, how many white lives have been scarred by fear, because we have wasted our energy and our substance to maintain the barriers of hatred and terror?

So I say to all of you here, and to all in the Nation tonight, that those who appeal to you to hold on to the past do so at the cost of denying you your future.

This great, rich, restless country can offer opportunity and education and hope to all: black and white, North and South, sharecropper and city dweller. These are the enemies: poverty, ignorance, disease. They are the enemies and not our fellow man, not our neighbor. And these enemies too, poverty, disease and ignorance, we shall overcome. . . .

My first job after college was as a teacher in Cotulla, Tex., in a small Mexican-American school. Few of them could speak English, and I couldn't speak much Spanish. My students were poor and they often came to class without breakfast, hungry. They knew even in their youth the pain of prejudice. They never seemed to know why people disliked them. But they knew it was so, because I saw it in their eyes. I often walked home late in the afternoon, after the classes were finished, wishing there was more that I could do. But all I knew was to teach them the little that I knew, hoping that it might help them against the hardships that lay ahead.

Somehow you never forget what poverty and hatred can do when you see its scars on the hopeful face of a young child.

I never thought then, in 1928, that I would be standing here in 1965. It never even occurred to me in my fondest dreams that I might have the chance to help the sons and daughters of those students and to help people like them all over this country.

But now I do have that chance—and I'll let you in on a secret—I mean to use it. And I hope that you will use it with me.

This is the richest and most powerful country which ever occupied the globe. The might of past empires is little compared to ours. But I do not want to be the President who built empires, or sought grandeur, or extended dominion.

I want to be the President who educated young children to the wonders of their world. I want to be the President who helped to feed the hungry and to prepare them to be taxpayers instead of taxeaters.

I want to be the President who helped the poor to find their own way and who protected the right of every citizen to vote in every election.

I want to be the President who helped to end hatred among his fellow men and who promoted love among the people of all races and all regions and all parties.

I want to be the President who helped to end war among the brothers of this earth. . . .

God will not favor everything that we do. It is rather our duty to divine His will. But I cannot help believing that He truly understands and that He really favors the undertaking that we begin here tonight.

Source: Public Papers of the Presidents of the United States, Lyndon B. Johnson, Containing the Public Messages, Speeches, and Statements of the President, 1965. Book I—January 1 to May 31, 1965 (Washington, D.C.: U.S. Government Printing Office, 1966), 281–287.

Document Five: President Johnson's News Conference, April 1, 1965

President Johnson spoke of the importance of education reform at his April 1, 1965, press conference.

. . . THE ELEMENTARY AND SECONDARY EDUCATION BILL [2.] Those Members of the Senate Education Subcommittee who today unanimously approved the administration's education bill are participating in one of the historic victories of the American Nation.

Once this bill becomes law, as I am confident it will, and I hope soon, those who shared in its enactment will have earned the gratitude of future generations of Americans. I am told that the leadership of the Senate—I was informed of this by Senator [Mike] Mansfield a little earlier—hopes to bring this bill before the Senate for debate and for action this coming Tuesday and Wednesday. If the full committee reports it Tuesday, it is hoped that they can take it up Wednesday, and it would be a wonderful thing for this country if we could have the bill passed before the end of the week. [The bill was passed by the Senate on April 9 and was approved by the President on April 11.]

This bill has a very simple purpose. Its purpose is to improve the education of young Americans. It will help them master the mysteries of their world. It will help them enrich their minds and learn the skills of work. These tools can open an entirely new world for them.

With education, instead of being condemned to poverty and idleness, young Americans can learn the skills to find a job and provide for a family. Instead of boredom and frustration they can find excitement and pleasure in their hours of rest. Instead of squandering and wasting their talents they can use these talents to benefit themselves and the country in which they live.

How many young lives have been wasted ? How many entire families now live in misery? How much talent has this great, powerful Nation lost because America has failed to give all our children a chance to learn?

Each day's delay in building an educational system means 2,700 school dropouts—2,700 wasted and blighted lives. Last year almost one out of every three draftees were rejected by the armed services because they could not read or write at the eighth grade level.

Today, as I speak, 8 million adult Americans have not finished 5 years of school; 20 million have not finished 8 years of school; and it is shocking that nearly 54 million have not finished high school at all.

This is a shocking waste of human resources. We can measure the cost in many other terms. We now spend about $450 a year per child in our public schools. But we spend $1,800 a year to keep a delinquent youth in a detention home; $2,500 for a family on relief; and $3,500 a year, almost $300 a month, for a criminal in a State prison. In other words, we are spending almost as much per month to keep a criminal in a State prison as it costs us to keep a child in our public schools.

Education is the most economical investment that we can make in this Nation's future.

From the very beginning, knowledge for all was the key to success in the American experiment. The duty to provide that knowledge has rested on each successive generation. It weighs most heavily on us. For as society has grown more intricate the need for learning has grown more intense. And the rapid growth of the Nation threatens to outdistance the capacities of the school systems we now have. The result is that millions of young Americans are denied their full right to develop their minds.

The administration bill reported by the Senate subcommittee under the leadership of Chairman [Wayne] Morse this morning is a bill that represents a national determination that this shall no longer be true. Poverty will no longer be a bar to learning, and learning shall offer an escape from poverty. We will neither dissipate the skills of our people nor deny them the fullness of a life that is informed by knowledge. We will liberate each young mind in every part of this land to reach to the farthest limits of thought and imagination. . . .

Source: Public Papers of the Presidents of the United States, Lyndon B. Johnson, Containing the Public Messages, Speeches, and Statements of the President, 1965. Book I—January 1 to May 31, 1965 (Washington, D.C.: U.S. Government Printing Office, 1966), 364–372.

Document Six: President Johnson, Address to the Nation Announcing Steps to Limit the War in Vietnam and Reporting His Decision Not to Seek Reelection, March 31, 1968

Convinced that the Vietnam War was at a stalemate, President Johnson told the American people in a televised address on March 31, 1968, that he would devote the remainder of his presidency to peace talks with the North Vietnamese and that he would not run for another term as president.

Good evening, my fellow Americans. Tonight I want to speak to you of peace in Vietnam and Southeast Asia. . . .

The Communists may renew their attack any day. They are, it appears, trying to make 1968 the year of decision in South Vietnam—the year that brings, if not final victory or defeat, at least a turning point in the struggle.

This much is clear: If they do mount another round of heavy attacks, they will not succeed in destroying the fighting power of South Vietnam and its allies. But tragically, this is also clear: Many men—on both sides of the struggle—will be lost. A nation that has already suffered 20 years of warfare will suffer once again. Armies on both sides will take new casualties. And the war will go on.

There is no need for this to be so.

There is no need to delay the talks that could bring an end to this long and this bloody war.

Tonight, I renew the offer I made last August—to stop the bombardment of North Vietnam. We ask that talks begin promptly, that they be serious talks on the substance of peace. We assume that during those talks Hanoi will not take advantage of our restraint.

We are prepared to move immediately toward peace through negotiations.

So, tonight, in the hope that this action will lead to early talks, I am taking the first step to deescalate the conflict. We are reducing—substantially reducing—the present level of hostilities. And we are doing so unilaterally, and at once.

Tonight, I have ordered our aircraft and our naval vessels to make no attacks on North Vietnam, except in the area north of the demilitarized zone where the continuing enemy buildup directly threatens allied forward positions and where the movements of their troops and supplies are clearly related to that threat.

The area in which we are stopping our attacks includes almost 90 percent of North Vietnam's population, and most of its territory. Thus there will be no attacks around the principal populated areas, or in the food-producing areas of North Vietnam.

Even this very limited bombing of the North could come to an early end—if our restraint is matched by restraint in Hanoi. But I cannot in good conscience stop all bombing so long as to do so would immediately and directly endanger the lives of our men and our allies. Whether a complete bombing halt becomes possible in the future will be determined by events.

Our purpose in this action is to bring about a reduction in the level of violence that now exists.

It is to save the lives of brave men—and to save the lives of innocent women and children. It is to permit the contending forces to move closer to a political settlement.

And tonight, I call upon the United Kingdom and I call upon the Soviet Union—as cochairmen of the Geneva Conferences, and as permanent members of the United Nations Security Council—to do all they can to move from the unilateral act of deescalation that I have just announced toward genuine peace in Southeast Asia.

Now, as in the past, the United States is ready to send its representatives to any forum, at any time, to discuss the means of bringing this ugly war to an end. . . .

I call upon President Ho Chi Minh to respond positively, and favorably, to this new step toward peace.

But if peace does not come now through negotiations, it will come when Hanoi understands that our common resolve is unshakable, and our common strength is invincible. . . .

We applaud this evidence of determination on the part of South Vietnam. Our first priority will be to support their effort.

We shall accelerate the reequipment of South Vietnam's armed forces—in order to meet the enemy's increased firepower. This will enable them progressively to undertake a larger share of combat operations against the Communist invaders.

On many occasions I have told the American people that we would send to Vietnam those forces that are required to accomplish our mission there. So, with that as our guide, we have previously authorized a force level of approximately 525,000. . . .

But let it never be forgotten: Peace will come also because America sent her sons to help secure it.

It has not been easy—far from it. During the past 4½ years, it has been my fate and my responsibility to be Commander in Chief. I have lived—daily and nightly—with the cost of this war. I know the pain that it has inflicted. I know, perhaps better than anyone, the misgivings that it has aroused.

Throughout this entire, long period, I have been sustained by a single principle: that what we are doing now, in Vietnam, is vital not only to the security of Southeast Asia, but it is vital to the security of every American.

Surely we have treaties which we must respect. Surely we have commitments that we are going to keep. Resolutions of the Congress testify to the need to resist aggression in the world and in Southeast Asia.

But the heart of our involvement in South Vietnam—under three different presidents, three separate administrations—has always been America's own security.

And the larger purpose of our involvement has always been to help the nations of Southeast Asia become independent and stand alone, self-sustaining, as members of a great world community—at peace with themselves, and at peace with all others.

With such an Asia, our country—and the world—will be far more secure than it is tonight.

I believe that a peaceful Asia is far nearer to reality because of what America has done in Vietnam. I believe that the men who endure the dangers of battle—fighting there for us tonight—are helping the entire world avoid far greater conflicts, far wider wars, far more destruction, than this one. . . .

Yet, I believe that now, no less than when the decade began, this generation of Americans is willing to "pay any price, bear any burden, meet any hardship, support any friend, oppose any foe to assure the survival and the success of liberty."

Since those words were spoken by John F. Kennedy, the people of America have kept that compact with mankind's noblest cause.

And we shall continue to keep it.

Yet, I believe that we must always be mindful of this one thing, whatever the trials and the tests ahead. The ultimate strength of our country and our cause will lie not in powerful weapons or infinite resources or boundless wealth, but will lie in the unity of our people.

This I believe very deeply.

Throughout my entire public career I have followed the personal philosophy that I am a free man, an American, a public servant, and a member of my party, in that order always and only.

For 37 years in the service of our Nation, first as a Congressman, as a Senator, and as Vice President, and now as your President, I have put the unity of the people first. I have put it ahead of any divisive partisanship.

And in these times as in times before, it is true that a house divided against itself by the spirit of faction, of party, of region, of religion, of race, is a house that cannot stand.

There is division in the American house now. There is divisiveness among us all tonight. And holding the trust that is mine, as President of all the people, I cannot disregard the peril to the progress of the American people and the hope and the prospect of peace for all peoples.

So, I would ask all Americans, whatever their personal interests or concern, to guard against divisiveness and all its ugly consequences.

Fifty-two months and 10 days ago, in a moment of tragedy and trauma, the duties of this office fell upon me. I asked then for your help and God's, that we might continue America on its course, binding up our wounds, healing our history, moving forward in new unity, to clear the American agenda and to keep the American commitment for all of our people.

United we have kept that commitment. United we have enlarged that commitment.

Through all time to come, I think America will be a stronger nation, a more just society, and a land of greater opportunity and fulfillment because of what we have all done together in these years of unparalleled achievement.

Our reward will come in the life of freedom, peace, and hope that our children will enjoy through ages ahead.

What we won when all of our people united just must not now be lost in suspicion, distrust, selfishness, and politics among any of our people.

Believing this as I do, I have concluded that I should not permit the Presidency to become involved in the partisan divisions that are developing in this political year.

With America's sons in the fields far away, with America's future under challenge right here at home, with our hopes and the world's hopes for peace in the balance every day, I do not believe that I should devote an hour or a day of my time to any personal partisan causes or to any duties other than the awesome duties of this office—the Presidency of your country.

Accordingly, I shall not seek, and I will not accept, the nomination of my party for another term as your President.

But let men everywhere know, however, that a strong, a confident, and a vigilant America stands ready tonight to seek an honorable peace—and stands ready tonight to defend an honored cause—whatever the price, whatever the burden, whatever the sacrifice that duty may require.

Thank you for listening. Good night and God bless all of you.

Source: Public Papers of the Presidents of the United States, Lyndon B. Johnson, Containing the Public Messages, Speeches, and Statements of the President, 1968–1969. Book I—January 1 to June 30, 1968 (Washington, D.C.: U.S. Government Printing Office, 1970), 469–476.

Richard M. Nixon

January 9, 1913–April 22, 1994

Thirty-seventh President of the United States
January 20, 1969–August 9, 1974

≈ RICHARD M. NIXON ≈

Place of Birth: Yorba Linda, California

Date of Birth: January 9, 1913

Places of Residence: California, New York

Class Background: modest

Father's Career: grocer

Mother's Career: homemaker

Number of Siblings: four

Religion: Quaker

Education: graduated Whittier College, 1934, graduated Duke University Law School, 1937

Political Party: Republican

Military Service: World War II: Commander, U.S. Naval Reserve, 1942–46

Spouse: Patricia Ryan Nixon

Spouse's Education: graduated from University of Southern California, 1937

Spouse's Career: teacher, price and economic analyst for the Office of Price Administration, homemaker

Number of Children: two

Sports and Hobbies: bowling, golf, piano

Career Prior to the Presidency: lawyer, businessman, World War II naval officer, member of the U.S. Congress, U.S. senator, vice president

Age upon Entering the White House: 56 years, 11 days

Reason for Leaving the White House: resigned as a result of the Watergate scandal

Career after the Presidency: writer, traveled extensively, elder statesman for the Republican Party

Date of Death: April 22, 1994

Cause of Death: cerebral hemorrhage

Last Words: unknown

Burial Site: Yorba Linda, California

Value of Estate at Time of Death: undisclosed

BIOGRAPHY OF NIXON

Richard Milhous Nixon was born on January 9, 1913, in Yorba Linda, California, the second of five boys born to Frank and Hannah Milhous Nixon. Hannah's family was Quaker, and had arrived in California in the 1880s, settling in a thriving community of coreligionists in Orange County. Quiet, devout, cultured, she had spent two years in college prior to taking a job teaching school. Frank Nixon left his native Ohio in the early 1900s and came west, working a variety of jobs before settling in Orange County. Frank had an intense work ethic, little formal education, and little money. He was a Methodist with strong beliefs and plenty of rough edges. Their many differences led friends and relatives to counsel Hannah against marrying Frank, but she did so nonetheless in 1908. The elder Nixon tried his hand at lemon growing, but this venture failed in 1922. The family moved to nearby Whittier that same year and the Nixons opened their next business—a small grocery and service station.

Entering school in 1918, Richard Nixon displayed a studious side and a precocious intellect. He excelled at music, playing both the piano and the violin by ear. He tried without much success to participate in sports. Young Richard had an encyclopedic memory, a voracious appetite for reading, and an ability to assimilate information about events of the day. He also worked hard in the family store. When the store closed for the day, he spent his evening hours reading or studying. In 1925, younger brother Arthur died of tuberculosis (TB) at the age of seven. For 12-year-old Richard the wrenching experience caused a week-long melancholy. Two years later, Nixon's older bother, Harold, contracted TB and began a six-year bout with the disease. Richard spent the summers of 1928 and 1929 with his mother and brother in far-off Arizona, where the climate was better for treating TB patients. Three childhood influences shaped Nixon as he grew up: his family's precarious economic situation, his father's temper and confrontational streak, and the death of two of his siblings.

Richard Nixon graduated high school in the summer of 1930. A gifted student leader of strong intellect, his potential attracted the attention of Harvard University, which granted him admission and a scholarship, but the Nixons could not afford living and transportation costs. Instead, in the fall of 1930, he entered nearby Whittier College, a small, formerly Quaker, liberal arts institution. Nixon thrived at Whittier. He went out for football, but was too slight to start for the team. The young collegian excelled at debate and acting. Males often belonged to an elite campus men's society called the Franklin. Nixon took a leading role in forming an alternative society named the Orthogonians. In 1933, Nixon won the student body presidency. Throughout his years at Whittier, he revealed a dogged determination to excel and achieve.

Fourteen-year-old Richard Nixon, a member of his high school orchestra at Fullerton, California, poses with his violin in 1927. *(Associated Press)*

In 1934, Nixon entered Duke University's law school. Duke offered generous scholarships to attract students. Nixon entered with a full-tuition scholarship that required a minimum "B" average. Always at the top of the heap at Whittier, the young Californian found himself surrounded by equally bright or even brighter students at Duke. At first, this new experience daunted him. He responded with a nearly monastic approach to study. Fellow law students remarked years later upon his withdrawn demeanor, but they also praised his work ethic. Classmates referred to the studious Nixon as "Iron Butt."

Even with a tuition scholarship, Nixon's living expenses while at Duke taxed the Nixon family finances. He took work in the Duke library with the National Youth Administration, a New Deal agency established to help cash-strapped students stay in high school and college. Law school represented Nixon's first extended experience with a region of the nation other than his own Southern California. He came to understand southern viewpoints, he later reflected. He got on well with most of his classmates. In 1936, they elected Nixon president of the Duke Student Bar Association. He served

PAT NIXON

(1912–1993) *first lady of the United States, January 20, 1969–August 9, 1974*

Born on March 16, 1912, to Katarina "Kate" Halberstadt Bender and William Ryan, Thelma Catherine "Pat" Ryan received her nickname when her father declared her to be his "St. Patrick's babe in the morn." She was the youngest of three children. Her mother was a German immigrant who was widowed with two children when she met and married Pat's father. William Ryan was a miner and truck farmer in Artesia (later renamed Cerritos), California. Kate Ryan was a homemaker, who died of cancer when her daughter was 14. When William Ryan died just before Pat's high school graduation she took the name Patricia in honor of his memory.

Patricia Ryan worked her way through Fullerton Junior College. She left school when offered a job chauffeuring an elderly couple to New York. There she got a job as an X-ray technician at Seton Hospital, where she worked for two years. She ultimately returned to California, matriculated the University of Southern California, and she graduated cum laude in 1937 with a marketing degree and a teaching certificate. She was hired to teach the business curriculum at Whittier High School, where she auditioned for a role in the local theater's production of *The Dark Tower*. She met a young attorney and actor, Richard Nixon.

Nixon was smitten, and he proposed marriage upon that first meeting. Pat Ryan was less sure; she rejected his initial overtures, but eventually the two began dating. They married in 1940, and moved to Washington, D.C. so Richard Nixon could begin working with the Office of Price Administration (OPA). Pat Nixon later obtained work with the agency. After he joined the navy and shipped out to the Pacific, Pat Nixon moved back to California, where she continued working for the OPA.

When he returned from the war, local Whittier Republican Party officials convinced Richard Nixon to run for Congress in 1946 against incumbent liberal Democrat Jerry Voorhis. Pat Nixon, pregnant with the couple's first child, Patricia, or "Tricia," who was born on February 21, 1946, agreed that her husband should run, and she encouraged him to use their savings of $7,000 to fund the race. She also helped with research on Voorhis's record and the production and distribution of campaign literature. She supervised the family's move to Washington, D.C. following her husband's victory in 1946. One year after moving to Washington, Pat Nixon gave birth to a second child, Julie, on July 5, 1948. Throughout the remainder of her husband's political career, Pat Nixon was a formidable presence in his various campaigns for office, critiquing his speeches, studying the efforts of his opponents, greeting voters, and giving speeches herself on his behalf. She earned the unflattering nickname "Plastic Pat" for her perfect grooming and manners at political functions, which she disliked, preferring to focus on her family.

Pat Nixon *(Library of Congress)*

on the law review and graduated third in his class in 1937. His studies earned him induction into the Order of the Coif, a prestigious legal honor society. Returning home, he prepared for the California bar, passed that examination, and was sworn in to the state bar in November 1937.

Nixon joined a local law firm, and he immersed himself in civil affairs. Though he impressed his boss and coworkers, the firm simply did not have enough work to go around. He joined local civic organizations and service clubs, gave speeches, and even took up acting in an area theater troupe.

He hoped to meet new people, he later explained. One of those he met was Patricia Ryan, an attractive *cum laude* graduate of the University of Southern California, who taught high school in Whittier. Though Nixon fell for her from the first, Pat Ryan repeatedly spurned him. The young lawyer tenaciously pursued her. He took up hobbies that interested her, though they made him uncomfortable. When she dated other men, he offered to drive her to and from her outings rather than compel her to ride in a streetcar. Eventually, he grew on her, and after two years of effort, Nixon won her

When Richard Nixon was the Republican nominee for vice president in 1952, he faced charges of maintaining a political slush fund. Some party operatives contended he needed to withdraw from the ticket, but Pat Nixon told her husband, "We both know what you have to do, Dick. You have to fight it all the way to the end, no matter what happens." He did, planning a television speech to explain their finances. Pat Nixon did not like that plan, asking "Why do we have to tell people how little we have and how much we owe?" Nevertheless, she appeared at her husband's side when he gave this speech, and in the process became a national figure. He had referred to her choice of a "good Republican cloth coat" over the mink coats commonly found on many Washington political wives. The speech was dubbed the "Checkers" speech for Nixon's reference to a dog given to his daughters that the family did not intend to return. It secured his place on the ticket and his political future.

As wife of the vice president, Pat Nixon often filled in for first lady Mamie Eisenhower at official functions. She also traveled the world with her husband. She acknowledged, "Everywhere I went, it helped women" but she also would have preferred the satisfaction of a job to the "useless gadding I am expected to do." In 1960, *Time* magazine called her "one of the U.S.'s most remarkable women—not just a showpiece Second Lady, not merely part of the best known team in contemporary politics, but a public figure in her own right." She was a helpful asset in her husband's losing race for the presidency in 1960 and the California governorship in 1962.

Though she had not wanted her husband to run again for the presidency in 1968, given the turmoil in the nation, she embraced her new responsibilities as first lady. Just as her husband spoke of the "silent majority," she welcomed reaching out to anonymous, average Americans, and she made sure each letter sent to her received a proper response. As first lady, she began a program of concerts for inner-city youth called "Evenings in the Park." She added to the fine arts and furniture collections of the White House when she renovated some of the home's state rooms. For the first time since the late 1940s, she opened the White House to public tours. She advocated volunteerism in America's communities. She practiced "personal diplomacy" on missions overseas with her husband, such as his historic visit to China in 1972. She traveled abroad without her husband to Africa, and when an earthquake hit Peru, she helped coordinate American relief efforts.

While first lady, Pat Nixon spoke out on pertinent women's issues. She declared abortion decisions were a "private matter." She pushed unsuccessfully for her husband to name a woman to the Supreme Court. She also was a forceful champion of the Equal Rights Amendment. She advocated the election of more women to public office, stating that she would vote for a woman who was not a Republican. Furthermore, while it might sound silly in the 21st century, she broke another significant barrier in that she was photographed wearing pants in public.

Finally, the White House years were filled with personal highs and lows for Pat Nixon. Her younger daughter Julie married David Eisenhower, the grandson of former president Dwight D. Eisenhower, between the 1968 election and the 1969 inauguration. Her older daughter Tricia married Edward Finch Cox in a White House garden wedding on June 12, 1971. Regarding Watergate, Pat Nixon routinely observed that she knew only what was in the newspapers. Initially, she opposed her husband's decision to resign the presidency in August 1974 out of concern that he would face a criminal indictment. Once the decision was final, she began packing personal belongings for transport back to their home in California, where she lived a quiet life socializing with friends and spending time with her daughters and their families.

Pat Nixon suffered strokes in 1976 and 1982, fully recovering from both. Other health problems plagued her, though, including emphysema, a degenerative spinal problem, and cancer of the mouth. The Nixons moved back to the East Coast in 1980 to be nearer their daughters, settling in Park Ridge, New Jersey. She made few public appearances in retirement, one at the July 1990 celebration of the Richard Nixon Birthplace and Library in Yorba Linda, California, and another at the September 1991 dedication of the Ronald Reagan Presidential Library. She died of lung cancer on June 22, 1993.

consent to wed. They were married in June 1940 and honeymooned in Mexico. The couple rented a duplex and went on with their lives.

With the coming of World War II, the Nixons moved to Washington, D.C. A former Duke law professor recruited Nixon for the Office of Price Administration (OPA), the newly created government agency in charge of rationing and combating inflation. The OPA position paid more than he had ever earned as a lawyer in Whittier, but he grew frustrated with the OPA's bureaucracy. He did not feel comfortable in Washington, still dominated by New Deal liberalism, and he later reflected that his experience at OPA made him more conservative. As a bureaucrat Nixon enjoyed a draft exemption, and (as a Quaker) arguably he could claim conscientious objector status. However, he had never considered himself a pacifist, and after talking it over with Pat, he joined the U.S. Navy in June 1942. From Nixon's stint in the navy, he learned to curse, drink, smoke cigars, and play poker. Indeed, Nixon's skill at poker earned him somewhere between $3,000 and $10,000 by 1945. His naval duties, even in the South Pacific,

Richard Nixon *(center)* as a member of the second string football team at Whittier College *(Associated Press)*

involved support work. In July 1944 the navy sent him back to California. He finished out the war stateside as an attorney for the navy, working on contracts with aircraft manufacturers.

In 1945, Orange County business leaders organized to recruit a highly qualified Republican candidate to oppose Democratic congressman Jerry Voorhis. They settled on Nixon. An aggressive attack against Voorhis, particularly his ties to organized labor and the CIO-PAC (Congress of Industrial Organizations Political Action Committee), represented the keystone of Nixon's strategy. The challenger hammered the congressman, implying that Voorhis's support of labor and the New Deal represented tacit support of communism. The young Republican also claimed the Democrat had done a poor job representing the district, citing Voorhis's inability to get his bills passed. Through four debates, played to ever larger audiences, Nixon bested Voorhis. Nixon enjoyed overwhelming support from the district newspapers. Editors actually went beyond endorsing the Republican to actively undermining his opponent. On November 6, 1946, Richard Nixon won election to the House of Representatives with 56 percent of the vote.

Just 33 years old, Nixon entered the 80th Congress as part of a Republican groundswell reflecting the increasingly conservative tenor of American politics and public dissatisfaction with President HARRY S. TRUMAN's handling of postwar economic adjustment. When the dust settled from the 1946 elections, Republicans controlled the House of Representatives 246-188 and the Senate 51-45. As a freshman representative, Nixon sat on the House Committee on Education and Labor as it considered legislation designed to rein in organized labor, which culminated in the Taft-Hartley Act of 1947. Though Nixon opposed the Truman administration on domestic policy, he supported the president's confrontation with the Soviet Union in the early cold war years. Nixon supported the massive aid program for Western Europe, the Marshall Plan, but he also wanted to include direct help for China. He panned the president's actions against the domestic communist menace as insufficient.

During his first term in Congress, none of his political responsibilities mattered as much to Nixon, his later political career, and his personal reputation, as his service on the House Un-American Activities Committee (HUAC). Republican House Speaker Joe Martin (R-MA) told Nixon that he would bring greater gravitas to the committee, which had never been considered a major force in Congress since its founding in the late 1930s. With a presidential election looming in 1948, Republicans expected to win the White House and expand their congressional majority. The issue of domestic communism appeared to be a winner.

Chaired by Representative J. Parnell Thomas (R-NJ), HUAC used its power during the 80th Congress to highlight the threat of communism in the federal government and critical areas of American culture, particularly the motion picture industry. The mere existence of the Communist Party of the United States of America (CPUSA) frustrated many members who hoped to see it outlawed. Representative Nixon, however, had rather different concerns. Though he coauthored a bill with Representative Karl Mundt (R-SD) requiring CPUSA members to register with the government, he felt an outright ban on the party served no purpose. The Nixon-Mundt bill passed the House easily enough, but it never got out of committee in the U.S. Senate.

Nixon limited his participation in HUAC hearings on communist influence in Hollywood. The freshman representative fretted about the wisdom of investigating Hollywood and relying too heavily on unreliable evidence and hearsay. However, his dogged pursuit of Alger Hiss, a former State Department official, demonstrated Nixon's ability to take some risks. The Hiss case helped create Nixon's national reputation, for better or worse, and it helped form an important part of his self-concept afterward. Whittaker Chambers, by 1948 an editor at *Time* magazine, but by his own admission a courier and spy for the Soviet government during the late 1930s, testified publicly before HUAC in the summer of 1948 and named Hiss as a spy. Hiss testified in August to refute the allegations. Nixon later recalled being impressed with Hiss's testimony, as were most in attendance. However, Nixon's suspicions had been heightened by the former diplomat's failure to categorically claim he did not know Chambers. Others on the committee felt that they had come to a dead end. Proving Hiss had spied would be hard, but to determine whether or not he had lied about knowing Chambers would not. Intensive questioning by a Nixon-led subcommittee in August revealed Chambers's extraordinary familiarity with Hiss. He had knowledge of his hobbies, his car, and even the pet names the diplomat and his wife had for one another.

Hiss met with Nixon's subcommittee on August 16 in executive session. He was not nearly as comfortable as before the whole committee. One by one, Chambers's detailed recollections of the Hiss family proved true. Then, the former diplomat admitted that he might have known Chambers after all, though by a different name—George Crosley. In December, news came that Chambers possessed documents passed by Hiss, through him, to the Soviets. But questions arose about his story, including whether the microfilm he claimed to have used even existed in 1938, when he claimed to have copied the documents. Chambers produced the purloined files for Nixon from their hiding place inside a pumpkin in his Maryland garden. However, the affair only heightened skepticism. This new information led the grand jury to indict Hiss for perjury. Decades later, the opening of Soviet archives revealed Hiss as a Soviet agent, but some still doubt this evidence, mistrusting the Soviet sources. However, in the context of the times, Hiss's guilt or innocence constituted a matter for partisan debate. The intensity of emotion over the Hiss affair made Nixon a hero in conservative circles, but a demon among liberals. These divisions of opinion influenced perceptions of Nixon's character well into the future.

Nixon was reelected to the House of Representatives in 1948. In an unexpected victory, President Truman also won reelection against Republican challenger Thomas E. Dewey. On November 3, 1949, Nixon announced his campaign for the U.S. Senate, and his efforts benefited from Hiss's conviction in January 1950. California Democrats ultimately selected Representative Helen Gahagan Douglas, a former actress and the wife of actor Melvyn Douglas to run against Nixon. She relied heavily upon the support of organized labor. Though critical of both the Soviet Union and the People's Republic of China, often referred to as "Red China," she had voted against funding HUAC and aid to Greece and Turkey in 1947. She had the support of Screen Actor's Guild president RONALD REAGAN, no ally of communism.

Nixon organized a ruthless campaign against Douglas, focusing on her association with liberal/leftist causes and personalities. Nixon referred to his opponent as the "pink lady," while Douglas pinned a long-lasting nickname on the Republican: "Tricky Dick." The Nixon campaign was better funded. The most infamous broadside of the campaign, the so-called pink sheet, dramatized the effectiveness of a statewide campaign based upon the issue of domestic communism. The pink sheet effectively cast the Democrat as a "fellow traveler"—someone who did not belong to, but sympathized with, the Communist Party. Originally a small run of broadsheets, Nixon campaign manager Murray Chotiner authorized 500,000 copies as the paper's efficacy became apparent. In November, Nixon won 2.2 million votes to Douglas's 1.5 million, the largest plurality for any Senate candidate in 1950.

When he entered the Senate, Nixon was only 38 years old. His successful pursuit of Hiss and his vigorous campaigning style and determined partisanship had made him a popular speaker in Republican circles. However, his expenses stretched his Senate salary. Off and on during his career in the House, Nixon had received contributions to help him defray these expenses; in late 1950, the arrangement was formalized into a designated fund and Southern California supporters were hit up for donations. With

BIOGRAPHICAL TIME LINE

1913
January 9 Richard Milhous Nixon is born in Yorba Linda, California.

1925
Nixon's younger brother Arthur dies of tuberculosis.

1928
Nixon and his mother spend the summer with older brother Harold, who has contracted tuberculosis.

1930
Nixon enters Whittier College in the fall.

1933
Nixon wins the student body presidency at Whittier College.

1934
Nixon enters Duke University Law School.

1936
Nixon is elected president of the Duke Student Bar Association.

1937
November Nixon passes the California state bar examination, and is sworn in.

1940
June Nixon marries Pat Ryan.

1942
June 21 Nixon joins the navy.

1946
November 6 Nixon defeats the sitting congressman to win election to the U.S. House of Representatives.

1950
November Nixon is elected to the U.S. Senate.

1952
July At the Republican National Convention Nixon wins the vice-presidential nomination.

1953
January 20 Nixon is sworn in as vice president of the United States.

1956
November 6 Nixon is reelected vice president of the United States.

1957
January 20 Nixon is sworn in as vice president of the United States for a second term.

1958
On a goodwill trip to South America Nixon is nearly killed by a mob in Caracas, Venezuela.

1959
On a trip to the Soviet Union while touring a U.S. exhibition, Nixon engages in the "Kitchen Debate" with Soviet premier Nikita Khrushchev.

1960
July 27 Nixon secures the Republican presidential nomination.

November 8 Nixon loses the presidential election to John F. Kennedy.

1962
November 6 Nixon loses the gubernatorial race in California to Pat Brown.

November 7 Nixon declares he has held his last press conference, and that his public career is over.

1968
November 5 Nixon is elected president of the United States.

1969
January 20 Nixon is inaugurated president.

1972
November 7 Nixon is reelected president.

1973
January 20 Nixon is inaugurated for a second term as president of the United States.

1974
August 9 Nixon resigns the presidency.

1994
April 22 Nixon dies in New York.

money fears relieved, Nixon traveled freely and widely, entertaining Republican crowds and lambasting the Truman administration.

The popular after-dinner speaker also became a sought-after ally for would-be Republican presidential nominees, including Ohio senator Robert Taft, California governor Earl Warren, and Minnesota governor Harold Stassen. Senator Nixon did all he could to avoid appearing too supportive of any one aspirant. Privately, Nixon believed the best Republican nominee would be General DWIGHT D. EISENHOWER, supreme commander of NATO.

The California senator's careful straddling of his party's factions served his own ambitions as well. Though relatively young, Nixon nurtured hopes for the vice-presidential slot. He met with East Coast party insiders, who agreed that Nixon would make a fine complement to the general on the ticket. His credentials as a conservative Californian would balance General Eisenhower's connections to the East Coast establishment. At the Republican National Convention in July 1952, General Eisenhower won the nomination, and Nixon received the vice-presidential nomination. They faced off against the Democratic ticket of Illinois governor Adlai Stevenson for president and Alabama senator John Sparkman for vice president.

Nixon's earliest speaking forays as a vice-presidential candidate focused upon the issue of corruption in the Truman administration, such as gifts of mink coats and refrigerators. Senator Nixon urged voters to support the Republican ticket to cleanse the nation's capital and its politics. In so doing, he invited a counterattack. On September 18, 1952, the *New York Post* published a story about Nixon's expense fund. Within days, the crisis escalated, and Nixon's place on the ticket appeared in question. Some of Eisenhower's closest advisers urged him to dump the senator. On September 21, Eisenhower suggested that Nixon explain the situation in a nationally televised address, including a careful recapitulation of his personal finances. When Nixon asked if that would be sufficient to remain on the ticket, the older man refused to answer directly.

Nixon took to the airwaves on September 23, 1952. With Pat at his side, the California senator offered a detailed, even embarrassing, account of the family's finances. The Republican vice-presidential candidate insisted that he had never taken any improper gifts. He did allow that a Texas supporter had given the Nixons a cocker spaniel, but he also refused to give back the dog, named Checkers, because his daughters loved it so. To solidify his own position, Nixon challenged Stevenson and Sparkman, and by extension, Eisenhower, to be as public about their finances as he had been. To this indirect challenge to Eisenhower, Nixon added another more formidable one. During the "Checkers Speech," as it became known, he told viewers who felt he should stay on the ticket to contact the Republican National Committee and not General Eisenhower. The responses ran 350-1 in favor of Nixon.

Richard Nixon sent this postcard to supporters who had written him after the "Checkers Speech." *(Richard Nixon Presidential Library and Museum)*

In the campaign, Nixon tied leading Democrats, including Stevenson, to Alger Hiss, and by extension, the internal communist menace. The November vote went decisively for the Republicans. The Eisenhower-Nixon ticket took 55 percent of the popular vote, racked up a significant Electoral College majority, and helped the Republicans regain control of the House of Representatives. With the U.S. Senate deadlocked at 48 seats for each party, Nixon held the tie-breaking vote as vice president, giving the Republican Party effective control over that chamber.

During his first term as vice president, Nixon emerged as an important player in the Eisenhower cabinet, particularly with regard to political strategy. Just as in the campaign, Nixon played hardball partisan politics while Eisenhower was the statesman. The vice president proved skilled at dealing with the most problematic of Republican politicos—Wisconsin senator Joseph McCarthy. Nixon got McCarthy to back off opposition to key presidential appointments and convinced him to drop a planned investigation of communist influence inside the CIA. The mercurial senator, however, remained a constant worry, making and then breaking agreements with the administration, staggering from one outrageous statement to another.

As the 1954 midterm elections approached, Vice President Nixon pressed for a political strategy that would build upon the Republican majority in the House and perhaps gain seats in the Senate. Nixon embarked upon a 48-day, 31-state campaign tour in which he delivered blunt, pugnacious speeches. The president himself did not step into the race until late October. The Democrats won control of Congress, though by slender margins in both houses.

Throughout early 1955, President Eisenhower refused to commit publicly to seeking a second term, and he privately toyed with the idea of retirement. This scenario became more complicated on September 24 when Eisenhower suffered a major heart attack while on vacation in Denver, Colorado. Until Eisenhower returned to work, Nixon supervised cabinet and National Security Council meetings, and he stayed on top of day-to-day affairs in Washington. The vice president obediently followed instructions and avoided creating perceptions that he was angling for power.

When Eisenhower did finally decide to run again, doing so did not determine the question of Nixon's place on the Republican ticket. In late 1955, President Eisenhower even suggested that the younger man consider leaving the vice presidency for a cabinet post in a second administration. To the president's way of thinking time spent serving in the cabinet would equip the 42-year-old Nixon with needed administrative experience. The idea mortified Nixon, who considered it a snub and a demotion. To make matters worse, Eisenhower told the press that Nixon's place on the ticket or in a second administration would be Nixon's own choice. Nixon finally told Eisenhower of his preference to stay on the ticket, and he left it to the president and party to determine. His decision was grounded upon the realization that the party leadership supported him, but also upon his own calculations about what was best for his career. Nixon survived and stayed on the ticket in 1956.

The president's health curtailed his activities in the campaign, so Nixon's role became that much more prominent. Unlike 1952, when Nixon, with Eisenhower's encouragement, played the part of attack dog, the 1956 race saw the emergence of a new and less partisan Nixon. The Republican administration had considerable economic achievements to trumpet, so Nixon focused upon these in his message to voters. Eisenhower's popularity combined with peace and prosperity made his reelection an easy one, with the Eisenhower-Nixon ticket winning by more than 10 million votes.

A second term as vice president stood to settle Nixon's place as the presumptive heir to Eisenhower. However, the president himself had to come around to that way of thinking. Nixon instead had to build his own following and establish himself in the next four years within the boundaries set by Eisenhower. Foreign travel, advocacy of important domestic issues and his own ability to take advantage of political opportunities allowed Nixon the chance to shine on his own and convince the general public of his presidential qualities. In both Latin America and Africa, Nixon worked to strengthen relationships and improve the perception of the United States among emerging and developing nations. While some in the administration failed to recognize the importance of these trips, Nixon understood that these regions loomed as a likely cold war battlefield in the future. On a trip to Latin America in 1958, he faced considerable criticism and even received death threats from hostile crowds. Nixon's near death at the hands of a mob in Caracas, Venezuela, represented a propa-

Senator Richard M. Nixon accepting the Republican vice-presidential nomination, 1952 *(Library of Congress)*

On a contentious trip to South America in 1958, Vice President Nixon shakes hands in Buenos Aires, Argentina. *(Associated Press)*

ganda victory for the United States. In the aftermath of the Caracas affray, political polls showed Nixon ahead of likely presidential opponents.

In 1959, Nixon drew considerable attention with a trip to the Soviet Union and a meeting with Soviet premier Nikita Khrushchev. He opened the United States Exhibition in Moscow, a cultural exchange event intended to demonstrate the strengths of American capitalism. The exhibition featured a mock-up of a typical American home, fitted out with the latest appliances, as well as a demonstration of color television. Nixon and Khrushchev toured the exhibit together, all the while debating the merits of capitalism and communism. While substantively the "Kitchen Debate" did little to shake the premier's faith in his own system, it did boost Nixon's profile at home just a little more than a year ahead of the 1960 presidential election.

On domestic issues Nixon played a critical role in administration deliberations. Of all high-ranking Eisenhower administration officials, he most firmly supported the cause of civil rights, advocating strong government action against segregation. Whereas Eisenhower privately disagreed with the Supreme Court's 1954 *Brown v. Board of Education* ruling, Nixon supported the decision. He also perceived that a strong stand by the administration might arrest the Republican Party's two-decades old loss of support among African Americans. Nixon supported passage of a strong civil rights bill in 1957. When the bill lost most of its teeth in the Democratic Senate, the vice president urged Eisenhower to fight for a tougher law. But, when the president appeared unwilling, he urged him to sign the Civil Rights Act of 1957 nonetheless, thinking—along with influential African-American leaders—that something was better than nothing.

As the 1960 presidential election neared, Eisenhower, an almost universally respected figure in the United States, consistently declined to publicly endorse either Nixon's conduct in office or his presidential aspirations. Nixon biographers suggest that the president's stinginess with praise troubled him greatly. Furthermore, Nixon's critics took it as a sign that Eisenhower had found Nixon's character lacking. At one point, when asked by reporters to identify an important idea of Nixon's that had been adopted as policy, the president offhandedly suggested that the press give him a week to think of

one. Privately, even at that late date, Eisenhower fretted about Nixon's maturity and readiness for the presidency.

Still, as preparations for the 1960 campaign began in 1958–59, Richard Nixon stood as the man to beat for the Republican nomination even if all in his party were not convinced. In a nation where Democrats significantly outnumbered Republicans, so partisan a figure as Nixon might harm the party's chances of retaining the White House. A number of those most concerned about Nixon looked to New York governor Nelson Rockefeller as an alternative. The

Republican convention in Chicago, 1960 *(Associated Press)*

New Yorker angled for Eisenhower's endorsement, which he withheld. Without this critical support for his campaign, the governor chose not to challenge Nixon, and Nixon secured planks in the Republican platform to suit Rockefeller on the issues of defense spending and civil rights. At the Republican National Convention in July 1960, with the Rockefeller threat neutralized, Nixon received the nomination without additional controversy. He took UN ambassador Henry Cabot Lodge of Massachusetts as his running mate. Lodge offered the possibility of boosting Republican chances in the Northeast against a strong Democratic showing expected there.

That summer, the Democrats nominated 43-year-old Massachusetts senator JOHN F. KENNEDY, scion of a wealthy Irish-Catholic Boston political dynasty. Kennedy's relative youth and inexperience could not undermine his personal appeal, his deep pockets, and his performance in key primaries. However, Democrats worried that his Catholicism might hurt his chances without a strong running mate. Texas senator LYNDON B. JOHNSON got the Democratic second slot to balance the ticket.

From the outset the Kennedy-Nixon race appeared likely to be close. Nixon determined early on to campaign in all 50 states, though it might not have been the most economical or wise use of his time and energy. He undertook an August campaign swing through the South, but he seriously injured his knee on a car door at a campaign stop in Greensboro, North Carolina, and a staph infection settled in, causing him great pain and a high fever. Laid up in hospital, he could do little in the way of campaigning, and only watch while an ally attacked Kennedy's Catholicism. Nixon had no intention of making his opponent's religion an issue. All he could do from his sickbed was wait. Even after two weeks of recuperation, the vice president refused to allow for any change to his 50-state plan.

The three televised debates between Nixon and Kennedy, a first in American history, served as the centerpiece of the 1960 campaign. Despite being advised by Eisenhower to avoid the debates, which the president thought trivial, the vice president agreed to participate. While the debates might enhance Kennedy's national recognition and force Nixon onto the defensive, debating was one of Nixon's great strengths. His showing against Khrushchev allowed him to think it would be easy to face Kennedy. The first debate was scheduled for Chicago, on September 26. The two weeks before the debate had been his first back on the campaign trail since his time in hospital. Nixon pushed himself too hard, and he came into Chicago weary. The night before the debate, he injured his knee again. By debate time the next evening, he was in pain and had a high fever, but Nixon insisted the show must go on.

The debate focused upon domestic issues, and with the country in recession, Nixon played defense. Furthermore, he looked awful, while Kennedy looked at ease, robust,

Candidates Kennedy *(left)* and Nixon *(right)* shake hands before their first nationally televised debate, September 26, 1960. *(© Bettmann/CORBIS)*

and sporting a healthy-looking tan. The vice president had refused to use make-up, his face was unshaven, and he sweated underneath the bright studio lights. Still he made a good showing, so far as the radio audience was concerned. Polls of radio listeners gave the victory to Nixon; but television created the impression of a Kennedy victory. October 7 brought the second debate, played out in Washington. The focus was foreign policy, a subject Nixon relished. The Republican candidate also felt better, the studio had been better air-conditioned, and the two thrust and parried more vigorously. Kennedy drew blood, however, with criticism of the administration's failure to stop communism in Cuba and its perceived weakness on national defense. The October 13 debate featured the candidates debating each other at a distance—each in different studios in different cities. The Democratic candidate continued to hit hard on foreign policy, mocking Nixon's readiness to defend the islands of Quemoy and Matsu, located between Taiwan and Red China, while being willing to do nothing about Castro's Cuba. Nixon, privately in administration talks, had backed much more vigorous action against Castro, and he knew a CIA-sponsored invasion was in the planning stages. Yet, he could not compromise that information, and so, he tried to portray Kennedy's approach as risky and unwise. Overall, substantively, the debates should have helped Nixon, but television was not kind to him as it had been in 1952, and the debates helped his opponent more.

Despite Kennedy's advantage in the debates, the race remained close, and both candidates sought the advantage.

A critical opportunity, but one fraught with potential risks, occurred on October 19. On that day, Atlanta police arrested civil rights leader Martin Luther King, Jr. during a sit-in at a downtown department store. The campaign that responded most carefully and effectively to the incident might gain traction with black voters in key battleground states. John F. Kennedy called King's wife to offer support in a widely publicized gesture. Robert Kennedy, who managed his brother's campaign, intervened quietly with the trial judge, a Democrat, and secured King's release. The Nixon campaign, however, did nothing. Nixon felt King had been treated unfairly, but he made no public statement to that effect, preferring simply to say it was inappropriate for him to comment upon a pending case. Kennedy's gesture gained him support in the black community, and the vice president's silence may have cost him the election.

The most important endorsement Nixon sought, that of President Eisenhower, remained elusive. Two weeks before the end of the race, Eisenhower began stumping for Nixon, but his campaign speeches were not promotions of Nixon. Instead, Eisenhower's efforts seemed primarily directed at refuting Kennedy's criticisms of the sitting president. But observers felt the old man's presence on the trail helped his vice president. When Mamie Eisenhower and the president's doctor urged Nixon to use his influence to get Ike to sit the campaign out, he did so. Eisenhower, put off by the strange request, stayed at home the rest of the race. Eight days remained before the election. Polling indicated a close race, but with Kennedy now holding a small lead.

On November 8, Nixon lost to Kennedy in the closest election of the 20th century. In the popular vote, Kennedy outpolled Nixon by less than 150,000 votes out of more than 68.8 million cast. Kennedy tallied 303 Electoral College votes to Nixon's 219. Even a minor change in votes in important states would have shifted the election in Nixon's favor. Accusations of fraud hovered over Kennedy's victory. The Democratic margin of victory in Illinois rested on returns from Cook County, which had a reputation for political cor-

After losing the 1960 election to John F. Kennedy, Richard Nixon returned to California with his wife Pat *(far right)* and two daughters, Tricia *(far left)* and Julie *(left)*. *(Library of Congress)*

ruption. The race had also been close, but less so, in Lyndon Johnson's Texas, with its own reputation for crooked politics. While Nixon refused to ask for recounts for fear of being seen as a sore loser, numerous individuals and state committees fought the election in court for a few weeks after the election. On January 20, 1961, John F. Kennedy became president and Richard Nixon became a private citizen.

A loss so close hurt Nixon, his wife, and family deeply. They returned to California. Nixon worked as a consultant in a Los Angeles law firm and began making more money than ever in his life. Throughout his political career, he had amassed little wealth. The Nixons built a large home in the city's Bel Air section. In 1961, he wrote a book, *Six Crises*, which focused upon six important moments in his political career: Alger Hiss, Checkers, Eisenhower's heart attack, the streets of Caracas, the kitchen debate with Khrushchev, and the 1960 race. *Six Crises* sold more than 250,000 copies, netting Nixon hundreds of thousands of dollars in royalties, and it appeared on bestseller lists for six months.

Seeking a political comeback, Nixon announced his candidacy for governor of California in September 1961. In doing so he challenged the sitting governor, Democrat Edmund G. "Pat" Brown, who had presided over an ongoing economic boom in the state. Democrats outnumbered Republicans in California, and Republicans were badly divided. For his part, Nixon worried about his long-shot candidacy. However, he believed President Kennedy would be unbeatable in 1964, and he needed to be in some position of political influence with his own following should the opportunity emerge to run for the White House in 1968. Not surprisingly, Nixon lost to Brown, and on the evening of the election, he refused to concede or speak to the press. Finally, the next day, a haggard and angry Nixon faced reporters, and he told his audience they would no longer "have Nixon to kick around any more."

With his defeat, Nixon left his home state and moved to the East Coast. Through the influence of friends, he signed on to the law firm of Mudge, Stern, Baldwin and Todd; when he passed the New York bar examination in late 1963, Nixon became a named partner. In New York, the Nixons moved in powerful circles. The former vice president socialized with old allies—such as former governor and presidential candidate Thomas Dewey—interacted with rivals, such as Governor Nelson Rockefeller, and made new friends, such as Henry Kissinger and John Mitchell. His legal work proved even more lucrative than with his Los Angeles firm. Despite the fire of his "last press conference" following his 1962 defeat, he kept his eyes open for political opportunities.

Nixon's law firm gave him plenty of time for politics. Throughout early 1964, he considered, but ultimately rejected, challenging the Republican front-runner, Senator Barry Goldwater of Arizona, whose views on Social Security, the Great Society, and civil rights were extreme. Goldwater lost badly

Richard Nixon, sitting with his dog Checkers in 1964 *(Photo by Bob Gomel/Time Life Pictures/Getty Images)*

to President Lyndon Johnson in 1964. Nixon had campaigned for the Republican ticket that fall and did so again in the 1966 congressional elections. Nixon sounded out the law-and-order themes that played a role in his own 1968 campaign for the presidency while also highlighting economic troubles on the horizon. Republicans made significant gains in the House in 1966, lesser ones in the Senate, and Nixon deserved a share of the credit. In 1967, Nixon attacked Johnson's Vietnam policy in an acclaimed article for *Foreign Affairs.* Nixon also published regularly in *Reader's Digest* during the mid-1960s. The former vice president emerged as the undisputed leader of his party and the likely nominee in 1968. As the war and domestic situation worsened, he looked forward to a campaign clash with the still formidable Lyndon Johnson.

The year 1968 was one of turmoil and division in the United States. This was true for all aspects of life in the country: social relations, culture, the economy, diplomacy and the military, and politics. It should be no surprise then that the presidential election that year was shaped by the rebellions of that fateful year. Incumbent president Lyndon Johnson had hoped to run for and win a second term in his own right, but public criticism of his administration's role in the Vietnam War made that increasingly difficult. He faced challenges from the left in his own party, barely winning the New Hampshire primary in March against an insurgent candidate, Senator Eugene McCarthy of Minnesota. That month Johnson dropped out of the race.

McCarthy's path to the nomination was not made easier by Johnson's decision. In fact, new challengers entered and complicated the contest. First, Senator Robert F. Kennedy announced his candidacy in March, promising a "new politics" of social justice at home and an end to the war abroad. Later Vice President Hubert Humphrey entered the race. Though he had a long record of liberal accomplishments, his association with the Johnson administration and the war complicated his candidacy.

Meanwhile the Republicans narrowed down their list of candidates fairly easily. Nixon was among the favorites because of the work he had done in the party to smooth over the discord following Goldwater's big defeat in 1964. None of the liberal and moderate challengers remained viable by the time the Republican National Convention met, and the conservative threats to Nixon were quickly dispatched, giving him his party's nomination.

The Democratic National Convention, which met in Chicago, was much less well organized and much more cha-

otic for both the party and the nation. Antiwar protesters converged on Chicago and a bloody melee resulted. Though Humphrey ultimately prevailed and won the nomination—his chief opponent, Senator Kennedy, had been assassinated in June—he led a bitterly divided party and his emphasis on the "politics of joy," an uplifting message, seemed out of sync with the times.

The third party candidacy of former Alabama governor George C. Wallace proved much more attractive to voters discontented with the Civil Rights movement and with the war protesters than was typically the case for minor candidates. Throughout the fall the contest remained close, but Nixon's ability to co-opt the Wallace message with more socially acceptable rhetoric about law and order helped assure him a victory that November in one of the closest races in American history. Nixon won 31.8 million votes (43.4 percent) to Humphrey's 31.3 million (42.7 percent) and Wallace's 9.9 million (13.5 percent). He won the electoral college 301–191, with Wallace receiving 46 electoral votes.

A supporter of Nixon, rock star Elvis Presley *(right)* met with the president in the Oval Office of the White House on December 21, 1970, offering to bring a more positive attitude to young people throughout the country. *(National Archives)*

Nixon was inaugurated on January 20, 1969. As president Nixon never quite escaped the turmoil of 1968. Still, his first term constituted a beehive of activity on both the foreign and domestic fronts. A significant and important series of environmental reforms were implemented. On the civil rights front his administration oversaw an expansion of AFFIRMATIVE ACTION POLICY and a major surge in school desegregation. He reversed course on economic policy when the country struggled financially, implementing WAGE AND PRICE CONTROLS. Although his administration introduced a significant initiative to reform welfare, he failed to achieve his objective on that front.

Foreign policy in the first Nixon term saw reduced U.S. troop commitments in Vietnam as the president introduced his program of "Vietnamization." While the public applauded this measure, questions were later raised about his decision to launch a secret war in Cambodia. His biggest foreign policy accomplishment in the first term was his program of DÉTENTE, which led him to visit China in February 1972. Later that year he also signed the ANTIBALLISTIC MISSILE SYSTEMS TREATY with the Soviet Union, which had resulted from the first round of Strategic Arms Limitation Talks.

The 1972 presidential election favored the Republicans. Though Nixon had his critics on the left and in the Democratic Party, he was popular with a majority of Americans, who agreed with his foreign and domestic policies. He faced no meaningful challenges for renomination in his own party. The Democrats seemed to be less sure of either their direction or the mood of the country. The party ultimately nominated the liberal antiwar South Dakota senator George McGovern, who campaigned for liberalized abortion rights, amnesty for Vietnam draft dodgers, and legalization of drugs, among other goals.

Given this context, it is difficult to understand why Nixon and his campaign staff burglarized and bugged the Democratic National Committee's headquarters at the Watergate Hotel in Washington, D.C. The facts behind "long national nightmare" of Watergate, as President GERALD FORD* later described it, were not known by the American people during the election campaign of 1972, and Richard Nixon was easily reelected to a second term, carrying 49 states and winning a landslide in the Electoral College, 520-17.

Nixon's second term was almost entirely consumed with the Watergate scandal. On June 17, 1972, five individuals later associated with the PLUMBERS unit in the White House had been arrested for burglarizing the Democratic National Committee's headquarters. Two reporters for the *Washington Post*, Robert Woodward and Carl Bernstein, stayed with the story. Simultaneously, the case of the burglars landed in the

courtroom of U.S. district judge John Sirica, who oversaw guilty verdicts in January 1973 and recommended that further investigations be conducted.

The following month, the Select Committee on Presidential Campaign Activities was established in the Senate with Sam Ervin, a North Carolina Democrat, as chairman. As Ervin's investigation progressed, more and more damning evidence against the White House was introduced, including testimony in March 1973 that high-ranking presidential aides and perhaps even the president had ordered the coverup of the Watergate scandal. Demands for a special prosecutor intensified, and Nixon named Harvard University law professor Archibald Cox to the post. At the same time, Ervin's committee began extended televised hearings, which lasted into November. A major breakthrough occurred on July 16, 1973, when testimony was received about the secret White House taping system. All parties investigating Watergate demanded access to the tapes, and to prevent access Nixon ordered Cox fired in October. The result was the SATURDAY NIGHT MASSACRE in which a number of Justice Department officials resigned or were fired.

In early 1974 more Nixon officials were indicted for their roles in Watergate, and in late July the Supreme Court ruled unanimously that the White House must turn over the tapes. Concurrently, the House Judiciary Committee had begun impeachment hearings. It voted out to the full House four articles of impeachment. Congressional insiders predicted that Nixon could not withstand either that vote or the Senate vote on conviction. As a result, President Nixon resigned his position on August 9, 1974, the only president ever to resign from office.

Many felt Nixon's disgrace would be permanent. However, only a few years later, he emerged to defend himself in television interviews and in his own writings, the most famous being the interviews he gave with British journalist David Frost in 1977 when he contended, regarding Watergate, "When the President does it, that means that it is not illegal." Critics assailed his performances as self-serving. Administration insiders and Watergate participants also propagated their versions of what happened from 1969 to 1974, often undercutting each other and Nixon at the same time. Psychoanalysts, film directors, novelists, historians, political scientists, and comedians labored in the years afterward to analyze and interpret his personality, motives, and actions. By the early 1990s, some academics hailed the liberal domestic achievements of his administration. For others the foresight and wisdom of certain of his foreign policy initiatives became gradually apparent. He traveled the world, speaking and writing copiously on foreign policy and the state of geopolitics. American and foreign politicians and diplomats sought his advice and counsel, and by the late 1980s he had secured a rehabilitation to a degree among a segment of the American public, although not among others.

* For more information on Gerald Ford, Richard Nixon's vice president, see the chapter on Ford, who was president from 1974 to 1977.

Articles by Bob Woodward *(left)* and Carl Bernstein of the *Washington Post* exposed the Watergate scandal that eventually led to President Nixon's resignation in 1974. *(Washington Post/Getty Images)*

Nixon died on April 22, 1994, in New York at age 81, a conflicted man with a conflicted reputation. His passing brought bipartisan response, praising his long record of public service and his foreign policy vision while expressing little acrimony regarding the Watergate scandal. Four former presidents attended his funeral, and Democratic president BILL CLINTON offered a eulogy. In his own eulogy, Kansas Republican senator Robert Dole described the last half of the 20th century as the "Age of Nixon."

PRESIDENTIAL ELECTION OF 1968

—ww—

By 1968, many traditionalists believed American society to be unraveling under the pressures of an overseas war, internal division, and cultural rot. The Civil Rights movement had essentially stagnated. Martin Luther King, Jr.'s attempt to export southern style nonviolent direct action to fight the north's de facto segregation had met stiff resistance. A more militant activism adopting the rhetoric of Black Power had emerged. Many American whites in the North, West, and Midwest—supportive of black demands while they had been directed at the white southern power structure—now bridled at demands for greater equality closer to home. Federal efforts to integrate northern neighborhoods and schools heightened tensions. For many African Americans, however, their gains came too slowly. The Great Society had dramatically reduced poverty, and the Johnson administration's efforts on behalf of civil rights had landed a killing blow against southern de jure segregation, but frustrations remained. Each summer from 1964 to 1968 race riots broke out in major American cities, with the worst coming in Detroit in 1967. Forty-three died in that city, and tensions could be calmed only by use of the National Guard. Black fury at continuing discrimination produced an equally determined white backlash among people who felt blacks had come too far too fast.

Young people, members of the huge generation born after World War II, also appeared in a state of revolt. The first American generation to be raised in middle-class comfort, they began to rebel, and that rebellion manifested itself in ways both ephemeral and long lasting. Clothes changed, as did hairstyles. Criticism of, and contrarian responses to, the norms and standards of middle-class America enraged parents and authority figures. Music celebrated defiance and demanded change. Drug use among white middle-class young people increased, with readily available alternatives ranging from marijuana to LSD. Premarital sexual activity, and its more open expression, flourished with improved methods of birth control and looser laws governing contraception and reproductive health. Though the politically active represented a distinct minority among this generation, youth protests grew from support of civil rights during the early 1960s into outright challenges to authority—free speech at universities and opposition to the draft and to the Vietnam War. The earliest protests against the war dated from the introduction of American combat forces in March 1965. By 1968, demonstrations often mustered tens of thousands in major American cities. In the first six months of 1968 alone, 101 American colleges and universities experienced protest demonstrations against either the war or local issues.

The war in Vietnam also took a dramatic turn for the worse. The government had told Americans that U.S. and South Vietnamese forces were winning the war. Progress was slow, but it was progress nonetheless, the Johnson administration assured Americans. At the end of January 1968, however, Vietcong and North Vietnamese Army forces launched a massive offensive, striking 100 different points throughout the whole of South Vietnam. It took until mid-March for the situation to stabilize, with communist forces suffering massive casualties. American deaths had also increased to nearly 300 a week in the first quarter of 1968. The Tet offensive proved a tactical defeat for the communists, but a strategic victory. Feeling deceived by their government, the American people turned decisively against the war, and against President LYNDON B. JOHNSON. Student protesters outside the White House regularly chanted, "Hey, hey, LBJ! How many kids did you kill today?" The previous summer, Johnson reversed himself and raised taxes to help pay for the war, while keeping Great Society spending on target. The result was public displeasure together with the first stirrings of inflation.

Still, as sitting president, Johnson appeared likely to hold on to the Democratic presidential nomination that year. However, a little-known contender, depending upon a volunteer staff and a shoestring budget, Minnesota senator Eugene McCarthy challenged LBJ on an antiwar platform in the party's early primaries. McCarthy entered the race in November 1967. Though an articulate liberal with 10 years of Senate service, McCarthy was not a strong candidate. He seemed more professorial than presidential. Nor had he amassed a significant record during his Senate service. Despite a disorganized campaign and a poor public speaking style, McCarthy made a strong showing in the New Hampshire primary on March 12. Events outside the campaign, namely the Tet offensive on January 30, 1968, thrust McCarthy into the role of a serious challenger to Johnson. Shedding their long hair and scruffy appearance, antiwar protesters suddenly decided they would be "Clean for Gene." Johnson still won in New Hampshire, but the divide was 49.4 percent to 42.2 percent when all had expected the president to win an easy victory.

McCarthy's showing encouraged New York senator Robert F. Kennedy, the late president's brother and bitter enemy of Johnson's to join the race. He announced his candidacy on March 16. Kennedy promised "new policies" on Vietnam and suggested he would expand social justice at home.

At the end of March, Johnson dropped out of the race and began peace overtures toward the North Vietnamese. He told a nationally televised audience, "I shall not seek and I will not accept the nomination of my party for another term as your President." He turned his support to Vice President Hubert Humphrey, a man of sterling liberal credentials, who was nonetheless hampered by his connection to Johnson and the war. Humphrey had a long record of success in U.S. politics, beginning as mayor of Minneapolis, then as U.S. senator from Minnesota, and finally as vice president. He had worked for civil rights throughout his career, and he was clearly identified with liberal causes. Still, he was at a disadvantage in the hunt for delegates with most of the primaries already over when he entered the race. Humphrey would have to find his backers from party bosses tied to Johnson. As a result, he would not be able to run against the war. As Humphrey observed, "If I run, Johnson's not going to make it easy." More important, Humphrey did not understand the national mood in 1968, running on the theme "politics of joy" in the midst of a year that was anything but joyous.

The Johnson announcement and the Humphrey candidacy made the contest for antiwar voters all the more important. McCarthy backers, generally middle-class liberals, were not at all willing to drop their man for the better-known Kennedy. Kennedy drew support away from McCarthy, mainly working class and minority voters, and as the summer neared, the Democratic nomination appeared a two-way battle between Humphrey and Kennedy, with McCarthy hanging on by a thread.

On April 4, Martin Luther King, Jr., was assassinated in Memphis, Tennessee. The deed unleashed a torrent of rage in the black community, as more than 100 cities experienced rioting. One of the only cities that did not riot was Indianapolis. Kennedy was campaigning there when he learned the news of King's death. He told his largely African-American audience what had happened in an impromptu speech in which he quoted the poet Aeschylus—"In our sleep, pain which cannot forget falls drop by drop upon the heart until, in our own despair, against our will, comes wisdom through the awful grace of God"—and he drew on his own personal pain from the assassination of his brother: "For those of you who are black and are tempted to be filled with hatred and distrust at the injustice of such an act, against all white people, I can only say that I feel in my own heart the same kind of feeling. I had a member of my family killed, but he was killed by a white man. But we have to make an effort in the United States, we have to make an effort to understand, to go beyond these rather difficult times." Kennedy's words helped ensure that Indianapolis remained calm.

The rioting nationwide only added to white backlash, and made more attractive the candidacy of a third-party contender, former Alabama governor George C. Wallace. Wallace's defiant support of segregation had endeared him to many southerners, but his masterful ability to capitalize on the chaos of the mid-1960s allowed him to make inroads elsewhere. As the candidate of the newly formed American Independent Party, he told supporters, "there's an awful lot of us rednecks in this country—and they're not all in the South!" In 1968, he attacked civil rights and antiwar protesters, suggesting that if an "anarchist" laid down in front of his car, it would be the last time.

In the aftermath of King's assassination, Kennedy prospered with voters, winning primaries in Indiana, Nebraska, and South Dakota but losing to McCarthy in Oregon. Kennedy's win in California meant that he would pose a serious challenge for the nomination. However, the nation's travails continued when Robert Kennedy fell to an assassin's bullet on

Senator Robert Kennedy meets with enthusiastic supporters in Indianapolis in May 1968. He would be assassinated one month later. *(Paul Shane/Associated Press)*

President Johnson *(right)* meets with Nixon in the White House in July 1968. *(Executive Office of the President of the United States)*

June 5 just after winning the California primary, and nearly locking up the Democratic nomination.

Nixon's own path toward the Republican nomination proved relatively smooth. Above all else, the party wanted to avoid a repeat of the ideological disaster of 1964, when Barry Goldwater challenged Johnson from the far right. Nixon's role as conciliator of the party's factions since 1964 did not assure him a coronation, but by doing so he had built up goodwill with important constituencies. New York governor Nelson A. Rockefeller, Michigan governor George Romney, and Illinois senator Charles Percy represented the center and left of the party. Of the three, Romney presented the most serious threat to Nixon. He was a former president of American Motors and a popular governor. In polling taken between late 1966 and mid-1967, Romney bested Johnson for the White House. Romney did himself in, though, with an ill-timed comment suggesting he had been "brainwashed" by military officials when he visited Vietnam in 1965. After that remark was publicized, journalists and pundits questioned whether Romney was able to think for himself. Romney abandoned his presidential bid on February 28, 1968.

Nixon had served two terms as vice president from 1953 to 1961 and had narrowly lost the presidential election of 1960 to JOHN F. KENNEDY. Two years later he failed in his bid to become governor of California. Nixon's defeats of 1960 and 1962 represented the best argument against the former vice president. To address this problem, Nixon entered the prima-

ries in early 1968. In New Hampshire in March, given Romney's withdrawal, Nixon bested Rockefeller's write-in effort by a seven-to-one margin, convincing the New Yorker to stay out of the contest. Conservatives, who had mistrusted Nixon since 1960, looked to a possible bid by first-term California governor RONALD REAGAN. By early May, however, a delegate count showed Nixon with enough pledged support to win the nomination. His strong showing in the mid-May Oregon primary solidified that lead all the more. In mid-July, former president DWIGHT D. EISENHOWER made a direct and firm endorsement of his former vice president for the Republican nomination, leading some to speculate what might have been had he been as forthright in 1960. The Republican National Convention in Miami Beach in late July 1968 held few surprises. Conservatives' best hopes to stop Nixon faded after South Carolina senator Strom Thurmond and other southern conservatives declined to back Reagan and threw their support to Nixon instead. Their support came at a price, however. As president, Nixon promised to go easy on integration of the region's schools and back away from busing as a means of achieving desegregation. As his running mate, the nominee chose Maryland governor SPIRO T. AGNEW. Agnew gained conservative plaudits for his hard line against black leaders, urban rioting, and student protests in his state.

Following Robert Kennedy's death in June, the Democratic Party lurched toward chaos. Kennedy's following scattered: Some returned to the establishment fold and

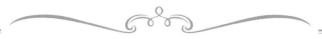

SPIRO T. AGNEW
(1918–1996) *vice president of the United States, January 20, 1969–October 10, 1973*

The son of a Greek immigrant father, Theodore Spiro Agnew (Anagnostopoulos in Greece) and Margaret Pollard Akers Agnew, Spiro Theodore Agnew was born on November 9, 1918. Theodore Agnew was a successful restaurateur until losing his business in the Great Depression. The family lived in Baltimore, Maryland, and after Spiro graduated high school, he matriculated Johns Hopkins University. After studying chemistry there for three years, he attended night classes at the University of Baltimore School of Law while working for a grocery chain and in the insurance business. He met and married Elinor Isabel Judefind, another worker in the insurance industry, in 1942. The couple had four children.

Agnew served as a tank commander in the army during World War II, fighting in the European theater. Once the war was over, he returned to school on the GI Bill and completed his LL.B. at the University of Baltimore in 1947 and his LL.D. at the University of Maryland in 1949. Although he had grown up in a Democratic family and had registered in that party, in 1946 he affiliated with the Republican Party in hopes of making a career in politics. His first political office was an appointed post with the Baltimore County Zoning Board of Appeals in 1957. In 1960, he ran for and lost a race for associate circuit judge. He also lost his seat on the zoning appeals board when the more powerful Democratic Party in Baltimore County decided to give the job to someone else. His protest against that decision was enough to secure his election as county executive, the first Republican to hold the post since 1895. He was elected governor of Maryland in 1966 against a segregationist Democrat, and he amassed a significant record of reform in his first year on the job. With time, he moved to the right, cutting state funds for welfare and health and striking back against civil rights protesters.

In the 1968 presidential campaign, Agnew had been an early supporter of New York governor Nelson Rockefeller, but when he dropped out, he shifted his allegiance to Richard Nixon. Nixon responded by selecting Agnew to be his running mate, a decision that caused many Americans to ask, "Spiro who?" While Agnew helped the ticket with white southerners, he created illwill among ethnic Americans with his frequent racist slurs, such as calling Polish Americans "Polacks" and a Japanese-American journalist a "fat Jap."

He used his office as vice president to speak critically about antiwar protesters and the "liberal media," calling the former "an effete corps of impudent snobs who characterize themselves as intellectuals" and the latter "a tiny and closed fraternity of privileged men, elected by no one, and enjoying a monopoly sanctioned and licensed by government." Among his more famous insults was his general characterization of Nixon critics as "pusil-lanimous pussyfooters." Historians have contended that White House speechwriters Pat Buchanan and William Safire scripted many of Agnew's remarks.

For conservative Americans, many who wore buttons proclaiming "Spiro Is My Hero," Agnew was a fresh new voice in American politics. Following the 1972 presidential election, though, he faced a scandal from which he could not recover. A federal grand jury in Maryland charged that he had taken bribes from construction companies while an official there. The panel also charged that the kickbacks continued into Agnew's vice-presidential years. The belligerent vice president responded angrily that he was innocent and that "I won't resign if indicted." However, veracity of the case was proven, and Agnew ultimately pleaded no contest to a charge of tax evasion. He was given a sentence of three years' probation and a $10,000 fine, and he was compelled to resign as vice president, effective October 10, 1973. He was the only vice president ever to resign from office. He was disbarred in Maryland, and 10 years later in a civil court action he was forced to repay the bribes with interest, which totaled $268,000. He lived quietly for the remainder of his life in Maryland. Spiro Agnew died on September 17, 1996.

Spiro T. Agnew *(Library of Congress)*

supported Vice President Humphrey, others departed for antiwar candidates such as McCarthy or dark horse South Dakota senator George McGovern. However, in reality the contest was a two-man struggle between Humphrey and McCarthy, who seemed to be losing interest in the struggle. As front-runner, Humphrey took on much of the venomous antiwar criticism that had been directed at President Johnson, with protesters chanting "Dump the Hump" and "Why Change the Ventriloquist for the Dummy?" when the Minnesotan appeared before crowds. The Democratic National Convention held that August in Chicago tapped Vice President Hubert Humphrey, though he had not won a single primary, by a delegate count of 1,760 to 601. Maine senator Edmund Muskie was nominated for vice president. The brokered convention embittered many, but rage was directed not solely toward Humphrey's nomination. Protesters were also irate that the strong antiwar plank was defeated. Anger spilled out onto the convention floor, as resolutions critical of the administration's conduct of the Vietnam War failed.

Humphrey, despite sterling liberal credentials, appeared badly tainted by his association with LBJ. Outside the convention hall, hundreds of thousands of protesters representing all walks of life gathered to demand an end to the war. Fringe elements among the demonstrators clashed violently with Chicago police, and the police attacked all those gathered outside the convention. The melee that followed appeared live on television on a split screen as Humphrey gave his acceptance speech, again calling for a "politics of joy." After the Democrats' brawl, Nixon took a big lead in the polls, but George Wallace's high level of support seemed capable of denying him a majority.

Throughout the campaign, the Wallace factor complicated calculations of the major party candidates and press observers. In September, polls showed the former Alabama governor with 20 percent support; early the next month, that number had risen to 22 percent. Though he could not win, the independent candidate stood to provoke a constitutional crisis by forcing the election into the House of Repre-

A smiling candidate Nixon, surrounded by Secret Service agents, greets supporters in Buena Park, California, on August 16, 1968. *(Associated Press)*

1968 Election Statistics

State	Number of Electors	Total Popular Vote	Elec Vote			Pop Vote			Margin of Victory	
			R	D	AI	R	D	AI	Votes	% Total Vote
Alabama	10	1,049,917			10	3	2	1	49,656	4.73%
Alaska	3	83,035	3			1	2	3	2,189	2.64%
Arizona	5	486,936	5			1	2	3	96,207	19.76%
Arkansas	6	609,590			6	2	3	1	4,161	0.68%
California	40	7,251,587	40			1	2	3	223,346	3.08%
Colorado	6	811,199	6			1	2	3	74,171	9.14%
Connecticut	8	1,256,232		8		2	1	3	64,840	5.16%
Delaware	3	214,367	3			1	2	3	7,520	3.51%
District of Columbia	3	170,578		3		2	1	-	108,554	63.64%
Florida	14	2,187,805	14			1	2	3	210,010	9.60%
Georgia	12	1,250,266			12	2	3	1	45,671	3.65%
Hawaii	4	236,218		4		2	1	3	49,899	21.12%
Idaho	4	291,183	4			1	2	3	76,096	26.13%
Illinois	26	4,619,749	26			1	2	3	134,960	2.92%
Indiana	13	2,123,597	13			1	2	3	261,226	12.30%
Iowa	9	1,167,931	9			1	2	3	142,407	12.19%
Kansas	7	872,783	7			1	2	3	175,678	20.13%
Kentucky	9	1,055,893	9			1	2	3	64,870	6.14%
Louisiana	10	1,097,450			10	3	2	1	52,080	4.75%
Maine	4	392,936		4		2	1	3	48,058	12.23%
Maryland	10	1,235,039		10		2	1	3	20,315	1.64%
Massachusetts	14	2,331,752		14		2	1	3	702,374	30.12%
Michigan	21	3,306,250		21		2	1	3	222,417	6.73%
Minnesota	10	1,588,510		10		2	1	3	199,095	12.53%
Mississippi	7	654,509			7	3	2	1	62,128	9.49%
Missouri	12	1,809,502	12			1	2	3	20,488	1.13%
Montana	4	274,404	4			1	2	3	24,718	9.01%
Nebraska	5	536,851	5			1	2	3	150,379	28.01%
Nevada	3	154,218	3			1	2	3	12,590	8.16%
New Hampshire	4	297,299	4			1	2	3	24,314	8.18%
New Jersey	17	2,875,395	17			1	2	3	61,261	2.13%
New Mexico	4	327,281	4			1	2	3	39,611	12.10%
New York	43	6,790,066		43		2	1	3	370,538	5.46%
North Carolina	13	1,587,493	12		1	1	3	2	163,079	10.27%
North Dakota	4	247,882	4			1	2	3	43,900	17.71%
Ohio	26	3,959,698	26			1	2	3	90,428	2.28%
Oklahoma	8	943,086	8			1	2	3	148,039	15.70%
Oregon	6	819,622	6			1	2	3	49,567	6.05%
Pennsylvania	29	4,747,928		29		2	1	3	169,388	3.57%
Rhode Island	4	385,000		4		2	1	3	124,159	32.25%
South Carolina	8	666,982	8			1	3	2	56,576	8.48%
South Dakota	4	281,264	4			1	2	3	31,818	11.31%
Tennessee	11	1,248,617	11			1	3	2	121,359	9.72%
Texas	25	3,079,406		25		2	1	3	38,960	1.27%
Utah	4	422,568	4			1	2	3	82,063	19.42%
Vermont	3	161,404	3			1	2	3	14,887	9.22%
Virginia	12	1,361,491	12			1	2	3	147,932	10.87%
Washington	9	1,304,281		9		2	1	3	27,527	2.11%
West Virginia	7	754,206		7		2	1	3	66,536	8.82%
Wisconsin	12	1,691,538	12			1	2	3	61,193	3.62%
Wyoming	3	127,205	3			1	2	3	25,754	20.25%
Total	538	73,199,999	301	191	46	1	2	3	511,944	0.70%

Nixon Republican		Humphrey Democratic		Wallace American Independent		Others	
146,923	13.99%	196,579	18.72%	691,425	65.86%	14,990	1.43%
37,600	45.28%	35,411	42.65%	10,024	12.07%	0	0.00%
266,721	54.78%	170,514	35.02%	46,573	9.56%	3,128	0.64%
189,062	31.01%	184,901	30.33%	235,627	38.65%	0	0.00%
3,467,664	47.82%	3,244,318	44.74%	487,270	6.72%	52,335	0.72%
409,345	50.46%	335,174	41.32%	60,813	7.50%	5,867	0.72%
556,721	44.32%	621,561	49.48%	76,650	6.10%	1,300	0.10%
96,714	45.12%	89,194	41.61%	28,459	13.28%	0	0.00%
31,012	18.18%	139,566	81.82%	0	0.00%	0	0.00%
886,804	40.53%	676,794	30.93%	624,207	28.53%	0	0.00%
380,111	30.40%	334,440	26.75%	535,550	42.83%	165	0.01%
91,425	38.70%	141,324	59.83%	3,469	1.47%	0	0.00%
165,369	56.79%	89,273	30.66%	36,541	12.55%	0	0.00%
2,174,774	47.08%	2,039,814	44.15%	390,958	8.46%	14,203	0.31%
1,067,885	50.29%	806,659	37.99%	243,108	11.45%	5,945	0.28%
619,106	53.01%	476,699	40.82%	66,422	5.69%	5,704	0.49%
478,674	54.84%	302,996	34.72%	88,921	10.19%	2,192	0.25%
462,411	43.79%	397,541	37.65%	193,098	18.29%	2,843	0.27%
257,535	23.47%	309,615	28.21%	530,300	48.32%	0	0.00%
169,254	43.07%	217,312	55.30%	6,370	1.62%	0	0.00%
517,995	41.94%	538,310	43.59%	178,734	14.47%	0	0.00%
766,844	32.89%	1,469,218	63.01%	87,088	3.73%	8,602	0.37%
1,370,665	41.46%	1,593,082	48.18%	331,968	10.04%	10,535	0.32%
658,643	41.46%	857,738	54.00%	68,931	4.34%	3,198	0.20%
88,516	13.52%	150,644	23.02%	415,349	63.46%	0	0.00%
811,932	44.87%	791,444	43.74%	206,126	11.39%	0	0.00%
138,835	50.60%	114,117	41.59%	20,015	7.29%	1,437	0.52%
321,163	59.82%	170,784	31.81%	44,904	8.36%	0	0.00%
73,188	47.46%	60,598	39.29%	20,432	13.25%	0	0.00%
154,903	52.10%	130,589	43.93%	11,173	3.76%	634	0.21%
1,325,467	46.10%	1,264,206	43.97%	262,187	9.12%	23,535	0.82%
169,692	51.85%	130,081	39.75%	25,737	7.86%	1,771	0.54%
3,007,932	44.30%	3,378,470	49.76%	358,864	5.29%	44,800	0.66%
627,192	39.51%	464,113	29.24%	496,188	31.26%	0	0.00%
138,669	55.94%	94,769	38.23%	14,244	5.75%	200	0.08%
1,791,014	45.23%	1,700,586	42.95%	467,495	11.81%	603	0.02%
449,697	47.68%	301,658	31.99%	191,731	20.33%	0	0.00%
408,433	49.83%	358,866	43.78%	49,683	6.06%	2,640	0.32%
2,090,017	44.02%	2,259,405	47.59%	378,582	7.97%	19,924	0.42%
122,359	31.78%	246,518	64.03%	15,678	4.07%	445	0.12%
254,062	38.09%	197,486	29.61%	215,430	32.30%	4	0.00%
149,841	53.27%	118,023	41.96%	13,400	4.76%	0	0.00%
472,592	37.85%	351,233	28.13%	424,792	34.02%	0	0.00%
1,227,844	39.87%	1,266,804	41.14%	584,269	18.97%	489	0.02%
238,728	56.49%	156,665	37.07%	26,906	6.37%	269	0.06%
85,142	52.75%	70,255	43.53%	5,104	3.16%	903	0.56%
590,319	43.36%	442,387	32.49%	321,833	23.64%	6,952	0.51%
588,510	45.12%	616,037	47.23%	96,990	7.44%	2,744	0.21%
307,555	40.78%	374,091	49.60%	72,560	9.62%	0	0.00%
809,997	47.89%	748,804	44.27%	127,835	7.56%	4,902	0.29%
70,927	55.76%	45,173	35.51%	11,105	8.73%	0	0.00%
31,783,783	43.42%	31,271,839	42.72%	9,901,118	13.53%	243,259	0.33%

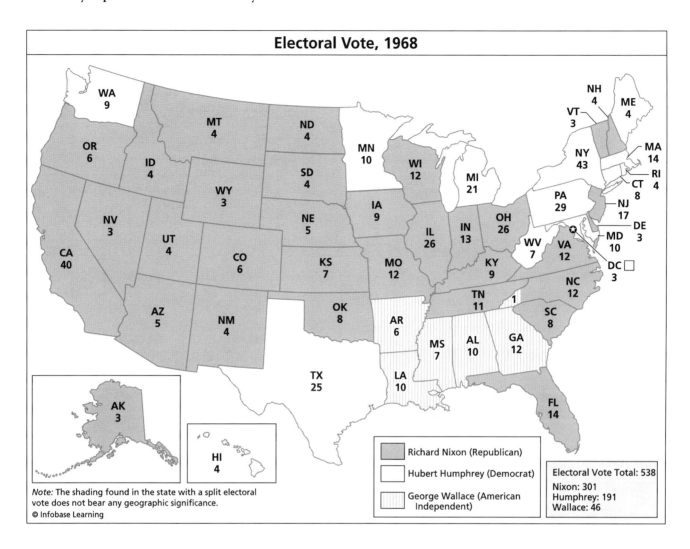

Electoral Vote, 1968

Richard Nixon (Republican)

Hubert Humphrey (Democrat)

George Wallace (American Independent)

Electoral Vote Total: 538
Nixon: 301
Humphrey: 191
Wallace: 46

Note: The shading found in the state with a split electoral vote does not bear any geographic significance.
© Infobase Learning

sentatives. Both Nixon and Humphrey worried that Wallace leeched support from them, though Nixon probably did so with more reason. The Alabamian depended upon middle- and working-class discontent for his support, exactly those elements that Nixon needed to woo. Republican strategist Kevin Phillips urged the Nixon campaign to carefully play upon the passions and hatreds unleashed in the last several years. Steal Wallace's thunder without sounding like Wallace, he urged. Nixon hit the right tone, and Wallace's support began to decline. Many later argued that the Republican nominee utilized almost a coded rhetoric to attract votes, playing upon simmering racial hostilities and fear of the disorder of the times. Certainly, Nixon knew what he was doing when he and his campaign took this tack in appealing to voters.

The race remained close, with none of the candidates receiving a majority in the polls throughout October. Nixon's lead over Humphrey widened, but its breadth was curbed by the refusal of Wallace's diehard supporters to migrate to the Republican. The war in Vietnam loomed as the main issue of the 1968 race. Nixon told voters that he had a secret plan to end the war, and that he alone was tough enough to force the com-

munists to grant "peace with honor." Wallace insisted that the war should be won at all costs, and his vice-presidential pick, former Air Force general Curtis LeMay, even suggested the use of nuclear weapons to bomb North Vietnam "back to the Stone Age." Humphrey could not move away from his support for administration policy on the conflict. If the vice president had a chance, it would have to be provided by his boss, President Lyndon Johnson. In secret, negotiations with the North Vietnamese for an American exit from the war had been ongoing since the spring. As October drew to a close, those seemed to be bearing fruit. For Johnson, the question was when, rather than whether, to announce these tidings. Both Nixon and Humphrey knew of the negotiations, and both had pledged to remain silent about them in order to avoid mishaps that might scuttle them. Both Nixon and Humphrey were kept informed about the talks by negotiator Henry Kissinger, a Harvard professor and protégé of Nelson Rockefeller.

On October 31, five days before the election, President Johnson announced a bombing halt in response to progress in the Paris negotiations. North Vietnam promised to keep its forces north of the demilitarized zone separating the two

Vietnams. Hanoi also agreed to not attack South Vietnamese cities and to participate in expanded talks, potentially including the South Vietnamese and Vietcong to begin the Wednesday after the American elections. Public response to the bombing halt was overwhelmingly positive, and Humphrey's support surged. The Nixon campaign reeled with the sudden shift of fortunes, but it quickly rebounded. Through contacts with South Vietnamese president Nguyen Van Thieu, Nixon sent assurances of his continued support for the South's independence and for U.S. military aid. Thieu, who had no intention of cooperating with the peace process, came away emboldened and he defied Johnson. The White House knew what Nixon was doing because of FBI surveillance, but administration officials could not communicate with the public Nixon's illegal behavior without revealing their own illegal activities. The South Vietnamese leader's rejection of talks dampened public hopes and Humphrey's likely chances in the bargain. Certainly Nixon helped create that image by blaming the failures on the Democrats. Nixon narrowly won the election with 43.4 percent of the popular vote (301 electoral votes); Humphrey posted 42.7 percent (191 electoral votes), and Wallace's threat peaked at 13.5 percent (46 electoral votes). The turmoil and bitterness of 1968 permeated the campaign, and from the beginning of his administration, the events of that year colored Nixon's approach to governing. Just as important, the vote in 1968 constituted a negative mandate. Voters had not chosen Nixon so much as they had rejected the status quo.

PRESIDENTIAL ELECTION OF 1972

—◊◊◊—

The 1972 presidential election by all accounts should have been a fairly simple affair for the incumbent president. During his first four years in office, Richard Nixon had acquitted himself well. His domestic policy, though more conservative than that of his predecessor, LYNDON JOHNSON, remained consistent with the trajectory of national politics established in the 1930s. Though he did try to shift a certain amount of budgetary control to the states, Nixon did not call for an elimination of any of the major reform programs enacted since the New Deal era. Regarding foreign affairs, Nixon's VIETNAMIZATION POLICY seemed to be working. At least American troop strength in Southeast Asia was being scaled back in meaningful ways. More important, he won bipartisan praise for his trip to China in which he began the process of DÉTENTE with that cold war enemy. For as many accomplishments as Nixon had on his record the eventual Democratic nominee, South Dakota senator George McGovern, seemed out of step with the ideological mood of the country, which was skewing rightward. He defended the legalization of abortion and illicit drugs while also calling for amnesty for Viet-

nam draft dodgers, leading some Republicans to dub him the candidate of "abortion, acid, and amnesty." Popular with liberals and many young people, McGovern generated something more akin to antipathy and animosity from long-term party activists. As such, Nixon would most likely have won his reelection contest with ease.

Richard Nixon's political paranoia led him and his campaign staff to make reckless, unwise, and illegal strategy decisions. The efforts of the president and his campaign staff, though, cannot be understood apart from the events of Nixon's first term in office. Fearful that he would have his reelection stolen from him, much as he believed had happened when he ran for and narrowly lost the presidency to JOHN F. KENNEDY in 1960, Nixon undertook an aggressive campaign. However, public opinion and the political milieu in 1972 suggested Nixon's strategy to be unnecessary.

The Democratic Party was not without a long list of contenders in 1972. Nixon's general popularity with the American people did not translate into favorable reviews from Democrats, who had viewed Nixon as a corrupt and contemptible figure since the 1950s. African-American representative Shirley Chisholm of New York, Senator Vance Hartke of Indiana, former vice president Hubert Humphrey, Washington senator Henry "Scoop" Jackson, New York City mayor John Lindsay, South Dakota senator George McGovern, Maine senator Edmund Muskie, Alabama governor George Wallace, and Los Angeles mayor Sam Yorty struggled to gain the upper hand. Of this large field, several of the candidates were never serious contenders: Chisholm, Hartke, Lindsay, and Yorty. Ironically, were it not for his nomination McGovern would also be on the list of second-tier candidates. Early in his campaign, he only polled 5 percent. His neo-populist tone and his liberal record made him a favorite with antiwar Democrats. Furthermore, he was associated with the McGovern-Fraser Commission, appointed in the aftermath of the 1968 Democratic convention to reform procedures within the Democratic National Committee and the presidential nominating process. That McGovern rose was due in part to his appeal to this constituency and in part to the weaknesses of other Democrats.

Humphrey suffered from his past support of the war. He was also late to enter the contest, serving only to show potential problems with McGovern, who had become the front-runner by the time the former vice president declared his candidacy. Hounded by press rumors about his wife's alleged infidelities and accused of using a derogatory term for French Canadians, Senator Muskie, the 1968 vice-presidential candidate, appeared to tear up under reporters questions, and he dropped out of the race shortly thereafter. Jackson ran as a cold war warrior without much success. Meanwhile, McGovern, campaigning as a strident opponent of the war and Nixon administration policy in Vietnam, found himself in a duel with Wallace for the nomination by late spring.

Representative Shirley Chisholm (D-NY) announcing her candidacy for the presidency *(Library of Congress)*

Wallace retained not only his strong stance on the war, but also found traction with the issue of busing. Not surprisingly, the Alabamian did well in southern primaries, but he augmented that base with wins and strong second-place finishes in the North and Midwest. On May 15, while campaigning in Washington, D.C.'s Maryland suburbs, Wallace was severely wounded and left paralyzed by a potential assassin. The next day, he handily won both the Maryland and the Michigan primaries, but the nomination ultimately went to McGovern. Wallace's health ultimately forced him to withdraw from the race.

Throughout the Democratic primaries, White House operatives, sometimes with President Nixon's approval and sometimes not, engaged in espionage against the various Democratic campaigns, resorting to dirty tricks in many cases in hopes of promoting discord. For example, when Muskie was still in the race and believed to be a front-runner, Nixon operatives placed orders for large amounts of alcohol and pizza for his campaign functions. Nixon officials

also appeared at Muskie rallies wearing signs that read "IF YOU LIKED HITLER YOU'LL LOVE WALLACE—VOTE MUSKIE." Though the only Democrat that posed a meaningful threat to Nixon's chances—Wallace—was out of the race in May, White House covert interference in the Democratic race continued, often crossing the line into illegality. These transgressions remained buried deep in the newspapers, but they would figure prominently later.

The Committee for the Reelection of the President, known more commonly as CREEP, most likely acting independently of the president's direct knowledge but, according to his general wishes, engaged in electronic surveillance of the Democratic National Committee's (DNC) offices, which were located in Washington, D.C.'s Watergate Hotel and office complex. In the early morning of June 17, 1972, five burglars were discovered and arrested in the DNC offices. That event, illegal in its own right, triggered a labyrinth of complex, devious activities designed to cover up the crime and White House knowledge of it. As a result the complicated series of events known as Watergate increased in severity with the passage of time. U.S. District judge John Sirica, into whose courtroom the case of the burglars fell, would pursue the Watergate affair with a vengeance.

Between the break-in and the election of 1972 four and a half months later, few people in Washington paid much attention to the crime or its larger meaning. Thus Nixon was easily reelected to the presidency over the unpopular McGovern. Furthermore, the president answered very few questions about the break-in, instead preferring to dissemble and deny. One of his most famous public comments came in an August 29, 1972, press conference when he declared, "what really hurts is if you try to cover it up." Privately, however, Nixon often instructed his staff that they should "stonewall" any unfriendly questions.

Ironically, McGovern had helped determine the key characteristics of his presidential nominating convention long before he became a front-runner for his party's ticket. As a result of the McGovern-Fraser Commission's work on party structure and delegate selection, the convention that was seated in 1972 at Miami Beach, Florida, was younger and more ethnically diverse than any previous major party convention. The delegation in 1972 was also less politically sophisticated and less tied to the hierarchy of the Democratic Party. Additionally, the O'Hara Commission redrew the rules for Democratic conventions, including time limits for speeches, bans on floor demonstrations, legalistic procedures for credentials challenges, and a lottery to determine floor seating.

One other aspect of rules changes from the McGovern-Fraser Commission's work threatened McGovern's nomination. While on the commission he had helped to draft new rules whereby delegates from each state would be determined proportionally as opposed to a winner-take-all system. Under this rule, he stood to have far fewer delegates from large states such as California, leaving him just short of assured nomination on the first ballot. Even though he had helped write the proportional rule, McGovern challenged it before the convention's credentials committee, which agreed with the proportional allocation. McGovern took his case to the floor of the convention where he prevailed, paving the way for a first ballot nomination on July 12. Because of inferior preparation on the campaign's part and because of the new rules, McGovern was not able to deliver his acceptance speech until 3 A.M. Eastern Daylight Time, long after many television viewers had gone to bed.

McGovern made other mistakes. He and his staff did not appropriately vet his choice for the vice-presidential nomination, Senator Thomas Eagleton from Missouri. At first glance Eagleton seemed like a wise pick: He was from a swing state, he was popular with labor unions, he was Catholic, and he was from an urban area. Just 11 days after his July 14 nomination, though, he admitted to reporters that he had been hospitalized in the 1960s for nervous exhaustion. Part of his treatment had involved electric shocks. McGovern gave a press conference at which he remained loyal to Eagleton, but the episode failed to put to rest controversy surrounding Eagleton. Two days after the press conference, a Washington columnist wrote that Eagleton had a long history of drunk driving arrests, which Eagleton denied. Many party and campaign insiders pressed McGovern to call for Eagleton's resignation from the ticket. When McGovern did so, and Eagleton withdrew on July 31, the Democratic nominee was still in trouble, but this time for vacillating on the Eagleton issue. Eagleton's replacement, Kennedy-in-law Sargent Shriver, could not rescue the Democratic ticket's hopes despite his record of success as director of the Peace Corps, director of the Office of Economic Opportunity, and U.S. ambassador to France.

The Republican convention met the following month also in Miami Beach, following a controversy over its original site of San Diego. The International Telephone and Telegraph Company, which owned Sheraton Hotels, had donated a significant amount of money to the convention, between $200,000 and $400,000, in hopes of gaining the goodwill of the government in an antitrust suit filed against the company. To avoid controversy, the Republican National Committee moved the convention to Miami Beach. There Nixon for the first time in his career as a presidential candidate was nominated without a protracted fight. His two challengers, Representative Paul N. McCloskey of California and Representative John Ashbrook of Ohio, came at him from opposite ends of the political spectrum. McCloskey was a liberal opposed to the Vietnam War and Ashbrook charged Nixon with being too liberal. Nixon secured the nomination on August 22, 1972, by a vote of 1,317 to one. The one vote against him was cast for McCloskey. There was a somewhat more energetic move to remove Agnew from the ticket, but

ultimately it came to naught. Nixon stood by his vice president and the convention followed the lead of the president.

Three minor party presidential candidates entered the race that fall. The American Party, derived from Wallace's 1968 American Independent Party, nominated Representative John G. Schmitz and Thomas J. Anderson for president and vice president. Schmitz was a member of Congress from California and Anderson, of Pigeon Forge, Tennessee, edited a farm magazine. Both were members of the right-wing John Birch Society. The famous pediatrician, Dr. Benjamin Spock, ran for the presidency on the People's Party ticket. He had become an outspoken critic of the Vietnam War in 1965, and that was the focus of his quixotic campaign. Finally, the Libertarian Party nominated John Hospers, a philosophy professor. None of these minor party candidates had any serious impact on the election.

Throughout the fall campaign, McGovern was running far behind Nixon. After the conventions, polling gave Nixon a lead of 72 percent to 28 percent. Part of McGovern's problem was his inability to stitch together the Democratic coalition that had dominated national politics since the 1930s. Key labor leaders, specifically George Meany, president of the American Federation of Labor–Congress of Industrial Organizations (AFL-CIO), withheld support from the Democratic ticket. Another McGovern problem was his strained relations with the old urban party bosses, such as Mayor Richard Daley of Chicago, who had not attended the convention in protest of the party's direction.

Nixon used his office and his incumbency to his advantage in the fall race. He interacted with the media on his own terms, usually issuing statements about foreign policy and the economy. On the other hand, McGovern was everywhere before the press. He advocated an immediate end to the Vietnam War, wealth redistribution, budget reductions for the Pentagon, and more programs to combat domestic poverty. While much was written about his domestic policy recommendations, his constant availability to the media made it easier for journalists to cover the faults in his campaign as well. Though journalists generally distrusted the president, most newspaper editorial boards endorsed Nixon for a second term as president. Furthermore, nagging distrust of Nixon among a minority of the electorate proved less important than its critical views of McGovern. A majority of 60 percent of the voters believed the president trustworthy. More important, Nixon extended his presidential prerogatives to include a refusal to debate with McGovern or even issue attacks against his opponent in the press. Nixon's only significant public comment about McGovern encapsulated the image of the Democrat as unreliable: "McGovern last year . . . this year . . . what about next year?"

What could have been the biggest issue for McGovern, Watergate and the corruption it represented, never became a front-page issue during the campaign. When Representative

1972 Election Statistics

State	Number of Electors	Total Popular Vote	Elec Vote			Pop Vote		Margin of Victory	
			R	D	L*	R	D	Votes	% Total Vote
Alabama	9	1,006,093	9			1	2	471,778	46.89%
Alaska	3	95,219	3			1	2	22,382	23.51%
Arizona	6	653,505	6			1	2	204,272	31.26%
Arkansas	6	647,666	6			1	2	246,852	38.11%
California	45	8,367,862	45			1	2	1,126,249	13.46%
Colorado	7	953,884	7			1	2	267,209	28.01%
Connecticut	8	1,384,277	8			1	2	255,265	18.44%
Delaware	3	235,516	3			1	2	48,074	20.41%
District of Columbia	3	163,421		3		2	1	92,401	56.54%
Florida	17	2,583,283	17			1	2	1,139,642	44.12%
Georgia	12	1,174,772	12			1	2	591,967	50.39%
Hawaii	4	270,274	4			1	2	67,456	24.96%
Idaho	4	310,379	4			1	2	118,558	38.20%
Illinois	26	4,723,236	26			1	2	874,707	18.52%
Indiana	13	2,125,529	13			1	2	696,586	32.77%
Iowa	8	1,225,944	8			1	2	210,001	17.13%
Kansas	7	916,095	7			1	2	349,525	38.15%
Kentucky	9	1,067,499	9			1	2	305,287	28.60%
Louisiana	10	1,051,491	10			1	2	388,710	36.97%
Maine	4	417,271	4			1	2	95,874	22.98%
Maryland	10	1,353,812	10			1	2	323,524	23.90%
Massachusetts	14	2,458,756		14		2	1	220,462	8.97%
Michigan	21	3,490,325	21			1	2	502,286	14.39%
Minnesota	10	1,741,652	10			1	2	95,923	5.51%
Mississippi	7	645,963	7			1	2	378,343	58.57%
Missouri	12	1,852,589	12			1	2	455,527	24.59%
Montana	4	317,603	4			1	2	63,779	20.08%
Nebraska	5	576,289	5			1	2	236,307	41.00%
Nevada	3	181,766	3			1	2	49,734	27.36%
New Hampshire	4	334,059	4			1	2	97,289	29.12%
New Jersey	17	2,997,229	17			1	2	743,291	24.80%
New Mexico	4	385,931	4			1	2	94,522	24.49%
New York	41	7,161,830	41			1	2	1,241,694	17.34%
North Carolina	13	1,518,612	13			1	2	616,184	40.58%
North Dakota	3	280,514	3			1	2	73,725	26.28%
Ohio	25	4,094,787	25			1	2	882,938	21.56%
Oklahoma	8	1,029,900	8			1	2	511,878	49.70%
Oregon	6	927,946	6			1	2	93,926	10.12%
Pennsylvania	27	4,592,105	27			1	2	917,570	19.98%
Rhode Island	4	415,808	4			1	2	25,738	6.19%
South Carolina	8	677,880	8			1	2	289,157	42.66%
South Dakota	4	307,415	4			1	2	26,531	8.63%
Tennessee	10	1,201,182	10			1	2	455,854	37.95%
Texas	26	3,472,714	26			1	2	1,144,605	32.96%
Utah	4	478,476	4			1	2	197,359	41.25%
Vermont	3	186,946	3			1	2	48,975	26.20%
Virginia	12	1,457,019	11		1	1	2	549,606	37.72%
Washington	9	1,470,847	9			1	2	268,801	18.28%
West Virginia	6	762,399	6			1	2	207,529	27.22%
Wisconsin	11	1,852,890	11			1	2	179,256	9.67%
Wyoming	3	145,570	3			1	2	56,106	38.54%
Total	538	77,744,030	520	17	1	1	2	17,995,488	23.15%

* One elector voted for Libertarian candidate John Hospers for president.

Nixon Republican		McGovern Democratic		Others	
728,701	72.43%	256,923	25.54%	20,469	2.03%
55,349	58.13%	32,967	34.62%	6,903	7.25%
402,812	61.64%	198,540	30.38%	52,153	7.98%
445,751	68.82%	198,899	30.71%	3,016	0.47%
4,602,096	55.00%	3,475,847	41.54%	289,919	3.46%
597,189	62.61%	329,980	34.59%	26,715	2.80%
810,763	58.57%	555,498	40.13%	18,016	1.30%
140,357	59.60%	92,283	39.18%	2,876	1.22%
35,226	21.56%	127,627	78.10%	568	0.35%
1,857,759	71.91%	718,117	27.80%	7,407	0.29%
881,496	75.04%	289,529	24.65%	3,747	0.32%
168,865	62.48%	101,409	37.52%	0	0.00%
199,384	64.24%	80,826	26.04%	30,169	9.72%
2,788,179	59.03%	1,913,472	40.51%	21,585	0.46%
1,405,154	66.11%	708,568	33.34%	11,807	0.56%
706,207	57.61%	496,206	40.48%	23,531	1.92%
619,812	67.66%	270,287	29.50%	25,996	2.84%
676,446	63.37%	371,159	34.77%	19,894	1.86%
686,852	65.32%	298,142	28.35%	66,497	6.32%
256,458	61.46%	160,584	38.48%	229	0.05%
829,305	61.26%	505,781	37.36%	18,726	1.38%
1,112,078	45.23%	1,332,540	54.20%	14,138	0.58%
1,961,721	56.20%	1,459,435	41.81%	69,169	1.98%
898,269	51.58%	802,346	46.07%	41,037	2.36%
505,125	78.20%	126,782	19.63%	14,056	2.18%
1,154,058	62.29%	698,531	37.71%	0	0.00%
183,976	57.93%	120,197	37.85%	13,430	4.23%
406,298	70.50%	169,991	29.50%	0	0.00%
115,750	63.68%	66,016	36.32%	0	0.00%
213,724	63.98%	116,435	34.85%	3,900	1.17%
1,845,502	61.57%	1,102,211	36.77%	49,516	1.65%
235,606	61.05%	141,084	36.56%	9,241	2.39%
4,192,778	58.54%	2,951,084	41.21%	17,968	0.25%
1,054,889	69.46%	438,705	28.89%	25,018	1.65%
174,109	62.07%	100,384	35.79%	6,021	2.15%
2,441,827	59.63%	1,558,889	38.07%	94,071	2.30%
759,025	73.70%	247,147	24.00%	23,728	2.30%
486,686	52.45%	392,760	42.33%	48,500	5.23%
2,714,521	59.11%	1,796,951	39.13%	80,633	1.76%
220,383	53.00%	194,645	46.81%	780	0.19%
478,427	70.58%	189,270	27.92%	10,183	1.50%
166,476	54.15%	139,945	45.52%	994	0.32%
813,147	67.70%	357,293	29.75%	30,742	2.56%
2,298,896	66.20%	1,154,291	33.24%	19,527	0.56%
323,643	67.64%	126,284	26.39%	28,549	5.97%
117,149	62.66%	68,174	36.47%	1,623	0.87%
988,493	67.84%	438,887	30.12%	29,639	2.03%
837,135	56.92%	568,334	38.64%	65,378	4.44%
484,964	63.61%	277,435	36.39%	0	0.00%
989,430	53.40%	810,174	43.72%	53,286	2.88%
100,464	69.01%	44,358	30.47%	748	0.51%
47,168,710	60.67%	29,173,222	37.52%	1,402,098	1.80%

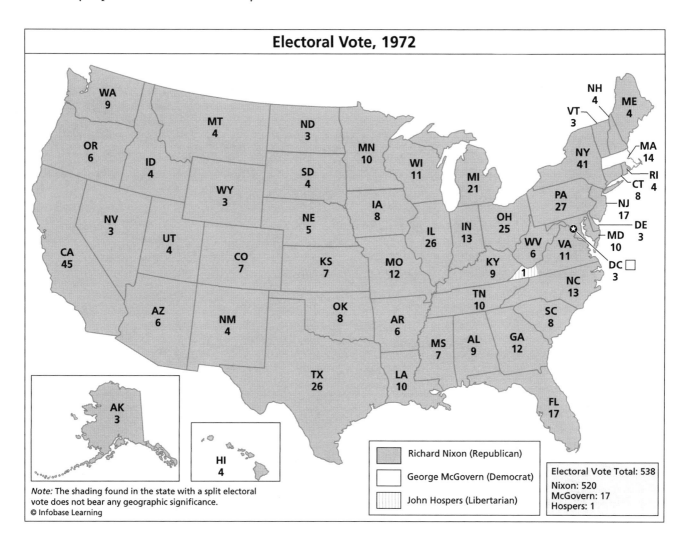

Electoral Vote, 1972

Note: The shading found in the state with a split electoral vote does not bear any geographic significance.
© Infobase Learning

Richard Nixon (Republican)
George McGovern (Democrat)
John Hospers (Libertarian)

Electoral Vote Total: 538
Nixon: 520
McGovern: 17
Hospers: 1

Wright Patman, the chair of the House Banking and Currency Committee, attempted an investigation before the election, arguing that failure to do so would be a corruption of democracy, his committee, including the Democratic majority, refused to vote for the subpoenas necessary to compel testimony. As events would later reveal, Nixon administration officials used leverage against several of the committee members, including suggestions that unrelated indictments against them would go unprosecuted if they cooperated with the president, to urge them to oppose their chairman on this partisan question. Beyond the failed Patman hearings, the only other public developments in the Watergate case that summer and fall included indictments by a federal grand jury against those involved with the initial Watergate break-in and a series of suits and countersuits for damages filed by the Democratic National Committee, the Republican National Committee, and individuals named in the case.

By using the trappings of his office, Nixon was able to frame the race and its questions about Vietnam and the future of the United States as a choice between his pledge of "peace with honor" and the risk of McGovern's search for "peace at any price." In 1972, voter turnout was lower than it had been since 1948, with just 55 percent of eligible voters casting a ballot. Additionally, ticket splitting was high. Nixon's victory did not translate into Republican gains down the ballot. Nixon carried all the states except Massachusetts and the District of Columbia. His popular vote margin of victory was 60.7 percent to 37.5 percent, one of the largest in American history. In the Electoral College the margin was much sharper, 520 to 17, with the one remaining vote going to Libertarian Party candidate John Hospers. The latter's Electoral College vote did not stem from his popularity, but rather from the action of one elector from Virginia, which had gone for Nixon, who was not willing to endorse the decision of his state. The American Party ticket polled just over 1 million votes, or 1.4 percent of the popular vote total. It earned no electoral votes, a decidedly worse performance than when Wallace headed the ticket in 1968. Spock performed even worse, polling only 78,801 votes, which was 0.1 percent of the popular vote total. The election results in 1972 reaffirmed the importance of centrism to American voters. For many, McGovern seemed too liberal, especially at a time when dis-

Richard Nixon in the back of a campaign motorcade in New York City. His wife Pat is beside him. *(National Archives)*

content was widespread over busing for school integration and the Vietnam War.

NIXON ADMINISTRATION (1969–1974)

—✹—

Nixon in Vietnam

During the 1968 presidential campaign, Republican candidate Richard Nixon told Americans that he had a secret plan for ending the Vietnam War and bringing "peace with honor." No such plan existed. Instead, Nixon and his national security advisor, Dr. Henry Kissinger, saw the Southeast Asian conflict as a sideshow that detracted from bigger for-eign policy ambitions. Vietnam, however, dominated the American political landscape, threatening to punish Nixon just as surely as it had helped elect him. Moreover, until some solution could be achieved, grander schemes would not matter much.

Though he had no plan going into office, Nixon's approach to Vietnam followed three basic threads. First, he kept up American military pressure, primarily through the use of airpower, in hopes of forcing concessions from the North Vietnamese and the Vietcong. Second, he began a phased withdrawal of American ground forces from the South, his VIETNAMIZATION POLICY, which led to a decline in casualties, and, third, he sought to diminish dissent and protest at home, which he and Kissinger felt weakened America's hand in world affairs. Behind this backdrop, negotiations

NIXON AND ELVIS: THE STORY BEHIND THE PICTURE

Among the most frequently requested items for reproduction from the National Archives is not something significant in the nation's founding or development as a democracy, such as the Constitution or the Bill of Rights. Rather, it is the photograph from rock star Elvis Presley's December 21, 1970, White House meeting with President Richard M. Nixon. Presley had written the president a handwritten, six-page letter requesting the meeting. The document was produced on American Airlines stationery. In it Presley stated, "I would like to introduce myself. I am Elvis Presley and admire you and Have Great Respect for your office. I talked to Vice President Agnew in Palm Springs 3 weeks ago and expressed my concern for our country. The Drug Culture, the Hippie Elements, The S.D.S., Black Panthers, etc do *not* consider me as their enemy or as they call it the Establishment. *I call it America and* I love it." He also asked to be made a federal agent at large in the Bureau of Narcotics and Dangerous Drugs. He told the president, "I have done an in depth study of Drug Abuse and Communist Brainwashing technique and I am right in the middle of the whole thing."

Presley personally delivered the letter to a security guard at the White House gates, and after a brief conversation convinced the guards and a White House aide that he was sincere. A meeting was arranged for later that day. A memorandum for the president explained the purpose of the meeting: "To thank Elvis Presley for his offer to help in trying to stop the drug epidemic in the country, and to ask him to work with us in bringing a more positive attitude to young people throughout the country." Soon after the two men met, Presley showed the president badges he had collected from local police departments around the country. Nixon told Presley that while he believed he could reach young people that to be effective the performer would have to remain credible. Presley countered that he did that by "just singing." Presley did not believe he would be effective if he tried to speak to the youth of the country. Running throughout the discussion at the meeting was a subtext revealing the shifts in rock and roll culture in the United States since Presley first became a sensation in the 1950s. According to the transcript of the meeting, the aging entertainer told the president that "the Beatles had been a real force for anti-American spirit. He said that the Beatles came to this country, made their money, and then returned to England where they promoted an anti-American theme." At the end of the meeting Presley stressed how much he supported the president and he even leaned in to give him a hug.

While the photograph of the two—Nixon in a business suit and Presley in one of the outfits he wore to perform—suggested a wide cultural chasm, many in Presley's audience were part of Nixon's "silent majority" of voters. Presley's last number one song, "Suspicious Minds," topped the charts on November 1, 1969. While it recounted a failing marriage, the chorus—"We can't go on together with suspicious minds (suspicious minds); / And we can't build our dreams on suspicious minds (suspicious minds)"—could have been the theme song for the Nixon presidency. Ironically, neither man realized how much they had in common: Both had risen from humble origins to the heights of their respective fields, both achieved great fame in the 1950s, and both drew their fan base from middle America. Most important, neither man was "cool" in 1970. All of this served as context for the major irony of Presley's fascination of himself as a drug enforcement agent. Indeed, Nixon was barely aware of who Presley was, and Presley was most interested in adding to his badge collection. By 1970, Presley had long been a regular user of a cornucopia of pharmaceutical products. He died in 1977 from cardiac arrhythmia resulting from long-standing abuse of drugs.

with North Vietnam and the Vietcong went on, both in public venues and in secret. "Peace with honor" amounted to acting upon a recognition that the war could not be won, while hoping that its end could be had on terms the American public might see as some measure of success. In reality, Nixon's efforts to end the war differed little from those of Johnson, whose poor choices in Vietnam had been driven in part by Nixon's sniping between 1965 and 1968. Nixon's own policy took four years to unfold, during which more than 20,000 more American personnel died in Vietnam.

Keeping the pressure on communist forces depended heavily upon the use of bombing. Attacks upon Hanoi, the capital, and other North Vietnamese cities intensified. In addition, American forces continued, and stepped up, aerial interdiction efforts against the Ho Chi Minh Trail, the long supply line from the North into the South that ran through Laos and Cambodia. In addition to bombing for tactical and strategic purposes, the president hoped to leverage the psychological impact of intensified bombardment. In what he called his "madman theory," Nixon actually encouraged talk that he might resort to the use of nuclear weapons in Vietnam. In this scenario, his reputation as an old cold warrior would stoke communist fears that he might use the ultimate weapon to secure more favorable terms. The communist North and Vietcong were not moved by either the threat of Nixon the "madman" or the prospect of an intensified bombing campaign. Though its success was questionable, the pummeling of communist targets continued because Nixon and Kissinger feared that relenting would signal a weakness of resolve. Official peace talks stalemated with Nixon's attempt to use bombing to force the North to accept the South's right to exist. Communist negotiators held firm to demands that the United States depart Vietnam and permit a government in the South without the presence of South Vietnamese president Nguyen Van Thieu. Secret efforts by Kissinger in 1969 and 1970 to get substantive concessions also failed.

The antiwar movement had been quiet after the August 1968 Democratic National Convention, but in the fall of 1969, two major protest events took place. October saw thousands in America's major cities participate in the Vietnam Moratorium; November 13–15 witnessed 250,000 to 800,000 protesters descend on Washington in a largely peaceful expression of opposition to Nixon's war policy.

Vietnamization, however, did not preclude the use of ground forces to keep pressure upon the North Vietnamese and Vietcong. South Vietnam's neighbor, Cambodia, had been unable to halt Vietcong attacks and resupply efforts into the South. Intelligence indicated that the Vietcong's central command for operations in South Vietnam functioned just inside Cambodia. Bombing had failed to demolish the Central Office for South Vietnam (COSVN), and consequently, Nixon ordered American forces to invade Cambodia in tandem with South Vietnamese troops on April 30, 1970. The

invasion enflamed campus protests across the nation, most notably at Kent State University in Ohio. Tensions at Kent State had already been high due to attacks by a radical antiwar minority upon ROTC facilities on campus. Ohio's governor sent in the National Guard to restore order. On May 4, guardsmen hemmed in by protesters opened fire, killing four students. The president commented that when "dissent turns to violence [it] invites tragedy" and refused to lower the White House flag in honor of the students he dismissed as "bums." Nixon's response no doubt pleased some of his supporters, but it only worsened campus unrest. COSVN proved an elusive target, modest caches of weapons were all that the invaders found, and eventually the operation came to an end. American casualties had been light, and casualties overall continued to decline as American disengagement and withdrawal began to take effect.

Nixon suffered by association with the growing distrust of government fueled by the war. In June 1971 the *New York Times* began to publish classified documents from the JOHN F. KENNEDY and Johnson administrations detailing America's growing involvement in Vietnam. The so-called Pentagon Papers, stolen by former Defense Department and RAND Corporation analyst Daniel Ellsberg, also revealed the deliberate efforts of both administrations to deceive the American public as to events in Southeast Asia. Though advisers pointed out that fallout from the Pentagon Papers would likely harm Democrats more, Nixon, already angry over government leaks and the perceived hostility of the press, moved to halt publication. The U.S. Supreme Court overruled him, and publication resumed. Efforts to prevent publication represented only one front in Nixon's efforts to deal with the Pentagon Papers incident. He also ordered, and his associates undertook on their own, illegal retaliatory action against Ellsberg and the press.

Despite the Cambodia incursion and an increasingly bitter effort against antiwar elements at home, the administration kept negotiating. In May 1971, Kissinger offered the North Vietnamese an American withdrawal within seven months of a cease-fire in exchange for the release of American POWs and the North's promise to stop sending its regular forces into the South. Hanoi's response proved promising and talks grew more earnest. In their counteroffer, the North Vietnamese sought fair elections in the South, which presumably would have meant the end of Nguyen Van Thieu's government. Later that year, the South did hold elections, but President Thieu so thoroughly rigged them that he obtained 94 percent of the vote. Americans grew impatient with democratic progress in Vietnam, which forced Nixon to attempt a defense of the obvious fraud. Democracy could not rise overnight in the South, he argued. The elections of 1971 represented a step. Thieu's continued presence in government, though, hardened the North Vietnamese position

(continues on page 498)

ADMINISTRATION TIME LINE

1969

January 20 Nixon is sworn in as president of the United States.

March 17 President Nixon orders a secret U.S. bombing campaign of neutral Cambodia.

April 30 Nixon calls for new legislation to consolidate federal assistance programs to states and cities.

July The Internal Revenue Service forms a Special Services Staff unit to handle White House requests for audits against perceived enemies.

July 20 At 4:17 P.M. EDT astronaut Neil Armstrong of *Apollo 11* becomes the first person to step on to the moon.

July 24 *Apollo 11* returns to Earth, landing in the Pacific Ocean.

July 25 The Nixon Doctrine is articulated, declaring that nations will be responsible for a greater share of their defense.

August 8 Nixon announces a plan for welfare reform, including the Family Assistance Plan, which would have provided direct payments to the working poor. The measure never became law because of Democratic opposition in Congress.

August 15–17 The Woodstock Music Festival occurs.

October 15 Two million protesters in American cities participate in the Vietnam moratorium demonstrations.

November 3 Nixon announces that North Vietnam has rejected secret U.S. entreaties for peace. He also introduces his plan for "Vietnamization" of the war whereby U.S. troops would be withdrawn, but U.S. dollars and equipment would still be made available to South Vietnam.

November 13–15 Protesters numbering between 250,000 to 800,000 descend upon Washington in a largely peaceful expression of opposition to Nixon's war policy.

November 26 Nixon signs the Selective Service Reform Act, implementing a lottery system for the draft.

December 30 Nixon signs the Tax Reform Act of 1969, preventing the very wealthy from dodging their income tax responsibilities either through establishment of private foundations or through use of excessive deductions; it also establishes the alternative minimum tax to prevent the wealthy from using questionable tax deductions.

1970

January 1 Nixon signs the National Environmental Policy Act of 1969 into law, requiring all federal construction projects to have an environmental impact study before initiation.

April 1 Nixon signs the Public Health Cigarette Smoking Act requiring a stronger warning be placed on cigarette packages and banning cigarette advertising on radio and television.

April 30 Nixon orders U.S. troops into Cambodia with South Vietnamese troops.

May 4 Four students are killed and nine wounded by Ohio National Guardsmen at a Kent State University protest over the Cambodian invasion by U.S. troops in Vietnam.

May 14 Two students are killed by Mississippi Highway Patrol officers at Jackson State College in Mississippi at a civil rights and antiwar protest.

July 9 Nixon announces plans for an Environmental Protection Agency and a National Oceanic and Atmospheric Administration.

October 15 Nixon signs the Organized Crime Control Act into law.

October 27 Nixon signs the Comprehensive Drug Abuse Prevention and Control Act, expanding the definition of "drug dependent person" to enable more people to gain treatment for addiction and other drug abuse problems.

October 30 Nixon signs the Railway Passenger Service Act, creating Amtrak to save passenger rail service in the United States.

December 21 Nixon meets with Elvis Presley in the White House.

December 26 Nixon signs Title X of the Public Health Service Act of 1970 providing for comprehensive family planning services to be administered by the Office of Family Planning.

December 29 Nixon signs the Occupational Safety and Health Act to protect employees from workplace hazards while also ensuring their overall health and safety.

December 31 Nixon signs into law the Clean Air Act of 1970.

1971

February 16 The White House taping system is activated.

April 18–24 An antiwar march in Washington, D.C., is led by the Vietnam Veterans Against the War.

April 20 The Supreme Court rules in *Swann v. Charlotte-Mecklenburg Board of Education* that the failure of districts to remedy violations of old mandates results in expanded authority for the federal courts.

May 18 Nixon signs legislation implementing wage and price controls.

June 13 The *New York Times* publishes the "Pentagon Papers," data from classified Defense Department studies into the history of U.S. involvement in Vietnam against the wishes of the Nixon administration.

June 30 The Supreme Court rules in *New York Times v. United States* that newspapers have the right to publish the material known as the Pentagon Papers.

July 9 Henry Kissinger secretly travels to China to work toward the easing of relations between the two nations.

July 15 Nixon announces he will visit China soon.

July 21 The Twenty-sixth Amendment to the Constitution is ratified, granting 18-year-olds the right to vote.

August 15 Nixon orders a 90-day halt to price, rent, and wage increases.

December 22 Nixon signs legislation extending the Economic Stabilization Act.

1972

February 7 Nixon signs the Federal Election Campaign Act of 1971, which attempts to fix several problems in operating elections from large donations to advertising in campaigns.

February 21–28 Nixon travels to China meeting with Mao Zedong and other Chinese leaders.

March 30 The North Vietnamese launch a 200,000-man offensive, prompting the Nixon administration to retaliate with a massive airpower bombing campaign.

May 26 While in Moscow for a summit Nixon signs the Strategic Arms Limitation Treaty (SALT I) together with Leonid Brezhnev of the Soviet Union.

June 17 Five burglars are discovered and arrested in the Democratic National Committee offices of the Watergate complex in Washington, D.C.

June 23 Nixon orders his chief of staff to use the five Watergate burglars' CIA connections as a means to halt the FBI probe into the break-in, commonly known as the "smoking gun" conversation that, when made public two years later, ultimately leads to his resignation.

Nixon signs into law the Education Amendments of 1972, including Title IX, which prohibits gender discrimination in education by those institutions that benefit from federal funding.

June 29 In *Branzburg v. Hayes,* the Supreme Court rules that journalists do not have the right to withhold the identity of their sources.

In *Furman v. Georgia,* the Supreme Court overturns all death penalty cases while the majority split on whether it is a cruel and unusual punishment in violation of the Eighth and Fourteenth Amendments to the Constitution.

August 22 Nixon wins the Republican presidential nomination for a second term with little opposition.

(continues)

ADMINISTRATION TIME LINE *(continued)*

August 29 During a press conference, Nixon asserts that no one currently employed in the White House was involved with Watergate.

September 5 Palestinian terrorists kill 11 Israeli athletes at the Olympic Games.

September 26 Nixon signs the Child Nutrition Act Amendments of 1972, establishing the Special Supplemental Food Program for Women, Infants, and Children (WIC) as a pilot program.

October 17 Nixon vetoes the Federal Water Pollution Control Act Amendments, but Congress overrides the veto, enacting the measure into law and giving the federal government increased jurisdiction over intrastate waterways, creating a system of federal permits for municipal sewage and industrial discharges, declaring a goal of zero pollution discharges by 1985, and providing $18 billion in federal grants.

Congress passes legislation providing for the Supplemental Security Income program, which shifts responsibility from the states to the federal government with regard to the aged, blind, and permanently and totally disabled.

October 20 More popularly known as general revenue sharing, the State and Local Fiscal Assistance Act of 1972 is signed into law, promising to share federal revenues with state and local governments, shifting power from Washington, D.C., to the states.

October 22 After a series of negotiations, National Security Advisor Henry Kissinger tells the world "peace is at hand" in the Vietnam War.

October 28 President Nixon signs the Coastal Zone Management Act, preserving and protecting the nation's coastal areas.

Nixon signs the Consumer Product Safety Act, establishing the Consumer Product Safety Commission.

November 7 Nixon wins reelection in a landslide.

November 8 Nixon asks for the resignation of all presidential appointees, department heads, and agency directors.

December 18 Nixon orders Operation Linebacker II, commonly known as the Christmas bombings, to get the North Vietnamese back to the negotiating table.

1973

January 20 Nixon is inaugurated for a second term in office.

January 22 The Supreme Court hands down its decision in *Roe v. Wade,* legalizing access to abortion in the first trimester.

January 27 A cease-fire in Vietnam takes effect with the signing of the Paris Peace Accords.

March 21 The Supreme Court decides in *San Antonio Independent School District v. Rodriguez* that there is no fundamental right to an education and that the Texas system of funding public education did not systematically discriminate against poor children.

March 29 The last U.S. troops leave Vietnam.

April 30 Nixon fires his counsel John Dean, and announces the resignations of both H. R. Haldeman and John Ehrlichman to try to distance himself from Watergate investigations.

May 14 The Supreme Court in *Frontiero v. Richardson* rules that a female soldier in the U.S. Air Force may claim her husband as a dependent in the same way that male soldiers claim their wives as dependents and receive dependent pay.

July 23 Nixon cites executive privilege when he refuses to turn over the White House tapes to the Senate committee investigating Watergate.

September 26 Nixon signs the Rehabilitation Act, the first federal initiative to give "rights" against discrimination to Americans with disabilities.

October 6 The Arab-Israeli War begins, also known as the Yom Kippur War. The United States provides material aid to Israel.

October 10 Vice President Spiro Agnew resigns after pleading no contest to bribery and tax evasion charges.

October 12 Nixon nominates Michigan representative Gerald Ford to be his new vice president. Ford is sworn in on December 6 following confirmation by the Senate.

October 17 The Organization of Petroleum Exporting Countries (OPEC) places an oil embargo against the United States in retaliation for its support of Israel.

October 20 To prevent the White House tapes from being released (by court order), President Nixon orders the firing of the Watergate special prosecutor by his attorney general, who refuses. The deputy attorney general also refuses. The solicitor general fires the Watergate Special Prosecutor. This episode becomes known as the "Saturday Night Massacre."

October 24 Nixon vetoes the War Powers Resolution, but Congress overrides the president on November 7.

November 16 Nixon signs the Trans-Alaska Pipeline Authorization Act into law.

November 27 Nixon signs the Emergency Petroleum Allocation Act, providing for an official federal government plan to allocate gasoline and home heating fuel.

December 21 Some of the White House tapes are made available to special prosecutor Leon Jaworski.

December 28 Nixon signs the Endangered Species Act into law.

Nixon signs the Comprehensive Employment and Training Act (CETA), establishing a program of block grants to state and local governments to assist and expand public and private job training programs for economically disadvantaged youth

1974

January 2 Nixon signs the Regional Rail Reorganization Act, providing for restructuring of the railroad industry according to new consolidated rail system, the elimination of unnecessary services, and minimal disruptions to rail services.

March 1 Jaworski's grand jury indicts seven campaign and White House aides relating to the Watergate scandal, and names Nixon as an "unindicted co-conspirator."

July 12 Nixon signs the Congressional Budget and Impoundment Control Act into law, providing for Congress to adopt annual budget resolutions with spending divided among 20 different functional categories.

July 24 In *United States v. Nixon,* the Supreme Court orders the complete release of the White House tapes, arguing that executive privilege does not trump an ongoing criminal investigation.

July 25 In *Milliken v. Bradley,* the Supreme Court rejects a comprehensive interdistrict plan to bring school desegregation to the Detroit, Michigan, public schools.

July 27 The House Judiciary Committee votes its first article of impeachment against Nixon.

July 29 The House Judiciary Committee votes its second article of impeachment against Nixon.

July 30 The House Judiciary Committee votes its third article of impeachment against Nixon.

August 5 Nixon finally relents and hands over the tapes, all the while insisting that his refusal to that point had been justified.

August 8 Nixon announces his resignation from the presidency effective the following day at noon.

August 9 Nixon resigns as president.

(continued from page 493)
again. Throughout 1971–72, President Nixon attempted to parlay better relations between the United States and both the Soviet Union and the People's Republic of China into leverage on the North Vietnamese. These hopes revealed American leaders' lack of understanding of the Vietnamese conflict; the North resented interference by these larger communist powers and it refused to budge.

On March 30, 1972, the North Vietnamese launched a 200,000-man offensive throughout the South, with the South's armies taking flight. With American forces in the country down to 140,000, with relatively few of those being "combat" forces, American airpower represented the best possibility of arresting North Vietnamese gains. Hitting the North hard from the air, striking strategic targets such as Haiphong and Hanoi, as well as offering tactical support to ground forces, American air units helped stem the tide. In June, 112,000 tons of American bombs fell on the North, the heaviest strikes of the war. American casualties in this most recent communist offensive remained relatively low, and con-

During his campaign for president in 1968, Nixon claimed he had a secret plan to end the Vietnam War. As this Herblock cartoon from 1972 acidly comments, the war continued for four more years, when President Nixon ran for reelection. *(A Herblock Cartoon, copyright by the Herb Block Foundation)*

sequently protests of the aerial escalation were muted. With most forces out of Vietnam, the draft undergoing modification, and economic worries mounting, the American public wished to forget Vietnam.

In 1972, the presidential campaign centered on the Vietnam War and its political impact. While the Republican nomination was never in doubt, the Democratic contest featured lingering bitterness and rivalries from 1968. Candidates from the right—George Wallace—the left—Edmund Muskie and George McGovern—and the center—Hubert Humphrey and Henry "Scoop" Jackson—vied for the nomination. McGovern prevailed in the end, but his liberal positions were out of step with the mood of the country. Progress on Vietnam, combined with continued successes in dealing with the Soviet Union and China, would solidify Nixon's lead over McGovern, whose campaign floundered.

Meanwhile, peace talks yielded an important breakthrough in October, less than a month before the election. Hanoi agreed to a cease-fire before launching steps to a political settlement, and to accept a temporary partition of South Vietnam into areas of Thieu and Vietcong control until a commission with South Vietnamese, Vietcong, and neutral representatives could determine the South's future. On October 22, National Security Advisor Henry Kissinger told the world that "peace is at hand." Kissinger's peremptory announcement enraged the president and his closest advisers. Moreover, it prompted South Vietnamese president Thieu to denounce the terms, and given his promises to Thieu, Nixon had to follow suit. Talks with the communists resumed, but Nixon sped shipment of $1 billion in military aid to the South and promised to interpose American force should the North break any future agreement. In the November election, Nixon crushed McGovern 520 electoral votes to 17; his popular vote majority was nearly 20 million of more than 70 million cast. But he had no significant congressional coattails. He emerged from his victory withdrawn and angry. Within a matter of days, Nixon notified most of his cabinet and staff that he wanted their signed resignations.

Peace negotiations stalled again in December, and, in rage, Nixon lashed out at the North with the most massive bombing to date, deliberately targeting civilian centers. The CHRISTMAS BOMBINGS lasted 12 days and they took place around the clock. American planes dropped more tonnage than in the whole period from 1969 to 1971. American and international newspapers decried the pointlessness of the gesture. The Soviets and the Chinese, who had been eager to help influence the North, now condemned Nixon and did little else to help the peace process. North Vietnamese resolve grew more steely under fire. After the beginning of the year talks resumed in Paris. A deal following the same broad outlines as the October peace that was at hand ended U.S. involvement in the war, and the cease-fire took effect on January 27, 1973, a week after Nixon's second inaugura-

A Vietnam veteran and head of Vietnam Veterans Against the War, John Kerry, future U.S. senator and presidential candidate, watches as President Nixon announces an agreement on a cease-fire in Vietnam in 1973. *(©Bettmann/CORBIS)*

tion. Soon American POWs began returning home, and in March, the last American combat forces in Vietnam departed the country. More than 55,000 American soldiers had died in Vietnam, nearly half of them on Nixon's watch. Just over two years later the war in Vietnam ended when communist forces finally entered Saigon.

Nixon and Foreign Policy

U.S. foreign policy under Nixon took new paths in response to America's changed status in world affairs. Vietnam drained the nation's military strength, and the war had badly hurt the nation's image abroad, particularly among its traditional allies. The Soviet Union had achieved relative parity with the United States in nuclear weapons. Economic factors increasingly influenced foreign policy considerations as the United States faced challenges to its global economic dominance. Despite his reputation as a hard-liner, Richard Nixon's travels, engagement with world leaders, and ruminations upon international developments during the 1960s led to an evolution in his thought. He had become more pragmatic and had

come to view a changed approach to cold war diplomacy as essential to preserving peace. The major communist powers, the Soviet Union and the People's Republic of China, might not be trustworthy, he believed, but cooperation with them was possible and essential.

In 1969, President Nixon appointed Henry Kissinger his National Security Advisor. Though quite different, the two men shared an appreciation of America's changed position, and they also took a realist view of policy options to meet that changed position. Both men were insecure; both wanted to change history; both loved secrecy and bold strokes in policymaking. The two were also intensely jealous and mistrustful of their own staffers, State Department bureaucrats, and each other. Together the two made American foreign policy, largely bypassing Secretary of State William Rogers. After 1973, Kissinger served as secretary of state. While their joint successes helped lay the groundwork for an updated American foreign policy, their methods helped pave the way for Nixon's eventual disgrace. In the years after Nixon left office, the two men, pundits, and historians have debated about who was most responsible for their foreign policy successes and failures.

Upon taking office in 1969, Nixon and Kissinger both sensed an opportunity to reconfigure cold war geopolitics. They sought advantage in the emerging rift between the Soviet Union and the People's Republic of China (PRC), which had emerged from ideological differences and traditional rivalries. In the mid-1960s, border clashes raised the stakes between the two nuclear powers. America stood to benefit if improved relations with China could prompt the Soviets to warm to the United States out of self-interest. The United States, however, had no diplomatic relationship with the PRC. Instead, since 1949 Washington had recognized the nationalist government of Taiwan—an island off the coast of mainland China—as the legitimate government of China. Nixon himself had stoked American hostility toward the PRC, and he refused to refer to the communist state by any term other than "Red China." Nixon gave subtle signals that he wanted a thaw. In 1970, he referred to the

"People's Republic of China" in a speech. That same year, the U.S. national table tennis team received an invitation to play exhibition matches in the PRC. Back-channel contacts with China continued with Pakistan as an intermediary, and in June 1971 Kissinger secretly traveled to China and met with its leadership. These talks opened the way for Nixon's own journey to China in February 1972. After he met with Mao Zedong and other Chinese leaders, the two nations agreed to continued exchanges, eventually bringing full diplomatic recognition in 1979.

Improvements in Sino-American relations worried the Soviet Union and provided Nixon with leverage in dealing with Soviet leaders. Constructive engagement and cooperation with the Soviet Union to ease tensions became known as DÉTENTE. While, the Soviet Union surpassed the United States in conventional forces and had reached parity in nuclear weapons, the buildup severely taxed that nation's economy. Soviet leaders governed a nation that could not feed itself. The United States stepped in with the sale of $750

President Nixon *(right)* meets with Leonid Brezhnev *(left)* during the Soviet leader's visit to the United States, June 19, 1973. *(Robert L. Knudsen/National Archives)*

million in much-needed grain. This gesture helped open talks on more significant concerns, such as both nations' massive arsenals of nuclear weapons. Beyond the 1963 limited test ban treaty few concrete steps had been taken to defuse the ability of the world's two greatest powers to destroy the planet. Both nations had the capacity to deploy nuclear weaponry by land, sea, and air. The arms race and the costs of supporting these arsenals taxed both nations' resources. The two powers began talks aimed at reducing nuclear arms in Geneva in 1969. Negotiations that led to drafting of the Strategic Arms Limitation Treaty (SALT I) continued in Washington through the remainder of the year as Nixon and Kissinger bargained with Soviet ambassador Anatoli Dobrinyn.

Later that year, President Nixon and Soviet premier Leonid Brezhnev signed the final treaty in Moscow amid champagne toasts. SALT I halted increases in sea and land-based missiles for five years and banned either power from attempting to construct an antiballistic missile defense system (ABM Treaty). The former provision, however, failed to address the development of multiple individual reentry vehicles (MIRVs), individually targeted warheads within individual missiles. The latter reflected mutual agreement that any development that undermined deterrence would create a greater danger of nuclear war. In 1973, both nations agreed to a timetable for SALT II talks with the aim to craft a treaty to take up where the first left off. SALT II, though, never came to fruition.

Although détente may have improved the direct relationship between the United States and the Soviet Union, cold war competition continued in Latin America, the Middle East, Africa, and Asia. The Middle East represented an area of particular sensitivity. American policy toward the Middle East in this period demonstrated Nixon's determination to be firm with the Soviets so as to gain other concessions, but it also highlighted the increasing role economic issues played in determining U.S. foreign relations. Since its founding in 1948, Israel, backed by the United States, had been both threatened and attacked by its Arab neighbors, particularly Syria and Egypt, backed by the Soviets. In the Six-Day War in 1967, the Israeli military thrashed Egyptian and Syrian armed forces, employing American-made military hardware to full effect and seizing territory from both Arab nations. Egypt and Syria plotted revenge and unleashed an attack against Israel in October 1973—the Yom Kippur War, also known as the Arab-Israeli War. The surprise Arab assault briefly caught Israeli defenders off guard, and Nixon ordered massive emergency shipments of arms to forestall defeat. Soviet leaders countered with a threat to send troops to Egypt, and President Nixon rejoined with an increase in American nuclear alert status to its highest level since the Cuban missile crisis in 1962. To ease tensions and to rein in its ally, the United States slowed arms shipments to Israel, and Kissinger began "shuttle diplomacy" among regional capitals to end hostilities. A cease-fire halted the fighting in November, and American diplomatic overtures in the region helped to engender a warming of U.S.-Egyptian relations in the following years.

However, as American aid flowed to Israel, Arab oil-producing states embargoed shipments of crude oil to the United States, provoking a spike in prices. Nixon envisioned a multipolar world emerging with the rise of China and the increased importance of energy and economics to geopolitics. His perceptive understanding of these developments influenced America's later role in the post–cold war world of the early 1990s, which the former cold warrior lived to see in his retirement. Whether he was influenced by Kissinger or the other way around, Nixon pursued a concept of superpower relations that stressed realism and national self-interest as the primary factors motivating policymaking, with less emphasis placed on ideology. Mistrust and tension remained, yet ideology would not be allowed to trump pragmatism when opportunities existed to make peaceful gains through negotiation. Conservative Republicans and Democratic cold warriors such as Senator Henry "Scoop" Jackson attacked Nixon-Kissinger foreign policy as too cozy with the communists. Liberal and moderate critics often criticized the administration's foreign policy's apparent lack of a moral dimension, particularly the lack of attention to human rights.

Nixon's Domestic Policies

The Nixon era saw the beginning of a period of long-term difficulties within the American economy. After a quarter century of robust economic growth following World War II, forces beyond the control of the administration played havoc with Americans' livelihoods, leaving President Nixon hard-pressed to respond. Inflation emerged first under President LYNDON JOHNSON in the late 1960s. Johnson refused to raise taxes or cut back federal domestic spending despite increasing expenditures on the war in Vietnam. Though LBJ finally agreed to a surtax on incomes to help fund the war in August 1967, inflation continued to present problems into 1968. Rising inflation coincided with new competitive pressures upon American industry. U.S. industries dominated the world market throughout the 1950s and 1960s, but American factories were in need of modernization. The Japanese and German economies, among others, had succeeded in fully recovering from World War II, ironically with American aid. Their exports, including automobiles, electronics, and appliances, were known for their high quality and durability. A strong dollar meant that imports could be purchased cheaply, and U.S. consumers rushed to buy them. The year 1971 witnessed the first American trade deficit since 1894. In 1973, when Arab nations embargoed oil in response to American support for Israel in the Yom Kippur War, oil prices rose up 400 percent. Amid this energy shortage, gas lines formed, and the cost of all products and services connected to or dependent upon fuel prices also increased, adding to inflation. That imported goods and autos often exceeded American products in fuel efficiency only added to the troubles of American industry.

The resulting phenomena of inflation combined with stagnant economic growth came to be defined by the term *stagflation*. American productivity declined significantly, and the nation's share of international trade fell off by half. As a result too few jobs were available for the maturing baby boom generation, resulting in increased unemployment and economic uncertainty. Four different presidential administrations wrestled with stagflation's effects into the early 1980s.

Nixon initially tried to combat inflation by cutting spending, particularly in the defense sector, which was made easier by Vietnamization. However, doing so only contributed to unemployment. He urged the Federal Reserve to increase interest rates to cool the inflationary spiral. However, these measures did little to ease the pressure. Congressional Democrats authorized President Nixon to impose WAGE AND PRICE CONTROLS to arrest inflation in 1970. Nixon, though, hesitated to use this power, remembering his days in the Office of Price Administration during World War II. But, as inflation continued to rise, he yielded to pressure to impose controls. In August 1971, Nixon ordered a 90-day halt to price, rent, and wage increases. At the end of the 90-day emergency, he limited wage increases to 5.5 percent per year, and he froze price and rent increases to 2.5 percent per annum. This turnabout signaled Nixon's willingness to sacrifice conservative principles to experimentation. Facing reelection in 1972, the president adopted a Keynesian approach to public spending to stimulate the economy. While increased spending allowed for modest improvements, it also stimulated more inflation. Hoping to improve the nation's trade deficit and boost exports Nixon devalued the dollar, allowing it to float against world currencies, essentially abrogating the postwar Bretton Woods Agreement on currencies and taking the nation off the gold standard. Early successes faded with the ARAB OIL EMBARGO. In 1973, the Dow Jones Industrial Average fell below 800. By the following year, inflation reached an annual rate of 11 percent.

On other domestic policy fronts, Nixon sought to distance himself from the legacy of the Johnson years, but just as often he ended up unable or unwilling to make strides in a new direction. One area in which the Nixon administration sought a different approach from the Democrats was civil rights, particularly school desegregation. The president had obtained the Republican nomination in 1968 in part because of the support from powerful southern politicians who hoped for a more conciliatory federal stance on desegregation. Reversing the landmark changes that had swept American race relations during the 1960s would not be possible. However, Nixon and his political appointees offered some real and symbolic gestures to reward southern Republicans for their support and broaden the party's base in the region.

Attorney General John Mitchell, for example, opposed extension of the 1965 Voting Rights Act in the early 1970s and he also took a less aggressive stance in enforcing the 1968 Fair Housing Act. The Justice Department attempted to delay school integration in certain districts in Mississippi, but it was rebuffed by the U.S. Supreme Court in *Alexander v. Holmes County* (1969). The Court reiterated earlier rulings demanding more immediate compliance with the 15-year-old *Brown* decision. Throughout the first Nixon administration tensions concerning desegregation persisted between politics and policy. Many Republican moderates and liberals had found important positions in the Department of Justice, and especially in the Department of Heath, Education and Welfare, where they pressed vigorously for promotion of civil rights, long part of the party's heritage. However, Nixon's attorney general, together with White House staffers and other appointees, worked just as hard to reap the political benefits of slowing the pace on desegregation. By late 1970, many moderate and liberal appointees had been purged or reassigned. However, the laws did not change, and desegregation proceeded, with or without Nixon's support.

In 1968, 68 percent of African-American school children in the South and 40 percent nationwide attended single-race schools; by 1972, only 8 percent of southern black children and 12 percent of black children nationally attended single-race schools. Budgets for civil rights enforcement under Nixon, in real dollars, eclipsed those under Johnson. Efforts to promote equal employment opportunity through AFFIRMATIVE ACTION POLICY became even more determined under Nixon. But the Nixon administration is remembered by many as hostile to desegregation because of symbolic efforts by the president and his allies. In 1971, he denounced the Supreme Court's SWANN v. CHARLOTTE-MECKLENBURG ruling favoring busing to achieve school desegregation. Nixon's SUPREME COURT APPOINTMENTS bear further consideration. Twice Nixon nominated southern judges to the Supreme Court with segregationist pasts only to have both rejected by the Senate. On both occasions Nixon feigned shock that senators rejected the southern jurists. Southerners responded to these overtures, with every southern state joining in the reelection tidal wave of 1972. This courting of the South by Nixon and the Republican Party was deliberate.

It would be too easy to dismiss Nixon's domestic record as reactionary. He at times showed an impulse toward innovation and even occasional tendencies seen as liberal by later scholars. Influenced by sociologist Daniel Patrick Moynihan, a liberal Democrat, serving on the White House staff, Nixon flirted with a major overhaul of welfare early in his first administration. As head of the Urban Affairs Council, Moynihan proposed the government guarantee an income of $1,600 for a family of four along with food stamps, arguing that putting cash in the hands of the poor would ener-gize their economic rise. Moynihan had gained fame, or notoriety, for his criticism of Johnson's War on Poverty and his assertion that the welfare system had contributed to a culture of poverty. The guaranteed income proposal, known as the Family Assistance Plan (FAP), promised to replace the existing welfare system. It passed the House of Representatives in 1969, but died in the Senate, where southern senators together with liberal Democrats teamed up to stop the measure. The FAP's failure also stemmed from Nixon's refusal to salvage his own program once it became apparent that liberal support would require commitment to higher payments.

Nixon also experimented with returning federal money to the states, on the assumption that federal programs might be more effectively and efficiently administered and funded at the state and local levels. In October 1972 on the eve of the presidential election, Democrats in Congress approved Nixon's proposed $30 billion revenue sharing plan. The plan would distribute funds to the states across five years. Assuming that states would use the new money to take up the slack, Congress and the administration authorized cuts in federal welfare expenditures. However, as inflation and energy prices rose, states, counties and cities found the federal dollars did not stretch far enough, and revenue sharing failed to live up to Nixon's original vision.

Watergate and Nixon's Fall

The pathway to scandal and resignation began early in the first administration and was inextricably linked to Nixon's Vietnam policy and the wide rift in American society over the war. What eventually came to be known as "Watergate" represented a pattern of illegal activities conducted by the White House from the outset of the first administration. In addition to being tightly linked to the controversy over Vietnam, the administration's crimes stemmed from its own internal dynamics, Nixon's management style, and long-established patterns of questionable behavior on the part of important government agencies and officials. The president and his defenders, then and later, were always quick to point out misdeeds of previous presidents. However, the sweep and boldness of the Nixon administration's actions set it apart from all immediately preceding presidencies.

The pattern of illegal activity that came to be known as Watergate emerged from several different strands of activity that began shortly after the start of the administration in January 1969 and developed both independently and inter-dependently through the next four years. By the summer of 1969, Counsel to the President John Ehrlichman, who had worked for Nixon periodically since 1960, hired former New York policeman John Caulfield to serve as a coordinator of presidential security, assisting the Secret Service's work with local law enforcement during presidential visits.

Shortly thereafter, Caulfield, who had some experience as a detective, began doing investigations on behalf of the White House, sometimes conducting surveillance. One of his earliest and most important jobs involved examining potentially useful information surrounding Massachusetts senator Edward M. Kennedy's 1969 auto accident at Chappaquiddick, which had led to the death of one of the senator's young female aides. Caulfield's activities, and subsequent value, to Ehrlichman and the administration increased in scope and value over time.

A road to Watergate also developed in response to the unrest surrounding the war in Vietnam. Some observers detected revolutionary undertones to the disorder in the United States, and they feared for the nation's stability. One young conservative White House staffer, Tom Charles Huston, proposed a change in American domestic intelligence policy in early 1970. The Huston Plan, as it came to be known, suggested that domestic intelligence gathering be separated from the promulgation of policy stemming from that intelligence. Huston argued that responsibility for the former should remain with the FBI and other bureaucratic agencies, but that the latter ought to be reserved to the White House. The president's need to act decisively against subversive elements, or political enemies, was inhibited by the existing system that left much leeway to bureaucracies, notably the FBI. Certainly, the FBI under longtime director J. Edgar Hoover did not coddle subversives, but its response was not always as robust as the White House might have wanted. Hoover, CIA director Richard Helms, and other agency heads balked. Hoover offered to implement the Huston scheme only if Nixon signed off on the measure. Nixon and his staff backed off, but demands persisted for an in-house organization to deal with sensitive problems quickly and effectively.

In 1969, the Nixon administration began a program of sporadic harassment of its perceived opponents, which, by 1971, had developed into a more systematic approach. The administration began to put pressure on the Internal Revenue Service (IRS) to audit and investigate antiwar and radical groups. Tom Huston coordinated White House contact with the IRS, and the agency formed a Special Services Staff (SSS) in July 1969 specifically to comply with White House requests. Eventually, liberal politicians, organizations, and celebrities were added to those subject to SSS investigations. The Department of Justice began supplying names of potential IRS targets shortly thereafter. In 1970, the IRS conducted a politically motivated investigation of former Alabama governor George C. Wallace's brother. Wallace had begun a campaign to reclaim the Alabama governor's mansion in hopes of securing a powerbase for a 1972 bid for the Democratic nomination. These efforts to spur IRS action against real and imagined enemies eventually evolved into a coordinated effort to compile a list of the administration's opponents against whom active retaliation could be launched.

Whether on his own initiative or at the request of chief of staff H. R. Haldeman and Ehrlichman, White House counsel John Dean started the so-called Enemies List in 1971. The list eventually included thousands of individuals and organizations, growing from Dean's own originally modest collection of names. Over time, White House staffers, including Charles Colson, Harry Dent, Patrick Buchanan, and others, added names. These names, in turn, were added to still more lists. White House–sponsored actions against those on the list ranged from surveillance and harassment to IRS audit and career sabotage. The Enemies List and the varied eventual and proposed strikes against those on the list represented a nexus of administration management style and individual ambition. Nixon believed in fostering intense competition among aides and advisers in hopes of bringing out their best work. Pitting staffers against one another frequently brought out wild ideas, such as Charles Colson's 1971 proposal to firebomb the Brookings Institution, a liberal think-tank. Sometimes ideas came as a direct result of Nixon's own musings. Young, ambitious aides heard and acted upon ideas that those who were closer to Nixon would have interpreted as dark fantasies. By 1971, however, a host of illegalities were ongoing and in the planning stages.

The nature and extent of President Nixon's awareness of these "White House horrors," as Attorney General John Mitchell termed them, and when and under what circumstances he came to know about them, varied. Nixon himself had ordered many of the individual IRS audits, notably actions against George Wallace's family. He certainly knew after the fact of Jack Caulfield's delving into Edward Kennedy's problems. He sometimes inspired, ordered, or heard about retaliation against various parties on the Enemies List after action had been taken.

A fifth catalyst to this pattern of illegal activities was Nixon and his advisers' concern about leaks of sensitive information relative to Vietnam and other diplomatic initiatives. Information leaks had plagued the Johnson White House, and the president's desperate efforts to stop them had reached fever pitch by the time he left office. He personally warned Nixon of the loss of control over such information. By May 1969, Nixon later recalled, the more than 20 incidents yielded significant press coverage. Most came from the National Security Council (NSC). Investigations to determine their source discovered links between reporter Jack Anderson and Senate leaders. In addition, Nixon's bold foreign policy moves had aroused the concern and suspicion of other elements of the Washington establishment. The Joint Chiefs of Staff, for example, grew worried about their apparent exclusion from decision making. They undertook a spying operation against National Security Advisor Henry Kissinger, using a young Navy yeoman, Charles Radford, who served as an NSC staffer. The administration retaliated by spying on the chiefs. Eventually, worries about leaks from the

NSC led Kissinger to order wiretaps and surveillance against his own subordinates. These were eventually extended to bureaucrats in the State, Defense and Justice Departments. Certainly, some control over sensitive information is necessary to conduct the business of the executive branch and to manage foreign policy. Other leaks are relatively innocuous. The volume of these disclosures angered Nixon to the extent that he lost awareness of the distinction. The most critical of these leaked stories involved the Pentagon Papers.

As related earlier, these Kennedy-Johnson era Defense Department documents revealed a pattern of deception leading to American intervention in Vietnam, and subsequently, a lack of truthfulness from the Johnson administration about the war's conduct. They were stolen and then passed to the *New York Times*, and other newspapers, by former Defense Department analyst Daniel Ellsberg. Some in Nixon's circle argued that the documents only stood to harm the Democrats; others even argued that most of them could be safely declassified. Nixon refused, however, to allow the story to play itself out. Convinced that essential secrecy in other areas might be compromised by allowing these relatively old secrets to be made public, the president moved to halt the *Times* planned serialized publication of the documents. That very public effort to censor the press became an issue before the Supreme Court. Illegal responses to the leak, aimed at harming Ellsberg and discrediting him, went on behind the scenes even as the case was fought in court.

The Ellsberg case led to the creation of the PLUMBERS, an in-house organization designed to deal with leaks and undertake operations reminiscent of the Huston Plan, though on a lesser scale. The Plumbers facilitated the administration's efforts to covertly police the bureaucracy, gather information useful in attacking enemies, and otherwise harass opponents. The group answered to John Ehrlichman, and it included Egil "Bud" Krogh, David Young, E. Howard Hunt and G. Gordon Liddy. Hunt in the CIA and Liddy in the FBI had been involved in similar activities. In addition, the Plumbers periodically brought in outside assistance, frequently drawn from CIA, FBI, and Cuban dissident connections. On Ehrlichman's verbal orders, Krogh initiated an operation to break into the office of Ellsberg's psychiatrist in hopes of finding information damaging to the former Defense Department analyst. The break-in to Dr. Lewis Fielding's office produced nothing, and the burglars ransacked the premises to give the impression that a random crime aimed at obtaining drugs had taken place.

With the 1972 election approaching, the Plumbers stepped up their activities concentrating on so-called dirty tricks. Conceptually, Nixon was aware of these efforts, having urged their use against real and potential opponents. Two broad paths of attack emerged early in 1972. The first, known as Operation Sandwedge, involved disruptions of the Democratic Party's nominating process through rumor, sabotage,

Shortly after giving classified Pentagon documents to the *New York Times,* Daniel Ellsberg appears on a television program in a filmed interview, June 23, 1971. *(CBS/Associated Press)*

and "black bag" jobs. Jack Caulfield originated this scheme and Ehrlichman approved it. The second, Operation Gemstone, conceived by Gordon Liddy, involved direct electronic surveillance of leading Democratic operatives, notably of Democratic National Committee (DNC) headquarters and the DNC's chairman, Lawrence O'Brien. These operations would require considerable funding, and the Committee to Reelect the President (CREEP), Nixon's campaign organization chaired by Attorney General John Mitchell, provided it, albeit on the sly.

Operation Gemstone's failure led to the outbreak of scandal. Sometime in late May 1972 burglars recruited by E. Howard Hunt and G. Gordon Liddy entered the DNC headquarters at the Watergate building in Washington. They placed listening devices, and shortly thereafter the first reports of DNC conversations reached White House chief of staff H. R. Haldeman. Not all the bugs worked properly, and a five-person team, again coordinated by Hunt and Liddy, led by former CIA agent and CREEP operative James W.

McCord, Jr. entered Democratic headquarters again on the night of June 17. The unarmed burglars were discovered by building security and arrested by District of Columbia police. All five gave false names; four were Cuban exiles with CIA ties. At arraignment, the five were ordered held without bond. Haldeman kept Nixon, on vacation in Florida, posted throughout the day. Shortly afterward, Liddy and Hunt's connections with the break-in were discovered, and they were arrested. The FBI soon took over the investigation.

The coverup began in earnest. Though Nixon's press secretary dismissed the event as a "third-rate burglary attempt," the White House began efforts to mitigate damage to Nixon. Attorney General Mitchell, who as chairman of CREEP was connected to the break-in, resigned for family reasons. His successor as attorney general, Richard Kleindienst, promised a full investigation. In an attempt to thwart that investigation, on June 23, President Nixon ordered his chief of staff to use the burglars' CIA connections as a means of halting the FBI probe. Nixon and his staff worked to keep the atten-

CABINET, COURT, AND CONGRESS

Cabinet Members

Secretary of State
William P. Rogers, 1969–73
Henry Kissinger, 1973–74

Secretary of Defense
Melvin R. Laird, 1969–73
Elliot L. Richardson, 1973
James R. Schlesinger, 1973–74

Secretary of the Treasury
David M. Kennedy, 1969–71
John B. Connally, 1971–72
George P. Shultz, 1972–74
William E. Simon, 1974

Postmaster General
Winton M. Blount, 1969–71

Attorney General
John N. Mitchell, 1969–72

Richard G. Kleindienst, 1972–73
Elliot L. Richardson, 1973
William B. Saxbe, 1974

Secretary of the Interior
Walter J. Hickel, 1969–70
Rogers C. B. Morton, 1971–74

Secretary of Agriculture
Clifford M. Hardin, 1969–71
Earl L. Butz, 1971–1974

Secretary of Commerce
Maurice H. Stans, 1969–72
Peter G. Peterson, 1972–73
Frederick B. Dent, 1973–74

Secretary of Labor
George P. Shultz, 1969–70
James D. Hodgson, 1970–73
Peter J. Brennan, 1973–74

Secretary of Health, Education and Welfare
Robert Finch, 1969–70
Elliot L. Richardson, 1970–73
Caspar Weinberger, 1973–74

Secretary of Housing and Urban Development
George W. Romney, 1969–73
James T. Lynn, 1973–74

Secretary of Transportation
John A. Volpe, 1969–73
Claude S. Brinegar, 1973–74

Supreme Court Appointments

*(Nominated for Chief Justice)

Name	Confirmation Vote	Dates of Service
*Warren Burger	74–3, Confirmed	1969–86
Clement Haynsworth, Jr.	45–55, Rejected	
G. Harrold Carswell	45–51, Rejected	
Harry Blackmun	94–0, Confirmed	1970–94
Lewis Powell, Jr.	89–1, Confirmed	1972–87
William Rehnquist	68–29, Confirmed	1972–2005

tion focused on, and the investigation confined to, the five burglars, plus Hunt and Liddy. At the end of September, a Washington grand jury indicted all seven for offenses including and related to the break-in.

Meanwhile, the election campaign was ongoing and Nixon's Democratic opponent, George McGovern, drew attention to the break-in and other dirty tricks throughout the fall. The public by and large, and the nation's press as well, paid little attention. However, *Washington Post* reporters Bob Woodward and Carl Bernstein followed the ongoing FBI investigation into the break-in and they became convinced that a wider conspiracy existed. Woodward and Bernstein faced considerable skepticism early on, though their investigation benefited from inside information from

Legislative Leaders

Congress	Speaker of the House	State	Party
91st Congress (1969–71)	John W. McCormack	Massachusetts	Democrat
92nd Congress (1971–73)	Carl B. Albert	Oklahoma	Democrat
93rd Congress (1973–74)	Carl B. Albert	Oklahoma	Democrat

Congress	House Majority Leader	State	Party
91st Congress (1969–71)	Carl B. Albert	Oklahoma	Democrat
92nd Congress (1971–73)	Hale Boggs	Louisiana	Democrat
93rd Congress (1973–74)	Thomas P. O'Neill, Jr.	Massachusetts	Democrat

Congress	House Minority Leader	State	Party
91st Congress (1969–71)	Gerald R. Ford	Michigan	Republican
92nd Congress (1971–73)	Gerald R. Ford	Michigan	Republican
93rd Congress (1973–74)	Gerald R. Ford	Michigan	Republican
93rd Congress (1974)	John J. Rhodes	Arizona	Republican

Congress	House Democratic Whip	State	Party
91st Congress (1969–71)	Hale Boggs	Louisiana	Democrat
92nd Congress (1971–73)	Thomas P. O'Neill, Jr.	Massachusetts	Democrat
93rd Congress (1973–74)	John J. McFall	California	Democrat

Congress	House Republican Whip	State	Party
91st Congress (1969–71)	Leslie C. Arends	Illinois	Republican
92nd Congress (1971–73)	Leslie C. Arends	Illinois	Republican
93rd Congress (1973–74)	Leslie C. Arends	Illinois	Republican

Congress	Senate Majority Leader	State	Party
91st Congress (1969–71)	Mike Mansfield	Montana	Democrat
92nd Congress (1971–73)	Mike Mansfield	Montana	Democrat
93rd Congress (1973–74)	Mike Mansfield	Montana	Democrat

Congress	Senate Minority Leader	State	Party
91st Congress (1969)	Everett McKinley Dirksen	Illinois	Republican
91st Congress (1969–71)	Hugh D. Scott, Jr.	Pennsylvania	Republican
92nd Congress (1971–73)	Hugh D. Scott, Jr.	Pennsylvania	Republican
93rd Congress (1973–74)	Hugh D. Scott, Jr.	Pennsylvania	Republican

an informant they called "Deep Throat," many years later revealed to be FBI second-in-command Mark Felt. An investigation undertaken by the House Banking and Currency Committee failed to find traction because the White House bribed committee members, who were facing their own legal problems, to vote against the issuance of subpoenas. The committee chairman, Representative Wright Pat-man, a Texas Democrat, was an avowed partisan, and the White House easily dismissed Patman's efforts. When Nixon was overwhelmingly reelected in November, few sensed the import of the failed burglary that summer.

However, the Watergate burglars, plus Hunt and Liddy, had time to think as they awaited trial. Anxiously hoping to keep them quiet, the White House, represented by White

House counsel John Dean, had begun funneling hush money to the defendants. Just over a month before the Watergate trials began, this effort began to unravel when E. Howard Hunt's wife, Dorothy, died when a United Airlines jet crashed in Chicago. Her purse contained $10,000 in cash and questions immediately arose about the possibility that the Hunts accepted the money in exchange for their silence. On January 10, 1973, Hunt, Liddy, and the burglars went on trial before U.S. district judge John Sirica, known as "Maximum John" for his tough sentences. Ten days later the trial ended with all but James McCord and G. Gordon Liddy having pled guilty. After only an hour and a half of deliberations, the jury convicted both on all counts. As he awaited sentencing, McCord wrote to Sirica, insisting that his former agency, the CIA, had nothing to do with the break-in and that the defendants had been pressured to keep silent. At the end of March, Sirica passed sentence, the harshest possible for the other defendants. The White House began to realize that its control of the Watergate affair was unraveling.

McCord's letter alone did not produce this result. Nixon's own appointment of L. Patrick Gray to head the FBI brought about disastrous Senate confirmation hearings. Gray had been installed as interim FBI director after J. Edgar Hoover's death in May 1972, despite the fact that bureau insiders slipped damaging information about Gray to the Senate committee considering his nomination. These revelations included contacts between White House counsel John Dean and Gray and the possible destruction of evidence. These disclosures torpedoed Gray's nomination, though none of the remaining leadership in the bureau regarded Gray as a worthy successor. Certainly, one of them, Mark Felt, had worked to undermine the administration by helping to keep the Watergate story alive in the newspapers.

Amid these growing revelations, the U.S. Senate created a special committee to further investigate the irregularities in the 1972 campaign. Headed by conservative North Carolina Democrat Sam Ervin, the Senate's Special Committee on Presidential Campaign Activities began meeting in early 1973. The committee's questioning drew closer to the president throughout March, prompting Nixon's counsel John Dean to warn that a "cancer" was growing on the presidency and had to be dealt with soon. With his own tampering with an FBI investigation becoming more and more evident, Dean approached the committee and prosecutors, indicating a willingness to testify. As the ring closed more tightly around the White House, President Nixon moved against his own staff in an attempt to save himself. On April 30, he fired Dean and announced both Haldeman and Ehrlichman's resignations. Shortly thereafter, Attorney General Richard Kleindienst, Mitchell's replacement who was himself implicated in the scandal, was pushed aside by Nixon in favor of Elliot Richardson.

Richardson appointed a special prosecutor, Harvard law professor Archibald Cox, to handle the Watergate case in a move designed to reassure the public of the president's determination to get to the bottom of the scandal. A noted scholar with links to the Kennedys and the national Democratic Party, Cox took over the case in May. His appointment coincided with the beginning of televised hearings by the Senate special committee. These events brought administration officials and other witnesses into American living rooms, and the precise breadth and depth of Watergate into public awareness. Former White House counsel John Dean's testimony dominated the proceedings. Dean carefully sketched a detailed narrative of Nixon's control over the coverup from its inception. His version of events proved easily corroborated by emerging evidence. However, Dean alone testified against the president's version of events. It remained his word against Nixon's. As the ranking Republican on the Senate special committee, Tennessee's Howard Baker, famously observed, the president's awareness of the coverup remained in question: What did the president know and when did he know it?

Then, in July, White House staffer Alexander Butterfield revealed to the Senate Watergate committee the existence of an extensive tape-recording system in the executive mansion, including in the Oval Office. If Nixon's involvement remained unclear, the tapes might clarify the situation. Both the Senate special committee and Special Prosecutor Cox sought the audio tapes, but Nixon refused to release them. The president reasoned that topics on the tapes relating to national security made them too sensitive. The president also insisted that "executive privilege" covered the tapes and that releasing them to the committee or the prosecutor would inappropriately weaken the presidency. A long legal and political battle ensued over access to the only definitive evidence of Nixon's conduct. When an October 1973 court order mandated their release to Cox and his investigative team, President Nixon ordered Richardson to dismiss the special prosecutor. Richardson and his deputy, William Ruckelshaus, resigned rather than carry out Nixon's orders, leaving Solicitor General Robert Bork to fire Cox on Saturday, October 20. The so-called SATURDAY NIGHT MASSACRE significantly damaged Nixon's standing with the public.

Though impeachment talk circulated widely, Nixon's likely successor, Vice President SPIRO AGNEW, was even less popular. Many felt impeachment unlikely given the prospect of Agnew becoming president. But Agnew had his own troubles. In September 1973 he was accused of engaging in bribery and tax evasion during his years as Baltimore County executive and Maryland governor. On October 10 he pled no contest to the charges and stepped down—the only vice president to ever resign from office. Under the recently enacted Twenty-fifth Amendment, President Nixon nominated a replacement, House minority leader GERALD FORD of Michigan. Though Nixon had privately described him as a "dope" and a "jerk," Ford was liked and respected by members of

Tourists read headlines in front of the White House, August 8, 1974. The next day, Nixon became the first U.S. president to resign from office. *(© Bettmann/CORBIS)*

both parties and in both houses of Congress. Ford easily won approval and became vice president. His presence at the post made Nixon's impeachment and removal from office more palatable to many. As autumn wore on, pressure mounted for release of the tapes and public approval ratings of the president slumped to new lows while Nixon traveled abroad in undertaking diplomatic offensives to deflect criticism.

Nixon appointed a new special prosecutor, Leon Jaworski, a Texas lawyer and ally of former president Johnson. If Nixon felt this change would ease the problems he faced, he was mistaken. Jaworski resumed demands for the tapes, and the president was forced to release a number of them in November. The tapes, though failing to provide a full disclosure, led Jaworski to conclude that the president had been involved in criminal activity. One tape revealed an 18-minute gap, which ignited additional controversy.

The House voted overwhelmingly in February 1974 to grant the Judiciary Committee full subpoena powers in its efforts to investigate Watergate. A Washington, D.C., grand jury working under Judge John Sirica indicted Haldeman, Ehrlichman, Mitchell, and several others the next month. The charges included multiple counts of obstruction of justice relating to the break-in and coverup. The

grand jury described Richard Nixon as an "unindicted co-conspirator," in the report that Judge Sirica forwarded to the House Judiciary Committee. Impeachment hearings began in May, though the full number of the WHITE HOUSE TAPES remained mired in litigation. Nixon engaged in piecemeal resistance to court orders to release the recordings. When Judge Sirica demanded 64 post-burglary tapes in April, the president submitted 42 highly edited tape transcripts, which did not match later releases of the actual recordings. Even these highly doctored transcripts revealed evidence of the plotting and conniving engaged in by the administration and also hinted at more venial sins—with their frequent use of the phrase "expletive deleted." Sirica renewed his demands for the actual recordings in May. Nixon insisted that regardless of what the House Judiciary Committee wanted or federal judges ordered, he would release only what he pleased. On July 24, the U.S. Supreme Court in *UNITED STATES v. NIXON* finally ordered the tapes' complete release, arguing that executive privilege did not trump an ongoing criminal investigation. Three days later, on July 27, the Judiciary Committee voted its first article of impeachment, and two others followed, attracting bipartisan support from committee members.

Just over a week later, on August 6, President Nixon finally relented and handed over the tapes, all the while insisting that his refusal to that point had been justified. A conversation between Nixon and Haldeman recorded on June 23, 1972, made plain that Nixon had ordered his chief of staff to use the CIA to obstruct the FBI investigation of the break-in. This so-called smoking gun established his guilt, but, by this time, two-thirds of Americans favored impeachment. The next day, key Republican congressional leaders went to the White House to advise Nixon that impeachment and removal from office could not be avoided. On August 9, 1974, Richard Nixon resigned as president at noon, and Gerald R. Ford became president. Nixon is the only president to ever resign from office. Citing a duty to end a "long national nightmare," President Ford pardoned Nixon a month later. The pardon played a major role in his defeat in the 1976 presidential election.

MAJOR EVENTS AND ISSUES

Affirmative Action Policy   Late in LYNDON JOHNSON's presidency (1963–69), the Philadelphia Plan, a quota system for African-American employment, was first developed. Policymakers did not push hard for its implementation, though. When Richard Nixon assumed office in 1969, having campaigned on a slogan to "Bring Us Together," he revived the Philadelphia Plan and the concept of affirmative action generally. Under President Nixon, affirmative action policies came to mean the pursuit of racial and ethnic proportionality in the workplace. Initially, the Philadelphia Plan applied only to construction contracts let by the federal government. The program was run through the Office of Federal Contract Compliance, and it evolved to encompass all federal contracts as well as protections for women. The Nixon administration's affirmative action policies withstood court challenges brought by litigants who claimed that it violated the equal protection clause of the Fourteenth Amendment and Titles VI and VII of the Civil Rights Act of 1964. The issue became more controversial with the passage of time and the broadening of affirmative action to include admission to higher education as well as employment.

Antiballistic Missile Systems Treaty (1972)   The most important outcome of the first round of Strategic Arms Limitation Talks (SALT I), the Antiballistic Missile Systems Treaty, was signed in Moscow on May 26, 1972, by the United States and the Soviet Union. The principal signatories were President Richard Nixon and Soviet premier Leonid Brezhnev. The SALT I talks followed completion of the Nuclear Nonproliferation Treaty in 1968, when both sides agreed to develop plans to limit nuclear stockpiles. Negotiations

proceeded slowly until Nixon asked Congress to approve legislation for an antiballistic missile shield. Democratic lawmakers were skeptical, but the White House used the move, in actuality, as a tactic to force the Soviets, concerned about the costs of a nuclear arms race, back to the bargaining table. This treaty limited the United States and the Soviet Union to just two antiballistic missile deployment sites, one to protect the national capital and one to protect the launch site for intercontinental ballistic missiles. Additional limits were placed on the number of launch systems and missiles at each site. The U.S. Senate ratified the treaty on August 3, 1972, and it became operative on October 3, 1972.

Antiwar March, Washington, D.C. (1971)   In April 1971, the Vietnam Veterans Against the War, an organization founded in 1967 that included 6,000 members by 1971, held a week-long protest in Washington, D.C. The protest was named Operation Dewey Canyon III after the first two Operation Dewey Canyon incursions into Laos with organizers contending that this was a "limited incursion into the foreign country of Congress." The protest lasted from April 18 through April 24 and it featured 800 veterans throwing their medals over a wire fence encircling the U.S. Capitol. One veteran declared, "I pray that time will forgive me and my brothers for what we did. Spec. 4, army, retired. I'm taking nine purple hearts, Distinguished Cross, Silver Star, Bronze Star and a lot of other shit. This is for my brothers." Another contended, "I symbolically return all Vietnam medals and other service medals given me by the power structure that has genocidal policies against non-white peoples of the world!" On April 19, a group of mothers who had lost their sons in Vietnam led the 1,200 or so war-injured veterans, some in wheelchairs and on crutches, on a march across the Lincoln Memorial Bridge to Arlington National Cemetery. The veterans camped out on the Mall despite Nixon administration efforts to secure court orders blocking their use of the public space. Senator Edward Kennedy (D-MA) spent an hour with the veterans on the first night they spent in defiance of a court order against sleeping on the mall. John Kerry, later a U.S. senator and Democratic candidate for president, was one of the leaders of this group. Protest actions included the testimony from approximately 200 veterans, who decried the war before the Senate Foreign Relations Committee. The veterans were not happy with the slow pace of U.S. withdrawals from Vietnam, wanting all soldiers to come home immediately. After calling the veterans "horrible" and "bastards," President Nixon joined with his inner circle in attempting to dismiss their protests as insignificant and unimportant. Kerry disproved the arguments from Henry Kissinger that the protesters were "inarticulate" when he told the Senate committee, "Someone has to die so that President Nixon won't be, and these are his words, 'the first President to lose

Vietnam War protesters demonstrate near the U.S. Capitol after a march along Pennsylvania Avenue, April 24, 1971. *(Associated Press)*

a war.'" Kerry concluded, "How do you ask a man to be the last man to die for a mistake?" On April 21, approximately 50 veterans marched to the Pentagon, where they tried, but failed, to turn themselves in as war criminals for actions taken in Vietnam. Kerry was one of several who addressed a large rally of 500,000 protesters at the end of the week on April 24: "This is a government that cares more about the legality of where men sleep than the legality of where we drop bombs and why men die."

***Apollo 11* Lands on the Moon (1969)**   The *Apollo 11* space mission marked the first time human beings landed on the moon. At 9:32 A.M. EDT on July 16, 1969, *Apollo 11* was launched from Cape Kennedy in Florida. Commanding the mission was Neil Armstrong. The command module pilot was Michael Collins. The lunar module pilot was Edwin "Buzz" Aldrin. The spaceship remained in Earth's orbit for just over two and half hours when its engines were reignited so as to escape Earth's gravity and proceed on its voyage to the moon. After *Apollo 11* entered a lunar orbit pattern, it took two hours to orbit the moon, and astronauts aboard the craft took many pictures to assist in the study of regional lunar geology. Astronauts Armstrong and Aldrin boarded the lunar module, dubbed the *Eagle,* undocked from the main

spacecraft, and landed on the moon in the Sea of Tranquility on July 20 at 4:17 P.M. EDT. Armstrong reported to NASA's mission control: "Houston, Tranquility Base here—the *Eagle* has landed." They had less than 30 seconds of fuel remaining for this portion of their journey. Their first order of business was to ready the lunar module for liftoff. Next they ate a meal but postponed a sleep period so they could descend to the lunar surface. Armstrong was the first to exit the craft and walk on the moon on July 20 at 10:56 P.M. EDT. He declared, "That's one small step for man, one giant leap for mankind." He released the equipment necessary to photograph the historic event, collected samples of moon rocks and material, took panoramic and closeup photographs of the moon, and undertook other scientific studies. Aldrin joined Armstrong for much of this work. They collected 46 pounds of lunar rocks. Their moon walk lasted about two and a half hours. They left a plaque on the moon that read: "HERE MEN FROM THE PLANET EARTH FIRST SET FOOT UPON THE MOON JULY 1969 A.D. WE CAME IN PEACE FOR ALL MANKIND." They slept before returning to the *Apollo 11* spacecraft. Aldrin and Armstrong were on the moon for a total of 21 hours and 38 minutes. Upon their return, *Apollo 11* began its return journey to Earth, landing in the Pacific Ocean on July 24, 1969, at 12:50 P.M. EDT.

President Richard Nixon speaks to *Apollo 11* astronauts *(left to right)* Neil A. Armstrong, Michael Collins, and Edwin E. Aldrin, Jr., shortly after their return from the moon on July 24, 1969. *(NASA)*

Assassination Attempt Against George Wallace (1972)

During his third consecutive bid for the presidency, Alabama governor George Wallace was the target of an assassination attempt on May 15, 1972 in Laurel, Maryland. He had previously commented, "Somebody's going to get me one of these days. I can just see a little guy out there that nobody's paying any attention to. He reaches into his pocket and out comes the little gun, like that Sirhan guy that got [Robert] Kennedy [in 1968]." As a result, Wallace used a bulletproof podium for his speeches, but this measure proved inadequate largely because Wallace liked to mingle with the crowds. The gunman was Arthur Herman Bremer, a mentally ill man. Wallace had already won the Florida, North Carolina, and Tennessee primaries in a campaign that had as its slogan, "send them a message." Wallace routinely told crowds that it was wrong for "briefcase-carrying bureaucrats" to "run your lives" when they "can't even park their bicycles straight." Wallace focused his major criticism on the issue of forced busing. Permanently paralyzed from the waist down, Wallace dropped out of the race, but he won the Maryland and Michigan primaries the day after the shooting.

"Battle of the Sexes" (1973)

The "Battle of the Sexes" was fought on a tennis court erected in the Astrodome in Houston, Texas, on September 20, 1973, between tennis players Bobby Riggs and Billie Jean King. Riggs was 55, and had already moved beyond the peak of his career when he won

Tennis champ Billie Jean King *(foreground)* defeated Bobby Riggs in the "Battle of the Sexes" at the Houston Astrodome on September 20, 1973. *(Associated Press)*

Wimbledon in 1939. By the early 1970s, he was more a hustler than an athlete. King was then a rising star on the women's tour at the age of 29. She was interested most especially in winning tournaments and promoting equality for women in sport. Riggs hoped to prove women as being unworthy of the public's consideration as serious athletes. He had defeated Margaret Court in a match on Mother's Day in 1973. King had previously turned down invitations from Riggs to play a match, but now she felt she had no choice. She explained, "I thought it would set us back 50 years if I didn't win that match. It would ruin the women's tour and affect all women's self esteem." The match in the Astrodome was watched by Americans whether or not they were tennis fans. It encapsulated the arguments around which women's rights issues were then swirling throughout the nation. The two players entered the court in bizarre ways. King was carried in like Cleopatra on a golden litter by four well-sculpted men dressed like slaves from the ancient world. Scantily clad women, dubbed "Bobby's Bosom Buddies," pulled Riggs in a rickshaw. King dominated the match, winning 6–4, 6–3, 6–3, after running Riggs all over the court. The *London Sunday Times* wrote that the match proved to be "the drop shot and volley heard around the world."

Branzburg v. Hayes (1972)

In a 5-4 ruling, the majority opinion written by Justice Byron White, the Supreme Court ruled in *Branzburg v. Hayes* in 1972 that journalists do not have the right to withhold the identity of their sources. White contended that the public interest trumped First Amendment protections of freedom of the press. White also contended that minimal damage would accrue to the press from such requirements. The case resulted from Paul M. Branzburg's reporting of local drug trafficking for the *Louisville Courier-Journal*, a Louisville, Kentucky, newspaper. Branzburg was asked, but refused, to testify before a grand jury. More than 30 years later, in 2006, this case was cited pertinent in the judicial determination that compelled journalists to testify about the Valerie Plame leak in federal proceedings against Vice President Dick Cheney's aide, Lewis "Scooter" Libby, during the administration of President GEORGE W. BUSH.

Cambodian Bombings and Invasion

President Nixon ordered a secret U.S. bombing campaign of neutral Cambodia in March 1969. Cambodia was located directly to the west of Vietnam, and it had steadily maintained its neutrality in the Vietnam War. Nevertheless, U.S. military policymakers argued that North Vietnamese leader Ho Chi Minh and the Vietcong were using Cambodian territory for the transport of troops and supplies and had located within the neutral country five sanctuaries for their troops, making the bombings unavoidable. The exact number of Cambodian casualties from these bombings remains unknown, but the best estimates suggest 100,000 Cambodian people were killed while another 2 million were made homeless. Nixon followed the bombing campaign with a televised announcement of an invasion of Cambodia on April 30, 1970, which both stunned and infuriated many Americans, who were looking for the VIETNAMIZATION POLICY to bring U.S. troops home. Many feared that this action would result in a widening and lengthening of the war. When Nixon addressed the nation to announce the invasion, he stood over a map, which he used as a prop to justify his argument. At one point while reading from his prepared remarks, Nixon lost his place. When he was stammering and trying to figure out what to say next his performance gave the occasion a surreal feel. Nixon denied that the U.S. military actions constituted an invasion of Cambodia, since the communists held the territory being attacked and not the peaceful Cambodians in contradiction to the facts of the bombings, which were still secret. A week into the invasion, 398 North Vietnamese were killed. Ultimately the U.S. House and Senate voted to eliminate funding for the carpet bombings in 1973 over the protests of the White House. The 1970 invasion announcement launched a newly charged wave of antiwar protests, the most notorious occurring at Kent State University and at Jackson State College. Four students were killed by National Guard troops at Kent State and two were killed by police officers at Jackson State. Opposition to the invasion was not limited to college campuses. Later in the year, Congress banned the use of combat troops in Cambodia and Laos. Most tragic of all, the U.S. actions in Cambodia destabilized the government of that country, which culminated in the brutal dictatorship of Pol Pot and the Khmer Rouge, which killed 2 million people in a genocide later in the decade.

Charles Manson Murders (1969)

Charles Manson was a gruesome serial killer who fed into social fears about the counterculture. He became a criminal at age 13, and he was released from prison in California in 1967. Manson was a hippie who had attracted a following of flower children. They were termed his family, and Manson preached to his followers about the Beatles and the coming of Helter Skelter. Life in the family was characterized by orgies and hallucinogenic drug usage. Manson presented himself as a "Christ-like" figure to his followers. On August 8, 1969, Manson told his family of followers that the Helter Skelter operation would be put into operation with the killing of actress Sharon Tate, who had recently appeared in the movie *Valley of the Dolls*, was married to director Roman Polanski, and was pregnant. Three female family members—Susan Atkins, Patricia Krenwinkel, and Linda Kasabian—and one male family member—Charles "Tex" Wilson—were tapped to execute the murders. In all, five people were killed that night. Manson was unhappy that the crime was so bloody and messy. He scheduled another Helter Skelter murder for the next night. Manson, Clem Tufts, and Leslie Van Houten joined the four

Charles Manson *(© Everett Collection, Inc./Alamy)*

individuals involved in the murders at the Tate home. Rosemary and Leno LaBianca were murdered, and as at the Tate crime scene bloody, hate-filled messages were left behind. A grand jury indicted the five people who actually participated in the murders—Watson, Krenwinkel, Atkins, Kasabian, and Van Houten—as well as Manson, who orchestrated the attacks. The four who were in custody in California—Manson, Krenwinkel, Atkins, and Van Houten—were tried jointly, and Watson was tried separately. All were convicted and sentenced to death, but the 1972 California Supreme Court ruling that the death penalty was unconstitutional meant that these sentences were commuted to life imprisonment.

Chicago 8 Trial (1969–1970)   In March 1969, the Nixon administration Justice Department used a provision of the 1968 Civil Rights Act, making it a federal crime to cross state lines to incite a riot, to bring charges against New Left activists. One such prosecution involved the eight radical political leaders in the protests that occurred at the 1968 Democratic National Convention in Chicago: Rennie Davis, David Dellinger, John Froines, Tom Hayden, Abbie Hoffman, Jerry Rubin, Bobby Seale, and Lee Weiner. The case against Seale

was weak; he had not been in Chicago more than 24 hours, nor had his participation in these particular protests been significant. He was targeted for his activism with the Black Panther Party. The defendants did not have a unified strategy. Whereas Hayden wanted to use the occasion to debate substantive issues, Rubin and Hoffman treated the trial as another opportunity for outlandish protests. Seale expressed his anger against the state during the trial, accusing the judge of racist and fascist behavior. His case was ultimately separated from those of the other defendants. The jurors had little sympathy for the defendants. One claimed they should be convicted for "their appearance, their language, and lifestyle" and another argued that the protesters "should have been shot down by police." Ultimately, the jury dismissed all the charges of conspiracy, but found Davis, Dellinger, Hayden, Hoffman, and Rubin guilty of crossing state lines to incite a riot, and sentenced them to five years of jail time and a $5,000 fine. The following year, an appellate court reversed the verdicts.

Child Nutrition Act Amendments (1972)   The Child Nutrition Act Amendments of 1972 established the Special Supplemental Food Program for Women, Infants, and Children (WIC) as a pilot program. It was made permanent in 1974, and administered by the Food and Nutrition Service of the U.S. Department of Agriculture. The program aims to protect the health of low-income women, infants, and children under the age of five by providing healthy food, information on eating properly, and health care referrals.

China   *See* VISIT TO CHINA (1972)

Christmas Bombings (1972)   President Nixon responded in anger to the failure of peace talks to end the Vietnam War during the winter of 1972 with Operation Linebacker II, commonly known as the Christmas bombings, a two-week campaign in late December, exclusive of Christmas day when no missions were flown. Some additional context about the peace talks is necessary to understand the rationale for the bombing campaign. National Security Advisor Henry Kissinger had been negotiating with the Democratic Republic of Vietnam, the official name of North Vietnam, and had reached preliminary terms. When other parties involved in the war—the South Vietnamese government in Saigon and the National Liberation Front—objected to the pending deal, this peace initiative fell apart. Because Congress would likely halt funding for the war in January 1973 the administration felt additional pressure to force a peace settlement.

Nixon justified the bombings by arguing that they would finally bring a speedy release of U.S. prisoners of war. Key North Vietnamese cities and military targets were selected. Nixon told the chairman of the Joint Chiefs of Staff: "I don't want any more of this crap about the fact that we couldn't hit this target or that one. This is your chance to use military power to win this war, and if you don't, I'll consider you responsible." The U.S. B-52s and F-4s deployed over 36,000 tons of bombs, more than in the period between 1969 and 1971. The attack destroyed a quarter of North Vietnam's oil reserves and 80 percent of its electrical capacity. Almost 2,000 civilians were killed. The United States lost 26 planes and 93 pilots in its assault on Hanoi. Reaction was swift and critical. Nixon was termed a "madman" for using "a Stone Age tactic," by Senate majority leader Mike Mansfield (D-MT). Nixon did not care, hoping that he could terrify the North to resume peace talks. On December 26, Hanoi asked for a resumption of peace talks.

Clean Air Act (1970)   Congress passed the first Clean Air Act in 1963, which for the first time gave the federal government responsibility for protecting air quality. That bill was more significant for what it symbolized than for what it accomplished. In 1970, Congress passed a much stronger Clean Air Act, which in conjunction with the newly created Environmental Protection Agency, established nationwide ambient air-quality standards. The 1970 law also provided for pollution emission standards for all types of motor vehicles. Human health protection was the primary consideration in the development of these standards. The best available technologies were required to implement the standards. Finally, compliance deadlines were included in the law. On signing the bill on December 31, 1970, President Nixon declared: "I think that 1970 will be known as the year of the beginning, in which we really began to move on the problems of clean air and clean water and open spaces for the future generations of America."

Coastal Zone Management Act (1972)   The Coastal Zone Management Act of 1972 provided for a program of preserving and protecting the nation's coastal areas. It also called for the various federal agencies with coastal responsibilities to cooperate. States were charged with developing plans to protect coastal wetlands. An additional feature of the law was the creation of the National Estuarine Research Reserve System to engage in additional study of estuarine areas. President Nixon signed the Coastal Zone Management Act on October 27, 1972, even though he was unhappy with placement of responsibility for the program with the Department of Commerce, not the Department of Interior as he had advised. He argued, "This action is not sufficient reason in my judgment for vetoing the bill, but it does underscore once again the importance of creating a new Department of Natural Resources, as I have recommended, so that we can reverse the trend toward fragmentation and fractionalization of Federal programs and begin to coordinate our environmental efforts more effectively." This law became a model for other nations seeking legislation by which to protect their coastlines.

Comprehensive Drug Abuse Prevention and Control Act (1970)   The Comprehensive Drug Abuse Prevention and Control Act of 1970 expanded the definition of "drug dependent person" to enable more people to gain treatment for addiction and other drug abuse problems. It also authorized the secretary of the Department of Health, Education and Welfare (now the Department of Health and Human Services) to make both scientific and medical decisions regarding controlled substances. Creation of a single control system for narcotic and psychotropic drugs promised greater control over the drug problem in the United States.

Comprehensive Employment and Training Act (1973)   The Comprehensive Employment and Training Act of 1973, often known as CETA, established a program of block grants to state and local governments to assist and expand public and private job training programs for economically disadvantaged youth. Upon signing the law, President Nixon celebrated the end of "the patchwork system of individual, rigid, categorical manpower programs." The state services to be funded with these block grants included classroom education and job skills training, job counseling, on-the-job training, supportive services, transitional public service employment, and work experience. Since the funding came in the form of block grants, no "federal strings" were imposed on the services to be provided by each state and local program.

Congressional Budget and Impoundment Control Act (1974)   For much of the Nixon administration, the president and the Congress wrangled over the budget. Because Democrats controlled Congress and because, in his second term, Watergate preoccupied the president's attention, lawmakers looked for ways to assert greater budgetary independence, especially after President Nixon refused to spend billions of dollars that Congress had appropriated for a host of different programs. Nixon signed the Congressional Budget and Impoundment Control Act into law on July 12, 1974. The law provided for Congress to adopt annual budget resolutions with spending divided among 20 different functional categories. While the president retained the authority under the law to submit an annual budget, the law also provided for a formal congressional budget document to be prepared by the newly created Congressional Budget Office, one provision of the law. Seemingly in denial of what the law meant, the president said of the measure: "Prior to the enactment of this bill, the Congress has had to consider a large number of separate measures with no system for establishing priorities relating to an overall spending goal. This system did not impose sufficient disciplines on the Congress to stop the passage of pork-barrel legislation or to resist the pressure of special interest groups seeking a disproportionate share of the tax dollar." The most important legacy of the 1974 legislation was to engender increased disagreement between the executive and legislative branches over the budget.

Consumer Product Safety Act (1972) The Consumer Product Safety Act of 1972 established the Consumer Product Safety Commission (CPSC) and determined its authority and jurisdiction. The CPSC was authorized to ban products without feasible standards for safety. Furthermore, it was given the authority to conduct recalls of unsafe products. The CPSC did not have jurisdiction over aircraft, boats, cosmetics, drugs, firearms and ammunition, fixed site amusement rides, food, medical devices, motor vehicles, pesticides, and tobacco products. When he signed the law, President Nixon criticized elements of the law that he believed would "weaken budget control" and threaten inflation. He contended such "unfortunate" provisions should not be viewed as precedents. He did praise the larger purpose of the law: "The most important thing about this bill, however, is its recognition that a defective lawn mower or electric heater can be just as dangerous to the consumer and his family as contaminated food or improperly packaged drugs. It is high time that the Government provided for comprehensive regulation of the many potentially dangerous products commonly used in and around American households."

Détente Perhaps the most significant component of President Richard Nixon's foreign policy was his move toward détente, a thawing of tensions in the cold war. Several significant developments characterized détente, including increased arms control talks with the Soviet Union and the opening of relations with mainland China, including Nixon's historic VISIT TO CHINA in 1972. The height of the cold war with the Soviets, at least in terms of the potential for nuclear war, came in 1962 with the Cuban missile crisis. In 1963, the two nations, having stepped back from the precipice, signed the Limited Test Ban Treaty. Vietnam slowed this progress toward détente, but during the Nixon administration conditions were ripe for a more meaningful pursuit of peace between the world's two superpowers. The most important signal of this readiness was the Nuclear Nonproliferation Treaty of 1968, ratified by the Senate and signed by President Nixon in 1969. Equally important to the success of détente early in the decade is that the approach fit with Nixon's preferred means by which to pursue foreign policy. Along with his National Security Advisor Henry Kissinger, the president pursued a pragmatic and flexible strategy in which emphasis on maintaining the balance of power prevailed. This was followed with the ANTIBALLISTIC MISSILE SYSTEMS TREATY of 1972, a product of the Strategic Arms Limitation Talks (SALT I). European security measures also constituted a part of détente as Chancellor Willy Brandt of West Germany pursued his own policy of détente with the Soviet Union, which included the recognition of political borders, improved trade and cultural exchanges, and improved human rights. Détente collapsed by the end of the decade when the second major round of arms reduction talks, SALT II, resulted in a signed agreement but no treaty.

Easter Offensive (1972) The Easter offensive began with a North Vietnamese attack on U.S. positions on March 30, 1972. It constituted the biggest engagement in the war since Nixon took office, and certainly since the invasion of Cambodia. Furthermore, because of President Nixon's VIETNAMIZATION POLICY U.S. troop strength was reduced 85 percent from its high mark of 549,500 in the spring of 1969. Meanwhile, U.S. troop morale had deteriorated to dangerous levels, and U.S. involvement in responding to the Easter offensive was limited to advisers working with South Vietnamese troops, U.S. airpower, the mining of Haiphong harbor, and logistical support. The equivalent of 20 divisions bore down on key South Vietnamese positions in a three-pronged attack designed to end the war. South Vietnamese units were pushed back but they did not crumble, leaving space for the U.S. to use massive air strikes and prevent a major defeat. North Vietnamese officials called the decision to mine Haiphong harbor, and other ports, the "gravest step in the escalation of the war to date."

Education Amendments *See* TITLE IX OF THE EDUCATION AMENDMENTS (1972)

Election Campaign Act *See* FEDERAL ELECTION CAMPAIGN ACT (1971)

Emergency Petroleum Allocation Act (1973) Drafted as a response to the OPEC OIL EMBARGO of 1973, the Emergency Petroleum Allocation Act of 1973 was signed into law by President Nixon in November. It provided for an official federal government plan to allocate gasoline and home heating fuel. Relationships between suppliers and purchasers were frozen and replaced by one based on a determination of priority users. Finally, the law authorized the president to implement price controls on petroleum, with oil not to exceed $7.66 a barrel. In 1974, Congress created the Federal Energy Administration to oversee the regulations put in place under this law.

Endangered Species Act (1973) The Endangered Species Act of 1973 built on the legislative foundation of the Endangered Species Conservation Act of 1969. The legislation passed in 1973 might well be understood as the apex of environmentalism, at least from a congressional perspective. The legislation privileged the rights and need for protection of endangered species of animals over the wants and needs of human beings. When President Nixon signed the Endangered Species Act on December 28, 1973, he declared, "Noth-

A pile of American bison skulls waiting to be ground for fertilizer. Due to commercial hunting and slaughter in the 19th century, the American bison nearly went extinct and is today restricted to a few national parks and other reserves. It is one of the species currently on the endangered species list, protected by the Endangered Species Act of 1973. *(Burton Historical Collection/Detroit Public Library)*

ing is more priceless and more worthy of preservation than the rich array of animal life with which our country has been blessed. It is a many-faceted treasure, of value to scholars, scientists, and nature lovers alike, and it forms a vital part of the heritage we all share as Americans." The legislation called for the protection of not only endangered species, but also the ecosystems in which they lived. Just under 2,000 species have been included in the program, which is jointly administered by the U.S. Fish and Wildlife Service and the National Marine Fisheries Service.

Environmental Policy Act   *See* NATIONAL ENVIRONMENTAL POLICY ACT (1969)

Equal Credit Opportunity Act (1974)   Prior to the 1970s, women faced significant discrimination from banks and other financial service institutions when they tried to borrow

money either for personal or for business reasons. Feminist organizations such as NOW had lobbied hard for remedial legislation. President Nixon also supported the reform. His National Commission on Consumer Finance, appointed in 1972, publicized many inequities in credit and banking. Congress had another reason to support the measure; it was revenue neutral in that it did not draw on the federal treasury. Support for the Equal Credit Opportunity Act cut across party and ideological lines. The law, which passed easily in 1974, forbade using gender to determine creditworthiness.

Family Educational Rights and Privacy Act (1974)   The Family Educational Rights and Privacy Act (FERPA) ensured that student education records remained private. It was one of the first privacy laws enacted by Congress. The sponsor, Senator James L. Buckley (Conservative-NY), introduced the measure as an amendment to a pending education bill because he was concerned that parents' rights were being violated when schools denied them access to their children's records. All educational institutions receiving federal funds were required to comply under the law, which was administered by the U.S. Department of Education. Parents were custodians of these privacy rights until their children turned 18, then all privacy rights redounded to the student. Under the law, parents or eligible students have the right of review over student records. Parents or eligible students have the right to request corrections to incorrect records. Parents or eligible students must provide written permission for the release of student records. President GERALD FORD signed FERPA into law in August 1974, less than two weeks after Richard Nixon resigned from the presidency.

Federal Election Campaign Act (1971)   The Federal Election Campaign Act of 1971 attempted to fix several problems in the functioning of U.S. elections. First, it addressed the problem of very wealthy candidates using their financial advantage to "buy" a victory. It also tackled the increasing tendency to rely on advertising to advance a political message by limiting media expenditures. Finally, the law required more stringent disclosure of campaign donations and expenditures. The law was more incremental than revolutionary in substance, and reformers continued to fight for even stronger measures. An attempt to amend this law came in 1974, after the first election conducted under terms of the 1971 law and, more important, the revelation of the Watergate scandal. The amendments passed in 1974 over President Nixon's veto provided for limits of $1,000 on individual contributions to any campaign in a single election year. It also capped total individual donations in a particular election to $25,000. Political action committee (PAC) donations were capped at $5,000 per campaign. Stricter reporting and disclosure requirements were implemented.

Federal Water Pollution Control Act Amendments (1972)   In 1970, President Nixon advocated stricter protections against water pollution. When Congress went to work on Nixon's proposal, the lawmakers produced a bill that did much more than the president recommended. It gave the federal government more jurisdiction over intrastate waterways, created a system of federal permits for municipal sewage and industrial discharges, declared a goal of zero pollution discharges by 1985, and provided $18 billion in federal grant money to fund more technologically sophisticated sewage disposal systems. After acknowledging that the "pollution of our rivers, lakes and streams degrades the quality of American life," President Nixon nonetheless vetoed the Federal Water Pollution Control Act Amendments of 1972 because he contended the legislation "ignore[d] other very real threats to the quality of life, such as spiraling prices and increasingly onerous taxes." At issue for the president was the

cost of the measure at $24 billion. Congress easily overrode the veto, and the measure became law.

Frontiero v. Richardson (1973)   An important Supreme Court case for gender equality, *Frontiero v. Richardson* (1973) resulted when a female soldier, Sharon Frontiero, a lieutenant in the U.S. Air Force, was denied the right to claim her husband as a dependent in the same way that male soldiers claimed their wives as dependents and who were thus liable to receive dependant pay. Existing federal law termed wives as automatic dependents but charged that husbands had to prove their dependency defined as meaning their wives paid for more than half of their support. She brought suit against Secretary of Defense Elliot L. Richardson. A plurality of the justices ruled 8–1 in favor of the plaintiff, arguing that the law in question violated the Fifth Amendment's Due Process Clause in that it resulted in "dissimilar treatment for men and women who are similarly situated."

Furman v. Georgia (1972)   The case of *Furman v. Georgia* offered the Supreme Court an opportunity to decide whether the death penalty was a cruel and unusual punishment in violation of the Eighth and Fourteenth Amendments of the Constitution. On August 11, 1967, William Henry Furman burglarized a Savannah, Georgia, home, killing one of the residents in the process. He was sentenced to death for his crime, and his case was appealed to the Supreme Court. The five-member majority in this 5-4 decision issued in 1972 could not agree on the reasoning for an opinion. Justices Thurgood Marshall and William Brennan contended that all capital punishment was wrong, with Brennan arguing, "a punishment may not be so severe as to be degrading to the dignity of human beings." Justice William O. Douglas found that the death penalty was "not compatible with the idea of equal protection of the laws" because it was assessed disproportionately against the poor. Marshall added that it was not an effective deterrent. Justices Potter Stewart and Byron White found that the current practices of implementing the death penalty were cruel without commenting on whether the punishment was ipso facto cruel. The *Furman* decision overturned all the death penalty statutes in the country.

General Revenue Sharing   More popularly known as general revenue sharing, the State and Local Fiscal Assistance Act of 1972 marked an important departure from trends in the political economy put in place in the 1930s. The program promised to share federal revenues with state and local governments, shifting power from Washington, D.C., to the states and thus curtailing federal involvement in the lives of the American people. The program was more innovative in its design than in its practice as it functioned more as just another federal program. It did so partly because, while a popular idea for Republicans, revenue sharing was never a major priority for the Nixon administration in being viewed rather as a secondary concern. The administration played smart politics to gain passage of the law, working in tandem with big city mayors and public interest groups to pressure the Democratic Congress. Furthermore, Nixon argued in his 1971 State of the Union address: "The time has now come in America to reverse the flow of power and resources from the States and communities to Washington, and start power and resources flowing back from Washington to the States and communities and more important, to the people all across America." Although popular with state and local governments, general revenue sharing was eliminated in 1986.

Hanoi Hilton   Hanoi Hilton was the name U.S. prisoners of war (POWs) in Vietnam gave to the Hoa Lo prison, originally constructed by France in the center of Hanoi, where many POWs were held. The structure filled a city block, and POWs nicknamed subdivisions: "New Guy Village," "Heartbreak Hotel," "Little Las Vegas," and "Camp Unity." The structure was well fortified, with walls 20 feet high, plus five feet of electrified barbed wire, and four feet thick. Conditions were predictably atrocious: concrete beds with stocks, poor sanitation, infestations of rats and insects, inedible food, no real medical care, incessant psychological abuse to try to gain confessions, and torture. The average age of POWs was 34, significantly older than the average age of U.S. troops in Vietnam, and most were college educated, again unlike the average soldier. Initially, POWs had been held in a number of different locations (other camps in or near Hanoi included Alcatraz, the Plantation, the Powerplant, and the Zoo; three other camps were approximately 35 miles from Hanoi: the Briarpatch, Camp Faith, and Camp Hope), but after a failed U.S. rescue attempt at one POW camp in November 1970, the North Vietnamese relocated all the POWs to the Hanoi Hilton. As a result of increased U.S. bombing in 1972 following the EASTER OFFENSIVE, approximately 200 POWs were moved to a camp near the border with China to make sure not all POWs were killed should the U.S. planes hit the Hanoi Hilton. The Hanoi Hilton operated as a POW camp from August 1964 through February 1973, and it housed over 700 U.S. soldiers.

Hearst, Patricia   *See* KIDNAPPING OF PATRICIA HEARST (1974)

Housing and Community Development Act (1974)   The Housing and Community Development Act of 1974 replaced the rigid housing policies enacted from 1945 until the 1960s, such as urban renewal and the Model Cities program of the Great Society, with a block grant program for community development. These block grants were provided to local governments. Because the law identified low-income families as intended beneficiaries of the program, many of the block grants were devoted to the inner cities. Another provision of the law put in place the Section 8 housing program whereby landlords received federal dollars in exchange for offering low-income tenants lower rents. The Section 8 program also provided developers with the use of tax-exempt bonds for financing the construction or renovation of apartment houses for low-income tenants. The new policy promised to give communities greater autonomy over the spending of federal dollars on housing programs.

Impeachment Hearings and Resignation of President Nixon (1974)   Simultaneous with the Supreme Court deliberations in UNITED STATES V. NIXON, the House Judiciary Committee met to debate a bill of impeachment against President Nixon. On July 27, 1974, the committee voted 27-11 in favor of the first of three articles of impeachment against Nixon. The first article looked at the facts of the Watergate break-in, charging that Nixon had "prevented, obstructed, and impeded the administration of justice" in "violation of his constitutional duty to take care that the laws be faithfully executed." The second article dealt with Nixon's abuses of power in "violati[on of] the Constitutional rights of citizens, impairing the due and proper administration of justice," and "contravening the laws governing agencies of the executive

After resigning the presidency on August 9, 1974, Richard Nixon *(right)* and his wife Pat leave the White House. Incoming president Gerald Ford *(left)* and first lady Betty Ford see them off. *(Oliver F. Atkins/Nixon Presidential Materials Project)*

branch" specifically with regard to his exploi tation of the Internal Revenue Service, his mishandling of the FBI, and his creation of the PLUMBERS unit and its improper association with the CIA. The House Judiciary Committee approved the article by a vote of 28-10 on July 29. The next day the committee approved the third article 21-17. It charged that Nixon had ignored subpoenas from the House Judiciary Committee. The committee had considered but rejected two other charges, dealing with the bombings in Cambodia and corruption with regard to his personal and political funds. The committee had hoped its case would prove Nixon should be impeached because he had acted in ways that threatened the constitutional order. Actually, the case rested more on the concept of an indictable offense, so clear was the evidence of Nixon's criminal behavior. After the Supreme Court ruling in the tapes case, Nixon's attorneys reviewed the tapes, especially a conversation on June 23, 1972, when Nixon ordered his aides to use the CIA to block any FBI investigation of Watergate, irrefutable evidence of obstruction of justice. Nixon met with leading House and Senate Republicans and they told him he could not withstand an impeachment vote. With an impeachment vote in the House and conviction in the Senate almost certain, Nixon announced his resignation from the presidency on August 8, 1974, effective the following day at noon. In his farewell address to his staff, Nixon declared: "Those who hate you don't win unless you hate them. And then you destroy yourself."

Jackson State College Shootings (1970) On May 14, 1970, 10 days after four white college students were killed by National Guard troops at Kent State University in 1970, two African-American students were killed by Mississippi Highway Patrol officers at Jackson State College, located in Jackson, Mississippi. Like the incident at Kent State, this tragedy began as an antiwar protest, but it was also a civil rights protest. Previously there had been very little campus unrest at Jackson State, and during the May 1970 demonstrations officials overreacted. The officials marched onto campus behind a 23-foot-long armored vehicle. The 10 men inside the tank were armed with Thompson submachine guns and shotguns capable of emitting tear gas. In this attack an additional 12 students were injured. Over 150 rounds were shot into the dormitory were the students were congregated when the attack began. The local medical center, Baptist Hospital, refused to treat the wounded African-American students for reasons of segregation. The media and the public paid much less attention to this event at a historically black college. Ultimately, a presidential commission, two grand juries, and a civil court deliberated these events. One of the county grand juries ruled that the shootings of unarmed students were "justified" because protesters "must expect to be injured or killed when law enforcement officers are required to reestablish order." The presidential commission, though, argued

that the police in Mississippi perpetrated an "unreasonable, unjustified, overreaction" in shooting the students.

Kennedy Center for the Performing Arts Opens (1971)
The Kennedy Center for the Performing Arts, an enduring memorial to President JOHN F. KENNEDY, opened on the banks of the Potomac River in Washington, D.C., on September 8, 1971, with the world premiere of a requiem mass in honor of Kennedy composed by Leonard Bernstein. Establishment of the center reiterated the importance of Washington, D.C., as a cultural as well as a political center of the nation. Planning for such a facility dated back to 1958 when President DWIGHT D. EISENHOWER signed a law to create a National Cultural Center to offer both classical and contemporary entertainment and education. It also provided that the center should be privately funded. A major funding drive began during the Kennedy administration. Two months after Kennedy's death in 1963, Congress named the center after the slain president and funded $23 million for its construction.

Kent State University Shootings (1970) Four students were killed and nine more were wounded when the Ohio National Guard fired into a crowd of demonstrators at Kent State University on May 4, 1970. College students across the nation went on strike in protest against the brutality, and hundreds of universities had to close temporarily as a result. The killings at Kent State took place in the context of increased antiwar activity following President Nixon's April 1970 announcement of an invasion of Cambodia, which angered many Americans. In response, on Friday, May 1, a rally was staged on the Commons, an outdoor area in the middle of campus and the site of many demonstrations and protests over the years. During this protest, the Nixon administration was criticized and a copy of the Constitution was buried to symbolize the illegality of the war being fought without congressional approval. Plans for another rally on May 4 were announced. Additionally on that Friday several thousand students at Kent State took their antiwar protests off campus and into the local business district of downtown Kent. There they collided with the local police, and the Ohio governor called in the National Guard. Next the ROTC building at Kent State was set on fire. Despite efforts on the part of the university administration to ban the May 4 rally before it began, 500 students rallied to protest the guard's presence on campus. A total of 3,000 students turned out to watch the protest. Guardsmen ordered the crowd to disperse, but they failed to move. A second attempt to break up the protest led some in the crowd to throw rocks and bottles; the troops responded with tear gas. The core group of 500 protesters moved to Blanket Hill and on to the Prentice Hall parking lot and the football practice field. Guardsmen followed the students, and some pointed, but did not fire, their weapons. Guardsmen next retreated following the same route. At the top of Blanket Hill, 28 of the 70 soldiers fired between 61 and 67 shots in a 13 second period of time, killing four and wounding nine. Scholars who have studied the events have argued that the troops were culpable. Guardsmen, however, contended that they shot because they feared for their lives. Court cases have largely upheld this position, finding the soldiers not legally responsible for the injuries and the deaths. A civil case was ultimately settled out of court with the 28 guardsmen signing a statement of regret, not an admission of guilt. A monetary settlement of $675,000 was provided to the wounded students and the parents of the deceased students. The money was paid by the state of Ohio and not the National Guard and sums amounted to the equivalent of what it would have cost to stage another trial. Public opinion polls suggested support rested with the National Guard at least in working-class communities where support for the student protesters was diminishing. The incident served to inspire an important antiwar song, "Ohio," by Neil Young.

Kidnapping of Patricia Hearst (1974)   On February 5, 1974, Patricia Hearst, the 19-year-old daughter of millionaire publisher Randolph Hearst, was kidnapped. The crime occurred at her Berkeley, California, apartment. Hearst

Patricia Hearst with weapon posing in front of SLA emblem, April 1974 (© Everett Collection, Inc./Alamy)

was entertaining her fiancé, Steven Weed. Two men and a woman rushed into the room after Hearst answered a knock at her door. Weed was attacked and tied up while Hearst was carried away. The kidnappers were affiliated with an unknown revolutionary group, the Symbionese Liberation Army (SLA). Over time, Hearst came to identify with her kidnappers. In April, a closed circuit television system showed her participating in a bank robbery with her kidnappers. Hearst ran away, but she was captured by the FBI. She was tried, convicted, and sentenced to seven years in jail, but she was released in 1979. President BILL CLINTON pardoned her in 2001.

Manson Murders   *See* CHARLES MANSON MURDERS (1969)

***Milliken v. Bradley* (1974)**   In a 5-4 decision in the case *Milliken v. Bradley* (1974), the Supreme Court rejected a comprehensive interdistrict plan to bring school desegregation to the Detroit, Michigan, area public schools. The plan affected 800,000 students. A district court had earlier ruled that de jure segregation existed in Detroit. Consequently, a plan was developed to integrate the Detroit public schools, which were 75 percent African American in student composition, with the overwhelmingly white suburban school districts, 53 in all. The Court of Appeals argued in the case that busing only in the city of Detroit would have resulted in "an all black [city] school system immediately surrounded by practically all white suburban school systems, with an overwhelmingly white majority population in the total metropolitan area." There was no finding of segregation, de jure or otherwise, in the suburban schools but these schools were included in the plan because it was found that doing so was the only practicable means by which to integrate the Detroit schools. Writing for the Court, Chief Justice Warren E. Burger contended: "While boundary lines may be bridged in circumstances where there has been a constitutional violation calling for inter-district relief, school district lines may not be casually ignored or treated as a mere administrative convenience; substantial local control of public education in this country is a deeply rooted tradition."

Moratorium Demonstrations (1969)   Staged on October 15, 1969, the moratorium demonstrations, alternatively known as the Vietnam moratorium or the peace moratorium, attracted 2 million protesters throughout the nation and the world, and it constituted the largest protest to date in U.S. history. The Vietnam Moratorium Committee, founded on June 30, 1969, sponsored the demonstrations. Organizers hoped to counter the lawless and chaotic tone of the protests at the 1968 Democratic National Convention in Chicago. They also wanted to make sure that people throughout the country could participate in community-level protests. Another group, the New Mobilization Committee to End the War in Vietnam, was also hoping to intensify antiwar protests.

The two groups arranged for a series of moderate and mainstream demonstrations throughout the country. For example, in Portland, Oregon, a struggle broke out between 400 protesters and local police when the antiwar activists tried to block entrance at an army induction center. Furthermore, 300 protesters gathered outside the U.S. embassy in London. Participants donned black armbands to show their solidarity and resolve to end the war. They also wanted to signal their remorse for the U.S. soldiers killed in the war since 1961.

The largest march was in Washington, D.C., where 250,000 demonstrators protested. At one rally, leading child care guru Dr. Benjamin Spock argued that the war was "a total abomination." Coretta Scott King, wife of slain civil rights leader Martin Luther King, Jr., led a candlelight vigil in Washington, D.C. New York City's mayor, John Lindsay, supported the day of mourning as did two large unions. The chairman of the Joint Chiefs of Staff, though, criticized the protesters, describing them as "interminably vocal youngsters, strangers alike to soap and reason." The Nixon administration issued a release from the North Vietnamese premier indicating support for the moratorium demonstrations in an attempt to squelch the impact of the protests at home. Soon thereafter, President Nixon gave his "silent majority" speech, but his strategy had little impact on public opinion. Another round of moratorium demonstrations in November 1969 drew larger crowds than the October protests. In April 1970, the Vietnam Moratorium Committee disbanded following Nixon's announcement in March 1970 that he would be bringing 150,000 more troops home.

Napalm   Developed during World War II by Harvard University professor Louis Fieser, napalm was first made of metallic soaps gelled with gasoline. The formula was later changed to consist of 50 percent polystyrene, gasoline, and benzene. When napalm comes into contact with the skin it burns both flesh and bone. Napalm bombs caused the deoxygenation of the air and an upsurge of carbon monoxide, which induced suffocation in people in the area of the bomb blast. First used to bomb a French fuel depot, American forces regularly employed napalm in bombs against Japanese cities and in flamethrowers against Japanese troops. More than 32,000 tons of napalm were dropped in the Korean War. In the Vietnam War, use of napalm surged to 400,000 tons, or 10 percent of all weapons deployed.

National Environmental Policy Act (1969)   Passed in response to an oil well explosion off the coast of Santa Barbara, California, in 1969, the National Environmental Policy Act of 1969 and signed into law by President Richard Nixon on January 1, 1970, was sponsored by two Democratic sena-

tors, Edmund Muskie of Maine and Henry Jackson of Washington. The legislation created a Council on Environmental Quality. The law required all federal construction projects to have an environmental impact study before initiation. This stipulation constituted the most important feature of the bill, and it became an important tool for environmentalists, who then proceeded to use the court system, which with its requirement that environmental impact studies be completed, could prove time consuming and so block work on questionable projects.

National Mass Transportation Assistance Act (1974)   In the words of President Nixon when he signed the National Mass Transportation Assistance Act in 1974, "this marks a long-term and vital major Federal commitment to mass transportation." Nixon noted that the law would help ease U.S. dependence on petroleum while also curbing pollution and congestion, especially in the nation's cities. The act provided $11.8 billion in federal funding to states and cities in meeting their transportation needs for the remainder of the decade.

***New York Times Co. v. United States* (1971)**   Commonly dubbed the "Pentagon Papers Case," *New York Times Co. v. United States* was an important 1971 Supreme Court decision pertaining to publication of information about the Vietnam War and indirectly the culture of secrecy that resulted in Watergate. Two leading national newspapers, the *New York Times* and the *Washington Post,* had tried to publish data from classified Defense Department studies into the history of U.S. involvement in Vietnam. The *New York Times* began publishing from these Pentagon documents on June 13, 1971, ignoring a plea from the Justice Department to withhold the documents from the public. The story ran on the front page just to the right of a picture of President Nixon with his daughter Tricia at her wedding. The *Post* followed suit. President Nixon contended that publication must be prevented to protect national security, and the attorney general gained a favorable ruling from a lower court to stop publication in the two newspapers. The case was heard in oral argument on June 26 in the high court. The question before the Court was whether the administration's efforts violated the First Amendment. In a 6-3 decision on June 30, the Court ruled that it was a violation and that the newspapers had the right to publish the material. Justices Hugo Black and William O. Douglas rejected the government's logic: "we are asked to hold that, despite the First Amendment's emphatic command, the Executive Branch, the Congress, and the Judiciary can make laws enjoining publication of current news and abridging freedom of the press in the name of 'national security.' The Government does not even attempt to rely on any act of Congress. Instead, it makes the bold and dangerously far-reaching contention that the courts should take it upon themselves to 'make' a law abridging freedom of the press in the name of equity, presidential power and national security, even when the representatives of the people in Congress have adhered to the command of the First Amendment and refused to make such a law."

Nixon's Visit to China   *See* VISIT TO CHINA (1972)

Occupational Safety and Health Act (1970)   The Occupational Safety and Health Act of 1970 was a comprehensive reform initiative to protect employees from workplace hazards while also ensuring their overall health and safety. Under the terms of this law, employers had to make sure no physical dangers were in place within the workplace while also providing safety training to employees about their job duties and the operations of the workplace. Additionally, employers had to notify employees about hazardous chemicals necessary to the workplace. When workplace accidents occurred, employers were required to keep safety records and report to the federal government problems encountered. In signing the bill, President Nixon credited all interested parties: Republicans, Democrats, Congress, the White House, labor unions, and workers. He contended that the new law "deals with the environment in which the people—the 55 million Americans who are covered by it— will be working. And it provides for an institute which will look into the problems of the environment, the problems of noise, the problems of cleanliness, all of these things that can affect health in an indirect way."

Oil Embargo (1973–1974)   As a result of U.S. support for Israel during the 1973 Yom Kippur War, also known as the Arab-Israeli War, the Organization of Petroleum Exporting Countries (OPEC) implemented an oil embargo against the United States. The embargo cannot be understood apart from a brief consideration of the war. The war resulted when Syria and Egypt attacked Israel to regain territory these nations had lost during the Six-Day War of 1967. The first attack occurred on October 6, or Yom Kippur, a date intentionally chosen as the holiest day of the Jewish calendar. Initially, the war proved successful for Syria and Egypt, but when the United States began actively supporting Israel, the tide turned. On October 10, the United States provided Israel with a full-scale airlift of military supplies.

In retaliation, OPEC instituted an oil embargo. The embargo hurt the United States in a way that could not have been possible as recently as the 1960s, when the country was still self-sufficient with regard to energy production. That independence had been lost by the early 1970s. OPEC extended the embargo to all nations backing Israel, notably the Netherlands, and it remained in effect until March 1974. In addition to the embargo, OPEC also cut its production of oil. The embargo led to a dangerous spike in oil prices with worldwide implications for the economy and energy policy. The price of a barrel of oil soared from approximately $3 to $12. The embargo's implementation, simultaneous with the devaluation of the dollar, helped generate a recession in the United States.

Economic consequences led to divisions among the United States, Japan, and the European nations as countries looked out for their own economic interests first. President Nixon announced Project Independence to encourage the nation to become more energy independent. The administration also used diplomacy to end the embargo, negotiating with Middle Eastern producers and with Egypt and Syria as well as with Israel, which it urged to retreat from the Sinai Peninsula and the Golan Heights in the interest of securing peace in the region. U.S. secretary of state Henry Kissinger had convinced Israel to withdraw from part of the Sinai by January 18, 1974, which proved sufficient for OPEC to lift the embargo in March. Two months later in May, Israel announced it would withdraw from the Golan Heights.

Organized Crime Control Act (1970)   The Organized Crime Control Act became law on October 15, 1970. The genesis of this law was the 1968 President's Commission on Law Enforcement and Administration of Justice. It included the Racketeer Influenced and Corrupt Organizations Statute, more commonly known as RICO. RICO was enacted in an effort to prevent organized crime from infiltrating legitimate interstate business operations and to provide a means of prosecuting the same, but the broadly worded statute has fostered prosecutions against a wide range of illegal activities involving interstate or foreign commerce. Charges of RICO violations have been brought in both criminal and civil cases. For RICO charges to apply to a case, an underlying lesser crime such as racketeering must also be established.

Paris Peace Talks   The first peace talks to end the Vietnam War began in Paris in 1968 during the last year of LYNDON B. JOHNSON's presidency. Very little progress was made. When Richard Nixon became president in 1969, the only accomplishment at the Paris talks was a decision about the shape of the table where diplomats would sit. The Nixon team fared no better for the first three and a half years of his presidency. The biggest challenges were U.S. demands that all North Vietnamese troops be removed from South Vietnam and North Vietnam's demand that South Vietnamese leader Nguyen Van Thieu not be part of a reorganized South Vietnamese government. Because the formal talks were not productive, National Security Advisor Henry Kissinger negotiated in secret with Le Duc Tho, a North Vietnamese official, outside of Paris, beginning in February 1970. Even those talks generated few tangible results.

Nixon's goal to win reelection in 1972, his initiative on behalf of DÉTENTE with the Soviets and the Chinese, and

North Vietnam's desire to end the U.S. bombing campaigns all combined to give the peace talks new energy. Kissinger agreed that troops from the North could remain in the South while also pulling back from U.S. support for the Thieu government. In October 1972, Kissinger declared "peace is at hand" when a tentative cease-fire was negotiated. According to this proposed deal, the United States would withdraw all of its forces from Vietnam, U.S. prisoners of war would be released, a political settlement would be reached for South Vietnam, and the United States would send economic aid to help Vietnam rebuild. To support the peace deal, Nixon ordered a halt to all bombing north of the 20th parallel.

This deal failed, though, because South Vietnamese officials, including Thieu, had been left out of the process. Thieu would not go along with the deal and by December 13 the negotiations fell apart. An aide to Thieu explained, "We say, fine, you know, thank you, could, could we see the text? And, we want to have time to study the text. Of course, they gave us the text in English, and at that time I thought I say, if our opposition knew that, that right this moment we were discussing the fate of a country in a text in English, boy, you know, it would be so bad that we shouldn't even think about it! So I ask, I say, where is the Vietnamese text? Oh, we forgot, and I say, what do you mean, you forgot? . . . We want to see the Vietnamese text." In response, Nixon promised Thieu a billion dollars in military aid and a reinvigorated war if the North did not agree to peace. To encourage the North to accept a peace deal, Nixon also began the very brutal and destructive CHRISTMAS BOMBINGS. On January 8, 1973, peace talks resumed in Paris, and a deal was struck on January 27, 1973, which was very similar to the October proposal.

Pentagon Papers   *See* NEW YORK TIMES CO. V. UNITED STATES (1971)

Plumbers   One result of the PENTAGON PAPERS case in 1971 was the development of an adversarial relationship between President Nixon and the media. One reaction to this development within the administration was the creation of the "Plumbers," a group of White House operatives who were deployed to handle political problems for the administration by preventing further leaks of classified information to the media by whatever means necessary. This group came to symbolize two things: the embrace of illegal tactics within the White House and the desire by the Nixon administration to control the federal bureaucracy by whatever means necessary. Nixon told some of his key aides after the first story from the Pentagon Papers appeared in the *New York Times*, "If we can't get anyone in this damn government to do something about the problem that may be the most serious one we have, then, by God, we'll do it ourselves. I want you to set up a little group right here in the White House. Have them

get off their tails and find out what's going on and figure out how to stop it."

In addition to general investigation, Nixon envisioned using the Plumbers against the Democratic Party. Because 1972 was an election year, Nixon wanted ammunition against his political opponents, especially what he believed to be their culpability for the Vietnam War since he feared they would try to use failures in Southeast Asia against him. Egil Krogh, a young attorney in the White House, was tapped to direct the Plumbers. Other key players included David Young, an attorney and aide to Henry Kissinger; former CIA agent Howard Hunt; and former FBI agent G. Gordon Liddy. Young gave the group its informal name when he told his mother-in-law that he had been charged with preventing leaks of sensitive information. Confused, she told friends and relatives there was a plumber in the family.

The Plumbers, or the Special Investigations Unit as they were formally known, set up an office in Room 16 in the basement of the Executive Office Building. John Ehrlichman, a key aide to the president, ordered the Plumbers to discern

This 1973 Herblock cartoon captioned "Nixon Awash in His Office" shows the Watergate scandal inundating the Nixon White House. *(A Herblock Cartoon, copyright by the Herb Block Foundation)*

the source of the leak of the Pentagon Papers and any other relevant information about that matter. The Plumbers were also used to burglarize the Democratic National Committee's headquarters at the Watergate Hotel in Washington, D.C. Their discovery on a second break-in attempt on June 17, 1972, ultimately led to the Watergate coverup and investigation and the downfall of the Nixon presidency.

Public Health Cigarette Smoking Act (1970)   The Public Health Cigarette Smoking Act of 1970 required a stronger warning be placed on cigarette packages than the one mandated in the Cigarette Labeling and Advertising Act of 1965. The new warning read "Warning: The Surgeon General Has Determined that Cigarette Smoking Is Dangerous to Your Health" whereas the old warning had read "Caution: Cigarette Smoking May Be Hazardous to Your Health." The 1970 legislation banned cigarette advertising on radio and television, and prohibited states and localities from interfering with the cigarette warnings.

Public Health Service Act   See TITLE X OF THE PUBLIC HEALTH SERVICE ACT (1970)

Racketeer Influenced and Corrupt Organizations Statute (1970)   See ORGANIZED CRIME CONTROL ACT (1970)

Railway Passenger Service Act (1970)   Beginning in the 19th century railroads became the preferred method of traveling great distances within the United States, but by the middle of the 20th century, new methods of transportation, specifically the automobile and the airplane, displaced the trains as preferred methods of travel. To save passenger rail service in the United States, Congress passed the Railway Passenger Service Act in October 1970. This law created Amtrak, a quasi-private company endowed with federal funding, to operate a nationwide passenger rail system. Amtrak commenced operations on May 1, 1971.

Regional Rail Reorganization Act (1973)   This law addressed the changed economic circumstances in the Northeast and Midwest as they affected the railroad industry. Seven large railroads operating in those regions were in bankruptcy, and one of the largest, the Penn Central, faced court-ordered liquidation. The railroads needed federal help because they had not been able to change their business model to meet the new economic environment of the 1970s; rather, they were still using models from early in the 20th century. The Regional Rail Reorganization Act of 1973 provided for restructuring the railroad industry to establish a new consolidated rail system, the elimination of unnecessary services, and minimal disruptions to rail services. The law also provided funding to the railroads in two ways: $500 million in direct payments to help the bankrupt railroads and

their employees and up to another $1.5 billion in federally guaranteed loans.

Rehabilitation Act (1973)   The Rehabilitation Act of 1973 marked the first federal initiative to give "rights" against discrimination to Americans with disabilities. The law applied to programs and agencies receiving federal funding and banned such discrimination from the same. It also prohibited employment discrimination against the disabled by either the federal government or federal government contractors.

RICO   See ORGANIZED CRIME CONTROL ACT (1970)

***Roe v. Wade* (1973)**   In the case of *Roe v. Wade,* the U.S. Supreme Court ruled in 1973 that women had the right to abortion during the first trimester of pregnancy. The case constituted a class action filing from Texas on behalf of Norma McCorvey, a woman described as Jane Roe in the court papers. While she has since come forward and identified herself as Roe, at the time McCorvey argued, "I consider the decision of whether to bear a child a highly personal one and feel that the notoriety occasioned by the lawsuit would result in a gross invasion of my personal privacy." Divorced, McCorvey already had a five-year-old daughter and was living with her parents. When she became pregnant in 1969 she did not wish to have a second child. At the time, Texas law outlawed abortion unless the mother's life was in jeopardy. McCorvey sought, but could not find, access to an illegal abortion. Instead, she met a young Texas attorney, Sarah Weddington, who was already interested in challenging the nation's abortion laws.

To get McCorvey's case into court, Weddington faced two major problems. First, Texas law penalized abortion providers and not the women seeking them; consequently, the question remained whether or not McCorvey had standing to sue. Second, McCorvey's pregnancy would in all likelihood proceed faster than the justice system, so the complaint had to be written on behalf of all pregnant women. If McCorvey was the only defendant and she gave birth prior to adjudication of the case, then her complaint would be moot. The case was filed at the federal courthouse in Dallas on March 3, 1970. Weddington drew on her own abortion experience in pursuing McCorvey's case in arguing that abortion laws in Texas violated the constitutional rights of pregnant women. The defendant in the case was Dallas County district attorney Henry B. Wade. When the case was heard most states had similar statutes.

The case was first argued before the Supreme Court on December 13, 1971, but only seven justices were serving at the time. As such, arguments were heard again in October 1972, and a ruling was handed down on January 22, 1973. Writing for a 7-2 majority, Justice Harry A. Blackmun asserted that the right to privacy was "broad enough to encompass a woman's decision whether or not to terminate her pregnancy." The *Roe* decision overturned all laws restricting abortion in the first trimester. Laws restricting second and third trimester abortions remained valid only if they were written to protect the health of pregnant women. In his decision, Blackmun dismissed the controversial question of when life begins: "We need not resolve the difficult question of when life begins. When those trained in the respective disciplines of medicine, philosophy, and theology are unable to arrive at any consensus, the judiciary, at this point in the development of man's knowledge, is not in a position to speculate as to the answer." The *Roe* decision was hailed as a major victory for women's rights, but it has remained a highly charged political symbol for the conservative political movement that gained in power in the last three decades of the 20th century.

Safe Drinking Water Act (1974) Passed in 1974, the Safe Drinking Water Act was a public health measure to regulate the nation's drinking water supply. The law provided for protection of drinking water at its sources, including rivers, lakes, reservoirs, springs, and groundwater wells. The law authorized the Environmental Protection Agency (EPA) to enforce safeguards against both natural and man-made contaminants, including chemicals, animal waste, pesticide runoff, and human waste. The law stressed water treatment as the best means to ensure safe drinking water. More important, the EPA was charged with establishing safety standards for all public water systems serving 25 or more people. Amendments to the law were passed in 1986 and 1996.

SALT I Agreement *See* ANTIBALLISTIC MISSILE SYSTEMS TREATY (1972)

***San Antonio Independent School District v. Rodriguez* (1973)** The Supreme Court case of *San Antonio Independent School District v. Rodriquez* (1973) examined the use of the property tax as a funding mechanism for public education. Demetrio Rodriguez represented the appellees in the case, the largely minority and impoverished residents of the Edgewood Independent School District in San Antonio, Texas. His class action case argued that the property tax unfairly discriminated against poor children in violation of the Fourteenth Amendment's Equal Protection Clause because funding for public education was not equally distributed among school districts. Property per pupil in this metropolitan district was assessed at $5,900 whereas property per pupil in nearby Alamo Heights School District was assessed at $49,000 per pupil. The Edgewood district charged the highest property taxes in San Antonio, $1.05 per $100 of property value in seeking to fund $26 per child while the Alamo Heights district charged $0.85 per $100 of property value in seeking to fund $333 per child. Once state and federal monies were added, $356 per child was spent in the Edgewood

district while $594 per child was spent in the Alamo Heights district. Supreme Court justice Lewis F. Powell, Jr., wrote for the 5-4 majority, which elected not to give the property tax method of school funding strict scrutiny because, as he argued, the Constitution provided for no fundamental right to education and because there was no systematic discrimination against all poor children in Texas. Furthermore, the Court found the similarity of the Texas funding mechanism with other states to be proof that it was not "so irrational as to be invidiously discriminatory."

Saturday Night Massacre (1973) On Saturday, October 20, 1973, President Richard Nixon and his lawyers determined that Archibald Cox, the Watergate special prosecutor, was a threat to the administration and had to be removed from office. He had drawn Nixon's ire because of his independence from the White House and because of his repeated demands for release of the WHITE HOUSE TAPES, which potentially contained evidence relating to the Watergate scandal. The clash between Cox and Nixon proved especially difficult for Attorney General Elliot Richardson. On the one hand, it was his sworn duty to protect the president's executive privilege but on the other his position required that he gather all pertinent evidence of criminal activity. Furthermore, Richardson grew concerned about Nixon's increasingly negative attitude toward Cox, especially after the president suggested dismissing the special prosecutor.

Tensions increased even further when the Circuit Court of Appeals ruled that Nixon must relinquish the tapes first to U.S. district judge John Sirica and then to Cox. From that point, Nixon never seriously considered further legal action, which would have involved an appeal to the Supreme Court. Instead he fixated on his goal to force Cox from office and thus, he hoped, quell all calls for the tapes. (After the Court of Appeals ruling Sirica decided that he could not force Nixon to give the tapes to the Senate Special Committee on Presidential Campaign Activities investigating Watergate, and so, for the moment, he was not a danger to the White House.)

The White House, which preferred to negotiate with the attorney general, presented Richardson with several scenarios, though none were favorable to Cox. At one point Nixon indicated that he was willing to provide "authenticated" tapes; later, he suggested using Senator John Stennis, a conservative Mississippi Democrat, to verify the Nixon edits. Cox disregarded the scheme. Much White House maneuvering resulted with most of the action focused on devising strategy that would force Cox's hand and justify the president in firing him. On Saturday, October 20, 1973, Cox gave a press conference in which he discounted the legality of replacing actual evidence—the tapes—with summaries of that evidence. He made clear that he would not retreat from his demand for the tapes.

Soon after the Cox press conference Richardson received a phone call instructing him to fire Cox. The attorney general

Attorney General Elliot Richardson *(right)* swears in Archibald Cox as special prosecutor investigating the Watergate scandal on May 25, 1973. Both would be gone five months later, victims of the Saturday Night Massacre. *(© Everett Collection, Inc./Alamy)*

responded by asking for, and obtaining, a meeting with the president at which time he resigned his post. William Ruckelshaus, the deputy attorney general, followed a similar course. (The White House, though, claimed that Ruckelshaus had been fired.) The third in command, Robert Bork, was left to fire Cox. The firing and resignations of Richardson, Ruckelshaus, and Cox became known as the Saturday Night Massacre. Although Cox was now gone, Nixon did not gain his larger objective of ending speculation about the content of the tapes, or even worse, demands for release of the tapes.

Cox's staff continued their work unabated in part because public criticism of Nixon intensified. A significant majority of the mail to even the most conservative members of Congress demanded Nixon's impeachment. While Nixon declared in an October 26 press conference that the investigation must move forward, Congress responded by introducing more than 20 impeachment resolutions. Indeed, pressure on the White House grew with much of it coming from individuals who had previously been friendly to the president. Congressional Republicans and southern Democrats raised

questions about Nixon's ethics. Leon Jaworski, a conservative Texas Democrat who would ultimately become the next special prosecutor, compared the events to those of the Nazi Gestapo in World War II. Indeed, Hitler analogies were rampant in the media.

The White House was forced to reinstate the Special Prosecutor's Office, and Jaworski was named to that post on November 1. He conducted a spirited investigation that helped ensure Nixon's downfall. While neither the start nor the end of the Watergate imbroglio, the Saturday Night Massacre proved to be a crucial turning point in official, public, and media reaction to Watergate. A full recounting of the background to the Saturday Night Massacre would fill hundreds of pages, but the essential facts disclose an executive branch mired in chaos and paranoia ready to take whatever action necessary, legal or not, to ensure its survival. This episode highlights the extent of the crisis over political ethics and executive privilege that permeated the federal government in the early 1970s.

Skylab Mission (1973) Lacking strong presidential leadership in the late 1960s, NASA became something of an independent operator, seeking whatever congressional funding could be had to continue space exploration and the ultimate establishment of a space station. Skylab was the realization of the latter goal even though the structure was much smaller than that originally sought by NASA. On May 14, 1973, NASA launched the first U.S. space station, Skylab, into orbit as part of the Apollo program. It was unmanned, and it was the last launch to use the old *Saturn V* launch vehicle. There were problems with the launch. The meteoroid shield fell off 63 seconds after launch. The screen was also designed to protect the work area in the spacecraft from the sun's rays. As a result, temperatures in the workshop reached 126 degrees Fahrenheit. Because of this problem the second launch with astronauts to man the station was delayed. Skylab weighed 91 metric tons and was four stories high. It orbited 270 miles above the Earth.

Skylab's mission lasted for nine months, and during that time, three different crews of astronauts manned the craft and conducted the scientific experiments central to the initiative. The program established that humans could live and work in space for extended periods of time. It also conducted substantial research on solar astronomy. After the third manned mission to Skylab, NASA had planned to keep the space station in orbit for approximately 10 more years as an unmanned craft, but solar problems with the orbit caused Skylab to crash into the Indian Ocean and over unsettled parts of western Australia on July 11, 1979. There was much public criticism about the risks of space debris to human life on Earth. This first U.S. manned space station did not end well, but NASA hoped to build on what had been learned and establish a permanent space station.

A view of Skylab from the departing Skylab 4 mission *(NASA)*

State and Local Fiscal Assistance Act (1972)   *See* Gen-eral Revenue Sharing

Stonewall Inn Riots (1969)   The Stonewall Inn was a popu-lar gay bar in Greenwich Village in New York City. On June 27, 1969, the New York City tactical police force conducted a raid there. Such raids were common at gay bars in the 1960s, but typically the operators of the bars were warned in advance so that the clientele could be advised not to engage in same-sex behaviors that might lead to arrest. No such warning was given on June 27; rather, this time the police went with the idea of provoking a conflict. Officers backed a paddy wagon up to the door of the establishment. All the patrons were frisked in an ostensible search for drugs. The officers yelled epithets at the clientele. After demanding to see the liquor license of the Mafia-run establishment, the police arrested as many people as they could on charges ranging from public lewdness to resisting arrest. Several nights of rioting resulted. The Stone-wall Inn riots constituted an important event in the emergence of the gay liberation movement. The Gay Liberation Front was formed in July 1969. This new civil rights group announced its rejection of society's "attempt to impose sexual roles and defi-nitions of our nature. We are stepping outside these roles and simplistic myths. We are going to be who we are."

Supplemental Security Income Program   Established under the Social Security Act Amendments of 1972, the Sup-plemental Security Income program (SSI) shifted responsibil-ity from the states to the federal government with regard to the aged, blind, and permanently and totally disabled. This program constituted a significant burden for the Social Secu-rity Administration (SSA) because, under the original Social Security Act of 1935, benefits were paid through a program of grants-in-aid to the state governments. Under the new SSI,

the SSA gained additional responsibility. Still, the new rules proved advantageous to beneficiaries because the grants-in-aid allowed for a patchwork system by which different states set different eligibility levels and benefits levels. This program redirection marked a major part of a larger trend in Medicaid to ensure that a federally determined floor for benefits was in place. By raising income eligibility levels the new SSI pro-gram broadened access to Medicaid and ensured that benefits were level across state lines. The only exception was the pos-sibility that states could offer additional benefits. Most of the states—42 in all—supplemented SSI payments with one state paying an additional $252 per person. Thus, the practical result of SSI was to set a floor, and not a ceiling, for benefits.

Supreme Court Appointments   President Richard Nixon had occasion to make two Supreme Court appointments very early in his first term. Chief Justice Earl Warren, concerned that Nixon, his lifelong political enemy, would be elected to the presidency in 1968, had announced his plans to retire early in the summer of 1968. He wanted President Lyndon Johnson to be able to appoint his successor. Johnson used the opportunity to try to elevate Associate Justice Abe Fortas to the chief justiceship and to appoint Judge Homer Thorn-berry, a Texas ally, to Fortas's seat. Though the Senate Judi-ciary Committee approved the Fortas nomination, Senate Republicans hoped to block elevation of a liberal to the chief justiceship on the floor. A three-month long debate ended in a filibuster, and Fortas withdrew his nomination.

In 1969, the Nixon administration forced him to resign from the Court because of a financial scandal. Nixon's appointment of Warren E. Burger to replace Earl Warren as chief justice was well received in the Senate. Nixon also had to replace Fortas. He wanted to fill the seat with a south-erner in gratitude to a region that had been important to his election. He first tapped Fourth Circuit chief judge Clement Haynsworth of South Carolina for the seat. His appoint-ment drew immediate protests from labor and civil rights groups, who viewed him as too conservative for the Court. What ended his bid for a seat on the high court, though, was a financial conflict of interest problem similar to the one that felled Fortas. Seventeen Republicans, including many in the leadership, joined with Democrats to reject the nomination so as to avoid any hint of ethical impropriety. While Nixon condemned the attacks on Haynsworth as unfair, Democratic leaders in the Senate argued that had a local judge rendered a verdict in a case where he had financial interests the citizens of the town would protest. Senators used that analogy as jus-tification for their decision.

Because Nixon remained intent on naming a strict con-structionist to the seat, he next tapped another southerner, Judge G. Harrold Carswell, from the Court of Appeals for the Fifth Circuit, located in the Deep South. Carswell's career on the bench had been short and undistinguished. One Republican senator, Roman Hruska of Nebraska, tried to turn this vice into a virtue: "Even if he is mediocre, there are a lot of mediocre judges and people and lawyers, and they are entitled to a little representation, aren't they? We can't have all Brandeises and Cardozos and Frankfurters and stuff like that." Carswell's defense of white supremacy in his 1948 campaign for the Georgia legislature together with his efforts to keep a public golf course in Florida segregated were enough for the Senate to reject his appointment 51-45.

Next, Nixon turned to Harry A. Blackmun, a judge on the Eighth Circuit Court of Appeals and a long-time friend of the new chief justice, upon the recommendation of Burger. His appointment sailed through the Senate Judiciary Committee and the full Senate approved him unanimously on May 12, 1970. Because of the circumstances of his nomination, Blackmun referred to himself as "Old No. 3."

Two more appointments came Nixon's way with the retirements of Hugo Black and John M. Harlan in 1971. Lewis F. Powell of Virginia was selected to replace Black. He had previously served as president of the American Bar Association, and following an easy confirmation process with just one negative vote on the floor of the Senate he assumed a position in the center of the Court. To replace Harlan, Nixon named conservative William H. Rehnquist. As a young Phoenix, Arizona, lawyer he had attacked the Warren Court and Justices Earl Warren and Hugo Black as "left-wing philosophers." In his early years on the Court, which remained left of center in the 1970s, Rehnquist was dubbed the "Lone Ranger" for his position as the only negative vote in a series of 8-1 decisions.

All told, the individuals who secured appointment to the Court from Nixon's several nomination attempts had significant judicial heft. Blackmun emerged as the most liberal of the appointees with Powell a centrist. Burger was to the right of center, and Rehnquist was a pure conservative. Rehnquist proved to be the most important of the appointments because he was later elevated to the chief justiceship. In that capacity, he remade the Supreme Court in significant ways and that constituted the mirror opposite of what Warren had done in the 1950s and 1960s.

Swann v. Charlotte-Mecklenburg Board of Education (1971)

Filed by the NAACP Legal Defense Fund on behalf of James Swann, a young boy, the case of *Swann v. Charlotte-Mecklenburg Board of Education* (1971) revealed how little progress had been made since the 1954 Supreme Court decision in *Brown v. Board of Education* with regard to school desegregation. The school system in Charlotte-Mecklenburg, North Carolina, contained 84,000 students while the 24,000 African-Americans in the district attended schools that were at least 99 percent black. This district included the city of Charlotte together with the county of Mecklenburg, where Charlotte was located. The question before the Court was whether the federal courts were responsible for overseeing remedies for de jure segregation in the states. Chief Justice

Warren E. Burger wrote for a unanimous Court. He argued that the failure of districts to remedy violations of old mandates resulted in expanded authority for the federal courts. The four part ruling found that (1) remediation plans would be judged by their results, including the effectiveness of quotas, although a strict quota system was rejected; (2) the courts would give schools with overwhelming African-American student bodies extra scrutiny; (3) noncontiguous attendance zones were permissible at least as temporary solutions; and (4) most important, busing could be used as a remedy to solve the problem of segregated education.

Tax Reform Act (1969)

The Tax Reform Act of 1969 marked the first major tax reform legislation in 15 years. President Nixon had asked Congress to work on this bill upon assuming the presidency. It accomplished significant policy changes, specifically preventing the very wealthy from dodging their income tax responsibilities through either the establishment of private foundations or the use of excessive deductions. The law differentiated between public charities and private foundations for the purpose of taxation. It also established the alternative minimum tax to prevent the wealthy from using questionable tax deductions. Because the alternative minimum tax was not tied to inflation, by the end of the 20th century it began to affect the upper middle class as well as the super wealthy. The law also carried benefits for the working poor who lived at or below the poverty line. These individuals were dropped from the tax rolls. The law provided for a single, standard deduction to make the filing of taxes easier. Nixon's only complaint about the law was the failure of Congress to cut spending in accordance with the new tax code. He feared the results would be damaging to the economy in stating: "We cannot reduce taxes and increase spending at a time and in a way that raises prices. That would be robbing Peter to pay Paul."

Title IX of the Education Amendments (1972)

In 1972, Congress considered and passed what were for the most part routine amendments to the education code. Very little debate took place on the floor of either chamber. The only exception was Title IX, which provided that "[n]o person . . . shall, on the basis of sex, be excluded from participation in, be denied the benefits of, or be subjected to discrimination under any education program or activity receiving Federal financial assistance." Exempt from the provisions of Title IX were military schools, nonvocational elementary and secondary schools, private undergraduate college admissions, and traditionally single-sex public undergraduate colleges. No one paid any attention to the implications of Title IX for college athletics generally or college football specifically.

Two factors explain the ease of Title IX's passage: It flew under the radar because of the Civil Rights movement and the busing controversy and it seemed to be the right thing to do. Even Nixon administration officials supported the measure during congressional hearings in 1970. When President Nixon signed the Education Amendments, he had nothing to say about Title IX; instead, he praised the financial aid provisions and criticized the antibusing components as "inadequate, misleading, and entirely unsatisfactory." He wanted firmer limits on court-ordered school busing than the amendments provided. It was only later after passage and during the implementation phase of Title IX that Nixon called this feature of the law a "monstrosity." It took the efforts of the Department of Health, Education, and Welfare (HEW) to determine what Title IX meant. Officials in HEW used the race integration guidelines as a vague outline for Title IX policies to avoid sex discrimination in public education. After Title IX entered into force, criticism in government circles mounted, but it was too late. Requirements for gender equity in education was now the law of the land.

Title X of the Public Health Service Act (1970) Title X of the Public Health Service Act of 1970 provided for comprehensive family planning services to be administered by the Office of Family Planning. It was the only federal grant program for such matters. The program provided for contraceptive services, supplies, and provision of information to low-income Americans. The program remained operative in the early 21st century. A range of preventative health services are available through these clinics, including patient education, breast and pelvic examinations, breast and cervical cancer screenings, STD and HIV education and testing, and pregnancy diagnosis and counseling. Later amendments to the law blocked the expenditure of Title X funds at clinics were abortion services were provided.

Trade Act (1974) The Trade Act of 1974 had its origins in fears engendered by the recession that ensued after the 1973 OPEC oil embargo. The law established the Trade Adjustment Assistance Program (TAA). The TAA assisted workers who either lost their jobs or saw their hours or wages reduced as a result of increased imports. In addition to temporary benefits, the TAA offered training, reemployment services, and relocation allowances. The law also authorized the president to consider fair labor standards in negotiating GATT trade deals for the first time in history. Furthermore, when unfair trade policies were detected, the law authorized the president to restrict imports. Finally the law granted the president "fast track authority" to negotiate reciprocal tariff reductions, eliminating the threat of Senate amendments and filibusters of such deals.

Trans-Alaska Pipeline Authorization Act (1973) President Nixon signed the Trans-Alaska Pipeline Authorization Act into law on November 16, 1973, to promote U.S. energy independence. The proposed 800-mile-long pipeline was to connect the Prudhoe Bay, Alaska, oil fields with the port at Valdez, Alaska. Ever since the 1968 discovery of oil on

Trans-Alaska pipeline system, running from the Arctic Ocean to the Gulf of Alaska at Valdez *(Luca Galuzzi-www.galuzzi.it)*

Alaska's North Slope a consortium of oil companies had been trying to build this pipeline, but they had met numerous challenges from environmentalists, who feared the impact of construction on the natural habitat. Congress legislated the disagreement because of the growing oil crisis engendered by the inability of U.S. production to keep up with U.S. demand. Lawmakers believed that the construction of a pipeline from Alaska would make oil production there more cost effective. Upon signing the law Nixon told a television audience: "Throughout history, America has made great sacrifices of blood and also treasure to achieve and maintain its independence. In the last third of this century, our independence will depend on maintaining and achieving self-sufficiency in energy." The pipeline was completed in 1977.

Twenty-sixth Amendment (1971)   Ratified on July 1, 1971, the Twenty-sixth Amendment to the U.S. Constitution granted 18-year-olds the right to vote. The voting age in most states had been 21. Passage of this amendment should be understood in the context of the antiwar movement and the student movement of the 1960s and 1970s. Student protesters had noted the hypocrisy of being old enough to go to war and die but not old enough to vote. A federal law had earlier authorized lowering the voting age to 18, but the Supreme Court overturned that legislation in *Oregon v. Mitchell* (1970). To address this failure, this constitutional amendment was introduced and ratified.

***United States v. Nixon* (1974)**   The case of *United States v. Nixon* was argued before the Supreme Court on July 8, 1974, and a decision was rendered on July 24, 1974. The case stemmed from the indictment by a grand jury of seven aides to the president for obstruction of justice in the Watergate scandal when the administration would not release the recorded telephone conversations to Special Prosecutor Leon Jaworski, or any of the other jurisdictions that sought access to the WHITE HOUSE TAPES. The president and his attorneys argued that the subpoena violated "executive privilege," or the right to protect confidential executive branch communications and material pertaining to national security. The question before the Court was whether the president's executive privilege rendered him exempt from all judicial review. In an 8-0 decision, the Court said no and it ordered President Nixon to release the tapes and all related documents. Writing for the Court, Chief Justice Warren Burger contended that the Court did have jurisdiction over intraexecutive disputes and that the special prosecutor did have authority to sue on behalf of the country. Burger wrote: "We conclude that, when the ground for asserting privilege as to subpoenaed materials sought for use in a criminal trial is based only on the generalized interest in confidentiality, it cannot prevail over the fundamental demands of due process of law in the fair administration of criminal justice. The generalized assertion

of privilege must yield to the demonstrated, specific need for evidence in a pending criminal trial." The president released the tapes.

U.S. Troops Evacuate Vietnam (1973)   President Nixon had campaigned in 1968 on the promise of pulling U.S. troops out of Vietnam, and throughout his presidency the number of troops declined. From 584,000, the number of troops in Vietnam when he took office in 1969, more than half that number were withdrawn by the end of 1970. In January 1972, he announced another phase of the withdrawal, noting that 70,000 troops would be out by summer. He also declared that a small force of approximately 25,000 to 35,000 troops would remain until all U.S. prisoners of war were released. The last contingent of U.S. troops was removed from Vietnam on March 29, 1973, with Nixon declaring, "the day we have all worked and prayed for has finally come."

Vietnamization Policy   The process of gradual withdrawal of American forces from Vietnam, known as Vietnamization, succeeded in bringing down U.S. troop levels from 584,000 in January 1969 to 280,000 at the end of 1970 to half that number the following year. American deaths in Vietnam dropped from more than 200 per week in early 1969 to 35 per week two years later. It took time for Vietnamization to make an impact upon American public opinion, and for many the phased withdrawal was too slow. Vietnamization gave hope to those U.S. troops seeking to return home, but it also signaled acceptance of defeat. Morale and discipline among American forces declined according to military observers. Instances of insubordination, attacks upon officers, and drug use increased.

Visit to China (1972)   President Richard Nixon's February 21–28, 1972, visit to China marked the first time a sitting U.S. president visited China. Since the Communist Chinese succeeded in their revolution in 1949, relations between the two countries had been minimal, and the visit helped to calm tensions on both sides. Nixon's visit mixed public relations with diplomacy and he achieved excellent results on both fronts. It would not have been possible had it not been for the secret missions National Security Advisor Henry Kissinger had earlier made to China in a long-term effort to bring DÉTENTE in relations between these two major world powers. Nixon called his visit, "the week that changed the world." To ensure favorable media coverage, the president made sure that the press corps traveling with him was skewed heavily toward television journalists. Nixon had long disliked print journalists. He also studied the briefing books for the trip well in advance of his departure to make sure that he would get the best press possible.

When Nixon exited Air Force One in Beijing on February 21, he demonstrated an awareness of the history of U.S.-

Richard Nixon shaking hands with armed forces in Vietnam, July 1969 *(National Archives)*

Chinese relations. In 1954, Secretary of State John Foster Dulles had refused to shake hands with Premier Zhou Enlai (Chou En-lai). Since Zhou would be greeting Nixon, the president wanted to make sure no one in his delegation would block the handshake. He made sure that Secret Service agents prevented Kissinger and Secretary of State William Rogers from deplaning until he had shaken hands with Zhou. A private meeting with Chairman Mao Zedong featured "serious and frank discussion." American television stations carried live the formal banquet of welcome that Zhou hosted. This celebration featured multiple courses and the People's Liberation Army band playing musical selections that included "America the Beautiful" and "Home on the Range." Symbolic of the new diplomatic era in U.S. relations with China, the end of the banquet featured multiple toasts, with Nixon quoting from Mao, "'Seize the hour! Seize the day!'" The president also declared, "There is no reason for us to be enemies." "Neither of us seeks the territory of the other; neither of us seeks domination over the other; neither of us seeks to stretch out our hands and rule the world." The remainder of the week featured numerous other travels to historic sites in China, including the Great Wall, together with talks among government officials. The chief diplomatic accomplishment came at the end of the week with the announcement of the Shanghai joint communiqué stating that Taiwan was part of China. Seven years later, in 1979, the United States established formal diplomatic relations with China.

Wage and Price Controls (1971)   During his presidency, Richard Nixon faced the challenge of inflation and the role of the rising cost of government in generating that threat. He had long been opposed to government intervention in the marketplace, developing a strong distaste for wage and price controls while working as an attorney in the Office of Price Administration during World War II. Furthermore, he was not greatly interested in pursuing the minutia of economic policy, foreign or domestic. Yet, on January 4, 1971, in an interview with Howard K. Smith of ABC News, Nixon made a surprising observation off air, which quickly became the talk of Washington, D.C.: "I am now a Keynesian in economics." Smith was so surprised to hear the Republican Nixon accept what had been Democratic dogma for decades, namely, that unbalanced budgets were desirable in a sluggish economy, that he replied, "That's a little like a Christian crusader saying, 'All things considered, I think Mohammed was right.'"

That month, President Nixon introduced a Keynesian budget to Congress, complete with deficit spending to tackle unemployment, which had risen from 3.5 percent in the late 1960s to 5 percent. Inflation also emerged as a problem in the early 1970s, having grown from 1.5 percent in the 1960s to 5 percent. Arthur Burns, whom Nixon had appointed to chair the Federal Reserve Board, advised the president that monetary and fiscal policy was not sufficient to deal with the nation's economic problems. Burns contended that the power of corporations and labor unions was such that they caused wages and prices to spiral and could not be checked by traditional methods. As such, Burns counseled the president to implement a wage-price review board with authority to make recommendations on the economy. Nixon's new treasury secretary, John Connally, the former Texas Democratic governor who had recently switched to the Republican Party, had no ideological commitments, seeking solely to make a bold move.

A related concern was the growing crisis concerning the balance of payments. While the price of gold had been fixed at $35 an ounce since the 1930s, the dollar was declining in foreign trade. Put simply, foreign governments had more U.S. dollars than there was gold in the treasury, and in August 1971, the British ambassador demanded the conversion of $3 billion in U.S. currency into gold. Despite these realities, Nixon resisted wage and price controls throughout the first half of 1971.

The economic problems did not abate and, on August 13–15, Nixon and 15 key economic advisers went to Camp David to review the issue. When the president returned to Washington, he announced his New Economic Policy, which froze wages and prices for 90 days. Administration Republicans hoped this would be sufficient to redress the most serious problems of inflation and unemployment and would provide sufficient time during which to develop and implement a noninflationary employment policy. Another component of the Nixon plan was cessation of the gold standard, a move that Burns disdained, "Pravda [the official Soviet newspaper] would write that this was a sign of the collapse of capitalism."

One telling sign about the potential for success of Nixon's wage and price freeze was the amount of time spent discussing when and how to present the plan to the American people—ultimately it was decided that a Sunday evening address during primetime, preempting the popular television program *Bonanza*, was necessary before the opening of the markets on Monday—and the considerably less attention given to how to transition away from the freeze once the 90 days were over. The speech was well received by the media, the public, and the markets. The Cost of Living Council was charged with operating the freeze, which helped restrain soaring prices but did little to lower unemployment. At the end of the 90-day period the freeze was gradually phased out. Inflation and unemployment remained concerns, and Nixon was forced to impose another wage and price freeze in June 1973. This freeze was much less successful. Farmers and ranchers refused to market their produce, for example. Most of these controls were removed by April 1974. George Shultz, the director of the Office of Management and Budget, observed: "At least we have now convinced everyone else of the rightness of our original position that wage-price controls are not the answer."

War Powers Act (1973)   The War Powers Act of 1973, also known as the War Powers Resolution, emerged as an outgrowth of domestic political conflict over the handling of the Vietnam War. Liberal New York Republican senator Jacob Javits sponsored the measure, which was described as "fulfill[ing] the intent of the framers of the Constitution of the United States and insur[ing] that the collective judgment of both Congress and the President will apply to the introduction of United States Armed Forces into hostilities." By the early 1970s, lawmakers were convinced that Presidents JOHN F. KENNEDY, LYNDON B. JOHNSON, and Richard M. Nixon had all overstepped their constitutional authority in sending troops to Vietnam. At issue was the failure to ask Congress for a formal declaration of war. Under the terms of the War Powers Act, presidents were given a timetable of 48 hours during which they had to inform Congress in writing when U.S. troops were sent abroad in situations that would likely result in combat. Furthermore, the legislation mandated that such troops must be removed within 60 days if, by congressional vote, legislators failed to approve their retention.

Nixon vetoed the measure, describing it as "Marquis of Queensberry rules in a world where good manners are potentially fatal hindrances," but a belligerent Congress overrode him. The law has had little practical effect. Presidents have worked diligently to skirt its requirements and Congress has too often failed to assert its prerogatives under the law, instead letting presidents operate as they have seen fit and bear the responsibility for missions that might not go as planned. Instead, the legislative and executive branches have negotiated vaguely worded authorizations of force that, according to some critics, have allowed the White House too much independence. The first crucial test of the War Powers Act came in 1990 when President GEORGE H. W. BUSH sought to use force to compel Saddam Hussein to move out of Kuwait.

Water Pollution Control Act Amendments   *See* FEDERAL WATER POLLUTION CONTROL ACT AMENDMENTS (1972)

White House Tapes   By July 1973, Archibald Cox in the Special Prosecutor's Office, U.S. district judge John Sirica, and Senator Sam Ervin (D-NC), chairman of the Senate Select Committee investigating Watergate had one common target—procurement of Nixon's secret White House tapes of his Oval Office conversations. Alexander Butterfield, a former White House aide who worked closely with the president, testified that month before Ervin's committee about the existence of a White House taping system. Nixon had had a voice-activated taping system installed in the Oval Office in February 1971. Knowing that FRANKLIN D. ROOSEVELT, DWIGHT D. EISENHOWER, JOHN F. KENNEDY, and LYNDON B. JOHNSON had all used secret recording devices in varying

degrees during their presidencies, Nixon nevertheless initially rejected such measures, but after his aides convinced him otherwise Nixon acquiesced.

When news of the tapes became public, the charges of political corruption relating to the Watergate break-in and coverup that had circulated since the summer of 1972 gained in legitimacy. All the Nixon investigators realized the strong likelihood that the tapes would provide clear-cut proof of what Nixon knew, when he knew it, and the degree of his involvement in the crime and its coverup. Historians of Watergate have argued that the ferocious battle waged by Nixon to preserve his executive privilege over the recordings and thus deny access to the tapes proved their significance.

The most important aspect of Nixon's year-long battle to control the tapes was the conflict with Archibald Cox, which ultimately led to the SATURDAY NIGHT MASSACRE in 1973 in which Nixon fired Cox, Attorney General Elliot Richardson, and Deputy Attorney General William Ruckelshaus. Both Cox and Ervin demanded immediate access to all relevant tapes and corresponding documentation. Nixon refused the two requests, telling Cox that his employment with the executive branch meant that he operated under presidential jurisdiction and thus could have the tapes only if Nixon deemed it necessary. Ervin and Cox responded with separate subpoenas for the materials. Judge Sirica heard the case and requested that he be allowed to review the tapes before rendering his decision.

Nixon thus had two choices beyond compliance: ignore the situation or appeal to a higher court. He ultimately chose the latter, taking the matter to the Supreme Court in *UNITED STATES V. NIXON*. In retrospect the Saturday Night Massacre that occurred can be characterized as a significant turning point in the Watergate debacle. It heightened questions about political corruption and suggested the lengths to which the White House would go to quiet its perceived enemies.

The tapes that Cox sought so zealously were not made available to the new special prosecutor, Leon Jaworski, until December 21, 1973, and those supplied were not comprehensive. Nevertheless, Jaworski's grand jury indicted seven campaign and White House aides on March 1, 1974, naming Nixon as an "unindicted co-conspirator." By that time, the House Judiciary Committee was also debating the merits of impeachment. By April 30, 1974, Nixon had agreed to the release of only 1,300 pages of edited transcripts from the White House tapes. The Supreme Court disagreed when Nixon asked it to rule in favor of his claim to executive privilege, and on July 24, 1974, the high court ordered the release of all tapes in what it affirmed was a criminal investigation. After hearing the June 23, 1972, conversation in which Nixon ordered the CIA to halt the FBI investigation of the Watergate break-in, Nixon's own lawyers along with leading Republicans suggested that resignation was the only option left to the president. The nation concurred after the tapes were

Official poster and logo of the 1969 Woodstock Music Festival designed by Arnold Skolnick *(Library of Congress)*

made public on August 5, 1974. Knowing that impeachment and removal from office were inevitable, Nixon resigned the presidency on August 9, 1974.

Woodstock Music Festival (1969)   Few believed that the promoters of the Woodstock Music Festival, scheduled for August 15–17, 1969, could stage a successful and peaceful event. Several other rock festivals that summer had turned violent, and the public attributed such events to the supposedly toxic combination of hippies, drugs, loud music, and radical politics. Still, some small music festivals had been successful that summer, including one in Atlanta where Paul Butterfield, Credence Clearwater Revival, Janis Joplin, and Led Zeppelin played. When the Woodstock promoters approached officials in Walkill, New York, about staging a festival there, they were denied the permits required for the performances. Max Yasgur, who owned a 600-acre farm near Bethel located approximately 60 miles south of Woodstock, decided to lease the promoters his land for the event. A wooden stage was erected, and helicopters were used to bring the performers in to Woodstock. Acts appearing at Woodstock included Joan Baez; The Band; Joe Cocker; Country Joe McDonald and the Fish; Credence Clearwater Revival; Crosby, Stills, and Nash; The Grateful Dead; Arlo Guthrie; Richie Havens; Jimi Hendrix; Jefferson Airplane; Janis Joplin; Santana; Sly & the Family Stone; The Who; and Neil Young.

Given the location of the event, confrontations with local police were not expected, but to provide protection and security the promoters employed members of the Hog Farm (a collective founded by Hugh Romney, known as Wavy Gravy) to deal with an estimated crowd of 50,000, who would pay $18 a ticket for admission. The Hog Farm security forces were provided with provisions sufficient to deal with the expected medical situations such as drug overdoses, and arrangements were made for food, portable toilets, and general medical supplies for as many as 150,000. Additionally, the promoters hired 300 New York City police officers to serve on standby, but they did not show up. New York City officials did not want the police associated with this countercultural event.

Attendance at Woodstock outstripped even the wildest predictions and no accurate headcount has ever been produced. At least 400,000 were in attendance at the festival and perhaps as many as half a million. Heavy traffic encumbered the roads leading to Yasgur's farm such that the state police turned drivers back. Given the size of the crowd, the toilets quickly overflowed and the food disappeared well before the festival ended. An additional level of discomfort resulted from the rains, which turned the fields into a muddy mess. Still, no incidents of violence occurred. At one point, an announcer told the crowds: "We are going to need each other to help each other work this out, because we are taxing the systems we've set up. We are going to be bringing the food in. But the one major thing that you have to remember tonight is that the man next to you is your brother." The three fatalities at Woodstock resulted from accidental causes. Perhaps more amazingly and symbolic of what Woodstock meant to the 1960s generation, three babies were born at the festival.

Woodstock was less about political protest and more about the music and the celebration of a way of life that would fast disappear. The white male participants that dominated both the audience and the stage at Woodstock revealed, according to Yasgur, "that half a million kids can get together for fun and music and have nothing but fun and music." Still, Woodstock is often juxtaposed against the music festival staged at the Altamont Speedway four months later in California. The Rolling Stones headlined that performance during which the Hells Angels motorcycle gang provided security for $500 worth of beer. Violence broke out near the stage even though most attendees recalled it as a good musical show. The clichéd criticisms of Altamont have been overblown. The more significant forces changing the nature of live music in the 1960s was the emergence of rock and roll as big business in departing from its status heretofore as a component exclusively of the counterculture.

Ricky F. Dobbs

Further Reading

Ambrose, Stephen E. *Nixon.* 3 vols. New York: Simon and Schuster, 1987–1991.

Berman, Larry. *No Peace, No Honor: Nixon, Kissinger, and Betrayal in Vietnam.* New York: Free Press, 2001.

Bernstein, Carl, and Bob Woodward. *All the President's Men.* New York: Simon and Schuster, 1974.

Carter, Dan T. *George Wallace, Richard Nixon, and the Transformation of American Politics.* Waco, Tex.: Markham Press Fund, 1992.

Casey, Shaun. *The Making of a Catholic President: Kennedy vs. Nixon 1960.* New York: Oxford University Press, 2009.

Dallek, Robert. *Nixon and Kissinger: Partners in Power.* New York: HarperCollins, 2007.

Dean, John W. *The Rehnquist Choice: The Untold Story of the Nixon Appointment That Redefined the Supreme Court.* New York: Free Press, 2001.

Donaldson, Gary. *The First Modern Campaign: Kennedy, Nixon, and the Election of 1960.* Lanham, Md.: Rowman and Littlefield, 2007.

Feeney, Mark. *Nixon at the Movies: A Book about Belief.* Chicago: University of Chicago Press, 2004.

Flippen, J. Brooks. *Nixon and the Environment.* Albuquerque: University of New Mexico Press, 2000.

Frick, Daniel E. *Reinventing Richard Nixon: A Cultural History of an American Obsession.* Lawrence: University Press of Kansas, 2008.

Garrison, Jean A. *Games Advisors Play: Foreign Policy in the Nixon and Carter Administrations.* College Station: Texas A&M University Press, 1999.

Gellman, Irwin F. *The Contender: Richard Nixon: The Congress Years, 1946–1952.* New York: Free Press, 1999.

Greenberg, David. *Nixon's Shadow: The History of an Image.* New York: W.W. Norton, 2003.

Greene, John Robert. *The Limits of Power: The Nixon and Ford Administrations.* Bloomington: Indiana University Press, 1992.

Hoff, Joan. *Nixon Reconsidered.* New York: BasicBooks, 1994.

Kimball, Jeffrey P. *Nixon's Vietnam War.* Lawrence: University Press of Kansas, 1998.

———. *The Vietnam War Files: Uncovering the Secret History of Nixon-Era Strategy.* Lawrence: University Press of Kansas, 2004.

Kutler, Stanley I., ed. *Abuse of Power: The New Nixon Tapes.* New York: Free Press, 1997.

———. *The Wars of Watergate: The Last Crisis of Richard Nixon.* New York: Knopf, 1990.

Lungren, John C. *Healing Richard Nixon: A Doctor's Memoir.* Lexington: University Press of Kentucky, 2003.

MacMillan, Margaret. *Nixon and Mao: The Week That Changed the World.* New York: Random House, 2007.

Matthews, Christopher. *Kennedy & Nixon: The Rivalry That Shaped Postwar America.* New York: Simon and Schuster, 1996.

Matusow, Allen J. *Nixon's Economy: Booms, Busts, Dollars, and Votes.* Lawrence: University Press of Kansas, 1998.

McGinniss, Joe. *The Selling of the President, 1968.* New York: Trident Press, 1969.

Mitchell, Greg. *Tricky Dick and the Pink Lady: Richard Nixon vs. Helen Gahagan Douglas—Sexual Politics and the Red Scare, 1950.* New York: Random House, 1998.

Mollenhoff, Clark R. *Game Plan for Disaster: An Ombudsman's Report on the Nixon Years.* New York: Norton, 1976.

Morris, Roger. *Richard Milhous Nixon: The Rise of an American Politician.* New York: Henry Holt, 1989.

Morrow, Lance. *The Best Year of Their Lives: Kennedy, Johnson, and Nixon in 1948: Learning the Secrets of Power.* New York: Basic Books, 2005.

Nixon, Richard M. *Beyond Peace.* New York: Random House, 1994.

———. *The Challenges We Face.* New York: McGraw-Hill, 1960.

———. *Four Great Americans.* Garden City, N.Y.: Doubleday, 1973.

———. *From the President: Richard Nixon's Secret Files.* Edited by Bruce Oudes. New York: Harper and Row, 1989.

———. *In the Arena: A Memoir of Victory, Defeat, and Renewal.* New York: Simon and Schuster, 1990.

———. *Leaders.* New York: Warner Books, 1982.

———. *A New Road for America; Major Policy Statements, March 1970 to October 1971.* Garden City, N.Y.: Doubleday, 1972.

———. *1999: Victory without War.* New York: Simon and Schuster, 1990.

———. *The Nixon Presidential Press Conferences.* New York: E. M. Coleman Enterprises, 1978.

———. *Nixon Speaks Out: Major Speeches and Statements.* New York: Nixon-Agnew Campaign Committee, 1968.

———. *No More Vietnams.* New York: Arbor House, 1985.

———. *The Presidential Transcripts.* New York: Delacorte Press, 1974.

———. *Real Peace.* Boston: Little, Brown, 1984.

———. *The Real War.* New York: Warner Books, 1980.

———. *Richard Nixon: Speeches, Writings, Documents.* Edited by Rick Perlstein. Princeton, N.J.: Princeton University Press, 2008.

———. *RN, The Memoirs of Richard Nixon.* New York: Grosset and Dunlap, 1978.

———. *Seize the Moment: America's Challenge in a One-Superpower World.* New York: Simon and Schuster, 1992.

———. *Setting the Course, The First Year; Major Policy Statements by President Richard Nixon.* New York: Funk and Wagnalls, 1970.

———. *Six Crises.* Garden City, N.Y.: Doubleday, 1962.

———. *Submission of Recorded Presidential Conversations to the Committee on the Judiciary of the House of Representatives, by Richard Nixon.* Washington, D.C.: U.S. Government Printing Office, 1974.

Parmet, Herbert S. *Richard M. Nixon: An American Enigma.* New York: Pearson Longman, 2008.

Perlstein, Rick. *Nixonland: The Rise of a President and the Fracturing of America.* New York: Scribner, 2008.

Public Papers of the Presidents of the United States, Richard M. Nixon, Containing the Public Messages, Speeches, and Statements of the President, 1969–1974. 6 vols. Washington, D.C.: U.S. Government Printing Office, 1971–1975.

Randolph, Stephen P. *Powerful and Brutal Weapons: Nixon, Kissinger, and the Easter Offensive.* Cambridge, Mass.: Harvard University Press, 2007.

Reeves, Richard. *President Nixon: Alone in the White House.* New York: Simon and Schuster, 2001.

Reichley, A. James. *Conservatives in an Age of Change: The Nixon and Ford Administrations.* Washington, D.C.: Brookings Institution Press, 1981.

Rorabaugh, W. J. *The Real Making of the President: Kennedy, Nixon, and the 1960 Election.* Lawrence: University Press of Kansas, 2009.

Safire, William. *Before the Fall: An Inside View of the Pre-Watergate White House.* Garden City, N.Y.: Doubleday, 1975.

Seaborg, Glenn T., with Benjamin S. Loeb. *The Atomic Energy Commission under Nixon: Adjusting to Troubled Times.* New York: St. Martin's Press, 1993.

Small, Melvin. *The Presidency of Richard Nixon.* Lawrence: University Press of Kansas, 1999.

Sorley, Lewis. *Arms Transfers under Nixon: A Policy Analysis.* Lexington: University Press of Kentucky, 1983.

Wicker, Tom. *One of Us: Richard Nixon and the American Dream.* New York: Random House, 1991.

Wills, Garry. *Nixon Agonistes: The Crisis of the Self-Made Man.* Boston: Houghton Mifflin, 1970.

Woodward, Bob. *The Final Days.* New York: Simon and Schuster, 1976.

DOCUMENTS

—⚬⚬—

Document One: President Richard M. Nixon, Telegram to the Crew of *Apollo 9,* March 13, 1969

Following the successful Apollo 9 *space mission in March 1969 that performed tests critical to the* Apollo 11 *moon landing four months later, President Nixon invited crew members to the White House.*

March 13, 1969

THE EPIC FLIGHT of Apollo Nine will be recorded in history as ten days that thrilled the world. You have by your courage and your skill helped to shape the future of man in space. The three of you and the great team which enabled you to complete your successful mission have shown the world that the spirit of man and his technological genius are eager to begin an age of adventure, an age which will benefit all the people on this good earth. Knowing that the dining in Apollo Nine, while nourishing, lacked some of the amenities of earth-bound dining, Mrs. Nixon and I invite you and your wives to have dinner with us at the White House at 8:00 Thursday evening, the twenty-seventh of March.

RICHARD NIXON

———————————⬦———————————

Source: Public Papers of the Presidents of the United States, Richard M. Nixon, Containing the Public Messages, Speeches, and Statements of the President, 1969 (Washington, D.C.: U.S. Government Printing Office, 1971), 207–208.

Document Two: President Nixon, Letter to President Ho Chi Minh of the Democratic Republic of Vietnam, November 3, 1969

On November 3, 1969, President Nixon wrote the North Vietnamese leader, Ho Chi Minh, about his desire for peace in the Vietnam War.

Dear Mr. President:

I realize that it is difficult to communicate meaningfully across the gulf of four years of war. But precisely because of this gulf, I wanted to take this opportunity to reaffirm in all solemnity my desire to work for a just peace. I deeply believe that the war in Vietnam has gone on too long and delay in bringing it to an end can benefit no one—least of all the people of Vietnam. My speech on May 14 laid out a proposal which I believe is fair to all parties. Other proposals have been made which attempt to give the people of South Vietnam an opportunity to choose their own future. These proposals take into account the reasonable conditions of all sides. But we stand ready to discuss other programs as well, specifically the 10-point program of the NLF.

As I have said repeatedly, there is nothing to be gained by waiting. Delay can only increase the dangers and multiply the suffering.

The time has come to move forward at the conference table toward an early resolution of this tragic war. You will find us forthcoming and open-minded in a common effort to bring the blessings of peace to the brave people of Vietnam. Let history record that at this critical juncture, both sides turned their face toward peace rather than toward conflict and war.

Sincerely,

RICHARD NIXON

———————————⬦———————————

Source: Public Papers of the Presidents of the United States, Richard M. Nixon, Containing the Public Messages, Speeches, and Statements of the President, 1969 (Washington, D.C.: U.S. Government Printing Office, 1971), 910–911.

Document Three: President Nixon, Statement on the Deaths of Four Students at Kent State University, May 4, 1970

President Nixon issued a brief statement on May 4, 1970, following the shooting of four students during an antiwar protest at Kent State University in Kent, Ohio.

THIS should remind us all once again that when dissent turns to violence, it invites tragedy. It is my hope that this tragic and unfortunate incident will strengthen the determination of all the Nation's campuses—administrators, faculty, and students alike—to stand firmly for the right which exists in this country of peaceful dissent and just as strongly against the resort to violence as a means of such expression.

———————————⬦———————————

Source: Public Papers of the Presidents of the United States, Richard M. Nixon, Containing the Public Messages, Speeches, and Statements of the President, 1970 (Washington, D.C.: U.S. Government Printing Office, 1971), 411.

Document Four: President Nixon, Address to the Nation Outlining a New Economic Policy: "The Challenge of Peace," August 15, 1971

Because of a sour national economy, President Nixon addressed the American people on August 15, 1971, about his new plans for bringing recovery. His advocacy of price controls was startling given his prior opposition to government intervention in the economy, and he also announced that the country would abandon the gold standard.

. . . Prosperity without war requires action on three fronts: We must create more and better jobs; we must stop the rise in the cost of living; we must protect the dollar from the attacks of international money speculators.

We are going to take that action—not timidly, not half-heartedly, and not in piecemeal fashion. We are going to move forward to the new prosperity without war as befits a great people—all together, and along a broad front.

The time has come for a new economic policy for the United States. Its targets are unemployment, inflation, and international speculation. And this is how we are going to attack those targets.

First, on the subject of jobs. We all know why we have an unemployment problem. Two million workers have been released from the Armed Forces and defense plants because of our success in winding down the war in Vietnam. Putting those people back to work is one of the challenges of peace, and we have begun to make progress. Our unemployment rate today is below the average of the 4 peacetime years of the 1960's.

But we can and we must do better than that.

The time has come for American industry, which has produced more jobs at higher real wages than any other industrial system in history, to embark on a bold program of new investment in production for peace.

To give that system a powerful new stimulus, I shall ask the Congress, when it reconvenes after its summer recess, to consider as its first priority the enactment of the Job Development Act of 1971. . . .

The second indispensable element of the new prosperity is to stop the rise in the cost of living.

One of the cruelest legacies of the artificial prosperity produced by war is inflation. Inflation robs every American, every one of you. The 20 million who are retired and living on fixed incomes—they are particularly hard hit. Homemakers find it harder than ever to balance the family budget. And 80 million American wage earners have been on a treadmill. For example, in the 4 war years between 1965 and 1969, your wage increases were completely eaten up by price increases. Your paychecks were higher, but you were no better off.

We have made progress against the rise in the cost of living. From the high point of 6 percent a year in 1969, the rise in consumer prices has been cut to 4 percent in the first half of 1971. But just as is the case in our fight against unemployment, we can and we must do better than that.

The time has come for decisive action—action that will break the vicious circle of spiraling prices and costs.

I am today ordering a freeze on all prices and wages throughout the United States for a period of 90 days. In addition, I call upon corporations to extend the wage-price freeze to all dividends.

I have today appointed a Cost of Living Council within the Government. I have directed this Council to work with leaders of labor and business to set up the proper mechanism for achieving continued price and wage stability after the 90-day freeze is over.

Let me emphasize two characteristics of this action: First, it is temporary. To put the strong, vigorous American economy into a permanent straitjacket would lock in unfairness; it would stifle the expansion of our free enterprise system. And second, while the wage-price freeze will be backed by Government sanctions, if necessary, it will not be accompanied by the establishment of a huge price control bureaucracy. I am relying on the voluntary cooperation of all Americans—each one of you: workers, employers, consumers—to make this freeze work.

Working together, we will break the back of inflation, and we will do it without the mandatory wage and price controls that crush economic and personal freedom.

The third indispensable element in building the new prosperity is closely related to creating new jobs and halting inflation. We must protect the position of the American dollar as a pillar of monetary stability around the world.

In the past 7 years, there has been an average of one international monetary crisis every year. Now who gains from these crises? Not the workingman; not the investor; not the real producers of wealth. The gainers are the international money speculators. Because they thrive on crises, they help to create them.

In recent weeks, the speculators have been waging an all-out war on the American dollar. The strength

Richard M. Nixon   541

of a nation's currency is based on the strength of that nation's economy—and the American economy is by far the strongest in the world. Accordingly, I have directed the Secretary of the Treasury to take the action necessary to defend the dollar against the speculators.

I have directed Secretary Connally to suspend temporarily the convertibility of the dollar into gold or other reserve assets, except in amounts and conditions determined to be in the interest of monetary stability and in the best interests of the United States.

Now, what is this action—which is very technical—what does it mean for you?

Let me lay to rest the bugaboo of what is called devaluation.

If you want to buy a foreign car or take a trip abroad, market conditions may cause your dollar to buy slightly less. But if you are among the overwhelming majority of Americans who buy American-made products in America, your dollar will be worth just as much tomorrow as it is today.

The effect of this action, in other words, will be to stabilize the dollar.

Now, this action will not win us any friends among the international money traders. But our primary concern is with the American workers, and with fair competition around the world.

To our friends abroad, including the many responsible members of the international banking community who are dedicated to stability and the flow of trade, I give this assurance: The United States has always been, and will continue to be, a forward-looking and trustworthy trading partner. In full cooperation with the International Monetary Fund and those who trade with us, we will press for the necessary reforms to set up an urgently needed new international monetary system. Stability and equal treatment is in everybody's best interest. I am determined that the American dollar must never again be a hostage in the hands of international speculators.

I am taking one further step to protect the dollar, to improve our balance of payments, and to increase jobs for Americans. As a temporary measure, I am today imposing an additional tax of 10 percent on goods imported into the United States. This is a better solution for international trade than direct controls on the amount of imports. . . .

As there always have been in our history, there will be voices urging us to shrink from that challenge of competition, to build a protective wall around ourselves, to crawl into a shell as the rest of the world moves ahead.

Two hundred years ago a man wrote in his diary these words: "Many thinking people believe America has seen its best days." That was written in 1775, just before the American Revolution—the dawn of the most exciting era in the history of man. And today we hear the echoes of those voices, preaching a gospel of gloom and defeat, saying the same thing: "We have seen our best days."

I say, let Americans reply: "Our best days lie ahead."

As we move into a generation of peace, as we blaze the trail toward the new prosperity, I say to every American: Let us raise our spirits. Let us raise our sights. Let all of us contribute all we can to this great and good country that has contributed so much to the progress of mankind.

Let us invest in our Nation's future, and let us revitalize that faith in ourselves that built a great nation in the past and that will shape the world of the future.

Thank you and good evening.

❖

Source: Public Papers of the Presidents of the United States, Richard M. Nixon, Containing the Public Messages, Speeches, and Statements of the President, 1971 (Washington, D.C.: U.S. Government Printing Office, 1972), 886–891.

Document Five: President Nixon, Question-and-Answer Session at the Annual Convention of the Associated Press Managing Editors Association, November 17, 1973

In this press conference at the Associated Press Managing Editors Association in Orlando, Florida, on November 17, 1973, President Nixon faced a host of questions about the Watergate scandal.

. . . Q. Paul Poorman from the Detroit News. Are you personally satisfied, sir, that the investigation of the Watergate matter is complete, to your satisfaction, and if so, could you tell us what your plans are to tell the American people about the facts of the case with regard, again, to your credibility on this matter?

THE PRESIDENT. First, with regard to whether the investigation is complete, as you know, there is now a new Special Prosecutor, Mr. Jaworski. He is a Democrat. He has always supported the Democratic ticket. He is a highly respected lawyer, a former president of the ABA in the year 1971. I may have met him. I have never talked to him personally and certainly have never talked to him about this matter. I refuse to because I want him to be completely independent.

He cannot be removed unless there is a consensus of the top leadership of both the House and the Senate,

Democrat and Republican: the Speaker and the majority and minority leaders of the House and the President pro tem, the majority and minority leaders of the Senate and the ranking two members of the Judiciary Committees of both the House and the Senate, which, incidentally, gives you, as you can see, a very substantial majority as far as the Democrats are concerned.

The second point, and the point I am trying to make is: one, he is qualified; two, he is independent and will have cooperation; and three, he will not be removed unless the Congress, particularly the leaders of the Congress and particularly the Democratic leaders who have a strong majority on this group that I have named, agree that he should be removed, and I do not expect that that time will come.

As to what I can tell the American people, this is one forum, and there may be others. As to what the situation is as to when it can be done, it is, of course, necessary to let the grand jury proceed as quickly as possible to a conclusion. And I should point out to you, as you may recall, Mr. Petersen testified before the Ervin committee that when he was removed from his position—you recall he was removed in April, and a Special Prosecutor was put in—that the case was 90 percent ready. For 6 months, under the Special Prosecutor who was then appointed, the case has not been brought to a conclusion.

And I think that now, after 6 months of delay, it is time that the case be brought to a conclusion. If it was 90 percent finished in April, they ought to be able to finish it now.

Those who are guilty, or presumed to be guilty, should be indicted. Those who are not guilty at least should get some evidence of being cleared, because in the meantime, the reputations of men, some maybe who are not guilty, have been probably irreparably damaged by what has happened in the hearings that they have appeared before publicly. They have already been convicted and they may never recover. And that isn't our system of government.

The place to try a man or a woman for a crime is in the courts and not to convict them either in the newspapers or on television before he has a fair trial in the courts. . . .

Q. Do you feel that the executive privilege is absolute?

THE PRESIDENT. I, of course, do not. I have waived executive privilege with regard to all of the members of my staff who have any knowledge of or who have had any charges made against them in the Watergate matter. I have, of course, voluntarily waived privilege with regard to turning over the tapes, and so forth.

Let me point out it was voluntary on my part, and deliberately so to avoid a precedent that might destroy the principle of confidentiality for future Presidents, which is terribly important.

If it had gone to the Supreme Court—and I know many of my friends argued, "Why not carry it to the Supreme Court and let them decide it?"—that would, first, have had a confrontation with the Supreme Court, between the Supreme Court and the President. And second, it would have established very possibly a precedent, a precedent breaking down constitutionality that would plague future Presidencies, not just [this] President.

I could just say in that respect, too, that I have referred to what I called the Jefferson rule. It is the rule, I think; that we should generally follow—a President should follow—with the courts when they want information, and a President should also follow with committees of Congress, when they want information from his personal files.

Jefferson, as you know, in that very, very famous case, had correspondence which it was felt might bear upon the guilt or innocence of Aaron Burr. Chief Justice Marshall, sitting as a trial judge, held that Jefferson, as President, had to turn over the correspondence. Jefferson refused.

What he did was to turn over a summary of the correspondence, all that he considered was proper to be turned over for the purposes of the trial.

And then Marshall, sitting as Chief Justice, ruled for the President.

Now, why did Jefferson do that? Jefferson didn't do that to protect Jefferson. He did that to protect the Presidency. And that is exactly what I will do in these cases. It isn't for the purpose of protecting the President; it is for the purpose of seeing that the Presidency, where great decisions have to be made—and great decisions cannot be made unless there is very free flow of Conversation, and that means confidentiality—I have a responsibility to protect that Presidency.

At the same time, I will do everything I can to cooperate where there is a need for Presidential participation. . . .

Source: Public Papers of the Presidents of the United States, Richard M. Nixon, Containing the Public Messages, Speeches, and Statements of the President, 1973 (Washington, D.C.: U.S. Government Printing Office, 1975), 946–964.

Document Six: President Nixon, Address to the Nation Announcing His Decision to Resign the Office of President of the United States, August 8, 1974

Facing imminent impeachment in the House of Representatives and almost certain conviction in the Senate, President Nixon announced his decision to resign as president of the United States on August 8, 1974, effective the following day at noon.

Good evening:

This is the 37th time I have spoken to you from this office, where so many decisions have been made that shaped the history of this Nation. Each time I have done so to discuss with you some matter that I believe affected the national interest.

In all the decisions I have made in my public life, I have always tried to do what was best for the Nation. Throughout the long and difficult period of Watergate, I have felt it was my duty to persevere, to make every possible effort to complete the term of office to which you elected me. . . .

From the discussions I have had with Congressional and other leaders, I have concluded that because of the Watergate matter, I might not have the support of the Congress that I would consider necessary to back the very difficult decisions and carry out the duties of this office in the way the interests of the Nation will require.

I have never been a quitter. To leave office before my term is completed is abhorrent to every instinct in my body. But as President, I must put the interests of America first. America needs a full-time President and a full-time Congress, particularly at this time with problems we face at home and abroad.

To continue to fight through the months ahead for my personal vindication would almost totally absorb the time and attention of both the President and the Congress in a period when our entire focus should be on the great issues of peace abroad and prosperity without inflation at home.

Therefore, I shall resign the Presidency effective at noon tomorrow. Vice President Ford will be sworn in as President at that hour in this office. . . .

⊰◇⊱

Source: Public Papers of the Presidents of the United States, Richard M. Nixon, Containing the Public Messages, Speeches, and Statements of the President, 1974 (Washington, D.C.: U.S. Government Printing Office, 1975), 626–630.